READER'S DIGEST

How to Increase
Your Word Power

READER'S DIGEST

How to Increase Your Word Power

*Prepared in Association
with Stuart B. Flexner*

The Reader's Digest Association [Canada] Ltd., Montreal

ACKNOWLEDGMENT

The editors of the Reader's Digest gratefully acknowledge the assistance of Donald Berwick, professor of English, Hofstra University, and Charles Rittenhouse, former Senior English Consultant for the Protestant School Board of Greater Montreal, in preparing and reviewing the manuscript of this book.

SBN: 0-88850-036-X

Printed in Canada
3 2 1

CONTENTS

Fun With Words:

Quickie Quizzes:

Exploring Words:

PART TWO: SPELL IT RIGHT

Fun With Words:

Quickie Quizzes:

Spelling Tests:

PART THREE: SAY IT RIGHT

PART FOUR: PUNCTUATE IT RIGHT

INTRODUCTION

The purpose of this book is very simple: to help you master the English language quickly, easily, and thoroughly. If you are a poor speaker or writer, this book will help you become a good one. If you are a good speaker and writer, it will help you become a better one. It will help you to increase that vital asset—your word power.

Starting with the very first chapter, How To INCREASE YOUR WORD POWER teaches you thousands of words to add to your vocabulary and gives you all the clear explanations, simple rules, and professional tips for vocabulary building, perfect spelling, correct pronunciation, proper punctuation, correct usage, and good grammar.

Research has shown that a person's success is very often closely related to his or her vocabulary and language skills. Such tests show that successful executives, students, scientists, secretaries, housewives, doctors—successful people in all walks of life—all have in common a skill with words. That is why How To INCREASE YOUR WORD POWER can be important to you. It can teach you to use your language far more easily, correctly, and effectively than you now do. It offers you the kind of self-training that can make you a confident, persuasive speaker and writer.

What This Book Contains

To do all these things, this book is actually two volumes in one. The first contains six parts, which form a complete self-teaching and review book on vocabulary building and good English. The second is the *Lexoguide* section, which is your own quick A-to-Z reference guide to over 4,000 of the most troublesome but useful words in the English language.

The first six parts of the book are *Three Keys to Greater Word Power, Spell It Right, Say It Right, Punctuate It Right, Practical Grammar,* and *Using Your Word Power.* Each contains step-by-step chapters that give you important vocabulary words and all the facts and easy-to-remember rules, hints, and tips you need to know. Each teaches you vocabulary building and the do's and don't's of good English. Each is complete, authoritative, and full of information, word lists, and entertaining special features. These special features include

1

over 100 tests, quizzes, and word games. Scattered throughout the entire book, these features include *Fun With Words* to test your vocabulary, *Quickie Quizzes* for speedy review, *Exploring Words* to tell you the fascinating stories behind many of the words we use every day, and spelling, pronunciation, punctuation, usage, and grammar exercises to sharpen your skills. (The correct answers immediately follow all vocabulary tests, review quizzes, and exercises so that you can check yourself quickly.)

Every chapter in the first section of the book gives you concise, easy-to-remember explanations of one basic group of vocabulary words or of one basic problem in English. Most chapters contain lists of words to add to your vocabulary or of spelling, pronunciation, or usage demons for you to learn or review. And finally, of course, many chapters end with an entertaining vocabulary test, review quiz, or even a word game to stump your family and friends.

Remember that just because this section is divided into six parts does not mean that you should separate vocabulary building, spelling, pronunciation, punctuation, usage, and grammar in your own mind. The divisions are intended only to make learning easy by letting you concentrate fully on a single vocabulary list or language problem at a time. Even though each part is a unit by itself, all six have been thoroughly integrated into the overall plan of How To INCREASE YOUR WORD POWER. Here's what you will find in each of them.

THREE KEYS TO GREATER WORD POWER This is the longest and one of the most important parts of the book, because a large, useful vocabulary is the basis of word power. It takes up the three keys to vocabulary building by teaching you to recognize the basic building blocks of words, while at the same time teaching you thousands of words using these building blocks. Every chapter in this part explains one or more basic word elements or building blocks and then lists, defines, and teaches the most useful, typical, and interesting core words based on them. Since the lists of vocabulary words taught in each chapter are grouped together and related in meaning, spelling, and pronunciation, they are easy to learn and remember. This part of the book also lists further related words to study. Many chapters are followed by vocabulary tests and drills.

SPELL IT RIGHT Step by step this part of the book teaches you all the facts, rules, tricks, and tips you need to spell perfectly—*and* it actually lists and tells you how to spell all of the most commonly misspelled words. It includes spelling lists from high schools and colleges, business firms, and government agencies. Almost every chapter in this section takes up one familiar spelling problem, such as double letters; *-able* or *-ible; -ie* or *-ei; -ceed, -cede,* or *-sede; -ance* or *-ence,* and tells you how to solve the problem. Helpful lists of all the most troublesome words in a specific problem category make it easier for you to learn all the related facts, rules, and tips.

SAY IT RIGHT This part teaches you to pronounce words properly. Almost every chapter in this part deals with one common pronunciation problem, such as avoiding slovenly speech, accenting the right syllable, long and short *a* sounds, silent letters, tricky *c* and *k* sounds, what words end in the confusing *-ate* or *-it* sounds and in the *-ile* or *-il* sounds. Each of these chapters contains lists of pronunciation demons, telling you exactly how to pronounce the words properly, and gives you rules and tips on pronouncing new words as you encounter them.

PUNCTUATE IT RIGHT This part of the book gives simple but complete explanations of all the punctuation marks and how, why, and where to use each—*plus* hundreds of examples for you to study or refer to at any time. Separate chapters cover the use of every punctuation mark and formality, including capital letters, the period, the comma, the semicolon, quotation marks, question marks, exclamation points, and parentheses. There are punctuation exercises and drills to give you practice and the *Fun With Words* vocabulary tests, quizzes, and word games that appear throughout the book.

PRACTICAL GRAMMAR This part of the book confines itself for the most part to everyday grammar, the grammar you must know and use to speak and write well in normal situations. It tells what good grammar is and how to know and use it easily and quickly. It takes up only the most common mistakes and problems in grammar and tells you how to recognize and avoid them. There are thorough, up-to-date discussions of such old puzzlers as *It is I* or *It is Me, Who* or *Whom,* split infinitives, ending sentences with prepositions. There are many examples, showing you exactly what to do and how to do it.

USING YOUR WORD POWER This part explains the various levels of speech and writing (formal and informal, slang, nonstandard) and when and how to use or avoid them. Most of the chapters in this section list the most commonly confused, misused, and abused words in the English language, point out causes of error, tell you how to avoid embarrassing mistakes, and show you how to use the proper word in the proper place.

Thus, the six parts which make up the first section of How To InCREASE YOUR WORD POWER can increase your vocabulary by thousands of words and teach you perfect spelling, correct pronunciation, perfect punctuation, correct usage, and good grammar. They will increase your word power and help you master English.

The Lexoguide

The second major section of this book is the *Lexoguide,* an easy-to-use A-to-Z list of over 4,000 of the most troublesome but useful words in the English language. It gives you quick answers to their correct spelling, hyphenation, pronunciation, meaning, and use—along with thousands of sample sentences showing how the words are used; tips on their spelling, pronunciation, and usage problems; and thousands of synonyms and antonyms. Thus, the *Lexoguide* is your personal language reference book, a combined short dictionary, thesaurus, and usage book of the words most likely to be looked up in home, school, or office. The *Lexoguide,* along with the many word lists and tips throughout the first six sections of this book, can serve as a permanent guide book to answer your language questions and solve your language problems at a glance.

How This Book Was Written

How To INCREASE YOUR WORD POWER combines the "tried-and-true" methods of teaching with the latest modern methods of vocabulary building and English instruction. All of the text, all the words taught and examples given, and all the tests, quizzes, exercises, and word games have been carefully selected to help you master a large vocabulary and the rules of good English.

In order that this book be complete, it teaches you both the most effective and the most troublesome words in the English language, as shown by thousands of careful tests and major word lists. For example, spelling word lists from grade-school tests, high-school tests, Regents and college-entrance exams, remedial-reading courses, college-board and placement exams, secretarial and business schools, large business firms, government agencies, and research bureaus have

4

been checked to insure that all the most important, useful spelling words, rules, and tips are given in this book. The same care has been taken with all the other sections to insure that the word lists, rules, tips, and tests given in the vocabulary, spelling, pronunciation, punctuation, usage, and grammar sections include all the most important, practical, easy-to-use information, all the demon words, and all the answers to the questions and problems you may have.

How To Use This Book

How much time you should spend on building your vocabulary and your mastery of good English depends on your present level of skill and your own need and desire to learn. Fifteen minutes a day may be enough to achieve what you want, or you may want to put in as much as an hour a day if you need to make more rapid progress. You can learn the material in How To Increase Your Word Power in 30 days or you can enjoy learning from it at your leisure over a period of several months.

To get the most out of this book be sure to master the simple rules, easy tips, and problem words from each chapter before starting the next. Do all the tests, quizzes, and word games, too—they are fun and you will learn something from all of them. In other words, don't just let your eyes passively read this book—get your mind actively involved in it, chapter by chapter and quiz by quiz. Concentrate on your own language problems. If you already know and use a word properly or don't have a problem with this or that spelling, pronunciation, punctuation, usage, or grammar rule, then just review the chapter that covers it and spend more time on the words and chapters that you, as an individual, need to work on.

However much time you take to study, read, browse in, or refer to this book, remember one thing: you'll be mastering the English language—there aren't many more profitable or satisfying ways to spend your time.

HOW TO USE THE PRONUNCIATION KEY

One problem of teaching proper pronunciation in a book is that the reader *sees* the printed words but cannot *hear* them. All dictionaries and language books, including this one, overcome this problem in a very simple way: We "respell" the words within brackets or parentheses so that they are written exactly as they should sound. For example, if the word *cat* were a pronunciation demon that we wanted to show you how to pronounce, we would respell it [kat].

Why is such respelling necessary to show correct pronunciation? First, because the English language uses over 45 basic sounds but has only 26 letters in the alphabet to represent them. Thus, some letters must do double duty and stand for more than one sound (all vowels, *a, e, i, o,* and *u,* do double duty as does *y,* which is both a consonant and a vowel). Second, because our normal, correct spelling does not always indicate the way words are pronounced today.

Thus, the letter *c* can be represented by a *k* to show that *cat* is pronounced [kat] or it can be represented by an *s* to show that the word *city* is pronounced [sit′ē]. This is simple for all the letters except the vowels *a, e, i, o,* and *u* and the letter *g* when it is pronounced[j] in such words as *gentleman, gem, gelatin,* and *genius.* Each vowel can be pronounced in two or more ways (the letter *o* can be pronounced in at least seven different ways!). So to show you exactly how an *a, e, i,* or *u* should be pronounced in any given word, certain simple marks (called diacritical marks) may be placed over the letter. For example, if a vowel in any word should be pronounceed like the *a* in *ace,* then that vowel is represented by ā. Thus, if the word *age* were a pronunciation demon we would respell it for you as [āj].

You never really have to memorize the letters and symbols used in such respellings. You already know exactly what *k* and *s* sound like; so that, if *cat* is respelled [kat] and *city* is respelled [sit′ē], you just pronounce them exactly as you see them. But suppose you don't know how the ē in the respelling [sit′ē] should be pronounced? It's simple. You turn to the PRONUNCIATION KEY (a list of all the letters, symbols, and marks used to indicate pronunciation) and find that the e is pronounced as the first *e* in *even* or the *ee* in *tree.* Thus, by already knowing how to pronounce the letters in a respelled word or by looking up any unusual symbols, combinations, or marks (such as an *a, e, i, o,* or *u* with diacritical marks) in the pronunciation key, you can pronounce the word properly—because it has been respelled for you exactly as it sounds.

Are there any other letters or marks used in respelling words so that they read the same way they sound? Yes, three easy ones. A primary stress mark (′) is placed after the group of letters forming a syllable that should be "stressed" or said loudest. Thus, *city* is respelled [sit′ē] and the primary stress mark shows that it is stressed or accented on the first syllable, said as SITe rather than as sitE. Some longer words will have both a primary stress mark (′) over the syllable to have the greatest emphasis and a secondary stress mark (′) over the syllable to have slightly less emphasis. Thus, the word *commendation* is respelled as [kom′ən·dā′shən], which shows you that the first syllable, kom, has the greatest emphasis and the third syllable, dā, has slightly less emphasis. So the primary stress mark (′) and the secondary stress mark (′) are two marks you should remember to help you pronounce the respelled words properly.

The third unusual mark or symbol you will see in respelled words looks like this: ə. Linguists call this ə symbol the "schwa" and it merely indicates the very common "uh" sound in English. So when you see the symbol ə in a respelled word, it is pronounced "uh." Amazingly enough, all five of our English vowels, *a, e, i, o,* and *u,* are often pronounced as ə or "uh." For example:

> the *a* in *above* respelled [ə·buv′]
> the *e* in *sicken* respelled [sik′ən]
> the *i* in *clarity* respelled [klar′ə·tē]
> the *o* in *melon* respelled [mel′ən]
> the *u* in *focus* respelled [fō′kəs]

That's all you need to know about how words are respelled in this book when it is necessary to show you how they are actually pronounced. The respelling system is simple: it uses common letters like k to respell *cat* [kat] and a few special combinations and marks to respell the *a, e, i, o,* and *u* vowel sounds, like the e sound in *city* [sit′ē], or like the combined th sound in *this* [this]. It also uses primary (′) and secondary (′) stress marks and the ə symbol to represent the common "uh" sound.

On the following page is a complete pronunciation key for you to refer to whenever you see a word respelled to indicate its proper pronunciation and aren't sure what the letters, symbols, or marks stand for. (This pronunciation key is based on that used in the Reader's Digest GREAT ENCYCLOPEDIC DICTIONARY.)

PRONUNCIATION KEY

The primary stress mark (′) is placed after the syllable having the heavier stress; the secondary stress mark (′) follows a syllable having a somewhat lighter stress, as in **com·men·da·tion** (kom′ən·dā′shən).

a	add, map	m	move, seem	u	up, done
ā	ace, rate	n	nice, tin	û(r)	urn, term
â(r)	care, air	ng	ring, song	yōo	use, few
ä	palm, father				
b	bat, rub	o	odd, hot	v	vain, eve
ch	check, catch	ō	open, so	w	win, away
d	dog, rod	ô	order, jaw	y	yet, yearn
		oi	oil, boy	z	zest, muse
e	end, pet	ou	out, now	zh	vision, pleasure
ē	even, tree	ōo	pool, food		
f	fit, half	ŏo	took, full	ə	the schwa, an un-
g	go, log				stressed vowel
h	hope, hate	p	pit, stop		representing the
		r	run, poor		"uh" sound spelled
i	it, give	s	see, pass		*a* in *above*
ī	ice, write	sh	sure, rush		*e* in *sicken*
j	joy, ledge	t	talk, sit		*i* in *clarity*
k	cool, take	th	thin, both		*o* in *melon*
l	look, rule	th	this, bathe		*u* in *focus*

FOREIGN SOUNDS

à as in French *ami, patte*. This is a vowel midway in quality between [a] and [ä].

œ as in French *peu*, German *schön*. Round the lips for [ō] and pronounce [ā].

ü as in French *vue*, German *grün*. Round the lips for [ōo] and pronounce [ā]

kh as in German *ach*, Scottish *loch*. Pronounce a strongly aspirated [h] with the tongue in position for [k] as in *cool* or *keep*.

ṅ This symbol indicates that the preceding vowel is nasal. The nasal vowels in French are œṅ [*brun*], aṅ [*main*], äṅ [*chambre*], ôṅ [*dont*].

′ This symbol indicates that a preceding (l) or (r) is voiceless, as in French *fin-de-siècle* [faṅ·de·sye′kl′] or *fiacre* [fyà′-kr′]; that a preceding [y] is pronounced consonantly in a separate syllable followed by a slight schwa sound, as in French *fille* [fē′y′]; or that a consonant preceding a [y] is palatalized, as in Russian *oblast* [ô′bləsty′].

8

PART ONE

Three Keys
To Greater
Word Power

1 ROOTS—YOUR FIRST KEY TO WORD POWER

The quickest, most useful, and easiest way to increase your word power is to analyze and understand how words are put together. Once you learn to recognize the building blocks with which words are made, many previously unfamiliar words become meaningful and useful. You will see that many words are actually made up of related or identical parts that you already know. For example, most people use the word *salary* and its plural form, *salaries*. They also recognize the word *salaried*, meaning "paying a salary"—*He has a salaried job at the orphanage*—or "receiving a salary"—*How many salaried salesmen does the firm employ?*

Now here is something interesting. The word *salary* is based on the Latin root *sal-* meaning "salt" (Roman soldiers were given a special allowance to buy their own salt). Now you understand why the expression "He's not worth his salt" means "He's not worth his pay."

Let's have some fun with this root *sal-*. What do we put salt on? SALads. What is a highly salted, spiced meat? SALami. What do chemists call water, soil, or a solution containing salt? They call it SALine. So, if you learn one basic word or one basic root, you can instantly increase your sight vocabulary.

English has hundreds of thousands of words built up from two or more distinct parts taken mostly from Latin or Greek. It would be impossible to learn and remember them all individually. But the parts, or building blocks, are limited in number and simple in meaning. With them you can analyze, understand, and use thousands of words almost on sight. These simple units are often not words themselves but are combined with other elements to form words.

You've seen a few words derived from the root *sal-*. Here's another example of how words are built. Notice what the following words have in common:

revive	vitamin	viviparous
vital	vivacious	vivid

Although you may not know the meaning of every word on this list, you can easily see that they all have something in common: each of them is built on the building block of *vit-* or *viv-* meaning "life" or "to live." This part is called a root.

A root is the part of any word that reveals its essential meaning, a meaning that never changes, even though other letters or word parts may be added at the beginning or end. Note in the above list that roots are used in combination with other word-building blocks such as prefixes, which come at the beginning of a word (*re-* meaning "again" in the first word *revive*), and suffixes, which come at the end of a word (*-al, -amin,* and *-acious* as in the words *vital, vitamin,* and *vivacious*). Many roots will vary slightly in spelling, as do *viv-* and *vit-*. In each word the root is the foundation, the basic building block.

The root *vit-* comes from a Latin noun meaning "life," and its variant spelling *viv-* comes from a Latin verb meaning "to live." Let us analyze the words formed from the root *viv-* or *vit-* to see how they are all built up from the basic meaning "life" or "to live."

revive comes from the prefix *re-* meaning "again" and the Latin root *viv-* meaning "to live." Thus, *revive* means "to live again or make live again; to bring back to life, strength, health, or consciousness."

> *The lifeguard revived the man by artificial respiration.*
> *After a hard day's work, a hot meal revived him.*
> *The stock company has revived several old plays.*

vital is formed from the Latin root *vit-* meaning "life" and the suffix *-al* meaning "pertaining to" or "full of." Thus, *vital* means (1) pertaining to (or necessary for) life; (2) full of life.

> *Oxygen is vital for all animals.*
> *She is a happy, vital person.*
> *Vital statistics relate to births, deaths, marriages, etc.*

vitamin is formed from the Latin root *vit-* meaning "life" and the suffix *-amin* meaning "amine" (an organic chemical compound). Thus, *vitamin* means "an organic substance found in most foodstuffs that is necessary for normal life functions in man and animals."

> *Vitamin C, found in citrus fruits, prevents scurvy.*

vivacious comes from the Latin root *viv-* meaning "to live" and the suffix *-acious* meaning "abounding in; given to." Thus, *vivacious* means "full of life; lively; active."

> *The young actress was charming and vivacious.*
> *Nick and Sue engaged in a vivacious, witty conversation.*

11

vivid stems from the Latin root *viv-* meaning "to live" and the suffix *-id* meaning "having a certain quality." Thus, *vivid* means "having the quality of life; lifelike; lively; not dull."

> *The boy had a vivid imagination.*
> *She loved to wear vivid colors.*
> *Dickens' novels are full of vivid characterizations.*

viviparous derives from the Latin root *viv-* meaning "to live" and another Latin root *par-* meaning "to bring forth" plus the suffix *-ous* meaning "given to; characterized by." Thus, the scientific word *viviparous* means "characterized by giving birth to live offspring" (as opposed to laying and hatching eggs).

> *Man and most other mammals are viviparous.*
> *Chickens are not viviparous.*

Once you know a root and some of the words built on it, you can keep building. For example, you can take *revive* and build *revival* meaning "the act of reviving; recovery" and *revivify*, which has much the same meaning as *revive*. From *vital* you can build *vitality*, which means "vigor; energy." *Survive* will give you *survivor* and *survival*. And you can also figure out that the phrase *vital organs* and the word *vitals*, which has the same meaning, refer to parts of the body that are necessary to sustain life.

This section of How To INCREASE YOUR WORD POWER gives you 72 of the roots that are most basic to the English language and shows you how to base words upon them. From these words in the text you can learn to recognize, analyze, build, and use many related words easily and quickly.

One of the most effective and enjoyable ways to increase your word power is to take the vocabulary tests, called "Fun With Words," and the shorter tests, called "Quickie Quizzes," that appear throughout the section dealing with roots. You will notice that a few of the tests do not relate directly to roots you may have just learned in the pages that precede them; however, they will help you to a better understanding of the function of roots as building blocks toward a greater vocabulary. In addition, the tests will introduce you to hundreds of new words. You will no doubt recognize a large number of these words but feel that you are unsure of the exact meanings of some of them. Take the tests several times if necessary to fix the definitions firmly and permanently in your mind.

ROOT: ACU-, ACR-

The Latin root *acu-* or *acr-* means "sharp." You should sharpen your vocabulary with the five core words in which the root *acu-* or *acr-* appears: *acrid, acrimony, acuity, acumen, acute.*

acrid comes from *acr-* meaning "sharp" and the Latin suffix *-id* meaning "having a particular quality." Thus, *acrid* means "having a sharp quality in taste or smell; bitter or burning to the senses."

The acrid smoke hurt our eyes.

A word based on *acrid* is *acridity*, meaning "the state or quality of being acrid; acridness."

The acridity of the smoke made our eyes water.

acrimony comes from *acr-* meaning "sharp" and the Latin suffix *-mony* which means "quality of being." Specifically, *acrimony* means "sharpness of speech or temper."

Our quarrel was full of acrimony.

A word based on *acrimony* is *acrimonious*, meaning "full of bitterness; sharp; sarcastic."

Their discussion turned into an acrimonious debate.

acuity is made up of *acu-* meaning "sharp" and the Latin suffix *-ity* which means "the state, condition, or quality of being." Thus, *acuity* means "the state or condition of being sharp," but it is applied to sharpness or acuteness of the mind or senses.

The professor has great mental acuity.

acumen comes directly from a Latin word meaning "point" or "sharpness (of mind)." It has come to mean "keenness," "quickness of insight."

John has shown great business acumen.

acute stems from a Latin word meaning "to sharpen." *Acute* means "sharp" or "coming to a sharp point," and thus it has also come to mean "reaching a crisis; critical; keen; intense; violent." Note carefully these various meanings in the following sentences:

An acute angle is an angle of less than 90 degrees.

He is suffering from acute appendicitis.
The food shortage in India is becoming acute.
The boy has a quick, acute mind.
His toothache was causing acute pain.

A word based on *acute* is *acutely,* meaning "intensely; extremely; keenly; highly."

He was acutely conscious of their disapproval.

REMEMBER: When you see *acu-* or *acr-* it means "sharp."

ROOT: AG-, ACT-

The Latin *ag-* or *act-* means "to do; drive." This root forms some of the most frequently used words in the English language. You already know some common words based on it, such as *act* and *action.* Here are seven more core words based on the root *ag-* or *act-* that you should know: *agenda, agent, agile, active, actor, actual, enact.*

agenda comes directly from a Latin word based on *ag-* meaning "to do" and means "a list of things to be done; a list of things to be discussed or decided upon."

There were three items on the agenda for the business meeting.

agent comes from *ag-* meaning "to do" plus the Latin suffix *-ent* which means "a person who." Thus, *agent* means "a person who does something." This word is applied to someone who does a specific action or job, or who works for or represents an individual, company, or government bureau.

He is an FBI agent.
Does the actor have a press agent?
Does that company have a sales agent in our town?

A word based on *agent* is *agency,* meaning "a company, department, or bureau that does a specific job or that represents other people or companies."

She works for an employment agency.

14

90-SECOND QUICKIE QUIZ

FOR MEN ONLY

Can you match the type of woman in the left-hand column with her description in the right-hand column? Answers follow.

1. winsome [win′səm]	(a) little
2. virago [vi·rä′gō *or* vi·rā′gō]	(b) a pert, saucy girl
3. hoyden [hoid′n]	(c) a sharp-tongued scold
4. prima donna [prē′mə don′ə]	(d) a temperamental woman
5. coquette [kō·ket′]	(e) a tomboy
6. petite [pə·tēt′]	(f) coy
7. minx [mingks]	(g) slender
8. svelte [svelt]	(h) a nag
9. shrew [shrōō]	(i) charmingly or shyly pleasing
10. demure [di·myŏŏr′]	(j) a flirt

ANSWERS:

1. **winsome**—(i) charmingly or shyly pleasing. 2. **virago**—(c) a sharp-tongued scold. 3. **hoyden**—(e) a tomboy. 4. **prima donna**—(d) a temperamental woman. 5. **coquette**—(j) a flirt. 6. **petite**—(a) little. 7. **minx**—(b) a pert, saucy girl. 8. **svelte**—(g) slender. 9. **shrew**—(h) a nag. 10. **demure** —(f) coy.

agile is made up of *ag-* meaning "to do" and the Latin suffix *-ile* which means "pertaining to; like; having the character or quality of." Thus, *agile* means "having the quality of doing or acting" or "able to do or move quickly and easily; nimble."

> *Charles is agile and athletic.*

A word based on *agile* is *agility*, meaning "the ability to move quickly and easily."

> *The quarterback had remarkable agility.*

active comes from *act-* meaning "to do" plus the Latin suffix *-ive* meaning "inclined to; tending to; having the character or quality of." Thus, *active* means "inclined to action; working; busy; lively."

> *She leads an active social life.*
> *This is an active volcano.*

Two words based on *active* are *activity* and *activate*. *Activity* means

15

(1) the state of being active; (2) a particular action. *Activate* means "to make active or make capable of action."

> *There was little activity on the stock market today.*
> *Can you activate this machine?*

actor is formed from *act-* meaning "to do" and the Latin suffix *-or* meaning "a person who or a thing that performs an action." An *actor* is thus "a person who does something," or "a person who acts."

> *My son was an actor in the struggle, not an onlooker.*
> *He was an actor in the play.*

A word related to *actor* is its female form, *actress*.

actual comes from the Latin word *actus*, "a doing," which is based on *act-* meaning "to do," and the Latin suffix *-al* which means "pertaining to; characterized by." *Actual* means "pertaining to something that is in action or in existence now"; thus, it means "existing; real."

> *What were his actual words?*

Two words based on *actual* are *actually*, meaning "really" or "truly," and *actuality*, which means "reality; truth; fact."

> *What did he actually say?*
> *Our dream of reaching the moon has become an actuality.*

enact stems from the Latin prefix *en-* meaning "to make; cause to be" plus the Latin root *act-* meaning "to do." Thus, *enact* means "to cause to be done" or, specifically, "to make into a law."

> *The Federal Government enacted a bill against air pollution.*

A word based on *enact* is *enactment*, meaning "the passing of a law" or "a law that has been passed."

> *The Legislature's enactment of the air-pollution bill goes into effect today.*

◊ Look up the following words in your dictionary. Does knowing the meaning of the root *act-* help you to understand their dictionary meanings?

> inactive   transact   interact   react

What other words are based on these words? Can you think of any besides *transaction* and *reaction?*

Fun With Words

SHORT WORDS

The various tests throughout this book will not only review material covered in the text, but will introduce you to many new words. Below is a vocabulary test on short words. Check the word or phrase you believe is closest in meaning to the key word. Answers follow.

1. **aura** [ôr′ə]—(a) oppressive heat. (b) a characteristic atmosphere. (c) pertaining to the sense of hearing. (d) by word of mouth.
2. **avid** [av′id]—(a) stingy. (b) rapid. (c) greedy. (d) bitter.
3. **aver** [ə·vûr′]—(a) to postpone. (b) to turn aside. (c) to declare positively. (d) to dismiss.
4. **avow** [ə·vou′]—(a) to deny. (b) to curse. (c) to swear allegiance to. (d) to declare openly.
5. **allay** [ə·lā′]—(a) to spread out flat. (b) to procrastinate. (c) to connect with. (d) to lessen.
6. **averse** [ə·vûrs′]—(a) unpleasant. (b) opposed. (c) unfortunate. (d) in the opposite order.
7. **arch** [ärch]—(a) playfully sly or roguish. (b) incriminating. (c) patriotic. (d) wandering.
8. **bask** [bask]—(a) any large receptacle. (b) a native of Spain. (c) to luxuriate in pleasant warmth. (d) to swim slowly.

9. **crass** [kras]—(a) irritating. (b) vulgarly stupid. (c) bitter. (d) noisy.
10. **carp** [kärp]—(a) to be boisterous. (b) to wander about. (c) to find fault unreasonably. (d) to insult.
11. **coy** [koi]—(a) shy or coquettish. (b) vain. (c) quiet. (d) authentic.
12. **cull** [kul]—(a) to strip the leaves off. (b) to explain. (c) to select or pick out. (d) to gather.
13. **chide** [chīd]—(a) to scold or admonish. (b) to insult. (c) to scream. (d) to compensate for.
14. **chic** [shēk]—(a) stylish. (b) impudent. (c) youthful. (d) merry.
15. **crux** [kruks]—(a) a laboratory report. (b) cleavage. (c) a problem. (d) the pivotal point.
16. **dire** [dīr]—(a) very poor. (b) cold and damp. (c) angry. (d) dreadful or calamitous.

ANSWERS:

1. **aura**—(b) a characteristic atmosphere. 2. **avid**—(c) greedy. 3. **aver**—(c) to declare positively. 4. **avow**—(d) to declare openly. 5. **allay**—(d) to lessen. 6. **averse**—(b) opposed. 7. **arch**—(a) playfully sly or roguish. 8. **bask**—(c) to luxuriate in pleasant warmth. 9. **crass**—(b) vulgarly stupid. 10. **carp**—(c) to find fault unreasonably. 11. **coy**—(a) shy or coquettish. 12. **cull**—(c) to select or pick out. 13. **chide**—(a) to scold or admonish. 14. **chic**—(a) stylish. 15. **crux**—(d) the pivotal point. 16. **dire**—(d) dreadful or calamitous.

ROOT: AM-

The Latin *am-* means "to love." You should learn these six core vocabulary words that are built on the root *am-: amateur, amatory, amiable, amicable, amorous, enamored.*

amateur comes from *am-* meaning "to love" and the French suffix *-ateur* which means "a person who." Thus, an *amateur* is "a person who does something for the love of it rather than for money; a person who practices an art, sport, or science for his own pleasure, rather than as a profession." *Amateur* may also mean "one who lacks professional skill."

> *The painter was a gifted amateur.*
> *Some amateur golfers are as good as professionals.*

Two words based on *amateur* are *amateurish* and *amateurishly.*

BEWARE: If you call an athlete or artist an *amateur,* you may not be criticizing him since you may mean only that he does not receive pay for what he does. But if you say that he is *amateurish* or that he does something *amateurishly* you are being critical. You mean that he lacks skill or that what he has done is not as good as it should be.

amatory comes from a Latin word based on the root *am-* meaning "to love" and the Latin suffix *-ory* meaning "related to; like; resembling." Thus, *amatory* means "relating to love; expressing love."

> *The girl gave him an amatory glance.*

amiable derives from *am-* meaning "to love" plus the Latin suffix *-able* meaning "able to; capable of; worthy of." *Amiable* means "able to love; capable of kindness or friendliness"; hence, it means "kindly; friendly."

> *He is an amiable person.*
> *The two friends had an amiable disagreement.*

A word based on *amiable* is *amiability* meaning "the quality or state of being amiable; friendliness."

> *The amiability of their rivalry impressed us.*

18

amicable comes from the same Latin word as *amiable* and contains the same root and suffix, although the spelling is different. *Amicable* also means "friendly," but it is used in a slightly different way. It means "peaceable."

> *The lawyer arranged an amicable settlement of the lawsuit.*

Two words based on *amicable* are *amicably*, meaning "in a friendly, peaceable manner," and *amicability*, meaning "the quality or state of being amicable; friendliness; peaceableness."

> *They ended their partnership amicably.*
> *The amicability of their parting was remarkable.*

amorous is a combination of *am* meaning "to love" and the Latin suffix *-ous* meaning "full of, given to, having, or like." *Amorous* thus means "tending to fall in love; showing love; in love."

> *He has a very amorous nature.*
> *The girl gave him an amorous glance.*

Either *amatory* or *amorous* may be used in the second example above, since both words can mean "showing or expressing love."

enamored comes from the Latin prefix *en-* meaning "to make; cause to be" plus the root *am-* meaning "to love" and the suffix *-ed* meaning that the word is a past participle. To be *enamored* means "to be in love; to be fascinated or enchanted."

> *The boy is enamored of the girl next door.*

ROOT: ANIM-

The Latin root *anim-* means "life; mind; soul; spirit." This root appears in several very important words. Learn the following six core vocabulary words based on *anim-: animal, animate, animosity, equanimity, magnanimity, unanimous.*

animal comes from *anim-* meaning "life" plus the Latin suffix *-al* meaning "pertaining to; characterized by." *Animal* means "that which

19

is characterized by life; a living being." Of course, this meaning
has been enlarged so that *animal* has other connotations, too, such
as "any creature other than man" or even "any creature other than a
man, bird, fish, or insect."

> *Is it animal, vegetable, or mineral?*
> *How many animals are in the zoo?*
> *Both men and dogs are animals.*

Two words based on *animal* are *animality* and *animalistic*. *Animality* means "animal nature; the nature and qualities of an animal."
Animalistic means "resembling an animal; like an animal."

> *Some men should subdue the animality in their natures.*
> *His rude behavior was more animalistic than human.*

animate comes from *anim-* meaning "life" plus the Latin suffix *-ate*,
which means "having; being." Pronounced one way, *animate* means
"to give life to; to make alive." Pronounced a different way, it means
"having life; living; full of life."

> *He tried to animate* [an′ə·māt] *the conversation by telling jokes.*
> *Man is an animate* [an′ə·mit] *being.*

Three words based on *animate* are *animated, animation,* and *inanimate*. *Animated* means "full of life; moving or seeming to move as if
alive." *Animation* means "vivacity or liveliness." *Inanimate* means "lifeless."

> *She was a happy, animated person.*
> *The children enjoy animated cartoons.*
> *She spoke with animation.*
> *A desk is an inanimate object.*

animosity is formed from the root *anim-* meaning "mind; spirit" and
the Latin suffix *-ity* meaning "the state, condition, or quality of."
Animosity originally meant "the condition of having a high spirit,"
but now it is restricted to one specific meaning, "hatred."

> *There is a great deal of animosity between us.*

equanimity comes from the Latin root *equ-* meaning "equal; even" and
the root *anim-* meaning "mind" plus the Latin suffix *-ity* meaning
"the state, condition, or quality of." Thus, *equanimity* means "evenness of mind; calmness; composure, especially steadiness under stress
or trying circumstances."

The mayor listened to their insults with equanimity.
The equanimity of the condemned man was remarkable.

A word based on *equanimity* is *equanimous*, meaning "even-tempered."

The judge was a good-natured, equanimous man.

magnanimity is made up of the Latin root *magn-* meaning "great" and the root *anim-* meaning "mind; spirit" plus -*ity* meaning "the state, condition, or quality of." Thus, *magnanimity* means "greatness of mind or spirit; the quality of being high-minded."

He shows magnanimity in forgiving his enemies.

A word based on *magnanimity* is *magnanimous*, meaning "high-minded; generous in forgiving."

After the war, the victors were magnanimous, not revengeful.

unanimous comes from the Latin root *un-* meaning "one" and the root *anim-* meaning "mind" plus the Latin suffix -*ous* which means "having; being." Thus, *unanimous* means "being of one mind; sharing the same views; showing the assent of all concerned."

There was a unanimous vote in favor of adjourning the meeting.
The committee was unanimous in favoring adjournment.

A word based on *unanimous* is *unanimity*, meaning "the state of being unanimous; complete agreement."

The jury reached unanimity on the question of his guilt.

ROOT: ANNU-, ENNI-

The Latin root *annu-* or *enni-* means "year." Five common core vocabulary words are formed from this root. They are: *annals, annual, perennial, centennial, annuity.*

annals comes from the root *annu-* meaning "year" and the Latin suffix -*al* meaning "of; pertaining to." Basically, *annals* means "yearly

21

records," but its use has expanded to mean "records in general," and especially "historical records."

Mr. Johnson compiles the annals of the Historical Society.
The professor has read all the annals of early American history.

annual also comes from *annu-* meaning "year" and the Latin suffix *-al* meaning "of; pertaining to." *Annual* means "of one year; yearly; occurring every year." As a noun *annual* means "a book or pamphlet issued once a year." In agriculture and gardening, it means "lasting only one year," and is applied to a plant living for only one year or growing season and not blooming again.

We have an annual vacation of two weeks.
Here is a picture of Tom in his high-school annual.
Beans and corn are annuals; you have to plant a new crop every year.

perennial derives from the Latin prefix *per-* meaning "through" plus *enni-* meaning "year." *Perennial* means "continuing or lasting through the year," but its use has expanded to mean "lasting through the years; everlasting." In agriculture and gardening, it means "a plant that lives for three or more years, usually blooming each year."

I'm tired of your perennial nagging!
These flowers are perennials; you don't have to plant new seeds every year.

centennial is formed from the Latin root *cent-* meaning "one hundred" and *enni-* meaning "year." Thus, *centennial* means (1) lasting for a hundred years; (2) marking a period of a hundred years; (3) happening once every hundred years.

This is the centennial anniversary of the founding of our town.
The centennial of Confederation occurred in 1967.

annuity comes from *annu-* meaning "year" and the Latin suffix *-ity* meaning "the state, condition, or quality of being." *Annuity* means "a yearly allowance or income."

How much is the annuity from this life insurance?

◊ Another word based on the root *annu-* or *enni-* is *biennial*. Look up the word in your dictionary. What does it mean? What does the prefix *bi-* mean? You'll learn more about the prefix *bi-* later on in this section.

EXPLORING WORDS

THE ANIMAL KINGDOM

Did you know that you are a viviparous mammalian biped? The following fourteen words describe some of the major types of animal that inhabit the earth, characterizing them according to the class they belong to, their physical make-up, their habits, or the way they bring forth young.

amphibian (1) in popular use: an animal that can or seems to live both in the water and on land, as a crocodile, seal, etc. (2) in scientific use: a class of animal that lives in the water at one stage of its life and on land at another, as the land-living frog, which starts life as a water-living tadpole.

aquatic living in or near water, as fish, whales, ducks, etc.

arboreal living in trees, as most birds, monkeys, etc.

biped an animal having only two feet, as man, apes, and birds.

carnivorous describing an animal that feeds chiefly or exclusively on meat, as dogs, wolves, lions, tigers, etc.

diurnal more active during the day than at night, as man, apes, birds, grazing animals, etc.

herbivorous describing an animal that feeds mainly on vegetable matter; plant-eating.

mammalian describing an animal that suckles its young with milk from breasts.

marsupial a member of an order of mammals whose females nourish and protect their newborn in a pouch in the abdomen, as kangaroos and opossums.

monotreme a member of the lowest order of mammals whose females lay and hatch eggs, as the duck-billed platypus.

nocturnal more active during the night than in the daytime, as bats, certain insects, some cats, etc.

oviparous belonging to a class of animals whose females lay and hatch eggs, as birds, most fishes, and reptiles.

pachyderm any of certain thick-skinned, nonruminant, hoofed animals, as the elephant, hippopotamus, and rhinoceros.

prehensile capable of or adapted for grasping or holding, as the hands or paws of man and some apes, monkeys, bears, opossums, etc., and the tails of certain monkeys.

ROOT: ANTHROP-, ANTHROPO-

The Greek root *anthrop-* or *anthropo-* means "man; human." This root appears in the following three core vocabulary words: *anthropology, philanthropist, misanthrope.*

anthropology comes from *anthropo-* meaning "man; human" plus the Greek root *-logy* meaning "the science or study of." Thus, *anthropology* is literally "the science or study of man"; that is, "the science dealing with the physical, social, and cultural development of man."

In college Steve majored in anthropology and sociology.

A word based on *anthropology* is *anthropologist,* meaning "a person whose profession or study is anthropology."

philanthropist comes from the Greek root *phil-* meaning "love" and *anthrop-* meaning "man; human" plus the Greek suffix *-ist* meaning "a person who believes in; a person engaged in." Thus, a *philanthropist* is "a person who loves his fellow men; especially, a person who is engaged in promoting the happiness or social progress of mankind by supporting charities, making donations to colleges, etc."

The philanthropist gave a million dollars for the building of a public library.

Two words based on or related to *philanthropist* are *philanthropy* and *philanthropic. Philanthropy* means "love of mankind; especially, a deed or deeds of charity for mankind." *Philanthropic* means "showing love for mankind, especially by supporting charities, making donations, etc."

misanthrope [mis'ən·thrōp] is made up of the Greek root *mis-* meaning "hate; hatred" and *anthrop-* meaning "man; human." Thus, a *misanthrope* is "a person who hates his fellow men."

It is impossible for a misanthrope to be a philanthropist.

Three words based on or related to *misanthrope* are *misanthropist* [mis·an'thrə·pist], which means exactly the same thing (a person who hates his fellow men); *misanthropic,* meaning "feeling or showing hatred for one's fellow men"; and *misanthropy,* which means "hatred of mankind."

ROOTS: ARCHEO-, ARCHI-, -ARCH, -ARCHY

Several common words are built on the roots *arche(o)-*, *arch(i)-*, *-arch*, and *-archy*. These roots look alike but are actually quite different. Let's take up each one in order.

The Greek root *arche-* or *archeo-* means "ancient." The most common word that it appears in is *archeology*.

archeology [är′kē·ol′ə·jē] comes from *archeo-* meaning "ancient" and the Greek suffix *-logy*, which means "the science or study of." Thus, *archeology* is "the study of history from the remains of ancient human cultures."

> *The discovery of the buried city of Troy was a great event in archeology.*

Two words based on *archeology* are *archeological*, meaning "of or pertaining to archeology," and *archeologist*, meaning "a person whose profession or specialty is archeology."

The second Greek root, *arch-* or *archi-*, means "chief; principal." (Note that there is no *e* in this root.) Many of the words in which *arch-* or *archi-* appear should be familiar to you, but be sure you know the meaning of the following four core words: *archangel, archbishop, archenemy, architect*.

archangel [ärk′ān′jəl] is made up of the Greek root *arch-* meaning "chief; principal" and the word *angel*. An *archangel* is "a chief or principal angel."

> *Gabriel is an archangel.*

archbishop [ärch′bish′əp] comes from the Greek root *arch-* meaning "chief; principal" and the word *bishop*. An *archbishop* is "the chief bishop of a province."

> *The bishop was elevated to archbishop.*

archenemy [ärch′en′ə·mē] is formed from the Greek root *arch-* meaning "chief; principal" and the word *enemy*. An *archenemy* is "a chief enemy."

> *Satan is often called the archenemy of mankind.*

25

architect comes from the Greek root *archi-* meaning "chief; principal" and the Greek root *tekt-* meaning "worker." An *architect* is literally "the chief worker"; he is "a person who designs and draws up plans for buildings and supervises their construction."

We will require the services of an experienced architect.

A word based on *architect* is *architecture*, which means "the design and construction of buildings; the style of a building."

Have you seen much colonial American architecture?
John took evening courses in architecture.

The final two roots, *-arch* and *-archy*, can be treated together. These roots appear at or toward the end of words and thus resemble suffixes. The Greek root *-arch* means "a ruler; a person who rules." The Greek root *-archy* means "a particular kind of rule or government." The roots *-arch* and *-archy* appear in the following four core words: *monarch, monarchy, matriarch, matriarchy.*

monarch comes from the Greek root *mon-* meaning "one; single" plus *-arch* meaning "a ruler." Thus, a *monarch* is "a person who rules alone; a king or sovereign."

Both kings and queens are called monarchs.

monarchy derives from the Greek root *mon-* meaning "one; single" and *-archy* meaning "rule; government." Thus, *monarchy* means (1) rule or government by a monarch; (2) a land ruled by a monarch.

France was once a monarchy.

matriarch comes from the Latin root *matri-* meaning "mother" and *-arch* meaning "a ruler." A *matriarch* is "a woman who rules or leads a large family or tribe by hereditary right."

Matriarchs ruled in some ancient societies.

matriarchy stems from the Latin root *matri-* meaning "mother" plus *-archy* meaning "rule; government." A *matriarchy* is "a society or culture ruled by a woman."

Some ancient societies were matriarchies.

The Latin root *patri-* means "father." What, then, is the meaning of the word *patriarchy?*

Fun With Words

SOME BIG A'S

Here are fourteen words beginning with the first letter of the alphabet. Check the word or phrase you believe is closest in meaning to the key word. Answers follow.

1. **allusion** [ə·lōo′zhən]—(a) a false mental image. (b) an indirect reference. (c) a claim. (d) a temptation.

2. **apprehension** [ap′rə·hen′shən]—(a) approval. (b) fear of the past. (c) information. (d) dread of the future.

3. **affinity** [ə·fin′ə·tē]—(a) daintiness. (b) on and on without an end. (c) close relationship (d) strength.

4. **appropriate** [ə·prō′prē·āt]—(a) to take for one's own use. (b) to make fitting and suitable. (c) to express a favorable opinion. (d) to give away.

5. **adaptation** [ad′əp·tā′shən]—(a) imitation. (b) act of fitting into an environment. (c) surrender or yielding. (d) act of taking for one's own.

6. **abridge** [ə·brij′] (a) to shorten or cut off. (b) to delay. (c) to express resentment. (d) to bind together.

7. **append** [ə·pend′]—(a) to shorten. (b) to judge. (c) to add to or attach. (d) to scold.

8. **affix** [ə·fiks′]—(a) to spread about. (b) to interfere with. (c) to make temporary. (d) to fasten on or attach.

9. **accentuate** [ak·sen′chōo·āt]—(a) to emphasize or intensify. (b) to speak in a dialect. (c) to collect. (d) to increase the cost of.

10. **aspiration** [as′pə·rā′shən]—(a) breathing. (b) discouragement. (c) facial expression. (d) ambition or lofty aim.

11. **align** [ə·līn′]—(a) to join with others in a cause. (b) to accuse or slander. (c) to measure. (d) to defame.

12. **appurtenance** [ə·pûr′tə·nəns]—(a) nasty remark. (b) accessory. (c) unnecessary detail. (d) projecting corner.

13. **admonitory** [ad·mon′ə·tôr′ē]—(a) gloomy. (b) death-dealing. (c) terrifying. (d) warning.

14. **appreciable** [ə·prē′shē·ə·bəl]—(a) perceptible. (b) grateful. (c) pleasant. (d) very small.

ANSWERS:

1. **allusion**—(b) an indirect reference. 2. **apprehension**—(d) dread of the future. 3. **affinity**—(c) close relationship. 4. **appropriate**—(a) to take for one's own use. 5. **adaptation**—(b) act of fitting into an environment. 6. **abridge**—(a) to shorten or cut off. 7. **append**—(c) to add to or attach. 8. **affix**—(d) to fasten on or attach. 9. **accentuate**—(a) to emphasize or intensify. 10. **aspiration**—(d) ambition or lofty aim. 11. **align**—(a) to join with others in a cause. 12. **appurtenance**—(b) accessory. 13. **admonitory**—(d) warning. 14. **appreciable**—(a) perceptible.

ROOT: AUD-, AUDIT-

The Latin root *aud-* or *audit-* means "to hear." *Audit-* is a root that we use by itself to form a word, *audit*. An *audit* is "an examination of something, especially of financial records or accounts." It originally meant "a hearing" but later came to mean "any examination or inspection." (In universities, a student who attends a course of lectures but does not take tests or receive a grade is said to *audit* the course—to give it a hearing.)

Numerous other words are based on *aud-* or *audit-*. Learn the following six important core words in which this root appears: *audible, audience, audio, audition, auditor, auditorium.*

audible comes from the root *aud-* meaning "to hear" and the Latin suffix *-ible* meaning "able; capable of." Thus, *audible* means "capable of being heard; loud enough to be heard."

> *The teacher's voice was barely audible.*

Two words based on *audible* are *audibility*, which means "the ability to be heard," and *inaudible*, which means "not loud enough to be heard."

> *The audibility of the speaker's voice was poor.*
> *The speaker's voice was inaudible.*

audience derives from *aud-* meaning "to hear" and the Latin suffix *-ience* meaning "the state or condition of." *Audience* originally meant "a hearing with someone else"; that is, "an interview or conference." Now it also means "the people assembled to hear something."

> *The ambassador had an audience with the Pope.*
> *The audience applauded the musicians.*

audio comes directly from the Latin root *aud-* meaning "to hear." *Audio* means "pertaining to hearing or to sound waves." In some modern uses, it means "electronically broadcast or reproduced sound."

> *I bought my record player in the audio department of the store.*
> *My television set has a good picture but weak audio.*

Audio is also often used in combination with other words. Make

90-SECOND QUICKIE QUIZ

FOR WOMEN ONLY

Can you match the type of man in the left-hand column with his description in the right-hand column? Answers follow.

1. **tycoon** [tī·kōōn′]	(a) smoothly pleasant; ingratiating.
2. **suave** [swäv]	(b) a gruff, irritable old man.
3. **philanderer** [fi·lan′dər·ər]	(c) a rake or seducer.
4. **lout** [lout]	(d) an awkward, rough fellow.
5. **curmudgeon** [kər·muj′ən]	(e) an idler or loafer.
6. **Don Juan** [don wän′]	(f) a courtly gentleman; gallant
7. **cavalier** [kav′ə·lir′]	(g) a handsome man.
8. **wastrel** [wās′trəl]	(h) a fickle suitor.
9. **debonair** [deb′ə·nâr′]	(i) a powerful businessman.
10. **Adonis** [ə·don′is]	(j) nonchalant; urbane.

ANSWERS:

1. **tycoon**—(i) a powerful businessman. 2. **suave**—(a) smoothly pleasant; ingratiating. 3. **philanderer**—(h) a fickle suitor. 4. **lout**—(d) an awkward, rough fellow. 5. **curmudgeon**—(b) a gruff, irritable old man. 6. **Don Juan** —(c) a rake or seducer. 7. **cavalier**—(f) a courtly gentleman; gallant. 8. **wastrel**—(e) an idler or loafer. 9. **debonair**—(j) nonchalant; urbane. 10. **Adonis**—(g) a handsome man.

vocabulary building a lifetime habit. Look up the following words in your dictionary. Do you see how they are all based on the word *audio?*

audiology	audio-visual
audiometer	audiophile

audition is made up of *audit-* meaning "to hear" and the Latin suffix *-ion* meaning "the act of, state of, or result of." Thus, *audition* means "the act of hearing something or someone," and especially "a hearing that serves as a test or trial, as of a singer or any actor trying out for a part."

> *The actress was late for her audition.*
> *The tenor auditioned for a role in the opera.*

auditor is made up of *audit-* meaning "to hear" and the Latin suffix *-or* meaning "one who or that which does something." An *auditor* is "one who hears; a hearer or listener."

He was an attentive auditor at the lecture.

Auditor also has the meaning of "one who examines accounts, verifies balance sheets, and the like." In this sense, an *auditor* inspects (that is, gives a hearing to) statements of account.

Mr. James was an auditor for an accounting firm.

auditorium comes from *audit-* meaning "to hear" and the Latin suffix *-orium* meaning "a place for." Thus, an *auditorium* is "a place for hearing; a building or room for concerts, plays, public meetings, etc."

The play was presented in the high-school auditorium.

ROOT: AUT-, AUTO-

The Greek root *aut-* or *auto-* means "self." This root appears in a large number of English words. Its basic meaning is always "self," although sometimes you may have to analyze the entire word carefully to see how the meaning "self" enters into it. Four of the common core *auto-* words are given below: *autocrat, autograph, automatic, automobile.* Be sure that you learn these and the words based on them.

autocrat comes from the Greek roots *auto-* meaning "self" and *-crat* meaning "rule; power." An *autocrat* is "a ruler with unrestricted power"; hence, "any arrogant, dictatorial person."

Grandfather was quite an autocrat at the dinner table.

A word based on *autocrat* is *autocracy,* meaning (1) rule by an autocrat; (2) a state ruled by an autocrat.

Under Hadrian, Rome was an autocracy.

autograph derives from *auto-* meaning "self" and the Greek root *-graph* meaning "a writing." An *autograph* is "the signature or handwriting of a particular person"; that is, "the handwriting of the person himself." To *autograph* something is "to sign one's own signature to it" or "to write it in one's own handwriting."

She stood in line to get the singer's autograph.
The singer autographed the program for her.

A word based on *autograph* is *autography* [ô·tog′rə·fē], meaning "the writing of a document in one's own handwriting."

automatic comes from *auto-* meaning "self" plus the Greek root *matic-* meaning "acting; moving." Thus, *automatic* means "acting by itself; self-moving; self-regulating, like a machine."

The clothes dryer is automatic.

Two words related to *automatic* are *automat*, meaning "a restaurant in which food is made available automatically from a receptacle," and *automation*, meaning "an automatic operation or automatic production, as in a factory in which labor is performed by machines."

With increased automation, workers will need to work fewer hours.

automobile comes from *auto-* meaning "self" and the Latin word *mobile* meaning "moving." An *automobile* is literally "a self-propelled or self-moving vehicle."

ROOTS: BENE-, BENIGN-

These two Latin roots look alike and are closely related in meaning. They can be learned together. The Latin root *bene-* means "well; good." Here are six core vocabulary words in which *bene-* appears: *benefactor, benefit, benevolent, benediction, beneficial, beneficiary.*

benefactor comes from *bene-* meaning "well; good" plus the Latin word *factor* meaning "a person who does." Thus, a *benefactor* is "a person who does good; a patron; a backer."

Mr. Smith, the banker, is a benefactor of the museum.

benefit derives from *bene-* meaning "well; good" and *-fit* which comes from the Latin root *fac-* meaning "to do." Thus, a *benefit* is "a good deed; an act of kindness" or it may be "that which does someone good; an advantage." To *benefit* is "to help or profit."

The club gave the dance as a benefit to raise money for charity.
What are the benefits of learning new words?
I benefited from your advice.

benevolent is made up of *bene-* meaning "well; good" and the Latin *volent-* meaning "wishing; willing." Thus, *benevolent* means "well-wishing; disposed to do good; kindly."

The women formed a local Benevolent Aid Society.
The teacher has a benevolent attitude toward his students.

benediction comes from *bene-* meaning "well; good" and the Latin root *dic-* meaning "to say" plus the suffix *-ion* meaning "the act of." Thus, *benediction* means "the act of blessing, as at the close of religious worship; the calling down of divine favor on a person."

The priest gave the people his benediction.

beneficial comes from *bene-* meaning "well; good" and the Latin root *fic-* meaning "to do; make" plus the suffix *-ial* meaning "of; pertaining to." Thus, *beneficial* means "of or pertaining to that which does good; helpful; advantageous."

Sleep and proper food are beneficial to health.

beneficiary is formed from *bene-* meaning "well; good" and the Latin root *fic-* meaning "to do; make" plus the suffix *-ary* meaning "a person connected with." Thus, *beneficiary* means "a person connected with benefits"; that is, "a person who receives benefits or advantages from something."

He was the beneficiary of his father's life-insurance policy.

The Latin root *benign-* is a combination of *bene-* meaning "well" and the root *gen-* meaning "born." In English, *benign* is a word in itself, meaning "kind; kindly; gentle; mild; favorable." Hence, those who are *benign* are "well-born" in the sense of being kind and gentle in their treatment of others. A *benign* tumor is "mild" or "favorable" in the sense of being curable.

The benign old gentleman reminded her of her grandfather.

Fun With Words

REVIEW OF ROOTS

The best way to remember what you have learned is by review tests and actual practice. You have already learned all the roots and key words listed below. How well can you score on this review test? Choose the answer which is closest in meaning to each of the key words. Answers follow.

1. **inactive** [in·ak′tiv]—(a) passed into law. (b) containing charcoal. (c) not engaged in activity; idle. (d) in action; working.
2. **enact** [in·akt′]—(a) to be in action, to work. (b) to perform between two acts of a play. (c) to make into a law. (d) to do or perform again.
3. **interact** [in′ter·akt′]—(a) to act on each other. (b) to perform between two acts of a play. (c) to interrupt. (d) to be angry.
4. **react** [rē·akt′]—(a) to give off atomic rays. (b) to explode. (c) to be startled or surprised. (d) to act in response to something.
5. **transact** [trans·akt′ or tranz·akt′] —(a) to carry through; accomplish. (b) to sin. (c) to give or carry to someone else. (d) to move from one place to another quickly.
6. **matriarchy** [mā′trē·är′kē]—(a) a country, tribe, or family ruled by

a man or by male heirs. (b) a country, tribe, or family ruled by a woman or by female heirs. (c) lawless confusion and political disorder. (d) patriotic feelings.
7. **patriarchy** [pā′trē·är′ke]—(a) a country, tribe, or family ruled by a male or by male heirs. (b) a country, tribe, or family ruled by an elderly person. (c) lawless confusion and political disorder. (d) patriotic feelings.
8. **acuity** [ə·kyōō′ə·tē]—(a) bitterness; sharpness of taste. (b) an overabundance. (c) a lack or deficit. (d) acuteness, sharpness.
9. **acumen** [ə·kyōō′mən or ak′yōō·mən]—(a) bitterness; sharp in taste. (b) quickness of insight; keenness of intellect. (c) an overabundance. (d) a lack or deficit.
10. **enamored** [in·am′ərd]—(a) wearing protective armor. (b) inflamed with love; charmed. (c) conceited. (d) shy; modest.

ANSWERS:

1. **inactive**—(c) not engaged in activity; idle. 2. **enact**—(c) to make into a law. 3. **interact**—(a) to act on each other. 4. **react**—(d) to act in response to something. 5. **transact**—(a) to carry through; accomplish. 6. **matriarchy** —(b) a country, tribe, or family ruled by a woman or by female heirs. 7. **patriarchy**—(a) a country, tribe, or family ruled by a male or male heirs. 8. **acuity**—(d) acuteness, sharpness. 9. **acumen**—(b) quickness of insight; keenness of intellect. 10. **enamored**—(b) inflamed with love; charmed.

ROOT: BIO-

The Greek root *bio-* means "life." Learn the following three core vocabulary words based on *bio-*: *biochemistry, biography, biology.*

biochemistry comes from *bio-* meaning "life" and the word *chemistry.* Thus, *biochemistry* means "the branch of chemistry relating to the processes and physical properties of living organisms."

We plan to study biochemistry at college.

A word based on *biochemistry* is *biochemist,* meaning "a specialist in biochemistry."

biography is made up of *bio-* meaning "life" and the Greek suffix *-graphy* meaning "a writing." Thus, *biography* means "a writing about a life; a written account of a person's life."

This biography of President Kennedy is a best seller.

Three words based on *biography* are *autobiography,* meaning "a biography of a person written by the person himself," *biographer,* meaning "a writer of biography," and *biographical,* meaning "of or concerning a person's life."

Benjamin Franklin wrote a famous autobiography in which he describes his struggles to rise in the world.
The teacher gave a brief biographical account of the author we were studying.

biology comes from *bio-* meaning "life" and the Greek suffix *-logy* meaning "the science or study of." Thus, *biology* means "the science of life in all its manifestations, and of the origin, structure, reproduction, growth, and development of living organisms."

Zoology (the study of animals) and botany (the study of plants) are the main divisions of biology.

Two words based on *biology* are *biological* and *biologist. Biological* means (1) of or pertaining to biology; (2) used for or produced by biological research. *Biologist* means "a specialist in biology."

Biological warfare makes use of germs or bacteria that destroy life.
My uncle is a biologist at the state university.

ROOT: CAD-, CID-, CAS-

The Latin root *cad-*, *cid-*, or *cas-* means "to fall; befall; happen by chance." Even though it has three spellings, this is one root. This root is used to form several basic words in English. Learn the following six core vocabulary words and the words based on them: *accident, casual, decadent, incident, occident, occasion.*

accident is the most obvious *cid-* word. It comes from the Latin prefix *ad-* or *ac-* meaning "to; upon" and the root *cid-* meaning "to fall; befall; happen by chance" plus the Latin suffix *-ent*, which is the same as the English suffix *-ing.* Thus, *accident* means "something that happens to someone by chance; an unexpected happening without a cause or plan; a chance; a mishap."

> *He was hurt in the automobile accident.*
> *Our meeting wasn't planned; it was just an accident.*

casual comes from *cas-* meaning "to fall; befall; happen by chance" and the suffix *-al* meaning "of; like; pertaining to." Thus, *casual* means "like that which happens by chance; offhand; informal; not planned or serious."

> *He has a relaxed, casual manner.*
> *He was just a casual acquaintance.*
> *He wore casual clothing.*

A word based on *casual* is *casualty,* meaning (1) a person or thing that is hurt or destroyed by chance, as in an accident; (2) an accident.

> *How many highway casualties were there last weekend?*

decadent derives from the Latin prefix *de-* meaning "down" and the root *cad-* meaning "to fall" plus the suffix *-ent*, which is the same as the English suffix *-ing.* Thus, *decadent* means "falling into ruin; falling down morally; declining; decaying."

> *Roman society became decadent before the fall of the Empire.*

A word related to *decadent* is *decay,* meaning (1) a falling into ruin; (2) to decline, rot, or decompose.

> *There is decay in this tooth.*
> *The tooth had decayed badly before Sam saw his dentist.*

incident comes from the Latin prefix *in-* meaning "on; upon" and *cid-* meaning "to fall; happen by chance" plus the suffix *-ent*, which is the same as the English suffix *-ing*. Thus, *incident* means "something that happened (fell on a particular person or happened at a particular time); an event or occurrence."

> *The old man told about an interesting incident in his past.*
> *An incident at the border of the two countries led to war.*

Three words based on *incident* are *incidence, incidental,* and *incidentally*. *Incidence* means "the degree of occurrence; the frequency with which something happens." *Incidental* means "occurring in the course of something else; secondary; casual." *Incidentally* means "by the way."

> *There is a high incidence of crime here.*
> *You will have incidental expenses besides your plane fare.*
> *Incidentally, how old are you?*

occident comes from the Latin prefix *oc-* meaning "toward" and the root *cid-* meaning "to fall" plus the suffix *-ent*, which is the same as the English *-ing*. Thus, *occident* means "that which is toward the falling (or setting) sun"; hence, "the West; the Western Hemisphere." (For the use of capital letters in these words, see the section on punctuation in this book.)

> *The Occident is the opposite of the Orient.*

A word based on *occident* is *occidental*, which means "of or belonging to the West; belonging to the countries in the Western Hemisphere." It may also mean "a person born or living in a Western country."

> *Europe and America are Occidental continents.*
> *Marco Polo was an Occidental who visited the Orient.*

occasion is made up of the Latin prefix *oc-* meaning "toward" and *cas-* meaning "to fall." *Occasion* originally meant "a falling toward, as an opportunity"; it now means "a favorable time, the time of an event, the event itself, or the reason for it."

> *This seems like a good occasion for a get-together.*
> *She was happy on the occasion of her marriage.*
> *The wedding was quite an occasion.*
> *What, sir, is the occasion for this visit?* (This is *very* formal English.)

A word based on *occasion* is *occasional,* which means (1) happening irregularly or now and then; (2) suiting a particular occasion; (3) small and not part of a set.

> *He made an occasional trip abroad.*
> *He wrote an occasional poem in honor of the queen's birthday.*
> *This is my favorite occasional chair.*

ROOT: CAP-, CAPT-, CIP-, CEPT-, CEIV-

The Latin root *cap-, capt-, cip-, cept-,* or *ceiv-* means "to take; seize." All these various spellings make up just one root. The differing spellings are the result of linguistic history. For example, the spelling *ceiv-* is different from the others because it came into English through French, instead of directly from Latin. Thus, whenever you see a word with *ceiv-* in it, see if you can relate it to a similar word with *cip-* or *cept-*.

Below are six core vocabulary words based on this root: *capable, capture, deceive, except, incipient, receive.* Learn them all, along with the many other words related to them.

capable comes from *cap-* meaning "to take" and the Latin suffix *-able,* which means "able." Thus, *capable* literally means "able to take." Hence, it means "having ability; having the qualities needed for something."

> *Are you capable of solving this problem?*
> *Dr. Smith is a capable dentist.*

Three words based on *capable* are *capability,* meaning "ability; competence"; *capably,* meaning "in a capable manner; skillfully"; and *incapable,* which means "unable or incompetent."

> *No one doubts his capability as a dentist.*
> *The doctor performed the operation capably.*
> *He is incapable of solving the problem.*

capture is made up of *capt-* meaning "to take; seize" and the Latin suffix -*ure* meaning "the act or result of." Thus, *capture* means "the act or result of seizing; a seizure." It also means "to gain, win, or take by force."

> *The capture of the enemy town was a great victory.*
> *The police captured the thief.*
> *The contestants all tried hard to capture the prize.*

QUICKIEQUIZQUICKIEQUIZQUICKIEQUIZQUICKIEQUIZQUICKIEQUIZQUICKIEQUIZQUICKIEQUIZQUICKIE

90-SECOND QUICKIE QUIZ
RECOGNIZING ROOTS

Knowing the meanings of roots can help you to understand many words. Can you match these basic word elements with their meanings? Answers follow.

1. **pyro-** as in pyromaniac [pī′rō·mā′nē·ak]	(a) father
2. **patri-** as in patriarch [pā′trē·ärk]	(b) sleep
3. **pod-** as in podium [pō′dē·əm]	(c) fire
4. **socio-** as in sociology [sō′sē·ol′ə·jē]	(d) cut
5. **psycho-** as in psychoanalysis [sī′kō·ə·nal′ə·sis]	(e) foot
6. **phono-** as in phonograph [fō′nə·graf]	(f) false
7. **toxico-** as in toxicology [tok′sə·kol′ə·jē]	(g) mind
8. **somni-** as in somniferous [som·nif′ər·əs]	(h) sound
9. **-sect** as in bisect [bī·sekt′]	(i) poison
10. **pseudo-** as in pseudonym [sōō′də·nim]	(j) society

ANSWERS:

1. **pyro-** — (c) fire. A pyromaniac is a person who feels a compulsion to set things on fire.
2. **patri-** — (a) father. A patriarch is the fatherlike leader of a family, tribe, or race.
3. **pod-** — (e) foot. A podium is a small platform on which a speaker stands.
4. **socio-** — (j) society. Sociology is the science that studies human society.
5. **psycho-** — (g) mind. Psychoanalysis is concerned with the study of mental states.
6. **phono-** — (h) sound. A phonograph reproduces sound from a record.
7. **toxico-** — (i) poison. Toxicology is the science that treats of the detection, nature, and properties of poisons.
8. **somni-** — (b) sleep. Somniferous means tending to produce sleep, as certain drugs.
9. **-sect** — (d) cut. Bisect means to cut in two.
10. **pseudo-** — (f) false. A pseudonym is a fictitious name.

QUICKIEQUIZQUICKIEQUIZQUICKIEQUIZQUICKIEQUIZQUICKIEQUIZQUICKIEQUIZQUICKIEQUIZQUICKIE

Four words related to or based on *capture* are *captor, captive, captivity,* and *captivate*. A *captor* is "a person who takes a captive." *Captive* means (1) a person who is captured; (2) taken or held prisoner. *Captivity* is "the state of being held captive." *Captivate* means "to capture by means of charm; fascinate."

> *The prisoner was freed by his captors.*
> *The captive escaped.*
> *The doctor was held captive by the kidnapers.*
> *The circus owned the largest elephant in captivity.*
> *Harvey was captivated by Rhoda's smile.*

deceive comes from the Latin prefix *de-* meaning "away; down" and *ceiv-* meaning "to take." Thus, *deceive* means "to take away from the truth"; that is, "to mislead; trick; lead astray."

> *He was deceived by the friendliness of the thief.*

Four of the many words related to or based on *deceive* are *deceit, deceitful, deception,* and *deceptive*. *Deceit* means (1) the act of deceiving; (2) a trick; (3) falseness. *Deceitful* means "given to deceiving; treacherous; lying." *Deception* means "deceit." *Deceptive* means "having a tendency to deceive."

> *He was the victim of his friend's deceit.*
> *She is known as a very deceitful person.*
> *The magician fooled us with his quick deception.*
> *The surface of a highway can be deceptive in the rain.*

except is formed from the Latin prefix *ex-* meaning "out" and *cept-* meaning "to take." Thus, *except* means "taking out"; that is, "leaving out; omitting."

> *Everyone is going except me.*

Three words based on *except* are *exception, exceptional,* and *exceptionally*. *Exception* means (1) something excluded from a general rule or agreement; (2) an objection or criticism. *Exceptional* means "unusually good." *Exceptionally* means "uncommonly; extremely."

> *Your brothers are lazy, but you're an exception.*
> *He took exception to the announced plans.*
> *John is an exceptional student.*
> *This is an exceptionally cold day.*

incipient comes from the Latin prefix *in-* meaning "in" and *cip-* meaning "to take" plus the suffix *-ent,* which is the same as the English *-ing.* Thus, *incipient* means "taking into existence"; that is, "coming into existence; just beginning to be or to appear."

He has incipient influenza.

Two words based on *incipient* are *incipience,* which means "in the early state or beginning of something," and *inception,* meaning "the beginning or start."

The incipience of our trouble dates back to World War II.
He has worked for the company since its inception.

receive derives from the Latin prefix *re-* meaning "back" and *ceiv-* meaning "to take." Thus, *receive* means "to take back toward oneself; take into one's possession; get."

I received a letter from Wayne.
The Ti-Cats will kick off and the Stampeders will receive.

Six of the very many words related to or based on *receive* are *receiver, receipt, reception, receptionist, receptacle,* and *receptive. Receiver* means "a person or thing that receives." A *receipt* is "a written acknowledgment of something received." *Reception* means (1) the act or manner of receiving; (2) a formal social entertainment of guests. A *receptionist* is "a person who receives callers in an office." A *receptacle* is "something that contains (or receives) something else." *Receptive* means "able to or inclined to receive."

He acted as a receiver of stolen goods.
Here is the receipt for your money.
Were you given a cordial reception?
We have an attractive receptionist in the front office.
Put the garbage in the trash receptacle.
He is receptive to new ideas.

◊ There are still other words based on the root *cap-, capt-, cip-, cept-,* or *ceiv-.* Look up the following words in your dictionary. Notice how the root always means "to take or seize." Learn the meanings of these words and check their definitions against their etymologies in the dictionary. Can you see the relationship between the way these words are built and what they mean?

accept	conceive	concept	conception

EXPLORING WORDS

For better or for worse, people have given their names to many common words. Sometimes the reasons are scientific or practical, and sometimes not so serious. Here are nine words that grew from personal names, some famous and some forgotten.

August the eighth month of the year. Named after Augustus Caesar.

bloomers women's loose, baggy trousers drawn close at the ankles and worn under a short skirt, or a woman's undergarment resembling these. Bloomers were named after Mrs. Amelia Jenks Bloomer (1818–94), an American champion of women's rights.

bobby a British policeman. This word, the familiar form of Robert, came into use after Sir Robert Peel set up the police system in London early in the nineteenth century. These London policemen were first called "Bobby's men" and later just "bobbies."

bowdlerize to censor any kind of writing in a prudish manner. The word immortalizes an English editor, Dr. Thomas Bowdler, who produced a "family" edition (1818) of the works of Shakespeare by removing every word or passage that offended his sense of propriety.

boycott to refuse, as a group, to buy from or have any dealings with a person or organization, in order to reduce prices or bring about some change; also, an instance of this. The word comes from C. C. Boycott, a British army officer and landlord's agent in Ireland in the nineteenth century, who was the first victim of boycotting because of his unpopularity among tenants from whom he collected rents.

chauvinism militant glorification of one's country; vain patriotism. After Nicholas Chauvin, a devoted soldier and overzealous supporter of Napoleon Bonaparte.

dahlia A flower that takes its name from Anders Dahl, the eighteenth-century Swedish botanist who developed it.

epicure a person given to discriminating luxury; a fastidious devotee of good food and drink; a gourmet. After the Greek philosopher Epicurus, who taught that peace of mind, cultural interests, and a discriminating temperance in sensual pleasure lead to the good life.

guillotine a machine used for beheading a person by means of a heavy knife that drops between two posts. It was named after J. I. Guillotin, a French physician, who developed it. It was used especially on victims of the French Revolution.

41

ROOT: CED-, CEDE-, CEED-, CESS-

The Latin root *ced-*, *cede-*, *ceed-*, or *cess-* means "to go; yield." This root is used in many common and important English words. When you learn that words having *ced-*, *cede-*, *ceed-*, or *cess-* in them are closely related in meaning, you will be able to expand your vocabulary quickly. Here are nine core *ced-*, *cede-*, *ceed-*, or *cess-* words: *antecedent, concede, exceed, excess, precede, proceed, process, recede, recess.*

antecedent comes from the Latin prefix *ante-* meaning "before" and *ced-* meaning "to go" plus the Latin suffix *-ent*, which is the same as the English suffix *-ing*. Thus, *antecedent* means "going before" or "someone or something that goes before or precedes."

> *Henry IV was antecedent to Henry V.*
> *The Wright brothers' airplane was the antecedent of modern airplanes.*
> *A pronoun often has a noun as an antecedent.*

concede is formed from the Latin prefix *con-* meaning "thoroughly" and *cede-* meaning "to go; yield." Thus, *concede* means "to yield completely; give up." It also means "to grant; admit; acknowledge as true."

> *He was so far ahead in the chess game that his opponent conceded.*
> *Mary conceded that Susan had been right.*

A word based on *concede* is *concession*, meaning (1) the act of conceding; (2) something granted or admitted as true; (3) the right to operate a subsidiary business on certain premises, or the business so operated.

> *Both sides made concessions in order to reach an agreement.*
> *The tobacco store in the lobby is a concession.*

exceed comes from the Latin prefix *ex-* meaning "beyond" and *ceed-* meaning "to go." Thus, *exceed* means "to go beyond; surpass."

> *Your spending should not exceed your income.*

A word based on *exceed* is *exceedingly*, meaning "extremely."

> *This is an exceedingly good steak.*

excess is made up of *ex-* meaning "beyond" and *cess-* meaning "to go." Thus, *excess* means (1) a going beyond what is necessary or proper; (2) an immoderate amount; (3) a surplus. It also means "surplus; extra; excessive."

> *Avoid excess in all things.*
> *The government imposed an excess-profits tax.*
> *You must get rid of that excess weight.*

A word based on *excess* is *excessive*, meaning "too much or too great; extreme; inordinate."

> *There was an excessive amount of traffic last weekend.*

precede comes from the Latin prefix *pre-* meaning "before" and *cede-* meaning "to go." Thus, *precede* means "to go before or in front of."

> *A precedes B in the alphabet.*
> *Soldiers preceded the President in the parade.*
> *The nineteenth century preceded the twentieth.*

Two words based on *precede* are *precedence,* which means "the act or right of going before; priority"; and *precedent,* meaning "a past act or instance that can be used as a guide for future actions."

> *Work takes precedence over play.*
> *The rulings of the Supreme Court often establish legal precedents.*

proceed comes from the Latin prefix *pro-* meaning "forward" and *ceed-* meaning "to go." Thus, *proceed* means "to go on or go forward, especially after a stop; continue." It also means "to begin and carry on an action."

> *If there are no further questions, I shall proceed with the lecture.*
> *The lawyer proceeded to cross-examine the witness.*

Five words based on *proceed* are *proceeding, proceedings, proceeds, procedure,* and *procedural. Proceeding* means "a course of continuing action." *Proceedings* are "the records or minutes of the activities of a meeting; courtroom activities." *Proceeds* [prō′sēdz] are "the useful or material results of an action or course; the return or yield." *Procedure* means (1) manner of proceeding or going forward; (2) a course of action. *Procedural* means "of or pertaining to procedure."

> *That was a strange proceeding on his part.*
> *The secretary copied the proceedings of the last meeting.*

The proceedings in the court went on and on.
Our financial proceeds from the transaction were good.
What procedure do you follow in getting a driver's license?
There were many small procedural details.

BEWARE: Do not confuse *precede* and *proceed*. *Precede* contains *pre-* meaning "before," and means "to go before or in front of." *Proceed* contains *pro-* meaning "forward," and means "to go forward; continue or begin."

process is formed from the Latin prefix *pro-* meaning "forward" and *cess-* meaning "to go." Thus, *process* means (1) a forward movement or ongoing operation; (2) a method of producing something; (3) a series of actions that bring about a result.

The baking process takes forty minutes.
What is the process used for mining coal?
Do you understand the process of growth?

Process may also mean "to subject to a routine procedure."

Please process this application without delay.

Two words based on *process* are *procession,* meaning "a parade or continued forward movement of people, vehicles, or events"; and *processional,* which means (1) of or pertaining to a procession; (2) the music played or sung during a procession.

The wedding procession entered the church.
What is the name of the processional hymn?

recede comes from the Latin prefix *re-* meaning "back" and *cede-* meaning "to go." Thus, *recede* means "to go back; withdraw."

The waters receded after the flood.

A word based on *recede* is *receding,* which means "going or sloping back."

He has a receding hairline.

recess is made up of the Latin prefix *re-* meaning "back" and *cess-* meaning "to go." *Recess* literally means "a going back." Hence, a *recess* is "an indentation or cavity" or "a time of withdrawal." To *recess* is "to withdraw for a time."

` *She put her umbrella in a recess near the door.*

The court recess lasted for two hours.
The court recessed for two hours.

Two words based on *recess* are *recession* and *recessional. Recession* means (1) the act of receding; (2) a withdrawal from an economic peak; an economic setback; a slight depression. *Recessional* means (1) pertaining to a recession; (2) a hymn sung as the choir and clergy exit from the church.

The recession resulted in increased unemployment.
Kipling's "Recessional" is a splendid hymn.

There are many other words based on the root *ced-, cede-, ceed-,* or *cess-.* In all of them *ced-, cede-, ceed-,* or *cess-* means "to go; yield."

How good are you becoming at figuring out the meanings of words? For example, *inter-* means "between" and you know that *cede-* means "to go." Thus, if you did not know that *intercede* meant "to go between," especially "to mediate between two parties in a dispute," could you work out its meaning? Could you figure out that *intercession* means "a going between" or "an act of mediating between two parties"?

◊ Here is a list of *ced-, cede-, ceed-, cess-* words to practice on. Look them up in your dictionary and learn their meanings. Check the definitions of these words against their etymologies. Can you see how the words are built—how roots, prefixes, and suffixes affect their meanings?

abscess	intercede	succeed
accede	intercession	success
access	secede	successful
accessory	secession	succession

ROOT: CENT-

The Latin root *cent-* means "one hundred." Learn the following four core vocabulary words based on *cent-: centenary, centipede, century, percent.*

centenary comes from the root *cent-* meaning "one hundred" and the Latin suffix *-ary* meaning "pertaining to." Thus, *centenary* means "pertaining to a hundred; marking a period of a hundred years;

45

lasting for a hundred years; occurring every hundred years." It may also mean "a one-hundredth anniversary."

We planned a centenary celebration for our company.

centipede derives from *cent-* meaning "one hundred" and the Latin root *-pede* meaning "foot." Thus, *centipede* literally means "a creature with a hundred feet," although in fact this is an exaggeration.

BEWARE: Though *cent-* in *centipede* does mean "one hundred," the scientific root *centi-* means "one-hundredth." In any terms taken from the metric system, *centi-* means "a hundredth," not "a hundred." Look up *centimeter* (a hundredth of a meter) in your dictionary. Be sure not to confuse the meaning of *centi-* in the metric system with the root *cent-*.

century comes from a Latin word based on *cent-* meaning "one hundred." *Century* means "one hundred consecutive years," or "a period of a hundred years."

We live in the twentieth century.
Columbus lived more than four centuries ago.

percent comes directly from a Latin phrase meaning "by the hundred." *Percent* means "the number of parts in every hundred of something specified; hundredths."

More than 50 percent of the people are women.

Two words based on *percent* are *percentage* and *percentile*. *Percentage* means (1) the rate or proportion of anything per hundred; (2) a proportion in general. *Percentile* means "any in a series of one hundred points on a scale, each of which denotes the percentage of the total cases lying below it in the scale."

What percentage of the population is under thirty-five years of age?
Only a small percentage of the class attended the concert.
His College Board scores are in the second percentile.

◊ Here is a list of some less familiar *cent-* words to look up in your dictionary. Check the definitions against the etymologies. Can you see how the root *cent-* affects the meanings of the words?

centenarian	centurion
centuple	sesquicentennial

MORE KEY ROOTS

The following thirteen words contain important roots. Choose the word or phrase you believe is closest in meaning to the key word. Answers follow.

1. **antithesis** [an·tith′ə·sis]—(a) an expository essay. (b) the direct opposite. (c) the subject. (d) a tentative theory.

2. **antidote** [an′ti·dōt]—(a) an amusing story. (b) opposition to a plan or idea. (c) a story about times gone by. (d) a remedy to counteract the effects of poison.

3. **adduce** [ə·dyōōs′]— (a) to find a solution to. (b) to persuade. (c) to increase. (d) to cite or allege.

4. **amity** [am′ə·tē]—(a) a pardon granted to a political prisoner. (b) a truce. (c) soundness of mind. (d) good will.

5. **antecedent** [an′tə·sēd′nt]—(a) contemporary. (b) prior. (c) a future generation. (d) conflicting.

6. **antipathy** [an·tip′ə·thē]—(a) ancient times. (b) agreement. (c) deep dislike. (d) the opposite side of the earth.

7. **acoustics** [ə·kōōs′tiks] (a) the furniture and color scheme of a room. (b) a type of word puzzle. (c) the sound-reflecting qualities of a place. (d) shrewdness.

8. **Anglophobe** [ang′glə·fōb]—(a) one who hates England. (b) one who loves England. (c) a member of the Anglo-Saxon race. (d) an instrument used in examining the eyes.

9. **annuity** [ə·nyōō′ə·tē]—(a) a flower that blooms yearly. (b) a yearly celebration. (c) a life-insurance policy. (d) a yearly allowance or income.

10. **animate** [an′ə·māt]—(a) to enrage. (b) to cause to move or work faster. (c) to describe dramatically. (d) to make more alive.

11. **accredit** [ə·kred′it]—(a) to vouch for or authorize. (b) to sell. (c) to discount. (d) to find fault with.

12. **antagonism** [an·tag′ə·niz′əm]—(a) hatred toward women. (b) hostility. (c) boredom. (d) sympathy.

13. **aural** [ôr′əl]—(a) pertaining to speech. (b) a mountain range. (c) pertaining to the ear. (d) peaceful.

ANSWERS:

1. **antithesis**—(b) the direct opposite. 2. **antidote**—(d) a remedy to counteract the effects of poison. 3. **adduce**—(d) to cite or allege. 4. **amity**—(d) good will. 5. **antecedent**—(b) prior. 6. **antipathy**—(c) deep dislike. 7. **acoustics**—(c) the sound-reflecting qualities of a place. 8. **Anglophobe**—(a) one who hates England. (An *Anglophile* loves England.) 9. **annuity**—(d) a yearly allowance or income. 10. **animate**—(d) to make more alive. 11. **accredit**—(a) to vouch for or authorize. 12. **antagonism**—(b) hostility. 13. **aural**—(c) pertaining to the ear.

ROOT: CERN-, CRET-

The Latin root *cern-* or *cret-* means "to separate; see as being different; distinguish." Learn the three core vocabulary words based on this root —*concern, discern, secret*—and the additional words derived from them.

concern comes from the Latin prefix *con-* meaning "thoroughly" and *cern-* meaning "to see; distinguish." Thus, *concern* literally means "to see thoroughly in the mind." In practice, it may mean "to involve oneself" or "to relate to or affect." It may also mean "interest or worry" or "a business enterprise or firm."

> *He was concerned with improving himself.*
> *Don't concern yourself with small details.*
> *Emma expressed concern about Bob's health.*
> *What is the name of that new manufacturing concern?*

A word based on *concern* is *concerning,* which means "regarding; about."

> *The customer wrote to us concerning his bill.*

discern is made up of the Latin prefix *dis-* meaning "apart" and *cern-* meaning "to separate." Thus, *discern* means "to recognize as separate or apart from everything else; to perceive."

> *It was hard to discern the right road in the dark.*
> *Having seen through the lies, can you discern the truth?*

Three words based on *discern* are *discernible,* meaning "capable of being discerned; perceptible"; *discerning,* which means "quick to discern; discriminating; perceptive"; and *discernment,* meaning "insight."

> *There is no discernible difference between these two hats.*
> *Einstein had a discerning mind.*
> *Dr. Smith is a man of great discernment.*

NOTE: Two other words are based directly on *discern: discreet,* meaning "careful not to do or say the wrong thing; tactful"; and *discrete,* meaning "separated from others; distinct; totally different." You can tell they are related to *discern* by their roots. Learn the difference between these two words.

He maintained a discreet silence.
Sand is composed of tiny discrete grains of rocklike material.

secret is formed from the Latin prefix *se-* meaning "apart" and *cret-* meaning "to separate." Thus, a *secret* is "something separated or kept apart from others; something kept hidden; something not told or not to be revealed." *Secret* also means "concealed; hidden."

Don't tell your friend's secret.
This house is supposed to have a secret door.

Three words based on *secret* are *secretary*, meaning literally "a person who, dealing with the paperwork of an individual or business, can be trusted to keep business secrets"; *secretarial*, meaning "of or pertaining to a secretary or a secretary's work"; and *secretive*, which means "inclined to secrecy; close-mouthed."

The job involves some secretarial duties.
Mr. Thornton is unusually secretive about his business affairs.

ROOT: CLAM-, CLAIM-

The Latin root *clam-* or *claim-* means "to cry out; shout." Learn the three core vocabulary words based on this root—*declaim, exclaim, proclaim*—and the additional words derived from them.

declaim comes from the Latin prefix *de-* meaning "completely," and *claim-* meaning to "cry out; shout." Thus, *declaim* means "to cry out" or "to speak loudly and fully"; hence, "to give a formal speech, as opposed to speaking informally or softly."

The politician declaimed his speech to a large audience.

Two words based on *declaim* are *declamation*, meaning "a prepared, formal speech," and *declamatory*, meaning "characterized by declamation; bombastic."

The mayor delivered a long anniversary declamation.
What a boring, declamatory speech!

exclaim comes from the Latin prefix *ex-* meaning "out" and *claim-*

meaning "to cry out; shout." Thus, *exclaim* means "to cry out suddenly."

> *"Look! Look!" he exclaimed.*

Two words based on *exclaim* are *exclamation* and *exclamatory*. *Exclamation* means (1) a sudden cry or shout; (2) a phrase or sentence that expresses surprise, shock, fear, or otherwise serves as a cry or shout. *Exclamatory* means "pertaining to or expressing surprise, shock, fear, etc."

> *He gave an exclamation of surprise.*
> *The speech was full of angry, exclamatory sentences.*

An exclamation mark (!) is used to end an *exclamatory* sentence or phrase in writing, showing that it is to be read as a cry or shout or is to carry emphasis.

proclaim is made up of the Latin prefix *pro-* meaning "before" and *claim-* meaning "to cry out." Thus, *proclaim* means "to cry something out before the people; make known before the public; announce; make clear."

> *The President proclaimed a national holiday.*
> *His manner proclaimed his innocence.*

A word based on *proclaim* is *proclamation*, meaning "a public announcement."

> *The dying King issued a royal proclamation.*
> *The rooster's crowing is a proclamation of daybreak.*

◊ Words that have the root *clam-* or *claim-* always have a meaning that relates to declaring something—to crying out, speaking out, or saying something in a certain way. For example, the prefix *re-* means "back." From this hint you could guess that *reclaim* means something like "to call back." Now look up the definition of *reclaim* in your dictionary. Is the meaning of *reclaim* related to calling back something? Look up the following list of words in your dictionary. Learn the meanings of these words and then read their etymologies. Can you see how the meanings of these words are built up from their prefixes and roots?

acclaim	clamorous	proclaimer
acclamation	disclaim	proclamatory
clamor	disclaimer	reclamation

ROOT: CLUD-, CLUS-, CLOS-

The Latin root *clud-*, *clus-*, or *clos-* means "to shut; close." Learn the six core vocabulary words based on this root: *conclude, disclose, enclose, exclude, include, preclude.*

conclude comes from the Latin prefix *con-* meaning "thoroughly" and *clud-* meaning "to shut." Thus, *conclude* literally means "to shut off thoroughly." Hence, it means (1) to bring to an end or finish; (2) to settle or decide.

> *The speaker concluded her speech in ten minutes.*
> *From the evidence, they concluded that the suspect was guilty.*

Two words based on *conclude* are *conclusion*, meaning "the end of something; a final outcome or decision"; and *conclusive*, which means "putting an end to doubt; decisive."

> *He left at the conclusion of the meeting.*
> *After seeing the evidence, what's your conclusion?*
> *The judge's ruling was conclusive.*

disclose comes from the Latin prefix *dis-* meaning "not" and *clos-* meaning "to shut." Thus, *disclose* literally means "not to shut." Hence, it means "to expose to view; reveal; make known to the public."

> *Please disclose everything you know about the incident.*
> *The Premier will disclose his new tax program tonight.*

A word based on *disclose* is *disclosure*, which means either "the act of disclosing or making known to the public," or "that which is disclosed or revealed."

> *The disclosure that he was a fraud forced him to leave town.*
> *The witness's disclosure helped to convict the defendant.*

enclose is formed from the Latin prefix *en-* meaning "in" and *clos-* meaning "to shut." Thus, *enclose* means (1) to shut in, fence in, or surround; (2) to put something inside an envelope, package, or other container; (3) to contain or hold.

> *The garden was enclosed by a wall.*
> *I am enclosing my check for $27.*
> *He herded the cattle into the enclosure.*

exclude comes from the Latin prefix *ex-* meaning "out" and *clud-* meaning "to shut." Thus, *exclude* means (1) to shut out; keep from entering; bar; (2) to leave out; (3) to put out; expel.

> *The apartment building excluded pets.*
> *The guest list included the Smiths but excluded the Browns.*
> *After the scandal, he was excluded from the club.*

Five words based on *exclude* are *excludable, exclusion, exclusive, exclusively,* and *exclusiveness. Excludable* means "able to be left out." *Exclusion* means (1) the act of excluding or leaving out; (2) that which is left out or excluded. *Exclusive* means (1) leaving out many; (2) admitting only a select group; restricted to one or a few; not shared; sole. *Exclusively* means (1) in an exclusive manner; (2) solely. *Exclusiveness* is "the condition or character of being exclusive."

> *You owe no tax on your excludable income.*
> *He liked movies to the exclusion of all other amusements.*
> *He is the exclusive owner of the house.*
> *That club is very exclusive.*
> *This story is exclusively yours.*
> *That club is noted for its exclusiveness.*

include is made up of the Latin prefix *in-* meaning "in" and *clud-* meaning "to shut." Thus, *include* means "to shut into a place"; hence, (1) to place in a general group or category; (2) to contain or take in.

> *Have you included bread on the grocery list?*
> *This price includes the delivery charge.*

Three words based on *include* are *includable, inclusion,* and *inclusive. Includable* means "able to be included." *Inclusion* means (1) that which is included; (2) the act of including. *Inclusive* means "comprehensive; including all."

> *Hotel bills are includable on your expense account.*
> *Their inclusion of the newcomer was kind.*
> *All the items are covered in an inclusive list.*

preclude comes from the Latin prefix *pre-* meaning "before" and *clud-* meaning "to shut." Thus, *preclude* means "to shut out in advance; make impossible by doing something in advance; prevent."

> *The heavy rain precluded our having the picnic.*
> *Your sloppy work precludes my giving you a raise.*

Fun With Words

REVIEW OF ROOTS

Here is a review test of roots and words you have already learned. Choose the answer which is closest in meaning to each of the key words. Answers follow.

1. **accept** [ak·sept']—(a) a generalized idea, thought, or mental image. (b) a line connecting two other lines. (c) with the exclusion of; save for; but. (d) to receive with favor or consent.

2. **concept** [kon'sept]—(a) a specific idea. (b) a line connecting two other lines. (c) the circumference of a circle. (d) a generalized idea, thought, or mental image.

3. **conception** [kən·sep'shən]—(a) with the exclusion of; save for; but. (b) a beginning. (c) the circumference of a circle. (d) a specific idea.

4. **conceive** [kən·sēv']—(a) to understand; grasp. (b) to bear a child. (c) self-love. (d) a large valley.

5. **abscess** [ab'ses]—(a) admittance; a way of approach or entrance. (b) a pain in or around a tooth. (c) a collection of pus in any part of the body. (d) a

boil or blister on the skin.

6. **access** [ak'ses]—(a) too much; more than enough. (b) friendship with important people. (c) admittance; a way of approach or entrance. (d) a large valley.

7. **accessory** [ak·ses'ər·ē]—(a) a necklace. (b) a witness for the defense. (c) an amount that is too large. (d) any item added for convenience or display.

8. **accede** [ak·sēd']—(a) to agree; assent. (b) to be too much; be more than a limit. (c) to disagree; dissent. (d) to do more than one's share, as of work.

9. **secede** [si·sēd']—(a) to accomplish what is attempted. (b) to prepare ground for planting. (c) to withdraw from a union or organization. (d) to grow old.

10. **succeed** [sək·sēd']—(a) to accomplish what is attempted. (b) to prepare ground for planting. (c) to grow old. (d) to obtain wealth.

ANSWERS:

1. **accept**—(d) to receive with favor or consent. 2. **concept**—(d) a generalized idea, thought, or mental image. 3. **conception**—(b) a beginning. 4. **conceive**—(a) to understand; grasp. 5. **abscess**—(c) a collection of pus in any part of the body. 6. **access**—(c) admittance; a way of approach or entrance. 7. **accessory**—(d) any item added for convenience or display. 8. **accede**—(a) to agree, assent. 9. **secede**—(c) to withdraw from a union or organization. 10. **succeed**—(a) to accomplish what is attempted.

ROOT: CORD-

The Latin root *cord-* means "heart." Learn the following three important core vocabulary words that are based on *cord-: cordial, accord, record* and the additional words derived from them.

cordial comes from *cord-* meaning "heart" and the Latin suffix *-ial* meaning "pertaining to." Thus, *cordial* as an adjective means "pertaining to the heart"; hence, "warm and hearty; friendly and sincere." The noun *cordial* means "a stimulating drink, such as a liqueur," or "a medicine given as a stimulant for the heart or circulation."

> *We received a cordial welcome.*
> *I had a glass of blackberry cordial.*

A word based on *cordial* is *cordiality*, meaning "warmth of feeling."

> *He greeted the visitors with much cordiality.*

accord comes from the Latin prefix *ac-* (another spelling of *ad-*) meaning "to; at" and *cord-* meaning "heart." *Accord* literally means "at heart" or, as a verb, "to be of one heart or mind; to agree." It may also mean "to grant what is deserved." And as a noun it means "harmony; agreement."

> *My opinions accord with yours.*
> *The teacher accorded the student a prize.*
> *They all cheered with one accord.*
> *Our opinions are in accord.*

Three words based on *accord* are *accordance*, meaning "agreement; harmony; conformity"; *according*, which means "on the authority of; as stated by"; and *accordingly*, which can mean either (1) consequently, or (2) correspondingly.

> *I'll act in accordance with your wishes.*
> *According to the teacher, he was a good student.*
> *He was the best student and accordingly won the prize.*
> *The dinner is informal, so dress accordingly.*

record is formed from the Latin prefix *re-* meaning "back; again" and *cord-* meaning "heart." To *record* [ri·kôrd′] is "to put something in the heart or mind again, as by writing it down." Thus, *record* means

54

"to write down, as for preserving an account of something; register in permanent form." As a noun, *record* [rek'ərd] means "a written or other permanent account, as a grooved disk that reproduces sound."

Will you record your impressions of your trip?
Do you keep a record of your expenditures?
What is that record on the phonograph?

◊ Learn the meaning of the following *cord-* words from your dictionary. Read the etymology of each word and see if you can figure out how each word's meaning is based on its word-building units.

concord	concordant	discord
concordance	concordantly	discordant

ROOT: CORPOR-, CORP-

The Latin root *corpor-* or *corp-* means "body; flesh." The most obvious modern word based on this root is *corpse*, which means "the body of a dead person." Thus, the root *corpor-* or *corp-* always refers to "body" or "flesh" in one way or another. In learning the following three core vocabulary words based on this root, note carefully their proper spellings: *corpulent, corpuscle, incorporate.*

corpulent comes from *corp-* meaning "body; flesh" and the Latin suffix *-ulent* meaning "abounding in; full of." Thus, *corpulent* means "fat; fleshy."

He grew increasingly corpulent as he grew older.

A word based on *corpulent* is *corpulence*, meaning "fatness; obesity."

The corpulence of the sultan impressed his people.

corpuscle comes from *corp-* meaning "body" and the Latin suffix *-cle* meaning "little." Therefore, a *corpuscle* is literally "a little body," and the word means "one of the small particles (or little bodies) that form part of the blood."

There are red and white corpuscles in the blood.

55

incorporate is made up of the Latin prefix *in-* meaning "into; in" and *corpor-* meaning "body" plus the Latin suffix *-ate*, which is merely a word-ending used to form verbs. Thus, *incorporate* means "to form into a body," and specifically "to form a legal association or company which can act as an individual."

>He has just incorporated his business.

Two words related to or based on *incorporate* are *corporation*, meaning "a body of persons recognized by law as an individual person or entity," and *corporate* [kôr′pər·it], meaning "combined as a whole; collective."

>He is president of a large business corporation.
>Voting is our corporate responsibility.

QUICKIEQUIZQUICKIEQUIZQUICKIEQUIZQUICKIEQUIZQUICKIEQUIZQUICKIEQUIZQUICKIEQUIZQUICKIE

QUICKIE QUIZ
· COLORS

How good is your color vocabulary? Can you match the color in the left-hand column with its description in the right-hand column? Answers follow.

1. **cerulean** [sə·rōō′lē·ən]
2. **indigo** [in′də·gō]
3. **ocher** [ō′kər]
4. **azure** [azh′ər]
5. **cerise** [sə·rēs′]
6. **ecru** [ek′rōō]
7. **chartreuse** [shär·trōōz′]
8. **fuchsia** [fyōō′shə]
9. **sorrel** [sôr′əl]
10. **mauve** [mōv]

(a) pale yellowish green
(b) light yellowish brown
(c) vivid blue
(d) purplish rose
(e) dark yellow
(f) deep violet blue
(g) cherry red
(h) reddish or yellowish brown
(i) bright bluish red
(j) clear sky blue

ANSWERS:

1. **cerulean**—(c) vivid blue. 2. **indigo**—(f) deep violet blue. 3. **ocher**—(e) dark yellow. 4. **azure**—(j) clear sky blue. 5. **cerise** —(g) cherry red. 6. **ecru** —(b) light yellowish brown. 7. **chartreuse**—(a) pale yellowish green. 8. **fuchsia**—(i) bright bluish red. 9. **sorrel**—(h) reddish or yellowish brown. 10. **mauve**—(d) purplish rose.

QUICKIEQUIZQUICKIEQUIZQUICKIEQUIZQUICKIEQUIZQUICKIEQUIZQUICKIEQUIZQUICKIEQUIZQUICKIE

ROOT: CRE-, CRESC-, CRET-

The Latin root *cre-*, *cresc-*, or *cret-* means "to grow." Here are three core vocabulary words to learn that are based on this root: *crescent, increase, concrete.*

crescent comes from *cresc-* meaning "to grow" and the Latin suffix *-ent*, which is the same as the English *-ing*. *Crescent* literally means "growing." That is why it has now come to mean "the visible part of the moon during its first or last quarter (which 'grows' larger or smaller)" or "anything shaped like a crescent moon."

> *Turkey has a crescent on its flag.*

increase is derived from the Latin prefix *in-* meaning "in" and *cre-* meaning "to grow." Thus, *increase* means "to grow in size, amount, degree, or number; to become or cause to become greater or larger." It may also mean "growth" or "the amount of growth."

> *As his vocabulary grew, his confidence increased.*
> *What was the rate of increase?*

A word based on *increase* is *increment,* meaning "a quantity added to another to increase it; the amount of increase."

> *What increment did you receive on your investment?*
> *My salary has gone up by a weekly increment of $10.*

concrete comes from the Latin prefix *con-* meaning "together" and *cret-* meaning "to grow." Thus, *concrete* originally meant "grown or melded together; solidified." Today it means "relating to one solidified, definite idea, thing, or case; individual or particular, as opposed to general; real; specific." Of course, it also means "any mass of solidified particles, especially the material used in building."

> *Try to be less vague and more concrete in your statements.*
> *The floor is made of concrete.*

◊ Look up these *cre-*, *cresc-*, *cret-* "growth" words in your dictionary. Be sure to learn the meaning of each and try to relate the meaning to each word's etymology.

decrease	accretion
crescendo	excrescence

ROOT: CRED-

The Latin root *cred-* means "to believe; trust." Learn tne following four core vocabulary words based on the root *cred-: credit, accredit, credentials, discredit.*

credit comes from a French word based on the Latin root *cred-* meaning "to believe; to trust." Thus, the noun *credit* basically means "trust or faith." This basic meaning has enlarged to include (1) a reputation for being trustworthy, especially in paying debts; (2) a source of honor; (3) acknowledgment for having done something; (4) confidence in a person's ability to be trusted; (5) money in one's favor or money entrusted to one as in a loan. To *credit* is (1) to give credit for; (2) to accept as true; (3) to attribute to, as honor or intelligence.

> *He has good credit at the bank.*
> *She is a credit to her school.*
> *He was given full credit for the work he did.*
> *The store sold her the goods on credit.*
> *The bank credited my account with $50.*
> *I cannot credit that story.*
> *Don't credit him with the idea, credit it to her.*

NOTE: In financial matters the opposite of *credit* is *debit*. If you write a check for $5 the bank will *debit* your account for that amount. You will have a $5 *debit*.

Two words based on *credit* are *creditable*, meaning "deserving credit; praiseworthy"; and *creditor*, meaning "a person or organization to whom money is owed."

> *The pianist gave a creditable performance.*
> *If you owe money to a store, the store is your creditor.*

accredit comes from the prefix *ac-* meaning "to" and the word *credit*. Thus, *accredit* means (1) to give credit to, as by acknowledging the work, effort, good qualities, etc., of; (2) to authorize officially; (3) to certify as meeting official requirements.

> *He was accredited with a quick intelligence.*
> *The ambassador was accredited by his government.*
> *The school board accredited the school.*

58

A word based on *accredit* is *accreditation,* meaning "the granting of recognition to a school, college, or the like, that fulfills official requirements of a state or country."

Our college has full accreditation.

credentials comes from *cred-* meaning "to believe" and the Latin suffix *-ent,* which is the same as the English *-ing,* plus the Latin suffix *-al* meaning "pertaining to." Thus, *credentials* can be "a certificate, letter, or other proof that gives evidence of a person's authority, identity, honesty, experience, etc."

The ambassador presented his credentials.
To enter this building, you must show your credentials.
His credentials as a doctor are excellent.

discredit comes from the Latin prefix *dis-* meaning "not" and the word *credit.* Thus, *discredit* means (1) not to credit; not to believe; (2) to harm the credit or reputation of someone; (3) to cause someone or something to be doubted. It also means "loss of reputation."

The lawyer discredited everything the witness said.
His acceptance of the bribe discredited him.
His rude behavior worked to his discredit.

◊ Here are six additional *cred-* words to learn. Look them up in your dictionary and learn their meanings. Can you relate the meaning of each word to the root *cred-* or the word *credit,* meaning "to believe; to trust"?

credible	incredible	credulous
credibility	incredibility	incredulous

ROOT: CUMB-, CUB-

The Latin root *cumb-* or *cub-* means "to lie down." Learn the following four core vocabulary words: *cubicle, incubate, incumbent, succumb.*

cubicle comes from *cub-* meaning "to lie down" and the Latin suffix *-cle* meaning "small." A *cubicle* was originally "a small room to lie down in; a bedroom." Today, *cubicle* means not only "a bedroom" but also "any small room or enclosed space."

Libraries often have cubicles in which students may study.

incubate comes from the Latin prefix *in-* meaning "in; on" and *cub-* meaning "to lie down" plus the Latin suffix *-ate* which is used to form verbs. *Incubate* literally means "to lie on" and thus it now specifically means "to sit on eggs in order to hatch them." It also means "to give form to; develop."

A hen will try to incubate a wooden egg.
The prisoners were incubating a plan for escape.

A word based on *incubate* is *incubator*, meaning "a device used for hatching eggs." By extension, *incubator* has also come to mean "an apparatus for keeping warm a prematurely born baby."

There are five dozen eggs in the incubator.
The quintuplets were kept in an incubator for several weeks.

incumbent comes from the Latin prefix *in-* meaning "in; on" and *cumb-* meaning "to lie down" plus the Latin suffix *-ent,* which is the same as the English *-ing.* Thus, *incumbent* means "lying or resting on someone as an obligation." It also means "a person on whom an obligation rests—in other words, one who holds public office."

It is incumbent upon you to increase your vocabulary.
It is hard for a newcomer to beat an incumbent in an election.

A word based on *incumbent* is *incumbency,* meaning (1) the state of being incumbent; (2) the holding of an office; (3) the period in which an office is held.

The mayor's incumbency is for four years.

succumb comes from the Latin prefix *suc-* (a variant of *sub-*) meaning "underneath" and *cumb-* meaning "to lie down." *Succumb* literally means "to give way underneath, or under the weight of, something." Thus, it means (1) to give way; yield; (2) to die.

The exhausted child finally succumbed to sleep.
He succumbed to pneumonia at the age of eighty.

◇ Look up the word *recumbent* in your dictionary. Be sure you understand all its parts—the prefix, the root, and the suffix.

EXPLORING WORDS

Certain English words are based on the names of places. We all know that Panama hats originally came from Panama, Persian rugs from Persia, and French pastry from France. But do you know that the words *afghan, cantaloupe,* and *damask* are also based on place names? In some cases, the place name remains unchanged when it is used as a word, but at times it is hardly recognizable. How good are you at spotting words that come from places?

afghan a coverlet that is knitted or crocheted from soft woolen yarn. Such coverlets originally came from Afghanistan.

Argyle a plaid design of diamond-shaped blocks of solid color overlaid by a contrasting plaid. This design is the tartan of the clan Campbell of Argyll, a county of western Scotland.

bedlam a scene of wild uproar. The word is a corruption of Bethlehem, and comes from the name of a former insane asylum, the hospital of St. Mary of Bethlehem in London, England.

bologna [pronounced, and often spelled, baloney] a seasoned sausage of mixed meats. It was named after Bologna, Italy.

calico a cotton cloth printed in a figured pattern of bright colors. This word comes from Calicut cloth, named for the city where it was originally made, Calicut, India.

cantaloupe a variety of muskmelon. It was named after an Italian castle, Cantalupo, where this melon was first successfully grown in Europe.

champagne a sparkling white wine made in the region of Champagne, France, or wine made elsewhere in imitation of it.

cologne or **eau de cologne** a toilet water consisting of alcohol scented with aromatic oils. It was named for the city of Cologne in West Germany.

damask a silk or linen fabric with a woven pattern. Named after Damascus, Syria, where it was first made.

denim a heavy twilled cotton cloth used for work clothes. This word is shortened and changed from the French term for the cloth, *serge de Nîmes* (serge of Nîmes), after Nîmes, the French city where it was made.

frankfurter a smoked sausage made of beef or beef and pork, or one of these served on a long bun. This "American" dish comes from Frankfurt, Germany.

ROOT: CUR-, CURS-. COURS-

The Latin root *cur-*, *curs-*, or *cours-* means "to run; go." Learn the following four core vocabulary words based on this root: *concur, current, occur, recur.*

concur comes from the Latin prefix *con-* meaning "together" and *cur-* meaning "to run; go." Thus, *concur* literally means "to run together"; hence, (1) to agree or approve; (2) to happen at the same time.

> *The entire group concurred on what to do next.*

Two words based on *concur* are *concurrent*, meaning "happening together; simultaneous"; and *concourse*, which means "a coming together, as of streets, or a place where people, traffic, etc., come together."

> *The convict's two ten-year sentences were concurrent.*
> *The train station has a large concourse.*

current comes from *cur-* meaning "to run; go" and the Latin suffix *-ent*, which is the same as the English *-ing*. A *current* is literally "a going, running, or moving." Thus, *current* means "any continuous onward movement of something, as of water in a river or lake, or of electricity in an electric wire." *Current* as an adjective means "moving along with the times" or "belonging to the immediate present."

> *The current of the river is swift.*
> *This lamp works only on alternating current.*
> *Jane is a slave to current fashions.*

A word based on *current* is *currency*, meaning (1) money (that is, what is in *current* use as a medium of exchange); (2) general acceptance or circulation.

> *The dollar is the standard unit of currency of Canada.*
> *The rumor gained wide currency.*

occur comes from the Latin prefix *oc-* meaning "toward; against" and *cur-* meaning "to run; go." To *occur* is literally "to rush toward something or someone," as an event or an idea might do. Thus, *occur* means "to happen; come about; come to mind."

> *When did the auto accident occur?*
> *When did that idea occur to you?*

A word based on *occur* is *occurrence*, meaning (1) an event or instance; (2) the act or fact of occurring.

> *Let me tell you about a strange occurrence.*
> *This is the third occurrence of robbery here this year.*
> *The occurrence of a solar eclipse is rare.*

recur comes from the Latin prefix *re-* meaning "back; again" and *cur-* meaning "to run; go." Thus, *recur* literally means "to run or go again," or "to happen again; to happen repeatedly."

> *John's asthma recurs every summer.*

Two words based on *recur* are *recurrence*, meaning "a happening again," and *recurrent*, meaning "happening repeatedly."

> *After one bad attack, Harry has had no recurrence of malaria.*
> *John has recurrent attacks of asthma.*

◊ Look up the following words in your dictionary. Be sure to learn the meaning of each word. Can you relate the meaning of each word to the root *cur-, curs-,* or *cours-?*

discourse	excursive	precursor
discursive	incur	precursory
excursion	incursion	recourse

ROOT: DE-, DIV-

The Latin root *de-* or *div-* means "a god." Learn the following three core vocabulary words based on this root: *deify, deity, divine.*

deify comes from *de-* meaning "a god" and the Latin suffix *-ify* meaning "to make." Thus, *deify* means "to make a god of someone or something; to worship as a god."

> *In earlier times the Chinese deified their ancestors.*
> *Some people almost deify neatness.*

A word based on *deify* is *deification*, meaning "the act of making a god of" or "the state of being made a god."

> *The Japanese used to approve of the deification of their Emperor.*

63

deity comes from *de-* meaning "a god" and the Latin suffix *-ity* meaning "the state or quality of being." Thus, *deity* means "the state of being a god" or, simply, "a god."

> *Jupiter was a Roman deity.*

divine comes from the root *div-* meaning "a god" and the Latin suffix *-ine* meaning "pertaining to." Thus, *divine* means "pertaining to a god or to God; godlike; sacred."

> *Various churches have different forms of divine worship.*

Two words based on *divine* are *divinely* and *divinity*. *Divinely* means (1) in a divine manner; (2) by or through God. *Divinity* means (1) the state or quality of being divine; (2) a god; (3) theology.

> *The prophet was divinely inspired.*
> *Christians believe in the divinity of Christ.*
> *Zeus and Athena were Greek divinities.*
> *He is a divinity student.*

ROOT: **DICT-**

The Latin root *dict-* means "to say or speak." Learn the following four core vocabulary words based on this root: *contradict, dictate, diction, predict.*

contradict comes from the Latin prefix *contra-* meaning "against" and *dict-* meaning "to say or speak." Thus, to *contradict* is "to speak against something; to hold that the opposite of what someone has said is true; to deny the truth of a statement."

> *Children should not contradict their parents.*
> *He contradicted his own previous testimony.*

Two words based on *contradict* are *contradiction* and *contradictory*. *Contradiction* means (1) a denial; (2) a statement that denies another. *Contradictory* means "involving or given to contradiction."

> *His speech was confusing and full of contradictions.*
> *The two witnesses made contradictory statements.*

dictate comes from *dict-* meaning "to say or speak" and the Latin suffix *-ate*, which is used to form verbs. *Dictate* means "to say something aloud, so that it can be recorded; to say commands or lay down laws, etc., with authority."

>*He dictated three letters to his secretary.*
>*Hitler dictated German policy in World War II.*

Three words based on *dictate* are *dictation, dictator,* and *dictatorial.* *Dictation* means (1) the act of dictating letters, memos, etc.; (2) that which is dictated. A *dictator* is "one who dictates, especially a tyrant." *Dictatorial* means "of or like a dictator; over-authoritative."

>*The secretary took the dictation in shorthand.*
>*Mussolini was a dictator.*
>*Her parents were strict but not dictatorial.*

diction comes from *dict-* meaning "to say or speak" and the Latin suffix *-ion* meaning "the state or quality of." Thus, *diction* means "the quality of one's speech or of one's choice and use of words."

>*After her talk, the student was praised for her good diction.*

A word based on *diction* is *dictionary,* meaning "a reference book listing the words of a language with their definitions and usually with their pronunciations and etymologies."

>*Everyone should have a modern dictionary.*

predict comes from the Latin prefix *pre-* meaning "before" and *dict-* meaning "to say or speak." Thus, *predict* means "to say before the event; to foretell; to say what will happen in the future."

>*The weather report predicted rain for tomorrow.*

Two words based on *predict* are *predictable* and *prediction.* *Predictable* means "capable of being predicted; easily foretold." *Prediction* means "the act of predicting; a forecast."

>*Solar eclipses are always predictable.*
>*What's your prediction for tomorrow's weather?*

◊ Look up the following words in your dictionary. Learn their meanings and relate each meaning to the root *dict-*.

| addict | dictum | edict | interdict |

Fun With Words

WHICH ROOTS DO YOU KNOW?

The following words contain common roots. Check the word or phrase you believe is closest in meaning to the key word. Answers follow.

1. **anthropology** [an'thrə·pol'ə·jē] —(a) the science of animals. (b) the study of fossils. (c) the science of man. (d) the science of past geological periods.
2. **bilingual** [bī·ling'gwəl]—(a) stuttering. (b) speaking two languages. (c) tongue-tied. (d) a translator.
3. **credence** [krēd'ns]—(a) a religion or personal belief. (b) reliance on the truth of something. (c) gullible. (d) simplicity.
4. **anachronism** [ə·nak'rə·niz'əm]— (a) government by a group of people. (b) old-fashioned. (c) a perpetual-motion clock. (d) something out of its proper time.
5. **biennial** [bī·en'ē·əl]—(a) occurring once every two years. (b) occurring twice a year. (c) a plant that blooms twice a year. (d) composed or created by two people.
6. **circumstantial** [sûr'kəm·stan'-shəl]—(a) furnishing conclusive proof. (b) dependent on circumstances. (c) not accepted in court. (d) vague or without details.

7. **credulous** [krej'ŏŏ·ləs]—(a) unbelievable. (b) firm in believing. (c) easily deceived. (d) suspicious.
8. **chronically** [kron'i·kəl·ē]—(a) irritably. (b) sickly. (c) habitually. (d) due to a generally run-down condition.
9. **misanthropic** [mis'ən·throp'ik] —(a) hating mankind. (b) charitable. (c) pertaining to non-human organisms. (d) pessimistic.
10. **circumlocution** [sûr'kəm·lō·kyŏŏ'shən]—(a) a grammatical error. (b) a strolling around. (c) a roundabout expression. (d) sailing around the world.
11. **credo** [krē'dō]—(a) a disposition to believe on slight evidence. (b) doubt. (c) a set of professed beliefs. (d) a group to which a person owes allegiance.
12. **carnivora** [kär·niv'ə·rə]—(a) a very strong person. (b) the four pointed teeth on either side of the upper and lower incisors. (c) gypsies. (d) flesh-eating animals.

ANSWERS:

1. **anthropology**—(c) the science of man. 2. **bilingual**—(b) speaking two languages. 3. **credence**—(b) reliance on the truth of something. 4. **anachronism**—(d) something out of its proper time. 5. **biennial**—(a) occurring once every two years. 6. **circumstantial**—(b) dependent on circumstances. 7. **credulous**—(c) easily deceived. 8. **chronically**—(c) habitually. 9. **misanthropic**—(a) hating mankind. 10. **circumlocution**—(c) a roundabout expression. 11. **credo**—(c) a set of professed beliefs. 12. **carnivora**—(d) flesh-eating animals.

ROOT: DOC-, DOCT-

The Latin root *doc-* or *doct-* means "to teach." Here are four core vocabulary words based on the root *doc-* or *doct-*: *docile, doctor, doctrine, document.* Learn the meanings of these words and their derivatives.

docile comes from *doc-* meaning "to teach" and the Latin suffix *-ile* meaning "able to be." Thus, *docile* literally means "teachable"; hence, "easy to teach, train, or manage."

> *The horse was safe to ride because it was docile.*

A word based on *docile* is *docility*, meaning "the state or condition of being easy to manage, teach, etc."

> *This horse is noted for its docility.*

doctor comes from the root *doct-* meaning "to teach" and the Latin suffix *-or* meaning "a person who." Thus, the word *doctor* originally meant "a teacher." Now, of course, *doctor* means "a person who has an advanced diploma, degree, or license in a certain field, especially a person trained and licensed to practice medicine or dentistry, or a person who holds an advanced degree from a graduate school."

> *When Mimi fainted, we called the doctor.*
> *Andrew is a Doctor of Philosophy.*

Two words based on *doctor* are *doctoral*, which means "pertaining or leading to the graduate-school degree of doctor," and *doctorate*, which means "the degree or title of doctor."

> *Erik is writing his doctoral dissertation in history.*
> *He hasn't yet received his doctorate.*

NOTE: We usually use the term *doctor* as a title for a person who is trained and licensed to practice medicine or dentistry—a physician or dentist. But people who have the degree of Ph.D. (Doctor of Philosophy) may also be called *doctors*. After finishing the usual four years of college and obtaining a bachelor's degree, they have attended a graduate school where, after completing many special requirements, including those for a master's degree, they have earned the highest graduate degree, the *doctorate*. *Doctoral* degrees are given in almost all fields of the arts and sciences. Remember, a *doctor* can be anyone—

a historian, a chemist, a lawyer, etc.— who has a *doctoral* degree. All *doctors* are not M.D.'s (Doctors of Medicine), although that is the type of *doctor* most of us know best.

doctrine comes from a Latin word based on *doct-* meaning "to teach." *Doctrine* means "a teaching or a body of teachings or beliefs, especially those of a political or religious group; a principle or set of principles."

> *What are the basic doctrines of Christianity?*
> *Buddhist and Hindu doctrines are different.*
> *The Monroe Doctrine (1823) warned European powers not to interfere in the affairs of the Western Hemisphere.*

A word based on *doctrine* is *doctrinal*, which means "pertaining to doctrine."

> *There are doctrinal differences between Roman Catholicism and Protestantism.*

document comes from *doc-* meaning "to teach" and the Latin suffix *-ment* meaning "the result of" or "the means of." A *document* is "a means of teaching something or of giving information." Thus, *document* is defined as "something written that gives conclusive information or evidence about something."

> *The Declaration of Independence is a famous historical document.*
> *What documents do you need to get a passport?*

Two words based on *document* are *documentary* and *documentation*. *Documentary* means (1) pertaining to or based upon descriptive facts or documents; (2) a motion picture or television program dealing with events in a factual way. *Documentation* is "the preparation or use of documents, factual references, records, etc., as in support of an idea or as evidence."

> *I have documentary evidence of my citizenship.*
> *This movie isn't fiction; it's a real documentary.*
> *This author provides thorough documentation in support of his argument.*

◊ Learn the meaning of the word *indoctrinate* from your dictionary. Can you see how it is based on the root *doc-* or *doct-* meaning "to teach"?

ROOT: DUC-, DUCT-

The Latin root *duc-* or *duct-* means "to lead." Learn the following four core vocabulary words: *conduct, introduce, produce, reduce.*

conduct comes from the Latin prefix *con-* meaning "with; together" and *duct-* meaning "to lead." Thus, *conduct* [kən·dukt'] means "to go with someone in order to lead him; to guide, escort, or direct." It also means "to direct, guide, or behave oneself." Pronounced another way, *conduct* [kon'dukt] means "behavior."

> *Can you conduct me to the personnel office?*
> *Do you know how to conduct a business?*
> *The composer conducted the orchestra.*
> *John always conducts himself well in public.*
> *His conduct in school is excellent.*

A word related to *conduct* is *conducive,* which means "helping, guiding, or leading toward a result."

> *Lack of sleep is not conducive to alertness.*

introduce comes from the Latin prefix *intro-* meaning "within" and the root *duc-* meaning "to lead." Thus, *introduce* literally means "to lead someone within something or into something"; hence, (1) to make a person acquainted with something or with another person; (2) to present; (3) to insert; (4) to start or bring into use.

> *This course will introduce you to higher mathematics.*
> *Peter, may I introduce you to Sally?*
> *John introduced the main speaker.*
> *The speaker introduced some humor into his talk.*
> *The Spaniards introduced the horse to America.*

Two words based on *introduce* are *introduction* and *introductory.* *Introduction* means (1) the act of introducing; (2) a person's first knowledge of something; (3) something that leads up to what follows. *Introductory* means "serving as an introduction."

> *That course was my introduction to higher mathematics.*
> *The introduction to this book is twenty pages long.*
> *The book has a twenty-page introductory chapter.*

produce comes from the Latin prefix *pro-* meaning forward and *duc-* meaning "to lead." Thus, *produce* [prə·dōōs'] literally means "to lead forward"; hence, (1) to bring forth or bear; (2) to bring about, make, create; (3) to exhibit or show. The noun *produce* [prod'ōōs] means "something brought forth; a yield, as of fruits and vegetables."

> *The land produced grapes.*
> *From the grapes men produced wine.*
> *The speech produced much disagreement.*
> *Our school is going to produce a play.*
> *The farmers sold their produce at the market.*

Four of the many words based on *produce* are *product, production, productive,* and *productivity.* A *product* is (1) anything produced; (2) a result. *Production* means (1) the act of producing; (2) that which is produced. *Productive* means (1) tending to produce; (2) tending to produce profits; (3) causing or resulting in. *Productivity* means either (1) the state of being productive; or (2) the rate of producing.

> *Wine is a product of grapes.*
> *The story was a product of his imagination.*
> *The production of cars is increasing.*
> *Last year's production was two million cars.*
> *The workers in the company are very productive.*
> *Their experiments have been productive of new techniques.*
> *Productivity in the factory has risen.*

reduce comes from the Latin prefix *re-* meaning "back" and *duc-* meaning "to lead." Thus, *reduce* literally means "to lead back"; hence, (1) to bring from a higher to a lower condition; (2) to make less in size, amount, number, value, etc.; (3) to become less in any way.

> *He was reduced in rank from sergeant to corporal.*
> *He has reduced his daily quota of cigarettes.*
> *The fire reduced the building to ashes.*
> *She hopes to reduce by dieting.*

Two words based on *reduce* are *irreducible,* meaning "incapable of being reduced," and *reduction,* meaning (1) the act or process of reducing; (2) the result of reducing.

> *We have cut costs to an irreducible minimum.*
> *The management plans a reduction in staff.*
> *He objected to the reduction in pay.*

◇ Look up the following words in your dictionary. Notice how the meaning of each is based on the root *duc-* or *duct-* meaning "to lead."

abduct	deductive	seduce
abduction	induce	seduction
deduce	induction	seductive
deduction	inductive	traduce

QUICKIEQUIZQUICKIEQUIZQUICKIEQUIZQUICKIEQUIZQUICKIEQUIZQUICKIEQUIZQUICKIEQUIZQUICKIE

90-SECOND QUICKIE QUIZ
WORD BUILDING

Knowing the meanings of their parts can help you to understand many words. Can you match these roots and prefixes with their meanings in the right-hand column? Answers follow.

1. **dextro-** as in ambidextrous [am′bə·dek′strəs]
2. **ambi-** as in ambiguous [am·big′yoo·əs]
3. **anthropo-** as in anthropology [an′thrə·pol′ə·jē]
4. **bi-** as in bigamy [big′ə·mē]
5. **hemi-** as in hemisphere [hem′ə·sfir]
6. **auto-** as in automobile [ô′tə·mə·bēl′]
7. **derm-** as in dermatologist [dûr′mə·tol′ə·jist]
8. **cosmo-** as in cosmopolitan [koz′mə·pol′ə·tən]
9. **ethno-** as in ethnology [eth·nol′ə·jē]
10. **equi-** as in equilibrium [ē′kwə·lib′rē·əm]

(a) man
(b) self
(c) both
(d) two
(e) half
(f) right
(g) equal
(h) nation
(i) universe
(j) skin

ANSWERS:

1. **dextro-** —(f) right. Ambidextrous means being able to use both hands equally well. 2. **ambi-** — (c) both. Ambiguous means capable of being understood in two or more senses; hence, unclear. 3. **anthropo-** —(a) man. Anthropology is the science that studies man, his origin, evolution, customs, etc. 4. **bi-** —(d) two. Bigamy is the criminal offense of having two wives or husbands at the same time. 5. **hemi-** —(e) half. A hemisphere is half a sphere or half of the terrestrial or celestial globe, as either the Northern Hemisphere or the Southern Hemisphere. 6. **auto-** —(b) self. An automobile is a self-propelled vehicle. 7. **derm-** —(j) skin. A dermatologist is a doctor who specializes in treating diseases of the skin. 8. **cosmo-** —(i) universe. Cosmopolitan means at home in all parts of the world; not limited to local interests. 9. **ethno-** —(h) nation. Ethnology is the branch of anthropology dealing with racial and ethnic groups. 10. **equi-** —(g) equal. Equilibrium means a state of balance or the condition of being well-balanced.

QUICKIEQUIZQUICKIEQUIZQUICKIEQUIZQUICKIEQUIZQUICKIEQUIZQUICKIEQUIZQUICKIEQUIZQUICKIE

ROOT: EQU-

The Latin root *equ-* means "equal; even." Since this root appears even in its own definition, "equal," you can see how important it is to English. Keep *equal* in mind as your key word while you learn the three core vocabulary words: *adequate, equilibrium, equivocal.*

adequate comes from the Latin prefix *ad-* meaning "to" and *equ-* meaning "equal" plus the Latin suffix *-ate*, which is used to form adjectives. Thus, *adequate* means "equal to the job; equal to what is required."

> *She's not a perfect typist, but she's adequate.*
> *We had an adequate amount of money for a two-week trip.*

equilibrium comes from *equ-* meaning "equal; even" and the Latin word *libra* meaning "balance." Thus, *equilibrium* means "an even balance; a state of balance; physical, mental, or emotional balance."

> *How does a tight-rope walker keep his equilibrium?*
> *May was upset by the bad news but soon regained her equilibrium.*

equivocal comes from *equ-* meaning "equal" and the Latin root *voc-* meaning "voice" plus the Latin suffix *-al* meaning "pertaining to." Thus, *equivocal* literally means "pertaining to something of equal voice or significance"; hence, "having a double meaning; misleading; purposely vague."

> *I want all the facts, so stop giving me equivocal answers.*

Two words related to or based on *equivocal* are *unequivocal,* meaning "not doubtful or vague; straightforward"; and *equivocate,* meaning "to use vague language in an attempt to mislead."

> *He made an unequivocal denial of the charges against him.*
> *The politician equivocated about his campaign expenses.*

◊ Look up the following words in your dictionary. Notice how the meaning of each is based on *equ-* meaning "equal; even."

equable	equator	equipoise	equivalent
equate	equilibrist	equinox	inequitable
equation	equidistant	equitable	inequity

Fun With Words

COMMON ROOTS

The following twelve words contain common roots used in word building. Check the word or phrase you believe is closest in meaning to the key word. Answers follow.

1. **dexterity** [dek·ster′ə·tē]—(a) superabundant strength. (b) ability to use both hands equally well. (c) sweetness. (d) skill in using the hands or body.

2. **dermatology** [dûr′mə·tol′ə·jē]—(a) the study of insects. (b) heat treatment. (c) the study of infectious disease. (d) the study of the skin and its diseases.

3. **feline** [fē′līn]—(a) delicate. (b) catlike. (c) feminine. (d) to libel or slander.

4. **demagogic** [dem′ə·goj′ik]—(a) given to unprincipled political agitation. (b) the art of public speaking. (c) having only half knowledge. (d) the investigation of evil spirits.

5. **equilibrium** [ē′kwə·lib′rē·əm]—(a) seeing equally well with both eyes. (b) stability or balance. (c) one who rides horses. (d) skill or dexterity.

6. **edict** [ē′dikt]—(a) a correction. (b) an abbreviation. (c) an explanation. (d) any proclamation or command.

7. **ambidextrous** [am′bə·dek′strəs]—(a) able to use both hands equally well. (b) good handwriting skill. (c) cross-eyed. (d) very graceful.

8. **dictum** [dik′təm]—(a) enunciation. (b) a law. (c) an authoritative statement. (d) an autocratic ruler

9. **decimate** [des′ə·māt]—(a) to cut into small pieces. (b) to count in tens. (c) to extract the moisture from. (d) to destroy a large part of.

10. **endemic** [en·dem′ik]—(a) a contagious disease. (b) peculiar to a particular locale. (c) tending to produce vomiting. (d) a disease affecting children.

11. **enamored** [in·am′ərd]—(a) inflamed with love. (b) coated with a shellac. (c) faded. (d) endorsed.

12. **filial** [fil′ē·əl]—(a) faithful. (b) of a father or mother. (c) of a son or daughter. (d) frail.

ANSWERS:

1. **dexterity**—(d) skill in using the hands or body. 2. **dermatology**—(d) the study of the skin and its diseases. 3. **feline**—(b) catlike. 4. **demagogic**—(a) given to unprincipled political agitation. 5. **equilibrium**—(b) stability or balance. 6. **edict**—(d) any proclamation or command. 7. **ambidextrous**—(a) able to use both hands equally well. 8. **dictum**—(c) an authoritative statement. 9. **decimate**—(d) to destroy a large part of. 10. **endemic**—(b) peculiar to a particular locale. 11. **enamored**—(a) inflamed with love. 12. **filial** —(c) of a son or daughter.

ROOT: FAC-, FIC-, FACT-, FECT-

The Latin root *fac-, fic-, fact-,* or *fect-* means "to do; make." It is one of the most frequently used roots in English, probably because the ideas of doing and making are so important to us. Learn the five core vocabulary words based on this important root: *facile, fiction, efficient, infect, manufacture.*

facile comes from *fac-* meaning "to do; make" and the Latin suffix *-ile* meaning "able to be." Thus, *facile* means "able to be done"; hence, "easy; requiring little effort; so skilled or talented as to do something very easily." Note that *facile* can also mean "too smooth and superficial to be serious."

> *His writing is merely facile; it lacks depth.*
> *Being a facile speaker, she is an effective politician.*

A word based on *facile* is *facility,* which means (1) ready skill or ability; (2) a building, room, piece of equipment, etc., that is provided to make some action or operation easier.

> *Professor Smith speaks French with facility.*
> *The university has many research facilities.*

fiction comes from *fic-* meaning "to make" and the Latin suffix *-tion,* which is used to form nouns. Thus, *fiction* is literally "a making" or "a made-up piece of writing"; hence, "prose writing about imaginary characters and events."

> *Mr. Jones has written both history and fiction.*

Two words based on *fiction* are *fictional,* which means "pertaining or belonging to fiction; imaginary"; and *fictitious,* meaning "imaginary; not real; false."

> *The characters in the story are fictional.*
> *The criminal gave a fictitious address.*

efficient comes from the Latin prefix *ef-* (another spelling of *ex-*) meaning "out" and *fic-* meaning "to do; make" plus the Latin suffix *-ent,* which is the same as the English *-ing.* Thus, *efficient* means "making, or turning out results with little wasted effort."

> *Reading is an efficient way of building your vocabulary.*

A word based on *efficient* is *efficiency,* meaning "the quality of being efficient or of producing results; effectiveness."

A firm's success depends on its workers' efficiency.

infect comes from the Latin prefix *in-* meaning "in" and *fect-* meaning "to do; make." Thus, *infect* literally means "to do into or inside of"; hence, "to affect with a disease; contaminate."

Is the wound infected?

Two words based on *infect* are *infection,* meaning "an invasion of the body by disease germs; a disease"; and *infectious,* meaning (1) liable to produce infection; (2) contagious; spreading to others.

The infection was checked by penicillin.
He has an infectious disease.
Her laughter was infectious.

manufacture comes from the Latin root *manu-* meaning "hand" and *fact-* meaning "to do; make" plus the Latin suffix *-ure* meaning "the act of." Thus, *manufacture* originally meant "a making by hand; making handmade products." Of course the meaning of *manufacture* has now enlarged to mean (1) to make a product, especially on a large scale; (2) to make up or invent, as an excuse or alibi.

Many cars are manufactured in Detroit.
He was late and had to manufacture an excuse.

◊ Listed below are eighteen more common words based on the root *fac-, fic-, fact-,* or *fect-.* Learn their meanings from your dictionary and relate each to the common root *fac-, fic-, fact-,* or *fect-* meaning "to do; make."

affect	defective	factory
affective	effect	perfect
affection	effective	perfection
deficient	fact	proficient
defect	factual	proficiency
defection	factor	unification

NOTE: *Affect* and *effect* are confused by many people. Pay particular attention to the difference between these two words. The verb *affect* means "to influence or have an effect on." The verb *effect* means "to bring about or produce as a result." As a noun, *effect* means "a result or influence." The relationship between the noun and the two verbs may be seen in the sentence below:

> *The mountain air had a noticeable effect on the invalid; it affected his health for the better and helped to effect a cure.*

ROOT: FER-

The Latin root *fer-* means "to carry; bring." Here are four core vocabulary words based on *fer-: confer, differ, offer, transfer.*

confer comes from the Latin prefix *con-* meaning "together; with" and *fer-* meaning "to carry; bring." Thus, *confer* literally means "to carry or bring together"; hence, "to give or bestow" or "to consult together."

> *The school conferred an award on the student.*
> *The business executives conferred about costs.*

A word based on *confer* is *conference*, meaning "a formal meeting for discussion of some important matter."

> *The executives held a business conference.*
> *The annual conference of women's clubs was held in Chicago.*

differ comes from the Latin prefix *dif-* (another spelling of *dis-*) meaning "apart" and *fer-* meaning "to carry; bring." Thus, *differ* means "to carry oneself apart from someone else; to be unlike; to disagree."

> *These colors differ.*
> *My opinion differs from yours.*

A word based on *differ* is *difference*, meaning (1) the state or an instance of being unlike; (2) a distinguishing characteristic.

> *We had a slight difference of opinion.*
> *There is a difference between these two colors.*

offer comes from the Latin prefix *of-* (another spelling of *ob-*) meaning "before" and *fer-* meaning "to carry; bring." Thus, to *offer* means "to bring something before someone; to present something for acceptance or rejection; to propose." An *offer* is "that which is presented or proposed."

> *He offered to walk her home.*
> *He offered us a ride.*
> *We accepted his offer of a ride.*
> *Shall we make an offer of $20,000 for the house?*

Two words based on *offer* are *offering*, meaning "something offered, especially a gift or contribution made in church"; and *offertory*, meaning (1) the part of a religious service during which the offering is collected; (2) a hymn sung, a prayer said, or music played during this part of the service.

> *The ushers collected the congregation's offerings.*
> *The choir sang the offertory anthem.*

transfer comes from the Latin prefix *trans-* meaning "across" and *fer-* meaning "to carry; bring." Thus, to *transfer* means "to carry, move, or cause to go from one person, place, carrier, etc., to another."

> *The company transferred him from Toronto to Vancouver.*
> *He transferred his property to his wife.*
> *Take the bus and transfer at Chestnut Street.*

Three words based on *transfer* are *transferable*, meaning "capable of being transferred from one person to another"; *nontransferable*, meaning "incapable of or prohibited from being transferred"; and *transference*, meaning "the act of transferring or the state of being transferred."

> *Bonds may be either transferable or nontransferable.*
> *The transference of his property was handled by a lawyer.*

◊ Look up the following twelve frequently used *fer-* words in your dictionary. Be sure you know the true meaning and use of each. Can you relate the meaning of each to the root *fer-* meaning "to carry; bring"?

defer	preferential	referent
deferential	refer	suffer
prefer	reference	sufferance
preference	referendum	transferal

Fun With Words
REVIEW OF ROOTS

Here is another review vocabulary test containing roots and words you have already learned. Choose the answer nearest in meaning to the key word. Answers follow.

1. **credible** [kred'ə·bəl]—(a) owing money. (b) easily convinced. (c) capable of being believed. (d) despicable.
2. **credulous** [krej'oo·ləs]—(a) owing money. (b) easily convinced. (c) despicable. (d) surprised.
3. **crescendo** [krə·shen'dō]—(a) a gradual increase in volume of sound. (b) a loud noise. (c) a waterfall. (d) an oily liquid.
4. **recumbent** [ri·kum'bənt]—(a) reclining; leaning. (b) twisted; bent. (c) sleeping. (d) elected for a second term of office.
5. **discursive** [dis·kûr'siv]—(a) loud or raucous. (b) rude. (c) passing quickly from one subject to another. (d) decisive, coming to the point or making a decision quickly.
6. **incur** [in·kûr']—(a) to become angry. (b) to agree; give assent. (c) to get rid of. (d) to become subject to; bring on oneself.
7. **recourse** [rē'kôrs] *or* ri·kôrs']—

(a) that which precedes and suggests the course of future events. (b) that which follows. (c) access to a person or thing for help or aid. (d) an alternative.

8. **precursor** [pri·kûr'sər]—(a) that which precedes and suggests the course of future events. (b) that which follows. (c) one who has given help or aid. (d) one who introduces a speaker.
9. **edict** [ē'dikt]—(a) to cast out. (b) a secret meeting. (c) to judge guilty. (d) an official decree publicly proclaimed.
10. **indoctrinate** [in·dok'trə·nāt]— (a) to inject medicine, drugs, etc., with a hypodermic needle. (b) to instruct in principles of belief. (c) to punish severely. (d) to dilute or add impurities to.
11. **deduce** [di·doos' *or* di·dyoos']— (a) to entice to immoral acts. (b) to guess or suppose. (c) to gather facts. (d) to reach a conclusion by reasoning.

ANSWERS:

1. **credible**—(c) capable of being believed. 2. **credulous**—(b) easily convinced. 3. **crescendo**—(a) a gradual increase in volume of sound. 4. **recumbent**—(a) reclining, leaning. 5. **discursive**—(c) passing quickly from one subject to another. 6. **incur**—(d) to become subject to; bring on oneself. 7. **recourse**—(c) access to a person or thing for help or aid. 8. **precursor**—(a) that which precedes and suggests the course of future events. 9. **edict**—(d) an official decree publicly proclaimed. 10. **indoctrinate**—(b) to instruct in principles of belief. 11. **deduce**—(d) to reach a conclusion by reasoning.

ROOT: FIRM-

Can you guess what the Latin root *firm-* means? It's easy. It means what it says, "firm; strong." This root is used in three important core vocabulary words: *affirm, confirm, infirm.*

affirm comes from the Latin prefix *af-* (another spelling of *ad-*) meaning "to" and *firm-* meaning "firm; strong." Thus, *affirm* means "to make firm; declare positively; state something to be true."

> *He affirmed the truth of the statement while under oath.*
> *She affirmed her belief in God.*

Two words based on *affirm* are *affirmation*, which means "the act of affirming; assertion; confirmation"; and *affirmative*, which means "characterized by affirming; positive; accepting or agreeing."

> *The voters expressed affirmation of the platform by electing the party's candidate.*
> *His answer was affirmative.*
> *The majority of the votes were in the affirmative.*

confirm comes from the Latin prefix *con-* meaning "thoroughly" and *firm-* meaning "firm; strong." *Confirm* means "to make thoroughly strong; strengthen; verify; ratify." It also means "to admit to the privileges of a church after having been strengthened in religious faith by training in religious teachings."

> *Success confirmed him in his resolution to work hard.*
> *The results confirmed our suspicions.*
> *The Board confirmed the appointment of the new general manager for the plant.*
> *Will you confirm your order in writing?*
> *She was confirmed in church last week.*

A word based on *confirm* is *confirmation*, meaning (1) the act of confirming; (2) proof; (3) a religious rite in which a person who has been strengthened in his faith is admitted to the privileges of a church.

> *The evidence gave confirmation of his theory.*
> *After her confirmation she began to teach Sunday school.*

infirm comes from the Latin prefix *in-* meaning "not" and *firm-* meaning "firm; strong." Thus, to be *infirm* is "not to be strong; to be feeble or weak; to be sick or weak with sickness."

Arthritis has made my grandmother infirm.

A word based on *infirm* is *infirmary,* meaning "a place for the treatment of sick people."

They rushed the sick student to the college infirmary.

ROOT: FLECT-, FLEX-

Can you *flex* your muscles? Here's a chance to *flex* your mind on another Latin root. The root *flect-* or *flex-* means "to bend." The three common *flect-, flex-* words for your core vocabulary are: *deflect, flexible, reflect.*

deflect comes from the Latin prefix *de-* meaning "down; away" and *flect-* meaning "to bend." Thus, *deflect* means "to bend away; turn aside; swerve or cause to swerve."

> *He deflected the blow with his left hand.*
> *The warrior used his shield to deflect the enemy's spears.*

flexible comes from the root *flex-* meaning "to bend" and the suffix *-ible* meaning "capable of being." Thus, *flexible* means "capable of being bent, twisted, etc., without breaking; pliant." It also means "giving in to persuasion" or "able to adjust easily to change."

> *Radio aerials on cars are made of flexible metal.*
> *Our employer is open-minded and flexible.*
> *Let's keep our traveling plans flexible.*

Two words based on *flexible* are *flexibility,* meaning "the state or condition of being flexible," and *inflexible,* meaning "not flexible."

> *He's stubborn and shows no flexibility.*
> *He maintains an inflexible political stand.*

reflect comes from the Latin prefix *re-* meaning "back" and *flect-* meaning "to bend." *Reflect* means "to bend back; turn or throw back waves of light, sound, or heat." It also means "to think back; think again; review in the mind."

The water reflected the sunlight.

The mirror reflected his face.

Stop and reflect a minute before you act.

Phyllis sat and reflected on the events of the past year.

Two words based on *reflect* are *reflection* and *reflective*. *Reflection* means (1) the act of reflecting; (2) that which is reflected. *Reflective* means "given to mental reflection; thoughtful."

On reflection, I've decided not to go to Europe this year.

He saw his reflection in the mirror.

Charles has a calm, reflective nature.

◊ Look up these two words in your dictionary and learn their meanings: *inflection, reflex.*

QUICKIEQUIZQUICKIEQUIZQUICKIEQUIZQUICKIEQUIZQUICKIEQUIZQUICKIEQUIZQUICKIEQUIZQUICKI.

60-SECOND QUICKIE QUIZ

WORD BUILDING

Knowing the meanings of roots can help you understand many words. You have already learned the roots and words given below. Match each root in the left-hand column with its meaning in the right-hand column. Answers follow.

1. **fact-** as in manufacture [man′yə·fak′chər]   (a) hand
2. **manu-** as in manufacture [man′yə·fak′chər]   (b) equal; even
3. **equ-** as in equilibrium [ē′kwə·lib′rē·əm]   (c) to carry; bring
4. **fer-** as in transfer [trans′fər]   (d) to love
5. **am-** as in amateur [am′ə·choŏr]   (e) to do; make

ANSWERS:

1. **fact-** —(e) to do; make. To manufacture now means to make any product, especially on a large scale.
2. **manu-** —(a) hand. To manufacture originally meant "to make by hand."
3. **equ-** —(b) equal; even. Equilibrium means an even balance; physical, mental, or emotional balance.
4. **fer-** —(c) to carry; bring. Transfer combines the prefix *trans-* meaning across with the root *fer-*. Thus, *transfer* means to carry, bring, or move from one person, place or carrier to another.
5. **am-** —(d) to love. An amateur is someone who does something, such as paint or play golf, for the love of it rather than for money.

QUICKIEQUIZQUICKIEQUIZQUICKIEQUIZQUICKIEQUIZQUICKIEQUIZQUICKIEQUIZQUICKIEQUIZQUICKIE

ROOT: FLU-, FLUX-

Do you know what the word *flux* means? It means "a flow"—coming from the Latin root *flu-* or *flux-:* "to flow." Now how would you explain the meaning of the word *fluid?* If you explain it as "that which flows; a liquid," you are well on your way to understanding how words are formed and how to improve your vocabulary. The three core vocabulary words based on the root *flu-* or *flux-* are: *affluent, fluency, influence.*

affluent comes from the Latin prefix *af-* (another spelling of *ad-*) meaning "to" and *flu-* meaning "to flow" plus the Latin suffix *-ent*, which is the same as the English *-ing*. Thus, *affluent* literally means "flowing to a person"; hence, "abundant or wealthy."

> *We live in an affluent country.*
> *My uncle was the most affluent man in town.*

A word based on *affluent* is *affluence*, meaning "riches or wealth."

> *Some men are noted for their affluence, others for their good deeds.*

fluency comes from *flu-* meaning "to flow" and the Latin suffix *-ency* meaning "the state or condition of." Thus, *fluency* means "the state or condition of flowing," or, more precisely, "smoothness, especially smoothness or readiness of speech."

> *Professor Karl has great fluency in German.*

A word based on *fluency* is *fluent*, which means "showing smoothness or effortless ease, especially in speech."

> *Professor Karl is fluent in German.*

influence comes from the Latin prefix *in-* meaning "in" and *flu-* meaning "to flow" plus the Latin suffix *-ence* meaning "the state or condition of." Thus, *influence* means "a flowing in of one person's thought upon others"; hence, (1) the power to produce effects on others; (2) a person or thing possessing such power; (3) an effect produced by such power. As a verb, *influence* means "to produce or have an effect on; to affect or change."

> *I wish I had more influence on the boss's decisions.*
> *Gloria's father was a major influence on her life.*

Don't drive while under the influence of alcohol.
Someone has said that influence is the effluence of affluence.
People once believed that the planets influenced men's lives.

A word based on *influence* is *influential,* which means "having or using influence."

The mayor is the most influential man in our town.

◊ Here are three other *flu-, flux-* words you should learn. Look them up in your dictionary and learn their meanings. Be sure you can relate their meanings to the root *flu-* or *flux-* meaning "to flow."

fluctuation   effluence   influx

ROOT: FRANG-, FRING-, FRACT-, FRAG-

Can you see the relationship of these four core vocabulary words: *fraction, fragile, fragment, infringe?* They are all based on the Latin root *frang-, fring-, fract-,* or *frag-,* which means "to break."

fraction comes from *fract-* meaning "to break" and the Latin suffix *-ion,* which is used to form nouns. Thus, a *fraction* is "something broken off from the whole; a disconnected part; a small portion; a quantity less than a whole unit."

Five dollars was only a fraction of the money he owed.
One-half is a fraction.

A word based on *fraction* is *fractional,* meaning "relating to or being a fraction; small in size; partial."

He made a fractional payment, not a full one.

fragile comes from *frag-* meaning "to break" and the Latin suffix *-ile* meaning "able to be." Thus, *fragile* means "breakable; easily broken or damaged; frail."

Be careful; that vase is fragile!
The box contained glass and was marked "Fragile."
Mrs. Jones looks thin and fragile.

83

A word based on *fragile* is *fragility*, meaning "the state or condition of being easily broken or damaged; frailness."

> *I decided not to buy the vase because of its fragility.*
> *Emily's fragility worries the family.*

fragment comes from *frag-* meaning "to break" and the Latin suffix *-ment* meaning "the condition of being." Thus, a *fragment* is "something broken off; a part broken off; a small detached portion." *Fragment* can also mean "a small part of something that has been left unfinished."

> *He tried to glue together the fragments of the vase.*
> *I heard only fragments of the conversation.*
> *He had written a fragment of a symphony before his death.*

Two words based on *fragment* are *fragmentary*, meaning "made up of unconnected bits and pieces; broken"; and *fragmentation*, meaning "a breaking up into fragments."

> *We overheard fragmentary bits of the conversation.*
> *I dislike the fragmentation of society into self-seeking groups.*
> *A fragmentation bomb explodes into many small pieces.*

infringe comes from the Latin prefix *in-* meaning "in" and *fring-* meaning "to break." Thus, *infringe* means "to break in or into another person's time, rights, etc." Specifically, it means "to break the terms or requirements of something, such as a promise or a law; to violate; to trespass on."

> *Do not infringe on the rights of others.*
> *He was fined for infringing the law.*
> *You're infringing on my territory.*
> *This invention does not infringe on any other patent.*

A word based on *infringe* is *infringement*, meaning "the violation or breach of a law, right, etc."

> *Sparta was guilty of an infringement of its treaty with Athens.*

◊ Knowing that *fract-* means "to break," can you explain what the word *fracture* means? Look up these *fract-*, *frang-* words in your dictionary and learn their meanings:

fracture	infraction	refraction
frangible	refract	refractory

EXPLORING WORDS
IS THERE A DOCTOR IN THE HOUSE?

In the vast field of physical care almost every part and function of the body has its own specialist or therapist. If you were sent to the following specialists or practitioners (not all of whom, incidentally, are M.D.'s), would you know what they do?

1. anesthetist; 2. cardiologist; 3. chiropodist; 4. dermatologist; 5. gynecologist; 6. internist; 7. neurologist; 8. obstetrician; 9. ophthalmologist; 10. orthodontist; 11. orthopedist; 12. pediatrician; 13. podiatrist.

ANSWERS:

1. **anesthetist** a person trained to administer anesthetics.

2. **cardiologist** a heart specialist.

3. **chiropodist** a specialist in minor ailments of the foot.

4. **dermatologist** a physician who specializes in treating diseases of the skin.

5. **gynecologist** a specialist in diseases and functions peculiar to women.

6. **internist** a doctor who specializes in diseases of the internal organs. (Do not confuse *internist* with *intern*, a medical graduate receiving clinical training in a hospital.)

7. **neurologist** a specialist in disorders of the nervous system.

8. **obstetrician** a specialist in childbirth.

9. **ophthalmologist** a doctor who specializes in the anatomy, functions and diseases of the eye.

10. **orthodontist** a dentist who specializes in the prevention and correction of tooth irregularities.

11. **orthopedist** a specialist in the prevention and treatment of deformities and diseases of the spine, limbs and other parts of the skeleton.

12. **pediatrician** a specialist in the care of babies and young children.

13. **podiatrist** a therapist whose specialty is treating ailments of the feet.

ROOT: FUS-, FUND-, FOUND-

The Latin root *fus-*, *fund-*, or *found-* means "to melt; pour." Here are four core vocabulary words based on this root: *confuse, foundry, fusion, refund.*

confuse comes from the Latin prefix *con-* meaning "together" and *fus-* meaning "to melt; pour." *Confuse* literally means "to melt together." Thus, *confuse* means "to mix up mentally; to jumble."

> *He confused the names of his two new friends.*
> *He was confused about their names.*

Two words related to or based on *confuse* are *confound* and *confusion. Confound* means (1) to confuse, bewilder, or amaze; (2) to damn (used in mild oaths or curses). *Confusion* is "the state of being confused."

> *He was confounded by the noise and the crowds.*
> *Confound that young whippersnapper!*
> *Her screams threw the entire office into confusion.*

foundry comes from a word which is based on the root *found-* meaning "to melt; pour." Thus, *foundry* means "a place in which metal is cast (melted and poured)."

> *There are two steel foundries in town.*

fusion comes from *fus-* meaning "to melt; pour" and the Latin suffix *-ion* meaning "the state or process of." Thus, *fusion* means (1) a melting or blending together; (2) the result of a melting or combining.

> *He was elected by a fusion of the two political parties.*
> *Brass is formed by the fusion of copper and zinc.*

Two words related to or based on *fusion* are *infuse* and *fuse. Infuse* means (1) to pour in, instill, or inspire something; (2) to soak a substance in a liquid in order to extract its properties. *Fuse* means (1) to melt or to join by melting; (2) a device intended to melt or break an electric circuit before an overload causes a fire or other damage.

> *The captain infused courage into the troops.*
> *Tea leaves are infused, or steeped, in hot water.*

The two pieces of metal were fused by the heat.
He put a new fuse in the fuse box.

refund comes from the Latin prefix *re-* meaning "back" and *fund-* meaning "to pour." To *refund* is "to pour something back." Thus, *refund* means (1) to give or pay back; (2) a repayment.

If I'm not satisfied, will my money be refunded?
Did you get a refund for the damaged article?

◇ Can you now figure out why *transfusion* means what it does? What is a blood *transfusion?* Look up the following words in your dictionary and learn their meanings. Be sure that you can relate each meaning to the root *fus-* meaning "to melt; pour."

diffuse	profuse	suffuse
diffusion	profusion	suffusion
effusion	profusive	transfuse
effusive	refuse	transfusion

ROOT: GAM-

The Greek root *gam-* means "marriage." Three core vocabulary words relating to marriage are based on the root *gam-: bigamy, monogamy, polygamy.*

bigamy comes from *bi-* meaning "twice; doubly; two" and *gam-* meaning "marriage." Thus, *bigamy* means "marrying another person while one still has a legal, living husband or wife."

Bigamy is a crime in all states.

monogamy comes from the Greek prefix *mono-* meaning "one; single" and *gam-* meaning "marriage." Thus, *monogamy* means "the practice of having only one wife or husband at a time."

Monogamy is the type of marriage prevailing in most civilized countries.

polygamy comes from the Greek prefix *poly-* meaning "many" and *gam-* meaning "marriage." Thus, *polygamy* means "the practice of having more than one wife or husband at a time; plural marriage."

A sultan with three wives is practicing polygamy.

◊ Almost all the vocabulary words taught in this book are common words for your everyday vocabulary. However, it's fun to know a few uncommon words. Here are two uncommon words based on the root *gam-* that you may find in sociology books or even in crossword puzzles: *exogamy, endogamy.*

ROOT: GEN-, GENIT-

The Greek and Latin root *gen-* or *genit-* means "to produce; give birth to; beget." Learn the six core vocabulary words based on *gen-* or *genit-*: *genesis, genius, genial, genuine, genital, progenitor.*

genesis comes directly from a Greek word which is based on the root *gen-* meaning "to produce; give birth to." Hence, *genesis* means "creation; beginning; the birth or origin of anything."

> *The genesis of the universe may have been a big explosion.*
> *Genesis, the story of the Creation, is the first book of the Bible.*

genius comes directly from a Latin word based on *gen-* meaning "the inborn or guardian spirit of a person or place." Hence, *genius* came to mean "extraordinary inborn intelligence" or "an outstanding natural aptitude for doing something." It also means "a person who has a brilliant mind, especially one of great intellectual achievements."

> *Einstein had a genius for mathematics.*
> *Shakespeare was a genius.*

genial comes from the same Latin word as *genius* and literally means "of one's guardian spirit." Hence, *genial* means "showing inborn or natural kindliness or pleasantness; giving comfort, warmth, or life."

> *She has a friendly, genial personality.*

A word based on *genial* is *congenial,* meaning "sympathetic or agreeable" and used to describe people or situations that one is naturally happy with or suited to.

> *His colleagues are all congenial.*
> *She finds her job very congenial.*

genuine comes from a Latin word based on *gen-* meaning "natural; inborn; innate." Hence, *genuine* means "native; original; authentic; real."

> *He is a genuine New Englander.*
> *This is genuine leather, not an imitation.*

genital comes from *genit-* meaning "to give birth to; beget" and the Latin suffix *-al* meaning "pertaining to." Thus, *genital* means "pertaining to the birth-giving or reproductive organs or processes." The *genitals* are "the external sexual organs."

A word based on *genital* is *congenital,* meaning (1) existing at or before birth, but not inherited; (2) by nature; natural; born.

> *The baby had a congenital defect.*
> *That boy is a congenital liar.*

progenitor comes from the Latin prefix *pro-* meaning "before" and *genit-* meaning "to give birth to; beget," plus the suffix *-or* meaning "the person or thing performing the action." Thus, *progenitor* means "an ancestor, usually remote; forebear."

> *The woolly mammoth is a progenitor of the elephant.*

◊ Look up these *gen-* words in your dictionary. Notice how the meaning of each word is based on the root *gen-* or *genit-* meaning "to produce; give birth to."

genitive	ingenious	ingenuous
hydrogen	ingenuity	oxygen

NOTE: There is a difference in meaning between *ingenious* and *ingenuous.* If you have trouble distinguishing between these two words, study their different definitions and the following sample sentences:

> *That was an ingenious solution to the problem.*
> *The naive child asked many ingenuous questions.*

This vocabulary test contains roots and words you have already learned. Choose the answer nearest in meaning to the key word. Answers follow.

1. **deferential** [def'ə·ren'shəl]—(a) lazy; uncaring. (b) the total difference between two things. (c) a number that is subtracted from another. (d) respectful; courteous.

2. **preference** [pref'ər·əns]—(a) that which precedes or comes first in time. (b) the largest portion. (c) an indirect statement; hint. (d) a choosing of one thing over another.

3. **reference** [ref'ər·əns *or* ref'rəns] —(a) second choice. (b) direction of the attention to a person or thing. (c) praise; a compliment. (d) printed material, as a book.

4. **referendum** [ref'ə·ren'dəm]—(a) a period of waiting. (b) the submission of a proposed law to a popular vote. (c) a ballot. (d) the submission of a dispute to a mediator or judge.

5. **transferal** [trans·fûr'əl]—(a) a method or means of transfer. (b) an official document. (c) trespassing. (d) the state or process of growth.

6. **reflex** [rē'fleks]—(a) the main muscle of the upper arm. (b) an involuntary movement, such as sneezing. (c) any quick movement. (d) an inverted image, such as seen in a mirror.

7. **inflection** [in·flek'shən]—(a) a modulation of the voice. (b) any quick movement. (c) a physical defect. (d) the thigh bone.

8. **influx** [in'fluks']—(a) constant change. (b) magnetic force, as around the North Pole. (c) a continuous flowing in, as of people or things. (d) unyielding; stubborn.

9. **fluctuation** [fluk'choo·ā'shən]— (a) a flood. (b) a confusing situation. (c) the monthly cycle of the tides. (d) continual change; vacillation.

10. **effluence** [ef'loo·əns]—(a) power to effect by indirect means. (b) political power. (c) a flowing out; emanation. (d) an oily scum, as on water.

11. **infraction** [in·frak'shən]—(a) the breaking of a law or rule. (b) a minor fracture, as of a small bone. (c) reflected light, as from a mirror. (d) a number that is divided by another.

ANSWERS:

1. **deferential**—(d) respectful; courteous. 2. **preference**—(d) a choosing of one thing over another. 3. **reference**—(b) direction of the attention to a person or thing. 4. **referendum**—(b) the submission of a proposed law to a popular vote. 5. **transferal**—(a) a method or means of transfer. 6. **reflex** —(b) an involuntary movement, such as sneezing. 7. **inflection**—(a) modulation of the voice. 8. **influx**—(c) a continuous flowing in, as of people or things. 9. **fluctuation**—(d) continual change; vacillation. 10. **effluence**—(c) a flowing out; emanation. 11. **infraction**—(a) the breaking of a law or rule.

ROOT: GEO-

Can you think of what *geography* and *geology* have in common? They both apply to the earth. In fact, both words are based on the Greek root *geo-* meaning "earth." The root *geo-* appears chiefly in words for certain common and important sciences or branches of knowledge. Here are the three "earthy" core vocabulary words based on *geo-*: *geography, geology, geometry.*

geography comes from *geo-* meaning "earth" and the Greek root *-graphy* meaning "writing; description." Thus, *geography* is "the description of the earth"; that is, "the science that describes the surface of the earth, or of other planets, especially in terms of large areas and how they are related."

> *Everyone studies some geography in school.*
> *We have learned a great deal about the moon's geography.*

Three words based on *geography* are *geographic* and *geographical,* which mean "pertaining to geography," and *geographer,* meaning "a specialist in or student of geography."

> *He is a member of the local geographic society.*
> *What was the expedition's exact geographical location?*
> *The expedition included a geographer to map the region.*

geology comes from *geo-* meaning "earth" and the Greek root *-logy* meaning "the science or study of." Thus, *geology* means "the science that deals with the origin and structure of the earth, especially its rocks and rock formations."

> *Gold prospectors must have some knowledge of geology.*

Three words based on *geology* are *geologic* and *geological,* which mean "pertaining to geology," and *geologist,* meaning "a specialist in or student of geology."

> *This is a geologic textbook.*
> *This is a geological map, showing ore deposits and rock formations.*
> *A geologist could tell us what kind of rock this is.*

geometry comes from *geo-* meaning "earth" and the Greek root *-metry* meaning "measure; measurement." *Geometry* was originally thought of as a way to measure the earth. Today, of course, *geometry* means "the branch of mathematics dealing especially with the measurements of and the relationships between points, lines, angles, surfaces, and solids."

I found geometry harder than algebra.

Three words based on *geometry* are *geometric, geometrical,* and *geometrician. Geometric* and *geometrical* mean (1) pertaining to or according to the rules of geometry; (2) characterized by straight lines, crosses, zigzags, etc., as some designs or paintings. A *geometrician* is "a specialist in geometry."

What is the geometric relation between these two lines?
The wallpaper has a geometrical design.

◇ Here are three more words based on the root *geo-*. These words apply to important concepts; you will find them mentioned in your newspaper from time to time. Look up these words in your dictionary. If you know that *geo-* means "earth," you will learn and remember these words easily.

geochemistry   geophysics   geopolitics

ROOT: GER-, GEST-

Did you know that there is a relationship between the words *belligerent* and *digestion?* They are both based on the Latin root *ger-* or *gest-* meaning "to carry; carry on; produce." Learn the following three core vocabulary words based on this root—*belligerent, digest, gestate*—and the additional words derived from them.

belligerent comes from the Latin root *belli-* meaning "war" and *ger-* meaning "to carry on" plus the Latin suffix *-ent,* which is the same as the English ending *-ing.* Thus, *belligerent* means "carrying on in a warlike way; warlike; antagonistic; engaged in warfare." As a noun, *belligerent* means "a person or nation engaged in warfare or fighting."

He was belligerent toward strangers, always picking fights.

A mediator tried to reconcile the belligerent factions.
The belligerents are going to hold truce talks.

A word based on *belligerent* is *nonbelligerent*, meaning (1) not war-like or not at war; (2) a person or nation that is not at war.

Switzerland is a nonbelligerent country.
A nonbelligerent may aid one of the belligerents in a war.

digest comes from the Latin prefix *di-* meaning "away" and *gest-* meaning "to carry." *Digest* is "to carry away something inside; to take in." Thus, the verb *digest* [di·jest'] means (1) to take in and assimilate, especially food for the body; (2) to take in and understand mentally; (3) to take in and condense or summarize. As a noun, *digest* [dī'jest] means "a condensation or summary."

Are cucumbers hard to digest?
I need time to digest this new idea.
Please digest this long report into a two-page summary.
Have you read the digest of his latest book?

Four words based on *digest* are *digestion, indigestion, digestive,* and *indigestible. Digestion* is "the act or process of digesting." *Indigestion* is "faulty digestion; painful or imperfect digestion, as from overeating or from eating rich or unsuitable foods." *Digestive* means "pertaining to or aiding digestion." *Indigestible* means "hard or impossible to digest."

Father claims to have a good digestion.
Bart took bicarbonate of soda for his indigestion.
Where is the digestive tract?
He finds cucumbers indigestible.

gestate comes from *gest-* meaning "to carry" and the Latin suffix *-ate,* which is used to form verbs. *Gestate* is "to carry young inside the body." Thus, *gestate* means "to carry young in the uterus."

The human female gestates for nine months.

A word based on *gestate* is *gestation,* meaning "the growth and development of the young in the uterus; pregnancy."

Gestation in human beings requires nine months.

◊ Look up the following words in your dictionary and learn their meanings. Notice how each word is based on the root *ger-* or *gest-* meaning "to carry; carry on; produce."

congest	gesticulate	gesture
congestion	gesticulation	ingest

NOTE: In this chapter you learned that the Latin root *belli-* means "war," as in *belligerent*. Knowing what the root *belli-* means, can you figure out the meanings of *bellicose* and *antebellum?* If you don't know what *bellicose* and *antebellum* mean, look them up in your dictionary and note how both are based on the root *belli-* meaning "war."

ROOT: GRAD-, GRESS-

The Latin root *grad-* or *gress-* means either "a step" or "to step or go." Learn the following four core vocabulary words based on *grad-* or *gress-*: *aggression, gradual, graduate, progress*. Here are ten interesting words based on this root.

aggression comes from the Latin prefix *ag-* (another spelling of *ad-*) meaning "to; toward" and *gress-* meaning "to step or go" plus the Latin suffix *-ion* meaning "the act or state of." An *aggression* is literally "an act of going to, or an approach toward, someone." Thus, *aggression* means "an attack."

The warring nations accused each other of aggression.

Two words related to *aggression* are *aggressive*, meaning "characterized by vigorous activity; disposed toward a forceful approach or attack"; and *aggressor*, which means "one who commits aggression."

Tom is an aggressive salesman—a real go-getter.
The United Nations condemned the aggressors.

gradual comes from *grad-* meaning "a step" and the Latin suffix *-al* meaning "pertaining to." *Gradual* means "moving or changing slowly, as if by steps; little by little; step by step."

The change in the weather was gradual.
Gradually his broken bones began to mend.

A word based on *gradual* is *gradualism,* meaning "the principle of gradual change, especially in social or political matters."

The governor is not against change but practices gradualism.

graduate comes from the root *grad-* meaning "a step" and the suffix *-ate* meaning "to take or make." The verb *graduate* [graj'ōō·āt] literally means "to take a step." Hence, it means "to grant or receive a diploma or degree for completing a course of study at a school or college." A *graduate* [graj'ōō·it] is "a person who holds a diploma or degree, especially a bachelor's degree." In other senses, the verb *graduate* means "to mark off in measured units" or "to adjust or change by steps."

The school graduated him at the top of his class.
He graduated from college in June.
She is a graduate of the University of Michigan.
Thermometers are graduated for the measurement of temperature.
The income tax is graduated; the more a person earns, the higher his tax bracket.

A word based on *graduate* is *graduation,* meaning (1) the act of graduating; (2) a ceremony at which degrees or diplomas are given out; (3) an equal division or mark of measurement, as on a scale.

We attended the graduation exercises.
The graduations on this thermometer are hard to see.

progress comes from the Latin prefix *pro-* meaning "forward" and *gress-* meaning "to step or go." Thus, the noun *progress* [prog'res] means "a going forward; advancement; improvement." The verb *progress* [prə·gres'] means "to go forward; advance; improve."

Have you noticed progress in your vocabulary building?
We must progress to our final goal.

Two words based on *progress* are *progression* and *progressive.* *Progression* means (1) the act of progressing; (2) an advancing sequence of things. *Progressive* means (1) moving forward, proceeding, or increasing; (2) aiming at progress.

The series 2, 4, 8, 16 is a mathematical progression.
There has been a progressive worsening of air pollution.
He is a progressive politician.

◇ Look up the following words in your dictionary. Learn the meaning of each and note how it is based on the root *grad-* or *gress-* meaning "to step or go."

digress	regress	transgress
digression	regression	transgression
digressive	regressive	transgressor

QUICKIEQUIZQUICKIEQUIZQUICKIEQUIZQUICKIEQUIZQUICKIEQUIZQUICKIEQUIZQUICKIEQUIZQUICKIE

90-SECOND QUICKIE QUIZ

WORD BUILDING

Reviewing the meanings of roots you have learned will help you remember them. You have already learned the roots and words given below. Match each root in the left-hand column with its meaning in the right-hand column. Answers follow.

1. **geo-** as in geology [jē·ol′ə·jē]   (a) ancient
2. **anthropo-** as in anthropology [an′thrə·pol′ə·jē] (b) pleasing
3. **archeo-** as in archeology [är′kē·ol′ə·jē]   (c) a step
4. **flux-** as in influx [in′fluks′]   (d) a flow
5. **fract-** as in fraction [frak′shən]   (e) to melt; pour
6. **grad-** as in gradual [graj′ōo·əl]   (f) earth
7. **grat-** as in gratitude [grat′ə·tyōod]   (g) man; human
8. **fus-** as in fusion [fyōo′zhən]   (h) to break

ANSWERS:

1. **geo-** —(f) earth. Geology is the science that deals with the origin and structure of the earth, especially its rocks and rock formations.
2. **anthropo-** —(g) man; human. Anthropology is the science that deals with the physical, social, cultural, and material development of man; it is the study of mankind.
3. **archeo-** —(a) ancient. Archeology is the study of history from the remains of ancient human cultures.
4. **flux-** —(d) a flow. An influx is a flowing or coming in, as of a large number of people or things.
5. **fract-** —(h) to break. A fraction is something broken off from the whole; a small portion or part; a quantity less than a whole number or unit.
6. **grad-** —(c) a step. Gradual means moving or changing slowly; step-by-step, little-by-little.
7. **grat-** —(b) pleasing. Gratitude is the state of being pleased or thankful; thankfulness, appreciation.
8. **fus-** —(e) to melt; pour. A fusion is a melting or blending together; a combination.

QUICKIEQUIZQUICKIEQUIZQUICKIEQUIZQUICKIEQUIZQUICKIEQUIZQUICKIEQUIZQUICKIEQUIZQUICKIE

ROOT: GRAT-

The Latin root *grat-* means "pleasing." The five core vocabulary words based on this root are: *congratulate, grateful, gratify, gratitude, gratuity.*

congratulate comes from the prefix *con-* meaning "together" and a Latin word meaning "to rejoice," which is based on the root *grat-* meaning "pleasing." *Congratulate* means "to express one's pleasure at the success, joy, etc., of someone else."

> *We congratulated John when he won the prize.*

A word based on *congratulate* is *congratulation,* meaning "the act of expressing one's pleasure at another's success or good fortune."

> *We sent our congratulations when our neighbors had a baby.*

grateful comes from *grat-* meaning "pleasing" and the suffix *-ful* meaning "tending to; characterized by." Thus, *grateful* means "characterized by being well pleased"; hence, "thankful or appreciative."

> *She was grateful for our help.*

gratify comes from *grat-* meaning "pleasing" and the Latin suffix *-ify* meaning "to make." Thus, to *gratify* is "to make pleased; to give pleasure or satisfaction to." *Gratify* also means "to satisfy or indulge."

> *She was gratified by the response to her suggestion.*
> *He gratified his wife's every wish.*

A word based on *gratify* is *gratification,* meaning "pleasure or satisfaction."

> *What gratification do you get from studying?*

gratitude comes from *grat-* meaning "pleasing" and the suffix *-itude* meaning "the quality or state of." *Gratitude* means "the state of being pleased or thankful; thankfulness; appreciation."

> *We were full of gratitude for the help she gave us.*

A word based on *gratitude* is *ingratitude,* meaning "lack of thankfulness or appreciation."

> *Parents sometimes accuse their children of ingratitude.*

gratuity comes from *grat-* meaning "pleasing" and the Latin suffix *-ity* meaning "the quality or state of." Thus, *gratuity* means "something given for having pleased another; especially, a gift of money given in return for some service." In short, *gratuity* is a very formal word for a tip.

Do you think the doorman expects a gratuity at Christmastime?

A word based on *gratuity* is *gratuitous,* meaning (1) free; (2) lacking cause; unwarranted.

Some people like to give gratuitous advice.
That was a gratuitous insult.

◊ Look up the following words in your dictionary. Learn their meanings and relate each to the root *grat-* meaning "pleasing": *gratis, ingrate.*

ROOT: GRAV-

The Latin root *grav-* means "heavy." A key word to remember in learning the root *grav-* is our modern adjective *grave,* meaning "of great importance; solemn; dignified; somber."

The town banker always had a grave look on his face.
This is a grave political issue.

Add *grave* to your core vocabulary, along with two additional words based on the root *grav-: aggravate* and *gravity.*

aggravate comes from the Latin prefix *ag-* (another spelling of *ad-*) meaning "to" and *grav-* meaning "heavy" plus the Latin suffix *-ate,* which can be used to form verbs. Thus, *aggravate* means "to make heavy"; hence, "to make worse, more unpleasant, or more burdensome."

His cold was aggravated by the rainy weather.
He is aggravating his cold by going out in the rain.

NOTE: Precise writers and speakers do not use *aggravate* to mean "annoy" or *aggravating* to mean "annoying, provoking, or exasperating." These usages are informal.

gravity comes from *grav-* meaning "heavy" and the Latin suffix *-ity* meaning "the state or quality of." Thus, *gravity* means "heaviness," or more specifically, "the force that causes material objects to fall toward the center of the earth." In another sense, *gravity* means "seriousness."

Who discovered the force of gravity?
Are you aware of the gravity of the current political situation?

Three words related to or based on *gravity* are *gravitate, gravitation,* and *gravitational*. *Gravitate* means "to move or be attracted as if by the force of gravity." *Gravitation* is (1) the act or state of gravitating; (2) in physics, the force whereby any two bodies attract each other; (3) gravity. *Gravitational* means "of or having to do with gravity or gravitation."

He gravitates toward people his own age.
The gravitation of one suspended object toward another can be measured by delicate instruments.
The earth's gravitational pull is greater than that of the moon.

◊ Now that you know what *gravity* means and that it is based on the root *grav-* meaning "heavy," look up the scientific term *specific gravity* in your dictionary. Note the difference between mere *weight* and *specific gravity*.

ROOT: HER-, HES-

The Latin root *her-* or *hes-* means "to stick." Learn the two core vocabulary words based on *her-* or *hes-: adhere* and *cohere*.

adhere comes from the Latin prefix *ad-* meaning "to" and *her-* meaning "to stick." Thus, *adhere* means "to stick to; stick fast; be attached to."

This tape won't adhere to a slick surface.
He always adheres to his principles.
In spite of opposition he adhered to his plan.

Four words based on *adhere* are *adherence, adherent, adhesion,* and *adhesive*. *Adherence* means "firm or faithful attachment." An *adherent*

99

INCREASE YOUR WORD POWER

is "a follower or supporter of a cause, doctrine, or leader." *Adhesion* means (1) sticking fast; (2) firm attachment or fidelity. *Adhesive* means (1) sticky or designed to stick; (2) a substance that sticks things together, as glue.

> *Their strict adherence to their beliefs brought them persecution.*
> *He is an adherent of the philosophy of nonviolence.*
> *The tape holds the bandage in place by adhesion.*
> *Where is the adhesive tape?*
> *Animal glue is a strong adhesive.*

cohere comes from the Latin prefix *co-* meaning "together" and *her-* meaning "to stick." *Cohere* means "to stick together"; hence, "to be firmly or logically connected; to hold together or be consistent."

> *The snowball wouldn't cohere and flew apart when he threw it.*
> *The stories of the three witnesses don't cohere.*

Four words based on *cohere* are *coherence, coherent, cohesion,* and *cohesive. Coherence* means (1) a sticking together; (2) logical connection or consistency. *Coherent* means (1) sticking together; (2) logically connected and consistent; (3) understandable. *Cohesion* is "the act or state of sticking together." *Cohesive* means "sticking close together."

> *His speech lacked coherence; he rambled and digressed aimlessly.*
> *Did you think his speech was coherent?*
> *She was too terrified to speak coherently.*
> *The cohesion of their family group is remarkable.*
> *He belongs to a very cohesive group of friends.*

NOTE: Many people confuse the words *adhesive* and *cohesive* because both are based on the root *hes-* meaning "to stick." Remember that the prefix *ad-* means "to," so that *adhesive* means "sticking to something else." Remember that the prefix *co-* means "together," so that *cohesive* means "sticking together." Something that is *adhesive* sticks *to* something else. Something that is *cohesive* sticks *together* in a solid mass.
◊ Learn the meaning of the following *her-* or *hes-* words from your dictionary. All these words also have the prefix *in-*, which has two possible meanings: "in" or "into" and "not." In which of the following *her-, hes-* words does the prefix *in-* mean "in"? In which word does it mean "not"?

incoherent   inhere   inherent   inhesion

Fun With Words

TOUGHER ROOTS

Some of the roots you learned in the preceding pages are found in these twelve words. Choose the word or phrase you believe is closest in meaning to the key word. Answers follow.

1. **genocide** [jen′ə·sīd]—(a) the extermination of an entire race or people. (b) self-destruction. (c) the murder of one's father. (d) the assassination of a king.

2. **homogeneity** [hō′mə·jə·nē′ə·tē] —(a) longevity. (b) comfort. (c) uniformity or likeness in kind. (d) manliness.

3. **genealogy** [je′ne·al′ə·je]—(a) the study of genes and chromosomes. (b) the science of man. (c) the study of old age. (d) a record of family descent.

4. **misogyny** [mis·oj′·ə·nē]—(a) hatred of mankind. (b) hatred of women. (c) hatred of marriage. (d) rule by a woman or women.

5. **juxtaposition** [juks′tə·pə·zish′ən] —(a) wide separation. (b) fairmindedness. (c) stubborn opposition. (d) placement side by side.

6. **luminary** [lōō′mə·ner′ē]—(a) a famous person. (b) pertaining to the moon's atmosphere. (c) hopeful. (d) a person who is very vain.

7. **homonym** [hom′ə·nĭm]—(a) a word with the same sound as another word but with a different meaning. (b) in complete accord. (c) a false name. (d) internal secretion of the endocrine glands.

8. **heterogeneous** [het′ər·ə·jē′nē·əs] —(a) pertaining to men and women. (b) foreign. (c) consisting of different elements; unlike. (d) unorthodox opinions.

9. **misogamy** [mis·og′ə·mē]—(a) hatred of marriage. (b) hatred of human society. (c) rule by a woman or women. (d) hatred of women.

10. **linguistics** [ling·gwis′tiks]—(a) the study of diction and enunciation. (b) geometric patterns. (c) the science of light. (d) the science and study of language.

11. **iconoclast** [ī·kon′ə·klast]—(a) a type of spring flower. (b) a destroyer of images. (c) a revolutionist. (d) a pioneer.

12. **monogamous** [mə·nog′ə·məs]— (a) boring and tiresome. (b) all of the same kind. (c) womanhating. (d) having only one spouse.

ANSWERS:

1. **genocide**—(a) the extermination of an entire race or people. 2. **homogeneity**—(c) uniformity or likeness in kind. 3. **genealogy**—(d) a record of family descent. 4. **misogyny**—(b) hatred of women. 5. **juxtaposition**—(d) placement side by side. 6. **luminary**—(a) a famous person. 7. **homonym**—(a) a word with the same sound as another word but with a different meaning. 8. **heterogeneous**—(c) consisting of different elements; unlike. 9. **misogamy**—(a) hatred of marriage. 10. **linguistics**—(d) the science and study of language. 11. **iconoclast**—(b) a destroyer of images. 12. **monogamous**—(d) having only one spouse.

ROOT: JAC-, JECT-

The Latin root *jac-* or *ject-* means "to throw, lie, or be thrown down." Learn the three core vocabulary words based on *jac-* or *ject-*: *adjacent, inject, project.*

adjacent comes from the Latin prefix *ad-* meaning "near" and *jac-* meaning "to be thrown down" plus the Latin suffix *-ent* which is the same as our English ending *-ing. Adjacent* therefore means "thrown down, or lying, next to or near something else; situated or located next to or near one another; adjoining."

> *Mr. Green's farm is adjacent to ours.*
> *We took adjacent rooms at the hotel.*

inject comes from the Latin prefix *in-* meaning "into" and *ject-* meaning "to throw." To *inject* is "to throw or shoot something into something else." Thus, *inject* means "to force into, as when shooting a fluid, drug, etc., into the body with a syringe or hypodermic needle," or "to introduce into, as when throwing in a comment or bringing in a new element."

> *The doctor injected the vaccine into my arm.*
> *Simon injected a touch of humor into the conversation.*

A word based on *inject* is *injection,* meaning (1) the act of forcing or introducing something into something else; (2) that which is injected.

> *Have you had a typhoid injection?*

project comes from the Latin prefix *pro-* meaning "forward; before" and *ject-* meaning "to throw." Thus, the verb *project* [prǝ·jekt'] literally means "to throw forward or throw forth"; hence, "to put forth one's words, ideas, etc.; to make oneself heard or understood." Pronounced another way, the noun *project* [proj'ekt] means "something that is proposed; a plan."

> *The speaker projected his voice all the way to the back row.*
> *The business project was approved.*

Four words based on *project* are *projectile, projection, projector,* and *projectionist.* A *projectile* is "something that is thrown forward by force." *Projection* means (1) the act of throwing forward; putting forth or presenting something; (2) something that is projected, presented, or proposed. A *projector* is "a person or thing that projects; especially, a machine for throwing film images on a screen." A *projectionist* is "an operator of a motion-picture film projector."

> *Both spears and bullets are projectiles.*
> *The projection of the film was delayed because of a missing reel.*
> *This chart is a projection of next year's income and expenses.*
> *The film projector is broken, and the projectionist can't fix it.*

◊ Look up the following words in your dictionary. Learn the meaning of each word and be sure you understand how each is built on the root *jac-* or *ject-* meaning "to throw."

abject	ejaculate	object
adjective	eject	reject
dejection	interjection	subject

ROOT: JUNCT-, JOIN-, JOINT-

Can you guess what the Latin root *junct-*, *join-*, or *joint-* means? It is as easy as it looks. This root means "to join." Of course, *join* and *joint* are key words to remember with this root. We all know what *join* means, and it is obvious that a *joint* in the body is "a place where two bones are joined together." Learn the following four core vocabulary words based on the root *junct-*, *join-*, or *joint-*: *adjoin, conjunction, injunction, junction.*

adjoin comes from the Latin prefix *ad-* meaning "to" and *join-* meaning "to join." Thus, *adjoin* means "to join to"; hence, "to be next to and often connected with something."

> *Our farm adjoins the road.*

Note: *Adjacent* and *adjoining* both mean "lying next to," but *adjoining* sometimes carries the additional meaning of being connected. Thus, two *adjacent* hotel rooms are next to each other, while two *adjoining* hotel rooms are next to each other and are connected by a door.

A word related to *adjoin* is *adjunct,* meaning "something of less importance joined to something of greater importance."

> *The orchard is a valuable adjunct of the farm.*

conjunction comes from the Latin prefix *con-* meaning "together" and *junct-* meaning "to join" plus the Latin suffix *-ion* meaning "the act or result of." Thus, *conjunction* means "the act or result of joining together; association." It also means "an occurrence of events joined together in time; a simultaneous occurrence." In grammar a *conjunction* is a word that joins grammatical elements together.

> *Our club is giving a dance in conjunction with two other organizations.*
> *The conjunction of the two accidents at midnight was strange.*
> *The conjunction and may be used to join independent clauses together in a compound sentence.*

Two words based on or related to *conjunction* are *conjoin,* meaning "to join together; combine; unite"; and *conjunctive,* meaning "connective."

> *We believe in justice conjoined with mercy.*
> And *is a conjunctive word.*

injunction comes from the prefix *in-* meaning "in; into" and *junct-* meaning "to join" plus the suffix *-ion* meaning "the act or state of." Thus, *injunction* means "the act of legally joining in or butting in"; hence, (1) the act of ordering something authoritatively; (2) an authoritative order or direction, especially one issued by a court of law that forbids a party from taking a certain action.

> *The judge issued an injunction against the strike.*

junction comes from the root *junct-* meaning "to join" and the suffix *-ion* meaning "the act or state of." Thus, *junction* means "the act of joining or the state of being joined"; hence, "the place where lines or routes, such as roads, railways, streams, etc., come together or cross."

> *The railway junction is two miles from town.*

◊ Look up the following words in your dictionary. Learn their meanings and how they are based on the root *junct-, join-,* or *joint-.*

disjunctive	enjoin	juncture	subjunctive

ROOT: LEG-, LIG-, LECT-

The Latin root *leg-*, *lig-*, or *lect-* means "to choose" or "to read." It is the basic root of such common words as *lecture*, *elect*, and *collect*. Learn the following six core vocabulary words based on *leg-*, *lig-*, or *lect-*: *collect*, *elect*, *eligible*, *lecture*, *legible*, *select*.

collect comes from the prefix *col-* meaning "together" and *lect-* meaning "to choose." *Collect* originally meant "to choose together." Now, of course, *collect* means (1) to gather together or assemble; (2) to bring together for study or as a hobby; (3) to gather payments of money, donations, etc.; (4) to accumulate, as dust or dirt.

> *People collected in the street to see the fire.*
> *He collects coins and stamps.*
> *The state collects taxes every year.*
> *Dust collects on this windowsill.*

Three words based on *collect* are *collection*, *collective*, and *collector*. *Collection* means (1) the act of gathering together; (2) that which is gathered together or assembled; (3) a collecting of money, as for a church, charity, etc. *Collective* means (1) of, related to, or proceeding from a number of persons or things together; common; (2) a group enterprise. A *collector* is "a person who collects anything."

> *Have you seen my stamp collection?*
> *We made a collective effort to win the game.*
> *He works on a collective farm in Russia.*
> *She is a coin collector.*
> *He is a tax collector.*

elect comes from the Latin prefix *e-* (another spelling of *ex-*) meaning "out" and *lect-* meaning "to choose." Thus, the verb *elect* means "to pick out, or choose; especially, to choose for an office by vote; select." The adjective *elect* means "chosen; chosen for office but not yet installed." The noun *elect* means "those chosen or favored."

> *Linda elected to take a course in dramatics.*
> *This year we vote to elect a president.*
> *He is the president-elect.*
> *Leonardo da Vinci is among the elect in the fine arts.*

QUICKIE QUIZ
SOME FAMILIAR ROOTS

Here are some roots you have already learned. Can you match them with their meanings? Answers follow.

1. **cumb-** as in recumbent [ri·kum′bənt]	(a) to teach
2. **doct-** as in indoctrinate [in·dok′trə·nāt]	(b) to step
3. **cresc-** as in excrescence [iks·kres′əns]	(c) to grow
4. **grad-** as in gradation [grā·dā′shən]	(d) to lie

ANSWERS:

1. **cumb-**—(d) to lie. Recumbent means lying down. 2. **doct-**—(a) to teach. Indoctrinate means to instruct in principles or doctrines. 3. **cresc-**—(c) to grow. An excrescence is an unnatural outgrowth, as a wart. 4. **grad-**—(b) to stop. Gradation means a gradual change by steps.

Three words based on *elect* are *election, elector,* and *electorate.* *Election* means (1) the formal choice of a person or persons for any position, especially by ballot; (2) a popular vote on any question; (3) the act of choosing. An *elector* is "a person who elects; one who is qualified to vote in an election." The *electorate* is "the whole body of voters."

> *He is running in the provincial election.*
> *Many electors vote a straight party ticket.*
> *Twenty percent of the electorate voted for the losing candidate.*

eligible comes from the Latin prefix *e-* (another spelling of *ex-*) meaning "out" and *leg-* meaning "to choose" plus the Latin suffix *-ible* meaning "able to be." Thus, *eligible* means "able to be chosen or picked out for something; worthy of being chosen; qualified for a position, office, or function; suitable; qualified and desirable, as for marriage."

> *Mr. Jones is an eligible candidate for mayor.*
> *All adult citizens are eligible to vote.*
> *Tony is an eligible bachelor.*

A word based on *eligible* is *eligibility,* meaning "the quality of being eligible; suitableness."

> *Have you checked his eligibility to run for office?*

106

lecture comes from *lect-* meaning "to read" and the Latin suffix *-ure* meaning "the act of." Originally, *lecture* meant "the act of reading." Now, of course, a *lecture* is "a discourse, read or spoken, on a specific subject, given before an audience for information or instruction." To *lecture* is "to deliver a lecture or lectures."

> *The professor gave lectures twice a week.*
> *She lectured at the university.*

legible comes from *leg-* meaning "to read" and the Latin suffix *-ible* meaning "able; able to be." Hence, *legible* means "able to be read; readable; clear, as handwriting."

> *This scrawled note is barely legible.*
> *Please try to write legibly.*

A word based on *legible* is *illegible*, meaning "not able to be read, as the result of poor handwriting, smears, bad printing, etc."

> *Your handwriting is illegible.*

select comes from the Latin prefix *se-* meaning "apart" and *lect-* meaning "to choose." Thus, the verb *select* means "to choose something apart from the rest; pick out in preference to others." As an adjective, *select* means "set aside by having been chosen; choice or exclusive."

> *Have you selected the book you want to buy?*
> *These are our best, select tomatoes.*
> *That club has a select membership.*

Two words based on *select* are *selection* and *selective*. *Selection* means (1) the act of choosing; (2) a choice; (3) a collection chosen with care. *Selective* means (1) pertaining to selecting or that which is selected; (2) careful in choosing.

> *Have you made a selection of books to buy?*
> *The store had a good selection of shoes.*
> *She had a highly selective taste in clothes.*

◊ Look up the following words in your dictionary. Learn their meanings and relate each to the root *leg-*, *lig-*, or *lect-* meaning "to choose" or "to read."

elective	lectern	legend	selectivity
intelligent	lecturer	predilection	selectman

Fun With Words

STORIES BEHIND THE WORDS

Here is a vocabulary test of twenty words that have interesting etymologies. Check the word or phrase you believe is closest in meaning to the key word. Answers and etymologies follow.

1. **tantalize** [tan′tə·līz]—(a) to tease or torment by holding out false hopes. (b) to dance in a lively manner. (c) to make one's mouth water. (d) to inoculate.

2. **titan** [tīt′n]—(a) a large cloud formation. (b) a pale blue color. (c) a figure or person of gigantic size. (d) the presiding officer.

3. **mausoleum** [mo′sə·lē′əm]—(a) a museum. (b) a floor covering. (c) a stately tomb. (d) an enclosure for animals.

4. **hegira** [hi·jī′rə]—(a) departure. (b) deceit. (c) bargaining. (d) a burden.

5. **nemesis** [nem′ə·sis]—(a) a fearsome opponent or antagonist. (b) favoritism extended toward relatives. (c) a kidney disease. (d) a bad omen.

6. **hallmark** [hol′märk′]—(a) a disfigurement. (b) a proof of excellence. (c) a piece of furniture. (d) a decoration.

7. **Thespian** [thes′pē·ən]—(a) a tramp. (b) one who lisps. (c) an actor. (d) a gypsy.

8. **solecism** [sol′ə·siz′əm]—(a) comfort. (b) a factor in astronomy. (c) loneliness. (d) a grammatical error.

9. **meander** [mē·an′dər]—(a) to flirt. (b) to waste time. (c) to wander aimlessly. (d) to mumble.

10. **chauvinism** [shō′vən·iz′əm]—(a) exaggerated, vainglorious patriotism. (b) a vulgar display. (c) capitalism. (d) complete and utter defeat.

11. **shambles** [sham′bəlz]—(a) a scene of disorder or ruin. (b) a forest path. (c) aimless wandering. (d) an overcrowded area.

12. **pariah** [pə·rī′ə]—(a) a Hindu ruler. (b) an underling. (c) a diseased person. (d) a social outcast.

13. **shanghai** [shang′hī]—(a) to kidnap for service on a ship. (b) a fancy beverage. (c) to deceive. (d) to render incapable.

14. **maverick** [mav′ər·ik]—(a) an undomesticated animal. (b) a criminal. (c) an immigrant. (d) a nonconformist.

15. **churlish** [chûr′lish]—(a) childlike. (b) effeminate. (c) rude. (d) foolish.

16. **stentorian** [sten′tôr′ē·ən]—(a) infuriated. (b) dignified. (c) loud-voiced. (d) grim.

17. **behemoth** [bi·hē′məth]—(a) a colossal beast. (b) a tomb. (c) a human giant. (d) a heathen idol.

18. **Pyrrhic victory** [pir′ik]—(a) a victory gained by ruinous loss. (b) an overwhelming victory. (c) a quick victory. (d) a victory by a few over many.

19. **braggadocio** [brag′ə·dō′shē·ō]—(a) humor. (b) jargon. (c) empty boasting. (d) long-windedness.

20. **mecca** [mek′ə]—(a) any temple. (b) a small, high plateau. (c) a wasteland. (d) a place of pilgrimage.

STORIES BEHIND THE WORDS

1. **tantalize**—(a) to tease or torment by holding out false hopes. (Tantalus, according to Greek mythology, was punished for a misdeed by being made to stand in water that receded when he tried to drink it and under fruit-laden branches which he could not reach.)

2. **titan**—(c) a figure or person of gigantic size. (The Titans were a race of gigantic Greek gods.)

3. **mausoleum**—(c) a stately tomb. (The tomb of King Mausolus at Halicarnassus was one of the Seven Wonders of the World in ancient times.)

4. **hegira**—(a) departure. (Mohammed's flight from Mecca to Medina in 622 was called his Hegira, which means "departure" in Arabic.)

5. **nemesis**—(a) a fearsome opponent or antagonist. (Nemesis was the Greek goddess of vengeance.)

6. **hallmark**—(b) a proof of excellence. (In medieval times, a hallmark was an official mark stamped on genuine gold and silver articles at the Goldsmiths' Hall in London.)

7. **Thespian**—(c) an actor. (Thespis, an ancient Greek poet and actor, was considered the father of tragic drama.)

8. **solecism**—(d) a grammatical error. (Soloi was an ancient town in Asia Minor, whose inhabitants spoke a substandard dialect of Greek.)

9. **meander**—(c) to wander aimlessly. (The Meander—now called Menderes—is one of the most winding rivers in Asia.)

10. **chauvinism**—(a) exaggerated, vainglorious patriotism. (Nicholas Chauvin was a zealous patriot in Napoleonic France.)

11. **shambles**—(a) a scene of disorder or ruin. (From the Old English word *scamol*, a table on which butchers displayed meat for sale.)

12. **pariah**—(d) a social outcast. (In the caste system of India a pariah belonged to a very low caste, at the botton of the social scale.)

13. **shanghai**—(a) to kidnap for service on a ship. (Men used to be drugged, kidnapped, and forced into service on ships bound for Oriental ports such as Shanghai.)

14. **maverick**—(d) a nonconformist. (Samuel A. Maverick was a Texan who didn't brand his cattle, claiming that all unbranded cattle were his.)

15. **churlish**—(c) rude. (In Anglo-Saxon England a churl was a freeman of low birth.)

16. **stentorian**—(c) loud-voiced. (In Homer's *Iliad*, Stentor is a herald famous for his loud voice.)

17. **behemoth**—(a) a colossal beast. (The behemoth is a mighty Biblical beast described in Job 40: 15–24.)

18. **Pyrrhic victory**—(a) a victory gained by ruinous loss. (King Pyrrhus of Epirus defeated the Romans in battle in 279 B.C., but suffered such heavy losses that the better part of his army was wiped out.)

19. **braggadocio**—(c) empty boasting. (Braggadochio is a boastful character in Edmund Spenser's poem *The Faerie Queen*.)

20. **mecca**—(d) a place of pilgrimage. (Mecca, Mohammed's birthplace, is a holy city to which Moslems make pilgrimages.)

ROOT: LOQU-, LOCUT-

Since the ancient Romans loved to give speeches and orations, it is no surprise that they had an important root meaning "to speak." This Latin root is *loqu-* or *locut-*. Learn the four core vocabulary words based on this important root: *colloquial, eloquent, elocution, interlocutor.*

colloquial comes from the Latin prefix *col-* (another spelling of *com-*) meaning "together" and *loqu-* meaning "to speak" plus the Latin suffix *-ial* meaning "pertaining to." Thus, *colloquial* means "pertaining to speaking together or to conversation"; hence, "belonging to informal or conversational speech or writing; informal and conversational."

> *Some colloquial words should never be used in formal writing.*
> *This novel is written in a lively, colloquial style.*

A word based on *colloquial* is *colloquialism,* meaning "an expression or word that is used in or suitable for informal speech or conversation, as opposed to formal speech or writing."

> *"Hi" is a colloquialism for "hello."*

eloquent comes from the Latin prefix *e-* (another spelling of *ex-*) meaning "out" and *loqu-* meaning "to speak" plus the Latin suffix *-ent,* which is the same as the English ending *-ing.* Thus, *eloquent* literally means "speaking out fully"; hence, "making effective use of language, especially in public speaking; forceful or moving."

> *The Gettysburg Address is an eloquent speech.*
> *Sir Wilfred Laurier was noted as an eloquent speaker.*

A word based on *eloquent* is *eloquence,* meaning "highly effective use of language, especially in public speaking."

> *Were you moved by the eloquence of his speech?*

elocution comes from the Latin prefix *e-* meaning "out" and *locut-* meaning "to speak" plus the Latin suffix *-ion* meaning "the act of." Thus, *elocution* literally means "the act of speaking out"; hence, (1) the act or art of public speaking; (2) one's manner of speaking.

> *Some lawyers are masters of elocution.*
> *The nervous speaker was criticized for his poor elocution.*

interlocutor comes from the Latin prefix *inter-* meaning "between; among" and *locut-* meaning "to speak" plus the Latin suffix *-or* meaning "a person who." Thus, an *interlocutor* is literally "a person who speaks between others"; hence, "a person who takes part in a conversation or who keeps a conversation going by asking questions."

> *Dr. Harris was my interlocutor at dinner.*
> *The lawyer served as an interlocutor, trying to get the full story from the witnesses.*

◊ Look up the following words in your dictionary. Learn the meaning of each word and relate the meanings to the root *loqu-* or *locut-* meaning "to speak."

colloquy	locution	loquacious
interlocutory	circumlocution	loquacity

ROOT: MIT-, MISS-

The Latin root *mit-* or *miss-* means "to send; let go." Learn the eight core vocabulary words based on this root: *admit, commit, dismiss, emit, missile, omit, permit, transmit.*

admit comes from the Latin prefix *ad-* meaning "to" and *mit-* meaning "to send; let go." *Admit* literally means "to let go." In practice, *admit* means (1) to let in; let enter; (2) to allow to join; (3) to have or leave room for; (4) to grant something as true.

> *This ticket admits one person to the theater.*
> *The theater could admit only 500 people.*
> *This key will admit you to the office.*
> *Have you been admitted to the club?*
> *His impatience admits no delay.*
> *I admit you are right about that.*

Four words based on *admit* are *admissible, inadmissible, admission,* and *admittance. Admissible* means "allowable." *Inadmissible* means "not allowable." *Admission* is (1) the act of admitting; (2) permission to go in or enter; (3) the price charged for letting a person enter a

111

theater, stadium, etc.; (4) a confession. *Admittance* is "the right or power to enter a place; entrance or admission."

> *The gun was shown to the jury as admissible evidence.*
> *Since the gun had not belonged to the suspect for the last five years, it was judged inadmissible evidence.*
> *Did you gain admission to the college of your choice?*
> *The theater charged a lower admission for children than for adults.*
> *He stole the money by his own admission.*
> *Did you gain admittance through the front door?*

commit comes from the Latin prefix *com-* meaning "together" and *mit-* meaning "to send." *Commit* literally means "to send together." Thus, it actually means (1) to do; (2) to entrust to the care of something or someone; (3) to devote oneself to something; (4) to place someone in custody, as in a prison or mental institution.

> *Did he commit the crime?*
> *Jack committed the speech to memory.*
> *She committed herself to raising her family.*
> *He was committed to prison.*

Two words based on *commit* are *commission* and *committee*. *Commission* means (1) an entrusting; (2) an authorization to act as specified; (3) the act of doing or performing; (4) a body of persons acting under lawful authority to perform certain duties; (5) a fee given an agent or salesman for his services. A *committee* is "a group of people chosen to investigate, report, or act on a matter."

> *He has a commission from the president to take charge of this area.*
> *He was charged with the commission of the crime.*
> *A commission was appointed to investigate the assassination.*
> *The salesman's commission on his sales was $100.*
> *Congress has a large number of committees.*

dismiss comes from the Latin prefix *dis-* meaning "away" and *miss-* meaning "to send." Thus, *dismiss* means "to send away"; hence, (1) to discharge from a job; (2) to tell or allow to go; (3) to reject; (4) to get rid of or have done with quickly.

> *The boss dismissed him because of his laziness.*
> *The teacher dismissed the students for the day.*
> *The politician dismissed the charges against him as lies.*

A word based on *dismiss* is *dismissal*, meaning (1) the act of dismissing or the state of being dismissed; (2) a notice of discharge.

His dismissal from the job came as a shock.

emit comes from the Latin prefix *e-* (another spelling of *ex-*) meaning "out" and *mit-* meaning "to send." Thus, *emit* means "to send out; send forth or give off sound, light, heat, etc.; give expression to something."

The electric typewriter was emitting a low buzz.
The firecracker emitted sparks in all directions.
The radioactive material emitted electromagnetic radiation.
The injured man emitted a moan.

A word based on *emit* is *emission*, meaning (1) the act of emitting something; (2) that which is emitted.

Can you hear the emission of a low buzz from the radio?
Radioactive emissions can be very dangerous.

missile comes from *miss-* meaning "to send" and the Latin suffix *-ile* meaning "able to be." Thus, *missile* literally means "something that can be sent or let go"; hence, "any object intended to be thrown or discharged, such as a rock, spear, arrow, or bullet." In modern times, *missile* has come to mean "a guided rocket."

The boy was collecting missiles for his slingshot.
"Apollo 12" was the first missile to take man to the moon.

omit comes from the Latin prefix *o-* (another spelling of *ob-*) meaning "toward" and *mit-* meaning "to send." *Omit* originally meant "to send something toward another person." Now *omit* means "to let something go away from oneself; let go; leave out; fail to include or do something."

I omitted sugar from the shopping list.
Helen carefully omitted her age on her application form.

A word based on *omit* is *omission*, meaning (1) the act of leaving something out; (2) something that is left out.

The shopping list was complete except for the omission of sugar.
Sugar was not a serious omission.

permit comes from the Latin prefix *per-* meaning "through" and *mit-*

meaning "to send; let go." Thus, *permit* [pər·mit'] means "to send or let something go through"; hence, "to allow, consent to, authorize, or offer an opportunity for." A *permit* [pûr'mit] is "a written authorization to do something; any official document authorizing the performance of a specified activity."

The mother permitted the children to go to the movies.
You are not permitted to park here.
His explanation did not permit of any misunderstanding.
Do you have a learner's permit to drive?

Three words based on *permit* are *permissible, permission,* and *permissive. Permissible* means "allowable." *Permission* is (1) the act of allowing; (2) formal authorization or consent. *Permissive* means (1) granting permission; (2) not strict in discipline; lenient.

It is not permissible to park here.
Do you have permission to park here?
The teacher is permissive and allows some talking in the classroom.

transmit comes from the Latin prefix *trans-* meaning "across" and *mit-* meaning "to send." Thus, *transmit* means "to send something across"; hence, "to send something from one place to another; pass on anything, such as news, a disease, a message, etc."

The message was transmitted from New York to London by cable.
Influenza is easily transmitted from person to person.

Two words based on *transmit* are *transmitter* and *transmission.* A *transmitter* is "a person or thing that transmits; especially, the part of an instrument, such as a telephone or telegraph or a radio or television system, that sends messages or that transmits electrical waves." *Transmission* means (1) the act of transmitting or the state of being transmitted; (2) that which is transmitted; (3) the device in an automobile that transmits the power from the engine to the driving wheels.

The transmitter of a telephone changes sound waves to electrical waves.
The transmitter of this station is located on a hill near town.
The transmission of the TV program was interrupted by a power failure.
Does this car have an automatic transmission?

◊ Look up the following words in your dictionary. Learn the meaning

114

of each word and relate each meaning to the root *mit-* or *miss-* meaning "to send; let go."

intermittent	emissary	missive	remission
missionary	intermission	remiss	remit

ROOT: MON-, MONIT-

The Latin root *mon-* or *monit-* means "to warn; advise." Learn the four core vocabulary words based on this root: *admonish, monument, monitor, premonition.*

admonish comes from the Latin prefix *ad-* meaning "to" and *mon-* meaning "to warn; advise" plus the suffix *-ish,* which appears as a verb ending. Thus, *admonish* means "to warn or advise someone of a fault; caution someone about a danger; reprove someone about an error."

The teacher admonished the dozing student to pay attention.

A word based on *admonish* is *admonition,* meaning (1) the act of admonishing; (2) a mild warning or gentle reproof.

The student didn't hear the teacher's admonition.

monument comes from *mon-* meaning "to warn; advise" and the Latin suffix *-ment* meaning "the act or means of." A *monument* is literally "a means of advising or reminding people of something." Thus, *monument* means "something, such as a statue, arch, pillar, etc., built as a reminder of a person, event, or the like." In more specific senses, *monument* means "a tombstone," or "a work of art, literature, scholarship, etc., that is considered to be of lasting value."

Have you seen the Centennial Monument?
There are thousands of monuments in this cemetery.
Michelangelo's great fresco on the Sistine Chapel ceiling is a monument to Renaissance art.

115

A word based on *monument* is *monumental,* meaning (1) pertaining to, like, or serving as a monument; (2) of great importance; memorable; (3) larger than life; huge or massive.

> *This is a monumental day in the history of our town.*
> *The Peace Tower is of monumental size.*

monitor comes from *monit-* meaning "to warn; advise" and the Latin suffix *-or* meaning "a person who or a thing that does something." Thus, a *monitor* is literally "one who advises or warns"; hence, (1) a student chosen to answer the door, carry messages and perform other assigned duties; (2) an apparatus used to check radio and television broadcasts for quality, compliance with laws, etc. To *monitor* is "to listen to or check conversations, radio or television broadcasts, etc., for quality, compliance with the law, or for other specific information."

> *As school monitor, Gene has to act as receptionist and escort visitors to various parts of the building.*
> *We are going to monitor all news broadcasts to see which station gives the most local events.*

A word based on *monitor* is *monitory,* meaning "warning."

> *The teacher gave Jim a monitory look and he stopped whispering.*

premonition comes from the Latin prefix *pre-* meaning "before" and *monit-* meaning "to warn; advise" plus the Latin suffix *-ion* meaning "the state or result of." Thus, a *premonition* is "the state of being warned beforehand"; hence, "an instinctive sense of what is going to happen in the future, based on intuition, not information."

> *Carl had a premonition that he would be in an accident.*

A word based on *premonition* is *premonitory,* meaning "giving warning beforehand; giving or containing a premonition."

> *Headache and sore throat are the first premonitory symptoms of many infectious childhood diseases.*

◊ Look up *admonishment* and *admonitory* in your dictionary. Learn their meanings and note how they are based on the root *mon-* or *monit-* meaning "to warn; advise."

EXPLORING WORDS

FROM THE ART WORLD

Painting, sculpture, and drawing have a special vocabulary of their own. If you like art, know someone who does, or would like to know more about it, here are some useful terms.

abstract a painting that does not portray natural objects or figures, but uses lines, masses of color, and geometrical forms such as oblongs, squares, circles, etc.

bas-relief [bä′ri·lēf′] a piece of sculpture in which the figures are raised out only slightly from a background panel or wall, such as a frieze on a building.

chiaroscuro [kē·är′ə·skyoor′ō] (1) the distribution and treatment of light and shade in a picture; (2) a kind of picture using only light and shade and no definite lines.

fresco a painting made by applying colors to a wet plaster surface, so that they sink in deeply and dry with it.

frieze a long strip or band of decoration, as on a building, ornamented with lettering, sculpture, scrolls, etc.

gouache [gwosh] a painting using opaque colors mixed with water and gum.

impasto [im·päs′tō] a method of painting in which colors are applied thickly so that they stand out from the canvas.

impressionism a late nineteenth-century theory and style of painting that tried to produce the visual impression of the subject with the color values of light and air—sometimes purposely resulting in paintings that seem misty or vaguely out of focus.

mobile a piece of sculpture made of wire, strips of metal, etc., in such a way that it moves when touched or blown by the wind.

mural a painting applied directly to a wall or ceiling.

palette a flat, thin piece of wood, plastic, etc., which holds the different paints used by an artist, and which is often held in the hand.

pastel [pas·tel′] a drawing made with colored crayons, especially soft crayons made of pipe clay, pigment, and gum water.

study a preliminary sketch or exercise, as a preliminary rough sketch of an object or landscape that will later be the subject of a painting.

tempera (1) a fast-drying paint made of colors that are mixed with water and egg yolk; (2) a painting made from such paint.

water color (1) a painting made with pigments mixed in water; (2) paint having water as the medium.

ROOT: MOV-, MOT-

The Latin root *mov-* or *mot-* means "to move." The common words *move, movement,* and *motion* are all directly based on the Latin root *mov-* or *mot-*. Keep them in mind as you master four more core vocabulary words based on this root: *emotion, promote, remote, remove.*

emotion comes from the Latin prefix *e-* (another spelling of *ex-*) meaning "out" and *mot-* meaning "to move" plus the Latin suffix *-ion* meaning "the act or state of." *Emotion* is literally "the act of moving out or outward." Hence, *emotion* means "a strong surge of feeling that is expressed outwardly; any intense feeling, such as love or hate."

> *Fear is a powerful emotion.*
> *His voice was full of emotion as he told us his story.*

A word based on *emotion* is *emotional,* meaning "full of emotion; pertaining to an emotion or to the feelings in general."

> *We had an emotional meeting with old friends.*
> *The actor gave an emotional performance.*

promote comes from the Latin prefix *pro-* meaning "forward" and *mot-* meaning "to move." Thus, *promote* literally means "to move someone or something forward"; hence, (1) to contribute to the progress or growth of something; (2) to advance someone; (3) to work on behalf of something; (4) to seek to make a product popular or successful.

> *He is famous for promoting public education.*
> *Did your teacher promote you to the next grade?*
> *The company launched an advertising campaign to promote its new product.*

A word based on *promote* is *promotion,* meaning (1) advancement in rank, position, etc.; (2) work on behalf of something.

> *She got a promotion to a more responsible job.*
> *Did the company's promotion campaign succeed in selling the new product?*

remote comes from the Latin prefix *re-* meaning "back" and *mot-* meaning "to move." Something *remote* is "something moved back or away from the place specified." Thus, *remote* means "located far away from a specified place; distant." It also means "not obvious; slight." A third meaning of remote is "distant in manner; aloof."

The beach is remote from the city.
He is a remote cousin of mine.
There is a remote possibility that it may rain tonight.
My grandfather was a remote, silent man.

remove comes from the Latin prefix *re-* meaning "back" plus the English word *move*, which is directly based on the Latin root *mov-* meaning "to move." To *remove* is literally "to move back." Thus, *remove* means (1) to take or move away; (2) to dismiss; (3) to take off; (4) to take out; extract.

They removed the extra chairs after the meeting.
He was removed from his position as head of the bus company.
He removed his coat when he entered the house.
How is the wheat removed from the chaff?
Charlie's tonsils were removed last week.

A word based on *remove* is *removal*, meaning (1) the act of removing or the state of being removed; (2) dismissal.

The operation was for the removal of gallstones.
Brown's removal as head of the bus company was the result of local politics.

NOTE: You have probably already noticed that *remote* and *remove* are based on the same prefix and root, despite the difference in their spellings and in their modern meanings. Their meanings really are very close: Something *remote* is something that is far removed; to *remove* is to move something away.

◊ Look up the following words in your dictionary. Learn the meaning of each and note how each meaning is based on the root *mov-* or *mot-* meaning "to move."

commotion	immovable	remoteness
demobilize	mobile	unmoved
demote	mobilize	motivation
demotion	mobilization	motive
immobilize	motility	motor

119

Fun With Words

REVIEW OF ROOTS

Here are more roots and words you have already learned. Choose the answer that is nearest in meaning to the key word. Answers follow.

1. **digress** [di·gres′ *or* dī·gres′]—(a) to separate. (b) to ramble; wander away from the main topic. (c) to move sideways. (d) to stop suddenly.
2. **regress** [rē′gres *or* ri·gres′]—(a) to right a wrong. (b) to break a promise. (c) to go backward; revert to an earlier state. (d) to complain repeatedly.
3. **transgress** [trans·gres′ *or* tranz·gres′]—(a) to change sides in a debate or argument. (b) to sin; offend. (c) to forgive. (d) to transport over a specific route.
4. **gratis** [grat′is *or* grā′tis]—(a) served with melted cheese on top. (b) to cut up into small pieces. (c) worthless. (d) free of charge.
5. **inherent** [in·hir′ənt *or* in·her′ənt]—(a) pertaining to a male heir. (b) vital; necessary. (c) inborn. (d) the beneficiary of a will.
6. **incoherent** [in′kō·hir′ənt]—(a) lacking logical connection; disjointed; confused. (b) illegible; hard to read. (c) shared equally

by two or more heirs. (d) slick; smooth; not sticky.
7. **eject** [i·jekt′]—(a) to refuse to accept. (b) to throw out with sudden force; expel. (c) to sadden or depress. (d) to pull apart; disassemble.
8. **dejection** [di·jek′shən]—(a) anger; a stormy mood. (b) a pensive, reflective mood. (c) stubbornness. (d) lowness of spirits; depression.
9. **interjection** [in′tər·jek′shən]—(a) a command. (b) an action verb. (c) a one-word exclamation. (d) a question mark.
10. **enjoin** [in·join′]—(a) to share good times. (b) to order, direct, or prohibit authoritatively. (c) to settle a labor dispute. (d) to meet with in order to negotiate.
11. **juncture** [jungk′chər]—(a) a point in time, especially at which a critical decision must be made. (b) the place where two roads cross. (c) a break or rupture. (d) a short vacation or quick trip.

ANSWERS:

1. **digress**—(b) to ramble; wander away from the main topic. 2. **regress**—(c) to go backward; revert to an earlier state. 3. **transgress**—(b) to sin; offend. 4. **gratis**—(d) free of charge. 5. **inherent**—(c) inborn. 6. **incoherent**—(a) lacking logical connection; disjointed; confused. 7. **eject**—(b) to throw out with sudden force; expel. 8. **dejection**—(d) lowness of spirits; depression. 9. **interjection**—(c) a one-word exclamation. 10. **enjoin**—(b) to order, direct, or prohibit authoritatively. 11. **juncture**—(a) a point in time, especially at which a critical decision must be made.

ROOT: NASC-, NAT-

The Latin root *nasc-* or *nat-* means "to be born." Learn the four core vocabulary words based on *nasc-* or *nat-: nascent, nation, native, prenatal.*

nascent [nā′sənt] comes from *nasc-* meaning "to be born" and the Latin suffix *-ent*, which is the same as the English ending *-ing*. Thus, *nascent* means "being born; beginning to exist or develop; newly conceived."

> *The survey uncovered nascent discontent among students.*

nation comes from *nat-* meaning "to be born" plus the suffix *-ion* meaning "the state of." *Nation* literally means "the place of one's birth." Today, of course, *nation* means "a body of persons in a place organized under one government" or "a body of persons having a common origin and language."

> *At what date did Canada become a nation?*
> *He is a member of the Cherokee nation.*

Two words based on *nation* are *national,* meaning "of, belonging to, or representative of a nation," and *nationalism,* which means (1) devotion, often extreme devotion, to the interests of one's own nation; (2) a political belief that the welfare of human beings is best served by the nations acting independently rather than in collective or cooperative action.

> *How much is the national debt?*
> *Nazism was an extreme form of nationalism.*

native comes from *nat-* meaning "to be born" and the Latin suffix *-ive* meaning "tending to" or, in this case, "a person who is." Thus, the noun *native* means "a person or animal born in a particular place," or "something that was originated, developed, or grown in a particular place." The adjective *native* means "by birth or origin; not foreign; inborn or natural."

> *Clarence is a native of Alberta.*
> *These are native Quebec tomatoes.*
> *Nora has a lot of native charm.*

A word based on *native* is *nativity,* meaning "birth, especially in regard to its time, place, or circumstances." *The Nativity* refers to the birth of Christ, or to Christmas Day.

prenatal comes from the Latin prefix *pre-* meaning "before" and *nat-* meaning "to be born" plus the Latin suffix *-al* meaning "pertaining to." Thus, *prenatal* means "pertaining to the time before birth; prior to birth."

> *Good prenatal care produces healthy babies.*

◊ Look up the word *natal* in your dictionary. Learn its meaning and note how it is based on the root *nat-* meaning "to be born." If you have paid attention to the explanation of the word *prenatal,* you can probably figure out the exact meaning of *natal* without using your dictionary. What is someone's "*natal* day"?

ROOT: PEL-, PELL-, PULS-

The Latin root *pel-, pell-,* or *puls-* means "to drive; push." Learn the following three core vocabulary words: *compel, impel, repel.*

compel comes from the Latin prefix *com-* meaning "together" and the root *pel-* meaning "to drive; push." *Compel* originally meant "to drive together; herd." Now it means (1) to urge forcefully; (2) to force or require by law, threat, necessity, etc.

> *My conscience compels me to tell the truth.*
> *All children are compelled to attend school.*

Four words based on *compel* are *compelling, compulsion, compulsive,* and *compulsory. Compelling* means "forceful; overpowering." *Compulsion* is (1) the act of compelling or the state of being compelled; force; coercion; (2) an irresistible impulse or desire. *Compulsive* means (1) compelling; (2) moved by or involving compulsion. *Compulsory* means (1) required; (2) using compulsion.

> *You have no compelling need to leave now.*
> *Did he do it voluntarily or under compulsion?*
> *Lisa has a compulsion to change her clothing several times a day.*

She had a compulsive desire to buy too many clothes.
Many alcoholics are compulsive drinkers.
Every Canadian province has compulsory education.

impel comes from the Latin prefix *im-* meaning "on" and *pel-* meaning "to drive; push." Thus, *impel* means "to drive on; force or drive someone or something to an action; urge on."

His desire for more money impelled him to get more education.

Three words based on *impel* are *impulse*, *impulsion*, and *impulsive*. *Impulse* means "a sudden, unplanned inclination to some action." *Impulsion* means (1) the act of impelling or the state of being impelled; (2) an impulse. *Impulsive* means (1) brought about by impulse rather than by reason or planning; unpremeditated; (2) acting on impulse and without forethought.

He followed his impulse and gave the stranger a lift.
He acted under the impulsion of the moment.
His purchase of an expensive new car was impulsive.

NOTE: *Impel* means "to urge on." It differs from *compel* in that it does not contain the idea of force, law, or coercion. When a person is *compelled* to do something, he has no choice. When he is *impelled* to do something, he feels a strong urge to do it, but he can choose not to.

repel comes from the Latin prefix *re-* meaning "back" and *pel-* meaning "to drive; push." Thus, *repel* means (1) to drive or force someone or something back; (2) cause one to feel distaste or disgust; (3) push or keep away.

The soldiers repelled the enemy attack.
Snakes repel me.
Will this coat repel water?

Three words based on *repel* are *repellent*, *repulsion*, and *repulsive*. *Repellent* means (1) tending to repel; resistant; (2) offensive or disgusting. *Repulsion* is "aversion; a feeling of extreme dislike, horror, or disgust." *Repulsive* means "horrifying or disgusting; abhorrent."

Is this a water-repellent raincoat?
Their way of life was repellent to him.
I feel nothing but repulsion for snakes.
George doesn't think snakes are repulsive.

123

◊ Another important word based on the root *pel-, pell-,* or *puls-* is *propel,* from which the words *propeller* and *propulsion* are derived. Look up these words in your dictionary, along with the words that follow. Learn their meanings and be sure you can relate each word to the root *pel-, pell-,* or *puls-* meaning "to drive; push."

dispel	expulsion	pulsation
expel	pulsate	pulse

QUICKIEQUIZQUICKIEQUIZQUICKIEQUIZQUICKIEQUIZQUICKIEQUIZQUICKIEQUIZQUICKIEQUIZQUICKIE

90-SECOND QUICKIE QUIZ

WORD BUILDING

Here is another quick review quiz of roots and words you have already learned. Match the roots with their meanings. Answers follow.

1. **grav-** as in aggravate [ag′rə·vāt]
2. **lect-** as in election [i·lek′shən]
3. **nat-** as in nation [nā′shən]
4. **anim-** as in unanimous [yoō·nan′ə·məs]
5. **cord-** as in accord [ə·kôrd′]
6. **gam-** as in monogamy [mə·nog′ə·mē]
7. **loque-** as in eloquent [el′ə·kwənt]
8. **audit-** or **aud-** as in audible [ô′də·bəl]
9. **bio-** as in biography [bī·og′rə·fē]

(a) to speak
(b) to hear
(c) marriage
(d) life
(e) to choose; to read
(f) heavy
(g) to be born
(h) life, mind, spirit
(i) heart

ANSWERS:

1. **grav-** —(f) heavy. To aggravate is to make worse or more burdensome or unpleasant.
2. **lect-** —(e) to choose; to read. An election is the choosing of a person or persons by ballot or by popular vote.
3. **nat-** —(g) to be born. Originally nation meant the place of one's birth. Now it means a country or a body of persons having a common origin and language or organized under one government.
4. **anim-** —(h) life, mind, spirit. Unanimous combines the root *un-* meaning one and the root *anim-*. It means being of one mind, sharing the same views.
5. **cord-** —(i) heart. Accord means to be of one heart; agreement.
6. **gam-** —(c) marriage. Monogamy is the practice of having only one wife or husband at a time.
7. **loque-** —(a) to speak. Eloquent means making effective use of language; forceful or moving in public speaking.
8. **audit-** or **aud-** —(b) to hear. Audible means capable of being heard; loud enough to be heard.
9. **bio-** —(d) life. A biography is a written account of a person's life.

QUICKIEQUIZQUICKIEQUIZQUICKIEQUIZQUICKIEQUIZQUICKIEQUIZQUICKIEQUIZQUICKIEQUIZQUICKIE

ROOT: PEND-, PENS-

The Latin root *pend-* or *pens-* means "to hang, weigh, or pay." The reason this root has three meanings is that in Roman times it referred to the weighing of gold on scales. Since weights were hung on one side of the scale and gold was weighed to determine the amount of money to pay, the root *pend-* or *pens-* developed all three meanings: "to hang," "to weigh," and "to pay." Learn the following four core vocabulary words based on the root *pend-* or *pens-*: *depend, dispense, expend, suspend.*

depend comes from the Latin prefix *de-* meaning "down" and *pend-* meaning "to hang." *Depend* originally meant "to hang down." The modern meanings of *depend* came from the idea of something hanging down from, or being supported by, something else. Hence, *depend* means (1) to trust or rely on; (2) to rely for support on someone or something; (3) to be determined.

> *The children depend on their parents in many ways.*
> *Whether we have the picnic or not will depend on the weather.*

Three words based on *depend* are *dependable, dependence,* and *dependent. Dependable* means "trustworthy or reliable." *Dependence* is (1) the state of relying on someone or something for support; (2) the state of being determined by something else; (3) subjection to the control of another. *Dependent* means (1) conditioned by something else; (2) subject to outside control; (3) relying on someone else for support; (4) a person who depends on another for support.

> *Walter owns a dependable car.*
> *The youth disliked his long dependence on his parents.*
> *Your success is dependent on your luck and intelligence.*
> *The income tax form allows you a deduction for each dependent.*

dispense comes from the Latin prefix *dis-* meaning "away" and *pens-* meaning "to weigh." Thus, *dispense* literally means "to weigh and give away"; hence, (1) to give or deal out something in portions; (2) to administer, as laws; (3) to get along without.

> *A pharmacist dispenses medicines.*
> *The judge dispenses justice.*
> *Let's dispense with these wild accusations and discuss the facts.*

Three words based on *dispense* are *dispensable,* meaning "capable of being dispensed with; unnecessary; not essential"; *indispensable,* meaning "incapable of being done without; necessary; essential"; and *dispensary,* which is "a place where medicines and medical advice are given out."

> *During the emergency they cut off all dispensable services.*
> *A car is indispensable to a traveling salesman.*
> *She was a nurse at the school dispensary.*

expend comes from the Latin prefix *ex-* meaning "out" and *pend-* meaning "to pay." Thus, *expend* means "to pay out; spend; use up."

> *What did the firm expend on new equipment last year?*
> *Don't expend all your energy on one thing.*

Five words based on *expend* are *expendable, expenditure, expense, expenses,* and *expensive. Expendable* means (1) available for spending; (2) able to be used up or sacrificed: applied especially to military equipment or supplies that can be sacrificed if necessary. *Expenditure* means (1) the act of expending; outlay; (2) what is spent; expense. *Expense* means (1) cost, outlay, or expenditure; (2) something requiring the continued spending of money; (3) loss or sacrifice necessarily involved in doing something. *Expenses* are "funds provided, spent, or required to cover costs." *Expensive* means "costly."

> *The company has $50,000 in expendable funds.*
> *Rescue the crew and save the records; the ship is expendable.*
> *What were the firm's expenditures for new equipment?*
> *What was the total expense of your trip?*
> *Owning a car is an expense.*
> *Don't work fast at the expense of accuracy.*
> *He receives a salary plus traveling expenses.*
> *A mink coat is very expensive.*

suspend comes from the prefix *sus-* (another spelling of *sub-*) meaning "under" and *pens-* meaning "to hang." *Suspend* literally means "to hang something under, or from, a support above." Hence, *suspend* means (1) to hang from a support, so as to allow free movement; (2) to bar for a time from a privilege or function; (3) to withhold temporarily; (4) to defer action on.

> *The chandelier was suspended from the ceiling.*

The student was suspended from school for a term.
Todd suspended payments on the car until the company had corrected the mechanical defects.
The judge suspended the sentence.

Three words based on *suspend* are *suspenders*, *suspense*, and *suspension*. *Suspenders* are "a pair of straps worn over the shoulders for supporting the trousers." *Suspense* is (1) the state of being uncertain or undecided, usually accompanied by fear, worry, agitation, etc.; (2) an uncertain or doubtful situation. *Suspension* means (1) a debarring; (2) an interruption; (3) a putting off of an action; (4) a stopping of payments in business; (5) any device from which something is suspended; (6) any mechanical system, as the springs in an automobile, intended to support the body or chassis of the machine and insulate it from shocks.

He always wears suspenders instead of a belt.
The outcome of the election kept us in suspense.
Have you heard about Richard's suspension from school?
The road of a suspension bridge is hung from cables.

◊ Look up the following words in your dictionary. Learn their meanings and relate each to the root *pend-* or *pens-* meaning "to hang, weigh, or pay."

append	compensate	pendant
appendage	impending	pending
appendix	independent	pendulum

ROOT: PET-, PETIT-

The Latin root *pet-* or *petit-* means "to go; seek; strive." Learn the following five core vocabulary words based on this root: *appetite, compete, competent, petition, repetition.*

appetite comes from the Latin prefix *ap-* (another spelling of *ad-*) meaning "to" and *pet-* meaning "to seek; strive" plus the Latin suffix *-ite*, which is used to form nouns. Thus, *appetite* originally meant "a striving to satisfy a desire." In modern times *appetite* means (1)

127

a desire for food or drink; (2) a physical craving; (3) a strong liking for anything.

He lost his appetite from eating too much candy.
My wife can't satisfy her appetite for social activities and expensive clothes and furs.

Two words based on *appetite* are *appetizer*, meaning "something that arouses the appetite; especially, tidbits of food served before a meal"; and *appetizing*, which means "stimulating to the appetite; arousing hunger or desire."

Our hostess served nuts and cheese as appetizers.
There was an appetizing aroma coming from the kitchen.

compete comes from the Latin prefix *com-* meaning "together" and *pet-* meaning "to strive." Thus, *compete* means "to strive with others, as for a prize"; hence, "to take part in a contest" or "to be a rival, as in business."

The two teams competed for the championship.
These two stores always compete with each other.

Three words based on *compete* are *competition, competitive,* and *competitor. Competition* means (1) a contest, as for a prize or business; (2) rivalry; (3) a rival or rivals. *Competitive* means "characterized by competition; inclined to compete; competing aggressively." A *competitor* is "a person or organization that competes, as in games or in business; a rival."

Did you enter last week's crossword competition?
The two oil companies are in competition.
I think our football team can beat the competition.
Business in this town is highly competitive.
Japan is a strong competitor in the world's markets.

competent comes from the Latin prefix *com-* meaning "together" and *pet-* meaning "to go" plus the Latin suffix *-ent*, which is the same as our English ending *-ing. Competent* originally referred to "something that goes together with something else"; that is, "something that is proper or fitting." Hence, *competent* means "capable; qualified."

He is a competent worker.
She is competent to do the job.

Two words based on *competent* are *competence* and *incompetent*. *Competence* means (1) ability; skill; (2) sufficient means for a comfortable life. *Incompetent* means "not capable; inadequate."

> *His competence as a violinist is well known.*
> *The huge dairy farm provided the family with a competence.*
> *He is a totally incompetent bookkeeper.*

petition comes from *petit-* meaning "to seek" and the Latin suffix *-ion* meaning "the act or state of." A *petition* is "an act of seeking something." Hence, a *petition* is "a request, especially a formal request or application to a law court, authority, etc., asking that some entreaty or demand be granted." To *petition* is (1) to make or sign such a request; to ask for something; (2) to ask, plead, or appeal for something, especially from a higher authority.

> *Have you signed the petition against higher taxes?*
> *O, Lord, hear my petition.*
> *They petitioned the city for better transportation.*

A word based on *petition* is *petitioner*, meaning (1) a person who makes or signs a petition; (2) one who makes an appeal or a claim, especially a formal written request.

repetition comes from the Latin prefix *re-* meaning "again" and *petit-* meaning "to seek" plus the Latin suffix *-ion* meaning "the act of." Thus, *repetition* literally means "the act of seeking something again"; hence, (1) the act of repeating; a doing or saying of something over again; (2) that which is repeated; a repeated instance.

> *His writing is long-winded and full of repetition.*
> *This morning's traffic jam was a repetition of yesterday's.*

Two words based on *repetition* are *repetitious*, meaning "full of repetition, especially useless or tedious repetition," and *repetitive*, which means "involving, using, or like repetition; repetitious."

> *He gave a long, repetitious report at the meeting.*
> *Bad teaching can make the learning process dull and repetitive.*

◊ Look up *impetus* and *impetuous* in your dictionary. Learn their meanings and relate each to the root *pet-, petit-* meaning "to go; seek; strive."

Fun With Words

VOCABULARY BUILDING

The following fourteen words contain common roots. Check the word or phrase you believe is closest in meaning to the key word. Answers follow.

1. **matriarch** [mā′trē·ärk]—(a) a woman who rules a family or group. (b) an elderly and wise woman. (c) a wise old man. (d) a mother-in-law.

2. **magnification** [mag′nə·fə·kā′-shən]—(a) the process of beautifying. (b) extreme boldness. (c) generosity. (d) enlargement.

3. **matriculate** [mə·trik′yə·lāt]—(a) to come to maturity. (b) to join together. (c) to graduate. (d) to gain a diploma that entitles one to enter a university.

4. **manipulate** [mə·nip′yə·lāt]—(a) to handle skillfully. (b) to construct. (c) to write illegibly. (d) many times over.

5. **manifest** [man′ə·fest]—(a) boasting. (b) evident. (c) destined. (d) generous.

6. **malefactor** [mal′ə·fak′tər]—(a) a criminal or evildoer. (b) a witch. (c) a violent windstorm. (d) a bad omen.

7. **nomenclature** [nō′mən·klā′chər]—(a) pen names. (b) law records. (c) the history of names. (d) names used in classifications.

8. **nominal** [nom′ə·nəl]—(a) understood; known. (b) unnamed. (c) too small to be considered. (d) believable.

9. **omniscience** [om·nish′əns]—(a) threatening or foretelling evil. (b) infinite knowledge. (c) conceit. (d) wide popularity.

10. **omnivorous** [om·niv′ər·əs]—(a) meat-eating. (b) heartless. (c) all-seeing. (d) devouring indiscriminately.

11. **phonetics** [fə·net′iks]—(a) the science of grammar. (b) diacritical marks. (c) speech sounds. (d) a study of rhetoric.

12. **orifice** [ôr′ə·fis]—(a) an oral report. (b) an opening or aperture. (c) an overlord. (d) a device used in examining the ears.

13. **cognomen** [kog·nō′mən]—(a) a family title. (b) an alias. (c) a political-party nominee. (d) a surname or a nickname.

14. **permissive** [pər·mis′iv]—(a) ungrudging. (b) immoral. (c) lenient. (d) relaxed.

ANSWERS:

1. **matriarch**—(a) a woman who rules a family or group. 2. **magnification**—(d) enlargement. 3. **matriculate**—(d) to gain a diploma that entitles one to enter a university. 4. **manipulate**—(a) to handle skillfully. 5. **manifest**—(b) evident. 6. **malefactor**—(a) a criminal or evildoer. 7. **nomenclature**—(d) names used in classifications. 8. **nominal**—(c) too small to be considered. 9. **omniscience**—(b) infinite knowledge. 10. **omnivorous**—(d) devouring indiscriminately. 11. **phonetics**—(c) speech sounds. 12. **orifice**—(b) an opening or aperture. 13. **cognomen**—(d) a surname or a nickname. 14. **permissive**—(c) lenient.

ROOT: PLE-, PLET-

The Latin root *ple-* or *plet-* means "to fill." Learn the following four core vocabulary words based on this common root: *complete, deplete, implement, replete.*

complete comes from the Latin prefix *com-* meaning "thoroughly" and *plet-* meaning "to fill." Thus, the adjective *complete* means "filled thoroughly; full; with all the needed parts or items included; wholly finished; perfect." As a verb, *complete* means "to finish; conclude."

> *Did you order the complete dinner?*
> *The clothing store carries a complete range of sizes.*
> *The author said his book was finally complete.*
> *He completed the book after years of work and study.*

Three words based on *complete* are *completely,* meaning "totally; entirely"; *completion,* meaning "the act of completing or the state of being complete"; and *incomplete,* meaning "not complete; unfinished."

> *I am completely satisfied.*
> *The completion of the work took two years.*
> *He left his task incomplete at the end of the day.*

deplete comes from the Latin prefix *de-* meaning "not" and *plet-* meaning "to fill." *Deplete* literally means "not to fill" or "to reverse the process of filling"; hence, "to lessen by use or waste; to use up or empty."

> *We have depleted many of our natural resources.*
> *The child's energy was depleted by malnutrition.*

A word based on *deplete* is *depletion,* meaning (1) the act of lessening or reducing something by use or waste; a using up; (2) the state of being used up or lessened.

> *The depletion of oil reserves is a major problem.*

implement comes from the Latin prefix *im-* (another spelling of *in-*) meaning "in" or "up" and *ple-* meaning "to fill" plus the Latin suffix *-ment* meaning "the act of." To *implement* originally meant "to fill something up with what is needed"; hence, "to give or do what is necessary to accomplish something; supply what is needed." An *implement* is "something used to accomplish a purpose; especially, a tool or piece of equipment used in some form of work."

> *The Cabinet implemented the welfare program with federal funds.*
> *The farm implements are stored in the barn.*

A word based on *implement* is *implementation*, meaning "a putting of something into effect; a carrying through of something."

> *The implementation of the welfare program was successful.*

replete comes from the Latin prefix *re-* meaning "again" and *plet-* meaning "to fill." *Replete* originally meant "filled again" or "filled up again." Today, *replete* means "completely full; supplied in abundance; well-provided."

> *Cod-liver oil is replete with vitamins A and D.*

A word based on *replete* is *repletion,* meaning "the state of being completely or excessively full."

> *We have dined to repletion.*

ROOT: PLIC-, PLICIT-, PLEX-, PLY-

The Latin root *plic-, plicit-, plex-,* or *ply-* means "to fold; twist; bend; tangle; connect." Learn the seven core vocabulary words based on this important root: *complex, complexion, complicate, explicit, implicate, implicit, imply.*

complex comes from the Latin prefix *com-* meaning "together" and *plex-* meaning "to twist; connect." Thus, *complex* means (1) consisting of various parts connected together; composite; (2) complicated, as in structure; involved; intricate. A *complex* is "a whole made up of connected or interwoven parts."

> *A computer is a complex machine.*
> *This is a complex problem; there is no easy solution.*
> *Have you seen the new housing complex?*

A word based on *complex* is *complexity,* meaning "the state of being complex or involved."

The complexity of a computer is amazing.

complexion comes from the Latin prefix *com-* meaning "together" and *plex-* meaning "to twist; connect" plus the Latin suffix *-ion* meaning "the state of." *Complexion* originally meant "the state of things closely .connected in a whole," referring to the constitution of the human body. Today, of course, *complexion* means "the color and appearance of the skin, especially of the face," or "the general appearance, quality, or character of a person or thing."

She has a light, clear complexion.
What is the political complexion of the new legislature?

complicate comes from the Latin prefix *com-* meaning "together" and *plic-* meaning "to twist; tangle" plus the Latin suffix *-ate* meaning "to make." To *complicate* is literally "to make twisted or tangled together"; hence, "to make or become complex or difficult."

Don't complicate your life by worrying too much.
The strike complicates our production problems.

Two words based on *complicate* are *complicated,* meaning "difficult to understand; involved," and *complication,* which means (1) the act of complicating; (2) a complicated situation, condition, element, or structure; (3) anything that causes difficulty, as a problem added to one already existing.

This book is too complicated for children.
The complications of the job are more than one man can handle.
He had a slight case of the flu, but then complications set in.

explicit comes from the Latin prefix *ex-* meaning "out" and *plicit-* meaning "to fold." *Explicit* originally meant "folded out" or "unfolded." Hence, *explicit* means "clearly expressed; straightforward; direct."

He gave us explicit instructions on how to reach the house.
You explicitly told me I would get a raise.

implicate comes from the Latin prefix *im-* (another spelling of *in-*) meaning "in" and *plic-* meaning "to fold; twist; tangle" plus the Latin suffix *-ate* meaning "to make." Thus, to *implicate* literally means "to entangle someone in something, as in an accusation of guilt"; hence, "to show that someone is involved in something, such as a crime or plot."

The informer's testimony implicated five people in the robbery.

A word based on *implicate* is *implication*, meaning (1) the act of involving or implying; (2) a hint or suggestion.

There is an implication of hostility in his remarks.
Your implication that I am wealthy makes me laugh.

implicit comes from the Latin prefix *im-* (another spelling of *in-*) meaning "in" and *plicit-* meaning "to fold." *Implicit* originally meant "folded in." Hence, *implicit* means "understood or suggested but not directly expressed." It also means "complete or total; unreserved; unqualified."

The partners have an implicit understanding rather than a contract.
I have implicit trust in my partner's judgment.
That theologian believes implicitly in original sin.

NOTE: *Explicit* and *implicit* have opposite meanings. *Explicit* means "unfolded." When you unfold your ideas explicitly, you clearly and directly express them. *Implicit* means "folded in." When you fold in your ideas implicitly, you express them only indirectly; you suggest or hint things instead of stating them straightforwardly.

imply comes from the Latin prefix *im-* (another spelling of *in-*) meaning "in" and *ply-* meaning "to fold; twist." Thus, *imply* is closely related to *implicit*, literally meaning "to fold in." Hence, *imply* means (1) to suggest without stating; suggest or convey indirectly; (2) to indicate or involve as an obvious cause or consequence.

Her blushing implied that she was embarrassed.
Smoke implies fire.

◊ Look up the following words in your dictionary. Learn their meanings and be sure you can relate each to the root *plic-*, *plicit-*, *plex-*, or *ply-* meaning "to fold; twist; bend; tangle; connect."

complicity	duplicity	replica
duplex	multiply	reply
duplicate	ply	supplication

EXPLORING WORDS
WHAT KIND OF PERSON IS THAT?

There are many words that describe types of people and the ways they react to the world about them. Here are fourteen words that deal with human behavior, both normal and abnormal. Do you recognize yourself or any of your friends and acquaintances in this list?

aesthete (1) a person who is devoted to beauty in nature, art, painting, music, etc.; (2) a person who displays an extravagant or affected admiration for beauty and the arts.

altruist a person who is selflessly concerned with the welfare of others; one who puts the comfort and happiness of others before his own.

ascetic a person who leads a simple, austere life, avoiding luxury and pleasure, seeking solitude, practicing self-discipline, and devoting himself to contemplation or meditation.

conservative a person who wants to preserve the existing order of things, feeling content or safe with things as they are.

exhibitionist a show-off; a person who tries to attract attention to himself by exaggerated or inappropriate behavior.

hypochondriac a person who worries constantly—usually without any real reason—about the state of his health, believing that he has many ailments, taking extreme health precautions, etc.

kleptomaniac a person who has an irresistible desire to steal and shoplift—not because he is in need of what he steals, but because stealing gives him an emotional satisfaction.

megalomaniac a person who suffers from delusions of greatness.

optimist a person who tends to look on the bright side of things, or one who tends to think that the world is basically good and that what happens is for the best: the opposite of *pessimist*.

paranoid a person who believes that other people are always plotting against him, cheating and persecuting him, feeling hate for him, etc.

pessimist a person who tends to look on the darker side of things, or one who believes that the world is basically bad or evil.

pragmatist a person who believes that ideas have value only in terms of their practical consequence and that practical results are the sole test of the truth or validity of beliefs.

realist a person who believes in basing his life on facts and who dislikes anything that seems imaginary, impractical, theoretical, or utopian.

romantic a person who approaches everything in life emotionally and who enjoys adventures, falling in love, fighting for causes, etc.

ROOT: PON-, POSIT-, POUND-, POSE-

The Latin root *pon-, posit-, pound-,* or *pose-* means "to put; place." This is one of the most important roots you will ever learn; it is used in making a great many common English words. Learn carefully the core vocabulary words based on this root: *component, compose, composite, compound, depose, deposit, dispose, expose, exposition, expound, impose, oppose, positive, postpone, propose, suppose.*

component comes from the Latin prefix *com-* meaning "together" and *pon-* meaning "to put; place" plus the Latin suffix *-ent,* which is the same as our English ending *-ing.* Thus, the noun *component* means "a part used in putting together a whole." As an adjective, *component* means "helping to make up a whole."

> *Flour is a basic component of bread.*
> *Turntable, amplifier, and speakers are components of a phonograph.*
> *Sugar and water are component parts of syrup.*

compose comes from the Latin prefix *com-* meaning "together" and *pose-,* meaning "to put; place." Thus, *compose* literally means "to put something together"; hence, (1) to make up, or form as a whole, from different elements; (2) to create, as a literary or musical work; (3) to arrange, settle, or calm.

> *Water is composed of hydrogen and oxygen.*
> *Beethoven composed nine symphonies.*
> *Relax and compose yourself.*

A word based on *compose* is *composure,* meaning "calmness or serenity."

> *Though he was heckled, the speaker maintained his composure.*

composite comes from the Latin prefix *com-* meaning "together" and *posit-* meaning "to put; place." Thus, *composite* means "put together or made up of separate parts." A *composite* is "something made up of separate parts."

> *This composite photograph was made by combining halves of two different negatives.*
> *This jigsaw puzzle is a composite of 200 pieces.*

compound comes from the Latin prefix *com-* meaning "together" and *pound-* meaning "to put; place." Thus, a *compound* [kom'pound] is "a combination of two or more separate parts or ingredients." To *compound* [kom·pound'] means (1) to make by combining parts or ingredients; (2) to complicate something by bringing in a new element; (3) in finance, to compute interest on both the original principal and the accumulated interest.

> *Most drugs are compounds of several chemicals.*
> Blackberry *is a compound word made up of* black *and* berry.
> *The pharmacist compounded the prescribed medicine.*
> *Tom's uncooperative attitude compounded the difficulty.*
> *The bank compounds interest on savings accounts.*

depose comes from the Latin prefix *de-* meaning "down" and *pose-* meaning "to put; place." *Depose* originally meant "to put someone down in position or rank; demote." Today, *depose* means "to take an office, position, etc., away from the person holding it; oust, as a monarch." In law, *depose* has a special meaning: "to give testimony under oath, especially in writing."

> *The revolutionary mobs deposed the king.*

A word related to *depose* is *deposition*, meaning "the act of deposing." In law, a *deposition* is "the written testimony of a witness who is under oath."

deposit comes from the Latin prefix *de-* meaning "down" and *posit-* meaning "to put; place." To *deposit* is "to put or set something down." Thus, *deposit* also means (1) to put something down in the form of a layer, as of dirt; (2) to put down and entrust money to a bank; (3) to put down money as a partial payment on something.

> *As the ages passed, the Nile River deposited silt to form a delta.*
> *She deposited $25 in her savings account.*
> *He made a $500 deposit on the car.*

A word based on *deposit* is *depository*, meaning "a place where anything is deposited; a storehouse."

> *An arsenal is a depository for weapons.*

dispose comes from *dis-* meaning "apart" and the root *pose-* meaning "to put." *Dispose* literally means "to put apart or set aside." Hence,

137

dispose means (1) to get rid of; (2) to put in order, arrange, or settle; (3) to put into a receptive frame of mind for; (4) to condition toward something.

> *Have you disposed of your old car?*
> *He disposed the business affairs of his ailing brother.*
> *The news disposed them to accept our offer of help.*
> *Lack of sleep disposes some people to headaches.*

Two words based on or related to *dispose* are *disposal* and *disposition*. *Disposal* means (1) a transfer of something to another, as by sale or gift; (2) a getting rid of something. *Disposition* means (1) one's usual frame of mind; (2) a tendency or habit; (3) management or settlement, as of business affairs; (4) a particular ordering or arrangement, as of troops.

> *His will provided for the disposal of his property.*
> *This sink takes care of waste disposal.*
> *Amy has a cheerful disposition.*
> *What did you think of the disposition of the lawsuit?*
> *The map showed the disposition of troops in the area.*

expose comes from the Latin prefix *ex-* meaning "out" and *pose-* meaning "to put; place." Thus, *expose* means "to put something out so that it is seen or known"; hence, (1) to reveal something, especially something that was deliberately hidden; (2) to lay something open to ridicule or criticism; (3) to uncover; (4) to lay open to the effect of sunlight, the elements, etc.

> *The newspaper reporter exposed the corruption in government.*
> *When Mary tries to discuss baseball, she exposes her ignorance.*
> *If you expose yourself to the sun too long, you get burned.*

Two words based on *expose* are *exposé* and *exposure*. An *exposé* is "a making known publicly of something hidden, especially something evil or scandalous." *Exposure* means (1) the act of exposing or the state of being exposed; (2) position in relation to the sun, elements, or compass points; (3) the act of exposing film in order to make a photograph; (4) the time that a film is exposed; (5) a segment of film from which a single picture is made.

> *The newspaper ran an exposé of corruption in local government.*
> *The exposure of government corruption brought about reforms.*

This room has a southern exposure.
The photograph needed an exposure of ten seconds.
There are twelve exposures on this roll of film.

exposition comes from the Latin prefix *ex-* meaning "out" and *posit-* meaning "to put; place" plus the Latin suffix *-ion* meaning "the state or act of." Hence, *exposition* means "the act of setting out, explaining, or displaying one's facts, ideas, products, works of art, etc." More specifically, it means (1) a detailed presentation of a subject; (2) a public display, show, or exhibition; (3) the part of a literary work, as a play, that gives the background of the plot and characters.

The teacher gave a clear exposition of the contents of the course.
The museum has an exposition of new paintings.

A word based on *exposition* is *expository,* meaning "of or pertaining to exposition; explanatory."

The novel Moby Dick *is full of expository chapters about whales.*

expound comes from the Latin prefix *ex-* meaning "out" and *pound-* meaning "to put; place." Thus, *expound* means "to put something out in the form of words; to state, reveal, explain, or interpret something."

The professor expounded Einstein's theory of relativity.

impose comes from the Latin prefix *im-* meaning "on" and *pose-* meaning "to put; place." Thus, *impose* means "to put or force something upon others"; hence, (1) to force oneself or one's views on others; (2) to establish or enforce something by authority.

He imposed on our hospitality by staying two weeks.
The governor imposed martial law during the riots.

Two words based on or related to *impose* are *imposing,* meaning "impressive, grand, or stately," and *imposition,* which means (1) the act of imposing; (2) that which is imposed, as a tax or an excessive requirement.

The governor's mansion is an imposing edifice.
His unexpected visit was an imposition.

oppose comes from the Latin prefix *op-* (another spelling of *ob-*) meaning "against" and *pose-* meaning "to put; place." Thus, *oppose*

90-SECOND QUICKIE QUIZ

WORD BUILDING

Here is another short review quiz of roots and words you have already learned. Match the roots with their meanings. Answers follow.

1. **pend-** as in depend [di·pend']
2. **plex-** as in complex [kom'pleks]
3. **corp-** as in corpulent [kôr'pyə·lənt]
4. **dict-** as in contradict [kon'trə·dikt']
5. **cred-** as in credentials [kri·den'shəls]
6. **ag-** as in agenda [ə·jen'də]
7. **posit-** as in deposit [di·poz'it]
8. **acu-** as in acute [ə·kyo̅o̅t']

(a) to say or speak
(b) to hang, weigh, or pay
(c) to put, place
(d) to fold; connect
(e) to believe; trust
(f) body; flesh
(g) to do
(h) sharp

ANSWERS:

1. **pend-** —(b) to hang, weigh, or pay. To depend means to trust or rely on; to rely for support on.
2. **plex-** —(d) to fold; connect. Complex means consisting of various connected parts, not simple; a whole made up of connected parts.
3. **corp-** —(f) body; flesh. Corpulent means abounding in flesh; fat.
4. **dict-** —(a) to say or speak. To contradict means to say the opposite, as of what someone else has said.
5. **cred-** —(e) to believe; trust. Credentials are proof or evidence that cause others to believe the identity, experience, or authority of someone.
6. **ag-** —(g) to do. An agenda is a list of things to be done, discussed, or decided.
7. **posit-** —(c) to put, place. Deposit means (1) to put something down in the form of a layer, as of dust or mud; (2) to put down or entrust money to a bank; (3) to put down money as a partial payment on something.
8. **acu-** —(h) sharp. Acute means coming to a sharp point; reaching a crisis, critical; keen, intense.

means "to put oneself against something or someone; to be or act against; resist or fight."

The senator opposed new taxes.
Canada opposed Germany in both world wars.

Three words related to *oppose* are *opponent*, *opposite*, and *opposition*. An *opponent* is "a person who opposes someone or something." *Opposite* means (1) being on the other side or on each side of something; (2) facing or moving the other way; (3) contrary or different in character. *Opposition* means (1) the act of opposing or the state of being opposed; (2) that which opposes; especially, a political party in power.

> *The Liberal beat his opponent in the election.*
> *The two men shouted at each other from opposite ends of the room.*
> *My views are in opposition to those of Marx.*
> *The opposition voted against Bill 66.*

positive comes from *posit-* meaning "to put; place" and the Latin suffix *-ive* meaning "inclined to." Thus, *positive* means "definitely put forth and accepted; affirmative or affirmed; not open to doubt."

> *He gave positive proof of his innocence.*
> *I'm positive that I left my umbrella at your house.*

postpone comes from the Latin prefix *post-* meaning "after" and *pone-* meaning "to put; place." Thus, *postpone* means "to put off until later; delay."

> *We postponed our picnic because of rain.*

A word based on *postpone* is *postponement*, meaning "a putting off of something; a delay."

> *Bad weather caused a three-day postponement of our trip.*

propose comes from the Latin prefix *pro-* meaning "forward" and *pose-* meaning "to put; place." Thus, *propose* means (1) to put something forward for consideration; (2) to nominate; (3) to make an offer of marriage.

> *The Council proposed an increase in taxes.*
> *I proposed Tom Smith for president of the club.*
> *Jonathan proposed to Kate Friday night.*

Two words based on or related to *propose* are *proposal* and *proposition.* A *proposal* is (1) an offer proposing something to be accepted or adopted; (2) an offer of marriage; (3) something proposed, such as a plan. *Proposition* means (1) a plan or proposal; (2) a subject or statement presented for discussion.

> *He made two proposals at the business meeting.*
> *She accepted his proposal of marriage.*
> *The chairman read his proposition to the committee.*

suppose comes from the Latin prefix *sup-* (another spelling of *sub-*) meaning "under; secretly" and *pose-* meaning "to put; place." Thus, *suppose* means "to put something secretly to oneself"; hence, (1) to think or imagine something to oneself as true; (2) to believe probable; (3) to require or expect; (4) to assume to be true for the sake of argument.

> *He actually supposed that people were spying on him.*
> *I suppose you are right.*
> *What are you supposed to be learning?*
> *Suppose he arrives late; what will we do?*

Two words based on or related to *suppose* are *supposed,* meaning "accepted as genuine or true, though perhaps not so," and *supposition,* which means (1) the act of supposing; (2) a guess.

> *Her supposed remorse proved to be a sham.*
> *It is my supposition that he will arrive late.*

◇ Look up the following words in your dictionary. Learn the meaning of each, and be sure you can relate each meaning to the root *pon-, posit-, pound-,* or *pose-* meaning "to put; place."

composition	juxtaposition	purpose
deponent	preposition	repository
exponent	proponent	superimpose
interpose	propound	transpose

ROOT: PORT-

The Latin root *port-* means "to carry." Learn the following core vocabulary words based on this root: *deport, export, import, portable.*

deport comes from the Latin prefix *de-* meaning "away" and *port-* meaning "to carry." To *deport* is literally "to carry someone away." Hence, *deport* means "to expel or banish someone from a country, often for political reasons."

> *Most governments have the right to deport undesirable aliens.*

Two words based on *deport* are *deportation,* meaning "banishment," and *deportment,* meaning "behavior or conduct; bearing."

> *The deportation of the spy is scheduled for today.*
> *Grandfather was noted for his dignified deportment.*
> *When I was in school we were graded on our deportment.*

export comes from the Latin prefix *ex-* meaning "out" and *port-* meaning "to carry." Thus, to *export* is "to send merchandise or raw materials out of a country for sale or trade." An *export* is "an exported commodity."

> *Canada exports wheat.*
> *Wheat is a major export.*

import comes from the Latin prefix *im-* meaning "in" and *port-* meaning "to carry." Thus, to *import* [im·pôrt′] means "to bring merchandise or raw materials into a country for commercial use." An *import* [im′pôrt] is "an imported commodity."

> *Canada imports coffee.*
> *Coffee is a major import.*

Import also has the meaning of "implication, purport, or consequence."

> *John felt the import of the speaker's words.*
> *The article discussed matters of great import.*

portable comes from *port-* meaning "to carry" and the Latin suffix *-able* meaning "capable of being." Thus, *portable* means "capable of being carried; easily or readily movable." A *portable* is "something that can be moved easily, as a lightweight typewriter or a small radio."

> *Do you have a portable television set?*
> *I have an office typewriter, not a portable.*

◊ You already know the meanings of the nine words below. Can you relate the meaning of each word to the root *port-* meaning "to carry"? Check yourself by looking up the words in your dictionary.

disport	report	supporter
porter	reporter	transport
portfolio	support	transportation

143

Fun With Words
REVIEW OF ROOTS

Here are more roots and words you have learned. Choose the answer nearest in meaning to the key word. Answers follow.

1. **mobile** [mō′bəl or mō′bēl]—(a) movable; capable of being moved easily. (b) agile; nimble. (c) a small truck. (d) a small mob.

2. **motive** [mō′tiv]—(a) slow, deliberate motion or action. (b) mechanical force. (c) a reason for a person's action or behavior. (d) actions leading up to a crime.

3. **motivation** [mō′tə·vā′shən]—(a) slow, deliberate motion or action. (b) the act of providing an incentive; drive. (c) actions leading up to a crime. (d) political power.

4. **natal** [nāt′l]—(a) pertaining to one's mother's family. (b) happening before one's birth. (c) happening after one's birth. (d) of or pertaining to one's birth.

5. **dispel** [dis·pel′]—(a) to doubt. (b) to be certain; have no doubts. (c) to disperse. (d) to swear to an oath.

6. **expel** [ik·spel′]—(a) to breathe out. (b) to spit. (c) to gather in. (d) to force out; eject.

7. **expulsion** [ik·spul′shən]—(a) forcible ejection. (b) rate of movement or progress. (c) an oath or curse. (d) death.

8. **compensate** [kom′pən·sāt]—(a) sad; pensive. (b) thoughtful. (c) to counterbalance; make up for. (d) to pay more than something is worth.

9. **dispensation** [dis′pən·sā′shən]—(a) to sell drugs or medicine. (b) distribution; an orderly dealing out or administering. (c) an excuse. (d) a gift to a charity or religious order.

10. **pending** [pen′ding]—(a) officially registered or recorded, as a patent. (b) urgent; most necessary. (c) remaining to be finished or decided. (d) supported from above.

11. **impending** [im·pen′ding]—(a) about to occur; imminent. (b) urgent; most necessary. (c) foreboding; forecasting bad luck or disaster. (d) restricting; confining.

ANSWERS:

1. **mobile**—(a) movable; capable of being moved easily. 2. **motive**—(c) a reason for a person's action or behavior. 3. **motivation**—(b) the act of providing an incentive; drive. 4. **natal**—(d) of or pertaining to one's birth. 5. **dispel**—(c) to disperse. 6. **expel**—(d) to force out; eject. 7. **expulsion**—(a) forcible ejection. 8. **compensate**—(c) to counterbalance; make up for. 9. **dispensation**—(b) distribution; an orderly dealing out or administering. 10. **pending**—(c) remaining to be finished or decided. 11. **impending**—(a) about to occur; imminent.

ROOT: QUIR-, QUISIT-, QUEST-

The Latin root *quir-*, *quisit-*, or *quest-* means "to seek or ask." This root is the basis of many common English words such as *question* and *quest*. Learn the three core vocabulary words based on the root *quir-*, *quisit-*, or *quest-*: *acquire*, *inquire*, and *require*.

acquire comes from the Latin prefix *ac-* (another spelling of *ad-*) meaning "to; for" and *quir-* meaning "to seek or ask." Thus, *acquire* means "to seek something for oneself and get it; obtain something by one's own efforts; get."

> *He has acquired a house in the country.*
> *Where did you acquire that Southern accent?*

Three words based on *acquire* are *acquirement*, *acquisition*, and *acquisitive*. Both *acquirement* and *acquisition* mean (1) the act of acquiring; (2) something acquired. An *acquirement*, however, is a skill gained by study or practice, while an *acquisition* is usually an object that has been acquired. *Acquisitive* means "inclined to acquire things; grasping."

> *She is a person of notable scholarly acquirements.*
> *The library has a display of its recent acquisitions.*
> *His acquisitive nature makes him a compulsive shopper.*

inquire comes from the Latin prefix *in-* meaning "in; into" plus *quir-* meaning "to seek or ask." Thus, *inquire* means "to ask or seek into something; seek information by asking questions; make an investigation or search into something."

> *"Why are you staring at me?" he inquired.*
> *He inquired about your health.*
> *The police are inquiring into the circumstances of the crime.*

Three words based on *inquire* are *inquiry*, *inquisition*, and *inquisitive*. *Inquiry* means (1) the act of inquiring; investigation; (2) a question. An *inquisition* is "an official inquiry or investigation into the beliefs of individuals or groups, for the purpose of enforcing dominant social, political, or religious beliefs." (The Spanish Inquisition was a judicial court of the Roman Catholic Church set up in Spain in the fifteenth century for the purpose of discovering and punishing heretics.) *Inquisitive* means (1) given to questioning, especially when too curious about the affairs of others; (2) eager for knowledge.

> *Discoveries are made through scientific inquiry.*
> *She handles customers' inquiries about merchandise.*
> *That woman is an inquisitive old gossip.*
> *Bill has an inquisitive mind and will make a good scientist.*

require comes from the Latin prefix *re-* meaning "back; again" and *quir-* meaning "to seek or ask." *Require* literally means "to ask again"; that is, "to ask as if demanding something." Hence, *require* means "to demand, order, or insist upon" or "to have need of something."

> *The hotel requires guests to dress formally for dinner.*
> *English is a required course.*
> *The patient requires rest and quiet.*

Two words based on *require* are *requirement*, meaning "that which is required; an essential or demand"; and *requisite*, which means (1) required by the nature of things; necessary; (2) a necessity or requirement.

> *Good grades are a requirement for graduation.*
> *Have you done the requisite amount of work, fulfilling all the requisites for the degree?*

◊ Look up the following words in your dictionary. Learn the meaning of each, and be sure you can relate each to the root *quir-, quisit-,* or *quest-* meaning "to seek or ask."

> conquest   exquisite   perquisite   request

ROOT: RUPT-

The Latin root *rupt-* means "to break; burst." Learn the five core vocabulary words based on this root—*corrupt, disrupt, erupt, interrupt, rupture.*

corrupt comes from the Latin prefix *cor-* (another spelling of *con-*) meaning "thoroughly" and *rupt-* meaning "to break." Thus, to *corrupt* is "to ruin or destroy morally; to debase or spoil." As an adjective, *corrupt* means "dishonest; immoral."

Joe's dishonest friends corrupted him.
There is nothing worse than a corrupt politician.

A word based on *corrupt* is *corruption,* meaning (1) the act of corrupting, or the state of being corrupt; (2) dishonesty or bribery.

Several local politicians have been accused of corruption.

disrupt comes from the Latin prefix *dis-* meaning "apart" and *rupt-* meaning "to break; burst." Thus, *disrupt* means "to break apart or break up; throw into disorder; upset."

Some of the students tried to disrupt classes.

Two words based on *disrupt* are *disruption,* meaning "the act of disrupting, or the state of being disrupted," and *disruptive,* which means "causing or tending to cause disruption."

Guards were posted to prevent the disruption of the meeting.
The dean expelled the disruptive students.

erupt comes from the Latin prefix *e-* (another spelling of *ex-*) meaning "out" and *rupt-* meaning "to break; burst." Thus, *erupt* means "to burst forth with lava, steam, etc., in the manner of a volcano or geyser; burst out or burst open suddenly or violently."

The volcano erupted at midnight.
Their anger erupted into a fight.
Riots erupted in several countries last year.

A word based on *erupt* is *eruption,* which means (1) a breaking forth or outbreak; (2) a bursting forth of lava, steam, etc.

He suffers from a skin eruption similar to acne.

interrupt comes from the Latin prefix *inter-* meaning "between; in between" and *rupt-* meaning "to break; burst." Thus, *interrupt* means "to break into the continuity of something, such as conversation or speech; stop temporarily."

The heckler interrupted the speaker several times.
The regular train schedule has been interrupted by snow.

A word based on *interrupt* is *interruption,* meaning (1) the act of interrupting or state of being interrupted; (2) something that interrupts.

The speaker tried to ignore the heckler's interruption.

rupture comes from *rupt-* meaning "to break; burst" and the Latin suffix *-ure* meaning "the act or state of." Thus, to *rupture* is "to break open or break apart." A *rupture* is "the act of bursting or breaking; a bursting or break; a breaking off, as of friendship or good relations between persons or countries."

His appendix ruptured.
He suffered a rupture of the appendix.
The rupture between England and Ireland has never been healed.

ROOT: SCRIB-, SCRIPT-

The Latin root *scrib-* or *script-* means "to write." Can you describe or scribble down two words containing this root? *Script,* you will note, is a word in itself, meaning "writing or a piece of writing, such as a copy of a play prepared for actors' use." With the addition of the letter *e,* *scrib-* becomes the word *scribe,* meaning "one who copies manuscripts." Learn the five core vocabulary words based on the root *scrib-* or *script-: describe, inscribe, prescribe, proscribe, subscribe, transcribe.*

describe comes from the Latin prefix *de-* meaning "down" and *scrib-* meaning "to write." *Describe* originally meant "to write something down." Today, *describe* means "to present something in spoken or written words; to give an account of something."

He described what he had seen on his trip.
Can you describe the burglar's appearance?

Two words based on *describe* are *description* and *descriptive. Description* is (1) an account that describes; (2) the act or technique of describing. *Descriptive* means "containing description or serving to describe."

He wrote a vivid description of the trip.
This is colorful, descriptive writing.

inscribe comes from the Latin prefix *in-* meaning "in; on" and *scrib-* meaning "to write." Thus, *inscribe* means (1) to write words, names, etc., on something for a public or formal purpose; (2) to write in a book or on a photograph, etc., as when autographing or dedicating it; (3) to enter a name on a formal or official list.

The monument was inscribed with the names of the war dead.
The author inscribed a copy of his book to his best friend.
He inscribed his name on the petition.

A word based on *inscribe* is *inscription*, meaning (1) the act of inscribing; (2) writing that has been inscribed on a tablet, statue, etc.; (3) an informal written dedication in a book.

The inscription on the old tombstone was hard to read.

prescribe comes from the Latin prefix *pre-* meaning "before" and *scrib-* meaning "to write." *Prescribe* literally means "to write before someone else acts, as when giving an order." Hence, *prescribe* means (1) to set something down as a rule to be followed; (2) to order the use of a medicine or treatment for a patient.

The engraved invitation prescribed formal dress.
The doctor prescribed an antibiotic.

Two words based on *prescribe* are *prescription* and *prescriptive*. A *prescription* is (1) a doctor's written formula authorizing a druggist to prepare a medicine; (2) a remedy recommended by a doctor. *Prescriptive* means "making strict rules."

Did the druggist fill your prescription?
Has the new prescription helped your allergy?
This book deals with prescriptive grammar.

proscribe comes from the Latin prefix *pro-* meaning "before" and *scrib-* meaning "to write." *Proscribe* originally meant "to write an outlaw's name in public." Today, *proscribe* means "to outlaw or banish; denounce or condemn someone or something; prohibit."

The nations agreed to proscribe germ warfare.

A word based on *proscribe* is *proscription*, meaning "a prohibition" or "banishment."

Nations should try to agree on a proscription of nuclear weapons.

NOTE: Be careful to learn the difference between *prescribe* and *proscribe*.

> *The doctor prescribed aspirin for my headache.*
> *Many states have proscribed the use of certain insecticides.*

subscribe comes from the Latin prefix *sub-* meaning "underneath" and *scrib-* meaning "to write." Thus, *subscribe* means (1) to write one's name underneath, or at the end of, a document, as to show agreement; sign; (2) to agree with, support, approve, or sanction; (3) to agree to pay money to a cause, or to a newspaper or periodical for its delivery.

> *I subscribe to everything the speaker said.*
> *Do you subscribe to the* Daily Record?

Two words based on *subscribe* are *subscriber,* meaning "a person who subscribes, as to a newspaper or magazine," and *subscription,* which means (1) the act of subscribing; (2) a signature; (3) the sale or purchase of prepaid orders for books, magazines, tickets, etc., as by mail or through a door-to-door salesman.

> *Are you a subscriber of your local newspaper?*
> *Tickets for some charity balls are sold only by subscription.*
> *When does your magazine subscription expire?*

transcribe comes from the Latin prefix *trans-* meaning "across; beyond; through" and *scrib-* meaning "to write." Thus, *transcribe* means (1) to copy or recopy from an original or from shorthand notes; (2) to adapt a musical composition for a change of instrument or voice.

> *It is difficult to transcribe another person's shorthand notes.*
> *The symphony was transcribed for two pianos.*

A word based on *transcribe* is *transcript,* meaning "a copy, especially of a student's academic courses and grades."

◊ Look up the following words in your dictionary. Learn the meaning of each, and be sure you can relate each to the root *scrib-* or *script-* meaning "to write."

ascribe	indescribable	scribble
circumscribe	manuscript	Scripture
conscript	postscript	scrip

SPOT THE SPECIALISTS

Do you know what profession or field of study the following people are associated with? The roots you are learning in this section will help you. Check the word or phrase you believe is closest in meaning to the key word. Answers follow.

1. **agronomist** [ə·gron′ə·mist]—(a) an expert in finance. (b) an expert in botany. (c) an expert in field-crop production. (d) an expert in home economics.

2. **antiquary** [an′ti·kwer′ē]—(a) a student of antiques. (b) a doctor who specializes in the care and treatment of elderly persons. (c) the curator of a zoo. (d) a stamp collector.

3. **etymologist** [et′ə·mol′ə·jist]—(a) a student of the meaning of words. (b) an expert in the pronunciation of words. (c) an expert in the derivation of words. (d) a student of insects.

4. **ichthyologist** [ik′thē·ol′ə·jist]— (a) one who studies religious characteristics. (b) an expert in fishes. (c) a professional hunter and fisherman. (d) one who grows herbs.

5. **philologist** [fi·lol′ə·jist]—(a) a handwriting expert. (b) a philosopher. (c) a student of words and languages. (d) an expert in map making.

6. **archeologist** [är′kē·ol′ə·jist]—(a) a student of medieval architecture. (b) a student of cathedrals. (c) a student of government. (d) one who uncovers and studies the remains of early human cultures.

7. **lexicographer** [lek′sə·kog′rə·fər] —(a) a printer. (b) one who writes or compiles a dictionary. (c) one who studies the science of law. (d) a map maker.

8. **anthropologist** [an′thrə·pol′ə·jist] —(a) one who studies the development of man. (b) a zoo attendant. (c) a geologist specializing in the study of coal and coal mines. (d) a professional boxer.

9. **zoologist** [zō·ol′ə·jist]—(a) a zoo keeper. (b) the curator of a museum. (c) a taxidermist. (d) one who studies the development and structure of animals.

10. **choreographer** [kôr′ō·og′rə·fər] —(a) one who devises dance movements and patterns. (b) a singer. (c) a priest. (d) a map maker.

ANSWERS:

1. **agronomist**—(c) an expert in field-crop production. 2. **antiquary**—(a) a student of antiques. 3. **etymologist**—(c) an expert in the derivation of words. 4. **ichthyologist**—(b) an expert in fishes. 5. **philologist**—(c) a student of words and languages. 6. **archeologist**—(d) one who uncovers and studies the remains of early human cultures. 7. **lexicographer**—(b) one who writes or compiles a dictionary. 8. **anthropologist**—(a) one who studies the development of man. 9. **zoologist**—(d) one who studies the development and structure of animals. 10. **choreographer**—(a) one who devises dance movements and patterns.

ROOT: SED-, SID-, SESS-

The Latin root *sed-*, *sid-*, or *sess-* means "to sit; settle." Learn the following four core vocabulary words based on this root: *preside, reside, sediment, session.*

preside comes from the Latin prefix *pre-* meaning "before" and *side-* meaning "to sit." Thus, *preside* means "to sit before others in the place of a leader; sit in authority; act as chairman."

> *Tom Smith presided at the meeting of the club.*

Three words based on *preside* are *president,* meaning "the person chosen to preside over any organization, group, nation, etc.; the chief executive"; *presidency,* meaning "the office of a president or the time that a president is in office"; and *presidential,* which means "of, for, or pertaining to a president, the presidency, or the election of a president."

> *World War II ended during Truman's presidency.*
> *Do you remember John Kennedy's presidential campaign?*

reside comes from the Latin prefix *re-* meaning "back" and *side-* meaning "to sit; settle." Thus, *reside* means "to settle back or stay at a place"; hence, (1) to make one's home at a particular place; (2) to exist as a quality in something; (3) to be vested in as a right.

> *The Governor-General resides at Rideau Hall.*
> *The power to confirm U.S. presidential appointments resides in the Senate.*

Three words based on *reside* are *residence, resident,* and *residential. Residence* means (1) the place or house where a person lives; (2) the fact of being officially present at a place. *Resident* means (1) a person who lives in a place; (2) having a residence; (3) staying in or being affiliated with a place in connection with one's official work. *Residential* means "of, pertaining to, or suitable for residences or homes."

> *Is your residence in Thunder Bay?*
> *Randall Jarrell was once writer in residence at my college.*
> *She is a resident of Kelowna, B.C.*
> *Dr. Jones is the resident physician at this hospital.*
> *The town has several beautiful residential districts.*

sediment comes from *sed-* meaning "to sit; settle" and the Latin suffix *-ment* meaning "the act or result of." Thus, *sediment* means "the result of something settling"; that is, "matter that settles or is settling to the bottom of a body of liquid."

> *The drinking water was full of sediment.*

session comes from *sess-* meaning "to sit; settle" and the Latin suffix *-ion* meaning "the act or state of." Thus, *session* means (1) the sitting together of a legislative body, a court, etc., for the purpose of doing business; (2) a single meeting of an organized group; (3) a school term.

> *Parliament is meeting for its winter session.*
> *The afternoon session of the conference lasted three hours.*
> *Did you attend the summer session at school?*

◇ Look up the following words in your dictionary. Learn the meaning of each, and be sure you can relate each meaning to the root *sed-*, *sid-*, or *sess-* meaning "to sit; settle."

dissident	residue	subside
obsession	sedate	subsidiary
residual	sedative	subsidy

ROOT: SPEC-, SPIC-, SPECT-

The Latin root *spec-*, *spic-*, or *spect-* means "to look; look at." Learn the five core vocabulary words based on this root: *conspicuous, expect, inspect, respect, spectacle.*

conspicuous comes from the Latin prefix *con-* meaning "together" and *spic-* meaning "to look; look at" plus the Latin suffix *-uous* meaning "tending to; inclined to." Something *conspicuous* tends to be looked at altogether, at once, and isn't hard to see. Hence, *conspicuous* means "easily visible; attracting attention."

> *The lighthouse was conspicuous for miles.*
> *She was wearing a loud, conspicuous dress.*

153

A word based on *conspicuous* is *inconspicuous,* meaning "not easily visible; not attracting attention; not noticeable."

> *The brown bird was inconspicuous among the branches.*
> *Mr. Burns is a quiet, inconspicuous man.*

expect comes from the Latin prefix *ex-* meaning "out" and *spect-* meaning "to look at." Thus, to *expect* is "to look out for something"; hence, "to look forward to something as certain or likely" or "to look for something as right or essential; require."

> *I expect that he will arrive tonight.*
> *He expected to be paid for his trouble.*
> *The teacher expected the students to write a paper every week.*

Three words based on *expect* are *expectancy, expectant,* and *expectation. Expectancy* is (1) the act or state of expecting; (2) something expected. *Expectant* means (1) expecting; (2) awaiting the birth of a child. *Expectation* is (1) the act of expecting or state of mind of a person who expects something; anticipation; (2) a prospect of some good to come.

> *What is the life expectancy of a 50-year-old Canadian?*
> *She is an expectant mother.*
> *Do you have any expectation of success?*
> *He has great expectations in life.*

inspect comes from the Latin prefix *in-* meaning "in; into" and *spect-* meaning "to look." Thus, to *inspect* is "to look into something; examine something carefully; examine or review something officially."

> *Holmes inspected the butterfly under a magnifying glass.*
> *The man was nervously inspecting his fingernails.*
> *The general inspected his troops.*

Two words based on *inspect* are *inspection,* meaning "a careful examination; an official examination or review"; and *inspector,* which means "a person who inspects, as an official examiner or a police officer ranking below a superintendent."

> *The fire department's inspection of the building was thorough.*
> *The troops stood inspection for the general.*
> *He is an inspector with Scotland Yard.*

respect comes from the Latin prefix *re-* meaning "back; again" and *spect-* meaning "to look; look at." *Respect* literally means "to look again at someone"; that is, "to treat someone with consideration." Hence, the verb *respect* means "to have regard for a person or to treat a person with consideration." The noun *respect* means "honor and esteem" or "a specific detail or aspect."

Children should respect their parents.
Parents should be held in respect.
In what respect do you feel we have failed in our mission?

Two words based on *respect* are *respectable,* meaning (1) deserving respect; having a good reputation; (2) fairly good or average; and *respectful,* which means "showing respect."

Her family is highly respectable.
He received a respectable raise.
Children should be respectful to their parents.

spectacle comes from a Latin word based on *spect-* meaning "to look; look at." *Spectacle* means "something exhibited to public view"— either "an unusual sight or grand display" or "a painful or embarrassing sight." The plural form of the word, *spectacles,* means "a pair of eyeglasses."

The three-ring circus was quite a spectacle.
John drank too much at the party and made a spectacle of himself.
Eloise is constantly breaking her spectacles.

A word based on *spectacle* is *spectacular,* meaning "of or like a spectacle; characterized by a grand display that excites wonder or amazement." A *spectacular* is "an impressive exhibition or production, as a show having a large cast, elaborate sets, exciting acts, etc."

We saw a spectacular display of fireworks at Expo.
The race ended in a spectacular neck-and-neck finish.
Did you see the television spectacular last night?

◊ Look up the following words in your dictionary. Learn the meaning of each. Be sure you can relate each meaning to the root *spec-, spic-,* or *spect-* meaning "to look; look at."

auspicious	perspicuity	speculate
despicable	specimen	suspect
perspective	spectator	suspicion

ROOT: TANG-, TING-, TACT-

The Latin root *tang-*, *ting-*, or *tact-* means "to touch." Here are eleven "touching" words. First learn the six core vocabulary words based on this root: *contact, contingent, intact, tact, tangent, tangible.*

contact comes from the Latin prefix *con-* meaning "together" and *tact-* meaning "to touch." Thus, the verb *contact* means (1) to come or bring together; touch; (2) to get in touch with someone. As a noun, *contact* means (1) the coming together or touching of two things; (2) a being in touch with someone or something; (3) a person with whom one is in touch and who can perhaps help one.

> *If these electric wires contact, the fuse will be blown.*
> *I think you should contact a good lawyer.*
> *It wasn't a collision; the two cars barely came into contact.*
> *Are you in contact with your brother?*
> *He has a contact in Washington who could help us.*

contingent comes from the Latin prefix *con-* meaning "together" and *ting-* meaning "to touch" plus the Latin suffix *-ent*, which is the same as our English ending *-ing*. *Contingent* literally indicates that two unrelated things are touching or happening together. Hence, *contingent* means (1) occurring by chance; accidental; (2) probable or liable to occur but not certain or logical; (3) dependent upon an uncertain event. A *contingent* is (1) a representative group in an assemblage; (2) a quota of something to be furnished, as troops.

> *Their budget allowed for contingent expenses as well as fixed costs.*
> *Our trip is contingent upon good weather.*
> *At the convention there was a large contingent from Chicago.*
> *A contingent of Australian troops joined the peace-keeping force.*

A word based on *contingent* is *contingency*, meaning "an unforeseen but possible occurrence, as an accident or emergency."

> *Before setting out, we tried to prepare for all contingencies.*

intact comes from the Latin prefix *in-* meaning "not" and *tact-* meaning "to touch." Thus, *intact* literally means "not touched or spoiled; remaining whole or unchanged; undamaged."

> *The fire destroyed the garage but left the house intact.*

tact comes directly from the root *tact-*. *Tact* means "just the right social 'touch'; a quick sense of what is appropriate, proper, or right; skill in avoiding what would offend."

> *An ambassador must have tact.*

Two words based on *tact* are *tactful*, meaning "having or showing tact; considerate"; and *tactless*, meaning "lacking tact; boorish."

> *An ambassador clearly has to be a tactful man.*
> *Jenny often makes tactless remarks to her friends.*

tangent comes from *tang-* meaning "to touch" and the Latin suffix *-ent*, which is the same as our English ending *-ing*. Thus, *tangent* means "touching." In geometry, the adjective *tangent* means "being in contact at a single point or along a line"; hence, a *tangent* is a "straight line that is in contact with a curved line at one point." The expression *to go off on a tangent* means "to make a sharp or sudden change in direction, especially when discussing a subject."

> *The line is tangent to the circle.*
> *The line is a tangent of the circle.*
> *He is an interesting speaker but tends to go off on tangents.*

A word based on *tangent* is *tangential*, meaning (1) of or pertaining to a tangent; (2) touching only slightly on something; (3) only slightly relevant to the main topic.

> *He kept introducing tangential questions into the debate.*

tangible comes from *tang-* meaning "to touch" and the Latin suffix *-ible* meaning "able to be; capable of being." *Tangible* literally means "capable of being touched; touchable." Hence, *tangible* means "perceptible by touch; having a definite shape; solid."

> *The oasis wasn't tangible; it was just a mirage.*
> *The storm seems to have had no tangible effect on our roofing.*

A word based on *tangible* is *intangible*, meaning "not tangible; real, but not material or concrete; hard to define or explain in words."

> *He cares more for material things than for intangible ideas.*
> *She has that intangible quality of good taste.*

◊ Sculptors may have more *tactile* sensitivity than most other people. Can you explain why?

Fun With Words

STUMP YOUR FRIENDS

Here are some fun words you might like to try on your friends. Check the word or phrase you believe is closest in meaning to the key word. Answers follow.

1. **amanuensis** [ə·man′yōō·en′sis]— (a) a magician. (b) stuttering. (c) a secretary. (d) one who hates men.
2. **bibelot** [bib′lō]—(a) a small object of art. (b) an old-fashioned neckpiece. (c) a marker for Holy Writ. (d) a love letter.
3. **bailiwick** [bā′lə·wik]—(a) a reed basket. (b) a prison. (c) one's own special place or province. (d) a whip.
4. **caravansary** [kar′ə·van′sə·rē]— (a) a traveling show. (b) an inn. (c) a camel train. (d) seeded bread from Arabia.
5. **cabalistic** [kab′ə·lis′tik]—(a) pertaining to black magic. (b) having a mystical meaning. (c) pertaining to those secretly united for intrigue. (d) pertaining to an acrostic.
6. **entrepreneur** [än′trə·prə·nûr′]— (a) a nightclub entertainer. (b) a person who is between jobs. (c) one who originates and conducts an enterprise. (d) an actor.

7. **furbelow** [fûr′bə·lō]—(a) a silly action. (b) a fussy or showy trimming. (c) a deep valley. (d) cheap jewelry.
8. **hoi polloi** [hoi′ pə·loi′]—(a) a Japanese emperor. (b) a Hawaiian fruit salad. (c) the common people. (d) a flowering shrub of the Pacific.
9. **leprechaun** [lep′rə·kôn]—(a) an elf in Irish folklore. (b) a disease of the skin. (c) a small leopard of the African highlands. (d) a medieval spell or charm.
10. **legerdemain** [lej′ər·də·mān′]— (a) a record of accounts. (b) magic tricks or sleight of hand. (c) witchcraft. (d) a chronicle of events.
11. **mountebank** [moun′tə·bangk]— (a) an area reserved for skiing. (b) a doctor. (c) an antelope of the African highlands. (d) a charlatan.
12. **nimrod** [nim′rod]—(a) an acrobat. (b) a fisherman. (c) a humorous character in puppet shows. (d) a hunter.

ANSWERS:

1. **amanuensis**—(c) a secretary. 2. **bibelot**—(a) a small object of art. 3. **bailiwick**—(c) one's own special place or province. 4. **caravansary**—(b) an inn. 5. **cabalistic**—(b) having a mystical meaning. 6. **entrepreneur**—(c) one who originates and conducts an enterprise. 7. **furbelow**—(b) a fussy or showy trimming. 8. **hoi polloi**—(c) the common people. 9. **leprechaun**—(a) an elf in Irish folklore. 10. **legerdemain**—(b) magic tricks or sleight of hand. 11. **mountebank**—(d) a charlatan. 12. **nimrod**—(d) a hunter.

ROOT: TEN-, TIN-, TENT-, TAIN-

The Latin root *ten-*, *tin-*, *tent-*, or *tain-* means "to hold." Learn the eight core vocabulary words based on this root: *contain, continent, detain, lieutenant, pertain, pertinacious, retain, tenacious.*

contain comes from the Latin prefix *con-* meaning "together" and *tain-* meaning "to hold." *Contain* literally means "to hold something together in a holder"; hence, (1) to hold or be able to hold; (2) to include; (3) to keep within bounds or restrain.

> *That bottle contains a quart of milk.*
> *This book contains useful information.*
> *A foot contains twelve inches.*
> *He was so angry he couldn't contain himself.*
> *Try to contain the enemy attack until reinforcements arrive.*

Three words based on *contain* are *container,* meaning "a box, carton, can, jar, etc., that holds or encloses something"; *containment,* meaning "the act or fact of containing; especially, the prevention of a nation from expanding its territories or political control"; and *content* [kon'tent], which means (1) that which a thing contains; (2) the amount of something contained; (3) subject matter.

> *She opened the container and removed the contents.*
> *We no longer have a policy of containment with regard to China.*
> *What is the silver content of the ore?*
> *They studied the style and content of the best-selling novel.*

continent comes from the Latin prefix *con-* meaning "together" and *tin-* meaning "to hold" plus the Latin suffix *-ent,* which is the same as our English ending *-ing.* Thus, a *continent* is "a mass of land that is holding together; one of the large land masses of the earth."

> *Africa is a continent.*
> *Englishmen and North Americans sometimes refer to Europe as "the Continent."*

A word based on *continent* is *continental,* meaning (1) of, on, or resembling a continent; (2) pertaining to Europe or Europeans.

> *Hawaii is not part of the continental United States.*
> *He has old-fashioned, Continental manners.*

detain comes from the Latin prefix *de-* meaning "away" and *tain-* meaning "to hold." *Detain* originally meant "to hold away from someone that which belonged to him; to withhold freedom from someone." Thus, *detain* means (1) to stop or delay; (2) to confine in jail.

> *I was detained by heavy traffic.*
> *The police detained the suspect for further questioning.*

A word based on *detain* is *detention,* meaning (1) the act of detaining or confining someone; (2) the state of being confined or delayed.

> *As a suspect, he was held in detention by the police.*

lieutenant comes from the French word *lieu* meaning "place" and the Latin root *ten-* meaning "to hold" plus the Latin suffix *-ant,* which is the same as our English ending, *-ing. Lieutenant* literally means "holding the place of another or acting in lieu of another." Hence, a *lieutenant* is (1) a person having the power to act for or represent his superior; (2) a commissioned officer ranking below a captain in the army and below a lieutenant commander in the navy.

> *His most reliable lieutenant managed the business in his absence.*
> *In the army, a second lieutenant ranks below a first lieutenant.*

pertain comes from the Latin prefix *per-* meaning "through; throughout" and *tain-* meaning "to hold." *Pertain* literally means "to have a hold throughout something"; hence, "to have to do with or have reference to something."

> *I don't see how your statement pertains to my question.*

Two words based on *pertain* are *pertinent,* meaning "related to the matter at hand; relevant" and *impertinent,* which means (1) disrespectful; unmannerly; impudent; (2) not pertinent; irrelevant.

> *His suggestion was pertinent; it was to the point.*
> *That child is rude and impertinent.*
> *Ed's wife has a way of breaking into serious conversations with impertinent small talk.*

pertinacious comes from the Latin prefix *per-* meaning "thoroughly; completely" plus the word *tenacious. Pertinacious* means "sticking stubbornly or with determination to a purpose or opinion."

> *The pertinacious detective tracked down the suspect.*

160

retain comes from the Latin prefix *re-* meaning "back" and *tain-* meaning "to hold." *Retain* literally means "to hold back something for oneself"; hence, (1) to keep or continue to keep something in one's possession; (2) to keep something in use, practice, etc.; (3) to keep in mind or remember; (4) to reserve the services of a lawyer or other representative by paying him a fee.

> *Mr. Smith retains complete control of the family business.*
> *Though he became famous, he retained his modesty.*
> *My mind doesn't retain facts as well as it used to.*
> *The firm retained a lawyer for any lawsuits that might arise.*

Three words based on *retain* are *retainer, retention,* and *retentive.* A *retainer* is (1) a servant; (2) a fee paid to engage or keep a representative, such as a lawyer. *Retention* means (1) the act of retaining or state of being retained or kept; (2) the ability to remember; memory. *Retentive* means "able to keep things, especially in memory."

> *The butler was an old family retainer.*
> *The lawyer collected his yearly retainer from the firm.*
> *The child has a retentive mind; his retention of new words is excellent.*

tenacious comes from *ten-* meaning "to hold" and the Latin suffix *-acious* meaning "tending to; inclined to." Thus, *tenacious* means "tending to hold something strongly, such as an opinion, belief, etc.; stubborn."

> *He is tenacious in his support of free speech.*
> *The wounded man clung to life tenaciously.*

A word based on *tenacious* is *tenacity,* meaning "the state or quality of holding firm; stubbornness; determination."

> *Though badly wounded, he clung to life with tenacity.*

◇ Look up the following words in your dictionary. Be sure you know the meaning of each. Relate each meaning to the root *ten-, tin-, tent-,* or *tain-* meaning "to hold."

abstain	entertain	sustenance
abstention	maintain	tenable
continuation	obtain	tenant
continue	sustain	tenancy

161

EXPLORING WORDS
MORE PEOPLE WHO BECAME WORDS

The name of each of the following men became a word in the English language. How many of the words and their meanings do you know or can you guess?

1. Julius Caesar, Roman general who introduced a calendar.

2. Jean Nicot, 16th-century courtier who introduced tobacco into France.

3. Henry Shrapnel, 19th-century British artillery officer.

4. Samuel A. Maverick, 19th-century Texan who refused to brand his cattle.

5. Vidkun Quisling, Norwegian Nazi.

6. Mary Magdalen, often pictured as weeping.

7. J. L. McAdam, 19th-century Scottish engineer.

8. François Mansard, 17th-century French architect.

9. Jean Martinet, 17th-century French general and drillmaster.

10. King Mausolus of Caria, 4th-century B.C., whose tomb was one of the Seven Wonders of the ancient world.

11. Louis Pasteur, 19th-century French chemist.

12. A. E. Burnside, Union general of the U.S. Civil War.

ANSWERS:

1. **July;** 2. **nicotine,** a poisonous alkaloid found in tobacco leaves; 3. **shrapnel,** a kind of shell containing pieces of sharp metal; 4. **maverick:** (i) an unbranded animal, (ii) one who refuses to follow the ways of his group; 5. **quisling,** a traitor who helps an invading enemy; 6. **maudlin,** easily moved to tears, sentimental; 7. **macadam,** a road made of crushed stone, oiled or tarred; 8. **mansard,** a flat roof with sharp, vertical slopes at the edges; 9. **martinet,** a strict taskmaster; 10. **mausoleum,** a large tomb; 11. **pasteurize,** to destroy germs in milk, wine, etc. by the use of high temperatures; 12. **sideburns.**

ROOT: **TRACT-**

The important Latin root *tract-* means "to drag; draw; pull." Learn the eleven core vocabulary words based on the root *tract-*: *attract, contract, detract, distract, extract, protract, retract, subtract, tract, traction, tractor.*

attract comes from the Latin prefix *at-* (another spelling of *ad-*) meaning "to; toward" and *tract-* meaning "to draw; pull." Thus, *attract* means (1) to draw something or someone to or toward oneself, as by magnetism; (2) to gain the admiration or attention of someone.

> *A magnet will attract iron.*
> *The pretty girl attracted the attention of all the men.*
> *The baby cried to attract attention.*

Two words based on *attract* are *attraction* and *attractive*. *Attraction* means (1) the act or power of attracting; (2) a characteristic or feature that attracts. *Attractive* means "having the quality of drawing interest or affection; pleasing."

> *Things fall downward because of the attraction of the earth's gravity.*
> *The girl's intelligence was her chief attraction.*
> *What is the main attraction at the local theater?*
> *The store's bargain prices were attractive.*
> *The girl has an attractive face.*

contract comes from the Latin prefix *con-* meaning "together" and *tract-* meaning "to draw; pull." Thus, *contract* [kən·trakt′] means (1) to draw together; to shrink or become more compact; (2) to cause something to draw together; (3) to take on or become affected with, as a debt or a disease; (4) to make a legal agreement. A *contract* [kon′trakt] is "a legal agreement that draws together two people or parties."

> *The pupils of his eyes contracted in the bright light.*
> *Cold contracts metals.*
> *Mr. Vernon contracted large debts in his business.*
> *He contracted pneumonia.*
> *The construction company contracted to build the new school.*
> *The lawyer drew up a contract for his clients.*

Three words based on *contract* are *contraction, contractor,* and *contractual. Contraction* means (1) a drawing or pulling together; a shrinkage or reduction; (2) a shortened form of a word. *Contractor* means "a person who makes a contract, especially one who agrees to supply certain materials or to perform a job for an agreed price." *Contractual* means "of or concerning a contract."

> *Cold causes the contraction of liquids.*
> *The word* can't *is a contraction of* cannot.
> *Mr. Smith is a building contractor.*
> *The business partners trusted each other so much that they did not have a contractual agreement.*

detract comes from the Latin prefix *de-* meaning "away" and *tract-* meaning "to draw." Thus, *detract* means "to draw or take away a part of something, as part of one's good reputation, enjoyment, etc."

> *His laziness detracts from his efficiency.*
> *The rainy weather detracted from our enjoyment of the scenery.*

Two words based on *detract* are *detractor,* meaning "a person who defames or disparages another"; and *detraction,* meaning "a taking away of something, such as someone's good reputation; slander."

> *He has always been one of the mayor's greatest detractors.*
> *He stood firm, despite the detractions of his critics.*

distract comes from the Latin prefix *dis-* meaning "away" and *tract-* meaning "to draw." Thus, *distract* means (1) to draw away or divert the mind, attention, etc., in a different direction; (2) to bewilder.

> *He went to a movie to distract his mind from his worries.*
> *The speed and roar of the traffic distracted the student driver.*

Two words based on *distract* are *distracted* and *distraction. Distracted* means (1) bewildered; confused; preoccupied with worry; (2) insane. *Distraction* means (1) a drawing away of the mind from an object or from cares; (2) anything that distracts, as a diversion or interruption; (3) extreme mental distress.

> *He was in a distracted, anxious frame of mind.*
> *He tries to avoid distractions such as telephone calls.*
> *A trip to the beach offered a welcome distraction for the children.*
> *The earsplitting noise of the drill is driving us to distraction.*

164

NOTE: Another word having almost the same meaning as *distracted* is *distraught*. Though it is spelled differently, *distraught* comes from the same Latin word as *distracted*. *Distraught* means "deeply agitated in mind; worried, tense, and bewildered."

Millie was distraught until her missing child was found.

extract comes from the Latin prefix *ex-* meaning "out" and *tract-* meaning "to draw; pull." Thus, *extract* [ig·strakt′] means (1) to draw or pull out; (2) to obtain something from a substance by squeezing it, distilling it, etc.; (3) to obtain or draw out pleasure, knowledge, a promise, etc., from something or someone; (4) to copy out information from a book. An *extract* [eks′trakt] is "anything drawn out of a thing or substance, as a passage or quotation copied out of a book or a preparation containing the essence of a substance in concentrated form."

The dentist extracted the bad tooth.
He extracted a big gold watch from his pocket.
This machine extracts juice from oranges.
Did you extract a promise of payment from the customer?
Dr. Lindon extracted a verse from the Bible for his sermon.
He read an extract from the Old Testament.
Don't forget to buy some vanilla extract.

A word based on *extract* is *extraction,* meaning (1) a drawing or pulling out of something; (2) a person's national origin or line of descent; ancestry.

The dentist charged $100 for the extraction of the wisdom tooth.
Mr. McLean is of Scottish extraction.

protract comes from the Latin prefix *pro-* meaning "forward" and *tract-* meaning "to draw." Thus, *protract* means "to draw forward in time"; hence, "to extend for a longer time than was expected; prolong."

The meeting should not be protracted beyond 5:00 P.M.

Two words based on *protract* are *protraction,* meaning "the act of prolonging something; an extension"; and *protractor,* meaning "an instrument for measuring and laying out angles."

The heated argument caused a protraction of the meeting.
A protractor is used in geometry.

retract comes from the Latin prefix *re-* meaning "back" and *tract-* meaning "to draw; pull." Thus, *retract* means (1) to draw and take something back, such as a remark, statement, promise, etc.; (2) to draw back in, as a cat draws in its claws.

He retracted the insult and apologized.
The landing gear retracted into the fuselage of the airplane.

Two words based on *retract* are *retractable*, or *retractible*, meaning "able to be taken back or drawn back in"; and *retraction*, meaning "a taking back of something, especially something said or written."

Are the wheels of all airplanes retractable?
He published a retraction of his unsupported accusations.

subtract comes from the Latin prefix *sub-* meaning "beneath; away from; under" and *tract-* meaning "to draw." Thus, *subtract* means "to take away from something by deducting a quantity, number, etc."

He subtracted the expenses from the profits.

A word based on *subtract* is *subtraction*, meaning "the act or process of taking a quantity, number, etc., away from something."

Addition and subtraction are taught in elementary school.

tract comes directly from the root *tract-* meaning "to draw." The word *tract* means (1) an extended area, as of land or water; (2) an extensive region of the body, especially a system of parts or organs. It can also mean "a short written discussion on some subject, especially a pamphlet on politics or religion."

This tract of land is about ten acres.
Food is digested in the alimentary tract.
Alexander Hamilton wrote a number of political tracts.

traction comes from *tract-* meaning "to draw; pull" and the Latin suffix *-ion* meaning "the act or result of." Thus, *traction* means (1) the act or result of a pulling force; (2) a pulling force itself; (3) the state or condition of being subject to a pulling force; (4) the ability to grip and move on a surface without slipping.

The broken leg was placed in traction to keep the parts of the fractured bone in place.
Trains used to be powered by steam traction.
It is hard for tires to get good traction on an icy road.

tractor comes from *tract-* meaning "to draw; pull; drag" and the Latin suffix *-or* meaning "a thing that does." Thus, a *tractor* is "a thing that pulls or draws something"; hence, "a vehicle used for pulling a piece of farm equipment, a trailer, etc."

QUICKIEQUIZQUICKIEQUIZQUICKIEQUIZQUICKIEQUIZQUICKIEQUIZQUICKIEQUIZQUICKIEQUIZQUICKIE

90-SECOND QUICKIE QUIZ

TEN MORE WORD BUILDING BLOCKS

Knowing the meaning of the roots that make up words can help you to define them. Can you match these word elements with their meanings? Answers follow.

1. **mono-** as in monocle [mon′ə·kəl]
2. **gam-** as in monogamy [mə·nog′ə·mē]
3. **matri-** as in matriarchy [mā′trē·är′kē]
4. **hydro-** as in hydroelectric [hī′drō·i·lek′trik]
5. **-graphy** as in photography [fə·tog′rə·fē]
6. **mega-** as in megaphone [meg′ə·fōn]
7. **gyn-** as in gynecologist [gī′nə·kol′ə·jist]
8. **icon-** as in iconoclast [ī·kon′ə·klast]
9. **omni-** as in omnipotent [om·nip′ə·tənt]
10. **hypno-** as in hypnosis [hip·nō′sis]

(a) sleep
(b) writing
(c) woman
(d) one
(e) image
(f) water
(g) mother
(h) marriage
(i) great
(j) all

ANSWERS:

1. **mono-** — (d) one. A monocle is an eyeglass for one eye.
2. **gam-** — (d) marriage. Monogamy is the practice of having only one marriage, or one husband or wife, at a time.
3. **matri-** — (g) mother. A matriarchy is a tribe, race, or family of which a woman is the head.
4. **hydro-** — (f) water. Hydroelectric refers to electricity generated by the energy of water, as a hydroelectric plant located near a dam or on a river.
5. **-graphy** — (b) writing. Photography literally means "writing with light."
6. **mega-** — (i) great. A megaphone is a funnel-shaped device for amplifying sound.
7. **gyn-** — (c) woman. A gynecologist is a doctor who specializes in diseases peculiar to women.
8. **icon-** — (e) image. An iconoclast seeks to destroy conventions and cherished beliefs (literally, to destroy the use of images in religious worship).
9. **omni-** — (j) all. Omnipotent means all-powerful; almighty.
10. **hypno-** — (a) sleep. Hypnosis is a trancelike condition resembling sleep.

QUICKIEQUIZQUICKIEQUIZQUICKIEQUIZQUICKIEQUIZQUICKIEQUIZQUICKIEQUIZQUICKIEQUIZQUICKIE

ROOT: VEN-, VENT-

The Latin root *ven-* or *vent-* means "to move toward; come." Learn the seven core vocabulary words based on *ven-* or *vent-*: *adventure, circumvent, convene, convenient, event, invent, prevent.*

adventure comes from the Latin prefix *ad-* meaning "to" and *ven-* meaning "to come" plus the Latin suffix *-ure* meaning "the act or state of." *Adventure* literally means "that which is about to come upon, or happen to, someone." Thus, *adventure* means "a thrilling experience; a risky or daring undertaking."

> *Huckleberry Finn's great adventure was sailing down the Mississippi on a raft.*

Two words based on *adventure* are *adventurer*, meaning "a person who takes part in adventures or who seeks them"; and *adventurous*, meaning "liking to seek adventures or take risks."

> *Explorers are all adventurers.*
> *The astronauts are adventurous men.*

circumvent comes from the Latin prefix *circum-* meaning "around" and *vent-* meaning "to come." Thus, *circumvent* means (1) to come around or get around something; (2) to avoid something, especially by using one's wits.

> *Many modern highways circumvent large towns.*
> *Don't try to circumvent the law!*

convene comes from the Latin prefix *con-* meaning "together" and *ven-* meaning "to come." Thus, *convene* means "to call or come together; assemble."

> *The Mayor convened an emergency session of the Council.*
> *The committee convened every Monday.*

Four words based on *convene* are *convent, convention, conventional*, and *unconventional*. *Convent* means (1) an assembly or community of nuns; (2) the building in which nuns live. *Convention* means (1) an assembly of delegates or members, meeting for political, professional, or other purposes; (2) a custom or rule that is generally followed by a group or by society as a whole. *Conventional* means (1) growing out of or following custom, established by general agreement; (2) lacking originality. *Unconventional* means "not following custom, tradition, or established rules."

> *Having chosen the religious life, she entered the convent.*
> *Where did the Elks' convention meet?*
> *According to convention, men wear coats and ties in business offices.*
> *An S.O.S. is a conventional signal for help.*
> *It is a rather dull, conventional movie, in which boy meets girl.*
> *Her teaching methods were unconventional but effective.*

convenient comes from the Latin prefix *con-* meaning "together" and *ven-* meaning "to come" plus the Latin suffix *-ient,* which is the same as our English ending *-ing.* Thus, *convenient* means (1) coming or fitting together so as to be proper or easy for a person; suited to what one needs; (2) within easy reach; handy.

> *Let's discuss this matter at a more convenient time.*
> *The house is in a convenient location for shopping.*

Two words based on *convenient* are *inconvenient* and *convenience.* *Inconvenient* means (1) not suitable for one's needs; troublesome; (2) not within easy reach; not handy. *Convenience* means (1) the quality of being suited to one's needs; (2) comfort; ease; (3) something that increases comfort or saves work, effort, or trouble.

> *The kitchen is poorly planned and inconvenient.*
> *It would be inconvenient for me to meet you for lunch.*
> *I'd like to discuss the matter with you at your convenience.*
> *A swimming pool was provided for the convenience of the guests.*
> *We don't really need a car, but it would be a convenience.*

event comes from the Latin prefix *e-* (another spelling of *ex-*) meaning "out" and *vent-* meaning "to come." Thus, *event* means (1) something that takes place; a situation or happening; (2) one of the items or "happenings" on a sports program.

> *He is interested in reading about historical events.*
> *The main event was the fight for the heavyweight championship.*

Four words based on *event* are *eventful,* meaning "marked by important events"; *eventual,* meaning "happening in the due course of time"; *eventuality*, meaning "a possible happening, situation, or outcome"; and *eventually*, meaning "finally; in due course."

> *The 1960s was an eventful decade.*
> *Their eventual victory made up for past defeats.*
> *If he keeps trying, he will eventually succeed.*
> *If you travel alone in the jungle, you must be prepared for any eventuality.*

invent comes from the Latin prefix *in-* meaning "on" and *vent-* meaning "to come." *Invent* literally means "to come on or come upon something." Hence, *invent* means "to think up or make something new; originate or create; make something up."

> *Edison invented the incandescent bulb.*
> *The author has invented some interesting characters in this book.*
> *Did you invent an excuse for your absence?*

Three words based on *invent* are *invention, inventive,* and *inventor.* *Invention* means (1) that which is invented or made up; (2) the act of inventing something. *Inventive* means (1) good at inventing things; (2) showing the power of invention. *Inventor* means "a person who invents something."

> *How many of Edison's inventions can you name?*
> *That story Donna told was pure invention.*
> *The invention of the airplane revolutionized transportation.*
> *She has an inventive mind.*
> *This is a very inventive solution to the problem.*
> *Thomas Edison was a famous American inventor.*

prevent comes from the Latin prefix *pre-* meaning "before" and *vent-* meaning "to come." Thus, *prevent* literally means "to make something come before something else in order to keep it from happening." Hence, *prevent* means "to keep something from happening or to keep someone from doing something, by taking measures beforehand."

> *You can help prevent forest fires by dousing your campfire.*
> *A snowstorm prevented them from driving home.*
> *A poor vocabulary prevented him from getting ahead.*

Two words based on *prevent* are *prevention* and *preventive.* *Prevention* means (1) the act of preventing; (2) a hindrance. *Preventive* means "intended or serving to prevent or ward off harm, disease, etc."

The prevention of forest fires is necessary for the protection of wildlife.
A proper diet helps in the prevention of disease.
Vaccines are a form of preventive medicine.

◊ Look up the following words in your dictionary. Learn the meaning of each. Be sure you can relate each meaning to the root *ven-* or *vent-* meaning "to move toward; come."

advent   intervene   venture   venturesome

ROOT: VERT-, VERS-

The Latin root *vert-* or *vers-* means "to turn." Learn the five core vocabulary words based on this root: *avert, convert, divert, reverse, subversive.*

avert comes from the Latin prefix *a-* (another spelling of *ab-*) meaning "away" and *vert-* meaning "to turn." Thus, *avert* means "to turn one's eyes or head away from something; to ward off a danger."

When he opened the furnace door, he averted his face.
He tried to avert the accident by slamming on his brakes.

A word based on *avert* is *aversion*, meaning "extreme dislike," literally, "that which makes one turn away."

She has an aversion to large crowds.

convert comes from the Latin prefix *con-* meaning "thoroughly; completely" and *vert-* meaning "to turn." Thus, *convert* [kən·vûrt′] means "to turn completely from one thing to another; change to another form, character, religion, etc.; transform." A *convert* [kon′vûrt] is "a person who changes his belief, especially his religious beliefs."

They converted the old barn into a summer house.
When I reached France, I had to convert my dollars to francs.
John Henry Newman converted to Catholicism.
Cardinal Newman was a Catholic convert.

171

Eight words based on *convert* are *conversant, conversation, conversational, conversationalist, converse, conversion, converter,* and *convertible. Conversant* means "familiar with." *Conversation* means "friendly talk or an exchange of ideas." *Conversational* means "having to do with or resembling conversation, especially informal conversation." *Conversationalist* means "a person who likes to talk or who is good at conversation." *Converse* means (1) to talk informally together; exchange ideas; (2) the opposite or "turned around" side of something; the contrary or reverse. *Conversion* means (1) the act of changing something into another form; (2) the act of changing to a new religion or way of thinking. *Converter* means "a person or thing that converts." *Convertible* means (1) capable of being converted or changed in character; (2) a convertible thing, especially an automobile with a folding top that can be lowered or raised.

> *He is conversant with many fields of study.*
> *We were having a conversation on politics.*
> *His style of writing is easy and conversational.*
> *He is too shy to be a good conversationalist.*
> *The old friends conversed late into the night.*
> *I believe that the converse of what he said is true.*
> *Extreme cold brings about the conversion of water into ice.*
> *Last year he experienced a conversion to Buddhism.*
> *A Bessemer converter is used to turn pig iron into steel.*
> *Checks are convertible into cash.*
> *Her father drives a sedan, and she drives a convertible.*

divert comes from the Latin prefix *di-* (another spelling of *dis-*) meaning "apart; in different directions" and *vert-* meaning "to turn." Thus, *divert* means (1) to turn in a different direction; turn aside from a set course; (2) to distract; (3) to entertain.

> *Traffic was diverted to a side road because of an accident.*
> *A loud noise diverted his attention from his book.*
> *The children were diverted by the puppet show.*

Three words based on *divert* are *diverse, diversion,* and *diversity. Diverse* means (1) marked by differences; not alike; (2) varied in kind or form. *Diversion* means (1) a turning aside; (2) an entertainment, amusement, or pleasant pastime. *Diversity* means (1) complete difference; (2) variety; multiplicity.

America is made up of people of diverse backgrounds.
His diverse interests range from baseball to classical music.
The dam caused a diversion of the river from its natural bed.
A visit to the zoo was a diversion for the children.
There was a diversity of opinions at the political convention.
Big cities offer a diversity of amusements.

reverse comes from the Latin prefix *re-* meaning "back" and *vers-* meaning "to turn." *Reverse* literally means "turned backward; having an opposite direction, character, etc." Hence, *reverse* means "to turn upside down, inside out, or in an opposite direction; set aside, overturn, or turn backward or to the rear." The *reverse* is "that which is directly opposite." A *reverse* means "a setback."

You may reverse this coat so that the fur is on the outside.
The Supreme Court reversed several lower court decisions.
He disagreed and took the reverse side of the argument.
The names were listed in reverse alphabetical order.
That is the reverse of the truth.
The business suffered reverses during the strike.

Four words based on *reverse* are *reversal, reversible, reversion,* and *revert. Reversal* means (1) the act of reversing; (2) something that is reversed; a setback. *Reversible* means "capable of being reversed." *Reversion* means "a return to a former condition, state, belief, practice, etc." *Revert* means "to go back to a former place, state, condition, etc."

Not getting the promotion was a major reversal in his career.
This raincoat is reversible—tan on one side and blue on the other.
After the war, industry underwent a reversion to peacetime products.
If the college does not use the money according to the will, the fund will revert to the family.

subversive comes from the Latin prefix *sub-* meaning "from beneath; up from under" and *vers-* meaning "to turn" plus the Latin suffix *-ive* meaning "tending to." Thus, *subversive* means "tending to overturn or overthrow something, especially a government, from its very foundations."

The British considered the Boston Tea Party a subversive act.

Two words based on *subversive* are *subversion,* meaning "the act of

173

overthrowing something or the state of being overthrown"; and *subvert*, meaning "to overthrow from the very foundation."

> *Dictatorship is a subversion of the rights of the people.*
> *Discontented people tried to subvert the new government.*

◇ Look up the following words in your dictionary. Learn the meaning of each. Try to relate each meaning to the root *vert-* or *vers-* meaning "to turn."

controversy   irreversible   traverse

ROOT: VID-, VIS-

When you noted this Latin root, perhaps you thought of *video, vision* or *television* and decided that the root meant "to see." If you did, you were right. Learn the five core vocabulary words based on the root *vid-* or *vis-*: *evident, provide, television, video, vision.*

evident comes from the Latin prefix *e-* (another spelling of *ex-*) meaning "out" and *vid-* meaning "to see," plus the Latin suffix *-ent*, which is the same as our English ending *-ing*. Thus, *evident* means "seeing something out in the open"; hence, "easily seen or recognized; clear."

> *It is evident that you are learning many new words.*
> *He was evidently in great pain.*

Two words based on *evident* are *self-evident*, meaning "requiring no proof of its truth; obvious in itself," and *evidence*, meaning "that which proves or disproves something; proof."

> *The thief was caught in the act; his guilt was self-evident.*
> *The evidence was overwhelming that the accused man was guilty.*
> *A gun was produced as evidence of the crime.*

provide comes from the Latin prefix *pro-* meaning "before" and *vid-* meaning "to see." Thus, *provide* literally means "to foresee"; hence,

(1) to prepare or supply beforehand; (2) to furnish necessary food, clothing, and shelter; support.

Who will provide the food for the picnic?
In case of your death, this life insurance policy will provide for your family.

Seven words based on *provide* are *provided, provider, providence, provident, provision, provisions,* and *provisional. Provided* means "if; depending on preparations or on expectations being fulfilled." A *provider* is "one who provides; especially, a person whose income supports a family." *Providence* means (1) concern for the future; foresight; (2) *spelled with a capital first letter* the care exercised by God over the universe. *Provident* means "preparing for future needs." *Provision* means (1) to supply with basic items or supplies of food; (2) the act of providing, or the state of being provided; (3) part of an agreement referring to one specific thing. *Provisions* are "supplies, especially of basic items of food." *Provisional* means "provided for a temporary need; adopted on a tentative basis or for lack of something permanent."

We'll have the picnic, provided the weather is good.
He was devoted to his family and was always a good provider.
The Puritans trusted in Providence.
He was provident and saved most of his earnings.
Napoleon provisioned his army well.
The treaty had no provision for settling the disputed boundary between the two nations.
Have you bought the provisions for the camping trip?
The general raised a provisional army to fight the invaders.

television comes from the Greek root *tele-* meaning "far; at a distance" and the word *vision. Television* means "the transmission of visual images over a distance as a series of electrical impulses." It can also mean "the television broadcasting industry" or "a television receiver."

Television has replaced radio in popularity.
Last night there was an old movie on television.

A word based on *television* is *televise,* meaning "to send or receive by television."

Wednesday night hockey games are usually televised.

video comes directly from a Latin word based on the root *vid-* meaning

"I see." In modern English, the adjective *video* means "the picture portion of television."

> *Television shows are filmed on video tape.*
> *How does the video news compare with newspaper and weekly magazine coverage?*
> *In our television set, the sound is good, but the video needs adjusting.*

vision comes from *vis-* meaning "to see" and the Latin suffix *-ion* meaning "the act, state, or result of." Thus, *vision* means (1) the sense of sight; (2) insight or imagination; (3) something seen as in a plan, dream, trance, etc.

> *She wears glasses to improve her vision.*
> *We need a man of vision to head the planning commission.*
> *He had a vision of owning a large ranch and raising cattle.*

Five words based on or related to *vision* are *visible, invisible, visionary, visual,* and *visualize. Visible* means (1) capable of being seen; (2) evident, obvious, or apparent. *Invisible* means "not capable of being seen." *Visionary* means (1) impractical or unreal; (2) a person who has visions of any kind, such as highly imaginative plans, unusual insight, dreams, trances, etc. *Visual* means "pertaining to, resulting from, or serving the sense of sight." *Visualize* means "to see in the mind; to form a mental image of something."

> *The camouflaged trucks were not visible from the airplane.*
> *The tramp had no visible means of support.*
> *A colorless gas such as oxygen is invisible.*
> *He lost money on several of his visionary schemes.*
> *Many Christian saints were visionaries.*
> *The school uses slides and movies as visual aids to learning.*
> *I can't visualize you as a lion hunter.*

◇ Look up the following words in your dictionary. You should know the meaning of each, but check to see how they are related to the root *vid-* or *vis-* meaning "to see."

advise	ill-advised	visibility
advisement	improvident	visit
adviser	proviso	visitation
advisory	visage	visitor

ROOT: VOC-, VOK-

The Latin root *voc-* or *vok-* means "voice" or "to call." Two simple words that you already know, *voice* and *vocal*, are based on this root. Learn the seven core vocabulary words based on *voc-* or *vok-*: *advocate, evoke, invoke, provoke, revoke, vocabulary, vocation.*

advocate comes from the Latin prefix *ad-* meaning "to" and *voc-* meaning "to call" plus the suffix *-ate*, which is used to form verbs. *Advocate* originally referred to someone who is "called to" another person in order to give assistance. Hence, to *advocate* [ad′və·kāt] means "to speak or write in favor of someone or something." An *advocate* [ad′və·kit] is "a person who pleads the cause of another or who defends a cause."

> *He advocates free speech.*
> *Dr. Smith is an advocate of strenuous exercise.*

evoke comes from the Latin prefix *e-* (another spelling of *ex-*) meaning "out" and *vok-* meaning "to call." Thus, *evoke* means (1) to call out or summon forth something, such as memories; (2) to produce a reaction, response, etc.

> *The writer evoked the days of his youth.*
> *His sarcastic letter evoked an angry reply.*

Two words based on *evoke* are *evocation*, meaning "the act of calling something forth, as memories," and *evocative*, meaning "tending to call something forth, as memories."

> *The author was praised for his moving evocation of a bygone era.*
> *He wrote an evocative description of his childhood.*

invoke comes from the Latin prefix *in-* meaning "on" and *vok-* meaning "to call." Thus, *invoke* means "to call upon someone or something, especially a spirit or god, for aid, protection, etc.; appeal to a law, power, etc., for aid or support; ask or call for something, especially a blessing."

> *The poet invoked the muses to inspire him.*
> *The chairman invoked the veto six times.*
> *The priest invoked God's blessing on the congregation.*

A word based on *invoke* is *invocation,* meaning "an appeal to a god, power, or other agent, for aid, protection, etc., especially a prayer said before and for a group."

> *The chaplain gave the invocation at the opening of the Legislature.*

provoke comes from the Latin prefix *pro-* meaning "forward; forth" and *vok-* meaning "to call." Thus, *provoke* means (1) to call forth or arouse anger in someone; irritate; stir up; (2) to arouse or cause some action or reaction.

> *He was provoked by the waiter's lack of attention.*
> *Their disagreement over politics provoked a serious quarrel.*
> *His slip of the tongue provoked shouts of laughter.*

Two words based on *provoke* are *provocation,* meaning "an act that causes anger or irritation; an act calling forth an angry response"; and *provocative,* meaning "calling forth anger or any strong feeling; irritating or stimulating."

> *He started the fight without provocation.*
> *The country responded to the hostile nation's provocations by declaring war.*
> *Did his provocative remarks really justify your hitting him?*
> *The perfume had a provocative aroma.*

revoke comes from the Latin prefix *re-* meaning "back" and *vok-* meaning "to call." Thus, *revoke* means "to make something void by calling it back or recalling it; cancel."

> *The captain revoked the soldier's weekend pass.*
> *His driver's license was revoked because he had had several accidents.*

Two words based on *revoke* are *irrevocable,* meaning "incapable of being repealed, changed, or canceled," and *revocation,* meaning "a repeal, reversal, or cancellation."

> *Once in writing, his decision to resign was irrevocable.*
> *The past is irrevocable.*
> *Drunken driving will result in the revocation of one's driver's license.*

vocabulary comes from the Latin root *vocabul-* based on *voc-,* which means "a word," and *-ary* meaning "connected with." Thus, *vocabu-*

lary means "a list of words or phrases, especially one arranged alphabetically and including definitions or translations." It may also mean "all the words of a language," or "all the words known or used by a particular person or in a particular field."

The French vocabulary was printed in the back of the textbook.
The English vocabulary includes hundreds of thousands of words.
A scientific vocabulary includes many words from Greek.

NOTE: Remember these different meanings of vocabulary. Your vocabulary is made up of the words you know or use. The English vocabulary is made up of all the words that have been used by English writers and speakers. A foreign language vocabulary is compiled for the use of persons learning that language.

vocation comes from *voc-* meaning "to call" and the Latin suffix *-ation* meaning "the act or state of." *Vocation* literally means "the state of being called"; hence, "a calling; a regular occupation; one's main job or interest." *Vocation* may also refer to "fitness for a certain career, especially religious work."

He chose medicine as his vocation.
The student felt he had a vocation for the priesthood.

A word based on *vocation* is *vocational*, meaning "of or pertaining to a job or career."

He learned welding in a vocational school.
Most schools offer vocational guidance.

NOTE: *Avocation* is built on the prefix *a-* (a form of the prefix *ab-* meaning "away") and the word *vocation*. Literally, an *avocation* is something that takes or calls a person "away" from his occupation or main job or interest. Thus, an *avocation* is "a hobby or diversion; a secondary job or interest."

The doctor's vocation is medicine; his avocation is golf.

◊ Look up the following words in your dictionary. Learn the meaning of each. Try to relate each meaning to the root *voc-* or *vok-* meaning "voice" or "to call."

vocal	vocalize	vociferous
vocalist	vociferate	vox populi

179

ROOT: VOLV-, VOLUT-

The Latin root *volv-* or *volut-* means "to roll." Learn the four core vocabulary words based on this root: *evolve, involve, revolve, revolt.*

evolve comes from the Latin prefix *e-* (another spelling of *ex-*) meaning "out" and *volv-* meaning "to roll." Thus, *evolve* means (1) to roll out or unroll, hence: to unfold or expand; (2) to work out or develop something gradually; (3) to develop from a lower to a higher stage of organization; (4) to undergo the process of evolution.

> *He evolved a plan for increasing sales.*
> *Over the years, the small business evolved into a large corporation.*
> *The jet airliner has evolved from the Wright brothers' small airplane.*
> *Birds evolved from prehistoric reptiles.*

A word based on *evolve* is *evolution*, meaning "the process of developing from one state to another, usually slowly and by stages" or "anything that develops by such a process."

> *The evolution of the airplane is an example of technological development.*
> *The evolution of living things took place over millions of years.*

involve comes from the Latin prefix *in-* meaning "in" and *volv-* meaning "to roll." *Involve* literally means "to roll in or roll up." Thus, *involve* means (1) to include as a necessary part of something; (2) to take in or have an effect on; (3) to bring someone or something into trouble, difficulty, danger, etc.; (4) to take up the attention; engross.

> *Building a good vocabulary involves study.*
> *The depression involved almost everyone in the country.*
> *I don't want to get involved in your argument with him.*
> *The girl was completely involved in her work.*

Two words based on *involve* are *involved*, meaning "complicated; intricate," and *involvement*, meaning "an involving or being involved."

> *The directions he gave us were so involved that we were lost.*
> *They were having an involved scientific discussion.*
> *The nightclub owner's involvement with gangsters was well known.*

revolve comes from the Latin prefix *re-* meaning "back" and *volv-* meaning "to roll." *Revolve* literally means "to roll back to the starting point; roll around." Thus, *revolve* means (1) to move in a circle around a center; rotate; (2) to occur regularly again and again, as in cycles.

> *The earth revolves around the sun.*
> *Most large buildings have revolving doors.*
> *The whole movie revolved around the star.*
> *The seasons revolve every year.*

Three words based on *revolve* are *revolution, revolutionary, revolver*. *Revolution* means (1) the act or state of revolving; (2) the overthrow and replacement of a government, group, or system by its members; (3) any drastic change in something, as in a condition, plan, etc. *Revolutionary* means (1) a person who leads or joins a revolution or who brings about a drastic change; (2) of, pertaining to, or causing a revolution or drastic change. A *revolver* is "a hand gun having a revolving chamber to hold several cartridges."

> *One complete revolution of the earth around the sun takes 365 days.*
> *The American Revolution led to independence.*
> *The invention of the automobile caused a revolution in our way of life.*
> *William Lyon Mackenzie and Louis Riel were Canadian revolutionaries.*
> *Henry Ford introduced the revolutionary idea of mass production into car manufacturing.*
> *Was the bullet fired from a pistol or from a revolver?*

revolt comes from the Latin prefix *re-* meaning "back" and the root *volt-*, which is based on *volv-* meaning "to roll." *Revolt* literally means "to roll back on or turn against." Thus, *revolt* as a verb means (1) to rise in rebellion against the constituted authority; (2) to disgust or repel. As a noun, *revolt* means (1) an uprising; a rebellion against authority; (2) the state of a person or persons who revolt.

> *The colonists revolted against taxation without representation.*
> *She was revolted by the strong smell of garlic.*
> *Troops were dispatched to put down an armed revolt.*
> *The nation was in revolt.*

Fun With Words
REVIEW OF ROOTS

Here is another review test of roots and words you have already learned. Choose the answer nearest in meaning to each of the key words. Answers follow.

1. **ascribe** [ə·skrīb′]—(a) to attribute to a specific cause or source. (b) to write down officially. (c) to mark out the limits of; confine within bounds. (d) to slander or libel.
2. **circumscribe** [sûr′kəm·skrīb′]— (a) to write down officially. (b) to mark out the limits of; confine within bounds. (c) to sail around the world. (d) an accent mark placed over certain vowels to indicate their correct pronunciation.
3. **transcribe** [tran·skrīb′]—(a) to write down officially. (b) to keep a diary. (c) a person who can speak or write many languages. (d) to make a written copy, as of a speech, lecture, shorthand notes, etc.
4. **indescribable** [in′di·skrī′bə·bəl] —(a) too good to be true. (b) too complex or unusual to be described. (c) extremely beautiful. (d) extremely ugly.
5. **postscript** [pōst′skript′]—(a) money or checks sent through the mail. (b) the opening or initial greeting beginning a letter. (c) the closing or final line of a letter. (d) a sentence or paragraph added to a letter after the writer's signature.
6. **obsession** [əb·sesh′ən]—(a) a shadow, semidarkness, as at dusk. (b) high regard; esteem. (c) a persistent idea or emotion. (d) an irrational scheme.
7. **sedate** [si·dāt′]—(a) old or old-fashioned. (b) sickly or feeble. (c) calm; quiet; composed. (d) dignified; poised.
8. **sedative** [sed′ə·tiv]—(a) any means of soothing distress or allaying pain. (b) a deep sleep. (c) old or old-fashioned. (d) sick or feeble.
9. **sedentary** [sed′ən·ter′ē]—(a) incapable of moving; stationary. (b) a sleeping pill. (c) a layer of silt or mud, as in a river. (d) sitting; inactive.

ANSWERS:

1. **ascribe**—(a) to attribute to a specific cause or source. 2. **circumscribe** —(b) to mark out the limits of; confine within bounds. 3. **transcribe**—(d) to make a written copy, as of a speech, lecture, shorthand notes, etc. 4. **indescribable**—(b) too complex or unusual to be described. 5. **postscript**—(d) a sentence or paragraph added to a letter after the writer's signature. 6. **obsession**—(c) a persistent idea or emotion. 7. **sedate**—(c) calm; quiet; composed. 8. **sedative**—(a) any means of soothing distress or allaying pain. 9. **sedentary**—(d) sitting; inactive.

2 PREFIXES—YOUR SECOND KEY TO WORD POWER

A prefix consists of a letter or group of letters placed before a root or word to alter its meaning. The word *prefix* is derived from two Latin words meaning "to place or attach before." Prefixes rank next in importance to roots as building blocks for a greater vocabulary.

Sometimes the same building block may seem to fit two different categories. For example, the Latin *bene-* meaning "good" is typically a prefix in position, being attached to the beginning of a word, as in *benefactor*. But *bene-* actually is, and functions as, a root, since it furnishes half the basic meaning of any word it forms. A *benefactor* is not simply "one who does something" but "one who does good." The same thing occurs in the related words *benefit, benediction,* and *benefice.* Hence, the fact that *bene-* looks like a prefix does not mean that we may not refer to it as a root.

The prefixes discussed in the following pages generally fall into one of four groups. The first is made up of mostly Latin and Greek words that have the meaning of English prepositions. Here are a few of them:

ante- (*before*), as in *antechamber,* meaning "a room coming before or leading into another room."

circum- (*around*), as in *circumvent,* meaning "to go around or to avoid."

com- (*with; together*), as in *combine,* meaning "to bring together in close union; blend; merge; unite."

intra- (*within; inside of*), as in *intramural,* meaning "situated or occurring within the limits of a city, building, organization, etc."

sub- (*under*), as in *substandard,* meaning "below the standard; lower than the established rate or requirement."

super- (*above in position; over*), as in *superstructure,* meaning "the parts of a ship's structure above the main deck."

ultra- (*on the other side of; beyond*), as in *ultramodern,* meaning "extremely modern."

The second group of prefixes serve to give a negative meaning to a word or to reverse and undo an action: *dis-* (as in *disease,* literally "a state of being not at ease; illness"); *in-* (as in *incapable,* meaning "not capable; not able to"); *mal-* (as in *malfunction,* meaning "a failure to function properly"); *mis-* (as in *misinform,* which means to "inform incorrectly; to give wrong information to"); *non-* (as in *nonflammable,* meaning "not flammable; not apt to catch on fire easily"); *un-* (as in *unbend,* which means to "become straight again or to relax").

The third group of prefixes have to do with amount, number, or degree: *ambi-* (as in *ambidextrous,* which means "able to use both hands equally well"); *bi-* (as in *bicuspid,* which means "having two points or cusps"); *hypo-* (as in *hypothyroidism,* meaning "a condition in which the thyroid gland is underactive"); *hyper-* (as in *hypercritical,* meaning "overly critical; excessively faultfinding").

The last group consists of common English words such as *extra-* (as in *extraordinary*), *out-* (as in *outspoken*), *over-* (as in *overweight*), and *under-* (as in *underprivileged*). Since these prefixes are perfectly familiar, you will have no difficulty in working out their meanings.

As you will see later, a number of prefixes have "disguises"—that is, their spelling changes before roots or words beginning with certain letters. This occurs in order to make pronunciation easier and more musical. For example, *sub-* meaning "under" becomes *sug-* in *suggest; com-* meaning "with" becomes *col-* in *collect.*

Let us try "taking apart" a few terms containing prefixes so that you can see how prefixes change the meaning of words or roots.

antisocial is made up of the prefix *anti-* meaning "against" plus the word *social* meaning (1) disposed to having friendly relations with persons living in a society; (2) having to do with society and the general good. Therefore, *antisocial* means (1) not friendly or outgoing; unsociable; (2) disruptive of society and the general good.

> *Hermits are generally considered antisocial.*
> *Robbery and assault are antisocial acts.*

refund comes from the Latin prefix *re-* meaning "again or back," plus the Latin root *fund-* meaning "to pour." Thus *refund* means "to pay back money." It also means "the money to be paid back."

> *We received a refund for our unused theater tickets.*

submerge comes from the Latin prefix *sub-* meaning "under" and the Latin root *merg-* one of whose meanings is "to plunge." Thus, *submerge* means "to plunge or dive under the surface of water."

> *The flood submerged all of the farmland in the area.*
> *With a flick of his tail, the porpoise submerged.*

unsound comes from the prefix *un-* meaning "not; opposed to," and the word *sound,* which means "healthy or strong." Therefore, *unsound* means "not strong, healthy, or solid; weak."

> *The platform was rickety and unsound.*
> *He was adjudged unsound of mind.*

The prefix section of *How to Increase Your Word Power* gives you 38 of the most common prefixes in English. You will enjoy testing your knowledge of prefixes in the vocabulary tests, called "Fun With Words," and the "Quickie Quizzes" that are included in many of the chapters. All of the tests relate to prefixes discussed in the preceding pages; many of them will also go on testing your knowledge of roots and of the special vocabularies that have appeared earlier in this book.

PREFIX: AB-, ABS-

The Latin prefix *ab-* or *abs-* means "off; away; from." Learn these ten core vocabulary words in which *ab-* appears: *abduct, abhor, abjure, abnormal, abort, absent, absolve, absorb, abstain, abuse.*

abduct comes from *ab-* meaning "away" and the root *-duct* meaning "to lead." Thus, *abduct* means "to lead or carry away wrongfully; to kidnap."

> *The kidnaper abducted the baby.*

abhor is formed from *ab-* meaning "from" and the Latin word *horrere* meaning "to shudder." Thus, *abhor* means "to hate or loathe."

> *Jane abhors spiders.*

A word based on *abhor* is *abhorrent,* meaning "hateful; disgusting."

> *Snakes are abhorrent to Mary.*

abjure derives from *ab-* meaning "away" and the Latin word *jurare* meaning "to swear." Thus, *abjure* means "to swear away an opinion or belief; to renounce or repudiate something under oath."

> *The convert abjured his old beliefs.*

abnormal stems from *ab-* meaning "away" or "from" and the Latin root *norm-* meaning "rule." Thus, *abnormal* means "unusual; irregular."

A bodily temperature of 102° F is abnormal.

A word based on *abnormal* is *abnormality*, meaning (1) the condition of being abnormal; (2) an abnormal or unusual thing.

A harelip is a correctable abnormality.

abort is formed from *ab-* meaning "away" or "from" and the Latin root *ort-* meaning "to be born." *Abort* means "to be born away from the right time"; hence, "to miscarry" or "to end something prematurely or unsuccessfully."

The mother cat aborted after being frightened by a dog.
The space flight was aborted after only one orbit.

Two words based on *abort* are *abortion*, which means "a miscarriage, especially one that is artificially induced," and *abortive*, meaning "coming to nothing; fruitless."

After many abortive attempts, they finally launched the boat.

absent comes from *abs-* meaning "away" and a form of the Latin verb *esse* meaning "to be." As an adjective, *absent* [ab'sənt] means "away; not present." Thus, the verb *absent* [ab·sent'] means "to take or keep oneself away."

Many workers were absent because of sickness.
Try not to absent yourself more than necessary.

Two words based on *absent* are *absenteeism*, meaning "habitual or frequent absence," and *absent-minded*, meaning "inattentive to what is going on; forgetful."

Absenteeism has been a problem at the factory.
Brian absent-mindedly wore bedroom slippers to the party.

absolve is derived from *ab-* meaning "from" and the Latin word *solvere* meaning "to loosen." Thus, *absolve* means "to free from something, as guilt or a mistake; forgive or acquit."

The youth confessed his sins and was absolved.
One motorist involved in the accident was absolved from blame.

186

QUICKIE QUIZ

PREFIX AB-, ABS-

Here are ten more words beginning with the prefix *ab-*, *abs-*. Check the word or phrase you believe is closest in meaning to the key word. Answers follow.

1. **absolute** [ab′sǝ·lōōt]—(a) positive; certain. (b) cleansing. (c) sympathetic. (d) careless.
2. **abstracted** [ab·strak′tid]—(a) emotionally upset. (b) lost in thought. (c) scholarly. (d) faithful.
3. **abstemious** [ab·stō′mō·ǝs] (a) squeamish. (b) dreary. (c) dignified. (d) eating and drinking sparingly.
4. **abstruse** [ab·strōōs′]—(a) abundant. (b) hard to understand. (c) negligent. (d) official.
5. **abscess** [ab′ses]—(a) a leavetaking. (b) the act of cutting. (c) a collection of pus in the body. (d) rudeness.

6. **abrade** [ǝ·brād′]—(a) to scrape away. (b) to frighten. (c) to annoy. (d) to scold.
7. **abrogate** [ab′rǝ·gāt]—(a) to question. (b) to repeal, as a law. (c) to deprive. (d) to condense or abridge.
8. **abscond** [ab·skond′] (a) to depart suddenly and secretly. (b) to steal. (c) to perjure. (d) to say farewell.
9. **abject** [ab′jekt]—(a) thrown aside. (b) miserable or despicable. (c) skillful. (d) exceptional.
10. **abstract** [ab·strakt′]—(a) used wrongly; misapplied. (b) forgiven. (c) theoretical; ideal. (d) traditional.

ANSWERS:

1. **absolute**—(a) positive; certain. 2. **abstracted**—(b) lost in thought. 3. **abstemious**—(d) eating and drinking sparingly. 4. **abstruse** (b) hard to understand. 5. **abscess**—(c) a collection of pus in the body. 6. **abrade**—(a) to scrape away. 7. **abrogate**—(b) to repeal, as a law. 8. **abscond**—(a) to depart suddenly and secretly. 9. **abject**—(b) miserable or despicable. 10. **abstract**—(c) theoretical; ideal.

Two words based on *absolve* are *absolution*, which means "forgiveness; especially, pardon from sin"; and *absolute*, meaning (1) unlimited; unrestricted; (2) perfect or positive.

He was given absolution by the priest.
Catherine the Great reigned as an absolute monarch.
We are in absolute agreement.

absorb is made up of *ab-* meaning "from" and the Latin word *sorbere*

187

meaning "to suck in." Thus, *absorb* means "to suck or drink in something; to take up or swallow; to take over or occupy completely."

Sponges absorb water.
The nearby towns were eventually absorbed by the expanding city.
The student was absorbed in his work.

Two words based on *absorb* are *absorbent* and *absorption*. *Absorbent* means (1) absorbing or tending to absorb; (2) a substance that absorbs. *Absorption* means (1) the act of absorbing; (2) assimilation, as by incorporation or the digestive process; (3) preoccupation of the mind.

Cotton is used as an absorbent in surgical dressings.
Technology is improved through the absorption of new techniques.

abstain is formed from *ab-*, or in this case *abs-*, meaning "from" and *-tain*, which comes from the Latin word *tenere* meaning "to hold." Thus, *abstain* means "to hold away from; to choose not to do something."

She decided to abstain from eating candy.
Since I can vote neither for nor against the issue, I will abstain.

Two words based on *abstain* are *abstention*, meaning "a refraining or abstaining from something," and *abstinence*, meaning "the act or practice of abstaining, as from food, drink, etc.; self-denial."

There were three votes for, two against, and one abstention.
Not having smoked in a week, Jack boasted of his abstinence.

abuse derives from *ab-* meaning "away" and the Latin root *us-* meaning "to use." Thus, to *abuse* [ə·byo͞oz'] means "to use away from what is proper or right; misuse; mistreat; injure by speech or action." The noun *abuse* [ə·byo͞os'] means "improper use; wrongful treatment; physical injury or verbal insults."

Do not abuse a friendship by asking too many favors.
If you abuse your privileges, they will be withdrawn.
Unlawful search is an abuse of police power.
The child had suffered abuse at the hands of his stepfather.

A word based on *abuse* is *abusive*, meaning "injurious or insulting."

She said that the man had used shocking and abusive language.

◊ The prefix *ab-* or *abs-* appears in many other words besides those listed above. Whenever you see an unfamiliar word beginning with *ab-* or *abs-*, remember that this prefix always means "away, off, or from." Sometimes, though, it may appear simply as *a-*, especially when it occurs before the letters *m, p,* or *v*. Now look up *avocation* in your dictionary. Note that this word is really *ab-* meaning "away from" plus the word *vocation*.

Look up the word *abscond* in your dictionary. Note that it comes from *abs-* meaning "away" and the Latin root *cond-* meaning "to hide or conceal." Thus, *abscond* means "to hide away"; hence, "to depart suddenly and secretly, especially in order to escape the law."

The thief absconded with the jewels.

Other words beginning with the prefix *ab-* include:

abdicate	abominate	abstemious
aberrant	abrogate	abstract
abject	abscess	abstruse

PREFIX: AD-

The Latin prefix *ad-* means "to; toward; near; at." Learn the three core vocabulary words beginning with *ad-*: *adapt, adjacent, admire.*

adapt comes from *ad-* meaning "to" and the Latin root *apt-* meaning "to fit." Thus, *adapt* means "to fit for a new use; adjust."

The author adapted his novel for the stage.
He adapted himself easily to his new job.

NOTE: Do not confuse the words *adapt* and *adopt*. *Adopt* comes from *ad-* meaning "to" and the Latin root *opt-* meaning "to choose." Thus, *adopt* means (1) to choose or take a new relationship or a new course of action; (2) to take up from someone else and use as one's own, as an idea; (3) to vote to accept, as a motion or committee report.

The Wilsons adopted two baby boys.
I've decided to adopt my wife's political views.
We willingly adopted the chairman's recommendations.

189

adjacent derives from *ad-* meaning "near; at" and the Latin root *jac-* meaning "to lie" plus the Latin suffix *-ent*, which is the same as the English ending *-ing*. Thus, *adjacent* means "lying or located near or next to something."

Alaska is adjacent to Canada.

admire is formed from *ad-* meaning "at" and the Latin root *mir-* meaning "to wonder." Thus, *admire* means "to have esteem for."

They admired the courage of the astronauts.

The following six words also use the prefix *ad-*. Study them and learn how the prefix enters into the meaning of the word.

addict a person who is enslaved by some habit, especially the use of narcotic drugs.

Drug addicts can be cured.

address (1) to speak to; (2) to direct. As a noun, *address* means (1) a speech; (2) a place of residence.

The chairman addressed the club.
She addressed the letter carefully.
The President was preparing his inaugural address.
What is your address?

adhere (1) to stick; (2) to follow closely.

The tape will not adhere to this slick surface.
We try to adhere to the principles of democracy.

administer (1) to manage; (2) to apply or supply.

The President administers the University.
The doctor administered the medicine to his patient.

adore literally, to pray to or worship; hence, (1) to honor as divine; (2) to love or honor with great devotion.

Gandhi's followers adored him.
George adores his wife.

advice a view or opinion on what should be done.

You should follow the doctor's advice.

The prefix *ad-* also has many disguises which you will learn next.

Fun With Words

FROM A TO AB

The following words all begin with the letter *a* or the prefix *a-* or *ab-*, meaning "away" or "from." Check the word or phrase you believe is closest in meaning to the key word. Answers follow.

1. **adipose** [ad′ə·pōs]—(a) fatty. (b) well-balanced. (c) avoiding excess. (d) emaciated.
2. **aversion** [ə·vûr′zhən]—(a) bitterness. (b) intense dislike. (c) interpretation. (d) unwillingness.
3. **addle** [ad′l]—(a) to unravel. (b) to spread out. (c) to confuse or muddle. (d) to accuse.
4. **avocation** [av′ə·kā′shən]—(a) a side interest. (b) the pleading of a legal cause. (c) a cancellation. (d) a main occupation or calling.
5. **abductor** [ab·duk′tər]—(a) a leader. (b) the usurper of a throne. (c) a kidnaper. (d) part of an electric circuit.
6. **abnegation** [ab′nə·gā′shən]—(a) self-denial. (b) humiliation. (c) contradiction. (d) escape.
7. **abortive** [ə·bôr′tiv]—(a) contorted. (b) explosive. (c) enraged. (d) resulting in nothing.
8. **agrarian** [ə·grâr′ē·ən]—(a) pertaining to birds. (b) favorably inclined. (c) pertaining to land and agriculture. (d) causing fear.

9. **aberration** [ab′ə·rā′shən]—(a) a deviation from the normal course. (b) an illusion. (c) trembling. (d) a falsehood.
10. **abjure** [ab·jōōr′]—(a) to denounce. (b) to take away a judicial decision. (c) to surrender. (d) to repudiate or renounce.
11. **abdicate** [ab′də·kāt]—(a) to give up formally. (b) to wander away. (c) to condense, as a novel. (d) to accompany.
12. **abstinence** [ab′stə·nəns]—(a) self-denial. (b) excessive use. (c) an eroding away. (d) self-righteousness.
13. **abrasive** [ə·brā′siv]—(a) unpleasant. (b) evasive. (c) harshsounding. (d) tending to wear away.
14. **albatross** [al′bə·trôs]—(a) a large sea bird. (b) a type of coal. (c) the white of an egg. (d) a chemical compound.
15. **amalgamate** [ə·mal′gə·māt]—(a) to gather. (b) to fill, as a tooth. (c) to astonish greatly. (d) to unite or combine.

ANSWERS:

1. **adipose**—(a) fatty. 2. **aversion**—(b) intense dislike. 3. **addle**—(c) to confuse or muddle. 4. **avocation**—(a) a side interest. 5. **abductor**—(c) a kidnaper. 6. **abnegation**—(a) self-denial. 7. **abortive**—(d) resulting in nothing. 8. **agrarian**—(c) pertaining to land and agriculture. 9. **aberration**—(a) a deviation from the normal course. 10. **abjure**—(d) to repudiate or renounce. 11. **abdicate**—(a) to give up formally. 12. **abstinence**—(a) self-denial. 13. **abrasive**—(d) tending to wear away. 14. **albatross**—(a) a large sea bird. 15. **amalgamate**—(d) to unite or combine.

PREFIX: AD- AND ITS DISGUISES

In the last section you learned that the Latin prefix *ad-* means "to; toward; near; at." This prefix appears in many disguises, with its last letter—*d*—changed in spelling to agree with the letter that follows it. This spelling change is natural; it happens simply because we pronounce the words in a certain way. For example, you would probably have trouble saying *adbreviate* instead of *abbreviate*. The *ad-* has been changed to *ab-* because it's easier and more natural to *say* the word that way.

Learn the ten core vocabulary words in which the last letter of the prefix *ad-* is changed to match the letter following it: *abbreviate, accord, affair, aggravate, alleviate, annex, appear, arrive, associate, attend.*

abbreviate is formed from the prefix *ad-* meaning "to" and the Latin root *breviat-* from *breviare* meaning "to shorten." Thus, *abbreviate* means "to shorten."

> *Mister is usually abbreviated "Mr."*

accord stems from *ad-* meaning "to; near" and the Latin root *cord-* meaning "heart." To *accord* originally meant "to be of one heart or mind." It now means (1) to agree or bring into agreement; (2) to grant in agreement with what is deserved. As a noun, *accord* means "agreement or harmony."

> *His views on the subject accord with mine.*
> *The general accorded the soldier the highest honors.*
> *Are our opinions in accord?*

Two words based on *accord* are *according* and *accordingly*. *According* means (1) as stated by; (2) in conformity with. *Accordingly* means (1) correspondingly; (2) consequently; so.

> *According to all reports, our population is growing.*
> *They lined up according to height.*
> *He advised caution, and we acted accordingly.*
> *The fighters were eager; accordingly, they sprang forward at the sound of the bell.*

affair is formed from *ad-* meaning "to" and a French word that comes from the Latin root *fac-* meaning "to do; make." Thus, *affair* means

(1) anything done or made; (2) concern or business; (3) an event.

The raft was a crude affair.
My private life is not your affair.
The ambassador is busy with affairs of state.
The masked ball was quite an affair.

aggravate comes from *ad-* meaning "to" and the Latin root *grav-* meaning "heavy." *Aggravate* has come to mean "to make worse," and some people use it informally to mean "antagonize or irritate."

His business troubles were aggravated by his partner's death.

alleviate is formed from *ad-* meaning "to" and the Latin root *lev-* meaning "light." *Alleviate* literally means "to make lighter"; hence, "to make easier to bear; to relieve." Note that *aggravate* and *alleviate* are exactly opposite in meaning.

The medicine alleviated his pain, which exercise had aggravated.

annex stems from *ad-* meaning "to; at" and the Latin root *nex-* meaning "tied together." Thus, to *annex* [ə·neks'] means "to bind one thing to something else; to add or attach an additional part or area to another." An *annex* [an'eks] is "an addition to a building."

The large nation annexed its small neighbor.
The choir director's office is in the church annex.

appear comes from *ad-* meaning "to" and the Latin root *par-* meaning "to come forth." Thus, *appear* means "to come forth to the eye or mind; to come into view; to seem."

The sun appeared after the rain.
You appear to be busy.

Three words based on *appear* are *appearance, apparent,* and *apparition. Appearance* means (1) the act of appearing; a coming into view; (2) outward show or physical aspect. *Apparent* means (1) readily perceived or obvious; (2) seeming. *Apparition* means "something that seems to appear out of nowhere, as a phantom or ghost."

Though he is poor, he keeps up an appearance of wealth.
Nora takes good care of her appearance.
His apparent boredom masked a keenly observant eye.
She looked so pale that I thought I was seeing an apparition.

arrive is made up of *ad-* meaning "to" and *-rive,* which comes from the Latin word *ripa* meaning "the shore." To *arrive* originally meant "to come to shore; to land." It long ago broadened in usage to mean "to reach a destination or goal."

> *The train arrived at the station on time.*
> *Helen's baby arrived at 3 A.M.*

associate stems from *ad-* meaning "to" and the Latin root *sociat-,* meaning "to join." Thus, to *associate* means "to join an idea or person to another or to bring or come into the company of others; to connect things mentally." An *associate* is "a companion or partner."

> *Don't associate with liars.*
> *We associate silk with China.*
> *The two men are business associates.*

A word based on *associate* is *association,* meaning (1) the act of associating or the state of being associates; (2) a group of people joined together; (3) the mental connection of two things or ideas.

> *The Robinsons belong to an association of homeowners.*
> *Do you make any association of silk with China?*

attend derives from *ad-* meaning "toward" and the Latin root *tend-* meaning "to stretch." Thus *attend* means (1) to stretch the mind toward or give attention to; (2) to be present at; (3) to go with, escort, accompany, or serve.

> *Did you attend to your duties?*
> *Are you going to attend the party?*
> *Two servants will attend the king.*

Two words based on *attend* are *attention* and *attentive. Attention* means (1) the concentrated direction of the mental powers; (2) care; (3) a soldier's position of readiness. *Attentive* means "thoughtful or considerate."

> *Pay attention!*
> *That cut on your hand needs attention.*
> *The soldiers stood at attention*
> *He is a very attentive husband.*

NOTE: The prefix *ad-* changes to *a-* before *sc, sp,* and *st,* as in *ascribe, aspect,* and *astringent.* It also changes to *ac-* before *q,* as in *acquire.*

PREFIX AD- AND ITS DISGUISES

The words in the following list begin with *ad-* or one of several other prefixes that mean "to, toward, near, or at." Check the word or phrase you believe is closest in meaning to the key word. Answers follow.

1. **abeyance** [ə·bā′əns]—(a) suspension or temporary suppression. (b) discipline. (c) reduction in number. (d) low tide.

2. **abate** [ə·bāt′]—(a) to increase. (b) to suppress. (c) to tease. (d) to reduce or diminish.

3. **adroit** [ə·droit′]—(a) skillful. (b) a game resembling checkers. (c) temporary. (d) destructive.

4. **advent** [ad′vent]—(a) an increase in numbers. (b) an approach or arrival. (c) a salesman or merchant of small wares. (d) a departure.

5. **abut** [ə·but′]—(a) to carve. (b) to hammer out. (c) to border on. (d) to protrude.

6. **aspirant** [ə·spīr′ənt]—(a) one eager for advancement. (b) one who holds a high rank or position. (c) a low, crackly voice. (d) a deep, resonant voice.

7. **affirmation** [af′ər·mā′shən]—(a) a code of laws. (b) denial. (c) a solemn assertion. (d) graduation from a religious school.

8. **assignment** [ə·sīn′mənt]—(a) a conflict of interests. (b) a pro-cessional. (c) a secret meeting. (d) a fixed task.

9. **annulment** [ə·nul′mənt]—(a) an annual growth. (b) a careful measurement. (c) a destruction of the force or validity of something. (d) a faking of documents.

10. **affability** [af′ə·bil′ə·tē]—(a) sense of humor. (b) pretense. (c) sociability. (d) talkativeness.

11. **adage** [ad′ij]—(a) the total amount. (b) a wise elder. (c) a familiar proverb. (d) a weight or mass.

12. **acquisition** [ak′wə·zish′ən]—(a) curiosity. (b) the act of obtaining. (c) a passive consent. (d) miserliness.

13. **aspersion** [ə·spûr′zhən]—(a) a distribution. (b) a compliment. (c) the act of diverting. (d) a slanderous remark.

14. **affront** [ə·frunt′]—(a) to advance abreast. (b) to offend purposely. (c) to bluff. (d) to display anger.

ANSWERS:

1. **abeyance**—(a) suspension or temporary suppression. 2. **abate**—(d) to reduce or diminish. 3. **adroit**—(a) skillful. 4. **advent**—(b) an approach or arrival. 5. **abut**—(c) to border on. 6. **aspirant**—(a) one eager for advancement. 7. **affirmation**—(c) a solemn assertion. 8. **assignment**—(d) a fixed task. 9. **annulment**—(c) a destruction of the force or validity of something. 10. **affability**—(c) sociability. 11. **adage**—(c) a familiar proverb. 12. **acquisition**—(b) the act of obtaining. 13. **aspersion**—(d) a slanderous remark. 14. **affront**—(b) to offend purposely.

PREFIX: AMBI:

The prefix *ambi-* means "both; on both sides; around." Here are three words that are typical of the use of this prefix: *ambidextrous, ambiguous, ambitious.*

ambidextrous is formed from *ambi-* meaning "on both sides; both" and the word *dextrous,* a variant of *dexterous* meaning "skillful." Thus, *ambidextrous* means "able to use both hands with equal skill."

> *A switch hitter in baseball is an ambidextrous batter.*

ambiguous is derived from the Latin word *ambigere,* meaning to wander around, which comes in turn from *ambi-* meaning "around" and *agere* meaning "to go." *Ambiguous* means (1) having a double meaning; (2) doubtful or uncertain; (3) unclear, indistinct.

> *The ambiguous testimony of the witness did not help to clarify the case.*
> *Chemists will test this ambiguous substance to determine its composition.*
> *He was frightened by the ambiguous shadows.*

ambitious comes from *ambi-* meaning "around" and the Latin root *it-* meaning "to go" plus the Latin suffix *-ous* meaning "given to." *Ambitious* originally meant "given to going around and getting votes, as a politician does." Thus, *ambitious* means "eager to succeed or to achieve fame, power, wealth, etc.; having a high goal."

> *Ambitious people work hard.*
> *The state had an ambitious highway-development program.*

◊ Two words that you should look up in your dictionary and relate to the prefix *ambi-* are *ambience* and *ambivalence. Ambience* means "the overall atmosphere or mood of a situation, place, etc." *Ambivalence* means "the state of feeling or thinking two different things toward the same person or situation at the same time; the condition of feeling both love and hate, like and dislike, or other contradictory emotions."

> *The ambience of the little French restaurant delighted Ellen.*
> *His attitude toward his family was marked by ambivalence—love and loyalty warring with deep resentment.*

EXPLORING WORDS

As our most widely read book, and the basis of the Jewish and Christian religions, the Bible has given many words and expressions to the English language. Which of these do you know?

Armageddon any great and decisive battle: from the name of the place where the Bible prophesies that the final battle between good and evil will be fought at the end of the world. *Revelation* 16:16.

calvary any great suffering: from the name sometimes associated with the hill where Christ was crucified; Golgotha. *Mark* 15:22.

Eden any delightful region or abode: from the Garden of Eden; Paradise. *Genesis* 2:8.

exodus a going forth or departure from a place or country by many people: from *The Exodus*, the departure of the Israelites from Egypt under the guidance of Moses, described in *Exodus*, the second book of the Old Testament. *Exodus* 13:18.

Gehenna any place of extreme torment or suffering; hell. Gehenna was the valley near Jerusalem where refuse was thrown and fires were kept burning to purify the air; in ancient times, it was likened to hell.

golden calf money or material goods as opposed to spiritual values: from the name of a molten image made by Aaron and worshiped by the Israelites. *Exodus* 32.

jeremiad a lament or tale of woe: from *Jeremiah*, a Judean prophet who lamented the ruin of Jerusalem.

Jezebel a bold, vicious woman: from the name of Ahab's wife, who was notorious for her evil actions. *I Kings* 16:31.

Judas a betrayer or traitor: from the name of the disciple of Christ who betrayed him with a kiss. *Matthew* 26:49.

magdalen a reformed prostitute: from Mary Magdalene, a penitent sinner whom Christ forgave. *Luke* 7:36–50.

pharisee a formal, sanctimonious, hypocritical person: from the name of an ancient Jewish sect that practiced strict observance of Mosaic law and religious ritual.

shibboleth password, watchword, pet phrase, or distinguishing custom. The word was used by Jephthah as a test word to distinguish his own men from the Ephraimites, who could not pronounce the *sh* sound. *Judges* 12:4–6.

widow's mite a small contribution given with good will by someone who is poor. This phrase refers to a poor woman whom Christ praised for her selfless spirit of giving. *Mark* 12:42.

PREFIXES: ANTE-, ANTI-

The prefixes *ante-* and *anti-* look somewhat alike and are usually pronounced alike. But their meanings are very different. Be sure that you learn the difference between *ante-* and *anti-*, since these prefixes appear in many words.

The Latin prefix *ante-* means "before" or "in front of." Here are five core vocabulary words beginning with *ante-*: *antebellum*, *antecede*, *antechamber*, *antedate*, *anteroom*.

antebellum comes directly from Latin and is made up of *ante-* meaning "before" and the Latin word *bellum* meaning "war." Thus, *antebellum* means "before the war." In the United States it often means "before the Civil War" or "made or done before the Civil War."

> *Many beautiful antebellum mansions still stand in the South.*

antecede is formed from *ante-* meaning "before" and the Latin root *cede-* meaning "to go." Thus, *antecede* means "to go before, in time, rank, order, etc." This verb is seldom used, however. Much commoner is the form *antecedent*, which means (1) going before; (2) a person or thing that goes before in time.

> *World War II was antecedent to the Korean War.*
> *They knew nothing of the stranger's antecedents (his ancestors or his early life).*

antechamber derives from *ante-* meaning "before" and the word *chamber*. Thus, *antechamber* means "a chamber or room coming before or leading to another room."

> *The duke waited in the king's antechamber.*

antedate comes from *ante-* meaning "before" and the word *date*. Thus, *antedate* means "to come or happen before something else."

> *Radio antedates television.*

anteroom is formed from *ante-* meaning "before" and the word *room*. Thus, *anteroom* means "a room that leads to another room; a waiting room." *Anteroom* is a modern form of *antechamber*.

> *The patient waited in the doctor's anteroom.*

The Greek prefix *anti-* means "against; opposed to." Learn these three core vocabulary words beginning with *anti-: antiaircraft, antidote, antipathy*.

antiaircraft is a common and obvious *anti-* word. It comes, of course, from *anti-* meaning "against" plus *aircraft*. This use of *anti-* meaning "for use as a weapon or defense against" is common, and we have *antisubmarine* warfare, *antitank* guns, *antiballistic* missiles, *antiwar* protests, etc.

antidote is formed from *anti-* meaning "against" and the Greek root *dot-* meaning "given." An *antidote* is literally "something given against something else." Thus, *antidote* means "anything that will counteract the effects of a poison or other evil."

> *What is the antidote for arsenic?*
> *Work is a good antidote for self-pity.*

antipathy derives from *anti-* meaning "against" and the Greek root *path-* meaning "to feel." An *antipathy* is "a feeling against someone or something; an instinctive dislike, or the object of such a dislike."

> *She had a strong antipathy for cats.*

A word based on *antipathy* is *antipathetic*, meaning "naturally opposed" or "arousing instinctive dislike."

> *The climate of Quebec is antipathetic to the growth of palm trees.*
> *Even harmless snakes are antipathetic to her.*

◊ There are hundreds of other *anti-* words in English. For example:

antibiotic a substance "used against" or to arrest or destroy microorganisms that infect the body.

> *Penicillin is an antibiotic.*

anticlimax a disappointing shift from something important, impressive, or moving to something petty or trivial.

> *The last chapter of detective novels is often an anticlimax.*

antiseptic a substance used in order to prevent the growth of certain harmful bacteria.

> *You'd better put some antiseptic on that scratch.*
> *Some people believe that antiseptic mouth washes prevent colds.*

antitrust opposing or attacking trusts, cartels, or monopolies in business.

The government filed an antitrust suit in court.

Open your dictionary and see how many *anti-* words are listed. You should learn many of these words and be able to use them when necessary. Notice that many of the *anti-* words are simple and obvious: *anticommunist, antifreeze, antiknock, antiperspirant, antisocial, antislavery,* and *antitoxic.* Other *anti-* words are based on less obvious Greek and Latin roots, but *anti-* almost always means "against; opposed to." Your dictionary will give you all meanings and etymologies.

REMEMBER: The prefix *ante-* means "before; in front of," whereas *anti-* means "against; opposed to."

PREFIX: BI-

The Latin prefix *bi-* means "twice; doubly; occurring twice or having two." Here are seven core vocabulary words formed with the prefix *bi-*: *biannual, bicameral, bicycle, bigamy, bilateral, bilingual, binoculars.*

biannual comes from *bi-* meaning "occurring twice" and the word *annual* meaning "yearly." Thus, *biannual* means "occurring twice a year; semiannual."

Our club has a biannual meeting.

BEWARE: Look up the word *biennial* in your dictionary. This word is made up of exactly the same word-building parts as *biannual.* But notice the difference in meaning. Whereas *biannual* means "two times every year," *biennial* means "once every two years." Learn this difference.

bicameral comes from *bi-* meaning "having two" and the Latin word *camera* meaning "chamber" plus the Latin suffix *-al* meaning "of or pertaining to." Thus, *bicameral* means "consisting of two legislative chambers, houses, or branches."

Our Parliament is bicameral.

bicycle is the most obvious *bi-* word. It is made up of *bi-* meaning "having two" and the Greek root *cycl-* meaning "wheel." A *bicycle* is, literally, "a two-wheeled vehicle."

bigamy comes from *bi-* meaning "twice; doubly" and the Greek root *gam-* meaning "marriage." Thus, *bigamy* means "the act of being doubly married; the offense of being married to two wives or two husbands at the same time."

Bigamy is a crime.

bilateral is formed from the prefix *bi-* meaning "having two" and the Latin *latus* meaning "side." Thus, *bilateral* means "having two sides; arranged symmetrically on two sides; binding on two parties (as an agreement)."

The Senator proposed a bilateral system of wage and price controls.
Our biology teacher explained that starfish show radial symmetry, but animals and insects show bilateral symmetry.
The two countries signed a bilateral disarmament pact.

bilingual derives from the prefix *bi-* meaning "having two" and the Latin root *ling-*, which means "tongue." Thus, *bilingual* means "having two tongues; able to speak two languages with ease; in two languages."

Many people in Quebec are bilingual; they speak both English and French.
The bilingual edition of the magazine was in English and Spanish.

binoculars comes from *bin-* (the form of the prefix *bi-* that is used before a vowel) meaning "having two" and the Latin root *ocular-* meaning "of the eyes." *Binoculars* are "telescopes or opera glasses that are made to be used with both eyes at once."

◊ There are numerous other important words based on *bi-* meaning "twice" or "having two." Look up the following words in your dictionary and learn their meanings:

bifocal	bimonthly	bipartisan
bifurcate	binomial	bipartite

BEWARE: Do not confuse the prefix *bi-* with the root *bio-*. *Bi-* means "twice" and *bio-* means "life." The two usually have nothing to do with each other in meaning.

PREFIX: CIRCUM-

The prefix *circum-* means "around; on all sides." Here are two typical words in which *circum-* appears: *circumambulate, circumlocution*.

circumambulate is formed from *circum-* meaning "around" and the word *ambulate* meaning "to walk." Thus, *circumambulate* means "to walk around; especially, to walk around an object as part of a religious ritual or as a form of worship."

> *The pilgrims circumambulated the holy shrine.*

circumlocution is formed from *circum-* meaning "around" and the word *locution* meaning "a phrase or saying; an expression." Thus, *circumlocution* means "an indirect, roundabout way of saying something."

> *The speech was full of ponderous circumlocutions.*

Learn the following seven words, all of which have the prefix *circum-*. You will already know several of them.

circumference (1) the boundary line of a circle or any closed curve; (2) the length of such a line or the distance around it.

> *The equator is the largest circumference that can be drawn around the earth.*

circumflex a mark written over a letter, to indicate pronunciation.

> *The letter "e" often has a circumflex over it in French, as in the word "fête."*

circumnavigate to sail around something, such as an island, the world, etc.

> *Magellan died before he could finish circumnavigating the globe.*

circumscribe (1) to draw a line around something; (2) to mark the limits of or restrict something.

> *The triangle was circumscribed by a circle.*
> *For months after John's illness, his activities were severely circumscribed.*

circumspect watchful in all directions, as for danger or error; being careful about one's reputation.

Politicians should be quite circumspect in their behavior.

circumstance a detail or factor that is part of a surrounding condition; a factor connected with an act, event, or condition.

Under what circumstances did you leave your last job?

circumvent (1) to "get around" or outwit; (2) to surround or trap, as an enemy.

It's foolhardy to try to circumvent the law.

PREFIX: COM- AND ITS DISGUISES

The prefix *com-* means "with; together; thoroughly." Like the prefix *ad-*, *com-* sometimes changes its spelling depending on the letters that follow it. Thus, *com-* may appear as *co-*, *col-*, *con-*, or *cor-*. Of these different spellings, *co-* is the most frequent and important.

Here are three typical words using *com-* or a variant of it: *combat, compatriot, concede.* Learn all the words in this section, and remember that all are based on the prefix *com-* meaning "with; together; thoroughly."

combat is derived from *com-* meaning "with" and the Latin root *bat* meaning "to fight." Thus, to *combat* [kəm-bat'] means "to fight with; fight against; oppose in battle; resist." As a noun, *combat* [kom'bat] means "battle; fighting" or "a battle or fight."

We must combat disease with better health programs.
Did you see much combat during the war?

compatriot is formed from *com-* meaning "together" and the Latin word *patriota*, meaning "countryman." Thus, *compatriot* means "a fellow countryman."

I saw many of my compatriots in Europe last summer.

concede comes from *con-* meaning "thoroughly" and the Latin root *ced-* meaning "to yield; withdraw." Thus, *concede* means "to yield thoroughly on some point; to admit; to give up or grant as a right or privilege."

> *After a long argument, Bob conceded that Jim was right.*
> *Even before the votes were counted, the mayor conceded the election to his opponent.*

The following words use one of the variants of the prefix *com-*. Study the meanings and select the sentence into which the word fits most appropriately.

coequal of the same value, size, rank, etc.

coerce to force by means of intimidation, authority, etc.

coeval belonging to the same age, time or era.

coexist to exist together at the same place or time.

cohere to stick or hold firmly together; be consistent.

cohort one of a band of followers.

collaborate to work with some person or group.

colleague a fellow member of a profession, organization, etc.

collide to come together with violent impact.

1. *The bully and his* . . . . *started the brawl.*
2. *The Aztec empire was* . . . . *with the reign of Henry VIII.*
3. *Although the players* . . . . *headlong, they are seldom injured.*
4. *In the U.S. Senate the smallest and the largest states are* . . . .
5. *The musician and the lyricist* . . . . *on writing songs.*
6. *The blackmailer* . . . . *his victim into paying $2,000.*
7. *Dr. Martin and his* . . . . *worked hard during the epidemic.*
8. *Can democracy and communism* . . . . *?*
9. *His speech was not* . . . . *(Use the adjectival form).*

ANSWERS:

1. **cohorts;** 2. **coeval;** 3. **collide;** 4. **coequal;** 5. **collaborate;**
6. **coerced;** 7. **colleagues;** 8. **coexist;** 9. **coherent.**

QUICKIE QUIZ

PREFIX COM-

Here are six more words beginning with the prefix *com-*. Check the word or phrase you believe is closest in meaning to the key word. Answers follow.

1. **complaisant** [kəm·plā′zənt]—(a) careless. (b) showing a desire to please, as by yielding. (c) not energetic or active. (d) immoral.
2. **compile** [kəm·pīl′]—(a) to compromise. (b) to store. (c) to bring together. (d) to force.
3. **compliance** [kəm·plī′əns]—(a) conformance or obedience. (b) solicitation. (c) faithfulness. (d) limitation.
4. **commendable** [kə·men′də·bəl]—(a) advisable. (b) tentative. (c) satisfactory. (d) praiseworthy.
5. **commotion** [kə·mō′shən]—(a) violent anger. (b) despair. (c) monotony. (d) excitement.
6. **complacent** [kəm·plā′sənt]—(a) sympathetic. (b) constantly complaining. (c) self-satisfied. (d) all-knowing.

ANSWERS:

1. **complaisant**—(b) showing a desire to please, as by yielding. 2. **compile** —(c) to bring together. 3. **compliance**—(a) conformance or obedience. 4. **commendable**—(d) praiseworthy. 5. **commotion**—(d) excitement. 6. **complacent**—(c) self-satisfied.

Check each of these words in a dictionary to find the meaning of the root or source:

combine to bring or come together into a close union; blend; unite.

> *Oil and water won't combine.*
> *Let's combine our efforts and get the work done.*

commerce the exchange of materials, products, etc.

> *Is there much commerce between Japan and Italy?*

commit (1) to do; (2) to place someone or something in the trust of another; (3) to devote oneself to something.

> *The gangster committed many crimes.*
> *The murderer was committed to a hospital for the mentally ill.*
> *I am committed to my ideals.*

community (1) a group of people living together in one location, sub-

205

ject to the same laws, having similar interests, etc.; (2) any group united by a common characteristic or common interests.

Our small town is a pleasant community.
A university is a community of scholars.
The business community favors this law.

compact (1) pressed together; firmly united; made small or packed into a small space; (2) an agreement or contract.

A snowball must be compact if it's to be any good.
He bought a compact car.
Japan and Italy have a commercial compact.

compassion pity for the suffering of another; fellow feeling.

She feels genuine compassion for the old and infirm.

compatible capable of existing together; able to get along peacefully.

Your ideas are not compatible with mine.
To have a happy marriage, a couple must be compatible.

compel (1) to force or urge irresistibly; (2) to obtain by force.

The general was compelled to surrender.
Duty compels me to go.
They compelled a confession at gunpoint.

compete to take part in a contest.

He will compete in the broad jump.

complete (1) having all needed parts; lacking nothing; (2) to add a needed part or parts to; to finish.

I'm going to order the complete dinner.
John completed the painting job that Mary had started.

complex [kəm·pleks'] having many related parts; complicated or intricate. As a noun, *complex* [kom'pleks] means "an intricate whole made up of many different but related parts."

Computers are complex machines.
This is a complex problem.
The manufacturing complex covered fifty acres.

composition (1) a putting together of different parts, ingredients, etc., to form a whole; (2) a whole formed in this way; (3) a written theme, essay, or piece of music.

This flooring is a composition of cork and wood fibers.
The student's composition was entitled "How I Spent the Summer."

compress (1) to condense; (2) to press together or into a smaller space. As a noun *compress* means "a cloth used to apply cold, heat, or pressure to a part of the body."

Compress this report into two pages.
The machine compresses cotton into bales.
Louise placed a compress on the cut.

concave hollow and curving inward. The opposite of *concave* is *convex*, meaning "curving outward."

The old man had a concave chest.
A baseball has a convex surface.

confide (1) to trust with one's secrets; (2) to reveal something in trust.

I asked Cathy to confide in me, and she confided that she was going to elope.

congregate to come together in a crowd; assemble.

The passers-by congregated around the shouting man.

correspond (1) to be in agreement; (2) to be similar in character; (3) to exchange letters with another person.

Your version of the accident corresponds with mine.
The claws of a cat correspond to the nails of a person.
We've been corresponding for fifteen years.

◊ How many additional words can you build from the words listed above? If you now know what *coerce* means, can you use *coercion* in a sentence? You have learned *coexist;* what does *coexistence* mean? Does the word *collaborate* remind you of *collaborator?* How many words can you build from *cohere, collide, combine, commit?* What does *compassionate* mean? *Incompatible? Competitor? Congregation? Correspondence?*

Many, many more words begin with the prefix *com-* or one of its variants. You will find scores of them in your dictionary. How many are familiar to you?

Fun With Words

TOGETHERNESS WORDS

Here are twelve words beginning with the prefix *con-*, meaning "with; together; thoroughly." Check the word or phrase you believe is closest in meaning to the key word. Answers follow.

1. **conclave** [kon'klāv]—(a) a secret council. (b) a church law. (c) any body of people meeting in council. (d) one of the sustaining arches of a cathedral.
2. **concomitant** [kon·kom'ə·tənt]—(a) an agreeable friend. (b) something that accompanies or attends. (c) a contestant. (d) a collaborator.
3. **concurrent** [kən·kûr'ənt]—(a) happening in sequence. (b) meeting by accident. (c) unexpected. (d) occurring or acting together.
4. **congenital** [kən·jen'ə·təl]—(a) idiotic. (b) natural, as though from birth. (c) diseased. (d) prolific.
5. **contrite** [kən·trīt']—(a) penitent. (b) accompanying. (c) hackneyed. (d) irritable.
6. **conjoin** [kən·join']—(a) to be awkward. (b) to follow. (c) to unite. (d) to distort.
7. **concordant** [kon·kôr'dənt]—(a) harmonious. (b) following one

after another. (c) occurring together. (d) combative.
8. **connotation** [kon'ə·tā'shən]—(a) earnest thought. (b) notes added by way of explanation. (c) an implied, additional meaning of a word. (d) the direct, basic meaning of a word.
9. **conviviality** [kən·viv'ē·al'ə·tē]—(a) foolishness. (b) sociability or good fellowship. (c) superficiality. (d) wit and lightheartedness.
10. **consanguinity** [kon'sang·gwin'ə·tē]—(a) a succession of mutually dependent events. (b) friendship. (c) a simultaneous occurrence. (d) blood relationship.
11. **conglomerate** [kən·glom'ər·it]—(a) pertaining to the total. (b) inherent. (c) a cluster or collection of various parts or materials. (d) gluey.
12. **convocation** [kon'vō·kā'shən]—(a) a speech. (b) an opening prayer. (c) an agreement. (d) a meeting.

ANSWERS:

1. **conclave**—(a) a secret council. 2. **concomitant**—(b) something that accompanies or attends. 3. **concurrent**—(d) occurring or acting together. 4. **congenital**—(b) natural, as though from birth. 5. **contrite**—(a) penitent. 6. **conjoin**—(c) to unite. 7. **concordant**—(a) harmonious. 8. **connotation**—(c) an implied, additional meaning of a word. 9. **conviviality**—(b) sociability or good fellowship. 10. **consanguinity**—(d) blood relationship. 11. **conglomerate**—(c) a cluster or collection of various parts or materials. 12. **convocation**—(d) a meeting.

PREFIX: CONTRA-, COUNTER-

The prefix *contra-* or *counter-* means "against; opposite; contrary; opposing." Here are two typical *contra-, counter-* words: *contraband, counterclockwise.*

contraband comes from *contra-* meaning "against" and the root *band-*, which goes back to a Latin word meaning "law." Thus, *contraband* means "articles brought into a country against the law; smuggled articles." It also means "the act of smuggling."

> *The customs agents seized $500,000 worth of contraband goods.*
> *To engage in contraband is to defy international law.*

counterclockwise comes from *counter-* meaning "opposite" and the word *clockwise* meaning "in the direction taken by the hands of a clock; in a circle, from left to right." Thus, *counterclockwise* means "opposite to the direction taken by the hands of a clock; in a circle from right to left."

> *Most horse races are run counterclockwise around the track.*

Other words using *contra-* or *counter-* include:

contraceptive (1) used against conception, to prevent pregnancy; (2) a device or medicine for preventing conception.

contradict (1) to say the opposite, or to maintain the opposite of a statement; (2) to be inconsistent with.

counterattack an attack made against and in answer to an enemy's attack.

counterbalance to oppose something with an equal weight or force.

counterespionage measures taken against enemy spying; operations and measures carried out by intelligence agents or spies against enemy spying.

counterfeit (1) to make an imitation of money, stamps, a feeling, etc., with the intent to defraud or mislead; (2) false; fraudulent; feigned; pretended; (3) a false imitation or copy.

counterpart someone or something closely resembling another person or thing in a different or "opposite" country, firm, region, etc.

counterpoise (1) to bring to a balance by opposing with an equal weight or force. (2) a counterbalancing weight.

countersign to sign a document already signed by another person in order to establish the authenticity of the first signature; to sign "against" another's signature as proof of its authenticity.

counterstatement a statement opposing or denying another statement.

There are many more words using the prefix *contra-* or *counter-*. Look them up in your dictionary. How many of them can you define?

PREFIX: DE-

The prefix *de-* means (1) away; off; (2) down; a lessening; (3) completely; (4) undoing or reversal of an action. Here are four typical words that make use of *de-: debar, debark, declare, dehumidify.*

debar comes from *de-* meaning "away; off" and the word *bar* meaning "to shut." Thus, *debar* means "to shut out; to exclude."

He was debarred from club membership because of the scandal.

debark is derived from *de-* meaning "away; off" and the old word *bark* meaning "a ship." Thus, *debark* means "to go away from, or off, a ship; to put something off a ship; to go ashore; to unload."

The ship docked at noon and we debarked immediately.

declare is formed from *de-* meaning "completely" and the Latin root *clar-* meaning "to make clear." Thus, *declare* means "to make completely clear"; hence, "to say something emphatically; to reveal or prove."

He declared that he was completely innocent.
The judges declared Sam the winner of the race.

dehumidify is made up of *de-* meaning "the reversal of an action" and the word *humidify* meaning "to make humid." Thus, *dehumidify* means "to make less humid."

An air conditioner both cools and dehumidifies the air.

Match each of these words with one of the definitions that follow.

1. decentralize; 2. decipher; 3. declaim; 4. decline; 5. decrease;
6. defend; 7. defer; 8. deflect; 9. deform; 10. deliver; 11. demote;
12. deplete; 13. depopulate; 14. depreciate; 15. descend; 16. detract.

a.   to come down; to lower oneself; to be derived by heredity.

b.   to put off or delay; to yield to someone else's opinion.

c.   to bring down or lower in rank.

d.   to reorganize into smaller parts away from the center.

e.   to take away a part of something; to lessen.

f.   to speak loudly and in a set, formal way.

g.   to reduce a supply of something as by use or waste.

h.   to set free from something; to hand over; to carry and distribute;
     to give or send forth.

i.   to determine the meaning of something that is hard to read, such as
     a code.

j.   to turn away injury, danger, etc.; to protect.

k.   to lessen the value of; to lose value.

l.   to grow less or smaller; to take away a part, quantity, rank, etc.

m. to turn something away; to swerve.

n.   to bend downward; to fail in health; to turn down or refuse.

o.   to distort the shape of something; to mar the beauty of something.

p.   to take away the inhabitants of a place, as by death, war, disaster.

ANSWERS:

1 d; 2 i; 3 f; 4 n; 5 l; 6 j; 7 b; 8 m; 9 o; 10 h; 11 c; 12 g; 13 p; 14 k; 15 a; 16 e.

PREFIX DE-

The fifteen words below begin with the prefix *de-*, which can mean "away, off, down, a lessening, or completely." Check the word or phrase you believe is closest in meaning to the key word. Answers follow.

1. **decant** [di·kant′]—(a) to talk insincerely. (b) to narrate at great length. (c) to pour off gently. (d) to complain.

2. **depredate** [dep′rə·dāt]—(a) to express disapproval of. (b) to disparage. (c) to despoil or plunder. (d) to make humble statements.

3. **deduce** [di·dyōōs′]—(a) to influence. (b) to infer or conclude. (c) to persuade. (d) to lead on.

4. **demise** [di·mīz′]—(a) modesty. (b) a plan. (c) death. (d) a legal oath.

5. **decadent** [dek′ə·dənt]—(a) evil. (b) a successor in office. (c) characterized by deterioration. (d) recently deceased.

6. **deterrent** [di·tûr′ənt]—(a) something that prevents or discourages. (b) a soap or cleansing agent. (c) a separation. (d) a heavy rainfall.

7. **delegate** [del′ə·gāt]—(a) to demote. (b) to give over authority to another. (c) to dismiss. (d) to point out.

8. **defile** [di·fīl′]—(a) filth. (b) a long, narrow pass. (c) a dry river bed. (d) the pattern of troops marching side by side.

9. **defunct** [di·fungkt′]—(a) not working properly. (b) putrid. (c) cowardly. (d) dead.

10. **deprecate** [dep′rə·kāt]—(a) to argue. (b) to lose value. (c) to implore. (d) to express disapproval of or regret for.

11. **detraction** [di·trak′shən]—(a) mental distress. (b) something that diverts the attention. (c) defamation. (d) a mountain path.

12. **derision** [di·rizh′ən]—(a) origin. (b) failure in duty. (c) act of throwing into disorder. (d) ridicule or scorn.

13. **defray** [di·frā′]—(a) to tear to tatters. (b) to postpone. (c) to pay. (d) to avoid.

14. **debase** [di·bās′]—(a) to lower in character or quality. (b) to lighten in color. (c) to remove troops from. (d) to benefit from.

15. **declivity** [di·kliv′ə·tē]—(a) a crack in a glacier. (b) an unwillingness to continue. (c) loyalty. (d) a downward slope.

ANSWERS:

1. **decant**—(c) to pour off gently. 2. **depredate**—(c) to despoil or plunder. 3. **deduce**—(b) to infer or conclude. 4. **demise**—(c) death. 5. **decadent**—(c) characterized by deterioration. 6. **deterrent**—(a) something that prevents or discourages. 7. **delegate**—(b) to give over authority to another. 8. **defile**—(b) a long, narrow pass. 9. **defunct**—(d) dead. 10. **deprecate**—(d) to express disapproval of or regret for. 11. **detraction**—(c) defamation. 12. **derision**—(d) ridicule or scorn. 13. **defray**—(c) to pay. 14. **debase**—(a) to lower in character or quality. 15. **declivity**—(d) a downward slope.

The prefix *dis-*, *di-*, or *dif-* means (1) away from; apart; in different directions; (2) the reversal or undoing of an action; (3) not. The meaning of the prefix *dis-* is close to that of the prefix *de-*. The important difference is: The prefix *de-* most often has the meaning "down" (and the associated meanings of "less; making smaller or less important"), whereas *dis-* has the stronger negative meaning of "not."

Here are seven words formed with the prefix *dis-* or its variants, *dif-* or *di-*:

diffuse [di·fyōōz′] comes from *dif-* meaning "in different directions" and the Latin root *fus-* meaning "to pour." Thus, *diffuse* means "to pour or send out something so that it spreads in all directions." The adjective *diffuse* [di·fyōōs′] means "widely spread out" or "wordy."

The cloud cover diffused the light of the sun.
His argument lacked force because it was diffuse.

disable derives from *dis-* meaning "not" and the word *able*. Thus, *disable* means "to make unable; to cripple."

He was disabled by the car accident.

disconnect is made up of *dis-* meaning "the reversal or undoing of an action" and the word *connect*. Thus, *disconnect* means "to break the connection of, or between, things or persons."

Operator, we've been disconnected!
He spoke in disconnected sentences.

discontinue is formed from *dis-* meaning "not" and the word *continue*. Thus, *discontinue* means "to break off or cease from doing, using, producing, etc.; to stop."

They have discontinued publication of the paper.
With regret the two men discontinued their friendship.

dislocate is a combination of *dis-* meaning "away from; apart" and the word *locate*. Thus, *dislocate* means "to put something out of its proper place."

Thousands of flood victims were dislocated last spring.
The quarterback dislocated his shoulder during the game.

disloyal is derived from *dis-* meaning "not" and the word *loyal.* Thus, *disloyal* means "not loyal."

A disloyal general caused the downfall of the government.

divert is made up of *di-* meaning "away from; apart" and the Latin root *vert-* meaning "to turn." Thus, *divert* means (1) to turn aside, as from a set course; (2) to distract the attention of; (3) to amuse.

The dam diverted the river.
The clowns diverted the children.

Now that you know the seven preceding words, learn the following words beginning with *dis-*:

disarm (1) to take away the weapons of a person or nation; (2) to allay or reduce suspicion, antagonism, etc.

The Allies forced Germany to disarm.
She was frowning angrily, but his smile disarmed her.

discomfit (1) to defeat someone's plans or purposes; (2) to throw into confusion.

A sudden hailstorm discomfited the picknickers.
The teacher's unexpected arrival discomfited the mischievous students.

discriminate (1) to act toward someone with partiality or prejudice; (2) to draw a clear distinction between things.

Many colleges used to discriminate against Negroes.
A true critic can discriminate between good and bad art.

disfigure to mar or destroy the appearance of something.

Deep scratches disfigured the surface of the table.

dishearten to weaken someone's spirit or courage.

Two quick touchdowns by Queen's disheartened the Toronto team.
News of the general's death disheartened the troops.

disintegrate (1) to destroy the wholeness of something; (2) to become reduced to fragments.

Heat disintegrates many substances.
The sand castle disintegrated before the waves.

dismantle (1) to strip something of its furniture or equipment; (2) to take apart.

Movers dismantled the apartment efficiently.

The maintenance crew dismantled the plane's engines for inspection.

disorient to confuse someone's sense of direction or perspective.

Heavy fog disoriented the ship's navigator.

disown to refuse to acknowledge or admit responsibility for something or someone.

When the industrialist heard of his daughter's elopement, he disowned her.

dissect (1) to cut apart, as a plant or a dead animal in a laboratory, in order to examine the structure; (2) to analyze in detail.

Our biology class dissected frogs last week.
A good debater can dissect his opponent's argument.

disseminate to scatter something far and wide, as if sowing, especially ideas, knowledge, etc.

dissipate (1) to drive away or dispel; (2) to spend wastefully or squander.

Gusts of wind quickly dissipated the smoke.
The young playboy dissipated his father's fortune in gambling and entertaining lavishly.

dissuade to persuade someone not to do something.

Can't I dissuade you from eating so much candy?

◊ How many words can you build from the above list? Knowing the meanings of these words, can you define the words below, which are built on them?

disarmament	disintegration	dissemination
discrimination	dissection	dissuasion

If you are in doubt about the meanings or uses of these additional words, look them up in your dictionary.

Many other words are built on the prefix *dis-*. Look them up in your dictionary. How many do you know?

NOTE: A knowledge of word building will also help you perfect your spelling. Knowing that the prefix *dis-* is added to *own* to form the word *disown*, you know why *disown* has only one *s*. Now, can you figure out why *dissect* and *dissuade* have two *s*'s?

PREFIX DIS-

These fifteen words begin with the prefix *dis-*, which has a variety of meanings: "apart; away from; not," etc. Check the word or phrase you believe is closest in meaning to the key word. Answers follow.

1. **dissonance** [dis′ə·nəns]—(a) keen dislike. (b) harshness of sound. (c) immorality. (d) discouragement.
2. **dissemble** [di·sem′bəl]—(a) to scatter. (b) to conceal or disguise. (c) to unravel. (d) to be embarrassed.
3. **dispense** [dis·pens′]—(a) to end. (b) to disagree. (c) to distribute. (d) to solve quickly.
4. **disparate** [dis·par′ət *or* dis′par·it] —(a) dissimilar. (b) discouraged. (c) reckless. (d) insufficient.
5. **dispensation** [dis′pən·sā′shən]— (a) a delaying. (b) a special exemption from an obligation. (c) a surrender of power. (d) a scattering.
6. **disingenuous** [dis′in·jen′yōō·əs] —(a) clever. (b) innocent. (c) dumb. (d) not sincere.
7. **disconsolate** [dis·kon′sə·lit]—(a) disorganized. (b) shabby. (c) forlorn. (d) untrustworthy.
8. **disclaim** [dis·klām′]—(a) to deliver an oration. (b) to avoid a direct statement. (c) to shout out. (d) to deny connection with.
9. **disavow** [dis′ə·vou′]—(a) to swear to. (b) to denounce. (c) to disclaim. (d) to apologize.
10. **distend** [dis·tend′]—(a) to expand. (b) to care for. (c) to wander aimlessly. (d) to keep away from.
11. **disdain** [dis·dān′]—(a) to be proud. (b) to flatter. (c) to dislike. (d) to scorn.
12. **distraught** [dis·trôt′ *or* dis·trot′] —(a) greatly agitated. (b) instinctive. (c) gullible or easily influenced. (d) morally binding.
13. **dismantle** [dis·man′təl]—(a) to upset. (b) to disillusion. (c) to shatter. (d) to strip or take apart.
14. **disinter** [dis′in·tûr′]—(a) to exhume. (b) to spread apart. (c) to become less active. (d) to question thoroughly.
15. **disparity** [dis·par′ə·tē]—(a) unjust criticism. (b) dissimilarity. (c) discouragement. (d) distaste.

ANSWERS:

1. **dissonance**—(b) harshness of sound. 2. **dissemble**—(b) to conceal or disguise. 3. **dispense**—(c) to distribute. 4. **disparate**—(a) dissimilar. 5. **dispensation**—(b) a special exemption from an obligation. 6. **disingenuous**—(d) not sincere. 7. **disconsolate**—(c) forlorn. 8. **disclaim**—(d) to deny connection with. 9. **disavow**—(c) to disclaim. 10. **distend**—(a) to expand. 11. **disdain**—(d) to scorn. 12. **distraught**—(a) greatly agitated. 13. **dismantle**—(d) to strip or take apart. 14. **disinter**—(a) to exhume. 15. **disparity**—(b) dissimilarity.

PREFIX: EX- AND ITS DISGUISES

The prefix *ex-* and its disguises *e-* or *ef-* means (1) out, out of, or from; (2) former; (3) thoroughly or completely. Learn the following core words in which *ex-*, *e-*, or *ef-* appears:

effervesce is formed from *ef-* meaning "out" and the Latin root *fervesc-* meaning "to boil." Thus, *effervesce* means (1) to give off bubbles of gas, as carbonated drinks; (2) to be exhilarated or vivacious.

> *The soda water is stale and doesn't effervesce.*
> *Mary has an effervescent way of speaking.*

evade derives from *e-* meaning "out" and the Latin root *vad-* meaning "to go." Thus, *evade* means "to go or get out of something; hence, to avoid or escape."

> *The witness tried to evade the lawyer's question.*
> *You can circumvent the law, but you can't evade it forever.*

exclude is made up of *ex-* meaning "out" and the Latin root *clud-* meaning "to shut." Thus, *exclude* means "to shut someone or something out, as from a group or place."

> *His poor grade in math excluded him from the honor roll.*

excruciate comes from *ex-* meaning "completely; thoroughly" and the Latin root *cruciat-* meaning "to torture." Thus, *excruciate* means "to inflict extreme pain on someone; to rack with pain."

> *Walking was excruciatingly painful for the wounded man.*

exhume stems from *ex-* meaning "out of; from" and the Latin root *hum-* meaning "the ground." Thus, *exhume* means "to dig up a corpse or other buried thing."

> *The soldier's body was exhumed and shipped home after the war.*

Learn these additional words that use the prefix *ex-*, *e-*, or *ef-*:

excavate (1) to hollow or dig out; (2) to make a tunnel or hole by digging out the earth.

> *Indians excavated the cores of fallen trees to make dugout canoes.*
> *Blasting crews will excavate a tunnel under the Alps.*

excerpt a passage picked out from a book, speech, etc., and used or quoted separately.

Several newspapers printed excerpts from the president's memoirs.

excommunicate to cut someone off from membership in a church.

exhale (1) to breathe out; (2) to breathe something out, such as tobacco smoke.

exonerate to free someone from blame; to acquit.

The court completely exonerated the defendant from charges of negligence.

expedite to speed up the progress of something.

Our new computer has expedited the company's billing operation.

expire (1) to breathe out one's last breath; to die; (2) to come to an end, as a contract or license.

The old woman expired peacefully in her sleep.
I hope you'll renew my lease when it expires next year.

exterminate to destroy; to wipe out a living thing or things.

extinguish (1) to put out or quench, as a fire; (2) to wipe out.

extort to wrest money, etc., from a person by threats or violence.

extricate to free from entanglements or other difficulties.

◊ Make up a sentence using each of the words in the preceding list. Now let's see how many of the following words you can figure out.

evasive	exhortation	ex-president
excrescent	expel	exterminator
exhaust	expiration	extortion

Many, many other words begin with the prefix *ex-*. Check under *ex-* in your dictionary; see how many of these words you know. What additional *ex-* words are you going to learn by reading the definitions and etymologies?

Fun With Words

PREFIX EX- AND ITS DISGUISES

Here are fifteen words beginning with the prefix *ex-*, *e-*, or *ef-* meaning "out, out of, former, or thoroughly." Check the word or phrase you believe is closest in meaning to the key word. Answers follow.

1. **emanate** [em′ə·nāt]—(a) to conspire. (b) to experience. (c) to flow forth. (d) to embrace.
2. **excoriate** [ik·skôr′ē·āt]—(a) to wipe out. (b) to strip off the skin or cover of. (c) to make clean and bright by friction. (d) to expel from a church.
3. **extenuate** [ik·sten′yōō·āt]—(a) to stretch out. (b) to become inactive. (c) to obtain by force. (d) to excuse the faults of.
4. **exonerate** [ig·zon′ə·rāt]—(a) to praise. (b) to free from blame. (c) to elevate. (d) to accuse.
5. **evolve** [i·volv′]—(a) to work out or develop gradually. (b) to entangle. (c) to explain and make clear. (d) to transmit or hand down.
6. **exacerbate** [ig·zas′ər·bāt]—(a) to encourage. (b) to overstate. (c) to bring to a high polish. (d) to aggravate.
7. **emit** [i·mit′]—(a) to leave out. (b) to forget. (c) to give out. (d) to let in.
8. **evasive** [i·vā′siv]—(a) gentle.

(b) abrasive. (c) elusive. (d) fleeting.
9. **exaction** [ig·zak′shən]—(a) a demand or requirement. (b) an inspection. (c) exhilaration. (d) the process of development.
10. **elide** [i·līd′]—(a) to omit a vowel or syllable in pronunciation. (b) to slip or fall. (c) to escape detection. (d) to wear away or be used up.
11. **evince** [i·vins′]—(a) to conquer. (b) to carry away. (c) to delay. (d) to make evident.
12. **extirpate** [ek′stər·pāt]—(a) to root out or eradicate. (b) to disturb. (c) to make extra work for someone. (d) to raise in rank.
13. **efface** [i·fās′]—(a) to be smug about something. (b) to mask. (c) to be friendly toward. (d) to obliterate.
14. **effeminate** [i·fem′ə·nit]—(a) opposed to women. (b) womanish. (c) harsh and disagreeable. (d) happy-go-lucky.
15. **egregious** [i·grē′jəs]—(a) conspicuously bad. (b) egg-shaped. (c) like a chant. (d) very poor.

ANSWERS:

1. **emanate**—(c) to flow forth. 2. **excoriate**—(b) to strip off the skin or cover of. 3. **extenuate**—(d) to excuse the faults of. 4. **exonerate**—(b) to free from blame. 5. **evolve**—(a) to work out or develop gradually. 6. **exacerbate**—(d) to aggravate. 7. **emit**—(c) to give out. 8. **evasive**—(c) elusive. 9. **exaction**—(a) a demand or requirement. 10. **elide**—(a) to omit a vowel or syllable in pronunciation. 11. **evince**—(d) to make evident. 12. **extirpate**—(a) to root out or eradicate. 13. **efface**—(d) to obliterate. 14. **effeminate**—(b) womanish. 15. **egregious**—(a) conspicuously bad.

PREFIX: EXTRA-

The prefix *extra-* means "outside of; beyond or outside the range, scope, or limits of something." As a word *extra* is used to mean "being over and above what is required; additional."

Here are two core vocabulary words beginning with the prefix *extra-*: *extraordinary, extrasensory.*

extraordinary is made up of *extra-* meaning "outside of; beyond" and the word *ordinary.* Thus, *extraordinary* means "being beyond or out of the ordinary; exceptional or remarkable."

She showed extraordinary presence of mind during the emergency.

extrasensory derives from *extra-* meaning "beyond the scope or range of" and the word *sensory* meaning "having to do with sensation or the sense impulses." Thus, *extrasensory* means "beyond the range of normal sense perception; perceived by unknown or unexplained senses beyond the ordinary ones of touch, sight, hearing, etc."

Do you believe in extrasensory perception?

◇ What is meant by *extracurricular* activities? You will find many words beginning with *extra-* listed in your dictionary. Study them and learn the ones that seem most useful. Their meanings should be obvious if you know the meaning of the words to which *extra-* is prefixed.

PREFIX: HYPER-

The prefix *hyper-* means "over; excessive or excessively." Learn the following three core vocabulary words that begin with *hyper-*: *hyperacidity, hypercorrect, hypersensitive.*

hyperacidity is formed from *hyper-* meaning "excessive" and the word *acidity.* Thus, *hyperacidity* means "an excess of stomach acid."

hypercorrect comes from *hyper-* meaning "excessively" or "over" and the word *correct.* Thus, *hypercorrect* means "excessively correct or finicky, especially in regard to such things as manners, appearance, writing, speaking, etc."

A hypercorrect person can be hard to live with.

hypersensitive derives from *hyper-* meaning "over" or "excessively" and the word *sensitive*. Thus, *hypersensitive* means "excessively sensitive or touchy; too easily insulted, angered, disappointed, etc."

Nancy is so hypersensitive that a tiny rebuke makes her cry.

◊ Look up the words listed under *hyper-* in your dictionary. How many of them can you define?

PREFIX: **HYPO-**

Believe it or not, a hypodermic needle and the hypotenuse of a triangle are related. The prefix *hypo-* means "under or beneath; less than." Do not confuse *hypo-* and *hyper-;* they are almost opposite in meaning. *Hyper-* means "over"; *hypo-* means "under." So remember the two core vocabulary words beginning with the prefix *hypo-: hypodermic, hypotenuse.*

hypodermic is formed from *hypo-* meaning "beneath" and the Greek root *derm-* meaning "skin" plus the Latin suffix *-ic* meaning "pertaining to." Thus, *hypodermic* means "of or pertaining to the area under the skin." As a noun, *hypodermic* means "a syringe for giving under-the-skin injections."

The doctor sterilized the hypodermic needle before giving me the flu shot.

hypotenuse comes from *hypo-* meaning "under" and the Greek root *tenus-* meaning "stretching." Thus, *hypotenuse* means "the side of a right triangle that stretches under (or lies opposite) the right angle."

Now learn three more words that begin with the prefix *hypo-:*

hypochondria persistent anxiety about one's health. *Hypochondria* literally means "under the cartilage of the breastbone"; this spot was once thought to be the physical seat of morbidity.

hypothesis an assumption that lies beneath or supports a line of reasoning, and that is therefore accepted as a basis for investigation, argument, or further reasoning.

> *On the hypothesis that the world was round, Columbus hoped to reach the East Indies by sailing westward.*

hypothetical pertaining to or of the nature of a hypothesis; based on an assumption.

> *There is no longer anything hypothetical about man's ability to reach the moon.*

PREFIX: IN- AND ITS DISGUISES

Like the prefix *ad-*, the prefix *in-* changes spelling depending on the letter that follows it. Thus, *in-* may also be spelled *em-*, *en-*, *il-*, *im-*, and *ir-*.

The prefix *in-* has two basic meanings: (1) not; without; un-; non-; (2) in; into; within. *In-* is one of the most important prefixes of the English language. It appears in hundreds of English words, many of which you know, but you may not know how the prefix *in-* always adds its own particular meaning. Study the following *in-* words carefully. Learn the six core vocabulary words beginning with *in-* (or one of its variants): *embrace, enclose, illiterate, imbalance, incarnate, irresistible.*

embrace is derived from *em-* meaning "in" and the root *brac-*, which comes from a Latin word meaning "arm." Thus, *embrace* means (1) to clasp in one's arms; (2) to accept a concept or belief willingly, as if by hugging it; (3) to include or contain. An *embrace* is, of course, "a hug."

> *Bob embraced his wife at the airport.*
> *Why do you embrace all the new fads?*
> *This plan embraces the major ideas you suggested.*

NOTE: Now that you know that the root *brac-* comes from a Latin word meaning "arm," can you figure out the etymology of the word *bracelet?*

enclose is formed from *en-* meaning "in" and the root *clos-*, which

QUICKIE QUIZ
"NOT" WORDS

These ten words begin with the prefix *in-*, meaning "without" or "not." Check the word or phrase you believe is closest in meaning to the key word. Answers follow.

1. **intestate** [in·tes′tāt]—(a) sick. (b) between states. (c) having gone bankrupt. (d) not having made a valid will.
2. **inviolate** [in·vī′ə·lit]—(a) calm. (b) excited. (c) brutal. (d) pure.
3. **insatiable** [in·sā′shə·bəl]—(a) greedy. (b) insecure. (c) unsatisfactory. (d) hungry.
4. **invalidate** [in·val′ə·dāt]—(a) to marry secretly. (b) to annoy. (c) unheroic. (d) to make void.
5. **inexorable** [in·ek′sər·ə·bəl]—(a) formidable. (b) inexcusable. (c) cruel. (d) relentless.
6. **incongruous** [in·kong′grōō·əs]— (a) not logical. (b) out of place. (c) foolish. (d) debatable.

7. **incessant** [in·ses′ənt]—(a) continuing without interruption. (b) unbelievable. (c) not cautious. (d) incomplete.
8. **insufferable** [in·suf′ər·ə·bəl]— (a) unqualified. (b) shameful or horrifying. (c) not enough. (d) not to be endured.
9. **indemnity** [in·dem′nə·tē]—(a) a compensation for loss or damage. (b) to owe money to. (c) damaging evidence. (d) a trivial amount.
10. **indomitable** [in·dom′i·tə·bəl]— (a) not intelligent. (b) domineering. (c) arch-shaped. (d) not easily defeated.

ANSWERS:

1. **intestate**—(d) not having made a valid will. 2. **inviolate**—(d) pure. 3. **insatiable**—(a) greedy. 4. **invalidate**—(d) to make void. 5. **inexorable**—(d) relentless. 6. **incongruous**—(b) out of place. 7. **incessant**—(a) continuing without interruption. 8. **insufferable**—(d) not to be endured. 9. **indemnity**—(a) a compensation for loss or damage. 10. **indomitable**—(d) not easily defeated.

derives from a Latin word meaning "to shut." Thus, *enclose* means (1) to shut in on all sides; (2) to send something inside an envelope; (3) to contain.

> *He enclosed the yard with shrubs.*
> *I enclose a cheque for $10.*
> *Her clenched fist enclosed the coins.*

illiterate comes from *il-* meaning "not" and the word *literate* meaning "able to read and write; educated." Thus, *illiterate* means "unable to read and write; uneducated." An *illiterate* is "a person who is unable to read and write." *Illiterate* is also used to describe incorrect language that shows a lack of education.

Twenty percent of the population are virtually illiterate.
Can you imagine what it's like to be an illiterate?
"Drownded" is an illiterate word.

imbalance is formed from *im-* meaning "not; without" and the word *balance.* Thus, *imbalance* means "the state or condition of being out of balance; inequality."

There is an imbalance between our exports and imports.

incarnate derives from *in-* meaning "in" and the root *carnat-*, which comes from a Latin verb meaning "to make flesh; to give a body to." Thus, to *incarnate* [in·kär′nāt] means "to give a bodily form to." As an adjective, *incarnate* [in·kär′nit] means "embodied in a human form."

He was the Devil incarnate!

irresistible is made up of *ir-* meaning "not" and the word *resistible.* Thus, *irresistible* means "not capable of being resisted." Specifically, it may mean "fascinating or enchanting."

The criminal said he'd had an irresistible impulse to steal.
Rhoda's irresistible smile won me over.

Learn these additional words that make use of the prefix *in-:*

inarticulate (1) said or expressed without distinct words, as a cry or yell; said incoherently; (2) unable to express oneself fully or understandably; (3) incapable of speech; dumb.

inconsequential having little or no importance.

inequitable not just; unfair.

infamous having a bad reputation; notoriously bad.

insatiable not capable of being satisfied; extremely greedy.

insuperable not to be overcome or surmounted.

◇ Make up a sentence using each of the above words. Look up the many other *in-* words in your dictionary and learn the definitions of those you have heard most often. While studying them, remember the two basic meanings of *in-:* (1) not; without; (2) in; into; within.

EXPLORING WORDS

HOW MANY LANGUAGES DO YOU SPEAK?

English has constantly borrowed words and expressions from other languages. Learn the following foreign expressions, which are often used in American speech and writing.

ad hoc [ad hok′]—*Latin* pertaining to this (particular thing); designating a committee formed for a specific purpose in a specific situation.

aficionado [ə·fē′syō·nä′dō]—*Spanish* an enthusiast; a devotee, as a fan of bullfights.

à la carte [ä′ lə kärt′]—*French* by the menu: applied to a meal in which each item on the menu has a separate price, as opposed to a complete meal for an all-in-one price.

à la mode [ä′ lə mōd′]—*French* in the latest fashion; generally, with ice cream on top (which was once a new way to serve pie and cake).

alter ego [ôl′tər ē′gō]—*Latin* a second self; a close friend; a confidant.

auf Wiedersehen [ouf vē′dər·zä′ən]—*German* till we meet again; good-by.

bona fide [bō′nə fīd′]—*Latin* in good faith; genuine.

canapé [kan′ə·pā]—*French* a small piece of bread or a cracker, spread with cheese, caviar, etc., usually eaten as an appetizer.

carte blanche [kärt′ blänsh′]—*French* unrestricted authority; permission to do whatever one wishes.

coup d'état [kōō′ dä·tä′]—*French* an unexpected stroke of policy; especially, a sudden seizure of government.

cul-de-sac [kul′də·sak′]—*French* a blind alley; a dead end.

de facto [dē fak′tō]—*Latin* existing in fact, with or without legal sanction.

en rapport [än rä·pôr′]—*French* in sympathetic relation or harmonious agreement.

e pluribus unum [ē plŏŏr′ə·bəs yōō′nəm]—*Latin* out of many, one: the motto of the United States (because it is one country made up of many states).

esprit de corps [es·prē′ də kôr′]—*French* a spirit of devotion to one's group and its goals.

225

PREFIX: INTER-

The prefix *inter-* means "among; between; with each other." Here are four core vocabulary words beginning with *inter-*: *interbreed, interfere, interject, interlude.*

interbreed is formed from *inter-* meaning "between; with each other" and the word *breed.* Thus, *interbreed* means "to breed different stocks of animals with each other; crossbreed; hybridize."

> *He stocked his farm by interbreeding Jersey and Guernsey cattle.*

interfere derives from *inter-* meaning "between" and the Latin root *fer-* meaning "to strike." Thus, *interfere* literally means "to strike (or come forcefully) between"; hence, "to get in the way; to take part in the affairs of others, especially when uninvited to do so; to meddle."

> *If you'll stop interfering, I'll finish the job faster.*

interject is made up of *inter-* meaning "between" and the Latin root *ject-,* which comes from a Latin verb meaning "to throw." Thus, *interject* means "to throw in a comment or a remark between other things; to introduce something abruptly."

> *I'd like to interject a few words before you go on.*

interlude comes from *inter-* meaning "between" and the Latin root *lud-* meaning "a play or game." *Interlude* originally meant "a short dramatic or comic act or a transitional piece of music performed between the acts of a play." Today, *interlude* also means "something that occurs in and divides up a longer, more important process; a feature that is put into a larger whole to break up the monotony; a short episode in one's life, history, etc."

> *Their love turned out to be only a brief interlude.*
> *The essay chapters of* Tom Jones *serve as interludes between the narrative portions.*

Here are some other important *inter-* words that you should learn:

intercept to seize or stop something or someone and prevent it or him from reaching a destination.

> *He intercepted the pass and ran for a touchdown.*

QUICKIE QUIZ
"IN" WORDS

The prefix *in-* sometimes means "in; into; within," as in the following ten words. Check the word or phrase you believe is closest in meaning to the key word. Answers follow.

1. **incarnate** [in·kär′nit]—(a) vulgar. (b) personified. (c) appearing again. (d) crimson.
2. **innate** [i·nāt′]—(a) inside. (b) inborn. (c) inhibited. (d) intimate.
3. **incarcerate** [in·kär′sə·rāt]—(a) to flay. (b) to visit scorn upon. (c) to imprison. (d) to forgive.
4. **incumbency** [in·kum′bən·sē]—(a) clumsiness. (b) ownership of possessions. (c) involvement in crime. (d) the holding of an office.
5. **inhibit** [in·hib′it]—(a) to set free. (b) to weaken. (c) to hinder or restrain. (d) to insist upon.
6. **ingratiate** [in·grā′shē·āt]—(a) to place oneself in a favorable position. (b) to cut into small pieces. (c) to be in debt to. (d) to act unkindly toward.
7. **infringe** [in·frinj′]—(a) to surround. (b) to decorate. (c) to limit. (d) to encroach.
8. **inherent** [in·hir′ənt]—(a) restrained. (b) possessive. (c) calm. (d) inborn or innate.
9. **incipient** [in·sip′ē·ənt]—(a) just beginning to appear. (b) maladjusted. (c) humble. (d) unthinking.
10. **incursion** [in·kûr′zhən]—(a) to swear at. (b) an invasion. (c) an agreement. (d) an exploration.

ANSWERS:

1. **incarnate**—(b) personified. 2. **innate**—(b) inborn. 3. **incarcerate**—(c) to imprison. 4. **incumbency**—(d) the holding of an office. 5. **inhibit**—(c) to hinder or restrain. 6. **ingratiate**—(a) to place oneself in a favorable position. 7. **infringe**—(d) to encroach. 8. **inherent**—(d) inborn or innate. 9. **incipient**—(a) just beginning to appear. 10. **incursion**—(b) an invasion.

intercollegiate involving two or more colleges, as in sports.

Intercollegiate baseball is less glamorous than football.

interdenominational of, for, or pertaining to two or more religious denominations.

There will be an interdenominational prayer meeting tonight.

interdependent dependent on each other.

intermezzo [in′tər·met′sō] (1) a short musical or dramatic offering given between the acts of a play or opera; (2) a short movement connecting the main parts of a long musical composition.

A melodious intermezzo precedes Act III of the opera Manon Lescaut.

internecine [in'tər·nē'sin] (1) destructive to both sides, as in a war; (2) of or pertaining to a divisive conflict within a group.

Both armies withdrew after the internecine battle.
A bitter internecine feud split the party into factions.

Many other words begin with the prefix *inter-*. Look under *inter-* in your dictionary to see how many words you know. Be sure to study the definitions and learn the words that you don't yet know.

PREFIX: **INTRA-**

What do an intramural football game and an intravenous injection have in common? What is the difference between intramural sports and intercollegiate sports? The Latin prefix *intra-* means "inside; within." Thus, *intra-* is opposed in meaning to both the prefix *extra-* meaning "outside; beyond" and the prefix *inter-* meaning "among; between."

Here are two core vocabulary words that begin with *intra-*: *intramural, intravenous.*

intramural is formed from *intra-* meaning "inside; within" and the word *mural* meaning "having to do with a wall or walls." Thus, *intramural* means "occurring within the walls or confines of one place, such as a city, organization, school, etc."

The coach scheduled an intramural football game between the freshmen and sophomores.

intravenous derives from *intra-* meaning "inside of" and the word *venous* meaning "of or having to do with a vein or veins." Thus, *intravenous* means "inside of or affecting the inside of a vein."

Have you ever had an intravenous injection?
The patient had to be fed intravenously.

◇ Several words beginning with the prefix *intra-* appear in your dictionary. Note that many of these are medical terms and have to do with internal medicine and parts of the body. Read the definitions for these words in your dictionary; learn any that you have heard frequently.

PREFIXES: **MAL- or MALE- and MIS-**

The prefix *mal-* or *male-* means "bad; ill; evil; wrong." Here are four typical words beginning with *mal-* or *male-*: *maladroit, malcontent, malediction, malignant.*

maladroit comes from the prefix *mal-* meaning "bad or badly" and the word *adroit* meaning "skillful or expert." Thus, a *maladroit* person is clumsy or lacking in skill. Something awkward can also be termed *maladroit.*

> *That waiter is so maladroit that he dropped the ashtray into my soup.*
> *The young man's maladroit remarks about the hostess embarrassed everyone at the party.*

malcontent is formed from *mal-* meaning "bad or badly" and the word *content.* Thus, *malcontent* means "barely content or not at all content with the existing state of things." A *malcontent* is "a discontented or dissatisfied person, especially a habitually discontented person."

> *Booth allied himself with a malcontent political faction.*
> *A group of malcontents tried to disrupt the meeting.*

malediction is made up of *male-* meaning "ill or evil" and the Latin root *dict-* meaning "to say or speak" plus the suffix *-ion* meaning "the act of." Thus, *malediction* means "the act of speaking ill"; hence, "a curse or slander."

> *Shylock heaped maledictions on the head of his daughter's lover.*

NOTE: *Malediction* is the opposite of *benediction,* meaning "the act of speaking well; a blessing." *Malediction* is pronounced [mal′ə·dik′shən]. Do not confuse the prefix *male-* [mal′ɔ] with the word *male.*

malignant comes from a Latin word based on *mal-* and meaning "to act maliciously or spitefully." Hence, *malignant* means "tending to produce or inflict evil; tending to do great harm; deadly."

A cancer is a malignant growth.

NOTE: *Malignant* is the opposite of *benign*, meaning "kindly" or "harmless." Two other words based on *mal-* or *male-* are *malnutrition* and *malefactor.* Can you figure out what they mean? Look them up in your dictionary.

The prefix *mis-* means (1) bad; badly; wrongly; (2) hating; hatred. Here are four words beginning with *mis-: misanthrope, misrepresent, misspell, mistake.*

misanthrope comes from *mis-* meaning "hating" and the Greek root *anthrop-* meaning "mankind." Thus, a *misanthrope* is "a person who hates mankind; one who hates or does not trust his fellow men."

Some misers are also misanthropes.

misrepresent is formed from the prefix *mis-* meaning "wrongly" and the word *represent,* meaning "to symbolize, describe, or express." *Misrepresent* thus means "to represent something falsely or poorly."

Your salesman misrepresented the terms of the warranty on my new car.
John Smith's stand on the tax bill misrepresents the wishes of the voters in his riding.

misspell comes from *mis-* meaning "wrongly" and the word *spell.* Thus, *misspell* means "to spell a word or words incorrectly."

If you look up unfamiliar words, you won't misspell them.

mistake comes from *mis-* meaning "wrongly" and the word *take.* *Mistake* literally means "to take (or understand) something wrongly." Hence, *mistake* means "to identify someone or something wrongly or to misinterpret." A *mistake* is "an error in action, judgment, knowledge, perception, understanding, etc."

I mistook you for someone else.
Do not mistake silence for consent.
Did you make any mistakes on the test?

Other words you should learn that begin with *mis-* include *misapprehension, misnomer,* and *misunderstand.* Look up these words in your dictionary and relate the meaning of each to the prefix *mis-*.

Fun With Words

PREFIXES MAL-, MALE-, MIS

Here are fourteen words beginning with the prefix *mal-*, *male-*, or *mis-*, which can mean "bad, ill, or wrong." Check the word or phrase you believe is closest in meaning to the key word. Answers follow.

1. **malodorous** [mal·ō′dər·əs]—(a) wicked. (b) musically pleasing. (c) ugly. (d) ill-smelling.
2. **malfeasance** [mal·fē′zəns]—(a) an illegal deed. (b) a failure. (c) a disappointment. (d) an unpleasant manner.
3. **misconstrue** [mis′kən·strōō′]— (a) to scatter about. (b) to be defeated. (c) to demolish. (d) to misunderstand.
4. **miscreant** [mis′krē·ənt]—(a) a slanderer. (b) an evildoer. (c) a misunderstood command. (d) an error.
5. **malcontent** [mal′kən·tent]—(a) unmixed. (b) playful. (c) dissatisfied. (d) incorrect.
6. **misdemeanor** [mis′di·mē′nər]— (a) a minor offense. (b) a doubting look. (c) bad luck. (d) a medley.
7. **misnomer** [mis·nō′mər]—(a) a wicked person. (b) a misrepresentation. (c) a wrong turn. (d) a name wrongly applied to someone or something.
8. **misconception** [mis′kən·sep′-shən]—(a) poor management.

(b) a false notion or idea. (c) failure to fertilize. (d) wicked thoughts.
9. **malediction** [mal′ə·dik′shən]— (a) a curse against someone. (b) an opening prayer. (c) a closing prayer. (d) an unintelligible speech.
10. **malefactor** [mal′ə·fak′tər]—(a) poor addition. (b) a miser. (c) a criminal. (d) to misunderstand.
11. **misapprehension** [mis′ap·ri·hen′-shən]—(a) fear or dread. (b) an illegal act. (c) misunderstanding. (d) an escape.
12. **malaise** [mal·āz′]—(a) uneasiness. (b) hatred. (c) discouragement. (d) acute pain.
13. **malevolent** [mə·lev′ə·lənt]—(a) extremely violent. (b) wishing evil toward others. (c) in poor voice. (d) insane.
14. **mishap** [mis′hap]—(a) poor behavior. (b) to do something incorrectly. (c) to tear down or destroy. (d) an unfortunate accident.

ANSWERS:

1. **malodorous**—(d) ill-smelling. 2. **malfeasance**—(a) an illegal deed. 3. **misconstrue**—(d) to misunderstand. 4. **miscreant**—(b) an evildoer. 5. **malcontent**—(c) dissatisfied. 6. **misdemeanor**—(a) a minor offense. 7. **misnomer**—(d) a name wrongly applied to someone or something. 8. **misconception**—(b) a false notion or idea. 9. **malediction**—(a) a curse against someone. 10. **malefactor**—(c) a criminal. 11. **misapprehension**—(c) misunderstanding. 12. **malaise**—(a) uneasiness. 13. **malevolent**—(b) wishing evil toward others. 14. **mishap**—(d) an unfortunate accident.

PREFIX: NON-

The Latin prefix *non-* means "not." *Non-* is one of the easiest of prefixes to learn, since it is a simple negative that behaves exactly like a minus sign; it negates the word that follows. Many other prefixes have a similar negative function— for example, *dis-, de-, in-,* and *un-.* However, these other negative prefixes have various other meanings as well, whereas *non-* means "not" and only "not."

Here are four core vocabulary words that show how *non-* is used: *nonchalant, nonconformist, nonentity, nonsense.*

nonchalant is a French word made up of *non-* meaning "not" and *chalant* meaning "to be warm; to be desirous." Thus, *nonchalant* means "showing a lack of interest or excitement; casually indifferent; self-confidently cool."

> *You take a very nonchalant attitude toward your work.*
> *Nonchalantly, unemotionally, he waited for the first question.*

nonconformist is formed from *non-* meaning "not" and the word *conformist* meaning "a person who follows conventional behavior." Thus, *nonconformist* means "a person who does not think or behave like most other people."

> *Many writers and artists are nonconformists.*
> *A Nonconformist is an English Protestant who refuses to conform to the Church of England.*

nonentity comes from *non-* meaning "not" and the word *entity* meaning "something that really exists; a real being." Thus, *nonentity* means "a mere nothing; a person or thing of very little account."

> *Tom brags about his work, but his boss considers him a nonentity.*

nonsense derives from *non-* meaning "not" and the word *sense.* Thus, *nonsense* means "anything that does not make sense; anything meaningless or absurd."

> *Tom's bragging is a lot of nonsense.*
> *Most children love nonsense rhymes.*

◇ How many words beginning with *non-* can you think of? There are literally hundreds of *non-* words listed in your dictionary. Look them up.

PREFIX: OB- AND ITS DISGUISES

The prefix *ob-* means "toward; to; against; completely; over." As in the case of *ad-* and *in-*, the spelling of this prefix may change depending on the letter that follows it. Thus, *ob-* may be spelled *oc-*, *of-*, or *op-*.

Here are six common words beginning with *ob-* or one of its variant spellings: *obese, object, obtrude, occupy, offend, oppress.* Start with these and then learn all the other words in this chapter.

obese comes from a Latin word meaning "fat," made up of *ob-* meaning "completely" or "over" and a verb meaning "to eat." Thus, *obese* means "fat from overeating; very fat."

> *She used to be only a bit overweight, but now she's obese!*

object is formed from *ob-* meaning "against" and the Latin root *ject-* meaning "to throw." Thus, to *object* [əb·jekt'] is "to throw criticism against something; to oppose something, especially with words." An *object* [ob'jikt] is literally "something thrown in the way." Hence, the noun *object* means (1) something that can be seen or touched; (2) something that is sought for; a purpose or goal.

> *Mr. Harris objected to the noise.*
> *They spotted an unidentified flying object.*
> *The object of the meeting was to elect a new president.*

obtrude comes from *ob-* meaning "against" or "toward" and the Latin root *trud-* meaning "to thrust." Thus, *obtrude* means "to force or thrust oneself, an opinion, etc., upon another person without being asked."

> *Anne loudly obtrudes her beliefs into every conversation.*

occupy is derived from *oc-* (another spelling of *ob-*) meaning "against" and the root *-cupy*, which is related to the Latin root *cap-* meaning "to take." Thus, *occupy* means (1) to take and hold possession of something, as by force or conquest; (2) to hold or fill, as an office or post; (3) to keep oneself busy at doing something.

> *Germany occupied France during World War II.*
> *He occupied the mayor's office for four terms.*
> *Can't you find something worthwhile to occupy your mind?*

offend stems from *of-* (another spelling of *ob-*) meaning "against" and the Latin root *fend-* meaning "to hit." Thus, *offend* literally means "to hit against or collide with"; hence, (1) to displease or anger someone; (2) to be disagreeable to the sense of smell, sight, etc.; (3) to commit a crime or sin, or to err in some other way.

> *I'm sorry if I've offended you.*
> *The blaring music offended Sue's ears.*
> *Nonconformists often offend against the customs of society.*

oppress is derived from *op-* (another spelling of *ob-*) meaning "against" and the word *press*. Thus, *oppress* means (1) to press or lie heavily upon someone, as a burden; (2) to keep in subjugation by harsh use of force or authority.

> *The atmosphere of uncertainty oppressed our spirits.*
> *They were an oppressed people, enslaved by conquerors.*

Learn the following thirteen additional words beginning with the prefix *ob-* or its disguises.

obfuscate (1) to confuse or perplex; (2) to darken or obscure something.

obligate to bind or force someone, as with a contract, promise, etc., that necessitates some action, such as the return of a favor or the performance of a duty.

oblique not following the perpendicular or horizontal; slanting.

oblong longer in one direction than in another.

obnoxious highly disagreeable; objectionable.

obsolete out of fashion; no longer used or done.

obstacle that which stands in the way; a hindrance.

obstetrics the branch of medicine dealing with pregnancy and childbirth; literally, the branch of medicine that "stands by" during the process.

obstreperous noisy and unruly; literally, making noise "against" a speaker, someone in authority, etc.

obtuse not quick in mind or feeling; stupid.

occult pertaining to various magical arts or practices, such as astrology, alchemy, and witchcraft, which are "hidden against" the light of reason.

opportune timely or favorable; literally, blowing "toward port," as a ship or a favorable wind.

opprobrium (1) the state of being reproached or scorned; (2) reproach mingled with disdain.

◊ You should be able to build many words from the ones presented in this chapter. Remembering the definitions given above, how would you define the words below?

obesity	offensive	obligatory
occupant	oppressive	opportunity

FOUR NATIVE ENGLISH PREFIXES: ON-, OUT-, OVER-, UNDER-

Latin and Greek are not only the only languages that give us prefixes. English has its own set of native prefixes. These are often simple words we all know—such as the words *on, out, over,* and *under*—which we prefix to other words (roots) in order to form new words. This simple manufacturing process is exactly how words are made from Greek and Latin prefixes and roots. The difference is that you need to learn the meaning of Greek and Latin prefixes and roots, whereas you already know the English words used in word building.

Here are eleven words that illustrate the way we use our own English words *on, out, over,* and *under* as prefixes to form new words:

onset a start or attack; literally, "the starting on" of something.

I've been suffering from the onset of a cold.

onslaught a strong attack on someone or something.

The troops fought back an onslaught of enemy soldiers.

outermost farthest out; farthest away from the center.

The submarine sank the outermost ship in the convoy.

outset the beginning or start.

> *We were seasick from the very outset of the voyage.*

outside (1) the outer side, part, surface, etc.; (2) the space beyónd an enclosure; (3) being, acting, etc., beyond an enclosure, limit, etc.

> *The outside of the car was muddy.*
> *Sounds of music came from outside.*
> *Robin Hood's activities were outside the law.*

oversight failure to notice; an error caused by carelessness.

> *Because of an oversight, our baggage was left in the plane.*

overweight weighing more than normal.

> *No one should be more than ten pounds overweight.*

overwrought excessively worked up; overstrained.

> *Overwrought young mothers need time away from their children.*

underhanded not open and honorable; secret and sly.

> *He made a fortune in underhanded business deals.*

underwear clothing worn under the outer clothes.

underweight weighing less than normal.

PREFIX: PER-

What do a percolator, a perambulator, and a perjurer have in common? The prefix *per-* means (1) through; throughout; by means of; by; (2) thoroughly; completely; (3) wrongly. Here are four core vocabulary words that begin with *per-: perambulate, percent, perfect, perjure.*

perambulate derives from *per-* meaning "through" and the word *ambulate* meaning "to walk." Thus, to *perambulate* means "to walk through or around; to stroll."

> *Their vast garden is marvelous for perambulating.*

percent is a combination of the prefix *per* meaning "by" and the Latin root *cent-* meaning "hundred." Thus, *percent* means "the number of parts in every hundred of something."

He lost nearly ten percent of his accounts.

perfect comes from *per-* meaning "thoroughly" and the Latin root *fect-*, meaning "to make or do." Thus, *perfect* [pûr'fikt] means "done thoroughly; without fault or blemish; completely suitable." To *perfect* [pər·fekt'] is "to make flawless; to improve, refine, or complete."

It's a perfect day for a picnic.
Our architect has been perfecting plans for the new house.

perjure is formed from *per-* meaning "wrongly" and the Latin root *jur-* meaning "to swear." Thus, to *perjure* means "to be guilty of swearing falsely or of giving false testimony while under oath."

If you falsify your tax return, you're guilty of perjury.

Learn these fourteen additional *per-* words:

percolate to pass a liquid or cause a liquid to pass through a filter or strainer; especially, to cause boiling water to filter down through ground coffee.

percussion (1) the sound produced by means of striking one thing against another; (2) musical instruments, such as drums, cymbals, etc., whose sound is caused in this manner.

perdition eternal damnation.

perfidious breaking faith, trust, or allegiance, especially through treachery.

permeate (1) to spread thoroughly through; (2) to pass through the pores of something, as of a filter or membrane.

pernicious having the power to destroy thoroughly; highly injurious; wicked.

perpendicular at right angles to or through the horizontal plane; vertical.

perpetual lasting forever.

perplexity doubt, confusion, or bewilderment.

persevere to continue striving for a purpose in spite of difficulties.

persist (1) to continue firmly in some course of action; (2) to be insistent, as in repeating an action.

perspective (1) the effect that distance has upon the appearance of objects, by means of which the eye judges spatial relationships; (2) the art or theory of portraying objects on a flat surface so that there is an effect of depth and distance, as in a painting; (3) judgment of facts, circumstances, etc., in regard to their proportional importance.

pertain (1) to have reference to; relate; (2) to belong to something, as a quality, function, adjunct, etc.

pervade to spread through every part of something.

An odor pervades a room by permeating the air in the room.

◇ Make up a sample sentence using each of the preceding words. Look up all the *per-* words listed in your dictionary. How many do you know? Learn any new *per-* words that seem especially *pertinent* to your own interests.

PREFIX: **POST-**

The word *postmeridian* may sound strange to you, but you use it—in a shortened form, to be sure—all the time!

The Latin prefix *post-* means "after; behind." Here are three core vocabulary words using the prefix *post-*: *postgraduate, postmeridian, postpone.*

postgraduate comes from *post-* meaning "after" and the word *graduate.* Thus, *postgraduate* means "pertaining to academic studies that are taken up after a degree has been received."

I took my B.A. at U.B.C. and did postgraduate work at McGill.

postmeridian comes from *post-* meaning "after" and the word *meridian* meaning "a great circle or dividing line drawn from any point on the earth's surface and passing through both poles." Thus, *postmeridian* means "after the sun has passed the dividing line at noon." Our abbreviation P.M. is taken from the Latin form of this word (*post meridiem*) and, of course, means "in the afternoon" or "in the second half of the day, from noon to midnight."

He works from 3 P.M. to 11 P.M.

postpone comes from *post-* meaning "after" and the Latin root *pon-* meaning "to put; place." Thus, to *postpone* means "to put off until afterward; delay."

The game was postponed because of rain.

Learn these additional *post-* words:

posterior (1) situated behind something else; (2) coming after another in time or order; (3) the rump.

posterity generations that come after; future generations taken as a whole.

posthumous [pos′chŏo·məs] (1) arising or continuing after one's death; (2) born after the father's death, as a child; (3) published after the author's death, as a book.

Most of Emily's poems were published posthumously.

post-mortem (1) happening or performed after death; (2) a medical examination of a body performed after death.

postprandial after-dinner.

postscript a sentence or more added to a letter after the writer's signature. The familiar abbreviation of *postscript* is *P.S.*

◊ Other words formed with the prefix *post-* range from simple terms like *postwar* and *postdate* to specialized terms like *postdiluvian*. Look up *post* referring to *mail*. This is not the same as the prefix *post-* meaning "after." Obviously, *postcard* and *poster* are based on the root *post*, not the prefix. From the *post* words in your dictionary, see if you can figure out which are based on the prefix *post-* meaning "after; behind" and which on the root *post*, referring to mail.

ALL, AROUND, AND BESIDE

The following ten words begin with three little-used but interesting Greek prefixes: *pan-* meaning "all," *peri-* meaning "around," and *para-* meaning "beside." Check the word or phrase you believe is closest in meaning to the key word. Answers follow.

1. **pandemonium** [pan'də·mō'nē·əm]—(a) a large area. (b) wild uproar. (c) plague. (d) a disease of the respiratory tract.
2. **peripatetic** [per'i·pə·tet'ik]—(a) talkative. (b) permissive. (c) amusing. (d) walking about from one place to another.
3. **panacea** [pan'ə·sē'ə]—(a) everywhere. (b) a cure-all. (c) equality. (d) a bodily organ of digestion.
4. **panoply** [pan'ə·plē]—(a) a magnificent array, especially of armor. (b) a covering for a four-poster bed. (c) a harplike musical instrument. (d) a fruit.
5. **periphery** [pə·rif'ər·ē]—(a) a straight line. (b) the diameter. (c) the outer bounds. (d) a diagonal line.
6. **paragon** [par'ə·gon]—(a) away. (b) an advocate. (c) a large building. (d) a model of excellence.
7. **perimeter** [pə·rim'ə·tər]—(a) an area bounded by certain limits. (b) the outer boundary. (c) a straight line through the center of an object. (d) a measurement of distance.
8. **paranoia** [par'ə·noi'ə]—(a) a mental disorder characterized by delusions of persecution. (b) double talk. (c) a disease of the nervous system. (d) a mental disorder characterized by lapses of memory.
9. **paraphernalia** [par'ə·fər·nā'lē·ə]—(a) a mental disorder characterized by alternating periods of anger and withdrawal. (b) a large suitcase. (c) abnormal sleep. (d) personal effects.
10. **panorama** [pan'ə·ram'ə]—(a) a comprehensive view of a subject. (b) a metropolis. (c) a confused state of mind. (d) a large screen to project pictures on.

ANSWERS:

1. **pandemonium**—(b) wild uproar. 2. **peripatetic**—(d) walking about from one place to another. 3. **panacea**—(b) a cure-all. 4. **panoply**—(a) a magnificent array, especially of armor. 5. **periphery**—(c) the outer bounds. 6. **paragon**—(d) a model of excellence. 7. **perimeter**—(b) the outer boundary. 8. **paranoia**—(a) a mental disorder characterized by delusions of persecution. 9. **paraphernalia**—(d) personal effects. 10. **panorama**—(a) a comprehensive view of a subject.

PREFIX: PRE-

What does the preface of a book have in common with a prefabricated house? The prefix *pre-* means "before in time or order; preceding; prior to; in front of." Here are four core vocabulary words beginning with *pre-: precaution, precursor, prefabricate, premolar.*

precaution is formed from *pre-* meaning "before" and the word *caution.* Thus, *precaution* means "caution taken as a preparation for a possible emergency."

Take the precaution of fastening your seat belt before starting.

precursor comes from *pre-* meaning "before" and the Latin root *curs-* meaning "to run" plus the suffix *-or* meaning "a person who." Thus, a *precursor* is literally "a person who runs before; a forerunner"; hence, "a person or thing that precedes and suggests the course of events to come."

The first robin you see is a precursor of spring.

prefabricate derives from *pre-* meaning "before" and the word *fabricate* meaning "to make; manufacture; build." Thus, to *prefabricate* is "to manufacture something beforehand; especially, to manufacture the parts of a house in standard sections that can be put together rapidly."

The workers erected the prefabricated house in three days.

premolar derives from *pre-* meaning "in front of" and the word *molar.* Thus, *premolar* means "one of the teeth situated in front of the molars; a bicuspid."

The dentist filled one of my premolars.

Learn these seventeen additional words that include the prefix *pre-:*

precept (1) a rule prescribing a particular kind of conduct; (2) a proverb.

precinct (1) an election district or a police district; (2) a place or enclosure marked off by fixed limits.

precipice the brink of a cliff; a high vertical or overhanging face of rock.

241

precipitate to bring something about suddenly and unexpectedly.

precipitation rain, snow, sleet, etc.

precise strictly accurate (originally, *precise* meant "to be sure before cutting or acting").

precocious (1) unusually developed or advanced for one's age; (2) developed before the usual time or age.

preface a brief, introductory statement or essay in the front of a book.

prelate [prel'it] a clergyman of high rank, as a bishop, archbishop, etc.

preliminary before or introductory to the main event, business, etc.

premeditate to plan or consider beforehand.

preposterous absurd; contrary to nature, reason, or common sense.

(Note that this word contains both the prefix *pre-* meaning "before" and the prefix *post-* meaning "after." Combining "before" and "after" is absurd, and that is how *preposterous* got its meaning.)

prerequisite something required before or necessary to something that follows, such as an academic course that must be taken before another, more advanced course.

prerogative an exclusive right or privilege belonging to a person or group; a right so obvious that it is given before it is asked for.

It is a prelate's prerogative to officiate at some functions.

presage (1) as a noun [pres'ij], an indication of something to come; an omen; (2) as a verb [pri·sāj'], to give an indication of something to come; to foreshadow.

presume (1) to take for granted beforehand; (2) to take an unwarranted liberty; dare; (3) to seem to prove; (4) to make excessive demands on or rely too heavily on.

prevaricator a person who acts or speaks in a deceptive manner (literally, "a person who walks crookedly before another").

◊ Make a sample sentence using each of the preceding words. You will find a long list of words beginning with *pre-* in your dictionary. How many of these words do you know? Learn any additional *pre-* words that you have heard frequently.

EXPLORING WORDS
CHEERS, OLD CHAP

People in Britain and on our side of the Atlantic speak the same language—almost. Some of the thirty-one British words listed below are rarely used in our speech. We use others, sometimes with different meanings. If you read British books, see British movies, or talk to British people, you might like to know the meanings of the British words listed below.

biscuit a cracker.
bonnet the hood of an automobile.
boot the trunk of an automobile.
braces a pair of suspenders.
cab rank taxi stand.
chemist a pharmacist or druggist.
chips French-fried potatoes.
circus a traffic circle.
cotton wool absorbent cotton.
crumpet a muffin or light biscuit.
draper's haberdashery.
dustbin a garbage can.
egg whisk eggbeater
flat apartment.
greengrocer a fruit-and-vegetable store, or the proprietor of one.
lift an elevator.
lorry a truck.
mute pallbearer.
nappy a baby's diaper.
petrol gasoline.
pram a baby carriage (short for *perambulator*).
pub a bar or tavern (short for *public house*).
spanner a wrench.
subway an underpass, especially one for pedestrians.
tin a can, as of food.
treacle molasses.
underground a subway or subway system.
vest an undershirt.
waistcoat [wes'kit] a vest.
windscreen the windshield of an automobile.
works factory.

PREFIX: PRO-

Such very different words as *promiscuous, propaganda, prodigal,* and *pronoun* have in common the Latin prefix *pro-* which means (1) forward; forth; (2) before; (3) in place of or on behalf of; for. Here are five core vocabulary words formed with the prefix *pro-: proceed, produce, profane, profess, pronoun.*

proceed derives from the prefix *pro-* meaning "forward" and the Latin root *ceed-* meaning "to go." Thus, to *proceed* means "to go on or go forward, especially after a stop or interruption."

> *If there are no more questions, I'll proceed with the lecture.*

produce is formed from *pro-* meaning "forward" and the Latin root *duc-* meaning "to lead." Thus, to *produce* means "to lead or bring forth; to yield, make, or bring about; to lead forward into view; to show or display."

> *An accusation of treachery always produces a violent reaction.*
> *It was hard to produce evidence of the man's innocence.*

profane comes from *pro-* meaning "before" and the Latin root *fan-* meaning "temple." Thus, *profane* literally means "outside the temple"; hence, (1) not religious or concerned with religious things; (2) irreverent; (3) coarse, as language. To *profane* something sacred is to treat it with irreverence.

> *Cursing is sometimes called profane language.*
> *The church was profaned by vandals who turned over the altar.*

A word based on *profane* is *profanity,* meaning "profane speech or action; disrespect for religious things."

> *His speech was coarse and full of profanity.*

profess is formed from *pro-* meaning "before" and the Latin root *fess-,* meaning "to confess; declare." Thus, to *profess* means (1) to declare before others; (2) to declare faith in; (3) to pretend.

> *The accused man professed his innocence.*
> *The young singer professed Islam and became a Muslim.*
> *People often profess to despise what they actually envy.*

244

Two words based on *profess* are *profession* and *professor*. *Profession* means (1) an occupation calling for education and involving mental rather than manual labor, as law, medicine, or theology; (2) the act of declaring openly. *Professor* means (1) a college or university teacher of the highest rank; (2) one who professes opinions or beliefs.

Dr. Smith, who is a professor of English, is proud of his profession.

pronoun is made up of *pro-* meaning "for; in place of" and the word *noun* meaning "the part of speech that names a person, place, or thing." Thus, *pronoun* means "a word used in place of a noun."

He, she, and *it are pronouns.*

Match each word with one of the definitions that follow.

1. **proclivity;** 2. **procure;** 3. **prodigal;** 4. **promiscuous;**
5. **promulgate;** 6. **propaganda.**

a.   to announce officially and formally before the people.

b.   to obtain by some means or effort; to bring about.

c.   indiscriminate, especially in sexual relations.

d.   an effort to persuade people to adopt a particular belief, attitude, course of action, etc.; the statements and printed material used in such an effort.

e.   a natural disposition or tendency.

f.   wasteful of money or time; a spendthrift.

Check your answers in a dictionary.

Remembering the definitions of the words you have just learned, can you figure out meanings for the six words that follow?

proceeds [prō'sēdz]   professoriate
procurement   promiscuity
production   propagandist

NOTE: The prefix *pro-* can also mean "in favor of," as opposed to *anti-* meaning "against." The word *pro* means "for" or "an argument in favor of something," as opposed to *con*, which means "against" or "an argument against something."

Some colonists were pro-British during the Revolutionary War. Before deciding, let's consider all the pros and cons.

Fun With Words

PREFIXES PRO- AND PRE-

The following thirteen words begin with the prefix *pro-* meaning "forward; before; for" or the prefix *pre-* meaning "before; prior to." Check the word or phrase you believe is closest in meaning to the key word. Answers follow.

1. **prescient** [prē'shē·ənt]—(a) prophetic. (b) patient. (c) pure. (d) peaceful.

2. **premonitory** [pri·mon'ə·tôr'ē]—(a) a headland. (b) sad. (c) giving warning of something to come. (d) resounding.

3. **promulgate** [prom'əl·gāt]—(a) to proclaim. (b) to thrash. (c) to intend. (d) to force upon others.

4. **propitiate** [prō·pish'ē·āt]—(a) to weaken. (b) to encourage. (c) to rain or snow. (d) to appease or win the favor of.

5. **propensity** [prə·pen'sə·tē]—(a) feebleness. (b) ability. (c) a tendency. (d) miserliness or penny-pinching.

6. **predilection** [prē'də·lek'shən]—(a) in the neighborhood of. (b) a preference for something. (c) an introduction. (d) an implication.

7. **precocity** [pri·kos'ə·tē]—(a) impetuousness. (b) perverseness. (c) a state of being mentally developed earlier than usual. (d) a state of being mentally developed later than usual.

8. **prestige** [pres·tēzh']—(a) pride. (b) performance. (c) distinction. (d) wealth.

9. **proviso** [prə·vī'zō]—(a) a condition or stipulation. (b) a supply. (c) a definite command. (d) a prophecy.

10. **provocation** [prov'ə·kā'shən]—(a) a narrow-minded viewpoint. (b) a cause of anger or resentment. (c) willingness to work. (d) an alliance.

11. **prognostication** [prog·nos'tə·kā'shən]—(a) mental absorption. (b) the act of prolonging. (c) diagnosis. (d) a prediction or forecast.

12. **pretext** [prē'tekst]—(a) a rule. (b) a promise. (c) an excuse. (d) a preface.

13. **profess** [prə·fes']—(a) to become expert at. (b) to proclaim or declare. (c) to plan or teach. (d) to foretell.

ANSWERS:

1. **prescient**—(a) prophetic. 2. **premonitory**—(c) giving warning of something to come. 3. **promulgate**—(a) to proclaim. 4. **propitiate**—(d) to appease or win the favor of. 5. **propensity**—(c) a tendency. 6. **predilection**—(b) a preference for something. 7. **precocity**—(c) a state of being mentally developed earlier than usual. 8. **prestige**—(c) distinction. 9. **proviso**—(a) a condition or stipulation. 10. **provocation**—(b) a cause of anger or resentment. 11. **prognostication**—(d) a prediction or forecast. 12. **pretext**—(c) an excuse. 13. **profess**—(b) to proclaim or declare.

What do a rebel, a refrigerator, and a reconnaissance plane have in common?

The Latin prefix *re-* means "back; again, thoroughly." Here are four core vocabulary words using *re-: rebel, recall, refresh, refrigerate.*

rebel is formed from the prefix *re-* meaning "again" and the Latin root *bel-* meaning "to make war." The verb *rebel* [ri·bel'] literally means "to make war again; resume fighting." Hence, to *rebel* is (1) to rise in resistance against the established government of one's country; (2) to resist or disobey any authority; (3) to react with strong opposition or disapproval. A *rebel* [reb'əl] is "a person who refuses to submit to the established authority or conventions."

> *The army rebelled against the dictator.*
> *Billy rebelled against his parents' way of life.*
> *The student rebels demanded an end to the grading system.*

recall derives from *re-* meaning "back" and the word *call*. Thus, *recall* means (1) to call back; order to return or be returned; (2) to take back; revoke; (3) to call back to mind; remember.

> *The retired general was recalled to duty.*
> *The manufacturer recalled the defective cars.*
> *Can you recall the date of the Battle of Waterloo?*

refresh is formed from *re-* meaning "again" and the word *fresh*. Thus, *refresh* means (1) to make fresh or vigorous again; revive; (2) to stimulate, as the memory.

> *He refreshed himself with a short nap.*
> *The old snapshots refreshed Sally's memory of her first teacher.*

refrigerate is made up of *re-* meaning "thoroughly" and the Latin root *frigerat-*, meaning "to cool." Thus, *refrigerate* means "to make or keep thoroughly cool."

> *Refrigerate the milk so that it won't spoil.*

Learn these eighteen additional *re-* words:

rebuff (1) to reject or refuse abruptly or rudely; snub; (2) an abrupt or rude rejection, denial, or defeat.

recalcitrant defying or resisting a request or command; obstinate, stubborn; rebellious (literally, "kicking back" at a request).

reciprocal done or given by each of two persons, things, parties, etc., to the other; mutual.

reconnaissance [ri·kon′ə·səns] (1) a preliminary survey or examination, as of an area of a country, for information; (2) the act of obtaining information of military value, especially regarding the position, strength, and movement of the enemy.

reconnoiter to survey or examine, as for military, engineering, or geological purposes.

recoup to get something back; recover or make up, as a loss.

recriminate to accuse in return; meet one accusation by making another.

recuperate to get back one's health or strength.

reiterate to say or do again and again, as for emphasis; repeat.

relapse (1) to lapse back, as into a disease, after a partial recovery; (2) a lapsing back.

relegate (1) to send back or off, as to a less important person, position, or place; (2) to assign to a certain category.

relinquish to give up or leave behind; abandon.

reminiscence (1) the calling to mind of past events; (2) the telling of past experiences.

remunerate to make a just or adequate return to or for; pay back or pay for; compensate.

reprieve (1) to delay temporarily the execution of a sentence upon a condemned person (literally, "taken back"); (2) to relieve for a time from trouble, danger, or pain; (3) the temporary suspension of a sentence; especially, the commutation of a death sentence; (4) temporary relief or a respite.

rescind to take back; make void; repeal.

revile to attack with contemptuous language; to abuse.

revise (1) to read again or read over in order to correct errors, make changes, etc.; (2) to change.

QUICKIE QUIZ

BACK AGAIN

The following seven words begin with the prefix *re-* meaning "back; again; thoroughly." Check the word you believe is closest in meaning to the key word. Answers follow.

1. **reverberate** [ri·vûr′bə·rāt]—(a) to separate into the original parts. (b) to echo or resound. (c) to regain one's energy. (d) to resume a former habit.
2. **recessive** [ri·ses′iv]—(a) indented. (b) growing gradually greater. (c) tending to go back. (d) growing gradually smaller.
3. **retrenchment** [ri·trench′mənt] —(a) a strengthening of the foundations. (b) a forced withdrawal. (c) a cutting down of expenses. (d) a retraction of a promise.

4. **remiss** [ri·mis′]—(a) absentminded. (b) careless. (c) sinful. (d) sorrowful.
5. **redress** [ri·dres′]—(a) to make amends for. (b) to make neat. (c) to withdraw. (d) to make a reply.
6. **repletion** [ri·plē′shən]—(a) a state of weakness. (b) the act of doing something more than once. (c) a state of complete or excessive fullness. (d) an invitation.
7. **recompense** [rek′əm·pens]—(a) to remember. (b) to reconcile. (c) to resume. (d) to pay back.

ANSWERS:

1. **reverberate**—(b) to echo or resound. 2. **recessive**—(c) tending to go back. 3. **retrenchment**—(c) a cutting down of expenses. 4. **remiss**—(b) careless. 5. **redress**—(a) to make amends for. 6. **repletion**—(c) a state of complete or excessive fullness. 7. **recompense**—(d) to pay back.

◇ You can build many more words on the words just discussed. Remembering their meanings, can you figure out the meanings of the words that follow?

rebellious	recuperation
refreshment	reminiscent
refrigerator	remuneration
recrimination	revision

Hundreds of other words begin with the prefix *re-*. Look at the words beginning with this prefix in your dictionary (there will be several pages of them). How many do you know? Learn the meanings of the *re-* words that you hear or see most often. Study their etymologies to be sure that you know how the prefix *re-* is used in word building.

The Latin prefix *se-* means "aside; apart; away; without." This prefix occurs in only a few words, but they are important. A basic word containing the prefix *se-* is *separate*, which literally means "to prepare apart." Here are six core vocabulary words using the prefix *se-*: *secede, secure, sedition, seduce, segregate, select.*

secede stems from *se-* meaning "apart" and the Latin root *ced-* meaning "to go." Thus, *secede* means "to go apart"; hence, "to withdraw from an association, especially for political or religious reasons."

> *Quebec separatists want their province to secede from the rest of Canada.*

secure derives from the prefix *se-* meaning "without" and the Latin root *cur-* meaning "care." Thus, *secure* means "free from care, fear, etc."; hence, (1) safe; (2) certain; (3) fixed firmly or strongly in place; (4) so strong or well made as to make loss, breakage, escape, or defeat impossible; (5) to protect, fasten, or guarantee; (6) to obtain.

> *Little Joey feels secure only when he is with his parents.*
> *He was secure in his knowledge of the facts.*
> *Our nation rests on a secure foundation.*
> *They secured all the doors and windows before the full force of the hurricane hit.*
> *Have you secured the necessary supplies?*

sedition is made up of *sed-* (another spelling of *se-*) meaning "aside" and the Latin root *it-* meaning "a going" plus the suffix *-ion* meaning "the act or state of." Thus, *sedition* literally means "the act of going aside from law and order"; hence, "language or action directed against public order; the encouragement of disorder or revolt against the state."

> *In Stalin's Russia, sedition meant certain death.*

seduce is formed of *se-* meaning "apart; away" and the Latin root *duc-* meaning "to lead." Thus, *seduce* means "to lead astray; to lure into wrong, disloyalty, etc.; especially, to persuade a person to engage in illicit sexual intercourse."

Their offer of big money seduced him into joining the conspiracy.
The heroine of many an old movie was seduced and abandoned
by the villain.

segregate is derived from *se-* meaning "apart" and the Latin root *greg-*
meaning "the flock or herd" plus the suffix *-ate* meaning "to make."
Thus, to *segregate* is "to place a person, thing, or group apart from
the rest; to isolate; especially, to subject a racial group to the practice of using separate facilities."

A child with measles should be segregated from the rest of the
pupils.
Segregated schools were common in the southern United States.

select is formed from *se-* meaning "apart" and the Latin root *loot*
meaning "to choose." Thus, to *select* literally means "to choose something apart from others"; hence, "to make a choice." As an adjective,
select means (1) set aside as being the best; chosen for high quality;
(2) making careful, discriminating choices.

You may select any dress you wish.
These tomatoes are select.

◊ From the words discussed in this chapter you can build such additional words as *secession, security, seditious,* etc. See how many you
can think of, and consult your dictionary to find out whether you've
figured out the correct meanings for them.

PREFIX: SUB- AND ITS DISGUISES

The Latin prefix *sub-* means (1) under; beneath; below; (2) secondary; subordinate; (3) less than, almost, or imperfectly; (4) secretly.

NOTE: Like *ad-*, the prefix *sub-* changes spelling so that its last letter
will harmonize with the letter following it. Thus, *sub-* may be spelled
suc-, suf-, sug-, sum-, sup-, sur-, or *sus-,* as in *succumb, suffer, suggest,*
summon, support, surrogate, susceptible, suspect, sustain.

Here are six core vocabulary words beginning with *sub-: subcon-*
scious, submarine, submit, suborbital, subordinate, suborn.

subconscious is formed from *sub-* meaning "imperfectly" or "below" and the word *conscious*. Thus, *subconscious* means "not clearly or wholly conscious." The *subconscious* is "the part of the mind or the mind's activity of which a person is usually not aware; the workings of the mind just below the threshold of consciousness."

> *Some people have a subconscious desire for self-destruction.*
> *The psychoanalyst knew that Laura's problem was buried in her subconscious.*

submarine derives from *sub-* meaning "under" and the word *marine* meaning "of or having to do with the sea or ships; nautical." Thus, *submarine* means "existing or operating beneath the surface of the sea." A *submarine* is designed to operate below the surface of the sea.

> *Skin divers can study submarine life.*
> *An atomic submarine can sail around the world without surfacing.*

submit comes from *sub-* meaning "under; beneath" and the Latin root *mit-* meaning "to send or place." Thus, *submit* means (1) to place under or yield to the authority, will, or power of another; to surrender; (2) to present for consideration; (3) to present as one's opinion; suggest.

> *The English tribes submitted to Caesar's legions.*
> *Please submit your report to the board on Friday.*
> *I submit that we are in error and should change our ways.*

suborbital stems from *sub-* meaning "less than, almost, or imperfectly," and the word *orbital* meaning "having to do with an orbit." Thus, *suborbital* means "not going into orbit; falling short of a complete revolution around the earth or another heavenly body: said of rockets, artificial satellites, and spacecraft."

> *The missile had a suborbital flight, landing a thousand miles down-range from the launching pad.*

subordinate is derived from *sub-* meaning "under" and the Latin root *ordin-* meaning "to order" plus the suffix *-ate* meaning "characterized by." Thus, *subordinate* means "belonging to a lower position, class, or rank." A *subordinate* is a person or thing lower in rank or authority than another.

> *A captain is subordinate to a major.*

An officer is authorized to give orders to his subordinates.
A complex sentence has an independent clause and one or more subordinate clauses.

suborn is formed from *sub-* meaning "secretly" and the Latin root *orn-* meaning "to equip." Thus, to *suborn* means "to incite someone to an evil or criminal act; especially, to bribe someone to commit perjury or some other criminal act."

The lawyer was charged with suborning a witness.

Learn these eight additional words beginning with the prefix *sub-:*

subcutaneous situated, found, or applied beneath the skin.

The doctor gave Paul a subcutaneous injection.

subliminal perceived below the threshold of consciousness, as certain stimuli, images, etc., of too low an intensity to produce a clear awareness.

Subliminal advertising is sometimes used in television.

subservient adapted to promote some higher or more important purpose; useful as a subordinate; servile.

subsidiary (1) a company owned and controlled by another company; (2) functioning in a lesser or secondary capacity; auxiliary.

subsidy financial assistance, especially through government grants, for an individual or enterprise that is thought to be beneficial to the public; literally, money that "sits under" something in order to support it.

substantiate to establish as truth by evidence; to verify; literally, to "stand under" something with supporting evidence.

substitute (1) to put in the place of another; (2) a person or thing that takes the place of another.

subterranean situated or occurring underground.

◊ Look up the words beginning with *sub-* in your dictionary. How many do you know? Then look up the nine words listed at the beginning of this discussion that contain a disguised form of the prefix *sub-*. How does the meaning of the prefix contribute to the meanings of these nine words?

Fun With Words

PREFIX SUB-

The following fourteen words begin with the prefix *sub-* meaning "under" or "secretly." Check the word or phrase you believe is closest in meaning to the key word. Answers follow.

1. **suborn** [sə·bôrn′]—(a) to swear in. (b) to bribe or induce to commit perjury. (c) to summon. (d) to arrest for false testimony.
2. **sublimate** [sub′lə·māt]—(a) to refine or purify. (b) to reduce to slavery. (c) to dignify with great honors. (d) to sum up.
3. **substantiate** [səb·stan′shē·āt]— (a) to weaken. (b) to substitute one thing for another. (c) to verify. (d) to make wealthy.
4. **subservient** [səb·sûr′vē·ənt]— (a) fawning and servile. (b) second in command. (c) insincere. (d) unfaithful.
5. **subversive** [səb·vûr′siv]—(a) secret. (b) deceptive. (c) overly humble. (d) tending to overthrow.
6. **subjugate** [sub′jŏŏ·gāt]—(a) to conquer or subdue. (b) to define. (c) to confuse. (d) to cause to wither and decay.
7. **submerge** [səb·mûrj′]—(a) to walk on. (b) to sink. (c) to appear. (d) to join together.
8. **subordinate** [sə·bôr′də·nit]—(a) extraordinary. (b) secondary or minor. (c) rebellious. (d) tamely submissive.
9. **subliminal** [sub·lim′ə·nəl]—(a) equal. (b) attached at the end of a line. (c) below the threshold of consciousness. (d) close to the seashore.
10. **subconscious** [sub·kon′shəs]— (a) mental activity of which a person is usually not aware. (b) below the level of human. (c) under hypnosis. (d) unaware.
11. **subscribe** [səb·skrīb′]—(a) to scorn. (b) to continue to exist. (c) to classify. (d) to give sanction, support, or approval.
12. **subsidiary** [səb·sid′ē·er′ē]—(a) an associate. (b) secondary. (c) government aid. (d) rock strata below the earth's surface.
13. **subtle** [sut′l]—(a) unwilling. (b) unsympathetic. (c) sociable or amiable. (d) keen or discriminating.
14. **subside** [səb·sīd′]—(a) to resist. (b) to become strong. (c) to become less agitated. (d) aligned in rows.

ANSWERS:

1. **suborn**—(b) to bribe or induce to commit perjury. 2. **sublimate**—(a) to refine or purify. 3. **substantiate**—(c) to verify. 4. **subservient**—(a) fawning and servile. 5. **subversive**—(d) tending to overthrow. 6. **subjugate**—(a) to conquer or subdue. 7. **submerge**—(b) to sink. 8. **subordinate**—(b) secondary or minor. 9. **subliminal**—(c) below the threshold of consciousness. 10. **subconscious**—(a) mental activity of which a person is usually not aware. 11. **subscribe**—(d) to give sanction, support, or approval. 12. **subsidiary**—(b) secondary. 13. **subtle**—(d) keen or discriminating. 14. **subside**—(c) to become less agitated.

You don't have to be a superman to have a "super" vocabulary. Of course, the slang word *super,* meaning "first-rate," comes from the prefix *super-,* which is also used in *superman,* "a man possessed of superhuman powers; a superior being." The Latin prefix *super-* means (1) above; over; beyond; (2) more than; greater than; superior; (3) excessively. Here are three core vocabulary words that include the prefix *super-: superficial, superhighway, supernatural.*

superficial derives from *super-* meaning "over" and the root *fic-,* which comes from a Latin word meaning "the face; surface" plus the suffix *-ial* meaning "of or having to do with." Thus, *superficial* literally means "on or over the surface"; hence, "affecting only the surface; going no deeper than the ordinary or obvious."

> *It was a superficial wound, not a serious one.*
> *This student has only a superficial knowledge of his subject.*

superhighway is formed from *super-* meaning "greater than; superior" and the word *highway.* Thus, a *superhighway* is "a highway designed to handle more or faster traffic than a regular highway."

> *The new superhighway cuts our driving time by an hour.*

supernatural comes from *super-* meaning "above or beyond" and the word *natural.* Thus, *supernatural* means "existing or occurring through some agency beyond the known forces of nature; lying outside the natural order." *The supernatural* comprises "those forces, powers, or events that exist, operate, or occur outside the known or natural order."

> *Ghosts are supernatural beings.*
> *Poe wrote strange tales of the supernatural.*

Here are ten additional words that begin with the prefix *super-:*

superannuated (1) retired on a pension because one is over a certain age; (2) too old to be useful; obsolete; out-of-date.

supercilious comes from *super-* meaning "above" and *cilium,* Latin for "eyelid." Literally it means "with raised eyebrows," and thus *supercilious* means "showing contempt or indifference; arrogant."

255

TWO-MINUTE QUICKIE QUIZ
SUPER-WORDS

These five words begin with the prefix *super-*, meaning "above, over, or greater than." Check the word or phrase you believe is closest in meaning to the key word. Answers follow.

1. **superlative** [sə·pûr'lə·tiv]—(a) lavish. (b) everlasting. (c) surplus. (d) supreme.
2. **supercilious** [sōō'pər·sil'ē·əs]—(a) highly intelligent. (b) above reproach. (c) scornfully superior. (d) tending to be a social climber.
3. **supervene** [sōō'pər·vēn']—(a) to follow closely upon something. (b) to overcome. (c) to force out. (d) to come in between.
4. **supersonic** [sōō'pər·son'ik]—(a) characterized by a speed greater than that of sound. (b) high-velocity sound waves. (c) extremely loud and noisy. (d) of unusual size.
5. **superimpose** [sōō'pər·im·pōz']—(a) to force one's demand on others. (b) to lay or place on something else. (c) to find to be above suspicion. (d) to make superfluous.

ANSWERS:

1. **superlative**—(d) supreme. 2. **supercilious**—(c) scornfully superior. 3. **supervene**—(a) to follow closely upon something. 4. **supersonic**—(a) characterized by a speed greater than that of sound. 5. **superimpose**—(b) to lay or place on something else.

superfluous exceeding what is needed; unnecessary; surplus.

superintendent (1) a person who is placed over others to supervise them, as a person in charge of an office, department, etc.; (2) a person who supervises the upkeep and repair of an apartment building.

superlative (1) of supreme excellence or eminence; (2) in grammar, the form of an adjective or adverb expressing the highest degree of comparison.

supernumerary (1) an extra or unnecessary person or thing; (2) being beyond a fixed, standard, or necessary number.

supersede (1) to take the place of, by reason of superior worth, right, newness, etc.; (2) to supplant, replace, annul.

supersensitive excessively sensitive; too easily offended.

superstition (1) a belief based on irrational feelings, marked by a trust in or respect for charms, omens, signs, the supernatural, etc.; literally, "excessive fear of the gods"; (2) any irrational belief.

supervise to have charge of directing workers, a project, etc.; literally, "to oversee."

◊ Look up the many other words in your dictionary that begin with the prefix *super-*. If you remember what *super-* means, you should be able to figure out the meaning of many of these words. Check your own definitions against the dictionary definitions.

PREFIX: SYN- AND ITS DISGUISES

What do synchronized watches have in common with syllables and symphonies? The Greek prefix *syn-* means "together; with." This prefix may also be spelled *syl-*, *sym-*, or *sys-*, as in *syllable, sympathy,* and *system.* Here are eight core vocabulary words making use of the prefix *syn-* or one of its variants: *syllable, sympathy, symphony, synchronize, syncopate, syndrome, synonym, syntax.*

syllable is formed from *syl-* meaning "together" and the root *lab-* meaning "to take." Originally, *syllable* referred to letters or sounds that were "taken together." Hence, a syllable is "the part of a word that is spoken as a single unit, consisting of a vowel alone or with one or more consonants."

The word vocabulary *has five syllables:* vo·cab·u·lar·y.

sympathy derives from the prefix *sym-* meaning "with" or "together" and the Greek root *path-* meaning "to feel" plus the suffix *-y* meaning "the quality or state of being." Thus, *sympathy* means "the quality of feeling with or feeling for someone else; a feeling of compassion for another's suffering; fellow feeling."

The neighbors expressed their sympathy to the widow.

symphony comes from *sym-* meaning "together" and the Greek root *phon-* meaning "sound" plus the suffix *-y* meaning "the act or state of." *Symphony* literally means "the act of sounding together." Hence, a symphony is (1) a musical composition written for all the instruments of the orchestra playing together; (2) a large orchestra; (3) a harmonious blending, as of sounds.

A symphony usually has four movements.
Did you hear the Cleveland Symphony play last night?
Morning brings us a symphony of bird songs.

synchronize is made up of the prefix *syn-* meaning "together" and the Greek root *chron-* meaning "time" plus the suffix *-ize* meaning "to make." Thus, *synchronize* means "to time things together; to adjust two or more things so that they agree with respect to time or speed; to work or cause to work in unison."

Synchronize your watches before you go to your posts.
When a movie is dubbed, the words and lip movements of the actors must be synchronized.

syncopate derives from *syn-* meaning "together" and the Greek root *cop-* meaning "to strike; cut" plus the suffix *-ate*, which is a suffix used to form verbs. *Syncopate* originally meant "to shorten something by cutting part of it out and piecing the rest together." Now *syncopate* means "to place a tone in music so that its accent or beat does not coincide with the regular beat or accent of the music."

Modern jazz usually has syncopated rhythms.

syndrome comes from *syn-* meaning "together" and the Greek root *drom-* meaning "to run." Thus, *syndrome* literally means "something that runs along together with something else," hence "a set of symptoms that occur together and are characteristic of a certain disease or a social or psychological condition."

The delusion of being persecuted is one aspect of the paranoid's syndrome.
The dropout syndrome among students is characterized by increasing absenteeism and indifference to grades.

synonym derives from *syn-* meaning "together" and the Greek root *onym-* meaning "name." Thus, a *synonym* is "a word having the same or almost the same meaning as another word."

The words reply *and* answer *are synonyms.*

syntax is formed from *syn-* meaning "together" and the Greek root *tax-*

meaning "to arrange." Thus, *syntax* means "the arrangement and re-lationship of words in phrases and sentences; sentence structure."

When learning a foreign language, you must study syntax as well as vocabulary and grammar.

Match each *syn-* word with one of the definitions and check your an-swers in a dictionary.

1. **synagogue**; 2. **syndicate**; 3. **synod**; 4. **synopsis**; 5. **synthesis.**

a. a summary or outline, as of a piece of fiction.

b. an association of companies or persons united to pursue a business venture; an agency that sells articles, comic strips, etc. to a number of newspapers.

c. a church council.

d. a place where Jews worship and receive religious instruction.

e. the assembling of separate parts into a whole; a complex whole composed of separate parts.

◊ Various other words begin with the prefix *syn-* or its variants *syl-*, *sym-*, and *sys-* meaning "with" or "together"—for example: *syllogism*, *symmetrical*, *symposium*, *symptom*, *synthetic*, and *system*. Look up these words in your dictionary to be sure you know their meanings and how they are built with the prefix *syn-* or one of its variants.

PREFIX: TRANS-

The Latin prefix *trans-* means (1) across; over; beyond; through; on the other side of; (2) completely; (3) surpassing. Here are six core vocabulary words that make typical use of the prefix *trans-*: *transact*, *transatlantic*, *transcribe*, *transfer*, *transform*, *transmit*.

transact is formed from *trans-* meaning "through" and the Latin root *act-* meaning "to do; drive." Thus, to *transact* means "to carry through; accomplish."

> *It took Philip ten minutes to transact his business at the bank.*

transatlantic derives from *trans-* meaning "across, on the other side of" and the word *Atlantic*. Thus, *transatlantic* means (1) on the other side of the Atlantic Ocean; (2) across or crossing the Atlantic Ocean.

> *We've just heard from our transatlantic representative.*
> *The dispatch was sent by transatlantic cable.*

transcribe is made up of *trans-* meaning "over" and the Latin root *scrib-* meaning "to write." Thus, *transcribe* means "to write over; copy from an original or from notes." *Transcribe* may also mean "to record a radio or television program for later broadcasting."

> *The typist quickly transcribed the letter from her shorthand notes.*
> *This program isn't live; it was transcribed earlier for broadcast.*

transfer comes from *trans-* meaning "across" and the Latin root *fer-* meaning "to carry." Thus, to *transfer* is "to carry across; to move or convey from one person, place, possessor, vehicle, etc., to another." A *transfer* is (1) the act of transferring or state of being transferred; (2) a thing or person transferred; (3) a means of transfer, as a ticket permitting a passenger to change from one bus to another.

> *He transferred his keys from his right hand to his left.*
> *The stock transfer between the two corporations will take place on Friday.*
> *Some of the new students were transfers from other colleges.*
> *Be sure to ask for a transfer to a cross-town bus at Fifth Street.*

transform comes from *trans-* meaning "over, completely" and the word *form*. Thus, *transform* means (1) to give a different form or appearance to; (2) to change the character, nature, condition, etc., of.

> *The Greggs have transformed their garage into a guest house.*

transmit is made up of *trans-* meaning "across" and the root *mit-* meaning "to send." Thus, *transmit* means "to send from one place or person to another; to pass on news, information, etc.; to broadcast."

> *He transmitted your message to me.*
> *On what frequency does this radio station transmit?*

30-SECOND QUICKIE QUIZ
DOCTORS AND THEIR SPECIALTIES

Here's a short quickie quiz. Can you match the doctor with his specialty? Answers follow.

1. **dermatologist** [dûr′mə·tol′·ə·jist]
2. **gynecologist** [gī′nə·kol′ə·jist]
3. **pediatrician** [pē′dē·ə·trish′ən]
4. **podiatrist** [pə·dī′ə·trist]
5. **ophthalmologist** [of′thal·mol′ə·jist]

(a) children and infants
(b) eye diseases
(c) women's disorders
(d) skin
(e) feet

ANSWERS:

1. **dermatologist**—(d) skin. 2. **gynecologist**—(c) women's disorders. 3. **pediatrician**—(a) children and infants. 4. **podiatrist**—(e) feet. 5. **ophthalmologist**—(b) eye diseases.

Here are five additional words prefixed by *trans-:*

transcend (1) to rise above in excellence or degree; (2) to overstep or exceed a limit.

transfusion the transfer of blood from one person or animal to another.

transgress to break a law, oath, etc.; to pass beyond a limit; literally, "to step across a forbidden line."

transparent (1) easy to see through; (2) obvious; open.

transpose (1) to reverse the order or change the place of something; (2) to change music to a different key.

By transposing the letters of rat, you get tar and art.

◇ From the words defined, you can build many additional words. Remembering the definitions that have just been given, can you figure out the meanings of the words below?

transaction	transformer
transcription	transgression
transformation	transmission

Many other words also begin with the prefix *trans-*. How many can you list? Some suggestions: *transient, transistor* (which has a very interesting etymology), *transit, transition, transom, transpire, transplant.*

261

PREFIX: ULTRA-

The Latin prefix *ultra-* means "beyond; surpassing; excessively." It is similar in meaning to the prefixes *super-* and *trans-*. However, *ultra-* is less often used than the other two prefixes. When used in non-technical contexts, it usually means "excessively." Here are two core vocabulary words using the prefix *ultra-* that you should learn: *ultraconservative, ultraviolet.*

ultraconservative is formed from *ultra-* meaning "excessively" and the word *conservative*. Thus, *ultraconservative* means "excessively conservative, especially in politics; reactionary." An *ultraconservative* is "an excessively conservative person."

> *Ultraconservatives often believe that many changes are dangerous.*

ultraviolet comes from *ultra-* meaning "beyond" and the word *violet*. Thus, *ultraviolet* means "lying beyond the violet end of the visible spectrum: said of high-frequency wavelengths."

> *Sunburn is caused by exposure to the sun's ultraviolet rays.*

◇ Look up the words beginning with the prefix *ultra-* in your dictionary. One you will recognize is *ultramodern,* meaning "extremely modern." Are there any others that you should learn because you hear or see them frequently?

PREFIX: UN-

The prefix *un-* means "not; opposed to; lacking; back" and is often used to indicate the reversal of an action.

The prefix *un-* is the last and most important of several negative prefixes that you have learned. What is the difference between *un-* and *in-*, the two most important of these negative prefixes? Notice that *un-* may often indicate a simple lack of something, whereas *in-* is more likely to indicate a definite negative, or "not." For example, *unapproachable* means "hard to approach, as a person who is aloof." In other

QUICKIE QUIZ

Here are ten more words begining with the prefix *un-* meaning "not; opposed to; lacking." Check the word or phrase you believe is closest in meaning to the key word. Answers follow.

1. **unscathed** [un·skāthd′]—(a) innocent. (b) unharmed. (c) burned. (d) angered.
2. **uncompromising** [un·kom′prə·mī′zing]—(a) indifferent. (b) reserved. (c) strict or inflexible. (d) uneasy.
3. **unwonted** [un·wōn′tid]—(a) unaccustomed. (b) not desirable. (c) unable to do wrong. (d) inconsistent.
4. **unkempt** [un·kempt′]—(a) unknown. (b) unfurled. (c) untidy. (d) freed from a cage.
5. **untoward** [un·tôrd′]—(a) unfortunate. (b) moving away or retreating. (c) uncovered. (d) absent-minded.
6. **uncivilized** [un·siv′ə·līzd]—(a) illegal. (b) barbarous. (c) unaffected. (d) barely within the law.
7. **unintelligible** [un′in·tel′ə·jə·bəl] —(a) incapable of being understood. (b) unable to be translated. (c) mutterings. (d) stupid.
8. **unparalleled** [un·par′ə·leld]— (a) out of line. (b) unmatched. (c) following a crooked course of action. (d) premeditated.
9. **unmitigated** [un·mit′ə·gā′tid]— (a) not wise. (b) incorrect. (c) unscrupulous. (d) as bad as can be.
10. **unwieldy** [un·wēl′dē]—(a) unaccustomed. (b) immoral. (c) bulky or clumsy. (d) slowly or carefully.

ANSWERS:

1. **unscathed**—(b) unharmed. 2. **uncompromising**—(c) strict or inflexible. 3. **unwonted**—(a) unaccustomed. 4. **unkempt**—(c) untidy. 5. **untoward**— (a) unfortunate. 6. **uncivilized**—(b) barbarous. 7. **unintelligible**—(a) incapable of being understood. 8. **unparalleled**—(b) unmatched. 9. **unmitigated**—(d) as bad as can be. 10. **unwieldy**—(c) bulky or clumsy.

words, an *unapproachable* person lacks friendliness. *Inapproachable,* if used with precision, means "not approachable; incapable of being reached." An isolated place without a road is *inapproachable* by car.

Here are three core vocabulary words using the prefix *un-: un-American, unbend, uncouth.*

un-American comes from *un-* meaning "not; opposed to" and the word *American.* Thus, *un-American* means (1) out of keeping with

American character, spirit, ideals, etc.; (2) acting against the interests or objectives of the United States; (3) lacking patriotism toward America.

> *The conferring of aristocratic titles is un-American.*
> *Is it un-American to protest a war in which the United States is engaged?*

unbend stems from *un-* meaning "back," indicating the reversal of an action, plus the word *bend*. Thus, *unbend* means (1) to bend back into place again; straighten; (2) to relax, as after tension, exertion, restraint, or formality.

> *Can you unbend this crooked nail?*
> *I unbend after work by watching television.*

uncouth is formed from *un-* meaning "not" and an older English word that is no longer used: *couth*, meaning "known." *Uncouth* originally meant "unknown." Now, of course, *uncouth* means "unknowing"; hence, "lacking refinement; crude; awkward; boorish."

> *It is uncouth to eat peas with a knife.*
> *The peasant, though uncouth in manner and appearance, was nevertheless honest and hard-working.*

◊ There are literally hundreds of words in your dictionary that begin with the prefix *un-*. How many of them can you list in ten minutes? Here are a few to start with: *unable, unarmed, unavoidable, unbearable, unbelievable, uncertain, uncomfortable, undecided, undressed, uneven, unfaithful, ungrateful, unhappy, unjust, unknown, unnatural, unorganized, unprepared, unqualified, unsuccessful, untie, unusual, unwrap.*

Notice that *un-* can be prefixed to an almost endless variety of words. As is true with some other prefixes, you can easily make up a list of *un-* words yourself. Would you like to *uninvite* a guest who has made himself unwelcome, or *unpot* an unhealthy plant, or *uninvent* an unsuccessful excuse? How many valid *un-* words can you make up that are not in your dictionary? Few people know prefixes, roots, and suffixes well enough to make up intelligible words, but *un-* is a good place to start. English is a wonderful language when you know the building blocks! Make up an *un-* word and try it on your family or friends. The chances are good that they will understand exactly what you are trying to say.

EXPLORING WORDS
NUMBERING, COUNTING, AND MEASURING

English has borrowed many words, roots, and prefixes from Greek and Latin that are used in numbering, counting, and measuring. Here is a sample chart of such terms, showing the Greek and Latin forms and how we use them. Be sure you know the meaning of the words used as examples. Remember that September, October, November, and December were the seventh, eighth, ninth, and tenth months in the old Roman calendar.

MEANING	FROM THE GREEK	FROM THE LATIN
half	*hemi-* as in *hemisphere*	*semi-* as in *semicircle*
		demi- as in *demitasse*
one	*mono-* as in *monogamous, monologue*	*uni-* as in *union, unilateral*
first	*proto-* as in *prototype, protoplasm*	*prim-* as in *prime, primary, primitive*
two; twice; double; in two	*di-* as in *dichloride* *dicho-* as in *dichotomy*	*bi-* as in *bicycle, bigamy* *du-* or *duo-* as in *dual, duet, duplex, duodecimal*
three	*tri-* as in *tricycle, trigonometry, trimeter*	*tri-* as in *tricolor, trio* *ter-* as in *tercentenary*
four	*tetra-* as in *tetrameter*	*quadr-* as in *quadrangle, quadrilateral, quadruped*
		quart- as in *quarter, quartet*
five	*penta-* as in *pentagon, pentameter*	*quint-* as in *quintet, quintuplets*
six	*hexa-* as in *hexagonal, hexagram, hexameter*	*sex-* as in *sextet, sextuple*
seven	*hepta-* as in *heptameter*	*sept-* as in *September, septet*
eight	*oct-* as in *octopus, octagonal*	*oct-* as in *October, octave, octet*
nine	*ennea-* as in *ennead*	*Nov-* or *non-* as in *November, nonagon*
ten	*deca-* as in *decade*	*dec-* or *deci-* as in *December, decimal*

3 SUFFIXES—YOUR THIRD KEY TO WORD POWER

Suffixes are less important than roots and prefixes in vocabulary building because they are usually (though not always) added on to a root or word after the primary meaning of the word has been established by the basic root and prefix. In such cases, the suffix serves to indicate the function of the word (that is, its use or part of speech). You should be familiar with suffixes and know how they are used, but you need not learn them as fully as you learned roots and prefixes. The following chapters will tell you what you need to know about suffixes.

Remember what suffixes are and what they do. They are attached to the ends of words just as prefixes are attached to the beginnings. Suffixes can sometimes change the meaning of a word, but they are primarily used to reveal its function. Suffixes, for example, can indicate the number of a noun by changing the singular form to a plural form. Thus, the suffix *-s* added to the word *boy* forms *boys*—the suffix *-s* showing that *boy* is plural. For another example, suffixes can indicate the time of a verb by showing whether the action is in the past or the present. Thus, the suffix *-ed* added to the verb *walk* forms the past tense *walked.*

To state it another way, the meaning of many suffixes is general: they serve primarily to tell you whether a word is used as an action word (verb), a modifier (adjective or adverb), or the name of a person, place, or thing (noun); and they serve to distinguish between such things as number and tense.

NOUN SUFFIXES: ACTS, CONDITIONS, OR STATES

The following fifteen suffixes generally mean (1) the act, state, quality, means, process, result, or condition of (doing or being); (2) the beliefs, teachings, or system of; (3) devotion to.

-acity
> **audacity** the quality of being audacious; boldness.
> **capacity** (1) the ability to receive, hold, or contain; (2) mental ability; (3) specific character or office.

tenacity the quality of being tenacious; stubbornness; toughness.

-acy

celibacy the state of being unmarried.

confederacy the condition of being allied; hence, a union of persons or states for mutual support or action.

fallacy (1) the condition of being in error; hence, an erroneous or misleading notion; (2) any reasoning, argument, etc., that violates logical rules.

-al (or **-ial, -eal**)

betrayal the act of betraying or the state of being betrayed.

denial the act of denying.

refusal the act of refusing.

-ence (or **-ance, -ency, -ancy**)

influence the quality or condition of being able to produce effects on others.

acceptance the act of accepting or the state of being accepted.

-ion

audition (1) the act or sense of hearing; (2) a hearing, especially a trial hearing of a performer.

creation (1) the act of creating, or the fact of being created; (2) anything created, especially by human intelligence or imagination, as an artistic work; (3) everything created; the universe.

union (1) the act of uniting or the state of being united; (2) the joining of persons, parties, nations, etc., for a mutual purpose.

-ism

alcoholism an abnormal or diseased condition caused by excessive use of alcohol.

heroism the state or condition of being heroic; bravery.

skepticism the state or condition of being a skeptic.

-ment (or **-men**)

excitement the state of being excited.

monument literally, a means of remembering someone or something; hence (1) a memorial erected in memory of a person, event, etc.; (2) a tombstone.

specimen a person, animal, plant, or thing regarded as representative of its class or type; a sample.

-mony

matrimony (1) the state or condition of being married; (2) the act or ceremony of marriage.

parsimony the condition of being overly thrify; stinginess.

-ness

coldness (1) the state or condition of being cold; chill. (2) the state of being unenthusiastic or unfriendly.

sleeplessness the condition of not being able to sleep.

goodness the state or condition of being good.

-or

ardor the condition or quality of being eager or enthusiastic; warmth of feeling.

error (1) the condition of being wrong; (2) a mistake.

-sis (or **-sy, -sia**)

analysis (1) an examination of the parts of any complex whole; (2) the act of separating a whole into its parts.

autopsy a medical examination of a corpse.

amnesia partial or total loss of memory; the state of having no memory.

-tude

longitude literally, the quality of being long (like the lines of longitude on a globe); hence, the distance east or west on the earth's surface, measured from the prime meridian that runs through Greenwich, England.

multitude literally, the condition of being many in numbers; hence, a great number or crowd.

-ty (or **-ety, -ity**)

notoriety the state of being widely known and generally disapproved of.

novelty (1) the quality of being new; (2) something new or unusual.

superiority the quality of being superior; excellence.

-ure

aperture an opening.

curvature the state of being curved; a curving.

pressure the act or result of pressing or weighing down on something.

-y

inquiry the act of inquiring or seeking for facts or truth; investigation.

perjury the act of giving false testimony.

victory the state or condition of being a victor; the act or result of winning a contest, a war, etc.; success; triumph.

Fun With Words

COLORFUL ADJECTIVES

Below are sixteen colorful adjectives whose meanings you should know. Check the word or phrase that is closest in meaning to the key word. Answers follow.

1. **pristine** [pris′tēn]—(a) shining. (b) unspoiled or primitive. (c) priggish. (d) honest.
2. **raucous** [rô′kəs]—(a) boisterous. (b) flavorful. (c) strong and aggressive. (d) evil.
3. **mundane** [mun′dān]—(a) lazy. (b) pertaining to the moon. (c) sad or depressing. (d) routine or ordinary.
4. **nostalgic** [nos·tal′jik]—(a) wistfully sentimental. (b) harmless. (c) debonair. (d) nightmarish.
5. **aquiline** [ak′wə·līn]—(a) a blue-green color. (b) noble. (c) hooked or curved like an eagle's beak. (d) bulbous.
6. **dolorous** [dō′lər·əs]—(a) impoverished. (b) lazy. (c) foolish. (d) sad.
7. **lurid** [loor′id]—(a) black and blue. (b) sensational. (c) passionate. (d) enticing.
8. **innocuous** [i·nok′yoō·əs]—(a) empty. (b) immune. (c) simpleminded. (d) harmless.

9. **niggardly** [nig′ərd·lē]—(a) hot and humid. (b) cruel. (c) stingy. (d) gloomy.
10. **obstreperous** [əb·strep′ər·əs]—(a) disagreeable. (b) stubborn. (c) unruly. (d) conceited.
11. **precocious** [pri·kō′shəs]—(a) overconfident. (b) scholarly. (c) showing premature development. (d) conservative.
12. **sallow** [sal′ō]—(a) yellowish in color. (b) salty. (c) unused. (d) fertile.
13. **pallid** [pal′id]—(a) wise. (b) pale. (c) dull. (d) unused.
14. **callous** [kal′əs]—(a) sickly looking. (b) inexperienced. (c) nonchalant. (d) unfeeling.
15. **picaresque** [pik′ə·resk′]—(a) pertaining to a type of fiction with a rogue as a central character. (b) pertaining to a folk dance. (c) quaint. (d) pertaining to a bullfight.
16. **ribald** [rib′əld]—(a) hairless. (b) humorous and indecent. (c) jeering. (d) disrespectful.

ANSWERS:

1. **pristine**—(b) unspoiled or primitive. 2. **raucous**—(a) boisterous. 3. **mundane**—(d) routine or ordinary. 4. **nostalgic**—(a) wistfully sentimental. 5. **aquiline** —(c) hooked or curved like an eagle's beak. 6. **dolorous**—(d) sad. 7. **lurid**—(b) sensational. 8. **innocuous**—(d) harmless. 9. **niggardly**—(c) stingy. 10. **obstreperous**—(c) unruly. 11. **precocious**—(c) showing premature development. 12. **sallow**—(a) yellowish in color. 13. **pallid**—(b) pale. 14. **callous**—(d) unfeeling. 15. **picaresque**—(a) pertaining to a type of fiction with a rogue as a central character. 16. **ribald**—(b) humorous and indecent.

NOUN SUFFIXES: **PEOPLE, PLACES, AND THINGS**

The following ten suffixes of nouns all mean (1) a person or thing that does, practices, or is characterized by or connected with something; (2) a native, citizen, or inhabitant of; (3) a follower of; (4) a place or instrument for.

-an (or **-ian, -ean, -ane**)

    American a native or inhabitant of North America; specifically, an inhabitant or citizen of the United States.

    crustacean a type of animal characterized by crustlike shell, as a lobster or crab.

-ant (or **-ent**)

    inhabitant a person who lives in or inhabits a specific place.

    resident a person who resides in a specific house, city, state, etc.

-ar

    beggar a person who begs for his living.

    scholar a person connected with or characterized by knowledge or studying.

-ary

    dictionary literally, a book connected with speaking; hence, a reference book containing the words of a language, arranged alphabetically with meanings, pronunciations, etc.

    library a place for the collection and storage of books.

    secretary literally, a person who keeps secrets; hence, a person employed to handle the records, letters, etc.; of a business office or of an individual.

-er

    baker a person who bakes bread, cake, etc., for his living.

    golfer a person who plays golf.

    traveler a person who travels.

-ician

    electrician a person who designs, installs, operates, or repairs electrical wiring, equipment, etc.

    logician an expert in the use of logic.

-ist

    communist a person who believes in the doctrines of communism.

    druggist a person who prepares and deals in medical drugs.

    genealogist a specialist in the study of genealogy or family trees.

-ite

> **socialite** a person connected with fashionable social life.
> **suburbanite** a person who lives in the suburbs.

-or

> **agitator** a person or thing that agitates; especially, a person who persists in political or social agitation for change.
> **competitor** a person who competes against another.
> **donor** a person who gives or donates something.

-ory

> **dormitory** a large room with sleeping accommodations for many persons.
> **lavatory** a place for washing, as a bathroom or sink.

The following three suffixes of nouns all mean (1) the art, science, or study of; (2) speech or discourse.

-ics (or **-tics**)

> **dramatics** the art or study of drama, the theater, acting, etc.
> **linguistics** the science of language.

-logy (or **-logue, -ology**)

> **biology** the science of life in all its manifestations.
> **geology** the science that deals with the origin and structure of the earth.

QUICKIEQUIZQUICKIEQUIZQUICKIEQUIZQUICKIEQUIZQUICKIEQUIZQUICKIEQUIZQUICKIEQUIZQUICKIE

30-SECOND QUICKIE QUIZ
-OLOGIES

Can you match the *-ology* with the field of study it pertains to? Answers follow.

1. **theology** [thē·ol′ə·jē]
2. **anthropology** [an′thrə·pol′ə·jē]
3. **geology** [jē·ol′ə·jē]
4. **entomology** [en′tə·mol′ə·jē]
5. **meteorology** [mē′tē·ə·rol′ə·jē]

(a) the development of man
(b) insects
(c) the earth
(d) the weather
(e) religion

ANSWERS:

1. **theology**—(e) religion. 2. **anthropology**—(a) the development of man. 3. **geology**—(c) the earth. 4. **entomology**—(b) insects. 5. **meteorology**—(d) the weather.

QUICKIEQUIZQUICKIEQUIZQUICKIEQUIZQUICKIEQUIZQUICKIEQUIZQUICKIEQUIZQUICKIEQUIZQUICKIE

    catalogue a list of names, objects, etc., usually in alphabetical order and often with accompanying descriptions.

    dialogue a conversation between two or more people, actors, groups, etc.

    monologue a long speech by one person.

-nomy

    astronomy the science that deals with heavenly bodies, their motions, distances, etc.

    economy (1) a system for developing and managing material resources; (2) careful management of money; thrift.

FIVE FAMILIAR SUFFIXES

The following five noun and verb suffixes are widely used, but are not related in meaning as are those already discussed.

-cracy means "rule by; government."

    democracy literally, rule by the people; hence, a form of government in which political power is exercised by the people, either directly or through elected representatives.

    plutocracy (1) government by the wealthy; (2) a class that controls a government by means of its wealth.

NOTE: The suffix -*cracy* has a related suffix -*crat* meaning "a person who supports a type of government or who belongs to a social class," such as *democrat, plutocrat, aristocrat.*

-graph means (1) a writing or drawing; (2) an instrument for writing, describing, or making sounds.

    autograph (1) literally, a self-writing; hence, one's own signature; (2) to sign something with one's own signature.

    telegraph (1) literally, distance-writing; hence, a device using coded impulses that are sent by wire or radio waves as messages; (2) to communicate by telegraph.

    phonograph a motor-driven turntable with a pickup attachment for the playing of phonograph records.

NOTE: The suffix -*graph* has a related suffix -*graphy* meaning "the art of writing or drawing," as in *geography, photography, biography.*

-meter means (1) a measure; (2) an instrument for measuring.

    diameter (1) literally, the measure through; hence a straight line passing through the center of a circle and ending at the circumference; (2) the length of such a line.

    thermometer an instrument for measuring heat or temperature.

NOTE: The suffix *-meter* has a related suffix *-metry* meaning "the art or science of measuring," as in *geometry, trigonometry.*

-scope means "an instrument for viewing or observing."

    microscope literally, an instrument for viewing that which is smallest; hence, an instrument used for magnifying objects too small to be seen, or to be seen in detail, by the naked eye.

    stethoscope literally, an instrument for observing the chest; hence, a device for conveying the sounds of the chest to the doctor's ears.

    telescope literally, an instrument for viewing a distance; hence, an instrument for enlarging the image of a distant object.

-s (-es) indicates that the noun is in the plural form. It means that there are two or more persons, places, or things being spoken of.

    The chairs are on the porch.
    Mr. Smith owns several houses.
    Foxes have been stealing our chickens.

SUFFIXES THAT FORM VERBS

The seven suffixes discussed here are added to roots or words in order to form verbs (words indicating action) or to indicate the tense of a verb.

-ate, -fy, -ish, and **-ize** are verb suffixes that mean (1) to cause to be, become, have, or do; (2) to make; (3) to act or act upon; (4) to subject to; (5) to act in the manner of; practice. Here are some examples:

decimate literally, to act upon a whole so as to take away a tenth; to select a group by lot and kill one out of every ten; hence, to kill or destroy a large proportion.

273

nominate literally, to cause to be named; hence, to name or propose as a candidate.

terminate to cause to end or stop.

electrify literally, to make electric; hence, to install electricity.

gratify literally, to make pleasing; hence, (1) to please; (2) to satisfy or indulge.

pacify (1) to make peaceful; (2) to calm or soothe.

admonish literally, to cause to be warned; hence, (1) to advise someone of a fault; to reprove; (2) to caution against error or danger; to warn.

demolish (1) to tear down; (2) to destroy.

extinguish (1) to put out, as a fire; (2) to wipe out or destroy, as life.

Christianize to cause to become Christian.

terrorize to subject to terror.

criticize to act in the manner of a critic or to practice criticism.

-s indicates that the verb, or action word, is in the present tense. It means that the action is taking place in the present, or that it is habitual or takes place at a regular time. This suffix also indicates that the subject of the verb is the third person singular, that one person or thing—one *he, she,* or *it*—is responsible for the action.

> *Nanette comes to see us every Sunday.*
> *Mr. Smith goes to his office every day at nine.*
> *The young girl dances well.*
> *The late-morning train always arrives on time.*
> *It occurs to me that I made a mistake.*

-ed indicates that the verb is in some form of the past tense. It means that the action has taken place and is now either partly or completely finished.

> *He whisked out of sight as I approached.*
> *Jerry has already played in five professional football games.*
> *When he was in college, he played football.*
> *Before he entered Western, he had played football in high school.*

-ing indicates that the action word will appear with some form of the verb *to be* and will signify a continuing action. It means that *am,* *are, is, were, was, has been, have been,* or *had been* is part of the verb form.

> *I am depending on you.*
> *He was driving too fast.*
> *We have been trying to improve our vocabulary—and still are.*

TWENTY-NINE SUFFIXES THAT FORM MODIFIERS

All the suffixes listed here are added to roots or words in order to form modifiers; they indicate that the new word functions as an adjective or adverb.

Suffix: *-al* and Related Suffixes

-al (or its variant spelling **-ial**), **-ar, -ary, -ic, -id, -ile, -ine, -ish, -oid,** and **-ory** are adjective suffixes meaning (1) of, pertaining to, of the nature of, like; (2) having, related to, or serving for.

equal of the same size, quality, rank, character, etc.
filial of or pertaining to a son or daughter.
manual of or pertaining to the hand or hands; done by the hands.
postal pertaining to the mails.

popular (1) of or pertaining to the people at large; (2) liked by most people; (3) suited to the means of the people.
similar like something else or one another, but not identical.

honorary pertaining to an office, title, etc., bestowed as an honor, usually without powers, duties, or salary.
pecuniary consisting of or pertaining to money.
secondary of second rank, grade, influence, etc.; subordinate; subsequent.

academic pertaining to an academy, college, or university; scholarly.
chromatic pertaining to color or colors.
despotic of or like a despot; tyrannical.

gravid heavy with child; pregnant.
humid having much water vapor, as air.

lucid (1) having light; shining; bright; (2) clear; easily understood; (3) rational; mentally sound.

juvenile pertaining to the young; young; youthful.

volatile literally, flying; hence, (1) evaporating rapidly at ordinary temperature on exposure to the air; (2) easily influenced; fickle; changeable.

bovine belonging or pertaining to the family of animals that includes oxen, cows, etc.

canine (1) of or like a dog; (2) of the dog family.

feline (1) of or like a cat; (2) of the cat family.

boyish of or like a boy or boys.

greenish of or like green; somewhat green.

ovoid like an egg; egg-shaped.

spheroid similar to a sphere; nearly sphere-shaped.

compulsory (1) involving or using compulsion, or being coercive; (2) required.

introductory serving as an introduction.

laudatory of the nature of praise; complimentary.

Suffix: *-ate* and Related Forms

-ate, -fic, -ose, -ous, -ulent (and its variant spelling **-olent**), **-ulous,** and **-y** are adjective suffixes meaning "full of, like, having, making or causing, given to, or characterized by."

adequate equal to or having what is required.

caudate having a tail.

pinnate (1) like a feather; (2) having the shape or arrangement of a feather.

soporific causing or tending to cause sleep.

terrific literally, full of or causing terror; hence, (1) extreme, intense, or tremendous; (2) wonderful, great, or splendid.

grandiose (1) characterized by grandeur or producing an effect of grandeur; (2) pretentiously grand.

verbose wordy.

glorious (1) full of or deserving glory; (2) bringing glory or honor; (3) splendid; magnificent.

joyous full of joy; causing joy; joyful.

opulent having or showing great wealth; rich.
redolent full of a pleasant fragrance; giving off a scent.
violent (1) coming from or characterized by physical force; (2) harsh or severe; (3) extreme or intense.

credulous given to believing on slight evidence; gullible.
populous full of people; crowded.

feathery (1) covered with feathers; (2) light or airy.
risky characterized by risk; full of risk.

Suffix: -*able* and Related Forms

-able (and its variant spelling **-ible**), **-acious, -ile,** and **-ive** are adjective suffixes meaning (1) able, able to be, or capable of being; (2) given to, likely to, or tending to; (3) characterized by or having the character or quality of.

peaceable (1) given to keeping the peace; (2) peaceful or tranquil.
audible capable of being heard.
terrible (1) likely to arouse terror; appalling; (2) extreme; severe; (3) awe-inspiring; (4) inferior; very bad.

tenacious tending to hold on strongly; hence, (1) holding strongly to opinions, beliefs, etc.; (2) stubborn.
voracious (1) eating with greediness or given to devouring things; (2) greedy; (3) never satisfied.

agile able to move quickly and easily.
docile able to be taught; obedient.

attractive (1) tending to attract interest, admiration, or affection; (2) exerting physical attraction, as a magnet.
massive having the quality of mass; having great bulk and weight.
secretive given to secrecy; reticent.

Suffix: -*an*

-an (or its variant spellings **-ian, -ean, -ane**) is an adjective suffix meaning (1) of, pertaining to, belonging to, or living in; (2) following.
human of, belonging to, or characteristic of man.

Confucian of or pertaining to Confucius; following the teachings of Confucius.

Grecian of, from, or pertaining to Greece or its people; Greek.

European of, from, or pertaining to Europe or its peoples.

urbane literally, belonging to the city; hence, having the refinement or elegance of manner associated with city life; suave.

Suffix: *-less*

-less is an adjective suffix meaning (1) lacking or without; (2) not able to; (3) not susceptible to or capable of being.

lifeless without life; inanimate or dead.

countless not capable of being counted; too many to count.

priceless without a price; too valuable to have a price.

sleepless not able to sleep; wakeful.

stainless (1) without a stain or spot; (2) not susceptible to staining; easy to keep clean.

toothless (1) not characterized by teeth, as a bird; (2) having lost all of one's teeth.

Suffix: *-ent*

-ent (or its variant spelling **-ant**) is an adjective suffix meaning "having the quality of or performing the action of." In many cases *-ent* is equivalent to *-ing*.

incumbent (1) resting upon one as a moral obligation; obligatory; (2) resting, leaning, or weighing upon something.

stringent literally, drawing tight; hence, compelling adherence to strict requirements; severe.

dormant (1) sleeping or motionless through sleep; (2) inactive.

Suffix: *-ing*

-ing is used to form the present participle of verbs and to form adjectives based on these participles. Among other things, it can mean (1) now doing the action indicated; (2) for or used for; (3) that results in. It is used with these meanings in the following phrases:

a running man   a cooking apple   a winning number

Suffix: -ed

-ed is used to form adjectives based on the past participles of verbs. It means "one who or that which has been or was."

> an educated man an overrated book
> an interrupted journey a scratched table

The suffix **-ed** is also used to form adjectives based on nouns. When so used, it means "one who or that which has, is, or resembles."

> a four-footed animal a winged cupid
> a blue-eyed girl dogged determination
> a stoop-shouldered man an eared seal

Suffix: -er

-er may be used to form the comparative of both adjectives and adverbs. It means "more than another or others."

> colder higher smaller sooner
> greater longer shorter later
> brighter greener duller sleepier

Suffix: -est

-est may be used to form the superlative of both adjectives and adverbs. It means "the most; the most of any or of all."

> coldest highest smallest soonest
> greatest longest shortest latest

Suffix: -ly

-ly is a suffix added to words to form modifiers—sometimes forming adjectives from nouns, and sometimes forming adverbs from either nouns or adjectives. It can mean (1) being or acting as; (2) in a certain manner or time; (3) characterized by; (4) with respect to.

> a friendly man recently ill
> speaking quickly a perfectly lovely girl
> a daily delivery physically sound
> suddenly afraid mentally unbalanced

EXPLORING WORDS

SOME WORD MINIATURES

English has a number of suffixes that are called diminutives; they show that the word to which they are attached refers to a miniature-sized version of the object. The diminutive suffixes are: *-cle, -cule, -el, -et* (or *-ette*), *-il, -let, -ling,* and *-ule.* All these suffixes mean "small." Here are fourteen words using these diminutive suffixes:

booklet a small book.

capsule literally, a small box; hence, (1) a small soluble container for enclosing a dose of medicine; (2) a small, detachable compartment of an airplane or spacecraft.

cigarette literally, a small cigar; hence, a small roll of finely cut tobacco for smoking, wrapped in a cylinder of paper.

codicil [kod′ə·səl] literally, a small writing tablet; hence, a supplement to a will, changing or explaining something; an addition. A codicil is so called because it is brief.

darling literally, little dear (*dar-* is an ancient variant spelling of *dear*); hence, a person tenderly loved.

duckling a young duck.

globule [glob′yo͞ol] literally, a small globe; hence, a tiny sphere of matter or drop of liquid.

gosling a young goose.

islet a small island.

leaflet literally, a small leaf, as a leaf of folded paper; hence, a small printed sheet of paper or a brochure.

molecule literally, a small mass; hence, the smallest particle of an element or compound that can exist separately without losing its physical or chemical properties.

morsel literally, a small bite; hence, a small piece of anything.

particle (1) a small part or piece of matter; a speck; (2) a very small amount.

suckling literally, an unweaned young animal or child; hence, (1) an unweaned mammal; (2) an infant or very young child.

PART TWO

Spell It Right

SPELLING—A SKILL THAT CAN BE LEARNED

Do some people have an inborn talent for spelling that many of us lack? The answer is no. An ability to spell is not inherited, and neither is an inability to spell. Spelling is a skill that can be learned. If it seems to come easy for some people, it is because they have learned it. You can become an excellent speller if you want to.

There are four main reasons why many normal, intelligent adults have trouble with spelling: (1) They never acquire the habit of looking closely at words, of questioning the spelling as they read a word or write it down; (2) they learned to hate spelling at school because, instead of being taught helpful rules, they were forced to learn seemingly disorganized lists of words; (3) they lack the energy, will power, or ambition to succeed at spelling; (4) although they know they have bad spelling habits, they have not yet realized that they can change those habits by studying meaningful word lists and practical guides to spelling power. This section provides you with just such lists and guides. Study them carefully and you will soon discover that you have broken bad old habits and have acquired good new ones.

Let us begin by admitting that English is not an easy language to spell. There are twenty-six letters in our alphabet as against about forty-five basic sounds—and the letters seldom match the sounds! Thus, one specific sound can be (and often is) spelled in a number of different ways; and, to complicate the problem even further, a single letter may represent any one of a variety of sounds (for instance, *a* stands for one sound in *day*, another in *hat*, and still another in *call*). Similarly, two vowels used together can represent totally dissimilar sounds, as the *ou* in *bough* [bou], the *ou* in *tough* [tuf], and that in *through* [thro͞o].

Matching a letter of the alphabet with a familiar sound can sometimes stump even the best of spellers. Take, for example, the simple words *pArade, sickEn, clarIty, melOn,* and *focUs.* In those five words the letters *a, e, i, o,* and *u* are all pronounced precisely the same way, as "uh"[ə]. Is it any wonder that some people have a hard time getting the fourth letter right in *sepArate?* Or, for an even more striking example, say the following words out loud: *stAge, rAIn, gAUge, dAY, matinEE, brEAk, vEIl, rEIGn, wEIGH, thEY.* The very same sound in those ten words [ā] is spelled in ten entirely different ways—and there are others as well.

There is only one rule, therefore, that will solve all spelling problems for you: When in doubt, look up the word in your dictionary. You should always have a dictionary within easy reach—in school, in the office, and at home.

Remember, though, that a dictionary is a reference book, not a teaching book. It will tell you how to spell a hard word, but if you do not learn the word now, you'll probably have to look it up all over again next week. So, although you can rely on your dictionary in a pinch, you should not rely on it exclusively. There are dozens of useful and easy-to-learn rules and guides that can make you a competent speller without constant reference to the dictionary. In the following chapters you will find such spelling aids explained, along with lists of related words and tips on how to master individual words that are your own personal spelling demons. Even the best of spellers encounter a few stumbling blocks. The spellings of look-alike words with different meanings, such as *principal* and *principle,* have often been confused by writers who should know better.

The words in these pages have been chosen with care. They are the useful words most commonly misspelled, as revealed in hundreds of thousands of tests given to elementary-school, high-school, secretarial-school, and college students, to Civil Service and other government workers, to job applicants, and to employees and executives of large companies. The words also include spelling demons from the Fitzgerald Master List, the Remington Rand List, state-board and college-entrance examinations, Gregg Secretarial lists, *The American School Board Journal,* style books of newspapers, magazines, and book publishers, and even from the National Spelling Bee.

You will almost certainly find your personal spelling demons discussed here. Don't waste time on the many words whose spellings you have already mastered. Concentrate on the ones you aren't sure of. As with learning to drive a car, play a game, or bake a cake, learning to spell will take time and concentration. But if your heart is in it, you will succeed in teaching yourself to be a better speller by making the most of these rules, tips, and tests. You will find that it is fun to test yourself, the members of your family, and your friends.

Faulty spelling can hinder a person's progress in both business and social life. On the other hand, the man or woman who writes business reports, letters, club notes, and so on without mistakes in spelling is very often the person who gets ahead. Now is your chance. Be sure to take it. Perfecting your spelling will require some effort and practice on your part, but you will find it worthwhile.

1 THE MOST FREQUENTLY MISSPELLED WORDS

What is the most commonly misspelled word in the English language? No one knows for sure. But it may well be any of these four:

all right	receive
coming	separate

For school children, the most frequently misspelled word might be any of the above four or *bicycle, description, really, similar,* or *writing.*

For office workers, secretaries, and businessmen, the culprit might be any of these:

advertisement	envelope
correspondence	recommend
definite	schedule

Housewives might most frequently misspell any of these words:

acquaintance	pleasant
development	spinach

This chapter will concentrate on everyday words that cause more than eighty percent of all spelling mistakes. Learn these words, drill yourself on them, review them at every opportunity. After you master them, spelling should never again be a major problem for you.

Sixth-Grade Spelling Demons

Here is a list of some of the most common spelling demons of sixth-graders. Many well-educated adults still misspell some of them. Check yourself to see whether you need to relearn any of them.

accommodate	Christmas	minute
across	coming	missile
already (one word)	deceive	niece
arithmetic	description, describe	really
athletics, athlete	February	separate
balloon	forty	similar
bicycle	fourth	sincerely
business	good night (two words)	studying
ceiling	grammar	surprise
challenge	Halloween	writing, written

High-School Spelling Demons

The following list contains eighty-seven of the words that are most frequently misspelled by high-school seniors and graduates. It is based on classroom lists, studies in *The American School Board Journal,* state-board and regents' tests, college-entrance and placement exams, and job-application tests given by large firms. Thus, this list is based on tests given to more than 87,000 high-school seniors and graduates from 750 different American high schools. Note that the words in italics also appeared on the sixth-grade spelling list, and that high-school students have been misspelling them since the sixth grade!

absence	embarrass	occasion
absurd	environment	occurred
accidentally	equipped	occurrence
accommodate	escape	omitted
across	exaggerate	opportunity
advertisement	excellent	parallel
all right	existence	parliament
amateur	experience	performance
athletics	familiar	permanent
attendance	fascinate	pleasant
beginning	*February*	possess
believe	foreign	prejudice
business	*forty*	privilege
coming	government	professor
committee	*grammar*	receive
condemn	guidance	recommend
conscious	humorous	repetition
convenient	imaginary	restaurant
correspondence	immediately	rhythm
criticize	independent	schedule
definite	irresistible	*separate*
dependent	laboratory	*similar*
descend	lightning	success
description	losing	*surprise*
desperate	lovely	tragedy
develop	misspelled	truly
difference	necessary	villain
disappoint	neighbor	weird
dispensable	*niece*	*writing*

285

TWO-MINUTE QUICKIE QUIZ
EASY

Choose the correctly spelled word from each pair below. This quiz contains problems from the sixth-grade and high-school-graduate lists. Take the test repeatedly until you do not hesitate at any pair, and can give all the correct answers in two minutes. Answers follow.

1.	(a) separate	(b) seperate
2.	(a) cieling	(b) ceiling
3.	(a) schedual	(b) schedule
4.	(a) parliament	(b) parlament
5.	(a) comming	(b) coming
6.	(a) wierd	(b) weird
7.	(a) posess	(b) possess
8.	(a) condem	(b) condemn
9.	(a) missile	(b) missle
10.	(a) speech	(b) speach
11.	(a) truely	(b) truly
12.	(a) fourty	(b) forty
13.	(a) ninty	(b) ninety
14.	(a) writing	(b) writting
15.	(a) written	(b) writen
16.	(a) lovely	(b) lovly
17.	(a) Halloween	(b) Haloween
18.	(a) until	(b) untill
19.	(a) decieve	(b) deceive
20.	(a) restaurant	(b) resteraunt
21.	(a) accommodate	(b) acommodate
22.	(a) February	(b) Febuary
23.	(a) beseige	(b) besiege
24.	(a) balloon	(b) baloon
25.	(a) excellent	(b) excelent

ANSWERS:

1. (a) separate. 2. (b) ceiling. 3. (b) schedule. 4. (a) parliament. 5. (b) coming. 6. (b) weird. 7. (b) possess. 8. (b) condemn. 9. (a) missile. 10. (a) speech. 11. (b) truly. 12. (b) forty. 13. (b) ninety. 14. (a) writing. 15. (a) written. 16. (a) lovely. 17. (a) Halloween. 18. (a) until. 19. (b) deceive. 20. (a) restaurant. 21. (a) accommodate. 22. (a) February. 23. (b) besiege. 24. (a) balloon. 25. (a) excellent.

Could You Pass a Civil Service Exam?

Since many people who take written Civil Service exams are likely to be high-school graduates, the words most frequently misspelled on these exams are almost the same as those on the high-school spelling list. In addition, Civil Service exams show twenty-five more spelling demons related to government, finance, and office work. Here are those additional words:

accident	federal	salary
auxiliary	filing (vs. filling)	simplified
career	legality	society
catalogue	mechanism	supervisor
clerical	monetary	technical
county (vs. country)	municipal	tendency
comptroller [kən·trō′lər]	personnel (vs. personal)	yield
enforcement	president	
expedient	responsibility	

Two Years of College

This list contains seventy-six words most frequently misspelled by students after two years of college work. Note that forty-two of these, printed in italics, are carried over from the high-school list. Obviously these are words that many students cannot spell when they graduate from high school and still can't manage after two years of college. The list is based on spelling tests that were given to more than 27,000 students and adults who had completed two years of college at 135 institutions.

absence	cemetery	*dependent*	*environment*
accidentally	coming	descendant	*exaggerate*
achieve	*committee*	desirable	exceed
aggravate	competition	despair	exercise
all right	conscientious	*develop*	*existence*
amateur	*conscious*	dining	*foreign*
appearance	convenience	disappear	*forty*
argument	*correspondence*	*disappoint*	*government*
athlete	council	*dispensable*	grievance
believe	*criticize*	*embarrass*	*irresistible*
benefited	definitely	enforcement	knowledge

287

laboratory	*occurrence*	procedure	*rhythm*
losing	*omitted*	proceed	*schedule*
maintenance	*parallel*	pronunciation	*separate*
marriage	*permanent*	*receive*	superintendent
mischievous	permissible	*recommend*	supersede
noticeable	precede	*repetition*	*tragedy*
occasion	*prejudice*	responsibility	*villain*
occurred	*privilege*	*restaurant*	*weird*

Business and Professional People Often Have Spelling Problems

Many college graduates, business executives, and professional people still have spelling problems. Here are fifty-one words they misspell most often. In this list, the words printed in italics are carried over from the two-years-of-college list. The other words not printed in italics are "new."

accessible	*embarrass*	*permissible*
acquainted	envelope	perseverance
all right	*exceed*	*precede*
analyze	*existence*	*prejudice*
appearance	incidentally	*privilege*
assistant	insistent	*proceed*
burglar	intercede	recognize
campaign	*irresistible*	*recommend*
canceled	irritable	*repetition*
coming	*laboratory*	*restaurant*
conscientious	license	*schedule*
coolly	loneliness	seize
correspondence	mortgage	*superintendent*
desirable	*occasion*	*supersede*
develop	*occurred*	*villain*
dispensable	*occurrence*	*weird*
drunkenness	*omitted*	withhold

The typical high-school graduate can spell about half of the words in this list correctly. The typical college graduate can spell thirty-seven (73%) of them correctly. What is your score?

It is interesting that *coming* has been on all spelling-demon lists since the sixth-grade list. It is certainly not hard to learn, but it must be hard to remember. Twenty other words on the business and professional list were not only on the college-sophomore list but also on the high-school list. This indicates how difficult bad spelling habits are to break. Here's your chance. Learn every word on each of the above lists thoroughly; then wait two days and look at the list again. If you still can't spell every word without hesitation, restudy the words that stump you.

QUICKIEQUIZQUICKIEQUIZQUICKIEQUIZQUICKIEQUIZQUICKIEQUIZQUICKIEQUIZQUICKIEQUIZQUICKIE

TWO-MINUTE QUICKIE QUIZ
MEDIUM

Choose the correctly spelled word from each pair below. This quiz comes from the high-school, Civil Service, and college lists. Repeat the test until you can give all the correct answers in two minutes. Answers follow.

1. (a) rhythm	(b) rythm	13. (a) occassion	(b) occasion
2. (a) foreign	(b) foriegn	14. (a) professor	(b) proffesor
3. (a) equiped	(b) equipped	15. (a) committee	(b) commitee
4. (a) absence	(b) abcense	16. (a) permanant	(b) permanent
5. (a) criticise	(b) criticize	17. (a) independent	(b) independant
6. (a) priviledge	(b) privilege	18. (a) embarass	(b) embarrass
7. (a) prejudise	(b) prejudice	19. (a) escape	(b) excape
8. (a) omitted	(b) omited	20. (a) humourus	(b) humorous
9. (a) dependant	(b) dependent	21. (a) argument	(b) arguement
10. (a) irresistible	(b) irresistable	22. (a) performence	(b) performance
11. (a) recommend	(b) reccommend	23. (a) indifferance	(b) indifference
12. (a) occurred	(b) occured	24. (a) attendence	(b) attendance

ANSWERS:

1. (a) rhythm. 2. (a) foreign. 3. (b) equipped. 4. (a) absence. 5. (b) criticize. 6. (b) privilege. 7. (b) prejudice. 8. (a) omitted. 9. (b) dependent. 10. (a) irresistible. 11. (a) recommend. 12. (a) occurred. 13. (b) occasion. 14. (a) professor. 15. (a) committee. 16. (b) permanent. 17. (a) independent. 18. (b) embarrass. 19. (a) escape. 20. (b) humorous. 21. (a) argument. 22. (b) performance. 23. (b) indifference. 24. (b) attendance.

QUICKIEQUIZQUICKIEQUIZQUICKIEQUIZQUICKIEQUIZQUICKIEQUIZQUICKIEQUIZQUICKIEQUIZQUICKIE

How Do the Spelling Experts Do?

Some people are particularly good spellers—among them English teachers, editors, and writers. The following list consists of sixty-two reasonably plain, everyday words that are most commonly misspelled by even such experts. Those words in the list that are followed by an asterisk (*) have determined high-school-student winners—and losers —of the annual United States National Spelling Bee. How many of these words can you spell correctly? (Where a second spelling is termed "also acceptable," the first is nonetheless preferred.)

abscess*
accelerator
aggressor*
allotted
annihilate*
assassin
battalion*
besiege
broccoli*
catalyst*
category
chrysanthemum*
connoisseur*
demagogue
desiccate*
dilapidated
discriminate
disheveled
dissipate
ecstasy*
effervescent

exhilarate*
fission*
fricassee*
fuselage
gaiety
gynecologist
harebrained*
hippopotamus*
hypocrisy*
immaculate
innocuous
inoculate
liquefy*
millionaire
miscellaneous
moccasin*
paraffin
paralyze
pedagogue
penitentiary
perspiration

phlegm
picnicking
prairie
prescription
propeller
questionnaire*
raspberry
requiem*
rhinoceros
sacrilegious*
sheriff
sieve
solder [sod'ər]
subpoena*
tariff
tonsillitis
tyranny
vacillate
vanilla
victuals* [vit'lz]

Note that such "simple" words as *category, gaiety, raspberry,* and *vanilla* are on this experts' list. Are you surprised? Don't be. So-called "simple" words can be among the worst spelling demons.

No question about it: This last list is a tough one. Most college graduates can spell only about thirty-five (56%) of these words. Most experts get about fifty-three (85%) right. Use the experts' list for fun —to stump your family and friends and to hold your own spelling bees at home.

THREE-MINUTE QUICKIE QUIZ
HARD

Choose the correctly spelled word from each pair below. This quiz is from the college-graduate and experts' lists. Take the test repeatedly until you can give all the correct answers in three minutes. Answers follow.

1. (a) campagne	(b) campaign
2. (a) recognize	(b) reconize
3. (a) sherrif	(b) sheriff
4. (a) dissipate	(b) disippate
5. (a) genealogy	(b) geneology
6. (a) develope	(b) develop
7. (a) an envelop	(b) an envelope
8. (a) sieve	(b) seive
9. (a) ecstasy	(b) exstacy
10. (a) hypocracy	(b) hypocrisy
11. (a) proceed	(b) procede
12. (a) exceed	(b) excede
13. (a) preceed	(b) precede
14. (a) supercede	(b) supersede
15. (a) responsability	(b) responsibility
16. (a) desireable	(b) desirable
17. (a) assistant	(b) assistent
18. (a) seize	(b) sieze
19. (a) cemetary	(b) cemetery
20. (a) mischievious	(b) mischievous
21. (a) questionnaire	(b) questionaire
22. (a) millionnaire	(b) millionaire
23. (a) auxilliary	(b) auxiliary
24. (a) perscription	(b) prescription
25. (a) millennium	(b) millenium

ANSWERS:

1. (b) campaign. 2. (a) recognize. 3. (b) sheriff. 4. (a) dissipate. 5. (a) genealogy. 6. (b) develop. 7. (b) an envelope. 8. (a) sieve. 9. (a) ecstasy. 10. (b) hypocrisy. 11. (a) proceed. 12. (a) exceed. 13. (b) precede. 14. (b) supersede. 15. (b) responsibility. 16. (b) desirable. 17. (a) assistant. 18. (a) seize. 19. (b) cemetery. 20. (b) mischievous. 21. (a) questionnaire. 22. (b) millionaire. 23. (b) auxiliary. 24. (b) prescription. 25. (a) millennium.

2 SAYING IT AND SPELLING IT

Many simple words are misspelled because they are mispronounced. Thus, if you mispronounce *Feb·ru·ar·y* as *Feb·yoo·ar·y* or *ath·lete* as *ath·a·lete,* you are likely to misspell them, too. Here is a list of fourteen simple words that are often mispronounced. You will have no trouble with the spellings if you say the words correctly.

accidentALly	goverNment
arCtic	libRary
asparAgus	PERspiration
aTHlete	PREscription
envirONment	sophOmore
eScape	temperAment
FebRuary	temperAture

When Pronunciation Isn't Much Help

Sometimes, of course, proper pronunciation won't help you to spell a word properly. For example, the "uh" sound (the schwa or ə sound) can be spelled in many different ways: as the letter *a, e, i, o,* or *u.* You must learn which of these letters is used in spelling certain words. Pronunciation won't help.

Silent letters are also a problem. A silent letter is one that is necessary for the correct spelling of a word but that is not pronounced. Thus, the *g* in *gnat* and the *b* in *climb* are silent letters. *Gnat* and *climb* are not spelling demons, of course, but some words having silent letters are. Here is a list of words in which pronunciation doesn't help in spelling. The silent letters appear in parentheses.

han(d)kerchief	r(h)yme	recei(p)t
We(d)nesday	r(h)ythm	ai(s)le
poi(g)nant	parl(i)ament	vi(s)count
rei(g)n	a(l)mond	apos(t)le
ex(h)ibition	colum(n)	ches(t)nut
r(h)apsody	condem(n)	gris(t)le
r(h)eumatism	cor(ps) (silent *p*	mor(t)gage
r(h)inoceros	and silent *s*)	gun(w)ale
r(h)ubarb	(p)tomaine	(w)retch

Many other words have silent letters, such as *han(d)some, g(h)ost, (h)our, i(s)land, lis(t)en, (w)rong,* etc., but most of them are not spelling demons for most adults.

Thus, pronunciation can sometimes help your spelling (as with *Feb(R)uary* and *at(H)lete*) and can sometimes be of no help at all (as with *parl(i)ament* and *mor(t)gage*). When pronunciation can help you, use it. When it can't help, use the spelling tips, rules, and lists that you will learn in the following chapters.

QUICKIEQUIZQUICKIEQUIZQUICKIEQUIZQUICKIEQUIZQUICKIEQUIZQUICKIEQUIZQUICKIEQUIZQUICKIE

ONE-MINUTE QUICKIE QUIZ
SPELLING AND PRONUNCIATION

Choose the correctly spelled word from each pair below. Repeat the test until you can give all correct answers in one minute. Answers follow.

1. (a) apostle	(b) aposle	13. (a) temperament (b) temperment
2. (a) environment (b) enviroment	14. (a) aile	(b) aisle
3. (a) prespiration (b) perspiration	15. (a) poignant	(b) poinant
4. (a) perscription (b) prescription	16. (a) hankerchief (b) handkerchief
5. (a) morgage	(b) mortgage	17. (a) receipt	(b) receit
6. (a) lisle	(b) laile	18. (a) artic	(b) arctic
7. (a) condem	(b) condemn	19. (a) chessnut	(b) chestnut
8. (a) accidentally (b) accidently	20. (a) almond	(b) amond
9. (a) parlament	(b) parliament	21. (a) exhibition	(b) exibition
10. (a) athalete	(b) athlete	22. (a) asparagus	(b) aspargus
11. (a) rhubarb	(b) rubarb	23. (a) escape	(b) excape
12. (a) rhinestone	(b) rinestone	24. (a) tomaine	(b) ptomaine
		25. (a) rinoceros	(b) rhinoceros

ANSWERS:

1. (a) aposTle. 2. (a) enviroNment. 3. (b) PERspiration. 4. (b) PREscription. 5. (b) morTgage. 6. (a) liSle. 7. (b) condemN. 8. (a) accidentALly. 9. (b) pàrlIament. 10. (b) atHlete. 11. (a) rHubarb. 12. (a) rHinestone. 13. (a) temperAment. 14. (b) aiSle. 15. (a) poiGnant. 16. (b) hanDkerchief. 17. (a) receiPt. 18. (b) arCtic. 19. (b) chesTnut. 20. (a) aLmond. 21. (a) exHibition. 22. (a) asparAgus. 23. (a) eScape. 24. (b) Ptomaine. 25. (b) rHinoceros.

QUICKIEQUIZQUICKIEQUIZQUICKIEQUIZQUICKIEQUIZQUICKIEQUIZQUICKIEQUIZQUICKIEQUIZQUICKIE

3 WHICH IS IT: -ABLE or -IBLE?

Words ending in *-able* and *-ible* are spelling nightmares because their endings sound alike. Words such as *agreeable, comfortable, horrible, visible,* for example, usually cause problems. The *-able* words (adjectives) have related *-ably* forms (adverbs) and the *-ible* words (adjectives) have related *-ibly* forms, as in *agreeably, comfortably, horribly, visibly,* etc. Thus, whatever is said about *-able* and *-ible* in this chapter also applies to *-ably* and *-ibly.* Fortunately, two points about *-able* and *-ible* simplify the decision as to which spelling is correct. Here are the points:

Point 1: *-able* is the basic form. Many more words end in *-able* than in *-ible.* When in doubt, and if your dictionary is temporarily unavailable, use *-able* (or *-ably*).

Point 2: An *a* for an *a* and an *i* for an *i*: If the adjective is closely related to a noun that ends in *-ation,* the adjective is almost certain to end in *-able;* if a related noun ends in *-ion* instead of *-ation,* the adjective is pretty sure to end in *-ible.* To figure out that *demonstrable* should end in *-able,* think of the well-known noun *demonstration.* In like manner, you can figure out *considerable* from *consideration, impenetrable* from *penetration,* and so on for hundreds of *-able* (or *-ably*) words. Similarly, you can figure out *admissible* from *admission, destructible* from *destruction,* etc.

Here is a list of *-able* and *-ible* words that you will spell correctly every time if you remember Point 2 about *a* for an *a* and *i* for an *i*:

-ATION becomes -ABLE		-ION becomes -IBLE	
adaptation	adaptable	accession	accessible
adoration	adorable	admission	admissible
application	applicable	apprehension	apprehensible
commendation	commendable	audition	audible
consideration	considerable	coercion	coercible
demonstration	demonstrable	combustion	combustible
dispensation	dispensable	comprehension	comprehensible
duration	durable	compression	compressible
estimation	estimable	conversion	convertible
explication	explicable	corruption	corruptible

-ATION becomes -ABLE

imitation	imitable
impregnation	impregnable
inflammation	inflammable
irritation	irritable
justification	justifiable
lamentation	lamentable
navigation	navigable
penetration	penetrable
reparation	reparable
separation	separable
toleration	tolerable
transportation	transportable
valuation	valuable

-ION becomes -IBLE

deduction	deductible
destruction	destructible
digestion	digestible
division	divisible
exhaustion	exhaustible
expansion	expansible
extension	extensible
perception	perceptible
perfection	perfectible
permission	permissible
reduction	reducible
reprehension	reprehensible
repression	repressible
reversion	reversible
suppression	suppressible
transmission	transmissible
vision	visible

NOTE: (1) As this list shows, when a negative prefix, such as *un-, non-, dis-, im-, in-,* or *ir-,* is added to the adjective or adverb, the basic fact about *-able* or *-ible* and *-ably* or *-ibly* remains unaffected.

(2) Some of the words in the list have minor internal changes. For instance, *conversion* is related to *convertible, inflection* to *flexible, reduction* to *reducible,* etc. Such internal changes are not important; the basic *-able, -ible* fact remains the same: *a* for an *a* and *i* for an *i.*

(3) Remember that Point 2 is not a rule. It is a helpful guide to the spelling of a great many *-able* and *-ible* words, but there are others to which this interesting relationship does not apply. And, too, there are certain exceptions to the *a*-for-an-*a* and *i*-for-an-*i* guideline. *Correctable* and *detectable* are the preferred spellings of the adjectives, for example, despite the noun forms *correction* and *detection. Sensible* is correct, in spite of *sensation;* and *predictable* is correct, in spite of *prediction.* These are only four major exceptions; there are several others.

-able Is Added to Whole Words, *-ible* to Stems

Here is another helpful guide to spelling these troublesome adjectives and adverbs: With some exceptions, provided later, the suffix *-able*

295

is often added to whole words such as *agree* (*agreeable*); to whole words minus their final *-e,* such as *cure* (*curable*); and to whole words whose final *-y* is changed to *-i,* such as *rely* (*reliable*). The suffix *-ible,* on the other hand, is often added to apparently meaningless groups of letters and to stems or roots that are not whole words, as in *horrible, terrible.* For example:

-ABLE
(added to whole words; to whole words minus a final *-e;* and to whole words whose final *-y* is changed to *-i*)

-IBLE
(added to meaningless groups of letters and to non-word roots or stems)

agree	agreeable	compat-	compatible
change	changeable	controvert-	controvertible
compar(e)	comparable	cred-	credible
deplor(e)	deplorable	cruc-	crucible
desir(e)	desirable	del-	indelible
enforce	enforceable	ed-	edible
env(y)	enviable	elig-	eligible
excus(e)	excusable	fall-	fallible
liv(e)	livable	feas-	feasible
marriage	marriageable	horr-	horrible
notice	noticeable	intellig-	intelligible
peace	peaceable	leg-	legible
pleasur(e)	pleasurable	neglig-	negligible
receiv(e)	receivable	ostens-	ostensible
rel(y)	reliable	plaus-	plausible
replace	replaceable	suscept-	susceptible
revok(e)	revocable	tang-	tangible
service	serviceable	terr-	terrible
trace	traceable	vinc-	invincible

-ABLE
(added to roots and stems)

-IBLE
(added to whole words)

ami-	amiable	collaps(e)	collapsible
cap-	capable	contempt	contemptible
despic-	despicable	defens(e)	indefensible
formid-	formidable	resist	irresistible
memor-	memorable	respons(e)	responsible

Spelling Test—Fourteen -able, -ible Spelling Mistakes

Add *-able* or *-ible* to complete the following words. These words are the fourteen most common *-able, -ible* spelling demons. Repeat this quiz as many times as you need until you can give all the correct answers.

1. convert_____
2. respons_____
3. suscept_____
4. depend_____
5. notice_____
6. change_____
7. contempt_____

8. desir_____
9. irresist_____
10. liv_____
11. compat_____
12. divis_____
13. irrit_____
14. indispens_____

ANSWERS:

1. convertIBLE. 2. responsIBLE. 3. susceptIBLE. 4. dependABLE. 5. noticeABLE. 6. changeABLE. 7. contemptIBLE. 8. desirABLE. 9. irresistIBLE. 10. livABLE. 11. compatIBLE. 12. divisIBLE. 13. irritABLE. 14. indispens-ABLE.

QUICKIEQUIZQUICKIEQUIZQUICKIEQUIZQUICKIEQUIZQUICKIEQUIZQUICKIEQUIZQUICKIEQUIZQUICKIEQUIZ

· QUICKIE QUIZ

STUMP YOUR FRIENDS

Stump your family and friends with this *-able, -ible* paragraph, or test yourself by having someone dictate it to you.

The Department of National Revenue said the form I filled out was *terribly illegible, incomprehensible,* and *noticeably implausible.* My financial records of *taxable* income were *accessible* to the tax bureau, but these records were said to be *undependable, unreliable, unsuitable, irresponsible,* and *inadmissible.* Though the tax bureau did not hold me *blamable,* its attitude made me *uncomfortable.* Thus, I hoped its attitude would be *changeable, revocable,* or *reversible.* My tax accountant was *irritable* and believed that such *horribly undesirable* and *unfavorable* objections were *insupportable, contemptible, intolerable, deplorable, reprehensible,* and *inexcusable.* The Income Tax Department was not *adaptable,* however. In fact, it was *predictably inflexible.*

QUICKIEQUIZQUICKIEQUIZQUICKIEQUIZQUICKIEQUIZQUICKIEQUIZQUICKIEQUIZQUICKIEQUIZQUICKIE

Fun With Words

-ABLE AND -IBLE

As you take this vocabulary test, use it to increase your knowledge of *-able* and *-ible* spellings. Choose the word or phrase you believe is closest in meaning to the key word. Answers follow.

1. **untenable** [un·ten′ə·bəl]—(a) not divisible by ten. (b) stubborn. (c) that cannot be maintained or defended. (d) not relaxed.

2. **irrevocable** [i·rev′ə·kə·bəl]—(a) stubborn. (b) temporary. (c) that cannot be recalled or changed. (d) unwritten.

3. **inestimable** [in·es′tə·mə·bəl]—(a) famous. (b) of little worth. (c) without esteem. (d) invaluable.

4. **inscrutable** [in·skroō′tə·bəl]—(a) incomprehensible. (b) unwholesome. (c) greedy. (d) Oriental.

5. **irrefutable** [i·ref′yə·tə·bəl]—(a) that can be conquered. (b) absurd. (c) that can be used as evidence. (d) that cannot be proved to be false.

6. **inalienable** [in·āl′yən·ə·bəl]—(a) that cannot be rightfully taken away. (b) not foreign. (c) inadmissible. (d) not transferable.

7. **implacable** [im·plā′kə·bəl]—(a) stubborn. (b) not to be appeased. (c) out of place. (d) given to violence.

8. **malleable** [mal′ē·ə·bəl]—(a) cheerful. (b) capable of being shaped by hammering. (c) prone to seasickness. (d) easily broken.

9. **negligible** [neg′lə·jə·bəl]—(a) trifling. (b) widespread. (c) sleepy. (d) unworthy.

10. **ostensible** [os·ten′sə·bəl]—(a) practical. (b) apparent. (c) obvious. (d) capable of being drawn into a wire between rollers.

11. **perceptible** [pər·sep′tə·bəl]—(a) agreeable. (b) helpful. (c) gradual. (d) visible.

12. **potable** [pō′tə·bəl]—(a) believable. (b) that can be carried. (c) drinkable. (d) edible.

13. **plausible** [plô′zə·bəl]—(a) worthy of applause. (b) deceitful. (c) contrived. (d) believable.

14. **personable** [pûr′sən·ə·bəl]—(a) human. (b) attractive. (c) gossipy. (d) insulting.

ANSWERS:

1. **untenable**—(c) that cannot be maintained or defended. 2. **irrevocable**—(c) that cannot be recalled or changed. 3. **inestimable**—(d) invaluable. 4. **inscrutable**—(a) incomprehensible. 5. **irrefutable**—(d) that cannot be proved to be false. 6. **inalienable**—(a) that cannot be rightfully taken away. 7. **implacable**—(b) not to be appeased. 8. **malleable**—(b) capable of being shaped by hammering. 9. **negligible**—(a) trifling. 10. **ostensible**—(b) apparent. 11. **perceptible**—(d) visible. 12. **potable**—(c) drinkable. 13. **plausible**—(d) believable. 14. **personable**—(b) attractive.

4 WHICH IS IT: -AL, -EL, or -LE?

No good rule has ever been devised that will help you to decide whether a word ends in *-al, -el,* or *-le.* Pronunciation will not help either, because all three endings sound alike. Although *-al, -el,* and *-le* words are troublesome, you undoubtedly mastered most of them in elementary school. You probably will find only two or three words in the following list that cause you trouble.

Here are the thirty-five words ending in *-al, -el,* and *-le* that are most frequently misspelled, especially by elementary-school students.

-AL		-EL	
accidental	essential	angel	label
acquittal	funeral	barrel	nickel
aerial	natural	colonel	squirrel
arrival	official		
chemical	principal (of a school;		
	capital for investment;		
	major)		
colonial	refusal		

-LE

angle	fiddle
assemble	marble
bangle	principle (a general
bauble	rule or truth)
candle	resemble
cradle	sample
dabble	trouble
double	whistle
example	wrestle

Don't Wrestle With Squirrels

One *-le* word, *wrestle,* is both a spelling and a pronunciation nuisance. It is spelled *wrestle* and pronounced [res'əl]. Do *not* spell or pronounce it as "rassle."

Another word in the above list, *squirrel,* bothers some spellers because they forget that it has two *r*'s.

Spelling Test— -al, -el, or -le?

Add *-al, -el,* or *-le* to complete the following sentences. Answers follow.

1. Can you assemb____ the baby's crad____?
2. Please lab____ this offici____ samp____.
3. The princip____ of the school said the boy behaved like an ang____.
4. She wears too many bang____s and baub____s.
5. Does Colon____ Smith live in a coloni____ house?
6. The boy borrowed a nick____ to buy a marb____.
7. It's not the troub____ he caused, it's the princip____ of the thing.
8. Put the cand____ on the barr____.
9. Nero fidd____d while Rome burned, but who kind____d the fire?
10. Whist____ while you wrest____ with the squirr____.

ANSWERS:

1. assembLE, cradLE. 2. labEL, officiAL, sampLE. 3. principAL, angEL.
4. bangLEs, baubLEs. 5. ColonEL, coloniAL. 6. nickEL, marbLE. 7.
troubLE, principLE. 8. candLE, barrEL. 9. fiddLEd. kindLEd. 10. whistLE,
wrestLE, squirrEL.

---

5 WHICH IS IT: -ANT or -ENT? -ANCE or -ENCE? -ANCY or -ENCY?

There has never been a rule to guide spellers when they hear words
in which they must choose either *-ant, -ance,* or *-ancy* versus *-ent, -ence,*
or *-ency.* If you know that a word ends in *-ant,* related words will
always end in *-ance* and *-ancy.* If a word ends in *-ent,* related words
will end in *-ence* and *-ency.* Thus, *abundant, abundance, abundancy;
consistent, consistence, consistency.* The best thing you can do is to
memorize the common words of this group.

The 20 Most Common *-ant, -ent* Puzzlers

Here are the twenty most troublesome *-ant* and *-ent* words, including

Fun With Words

WORDS ENDING IN -AL, -EL, AND -LE

Choose the word or phrase you believe is closest in meaning to each of the key words below. Also learn their proper spellings. Answers follow.

1. **trivial** [triv′ē·əl]—(a) amusing. (b) of little importance. (c) amateurish. (d) changeable.
2. **rankle** [rang′kəl]—(a) to be noisy. (b) to argue. (c) to cause continued resentment. (d) to confuse.
3. **arable** [ar′ə·bəl]—(a) capable of being plowed or cultivated. (b) healthy. (c) public. (d) praiseworthy.
4. **mettle** [met′l]—(a) stubbornness. (b) irritation. (c) foolhardiness. (d) courage and ardor.
5. **farcical** [fär′si·kəl]—(a) forlorn. (b) quaint. (c) very old. (d) ludicrous.
6. **tangible** [tan′jə·bəl]—(a) definite and real. (b) justifiable. (c) adjacent to. (d) capable of being hammered into shape.
7. **temporal** [tem′pər·əl]—(a) saintly. (b) warm. (c) worldly. (d) lasting a short time.
8. **lethal** [lē′thəl]—(a) painful. (b) sharp. (c) deadly. (d) a large quantity.
9. **fettle** [fet′l]—(a) a shackle. (b) state or condition. (c) good health. (d) courage.
10. **hurtle** [hûr′təl]—(a) to fling. (b) to jump over. (c) to overcome. (d) to rush headlong.
11. **staple** [stā′pəl]—(a) dependable. (b) a principal commodity (c) any starchy food. (d) strength.
12. **mercurial** [mər·kyōōr′ē·əl]—(a) humorous. (b) changeable. (c) mercenary. (d) hot.
13. **vernal** [vûr′nəl]—(a) truthful. (b) aged. (c) of the spring. (d) of the fall.
14. **rational** [rash′ən·əl]—(a) perceptive. (b) sensible. (c) scarce. (d) boring.
15. **sequel** [sē′kwəl]—(a) an agreement. (b) calm. (c) equality. (d) that which follows.
16. **sidle** [sīd′l]—(a) to move sideways. (b) to smile foolishly. (c) an oath. (d) a beer mug.
17. **insoluble** [in·sol′yə·həl]—(a) too salty. (b) not able to be dissolved. (c) lubricated. (d) not able to be defeated.

ANSWERS:

1. **trivial**—(b) of little importance. 2. **rankle**—(c) to cause continued resentment. 3. **arable**—(a) capable of being plowed or cultivated. 4. **mettle**—(d) courage and ardor. 5. **farcical**—(d) ludicrous. 6. **tangible** —(a) definite and real. 7. **temporal**—(c) worldly. 8. **lethal**—(c) deadly. 9. **fettle**—(b) state or condition. 10. **hurtle**—(d) to rush headlong. 11. **staple**—(b) a principal commodity. 12. **mercurial**—(b) changeable. 13. **vernal**—(c) of the spring. 14. **rational**—(b) sensible. 15. **sequel**—(d) that which follows. 16. **sidle**—(a) to move sideways. 17. **insoluble**—(b) not able to be dissolved.

some representative *-ance, -ancy* and *-ence, -ency* examples. Learn these spellings by heart.

-ANT, -ANCE, -ANCY	-ENT, -ENCE, -ENCY
acceptance	apparent
assistant, assistance	coincident, coincidence
attendant, attendance	conference
insurance	confident, confidence
maintenance	consistent, consistence, consistency
relevant, relevance, relevancy	correspondent, correspondence
resistant, resistance	dependent, dependence, dependency
tolerant, tolerance	existence
	occurrence
	persistent, persistence
	reference
	superintendent

NOTE: The word *descendant* is spelled correctly with an *a* when used as a noun meaning "offspring." As an adjective meaning "descending," the preferred spelling is *descendent*.

More *-ant, -ent* Words

Here are additional lists of *-ant, -ent* words with some representative *-ance, ancy,* and *-ence, -ency* examples. They are not major stumbling blocks for most people. Are any of them problems for you?

-ANT, -ANCE, -ANCY

abundant, abundance	ignorant
acquaintance	inheritance
appearance	observant, observance
clearance	perseverant, perseverance
defendant	radiant, radiance, radiancy
dominant, dominance	repentant, repentance
endurance	resemblance
entrant, entrance	restaurant
extravagant, extravagance	significant, significance
grievance	substance
guidance	sustenance
hindrance	tenant, tenancy

-ENT, -ENCE, -ENCY

abhorrent, abhorrence
absent, absence
abstinent, abstinence
adherent, adherence
antecedent
audience
coherent, coherence, coherency
competent, competence,
   competency
convalescent, convalescence
convenient, convenience
different, difference
diffident, diffidence
diligent, diligence
dissident, dissidence
divergent, divergence
efficient, efficiency
eminent, eminence
equivalent, equivalence
excellent, excellence, excellency
impertinent, impertinence
indulgent, indulgence
inference

insistent, insistence
insolent, insolence
intelligent, intelligence
magnificent, magnificence
obedient, obedience
opponent
opulent, opulence, opulency
penitent, penitence
permanent, permanence, permanency
pertinent, pertinence, pertinency
precedent, precedence
preference
proficient, proficience, proficiency
prominent, prominence
recurrent, recurrence
repellent
resident, residence, residency
reverent, reverence
subsistent, subsistence, subsistency
sufficient, sufficiency
tendency
violent, violence

Two Super Spelling Demons

Two words ending in *-ant* are difficult not only because of their endings but because they contain certain other letters. They are *lieutenant* and *sergeant*.

Lieutenant is an interesting word, the derivation of which will help you remember its proper spelling. *Lieutenant* is a combination of *lieu,* meaning "place," and *tenant,* which comes from the Latin verb "to hold." Thus, a *lieutenant* is someone who holds the place of another, especially someone who acts as a deputy in *lieu* of a higher officer, the king, or other superior.

The second letter in *sergeant* is *e* because the word is related to *serve,* which used to be pronounced [särv]. *Serve* is no longer pronounced that way, but the *är* sound remains in *sergeant*.

303

Spelling Test— -ant, -ance, -ancy or -ent, -ence, -ency

Complete the following sentences by adding *-ant, -ance, -ancy, -ent, -ence,* or *ency* in the blanks. Answers follow.

1. The descend_____ of the lieuten_____ was very effici_____.

2. The abs_____ of sunshine was a hindr_____ to her convales-c_____.

3. His mainten_____ of an opul_____ mansion is a personal indul-g_____.

4. An acquaint_____ left him an inherit_____ suffici_____ for all his needs.

5. At a clear_____ sale, a shopper needs endur_____, insist_____, and dilig_____.

6. The dog's tend_____ toward viol_____ was tempered by obedi-_____.

7. There is a signific_____ differ_____ in the guid_____ systems of the two missiles.

8. An observ_____ audi_____ saw the resembl_____ between the two actors.

9. A good employer should be consist_____ and compet_____ but toler_____ of the mistakes of others.

10. A good lawyer never makes irrelev_____, ignor_____, or imperti-n_____ statements in court.

11. The insur_____ office assist_____ is an extravag_____, ele-g_____ woman.

ANSWERS:
1. descendANT, lieutenANT, efficiENT.
2. absENCE, hindrANCE, convalescENCE.
3. maintenANCE, opulENT, indulgENCE.
4. acquaintANCE, inheritANCE, sufficiENT.
5. clearANCE, endurANCE, insistENCE, diligENCE.
6. tendENCY, violENCE, obediENCE.
7. significANT, differENCE, guidANCE.
8. observANT, audiENCE, resemblANCE.
9. consistENT, competENT, tolerANT.
10. irrelevANT, ignorANT, impertinENT.
11. insurANCE, assistANT, extravagANT, elegANT.

Fun With Words

-ANT AND -ENT

Choose the definition you believe is closest in meaning to each of the key words below. As you do this vocabulary test, notice the *-ant* and *-ent* spellings. Answers follow.

1. **rampant** [ram'pənt]—(a) noisy. (b) rising. (c) unrestrained. (d) gigantic.
2. **blatant** [blā'tənt]—(a) offensively loud. (b) cheap. (c) boastful. (d) notorious.
3. **aberrant** [ab·er'ənt]—(a) reformed. (b) confused. (c) wandering. (d) suffering.
4. **resplendent** [ri·splen'dənt]—(a) many-colored. (b) lustrous and shining. (c) famous. (d) luxurious.
5. **benignant** [bi·nig'nənt]—(a) wise. (b) religious. (c) old. (d) kindly.
6. **cognizant** [kog'nə·zənt]—(a) puzzled. (b) aware. (c) shrewd (d) modern.
7. **covenant** [kuv'ə·nənt]—(a) a solemn agreement. (b) a small bay. (c) a carefully guarded secret. (d) one of the Ten Commandments.
8. **coherent** [kō·hir'ənt]—(a) logically consistent. (b) very strong. (c) friendly. (d) slanderous.
9. **contingent** [kən·tin'jənt]—(a) continuous. (b) dependent upon an uncertain event. (c) side-by-side. (d) obligatory.
10. **consonant** [kon'sə·nənt]—(a) discordant. (b) consistent. (c) virtuous. (d) faithful.
11. **conversant** [kən·vûr'sənt]—(a) suave. (b) talkative. (c) intimately acquainted. (d) sophisticated.
12. **decadent** [di·kād'nt *or* dek'ə·dənt]—(a) evil. (b) a period of ten years. (c) deceased. (d) deteriorating.
13. **dormant** [dôr'mənt]—(a) extravagant. (b) modest. (c) inactive. (d) cruel.
14. **flamboyant** [flam·boi'ənt]—(a) charming. (b) blushing. (c) friendly. (d) showy or bombastic.
15. **extant** [ek'stənt]—(a) long and drawn out. (b) still existing. (c) far-reaching. (d) prominent.
16. **errant** [er'rənt]—(a) noble. (b) wandering. (c) eccentric. (d) serving a king.

ANSWERS:

1. **rampant**—(c) unrestrained. 2. **blatant**—(a) offensively loud. 3. **aberrant** —(c) wandering. 4. **resplendent**—(b) lustrous and shining. 5. **benignant**— (d) kindly. 6. **cognizant**—(b) aware. 7. **covenant**—(a) a solemn agreement. 8. **coherent**—(a) logically consistent. 9. **contingent**—(b) dependent upon an uncertain event. 10. **consonant**—(b) consistent. 11. **conversant** (c) intimately acquainted. 12. **decadent**—(d) deteriorating. 13. **dormant** (c) inactive. 14. **flamboyant**—(d) showy or bombastic. 15. **extant**—(b) still existing. 16. **errant**—(b) wandering.

WORDS ENDING IN -ANCE AND -ENCE

Choose the word or phrase you believe is closest in meaning to each of the key words below. As you do this vocabulary test, learn the spelling of these words that end in *-ance* or *-ence*. Answers follow.

1. **appurtenance** [ə·pûr′tə·nəns]— (a) an accessory. (b) an apt retort. (c) diligence. (d) disrespectfulness.

2. **irrelevance** [i·rel′ə·vəns]—(a) a divine disclosure. (b) the state of not being pertinent. (c) disrespect. (d) blasphemy.

3. **abeyance** [ə·bā′əns]—(a) obedience. (b) temporary inaction. (c) servile humility. (d) under consideration.

4. **diffidence** [dif′ə·dəns]—(a) disagreement. (b) respect. (c) self-confidence. (d) shyness.

5. **preponderance** [pri·pon′dər·əns] —(a) indebtedness. (b) superiority or excess of weight, influence, etc. (c) forethought. (d) an insufficient amount.

6. **turbulence** [tûr′byə·ləns]—(a) rage. (b) a violent disturbance. (c) muddiness. (d) quick-flowing water.

7. **resilience** [ri·zil′yəns]—(a) determination. (b) stupidity. (c) elasticity or buoyancy. (d) cleverness.

8. **dissonance** [dis′ə·nəns]—(a) shrillness. (b) anger. (c) discord. (d) disagreement.

9. **ordinance** [ôr′də·nəns]—(a) commonplace materials. (b) military supplies. (c) weapons and ammunition. (d) that which is decreed.

10. **sustenance** [sus′tə·nəns]—(a) believability. (b) moral support. (c) opportunity. (d) nourishment.

11. **clairvoyance** [klâr·voi′əns]—(a) the state of being lighter than water. (b) purity. (c) extraordinary insight. (d) transparency.

12. **incidence** [in′sə·dəns]—(a) anecdotes. (b) the range of occurrence. (c) stubbornness. (d) glowing with heat.

13. **inference** [in′fər·əns]—(a) a reasoned deduction. (b) inferiority. (c) an oversight. (d) inattention.

14. **pittance** [pit′əns]—(a) a small British coin. (b) a small amount. (c) alms. (d) punishment for sins.

ANSWERS:

1. **appurtenance**—(a) an accessory. 2. **irrelevance**—(b) the state of not being pertinent. 3. **abeyance**—(b) temporary inaction. 4. **diffidence**—(d) shyness. 5. **preponderance**—(b) superiority or excess of weight, influence, etc. 6. **turbulence**—(b) a violent disturbance. 7. **resilience**—(c) elasticity or buoyancy. 8. **dissonance**—(c) discord. 9. **ordinance**—(d) that which is decreed. 10. **sustenance**—(d) nourishment. 11. **clairvoyance**—(c) extraordinary insight. 12. **incidence**—(b) the range of occurrence. 13. **inference**—(a) a reasoned deduction. 14. **pittance**—(b) a small amount.

6 WHICH IS IT: -AR, -ER, or -OR? OR EVEN -RE or -OUR?

The word *beggar* (one who begs) ends in *-ar; purchaser* (one who purchases) ends in *-er;* and *collector* (one who collects) ends in *-or.* Obviously, the endings *-ar, -er,* and *-or* mean the same thing. Each is added to verbs (in these examples, to *beg, purchase,* and *collect*) to form nouns that mean "a person who or thing that" does what the verb says. Why do we have three different endings— *-ar, -er,* and *-or* —that mean the same thing?

The answer is that the English language was not created at one time or from one source. The standard ending *-er* is added to a verb to make it into a noun meaning "a person who or thing that," as in *farmer* (one who farms), *propeller* (that which propels), and *runner* (one who runs). The equivalent Latin ending is *-or.* Thus, in many Latin words taken into English, we keep the Latin *-or* spelling, as in *editor.*

The *-ar* ending originally meant "a person or thing like or connected with." A *scholar* is not "one who schools," but "one who is connected with learning." This original meaning has become blurred so that *-ar* is also a variant of *-er,* giving us a few words such as *beggar.*

Thus, *-ar, -er,* and *-or* can mean the same thing—and they sound alike! How, then, can we know which ending to use when spelling a word? Here are two tips on *ar, -er,* and *-or* words.

The first tip is this: The ending *-ar* is rare. All you need do is learn a few such common *-ar* words as *beggar, liar,* and *scholar.*

The more confusing endings are *-er* and *-or.* So, here's the second tip: For simple, common English words, the kind you learned to spell in elementary school, *-er* is usually the right ending. The Latin *-or* goes with more advanced words. Thus, very simple words like *doer, talker,* and *seller* tend to end in *-er.* More difficult words such as *administrator, orator,* and *vendor* tend to end in *-or.*

-ar, -er, and *-or* for Nouns Meaning "Doers" of Something

If the following lists of *-ar, -er,* and *-or* words seem easy to you, good! Some persons, though, have trouble with a few of these words.

-AR

beggar	registrar
liar	scholar

-ER

adjuster

advertiser

adviser (also acceptable: advisor)

amplifier

announcer

appraiser

baker

batter

bearer

beginner

believer

brewer

comptroller [kən·trō′lər]

consumer

defender

designer

digger

distiller

employer

eraser

examiner

executioner

invader

laborer

lecturer

manager

manufacturer

mourner

observer

passenger

peddler

producer

purchaser

subscriber

teller

traveler

treasurer

writer

-OR

accelerator

actor

administrator

advisor

auditor

bettor

calculator

collector

commentator

competitor

conductor

confessor

conqueror

conspirator

contractor

contributor

counselor

depositor

dictator

director

distributor

editor

educator

elector

escalator

executor

fumigator

governor

incinerator

incubator

indicator

inspector

inventor

investigator

investor	sculptor
legislator	speculator
mortgagor	sponsor
operator	successor
orator	supervisor
professor	surveyor
protector	survivor
radiator	translator
refrigerator	vendor
sailor	visitor

The endings -*ar*, -*er*, and -*or* also have other uses. Sometimes -*er* is used to form a noun that names a person according to the product he makes or sells: *hatter*, for instance, or *jeweler*. Or -*er* may indicate a person's place of birth or residence, as *villager*, *Westerner*, or *New Yorker*. Also, of course, any one of these endings may simply happen to be the last two letters of a word and have no special meaning at all. The following -*ar*, -*er*, and -*or* words are a mixed bag where meanings are concerned, but they have one thing in common: They are spelling problems for many people.

More -*ar*, -*er*, and -*or* Words

-AR

angular	insular
calendar (for dAtes)	jugular
cedar	molar
cellar	peculiar
circular	regular
collar	similar
dollar	singular
familiar	sugar
grammar	vicar
hangar (for plAnes)	vulgar

-ER

butler	character
calender (for papEr making)	confectioner
center	foreigner

309

grocer	milliner
haberdasher	miner (works in a minE)
hanger (in the closEt)	minister
jeweler	officer
lawyer	partner
ledger	stationer
meager	stenographer
messenger	theater

-OR

ancestor	inferior
anchor	janitor
ardor	major
author	minor (a yOung person)
aviator	motor
bachelor	neighbor
behavior	predecessor
captor	proprietor
creditor	realtor
debtor	rumor
doctor	senator
emperor	spectator
favor	superior
harbor	tailor
honor	tractor
humor	traitor
impostor	tremor
	vigor

When Is the Ending -re Used?

In English -re is not one of the more common endings, but it does appear quite often. You'll do well to learn the correct spellings of these six -re words:

acre	massacre
lucre	mediocre
macabre	ogre

Like the British, many Canadians prefer the ending -re for words that Americans spell with an -er. Thus, you will find such spellings as *centre, meagre, sabre, theatre,* etc., in our books and periodicals.

The only *-re* British spelling appearing frequently in the United States is *theatre.* Some Americans associate this British spelling with "elegance"; certain American theaters, especially those specializing in foreign films, classical drama, ballet, etc., are likely to call themselves *theatres.*

When Is the Ending *-our* Used?

The *-our* ending is distinctively British and many Canadians, too, prefer it for *colour, favour, glamour* (also preferred in the U.S.), *harbour, honour, labour, rumour, saviour,* etc. Few Canadians, though, object to the *-or* ending, and you will find it even in letters to the editor complaining about the "American takeover."

The *-our* spelling is also used in Canada for the derivatives of the above words, as *colourful, favourite, honourable.* Note, however, these important exceptions: *humorist, humorous, laborious.*

Spelling Test— -ar, -er, -or, or -re

Complete the following sentences by adding *-ar, -er, -or,* or *-re* where necessary. Answers follow.

1. The begg_____ told the passeng_____ that the peddl_____ was a li_____.
2. Schol_____s and educat_____s acted as advis_____s to the govern_____.
3. The sail_____'s superi_____ offic_____ had trouble with gramm_____.
4. The spectat_____s enjoyed the hum_____ous charact_____ that the act_____ portrayed.
5. Since the coal min_____ was a min_____, he could not vote for senat_____.
6. The jewel_____'s apprais_____ said the diamond was inferi_____.
7. The rum_____ was that the bachel_____'s butl_____ was an impost_____.
8. He was a debt_____ because he did not pursue the doll_____.

311

9. Beginn____s in gramm____ use many eras____s.

10. Refrigerat____ manufactur____s have many competit____s.

11. Burs____s, comptroll____s, and treasur____s use calculat____s and write figures in ledg____s.

12. The teetotal____s criticized distill____s with singul____ ard____.

13. The conquer____s were invad____s for their emper____.

14. Minist____s and vic____s have somewhat simil____ lives.

15. Do produc____s and direct____ hire min____ act____ for maj____ roles in the theat____?

16. Glam____ous foreign____s fav____ famili____ spons____s.

17. The og____'s farm consisted of a meag____ half ac____.

18. The trait____ helped to massac____ the troops.

19. The aviat____ landed the seaplane in the harb____.

20. The design____ designed an instant pancake batt____ for the consum____.

21. The elevat____ operat____ became a stenograph____ when the firm installed an escalat____.

ANSWERS:

1. beggAR, passengER, peddlER, liAR.
2. scholARs, educatORs. advisERs (or -ORs), governOR.
3. sailOR's, superiOR, officER, grammAR.
4. spectatORs, humORous, charactER, actOR.
5. minER, minOR, senatOR.
6. jewelER's, appraisER, inferiOR.
7. rumOR, bachelOR's, butlER, impostOR.
8. debtOR, dollAR, vigOR.
9. beginnERs, grammAR, erasERs.
10. refrigeratOR, manufacturERs, competitORs.
11. bursARs, comptrollERs, treasurERs, calculatOR, ledgERs.
12. teetotalERs, distillERs, singulAR, ardOR.
13. conquerORs, invadERs, emperOR.
14. ministERs, vicARs, similAR.
15. producERs, directORs, minOR, actORs, majOR, theatER.
16. glamORous, foreignERs, favOR, familiAR, sponsORs.
17. ogRE's, meagER, acRE.
18. traitOR, massacRE.
19. aviatOR, harbOR.
20. designER, battER, consumER.
21. elevatOR, operatOR, stenographER, escalatOR.

WORDS ENDING IN -AR, -ER, AND -OR

Choose the word or phrase you believe is closest in meaning to each of the key words below. These key words all end in *-ar, -er,* or *-or,* and you should also learn their proper spelling. Answers follow.

1. **welter** [wel′tər]—(a) heat. (b) a crowd. (c) turmoil or commotion. (d) suffering.

2. **caper** [kā′pər]—(a) to gamble. (b) to joke. (c) to trifle with. (d) to prance.

3. **garner** [gär′nər]—(a) to decorate. (b) to cut down. (c) to gather. (d) to scatter.

4. **render** [ren′dər]—(a) suffer. (b) rip apart. (c) contribute. (d) take back.

5. **banter** [ban′tər]—(a) playful teasing. (b) gossip. (c) very small. (d) memorable.

6. **provender** [prov′ən·dər]—(a) forethought. (b) supplies in general. (c) wealth. (d) feed for cattle.

7. **secular** [sek′yə·lər]—(a) following after. (b) wicked. (c) carefully chosen. (d) worldly.

8. **ulterior** [ul·tir′ē·ər]—(a) undisclosed. (b) evil. (c) false. (d) outside.

9. **titular** [tich′ōō·lər]—(a) famous. (b) in name only. (c) high in authority. (d) temporary.

10. **perpetrator** [pûr′pə·trāt·ər]—(a) a criminal. (b) one who performs an act. (c) an accomplice. (d) an interior decorator.

11. **engender** [in·jen′dər]—(a) to make angry. (b) to conspire. (c) to cause to develop. (d) to deceive.

12. **proffer** [prof′ər]—(a) to accumulate wealth. (b) to act skillfully. (c) to teach. (d) to offer for acceptance.

13. **roister** [rois′tər]—(a) to carouse. (b) to list. (c) a calendar of events. (d) a noisy gathering.

14. **squalor** [skwol′ər]—(a) noise. (b) poverty. (c) dirt and misery. (d) extravagance.

15. **insular** [in′sə·lər]—(a) proud. (b) narrow-minded. (c) insulting. (d) powerful.

16. **demeanor** [di·mē′nər]—(a) manner or deportment. (b) disgrace. (c) humility. (d) shrewdness.

17. **sinister** [sin′is·tər]—(a) unmarried female. (b) causing sadness. (c) murderous. (d) menacing.

ANSWERS:

1. **welter**—(c) turmoil or commotion. 2. **caper**—(d) to prance. 3. **garner** —(c) to gather. 4. **render**—(c) contribute. 5. **banter**—(a) playful teasing. 6. **provender**—(d) feed for cattle. 7. **secular**—(d) worldly. 8. **ulterior**— (a) undisclosed. 9. **titular**—(b) in name only. 10. **perpetrator**—(b) one who performs an act. 11. **engender**—(c) to cause to develop. 12. **proffer**— (d) to offer for acceptance. 13. **roister**—(a) to carouse. 14. **squalor**—(c) dirt and misery. 15. **insular**—(b) narrow-minded. 16. **demeanor**—(a) manner or deportment. 17. **sinister**—(d) menacing.

7 WHICH IS IT: -ARY or -ERY?

Because the word endings -*ary* and -*ery* sound alike, they can cause spelling problems. However, one fact will solve most of the problems: More than 300 words end in -*ary*; only a few words end in -*ery*. If you learn these few -*ery* words, you have the difficulty licked.

Here are seven -*ery* words that are easy to learn. First, let's look at the roots of these words:

baker	milliner
brewer	refiner
confectioner	stationer
distiller	

Note that these seven root words end in -*er*, a suffix meaning "a person who makes, sells, or does something." Thus, a baker bakes bread, a stationer sells stationery, and so forth. By adding a -*y* to this -*er* suffix, we get -*ery*. This new ending means "the product made or sold, or the place that makes or sells it." Thus, a *bakery* is the place where the baker's goods are made or sold, and *stationery* is the product sold by a stationer. In the seven -*ery* words that follow, the -*y* is merely added to an already existing -*er* ending:

bakery	millinery
brewery	refinery
confectionery	stationery
distillery	

Of these seven words, *confectionery, millinery,* and *stationery* are on many spelling-demon lists. Learn them well. In particular, remember that a stationER sells stationERY; his shop is stationARY because it stays in the same plAce.

A few other words also end in -*ery*. Some are no problem: *bribery, cutlery, finery, flattery, machinery, nunnery,* and *thievery*. However, five other -*ery* words do perplex some people:

artillery	dysentery
celery	monastery
cemetery	

Celery is on many high-school lists, and *cemetery* and *monastery* are on many college lists. Be sure you know how to spell them.

Are There Any -*ary* Puzzlers?

Although more than 300 words end in -*ary*, few of them are confusing. Some persons, however, find the following -*ary* words difficult to spell. If any of these words bother you, learn them now:

adversary	infirmary
auxiliary	library
boundary	necessary
commentary	revolutionary
contemporary	secondary
dictionary	secretary
elementary	stationary (in one plAce)
February	tributary
honorary	vocabulary
imaginary	voluntary

Spelling Test— -ary or -ery?

Complete the following sentences by adding -*ary* or -*ery* where needed. Answers will be found on the next page.

1. He fell from the distill_____ window, was sent to the infirm_____, and ended up in the cemet_____.
2. The volunt_____ artill_____ group received an honor_____ medal.
3. The bak_____ prepared a special confection_____.
4. The secret_____ bought millin_____ and other fin_____.
5. If the size of your vocabul_____ remains station_____, a diction-_____ may be necess_____ to improve it.
6. The brew_____ patented revolution_____ new machin_____.
7. In Febru_____, my advers_____ fled to a monast_____.
8. The auxili_____ libr_____ contains element_____ books.
9. The brib_____ attempt was written on pink station_____.
10. Cel_____ will not cure dysent_____, but remaining station_____ may help.

315

11. The monast_____ is on the St. Lawrence tribut_____.

12. In the Sahara it is necess_____ to ride a dromed_____.

13. People in sedent_____ jobs require salut_____ exercise.

14. Sir, my advers_____'s effront_____ is unbearable.

15. The rebels made incendi_____ and revolution_____ speeches.

16. Is the equator an imagin_____ bound_____?

17. Much thiev_____ goes on at the brew_____.

18. The comment_____ in the back of the book is element_____.

19. Every day the lapid_____ went to the bak_____ for rolls.

20. Flatt_____ is only second_____ to good will.

21. In Janu_____ she bought a propriet_____ medicine for colds.

22. Most people work for monet_____ gain.

ANSWERS:

1. distillERY, infirmARY, cemetERY.
2. voluntARY, artillERY, honorARY.
3. bakERY, confectionERY.
4. secretARY, millinERY, finERY.
5. vocabulARY, stationARY, dictionARY, necessARY.
6. brewERY, revolutionARY, machinERY.
7. FebruARY, adversARY, monastERY.
8. auxiliARY, librARY, elementARY.
9. bribERY, stationERY.
10. celERY, dysentERY, stationARY.
11. monastERY, tributARY
12. necessARY, dromedARY.
13. SedentARY, salutARY.
14. adversARY, effrontERY.
15. incendiARY, revolutionARY.
16. imaginARY, boundARY.
17. thievERY, brewERY.
18. commentARY, elementARY.
19. lapidARY, bakERY.
20. FlattERY, secondARY.
21. JanuARY, proprietARY.
22. monetARY.

WORDS ENDING IN -ARY AND -ERY

Choose the word or phrase you believe is closest in meaning to each of the key words below. These key words all end in *-ary* or *-ery,* and you should also learn their proper spelling. Answers follow.

1. **lapidary** [lap′ə·der′ē]—(a) a cutter of precious stones. (b) a roofer. (c) a mason. (d) an eskimo dog.

2. **supernumerary** [sōō′pər·nōō′mə·rer′ē]—(a) a servant. (b) an unknown person. (c) an unneeded extra person. (d) a very strong person.

3. **exemplary** [ig·zem′plər·ē]—(a) authoritative. (b) well-dressed. (c) fit to be imitated. (d) not subject to a rule or law.

4. **raillery** [rā′lər·ē]—(a) cruel ridicule. (b) complaints. (c) good-humored jesting. (d) absurdities.

5. **arbitrary** [är′bə·trer′ē]—(a) decisive but unreasonable. (b) sudden. (c) just and fair. (d) difficult.

6. **incendiary** [in·sen′dē·er′ē]—(a) angry. (b) ambitious. (c) inflammatory. (d) sweet-smelling.

7. **effrontery** [i·frun′tər·ē]—(a) lavish display. (b) humility. (c) false pride. (d) insolent boldness.

8. **commentary** [kom′ən·ter′ē]—(a) a long speech. (b) suggestions. (c) a list of questions. (d) anything serving to explain or illustrate.

9. **estuary** [es′chōō·er′ē]—(a) an inlet or arm of the sea. (b) a religious home. (c) a cluster of islands. (d) a large estate.

10. **sedentary** [sed′ən·ter′ē]—(a) unhurried. (b) inactive. (c) aged. (d) full of mud and silt.

11. **cutlery** [kut′lə·rē]—(a) implements for cutting and serving food. (b) a thin piece of meat. (c) small sleigh. (d) a peddler.

12. **lamasery** [lä′mə·ser′ē]—(a) a South American beast of burden. (b) a Tibetan monastery. (c) a sheepfold. (d) a poisonous shrub.

13. **dromedary** [drom′ə·der′ē]—(a) a date palm. (b) a racecourse. (c) a medieval ship. (d) a camel with a single hump.

14. **proprietary** [prə·prī′ə·ter′ē]—(a) proper behavior. (b) made and sold by exclusive legal right, as a medicine. (c) a scheme. (d) real estate.

ANSWERS:

1. **lapidary**—(a) a cutter of precious stones. 2. **supernumerary**—(c) an unneeded extra person. 3. **exemplary**—(c) fit to be imitated. 4. **raillery**—(c) good-humored jesting. 5. **arbitrary**—(a) decisive but unreasonable. 6. **incendiary**—(c) inflammatory. 7. **effrontery**—(d) insolent boldness. 8. **commentary**—(d) anything serving to explain or illustrate. 9. **estuary**—(a) an inlet or arm of the sea. 10. **sedentary**—(b) inactive. 11. **cutlery**—(a) implements for cutting and serving food. 12. **lamasery**—(b) a Tibetan monastery. 13. **dromedary**—(d) a camel with a single hump. 14. **proprietary**—(b) made and sold by exclusive legal right, as a medicine.

8 WHICH IS IT: C or CK?

C is one of the most useless letters in the language. It doesn't have its own sound but is sounded either like an *s* (as in *city*) or like a *k* (as in *cat*). In fact, every *c* could be completely replaced by an *s* or a *k*, as is done in dictionary pronunciations.

C is pronounced like an *s* before the vowels *e, i,* and *y* (as in *CEdar, CIty,* and *biCYcle*). When *c* is pronounced with this *s* sound, it is called a "soft c."

C is pronounced like a *k* either before the vowels *a, o,* and *u* (as in *CAt, COol,* and *CUt*), or at the end of a word (as in *froliC, paniC,* and *picniC*). When *c* is pronounced with a *k* sound, it is called a "hard c."

The fact that a *c* at the end of a word is normally hard and a *c* before an *e, i,* or *y* is normally soft can cause a minor spelling problem. With a word like *frolic* or *picnic,* the *c* must remain hard even when you add a suffix beginning with an *e, i,* or *y.* For example, if you add the suffix *-ing* to picnic, you form the word *picnicing.* But this spelling simply won't do, because the *i* after the *c* forces it into an *s* sound. And so, to keep the original hard *c* sound, we add a *k* to it. Thus, the proper spelling becomes *picniCKing.* This is a good example of how the requirements of pronunciation can result in unexpected spellings.

REMEMBER: If a word ends in a *c,* you must add a *k* to it before a suffix beginning with *e, i,* or *y.* The dash (—) used in the following list is a substitute for the word "becomes."

Root ends in a hard C (K) sound		Add a K to keep the C hard
bivouac	—	bivouacked, bivouacking
colic	—	colicky
frolic	—	frolicked, frolicking
mimic	—	mimicked, mimicking
mosaic	—	mosaicked, mosaicking
panic	—	panicked, panicking, panicky
picnic	—	picnicked, picnicking
politic	—	politicking
shellac	—	shellacked, shellacking
traffic	—	trafficked, trafficking

9 WHICH IS IT: C, S, or SC?

The letters *c, s,* and *sc* may all be pronounced alike, as in *competenCe, licenSe,* and *adoleSCence.* When you hear this sound, you have no way of knowing whether it is spelled *c, s,* or *sc.* Here are the most common words in which *c, s,* and *sc* may be confused:

C	S	SC
competenCe	apprehenSive	abSCess
evidenCe	comprehenSive	adoleSCent
negligenCe	incenSe	convaleSCent
violenCe	licenSe	irideSCent
	pretenSe	laSCivious
	reprehenSible	resuSCitate
	suspenSe	viSCera

In addition, *c* and *sc* may both be pronounced *sh,* as in *capricious* and *luscious.* Learn the following words, which can be troublesome because of the possible confusion of *c* and *sc:*

C	SC
capriCious	conSCience
defiCient	conSCious
maliCious	luSCious
suspiCion	omniSCient

QUICKIE QUIZ
STUMP YOUR FRIENDS

Stump your friends and family with this paragraph, or have someone dictate it to you as a spelling test:

The *convalescent* manager was *apprehensive* about his new *adolescent* employee. There was *evidence* that the lad lacked *competence, diligence, obedience,* and *intelligence,* although he never did anything *reprehensible, capricious,* or *malicious.* Nor was he *lascivious* or given to *violence.* But the manager was *suspicious* that the boy's *license* was under *suspension* for *negligence* in driving.

QUICKIE QUIZ

C, S, OR SC?

Choose the preferred spelling for each of the words below. Answers follow.

1. (a) reprehensable	(b) reprehenscible	(c) reprehensible
2. (a) concious	(b) consious	(c) conscious
3. (a) violense	(b) violance	(c) violence
4. (a) comprehension	(b) comprehencion	(c) comprehenscion
5. (a) negligensce	(b) negligence	(c) negligense
6. (a) competence	(b) competense	(c) compitence
7. (a) lisence	(b) license	(c) licence
8. (a) suspicion	(b) suspision	(c) suspiscion
9. (a) unconsious	(b) unconcious	(c) unconscious
10. (a) adolesent	(b) adolescent	(c) adolecent
11. (a) insense	(b) incence	(c) incense
12. (a) evidense	(b) evidance	(c) evidence
13. (a) convalescence	(b) convalesence	(c) convelesence
14. (a) caprecious	(b) capricious	(c) capriscious
15. (a) apprehencive	(b) apprehensive	(c) apprehenscive
16. (a) adolesence	(b) adolescence	(c) adolecense
17. (a) abscess	(b) abcess	(c) absess
18. (a) iridesent	(b) iridescent	(c) iridecent
19. (a) delicious	(b) deliscious	(c) delishius
20. (a) pretense	(b) pretence	(c) pretensce
21. (a) lucious	(b) luscious	(c) lusious
22. (a) malisous	(b) malicous	(c) malicious
23. (a) vicera	(b) viscera	(c) visera
24. (a) senesent	(b) senecent	(c) senescent
25. (a) offinse	(b) offense	(c) offensce

ANSWERS:

1. (c) reprehensible. 2. (c) conscious. 3. (c) violence. 4. (a) comprehension. 5. (b) negligence. 6. (a) competence. 7. (b) license. 8. (a) suspicion. 9. (c) unconscious. 10. (b) adolescent. 11. (c) incense. 12. (c) evidence. 13. (a) convalescence. 14. (b) capricious. 15. (b) apprehensive. 16. (b) adolescence. 17. (a) abscess. 18. (b) iridiscent. 19. (a) delicious. 20. (a) pretense. 21. (b) luscious. 22. (c) malicious. 23. (b) viscera. 24. (c) senescent. 25. (b) offense.

10 WHICH IS IT: -CEDE, -CEED, or -SEDE?

Since the endings *-cede, -ceed,* and *-sede* sound alike, poor spellers can be confused. However, only about a dozen basic words (all of them verbs) end in *-cede, -ceed,* or *-sede,* and these words are easy to learn. Here is all you need to know:

1. Only one common word in the English language ends in *-sede: supersede,* along with its forms *supersedes, superseded,* and *superseding.*

2. Only three common words end in *-ceed: exceed, proceed,* and *succeed,* along with their many forms, such as *exceeds, exceeding, proceeded, succeeding,* and so forth.

NOTE: The noun formed from the verb *proceed* is not spelled with a double *e*. It is spelled *procEdure.*

Here is a sentence worth memorizing: *When you sucCEED in remembering this exCEEDingly easy list of three words, proCEED to the next.*

3. All the other common words ending in this sound end in *-cede,* and there are only half a dozen or so of them: *accede, antecede, concede, intercede, precede, recede,* and *secede.* And, of course, the word *cede* itself "ends" in *cede.*

Spelling Test— *-cede, -ceed,* or *-sede*

Add *-cede, -ceed,* or *-sede* to the following to form complete words. Answers follow.

1. se_____
2. ac_____
3. ex_____
4. re_____
5. super_____
6. pre_____
7. pro_____
8. con_____
9. suc_____
10. inter_____
11. ante_____
12. retro_____

ANSWERS:

1. seCEDE. 2. acCEDE. 3. exCEED. 4. reCEDE. 5. superSEDE. 6. preCEDE. 7. proCEED. 8. conCEDE. 9. sucCEED. 10. interCEDE. 11. anteCEDE. 12. retroCEDE.

REVIEW: -ARY, -ERY, -CEDE, -SEDE

Choose the word or phrase that you believe is closest in meaning to each of the key words below. Answers follow.

1. **accede** [ak·sēd′]—(a) to be successful. (b) to give consent to. (c) to be more than. (d) to replace.
2. **replete** [ri·plēt′]—(a) generous. (b) dangerous. (c) filled to the utmost. (d) reiterated.
3. **commentary** [kom′ən·ter′ē]—(a) haughty. (b) qualification. (c) explanatory remarks. (d) basic facts.
4. **exemplary** [ig·zem′plər·ē]—(a) worthy of imitation. (b) plainly expressed. (c) true to type. (d) unusual.
5. **concede** [kən·sēd′]—(a) to admit as true. (b) to suggest. (c) to consider. (d) self-approval.
6. **rudimentary** [rōō′də·men′tər·ē] —(a) blunt. (b) nasty. (c) cud-chewing. (d) elementary.
7. **unsavory** [un·sā′vər·ē]—(a) dangerous. (b) disagreeable. (c) not sociable. (d) not suitable.
8. **supersede** [sōō′pər·sēd′]—(a) to supplant. (b) exceptional. (c) to overcome. (d) to admit as true.
9. **monetary** [mon′ə·ter′ē]—(a) fault-finding. (b) pertaining to money. (c) tedious. (d) a warning.
10. **vagary** [və·gâr′ē *or* vā′gər·ē]— (a) a wanderer. (b) an excuse. (c) vanity. (d) a wild fancy.
11. **corollary** [kə·rol′ər·ē or kôr′ə·ler′ē]—(a) a paradox. (b) something that naturally follows. (c) a maxim. (d) a heart ailment.
12. **recede** [ri·sēd′]—(a) to withdraw. (b) to sow again. (c) to rely on. (d) to take out an application.
13. **perfunctory** [pər·fungk′tər·ē]— (a) surrounding. (b) not functioning. (c) superficial. (d) at intervals.
14. **mercenary** [mûr′sə·ner′ē]—(a) sympathetic. (b) cruel. (c) warlike. (d) moved by love of money.
15. **votary** [vō′tər·ē]—(a) a petty official. (b) a sacrifice. (c) a devoted adherent. (d) an expert.
16. **trumpery** [trum′pər·ē]—(a) tasteful decorations. (b) worthless finery. (c) cheap boasting. (d) brazenness.

ANSWERS:

1. **accede**—(b) to give consent to. 2. **replete**—(c) filled to the utmost. 3. **commentary**—(c) explanatory remarks. 4. **exemplary**—(a) worthy of imitation. 5. **concede**—(a) to admit as true. 6. **rudimentary**—(d) elementary. 7. **unsavory**—(b) disagreeable. 8. **supersede**—(a) to supplant. 9. **monetary** —(b) pertaining to money. 10. **vagary**—(d) a wild fancy. 11. **corollary**— (b) something that naturally follows. 12. **recede**—(a) to withdraw. 13. **perfunctory**—(c) superficial. 14. **mercenary**—(d) moved by love of money. 15. **votary**—(c) a devoted adherent. 16. **trumpery**—(b) worthless finery.

11 WHICH IS IT: -CY or -SY?

As a final syllable, -cy is much more common than -sy. In fact, words ending in -sy may be considered exceptions. Here is a list of the most common words ending in -cy and -sy:

-CY Endings (frequent)	-SY Endings (rare)
accuracy	apostasy
bankruptcy	ecstasy
bureaucracy	heresy
democracy	hypocrisy
diplomacy	idiosyncrasy
expediency	
fallacy	
legacy	
literacy	
obstinacy	
secrecy	

Spelling Test— -cy or -sy?

Choose the correctly spelled words within the parentheses below. Answers follow.

1. All the motels had their "no (vacancy, vacansy)" signs on.
2. The firm went into (bankruptcy, bankruptsy) in 1970.
3. He was excommunicated for (heresy, herecy).
4. Some countries have only a 20% (literasy, literacy) rate.
5. Sleeping late on Sundays is sheer (ecstacy, ecstasy).
6. Do you have any memories of your (infansy, infancy)?
7. Eating banana sandwiches is one of Sam's (idiosyncrasies, idiosyncracies).
8. Eating banana sandwiches isn't an (idiosyncracy, idiosyncrasy); it's (lunacy, lunasy)!
9. We began our (occupansy, occupancy) of the house last May.
10. Can a (democracy, democrasy) also be a (bureaucrasy, bureaucracy)?

ANSWERS:

1. vacanCY. 2. bankruptCY. 3. hereSY. 4. literaCY. 5 ecstaSY. 6. infanCY. 7. idiosyncraSIES. 8. idiosyncraSY, lunaCY. 9. occupanCY. 10. democraCY, bureaucraCY.

WORDS ENDING IN -CY OR -SY

Choose the word or phrase you believe is closest in meaning to each of the key words below. These key words all end in *-cy* or *-sy* and you should also learn their proper spellings. Answers follow.

1. **intricacy** [in′tri·kə·sē]—(a) secret. (b) familiarity. (c) that which is deceitful. (d) that which is complicated.
2. **potency** [pōt′n·sē]—(a) suitability for drinking. (b) fertility. (c) good health. (d) power.
3. **ascendancy** [ə·sen′dən·sē]—(a) domination. (b) an inheritance. (c) ashes. (d) a staircase.
4. **constancy** [kon′stən·sē]—(a) hardheartedness. (b) temperateness. (c) faithfulness. (d) unending.
5. **idiosyncrasy** [id′ē·ō·sing′krə·sē] —(a) a personal oddity. (b) a country ruled by a committee. (c) a hobby. (d) a folk song.
6. **exigency** [ek′sə·jən·sē]—(a) effort. (b) urgency. (c) an extreme emergency. (d) an unneeded item.
7. **contingency** [kən·tin′jən·sē]— (a) a body of troops. (b) a defeat. (c) a dangerous situation. (d) a possible occurrence.
8. **expediency** [ik·spē′dē·ən·sē]— (a) that which is moral. (b) that which is advantageous or useful. (c) that which is evil. (d) that which is pleasing.
9. **fallacy** [fal′ə·sē]—(a) companionship. (b) a basic truth. (c) a mistaken notion. (d) deceit.
10. **magistracy** [maj′is·trə·sē]—(a) a king or queen. (b) the office or function of a magistrate. (c) a body of laws. (d) large and imposing.
11. **hypocrisy** [hi·pok′rə·sē]—(a) a theory. (b) a trancelike condition. (c) insincerity. (d) high blood pressure.
12. **apostasy** [ə·pos′tə·sē]—(a) desertion of one's faith or principles. (b) a chemical compound. (c) a digression. (d) a warding off of evil.
13. **heresy** [her′ə·sē]—(a) a person who lives in seclusion. (b) a belief contrary to established doctrine. (c) a future existence. (d) armorial bearings.
14. **literacy** [lit′ə·rə·sē]—(a) having to do with literature. (b) the ability to read and write. (c) a liquid measure. (d) actually; really.

ANSWERS:

1. **intricacy**—(d) that which is complicated. 2. **potency**—(d) power. 3. **ascendancy**—(a) domination. 4. **constancy**—(c) faithfulness. 5. **idiosyncrasy**—(a) a personal oddity. 6. **exigency**—(b) urgency. 7. **contingency**— (d) a possible occurrence. 8. **expediency**—(b) that which is advantageous or useful. 9. **fallacy**—(c) a mistaken notion. 10. **magistracy**—(b) the office or function of a magistrate. 11. **hypocrisy**—(c) insincerity. 12. **apostasy**— (a) a desertion of one's faith or principles. 13. **heresy**—(b) a belief contrary to established doctrine. 14. **literacy**—(b) the ability to read and write.

12 THE FINAL-E RULE

The final-*e* rule is one of the most important in spelling. Learn it now. A word ending in a consonant and a silent *e* (like *blame, confuse, hope*) usually drops the *e* before a suffix that starts with a vowel (like *-able, -ion, -ing*). Just using these examples, we get *blam(e)able, confus(e)ion,* and *hop(e)ing.*

This is just as easy every time. As you know, vowels are the letters *a, e, i, o, u,* and sometimes *y* (when it sounds like an *i*); all other letters are consonants. The rule says that the final *e* is normally dropped from a root word before a suffix when all three of the following facts apply:

1. The final *e* is silent, as in *ache, become, hope,* etc.
2. The final *e* is preceded by a consonant, as in the above examples.
3. The added suffix begins with a vowel, as *-able, -al, -er,* etc.

The Final-E Rule—Dropping the E

Here are some common words in which an understanding of the final-*e* rule will solve your spelling problems. The dash (—) used in the following list is a substitute for the word "becomes."

ache	—	aching	excite	—	exciting
achieve	—	achieving	grieve	—	grievance
admire	—	admirable	hope	—	hoping
adore	—	adorable	judge	—	judging
advertise	—	advertising	like	—	likable
advise	—	advisable	live	—	livable
arrive	—	arrival	love	—	lovable
believe	—	believable	move	—	movable
blame	—	blamable	noise	—	noisy
bone	—	bony	notice	—	noticing
care	—	caring	service	—	servicing
change	—	changing	size	—	sizable (also
come	—	coming			acceptable:
complete	—	completing			sizEable)
conceive	—	conceivable			
confuse	—	confusion	sponge	—	spongy
debate	—	debatable	stone	—	stony
deplore	—	deplorable	trace	—	tracing
deserve	—	deserving	trouble	—	troubling
			use	—	using

Hundreds of other words follow the final-*e* rule by dropping the silent *e* before a suffix beginning with a vowel. But there is another way in which the rule works. It also tells you when not to drop the *e*.

The Final-E Rule—Keeping the E

The final *e* normally is retained under any one of the following three circumstances:

1. The *e* is not silent but is pronounced, as in *be*, which becomes *being*.

2. It is preceded not by a consonant, but by a vowel, as in *shoe*, which becomes *shoeing*.

3. The added suffix begins with a consonant, as in the suffixes *-ful*, *-less*, *-ly*, *-ness*, *-ty*, etc.

The dash (—) used in the following list is a substitute for the word "becomes."

absolute	—	absolutEly	like	—	likEly
achieve	—	achievEment	live	—	livEly
advertise	—	advertisEment	lone	—	lonEly
bare	—	barEly	love	—	lovEly
care	—	carEful	mere	—	merEly
complete	—	completEly	move	—	movEment
decisive	—	decisivEness	nine	—	ninEty
definite	—	definitEly	rare	—	rarEly
dye	—	dyEing	replace	—	replacEment
encourage	—	encouragEment	severe	—	severEly
eye	—	eyEing	shoe	—	shoEing
hie	—	hiEing	sincere	—	sincerEly
hoe	—	hoEing	toe	—	toEing
immediate	—	immediatEly	use	—	usEful
immense	—	immensEly	whole	—	wholEsome

NOTE: In many pairs of words based on the same root word, the presence or absence of an *e* depends solely on whether the suffix starts with a vowel or a consonant. The final-*e* rule explains why English has such pairs as *advertising–advertisement, bony–boneless, hating–hateful, hoping–hopeful, lovable–lovely*, etc. In such pairs, the silent *e* of the root word is dropped before a suffix beginning with a vowel and kept before a suffix beginning with a consonant.

Exceptions to the Final-E Rule

Some words keep the silent *e* in spite of the rule. The usual reason is that the word might be mispronounced or misunderstood if the *e* were dropped. For instance, any word ending in -*ce* or -*ge* presents a special problem. The *c* and *g* are "soft" (that is, they are pronounced *s* and *j*, respectively) before the vowels *e* and *i*, but they are "hard" (pronounced *k* and *g*) before *a*, *o*, and *u*. For this reason, the final silent *e* often is retained before a suffix beginning with an *a*, *o*, or *u*. We drop the final *e* in *embracing*, but we keep it in *embraceable;* we drop the *e* in *charging*, but we keep it in *chargeable*. In that way the correct pronunciation is maintained.

For a different reason, we keep the *e* in *singeing* (meaning "burning slightly"). If we followed the final-*e* rule here, the resultant word could be confused with *singing* (meaning "making vocal music").

Here is a list of words you should have no trouble with if you remember why they are exceptions to the final-*e* rule. The *e* is kept for the sake of pronunciation or to avoid confusion. The dash (—) used in the following list is a substitute for the word "becomes."

acre	—	acrEage
advantage	—	advantagEous
change	—	changEable
charge	—	chargEable
courage	—	couragEous
embrace	—	embracEable
enforce	—	enforcEable
Europe	—	EuropEan
knowledge	—	knowledgEable
manage	—	managEable
marriage	—	marriagEable
notice	—	noticEable
outrage	—	outragEous
peace	—	peacEable
pronounce	—	pronouncEable
replace	—	replacEable
salvage	—	salvagEable
service	—	servicEable
singe	—	singEing
trace	—	tracEable

A number of words drop the silent *e* when, according to the rule, you would expect them to retain it. Learn the words in the following list now. Many of them can stump even the experts.

NOTE: The silent *e* is not dropped in some spellings which are preferred in Britain, and these spellings—as in *judgement, abridgement, acknowledgement* and *fledgeling*—are acceptable in Canada. We prefer, however, to drop the *e*, as *judgment*, etc.

argue	—	arguing (argument)	tie	—	tying
blue	—	bluish	true	—	truly
die	—	dying	value	—	valuable
lie	—	lying	vie	—	vying
nine	—	ninth	whole	—	wholly

In the above list, note that the *ie* of *die, lie, tie,* and *vie* changes to *y* before adding the *-ing*. And make a special point of learning how to spell *ninth* and *wholly*.

REMEMBER: *Ninth* has no *e*, but *ninety* does. *Wholly* has no *e*, but *wholesome* does!

NOTE: The preferred spelling for the word *mileage* retains the *e*, though *milage* is acceptable. And there are two correct ways to spell *line* plus the suffix *-age*. *Linage* without the *e* refers to the lines in a piece of written or printed matter, and it is pronounced [li′nij]. *Lineage*, which is pronounced [lin′ē·ij], means "ancestry or pedigree."

Spelling Test—The Final-E Rule

Combine the following root words and suffixes to form properly spelled words. Be sure you know when to keep or drop a final *e* from the root before adding the suffix. Answers follow.

1. safe + -ty
2. amuse + -ing
3. amuse + -ment
4. nine + -ty
5. judge + -ment
6. believe + -ing
7. come + -ing
8. become + -ing
9. mile + -age
10. change + -able

11. true + -ly
12. ache + -ing
13. rare + -ly
14. rare + -ity
15. courage + -ous
16. hope + -ing
17. bare + -ly
18. mere + -ly
19. argue + -able
20. argue + -ment

21. sale + -able
22. sue + -ing
23. bone + -y
24. knowledge + -able
25. acknowledge + -ment
26. advantage + -ous
27. nose + -y
28. adore + -able
29. die + -ing
30. dye + -ing

ANSWERS:

1. safEty. 2. amusing. 3. amusEment. 4. ninEty. 5. judgment. 6. believing.
7. coming. 8. becoming. 9. milEage or milage. 10. changEable. 11. truly.
12. achIng. 13. rarEly. 14. rarity. 15. couragEous. 16. hoping 17. barEly,
18. merEly. 19. arguable. 20. argument. 21. salable or salEable. 22. suing.
23. bony. 24. knowledgEable. 25. acknowledgmEnt. 26. advantagEous.
27. nosy. 28. adorable. 29. dying. 30. dyEing.

13 WHICH IS IT: -EFY or -IFY?—TestEFY or TestIFY? StupEFY or StupIFY?

The ending -ify is much more common than -efy. In fact, words ending in -efy may be considered exceptions. Here is a list of the most common words ending in -efy and -ify.

-IFY (the usual ending)	-EFY (the exceptions)
clarify	liquefy
codify	putrefy
deify	rarefy
fortify	stupefy
glorify	
intensify	
modify	
mortify	
purify	
ratify	
testify	
verify	

Spelling Test— -efy or -ify?

Choose the correctly spelled words within the parentheses below. Answers follow.

1. Should the Congress (ratefy, ratify) the new treaty?
2. The news (stupefied, stupified) me!
3. The witness for the prosecution will now (testefy, testify).
4. Please (clarify, clarefy) your last statement.
5. If Joe can't (verify, verefy) his facts, he will be (mortefied, mortified).
6. We must (intensify, intenscfy) our sales efforts.
7. Meat soon (putrifies, putrefies) if it is not refrigerated.
8. This milk is (fortefied, fortified) with vitamin D.
9. Would you care to (modify, modefy) your report?
10. (Liquefied, liquified) oxygen is used as a rocket fuel.

ANSWERS:

1. ratify. 2. stupefied. 3. testify. 4. clarify. 5. verify, mortified. 6. intensify.
7. putrefies. 8. fortified. 9. modify. 10. liquefied *or* liquified.

---

14 THERE IS NO DG IN PRIVILEGE

Some words are spelling problems because the *g* sound in them is pronounced as *j* or *dg*. The letters *g, j,* and *dg* sometimes sound alike in English. Thus: *jam, gem, knowledge.* Very few people make the mistake of spelling simple *g* words with a *j* instead of a *g*. But a common error is to spell these words with a *dg*. Don't!

Three Simple G Words
privilege
allege
pigeon

Three Difficult G Words
cortege
sacrilege
sortilege

Spelling Test— –ege or –edge?

Choose the preferred spelling for the words between the parentheses below. Answers follow.

1. Criminals hate stool (pidgeons, pigeons).
2. The store's (legers, ledgers) are checked by an accountant.
3. In my (judgment, judgement), this house isn't (liveable, livable).
4. Have you read the (abridgement, abridgment) of the best-selling novel?
5. What are the (privileges, priviledges) that go with being an adult?
6. There are millions of (college, colledge) students in America.
7. The (alledged, alleged) thief has been arrested.
8. She carried a (lace-eged, lace-edged) handkerchief.
9. The funeral (cortedge, cortege) passed slowly by.
10. The boy (mimiced, mimicked) the (fledgling's, flegling's) walk.

ANSWERS:

1. pigeons. 2. ledgers. 3. judgment, livable. 4. abridgment. 5. privileges.
6. college. 7. alleged. 8. lace-edged. 9. cortege. 10. mimicked, fledgling's.

---

15 I BEFORE E EXCEPT AFTER C

Spelling rules can be helpful if you bear in mind that there are exceptions to almost every rule. One of the best-known rules in English spelling is this:

> Write *I* before *E*
> Except after *C*,
> Or when sounded like *A*
> As in *neighbor* and *weigh*.

This jingle is catchy, easy to remember, and, as far as it goes, correct. It just isn't complete. In fact, there are almost more exceptions to the rule than words that fit it. Contrary to the rule, *I* can come before *E* after *C* if it is a sh-sounding *C*, as in *conscience*. And after establishing that the *I*-before-*E* rule refers to words having an *e* sound, as either of the *e*'s in *even*, what about *codeine* and *heifer?*

Your best bet with *IE* and *EI* words is to learn the rule, learn to apply it, and then learn the exceptions.

I before E (when the word has a long or short *e* sound)

achieve	frieze	piece	wield
apiece	frontier	priest	yield
believe	grieve	relieve	
brief	hygiene	reprieve	
chief	liege	retrieve	
fiend	lien	shriek	
fierce	mien	siege	
friend	niece	thief	

Exceptions:

caffeine	heifer	nonpareil	sheik
codeine	leisure	protein	weir
either	neither	seize	weird

E before I after (an ess-sounding) C

ceiling	deceive
conceit	perceive
conceive	receipt
deceit	receive

Exceptions (after a sh-sounding C):

ancient	omniscient
conscience	proficient
deficient	species
efficient	sufficient
glacier	

E before I (when sounded like A or air)

beige	freight	neighbor	skein
chow mein	heinous	obeisance	sleigh
deign	heir	reign	surveillance
eight	heirloom	rein	veil
feign	inveigh	reindeer	vein
feint	neigh	seine	weigh

There are no exceptions to this part of the rule!

E before I (when the word has a long or short *i* sound)

counterfeit	leitmotif
eiderdown	seismograph
fahrenheit	sleight
foreign	stein
forfeit	surfeit
height	

Exceptions:

handkerchief	mischievous
mischief	sieve

There is one word, *financier,* that follows no rules at all. It must be memorized.

QUICKIEQUIZQUICKIEQUIZQUICKIEQUIZQUICKIEQUIZQUICKIEQUIZQUICKIEQUIZQUICKIEQUIZQUICKIE

TWO-MINUTE QUICKIE QUIZ

IE OR EI?

Add *ie* or *ei* to each of the words in this list. Answers follow.

1. anc_____nt	13. glac_____r
2. hyg_____ne	14. f_____nd
3. caff_____ne	15. effic_____ncy
4. bes_____ge	16. s_____zure
5. w_____rd	17. s_____ve
6. dec_____tful	18. v_____n
7. financ_____r	19. ach_____vement
8. repr_____ved	20. l_____utenant
9. chow m_____n	21. rec_____ving
10. forf_____t	22. h_____rloom
11. cloth_____r	23. d_____ty
12. r_____ndeer	24. gr_____vous

ANSWERS:

1. anclEnt. 2. hyglEne. 3. caffEIne. 4. beslEge. 5. wEIrd. 6. decEItful. 7. financlEr. 8. reprIEved. 9. chow mEIn. 10. forfEIt. 11. clothIEr. 12. rEIndeer. 13. glacIEr. 14. fiEnd. 15. efficIEncy. 16. sEIzure. 17. sIEve. 18. vEIn. 19. achIEvement. 20. lIEutenant. 21. recEIving. 22. hEIrloom. 23. dEIty. 24. grIEvous.

QUICKIEQUIZQUICKIEQUIZQUICKIEQUIZQUICKIEQUIZQUICKIEQUIZQUICKIEQUIZQUICKIEQUIZQUICKIE

333

Spelling Test—ie or ei?

Add *ie* or *ei* to complete the following words. Answers follow.

1. The ch____f's chow m____n was s____zed on the front____r.
2. N____ther my n____ghbor nor my fr____nd is dec____tful.
3. What spec____s of r____ndeer did you see in the f____ld?
4. The sh____k r____gned at the ball.
5. Anc____nt Roman pleb____ans inv____ghed against for____gn finance____rs.
6. Sc____ntists use a s____smograph to record earthquakes.
7. The v____led queen d____gned to rev____w her tenant's f____fs.
8. H____fers need prot____n to gain w____ght.
9. The w____r across the stream y____lded ____ghty fish.
10. I gave my n____ce an ____derdown quilt when she married the L____utenant.
11. The magician's sl____ght of hand rec____ved careful surv____llance.
12. Bel____ve in your own ability and you will ach____ve the h____gts.
13. A h____nous th____f conc____ved that dastardly crime.
14. The cash____r's rec____pt reflected fr____ght charges.
15. We forf____ted the game in l____u of playing in the f____ry heat.
16. The ruthlessness of the sh____k brought gr____f to his people.
17. The w____rd hermit f____gned qu____t madness.
18. ____ther his consc____nce or his bel____fs made his behavior inconc____vable.
19. The propr____tor sold counterf____t h____rlooms.
20. The c____ling of the theater was p____rced to add a t____r of seats.

ANSWERS:

1. chIEf's, chow mEIn, sEIzed, frontIEr. 2. nEIther, nEIghbor, frIEnd, decEItful. 3. specIEs, rEIndeer, fIEld. 4. shEIk, rEIgned. 5. ancIEnt, plebEIans, invEIghed, forEIgn, financIErs. 6. scIEntists, sEIsmograph. 7. vEIled, dEIgned, revIEw, fIEfs. 8. hEIfers, protEIn, wEIght. 9. wEIr, yIElded, EIghty. 10. nIEce, EIderdown, lIEutenant. 11. slEIght, recEIved, survEIllance. 12. belIEve, achIEve, hEIghts. 13. hEInous, thIEf, concEIved. 14. cashIEr's, recEIpt, frEIght. 15. forfEIted, lIEu, fIEry. 16. shEIk, grIEf. 17. wEIrd, fEIgned, quIEt. 18. EIther, conscIEnce, belIEfs, inconcEIvable. 19. proprIEtor, counterfEIt, hEIrlooms. 20. cEIling, pIErced, tIEr.

Fun With Words

IE AND EI

Choose the definition you believe is closest in meaning to each of the key words below. (As you do this vocabulary test, notice the *ie* and *ei* spellings.) Answers follow.

1. **aggrieved** [ə·grēvd′]—(a) distressed. (b) massed together. (c) aroused. (d) rocky.
2. **cavalier** [kav′ə·lir′]—(a) graceful. (b) supercilious and haughty. (c) expert in horsemanship. (d) stylishly dressed.
3. **inconceivable** [in′kən·sē′və·bəl] —(a) unimportant. (b) unthinkable. (c) improbable. (d) impossible.
4. **obeisance** [ō·bā′səns]—(a) a musical instrument. (b) an Egyptian monument. (c) a large depression. (d) homage.
5. **inveigle** [in·vē′gəl *or* in·vā′gəl] —(a) to lead on by deceit. (b) to flatter. (c) to invite. (d) to steal from.
6. **reprieve** [ri·prēv′]—(a) suspension of a sentence. (b) the death penalty. (c) a repeated musical phrase. (d) to censure.
7. **weir** [wir] (a) a dam in a stream. (b) a fish net. (c) crazy. (d) a mine entrance.

8. **heinous** [hā′nəs]—(a) extremely wicked. (b) a king or queen. (c) funny. (d) renowned.
9. **nonpareil** [non′pə·rel′]—(a) unaligned. (b) a cable car. (c) misunderstood. (d) unrivaled.
10. **deign** [dān]—(a) to condescend. (b) a Scandinavian king. (c) to exalt. (d) to divert.
11. **specie** [spē′shē]—(a) a category of animals. (b) rare vegetation. (c) a ghost. (d) coined money.
12. **species** [spē′shēz]—(a) museum exhibits. (b) a monocle. (c) a category of animals. (d) coined money.
13. **irretrievable** [ir′i·trē′və·bəl]— (a) extremely valuable. (b) damaged. (c) full of holes. (d) gone forever.
14. **feint** [fānt]—(a) to exhaust. (b) to quarrel loudly. (c) to mislead by a false move. (d) to become unconscious.
15. **plebeian** [pli·bē′ən]—(a) military. (b) common. (c) unusual. (d) an ancient sailor.

ANSWERS:

1. **aggrieved**—(a) distressed. 2. **cavalier**—(b) supercilious and haughty. 3. **inconceivable**—(b) unthinkable. 4. **obeisance**—(d) homage. 5. **inveigle** —(a) to lead on by deceit. 6. **reprieve**—(a) suspension of a sentence. 7. **weir**—(a) a dam in a stream. 8. **heinous**—(a) extremely wicked. 9. **nonpareil**—(d) unrivaled. 10. **deign**—(a) to condescend. 11. **specie**—(d) coined money. 12. **species**—(c) a category of animals. 13. **irretrievable**—(d) gone forever. 14. **feint**—(c) to mislead by a false move. 15. **plebeian**—(b) common.

16 WHICH IS IT: -ISE, -IZE, or -YZE—AdvertISE or AdvertIZE? AnalIZE or AnalYZE?

The question of whether to spell a word with an *-ise, -ize,* or *-yze* stumps many people. All three endings are pronounced alike. The problem becomes a lot easier when you realize that the usual suffix is *-ize* and that *-yze* and *-ise* are rather rare exceptions. More than 400 common words end in *-ize.* Here is a list of a few of them:

agonize	emphasize	patronize
Americanize	equalize	philosophize
amortize	familiarize	plagiarize
antagonize	fertilize	pulverize
apologize	generalize	realize
authorize	harmonize	recognize
baptize	hypnotize	reorganize
brutalize	itemize	scandalize
capsize	jeopardize	scrutinize
cauterize	legalize	specialize
characterize	mechanize	subsidize
Christianize	memorize	symbolize
civilize	modernize	sympathize
colonize	monopolize	tantalize
criticize	moralize	terrorize
crystallize	nationalize	utilize
demoralize	neutralize	victimize
disorganize	normalize	visualize
dramatize	ostracize	vocalize
economize	oxidize	vulcanize

REMEMBER: *-ize* is a common English suffix added to words and roots.

Only Two Common Words End in *-yze* or *-yse*

There are two common words which end either in *-yze* or *-yse*—analyse and paralyse. There are some less common words that end with these letters (also interchangably); for example, *catalyse, dialyse, electrolyse* and *psychoanalyse.* But if you're in a field where you need to know such technical words, you no doubt already know how to spell them.

Only Thirty-Odd Common Words End in *-ise*

A final *-ise* is rare. If you learn to spell the following, you will know all the common *-ise* words you need.

advertise	devise	merchandise
advise	disguise	otherwise
apprise	enfranchise	premise
arise	enterprise	reprise
chastise	excise	revise
circumcise	exercise	rise
clockwise	exorcise	sidewise
comprise	guise	supervise
compromise	improvise	surmise
demise	lengthwise	surprise
despise	likewise	televise

Spelling Test— -yze, -yse, -ise, or -ize?

Add *-yze, -yse, -ise,* or *-ize* to complete the following words. Answers follow.

1. advert_____
2. apolog_____
3. real_____
4. exerc_____
5. familiar_____
6. Christian_____
7. surpr_____
8. item_____
9. paral_____
10. critic_____
11. lengthw_____
12. patron_____
13. compr_____
14. modern_____
15. special_____
16. psychoanal_____
17. bapt_____
18. comprom_____
19. desp_____
20. superv_____
21. general_____
22. util_____
23. telev_____
24. merchand_____

ANSWERS:

1. advertISE. 2. apologIZE. 3. realIZE. 4. exercISE. 5. familiarIZE 6. ChristianIZE. 7. surprISE. 8. itemIZE. 9. YSE or YZE. 10. criticIZE. 11. lengthwISE. 12. patronIZE. 13. comprISE. 14. modernIZE. 15. specialIZE. 16. YSE or YZE. 17. baptIZE. 18. compromISE. 19. despISE. 20. supervISE. 21. generalIZE. 22. utilIZE. 23. televISE. 24. merchandISE.

17 WHICH IS IT: -LY or -ALLY?

A common word-ending is -ly, which is often added to adjectives in order to form adverbs—*greatly, coolly, warmly,* etc. When the original ends in -ic, the adverb-making suffix sometimes is -ally instead of -ly. The extra syllable makes the adverb easier to pronounce.

Adverb Formed by Adding -ALLY

academicALLY	fantasticALLY
artisticALLY	lyricALLY
automaticALLY	systematicALLY

The -ally ending is not always used with adjectives ending in -ic. For instance, one very common -ic word that is made into an adverb by adding only -ly is *public;* the adverb is *publicly.*

Many adverbs that seem to have the -ally suffix do not really have an added syllable. In the following list, each of the basic adjectives ends in -al. So the suffix -ly simply is added to form the adverb.

Adverb Formed by Adding -LY

accidental + ly = accidentally	grammatical + ly = grammatically
critical + ly = critically	incidental + ly = incidentally
final + ly = finally	practical + ly = practically
general + ly = generally	typical + ly = typically

The above adverbs, and dozens similar to them, should be easy to spell. You merely have to remember that you are adding -ly to an adjective that already ends in -al to get the combination -ally.

18 WHICH IS IT: -OUS or -US?

Because -ous and -us sound alike, they can cause spelling problems. One easy way exists to tell when to end a word with -ous and when to end it with -us. Adjectives end in -ous and nouns end in -us. Thus, -ous is added to roots and other words to form adjectives: *advantage + ous = advantageous.* The ending -us is found only at the end of nouns. On page 340 are some of the most common -ous and -us words:

QUICKIE QUIZ

-LY OR -ALLY?

Choose the correctly spelled word from each pair below. Answers follow.

1. (a) exceptionally	(b) exceptionly
2. (a) cooly	(b) coolly
3. (a) incidentally	(b) incidently
4. (a) merrily	(b) merrilly
5. (a) criticly	(b) critically
6. (a) generly	(b) generally
7. (a) equaly	(b) equally
8. (a) anxiousally	(b) anxiously
9. (a) thoughtfully	(b) thoughtfuly
10. (a) typicly	(b) typically
11. (a) finally	(b) finaly
12. (a) logicly	(b) logically
13. (a) intentionly	(b) intentionally
14. (a) accidentally	(b) accidently
15. (a) publicly	(b) publically
16. (a) scholasticly	(b) scholastically
17. (a) pensivelly	(b) pensively
18. (a) academically	(b) academicly
19. (a) realy	(b) really
20. (a) practically	(b) practicly
21. (a) carefuly	(b) carefully
22. (a) happily	(b) happyly
23. (a) lackadaisicly	(b) lackadaisically
24. (a) usually	(b) usualy
25. (a) lyricly	(b) lyrically
26. (a) basically	(b) basicly
27. (a) elemently	(b) elementally
28. (a) prudentally	(b) prudently
29. (a) intrinsically	(b) intrinsicly
30. (a) demonicly	(b) demonically

ANSWERS:

1. (a) exceptionally. 2. (b) coolly. 3. (a) incidentally. 4. (a) merrily. 5. (b) critically. 6. (b) generally. 7. (b) equally. 8. (b) anxiously. 9. (a) thoughtfully. 10. (b) typically. 11. (a) finally. 12. (b) logically. 13. (b) intentionally. 14. (a) accidentally. 15. (a) publicly. 16. (b) scholastically. 17. (b) pensively. 18. (a) academically. 19. (b) really. 20. (a) practically. 21. (b) carefully. 22. (a) happily. 23. (b) lackadaisically. 24. (a) usually. 25. (b) lyrically. 26. (a) basically. 27. (b) elementally. 28. (b) prudently. 29. (a) intrinsically. 30. (b) demonically.

ADJECTIVES	NOUNS
ambitious	apparatus
callous (meaning "hardened or thickened")	cactus
	calculus
courageous	callus (meaning "a hardened or thickened area of skin")
dangerous	
fictitious	campus
generous	esophagus
humorous	genius
marvelous	hippopotamus
miscellaneous	humus
monstrous	impetus
outrageous	rumpus
pious	sarcophagus
righteous	status
serious	stimulus
wondrous	

19 WHEN IS A FINAL Y CHANGED TO I?

A simple rule tells you when to change a final *y* to an *i* at the end of a word before adding a suffix. Here is that rule:

If a word ends in *y* preceded by a consonant (any letter other than *a, e, i, o,* or *u*), change the *y* to an *i* when you add a suffix. Here are some examples. The dash (—) used in the following list is a substitute for the word "becomes."

accompany	—	accompanied, accompanies, accompaniment
ally	—	allied, allies
angry	—	angrily
beauty	—	beauties, beautified, beautiful (but beautEous)
busy	—	busier, busiest, busily, business
carry	—	carried, carrier, carries
city	—	cities, citified
cry	—	cried, crier, cries
dignify	—	dignified, dignifies
duty	—	duties, dutiful

easy	—	easier, easiest, easily
empty	—	emptier, emptiness
enemy	—	enemies
happy	—	happier, happiest, happily, happiness
heavy	—	heavier, heaviest
lazy	—	lazier, laziest, lazily, laziness
lively	—	livelier, liveliest, livelihood, liveliness
pity	—	pitiful
plenty	—	plentiful (but plentEous)
salary	—	salaried, salaries
steady	—	steadily, steadiness
try	—	tried, tries
worry	—	worrier, worries, worriment

EXCEPTIONS: There are three general exceptions to the above rule:

1. The English language does not like two *i*'s to come together. Thus, even when the final *y* is preceded by a consonant, this *y* does not change to an *i* before a suffix that begins with an *i*. For this reason, words like *babyish, carrying, pitying,* and *trying* have not changed their *y*'s to *i*'s.

2. A number of very simple short words containing a final *y* preceded by a consonant may keep the *y* unchanged before some suffixes. Here are some of the most common such words:

dry	—	dryly, dryness (but drIer)
lady	—	ladylike
shy	—	shyly, shyness (but shIes)
sly	—	slyly, slyness
spry	—	spryly, spryness
wry	—	wryly, wryness

3. The final *y* does not change to *i* before adding a suffix to proper names. Proper names are often exceptions to spelling rules because we respect a person's name and try to preserve its original spelling whenever possible. If a proper name ends in a *y* preceded by a consonant, keep the final *y* intact before adding any suffix—even including the plural -*s*. For example:

Harry	two Harrys	McCarthy	two McCarthys
Larry	two Larrys	O'Reilly	two O'Reillys
Mary	two Marys	Perry	two Perrys

341

WORDS ENDING IN -OUS OR -US

Choose the word or phrase you believe is closest in meaning to each of the key words below. These key words all end in *-ous* or *-us,* and you should also learn their proper spellings. Answers follow.

1. **nebulous** [neb′yə·ləs]—(a) tiny. (b) hazy. (c) foolish. (d) moist.
2. **opprobrious** [ə·prō′brē·əs]—(a) worthy of praise. (b) disgraceful. (c) oily. (d) quick.
3. **ostentatious** [os′tən·tā′shəs]— (a) wealthy. (b) talkative. (c) showy. (d) noisy.
4. **propitious** [prō·pish′əs]—(a) routine or ordinary. (b) impulsive. (c) unfavorable. (d) favorable.
5. **illustrious** [i·lus′trē·əs]—(a) famous. (b) illustrated. (c) wealthy. (d) gallant.
6. **emeritus** [i·mer′ə·təs]—(a) an honorary degree. (b) having seniority. (c) praiseworthy. (d) retired from active service.
7. **devious** [dē′vē·əs]—(a) divided. (b) illegal. (c) varying from a straight course. (d) insane.
8. **meticulous** [mə·tik′yə·ləs]—(a) quick. (b) humorous. (c) very small. (d) careful about details.
9. **portentous** [pôr·ten′təs]—(a) very heavy. (b) ominous. (c) overweight. (d) ridiculous.
10. **impetus** [im′pə·təs]—(a) cunning. (b) disagreeableness. (c) momentum. (d) prejudice.
11. **erroneous** [ə·rō′nē·əs]—(a) foolish. (b) passionate. (c) mistaken. (d) dishonest.
12. **hiatus** [hī·ā′təs]—(a) mobility. (b) a mountain peak. (c) vain pride. (d) a space or gap.
13. **arduous** [är′jōō·əs]—(a) brave. (b) involving great labor. (c) passionate. (d) intense and fervent.
14. **solicitous** [sə·lis′ə·təs]—(a) serene. (b) energetic. (c) bitter. (d) showing care and concern.
15. **ingenuous** [in·jen′yōō·əs]—(a) absolutely true. (b) candid or naive. (c) very wise. (d) native.
16. **onus** [ō′nəs]—(a) burden. (b) Latin word for "one." (c) proof. (d) blame.
17. **indigenous** [in·dij′ə·nəs]—(a) destitute. (b) native. (c) angry. (d) lazy.

ANSWERS:

1. **nebulous**—(b) hazy. 2. **opprobrious**—(b) disgraceful. 3. **ostentatious**—(c) showy. 4. **propitious**—(d) favorable. 5. **illustrious**—(a) famous. 6. **emeritus**—(d) retired from active service. 7. **devious**—(c) varying from a straight course. 8. **meticulous**—(d) careful about details. 9. **portentous**—(b) ominous. 10. **impetus**—(c) momentum. 11. **erroneous**—(c) mistaken. 12. **hiatus** —(d) a space or gap. 13. **arduous**—(b) involving great labor. 14. **solicitous** —(d) showing care and concern. 15. **ingenuous**—(b) candid or naive. 16. **onus**—(a) burden. 17. **indigenous**—(b) native.

When There Is No Consonant

Remember that the rule is: "If a word ends in a *y* preceded by a consonant, change the *y* to an *i* when you add a suffix." What if the final *y* is not preceded by a consonant? Then, obviously, the rule does not apply; the final *y* remains a *y*. Here are some common examples:

allay	—	allayed, allays
alley	—	alleys
annoy	—	annoyance, annoyed
array	—	arrayed, arrays
bray	—	brayed, brays
chimney	—	chimneys
cloy	—	cloyed, cloys
day	—	days, daytime
decay	—	decayed, decays
delay	—	delayed, delays
destroy	—	destroyed, destroys
dismay	—	dismayed, dismays
donkey	—	donkeys
employ	—	employed, employer, employment, employs
essay	—	essayed, essays
foray	—	forayer, forays
joy	—	joyous, joys
monkey	—	monkeys
pay	—	payment, pays
play	—	played, playful, plays
portray	—	portrayal, portrayed, portrays
pray	—	prayer, prays
stay	—	stayed, stays
tray	—	trays

EXCEPTIONS: There are a few common exceptions to the rule that a final *y* preceded by a vowel remains a *y*. All are simple words that most of us learned to spell in elementary school. In the following words the final *y* changes to an *i* even though preceded by a vowel.

day	—	daily
gay	—	gaily, gaiety
lay	—	laid
pay	—	paid
slay	—	slain

Spelling Test—y or i?

Insert *y* or *i* to complete the following words. Answers follow.

1. anno__ed	22. beautif__ed
2. ga__ety	23. dr__ly
3. ga__ly	24. dr__ness
4. necessit__es	25. dr__er
5. obe__ed	26. occup__ed
6. sl__ness	27. occup__ing
7. accompan__ment	28. portra__al
8. pr__ed	29. livel__hood
9. pr__ing	30. wr__ly
10. emplo__ee	31. comed__es
11. traged__es	32. merr__ment
12. laz__ly	33. wear__ness
13. laz__ness	34 co__ness
14. monke__s	35. donke__s
15. compl__ance	36. certif__ing
16. dut__ful	37. parod__es
17. pit__ful	38. penalt__es
18. jo__ful	39. joll__ty
19. jo__ous	40. foll__es
20. worr__ment	41. chimne__s
21. beautif__ing	42. jerse__s

ANSWERS:

1. annoYed. 2. gaIety. 3. gaIly. 4. necessitIes. 5. obeYed. 6. slYness. 7. accompanIment. 8. prIed. 9. prYing. 10. emploYee. 11. tragedIes. 12. lazIly. 13. lazIness. 14. monkeYs. 15. complIance. 16. dutIful. 17. pitIful. 18. joYful. 19. joYous. 20. worrIment. 21. beautifYing. 22. beautifIed. 23. drYly. 24. drYness. 25. drIer. 26. occupIed. 27. occupYing. 28. portraYal. 29. livelIhood. 30. wrYly. 31. comedIes. 32. merrIment. 33. wearIness. 34. coYness. 35. donkeYs. 36. certifYing. 37. parodIes. 38. penaltIes. 39. jollIty. 40. follIes. 41. chimneYs. 42. jerseYs.

Fun With Words

A ROUNDUP

The following sixteen words are among the spelling demons you have already studied. Check the word or phrase you believe is closest in meaning to the key word. Answers follow.

1. **remediable** [ri·mē′dē·ə·bəl]— (a) justifiable. (b) notable. (c) curable. (d) helpful to reading.
2. **severance** [sev′ər·əns]—(a) separation. (b) indignation. (c) deep respect. (d) final.
3. **addle** [ad′l]—(a) to increase. (b) to make strong. (c) to confuse. (d) to stir.
4. **exuberant** [ig·zoo′bər·ənt]—(a) breathless. (b) humorous. (c) striving to please. (d) full of joy and vigor.
5. **rancor** [rang′kər]—(a) tumult. (b) conceit. (c) sourness. (d) malice.
6. **tractable** [trak′tə·bəl]—(a) capable of being lengthened. (b) docile. (c) stubborn. (d) easily angered.
7. **chauvinist** [shō′vən·ist]—(a) a person who makes an extravagant show of patriotism. (b) an overly cautious scientist. (c) a person who finds fault with everything. (d) a musician.
8. **dissidence** [dis′ə·dəns]—(a) disagreement. (b) timidity. (c) nonconformity. (d) a result.

9. **parochial** [pə·rō′kē·əl]—(a) having to do with teaching. (b) ecumenical (c) monastic. (d) provincial.
10. **expedient** [ik·spē′dē·ənt]—(a) suitable and advantageous. (b) moral or ethical. (c) troublesome or costly. (d) a quick solution.
10. **surveillance** [sər·vā′ləns]—(a) slavelike obedience. (b) unusual wisdom. (c) deep respect. (d) close watch.
12. **nucleus** [noo′klē·əs]—(a) a core or central point. (b) a sailfish. (c) a root. (d) an outer part.
13. **somber** [som′bər]—(a) reluctant. (b) gloomy. (c) formal or unfriendly. (d) tranquil.
14. **archeology** [ar′kē·ol′ə·jē]—(a) the study of birds. (b) the study of history through excavations. (c) the study of theology. (d) the science of building.
15. **veritable** [ver′ə·tə·bəl]—(a) real. (b) old and honored. (c) abundant. (d) lively.
16. **flippant** [flip′ənt]—(a) flirtatious. (b) talkative. (c) joyous. (d) pert.

ANSWERS:

1. **remediable**—(c) curable. 2. **severance**—(a) separation. 3. **addle**—(c) to confuse. 4. **exuberant**—(d) full of joy and vigor. 5. **rancor**—(d) malice. 6. **tractable**—(b) docile. 7. **chauvinist**—(a) a person who makes an extravagant show of patriotism. 8. **dissidence**—(a) disagreement. 9. **parochial**—(d) provincial. 10. **expedient**—(a) suitable and advantageous. 11. **surveillance**—(d) close watch. 12. **nucleus**—(a) a core or central point. 13. **somber**—(b) gloomy. 14. **archeology**—(b) the study of history through excavations. 15. **veritable**—(a) real. 16. **flippant**—(d) pert.

Fun With Words

A SECOND ROUNDUP

The following fifteen words are among the spelling demons you have already studied. Check the word or phrase you believe is closest in meaning to the key word. Answers follow.

1. **echelon** [esh'ə·lon]—(a) a series of levels or grades in an organization. (b) a triangular flag. (c) a shade of blue. (d) a series of numbers.

2. **nonchalance** [non'shə·ləns]—(a) superiority. (b) nonconformity. (c) unconcern. (d) insanity.

3. **intermittent** [in'tər·mit'ənt]—(a) occurring at intervals. (b) obvious. (c) fragmented. (d) to come to a decision.

4. **feral** [fir'əl]—(a) manly. (b) containing iron. (c) straight. (d) wild.

5. **prior** [prī'ər]—(a) nearby. (b) just after. (c) just before. (d) higher up.

6. **extraneous** [ik·strā'nē·əs]—(a) unwanted. (b) abundant. (c) extremely loud. (d) external or foreign.

7. **arrogance** [ar'ə·gəns]—(a) boldness. (b) aristocracy. (c) overbearing pride. (d) sarcasm.

8. **gaucherie** [gōsh'ə·rē]—(a) awkward or tactless action or speech. (b) a South American cowboy.

(c) a small clothing shop for women. (d) ambition.

9. **strident** [strīd'nt]—(a) swaggering. (b) aggressive. (c) shrill. (d) selfish.

10. **Machiavellian** [mak'ē·ə·vel'ē·ən] —(a) politically unscrupulous or crafty. (b) wise. (c) inconsequential. (d) in a robot-like manner.

11. **susceptible** [sə·sep'tə·bəl]—(a) easily influenced. (b) convincing. (c) dignified. (d) contagious.

12. **termagant** [tûr'mə·gənt]—(a) a migratory sea bird. (b) a type of small rodent. (c) a gossipy woman. (d) a scolding woman.

13. **insatiable** [in·sā'shə·bəl]—(a) very tense. (b) flimsy. (c) incapable of being satisfied. (d) incapable of growing.

14. **pivotal** [piv'ə·təl]—(a) serving as a crucial factor. (b) the central core. (c) uplifting. (d) impressive.

15. **viable** [vī'ə·bəl]—(a) easily influenced. (b) powdery. (c) practicable. (d) land that can be plowed.

ANSWERS:

1. **echelon**—(a) a series of levels or grades in an organization. 2. **nonchalance**—(c) unconcern. 3. **intermittent**—(a) occurring at intervals. 4. **feral** —(d) wild. 5. **prior**—(c) just before. 6. **extraneous**—(d) external or foreign. 7. **arrogance**—(c) overbearing pride. 8. **gaucherie**—(a) awkward or tactless action or speech. 9. **strident**—(c) shrill. 10. **Machiavellian**—(a) politically unscrupulous or crafty. 11. **susceptible**—(a) easily influenced. 12. **termagant**—(d) a scolding woman. 13. **insatiable**—(c) incapable of being satisfied. 14. **pivotal**—(a) serving as a crucial factor. 15. **viable**—(c) practicable.

PART THREE

Say It Right

PRONUNCIATION—PART OF YOUR WORD POWER

Good pronunciation goes hand in hand with a good vocabulary. There is little use in learning the meanings of words unless you can pronounce them properly. To learn a new word, you must actually learn three things: its meaning, its spelling, and its pronunciation. That is why vocabulary building, spelling, and pronunciation are taught in the first three sections of this book. Correct pronunciation can be a help to your spelling. If you mispronounce a word, you are likely to misspell it as well. If you pronounce it correctly, you are more likely to spell it correctly. For example, if you pronounce *athlete* without adding an extra *a* sound, you will not be tempted to misspell it as *athalete* by adding that incorrect extra *a*. When you get in the habit of pronouncing all words with care, your spelling is bound to improve.

Your Right to Be Heard

Good pronunciation does not require everyone to speak alike. National accents and the tone of one's voice have nothing to do with saying words correctly. You may have an Irish, Scottish, Western Canadian or Newfoundland accent, and your voice may be full and deep or thin and high. No matter! What does matter is to say every word correctly in your own accent and natural voice.

How to Learn Pronunciation

From childhood on, we learn to say new words by imitating others. In that way, we learn to pronounce most words correctly—but we also repeat the mistakes of our friends and add a few of our own.

As we grow older, we enlarge our vocabulary by reading. Thus, we learn many new words by seeing them in print. The trouble is, however, that we see rather than hear them. The only sure way to learn the pronunciation of new words is to look them up in a good dictionary. And to understand what the dictionary tells us, we must learn how to interpret the symbols in its pronunciation key.

The pronunciation key of the Reader's Digest *Great Encyclopedic Dictionary* is used in this book as your guide to correct pronunciation.

It is thoroughly explained on pages 6–7 in the Introduction. Review these pages now, and refer to the key whenever you need to as you study the following chapters.

Those chapters will help to guide you along the path toward good, correct pronunciation. They will help you train yourself to listen to—and to reproduce—the modern accepted pronunciation of words by educated speakers. Good pronunciation, you'll find, is an easy habit to acquire; it is also one of the surest ways to improve your word power.

There are fewer pronunciation demons than spelling demons. If you have serious pronunciation problems, they probably turn up in only one or two sounds or in a few dozen words. In the following chapters we concentrate on the most common pronunciation difficulties chosen from the 2,500 most frequently mispronounced words. Don't spend your time on the many words you already pronounce correctly.

REMEMBER: A poor speaker is often considered a poor thinker. Improve your speech habits, and your words (which reflect your thoughts, feelings, and personality) will get the attention and respect they deserve.

1 SPEAK FOR YOURSELF

People judge you not only by what you say, but by how you say it. So it behooves you to give particular care to your pronunciation and how you sound to others.

Fads and fashions come and go in pronunciation; what was once considered cultured and preferred may now sound phony or exaggerated. A hundred years ago, almost every educated person in North America who spoke English pronounced *vase* as *vahz*, but today that pronunciation, while common in Canada, is considered "highbrow" by Americans who usually say *vayz*. Similarly, fifty years ago a *tune* was a *tyoon* almost everywhere; but now it is a *toon* to nearly all Americans and to some Canadians, to the regret of other Canadians and their British cousins. Do you consider it "more refined" to make the first syllable of *either* rhyme with *my* instead of *me*, and to make *been* rhyme with *bean* instead of *bin?* If so, change your mind. Both pronunciations are wholly acceptable in polite circles.

How Do You Sound to Others?

Pronunciation and speech should be natural, smooth-flowing, and unobtrusive. Don't leave your listeners wondering how long you've lived at Buckingham Palace or how many nights a week you attend Miss Prim's School of Diction. Remember that the purpose of good pronunciation is to speak like a warm, reasonably well-educated human being, to communicate ideas, emotions, and your true personality and beliefs—not to impress people with your superior "refinement." So if you were brought up to say *eyether* and *nyether* as naturally as any other word, continue to say them. They will match the rest of your speech patterns and sound perfectly normal and unaffected. If, however, you've schooled yourself to say *eyether* and *nyether* because you think they sound "high class," drop them fast. What is right for actors and actresses may be all wrong for you.

Uh and Thuh or A and Thee?

The words *a* and *the* are two of the simplest words in English; yet many people are confused about how to say them. The letter A is pronounced [ā] as in "He got an A in history" or *A-1*. But the word *a* is normally pronounced *uh* [ə]: *uh book*. Don't try to impress people by saying the letter *a* [ā] when you mean the word *a* [ə].

REMEMBER: The word *a* is pronounced *uh* [ə] in normal conversation. (The exception occurs when you want to stress the word *a*, as in "I didn't say 'the books,' I said 'a book.'")

The word *the* is pronounced either *thuh* [thə] or *thee* [thē] depending on its use. Many persons say *thuh* at all times, but most speakers follow an older pronunciation rule—which is good because it makes "the apple" easier, not harder, to say. The rule is that *the* should be pronounced *thuh* before a word beginning with a consonant (*thuh table*) and *thee* before a word beginning with a vowel (*thee apple*). "I ate *thee* apple, *thee* egg, and *thee* onion" is easier to say, you'll find, than "I ate *thuh* apple, *thuh* egg, and *thuh* onion." The long *ee* in *the apple* is not as long as it is in *me*; in fact, some linguists would say that it is closer to the *i* in *hit*. Listen to it in your own speech.

NOTE: *A* is an *indefinite article*, and *the* is the *definite article* in English. There are two indefinite articles, *a* and *an*. *A* is used before a word beginning with a consonant (*a table*) and *an* is used before a word beginning with a vowel (*an apple*). It is never acceptable to speak of *a* apple or *a* egg.

Vayz or Vahz, Tomayto or Tomahto?

If I say *tomayto* and you say *tomahto*, I say *vayz* and you say *vahz*, maybe we'll never get together—because the chances are that you're a hundred years older than I am!

Very few Canadians still use the British broad *a* for words like *tomato, ask, bath* and *half*. Those who do were probably educated in England or in British-type boarding schools in New England. But if you were brought up to pronounce *aunt* as *ahnt* instead of *ant* and *laugh* as *lahf* instead of *laff*, you don't need to change. Be yourself. Nor should you try to use the broad *a* if it doesn't come naturally to you. People will know it's a fake.

	Preferred Canadian Pronunciation
after	af′tər
ask	ask
aunt	ant
bath	bath
can't	kant
chance	chans
last	last
laugh	laf
pass	pas
patio	pat′ē·ō
plaza	plaz′ə
rather	rath′ər
tomato	tə·mā′tō or tə·ma′tō

EXCEPTIONS: *Lama* (a Tibetan monk) and *llama* (the South American animal) are pronounced exactly alike:

lama	lahma	[lä′mə]
llama	lahma	[lä′mə]

351

QUICKIE QUIZ

DEMONS AND DOUBLE DEMONS

Choose a pronunciation of the following key words. Some will have only one acceptable form; others will have two. A few of the words in this test are new and have been included as a challenge to you.

1. ignoramus	(a) ig′nə·ram′əs	(b) ig′nə·rā′məs
2. sacrifice	(a) sak′rə·fīs	(b) sak′rə·fis
3. radiator	(a) rā′dē·ā′tər	(b) ra′dē·ā′tər
4. tomato	(a) tə·mā′tō	(b) tə·mä′tō
5. Cupid	(a) kyōō′pid	(b) kōō′pid
6. verbatim	(a) vər·ba′tim	(b) vər·bā′tim
7. either	(a) ē′thər	(b) ī′thər
8. appreciate	(a) ə·prē′sē·āt	(b) ə·prē′shē·āt
9. llama	(a) la′mə	(b) lä′mə
10. illustrate	(a) i·lus′trāt	(b) il′ə·strāt
11. Tuesday	(a) tōōz′dē	(b) tyōōz′di
12. cement	(a) sē′ment	(b) si·ment′
13. patio	(a) pä′tē·ō	(b) pat′ē·ō
14. process	(a) pros′es	(b) prō′ses
15. ultimatum	(a) ul′tə·mä′təm	(b) ul′tə·mā′təm

ANSWERS:

1. **ignoramus**—(a) [ig′nə·ram′əs] *or* (b) [ig′nə·rā′məs] 2. **sacrifice**—(a) [sak′rə·fīs] 3. **radiator**—(a) [rā′dē·ā′tər] 4. **tomato**—(a) [tə·mā′tō] *or* (b) [tə·mä′tō] 5. **Cupid**—(a) [kyōō′pid] 6. **verbatim**—(b) [vər·bā′tim] 7. **either** —(a) [ē′thər] *or* (b) [ī′thər] 8. **appreciate**—(b) [ə·prē′shē·āt] 9. **llama**— (b) [lä′mə] 10. **illustrate**—(a) [i·lus′trāt] *or* (b) [il′ə·strāt] 11. **Tuesday**— (b) [tyōōz′di] 12. **cement**— (b) [si·ment′] 13. **patio**—(a) [pä′tē·ō] *or* (b) [pat′ē·ō] 14. **process**—(a) [pros′es] *or* (b) [prō′ses] 15. **ultimatum**—(a) [ul′tə·mä′təm] *or* (b) [ul′tə·mā′təm]

Datta or Dayta, Stattus or Staytus?

The long *a* sound [ā], as in *day, ray,* and *stay,* and the flat *a* sound [a] as in *at, cat,* and *rat,* cause some speakers to worry about their pronunciation. Does the first *a* in *data, aviator,* and *status* rhyme with the long *a* of *day* or with the flat *a* of *at?* In which of these two series do the *a*'s all rhyme:

day-date-data; ape-ate-aviator; stay-state-status

or

at-bat-data; add-at-aviator; rat-sat-status

The answer is that both pronunciations of the *a* in *data, aviator,* and *status* are correct. Relax! Years ago, speech teachers, actors, and radio commentators used the long *a* so that *day-date-data, ape-ate-aviator,* and *stay-state-status* all rhymed. Today, however, those concerned with pronunciation agree that the flat *a* is every bit as acceptable. Just stick to your natural pronunciation of *data, aviator,* and *status.*

In the following words either a long *a* or a flat *a* is acceptable:

apparAtus	ap'ə·rā'təs	*or*	ap'ə·rat'əs
Apricot	ā'pri·kot	*or*	ap'ri·kot
dAta	dā'tə	*or*	dat'ə
ignorAmus	ig'nə·rā'məs	*or*	ig'nə·ram'əs
pro rAta	prō rā'tə	*or*	pro rat'ə
stAtus	stā'təs	*or*	stat'əs
sAtrap	sā'trap	*or*	sat'rap

But isn't there a rule for pronouncing these words? Yes. The rule is: Be natural. Pronounce this *a* sound as do others in your locality.

BEWARE: *Again* [ə·gen'] and *against* [ə·genst'] are commonly pronounced to rhyme with *end-pen: end-pen-again, end-pen-against.* The long *a* sound of *agayn* [ə·gān'] and *agaynst* [ə·gānst'] is less common. Don't rhyme *day-gay-again* or *day-gay-against* just because you think it sounds better. It doesn't.

Radio and *radiator* have only one acceptable pronunciation: *Raydio* [rā'dē·ō] and *raydiator* [rā'dē·ā'tər]. Their first syllables should rhyme with *day* and *ray: day-ray-radio, day-ray-radiator.* To rhyme them with *bad* and *add* (*bad-add-radio, bad-add-radiator*) is considered unacceptable pronunciation. The words *fracas* and *verbatim* should also be pronounced with the long *a, fraycas* [frā'kəs] and *verbaytim* [vər·bā'tim].

NOTE: Another common word that can properly be pronounced in two different ways is *route,* either as *root* [rōot] or as *rout* [rout]. *Root* is preferred by many careful speakers, but *rout* is acceptable.

Is It Toon or Tyewn, Dooty or Dyewty?

By now, you probably know the answer to the above question. Teachers and careful speakers agree that pronouncing *tune* as *tyewn* or *duty* as *dyewty* is an affectation for most Americans but this is the pronunciation preferred by most Canadians. Note that this *u* sound may be spelled -*u* (tune), -*ue* (avenue) or -*ew* (dew).

	Preferred American Pronunciation	Preferred Canadian Pronunciation
avenue	av′ə·nōō	av′ə·nyōō
duration	dŏŏ·rā′shən	dyŏŏ·rā′shən
duty	dōō′tē	dyōō′tē
stew	stōō	styōō
stupid	stōō′pid	styōō′pid
tube	tōōb	tyōōb
Tuesday	tōōz′dē	tyōōz′di
tune	tōōn	tyōōn

NOTE: The sharp *u* sound is used everywhere in many words such as *beauty* [byōō′tē], *Cupid* [kyōō′pid], and *Hubert* [hyōō′bərt]. And a great many people pronounce *coupon* as [kyōō′pon], even though most authorities prefer [kōō′pon]. If [kyōō′pon] sounds better to you, go ahead and use it.

As we have discussed elsewhere, the way words are spelled changes: everyone once spelled *honor* as *honour* (some of us still do), and hundreds of years ago *wife* was written *wif*. Pronunciation also changes. *Appendicitis* [ə·pen′də·sī′tis] used to be pronounced [ə·pen′də·sē′tis]; and *vitamin* [vī′tə·min] used to be pronounced [vit′ə·min], which is still the correct British pronunciation. Other pronunciations are changing today. Your best guide is to say words as do the majority of careful speakers—that is, to follow the pronunciations given in a modern dictionary. Do you pronounce the words listed here in the preferred way? Modern pronunciation does not stress or draw out the final -*or* of the following six words or of similar words ending in -*or*:

	Preferred General Pronunciation		
actor	ak′tər	*not*	ak′tôr
debtor	det′ər	*not*	det′ôr
editor	ed′i·tər	*not*	ed′i·tôr
honor	on′ər	*not*	on′ôr
rumor	rōō′mər	*not*	rōō′môr
senator	sen′ə·tər	*not*	sen′ə·tôr

FOURTEEN PRONUNCIATION DEMONS

This test contains some words that are often mispronounced. Learn their proper meanings and pronunciations. When alternate pronunciations are given, both are acceptable, although the first is preferred. Check the word or phrase you believe is closest in meaning to the key word. Answers follow.

1. **lamentable** [lam′ən·tə·bəl *or* la·ment′ə·bəl]—(a) regrettable. (b) separable. (c) extremely noisy. (d) vicious.
2. **demise** [di·mīz′]—(a) result. (b) death. (c) apprehension. (d) an oath.
3. **tactile** [tak′tīl *or* tak′til]—(a) pertaining to the sense of touch. (b) a satiny material. (c) grasping. (d) silently understood.
4. **contest** [kən·test′]—(a) to ally with. (b) to challenge. (c) to agree to. (d) to strike.
5. **impious** [im′pē·əs]—(a) ape-like. (b) deceptive. (c) irreverent. (d) cruel.
6. **ignominy** [ig′nə·min′ē]—(a) a misconception. (b) a pseudonym. (c) complete ignorance. (d) disgrace.
7. **ignominious** [ig′nə·min′ē·əs]—(a) humiliating. (b) unknown. (c) glorious. (d) breathtaking.
8. **enigma** [i·nig′mə]—(a) a pale yellow color. (b) something that baffles. (c) a disease of the eye. (d) something ancient.
9. **clandestine** [klan·des′tin]—(a) calm. (b) friendly. (c) secret. (d) riotous.
10. **harass** [har′əs *or* hə·ras′]—(a) to torment. (b) to dispute. (c) to haggle. (d) to mimic.
11. **remonstrate** [ri·mon′strāt]—(a) to plead in protest. (b) to beg. (c) to renew. (d) to give up.
12. **incognito** [in·kog′nə·tō *or* in′kog·nē′tō]—(a) at home. (b) an assumed identity. (c) traveling first class. (d) devious.
13. **barrage** [bə·räzh′]—(a) an overwhelming attack. (b) fireworks. (c) a kind of balloon. (d) a deathblow.
14. **potentate** [pōt′n·tāt]—(a) a cure-all. (b) a very strong drink. (c) a person having great power. (d) seeming to be everywhere at once.

ANSWERS:

1. **lamentable**—(a) regrettable. 2. **demise**—(b) death. 3. **tactile**—(a) pertaining to the sense of touch. 4. **contest**—(b) to challenge. 5. **impious**—(c) irreverent. 6. **ignominy**—(d) disgrace. 7. **ignominious**—(a) humiliating. 8. **enigma**—(b) something that baffles. 9. **clandestine**—(c) secret. 10. **harass**—(a) to torment. 11. **remonstrate**—(a) to plead in protest. 12. **incognito**—(b) an assumed identity. 13. **barrage**—(a) an overwhelming attack. 14. **potentate**—(c) a person having great power.

2 "CORRECT PRONUNCIATION"

Just what is "correct pronunciation"? It is any pronunciation used by careful speakers and recorded in dictionaries. Frequently two or more different pronunciations are acceptable, depending on such factors as where people live or how they have learned a given word.

Don't Be a *Yeller Feller*

Some people pronounce words ending in *-ow, -o,* or *-a* as if they ended in *-er;* thus *yellow* becomes *yeller,* and *fellow* becomes *feller.* This may sound rustic or "folksy" in the movies, but in real life it is often just plain careless.

bellow	bel'ō	*not*	bel'ər
fellow	fel'ō	*not*	fel'ər
hollow	hol'ō	*not*	hol'ər
potato	pə·tā'tō	*not*	pə·tā'tər
vanilla	və·nil'ə	*not*	və·nel'ər
window	win'dō	*not*	win'dər

Don't Be a *Dese, Dem,* and *Dose* Guy

The voiced *th* [t͟h] sound is common in English, as in *this* and *bathe,* and it is often mispronounced as a *d* by slovenly speakers. You are probably not guilty of this fault, but many persons fall into careless speech patterns unintentionally. So listen to yourself the next time you say one of the following words, and make sure that you hear not even a hint of a *d* where the voiced *th* sound should be.

bother	both'ər
brother	bruth'ər
father	fä'thər
mother	muth'ər
that	that
them	them
these	thēz
this	this
those	thōz

Don't Say *Sawr*

Some speakers pronounce words ending in *-aw* as if they ended in *-awr*. This, too, is careless speech.

crawfish	krô′fish′	*not*	krôr′fish′
draw	drô	*not*	drôr
drawing	drô′ing	*not*	drô′ring
law	lô	*not*	lôr
raw	rô	*not*	rôr
saw	sô	*not*	sôr

Twenty-one other words often pronounced carelessly are given below. Be alert to them.

accept	ak·sept′	*not*	ə·sept′
accessory	ak·ses′ər·ē	*not*	a·ses′rē
audience	ô′dē·əns	*not*	ô′jens
bronchial	brong′kē·əl	*not*	bron′ə·kəl
chic	shēk	*not*	chik
escape	ə·skāp′	*not*	ek·skāp′
genuine	jen′yōō·in	*not*	jen′yōō·wīn
hearth	härth	*not*	hûrth
human	hyōō′mən	*not*	yōō′mən
Italian	i·tal′yən	*not*	ī·tal′yən
just	just	*not*	jist
larynx	lar′ingks	*not*	lar′niks
manufacture	man′yə·fak′chər	*not*	man′ə·fa′chər
modern	mod′ərn	*not*	mod′rən
perspiration	pûr′spə·rā′shən	*not*	pres′pə·rā′shən
picture	pik′chər	*not*	pit′chər
point	point	*not*	pûrnt
poison	poi′zən	*not*	⎧ pī′zən
		not	⎩ pûr′zən
something	sum′thing	*not*	⎧ sump′ən
		not	⎩ sum′thən
spoil	spoil	*not*	spûrl
wrestle	res′əl	*not*	ras′əl

357

Fun With Words

COLORFUL ADJECTIVES

This vocabulary test contains sixteen colorful adjectives that are pronunciation stumblers. Learn both their preferred pronunciations and their meanings. Check the word or phrase you believe is closest in meaning to the key word. Answers follow.

1. **sumptuous** [sum′chŏŏ·əs]—(a) luxurious. (b) accurate. (c) overflowing. (d) serious.
2. **svelte** [svelt]—(a) fashionable. (b) slender. (c) foreign. (d) theatrical.
3. **tacit** [tas′it]—(a) selfish. (b) unspoken. (c) shy. (d) talkative.
4. **piquant** [pē′kənt]—(a) pretty. (b) having a pungent taste. (c) irritated. (d) sweet.
5. **phlegmatic** [fleg·mat′ik]—(a) congested. (b) sluggish. (c) stern. (d) easily irritated.
6. **blasé** [blä·zā′]—(a) scholarly. (b) gracious. (c) bored. (d) brilliant.
7. **grisly** [griz′lē]—(a) white. (b) disheveled. (c) gruesome. (d) sordid.
8. **poignant** [poin′yənt]—(a) painful and distressing to the feelings. (b) poised. (c) repulsive. (d) poisonous.
9. **grandiose** [gran′dē·ōs]—(a) imposing. (b) ominous. (c) greedy. (d) very loud.
10. **flaccid** [flak′sid]—(a) flabby. (b) strict. (c) tart. (d) offensive.
11. **hoary** [hôr′ē]—(a) coarse. (b) cold and frosty. (c) unkempt. (d) gray with age.
12. **maladroit** [mal′ə·droit′]—(a) intentionally insulting. (b) feigning sickness. (c) witty and amusing. (d) clumsy and awkward.
13. **oblique** [ə·blēk′]—(a) complicated. (b) out-of-date. (c) slanting or indirect. (d) sarcastic.
14. **statuesque** [stach′ŏŏ·esk′]—(a) graceful and dignified. (b) lavish. (c) secluded. (d) demanding.
15. **posthumous** [pos′chŏŏ·məs]—(a) in the rear. (b) rich and fertile. (c) happening after death. (d) decayed.
16. **resilient** [ri·zil′yənt]—(a) elastic. (b) determined. (c) resolvable. (d) highly respected.

ANSWERS:

1. **sumptuous**—(a) luxurious. 2. **svelte**—(b) slender. 3. **tacit**—(b) unspoken. 4. **piquant**—(b) having a pungent taste. 5. **phlegmatic**—(b) sluggish. 6. **blasé**—(c) bored. 7. **grisly**—(c) gruesome. 8. **poignant**—(a) painful and distressing to the feelings. 9. **grandiose**—(a) imposing. 10. **flaccid**—(a) flabby. 11. **hoary**—(d) gray with age. 12. **maladroit**—(d) clumsy and awkward. 13. **oblique**—(c) slanting or indirect. 14. **statuesque**—(a) graceful and dignified. 15. **posthumous**—(c) happening after death. 16. **resilient**—(a) elastic.

3 DON'T LEAVE OUT LETTERS OR SOUNDS

If what you say is false, you may be forced to "eat your words." But don't be careless and swallow your words before you get them out.

Most poor pronunciations are due to the omission of a sound altogether or to the swallowing or slurring of sounds and syllables. Many persons just won't make the effort required to say words distinctly. Most of us, in fact, have "lazy lips."

Poor pronunciation can be corrected easily once you're aware of the problem. Some faults result from omitting or swallowing *g, d, t,* or *r* sounds, or the vowel sounds of *a, e, i, o,* and *u.* Other errors come from combining simple words into one swallowed mutter, as in *gonna* for *going to.*

Let's go down the following lists and make sure we say all of every word without "eating" a part of it.

Don't Drop Your *G*'s

Don't drop the final *g* in words ending in *-ing*. If you say the final *-ing* so that it sounds like *-in* or *-en* [ən] you are not pronouncing these words according to generally accepted standards. Pronounce *going* as *going* and not as *goin'.* (On the other hand, don't over-accent the final *g*—that is, don't close your throat or click the final *g*.)

Here are ten common *-ing* pronunciation hazards:

beginninG	bi·gin′ing	readinG	rē′ding
cryinG	krī′ing	talkinG	tô′king
doinG	doō′ing	walkinG	wô′king
eatinG	ē′ting	workinG	wûr′king
lovinG	luv′ing	writinG	rī′ting

Note that although the accent of these words is on the root and not on the *-ing*, the *-ing* must still get a full, unslurred pronunciation. Don't swallow your end-*ings*.

Particularly troublesome for many speakers are the *g*'s in the middle of words. You must not drop the *g* in the following words if you want to speak well:

lenGth	lengkth	*not*	lenth
recoGnize	rek′əg·nīz	*not*	rek′ə·nīz
strenGth	strengkth	*not*	strenth

359

Don't Omit the *D, K,* or *T* Sound

Careless speakers often omit other letters besides *g,* such as *d, k,* or *t.* Here are a few of the most bothersome words:

asKed	askd	*not*	ast
canDidate	kan'də·dāt	*not*	kan'ə·dāt
idenTify	ī·den'tə·fī	*not*	ī·den'ə·fī
kepT	kept	*not*	kep
parTner	pärt'nər	*not*	pär'nər
supposeD	sə·pōzd'	*not*	sə·pōs'
wiDth	width	*not*	with

Poor pronunciation is frequently caused by haste in speaking. Many persons ordinarily drop the final *d* in words like *used* and *told* or the final *t* in words like *compact, contradict, protect,* etc. For this reason, you'll find that one excellent way to improve your pronunciation is to talk less rapidly—hence, less carelessly.

EXCEPTIONS: Some common words have *t*'s that should not be pronounced. Those who try to be overly precise sometimes pronounce these *t*'s. This is as much an error as the omission of a *t* where it should be pronounced. For example:

chestnut	ches'nut'	*not*	chest'nut'
often	ôf'en	*not*	ôf'ten
soften	sôf'en	*not*	sôf'ten

Don't Omit the *R*

Some common words are pronounced carelessly by so many people that the mispronunciations may someday become the preferred pronunciations. Precise speakers today, however, do *not* drop the *r*'s in the following words:

FebRuary	feb'rōō·er'ē	*not*	feb'yōō·er'ē
libRary	lī'brer·ē	*not*	lī'ber·ē

Other words in which the *r* is often—but ought not to be—slurred or dropped are:

formeRly	govcRnment	particulaRly
geogRaphy	itineraRy	secRetary
goveRnor	laboratoRy	similaRly

Don't Omit or Slur the Vowel Sound

Poor speakers tend to leave out or swallow the vowel sounds in a great many words. If you pronounce with care, you give the vowels *a, e, i, o,* and *u* the attention they deserve, even when the sound is a rather weak one. Try saying the following words out loud, and pay attention to the vowels—even though they are usually pronounced merely as a quick *uh* [ə]:

accUrate	ak′yər·it	liAble	lī′ə·bəl
asparAgus	ə·spar′ə·gəs	magAzine	mag′ə·zēn′
authOrize	ô′thə·rīz	memOry	mem′ər·ē
barbArous	bär′bər·əs	motOrist	mō′tər·ist
bElieve	bi·lēv′	opErate	op′ə·rāt
cafEteria	kaf′ə·tir′ē·ə	particUlar	pər·tik′yə·lər
capItal	kap′ə·təl	peculIar	pi·kyōōl′yər
cOrrect	kə·rekt′	poEm	pō′əm
crimInal	krim′ə·nəl	poEtry	pō′i·trē
currEnt	kûr′ənt	prepAration	prep′ə·rā′shən
defInite	def′ə·nit	privIlege	priv′ə·lij
equivAlent	i·kwiv′ə·lənt	probAbly	prob′ə·blē
exhIbition	ek′sə·bish′ən	promInent	prom′ə·nənt
factOry	fak′tər·ē	regUlar	reg′yə·lər
favOrable	fā′vər·ə·bəl	restAurant	res′tər·ənt
favOrite	fā′vər·it	simIlar	sim′ə·lər
fedEral	fed′ər·əl	sophOmore	sof′ə·môr
finAlly	fi′nəl·ē	sUppose	sə·pōz′
gEography	jē·og′rə·fē	temperAment	tem′pər·ə·mənt
humOrist	hyōō′mər·ist	temperAture	tem′pər·ə·chər
irOny	ī′rə·nē	usuAlly	yōō′zhōō·əl·ē

EXCEPTIONS: There are two pronunciation demons with *e*'s in the middle that are *not* pronounced. The *e*'s are silent in *pomegranate* [pom′gran·it] and *vineyard* [vin′yərd].

Try Not to Say *Gonna* and *Wanna*

Certain two-word combinations combine so easily that most of us slur them into one word when we speak hastily and without care. Thus, *going to* becomes *gonna* and *want to* becomes *wanna*. Children do it, adults do it, grade-school dropouts do it, and Ph.D.'s do it. Here is a

361

list of the most common two-word combinations that do, nonetheless, sound better when pronounced as two words instead of being jammed together:

can't you	kant yo͞o	*not*	kan'chə
could you	ko͝od yo͞o	*not*	ko͝od'yə
don't you	dōnt yo͞o	*not*	dōn'chə
do you	do͞o yo͞o	*not*	dyə
glad to	glad to͞o	*not*	glad'tə
going to	gō'ing to͞o	*not*	gun'ə
got to	got to͞o	*not*	god'ə
has to	haz to͞o	*not*	has'tə
kind of	kīnd uv	*not*	kīnd'ə
let her	let hûr	*not*	let'ər
let him	let him	*not*	let'əm
let me	let mē	*not*	lem'ē
ought to	ôt to͞o	*not*	ôd'ə
want to	wont to͞o	*not*	won'ə
what did	hwot did	*not*	hwot'əd
what you	hwot yo͞o	*not*	hwot'yə
will he	wil hē	*not*	wil'ē
will you	wil yo͞o	*not*	wil'yə
would you	wo͝od yo͞o	*not*	wo͝od'yə

These and similar two-word combinations are so often slurred that a few of them together may combine to make sentences that no one understands or really listens to. Don't make a poor first impression on a new acquaintance by saying "Gladdameetcha." He may be tempted to ask "Whatchasay?"

Some Help With Your Aitches

Some Englishmen fail to pronounce the letter *h* at the beginning of words; they say *'elp, 'old, 'appiness,* and so on. This is a tradition that goes back to the beginnings of the English language. In fact, not until the eighteenth century, when scholars and teachers tried to make pronunciation conform more nearly to spelling, was the public advised to sound initial *h*'s. Is the Englishman who still drops his *h*'s guilty of poor pronunciation? Opinions vary. In Canadian English most *h*'s should be pronounced, but a few should never be. Is there a rule as to when you should and should not sound your *h*'s? No. However, to help you solve your *h* problems, here are two useful lists. In the following seven words the initial *h* should always be sounded:

Homage	hom′ij
Huge	hyōōj
Human	hyōō′mən
Humane	hyōō·mān′
Humble	hum′bəl
Humor	hyōō′mər
Humorous	hyōō′mər·əs

In the following ten words the *h* in parentheses is never sounded:

(h)eir	âr	shep(h)erd	shep′ərd
(h)onest	on′ist	T(h)ailand	tī′land
(h)onor	on′ər	t(h)yme	tīm
(h)our	our	ve(h)ement	vē′ə·mənt
pro(h)ibition	prō′ə·bish′ən	ve(h)icle	vē′ə·kəl

QUICKIE QUIZ

TEN KEY PUZZLERS

Choose the preferred pronunciation for each of the key words listed below. Answers follow.

1. **recognize**	(a) rek′ə·nīz	(b) rek′əg·nīz
2. **February**	(a) feb′yōo·er′ē	(b) feb′rōo·er′ē
3. **homage**	(a) hom′ij	(b) om′ij
4. **candidate**	(a) kan′ə·dāt	(b) kan′də·dāt
5. **pomegranate**	(a) pom′gran·it	(b) pom′ə·gran·it
6. **length**	(a) lengkth	(b) lenth
7. **dirigible**	(a) dir′ə·jə·bəl	(b) dir′jə·bəl
8. **herb**	(a) hûrb	(b) ûrb
9. **sophomore**	(a) sof′ə·môr	(b) sof′môr
10. **chestnut**	(a) ches′nut′	(b) chest′nut′

ANSWERS:

1. **recognize**—(b) [rek′əg·nīz] 2. **February**—(b) [feb′rōo·er′ē] 3. **homage** —(a) [hom′ij] 4. **candidate**—(b) [kan′də·dāt] 5. **pomegranate**—(a) [pom′- gran·it] 6. **length**—(a) [lengkth] 7. **dirigible**—(a) [dir′ə·jə·bəl] 8. **herb**— (b) [ûrb] is preferred but (a) [hûrb] is acceptable 9. **sophomore**—(a) [sof′- ə·môr] 10. **chestnut**—(a) [ches′nut′]

4 DON'T ADD LETTERS OR SOUNDS

A fault as bad as word-swallowing is its opposite—adding letters or syllables where they don't belong. This is like serving alphabet soup; your listener has to strain out the unrelated letters in order to make sense out of what you say.

The most common alphabet-soup mispronunciations are caused by adding a final -*t* or -*ed* where none belongs or by adding an additional vowel sound where none should be.

Note that many of the most commonly mispronounced words are also spelling demons. If you mispronounce *athlete* as "athalete" you are probably going to misspell the word, too. So learn the words in this chapter; they will improve your spelling as well as your pronunciation.

Don't Add an Extra *T* or -*Ed* Sound

This extra *t* or -*ed* is probably the most substandard speech habit of modern times. To correct it you need to know the proper pronunciation of only seven basic words.

across	ə·krôs′	*not*	ə·krôst′
attack	ə·tak′	*not*	ə·tak′t
attacked	ə·takd′	*not*	ə·tak′təd
drown	droun	*not*	dround
drowned	dround	*not*	droun′dəd
once	wuns	*not*	wunst
twice	twīs	*not*	twīst

Don't Add an Extra Vowel Sound

The following five words are on almost everyone's list of pronunciation demons. None of them has an *a* for a syllable.

athlete	ath′lēt	*not*	ath′ə·lēt
athletic	ath·let′ik	*not*	ath·ə·let′ik
burglar	bûr′glər	*not*	bûr′gə·lər
pamphlet	pam′flit	*not*	pam′fə·lit
translate	trans′lāt	*not*	trans′ə·lāt

The first, fifth, and last words listed below are often mispronounced by children and can make anyone sound a bit childish. Be especially careful of them.

chimney	chim′nē	*not*	chim′ə·nē *or* chim′blē
disastrous	di·zas′trəs	*not*	di·zas′tə·rəs
extraordinary	⎰ik·strôr′də·ner′ē *or* ⎱eks′trə·ôr′də·ner′ē	*not*	eks′tər·ôr′də·ner′ē
hindrance	hin′drəns	*not*	hin′dûr·əns
lightning	līt′ning	*not*	lī′tə·ning
remembrance	ri·mem′brəns	*not*	ri·mem′bûr·əns
umbrella	um·brel′ə	*not*	um·bə·rel′ə

The correct pronunciation of the following four words is one mark of a truly careful speaker. They are mispronounced by many college graduates!

accompanist	ɔ·kum′pə·nist	*not*	ə·kum′pə·nē·ist
electoral	i·lek′tər·əl	*not*	i·lek′tôr′ē·ɔl
grievous	grē′vəs	*not*	grē′vē·əs
mischievous	mis′chi·vəs	*not*	mis′chē·vē·əs

Two words especially bother elementary-school students. If you still pronounce them in a childish way, learn the proper pronunciation now.

| elm | elm | *not* | el′əm |
| film | film | *not* | fil′əm |

REVIEW: Note that by adding an extra sound in many of the above words, the speaker also adds an extra syllable. To help you remember the proper pronunciation of these words, keep in mind their correct number of syllables.

One syllable only

elm   film

Two syllables only

athlete	chimney	lightning
attacked	grievous	pamphlet
burglar	hindrance	translate

Three syllables only

athletic   disastrous   mischievous
                  remembrance
                  umbrella

Four syllables only

accompanist

If you learn to pronounce the above words correctly, you will have mastered seventeen of the most commonly mispronounced words in the English language.

Don't Pronounce Silent Consonants

One related danger to that of adding extra sounds is to pronounce silent letters. As you know, many English words have consonants (letters other than *a, e, i, o,* or *u*) that must be written but not pronounced. Examples of such "silent" consonants are the final *b* in words like *lamb* and *crumb;* the silent *d* in *handkerchief;* the silent *g* in *gnat* or *sign.*

Probably no native speaker of English has trouble with most words of this sort; they are too common to give us trouble. Certainly we are so accustomed to the silent letters in such words as *climb, know, pneumonia, psychology, island, whistle,* and *wrench* that there is no danger of our pronouncing the silent letter and thus mispronouncing the word. But there *are* a number of words with troublesome silent consonants. The following list contains some of them. It is best not to pronounce the silent letters within the parentheses in these words.

a(l)mond	ä′mənd	of(t)en	ôf′ən
bla(ck)guard	blag′ərd	poi(g)nant	poin′yənt
ches(t)nut	ches′nut′	(p)seudo	sōō′dō
cor(ps)	kôr	s(ch)ism	siz′əm
ex(h)ibition	ek′sə·bish′ən	sof(t)en	sôf′ən
glis(t)en	glis′ən	su(b)tle	sut′l
gun(w)ale	gun′əl	ve(h)ement	vē′ə·mənt
mor(t)gage	môr′gij	ve(h)icle	vē′ə·kəl

The word *parliament* is quite unusual in that its vowel *i* is silent. *Parliament* is pronounced [pär′lə·mənt]. And for good measure, don't forget the fine old nautical word that has five silent letters—*boatswain,* pronounced *bos'n* [bō′sən].

Fun With Words

SILENT LETTERS

These fifteen words contain silent letters. Learn both the meanings and pronunciation of these words. Check the word or phrase you believe is closest in meaning to the key word. Answers follow.

1. **archetype** [är′kə·tīp]—(a) an original pattern or model. (b) a villain. (c) a Greek column. (d) handwriting.
2. **wraith** [rāth]—(a) an apparition. (b) anger. (c) violent pain. (d) a very small creature.
3. **schism** [siz′əm]—(a) a reverberating noise. (b) a joining together. (c) a wearing out. (d) a division into hostile groups.
4. **jeopardize** [jep′ər·dīz]—(a) to mock. (b) to attack. (c) to joke. (d) to risk.
5. **imbroglio** [im·brōl′yō]—(a) complexity of design or structure. (b) a confusion of noises. (c) a kind of embroidery. (d) a troublesome situation.
6. **scintilla** [sin·til′ə]—(a) a spark or trace. (b) part of a flower. (c) a fleet of ships. (d) twinkling.
7. **euphoria** [yoo·fôr′ē·ə]—(a) a pastoral scene. (b) loss of speech. (c) loss of memory. (d) a sense of well-being.

8. **wrest** [rest]—(a) to snatch forcibly. (b) to travel slowly. (c) to slant. (d) to condescend.
9. **sovereign** [sov′rən]—(a) serious. (b) rich. (c) beautiful. (d) supreme.
10. **impugn** [im·pyoon′]—(a) to attack as false or untrustworthy. (b) to take away. (c) to dare. (d) to rub off by friction.
11. **exhortation** [eg′zôr·tā′shən]—(a) the act of obtaining by violence. (b) an expression of joy. (c) an earnest plea. (d) rapture.
12. **eulogistic** [yoo′lə·jis′tik]—(a) clear-minded. (b) laudatory. (c) hopeful. (d) thoughtful.
13. **wreak** [rēk]—(a) to inflict, as vengeance. (b) to smell. (c) to irritate. (d) to dwarf.
14. **vehemence** [vē′ə·məns]—(a) an eager wish. (b) noise. (c) loyalty. (d) great force or violence.
15. **realignment** [rē′ə·līn′mənt]—(a) a new division or grouping. (b) a cure-all. (c) resurgence. (d) an increase.

ANSWERS:

1. **archetype**—(a) an original pattern or model. 2. **wraith**—(a) an apparition. 3. **schism**—(d) a division into hostile groups. 4. **jeopardize**—(d) to risk. 5. **imbroglio**—(d) a troublesome situation. 6. **scintilla**—(a) a spark or trace. 7. **euphoria**—(d) a sense of well-being. 8. **wrest**—(a) to snatch forcibly. 9. **sovereign**—(d) supreme. 10. **impugn**—(a) to attack as false or untrustworthy. 11. **exhortation**—(c) an earnest plea. 12. **eulogistic**—(b) laudatory. 13. **wreak**—(a) to inflict, as vengeance. 14. **vehemence**—(d) great force or violence. 15. **realignment**—(a) a new division or grouping.

5 IS CH PRONOUNCED CH, SH, or K?

The letter combination *ch* can cause problems because it is pronounced in three distinct ways, depending on the word in which it occurs. Thus, *ch* is pronounced "ch" as in *chair* [châr], "sh" as in *champagne* [sham·pān'], and "k" as in *chaos* [kā'os].

The words in which *ch* is pronounced as "ch" (*chest, choose, chop, march*) give few native speakers any trouble. Many are simple words that we have known since childhood. However, some in which *ch* is pronounced as "sh" (*chalet, chaperon, chauffeur*) or as "k" (*archeology, chaos, zucchini*) give many of us trouble. Most of them are from our more complicated adult vocabulary, and probably we first saw them in print rather than hearing them from family or friends. (That is, we may have learned to recognize them without having learned how to say them.)

Is there any rule as to when *ch* is pronounced "ch," "sh," or "k"? No. In simple English words the *ch* often is pronounced as "ch" (*chair, cheese*); in borrowings from the French, the *ch* often is pronounced as "sh" (*champagne, chapeau*); and in words from the Greek or Italian, *ch* is generally pronounced as "k" (*Achilles, Chianti* wine).

Here is a list of the most common *ch* pronunciation demons. Pay special attention to those in which *ch* is properly pronounced as "sh" or as "k."

CH pronounced as "ch"

anchovy	an'chō·vē	chapter	chap'tər
arch	ärch	chard	chärd
chafe	chāf	chattel	chat'l
chaff	chaf	Cherokee	cher'ə·kē
chalice	chal'is	cherub	cher'əb
chancel	chan'səl	chide	chīd

CH pronounced as "sh"

cache	kash	charlatan	shär'lə·tən
chagrin	shə·grin'	chartreuse	shär·trōōz'
chalet	sha·lā'	chateau	sha·tō'
champagne	sham·pān'	chauffeur	shō'fər
chandelier	shan'də·lir'	Cheyenne	shī·en'
chaperon	shap'ə·rōn	chiffon	shi·fon'
charades	shə·rādz'	chivalrous	shiv'əl·rəs

CH pronounced as "k"

Achilles	ə·kil′ēz	chasm	kaz′əm
archaic	är·kā′ik	Chianti	kē·an′tē
archangel	ärk′ān′jəl	chimera	kə·mir′ə
archeology	ar′kē·ol′ə·jē	chiropodist	kə·rop′ə·dist
archetype	är′kə·tīp	chiropractor	kī′rə·prak′tər
archipelago	är′kə·pel′ə·gō	cholera	kol′ər·ə
bronchial	brong′kē·əl	choreographer	kôr′ē·og′rə·fər
Chaldea	kal·dē′ə	hierarchy	hī′ə·rär′kē
chameleon	kə·mēl′ē·ən	hypochondriac	hī′pə·kon′drē·ak
chaos	kā′os	machinations	mak′ə·nā′shənz
charisma	kə·riz′mə	zucchini	zŏŏ·kē′nē

Don't be fooled by the above lists of troublesome *ch* words. There are many more words in which the *ch* sound is pronounced "ch," but they are so common that we all pronounce them properly—for example, *champion, chamber, chance, change, channel, chart, charity, Charleston, checkers, cheek, cherish,* and so on.

6 THE HARD G, THE SOFT G, AND SOME OTHER G'S

As everyone who speaks English knows, the letter *c* has two common sounds, the hard *c* [k] sound before *a, o,* and *u* (*cat, canapé, cot, cocoon, cut, custard*); and the soft *c* [s] sound before *e, i,* and *y* (*cent, celebrate, city, cistern, Nancy, cylinder*).

The letter *g* follows the same pattern. The most common *g* sound is the hard *g* (or true *g*) sound usually found before *a, o, u, l, r,* and at the end of words, as in *gas, prodigal, go, asparagus, glow, grass,* and *log.* The less common *g* sound is the soft *g* sound, which is pronounced like a *j* and is usually found before *e, i,* and *y,* as in *gem, engine,* and *clergy.*

The fact that *g* has two distinct sounds usually causes native Americans no problems. We do not stumble when pronouncing *gem* and *get,* even though *gem* follows the general rule—soft *g* [j] sound before an *e*—and *get* does not. We have learned most of the frequently used words as children. However, the soft *g* [j] appears in a number of

369

Fun With Words

C, CH, OR K CHALLENGES

These are fourteen words with a *c, ch,* or *k* sound. Learn the meanings and pronunciations of these words. Check the word or phrase you believe is closest in meaning to the key word. Answers follow.

1. **archaic** [är·kā′ik]—(a) no longer in use. (b) having to do with an archway. (c) a type of suspension bridge. (d) high-ranking.

2. **archives** [är′kīvz]—(a) a place where historical and public documents are kept. (b) ancient temples. (c) small sailing vessels. (d) superior archers.

3. **hierarchy** [hī′ə·rär′kē]—(a) a grouping arranged in successive orders. (b) an archbishop. (c) a presidential cabinet. (d) the upper classes.

4. **chagrin** [shə·grin′]—(a) violent anger. (b) pride. (c) vexation. (d) foolishness.

5. **chaotic** [kā·ot′ik]—(a) disordered and confused. (b) calm. (c) a type of horse-drawn carriage. (d) very careful.

6. **debouch** [di·boosh′ *or* di·bouch′] —(a) to issue forth. (b) to humble. (c) to scold. (d) to scoff at.

7. **inchoate** [in·kō′it]—(a) unable to express oneself clearly. (b) in an elementary stage. (c) weak. (d) chaotic.

8. **chicanery** [shi·kā′nər·ē]—(a) petty evasion and trickery. (b) major fraud. (c) candor. (d) a perennial herb.

9. **lachrymose** [lak′rə·mōs]—(a) lazy. (b) tearful. (c) harmful. (d) stupid.

10. **pulchritude** [pul′krə·tood]—(a) beauty. (b) overabundance. (c) fighting ability. (d) flattery.

11. **machinations** [mak′ə·nā′shənz] —(a) complexities. (b) mechanical operations. (c) wild cherries. (d) artful schemes.

12. **choreography** [kôr′ē·og′rə·fē]— (a) arrangement of light and shade. (b) the art of arranging dances. (c) the art of making maps. (d) the art of group singing.

13. **pachyderm** [pak′ə·dûrm]—(a) therapeutic heat treatment. (b) something discarded. (c) a giant prehistoric fish. (d) a thick-skinned quadruped, as an elephant.

14. **chary** [châr′ē]—(a) cautious. (b) sticky. (c) cooked to a crisp. (d) aware.

ANSWERS:

1. **archaic**—(a) no longer in use. 2. **archives**—(a) a place where historical and public documents are kept. 3. **hierarchy**—(a) a grouping arranged in successive orders. 4. **chagrin**—(c) vexation. 5. **chaotic**—(a) disordered and confused. 6. **debouch**—(a) to issue forth. 7. **inchoate**—(b) in an elementary stage. 8. **chicanery**—(a) petty evasion and trickery. 9. **lachrymose**—(b) tearful. 10. **pulchritude**—(a) beauty. 11. **machinations**—(d) artful schemes. 12. **choreography**—(b) the art of arranging dances. 13. **pachyderm**—(d) a thick-skinned quadruped, as an elephant. 14. **chary**—(a) cautious.

words that are commonly mispronounced. Learn the following soft g
[j] pronunciation demons now:

gesticulate	jes·tik′yə·lāt	harbinger	här′bin·jər
gesture	jes′chər	longevity	lon·jev′ə·tē
gibbet	jib′it	manger	mān′jər
gibe	jīb	orgy	ôr′jē
gist	jist	turgid	tûr′jid

Words Ending in -age, -ege, and -ige

Some English words ending in -age, -ege, and -ige have been borrowed from the French; and in these the g is neither hard nor soft
but may keep its original French flavor. The French g sounds very much
like the s in *vision* or *pleasure*, and the common dictionary symbol for it
is *zh*. Here are eight examples where the g in -age, -ege, or -ige is preferably pronounced with the French g sound of *zh*:

barrage	bə·räzh′	garage	gə·räzh′
camouflage	kam′ə·fläzh	massage	mə·säzh′
corsage	kôr·säzh′	prestige	pres·tēzh′
cortege	kôr·tezh′	sabotage	sab′ə·täzh

NOTE: Many Canadians use the short a in the -age ending: [gə·razh′]
rather than [gə·räzh′].

The Final -ng Sound

The g of a final -ng (*ring, long*) always is softened somewhat or
slurred. Do not pronounce this g as hard as the g in *go* or *dog*. In the
following words do not click your throat shut; don't make a *guh* sound
to end a final -ng:

among	among	*not*	among-guh	long	long	*not*	long-guh
bring	bring	*not*	bring-guh	ring	ring	*not*	ring-guh
fling	fling	*not*	fling-guh	sing	sing	*not*	sing-guh
hang	hang	*not*	hang-guh	wrong	wrong	*not*	wrong-guh

This same softened or slurred g sound is usually kept when you add
an -er or -ing to one of these root words ending in -ng. For instance:

bringing	bring′ing	*not*	bring-ging
flinging	fling′ing	*not*	fling-ging
hanger	hang′er	*not*	hang-ger
hanging	hang′ing	*not*	hang-ging
nagging	nag′ing	*not*	nag-ging
ringing	ring′ing	*not*	ring-ging
singer	sing′er	*not*	sing-ger
singing	sing′ing	*not*	sing-ging

EXCEPTIONS: There are some exceptions to keeping a final -*ng* soft before adding an -*er*. In *English, finger, longer, stronger,* and *younger,* for example, the *g* is stressed a little more than in *hanger, ringer,* or *singer.* In fact, the proper pronunciations are [ing′glish], [fing′gər], [long′gər], and so forth.

QUICKIEQUIZQUICKIEQUIZQUICKIEQUIZQUICKIEQUIZQUICKIEQUIZQUICKIEQUIZQUICKIEQUIZQUICKIE

QUICKIE QUIZ

GETTING THE GIST OF G'S

In the list below, choose the proper pronunciation for each of the key words. Answers follow.

1. **gist**—(a) jist (b) gist
2. **singer**—(a) sing′gər (b) sing′ər
3. **prodigal**—(a) prod′ə·jəl (b) prod′ə·gəl
4. **gesture**—(a) ges′chər (b) jes′-chər
5. **bringing**—(a) bring′ing (b) bring′ging
6. **sabotage**—(a) sab′ə·täj (b) sab′ə·täzh
7. **longer**—(a) long′gər (b) lông′ər
8. **harbinger**—(a) här′bin·jər (b) här′bin·gər
9. **orgy**—(a) ôr′jē (b) or′gē
10. **asparagus**—(a) ə·spar′ə·gəs (b) ə·spar′gras
11. **stronger**—(a) strong′gər (b) strong′ər
12. **longevity**—(a) lon·gev′ə·tē (b) lon·jev′ə·tē
13. **gesticulate**—(a) ges·tik′yə·lāt (b) jes·tik′yə·lāt
14. **giblet**—(a) jib′lit (b) gib′lit

ANSWERS:

1. **gist**—(a) [jist] 2. **singer**—(b) [sing′ər] 3. **prodigal**—(b) [prod′ə·gəl] 4. **gesture**—(b) [jes′chər] 5. **bringing**—(a) [bring′ing] 6. **sabotage**—(b) [sab′ə·täzh] 7. **longer**—(a) [long′gər] 8. **harbinger**—(a) [här′bin·jər] 9. **orgy**—(a) [ôr′jē] 10. **asparagus**—(a) [ə·spar′ə·gəs] 11. **stronger**—(a) [strong′gər] 12. **longevity**—(b) [lon·jev′ə·tē] 13. **gesticulate**—(b) [jes·tik′-yə·lāt] 14. **giblet**—(a) [jib′lit]

QUICKIEQUIZQUICKIEQUIZQUICKIEQUIZQUICKIEQUIZQUICKIEQUIZQUICKIEQUIZQUICKIEQUIZQUICKIE

7 -ATE, -ILE, AND S

If a word of more than one syllable ends in -ate, as in *alternate, candidate, estimate, graduate*, etc., is the final -ate pronounced [it] or [āt]? Is it gradu*it* or gradu*ate*, estim*it* or estim*ate*?

Most such words are pronounced -ate [āt]. But, four common nouns that end in -ate are exceptions and generally are pronounced -it [it].

	[-āt]		[-it]
to alternate	ôl′tər·nāt	an alternate	ôl′tər·nit
to associate	ə·sō′shē·āt *or* ə·sō′sē·āt	an associate	ə·sō′shē·it *or* ə·sō′sē·it
a candidate	kan′də·dāt		
to concentrate	kon′sən·trāt		
to estimate	es′tə·māt	an estimate	es′tə·mit
to graduate	graj′ōō·āt	a graduate	graj′ōō·it
an inmate	in′māt		
a magnate	mag′nāt		

NOTE CAREFULLY: Four common words ending in -ate (*alternate, associate, estimate,* and *graduate*), which can be used as either verbs or nouns, should be pronounced -ate [āt] as verbs and -it [it] as nouns. Thus, these four words are doubly difficult because each has two pronunciations, depending on how it is used.

Is -ile Pronounced "isle" or "ill"?

Some words of two or more syllables that end in -ile are pronounced [īl] as in *smile, mile,* and *while.* Other words that end in -ile are pronounced [il] or even [ēl] or [əl]. Here are twelve words in which a final -ile may cause problems:

	[īl]		[īl, əl *or* il]	
Anglophile	ang′glə·fīl	docile	dos′əl	*or* dō′sīl
exile	eg′zīl *or* ek′sīl	fertile	fûr′təl	*or* fûr′tīl
infantile	in′fən·tīl	fragile	fraj′əl	*or* fraj′īl
profile	prō′fīl	futile	fyōō′təl	*or* fyōō′tīl
reconcile	rek′ən·sīl	hostile	hos′təl	*or* hos′tīl
turnstile	tûrn′stīl′	imbecile	im′bə·sil	*or* im′bə·sīl

Other words that end in *-ile* are pronounced properly either as [-īl] or as [-əl], [-il], or [-ēl]. In the following list the more common or slightly preferred pronunciation is given first:

agile	aj′īl	*or*	aj′əl
domicile	dom′ə·sīl	*or*	dom′ə·səl
juvenile	jōō′və·nīl	*or*	jōō′və·nəl
mercantile	mûr′kən·tīl	*or*	mûr′kən·til
mobile	mō′bīl	*or*	mō′bēl
puerile	pyōō′rīl	*or*	pyōō′ər·il
senile	sē′nīl	*or*	sē′nil
servile	sûr′vil	*or*	sûr′vīl
textile	teks′tīl	*or*	teks′til

NOTE: The British and many Canadians tend to pronounce all *-ile* endings as [īl], to rhyme with *smile*. This is not generally accepted American pronunciation.

The S—A Hiss or a Buzz?

The letter *s* has two main sounds, the *hissing s*, as in *see* and *pass*, and the *buzzing s* [z], as in *amuse* and *music*. Most words with *s* are simple to pronounce, but here are several that are not:

Hiss the S		*Buzz the S*	
crease	krēs	abysmal	ə·biz′məl
crisis	krī′sis	demise	di·mīz′
douse	dous	dismal	diz′məl
gasoline	gas′ə·lēn	houses	hou′zəz
grease	grēs	to house (a verb)	houz
house (a noun)	hous	preside	pri·zīd′
mausoleum	mô′sə·lē′əm	reside	ri·zīd′
Vaseline	vas′ə·lēn	resilient	ri·zil′yənt
vise	vīs	surprise	sər·prīz′
		visa	vē′zə

NOTE: *Advice* is a noun (*I will take your advice*) and is pronounced [ad·vīs′]. *Advise* is a verb (*to advise a friend*) and is pronounced [ad·vīz′]. Remember also that one *house* hisses; two *houses* buzz!

In the following words, you may either hiss or buzz it, since either is acceptable:

absorb	ab·sôrb′	or	ab·zôrb′
absorbent	ab·sôr′bənt	or	ab·zôr′bənt
absurd	ab·sûrd′	or	ab·zûrd′
absurdity	ab·sûr′də·tē	or	ab·zûr′də·tē
usurp	yōō·sûrp′	or	yōō·zûrp′
venison	ven′ə·sən	or	ven′ə·zən

QUICKIEQUIZQUICKIEQUIZQUICKIEQUIZQUICKIEQUIZQUICKIEQUIZQUICKIEQUIZQUICKIEQUIZQUICKIE

QUICKIE QUIZ

-ILE AND S SOUNDS

Choose the preferred pronunciation for each of the key words below. Some may properly be pronounced either way; see if you can decide which they are. Answers follow.

1. mobile	(a) mō′bēl	(b) mō′bīl
2. gasoline	(a) gas′ə·lēn	(b) gaz′ə·lēn
3. usurp	(a) yōō·zûrp′	(b) yōō·sûrp′
4. juvenile	(a) jōō′və·nəl	(b) jōō′və·nīl
5. abysmal	(a) ə·bis′məl	(b) ə·biz′məl
6. textile	(a) teks′til	(b) teks′tīl
7. bibliophile	(a) bib′lē·ə·fīl′	(b) bib′lē·ə·fil′
8. resilient	(a) ri·sil′yənt	(b) ri·zil′yənt
9. fragile	(a) fraj′īl	(b) fraj′əl
10. Anglophile	(a) ang′glə·fīl	(b) ang′glə·fil
11. mercantile	(a) mûr′kən·til	(b) mûr′kən·tīl
12. Vaseline	(a) vas′ə·lēn	(b) vaz′ə·lēn
13. agile	(a) aj′əl	(b) aj′īl
14. demise	(a) di·mīs′	(b) di·mīz′
15. virile	(a) vir′əl	(b) vir′ıl

ANSWERS:
1. **mobile**—(a) [mō′bēl] *and* (b) [mō′bīl] 2. **gasoline**—(a) [gas′ə·lēn] 3. **usurp**—(a) [yōō·zûrp′] *and* (b) [yōō·sûrp′] 4. **juvenile**—(a) [jōō′ve·nəl] *and* (b) [joo′və·nīl] 5. **abysmal**—(b) [ə·biz′məl] 6. **textile**—(a) [teks′til] *and* (b) [teks′tīl] 7. **bibliophile**—(a) [bib′lē·ə·fīl′] 8. **resilient**—(b) [ri·zil′-yənt] 9. **fragile**—(a) [fraj′īl] *and* (b) [fraj′əl] 10. **Anglophile**—(a) [ang′-glə·fīl] 11. **mercantile**—(a) [mûr′kən·til] *and* (b) [mûr′kən·tīl] 12. **Vaseline**—(a) [vas′ə·lēn] 13. **agile**—(a) [aj′əl] *and* (b) [aj′īl] 14. **demise**—(b) [di·mīz′] 15. **virile**—(a) [vir′əl]

QUICKIEQUIZQUICKIEQUIZQUICKIEQUIZQUICKIEQUIZQUICKIEQUIZQUICKIEQUIZQUICKIEQUIZQUICKIE

8 THE SHIFTY ACCENT

Long words have at least one syllable that is pronounced more strongly or more loudly than others. This is called the *accented* or *stressed syllable*. It is indicated in dictionaries by a *primary accent mark* (sometimes called a primary stress mark), usually boldface ('), placed after the syllable. Thus, the word *reader* is pronounced READer and may be shown in your dictionary as [rē'dər]. Some words have two accents. If one of the syllables in such a word is stressed more strongly than the other, the lesser takes a *secondary accent mark*. This secondary accent may be shown in your dictionary as a light-face mark (') or else with two marks ("). Thus, *realism* is pronounced [rē'əl·iz'əm].

In most words the problem is whether the primary accent falls on the first or second syllable. Of course, the primary accent need not fall either on the first or second syllable but may emphasize the third, fourth, fifth, or even sixth. Very long words are rare in English and cause few pronunciation problems to those who know and use them. The major problem is generally whether to place the primary accent on the first or second syllable.

The following fifteen pronunciation demons should always be accented (stressed) on the first syllable:

AMicable	am'i·kə·bəl	*not*	ə·mik'ə·bəl
COMment	kom'ent	*not*	kə·ment'
COMparable	kom'pər·ə·bəl	*not*	kom·pâr'ə·bəl
DEFicit	def'ə·sit	*not*	def·ə·sit'
FORmidable	fôr'mi·də·bəl	*not*	for·mid'ə·bəl
IMpious	im'pē·əs	*not*	im·pī'əs
IMpotent	im'pə·tent	*not*	im·pō'tənt
INfamous	in'fə·məs	*not*	in·fām'əs
INfluence	in'flōō·əns	*not*	in·flōō'əns
INtricate	in'tri·kit	*not*	in·trik'ət
PREFerable	pref'ər·ə·bəl	*not*	prē·fûr'ə·bəl
REParable	rep'ər·ə·bəl	*not*	rē·pâr'ə·bəl
REPutable	rep'yə·tə·bəl	*not*	rē·pyōōt'ə·bəl
REVocable	rev'ə·kə·bəl	*not*	rē·vōk'ə·bəl
THEater	thē'ə·tər	*not*	thē·ā'tər

Note that careful speakers accent the first syllable of many words ending in *-able:* AMicable, COMparable, FORMidable, PREFerable,

REParable, REPutable, and REVocable. If a prefix such as *in-*, *dis-*, or *ir-* is added to form the negative of such words, the primary accent is still kept on the same syllable as it was without the prefix, as in:

inCOMparable	in·kom′pər-ə·bəl
irREParable	ir·rep′ər-ə·bəl
disREPutable	dis·rep′yə·tə·bəl
irREVocable	i·rev′ə·kə·bəl

Always accent the following words on the second syllable:

clanDEStine	klan·des′tin	*not*	klan′dəs·tin
cruSADE	krōō·sād′	*not*	krōō′sād
deCLINE	di·klīn′	*not*	dē′klīn
disPATCH	dis·pach′	*not*	dis′pach
eLITE	ā·lēt′	*not*	ē′lēt
eNIGma	i·nig′mə	*not*	en′ig·mə
reCRUIT	ri·krōōt′	*not*	rē′krōōt
reMONstrate	ri·mon′strāt	*not*	rem′ən·strāt

This Is Easy—You're Right Either Way

Some words may rightly be accented on either the first or second syllable. No matter which syllable you stress, you are safe; dictionaries accept both pronunciations.

abdomen	ab′də·mən	*or*	ab·dō′mən
acclimate	ak′lə·māt	*or*	ə·klī′mit
adult	ad′ult	*or*	ə·dult′
applicable	ap′li·kə·bəl	*or*	ə·plik′ə·bəl
chauffeur	shō′fər	*or*	shō·fûr′
despicable	des′pi·kə·bəl	*or*	di·spik′ə·bəl
exquisite	eks′kwi·zit	*or*	ik·skwiz′it
gondola	gon′də·lə	*or*	gon·dō′lə
grimace	grim′əs	*or*	gri·mās′
harass	har′əs	*or*	hər·as′
hospitable	hos′pi·tə·bəl	*or*	hos·pit′ə·bəl
inquiry	in′kwər·ē	*or*	in·kwīr′ē
lamentable	lam′ən·tə·bəl	*or*	lə·ment′ə·bəl
perfume	pûr′fyōōm	*or*	pər·fyōōm′
robust	rō′bust	*or*	rō·bust′
romance	rō′mans	*or*	rō·mans′

The word *calliope* is a rather special case. It may be accented acceptably on either the first or second syllable, but the pronunciation of the word changes according to your choice of stress: callIope [kə·lī′ə·pē]; CALLiope [kal′ē·ōp]. Note the final long *e* in the first pronunciation of the word.

Two additional words, *advertisement* and *incognito,* are easy to pronounce because the accent is correct on either the second or the third syllable. You may safely say either adVERtisement [ad·vûr′tis·mənt] or adverTISEment [ad′vər·tīz′mənt] and either inCOGnito [in·kog′nə·tō] or incogNIto [in′kog·nē′tō].

This Is Hard—You May Be Wrong Either Way

In some words the accent changes depending on the use. Thus, a child who conDUCTS himself well has good CONduct. In general, two-syllable words that can be used either as nouns or as verbs have the first syllable accented when they are used as nouns and the second syllable accented when they are used as verbs.

This is not as involved as it sounds. For example, when *conduct* is used as a noun, its first syllable is accented: *The child's CONduct was good.* When *conduct* is used as a verb, its second syllable is accented: *He will conDUCT the orchestra.*

Here are further examples of the shift in stress from noun to verb:

NOUN	VERB
a CONscript [kon′skript]	to conSCRIPT [kən·skript′]
He is a military CONscript.	*He was conSCRIPTed.*
a CONtest [kon′test]	to conTEST [kən·test′]
She entered the CONtest.	*I will conTEST the decision.*
CONverse [kon′vûrs]	to conVERSE [kən·vûrs′]
The CONverse is true.	*Let's conVERSE awhile.*
a CONvict [kon′vikt]	to conVICT [kən·vikt′]
The CONvict escaped from jail.	*He was conVICTed for robbery.*
a DESert [dez′ərt]	to deSERT [di·zûrt′]
He rode through the DESert.	*He deSERTed his family.*
an INsult [in′sult]	to inSULT [in·sult′]
I'll stand for no INsults.	*He inSULTed me.*

an OBject [ob'jikt]
What's that OBject?

to obJECT [əb·jekt']
Your Honor, I obJECT.

PROGress [prog'res]
We're making PROGress.

to proGRESS [prə·gres']
You may proGRESS.

a PROJect [proj'ekt]
Our PROJect succeeded.

to proJECT [prə·jekt']
Try to proJECT your voice.

a PROtest [prō'test]
The lawyer filed a PROtest.

to proTEST [prə·test']
They proTESTed vehemently.

REFuse [ref'yōōs]
Throw your REFuse in that bag.

to reFUSE [ri·fyōōz']
I reFUSE to go.

a SUBject [sub'jikt]
Math is a hard SUBject.

to subJECT [səb·jekt']
He was subJECTed to insults.

EXCEPTIONS: Some words are always accented on the first syllable no matter how they are used, others on the second syllable.

Accent the First Syllable		Accent the Second Syllable	
a COMment to COMment	[kom'ent]	a deCLINE to deCLINE	[di·klīn']
a PREFace to PREFace	[pref'is]	a disPATCH to disPATCH	[dis·pach']

A Hint to the Wise

Address is an interesting word. You must always accent the second syllable, adDRESS [ə·dres'], when you use the word as a verb: *The speaker adDRESSed the audience; She adDRESSed the envelope.* Preferably, too, you accent the second syllable when you use the word as a noun meaning a speech or talk: *The speaker delivered the commencement adDRESS.*

You may accent either syllable to mean a person's place of residence —either adDRESS [ə·dres'] or ADdress [ad'res]: *What is Bob Smith's adDRESS?* or *What is Bob Smith's ADdress?*

Since you must say adDRESS in some instances but may say either adDRESS or ADdress in others, when in doubt you will never go wrong if you accent the second syllable: adDRESS.

379

Fun With Words

THE SHIFTY ACCENT

Choose the proper pronunciation or pronunciations of the key words given in the list below. This is tricky because some have two acceptable pronunciations; others have shifty accents, depending on whether they are nouns (a CONvict) or verbs (to conVICT). Answers follow.

1. **grimace**—(a) grim′əs (b) gri·mās′
2. **conduct** (*verb*)—(a) kon′dukt (b) kən·dukt′
3. **conduct** (*noun*)—(a) kon′dukt (b) kən·dukt′
4. **infamous**—(a) in′fə·məs (b) in·fām′əs
5. **gondola**—(a) gon′də·lə (b) gon·dō′lə
6. **incognito**—(a) in′kog·nē′tō (b) in·kog′nə·tō
7. **abdomen**—(a) ab′də·mən (b) ab·dō′mən
8. **chauffeur**—(a) shō′fər (b) sho·fûr′
9. **preferable**—(a) pref′ər·ə·bəl (b) pref·ər·a′bəl
10. **incomparable**—(a) in·kom·par′ə·bəl (b) in·kom′pər·ə·bəl
11. **reparable**—(a) rep′ər·ə·bəl (b) rep′rə·bəl
12. **permit** (*noun*)—(a) pər·mit′ (b) pûr′mit
13. **permit** (*verb*)—(a) pûr′mit (b) pər·mit′
14. **romance**—(a) rō·mans′ (b) rō′·mans
15. **acclimate**—(a) ak′lə·māt (b) ə·klī′mit
16. **irrevocable**—(a) i·rev′ə·kə·bəl (b) ir·rə·vō′kə·bəl
17. **elite**—(a) ā·lēt′ (b) ə·lēt′
18. **inhospitable**—(a) in·hos′pi·tə·bəl (b) in′hos·pit′ə·bəl
19. **clandestine**—(a) klan·də·stin′ (b) klan·des′tin
20. **crusade** (*noun*)—(a) kroō·sād′ (b) kroō′sād
21. **crusade** (*verb*)—(a) kroō·sād′ (b) kroō′sād
22. **adult**—(a) ə·dult′ (b) ad′ult
23. **contest** (*noun*)—(a) kən·test′ (b) kon′test

ANSWERS:

1. **grimace**—(a) [grim′əs] or (b) [gri·mās′] 2. **conduct** (verb)—(b) [kən·dukt′] 3. **conduct** (*noun*)—(a) [kon′dukt] 4. **infamous**—(a) [in′fə·məs] 5. **gondola**—(a) [gon′də·lə] *or* (b) [gon·dō′lə] 6. **incognito**—(a) [in′kog·nē′tō] *or* (b) [in·kog′nə·tō] 7. **abdomen**—(a) [ab′də·mən] *or* (b) [ab·dō′·mən] 8. **chauffeur**—(a) shō′fər] *or* (b) [shō·fûr′] 9. **preferable**—(a) pref′·ər·ə·bəl] 10. **incomparable**—(b) [in·kom′pər·ə·bəl] 11. **reparable**—(a) rep′·ər·ə·bəl] 12. **permit** (*noun*)—(b) [pûr′mit] 13. **permit** (*verb*)—(b) [pər·mit′] 14. **romance**—(a) [rō·mans′] *or* (b) [rō′mans] 15. **acclimate**—(a) [ak′lə·māt] *or* (b) [ə·klī′mit] 16. **irrevocable**—(a) i·rev′ə·kə·bəl] 17. **elite**—(a) [ā·lēt′] 18. **inhospitable**—(a) [in·hos′pi·tə·bəl] *or* (b) [in′hos·pit′ə·bəl] 19. **clandestine**—(b) [klan·des′tin] 20. **crusade** (*noun*)—(a) [kroō·sād′] 21. **crusade** (*verb*)—(a) [kroō·sād′] 22. **adult**—(a) [ə·dult′] *or* (b) [ad′ult] 23. **contest** (*noun*)—(b) [kon′test]

9 WHERE ARE YOU?

The pronunciation of the names of countries, cities, rivers, mountains, streets, etc., can cause many problems. Place names may be derived from various American Indian languages, from Chinese, Japanese, Russian, or any of hundreds of other languages that the average person does not know. These may also be pronounced differently in different countries. Thus, the city we know as *Vienna* [vē·en'ə] is *Wien* [vēn] in Austria, and the country we know as *Mexico* [mek'sə·kō] is written *México* in Latin-American countries and pronounced [mā'hē·kō].

North American place names can be difficult. *Beaufort* is [byōō'fərt] in South Carolina, but [bō'fərt] in North Carolina. *Quincy* is [kwin'zē] in Massachusetts but [kwin'sē] in Florida and other states. And *Natchitoches*, Louisiana, is pronounced [nak'i·tush]. English-speaking people will say [kwə·bek'], [kə·bek'] or [kwē'bek] for *Québec*, while the French-speaker will say [kā'bek]. *Caribbean* (which comes from the Spanish *caribe*—cannibal) is pronounced both [kərib'ēyn] and [ka'rə·bēyn].

No wonder, then, that a Canadian finds impossible the pronunciation of the capital of Slovenia in Yugoslavia, Ljubljana [lyōō'blyä·nä], or the famous Welsh town with the longest name on record: Llanfairpwllgwyngliigogerychwyrndrobwllllantysiliogogogoch [hlan·vīr'pōōhl· gwin'gahl·gô·ge'rōōn·wōoym·drōob'ōohl·hlan·tē·sē'lē·ô'gô·gô·gôn'], which means "St. Mary's Church in a hollow by the white hazel close to the rapid whirlpool by the red cave of St. Tysilio." And the second longest place name in English belongs to a lake in Massachussets—Chargoggagoggmanchauggagoggchaubunagungamaugg—which means "fishing place at the boundaries; neutral meeting grounds." Natives of the Welsh town call it simply *Llanfair*, while Massachusetts folk call their lake *Chargogg*.

What to do about difficult place names? Learn the correct way to pronounce the more common ones and look up the others in your dictionary when you encounter them. Some frequently used demons are:

Albuquerque, New Mexico	al'bə·kûr'kē
Ankara, Turkey	äng'kə·rə
Beirut, Lebanon	bā'rōōt *or* bā·rōōt'
Cairo, Egypt	kī'rō
Cairo, Illinois	kâr'ō
Cannes, France	kan *or* kanz
Champs Elysées, a Paris boulevard	shän'zā·lē·zā'

Des Moines, Iowa	də·moin′
Edinburgh, Scotland	ed′ən·bûr′ə
Eire	âr′ə
Gloucester	glos′tər or glôs′tər
Greenwich	gren′ich
Lachine, Québec	lə·shēn
Guiana	gē·an′ə
Hawaii	həwä′ē or hə·wī′yə
Himalayas, the Asian mountain range	him·ē·lā′əz or hi·mäl′yəz
Houston, Texas	hyōōs′tən
La Jolla, California	lə·hoi′yə
Laos	lä′ōs
Mojave Desert	mō·hä′vē
Monaco	mon′ə·kō or mə·nä′kō
Moscow	mos′kou or mos′kō
Oahu	ō·ä′hōō
Okinawa	ō′ki·nä′wä
Palestine	pal′is·tīn
Rio de Janeiro, Brazil	rē′ō də jə·nâr′ō
Rio Grande river	rē′ō grand′
Salisbury	sôlz′bər·ē

NOTE: *Salisbury steak* (a hamburger steak) is pronounced the same way! Do not pronounce it *Sal-is-bury*.

Saint-Joachim, Québec	sän·jōə·shen′
San Joaquin Valley, California	san′ wô·kēn or san′ wä·kēn′
San Jose, California	san′ hō·zā′
San Juan, Puerto Rico	sän hwän′
Sault Sainte Marie	sōō′ sānt′ mə·rē′
Schenectady, New York	skə·nek′tə·dē
Thailand	tī′land
Tokyo	tō′kē·ō
Tucson, Arizona	tōō·son′ or tōō′son
Versailles	ver·sī′

NOTE: Eight U.S. towns called Versailles are pronounced [ver·sālz].

Vietnam	vē·et·näm′
Waco, Texas	wā′kō
Worcester, Worcestershire	wŏŏs′tər, wŏŏs′tər·shir

NOTE: *Worcestershire sauce* is pronounced exactly the same way.

Yosemite National Park	yō·sem′ə·tē

THREE-MINUTE QUICKIE QUIZ

IT'S A GREAT PLACE TO VISIT, BUT . . .

From the choices given below, choose the proper spelling of each place name. Answers follow.

1. (a) Edinburg   (b) Edinburgh   (c) Edinborough
2. (a) Rio de Janero   (b) Rio de Janeiro   (c) Rio de Janiero
3. (a) Tailand   (b) Thiland   (c) Thailand
4. (a) Salisberry   (b) Salisbury   (c) Salesbury
5. (a) Hawaii   (b) Hawai   (c) Hawaai
6. (a) Tucson   (b) Tuscon   (c) Tuscan
7. (a) Alburquerque   (b) Albuquerque   (c) Albuqueque
8. (a) Champs Élysées   (b) Champs de Eylsoes   (c) Champs Elyse
9. (a) Canne   (b) Canes   (c) Cannes
10. (a) Himmalayas   (b) Himalayas   (c) Himallayas
11. (a) Worcestershire   (b) Woostershire   (c) Wocestershir
12. (a) Schenectady   (b) Scenecktady   (c) Schenectedy
13. (a) Soo Saint Marie   (b) Salt Sant Marie   (c) Sault Sainte Marie
14. (a) San Wakeen   (b) San Joaquin   (c) San Jacquin
15. (a) Glocester   (b) Gloucster   (c) Gloucester
16. (a) Sioux Falls   (b) Soo Falls   (c) Siox Falls
17. (a) Shillo   (b) Shiloh   (c) Shylo
18. (a) Placamine   (b) Plackmine   (c) Plaquemine
19. (a) Apomattox   (b) Appomattox   (c) Appomatox
20. (a) Berchtesgaden   (b) Birchtesgarden   (c) Berktesgaden
21. (a) Galaupagos   (b) Galápagos   (c) Gallapagos
22. (a) Wilkes-Barry   (b) Wilks-Barre   (c) Wilkes-Barre
23. (a) Seatle   (b) Seattle   (c) Settle
24. (a) Guadalahara   (b) Guadalara   (c) Guadalajara
25. (a) Torquay   (b) Torkay   (c) Torquey

ANSWERS:

1. (b) Edinburgh. 2. (b) Rio de Janeiro. 3. (c) Thailand. 4. (b) Salisbury. 5. (a) Hawaii. 6. (a) Tucson. 7. (b) Albuquerque. 8. (a) Champs Élysées. 9. (c) Cannes. 10. (b) Himalayas. 11. (a) Worcestershire. 12. (a) Schenectady. 13. (c) Sault Sainte Marie. 14. (b) San Joaquin. 15. (c) Gloucester. 16. (a) Sioux Falls. 17. (b) Shiloh. 18. (c) Plaquemine. 19. (b) Appomattox. 20. (a) Berchtesgaden. 21. (b) Galápagos. 22. (c) Wilkes-Barre. 23. (b) Seattle. 24. (c) Guadalajara. 25. (a) Torquay.

All countries "borrow" words from other countries and languages. We have such foreign expressions as *status quo* (Latin), *hors d'oeuvre* (French), *ersatz* (German), *intermezzo* (Italian), *cabana* (Spanish), *sputnik* (Russian), *hara-kiri* (Japanese), and *aloha* and *ukulele* (Hawaiian).

Foreigners borrow from English. Indeed, foreign countries now adopt more words from American English than from any other language. The French, Germans, Italians, Latin Americans, Russians, Japanese, etc., have incorporated into their languages such typical American words as *supermarket, cocktail, astronaut,* and *gasoline.* Of course, foreign peoples often spell and pronounce these borrowings in their own way, just as we do when we take from them.

Common foreign imports are bound to cause pronunciation problems for many of us. Who has not been intimidated by French words on a menu? No one is expected to know French, Italian, German, Spanish, Latin, etc., just to be able to pronounce imported "English" properly. Still, it's nice to know the generally accepted Anglicized pronunciation of some foreign words that are used widely in Canada. Let's learn a few of those words now.

Parlez-Vous English?

We have borrowed thousands of expressions from the French. Most of them have become so common that we have little trouble saying them. Here are sixty-three words of French origin that retain their French flavor even after they have been somewhat Anglicized in sound or spelling. Learn the ones you aren't already sure of.

amour [ə·mŏor′]—a love affair; love; a lover.
au courant [ō kōo·rän′]—up-to-date.
au gratin [ō grat′ən]—sprinkled with bread crumbs or grated cheese and baked.
au jus [ō zhü′]—served with its own natural juice or gravy.
au lait [ō lā′]—with milk, as coffee.
au revoir [ō rə·vwär′]—good-by.
billet-doux [bil′ā·dōo′]—a love letter.
blasé [blä·zā′]—bored, as from having seen or done too much.
bourgeois [bŏor′zhwä]—middle-class.

brassiere [brə·zir′]—a woman's undergarment.

buffet [boŏ·fā′]—a sideboard; a light meal.

canapé [kan′ə·pā]—an appetizer, usually a cracker topped with caviar, cheese, etc.

cliché [klē·shā′]—a trite expression.

coiffure [kwä·fyŏor′]—a style of arranging the hair.

coupe [koōp or koō·pā′]—a two-door automobile.

crouton [kroō′ton or kroō·ton′]—a small cube of toast used as a garnish in soups or salads.

cuisine [kwi·zēn′]—a style or quality of cooking.

cul-de-sac [kul′də·sak′]—a blind alley; especially, a trap with only one means of escape.

décolletage [dā·kôl·täzh′]—a garment with a low-cut neckline.

dishabille [dis′ə·bĕl′]—the state of being partially or negligently dressed.

dossier [dos′ē·ā]—a collection of documents relating to a particular person or matter.

éclair [ā·klâr′ or i·klâr′]—an oblong pastry filled with custard or whipped cream.

entrée [än′trā]—the principal dish (or main course) at a meal.

faux pas [fō pä′]—a social mistake or breach of etiquette.

fete [fet]—(1) a festival; (2) an outdoor celebration.

fiancé [fē·än′sā]—a man to whom a woman is engaged.

fiancée [fē·än′sā]—a woman to whom a man is engaged.

finesse [fi·nes′]—delicate skill or tact.

gauche [gōsh]—awkward; boorish.

gourmand [goŏr′mənd]—a big eater.

gourmet [goŏr′mā or goŏr·mā′]—a judge or lover of fine food and drink.

habitué [hə·bich′oō·ā]—a person who frequents a specific place.

hors d'ocuvre [ôr dûrv′]—an appetizer or appetizers.

ingénue [an′zhə·noō′]—an innocent young girl (chiefly as played by an actress).

liaison [lē′ā·zon′ or lē·ā′zon]—(1) a bond or link; (2) a person who coordinates activities between two groups.

lingerie [län′zhə·rē or län′zhə·rā′]—women's light undergarments.

loge [lōzh]—a box or a balcony section in a theater.

macabre [mə·kä′brə]—gruesome.

mal de mer [mal′ də mâr′]— seasickness.

marquee [mär·kē′]—a canopy over the sidewalk in front of a hotel or theater.

melee [mā′lā *or* mä·lā′]—a brawl or noisy free-for-all.

milieu [mē·lyœ′]—environment; surroundings.

motif [mō·tēf′]—the underlying theme or design in a literary or artistic work.

naive [nä·ēv′]—unsophisticated, artless.

naiveté [nä·ēv′tā]—the quality of being naive.

negligée [neg′li·zhā′]—a dressing gown for women.

nuance [nyo͞o·äns′ *or* no͞o′äns]—subtle variation in color, tone, or meaning.

passé [pa·sā′]—(1) past the prime; faded; (2) old-fashioned.

patois [pat′wä]—a type of local dialect.

piquant [pē′kənt]—peppery or pungent in taste; agreeably stimulating.

pique [pēk]—a feeling of irritation or resentment.

potpourri [pō·po͞o·rē′ *or* pot·po͝or′ē]—a mixture of incongruous or miscellaneous elements.

ragout [ra·go͞o′]—a meat and vegetable stew.

rendezvous [rän′dä·vo͞o]—a prearranged meeting or the appointed place for a meeting.

repartee [rep′ər·tē′ *or* rep′är·tā]— a witty or quick reply.

résumé [rez′o͝o·mā′]—a summary or recapitulation, as of one's background and job experience.

ricochet [rik′ə·shā′]—to glance from a surface, as a ball or bullet.

roué [ro͞o·ā′ *or* ro͞o′ā]—a man who devotes his time to sensual pleasure.

sachet [sa·shā′]—an ornamental bag of perfumed powder.

salon [sa·lon′]—a drawing room.

savoir-faire [sa·vwär fâr′]—the ability to say and do the right thing; tact.

tête-à-tête [tāt′ə·tāt′]—a private chat; confidential, as between two persons only.

valet [val′ā *or* val′it]—a gentleman's personal servant.

Note that the *i* in many of these French words is pronounced as [ē]: *cliché, fiancé, naive, piquant.*

Most words of several syllables that end in *-et* derive from the French. Many of these words have been Anglicized completely so that the *-et* is pronounced "et," as in *bayonet, cadet, coronet, martinet,* and *tourniquet.* These cause no problems. However, other French borrowings ending in *-et* have not yet been Anglicized completely. The *-et* sound keeps some of its Gallic flavor and is pronounced [ā], as in *bouquet, cabaret, chalet, gourmet,* and *sachet.*

Fun With Words
FROM THE FRENCH

These fifteen words have been taken into English from French. Learn their proper meanings and pronunciations. Check the word or phrase you believe is closest in meaning to the key word. Answers follow.

1. **potpourri** [pō·pōō·rē' *or* pot·poŏr'ē]—(a) a Spanish gypsy dance. (b) a dialect. (c) the common people. (d) a medley or mixture.

2. **patois** [pat'wä]—(a) a local dialect. (b) the language of a nation. (c) a foreign accent. (d) a dish in cookery.

3. **ingénue** [an'zhə·nōō']—(a) a young woman of simplicity and innocence. (b) indifference. (c) a shade of blue. (d) boredom.

4. **gasconade** [gas'kə·nād']—(a) a coward. (b) a torrent of water. (c) bragging talk. (d) a kind of soufflé.

5. **portmanteau** [pôrt·man'tō]—(a) large overcoat. (b) a cape. (c) a curtain. (d) a suitcase.

6. **milieu** [mē·lyœ']—(a) grace. (b) environment. (c) softness. (d) one's special occupation.

7. **fete** [fet]—(a) a festival. (b) overflowing. (c) a bouquet. (d) an accomplished deed.

8. **finesse** [fi·nes']—(a) completion.
(b) slenderness. (c) clumsiness. (d) tact or skill.

9. **macabre** [mə·kä'brə]—(a) a type of corn. (b) a Spanish gypsy dance. (c) envious. (d) gruesome.

10. **métier** [mā·tyā']—(a) a person's special calling. (b) a measure or norm. (c) a weapon. (d) average.

11. **habiliments** [hə·bil'ə·mənts]—(a) articles of clothing. (b) habits. (c) residences. (d) fortifications.

12. **éclat** [ā·klä']—(a) abundance. (b) brilliance of action or effect. (c) a kind of pastry. (d) a creamy filling for cakes.

13. **dossier** [dos'ē·ā]—(a) a briefcase. (b) a festival. (c) a collection of papers, documents, etc. (d) a tapestry.

14. **hauteur** [hō·tûr']—(a) polite anger. (b) style. (c) a well-bred manner. (d) disdainful pride.

15. **esprit** [es·prē']—(a) lively wit. (b) a group of dancers. (c) a ghost. (d) talkativeness.

ANSWERS:

1. **potpourri**—(d) a medley or mixture. 2. **patois**—(a) a local dialect. 3. **ingénue**—(a) young woman of simplicity and innocence. 4. **gasconade**—(c) bragging talk. 5. **portmanteau**—(d) a suitcase. 6. **milieu**—(b) environment. 7. **fete**—(a) a festival. 8. **finesse**—(d) tact or skill. 9. **macabre**—(d) gruesome. 10. **métier**—(a) a person's special calling. 11. **habiliments**—(a) articles of clothing. 12. **éclat**—(b) brilliance of action or effect. 13. **dossier**—(c) a collection of papers, documents, etc. 14. **hauteur**—(d) disdainful pride. 15. **esprit**—(a) lively wit.

387

Watch Out for the French *en-*

The French word and syllable *en-* can cause pronunciation problems. In many words it has been Anglicized to our own *en* sound. Others, however, keep the French *ahn* or *on* sound, a nasalized vowel with just a suggestion of *n*:

en garde [än·gärd′]—on guard (a fencing position).
ennui [än′wē]—boredom.
en rapport [än ra·pôr′]—in sympathetic agreement.
en route [än rōōt′]—on or along the way.
ensemble [än·säm′bəl]—a unified whole, as a matching costume or group of musical performers.
entente [än·tänt′]—an understanding or agreement, as between governments.
entourage [än′tŏŏ·räzh′]—a group of followers; retinue.
entr′acte [än·trakt′]—the interval between the acts of a play, opera, etc.
entrée [än′trā]—(1) the main course of a meal; (2) a means of obtaining entry, as into a special group.
entrepreneur [än′trə·prə·nûr′]—a person who starts or conducts a business enterprise.

NOTE: *Envelope* preferably is pronounced with the English *en* sound [en′və·lōp], but the French *en* sound [än′və·lōp] is acceptable.

Sprechen Sie English?

English has also borrowed from the German. The following list includes words that cause pronunciation trouble. Learn the Anglicized pronunciation of these words now.

blitzkrieg [blits′krēg]—a swift, sudden attack.
ersatz [er·zäts′ *or* er′zäts]—a substitute, usually an inferior one.
glockenspiel [glok′ən·spēl]—a musical instrument consisting of tuned metal bars played by striking with a small hammer.
kindergarten [kin′dər·gär′tən]—a school or class for small children.
knockwurst [näk′wûrst]—a highly seasoned sausage.
lieder [lē′dər]—German songs, especially ballads or love poems set to music.
rathskeller [rats′kel·ər]—a beer hall or restaurant.
sauerbraten [sour′brä·tən]—beef marinated in vinegar and cooked.

How About Spanish, Italian, and Latin?

Here are eleven words we have borrowed from Spanish along with a generally accepted pronunciation for each:

aficionado [ə·fē′syō·nä′dō]—an enthusiast; devotee, as of bull fights.
amontillado [ə·mon′tə·lä′dō]—a pale dry Spanish sherry.
cabana [kə·ban′ə]—literally, a small cabin; a beach bath house.
castanet [kas′tə·net′]—one of a pair of wood or ivory disks clapped together in the fingers to accompany a dance or song.
flamenco [flə·meng′kō]—a style of singing and dancing developed by Spanish gypsies.
guava [gwä′və]—a tropical tree, the fruit of which is used in jellies.
hacienda [hä′sē·en′də]—a large ranch, or its main house.
iguana [i·gwä′nə]—a tropical American lizard.
jai alai [hī ə·lī′]—a popular Latin-American game somewhat similar to handball but played with a curved wicker basket strapped to the arm.
junta [jun′tə]—(1) a secret political faction; (2) a legislative body.
tortilla [tôr·tē′yä]—a round, flat cornmeal cake used in place of bread in Mexico.

Many imports from Italy are listed below. Note how many of them relate either to music or food. Can you pronounce them all correctly?

alfresco [al·fres′kō]—out of doors.
antipasto [än′tē·päs′tō]—a variety of appetizers.
cadenza [kə·den′zə]—a musical flourish for a solo performer.
Chianti [kē·an′tē]—a dry red wine.
coloratura [kul′ər·ə·tŏŏr′ə]—(1) a soprano with an unusually wide range and flexibility; (2) runs or trills in vocal music.
crescendo [krə·shen′dō]—a gradual increase in volume in music.
finale [fi·nal′ē]—the last part of a performance.
fortissimo [fôr·tis′ə·mō]—very loud: a musical direction.
grotto [grot′ō]—a cave.
intermezzo [in′tər·met′sō]—a short musical, dramatic, or ballet offering given between the acts of a play or opera.
lasagne [lə·zän′yə]—a dish comprising pasta, ground meat, tomato sauce, and cheese.
obbligato [ob′lə·gä′tō]—an accompanying part of a musical composition.

pasta [päs′tə]—any type of spaghetti, macaroni, etc.

pianissimo [pē′ə·nis′i·mō]—very soft: a musical direction.

piazza [pē·äz′ə]—a veranda or porch.

pizza [pēt′sə]—a doughy crust covered with cheese, tomatoes, spices, anchovies, etc., and baked.

pizzicato [pit′sə·kä′tō]—music made by plucking strings rather than by using a bow.

vendetta [ven·det′ə]—a blood feud.

zucchini [zōō·kē′nē]—a green summer squash.

We call Latin a "dead" language, but it lives on in many English expressions, especially scientific, legal, medical, and business terms. The list of Latin terms below includes words that every educated person should be able to pronounce properly and easily.

ad hoc [ad hok′]—a term for any group or committee formed for a specific purpose in a specific situation.

ad hominem [ad hom′ə·nəm]—appealing to one's individual passions or prejudices.

agenda [ə·jen′də]—program of business.

angina [an·jī′nə]—a pain in the chest and arm caused by insufficient coronary circulation.

aurora borealis [ô·rôr′ə bôr′ē·al′is]—the northern lights.

bona fide [bō′nə fīd′]—genuine.

de facto [dē fak′tō]—existing in fact, with or without legal sanction.

erratum [i·rä′təm]—an error.

finis [fin′is or fī′nis]—the end.

ibidem [i·bī′dem]—in the same place.

non sequitur [non sek′wə·tər]—an irrelevant comment or remark.

per se [pûr sā′ or pûr sē′]—by itself.

quasi [kwā′zī or kwā′sī; kwä′zē or kwä′sē]—similar, but not precisely the same.

rara avis [râr′ə ā′vis]—an unusual or rare person or thing.

status quo [stā′təs or stat′əs kwō]—an existing condition or state.

stet [stet]—let it stand: a proofreader's direction.

BEWARE: Many foreign words in this chapter are also spelling and vocabulary demons as well. Many speakers avoid these useful words because they don't know how to pronounce or spell them or exactly how to use them. Don't let such difficulties stand in your way. Study the above lists with care, and consult your dictionary for further help.

390

PART FOUR

Punctuate
It Right

PUNCTUATION MARKS—CLUES TO CLEARER MEANING

Why do we have punctuation? When you talk, you do not depend on words alone to tell your listener what you mean. The tone and stress of your voice affect the meanings of the words you use: You speak calmly or angrily; you whisper or yell. Facial movements and body gestures add meanings: You grin or grimace, nod or shake your head, wiggle a finger, shrug, or raise an eyebrow. The true meaning of conversation is affected by pauses and halts that are as significant as words themselves.

When you write, what you are really doing is "talking" to someone who is not there. That is why your full meaning, pauses, emphases, and emotional states must be suggested by punctuation marks. The primary aim of every punctuation mark is to make unmistakable the meaning of written words. Every mark of punctuation is a road sign set up to help the reader grasp what the writer intended to convey. Punctuation is effective if it helps a reader to understand; it is ineffective and even harmful if it gets in the way of his understanding.

Punctuation marks serve four general purposes: (1) to terminate; (2) to introduce; (3) to separate; and (4) to enclose. They do more than mark such obvious facts of language as "This is a question." They help group related ideas; they set off words for emphasis; they affect the mood and the tempo of what you write; they indicate which words are to be taken together and which are to be kept separate. Thus, punctuation points up the relationships and the relative importance of words and groups of words.

Words Without End

The right words in the right places will convey our ideas, but only the right punctuation can organize them into meaningful patterns for the eye. We cannot hope to communicate with a reader in this way:

> andsoshesaidtohimyesisupposethatsallrightbutireally
> thinkthatyououghttocheckwithmarty

For clarity, we must separate, punctuate, and organize written words into groups. We do this with some standard devices—actually writing "tricks." Some of these punctuation "tricks" are almost as natural to us as speech itself. Others are more complex and can cause us trouble.

First, we use spaces between words as the initial step in reducing the jumble of letters to an understandable pattern. Even a child just beginning to write does this almost automatically. The space between words is our most basic "punctuation mark"; it takes the place of natural pauses between words in speaking. Spacing in general is used to group written words into understandable patterns.

Thus, we group the elements of a thought, or closely related thoughts, into a series of paragraphs. We also group the smaller elements of single thoughts into sentences. We mark the start of the sentence with a capital letter—or beginning punctuation—and mark the end of it with a period, question mark, or exclamation point, which tells the reader whether our written "voice" is falling, rising, or expressing strong emotion.

We give the reader further help in understanding the individual parts of an idea and their relationships by using commas, colons, semicolons, dashes, parentheses, and quotation marks. And some of these punctuation marks also help the reader to "hear" our pauses and tone of voice.

In this part of the book you will learn all about these easy devices—the tricks of written communication called *punctuation marks*. Since capitalization and hyphenation are so closely related to punctuation, they will be discussed here, too.

Modern Punctuation

All punctuation in the Western world began with the little dot that we call a *period*. In fact, the very word "punctuation" comes from the Latin word *punctum,* meaning "a point or dot." Gradually, through the centuries, other punctuation marks have been developed in order to signify a variety of changes in mood and tempo within sentences, as well as to clarify the relationships between various elements within a given sentence. Punctuation marks were particularly necessary in the nineteenth century because writers in those days often wrote long, complex sentences, and punctuation helped make them easier to read and to understand.

In our own century most writers and their readers have come to prefer simpler, shorter sentences—sentences with just one subject and one predicate and with few qualifying expressions. Thus, there is less need today than there used to be for internal (within a sentence) punctuation—commas, semicolons, and colons—to separate complex

393

clauses and phrases from one another. And since there are more short sentences, the period tends to occur more often than it used to.

The modern tendency toward streamlining has also caused punctuation marks to be dropped from the ends of lines in addresses on letters; and we no longer put periods at the end of newspaper headlines, chapter headings in books, and the like. Today, we think of punctuation and its allies—capitalization and hyphenation—as purely functional rather than as having to conform to hard-and-fast rules. When you finish this part of the book, you should know all you need to know about the reasonable use of punctuation marks in modern writing.

REMEMBER: Without punctuation, written words would be difficult to understand. Punctuation can help you to a more effective use of your vocabulary. It can save you time and effort in writing clearly what you have to say. Much of what follows may be merely a review of what you already know, but the rest of it will help you sharpen your use of punctuation power to a fine point. Do all the tests and quizzes, even if you find them easy.

---

1 CAPITALIZATION

As in spacing between words and indenting before paragraphs, capitalization is a simple visual trick that helps make our writing intelligible. A capital letter (A, B, C) sticks out because it is bigger than other letters. It is used to direct attention to a new sentence or group of words, or to indicate the proper name of a person, place, or thing.

Capitalization is not difficult. You probably capitalize correctly most of the time without giving it a thought, even if you don't always know the rules. This chapter will tell you some things you need to know in order to capitalize correctly all of the time.

(a) Use a capital letter at the beginning of every sentence or of every word or group of words that has the force of a sentence.

> *He came to work.*
> *What time did he come to work?*
> *Eight.*
> *That early? Nonsense!*

This rule also applies to quoted matter. Every sentence in a direct quotation starts with a capital letter.

Bob asked, "What time did he come to work?"
Pete shouted, "Go!"
John said, "No. You can't make me go."

EXCEPTION: A sentence within a sentence does not start with a capital letter if it is enclosed in parentheses.

The meeting will start at noon (please be on time!) and will end at four.

Remember that the salutation and the complimentary close of a letter have the force of a sentence and therefore must begin with a capital letter.

Dear Mr. Jones:	Dear Mary,
Gentlemen:	Sincerely,

(b) Use a capital letter for the pronoun "I" and for the letter "O" when used as an interjection (generally only in religious contexts).

May I go with you?   *Hear us, O Lord!*

(c) Use a capital letter for proper nouns. A proper noun is the name of a particular person, place, or thing—for instance, Elizabeth, Halifax, Conservative Party. A "person" or "place" will probably give you no trouble, but remember that a "thing" is construed very broadly to include monuments (Peace Tower), school subjects (Geography, Business Administration), book titles (*Paradise Lost*), and political parties (Liberal).

All the major types of proper noun are discussed below. Study them until you are sure that you know when to begin—and when not to begin—a noun with a capital letter.

Proper Nouns That Name Persons or Animals

(1) Capitalize any part or form of a name, including a nickname, epithet, title, initial, or term of address. This rule applies both to real and fictitious names, whether of people or animals.

Robert Brown	Queen Elizabeth	Premier Smythe
Bob Brown	the Queen (*but:* a queen)	Senator Croll

Mr. Brown	Your Highness	the Mayor
R. B.	Henry the Eighth	Assemblyman Smith
Battlin' Bob Brown	Sir Walter Raleigh	Professor Jones
Uncle Bob (*but:* He's my uncle.)	Lady Jane Grey	Father Flanagan
	the Prince of Wales	Mr. and Mrs. Brown

EXCEPTIONS: A small, unimportant word in a person's name or title (such as *the, of, and,* etc.) is not capitalized unless it begins a sentence. (Note, above, Henry *the* Eighth and *the* Prince *of* Wales.)

Designations of rank without an accompanying name are capitalized when they stand for a specific person: *the President* (referring to a specific president of the United States, a university, a corporation, etc.). But such words are not capitalized when they simply refer to a class or type of person: *a senator; a president.* Note, too, that titles of rank that follow the name are usually capitalized only when the title is one of very great distinction:

> Abraham Lincoln, the President of the United States
> H. R. Jones, president of the Highland Bowling Club

Titles of family relationship are capitalized only when used with a name or in place of a name. They are not capitalized when used with a possessive pronoun such as *my* or *your.*

> *We'll have to ask Mother.*
> *We'll have to ask our mother.*

(2) Capitalize the name of a thing or idea when it is treated as though it were a person.

> Dame Rumor
> Jack Frost
> Mother Nature

(3) Capitalize all names for supernatural figures or powers, including pagan deities. Note that words referring to sacred persons, such as epithets or terms of address, are also capitalized. Some pronouns referring to God and Christ (usually *He, Him,* and *His; Thee* and *Thou*) are generally capitalized. But when pagan deities are referred to in general terms, they are known as *gods* with a small *g.*

God (*but:* a pagan god)	Zeus
Allah	Providence
the Holy Trinity	the Almighty

Proper Nouns That Name Specific Places

(1) Capitalize the standard or accepted name of a geographical place, area, or feature, whether real or fictitious.

Medicine Hat	the Grand Canyon
Westchester County	the North Pole
New Brunswick	the Temperate Zone
the West	Lake Huron
the New World	the Promised Land
the Western Hemisphere	Camelot
the Mississippi River	the Happy Hunting Ground
the Pacific Ocean	the Rockies

NOTE: Capitalize *North, South, East,* and *West* only when you are referring to a part of the country. Do not capitalize them when you mean a compass direction, such as *north, south,* or *north by northwest.*

> *Calgary is in the West.* (a section of the country)
> *Turn right and drive ten miles west.* (a compass direction)

West and *East* are also capitalized when you mean a section of the world, referring to the Occident or Orient.

> the mystery of the East (the Orient)
> the technology of the West (the Occident)

(2) Capitalize the name of a celestial body or system, such as a planet or galaxy, or of any specific place on a celestial body, such as a valley on the moon.

Mars	the Milky Way
the North Star	the Big Dipper
the Great Bear	the Sea of Tranquillity

EXCEPTIONS: The words *sun, moon,* and *solar system* are not capitalized. And *earth* is generally capitalized only when used as a planetary name: *Mars, Jupiter,* and *Earth* revolve around the sun.

(3) Capitalize the name of a specific location, as a street, road, square, or park.

Marymount Road	the Trans-Canada Highway
Route 95	Banff National Park

Proper Nouns That Name Specific Things

The category of "things" is broad enough to include any one-of-a-kind thing with a proper name—for instance, buildings, companies, products, and the like.

(1) Capitalize any one-of-a-kind object with a proper name, as a ship, plane, bridge, tunnel, document, or award.

the Titanic
the Apollo 11
the Château de Ramezay

the Quebec Bridge
the British North America Act
the Victoria Cross

(2) Capitalize the names of days, months, divisions of history, holidays, and important events.

Monday
September
Labor Day

World War II
the Crusades
the Battle of Ypres

the Depression
the Victorian Period
the Stone Age

EXCEPTION: Designations of centuries—*the nineteenth century, the twentieth century*—and the names of seasons—*spring, summer,* etc.— are not usually capitalized.

(3) Capitalize all names for religions, sacred writings, religious orders and denominations, and their members.

Christianity
Judaism
a Buddhist
the Bible
the Koran

the Old Testament
the Talmud
the Sermon on the Mount
Genesis
Anglican

Catholic
Protestant
Methodist
Franciscan
Islam

(4) Capitalize all names for peoples, races, tribes, nationalities, etc.

Indian
Anglo-Saxon
Norwegian

Eskimo
Cherokee
Finn

Spaniard
New Englander
Italian

Québecois
Neanderthal man
Newfoundland

NOTE: Although the words *black* and *white* as designations of skin color are usually not capitalized, there is an increasing tendency toward capitalizing them and using them as racial terms.

(5) Capitalize the names of languages.

English   German   Yiddish   Swahili

(6) Capitalize the names of political parties or movements and their members. Also capitalize the names of executive, legislative, and judicial bodies.

the Agrarian Movement	County Assessor's Office
a New Democrat	Toronto Board of Education
the Department of Defense	the Senate
the Supreme Court	the United Nations

NOTE: Use small letters for terms that refer generally to social ideologies: *fascism, socialism, communism, democracy*. But capitalize such words when referring to specific political systems and their members.

Bill Robinson is a born democrat. (The reference is to his belief in democracy.)
Jack Meredith has been a Democrat since 1960. (The reference is to his party affiliation.)

(7) Capitalize the names of organizations, including their identifying initials, branches, departments, and members.

York Public School
Simon Fraser University
the Y.M.C.A.
the Boy Scouts
a Girl Guide
a Mason

(8) Capitalize the names of companies, trademarks, and brand names.

General Motors	the Royal Bank of Canada
Coca-Cola	the Palace Theater
National Biscuit Company	the Metropolitan Opera

(9) An unimportant word like *a, the, of, and,* etc., should not be capitalized unless it begins a sentence or is the first word of the full title.

Handel's oratorio *The Messiah*
Steinbeck's *Of Mice and Men*

A preposition or conjunction is often capitalized, however, when it is at least four letters long: for example, *Rebel Without a Cause.*

399

(10) Capitalize every important word in the title of a book, chapter, poem, movie, comic strip, painting, musical composition, document, legislative act, treaty, and the like.

Gone With the Wind	the Gettysburg Address,
"Jack and the Beanstalk"	Beethoven's Ninth Symphony
the *Mona Lisa*	the Fifth Amendment
"Terry and the Pirates"	the Treaty of Versailles

NOTE: You've probably noticed that some titles are generally italicized, while others are enclosed in quotation marks. Briefly, titles of full-length works of literature, as well as of most other works of art, are generally italicized; titles of *parts* of books and of such shorter works as short stories and poems (or of comic strips, TV programs, etc.) are usually put in quotation marks. Other kinds of titles—for example, the Bible and its various parts—are neither italicized nor put in quotation marks.

Our class is reading *Robinson Crusoe, Hamlet,* and Kipling's poem "Recessional."
The last book of the New Testament is Revelation.

How do you indicate italics in a handwritten or typewritten manuscript? It's easy! You underline the word or words this way, and the printer will print them *this way.*

(11) Capitalize the name of a specific course in school.

He took Biology, English Composition, and Music last year.

Note that these are specific courses; otherwise, only the word *English* (a language) would be capitalized.

He studied biology, English, and music in school.

Proper Adjectives

Capitalize proper adjectives. A proper adjective is either formed from a proper noun, or is a proper noun used as an adjective. The proper adjectives *American* and *Jeffersonian,* for example, are formed from the proper nouns *America* and *Jefferson.* The proper adjective *Montana* in *a Montana law* is a proper noun used as an adjective.

Paris fashions (proper noun used as adjective)
Parisian glamour (adjective formed from proper noun)

EXCEPTIONS: A number of adjectives formed from proper names have become words in their own right and are no longer capitalized.

a platonic relationship (from Plato)
a quixotic outlook (from Don Quixote)

Punctuation Test—Capital Letters

Supply capital letters where needed in the following sentences.

1. john collins was pleased to learn that an ancestor of his had helped to settle the prairie provinces.
2. you were born in the northwest, weren't you? in whitehorse?
3. where does the chairman of the parliamentary committee on federal pollution control live?
4. the flier won a d.s.o. in the battle of britain.
5. all points on the map are south of the north pole.
6. this young man, al jenkins, was graduated from lane technical institute.
7. were you in regina when the roughriders played the alouettes?
8. thank you, mr. chairman, for that gracious introduction.
9. to reach fort brown, drive west on highway 62 and then turn right on route 19.
10. pierre elliott trudeau was born in montreal, did postgraduate work at harvard and the london school of economics and became prime minister in 1968.

ANSWERS:
1. John Collins was pleased to learn that an ancestor of his had helped to settle the Prairie Provinces.
2. You were born in the Northwest, weren't you? In Whitehorse?
3. Where does the Chairman of the Parliamentary Committee on Federal Pollution Control live?
4. The flier won a D.S.O. in the Battle of Britain.
5. All points on the map are south of the North Pole.
6. This young man, Al Jenkins, was graduated from Lane Technical Institute.
7. Were you in Regina when the Roughriders played the Alouettes?
8. Thank you, Mr. Chairman, for that gracious introduction.
9. To reach Fort Brown, drive west on Highway 62 and then turn right on Route 19.
10. Pierre Elliott Trudeau was born in Montreal, did postgraduate work at Harvard and the London School of Economics and became Prime Minister in 1968.

2 THE PERIOD

The little dot from which all punctuation grew is still our most common punctuation mark. Its chief function, of course, is as a stop sign: We use it to end a sentence, to bring a single thought to a full stop. Indeed, "full stop" is another name for the period. It can perform a number of functions, but here are its two major uses:

(1) Use a period to end a declarative or an imperative sentence—that is, a sentence that makes a statement or gives a command or request.

> *You left your book on the chair next to your purse and gloves.* (A statement.)
> *Leave your book, please.* (A request.)
> *Good-by. Yes.* (Each of these, even though very short, is a statement.)

Most people think of a sentence as something that must have a subject (such as "I"), a predicate (such as "will buy"), and perhaps an object (such as "an apple"); but this is not always the case. The only true requirement of a sentence is that it must express a complete thought. Therefore, "Yes" and "Good-by" are sentences, for in context they express complete thoughts.

(2) Use a period after initials and most abbreviations.

W. C. Fields	Dr. Edwards	ten ft. wide
Mr. and Mrs. Bolton	William C. Jonas, Ph.D.	Denver, Colo.
the Lessing Co.	Joyce Brown, M.A.	five ft. tall

ONE PROBLEM: Is it U.S.A. or USA, P.M. or PM, F.B.I. or FBI? In many cases either form will do. But since there are hundreds of abbreviations, the best thing to do is to consult your dictionary.

USAGE NOTE: Do not put two periods together. If a sentence ends in an abbreviation with a period, that period suffices to end the sentence; do not add a second period unless a parenthesis intervenes.

> *It took him seven years to earn his Ph.D.*
> *Enclosed are the stamps, coupons, clippings, etc.*
> *I like everything I have (house, family, job, etc.).*
> *The sign read "John Knowles, M.D."*

MORE FOREIGN WORDS

Here are fifteen foreign words to learn or review. Check the word or phrase you believe is closest in meaning to the key word. Answers follow. And while you're at it, be sure that you know the proper pronunciation of these words.

1. **a priori** [ā' prī·ō'rī]—(a) prior to experience. (b) to the rear. (c) after careful examination. (d) the most important.
2. **ex cathedra** [eks' kə·thē'drə]— (a) a sermon. (b) highly secret. (c) with authority. (d) contrary to accepted belief.
3. **non sequitur** [non sek'wə·tər]— (a) foolishness. (b) an irrelevant remark or conclusion. (c) sound logic. (d) a connected series.
4. **quid pro quo** [kwid' prō kwō'] —(a) a puzzle. (b) a proposition. (c) something for nothing. (d) one thing in return for another.
5. **in toto** [in tō'tō]—(a) impatiently. (b) strongly. (c) entirely. (d) bluntly.
6. **cadenza** [kə·den'zə]—(a) a musical flourish. (b) a fast dance. (c) a woman soloist. (d) a concert.
7. **vendetta** [ven·det'ə]—(a) a light opera. (b) a feud. (c) a weapon. (d) a cape.

8. **crescendo** [krə·shen'dō]—(a) crisis. (b) an opera score. (c) gossip. (d) increase in volume of sound.
9. **inamorata** [in·am'ə·rä'tə]—(a) a beloved woman. (b) a clandestine affair. (c) immortal. (d) infatuated.
10. **piazza** [pē·az'ə]—(a) a pie. (b) a veranda. (c) a country fair. (d) a fish.
11. **cupola** [kyoō'pə·lə]—(a) a small dome. (b) a bay window. (c) a terrace. (d) trimming.
12. **fiasco** [fē·as'kō]—(a) an altercation. (b) a fistfight. (c) a humiliating failure. (d) a mistake.
13. **libretto** [li·bret'ō]—(a) free and easy. (b) the text or words of an opera. (c) a light opera score. (d) a song.
14. **inferno** [in·fûr'nō]—(a) summer heat. (b) a hot oven. (c) hot-blooded. (d) a hellish place.
15. **flotilla** [flō·til'ə]—(a) a fleet of small ships. (b) a floating dry dock. (c) floating objects. (d) a baking process.

ANSWERS:

1. **a priori**—(a) prior to experience. 2. **ex cathedra**—(c) with authority. 3. **non sequitur**—(b) an irrelevant remark or conclusion. 4. **quid pro quo**— (d) one thing in return for another. 5. **in toto**—(c) entirely. 6. **cadenza**— (a) a musical flourish. 7. **vendetta**—(b) a feud. 8. **crescendo**—(d) increase in volume of sound. 9. **inamorata**—(a) a beloved woman. 10. **piazza**—(b) a veranda. 11. **cupola**—(a) a small dome. 12. **fiasco**—(c) a humiliating failure. 13. **libretto**—(b) the text or words of an opera. 14. **inferno**—(d) a hellish place. 15. **flotilla**—(a) a fleet of small ships.

3 THE QUESTION MARK

The question mark (or interrogation point), the second most common punctuation mark, is used at the end of a word or group of words to indicate that a question is being asked, or, less frequently, to indicate doubt. There are three main ways in which you can make it do its job for you:

(1) Use the question mark to end a direct question.

> *When will you arrive?*
> *Why not?*
> *You left at noon?*

Note that the first two examples above begin with *when* and *why*, which indicate to the reader that the sentence is going to be a question. But the last example depends completely on the question mark to tell the reader that a question is being asked. If you were putting the question to someone in this form, your voice would rise at the word *noon*. It is the question mark that tells the reader how to "think" the sentence correctly.

(2) Use a question mark after each question in a series of questions within a sentence.

> *When will you arrive? on what airline? on what flight?*
> *Can we depend on Bob? on Jim? on Al?*

Question marks used within a sentence in this way call for a series of halts so that extra stress is placed on each element.

(3) Use a question mark to express doubt. Such a question mark is usually put inside parentheses after a date, word, or figure, to show that the writer is not sure that it is correct.

> *Columbus was born in 1446 (?) and died in 1506.* (The date of his death has been firmly established, but the year of his birth is not entirely certain.)
> *At the party, you'll meet the Browns, Bob Pearce (?), and Frank Harrison.* (This means either that the writer is not sure that Bob Pearce will be there or that he is not sure of the correct spelling of Bob's last name.)

404

WARNING: Such parenthetical question marks are *not* to be used to show the reader that you are too lazy to use your dictionary. In other words, never use a question mark to express doubt over a fact or spelling that you could easily verify if you tried. Don't do this: "Our cruise to the Caribbean (?) was wonderful."

TWO MINOR PROBLEMS: First, when is a sentence a statement or request, and when is it a true question? In other words, is a sentence that starts out as a statement but ends up as a question a statement or a question? And, secondly, should you use a period or a question mark after a polite request put in the form of a question or after a rhetorical question (one for which no answer is expected)? The following examples should help solve these problems for you.

> *She asked me how long I'd been away.* (Here the period is required. The question is only an indirect one.)
> *The point at issue is this: Am I right or wrong?* (The question mark is correct because it follows a direct question.)
> *Won't you please come in.*
> *You think you're pretty smart, don't you.*
> *Who knows when the rain will stop.*

The first of these last three sentences is a polite request. The other two are rhetorical questions—that is, they are put in the form of questions, but the speaker does not expect an answer; he is merely giving vent to his feelings. In all three cases most good writers do not use a question mark, but it is not incorrect to use one. The choice is yours.

4 THE EXCLAMATION POINT

The exclamation point is the third and final mark of terminal punctuation, but it appears less often than the period and the question mark.

The exclamation point is used after a word or group of words to indicate that the writer is making some kind of strong exclamation or interjection. In many instances, you can think of this punctuation mark as a shout from the writer or one of his characters. Here are its two main uses:

(1) Use an exclamation point to end a sentence or phrase expressing

405

strong emotion, shock, surprise, sarcasm, etc., or after an interjection (that is, a single word expressing strong emotion, shock, etc.).

> *"You'll never catch me alive!"* he screamed.
> *Fancy meeting Jane in Mexico! And she's getting married there!*
> *Hot dogs! Peanuts and popcorn!* (These exclamation points merely let the reader know that the vendor is "shouting" his wares.)
> *Oh!* (This exclamation point shows shock, surprise, or delight.)
> *You're a fine one to tell me how to diet!* (Here the exclamation point shows sarcasm.)

(2) Use the exclamation point after some commands.

> *Column right, march!*
> *Run for your life!*

These commands are literally shouted—or, at least, they are so urgent that they'd better be obeyed. Simple commands or polite requests are best followed by either a period or a question mark.

WARNING: Exclamation points lose their effectiveness when overused. Save them for cases of extreme amazement, shock, etc. Too many people try to make up for a dull or uncertain style of writing by using exclamation points to show emotion, as in these two examples:

> *"I love you, Mary!"* he whispered.
> *"Oh, John!"* she replied.

The really competent writer shows feeling in his handling of words, not in the way he punctuates.

A MINOR PROBLEM: Even though you know the common uses of the period, question mark, and exclamation point, there are times when you must rely on your knowledge of the true meaning of the sentence in order to decide which punctuation mark it should end with. At such times ask yourself whether you want the reader to read it as a flat statement, as a question, or as a kind of shout. For example, the short sentence "Sit down" can be punctuated in the following three ways:

> *Sit down.*
> *Sit down!*
> *Sit down?*

The first is a mild command or polite request. The second is an urgent command; it may indicate extreme irritation or anger, or it may be a warning to someone about to fall overboard from a rowboat. The last has a question built into it. It may mean "How can I, since there's no place to sit?" Or perhaps it means "Do you really want me to sit down?"

In any case, as these three examples show, terminal punctuation marks can do a great deal to set the tone or shift the meaning of a sentence.

Punctuation Test—Periods, Exclamation Points, and Question Marks

Supply the punctuation needed in the following sentences. The answers that follow are not necessarily the only possible ones. Can you improve on them?

1. The Pierre Laporte Bridge can't be a mile long, can it
2. The crash caused me to cry out in horror
3. Ouch that's hot
4. When will your sister arrive I hope she is enjoying her trip
5. That electrician Do you know what he charged Fifty dollars
6. What a shame Mrs. Baker won't be here for the party How disappointed she must be
7. I wonder why the play doesn't begin Oh Now the curtain is rising
8. We should make an early start Can you be ready to leave at 6 A.M.
9. I asked the salesman, "For how long is this article guaranteed" He exclaimed, "Forever"
10. When it's 6 P.M. in Regina, what time is it in Charlottetown, P E I

RECOMMENDED PUNCTUATION:

1. The Pierre Laporte Bridge can't be a mile long, can it?
2. The crash caused me to cry out in horror.
3. Ouch! That's hot!
4. When will your sister arrive? I hope she is enjoying her trip.
5. That electrician! Do you know what he charged? Fifty dollars.
6. What a shame Mrs. Baker won't be here for the party! How disappointed she must be!
7. I wonder why the play doesn't begin. Oh! Now the curtain is rising.
8. We should make an early start. Can you be ready to leave at 6 A.M.?
9. I asked the salesman, "For how long is this article guaranteed?" He exclaimed, "Forever!"
10. When it's 6 P.M. in Regina, what time is it in Charlottetown, P.E.I.?

5 THE COMMA

Commas are the workhorses of English pronunciation and are the punctuation marks used most frequently within sentences. One of the comma's main functions is to keep the meaning of a sentence clear by indicating which of its parts are necessary for the basic sense and which parts are not quite as essential. Another important function of the comma is to show the reader which parts of a sentence belong together, and which should be read as separate, though closely related, elements of the sentence.

More specifically, the comma has the following principal uses:

(1) It may be used to separate the components of a date, of an address, of a large number, or of a series of three or more items, words, or groups of words.

> July 4, 1776
> Thursday, November 12
> Winnipeg, Manitoba
> 107 Patterson Ave., Victoria, British Columbia
> 2,841
> $5,322,476
> *She won the bingo game by covering B3, I27, N42, G78, and O93.*
> *On our vacation we visited friends in Kingston, Peterborough, and Cornwall.*
> *Mr. and Mrs. Snyder, Dr. and Mrs. Brewster, and Mrs. Green were at the party.*

NOTE: In lists or series such as those illustrated in the last three sentences above, many writers omit the last comma (the one that immediately precedes *and*). Both ways of punctuating lists or series are acceptable. Just be sure you are consistent. Do not include the final comma in one instance and drop it in another.

(2) A comma may be used after the salutation (greeting) and after the conventional closing phrase of a letter. A colon (:) is preferred for the salutations in business or other formal letters.

> Dear Jim,
> Dear Mom, (*but* Dear Sir:)
> Best regards,
> Sincerely yours,

(3) A comma is always used to set off the name or title of a person you address directly in writing, or to set off a person's name from his title, academic degree, or the like.

Well, Tom, that's about the end of the story.
I'm very happy to tell you this news, Aunt Jane.
The project chief was Gordon French, Ph.D.

(4) A comma is used to separate the two parts of any sentence that begins as a statement but ends as a question.

He's a devil, isn't he?
That wasn't too much to spend for this dress, was it?

(5) Expressions such as *she said, he wrote,* etc., that either introduce or follow quoted dialogue are usually set off by commas.

George said, "Let's start now."
"Let's start now," said George.
"By tomorrow," Cynthia wrote, "I'll be in Saskatoon again."

(6) A comma is used between each of two or more adjectives that modify the same noun.

We kept up a brisk, steady pace on the hike.
Queechy Lake is a deep, blue, calm body of water.

NOTE: To test whether the modifiers all modify the same noun, substitute the word *and* for the commas: "brisk *and* steady pace"; "deep *and* blue *and* calm body of water." If the word *and* cannot be meaningfully inserted, commas should not be used. Consider, for instance, the sentence "She wore brown leather gloves." Here the gloves are not really brown *and* leather; the two words *brown leather* are a unit that cannot be meaningfully separated. Hence, no comma.

Similarly, if you write "Queechy Lake is a deep blue color," you do not mean that the color is both deep *and* blue; it is *deep blue*, without a comma.

(7) Commas are always used to set off *appositives*—that is, words or phrases that rename, identify, or explain the preceding word or phrase.

I, John Lovell, do make this last will and testament.
The captain of the football team, a senior from Verdun, scored the first touchdown.
Why should this have happened to him, honest fellow that he is?

409

NOTE: Except at the end of a sentence (as in the last of the preceding examples) a pair of commas is always used in such situations, one before and one after the appositive word or words.

(8) Commas may be used to set off an introductory phrase or clause that tells how, when, where, why, etc., the following statement has happened, is happening, or will happen.

> *When the war was over, Jerry returned to Hull.*
> *In Puerto Rico, it never gets this cold.*
> *Even if it rains cats and dogs tomorrow, we won't call off our picnic.*

NOTE: If the introductory group of words is very short, many writers feel that no comma is needed. It would not be incorrect, for example, to write "In Puerto Rico it never gets this cold." Note, too, that a comma is not generally used to set off a clause or phrase that follows the main statement instead of preceding it:

> *Jerry returned to Hull when the war was over.*
> *We won't call off our picnic even if it rains cats and dogs tomorrow.*

(9) Commas are often used to separate almost unnecessary words or groups of words (parenthetical expressions) from the rest of the sentence.

> *I appreciate your offer but cannot, however, accept the position.*
> *You are, therefore, the only person who can do the job.*
> *He is, unfortunately, a rather poor sport.*
> *Nancy knew, of course, that the party started at eight.*
> *Yes, you're absolutely right.*
> *You look a little pale, to tell the truth.*

In all the above sentences, the words set off by commas serve mainly as personal emphasis, personal asides, word bridges, or nonessential introductions or conclusions to the major statement. Note that except at the beginning or end of a sentence, the commas are always paired around the parenthetical expression so that it is entirely separated from the essential parts of the sentence.

(10) A comma usually precedes the coordinating conjunction in a compound sentence. A compound sentence is a sentence that is really composed of two or more sentences joined together (that is, coordinated) by a conjunction such as *and, but, for,* or *or.*

A boy gave us directions, but they were so complicated we couldn't follow them.

I returned the book to Jane, and she took it right back to the library.

We could hardly hear the speaker, for we sat in the last row of the auditorium.

If the compound sentence is very brief, you may safely omit the comma before the conjunction.

Henry thought he knew his way but he didn't.

At night the children play checkers or I read to them.

(11) Commas should always be used to set off *nonrestrictive clauses*. A nonrestrictive clause is a group of words that describes something or someone without being absolutely necessary for identifying the thing or person. In other words, you can drop a nonrestrictive clause from the sentence without changing the meaning.

Peter's new fishing rod, which is an eleven-footer, cost him a small fortune. (The clause *which is an eleven-footer* is nonrestrictive and must be set off by commas because it merely adds some information about the rod; the rod has already been clearly identified as *Peter's new fishing rod.* Compare this with the following sentence: *The fishing rod which Peter just bought cost him a fortune.* Here the clause *which Peter just bought* is restrictive: It is essential to the meaning of the sentence because it tells the reader which one of Peter's rods the writer is referring to, and so it should not be enclosed in commas.)

My favorite niece, whom I almost never see, lives in Honolulu. (No question about which of my nieces lives in Honolulu, is there? Compare this with the following sentence: *The niece whom I see least often lives in Honolulu.*)

Our house, where three generations have been born and died, stands on a high hill. (Compare *Any house where three generations have been born and died is worth preserving.*)

NOTE: Some writers pepper their sentences too heavily with commas, and others use too few. Remember that the comma is not just a decoration on the page; it has an important job to do in sorting out, separating, and combining the various parts of a sentence. When you are in doubt about whether or not you need a comma at a certain place, try saying the sentence out loud. If it seems natural for you to pause, no matter how briefly, at that spot, a comma may well be in order. If, on the other hand, a pause seems to break into the middle of a tight cluster of words and to make you sound as if you're gasping for breath, do not insert a comma.

Thus, for example, you would not normally say "John and Mary (*pause*) have gone out for a walk." But you would pause for at least an instant at the places where commas are inserted in the following sentence: *John and Mary, who felt they needed a breath of fresh air, have gone out for a walk.*

This is not, of course, a sure-fire way to test your use of commas, but it may often help to resolve your doubts.

6 THE COLON

Once you have learned how to use capital letters, periods, question marks, exclamation points, and commas properly, you have mastered the hardest and most common punctuation marks. Although everyone should understand them, the remaining punctuation marks are used much less frequently.

The colon (:) indicates a division in writing or a pause in speech greater than that of a comma and less than that of a period. It usually separates a general, introductory item from a specific explanation, list, quotation, number, or the like. It often indicates to the reader: "I've told you my overall plan; now look at the details."

The colon has four principal uses:

(1) Use a colon to follow the salutation (greeting) of a formal or business letter, speech, or report.

Dear Dr. Loomis: To Whom It May Concern:
Gentlemen: Mr. Chairman, Honored Guests, Ladies
                          and Gentlemen:

When is a letter formal enough to require a colon after the greeting? Usually, when you address the reader by his or her business, professional, or other official title or by an impersonal term of address like *Sir* or *Madam*. The trend, especially in some kinds of business letters, is toward the more informal comma rather than the colon.

412

(2) Use a colon after a word, phrase, or statement that introduces a list or an item.

> *Grocery list: bread, milk, orange juice, hamburger.*
> *On duty tonight: Jones, Brown, Johnson.*
> *For rent: large 6-room apartment.*
> *Bob excels in the following sports: baseball, basketball, and hockey.*

WARNING: The colon is correctly used after a phrase such as "including the following," "as follows," etc. Do *not* use a colon, however, if the verb in a statement leads directly into a list—that is, if you would *not* pause in saying the sentence. Thus:

> *Bob excels in baseball, basketball, and hockey.*

One simple way to tell when to use the colon and when not to use it is to say the sentence out loud. If you normally take a breath before the list, then use a colon to indicate the pause. If you wouldn't pause when saying the sentence, then don't use a colon.

(3) Use a colon after a statement that introduces a quotation, another statement, or an explanation or amplification of what has just been said.

> *He began the meeting with this warning: "Gentlemen, we're in trouble."*
> *My conclusion is: The dog is not man's best friend.*
> *I have three objections to the plan: It would take too long, it would cost too much, and it would be too risky.*

NOTE: Use the colon in this way only when you want to emphasize the quotation, the second statement, or the amplification by setting it off from the rest of the sentence. If you don't want such strong emphasis, you can link the introductory words and the following statement in some less emphatic fashion.

> *He began the meeting by saying, "Gentlemen, we're in trouble."*
> *My conclusion is that the dog is not man's best friend.*
> *I object to the plan because it would take too long, cost too much, and be too risky.*

(4) A colon is often used to separate the hour from the minutes in a numerical writing of the time of day (12:15), or the volume number from the page number in a citation from a publication (*The Congressional Record* 65:832).

Fun With Words

MORE SHORTIES

Too many vocabulary-building programs concentrate on long, complicated words—the kind few people find useful for everyday business or conversation. Here's a test of vocabulary shorties, of words having only three letters. Check the word or phrase you believe is closest in meaning to the key word. Answers follow.

1. **nib** [nib]—(a) point of a pen. (b) a fleshy part. (c) cream. (d) a slight cut.
2. **van** [van]—(a) to excommunicate. (b) forefront. (c) highest point. (d) background.
3. **yaw** [yô]—(a) an African antelope. (b) to quarrel. (c) to cast aspersions at. (d) to move wildly off course.
4. **wan** [won]—(a) pale. (b) a storage place. (c) ghastly. (d) to diminish.
5. **wry** [rī]—(a) an incorrect decision. (b) wrong. (c) twisted. (d) very common.
6. **eke** [ēk]—(a) to piece out or supplement. (b) to yell or scream. (c) to trickle forth. (d) to throw out.
7. **con** [kon]—(a) to end abruptly. (b) to read with care. (c) to go with someone. (d) to forfeit.
8. **nub** [nub]—(a) a baby. (b) the hilt. (c) the gist or point. (d) the conclusion.
9. **oaf** [ōf]—(a) a dark horse. (b) a blockhead. (c) a sacrificial offering. (d) an elf.
10. **vie** [vī]—(a) vigor. (b) to compete with. (c) to consider. (d) to pledge allegiance.
11. **fen** [fen]—(a) to duel with. (b) to keep away from. (c) a marsh or swamp. (d) an oasis.
12. **don** [don]—(a) to put on, as a garment. (b) a lover. (c) to dance lightly. (d) an infatuation.
13. **dun** [dun]—(a) to annoy. (b) to chew or bite on. (c) to notify. (d) to press for payment.
14. **rue** [rōō]—(a) to regret extremely. (b) to wander. (c) to tint with a red dye. (d) to pine away.
15. **ebb** [eb]—(a) to fuss over. (b) to study. (c) to reach a peak. (d) to wane.
16. **eon** [ē'on]—(a) a vast number. (b) an atomic particle. (c) an incalculably long period of time. (d) several years.

ANSWERS:

1. **nib**—(a) point of a pen. 2. **van**—(b) forefront. 3. **yaw**—(d) to move wildly off course. 4. **wan**—(a) pale. 5. **wry**—(c) twisted. 6. **eke**—(a) to piece out or supplement. 7. **con**—(b) to read with care. 8. **nub**—(c) the gist or point. 9. **oaf**—(b) a blockhead. 10. **vie**—(b) to compete with. 11. **fen**—(c) a marsh or swamp. 12. **don**—(a) to put on, as a garment. 13. **dun**—(d) to press for payment. 14. **rue**—(a) to regret extremely. 15. **ebb**—(d) to wane. 16. **eon**—(c) an incalculably long period of time.

414

7 THE SEMICOLON

The semicolon (;) has two basic uses:

(1) The first is to join two or more closely related sentences together into one sentence.

> *The car stopped; Joe got in.*
> *I went to work; I had a quick lunch; I came straight home.*

Notice that *The car stopped* and *Joe got in* as well as *I went to work, I had a quick lunch,* and *I came straight home* are all complete statements by themselves. It would therefore be correct to separate them by means of periods. But in each of the above sentences the complete statements are short and closely related. So it makes sense to tie them together with semicolons. Notice, too, that you could also combine the short independent clauses by means of conjunctions or by means of commas along with conjunctions.

> *The car stopped and Joe got in.*
> *I went to work, had a quick lunch, and came straight home.*

Why not write the sentences this way? You could. But you get a slightly different shade of meaning when you use semicolons instead of conjunctions. The semicolons show that the actions are not quite as closely related to each other as they would seem to be if they were connected by "and."

NOTE: Sometimes the semicolon joins sentence parts that are not complete statements but that would be complete statements if certain words were repeated instead of being left out. The omitted words are, in effect, "carried over" from the first statement in the series and are "understood" in the later statements.

> *In France, we bought perfume; in Ireland, sweaters; in England, shoes.*

It is also correct to use a semicolon before such words and expressions as *nevertheless, accordingly, therefore, however, hence, instead, yet, thus, for example,* and *consequently* when they join two closely related independent clauses. In the following examples a period could be substituted for the semicolon, but the semicolon makes the relationship between the parts more apparent.

415

We got a late start; nevertheless, we got to the airport on time.
The child was bright; for example, he could do long division.
The weather did not clear; instead, the rain increased.
He was the eldest son; consequently, he inherited everything.

WARNING: In these and similar sentences, either a period or a semicolon may acceptably precede the words *therefore, nevertheless,* and so on. But a comma would not be acceptable. Two independent clauses (complete statements) should not be joined by a comma without the addition of *or, and,* or *but.*

(2) A semicolon may replace a comma when a sentence is very long or already has too many commas. This does not mean that a semicolon may substitute for just any comma. The semicolon may be used to separate the items of a list; or to separate one related group of words from another group of words if there are already commas within the group; or to separate the various self-contained parts of a very long sentence. Study each of the following examples:

Important nutrient groups include: milk, butter, and cheese; meat, poultry, and eggs; green or yellow vegetables; cereals.
You will find references to herb gardens on pages 4, 38, 43, and 72; to wild herbs on pages 18, 37, and 42.
The winning numbers were 1,273; 3,663; 8,462; and 2,370.

Since the numbers already have commas in them, it would confuse the reader if you used more commas instead of semicolons to separate the numbers.

Mr. Green, the plumber; George Crompton, the painter; and Joe Brown were at the party.

Here, too, semicolons are used to help out the reader. If commas were used, we would have *Mr. Green, the plumber, George Crompton, the painter, and Joe Brown were at the party.* The reader would wonder whether five people are mentioned: (1) *Mr. Green,* (2) *a plumber,* (3) *George Crompton,* (4) *a painter,* and (5) *Joe Brown;* or perhaps he would assume that two of the people are *Mr. Green* and *the plumber George Crompton.* Only the use of the semicolon makes it clear who's who at this party.

The bus stop, worse luck, was three blocks away; and Jim, thoroughly drenched by the rain, headed for it at a trot.

If there were no internal commas within the two independent clauses, a comma would, of course, be used before *and: The bus stop was three blocks away, and Jim headed for it at a trot.* In this case, only a comma would be needed to organize the sentence into two parts. In the longer sentence, however, commas are already used around *worse luck* and *thoroughly drenched by the rain.* And so we show where the two major parts of the sentence are separated by using a "louder" or "longer" pause at that point: the semicolon.

Punctuation Test—Commas, Semicolons, and Colons

Add commas, semicolons, and colons where necessary to the following letter. Recommended punctuation—though not necessarily the only correct punctuation—follows.

Monday August 30, 1971

Dear Sir

On May 15th I ordered the following from your store 4 chairs your model number 1407-B 1 table your model number M-607 and 2 lamps your model number 1703. These items were to be delivered before 430 P.M. June 25th to me Mr. Charles Bolland 1867 West Street London Ont. To date the furniture has not been delivered and I have had no word from you. Please let me know when I can expect delivery on the chairs the table and the lamps. I do want them as soon as possible.

Very truly yours

RECOMMENDED PUNCTUATION:

Monday, August 30, 1971

Dear Sir:

On May 15th I ordered the following from your store: 4 chairs, your model number 1407-B; 1 table, your model number M-607; and 2 lamps, your model number 1703. These items were to be delivered before 4:30 P.M., June 25th, to me, Mr. Charles Bolland, 1867 West Street, London, Ont. To date, the furniture has not been delivered, and I have had no word from you. Please let me know when I can expect delivery on the chairs, the table, and the lamps. I do want them as soon as possible.

Very truly yours,

417

Fun With Words

ONE-SYLLABLE WORDS

Here are some short words to learn. They aren't as short as the three-letter words in an earlier vocabulary test, but they all contain only one syllable. Check the word or phrase you believe is closest in meaning to the key word. Answers follow.

1. **feat** [fēt]—(a) an act of unusual skill or courage. (b) a gala party. (c) a heavy task. (d) a mission of mercy.
2. **rift** [rift]—(a) sediment. (b) a cloud formation. (c) a split or cleft. (d) to manipulate.
3. **filch** [filch]—(a) to strain or filter. (b) to adorn with gold. (c) to cross into enemy lines. (d) to steal small amounts slyly.
4. **harp** [härp]—(a) to dislike violently. (b) to pillage. (c) to dwell on a subject tediously. (d) to argue.
5. **trice** [trīs]—(a) an instant or moment. (b) to bind up. (c) three-fold. (d) a predicament.
6. **curt** [kûrt]—(a) extremely polite. (b) abrupt or brusque. (c) persuasive. (d) coy.
7. **cult** [kult]—(a) to sort or select. (b) a system of zealous devotion to a person or object. (c) to refine. (d) the elite.
8. **staid** [stād]—(a) theatrical. (b) a wide variety. (c) dull. (d) sedate.
9. **crux** [kruks]—(a) the ending. (b) a fork in the road. (c) the pivotal or critical point. (d) a heavy load.
10. **gloss** [glos]—(a) to give plausible explanations to cover a fault. (b) to act foolishly. (c) to explain thoroughly. (d) to ignore.
11. **flex** [fleks]—(a) to bend, as the arm. (b) to shake. (c) to gather up one's strength. (d) to free from bondage.
12. **waft** [waft]—(a) to relinquish. (b) to sing softly. (c) to wade. (d) to convey by floating, as in air or water.
13. **pent** [pent]—(a) uncooperative. (b) confined; penned up or in. (c) awaiting trial. (d) awaiting approval.
14. **crop** [krop]—(a) to cut or eat off the stems, as of grass. (b) to default. (c) to disappear. (d) to destroy.

ANSWERS:

1. **feat**—(a) an act of unusual skill or courage. 2. **rift**—(c) a split or cleft. 3. **filch**—(d) to steal small amounts slyly. 4. **harp**—(c) to dwell on a subject tediously. 5. **trice**—(a) an instant or moment. 6. **curt**—(b) abrupt or brusque. 7. **cult**—(b) a system of zealous devotion to a person or object. 8. **staid**—(d) sedate. 9. **crux**—(c) the pivotal or critical point. 10. **gloss**—(a) to give plausible explanations to cover a fault. 11. **flex**—(a) to bend, as the arm. 12. **waft**—(d) to convey by floating, as in air or water. 13. **pent**—(b) confined; penned up or in. 14. **crop**—(a) to cut or eat off the stems, as of grass.

8 THE DASH

The dash(—)is both a true punctuation mark and a mark used to indicate an omission of letters or words from a sentence. Since we're learning about the dash in this chapter, we'll take up all its uses.

(1) Use a dash to represent the omission of a word or part of a word, as all or part of a person's name to avoid identifying him, or all or some of the letters of a word that you'd rather not spell out in full.

> *Mrs. S—, who is suspected of stealing, has left town.*
> *"D—n you, you can go to—!" he shouted.*

There is no rule as to which words are considered too blasphemous or obscene to spell out; it depends on your own feelings and on who might read what you write. Modern writers and readers have lost much of their squeamishness about words. Thus, this use of the dash is decreasing.

Similarly, it used to be quite common for the members of certain denominations to avoid spelling out the word *God* by substituting a dash for the letter *o*. This custom stemmed from the belief that the word was too sacred to be written out in anything but a religious work. Here, too, however, modern writers no longer use the dash.

(2) Use a dash between numbers or words to mean "to," "until," or "through," indicating inclusion of all the intervening time, numbers, distances, etc.

> *Benjamin Franklin (1706–90) was a great American.*
> *Visiting hours are 2:30 P.M.–4 P.M.*
> *For tonight's homework, read chapters 20–25.*

There is a danger in this last sentence: Does it mean *from 20* or *including 20? to 25* or *through 25?* Because the answer is not entirely clear, it is often best to avoid the dash and to write out such words as *to, through, inclusive,* etc.

NOTE: The dashes in the above three examples are only half as long as the others in this chapter. Nonetheless, they are dashes and should not be confused with *hyphens.* (For the use of the hyphen, see page 433.) When you type, you indicate the longer form of the dash by typing two short dashes side by side (--). The short dash (–) and the hyphen do, of course, look somewhat alike.

(3) Use a dash to set off a word or group of words introduced unexpectedly into a sentence, especially a word or phrase that is not structurally related to the rest of the sentence.

That looks like smoke coming from the—help! Fire!
Jerry has a clever idea here—but read his report yourself.
Mountain air is good for you—if, that is, you have strong lungs.

Note that in the first two examples, the dash indicates an abrupt breaking off of one thought and the beginning of another. In the third, there is an added, unexpected thought; the importance of this added thought is emphasized by the use of the dash.

When we see Ann—here she comes now—act as if nothing had happened.
If you like pot roast—you do, don't you?—you'll love this recipe.

Note that in each of these examples a dash is used both before and after an interruption of the normal flow of words; the two dashes set off a thought that only temporarily interrupts the sentence. Note, too, that a question mark may be used before the closing dash to punctuate the interruption. This is equally true of an exclamation point. But a period is never used after declarative interruptions.

(4) Use a dash to separate two identical or almost identical words or expressions when you want to use repetition or to sum something up.

I can do the job—the job you want done.
Laurier and King—these men were his idols.

These sentences could have been written *I can do the job you want done* and *Lincoln and Wilson were his idols.* But they would have lost the extra force gained through the use of the dash (a pause) followed by repetition or a summing up.

The roar of the surf, the shouts of small children, a woman's laughter—these are the sounds I like best.

(5) Use a dash before a specific list or example that explains in detail some word or phrase in the first part of a sentence.

Two members of the committee called on me—specifically, Gorman and Lewis.
Bring some warm clothes—among other things a sweater and wool socks.

Either a colon or a semicolon could be used in place of the dash in both these sentences. But the recent trend in informal writing is toward the dash in such cases. A colon might be better, perhaps, in a very formal sentence (*This nation finds comfort and support in two great principles: liberty and justice for all*). The semicolon is less formal than the colon, but somewhat more formal than the dash (*After careful deliberation, he decided to plant only perennials; for example, peonies, asters, and delphiniums*). You will not go wrong if you use the punctuation mark that seems most appropriate to you for the type of sentence you are writing.

NOTE: Be careful not to overdo your use of dashes. A mark of the inexperienced, hurried writer is the use of dashes to replace almost all punctuation. We've all read breathless, disorganized writing of this sort:

> *Dear Joe—*
>
> *Just a note—I know I owe you a letter—to say I'll be in Chicago next week—probably Thursday or Friday. Can you meet me at the station—or are you too busy?*

Dash it all, don't dash it all! Write words and sentences and use proper punctuation. The dash is a splendid punctuation mark—but only when it is used properly.

9 QUOTATION MARKS AND ITALICS

There are double quotations marks (" ") and single quotation marks (' '). Note that each kind is always used in pairs. Double quotation marks are by far the most frequently used.

Double Quotation Marks

(1) Use double quotation marks to set off a direct quotation—that is, the exact words of a speaker or writer—whether or not your own explanatory words intervene.

421

"Mary gave me a bowling ball for Christmas," Ed said.
"Next year," the sales manager continued, "we'll do better."
He finally admitted, "Dan's not such a bad worker."
He wrote "300 red chairs" on his order, and that's what he wants.

EXCEPTIONS: Long quotations, as from a speech, report, or book, are often typed or printed in a different way: Instead of being set off by quotation marks, they are indented and printed in smaller type. (In typing, you would indent each typed line of the quoted material and indicate the smaller type by single-spacing.) If you prefer to use quotation marks, however, remember that for a quotation that runs into several paragraphs of prose, the marks are placed at the *beginning* of each paragraph and at the end of only the *final* paragraph.

Constitutional Amendments VIII and IX read as follows:

> Excessive bail shall not be required, nor excessive fines imposed, nor cruel and unusual punishments inflicted.
> The enumeration in the Constitution, of certain rights, shall not be construed to deny or disparage others retained by the people.

NOTE: When conversation is quoted, each speaker is given a paragraph of his own, no matter how little he says.

"John," Peter called, "do you remember where you put the fishing rods?"
"In the garage, I think," John answered. He entered the room from the kitchen, stretching lazily. "Or maybe it was in the attic." He yawned, then sank into a chair. "Or was it the basement?"
"Well, try to remember," Peter insisted.
"I am trying."

Notice that descriptive material and additional remarks by the same speaker are included in the same paragraph. But the paragraph changes when the speaker changes.

(2) Use double quotation marks to set off the title of a short or subordinate work, as a book chapter, a newspaper or magazine article, a report, a short story or short poem, a song, a one-act play, and so on. The quotation marks indicate the title of a short work or of part of a longer work or collection. The name of an entire book or other long work and of newspapers or magazines is generally italicized. (To italicize in typing or writing by hand, you simply underline.)

Read Chapter 2, "Early Childhood," of Thompson's *My Life and Times*.

You should read the editorials in the daily *Globe*.

They sang the song "Oklahoma!" from the musical *Oklahoma!*

I have read Hemingway's short story "The Killers" and his novel *The Old Man and the Sea*.

NOTE: Certain other titles, such as the names of art works or of ships and planes, are usually italicized.

Rembrandt's *Night Watch*
Lindbergh's plane, *The Spirit of St. Louis*

EXCEPTIONS: The Bible and the names of its books, sections, and verses are never put in italics or quotation marks.

John 3:16   the Old Testament   the Apocrypha

(3) Use double quotation marks to set off any word or group of words that you are using in a special way, and to which you want to call attention. There are four classes of terms that can be pointed out in this manner:

(a) Out-of-date or slang expressions, jargon, made-up words, or unusual word combinations. (But use such quotation marks sparingly! They tend to seem affected.)

That restaurant you took us to was "groovy."
I have a cold now—or, more expressly, a "slight catarrh."

(b) Mottoes, clichés, and popular sayings.

Do you believe that "love conquers all"?
I still think we should fight "to make the world safe for democracy."

(c) Nicknames, epithets, or other designations that represent true names or personified objects. (But remember that familiar or common nicknames—such as *Jack* or *Bill* or *Honest Abe* or *Stonewall Jackson*—are *not* set off by quotation marks.)

Robert Johnson—"Big Bob" to his friends—now heads the firm.
Throughout the Southwest he was known as "The Purple Avenger."

NOTE: When a word (or phrase) is pointed out *as* a word, whether it is defined or simply mentioned, it should be written in italics rather than placed within quotation marks.

423

Your opening paragraph is cluttered with *I believe*'s and *in my opinion*'s.
Bottle has two syllables.

Here the meaning of the italicized words is of no importance; they are quoted simply as words.

A *soft drink* may be defined as a drink that contains no alcohol.

Here the term *soft drink* is being defined, although its meaning is not being used.

Single Quotation Marks

Use single quotation marks to set off a quotation within a quotation.

> *General Granger said, "Remember the words of Colonel Prescott at Bunker Hill: 'Don't fire until you see the whites of their eyes.' "*

This sentence quotes General Granger, who, in turn, is quoting someone else. Note that in this example both quotations end at the same place; so both a single and double closing quotation mark must be used.

> *He reported that "most Europeans like us 'Canucks.' "*
> *The chairman of the board announced: "Robert Johnson—'Big Bob' to his friends—has been made president of the firm."*

Usage Notes on Quotation Marks

(1) Capitalization: If quoted material begins with a capital letter (because it begins a sentence in the original, or because it is a name or title), keep the capital letter in your quotation.

> *The winning essay was called "How I Overcame Insomnia."*

(2) Punctuation: To separate a quoted remark from the part of the sentence that introduces it, use a comma or—somewhat more formally —a colon.

> *He said, "I'll be glad to vote for you."*
> *The report ends: "We conclude that life cannot exist on Mars."*

When either a comma or a period is needed at the end of a quotation or of any quoted matter, such as a title, the comma or period is *always* placed inside the closing quotation marks.

"Next year," said Ed, "we'll do even better."
This statement concludes the report "Is There Life on Mars?": "We believe that life as we know it cannot exist on Mars."
She said, "I remember that you asked whether my fudge was really 'fudgy.'"

The above examples all illustrate the most important fact about punctuation as it applies to quotation marks: Without exception, commas and periods go inside the closing quotation marks, even when there are single as well as double quotes, or when the comma or period logically applies to the whole sentence rather than to the quoted matter—in other words, always. This is a nice, easy American rule that Canadians would do well to follow.

But, as the above examples also help to show, all writers should follow the British rule for the placement of semicolons, colons, question marks, and exclamation points. These punctuation marks are placed inside the closing quotation marks if they belong to the quotation, but outside the quotation marks if they belong to the sentence proper.

Do you believe that "love conquers all"?
Spare us your "sympathy"!
She asked, "Does love conquer all?"
Joe said, "I have the answer"; Jim said, "I'll have it soon"; Bill said, "I never will!"

Note that no final period is required for the last two sentences above, even though they are declarative statements. The end of the sentence is adequately signaled by the closing quotation marks.

10 PARENTHESES AND BRACKETS

Parentheses, like quotation marks, come in pairs. The beginning or opening parenthesis [(] is placed before the first word of the material to be enclosed, and the ending or closing parenthesis [)] is put after the last enclosed word.

Parentheses are one of three principal ways to separate material in a sentence from the surrounding material: Paired commas make the least separation; paired dashes make a more forceful separation; and parentheses make the greatest separation in thought. They are also useful for separating an extra sentence or two of added, but not entirely essential, comment from the rest of a passage, so that the flow of the central idea is not interrupted.

(1) Use parentheses to set off nonessential—"parenthetical"—material or remarks that explain, question, illustrate, or comment upon the main idea. A parenthetical remark is a remark that is literally "thrown in," often as a helpful aside to the reader.

> *She met her uncle (her mother's brother) at the station.*
> *Eat a green vegetable (spinach, beans, peas, or the like) every day.*
> *You are to call Mr. Olafszyski (spelling?).*
> *The meeting will start at 10 (please be on time!) and end at noon.*

(2) Use parentheses to set off numbers and letters in an outline or list.

> *The company has four main divisions: (1) Research and Development, (2) Production, (3) Sales, (4) Advertising and Promotion.*

Usage Note: When you punctuate a sentence containing parentheses, place commas, semicolons, colons, etc., between the same words or the same parts of the sentence as you would do if there were no parentheses. Remember, however, that the punctuation marks are normally placed after, not before, the parenthesized material.

> *If you like to bake, here is a good recipe.*
> *If you like to bake (I hate to), here is a good recipe.*

Exception: When parentheses are used simply for setting off numbers or letters in a list, the commas are placed before the parenthesized numbers or letters.

> *He had three interests in life: (a) work, (b) golf, and (c) his son's career.*

If commas, semicolons, colons, etc., are needed within the parentheses, use them.

> *Pick an object from one category (animal, vegetable, or mineral).*

If the parenthetical remark within a sentence is a question or exclamation, put a question mark or exclamation point inside the closing parenthesis. But if the parenthetical remark within a sentence is itself a sentence, do not use a period within the parentheses.

You received a call from Mr. Smith (Smythe?).
The sales meeting will start at noon (we trust that it will begin on time) and end at 4.
That man (I hate the sight of him!) has gone.

Brackets [], which are also used in pairs, are actually squared-off parentheses. They furnish still another way to set off material within a sentence.

(1) Use brackets to enclose parenthetical material that is already within parentheses:

The low-lying region of the eastern United States, the Piedmont (literally, "lying at the foot of mountains" [in this case the Appalachian Range]), extends from New Jersey to Alabama.

(2) Use brackets to enclose explanatory material inserted into a quotation by someone other than the original author:

He told me that his boss said, "You'd better report your symptoms [fatigue and rapid loss of weight] to Dr. Samuels right away."

(3) Use brackets to correct an error in an edited sentence:

July 15 [14], Bastille Day, is a national holiday in France.

As you have no doubt noticed, brackets are used throughout this book and in many dictionaries to set off word pronunciations: **ad·mi·ra·tion** [ad′mə·rā′shən].

11 THE APOSTROPHE

The apostrophe (') and the hyphen (-) (which is the next subject discussed) differ from pure punctuation marks in that they do not indicate major divisions of your writing or help to organize your thoughts on paper. These two symbols are often part of a word itself, just as much a part as are any of the word's letters. Sometimes the apostrophe and the hyphen serve to distinguish completely different words, such as *can't* and *cant*, *we'll* and *well*, *it's* and *its*, *girls* and *girl's*, *old-fashioned* (out-of-date) and *old fashioned* (a cocktail). In such cases, using an apostrophe or hyphen in the wrong place, or leaving one out when it is needed, might just as reasonably be considered a spelling or usage mistake as a punctuation error.

The apostrophe is used in four basic ways:

(1) Use the apostrophe to take the place of an omitted letter or letters when writing a shortened form of a word or phrase. Shortened forms of words or of two-word combinations are called *contractions*.

(a) One-word combinations representing a pronoun (*I, you, he, she, it, they*) joined to a common verb form (such as *am, are, have,* etc.).

> I'd   he's
> you'll   we've

Here's (here is) and *there's* (there is) are formed in the same way, by adding *here* and *there* to the verb *is*.

(b) One-word combinations representing a common verb form (such as *is, are, could, did,* etc.) joined to *not*.

> aren't   doesn't
> couldn't   won't

(c) Other standard, familiar, or accepted shortened forms. For example:

> o'clock   o(*f the*) clock
> 'tis   (i)t is

In spelling a contraction, an apostrophe is as important as a letter. Without an apostrophe, *she'll* would be *shell, we'll* would be *well,* and *he'll* would be worse! Every contraction must have an apostrophe—at least until such time as the contraction becomes an accepted full form in its own right, as *plane* for *airplane, phone* for *telephone,* or *cello* for *violoncello*.

> *It's ten o'clock.* (it is)
> *Its tires need air.* (the possessive form of *it*)
> *They're late for work.* (they are)
> *Their house is big.* (the possessive form of *they*)

If you have trouble with such pairs of words—words with similar spellings or sounds—be sure to study the part of this book entitled "Using Your Word Power."

428

(2) Use the apostrophe to take the place of an omitted figure or figures when writing a shortened form of a number, as a date.

> the class of '72 (1972)
> the flappers of the '20's (1920's)
> the spirit of '76 (1776)

(3) Use the apostrophe to show possession in nouns.

  (a) To form the possessive case of a noun that does not end in *s* (or in an *s* or *z* sound), use the apostrophe with *s* (*'s*). This rule applies to all types of nouns, singular and plural.

> Joe's country
> the man's job
> the men's jobs
> Chicago's weather
> Madeline's new coat

  (b) To form the possessive case of a plural noun that already ends in *s*, add only an apostrophe (*'*).

> the Joneses' house (two or more people named Jones)
> the bosses' daughters (several bosses)
> boys' games (all boys)

  (c) To form the possessive case of a singular noun that ends in *s* (or in an *s* or *z* sound), use the apostrophe with *s* (*'s*) if the noun has only one syllable, to show that an extra *s* sound [əz] is pronounced.

> the boss's daughter   the mouse's cheese
> Jones's job   Yeats's poetry
> the house's value   Marx's teachings

But use the apostrophe alone if the noun has more than one syllable, unless you prefer to think of the extra *s* or *z* sound [əz] as being pronounced.

> Socrates' wisdom   Rodriguez' car
> Moses' people   Thomas's (*or* Thomas') hat
> for goodness' sake   Dickens's (*or* Dickens') works

USAGE NOTES: In cases where more than one possessive word is involved, you may still wonder where to put the apostrophe or the apostrophe and *s*. Here are some helpful hints:

When adding a possessive ending to a compound, add it to the part that is closest to the thing possessed.

his mother-in-law's car
Senator Jones of Texas' speech

When joint possession of something is involved, you may add the possessive ending to the last noun only.

Jack and Jill's pail
a dogs and cats' shelter

When separate possession is involved, add the possessive ending to each noun separately.

Jack's and Jill's injuries (Each one has different injuries.)
England's or France's museums (Each country has its own museums.)

Sometimes a double possessive is acceptable—that is, the preposition *of* plus a possessive ending.

a friend of my brother's
a letter of Carol's

EXCEPTIONS: The apostrophe is often used in certain cases where true possession is not involved but where custom calls for a possessive form.

In certain familiar expressions:
a month's pay
a week's vacation
an hour's drive

With nouns ending in *-ing* (such as *working, playing, doing, seeing, acting, thinking,* etc.):

Roger's traveling is part of his job. (*not* Roger traveling)
I don't approve of your going. (*not* you going)

REMEMBER: Never use an apostrophe with personal pronouns that are already in the possessive case, such as *his, hers, yours, ours, theirs, its,* and *whose.*

Whose hat is this?
It's hers. It isn't Mary's or yours.
Who's to blame? (a contraction)
The man whose dog barked is a neighbor. (a possessive)

430

(4) The apostrophe is often used with *s* (*'s*) to form the plural of a figure, a letter, an abbreviation, or a word that is referred to as a word.

Two 12's are 24.
She's at least in her 40's.
He was born in the early '50's. (Here, the first apostrophe indicates the omission of the century numerals. The second apostrophe forms the plural of a figure.)
There are no if's, and's, or but's about it.
During the blizzard the temperature remained in the 20's.
Do all the instructors have Ph.D.'s?
There are many maybe's in our vacation plans.

Punctuation Test—The Apostrophe

1. When (it's, its) eight o'clock, give the dog (it's, its) food.
2. The (Kimberley's, Kimberleys') old car can reach a top speed in the (50s, 50's, 50s').
3. The Ten Commandments are sometimes called (Mose's, Moses', Moses's) laws.
4. The (womens, women's, womens') bridge club will meet at 8 (o'clock. oclock).
5. Write your (s'es, s's, ss') bigger.
6. Yes, (their, there, they're) pleased with (their, there, they're) new house.
7. (Here's, Heres', Hears) to you. Good luck!
8. (There's, Theres, Theirs, Theirs') room for two (2s, 2's, 2s') at a table for 4.
9. Now (you're, your) late for (you're, your) lesson.
10. I like (San Diego's, San Diegos', San Diegoe's, San Diegoes') climate.
11. Three (7s, 7's) equal 21.
12. (Its, It's) true that the dog lost (it's, its) collar.

ANSWERS:

1. it's, its. 2. Kimberleys', 50's. 3. Moses'. 4. women's, o'clock. 5. s's 6. they're, their. 7. Here's. 8. There's, 2's. 9. you're, your. 10. San Diego's. 11. 7's. 12. It's, its.

REVIEW OF PREFIX PRE-

How well do you remember the words beginning with the prefix *pre-* that were taught in the vocabulary-building part of this book? The test below will help you to review the *pre-* words. Check the word or phrase you believe is closest in meaning to the key word. Answers follow.

1. **prerogative** [pri·rog′ə·tiv]—(a) superior power. (b) special privilege. (c) questionable procedure. (d) higher rank.

2. **preempt** [prē·empt′]—(a) to appropriate. (b) to order bluntly. (c) to contradict. (d) to obstruct or block.

3. **predilection** [prē′də·lek′shən]—(a) a preference or predisposition. (b) an extemporaneous speech. (c) a great liking for someone. (d) a slate of candidates for office.

4. **precursor** [pri·kûr′sər]—(a) an attacker. (b) a pursuer. (c) a forerunner. (d) a fugitive.

5. **preferential** [pref′ə·ren′shəl]—(a) favored. (b) of little value. (c) discriminated against. (d) humble.

6. **presentiment** [pri·zen′tə·mənt]—(a) a gift. (b) a premonition. (c) tender sensibility. (d) strangeness.

7. **prevail** [pri·vāl′]—(a) to overthrow. (b) to adhere to. (c) to be widespread or common. (d) to prevent.

8. **presumptive** [pri·zump′tiv]—(a) affording reasonable grounds for belief. (b) seeking admiration. (c) taking undue liberties. (d) garish.

9. **predictive** [pri·dik′tiv]—(a) commanding. (b) vengeful. (c) pertaining to a grammatical term. (d) foreshadowing the future.

10. **preamble** [prē′am·bəl]—(a) an introductory statement. (b) a constitutional amendment. (c) a short walk. (d) a winding lane.

11. **prefatory** [pref′ə·tôr′ē]—(a) the front of a cathedral. (b) introductory. (c) something more desirable. (d) high esteem.

12. **presumptuous** [pri·zump′chōō·əs]—(a) offensively bold. (b) giving reasonable ground for belief. (c) insincere. (d) luxurious.

13. **presage** [pri·sāj′]—(a) to predict. (b) to guess. (c) to terrify. (d) to brag.

ANSWERS:

1. **prerogative**—(b) special privilege. 2. **preempt**—(a) to appropriate. 3. **predilection**—(a) a preference or predisposition. 4. **precursor**—(c) a forerunner. 5. **preferential**—(a) favored. 6. **presentiment**—(b) a premonition. 7. **prevail**—(c) to be widespread or common. 8. **presumptive**—(a) affording reasonable grounds for belief. 9. **predictive**—(d) foreshadowing the future. 10. **preamble**—(a) an introductory statement. 11. **prefatory**—(b) introductory. 12. **presumptuous**—(a) offensively bold. 13. **presage**—(a) to predict.

12 THE HYPHEN

The hyphen (-) may serve to join several words into one whole word or to divide a single word into separate parts. It is used to connect the parts of certain compound words and phrases, and to show word divisions at the end of a line of type or writing.

If you look for total logic in hyphenation, you are doomed to disappointment. Rules for hyphenation can seem complicated and confusing, but the basic guidelines discussed in this chapter, together with your dictionary, will serve to keep you on the right track.

The Hyphen and Compound Words

A hyphen may be used to join the parts of certain compound words. Some compound words are normally written as two separate words; some are usually joined with hyphens; and some are written "solid" as one word. Many a solid compound was originally written as two words. Then, as the combination grew more common, writers began to recognize it as a unit and to hyphenate it. Finally, the hyphen was dropped, and the two words became one. This happened with *gentleman, bloodthirsty, dressmaker,* and *loudspeaker,* to name but a few.

It is still happening as the language changes and grows. Only a few years ago, *teen-ager* used to be written *teen ager;* now it is normally written *teenager.*

How do you know which words to hyphenate? How do you know whether a term is still written as two words, as a hyphenated compound, or as a solid word? The only way to feel secure is to use an up-to-date dictionary.

Often hyphenation is logical, but sometimes it is not. For example, only your dictionary can tell you that *pre-shrunk* is preferably hyphenated and *preconceived* is never hyphenated; that *snow cloud* is commonly written as two words, *snow-blind* is usually hyphenated, and *snowflake* is always written solid; *stronghearted* is always one word but *strong-armed* is preferably hyphenated. When in doubt, therefore, use your dictionary. But remember that even dictionaries do not always agree on questions of hyphenation. This is an area in which English usage changes very rapidly. So don't be shocked if you pick up a good book and find the words *preshrunk, snowblind,* and *strongarmed* without their prescribed hyphens.

Here are some familiar compound words that are regularly written with hyphens:

a free-for-all	a sit-in
a passer-by	a has-been
a go-between	out-of-date
a know-it-all	first-rate
make-believe	court-martial
to second-guess	know-how

There are a few dependable guides for hyphenating certain types of compound words—guides that can help you to avoid unnecessary trips to the dictionary. Learn these guides and you will save yourself much time and trouble.

(1) Use a hyphen to join written compound numbers from twenty-one to ninety-nine.

forty-eight   eighty-fifth

(2) Use a hyphen to join the two parts of a written fraction.

three-fourths   twenty-five forty-thirds

(3) Use a hyphen to join a number to a noun, a letter to a noun, or a number to a letter in a compound.

a six-cylinder car	an X-ray machine
a 50-foot span	an A-bomb
BU8-8598	a U-turn
a two-base hit	

(4) Use a hyphen to join the words *great* and *in-law* to nouns expressing family relationships.

mother-in-law	son-in-law
stepdaughter-in-law	great-grandson

Note that we do not hyphenate compound words expressing *grand* or *step* family relationships, such as *grandmother, grandson, stepmother.*

(5) Use a hyphen to join the prefixes *ex-* and *self-* or the suffix *-elect* to another word in a compound.

an ex-president	self-reliance
the president-elect	self-employed
his ex-wife	a self-addressed envelope

There are a few exceptions, such as *selfhood, selfless,* and *selfsame.* But almost all the *self-* words are hyphenated: *self-help, self-respect, self-sacrifice,* etc.

(6) Use a hyphen to join together two or more words that combine into a compound adjective. This holds true whether the adjective is a made-up compound (as in *a never-to-be-forgotten day*) or a regularly hyphenated word (as in *a narrow-minded man*).

out-of-town guests	a broad-minded judge
a grin-and-bear-it attitude	German-American cooking
a chauffeur-driven limousine	well-aimed shots

But the hyphen is omitted when an adjective which is made up of *well* combined with another word follows the verb instead of preceding the word it modifies.

What a well-bred child he is!
Yes, he is well bred.
Sandy is a well-dressed girl.
She's always well dressed.

There is a good reason for hyphenating compound adjectives: Without the hyphen there is often a possibility of misunderstanding. For example, the *deep blue sea* can mean either a sea that is both deep and blue or a sea whose color is deep blue. If you mean that the color is deep blue, you make that meaning clear by writing *the deep-blue sea.* But do not hyphenate combinations of an adjective and an adverb ending in *-ly: a happily married couple; a highly successful policy.* Here there is no chance of confusion.

(7) Use a hyphen to connect a compound that is a single unit of measurement.

kilowatt-hour	foot-pound	light-year

(8) Use a hyphen to connect the elements of certain compound titles.

ambassador-at-large	owner-manager	secretary-treasurer

(9) Use a hyphen to separate a prefix from a word that starts with a capital letter.

pro-American	a very un-British thing to do
a trans-Canada highway	mid-Atlantic

(10) In general, use a hyphen to keep two *i*'s or two *o*'s from coming together when one of them ends a prefix and the other starts a root word.

anti-intellectual co-occupy
semi-independent co-owner

In the recent past, the hyphen was commonly used to keep two *e*'s from coming together. Not too long ago, such words as *reentry, reenact, reevaluate, reexamine,* and *preeminent* were spelled with hyphens, the prefixes *re-* and *pre-* being separated from the root words starting with *e.* Although some people still hyphenate such words, modern usage favors the solid form. A hyphen is still generally used, however, with the prefix *de-*, as in *de-emphasize* and *de-escalate.*

Even the rule that two *o*'s should be separated by a hyphen has been greatly modified in recent years. We still hyphenate *co-occupy, co-owner,* and many others; but certain *o-o* words are now preferred in solid form—for instance, *cooperation, coordinate,* and *microorganism.*

(11) Use a hyphen to keep three identical consonants from coming together in compound words.

cross-stitch shell-like bell-like hull-less

(12) Use a hyphen to distinguish a compound from a solid word with a different meaning.

> *Please re-sign this bill.* (Here, the hyphen is necessary to distinguish *re-sign*—to sign again— from *resign*—to give up a job.)

> *We will re-cover the chair.* (Without the hyphen, *re-cover*—to cover again—would look like *recover*—to get well or get something back.)

(13) Use a hyphen to show word division at the end of a line of type or writing. In this instance, the hyphen follows that portion of an incomplete word that ends a line, showing the reader that the word is continued on the next line.

When writing, you may often be faced with the question: "Where can I break a word at the end of a line?" Here is the rule: You can break a word only between syllables. You may not break a one-syllable word at all, no matter how long it is. If you are not certain of the number or correct division of syllables in a word, consult your dictionary. In most dictionaries, each boldface entry word is printed with its syllables separated in some manner—often by dots, like this: **tick·et, fla·vor·ful, Mis·sis·sip·pi.** The dots show you the only points where you may break the word at the end of a line.

Punctuation Test—The Hyphen

In the paragraphs below, combine words or word parts into single, solid words or into hyphenated words when advisable. Recommended hyphenation follows.

Last summer, my sister in law and I took a fly now, pay later, 21 day excursion to our dream city, Paris. Paris was a never to be forgotten, once in a life time experience. We visited the birth place of my great grand mother, bought honest to goodness French wine at ninety five cents a bottle, and ate snails, frog's legs, and a shell like pastry the name of which I can't remember.

I learned some schoolgirl French and can now mispronounce the "Marseillaise"! I sang this national anthem of France for the first time under the Eiffel Tower, to the accompaniment of a one man band. What a self satisfied musician he was!

As we re entered Canada, both my sister in law and I were happy to be home again. However, we vowed to put on our seven league boots and cross the ocean again next year.

ANSWER:

Last summer, my sister-in-law and I took a fly-now, pay-later, 21-day excursion to our dream city, Paris. Paris was a never-to-be-forgotten, once-in-a-lifetime experience. We visited the birthplace of my great-grandmother, bought honest-to-goodness French wine at ninety-five cents a bottle, and ate snails, frog's legs, and a shell-like pastry the name of which I can't remember.

I learned some schoolgirl French and can now mispronounce the "Marseillaise"! I sang this national anthem of France for the first time under the Eiffel Tower, to the accompaniment of a one-man band. What a self-satisfied musician he was!

As we reentered Canada, both my sister-in-law and I were happy to be home again. However, we vowed to put on our seven-league boots and cross the ocean again next year.

A Hard Final Examination on Punctuation

Now that you have completed your study of punctuation, test your punctuation power. Before you begin, you may want to make a quick review of the rules for beginning punctuation (capitalization), end punctuation (the period, question mark, and exclamation point), and internal punctuation (the comma, colon, semicolon, dash, quotation marks, italics, parentheses, apostrophe, and hyphen). If you have studied these punctuation marks, see how high a mark you can make on punctuation! Supply the missing punctuation in the following sentences. Recommended answers follow.

1. the ingredients are as follows eggs celery bread crumbs and parsley
2. tell me i said where will you go from here
3. its about to explode run for your lives
4. the manager was impatient for the new branch office to open but the lobby was not yet ready
5. riding through the peaceful shenandoah valley who i ask could imagine that once cannon roared here and many men died in a single afternoon
6. hes a boor i wont say an out and out liar and i dont know what sally sees in him
7. jerry and i can go now cant we
8. courage patience and hope of these was his resolution compounded
9. youll never learn i guess
10. the games at 830 mary asked
11. jack called harry fatso said bill and thats how the fight started
12. stop the grocer yelled but the man ran out with an armful of canned goods and got away in broad daylight mind you
13. please send a telegram to mr t w brewster vancouver b c asking if he can speak at our sales conference and if so on which day
14. on may 6 1970 against the fortune tellers advice she embarked on a long hazardous journey
15. jennifer bowled 110 george 156 and henry 161
16. captain morton the company commander and major criswell are both haligonians arent they

17. the smiths who had the bungalow next door were related to the smiths who rented the cabin near the creek

18. please send me my red dress in the large closet eddys zippered jacket behind his door and dicks copy of robinson crusoe on his desk

19. dont forget to bring your tennis racket your tennis shoes you forgot them last time and but you know what else youll need here

20. wheres the fire i shouted but the boy kept running

21. according to a book review the presidents girl takes place in 1881 just after the inauguration of americas first bachelor president but the reviewer and perhaps the novel which i havent read is wrong president james buchanan also was a bachelor

22. he may have a soft as silk voice girls but those muscles

23. dr greenspan when if you had to make a guess would you anticipate a landing on jupiter

24. mary id like you to meet my sister mrs larson

25. the introductions over the girls and the boys retreated to opposite ends of the gymnasium the dance was off to a slow start to put it mildly

26. a philanthropist my nephews not

27. i cant believe that tom asked that joe said knowing how devilishly frighteningly well informed he is but you insist he did eh

28. you say you resent the letter when it came back with postage due

29. shall we go by bus by train by helicopter

30. the antiicer wasnt working and the windshield was freezing up fast

ANSWERS:

1. The ingredients are as follows: eggs, celery, bread crumbs, and parsley.
2. "Tell me," I said, "where will you go from here?"
3. It's about to explode! Run for your lives!
4. The manager was impatient for the new branch office to open, but the lobby was not yet ready.
5. Riding through the peaceful Shenandoah Valley, who, I ask, could imagine that once cannon roared here and many men died in a single afternoon?
6. He's a boor (I won't say an out-and-out liar), and I don't know what Sally sees in him.

439

7. Jerry and I can go now, can't we?
8. Courage, patience, and hope—of these was his resolution compounded.
9. You'll never learn, I guess.
10. "The game's at 8:30?" Mary asked.
11. "Jack called Harry 'fatso,'" said Bill, "and that's how the fight started."
12. "Stop!" the grocer yelled, but the man ran out with an armful of canned goods and got away—in broad daylight, mind you!
13. Please send a telegram to Mr. T. W. Brewster, Vancouver, B.C., asking if he can speak at our sales conference and, if so, on which day.
14. On May 6, 1970, against the fortuneteller's advice, she embarked on a long, hazardous journey.
15. Jennifer bowled 110; George, 156; and Henry, 161.
16. Captain Morton, the company commander, and Major Criswell are both Haligonians, aren't they?
17. The Smiths who had the bungalow next door were related to the Smiths who rented the cabin near the creek.
18. Please send me my red dress (in the large closet), Eddy's zippered jacket (behind his door), and Dick's copy of *Robinson Crusoe* (on his desk).
19. Don't forget to bring your tennis racket; your tennis shoes (you forgot them last time); and—but you know what else you'll need here.
20. "Where's the fire?" I shouted, but the boy just kept running.
21. According to a book review, *The President's Girl* takes place in 1881, just after the inauguration of America's first bachelor President. But the reviewer (and perhaps the novel, which I haven't read) is wrong: President James Buchanan also was a bachelor.
22. He may have a soft-as-silk voice, girls, but those muscles!
23. Dr. Greenspan, when, if you had to make a guess, would you anticipate a landing on Jupiter?
24. Mary, I'd like you to meet my sister, Mrs. Larson.
25. The introductions over, the girls and boys retreated to opposite ends of the gymnasium; the dance was off to a slow start, to put it mildly.
26. A philanthropist my nephew's not.
27. "I can't believe that Tom asked that," Joe said, "knowing how devilishly, frighteningly well-informed he is, but you insist he did, eh?"
28. You say you re-sent the letter when it came back with postage due?
29. Shall we go by bus? by train? by helicopter?
30. The anti-icer wasn't working, and the windshield was freezing up fast.

PART FIVE

Practical Grammar

PUTTING GRAMMAR TO WORK

If your native tongue is English, you can be certain that you obey the basic rules of English grammar even if you do not know them. Can you imagine yourself saying "I the woman take the saw boy house his from"? Of course not. It makes no grammatical sense; the words do not relate to one another so as to communicate a clear thought. Put the same words together differently—"I saw the woman take the boy from his house"—and you have turned nonsense into grammatical English. Positioning of words in a sentence is the essence of English grammar.

Nobody needs to teach you how to place words in relation to one another in order to make sense. You learned that by yourself, almost miraculously, when you were a small child. What the grammar books and teachers do is this: (1) They analyze and explain how English is built, so that our comprehension of the whys and wherefores is broadened; and (2) they help us to use the language more effectively by pointing out some of its refinements—some of the ways in which we can come closer to expressing our thoughts not just adequately but precisely and attractively.

This section is called "Practical Grammar" because it concentrates mainly on the useful aspects of grammar rather than on rules or ideals. It simply deals with common mistakes—the mistakes that are most often made by careless or uninformed speakers and writers. Some of these errors are particularly serious ones, because they blur the meaning of the statement in which they occur. For example, consider this sentence: "Walter was the first to tell Bill that he had been fired." Do you see why that is unclear, even though it may look right at first?

Who had been fired? Had Walter been fired? Or had Bill been fired? We cannot answer the question; the sentence is unclear because of a basic flaw in grammar: the writer's failure to provide the pronoun *he* with a single noun to which it directly refers.

Other errors may not necessarily result in confusion. Take, for instance, the sentence we started out with: "I saw the woman take the boy from his house." A fairly common mistake would be to substitute the word *seen* for *saw:* "I *seen* the woman take the boy . . . ." The meaning of the sentence still comes through clearly. Yet *seen* is ungrammatical; the past tense of the verb *to see* is *saw*, not *seen*. More important, *seen* is an unsuitable usage unless the intent is to portray the speaker as ill-educated. No competent speaker or writer would find it acceptable. Anyone who makes such a mistake is advertising his lack of word power.

442

1 WRONG PRONOUNS

WHY YOU SHOULDN'T SAY: *Between you and I, him and me did it.*

This kind of mistake is the result of using the *wrong pronouns. I* should be *me; him* and *me* should be *he* and *I.* Why?

Nouns, as you remember, are words that stand for things or people. *Man, books,* and *Chicago* are all nouns. Pronouns are words that stand for nouns. *He, they,* and *it* are all pronouns. And just as all nouns can act either as the subject of a sentence (the person or thing doing something) or as the object of a sentence (the person or thing to which something is done), so it is with the pronouns that stand for them. "John gave the book to Mary" is a sentence that contains three nouns. If you used the proper pronouns instead, you would say, "He gave it to her."

In addition to acting as subject or object, some pronouns indicate possession. But practically no one worries about this use; it is obvious that *our* house is not *yours* and that *her* pocketbook is not *mine.*

Many people, however, confuse the subjective and objective forms of pronouns. They say "Pass the ball to John and I," or "John and me were playing football," or "Her daughter looks a lot like she," and they hope that they have used the correct pronouns.

Well, they haven't used the correct pronouns. Here's why: The subjective form of a pronoun (*I, you, he, she, it, we, they*) should always be used as the subject of a verb, and the objective form (*me, you, him, her, it, us, them*) should always be used as the object of a verb or of a preposition (*after, against, before, except, like, to, with,* etc.).

An interesting thing about the above rule is that people seldom break it when they are using just a single pronoun. They may be tempted to use the subjective case after one or two such prepositions as *except* and *like,* but they usually manage to resist the temptation. Most of the time, they know almost by instinct which pronoun to use. For instance, a glance at each of the following sentences will be enough to tell you that it is ungrammatical. Moreover, your immediate reaction—and a correct one—will be disbelief that anyone whose native language is English could speak or write this way:

> *Pass the ball to I.*
> *I'm worried about she.*
> *Me was playing football.*
> *Let's drop in on he tonight.*

443

Those are ridiculous sentences, are they not? Yet note that when two pronouns or a noun plus a pronoun is substituted for the obviously ungrammatical single pronoun, the sentences no longer sound so silly.

Incorrect	Correct
Pass the ball to he and I.	*Pass the ball to him and me.*
I'm worried about her family and she.	*I'm worried about her family and her.*
John and me were playing football.	*John and I were playing football.*
Let's drop in on Mary and he tonight.	*Let's drop in on Mary and him tonight.*
The Smiths and them had fun together.	*The Smiths and they had fun together.*

For the most part, then, you do not really have to know what a preposition is, or what the difference is between the objective and the subjective case, in order to get your pronouns right. Since you are likely to get them wrong only when they are paired with some other pronoun or a noun, there is an easy way to test your grammar. Simply drop the second word for a moment and see how the sentence looks— or hear how it sounds—with just the single pronoun. *Pass the ball to he? Pass the ball to I?* Nonsense! Only *him* and *me* in those two sentences will satisfy your basic knowledge of grammar. Thus, the correct pronouns when combined must both be in the objective case *(Pass the ball to him and me).*

Many speakers carelessly say *between you and I.* But if you omit the *you and* and consider the *I* alone after *between,* you will realize at once that the *I* must be changed to *me. Between I* is not English because the preposition *between* is always followed by an object not a subject.

NOTE: Traditional grammar once prescribed the use of the subjective form for a pronoun that follows such verbs as *is, are, was,* and *were* (in other words, most forms of the verb *to be*). Teachers used to insist that their pupils say "It's *I*," or "It was *she*," and so on. But in spite of the grammarians, even such careful speakers as Sir Winston Churchill persisted in saying "It's *me* (or *her* or *him*)" until finally the grammarians gave up. Today it is preferable to say "It's him" in conversation; in a formal essay, however, one should say "It was *he* (or *she* or *we* or *they*)."

Grammar Test—*I or ME? SHE or HER? HE or HIM? WE or US? THEY or THEM?*

Choose the word or words from each pair in the parentheses to make a correct sentence. This test is a drill. Repeat it as many times as necessary until you can give the correct answers quickly and automatically. Answers follow.

1. This is a secret between you and (I, me).
2. Will you go shopping with Jane and (I, me)?
3. He gave the gift to my wife and (me, I).
4. What has she got against Walter and (me, I)?
5. You come next, after (I, me).
6. Please buy a book for (she and I, her and me).
7. Stand between Betty and (me, I).
8. He arrived before (me, I).
9. Everyone ate dessert except (I, me).
10. You arrived after (her, she).
11. Mrs. Lanier's daughter looks just like (she, her).
12. That's a personal matter between you and (her, she).
13. Your sister is cute, and I wish you were more like (her, she).
14. Why do you try to dress like (her, she)?
15. Everyone but Sally and (her, she) is waiting on tables.
16. Have you called all the members except (she, her)?
17. Try to talk like (him, he).
18. I gave them to you and (him, he).
19. She asked his name right in front of Bill and (he, him).
20. This should be settled between the lawyer and (we, us).
21. What would you men do without (us, we) women?
22. Everyone was invited to the party but (we, us).
23. Will our children grow up to be like (we, us)?
24. The Smiths couldn't come, but everyone is here except (they, them).
25. All the neighbors but (them, they) grow roses.

ANSWERS:

1. between you and *me*. 2. with Jane and *me*. 3. to my wife and *me*. 4. against Walter and *me*. 5. after *me*. 6. for *her* and *me*. 7. between Betty and *me*. 8. before *me*. 9. except *me*. 10. after *her*. 11. like *her*. 12. between you and *her*. 13. like *her*. 14. like *her*. 15. but Sally and *her*. 16. except *her*. 17. like *him*. 18. to you and *him*. 19. in front of Bill and *him*. 20. between the lawyer and *us*. 21. without *us* women. 22. but *us*. 23. to be like *us*. 24. except *them*. 25. but *them*.

Fun With Words

MORE -ABLE, -IBLE WORDS

Choose the word or phrase which is closest in meaning to each of the key words. As you do this vocabulary test, note the *-able* and *-ible* spellings. Answers follow.

1. **amicable** [am'i·kə·bəl]—(a) amusing. (b) easy to clean. (c) cheerful. (d) friendly.
2. **amenable** [ə·mē'nə·bəl]—(a) unpleasant. (b) capable of being persuaded. (c) praiseworthy. (d) capable of amusing.
3. **feasible** [fē'zə·bəl]—(a) afraid. (b) practicable. (c) understandable. (d) easy to do.
4. **credible** [kred'ə·bəl]—(a) meritorious. (b) bordering on the impossible. (c) financially secure. (d) believable.
5. **creditable** [kred'it·ə·bəl]—(a) financially secure. (b) meritorious. (c) bordering on the impossible. (d) guaranteed.
6. **culpable** [kul'pə·bəl]—(a) perceptible to the senses. (b) conscience-stricken. (c) slanderous. (d) blameworthy.
7. **delectable** [di·lek'tə·bəl]—(a) delightful. (b) fussy. (c) carefully selected. (d) capable of great speed.
8. **equable** [ek'wə·bəl]—(a) steady or even. (b) near the equator.

(c) capable of being compared. (d) fair or just.
9. **estimable** [es'tə·mə·bəl]—(a) careless. (b) popular. (c) worthy of high regard. (d) capable of being counted.
10. **execrable** [ek'sə·krə·bəl]—(a) painful. (b) pugnacious. (c) detestable. (d) responsive.
11. **habitable** [hab'it·ə·bəl]—(a) customary. (b) endurable. (c) well-mannered. (d) capable of being lived in.
12. **impeccable** [im·pek'ə·bəl]—(a) faultless. (b) mysterious. (c) in bad taste. (d) pure.
13. **irreparable** [i·rep'ər·ə·bəl]—(a) that cannot be repaired. (b) damaging or dangerous. (c) that cannot be forgotten. (d) deserving blame.
14. **imponderable** [im·pon'dər·ə·bəl]—(a) soft and light. (b) heavy. (c) that cannot be calculated or valued. (d) thoughtful.
15. **incomparable** [in·kom'pər·ə·bəl]—(a) irrelevant. (b) unworthy. (c) hard to understand. (d) unequaled.

ANSWERS:

1. **amicable**—(d) friendly. 2. **amenable**—(b) capable of being persuaded. 3. **feasible**—(b) practicable. 4. **credible**—(d) believable. 5. **creditable**—(b) meritorious. 6. **culpable**—(d) blameworthy. 7. **delectable**—(a) delightful. 8. **equable**—(a) steady or even. 9. **estimable**—(c) worthy of high regard. 10. **execrable**—(c) detestable. 11. **habitable**—(d) capable of being lived in. 12. **impeccable**—(a) faultless. 13. **irreparable**—(a) that cannot be repaired. 14. **imponderable**—(c) that cannot be calculated or valued. 15. **incomparable**—(d) unequaled.

2 SINGULAR AND PLURAL FORMS

WHY YOU SHOULDN'T SAY: *He don't know if everybody is in their proper places.*

This is a mistake because the speaker has mixed up his singular and plural forms.

You will remember that when a singular noun or pronoun (*boy, parrot, it*) is the subject of a sentence, you must also use the singular form of the verb—the action word in the sentence. You say, "The boy *does* his homework; the parrot *flies;* it *grows* bigger." If the noun or pronoun that is the subject of the sentence is a plural (representing more than one person or thing) you must use a plural verb form: "The boys *do* their homework; the parrots *fly;* they *grow* bigger." This matching of singular nouns and pronouns with singular predicates, and plurals with plurals, is what is called "agreement in number."

There are two common errors that cause listeners or readers to wince. The first of these errors is to be found in its simplest form in the expression *he don't. Don't* is, of course, a contraction of *do not.* You would not say "He do not," would you? Then why permit yourself to say "He don't"? You will not make this mistake if you constantly remind yourself that *don't* is a plural verb and that its subject must therefore also be plural.

Wrong	Right
He don't.	*He doesn't.*
She don't.	*She doesn't.*
It don't.	*It doesn't.*

The problem of agreement of subject and predicate becomes more confusing, to be sure, when there is some doubt in your mind whether the subject of a sentence is actually singular or plural. This often happens when the singular subject is separated from its verb by several words that have a plural sound to them. For instance, which is the correct verb form in each of the following sentences?

The smell of garlic and onions (was or were) overpowering.
A touch of money and success (has or have) spoiled her.
Each of the twelve men, not to mention their wives, (is or are) going on a trip.
Everything except the cups (is or are) in the dishwasher.

447

The correct verb for the preceding sentences is the singular one (*was, has, is*). If you are not quite sure how to find the subject so as to determine its number, try saying the sentence without the words (beginning with the preposition *of* or *except*) that intervene between the first noun and the verb:

> *The smell . . . was overpowering.*
> *A touch . . . has spoiled her.*
> *Each . . . is going on a trip.*
> *Everything . . . is in the dishwasher.*

Now it becomes clear, you see, that the real subject is singular and that the verb must also be singular. Remember, too, that intervening phrases like *in addition to* and *together with* do not affect the number of the subject. Here are a few correct sample sentences using *in addition to, together with,* and similar phrases. In each sentence, note the use of the singular verb.

> *Joe, accompanied by Bill, is going fishing.*
> *Mary, along with Jane, has taken on the job.*
> *The cup, in addition to the plate, was broken.*
> *Mr. Hays, together with the whole office staff, is getting a bonus.*

Each and *Everybody* Are Singular

The second common error in the wrong-number category arises from the feeling that many people have that such nouns as *anybody, each, everybody,* and *everyone* are, or ought to be, plural. These words are not plural; each of them refers to one person or thing and should be followed by the singular pronouns *he, his, him; she, her; it, its.* The use of *their* and *they* instead of *his* and *he* when the antecedent is everybody, everyone, none, etc., has been defended and adopted by many writers and linguists. But until you become expert, you would be wise to follow the simple rule—*use the singular.* The plural pronouns *them* and *their* are grammatically incorrect in the following sentences.

> *If anybody calls, tell them I've gone to lunch.* (The correct pronoun here would be *him,* which may acceptably refer to one person of either sex.)

> *Each of the children memorized their telephone numbers.* (The correct phrase would be *his telephone number.*)

NOTE: Some nouns may be considered either singular or plural, depending on the context in which they are used. Do not waste your time and energy in worrying about which verb or pronoun to use with such collective nouns as *audience, class, committee, crew, crowd, group, jury, team,* and so on. *The audience were very attentive* is as correct as *The audience was very attentive;* and *The team did its best* is as correct as *The team did their best.* A sensible practice to follow with a collective noun is to treat it as a singular noun if you think of it as a unit, and to treat it as a plural noun if you think of it as composed of a number of individuals. Thus, for example: *The jury has done a good job,* but *The jury have all returned to their homes.*

3 WRONG PRONOUNS

WHY YOU SHOULDN'T SAY: *If your child dislikes spinach, try boiling it in milk.*

The *pro-* in *pronoun* means "in place of." Thus, every pronoun stands in place of a noun; the meaning of a sentence with a pronoun in it is clear only when there is no doubt in the reader's mind about which noun the pronoun stands for. If you use a pronoun that might possibly refer to any one of two or more people, places, or things, you risk being misunderstood by your reader.

No reader can be sure of the meaning of the sentence quoted on the first page of this part of the book: "Walter was the first to tell Bill that he had been fired." Because the order of the words within an English sentence is so important for getting the meaning across, competent writers usually try to place pronouns as close as possible to their antecedents. Similarly, readers tend to assume that the nearest noun preceding a pronoun is the one it refers to. If everything in sentence construction always fitted together tidily, we could take it for granted that the noun represented by *he* in the above sentence is *Bill,* and that Bill is the one who has lost his job. But, any reader may well wonder: Isn't it likely that the writer intends the *he* to refer back to *Walter* rather than to *Bill?*

For the sake of total clarity, the writer should have said "Walter was the first to tell Bill that Bill (*or* Walter) had been fired." It is much better to repeat the noun than to leave the reader in doubt.

The following sentences should also be rewritten to avoid confusion:

> *As soon as their husbands bring home the Christmas trees, the wives drop everything to attend to them.*
> *If your child does not like spinach, try boiling it in milk.*
> *Margaret went to visit Anne because she was lonely.*
> *Since the cats seem frightened by the dogs, I think we should get rid of them.*

Grammar Test—The Numbers Game

Choose the proper word from each pair in the parentheses below to make a correct sentence. Use this test as a drill to perfect your use of proper verb and pronoun forms. Repeat it as many times as necessary until you can give the correct answer quickly and easily. Answers follow.

1. The aim of the sales manager and his assistant (is, are) to increase sales.
2. The taste of honey, sugar, and chocolate (was, were) too sweet.
3. His job, even with good wages and short hours, (is, are) tedious.
4. The purpose of all these chapters and tests (is, are) to teach you correct grammar.
5. The output of the three clothing factories and their 800 employees (is, are) 200 suits a day.
6. This desk and typewriter, together with the chair, (belong, belongs) to me.
7. Your clothes, including your shirt, (is, are) in the closet.
8. Joe, along with his brother, (run, runs) the family business.
9. The plate, as well as the glass, (was, were) on the table.
10. The teacher and his assistant, along with the principal, (grade, grades) the final exams.
11. Each of the workers must bring (their, his) own lunch.
12. Will any member who has not done so please cast (his, their) vote now?
13. Doesn't anybody have (his, their) driver's license?
14. Every day has (its, their) problems.
15. If somebody lost a wallet, (he, they) should let me know.
16. When someone sneezes, (they, he) should cover (their, his) mouth.
17. None of the women will admit that (they, she) broke the cup.

18. None of the workers will accept the same salary (he, they) made last year.
19. Nobody is going to improve (her, their) bridge game unless (she, they) tries.
20. Everyone must bring (their, his) own bicycle.

ANSWERS:

1. The aim . . . *is.* 2. The taste . . . *was.* 3. His job . . . *is.* 4. The purpose . . . *is.* 5. The output . . . *is.* 6. This desk and typewriter . . . *belong.* 7. Your clothes . . . *are.* 8. Joe . . . *runs.* 9. The plate . . . *was.* 10. The teacher and his assistant . . . *grade.* 11. Each . . . must bring *his.* 12. Will any member . . . cast *his.* 13. Doesn't anybody have *his.* 14. Every day has *its.* 15. If somebody lost a wallet, *he.* 16. When someone sneezes, *he . . . his* mouth. 17. None . . . will admit that *she.* 18. None . . . will accept the same salary *he.* 19. Nobody is going to improve *her . . .* unless *she.* 20. Everyone must bring *his.*

---

4 MISPLACED MODIFIERS

WHY YOU SHOULDN'T SAY: *When only four, my mother taught me to read.*

The reason is, of course, that you're not saying what you mean to say. Your mother didn't teach you to read when *she* was only four, yet that's what the statement seems to say. These sentences illustrate the same kind of error.

> *The teacher only knows the square root of 81.*
> *The girl who had been kissed quickly left.*
> *While sitting comfortably indoors, a storm blew up.*
> *Lincoln wrote the Gettysburg Address while riding through Pennsylvania on the back of an envelope.*

These sentences can be interpreted to mean that the teacher knew nothing except the square root of 81, that the girl left because she had been kissed quickly, that the storm was sitting indoors, or that Lincoln rode on an envelope. In each case the misinterpretation is due to the fact that an important word of phrase has been put in the wrong place, so that it seems to describe (or *modify*) the wrong thing. Note how simple it is to rearrange the words, or to add a word or two, so as to resolve all doubts about meanings:

> *Only the teacher knows the square root of 81.*
> *The girl who had been kissed left quickly.*
> *While we were sitting comfortably indoors, a storm blew up.*
> *While riding through Pennsylvania, Lincoln wrote the Gettysburg Address on the back of an envelope.*

It is because the placement of words determines the meaning of a sentence that the error of misplaced modifiers is so serious. You will not be guilty of such mistakes if you remember the following facts:

(1) A word or phrase that *modifies* something in a sentence changes the meaning of the word or phrase it modifies—usually by describing it in more detail. Thus, an *only* child is not just any child; he is a child who has no brothers or sisters. The modifier must be kept as close as possible to the part of the sentence that it modifies, and it must not be placed in a position where it seems to modify some other word instead of the right one.

It is essential that you place these descriptive words—or modifiers—where they belong. To see just how much difference in meaning results from a different placement, let us look once more at that phrase *an only child.* In it, *only* clearly modifies (changes the meaning of) *child.* But suppose you shift the order of the words so that the phrase reads *only a child.* Instantly, the meaning again changes. Or try shifting the words once more: *a child only.* Here are three sentences containing those three words in the three arrangements. Note the difference in meanings.

> *An only child, having no brothers or sisters, is sometimes spoiled.*
> *Only a child, not a grown person, could enjoy such a show.*
> *In our family, a parent gives orders; a child only listens and obeys.*

Now you know why it may be questionable to say "I only see my father on Saturdays." Do you really only *see* him, not hear him or talk to him? Or do you see only your *father*, not your mother? Or do you see your father only on *Saturdays?* Unless you put the modifier in the right position, no one can be sure of your intended meaning!

452

(2) Misrelated or wrongly attached modifiers are among the commonest and most ludicrous of grammatical errors. One familiar type is the carelessly written opening phrase that attaches itself willy-nilly to the noun or pronoun that follows it. This error is often good for a laugh as you will see from these examples:

Dashing madly through the crowd at the station, the train went off without me.
After brushing his teeth, the coffee tasted better.
On his first safari, a lion was killed.
When only four, my mother taught me to read.
While asleep in the park, somebody stole her pocketbook.
Walking across the field, a light appeared in the distance.

Those sentences are all boners because the opening phrases are misrelated. As a result, the reader gets the absurd picture of a train dashing madly through a crowd, coffee brushing someone's teeth, a four-year-old mother teaching her child, and so on. Here are suggested corrections:

I dashed madly through the crowd at the station only to see the train go off without me.
After Henry brushed his teeth, the coffee tasted better.
On his first safari, Peter killed a lion.
When I was only four, my mother taught me to read.
While she was asleep in the park, somebody stole her pocketbook.
As I walked across the field, I saw a light in the distance.

REMEMBER: When you start a sentence with a phrase that begins with such words as *after, before, on, when,* or *while,* or with a verb form ending in *-ing,* don't forget to provide this modifying phrase with something to modify. Be sure that you (1) state the true subject and (2) place the true subject correctly in order to avoid confusion.

Grammar Test—Just for Fun

Here are some more humorous examples of misplaced and misrelated modifiers. Practice correcting these sentences, each of which may be restated in any of several ways, so that you will never be tempted to say or write such bloopers. Correct the sentences to suit yourself. Just be sure your finished sentences are clear and not ridiculous. No answers are given.

1. While in the bathtub, the telephone rang.
2. After fixing the motor, the car started again.
3. While visiting in Denver, the snowstorm struck.
4. To read well, good light is needed.
5. If your shoes don't fit your feet, get a new pair.
6. When in a hurry to get to Chicago, a jet plane leaves at 9 A.M.
7. Reading the book, the cat sat in her lap.
8. Having been built in 1920, I had to remodel the house.
9. Fighting among themselves, the mothers separated the boys.
10. Waiting impatiently for the mail, the mailman finally came.
11. Walking down the path, the cabin came into view.
12. He watched the parade sitting by the television set.
13. The church was designed by J. T. Smith, whose belfry is full of bats.
14. I spoke to the man with the dog in the blue suit.
15. I heard the bird near the nest that was singing.
16. He waved to me as I left with his right hand.
17. The policeman shot the kidnaper who was fleeing with his gun.
18. The hostess was escorted by her husband wearing a red gown.
19. Gulping down the food, mother warned us to eat slower.
20. On rereading these sentences, the answers are easy.

5 WRONG VERB FORM

WHY YOU SHOULDN'T SAY: *She had broke it, but I said that I done it.*

In this example the writer used the wrong forms of the verbs *to break* and *to do* in a sentence.

Every verb has three basic forms, called the "principal parts," and all the *tenses* are built up from these parts. The tenses are the specific forms of the verb that show when the action it describes is taking place: if it is now taking place, has taken place in the past, or will take place in the future. Take the verb *walk:* The present and future tenses are formed from the present infinitive *walk* (you *walk*, he *walks*, they *will walk*); the simple past tense is formed from the past tense *walked* (you *walked*, they *walked*); and the so-called "perfect" tenses are formed from the past participle *walked* (you *have walked*, he *has walked*, they *had walked*). There are several other tenses, of course, to indicate a variety of times before, after, or during an action, but all of them are built in one way or another upon those three basic forms: the present infinitive, the past, and the past participle. A fourth form, the present participle, is made by adding the suffix *-ing* to the present infinitive. It is used in such compound verb forms as *is walking, were walking, had been walking*, etc.

No one is likely to make bad mistakes in tense with such verbs as *walk*. Such verbs are called regular verbs, and they all form both their past tense and past participle simply by adding *-d* or *-ed* to the present infinitive. Thus:

Present Infinitive	Past Tense	Past Participle
walk	walked	walked
hear	heard	heard
vote	voted	voted

Most verbs follow this simple pattern. You learned the pattern and how to form tenses when you were very young. Many people, however, have trouble with the tenses of a different kind of verb: the *irregular* verb. Irregular verbs form their pasts and past participles in a number of different ways, and so their principal parts must be memorized. A child will say "I swim," "I swimmed," and "I have swimmed" because, believe it or not, he knows the language so well that it is second nature to him to form all tenses in the regular, logical way. What he learns as he grows up is that logic does not always work with language. *Swim* is an irregular verb, and its principal parts are *swim, swam, swum.*

It is because irregular verbs are so often used that expressions such as *I done it, I seen it, I have went,* and *I got took* grate upon the ear with such force. The past tense of *do* is *did; done* is its past participle—which means that it may be used only in combination with *have, has, had, was, were,* or (sometimes) *got* or *gotten; I have done it, He has done it, We have done it, They were soon done with their work,* or *The roast got done too fast,* etc. And just as *done* may be used only in tenses formed by adding *have, has,* etc., so *did* may be used only by itself, in the simple past tense: *I did it, He did it, They did it.*

Irregular verbs follow no consistent pattern. Each is irregular in its own way. This means that we must know their principal parts by heart (and, of course, we do know most of them because we have used them constantly all our lives). It also means, though, that we must never forget that the simple past tense is always used alone, whereas the past participle is always combined with a short word like *have* or *had*. Here is a list of seventy-nine of the most common irregular verbs. Learn the ones you are not quite sure of. And remember to use them correctly from now on.

Principal Parts of Irregular Verbs

Present Infinitive	Past Tense	Past Participle
	(*never* used with *have, has, had, was, were,* or *got*)	(*always* used with *have, has, was, were,* or *got*)
arise	arose	arisen
awake	awoke	awake *or* awakened
bear	bore	borne
beat	beat	beaten *or* beat
become	became	become
begin	began	begun
bite	bit	bitten *or* bit
bleed	bled	bled
blow	blew	blown
break	broke	broken
bring	brought (not "brang")	brought (not "brung")
build	built	built
burst	burst	burst
catch	caught	caught
choose	chose	chosen
come	came	come
dig	dug	dug
do	did	done
draw	drew	drawn
drink	drank	drunk
drive	drove	driven
eat	ate	eaten
fall	fell	fallen
fight	fought	fought

Present Infinitive	Past Tense	Past Participle
	(*never* used with *have, has, had, was, were,* or *got*)	(*always* used with *have, has, was, were,* or *got*)
fly	flew	flown
forbid	forbade	forbidden
forget	forgot	forgotten *or* forgot
forsake	forsook	forsaken
freeze	froze (not "freezed")	frozen
get	got	got *or* gotten
give	gave	given
go	went	gone
grow	grew (not "growed")	grown
hang	hung (for pictures)	hung (for pictures)
	hanged (for men)	hanged (for men)
have	had	had
hide	hid	hidden *or* hid
hurt	hurt	hurt
know	knew (not "knowed")	known
lay (meaning "place" or "put")	laid	laid
lead	led	led
leave	left	left
lend	lent	lent
let	let	let
lie (meaning "recline")	lay	lain
make	made	made
pay	paid	paid
put	put	put
ride	rode	ridden
ring	rang	rung
rise	rose	risen
run	ran	run
say	said	said
see	saw	seen
seek	sought	sought
sell	sold	sold
set	set	set

Present Infinitive	Past Tense (*never* used with *have, has, had, was, were,* or *got*)	Past Participle (*always* used with *have, has, was, were,* or *got*)
shake	shook	shaken
shrink	shrank *or* shrunk	shrunk *or* shrunken
sing	sang	sung
sink	sank	sunk
sit	sat	sat
slay	slew (not "slayed")	slain
sling	slung (not "slang")	slung
speak	spoke	spoken
spin	spun	spun
spring	sprang	sprung
steal	stole	stolen
sting	stung (not "stang")	stung
strike	struck	struck
swear	swore	sworn
swim	swam	swum
swing	swung (not "swang")	swung
take	took	taken
teach	taught	taught
tear	tore	torn
think	thought	thought
throw	threw (not "throwed")	thrown
wear	wore	worn
write	wrote	written

NOTE: The most common of all verbs is also the most irregular. Do you know which verb it is? That's right: It is the verb *to be*. Unlike the irregular verbs in the above list, *be* does not have three dependable parts. Its forms change so drastically (for instance, from *am* to *are* to *is* to *was* to *were* to *been*) that no simple rule can cover them. Fortunately, most of us have no trouble with the word, because its many forms are so basic that constant practice has made us perfect. The only error that crops up frequently is the confusion of the singular *was* with the plural *were*. Make sure that you never say "we was," "you was," or "they was." Only the word *were* is correct; it is correct in the expression *you were* even when *you* refers to only one person.

Grammar Test—Correct Verb Forms

In the parentheses below, choose the proper word or words to make a correct sentence. Note that in a few cases either of the two choices is acceptable. This test is a drill. Take it over and over again until you can choose all the right verb forms quickly and easily. Answers follow.

1. I (done, have done) it.
2. They (came, come) yesterday.
3. Mary said she (thunk, thought) of it yesterday.
4. Four sailors (drowned, drownded) in the accident.
5. I (have seen, seen) it.
6. I (have saw, saw) it.
7. We (did, done) it when you told us to.
8. We have (did, done) it before.
9. You (wrote, have wrote) a good letter.
10. They (threw, throwed) out a lot of old magazines.
11. She (has broke, has broken) her promise.
12. The water pipe (burst, bursted) last week.
13. I (knowed, knew) he was right all along.
14. He (drank, drunk) his coffee.
15. He (has drunk, has drank) his coffee.
16. I (brang, brought) a friend along.
17. She has (wrote, written) us a nice note.
18. We have (driven, drove) 300 miles today.
19. The batter (slid, slud) into third base.
20. I'm sorry but I've (forgotten, forgot) his name.
21. You have (gone, went) and done it again!
22. Mrs. Brown has (chosen, chose) not to go.
23. He has been (bitten, bit) by the dog.
24. Just an hour ago she (laid, lay) down for a nap.
25. The farmer (dug, digged) the potatoes before noon.
26. I have (spoken, spoke) to the principal about your behavior.
27. Have you (ate, eaten)?
28. Yesterday a bee (stung, stang) her.
29. The water pipes have (froze, frozen).
30. St. George (slew, slayed) the dragon.
31. My son has (grown, growed) a lot this year.
32. My son (grew, growed) tomatoes in the back yard last summer.
33. Have you (drew, drawn) your pay yet?
34. Have you ever (swum, swam) in the ocean?

35. The birds have all (flown, flew) away.
36. Have you ever (ridden, rode) a horse?
37. She hasn't (drank, drunk) her milk this morning.
38. I'd have (thunk, thought) you knew better than that.
39. He picked up the rock and (slang, slung) it over the fence.
40. Have you (given, gave) him his share?
41. Who (built, builded) this cabin?
42. He (throwed, threw) the snowball at me!
43. We have all (sang, sung) the national anthem.
44. The cut on his finger (bleeded, bled) badly.
45. You have (broke, broken) Mother's favorite vase!
46. She (began, begun) the job yesterday.
47. She (began, has begun) the job already.
48. He (swimmed, swam) the river at its widest point.
49. You have (tore, torn) your dress.
50. Haven't I (seen, saw) you somewhere before?
51. Joe and Tom (begun, began) the job yesterday.
52. Joe and Tom have (begun, began) the job.
53. Have you (worn, wore) that dress before?
54. She (strove, strived) to improve herself.
55. The baseball team got (beat, beaten) badly.
56. Your shirt (shrunk, shrank) in the laundry.
57. Has the whistle (blew, blown)?
58. He had (run, ran) all the way to school.
59. I (done, did) it yesterday.
60. Mother has (hidden, hid) the cooky jar.
61. Have you (learned, learnt) how to fly a plane?
62. Last week he (sprang, sprung) a joke on us.
63. The telephone (rang, rung) while I was in the bathtub.
64. I (knew, knowed) you were going to visit us today!

ANSWERS:

1. have done. 2. came. 3. thought. 4. drowned. 5. have seen. 6. saw. 7. did. 8. done. 9. wrote. 10. threw. 11. has broken. 12. burst. 13. knew. 14. drank. 15. has drunk. 16. brought. 17. written. 18. driven. 19. slid. 20. forgotten *or* forgot. 21. gone. 22. chosen. 23. bitten *or* bit. 24. lay. 25. dug. 26. spoken. 27. eaten. 28. stung. 29. frozen. 30. slew. 31. grown. 32. grew. 33. drawn. 34. swum. 35. flown. 36. ridden. 37. drunk. 38. thought. 39. slung. 40. given. 41. built. 42. threw. 43. sung. 44. bled. 45. broken. 46. began. 47. has begun. 48. swam. 49. torn. 50. seen. 51. began. 52. begun. 53. worn. 54. strove *or* strived. 55. beaten *or* beat. 56. shrank *or* shrunk. 57. blown. 58. run. 59. did. 60. hidden *or* hid. 61. learned *or* learnt. 62. sprang. 63. rang. 64. knew.

Fun With Words

INTERESTING VERBS

The following sixteen words are interesting verbs that you should know. Check the word or phrase you believe is closest in meaning to the key word. Answers follow.

1. **ravage** [rav′ij]—(a) to enrage. (b) to plunder. (c) to devour. (d) to wear away.
2. **edify** [ed′ə·fī]—(a) to scold. (b) to praise. (c) to improve and enlighten. (d) to have exceptional pleasure from.
3. **haggle** [hag′əl]—(a) to wrangle or dispute. (b) to scold. (c) to lie. (d) to beg.
4. **curtail** [kər·tāl′]—(a) to curl or intertwine. (b) to deprive of. (c) to confuse. (d) to cut short.
5. **supplicate** [sup′lə·kāt]—(a) to strangle. (b) to grow weak. (c) to beg humbly. (d) to curse.
6. **extol** [ik·stōl′]—(a) to announce. (b) to collect. (c) to scold or harass. (d) to praise.
7. **facilitate** [fə·sil′ə·tāt]—(a) to tease. (b) to make easy. (c) to pretend. (d) to congratulate.
8. **cavort** [kə·vôrt′]—(a) to prance around. (b) to fling. (c) to find fault with. (d) to enjoy in a carefree manner.
9. **sully** [sul′ē]—(a) to keep hidden; make secret. (b) to hinder.

(c) to defile; soil. (d) to put the blame on someone.
10. **usurp** [yōō·zûrp′]—(a) to charge high interest rates. (b) to intrude upon. (c) to disturb. (d) to seize power or position.
11. **goad** [gōd]—(a) to annoy. (b) to incite or spur. (c) to argue. (d) to beg.
12. **augment** [ôg·ment′]—(a) to urge. (b) to dispute. (c) to promise. (d) to increase; add to.
13. **inundate** [in′un·dāt]—(a) to flood; deluge. (b) to break down. (c) to retreat. (d) to enter into an agreement.
14. **waive** [wāv]—(a) to forgo. (b) to demand. (c) to look for. (d) to be irresolute.
15. **confound** [kon·found′]—(a) to impress. (b) to bring together. (c) to frustrate. (d) to confuse; perplex.
16. **heed** [hēd]—(a) to agree to; accept. (b) to dispute. (c) to pay attention to; consider carefully. (d) to prepare for.

ANSWERS:

1. **ravage**—(b) to plunder. 2. **edify**—(c) to improve and enlighten. 3. **haggle**—(a) to wrangle or dispute. 4. **curtail**—(d) to cut short. 5. **supplicate**—(c) to beg humbly. 6. **extol**—(d) to praise. 7. **facilitate**—(b) to make easy. 8. **cavort**—(a) to prance around. 9. **sully**—(c) to defile; soil. 10. **usurp**—(d) to seize power or position. 11. **goad**—(b) to incite or spur. 12. **augment**—(d) to increase; add to. 13. **inundate**—(a) to flood; deluge. 14. **waive**—(a) to forgo. 15. **confound**—(d) to confuse; perplex. 16. **heed**—(c) to pay attention to; consider carefully.

6 CONFUSION OF ADJECTIVES AND ADVERBS

WHY YOU SHOULDN'T SAY: *My mother treats me real cruel when I shout too loud.*

This sentence is acceptable in conversation—unless you are talking to a strict grammarian. He would probably correct you for using an adjective, *real*, when you should have used the adverb *really*.

The rule is simple: Adjectives modify nouns or pronouns; adverbs modify verbs, adjectives, or other adverbs. In most cases, too, the rule is easy to follow. We all say "John is a *brave* man" or "Mary is a *happy* woman" without thinking twice. *Brave* and *happy* describe the nouns *man* and *woman*. They are adjectives. We also say correctly "John fought *bravely*" or "Mary smiled *happily*." *Bravely* and *happily* describe the verbs *fought* and *smiled*. They are adverbs.

Those are the most basic forms, uses, and placements of adjectives and adverbs, and they should cause little trouble. There are several common situations, however, in which mistakes are often made. The mistake is always the same—that is, an adjective is used where an adverb belongs, or an adverb is used instead of an adjective. This confusion generally happens for one of four different reasons:

(1) The sentence is phrased in such a way that the adverb is placed closer to a noun or a pronoun than to the verb it modifies; as a result, the writer is misled into substituting an adjective for the adverb.

> *Al treated his wife cruel.*
> *I saw the snake clear before it slithered away.*

In those sentences, the words *cruel* and *clear* explain how Al treated his wife and how I saw the snake. They do not describe the wife and the snake. You won't make this type of error if you remember that adverbs often answer the questions *how?*, *when?*, *where?*, etc., even when they follow a noun instead of a verb. The above sentences should read this way, of course:

> *Al treated his wife cruelly.*
> *I saw the snake clearly before it slithered away.*

(2) Many people tend to forget that adverbs modify *adjectives* as well as verbs. Thus, sentences like the following are questionable:

462

Al is real cruel to his wife.
You have to be awful brave to handle poisonous snakes.
It was plain thoughtless of him to forget his umbrella.

Really cruel, awfully brave, and *plainly thoughtless* (although they might sound rather stiff in conversation) are the expressions to use in writing and in formal speech.

(3) A third, extremely frequent reason for confusion stems from the fact that there is one kind of verb that should usually be followed by an adjective rather than an adverb. Not realizing this, many speakers and writers use adverbs instead of adjectives with these verbs (thus advertising their lack of word power). Consider the following sentences. Are they right or wrong?

Velvet feels smoothly to the touch.
Cindy looks gorgeously in her new dress.
These roses smell well.
That orchestra sounded too loudly for my ears.
The eggs tasted rottenly this morning.

Note that the verbs in these sentences are descriptive of the action of the five senses—sight, hearing, smell, taste, and touch. Such verbs are generally followed by adjectives, because it is not the verb that is being described; it is the subject. Thus, it is *velvet* that feels *smooth*, *Cindy* who looks *gorgeous*, the *roses* that smell *good*, and so on. The adverbial form instead of the adjectival is wrong in every one of the five sentences.

To clarify this distinction, think for a moment about the difference between *The dog smells bad* and *The dog smells badly*. In the first sentence, the dog has a bad odor, whereas in the second sentence his sense of smell is poor. In other words, the adjective *bad* modifies (that is, describes) the noun *dog*, but the adverb *badly* modifies the verb *smells*. Only if you want to say that the dog has a poor sense of smell can you say that he smells *badly*. Eggs have no sense of taste; therefore they can only taste *rotten*. Roses have no sense of smell; therefore they can smell only *good* or *bad*, not *well* or *badly*.

NOTE: Here is a good way to test your grammar in this type of sentence: The verb *to be* never takes an adverb; and so you can decide whether or not to use an adverb after a verb like *feel, look, smell*, etc., by substituting some form of *to be* for it. If the sentence sounds peculiar with *is, are, was,* or *were,* you should be using an adjective, not an adverb. Let's try this test on just two of the above five sentences:

> *Cindy looks (is?) gorgeously in her new dress.*
> *That orchestra sounded (was?) too loudly for my ears.*

It immediately becomes obvious that the adverbs are wrong and should be changed to adjectives. Remember the *to be* test, and you will have no further trouble with verbs relating to the five senses.

(4) People are sometimes confused by the fact that while most adverbs end in *-ly,* some do not. A good example of such an adverb is *hard.* As an adjective, *hard* may mean "violent," as in *a hard punch.* The adverbial form of this adjective, however, is not *hardly.* The word *hardly* means "scarcely or barely." The adverb meaning "violently or with great energy" is *hard,* without the *-ly:* "The boxer punched his opponent hard."

Some adverbs even have two forms, one with and one without the *-ly.* It is a common mistake of people who think they know more about grammar than they actually do to criticize highway signs that read "Drive Slow!" They insist that the only correct adverbial form is *slowly* —but they are wrong. Here is a list of some common adverbs that have two acceptable forms. The illustrative sentences are all correct.

Adverbs Without *-ly*		Adverbs With *-ly*	
bright	(*The sun shone bright this morning.*)	brightly	(*The sun shone brightly this morning.*)
deep	(*Drink deep.*)	deeply	(*She felt the loss deeply.*)
fair	(*Play fair.*)	fairly	(*We must deal fairly with him.*)
high	(*Aim high in life.*)	highly	(*He thinks highly of you.*)
loose	(*This collar fits too loose.*)	loosely	(*Tie the rope loosely to the post.*)
quick	(*Come quick!*)	quickly	(*He asked me to come quickly.*)
slow	(*Drive slow.*)	slowly	(*He drove slowly off.*)
soft	(*Speak soft, please.*)	softly	(*To speak softly is to speak well.*)
tight	(*Tie the rope tight.*)	tightly	(*He held her tightly by the hand.*)

464

If both *bright* and *brightly, deep* and *deeply, slow* and *slowly,* and so on are adverbs, how do you know which to use? It's simple. The *-ly* forms are generally best for formal speech or writing. The shorter forms without the *-ly* are used in less formal speech or writing, and especially in commands, requests, or instructions: *drink deep, play fair, aim high, come quick,* etc.

REMEMBER: Do not force the suffix *-ly* onto adverbs that should not or need not have it. When in doubt, consult your dictionary.

Grammar Test—WELL or GOOD? BAD or BADLY? SLOW or SLOWLY?

Choose the proper word from each pair in the parentheses below. Use this test as a drill to help you perfect your use of adverbs and adjectives. Repeat it until you can give all the correct answers quickly and easily. Answers follow.

1. You did (well, good) on your test.
2. The new quarterback passes the ball (well, good).
3. He did very (badly, bad) on the final exam.
4. He feels (sad, sadly) about the loss of his dog.
5. The shoes feel (badly, bad) on my feet.
6. The green chair looked (good, well) in the living room.
7. This stew tastes (horribly, horrible).
8. Even though I burned my tongue, I can still taste (well, good).
9. My chances for a raise look (slimly, slim).
10. The water feels (cold, coldly).
11. The doctor said her chances for a full recovery look (well, good).
12. The new quarterback looks (good, well) in practice.
13. The flowers look (beautiful, beautifully) in the yard.
14. This silk feels so nice and (softly, soft).
15. Her voice sounded very (harshly, harsh) to me.
16. That perfume smells (divine, divinely).
17. I did my homework (easily, easy).
18. He writes his papers more (legible, legibly) than I do.
19. This horse runs very (fastly, fast).
20. She takes everything too (serious, seriously).
21. I can see your mistake (plainly, plain) enough.
22. He plays chess (wonderful, wonderfully) well.

23. She treated him very (cruel, cruelly).
24. Let's do the job (different, differently) the next time.
25. You must go (straight, straightly) to bed.
26. You must play (fair, fairly).
27. Breathe (deep, deeply) and say "ah."
28. You must work (hardly, hard).
29. She sees (well, good) with her new glasses.
30. My sore hand feels (awfully, awful).

ANSWERS:

1. well. 2. well. 3. badly. 4. sad. 5. bad. 6. good. 7. horrible. 8. well. (Remember, you might taste *good* to a cannibal, but when you taste something yourself, you taste it *well*.) 9. slim. 10. cold. 11. good. 12. good. 13. beautiful. 14. soft. 15. harsh. 16. divine. 17. easily. 18. legibly. 19. fast. (There is no such word as *fastly*.) 20. seriously. 21. plainly. 22. wonderfully. 23. cruelly. 24. differently. 25. straight. 26. fair *or* fairly. 27. deep *or* deeply. 28. hard. 29. well. 30. awful.

---

7 THE DOUBLE NEGATIVE

WHY YOU SHOULDN'T SAY: *I can't hardly wait until Christmas.*

Almost everybody knows that *I don't want none* is frowned on. And almost everybody knows that this use of two negatives (*do not* and *none*) in a single statement is called a *double negative*. Many people believe, too, that a double negative is wrong because two *no's* add up to a *yes;* in other words, *I do not want none* means I *do want some*. This is only partly true, however. The trouble with double negatives is not that they cancel each other out and may therefore lead to misunderstandings, for nobody assumes that the person who says "I don't want none" means anything but an emphatic *no*. The real trouble with double negatives is that they are seldom permitted to creep into the English of careful speakers and writers. To use them, other than for special effect, is to display your lack of word power.

Obvious double negatives cause little trouble for most people who try to speak and write correctly; but there are several words that can be used in a negative sense without being recognized as negatives, and these are often combined with other words to form what might be called "subtle" double negatives. Below is a list of several such words. Note that the list does not include immediately recognizable negatives *never, not, no,* and such obviously negative contractions as *can't, don't, shouldn't,* etc. If you combine any of the following words with an obvious negative, you may be guilty of creating a double negative of the subtle kind that good writers are especially careful to avoid:

barely	neither
but (meaning "only")	nothing
ever	nowhere
except	only
hardly	rarely
just	scarcely
merely	seldom
nearly	

Here are some samples of sentences containing subtle double negatives:

Avoid	Use
They aren't barely old enough to vote.	*They're barely old enough to vote.*
I can't hardly wait until Christmas.	*I can hardly wait until Christmas.*
You can't go neither.	*You can't go either.*
We didn't scarcely have money enough.	*We had scarcely money enough.*
I haven't ever got time to read.	*I never have time to read.*
He isn't but ten years old.	*He is only ten years old.*
She just merely weighs ninety pounds.	*She weighs merely ninety pounds.*
He hasn't worked here except six months.	*He has worked here only six months.*
The curtains wouldn't barely cover the windows.	*The curtains would barely cover the windows.*
We seldom ever come here.	*We seldom come here.*

A Final Word About Grammar

The seven kinds of error we have talked about in the foregoing pages are not the only grammatical errors that people are likely to make. They are, however, the most frequent mistakes—the ones that modern writers are most careful to avoid. If you feel that your grammar needs improvement in certain areas that require a study of the basic rules and regulations, you can find those rules set forth in detail in any modern grammar book.

There are dozens of books available. They will provide answers for your questions about such intricate matters as, for example, the active and passive voices, the inflection of adjectives and adverbs, and the correct use of the subjunctive mood. Remember, however, that grammar and good usage can change from one generation to the next. So if you decide to study grammar, make sure that you get yourself a *modern* textbook.

Grammar is a living thing; like all living things, it never stops changing. Old-fashioned grammarians used to lay down the law as if English were a dead (and therefore unchanging) language. There are many laws, to be sure, but the modern grammar book does more than just spell them out: it helps you to interpret them and to understand why some of them are no longer fully in effect.

The more you increase your word power, including your knowledge of usage, punctuation, and grammar, the more you will realize that it is *you* who have power over *words*, not the other way around. By now you should be in command of your native language as never before. Your dictionary and your grammar book are helpful aids. They are guides to growth, not slave drivers. Use them wisely, and they will serve you well.

Always remember that language is a tool to be used. The better you can use this tool to express your ideas, thoughts, feelings, and emotions, the more successful you will be and the more complete and fulfilled a human being you will be. But language, including grammar, is merely a tool, not a religion or a way of life. It is better to make mistakes than to put this most powerful tool aside. You will improve your word power only by constant and careful use.

If you are not in the habit of writing, assign yourself the task of writing a letter every week, or of keeping a diary, taking notes for your club or business conferences, etc. As you listen to radio and TV newscasters, as you read magazines, newspapers, and books, note carefully how others use word power. Copy down new words you hear or see and learn how to spell, pronounce, and use them. Note how professional speakers and writers use words, punctuate their sentences, use or avoid split infinitives and double negatives, handle tricky sentences. Try to read at least one magazine a week and one book a month to keep alert to how professional writers use word power.

PART SIX

Using Your
Word Power

USE YOUR WORD POWER RIGHT

English, like many other languages, has several levels of usage, ranging from *standard* to *informal* to *dialect* to *slang* to *nonstandard*.

Standard usage refers to the words and expressions accepted as correct by authorities on the language as it is spoken and written today. *Standard* is the only level that is thoroughly acceptable in every situation—at a formal or informal gathering, in a carefully worded business report, or in a personal letter. It is always "good" usage.

Informal usage refers to words and expressions that are quite all right in casual talk and writing, but are not appropriate for formal social and business occasions. For example, "How do you do" and "Hello" are standard and may be used anywhere at any time. But "Hi" is acceptable only on an informal level; you wouldn't greet the President of the United States or a new employer with a "Hi."

Dialect refers to local words, expressions, pronunciations, and speech patterns of a specific region. It is most noticeable as a pronunciation or accent. We have all heard Cockney accents, Brooklyn accents, "hillbilly" accents, etc. Many expressions are unique to one area—*sowbelly* for *salt pork*, for instance—which may not be fully understood elsewhere. Dialect isn't "wrong." It simply isn't meaningful from coast to coast.

Slang is the vocabulary of special occupational, age, ethnic, or interest groups that has gained some popularity with the general public. *Cool* meaning "excellent" is a recent example. The difficulty of slang is that often its meaning is clear only to special groups, and it can quickly become out of date. Some years ago people were calling things they liked *hot stuff*. By the time you read these words, a new slang term may have forced *cool* back to its old, standard usage.

Nonstandard refers to certain "outlawed" written and spoken forms like *should of, ain't, didn't ought to, I done good,* and so on. *Non*-standard is so far removed from *standard* that it seems to say, "I ain't never been to school."

Who Determines Standard Usage?

Standard usage is determined by what the majority of highly regarded writers and speakers use. Dictionary makers and grammarians in America consider themselves reporters, not judges. They report what is being written and said by the experts. Thus, when your dictionary defines a word, or indicates a preference for one particular spelling, or labels a word "nonstandard," you are not bound by some old-fashioned pedantic decree. You are being told what standard usage actually is today.

In this section we will discuss usage as if *standard* were the only "correct" usage. This is not always true, of course. Many informal, dialect, and slang terms may be used "correctly" at some time or place. Once you have mastered standard usage, you will know when and how to deviate from it.

What Is Correct Usage?

What is wrong with the sentence "I ain't going"? *Ain't* is not a standard word. It is nonstandard usage. The standard, accepted way to say this is "I am not going." Nonstandard usages are discussed later.

What is wrong with the sentence "The witness raised his right handle and swore to tell the truth"? Obviously the word *handle* is used instead of the word *hand*. The speaker or writer (clearly a foreigner) has not yet learned the difference between *handle* and *hand* because they sound and look somewhat alike. Of course, you would not make such a mistake, but you might say or write *accede* for *exceed*, *emigrant* for *immigrant*, *principal* for *principle*, and *there* or *their* for *they're*. In this part of the book you will learn to distinguish between such pairs or groups of words that sound alike or look alike.

What is wrong with the sentence "He drove from here at Chicago yesterday"? Obviously, the word *at* should be *to*. Correct usage links *from* and *to* together—we say that one goes *from* somewhere *to* somewhere else. Certain words are always linked together to achieve specific meanings. No one whose native tongue is English will fail to link *from* and *to*. But some people do sometimes forget to link *either* with *or* and *neither* with *nor*; and they don't know whether to link *accompanied* with *by* or *with*, and *wait* with *on* or *for*. This part of the book will help you to learn what words are linked correctly together.

Thus, a discussion of usage may be divided into four categories: (1) bad usage that you should avoid; (2) sound-alike, look-alike word pairs that may snare you; (3) words whose meanings are confused even though they do not look or sound alike; and (4) words that must be linked together properly if the writer wants to use them in a standard, fully acceptable way. Learn the proper meanings and forms of all the usage hurdles in this section.

471

1 WRONG USAGE

Usage that is glaringly wrong includes nonstandard words such as *ain't* and *disremember,* incorrect forms such as *nowheres* for *nowhere,* and faulty combinations such as *the reason is because, where at,* and *hadn't ought.*

At certain times and places no common usage is actually wrong. Anything a child says on the playground to his playmates is perfectly all right there so long as his playmates do not object to it. In these pages, however, we use the words *wrong* and *incorrect* to indicate usages that would be grossly *out of place* in the careful writing and polite conversation of an educated adult.

ain't This word, of course, is popular but incorrect. Educated speakers sometimes use *ain't* in humorous contexts, as when mimicking uneducated speakers. But most of us will do well never to use the word, even in fun.

> WRONG *I ain't going.*   RIGHT *I'm not going*
> *He ain't got any.*   *He hasn't any.*

alongside of *Alongside* is complete by itself and the *of* is incorrect.
> WRONG *The black car pulled up alongside of Harry.*
> RIGHT *The black car pulled up alongside Harry.*

alright The correct expression is *all right*—two words.

REMEMBER: You would not write *alwrong;* so don't write *alright.*

altho, tho These shortened forms for *although* and *though* are being used more and more often, but they are still not accepted as standard English.
> WRONG *Altho the hour was late, I finished the work.*
> RIGHT *Although the hour was late, I finished the work.*

and, etc. *Etc.* is the abbreviation of *et cetera,* Latin for *and so forth.* Since the *and* is already there in *etc.,* don't add another *and* before it. If you do, you are actually saying *and and so forth.*
> WRONG *We played cards, checkers, and etc.*
> RIGHT *We played cards, checkers, etc.*

anyplace, everyplace, noplace, someplace These words are frequently used by modern writers and speakers and are not truly bad usage. But they are most at home in informal contexts. The words *any-*

where, everywhere, nowhere, and *somewhere* are preferred in formal writing.

INFORMAL *I can't find it anyplace.*
Well, it must be someplace!

STANDARD *I can't find it anywhere.*
Well, it must be somewhere!

anyways, someways These words do not exist in standard speech. Use *anyway* and *someway.*

WRONG *I never liked that job anyways.*
We'll have to convince him someways.

RIGHT *I never liked that job anyway.*
We'll have to convince him someway.

anywheres, everywheres, nowheres, somewheres These words do not exist in standard speech. Use *anywhere, everywhere, nowhere,* and *somewhere.*

WRONG *Anywheres you want to go is all right with me.*
There's nowheres I'd rather go than Hawaii.

RIGHT *Anywhere you want to go is all right with me.*
There's nowhere I'd rather go than Hawaii.

as how This is an awkward substitute for *that.* It should be avoided.

WRONG *Knowing as how you don't like to swim, let's just fish.*

RIGHT *Knowing that you don't like to swim, let's just fish.*

awful Despite what pedants may say, *awful* is no longer restricted to meaning "awesome" or "majestic." A common, accepted, now standard meaning of *awful* is "unpleasant"—*an awful party, an awful movie.* However, *awful* should not be used as an adverb except in very informal conversation; that is, it should not be used to mean *very* or *really.* The correct form for such use would be *awfully.*

WRONG *Mrs. Glenn is an awful good worker.*
Yet Mrs. Glenn is awful poor.

RIGHT *Mrs. Glenn is an awfully* (or *very*) *good worker.*
Yet Mrs. Glenn is awfully (or *very*) *poor.*

being as, being that These two word combinations should not be used as substitutes for *because, since,* or *as.*

WRONG *Being as she's going, so will I.*
Being that it rained, we did not go.

RIGHT *Since she's going, so will I.*
Because it rained, we did not go.

could of, should of, would of These are corruptions of abbreviated forms of *could have* (*could've*), *should have* and *would have*. Using *of* for *have* is one of the commonest of errors.

WRONG *That was a job he should of taken.*
Cora would of phoned if she had known the number.

RIGHT *That was a job he should have taken.*
Cora would have phoned if she had known the number.

didn't ought See *hadn't ought*.

disregardless, irregardless These two words don't exist in standard usage. They have the dubious distinction of being one-word double negatives. *Regardless* already means "heedless, having no regard for or consideration of"—so what else could *disregardless* or *irregardless* mean?

WRONG *Irregardless of the weather, I'm still going.*
RIGHT *Regardless of the weather, I'm still going.*

disremember This word does not exist in standard usage. Do not use it to mean *forget*.

WRONG *I disremember what Jerry said .*
RIGHT *I forget what Jerry said.*

enthuse This is a comparatively new verb, based on the standard noun *enthusiasm* and the standard adjective *enthusiastic*. It is used informally to mean "to be enthusiastic." But many good writers dislike the word, whether or not they consider it nonstandard.

DUBIOUS *He enthused about the project.*
STANDARD *He was enthusiastic about the project.*

equally as good This is an awkward blend of *equal to* and *as good as*. One or the other is better than a sloppy mixture of both.

WRONG *A picture is equally as good as a thousand words.*
RIGHT *A picture is equal to* (or *as good as*) *a thousand words.*

everyplace See *anyplace*.

everywheres See *anywheres*.

graduate A school *graduates* a student, but a student must *graduate from* a school.

WRONG *Frances graduated high school last month.*
RIGHT *Frances graduated* (or *was graduated*) *from high school last month.*

hadn't ought, didn't ought, had ought These are substandard; *ought not* or *ought* alone will say the same thing.

> WRONG *You hadn't ought to do that.*
> *You didn't ought to say that.*
> *He had ought to take the job.*
>
> RIGHT *You ought not to do that.*
> *You ought not to have said that.*
> *He ought to have taken the job.*

half a, a half, a half a A *half* is formal; *half a* is less formal but thoroughly acceptable. A *half a* contains an unnecessary *a.*

> WRONG *He bought a half a watermelon.*
> RIGHT *He bought half a watermelon.*
> *He bought a half watermelon.*

individual See *party.*

in back of This wordy phrase meaning "behind" may not be bad usage, but competent writers consider it awkward.

> AWKWARD *In back of the fence was an apple tree.*
> BETTER *Behind the fence was an apple tree.*

irregardless See *disregardless.*

is when, is where These expressions may be used correctly to indicate time or place, but they should never be used to define a word or idea.

> WRONG *Monotheism is when there is only one God.*
> *Monotheism is where there is only one God.*
>
> RIGHT *Monotheism is the belief that there is only one God.*
> *The time to be silent is when you have nothing to say.*
> *This is where I work.*

kind of, sort of; kind of a, sort of a The expressions *kind of* and *sort of* to mean *rather* or *somewhat* are entirely acceptable. But most people consider *kind of a* and *sort of a* as bad usage.

> INFORMAL *She looked kind of tired.*
> *I was sort of disappointed.*
>
> FORMAL *She looked rather tired.*
> *I was somewhat disappointed.*
>
> WRONG *What kind of a camera is that?*
> *What sort of a man was Woodrow Wilson?*
>
> RIGHT *What kind of camera is that?*
> *What sort of man was Woodrow Wilson?*

like to have, liked to These are definitely substandard substitutes for *almost* or *nearly.*

> WRONG *I like to have died in the accident.*
> *He liked to bought that house.*
> RIGHT *I nearly died in the accident.*
> *He almost bought that house.*

most *Most* means "more than half." It may not be used as a substitute for *almost.*

> WRONG *Most everyone came to the party.*
> RIGHT *Almost everyone came to the party.*

noplace See *anyplace.*

no sooner . . . when This combination is nonstandard; do not use it. The correct expression is *no sooner . . . than.*

> WRONG *He had no sooner sat down when the phone began to ring.*
> RIGHT *He had no sooner sat down than the phone began to ring.*

nowheres See *anywheres.*

off of This phrase is considered careless usage by precise speakers and writers. *Off* is all that is needed; the *of* is unnecessary.

> DUBIOUS *Get off of that bicycle.*
> *He jumped off of the dock and swam to the boat.*
> RIGHT *Get off that bicycle.*
> *He jumped off the dock and swam to the boat.*

NOTE: *Off* and *off of* do not mean "from." If you mean "from," use it.

> WRONG *I got this sweater off of my father.*
> *The thief stole $10 off Mr. Clark.*
> RIGHT *I got this sweater from my father.*
> *The thief stole $10 from Mr. Clark.*

party, individual, person A *party* means "a group of persons" (*The Coast Guard sent out a search party. We reserved a table for a party of four*). *Party* means "one person" only in the legal sense of "a person involved in a transaction" (*the party of the first part*) or in the unique telephone-operator use "Your party does not answer." In informal usage *party* may mean "one person," "a stranger," "a human being." Individual means "one person as distinguished from a group" (*This job doesn't need a committee; it needs one hard-working individual. He doesn't follow the crowd; he's a true individual*). Few speakers use *individual* to mean "a human being." *Person*, however, does mean "a human being" (*A person who likes history will like this book*).

INFORMAL   *Then this strange party asked me for a match.*
Who is the party who opened the door for us?
A certain party asked me for a date last night!
Any individual who likes football should watch tonight's game.

RIGHT   *Then the stranger asked me for a match.*
Who is the person who opened the door for us?
A certain person asked me for a date last night!
Anybody who likes football should watch tonight's game.
Another party has reserved this row of seats.
The party of the first part must sign the contract.
One individual can change the history of a nation.
I don't like him as a teacher, but he's a nice person.
There wasn't another person in the entire park.

real This word is an adjective. In informal speech it may be used as an adverb meaning "really" or "very," although most people dislike this usage.

INFORMAL   *Yesterday was a real nice day.*
RIGHT   *Yesterday was a really nice day.*

the reason is because Precise speakers and writers object strongly to this expression though some linguists defend it. *Because* means "for this reason." Thus, when you say "the reason is because," you're actually saying "the reason is for this reason," which is redundant. Standard usage calls for *the reason is that.*

DUBIOUS   *The reason we're late is because the car wouldn't start.*
RIGHT   *The reason we're late is that the car wouldn't start.*

should of See *could of.*

someplace See *anyplace.*

someways See *anyways.*

somewheres See *anywheres.*

sort of, sort of a See *kind of.*

sure This is an adjective that is informally used as an adverb instead of *surely*. Many people still object to this usage.
    WRONG   *That sure is a good product.*
    RIGHT   *That surely is a good product.*
                There's no sure way to make a profit in business.

these here, those there; this here, that there These four expressions are considered nonstandard. *These, those, this,* and *that* are adequate alone; *here* and *there* are neither needed nor wanted.
    WRONG   *These here pies are good compared with those there.*
                This here pie is tastier than that there one.
    RIGHT   *These pies are good compared with those.*
                This pie is tastier than that one.

tho See *altho*.

thusly This does not exist in standard speech. The word is *thus* and only *thus*. *Thus* is an adverb and does not need the added adverbial ending *-ly*.
    WRONG   *The pump is primed thusly.*
    RIGHT   *The pump is primed thus* (or, better, *this way*).

ways The only standard use of this word is as a plural of *way*, meaning "method, plan, or manner." Do not use it as a substitute for *way* or to mean "distance."
    WRONG   *It's a long ways from here to Tulsa.*
    RIGHT   *It's a long way from here to Tulsa.*

where . . . at Don't use *at* after *where*. *Where* means "at a place" and is complete by itself. The *where . . . at* combination is redundant.
    WRONG   *Where are you staying at?*
    RIGHT   *Where are you staying?*

would of See *could of*.

Usage Test—Avoiding Poor Usage

In the sentences below, choose the words or phrases in parentheses that are standard or preferred usage. Answers follow.

1. A certain (party, person) whom I won't mention says she likes you.
2. She (ought not, hadn't ought) to go.
3. (Being as, Because, Being that) it's late, I cannot go.

4. I'm not going (anywhere, anywheres).

5. (Regardless, Irregardless, Disregardless) of the price, I'll buy it.

6. Is everything (alright, all right)?

7. He worked only (a half, half a, a half a) day.

8. You should (of, have) voted for me.

9. Knowing (as how, that) you like cake, I've baked one for you.

10. When did your brother (graduate from, graduate) college?

11. I left the mower (in back of, behind) the garage.

12. He is (most, almost) always in a good mood.

13. He made an (awful, awfully) bad mistake.

14. Can you get the lid (off, off of) this jar?

15. Is she (enthused, enthusiastic) about the party?

16. Yes, I'm angry, and the reason (why is, is because, is that) you are late.

17. I (sure, surely) appreciate all you've done for us.

18. She prefers (this, this here) chair.

19. Put the blueprint (alongside, alongside of) the scale model.

20. (Most, Almost) anyone could have done better.

ANSWERS:

1. person. 2. ought not. 3. Because. 4. anywhere. 5. Regardless. 6. all right.
7. a half *or* half a. 8. have. 9. that. 10. graduate from. 11. behind. 12. almost.
13. awfully. 14. off. 15. enthusiastic. 16. is that. 17. surely. 18. this. 19.
alongside. 20. Almost.

2 PAIRS THAT SNARE

Some words sound and look nearly alike, but have different meanings.
Words that look or sound alike are often called *homonyms,* and we are
so used to such pairs that most of them do not trouble us. Thus, few
people confuse *ate* and *eight; know* and *no; pore* and *pour; wait* and
weight; or *bark* (of a dog) and *bark* (of a tree). Where problems of
usage do occur is with pairs or groups of words that are both similar
enough and different enough to be confused with one another.

Someone has described such usage problems as "pairs that snare"
—and we are using that phrase for the title of this chapter. The word
pairs or groups listed in alphabetical order are truly traps for the un-

wary. A good speaker or writer must distinguish between these sound-alike, look-alike words. Learn exactly what each word means in the following list and how to spell and use it exactly:

accede (1) to consent or agree; (2) to come into office.
I will accede to your plan.
The prince acceded to the throne.
exceed to surpass; to go beyond the limit of.
For safety's sake, don't exceed the speed limit.
This year's profits exceeded last year's.

accept to take something offered.
I accept your invitation.
Did you accept his resignation?
except to exclude or leave out; with the exception of.
When I say I like fruit, I except plums.
No one is going except Kenneth.

access a way of getting to something or someone.
Few people have access to the R.C.M.P.'s files.
excess surplus; overabundance.
This year there is an excess of eggs on the market.
The bill was in excess of $400.

adapt to adjust; to fit or make fit.
Eskimos learn how to adapt to the cold.
adopt to take as one's own.
We are going to adopt a child.
The club adopted a new set of rules.
REMEMBER: You go to an *adopt*ion agency to *adopt* a child, and he will learn to *adapt* to your way of life.

advice rhymes with *ice* and has a hissing *s* sound [ad·vīs′]. It is a noun and means "counsel, suggestion, or information."
People who give unsolicited advice are very tiresome.
Consider Mary's advice carefully before you take it.
advise rhymes with *eyes* and has a buzzing *z* sound [ad·vīz′]. It is a verb and means "to give advice to; counsel."
I advise you to try to stay in school.
REMEMBER: One seeks adv*ice* about pr*ice*. The w*ise* have a right to adv*ise*.

affect to influence.
> *Government decisions affect the future of us all.*
> *Your insults don't affect me in the slightest.*

effect (1) to bring about a result; to produce or accomplish something;
(2) a result or consequence.
> *The doctor will try to effect a cure.*
> *His medicine had a good effect on me.*
> *Saunders effected a total reorganization of the sales department.*

REMEMBER: To *affect* is merely to influence, but to *effect* is to produce a result.

aisle a passageway.
> *The bride and groom walked up the aisle.*

isle an island.
> *They vacationed on the Isle of Wight.*

all ready means that *all* or everything is *ready* or prepared.
> *The house is all ready for us to move in.*
> *I'm all ready for bed.*

already means "previously, earlier; by this time."
> *We had already left when the accident happened.*
> *It's already 10 o'clock.*

all together means that *all* or everything is *together,* in the same place
or at the same time.
> *The guests arrived all together.*

altogether means "completely; absolutely."
> *You are altogether wrong.*

allusion a reference or mention.
> *The preacher made an allusion to Homer.*

illusion a false impression; something that seems to be something else
or that actually does not exist.
> *The white walls create the illusion that the room is very large.*

altar a platform or raised area, as in a church.
> *The bride and groom stood before the altar.*

alter to change.
> *The tailor altered Debbie's dress.*
> *If it rains, we must alter our plans.*

481

anecdote a short narrative.
He told an anecdote about his childhood.
antidote something that counteracts a poison, disease, or bad mood.
What's the antidote for arsenic?
Laughter is the best antidote to disappointment.
REMEMBER: *Anti-* means "against." An *antidote* acts *against* a poison, disease, etc.

angel a heavenly being; an extremely beautiful or sweet person.
Hark! The herald angels sing.
Thanks; you're an angel.
angle (1) a geometric figure formed by two straight lines meeting; (2) a projecting corner; (3) a point of view.
a 90-degree angle
The dog disappeared around an angle of the house.
The problem must be studied from all angles.

assure to guarantee; state with confidence.
I assure you that his intentions are good.
ensure to make certain.
These measures will ensure the success of our program.
insure to guard against loss or harm.
When you mail this package, please insure it.

baited containing or holding bait, as a trap or a fishhook.
My poor dog fell into a baited trap.
bated held in.
He waited with bated breath.

beside at the side of, next to.
Walk beside me.
He lives in a house beside an enormous tree.
besides in addition to; moreover.
It was snowing; besides, it was below zero.

blond (1) a fair-haired person of either sex; (2) a golden color.
The brother and sister are both blonds.
Is the table made of blond wood?
blonde a blond woman or girl.
Many gentlemen prefer blondes.
REMEMBER: A *blonde* is a girl, like Ella, Eva, and Elinore.

482

brake (1) a device that stops or slows down; (2) to reduce the speed of.
> *The car needs new brakes.*
> *The boy braked his bicycle to a stop.*

break (1) to smash; (2) an opening.
> *Don't break the window.*
> *There is a break in the clouds.*

breath air from or in the lungs.
> *The air is so cold you can see your breath.*
> *Asthmatics are often short of breath.*

breathe to inhale and exhale.
> *Now that the danger is over, I can breathe easily.*

breadth width; the opposite of length.
> *What are the length and breadth of your property?*

bridal of or pertaining to a bride.
> *Her bridal gown was trimmed with lace.*

bridle (1) headgear attached to the reins to control a horse; (2) of or pertaining to horseback riding; (3) to draw in the chin through anger, pride, etc.
> *Put on the bridle and saddle.*
> *We galloped along the bridle path.*
> *Our probing questions made him bridle.*

brunet a dark-haired man, or the color of his hair.
> *My brother is a brunet.*

brunette a dark-haired girl or woman, or the color of her hair.
> *My sister is a brunette.*

REMEMBER: A brunette is a girl, like Ella, Eva, or Elinore.

canon a rule or law, especially of religious faith; sacred books.
> *This canon has been enacted by the church council.*

cannon a large gun, often mounted on wheels.
> *An old cannon stood at the entrance to the fort.*

canvas a sturdy cloth.
> *The tent is made of canvas.*

canvass to solicit votes, sales, opinions, etc., especially by going from house to house.
> *We canvassed the neighborhood selling magazines.*

QUICKIE QUIZ
PAIRS THAT SNARE

In the sentences below, choose the words in parentheses that are correct or preferred usage. Answers follow.

1. What's that (blond, blonde) hair doing on your coat?
2. His warning to drive carefully had no (affect, effect) at all.
3. I hoped the prescribed (anecdote, antidote) would (affect, effect) a cure.
4. Can we (adapt, adopt) this filing system to fit our files?
5. Now then, (all together, altogether), let's sing.
6. If I had the (capital, capitol), I'd go into business for myself.
7. There are no tickets available for two on the (aisle, isle).
8. We hope to (accede, exceed) last year's sales.
9. The Senate's duty is to (advice, advise) and consent.
10. Do you have (access, excess) to a good library?
11. It's (all ready, already) time to leave.
12. He has (allusions, illusions) of becoming famous.
13. I would (accept, except) the job (accept, except) for the late hours.
14. What is your (advice, advise)?
15. It's (all together, altogether) impossible!
16. The painting shows an (angel, angle) (beside, besides) the right hand of God.
17. Paris is the (capital, capitol) of France, and also its foremost—or (capital, capitol)—city.
18. According to the old joke, the cat put a piece of cheese in his mouth and waited by the mouse hole with (baited, bated) (breathe, breath).
19. Don't (accept, except) the package. Send it back.
20. The left rear tire blew out, and he (braked, breaked) the car to a stop.

ANSWERS:

1. blond (also acceptable: blonde). 2. effect. 3. antidote; effect. 4. adapt. 5. all together. 6. capital. 7. aisle. 8. exceed. 9. advise. 10. access. 11. already. 12. illusions. 13. accept; except. 14. advice. 15. altogether. 16. angel; beside. 17. capital; capital. 18. baited; breath. (*Baited* here is, of course, a pun on *bated*.) 19. accept. 20. braked.

capital (1) major or most important; (2) the city that is the seat of a central government; (3) money for investment; (4) a large letter, such as *A, B, C,* etc.

The Wright brothers began by having a capital idea.

Winnipeg is the capital of Manitoba.

My capital brings in only a small income.

capitol the main building of a government.

In Washington, the Smiths visited the Lincoln Memorial and the Capitol.

REMEMBER: A capitol building often has a dome. All other capitals are spelled with an *a.*

cede to grant; give up something.

Germany ceded territory to Poland in 1945.

seed that from which something is grown.

We planted watermelon seeds.

censer a vessel for burning incense, as in religious ceremonies.

The priest swung the censer.

censor (a) a person who examines books, plays, letters, etc., to prohibit what seems objectionable; (2) to prohibit, suppress, or remove allegedly objectionable material.

The censor cut a scene from the movie.

Every dictator censors the newspapers in his country.

The military censor examined mail from the war zone.

censure to reprimand, blame, or denounce.

The principal censured the students for their rude behavior.

REMEMBER: A censor decides what to leave in *or* take out.

chafe to irritate or make sore by rubbing.

The tight collar chafed my neck.

chaff (1) to tease or make fun of; (2) the husks of grain.

It is impolite to chaff a stranger.

Separate the wheat from the chaff.

chord (1) a combination of three or more musical tones; (2) a string or strings of a guitar, violin, etc.; (3) an emotional response; (4) in geometry, a straight line intersecting a curve or arc.

The opening chords of the symphony were very loud.

The chords of the guitar are made of nylon.

His sad words struck a responsive chord in her, and she began to cry.

Chord AB connects the ends of the arc AB of circle C.

cord (1) a string, rope, etc., used to tie something; (2) an insulated electric wire with a plug at one end; (3) a cubic measure for firewood; (4) a rib, as in fabric (a short form of the word *corduroy*); (5) a cordlike part of the body.

Tie the box with this cord.

The toaster needs a new electric cord.

We bought two cords of firewood.

Wear your cord jacket.

Shouting strains the vocal cords.

cite to quote or refer to.

I would like to cite Genesis 2:2.

sight (1) something seen; (2) vision; (3) an aiming device; (4) to see.

Lake Louise is one of the sights of Alberta.

He lost the sight in one eye.

The sight of that gun needs adjusting.

We sighted land on Tuesday, May 7, at 3 P.M.

site a place where something is located.

The tool company has found a new plant site.

The site of Lake Louise is Alberta.

clench to close tightly.

The angry boy clenched his fists.

The pain caused me to clench my teeth.

clinch (1) to secure firmly by bending down a protruding point, as of a nail or staple; (2) to make sure of; (3) the act of grasping.

Sam clinched the nails of the bookcase he was building.

He tried hard to clinch the sale.

The fighters went into a clinch.

coarse (1) composed of large particles; (2) vulgar.

Use coarse-grained sugar, not confectioner's sugar.

He made a coarse remark.

course (1) direction; (2) passage or duration of time; (3) progress; (4) a series of actions or events making up a unit.; (5) ground passed over; (6) a series of classes, or a curriculum of studies; (7) a portion of a meal; (8) a line of conduct.

Our course was due north.

In the course of a week he completed the job.

The disease must run its course.

My uncle is taking a course of treatments for arthritis.

John liked walking on the golf course.

He took a chemistry course in high school.

The main course was veal and potatoes.

You are following a wise course.

complement (1) to complete or perfect; (2) that which completes; (3) a complete number or amount.

A red scarf complemented her outfit.

A good dessert is always a complement to a fine meal.

The ship had a full complement of crewmen.

complementary (1) serving to complete; (2) referring to one of two colors that when mixed produce a third color.

Husbands and wives often make complementary remarks: One finishes what the other begins to say.

Blue and yellow are complementary colors.

compliment (1) an expression of praise or admiration; (2) to express praise or admiration.

Larry heaped compliments on Meg's cooking.

I would like to compliment you on your cooking.

complimentary (1) conveying or using praise; (2) given free.

To tell a woman she looks tired is hardly a complimentary remark.

The new shop handed out complimentary packs of chewing gum.

consul a foreign-based government official below the rank of ambassador.

Is there a Swedish consul in Omaha?

council (1) a group of people organized to deliberate or rule; (2) a meeting.

The city council meets on October 1.

The Council of Trent was held in Italy in the sixteenth century.

counsel (1) to advise; (2) advice; (3) a lawyer or adviser.

Will you listen to my counsel?

His guardian counseled him well.

Is the plaintiff's counsel in court?

487

core the center, especially of fruit.
    Jane threw an apple core into the wastebasket.
corps an organized unit of people.
    He joined the drum and bugle corps.

currant a small black or red berry.
    Try spreading currant jelly on your currant bun.
current (1) a continuous onward flowing, as of water or electricity; (2) belonging to the present.
    Tides and currents affect ships.
    Phil's electric razor works only on alternating current.
    Current events sometimes scare me.

dairy (1) a farm or barn where milk cows are kept; (2) a place where milk and milk products are prepared and sold.
    The Hopkinses run a dairy farm.
    We bought milk and ice cream at the local dairy.
diary a daily record or journal.
    I keep a diary of daily happenings.

decent suitable; respectable.
    Please wear a decent suit to the party.
    She was a decent woman of modest means.
descent the act of coming down.
    Our descent from the mountain was painfully slow.
dissent (1) to differ; disagree; (2) difference of opinion; disagreement.
    Three justices dissented from the Supreme Court's decision.
    Justice Holmes filed many notable dissents in the Supreme Court.

desert (1) an arid region [dez′ərt]; (2) to abandon or forsake [di·zûrt′].
    Lawrence rode a camel across the desert.
    He intended to desert his wife and children.
dessert [di·zûrt′] a sweet course at the end of a meal.
    Strawberry pie is my favorite dessert.

device [di·vīs′] a contrivance, as a tool or aid.
    He invented a device for cracking ice.
devise [di·vīz′] to invent or construct.
    He devised a new way to make bread rise.

ish.

(2) the coloring matter used.

een two people, usually with
veen two people.

y to move to another.
t at Naples.

immigrant a person who enters one country from another.
The immigrants to Canada got off the boat in Montreal.

eminent well-known; distinguished; highly respected.
Watson is an eminent biologist.
imminent about to happen; impending.
He predicted that an earthquake was imminent.

envelop [in·vel′əp] to wrap or enclose.
Fog often envelops the local airport.
envelope [en′və·lōp] a paper wrapper, as for a letter.
He addressed the envelope.

exceed—accede See *accede—exceed.*

except—accept See *accept—except.*

excess—access See *access—excess.*

faint (1) timid, feeble; (2) to lose consciousness briefly.
Alice felt faint with hunger.
Victorian ladies often fainted at the sight of a mouse.
feint a mock attack or blow; to make a mock attack in order to divert
attention from a real one.
He feinted with his left and hit me with his right.

489

farther This word may be used interchangeably with *further*, but precise writers prefer to restrict its use to mean "at a greater distance."
I can see farther than you can.

further This word may be used interchangeably with *farther*, but precise writers prefer to restrict its use to mean "more."
I have nothing further to report.

fiancé a man who is engaged to be married.
He is Helen's fiancé.

fiancée a woman who is engaged to be married.
Helen is his fiancée.

flaunt to make a gaudy display; to show off something.
Some hostesses like to flaunt their wealth.

flout to defy.
He flouts all the rules, but he'll get caught someday.

formally in a formal way.
Have you two been formally introduced?

formerly some time ago; previously.
West Virginia was formerly part of Virginia.

foul (1) disgusting; evil; (2) out-of-bounds; (3) something that is out-of-bounds or against the rules.
A foul smell arose from the swamp.
"Foul ball!" shouted the umpire.
The boxer was disqualified for committing a foul.

fowl a chicken, duck, turkey, or pheasant.
Jack has never eaten any kind of fowl.

idle not active.
The plant was idle during the strike.

idol an object or image of a god; a person who is greatly admired.
Pagan peoples often set up idols to worship.
Bobby Orr is every boy's idol.

idyl *or* **idyll** [īd'l] (1) a poem or prose work that concentrates on simple, pastoral scenes; (2) any very attractive, simple scene or event.
Tennyson's Idylls of the King *is a very long poem.*
Our summer in Nantucket was an idyl.

illusion—allusion See *allusion—illusion.*

QUICKIE QUIZ
REVIEW OF PAIRS THAT SNARE

In the sentences below, choose the words in parentheses that are correct usage. Answers follow.

1. It's hard to swim against the (currant, current).
2. One of my favorite songs is "The Lost (Chord, Cord)."
3. I hope we can (clench, clinch) the contract tonight.
4. He (deserted, desserted) from the army and hid out in the (desert, dessert).
5. She painted the room in (complementary, complimentary) colors.
6. To illustrate my point, I will (cite, sight, site) a line from Shakespeare.
7. The murder suspect refused to answer the questions on the advice of (consul, council, counsel).
8. This is a (dual-purpose, duel-purpose) tool, a combined screwdriver and wrench.
9. I want to (complement, compliment) you on your fine work.
10. Do you believe (censership, censorship, censureship) endangers freedom of speech?

ANSWERS:

1. current. 2. Chord. 3. clinch. 4. deserted; desert. 5. complementary. 6. cite. 7. counsel. 8. dual-purpose. 9. compliment. 10. censorship.

immigrant—emigrant See *emigrant—immigrant.*

imminent—eminent See *eminent—imminent.*

ingenious clever; imaginative.
> *Ingenious minds dream up ingenious plans.*

ingenuous naive; frank and open.
> *Gloria has an ingenuous way of believing everything she hears.*

isle—aisle See *aisle—isle.*

its the possessive form of *it.*
> *Give the dog its food.*

it's the contraction of "it is."
> *It's time to go.*

491

later [lā′tər] more late; after some time.
It's later than you think.
My father got home later than I did.
latter [lat′ər] the second of two.
I like both apples and pears but prefer the latter.
ladder [lad′ər] parallel steps for climbing.
Come down off that ladder!

lead (1) a metal (rhymes with *head*); (2) to be first or to conduct (rhymes with *need*).
He picked up a section of lead pipe.
Who's leading in the race?
Oliver wants to lead an orchestra when he grows up.
led This word also rhymes with *head*. It is the past tense of the verb *lead* (to be first or to conduct).
At first, he led in the race, but somebody passed him.
NOTE: The verb *lead* [lēd] becomes *led* [led] in the past tense. We lead to the *east*; we led to the *west*.

loose This word has a hissing *s* sound. It means "not tight; untied or free."
This shirt collar is too loose.
Let the dog loose.
lose This word rhymes with *ooze*; it has a buzzing *z* sound. It means (1) to misplace; to suffer the loss of; (2) to be beaten.
Did you lose your wrist watch in addition to losing the race yesterday?

material anything of which something can be made; fabric.
Building materials are expensive.
The dress was made of synthetic material.
materiel [mə·tir′ē·el′] supplies, especially military supplies.
The general needs more troops and materiel.

miner a person who works in a mine.
Lewis began as a coal miner.
minor (1) a person who is under age; (2) of little importance.
You're a minor until you're 18.
Even minor inconveniences infuriate Jane.

moral (1) adhering to the laws of God and man; (2) a point or lesson.
My father was a moral and just person.
The moral of the story is "Beware of flattery."
morale [mə·ral'] a state of mind in terms of confidence and courage.
The morale of our troops is high.

naval referring to a navy or ships.
Naval battles helped win World War II.
navel the sunken indentation in the abdomen, or any similar indentation.
I think a swimming suit should cover the navel.
She ate a navel orange for lunch.

passed This is the past tense of the verb *pass.* Hence, *pass + ed.* It means (1) to have gone by, got by, or moved through; (2) to have handed something to someone.
Beth passed the exam easily.
We passed the gate without seeing it.
Davie passed the salt to his aunt.
past having already happened; time gone by.
This past week was very warm.
The past is over, so don't worry about it.

peace freedom from war or disturbance.
Let us pray for peace in our time.
piece a part or portion.
I'll have a piece of pie.

pedal a foot-operated lever.
A pedal of the bicycle fell off.
peddle to sell at retail; to hawk.
Where do you plan to peddle these items?

personal of, for, or belonging to a particular person.
A man's letters are his personal property.
personnel [pûr'sə·nel'] (1) the people employed on a job; (2) of or having to do with workers.
The Coast Guard takes good care of its personnel.
Apply for a job in the company's personnel office.

precede (1) to go in advance of; (2) to come first.
The usher preceded us down the aisle.
A precedes B in the alphabet.
proceed to go on or go forward.
If there are no further questions, I will proceed with the lecture.

prescribe to recommend or set down a rule to be followed.
The doctor prescribed absolute rest for the patient.
proscribe to ban something, as by decree.
Cannibalism is proscribed in most societies.

principal (1) major; (2) a person who takes a leading part; (3) capital as opposed to interest.
Carelessness is a principal cause of highway accidents.
The principal of the school attended our concert.
The principal was $1,000 and the interest 5% a year.
principle a general rule or truth, as in ethics or morality.
It's not the money but the principle of the thing that matters.

quiet calm; still; silent.
This quiet, moonlit night fits my mood.
quit to stop doing something.
You can't fire me. I quit!
quite (1) entirely; (2) really; (3) noticeably.
That is, I assure you, quite true.
Mary felt quite ill during dinner.

rain liquid precipitation.
The forecast is for rain today.
rein a device used to guide a horse.
Adjust the saddle and reins.
reign (1) to rule, as a sovereign; (2) the rule of a sovereign.
Cromwell reigned over England like a king.
It happened in the reign of Queen Wilhelmina.

raise (1) to lift something; (2) to grow or breed something.
Raise your right hand.
He raises chickens.
raze to demolish.
The wreckers began to raze the building.

rise (1) to get up; (2) to grow higher.

I often rise when the sun rises.

When the snows melt, the river will rise in its banks.

NOTE: *Raise* is a transitive verb, which means that it must have an object: *Raise the table. Rise* is an intransitive verb, which means that it cannot take an object: *I rise at six.* Note this difference: *Melinda raised her hand; Melinda has risen from her chair.*

respectably in a worthy or proper manner.

The man seemed poor, but he was respectably dressed.

respectfully in a respectful or polite way.

Children should speak respectfully to their elders.

respectively in a specified order.

"Auf Wiedersehen," "au revoir," and "good-by" are, respectively, German, French, and English farewells.

stationary in a fixed position; standing still.

The population of France remained stationary for a century.

stationery writing paper and related materials.

Herbert bought a notebook at the stationery store.

straight not curved or crooked.

A straight line is the shortest distance between two points.

strait (1) a narrow passage of water connecting two larger bodies of water; (2) (plural) a restricted or distressing situation.

We passed through the Strait of Magellan.

That family next door is in dire financial straits.

suit [soot] (1) A coat with matching trousers or skirt; (2) a series of playing cards; (3) a proceeding in a law court; (4) the courting of a woman.

Grandfather still wears a blue suit every Sunday.

If hearts are trumps, why didn't you lead another suit?

Robert's lawyer argued his suit eloquently.

After the briefest of suits, Juliet said yes to Romeo.

suite [swēt] a set of rooms, of matching furniture, or related musical compositions, etc.

They reserved the bridal suite at the Ritz.

My cousin has a new living-room suite.

Everybody loves Tchaikovsky's "Nutcracker Suite."

than when compared with; except; but.
> *I am taller than you.*
> *I refer to none other than our president, Hugh Smith!*

then at that time; in that case; for that reason; also.
> *Life was easy in 1875; there were no cars then.*
> *If you won't go, then I will, and then you'll be sorry.*

their, theirs the possessive forms of *they.*
> *It is their house.*
> *The house is theirs.*

there at that place.
> *Put the box over there.*

there's the contraction of *there is.*
> *There's no reason to worry.*

they're the contraction of *they are.*
> *They're ready to start.*

REMEMBER: *There* is the opposite of *here,* and the two words are spelled almost alike. The apostrophe in *they're* stands for the missing *a* in *they are. Their* and *theirs* are possessive forms of the pronoun *they,* and possessive pronouns never include apostrophes. (See, for a similar snaring pair, *its* and *it's.*)

thorough complete.
> *Mrs. Curtis gave the room a thorough cleaning.*

threw the past tense of *to throw.*
> *Mrs. Grover threw another blanket on her sleeping child.*

through from one side or one end to the other.
> *Let's walk all the way through the woods.*

to toward; in the direction of.
> *He drove from Chicago to Indianapolis.*

too (1) also; (2) more than enough.
> *I, too, can solve hard problems.*
> *This candy is too sweet.*

two the number after one; two is 2.
> *Two and two are four.*

REMEMBER: *I, too, took the two twins to Tom's.* In this sentence, *too, two,* and *to* are used properly and are immediately followed by the identical letters that spell them correctly.

vain (1) conceited; (2) useless.
   That model is an unusually vain girl.
   Several vain attempts to find a job discouraged Charlie.

vane a direction pointer.
   The weekend farmers bought a new weather vane for the barn.

vein a blood vessel.
   The lumberman cut a vein, not an artery.

waist the narrow part of the body above the hips, or the corresponding part of a garment.
   Sarah has a 24-inch waist.

waste (1) needless consumption or destruction; (2) refuse.
   I think golf is a waste of time.
   The waste from the factory polluted the river.

weather day-to-day climate.
   What's the weather forecast for today?

whether if it be the case that; in case.
   I shall go whether or not you do.

whose the possessive of the pronoun *who.*
   Whose book is this?

who's the contraction of *who is.*
   Who's going to go with me?
REMEMBER: The apostrophe in *who's* stands for the missing *i* in *who is.* There is no apostrophe in *whose* because possessive pronouns never have apostrophes.

your the possessive of the pronoun *you.*
   Is this your book?

you're the contraction of *you are.*
   You're late for work.

Tests given to 15,000 college freshmen from more than 300 colleges show that one in every six still misuses *their–there–they're;* one in eight still has trouble with *to–too–two;* one in twenty still confuses *its–it's* and *than–then;* one in forty still confuses *principal–principle;* and one in fifty still confuses *accept–except, affect–effect,* and *quiet–quit–quite.* How do you compare with these college students? Review your personal usage demons over and over until they are no longer troublesome. You will enjoy the extra word power that this will give you.

QUICKIE QUIZ
MORE PAIRS THAT SNARE

In the sentences below, choose the words in parentheses that are correct usage. Answers follow.

1. What you don't eat goes to (waist, waste), but what you do eat goes to your (waist, waste)!
2. This country was founded on the (principal, principle) of individual freedom for all.
3. The secretary (proceeded, preceded) to take the minutes of the meeting.
4. How did your fiancé (propose, purpose) to you?
5. (You're, Your) late for (you're, your) appointment.
6. Have you read Tolstoy's novel *War and* (*Peace, Piece*)?
7. We sailed through the (Straight, Strait) of Gibraltar.
8. The sun will (rise, raise) at 5:45 tomorrow morning.
9. Please don't make (personal, personnel) phone calls during office hours.
10. (Who's, Whose) going to pay for all this?
11. He gave her a box of (stationary, stationery) for Christmas.
12. Give those (to, too, two) books (to, too, two) me (to, too, two).
13. It's already half (passed, past) eight.
14. We won even though the first three runs were (their's, theirs).
15. Name the three (principal, principle) cities in Canada.
16. I was hired by the (personal, personnel) manager.
17. We ate dinner and (than, then) saw a movie.
18. We will have the picnic (whether, weather) the (whether, weather) is good or bad.
19. Please be (quiet, quit, quite).
20. Put (their, there, they're) books over (their, there, they're).

ANSWERS:

1. waste; waist. 2. principle. 3. proceeded. 4. propose. 5. You're; your. 6. *Peace*. 7. Strait. 8. rise. 9. personal. 10. Who's. 11. stationery. 12. two; to; too. 13. past. 14. theirs. 15. principal. 16. personnel. 17. then. 18. whether; weather. 19. quiet. 20. their; there.

3 CONFUSED WORDS

Here begins an alphabetical list of "confused words." These are different from Pairs that Snare. Confused Words are usage problems because their meanings are related in some way. Thus, *allude* and *refer,* *flotsam* and *jetsam,* and *imply* and *infer* do not sound or look alike; yet many people confuse them because their meanings or uses are related.

To speak and write well you must keep these words straight in your mind. Many of these pairs are among the most interesting in our language. Once you are truly at home with them, you can have fun helping to settle the debates of those of your friends who are still unsure about the distinctions between these words.

WARNING: Not all definitions are given for every word in the following list. Many have several different meanings; we deal here only with meanings that might be confusing.

a use *a* before words beginning with a consonant sound (all sounds except *a, e, i, o, u*).
> *He drew up a chair and sat down.*
> *I ate a peach.*
> *He is not a union member.* (Even though *union* begins with a *u*, the sound is that of the consonant *y*.)

an use *an* before words beginning with a vowel sound (*a, e, i, o, u*).
> *I ate an orange.*
> *A policeman stopped Ernest at the bridge.*
> *Miss Adams has an M.A. in history.* (Even though *m* is a consonant, the sound is that of a vowel, *em*.)

aggravate to make worse.
> *His discomfort was aggravated by a toothache.*

irritate to annoy or vex.
> *Kitty's constant nagging irritated her husband.* (As a result, their little misunderstanding was enormously *aggravated*.)

allude to mention indirectly or in passing.
> *He alluded to his past job but didn't go into the details.*

refer to mention directly or in detail.
> *He referred bitterly to his most recent clash with the foreman.*

alumnus a male graduate.

Eisenhower was an alumnus of West Point.

alumni [ə·lum′nī] graduates, whether male or both male and female.

The West Point alumni were from the class of 1970.

My son and my daughter are both alumni of Ohio State.

alumna a female graduate.

She is an alumna of Sir George Williams University.

alumnae [ə·lum′nē] the plural of *alumna*.

Both my daughters are alumnae of Cliffbriar Women's College.

REMEMBER: *-us* is very often an ending of masculine names and words, such as G*us*, Cassi*us*, and alumn*us*. *-a* is very often an ending of feminine names and words, such as Alm*a*, Ann*a*, and alumn*a*.

among (1) refers to three or more things having some sort of loose relationship to one another; (2) in the midst of; amid.

He found the textbook he wanted among (or amongst) the many others on the shelf.

Steven relaxes only when he's among his friends.

between refers to two related things, or to more than two when each is being compared to or related to each of the others.

Susan sat down between her brother and his friend.

There was a bond between the members that held our whole group together.

NOTE: The old distinction between *among* or *amongst* (for more than two) and *between* (for only two) has become increasingly blurred. *Between* is now considered generally acceptable except in cases where *among* really means "in the midst of; amid."

amoral See *immoral—amoral—unmoral—immortal*.

amount quantity in mass or bulk.

He spent a small amount of money.

Charlie ate a large amount of mashed potatoes.

number quantity in terms of separate items or units.

The tenants filed a number of complaints against the landlord.

George owns a small number of books.

There is a large number of baked potatoes in the oven.

NOTE: *Number* always tells how many, 1, 2, 3, or 4, etc. *Amount* tells how much. See also the usage discussion of *fewer–less* later on in this chapter.

anxious distressed with worry.

The mother was anxious about her missing child.

eager happily expectant.

The mother was eager to visit her married daughter.

NOTE: *Anxious* may also be used to mean *eager;* but this has not yet become entirely standard usage.

apt (1) inclined to as a matter of course; usually expected to; (2) quick to learn.

It's apt to be hot in summer.

Henry is an apt student of the practical sciences.

likely probable; expected but not as a matter of course.

The weather report says it's likely to be hot tomorrow.

liable (1) responsible for the consequences; (2) in danger of experiencing something disagreeable.

A husband is liable for his wife's debts.

If you play tennis at high noon, you're liable to get a heat stroke.

NOTE: Many precise writers still differentiate between these three words, but more and more people are using them interchangeably.

as introduces a group of words containing a verb (in other words, a *clause*).

Taffy tastes sweet, as candy should.

My son eats as I ate when I was his age—rapidly.

as if introduces (1) contrary-to-fact or untrue comparisons; (2) non-comparative conjectures.

My son eats as if he were starving. (This is contrary to fact; he isn't starving.)

Molly insists on singing as if she were Barbra Streisand. (This, too, is obviously contrary to fact.)

It looks as if we'll all be fired. (This makes no comparison; it is a conjecture.)

like introduces a group of words without a verb (in other words, a *phrase*).

My son eats like a horse. (But: *My horse eats hay, as a horse should.*)

He sings like an Irish tenor—with his heart in every note.

NOTE: Vast numbers of persons use *like* where standard usage prescribes *as* or *as if*. Careful writers and speakers avoid this misuse of *like,* however. They remember that *like* is a preposition and that prepositions introduce phrases, whereas conjunctions introduce clauses. If you wish to write and speak proper English, whether formal or informal, you will learn the above distinctions and respect them.

avocation—vocation *See vocation— avocation.*

bad—badly *See well—good—bad—badly.*

because of by reason of; on account of.
>   *Because of my errors, we lost the match.*

due to has the same meaning as *because of,* but is preferably used only when you can substitute *caused by.*
>   *My absence was due to (caused by) illness.*

REMEMBER: When in doubt whether to use *because of* or *due to,* say the sentence to yourself and see if it continues to make perfect sense when you substitute *caused by.* If *caused by* sounds all right, *due to* is all right. If *caused by* sounds awkward—as it would in the sentence that begins "Because of my errors"—*due to* is not good usage in that context.

can to be able to.
>   *Frank, who is only thirteen, can drive a car.*

may to have permission to.
>   *Because of his youth, Frank may not drive a car even though he knows how.*

NOTE: The distinction between *can* and *may* is rapidly disappearing. Except in very formal English, you may (and can) correctly use *can* for both meanings.

compare One compares *like* things, things that are of the same class or kind.
>   *How does your new car compare with the old one?*

contrast One contrasts *unlike* things, things that are of different kinds or classes.
>   *Contrast a horse and buggy with a modern car.*

connotation what a word suggests or implies.
>   *The word "snake" has unpleasant connotations for most people.*

denotation the specific meaning of a word.
>   *The denotation of "snake" is simply this: a legless reptile with a long, thin body.*

contemptible deserving of contempt.
> *Hitler was a contemptible person.*

contemptuous showing or feeling contempt.
> *Churchill was always contemptuous of Hitler.*

continual over and over again; regular but interrupted.
> *We had a continual series of hot spells last summer.*

continuous nonstop; constant and not interrupted.
> *Many plants and animals thrive in the continuous jungle heat.*

credible believable.
> *His story, though unusual, is credible.*

creditable praiseworthy; to one's credit.
> *Roger's grades in school are very creditable.*

credulous gullible; too much inclined to believe.
> *Only a credulous person would fall for that old trick.*

disinterested impartial; unbiased.
> *An umpire must be an entirely disinterested but keen observer.*

uninterested not interested; uncaring.
> *I am uninterested in any TV program that lacks comedy.*

egoist a self-centered, selfish person.
> *An egoist lives only for his own pleasure.*

egotist a person who boasts about himself.
> *Marian is such an egotist that she talks about herself all the time.*

NOTE: These two words may be used interchangeably. But precise writers appreciate the distinction in meaning between the talkative egotist and the I-centered egoist.

elder, eldest Careful writers once used these synonyms for *older* and *oldest* in comparing ages, as of brothers and sisters. However, most people now use *older* and *oldest* exclusively, except in the expression "elder statesman."

older, oldest the comparative and superlative of *old*.
> *Jim's older brother is the oldest child in a family of six.*

explicit specifically said or written.
> *When we discussed your debt, you made me the explicit promise of repayment by January.*

implicit implied or understood but not directly stated.
> *Though we never discussed it openly, there was an implicit understanding between us that you'd return the money.*

503

fewer applies to number, to separate items, units, parts, or portions that can be counted. It tells how many.

Louise has fewer books than Marilyn.

He found fewer bargains at the sale than he had hoped for.

less applies to amount or quantity of nonseparable things.

Apples cost less money than lemons.

During a drought there is less water in the pond.

NOTE: One has a *fewer number* of things and a *less amount* of a thing than someone else. See the definitions of *amount* and *number* in this chapter and note how they correspond to *fewer* and *less*.

flotsam a ship's goods or parts found floating in the water.

jetsam a ship's goods or parts thrown overboard (jettisoned) in order to lighten a ship that is in danger of sinking.

NOTE: The literal distinction between these words is important only to marine lawyers and nautical writers. The rather hackneyed expression *flotsam and jetsam*, which derives from the literal meanings, generally refers to any worthless trifles found "floating" around on sea or land.

hanged put to death by hanging.

The spy was hanged at noon.

hung suspended or caused to be suspended from a wall, ceiling, etc.

We hung our reproduction of the "Mona Lisa" above the sideboard.

NOTE: People are sometimes—alas!—*hanged*. Pictures are *hung*.

historic famous in history.

The Constitutional Convention was a historic occasion.

historical concerned with history.

I read historical novels and often visit our local historical society.

if introduces a cause-and-effect relationship, or suggests doubt.

If it rains, we won't go to the races.

I wonder if it's raining in St. Louis.

whether introduces an indirect question or an alternative.

He asked whether we would go if it rained.

We'll go whether or not it rains.

NOTE: The distinction between *if* and *whether* is becoming increasingly blurred. Use the one that sounds right to you in a given context, and it will probably be right.

QUICKIE QUIZ
CONFUSED WORDS

In each of the sentences below, choose the word in parentheses that is correct or preferred usage. Answers follow.

1. The weather forecast says it is (apt, likely, liable) to rain today.
2. Her mother said that she (can, may) go.
3. She is an (alumnus, alumni, alumna, alumnae) of the local college.
4. Did you (compare, contrast) the price of meat at the two stores?
5. This salad is good but it needs (a, an) onion.
6. The word *red* has an unpleasant (connotation, denotation) for many people.
7. (Because of, Due to) the bad weather, we arrived late.
8. One could say that all cats are (egoists, egotists).
9. Milk that is kept in the sun is (apt, likely, liable) to turn sour.
10. Your story of catching a thirty-pound trout is (incredible, incredulous).
11. Let's keep this a secret (between, among) the three of us.
12. The whistle blew one long (continual, continuous) blast.
13. Who has the (fewest, less) chores to do?
14. The audience yawned and seemed (disinterested, uninterested) in the speech.
15. It looks (as if, like) it's going to rain.
16. Can sin and (immorality, immortality) be forgiven?
17. My small son is (anxiously, eagerly) looking forward to Christmas.
18. I don't fully understand the problem; please be more (explicit, implicit).
19. Do you and your wife belong to the (alumnus, alumni, alumna, alumnae) association?
20. He has a (contemptible, contemptuous) attitude toward sloppy work.
21. We expect a large (amount, number) of people at the dance.
22. (Can, May) you really do a hundred push-ups?
23. This painting is beautiful, (as, like) a painting should be.
24. This painting looks (as, like) a photograph.
25. My pocketbook tells me we (can, may) have steak for dinner if we want to.

ANSWERS:

1. likely (preferred). 2. may (preferred). 3. alumna. 4. compare. 5. an. 6. connotation. 7. Because of. 8. egoists (preferred). 9. apt (preferred). 10. incredible. 11. between *or* among. 12. continuous. 13. fewest. 14. uninterested. 15. as if. 16. immorality. 17. eagerly (preferred). 18. explicit. 19. alumni. 20. contemptuous. 21. number. 22. Can. 23. as. 24. like. 25. can.

immoral violating morality; sinful.
> *It is immoral to steal another man's wife.*

amoral not subject to moral judgment; lacking a knowledge of right and wrong.
> *Cats are amoral; they can't be censured for killing birds.*

unmoral not pertaining to morality; neither moral nor immoral.
> *Most scientists believe their research to be unmoral, no matter what the results.*

immortal never dying; eternal or remembered forever.
> *Christians believe in the immortal soul.*
> *Beethoven wrote nine immortal symphonies.*

imply to suggest or hint.
> *He implied that my friend John had stolen a necklace.*

infer to conclude or derive from.
> *From what he said, I inferred that he believed John had stolen a necklace.*

NOTE: You will often hear people use *infer* as an exact synonym for *imply* in the above sense. This is incorrect usage. Someone *implies* (hints or suggests) something, from which you *infer* (conclude) something. In other words, an inference correctly follows from an implication.

in indicates location, situation, or position.
> *I walked in the park for an hour.*
> *She held a child in her arms.*
> *The doctor is in his office.*

into indicates direction or motion to or toward a location or situation.
> *I walked into the park at 9:30.*
> *The doctor just went into his office.*

REMEMBER: *In* means you are there; *into* means you are on your way or have just arrived.

incomparable—uncomparable See *uncomparable—incomparable.*

incredible hard to believe.
> *It's incredible that you could have made such a mistake!*

incredulous skeptical; hard to convince.
> *I was incredulous when I heard that you—you, of all people!—had made such a mistake.*

learn to acquire knowledge or skills.
> *Students learn.*

teach to impart knowledge or skills.
> *Teachers teach.*

leave to go away from; to depart.
> *When does the next plane leave for Los Angeles?*

let to permit.
> *Will you let me go to Los Angeles?*

NOTE: *Leave* does not mean *let* or *permit*. Wrong: *Leave me go. Leave me do it.* Right: *Let me go. Let me do it.* There is one case, however, in which *leave* may be correctly substituted for *let:* when the verb is followed by an object plus the word *alone. Leave me alone* and *Leave Gerald and his sister alone* are as good usage as *Let me alone* and *Let Gerald and his sister alone.*

less—fewer See *fewer—less.*

liable—apt—likely See *apt—likely—liable.*

libel—slander See *slander—libel.*

lie to recline.
> *Lie down on the couch.*

lay to put something down.
> *Lay the plate on the table.*

NOTE: Confusion occurs because the past tense of *lie* is *lay.*
The present tense of *lie* is *lie: Lie down on the couch.*
The present tense of *lay* is *lay: Lay the plate on the table.*
The past tense of *lie* is *lay: He lay down on the couch yesterday.*
The past tense of *lay* is *laid: He laid the plate on the table.*
Note, moreover, that *lie* is an intransitive verb—which means that it does not have a direct object: *Lie down. Lay* is a *transitive* verb— which means that it must have an object: *Lay the plate down.* Study the difference between these two sentences, both of which are correct: (1) *Now I lie down to sleep;* (2) *Now I lay me down to sleep.*

like—as—as if See *as—as if—like.*

likely—apt—liable See *apt—likely—liable.*

luxurious characterized by luxury.
The governor lives in a luxurious mansion.
luxuriant growing lushly; abundant.
Alice has a luxuriant head of hair.

majority more than half.
He won the election by a clear majority: 60 of the 102 votes cast.
plurality more than any other, but not more than half the total.
Smith won by a plurality: forty votes against thirty for each of his two opponents.

mania a compulsive craving, enthusiasm, or love for something.
Some people have a mania for mountain climbing.
phobia a compulsive fear of something.
Dorothy has only one real phobia: Spiders terrify her.

may—can See *can—may.*

number—amount See *amount—number.*

oldest—eldest See *eldest—oldest.*

ophthalmologist a physician (M.D.) who specializes in diseases of the eye.
oculist an older word for *ophthalmologist.*
optician any person who makes or sells eyeglasses or other optical goods.
optometrist a technician who measures visual ability and provides lenses for eyeglasses.
NOTE: *Ophthalmologist* is a more complicated word than *optometrist,* and an ophthalmologist also has a more complicated medical education.

oral—verbal See *verbal—oral*

persecute to oppress; to harass persistently.
The Romans persecuted the early Christians.
prosecute to try by law.
The engineer of the wrecked train was prosecuted for criminal negligence.
NOTE: A *professional* lawyer *prosecutes* a person in court.

qualitative refers to *quality,* to the nature or value of something.
> *Qualitative analysis shows that water is made up of hydrogen and oxygen.*

quantitative refers to quantity, to the amount or size of something.
> *When you say that your state is "greater" than mine because of its high per-capita income, that's a purely quantitative judgment.*
> *Quantitative analysis shows that water has two atoms of hydrogen to one of oxygen.*

refer—allude See *allude—refer.*

shall This word is used with *I* and *we* (the "first person") to express the future tense of verbs. In formal speech the combination is usually *I shall, we shall.*
> *I shall be in Chicago next week.*
> *We shall be in Chicago next week.*

will This word is used with *you* (the "second person") and with *he, she, it,* and *they* (the "third person") to express the future tense of verbs. The correct combination is usually *you will, he will, she will, it will, they will.*
> *You will be in Chicago next week.*

NOTE: It makes no difference if *you* refers to one person, two people, or 300 people; the combination is still *you will.*
> *He* (or *she, it, they*) *will be in Chicago next week.*

EXCEPTIONS: The above rules are reversed in expressing determination or command.
> *I will go despite your disapproval.*
> *We will go despite your disapproval.*
> *You shall do as I say!*
> *He* (or *she, it,* or *they*) *shall do what the king orders!*

NOTE: The preceding rules for *shall* and *will* are still observed by formal writers and speakers. In ordinary use, however, more and more people accept the use of *will* almost all the time, and *shall* is relegated to a few specific uses in questions involving the first person, such as *shall we go?*

sit to seat oneself; to be seated.
> *Sit on the couch.*

set to put something down.
> *Set the plate on the table.*

slander a spoken defamation or unjustified attack on a person's reputation.

> *Three people heard him slander me by saying I can't hold down a job.*

libel a published written (or broadcast) defamation or unjustified attack on a person's reputation.

> *A newspaper or TV commentator can be sued for libel.*

stalagmite a tapering formation growing upward from the floor of a cave.

stalactite a tapering formation hanging down from the roof of a cave.

strategy an overall campaign or plan.

> *Our strategy was to concentrate on Europe before turning our attention to the Asian theater of war.*

tactics specific techniques and ploys.

> *Our sales tactics include daily newspaper advertising and 20% discount offers.*

teach—learn See *learn—teach.*

uncomparable not open to comparison, so different that comparison is impossible.

> *Horses and airplanes are uncomparable (or,* better, *not comparable).*

incomparable unique; in a class by itself or himself.

> *Bessie Smith was an incomparable singer.*

unconscious (1) not conscious, as a person who has fainted; (2) totally unaware; (3) that part of the mind not in the field of awareness.

> *Edna was unconscious for two hours after the accident.*
>
> *No psychiatrist can probe the unconscious.*

subconscious mental activity of which one is not aware, but which can sometimes be brought to the level of consciousness.

> *Oswald may have had a subconscious desire to injure his father.*
>
> *A psychiatrist can help some people to understand their subconscious urges.*

uninterested—disinterested See *disinterested—uninterested.*

unorganized without any plan or order.
> *An unorganized mob can accomplish nothing but chaos.*

disorganized having a bad, misused, or abandoned plan or order.
> *The office, where everything had worked so smoothly, became completely disorganized after Mr. Avery resigned.*

verbal communication in words, whether spoken or written.
> *These children rate very high in verbal skills.*

oral spoken as opposed to written communication.
> *John chose to give his teacher an oral rather than a written report.*

REMEMBER: *Verbal* does not distinguish between speech and writing; *oral* does.

vocation a person's main work.
> *Carpentry was Mr. Egan's vocation.*

avocation a person's hobby or diversion.
> *Stamp collecting was Mr. Egan's favorite avocation.*

warp the yarn that runs lengthwise in a loom.

woof the yarn that runs crosswise in a loom.

well (1) in a satisfactory or excellent manner; (2) in good health.
> *Mark plays soccer well, but he does badly at tennis.*
> *Kevin looks well in spite of his long illness.*

good satisfactory or excellent.
> *My grandmother's hearing is still good.*

bad (1) in poor health; (2) sorry; (3) unpleasant; spoiled.
> *After two sleepless nights, I feel pretty bad.*
> *I feel bad about having forgotten my wife's birthday.*
> *The eggs taste bad.*

badly not in a satisfactory manner.
> *Even when Mark feels well, he plays tennis badly.*
> *The child behaved badly in school.*

NOTE: Many people say "I feel badly" when they mean "I feel bad." This is not yet standard usage, however, and should be avoided. "I feel badly" actually means "My sense of touch is not good."

whether—if See *if—whether.*

will—shall See *shall—will.*

QUICKIE QUIZ
REVIEW OF CONFUSED WORDS

In each of these sentences choose the word in parentheses that is correct or preferred usage. Answers follow.

1. (Sit, Set) the teapot on the table before you (sit, set) down.
2. The Grand Canyon is of (incomparable, uncomparable) beauty.
3. My (ophthalmologist, optometrist) will soon be operating on the cataract in my left eye.
4. Golf is the (vocation, avocation) of a professional golfer.
5. (Shall, Will) it rain today?
6. A good judge should be somewhat (incredible, incredulous).
7. I taught the dog to (lay, lie) down and roll over.
8. I didn't mean to (infer, imply) that you're not a good worker.
9. I felt (badly, bad) when she thought I'd insulted her.
10. I don't know why you don't (leave, let) Diane go downtown by herself at her age.
11. He didn't put it in writing, but I had his (oral, verbal) approval.
12. Well, it's better to be (disorganized, unorganized) than not organized at all!
13. How did we get (in, into) this argument?
14. It's impossible to trip over a (stalactite, stalagmite).
15. The yard has a (luxuriant, luxurious) growth of weeds.
16. Your work for the committee has been most (credible, creditable, credulous).
17. This is the most (historic, historical) building in the town.
18. Cheating on a test is (contemptible, contemptuous).
19. I can't stand your (continual, continuous) interruptions.
20. Did he say (if, whether) he liked the plan or not?

ANSWERS:

1. Set; sit. 2. incomparable. 3. ophthalmologist. 4. vocation. 5. Will. 6. incredulous. 7. lie. 8. imply. 9. bad. 10. let. 11. oral. 12. disorganized. 13. into. 14. stalactite. 15. luxuriant. 16. creditable. 17. historic. 18. contemptible. 19. continual. 20. whether (preferred).

4 LINKED WORDS

In good usage, certain words go together in order to convey the right meaning. For example, certain verbs are usually followed by specific prepositions in standard speech and writing. *Wait on* and *wait for* are both correct, but in different situations. In some instances, *differ from* is correct; others, *differ with* sounds better. Know when to link *differ* with *from* or *with* if you are to master the fine points of usage. This section takes up the most common linked words that are used together.

accompanied by People are accompanied *by* other people or living creatures.
accompanied with Things are accompanied *with* other things.
> *Elston was accompanied by his wife and his youngest son.*
> *He accompanied his words with angry gestures.*

agree to People agree *to* a thing, a plan, a scheme, etc.
agree with Someone or something agrees *with* a person or people.
> *I agree to your terms.*
> *I agree with you.*
> *The climate seems to agree with you.*

NOTE: We may also use *agree on* in connection with a plan: *Our team agreed on a plan of action.*

compare to to liken one thing to another; to point out similarities.
compare with to examine and point out differences and similarities.
> *He compared her eyes to the blue Mediterranean.*
> *The doctor compared Irene's left eye with her right.*
> *Gretchen compared her answers with those in the book.*

correspond to to resemble in function or character.
correspond with to exchange letters.

QUESTIONABLE USAGE *Part A in the diagram corresponds with this red and blue plastic part.*
Man's hair corresponds with the fur of animals.

GOOD USAGE *Part A in the diagram corresponds to this red and blue plastic part.*
Man's hair corresponds to the fur of animals.
Carol and I have corresponded with Amanda.

QUICKIE QUIZ
LINKED WORDS

In each of the sentences below, choose the word in parentheses that is correct or preferred usage. Answers follow.

1. Please try (and, to) be on time.
2. If you have a cough accompanied (by, with) a fever, see a doctor.
3. How do this year's sales correspond (to, with) last year's?
4. He asked me to compare this year's sales (to, with) last year's.
5. We find that this year's sales are vastly different (from, than) last year's.
6. I am accusing neither Ronald (or, nor) Kate.
7. Oh, my love, shall I compare thee (to, with) a summer's day?
8. The president was accompanied (by, with) his son.
9. Do you agree (to, with) the plan or not?
10. How long did you have to wait (on, for) her at the airport?

ANSWERS:

1. to (preferred). 2. with. 3. to (preferred). 4. with. 5. from (preferred). 6. nor. 7. to. 8. by. 9. to. 10. for.

differ from to be different from, to be unlike.
differ with to disagree with in opinion.
> *This brand differs from that in price, if nothing else.*
> *When it comes to politics, I differ with him completely.*
> *Whether you differ with his ideas or not, you must work together.*

different from This is the standard two-word combination.
different than Though still considered unacceptable by some purists, this combination has gained wide currency. It can no longer be labeled as "substandard."

> PREFERRED *The outcome was different from what I had expected.*

> ACCEPTABLE *The outcome was different than I had expected.*

either . . . or These two words must go together.
neither . . . nor These two words must go together.

> WRONG *Neither you or your brother may go.*

> RIGHT *Neither you nor your brother may go.*
> *Either you or your brother may go.*
> *Neither the boy next door nor his friend can go with us.*

try and acceptable in speech and informal writing.
try to the formal, standard usage.

> INFORMAL   *Try and open this desk drawer.*

> PREFERRED   *Try to open this desk drawer.*

wait on to serve.
wait for to await.

> WRONG   *I'll be very late, so don't wait on me.*

> RIGHT   *Please ask the man who waited on us to bring us the check.*
> *I'll be very late, so don't wait for me.*

5 SIX KEY QUESTIONS ABOUT USAGE AND GRAMMAR

Most people are vague about the difference between good usage and good grammar. In fact, even grammarians and authorities on English usage disagree as to where usage ends and grammar begins—or vice versa. The simplest (and perhaps the most realistic) way to distinguish between usage and grammar is to say that grammar deals with the way words are put together in order to achieve *clear* communication, whereas usage is often a question of using the proper word and sometimes is only a matter of *polish* and *manners* rather than of *clarity*.

This is not a sharp distinction, however. Very often, a mistake in grammar does not obscure the meaning of a sentence; very often, too, what was once considered an ugly mistake becomes standard usage if it gains currency among well-informed speakers and writers. Thus, our great-grandparents would have rebuked anyone who said "Who are you looking for?" Most modern authorities, on the other hand, find that expression preferable to "For whom are you looking?" even though the latter is grammatically "correct."

In this final chapter of our discussion of usage and grammar, let us try to answer six questions that many people find puzzling. One particularly troublesome thing about some of these problems is that they show how good usage does not always coincide with good grammar in the traditional sense of the word *grammar*. Read each of the following questions carefully, and consider your own reaction to it before studying the answer.

QUESTION: How can you tell when to use *who* or *whom* (*whoever* or *whomever*) in a sentence?
ANSWER: You cannot go wrong by dropping the words *whom* and *whomever* from your vocabulary as objects except immediately after prepositions. Grammatically, *whom* is the objective form of *who; who* or *whoever* is correctly the subject of a verb, and *whom* or *whomever* is correctly the object of a verb or preposition. In modern English, however, *who* and *whoever* are acceptably used in both cases. Thus, only the most fastidious teachers and writers would consider the following incorrect:

> *Who do you want to see?*
> *I did not know who I was talking to.*
> *I don't know who you mean.*
> *My office hires whoever our supervisor recommends.*

Such usages as these are increasingly found even in the more formal style that some people consider best for such things as sermons, commencement addresses, and business reports.

If you want to be thoroughly correct do use *whom* and *whomever*—but just be sure you use them correctly. Where many people go wrong is in assuming that *whom* is somehow more "highbrow" than *who;* as a result they often use *whom* where *who* is the only correct grammatical form. The following sentences are all incorrect:

> *Whom shall I say is calling?*
> *Sally was a woman whom we thought could be trusted.*
> *A teacher whom I know is very fair flunked my son in math.*
> *Give the reward to whomever deserves it.*

On the other hand, it is still unacceptable to use *who* or *whoever* as the object of a preposition that precedes it. Note the following:

ACCEPTABLE	*Who are you going with?*
CORRECT	*With whom are you going?*
ACCEPTABLE	*Who do you want to speak to?*
CORRECT	*To whom do you want to speak?*

QUESTION: Is it always wrong to split an infinitive?

ANSWER: No. Most modern teachers, writers, and speakers agree that it is far better to do so than to rephrase a sentence into a self-conscious, awkward construction in order to avoid splitting an infinitive.

As you know, an infinitive is the verb form preceded by *to:* for instance, *to win, to eat, to understand.* You "split" the infinitive when you insert a word or group of words between *to* and the verb. Sometimes such insertions are unpleasant because they leave the listener or reader caught in midair waiting for the infinitive to be completed—as if waiting for the other shoe to drop. Here is an example of such a bad split infinitive:

> *We intend to, despite rain, sleet, hail, or snow, deliver the mail on time.*

This sentence is certainly improved by removing the "split" in some such fashion as this:

> *Despite rain, sleet, hail, or snow, we intend to deliver the mail on time.*

Most people naturally avoid long, awkward splits. What they are more likely to say is something like this:

> *I don't expect you to completely understand what I've been trying to tell you.*

How would you avoid splitting the infinitive in such a sentence? You could say "completely to understand" or "to understand completely," but either of those changes might weaken your point. In this case, therefore, the split infinitive is preferable to any alternative.

REMEMBER: If a split infinitive makes a sentence unclear or hard to read, rewrite the sentence. If the clearest, most forceful way of stating your idea seems to require a split infinitive, go ahead and split it.

QUESTION: Is it always wrong to end a sentence with a preposition?

ANSWER: No. The rule about not ending sentences with prepositions (*at, for, from, in, with,* etc.) was never really obeyed even in the days when schoolmarms tried to enforce it. A famous grammar book of a century or so ago stated the rule this way: "Never use a preposition to end a sentence with." That sentence itself ends with a preposition!

Modern writers believe that the natural order of words is the right order. Therefore the following sentences are all correct:

Fame is a goal worth working for.
Love is a force that we must reckon with.
Patsy tries to never do anything she'll be ashamed of.

Compare that last sentence with a rewritten version that avoids both the split infinitive and the final preposition: "Patsy tries never to do anything of which she'll be ashamed." This version, which might have been considered "better" fifty or sixty years ago, sounds stilted to modern ears.

QUESTION: May the possessive pronoun *whose* be used in place of *of which* to refer to things?
ANSWER: Yes. *Whose* may refer either to people or to things. Consider the following sentences:

Correct but Awkward	Preferable
This is the bicycle of which the chain is broken.	*This is the bicycle whose chain is broken.*
The one book of which the contents never grow stale is the Bible.	*The one book whose contents never grow stale is the Bible.*

Certainly the *whose* construction in the above sentences reads more smoothly than the *of which* construction. Therefore, since both are acceptable, the less awkward one is preferable.

QUESTION: In an adjective clause (a group of words that modify a noun or pronoun), when should the introductory relative pronoun be *which* rather than *that*—and vice versa?
ANSWER: When in doubt, use *which*. Many careful writers still prefer to use *which* to introduce a clause that can be omitted from the sentence without changing its basic meaning; and *that* to introduce a clause that is essential to the meaning. Thus:

San Francisco, which I visited last year, is my favorite city.
Our summer cottage, which is an hour's drive from Windsor, is right on the water.
The city that I like best is Victoria.
Only a cottage that is right on the water will suit my family.

In the first two of those sentences, the central idea would remain unchanged (*San Francisco is my favorite city* and *Our summer cottage is right on the water*) if the adjective clause were omitted. In the third and fourth sentences, the basic meaning is either lost or changed if the clauses are dropped (*The city is Victoria* and *Only a cottage will suit my family*).

NOTE: The substitution of *that* for *which* is generally not considered acceptable. So remember: when there is doubt as to which of the two words sounds better in a sentence, use *which*. It won't be wrong.

QUESTION: Is it permissible to begin a sentence with *and* or *but?*
ANSWER: Yes. *And* and *but* are coordinating conjunctions (which means that they are used to join closely related ideas to each other). If the ideas that they coordinate are briefly expressed or tightly linked, it is often best to combine these ideas into a single sentence by means of either a comma or a semicolon. Thus:

Jane took a walk, and Sally accompanied her.
Jane, who felt she needed a breath of fresh air, took a walk; and because the weather was so unusually warm, Sally accompanied her.

Sometimes, though, for the sake of emphasis or contrast or because the coordinated ideas are less closely connected than they are in the examples above, the second idea may seem to deserve a sentence of its own. It is not wrong to start such a sentence with *and* or *but*. The greatest writers in our language have often done so. But here is a word of warning (and note that this very sentence begins with *but*): A loose, uninteresting style of writing or speaking can result from the careless habit of beginning too many sentences with coordinating conjunctions. Don't permit yourself to write like this:

Jane took a walk, and Sally accompanied her. But I stayed home to mow the lawn. But I didn't do much, because of the heat. And so I sat down and picked up a magazine. And it was fun just doing nothing for a change. But soon I began to feel guilty. And so I went out to the kitchen to start supper. But the groceries hadn't been delivered and I had to wait. And so I . . .

REMEMBER: The reason some teachers advise against starting sentences with *and* or *but* is that they know how monotonous such loose structuring can become. *But* if you don't make a careless habit of starting sentences that way, don't be afraid to do it sometimes. *And*, even more important, don't think of it as a grammatical "mistake."

519

Fun With Words

REVIEWING THE SPECIALISTS

Here are eight words having to do with specialists in medicine and related fields. Choose the answer you believe is closest in meaning to each of the key words below. Answers follow.

1. **pediatrician** [pē′dē·ə·trish′ən]—
   (a) a specialist in foot diseases.
   (b) a physician specializing in the diseases and care of babies and small children. (c) a bone specialist. (d) a surgeon specializing in bone fractures.

2. **chiropractor** [kī′rə·prak′tər]—(a) a specialist in foot diseases. (b) a therapist who attempts to relieve pain and cure disease by manipulation of the spinal column. (c) a specialist in the diseases and care of children. (d) a heart specialist.

3. **physiotherapist** [fiz′ē·ō·ther′ə·pist]—(a) one who treats brain diseases. (b) one who treats injury and disability by external means such as massage, heat, exercise, etc. (c) a specialist in nerve diseases and psychic disorders. (d) one who treats kidney and liver diseases.

4. **cardiologist** [kär′dē·ol′ə·jist]—(a) a specialist in interpreting brain waves. (b) a doctor who treats stomach disorders. (c) a bone surgeon. (d) a doctor who specializes in the function and diseases of the heart.

5. **biologist** [bī·ol′ə·jist]—(a) a specialist in the study of plant and animal life. (b) a specialist in the treatment of diseases caused by bacteria. (c) a doctor of internal disorders. (d) a two-man surgical team.

6. **optometrist** [op·tom′ə·trist]—(a) a scientist who studies stars. (b) a technician who fits your eyes with glasses. (c) a doctor who examines your eyes. (d) a physician who treats diseases of the eye.

7. **ophthalmologist** [of′thal·mol′ə·jist]—(a) a technician who fits and prescribes eyeglasses. (b) a merchant who sells glasses. (c) a specialist in ear, nose, and throat diseases. (d) a medical doctor who treats eye disorders.

8. **podiatrist** [pə·dī′ə·trist]—(a) a bone doctor. (b) a children's doctor. (c) a therapist who treats foot ailments. (d) a nerve specialist.

ANSWERS:

1. **pediatrician**—(b) a physician specializing in the diseases and care of babies and small children. 2. **chiropractor**—(b) a therapist who attempts to relieve pain and cure disease by manipulation of the spinal column. 3. **physiotherapist**—(b) one who treats injury and disability by external means such as massage, heat, exercise, etc. 4. **cardiologist**—(d) a doctor who specializes in the function and diseases of the heart. 5. **biologist**—(a) a specialist in the study of plant and animal life. 6. **optometrist**—(b) a technician who fits your eyes with glasses. 7. **ophthalmologist**—(d) a medical doctor who treats eye disorders. 8. **podiatrist**—(c) a therapist who treats foot ailments.

Lexoguide

HOW TO USE THE LEXOGUIDE

This Lexoguide is a complete, easy-to-use reference book in itself. It is your handy guide to a carefully chosen list of over 4,000 of the most powerful and troublesome words—showing you at a glance their proper spelling, pronunciation, meaning, and use. You can use it to review what you have learned in the first part of this book. You can refer to it whenever you need to improve your word power or to answer questions about words.

The Lexoguide resembles a dictionary but is shorter, more selective, and easier to use. Each entry contains only the basic facts to help you increase your vocabulary and to help you spell, pronounce, and use the word correctly. A careful reading of the nine items that follow will help you to use this Lexoguide effectively.

1. The Main-Entry Word

Each main-entry word in the Lexoguide is printed in large, heavy type that projects into the left-hand margin of the column.

2. Division into Syllables

If the main-entry word has more than one syllable, the syllable divisions are marked by center dots (·). The center dots show where the word may be divided at the end of a line. They will also help you to pronounce the word correctly.

3. Pronunciation

Each main-entry word is followed by its proper pronunciation in parentheses. All letters and symbols used in the pronunciations are taken from the standard pronunciation key, which is given on page 8.

If the pronunciation of a word varies according to its part of speech, separate pronunciations are given and labeled, as: **ab·stract** (ab′strakt *adj., n.;* ab·strakt′ *v.*). If there is more than one accepted pronunciation, both may be listed, as: **ab·sorb** (ab·sôrb′ *or* ab·zôrb′).

4. Part of Speech

The part of speech of each entry word is given in italics after the pronunciation. If the main-entry word is used as more than one part of speech, all applicable labels are listed together after the pronunciation. Then each part-of-speech label is repeated at the left margin before the definition or definitions to which it applies. For example, under the entry for **dissent** you will find:

> *v.* To differ in thought, opinion, or belief . . .
>
> *n.* Difference of opinion

Parts of speech are labeled and abbreviated as follows: *n.* (noun), *v.* (verb), *pron.* (pronoun), *adj.* (adjective), *adv.* (adverb), *prep.* (preposition), *conj.* (conjunction), *interj.* (interjection). When shown, plurals of nouns are followed by the label *pl.* (plural).

5. Inflected Forms

Inflected forms are the special forms of words which make them into the past tense, past participle, and present participle of verbs, the plural of nouns, and the comparative and superlative degrees of adjectives and adverbs. Such forms are shown in this Lexoguide only when they are irregular—usually when some spelling change is involved other than the simple addition of *-ed*, *-ing*, *-s*, *-er*, or *-est* to the main-entry word.

When such inflected forms are shown, they, too, are divided into syllables and printed in heavy type after the part-of-speech label to which they apply. If alternative inflected forms are shown, the preferred form is listed first. Pronunciations are also given for inflected forms when they are unfamiliar or when they are pronounced differently from the main-entry word. For example:

crux (kruks) *n.*, **crux·es** or **cru·ces** (krōō′sēz) *pl.*

If the past tense and past participle of a verb are the same, the inflected form is listed only once, as *bus·ied* at *bus·y, bus·ied, bus·y·ing.* If they differ, the past tense is listed first, as *a·rose* at *a·rise, a·rose, a·ris·en, a·ris·ing.*

6. Definitions and Examples

The definitions in the Lexoguide are brief and to the point. They are often followed by examples—sample sentences or phrases in italics showing how the entry word is actually used in speech and writing. Sometimes a direction (in parentheses) or a label (in italics) precedes a definition. For example, one sense of *capitol* bears the direction: (Capital *C*). Separate meanings within the same part-of-speech category are numbered in heavy type.

7. Run-on Bonus Words

A Lexoguide entry may include one or more bonus words based on the main-entry word. These extra words are called run-ons because they are simply added on at the end, after the last definition or example. Run-on bonus words are also printed in heavy type and divided into syllables, with the accented syllables stressed. They are not defined because they are based on the main-entry words and their meanings will be obvious. For example, at **adept:**

> **a·dept** (ə·dept′) *adj.*
> Highly skilled; proficient: *He isn't adept at tennis.*—**a·dept′ly** *adv.*, **a·dept′ness** *n.*

8. Spelling Tips, Usage Notes, and Other Hints

Many spelling tips are included in the Lexoguide. These focus attention on tricky or deceptive spellings. Sometimes hints and pointers on pronunciation are also given.

Usage notes throughout the Lexoguide provide added information about correct word use. They give advice on how to choose words with care, how to use words correctly, and how to tell confusing words apart. For example, under the entry for **flaunt** you will read:

> **Usage:** *Flaunt* and *flout* are frequently confused. . . . The word flout means to express scorn or contempt for something. Note the difference between the two words in this sentence: *Teen-agers flaunt their youthful independence by flouting the authority of their parents.*

9. Synonyms and Antonyms

Many Lexoguide entries end with lists of synonyms and antonyms (abbreviated **Syn.** and **Ant.**). The synonyms mean substantially the same as the main-entry word. The antonyms mean the opposite. Thus you will continue to increase your vocabulary by relating words of like and opposite meanings.

Use this Lexoguide as your quick reference to learn new words and master old ones. Then, if you want fuller information, consult a dictionary.

A

a·ban·don·ment (ə·ban′dən·mənt) *n.*
1 The act of deserting or giving up a person, thing, or principle: *the abandonment of a baby on the church steps.* 2 Freedom from restraint or self-control: *At the carnival, the usually quiet people celebrated with abandonment.*
Syn. 1 desertion, leaving. 2 unrestraint.
Ant. 1 care, protection, concern. 2 propriety, constraint.

a·base (ə·bās′) *v.* **a·based, a·bas·ing**
To lower in position, rank, or estimation: *Their cowardice under fire abased the soldiers.*
Syn. humble, demean, degrade.
Ant. exalt, honor.

a·bash (ə·bash′) *v.*
To shame or embarrass: *He was abashed at his brother's rudeness.*
Syn. disconcert, faze.
Ant. encourage, embolden.

a·bate (ə·bāt′) *v.* **a·bat·ed, a·bat·ing**
To reduce in value, force, or intensity: *The next morning the storm abated.*
Syn. decrease, lessen, subside.
Ant. increase, intensify.

ab·bre·vi·ate (ə·brē′vē·āt) *v.* **ab·bre·vi·at·ed, ab·bre·vi·at·ing**
1 To shorten a word or expression by leaving out part of it: *"Mister" is abbreviated "Mr."* 2 To make shorter: *to abbreviate the visit.*
Syn. 1 reduce, curtail, abridge.
Ant. 2 increase, enlarge, extend.

ab·bre·vi·a·tion (ə·brē′vē·ā′shən) *n.*
1 A shortened form of a word or phrase, used to represent the full form: *"N.J." is the abbreviation for "New Jersey."* 2 The act of making briefer: *an abbreviation of a long speech.*
Usage: "U.S.A." is an *abbreviation*, but "NATO" is an *acronym.* An acronym is an abbreviation that may be pronounced as a word rather than as a series of letters. See ACRONYM.
Syn. 2 abridgement, reduction.
Ant. 2 extension, enlargement.

ab·di·cate (ab′də·kāt) *v.* **ab·di·cat·ed, ab·di·cat·ing**
To give up rights, as to a throne, power, or high position: *The king was forced to abdicate.*—**ab′di·ca′tion** *n.*
Syn. resign, renounce.
Ant. seize, usurp, retain.

ab·do·men (ab′də·mən *or* ab·dō′mən) *n.*
1 In man and in animals with backbones, the part of the body between the chest and the pelvis, containing the digestive tract. 2 In insects, the hindmost division of the body.
Usage: *Abdomen* is a more scientific and formal term than either *stomach* or *belly,* and it refers precisely to the front of the body between the diaphragm and the pelvis. Long ago, *belly* was the standard word to refer to the same region. Later on it was suppressed in favor of *stomach,* which is actually the internal digestive organ.
Syn. belly, stomach.

a·bet (ə·bet′) *v.* **a·bet·ted, a·bet·ting**
To give aid and encouragement, especially in wrongdoing: *to abet the kidnapers was a serious offense.*—**a·bet′tor, a·bet′ment, a·bet′tal** *n.*
Syn. help, promote, encourage.
Ant. hinder, stop, prevent.

a·bey·ance (ə·bā′əns) *n.*
A holding up or putting aside for future action: *He is holding his decision in abeyance until he has all the facts.*

ab·hor (ab·hôr′) *v.* **ab·horred, ab·hor·ring**
To feel repugnance or loathing for; hate: *Many people abhor spiders.*—**ab·hor′rence, ab·hor′rer** *n.;* **ab·hor′rent** *adj.*
Syn. detest, abominate, loathe.
Ant. love, like, admire, enjoy.

ab·ject (ab′jekt *or* ab·jekt′) *adj.*
1 Sunk to a low condition; despicable: *an abject coward.* 2 Hopelessly low; wretched: *abject poverty.*
Syn. 1 contemptible, degraded, shameful. 2 miserable, squalid.
Ant. 1 dignified, noble. 2 comfortable, prosperous.

ab·lu·tion (ə·blōō′shən) *n.*
A washing or cleansing of the body or part of the body, especially in a religious ceremony: *to perform one's morning ablutions; priestly ablutions before the altar.*
Usage: *Ablution* is usually in the plural. The word tends to sound high-flown and literary, but many people use it humorously as a synonym for *washing* or *bathing.*

a·bom·i·nate (ə·bom′ə·nāt) *v.* **a·bom·i·nat·ed, a·bom·i·nat·ing**
To dislike strongly; loathe: *to abominate dirt and untidiness.*—**a·bom′i·na′tion** *n.*
Syn. hate, abhor, detest.
Ant. like, admire.

ab·o·rig·i·nes (ab′ə·rij′ə·nēz) *n.pl.*
The original and earliest people, plants, or animals of a country or area: *The Maoris are the aborigines of New Zealand.*
Syn. native.
Ant. emigrant, outsider, alien.

a·bor·tive (ə·bôr′tiv) *adj.*
1 Resulting in nothing; failing: *an abortive revolt.* 2 Born too prematurely to be able to live: *an abortive fetus.*—**a·bor′tive·ly** *adv.*
Syn. 1 unsuccessful, futile. 2 miscarried.
Ant. 1 successful, fruitful, victorious. 2 full-term, viable.

a·brade (ə·brād′) *v.* **a·brad·ed, a·brad·ing**
To rub or wear off by friction: *The waves abraded the rocks.*
Syn. scrape, chafe, gall.

a·bra·sive (ə·brā′siv) *adj., n.*
adj. Tending to wear down or rub away: *the abrasive action of an emery board.*
n. A hard, coarse, or gritty material such as sand, that smooths or polishes.

a·brupt (ə·brupt′) *adj.*
1 Beginning, ending, or changing suddenly and unexpectedly: *an abrupt change of subject.* 2 Curt or rude: *his abrupt manner.*
Syn. 1 precipitous, impetuous. 2 brusque, bluff, unceremonious.
Ant. 1 gradual, prolonged. 2 courteous, genial.

ab·scess (ab'ses) n.
A collection of pus in some part of the body, resulting from an infection and often accompanied by painful inflammation: *an abscess in his gum.*
Spelling tip: Remember abscess has a *c* in the middle.

ab·scond (ab·skond') v.
To depart suddenly and secretly, especially to escape the law or to avoid punishment: *The overnight guest absconded with the family jewels.*
Syn. leave, disappear.
Ant. stay, remain.

ab·so·lute·ly (ab'sə·lōōt'lē, *emphatic* ab'sə·lōōt'lē) adv.
Completely or unconditionally: *I am absolutely sure.*
Spelling tip: *Absolute* + *-ly.*
Syn. totally, uncategorically.
Ant. partially, conditionally, tentatively.

ab·solve (ab·solv' *or* ab·zolv') v. **ab·solved, ab·solv·ing**
1 To free from a debt, obligation, promise, or ruling: *His illness absolved him from attending the meeting.* 2 To acquit, as of guilt or wrongdoing; forgive: *A priest absolves sinners.*
Syn. 1 excuse, exempt. 2 pardon, exonerate.
Ant. 1 oblige, bind. 2 condemn, convict.

ab·sorb (ab·sôrb' *or* ab·zôrb') v.
1 To drink in or soak up: *A blotter absorbs ink. Bright children absorb knowledge.* 2 To hold the attention completely; engross: *The man was absorbed in his newspaper.*
Syn. 1 take in, swallow, assimilate. 2 immerse, occupy.

ab·sorp·tion (ab·sôrp'shən *or* ab·zôrp'shən) n.
1 The act or condition of drinking in or soaking up: *the absorption of water by a sponge.* 2 Preoccupation of the mind; concentration: *his complete absorption in the baseball game.*
Spelling tip: Note the *p* in the second syllable of this word. But remember that absor*b*, the ver*b*, has a final *b.*

ab·sti·nence (ab'stə·nəns) n.
A refraining from or doing without certain foods, drinks, or pleasures: *He was proud of his abstinence from smoking and drinking.*
Syn. temperance, self-deprivation.
Ant. indulgence, intemperance.

ab·stract (ab'strakt adj., n.; ab·strakt' v.) adj., n., v.
adj. 1 Considered apart from matter or from particular examples: *abstract truth.* 2 Expressing a quality or thought that is apart from any real object having the quality: *"Bravery" and "blueness" are abstract nouns.* 3 *In art* Presented as a form or pattern rather than as a representation of a real object: *Many abstract paintings have been created by Picasso.*
n. A summary of the most important points of a book or document: *a three-page abstract.*
v. 1 To make a summary of, as a book or document: *to abstract the main points of the Constitution.* 2 To remove or take away, especially secretly: *Unnoticed, a thief abstracted*

the documents from the files.—**ab·strac'tion** n., **ab·stract'ly** adv.

ab·stract·ed (ab·strak'tid) adj.
Lost in thought; absent-minded: *He was so abstracted that he stumbled against a lamppost.*
Syn. inattentive, absorbed, preoccupied.
Ant. alert, attentive, watchful.

ab·struse (ab·strōōs') adj.
Difficult to understand: *For most people nuclear physics is an abstruse subject.*
Syn. obscure, complex, mysterious.
Ant. simple, plain, intelligible.

a·but (ə·but') v. **a·but·ted, a·but·ting**
To touch or join at the edge or side; border: *Our farm abuts our neighbor's property.*

a·bys·mal (ə·biz'məl) adj.
Too great to measure; without limit: *She was moved to tears by the abysmal wretchedness of the poor.*—**a·bys'mal·ly** adv.
Usage: *Abysmal* frequently implies being hopelessly beyond correction or redemption.
Syn. immeasurable, limitless.
Ant. limited, slight.

a·byss (ə·bis') n.
1 A bottomless gulf; chasm: *The mountain trail ran along the edge of an abyss.* 2 Any great depth or emptiness: *the abyss of time.*

ac·a·dem·ic (ak'ə·dem'ik) adj.
1 Pertaining to a school, college, or university: *Many people think of their academic years as the happiest of their lives.* 2 Offering or having to do with liberal arts or classical subjects rather than vocational or technical studies: *College preparatory courses are taught in an academic high school.* 3 Having little practical use or purpose: *It is academic to think about what might have been.*
Syn. 3 theoretical, impractical, speculative.

a·cad·e·my (ə·kad'ə·mē) n., **a·cad·e·mies** pl.
1 A private high school or secondary school. 2 A school giving instruction in some science or art: *an academy of music.* 3 A society of learned men for the advancement of arts or sciences.
Spelling tip: Remember that academy, like school, has one *c.*

ac·cel·er·ate (ak·sel'ə·rāt) v. **ac·cel·er·at·ed, ac·cel·er·at·ing**
1 To cause to act or move faster: *The car quickly accelerated to sixty miles per hour.* 2 To make happen more quickly: *Warm winds accelerate a thaw.*—**ac·cel'er·a'tion, ac·cel'er·a'tor** n.
Syn. hasten, speed, hurry.
Ant. delay, hinder, retard.

ac·cept (ak·sept') v.
1 To receive willingly: *They accepted our gift.* 2 To give an affirmative answer to: *We accepted their invitation.* 3 To take with good grace; submit to: *He accepts the future philosophically.* 4 To receive a person warmly: *The new boy was quickly accepted in the neighborhood.* 5 To believe in: *He accepts Buddhism.*
Usage: Do not confuse *accept* with *except.*

Except as a verb means to leave out: *Medicines are excepted from sales tax. Except* is more commonly used as a preposition meaning *but*, as in *Everyone except me drank coffee.*

ac·cess (ak′ses) *n.*
1 The act or opportunity to enter, come near, or obtain: *The child had access to the cookie jar.* 2 A way of entering; passage or path: *The mountain pass provided access to the valley.*
Usage: Do not confuse *access* with *excess*, which means too much of something.
Syn. 2 entrance, approach, entry.
Ant. 2 exit, egress.

ac·ces·si·ble (ak·ses′ə·bəl) *adj.*
1 Possible to reach or enter: *The small mountain settlement was accessible only by muleback.* 2 Easy to approach or speak with: *The chaplain was a friendly and accessible man.* 3 Attainable; obtainable: *The book is in the library, where it is accessible to all students.* 4 Open to the influence of: *Few policemen are accessible to bribery.*—**ac·ces·si·bil′i·ty** *n.*

ac·ces·so·ry (ak·ses′ər·ē) *n., adj.;* **ac·ces·so·ries** *pl.*
n. 1 Something added for display, convenience, decoration, etc.: *Purses and gloves are accessories to a woman's costume.* 2 Someone who encourages or helps another who commits a felony: *By hiding the criminal she became an accessory in the robbery.*
adj. Aiding or contributing to the main thing: *accessory benefits to an insurance plan.*
Syn. *n.* 1 detail, appurtenance. 2 confederate, accomplice. *adj.* supplemental, extra.
Ant. *n.* 2 opponent, rival, adversary. *adj.* essential, inherent.

ac·claim (ə·klām′) *v., n.*
v. 1 To proclaim or hail: *He was acclaimed the winner.* 2 Praise; applaud: *The fans acclaimed his heroic action.*
n. Enthusiastic approval: *He received worldwide acclaim for landing on the Moon.*

ac·cli·mate (ak′lə·māt) *v.* **ac·cli·mat·ed, ac·cli·mat·ing**
To adapt to a different climate or environment: *He acclimated himself to the arctic cold.*
—**ac′cli·ma′tion** *n.*
Syn. accustom, adjust.

ac·co·lade (ak′ə·lād′) *n.*
An honor or award: *They heaped accolades upon the astronaut.*
Syn. praise, tribute.
Ant. criticism, rebuke.

ac·com·pa·ny (ə·kum′pə·nē) *v.* **ac·com·pa·nied, ac·com·pa·ny·ing**
1 To go with: *A guide accompanied them on their tour.* 2 To play or sing the background music to or for: *A pianist was accompanying the singer.* 3 To supplement: *He accompanied his orders with threats.*
Spelling tip: The past tense (accompanied) changes the *y* to *i*.
Syn. 1 attend, escort, conduct.

ac·com·plice (ə·kom′plis) *n.*
A partner in crime: *His accomplice in the*

bank robbery was a safecracker.
Syn. accessory, confederate.

ac·com·plish (ə·kom′plish) *v.*
1 To get done: *How much can you accomplish in an hour?* 2 To finish: *I've accomplished my very secret mission.*—**ac·com′plish·ment** *n.*
Usage: *Accomplish* applies to things that are completed fully.
Syn. 1 do, perform, achieve. 2 complete, fulfill.

ac·cord (ə·kôrd′) *n., v.*
n. Agreement or harmony: *Punishment should be in accord with the severity of the crime. The treaty brought accord between the disputing nations.*
v. 1 To give or grant as due: *Accord him the respect that he deserves.* 2 To be in agreement or harmony with: *Their aims accord with ours.* Also **ac·cord′ance** *n.*
Usage: The phrase *in accordance with* means in agreement with: *to act in accordance with instructions.* However, *of one's own accord* means voluntarily, by one's own choice: *He confessed of his own accord.*
Syn. *n.* conformity, concord. *v.* 1 allow, award, concede. 2 agree, harmonize.
Ant. *n.* conflict, discord, disagreement. *v.* 1 deny. 2 disagree, clash, conflict.

ac·cord·ing·ly (ə·kôr′ding·lē) *adv.*
1 In agreement with what has come before: *He received the general's order and acted accordingly.* 2 Therefore; consequently: *The men's club voted to accept women, and accordingly the name was changed.*
Syn. 1 correspondingly. 2 so.

ac·cost (ə·kôst′) *v.*
To approach and speak to: *A beggar accosted him in the street.*
Usage: The word *accost* is unpleasant or threatening in tone. A person is *greeted* by someone he knows or is glad to meet. He is usually *accosted* by a stranger whom he would rather avoid.
Syn. address, hail, confront.
Ant. ignore, leave alone.

ac·cou·ter·ments (ə·kōō′tər·mənts) *n.pl.*
A soldier's equipment, other than clothing and weaponry: *knapsacks, canteens, gun belts, and other military accouterments.*
Spelling tip: This word may also be spelled **ac·cou·tre·ments** (ə·kōō′trə·mənts). Whichever way you spell it, "c" that "u" don't forget the two *c*'s and the *u*.
Syn. furnishings, accessories.

ac·cre·tion (ə·krē′shən) *n.*
1 Cumulative growth or increase, or the whole resulting from such a process of growth: *an accretion of unwritten laws.* 2 An addition from without: *Accretions of paint covered the original wood.*

ac·crue (ə·krōō′) *v.* **ac·crued, ac·cru·ing**
1 To come as a natural result, addition, or advantage: *Many benefits accrued to the nation when women became eligible to vote.* 2 To be added periodically: *One year's interest had accrued on his savings account.*
Syn. 2 accumulate, collect.

ac·cu·mu·late (ə·kyōōm′yə·lāt) v. **ac·cu·mu·lat·ed, ac·cu·mu·lat·ing**
To increase by regular additions: *Dust had accumulated on the mantel.*
Spelling tip: *Accumulate* the *c*'s and the *u*'s. You need two of each.
Syn. collect, amass, gather.
Ant. dissolve, dissipate.

ac·cu·rate (ak′yər·it) *adj.*
Free from errors: *Your addition is accurate.*—**ac′cu·ra·cy** *n.,* **ac′cu·rate·ly** *adv.*
Spelling tip: You'll *rate* high if you spell *accurate* accurately.
Syn. correct, precise, exact.
Ant. erroneous, wrong, incorrect.

ac·cus·tom (ə·kus′təm) *v.*
To adapt by custom or habit: *to accustom oneself to hardship.*
Spelling tip: *ac-* + *custom* = *accustom.*
Syn. habituate, inure, acclimate.

ac·cus·tomed (ə·kus′təmd) *adj.*
Habitual or usual: *The watchman went his accustomed rounds.*
Syn. appointed, scheduled, regular.
Ant. unscheduled, irregular.

ac·e·tate (as′ə·tāt) *n.*
A chemical compound containing acetic acid, such as cellulose acetate, which is used in making synthetic textile yarns and fabrics.

a·cet·y·lene (ə·set′ə·lēn) *n.*
A colorless gas burned to produce light or to give off heat for welding or for cutting metals: *an acetylene torch.*

a·chieve (ə·chēv′) *v.* **a·chieved, a·chiev·ing**
To accomplish or win, often through effort: *He has finally achieved fame.*—**a·chiev′er** *n.*
Spelling tip: In spelling *achieve,* remember the basic rule, *i* before *e* except after *c.*
Syn. attain, realize, obtain.

a·chieve·ment (ə·chēv′mənt) *n.*
1 The act of accomplishing: *the achievement of equal employment opportunity.* 2 Something accomplished: *an award for distinguished scholastic achievements.*
Spelling tip: Achieve + ment = achievement.
Syn. accomplishment, attainment.
Ant. failure.

ac·knowl·edge (ak·nol′ij) *v.* **ac·knowl·edged, ac·knowl·edg·ing**
1 To recognize and admit: *He acknowledged the good work done by his predecessors.* 2 To report receipt of or express thanks for: *to acknowledge a gift.*
Spelling tip: Display your *knowledge* when you spell *acknowledge.*
Syn. 1 confess, concede.
Ant. 1 deny, disavow, repudiate.

ac·knowl·edg·ment (ak·nol′ij·mənt) *n.*
1 Recognition or admission: *an acknowledgment of error.* 2 A response or reply: *They received the invitation and sent an acknowledgment.*
Spelling tip: When adding *-ing* or *-ment* to *acknowledge,* push the last *e* off the *ledge.*
Syn. 1 confession.
Ant. 1 denial, disavowal.

ac·me (ak′mē) *n.*
The highest point: *A Rolls Royce is considered the acme of automotive excellence.*
Syn. height, peak, summit.
Ant. depth, nadir.

a·cous·tics (ə·kōōs′tiks) *n.pl.*
The quality of a room or hall with respect to sound production: *Carnegie Hall has excellent acoustics.*

ac·qui·es·cent (ak′wē·es′ənt) *adj.*
Willing to go along with something: *Because there was a school dance that night, the teacher was acquiescent to their request for less homework.*—**ac′qui·es′cence** *n.*
Syn. compliant, agreeable.
Ant. opposed, adverse.

ac·quire·ment (ə·kwīr′mənt) *n.*
1 The act of acquiring: *the acquirement of knowledge.* 2 Something acquired, as a skill: *an accomplished young lady with many acquirements.* Also **ac·qui·si·tion** (ak′wə·zish′ən) *n.*
Usage: An *acquirement* is gained through study or practice rather than through natural talent. An *acquisition* is usually a material possession: *a prized acquisition for the rare-book room.*
Syn. attainment, accomplishment.

ac·quit (ə·kwit′) *v.* **ac·quit·ted, ac·quit·ting**
1 To declare innocent: *The accused was acquitted of the crime.* 2 To conduct oneself: *He acquitted himself like a gentleman.*
Spelling tip: When you add an ending to *acquit,* don't *quit* until you double the *t*: *acquittal, acquitter, acquittance.*

ac·rid (ak′rid) *adj.*
1 Disagreeably sharp, bitter, or pungent: *the acrid odor of rotten eggs.* 2 Sharp and biting in manner: *His acrid attack on his enemy included charging him with extortion, bribery, and deceit.*
Syn. 1 penetrating, irritating. 2 caustic, sarcastic, vitriolic.
Ant. 1 bland, mild. 2 kind, gentle.

ac·ri·mo·ni·ous (ak′rə·mō′nē·əs) *adj.*
Full of bitterness: *The political discussion turned into an acrimonious debate.*—**ac′ri·mo′ny** *n.*
Syn. sarcastic, caustic, stinging.
Ant. bland, mild, good-natured.

ac·ro·nym (ak′rə·nim) *n.*
An abbreviation that forms a word: *Radar* (*radio detection and ranging*) *is an acronym.*
Usage: An *acronym* is a combination of initial letters that may be pronounced as a word, such as NATO (*North Atlantic Treaty Organization*). An *abbreviation* is pronounced as separate letters, such as FBI (*Federal Bureau of Investigation*).

ac·tu·al (ak′chōō·əl) *adj.*
Real: *a story based on an actual case history.*
Syn. true, authentic, bona fide.
Ant. false, fictitious, made-up.

ac·tu·al·i·ty (ak′chōō·al′ə·tē) *n.*
Reality: *In his daydreams he did heroic deeds, but in actuality he was a coward.*

Syn. truth, verity, fact.
Ant. pretense, fantasy, illusion.

ac·tu·ar·y (ak'chōō·er'ē) *n.*, **ac·tu·ar·ies** *pl.*
A statistician who calculates and states risks, premiums, etc. for insurance purposes.—**ac'·tu·ar'i·al** *adj.*, **ac'tu·ar'i·al·ly** *adv.*

ac·tu·ate (ak'chōō·āt) *v.* **ac·tu·at·ed, ac·tu·at·ing**
1 To set into action or motion: *a lever actuated by an electric current.* 2 To influence or impel to action: *He was actuated by feelings of pity.*—**ac'tu·a'tion, ac'tu·a'tor** *n.*
Syn. move, drive, start, urge.
Ant. discourage, prevent, stop.

ad·age (ad'ij) *n.*
An old, widely known saying that expresses a common observation in a way that gives it the authority and force of a truth, such as: *"A man is known by the company he keeps."*

ad·a·mant (ad'ə·mənt) *adj.*
Immovable, unyielding, or unshakable: *The candidate was adamant in refusing to explain his campaign plans.*
Etymology: *Adamant* originally denoted a very hard, legendary mineral. The word is derived from the Latin *adamus,* which means the hardest metal (hence, unyielding).
Syn. pigheaded, stubborn.
Ant. adaptable, compliant, docile.

a·dapt (ə·dapt') *v.*
1 To change and make suitable for a new use or to fit new conditions: *He was assigned the job of adapting the play for television.* 2 Of living things, to adjust to a new situation or environment: *The children had some difficulty adapting to city life.*
Usage: Don't confuse *adapt* with *adopt.* *Adopt* means to take and follow as one's own without change: *adopted his predecessor's marketing plan.* *Adapt* means to take a thing and change it to fit new requirements and conditions.

ad·den·dum (ə·den'dəm) *n.*, **ad·den·da** (ə·den'də) *pl.*
1 A thing added or to be added: *addendum to the chairman's speech.* 2 A supplement, as to a book.
Syn. 1 addition, annex. 2 appendix.

ad·dic·tion (ə·dik'shən) *n.*
The state of being given over to some pursuit, practice, or habit, especially the compulsive use of habit-forming drugs: *Her craving for sweets amounted almost to an addiction.*
Syn. liking, craving, habit.
Ant. aversion, disinclination, dislike.

ad·di·tion (ə·dish'ən) *n.*
1 The act of joining or uniting so as to increase the quantity, importance, size, or scope. *Two plus two is a typical problem in addition. The addition of a new porch to our house was costly.* 2 That which is joined or united: *The music library is a most interesting addition to our town's cultural center.*—**ad·di'·tion·al** *adj.*, **ad·di'tion·al·ly** *adv.*
Syn. 1 annexation, accession, supplementation. 2 annex, appendage, accessory.

Ant. 1 subtraction, deduction, removal. 2 deduction, withdrawal.

ad·dress (ə·dres'; *also* ad'res *for n. defs. 2 and 3*) *v., n.*
v. 1 To speak to: *I addressed him by name.* 2 To deliver a set speech to: *The President addressed Congress.* 3 To write or mark a letter, etc., to whom and where it is to go.
n. 1 A set or formal speech: *an address to Congress.* 2 The writing on an envelope, etc., directing it to a person or place. 3 The name, place, residence, of a person etc., or organization.

ad·duce (ə·d(y)ōōs') *v.* **ad·duced, ad·ducing**
To bring forward examples, reason, or proof for consideration in a discussion or analysis: *to adduce evidence on automobile safety records.*
Usage: *Adduce* implies offering facts or other evidence to support something that has been stated.
Syn. cite, allege.

a·dept (ə·dept') *adj.*
Highly skilled; proficient: *He is adept at tennis.*—**a·dept'ly** *adv.*, **a·dept'ness** *n.*
Spelling tip: Sometimes *adept* is confused with *adapt.* Careful pronunciation of the second vowel in each word will help you avoid this error.
Syn. skillful, expert.
Ant. unskillful, inept.

ad·e·quate (ad'ə·kwit) *adj.*
Equal to what is required; suitable or sufficient for the case, occasion, or need: *Are his abilities adequate for such a responsible position?*—**ad'e·quate·ly** *adv.*
Syn. enough, satisfactory, sufficient.
Ant. unsatisfactory, insufficient.

ad·here (ad·hir') *v.* **ad·hered, ad·her·ing**
1 To stick fast or together: *The stamp would not adhere to the envelope.* 2 To be attached or devoted, as to a faith or political party: *He adheres to his ideals in spite of their impracticality.* 3 To follow closely or without deviation: *He adhered to the plan.*—**ad·her'ence, ad·her'ent** *n.*
Syn. 1 hold, cling. 2 follow, hold. 3 support, hold to.
Ant. 2 deny, waver, change.

ad·he·sive (ad·hē'siv) *adj., n.*
adj. Tending or prepared to stick; *adhesive tape.*
n. A substance that causes adhesion, as glue or paste.—**ad·he'sive·ly** *adv.*, **ad·he'sive·ness** *n.*
Syn. *adj.* sticky, gummed. *n.* cement, binder.

ad·i·pose (ad'ə·pōs) *adj.*
Of or pertaining to fat; fatty: *adipose tissue.* Also **ad·i·pous** (ad'ə·pəs) *adj.*

ad·ja·cent (ə·jā'sənt) *adj.*
Lying near or close at hand: *We bought land adjacent to the river.*—**ad·ja'cent·ly** *adv.*
Spelling tip: A newspaper *ad* is placed adjacent to the news—remember the silent *d* in this word.
Syn. adjoining, contiguous.
Ant. distant, remote, far.

ad·just (ə·just′) *v.*
1 To arrange so as to fit or match: *to adjust the height of a bicycle seat for a tall person.* **2** To regulate or make accurate for satisfactory use: *to adjust the sights of a gun.* **3** To harmonize or compose: *The two men had many differences to adjust before they could join forces in business.* **4** To adapt oneself, as to a new environment: *the difficulties of a country boy adjusting to the city.*
Syn. 1 adapt, fit. **2** alter, fix, set. **3** reconcile, settle. **4** conform.

ad·ju·tant (aj′ŏŏ·tənt) *n.*
A military staff officer who assists a commanding officer in administrative duties.

ad·min·is·tra·tion (ad·min′is·tra′shən) *n.*
1 Managing or directing, or being managed or directed: *administration of office routines.* **2** All the persons who compose a government, especially the executive department. **3** The term of office of such a government or of one of its officials: *The new Administration took office in January.* **4** All the persons who manage or supervise something, as a school system.—**ad·min′is·tra′tive** *adj.*
Syn. 1, 4 management, direction, control.

ad·mi·ral·ty (ad′mər·əl·tē) *n.*, **ad·mi·ral·ties** *pl.*
1 The office or functions of an admiral. **2** (Capital *A*) A department of the British government having supreme charge of naval affairs.

ad·mon·ish (ad·mon′ish) *v.*
1 To criticize mildly or talk to someone about a fault: *He admonished the inattentive student.* **2** To warn, especially in a friendly or sympathetic way: *The mother admonished her little boy about fibbing.*—**ad·mon′ish·er** *n.*
Syn. 1 chide, rebuke, reproach. **2** counsel, caution, advise.

ad nau·se·am (ad nô′zē·əm)
A Latin phrase meaning to the point of causing nausea or disgust, especially by continued repetition or prolonged duration: *At the dedication dinner, speeches went on ad nauseam.*

a·do·be (ə·dō′bē) *n.*
1 An unburnt, sun-dried brick. **2** The mixed earth or sandy clay from which such bricks are made. **3** A structure made of such bricks.

ad·o·les·cence (ad′ə·les′əns) *n.*
The period of life and growth from the beginning of puberty to the stage of adult development, roughly the ages twelve to twenty-one.
Spelling tip: Adolescence is a time for school—remember there is an *sc* in the middle of the word, as in *sc*hool.

a·dopt (ə·dopt′) *v.*
1 To take a child of other parents into one's own family as one's own child by legal measures. **2** To take from someone else and follow or use as one's own: *The politician adopted his foe's persuasive speaking style.* **3** To accept or choose: *to adopt a particular textbook for use in all schools.*—**a·dopt′a·ble** *adj.*, **a·dop′ter** *n.*
Usage: See ADAPT.

Syn. 2 appropriate, borrow. **3** embrace, support.
Ant. 2 reject, discard, renounce.

a·droit (ə·droit′) *adj.*
Skillful or prepared in the use of bodily or mental powers; dexterous or expert: *adroit in mathematics.*—**a·droit′ly** *adv.*, **a·droit′ness** *n.*
Syn. clever, deft, handy.
Ant. awkward, clumsy, dull.

a·dul·ter·ate (ə·dul′tə·rāt) *v.* **a·dul·ter·at·ed, a·dul·ter·at·ing**
To make impure or inferior by adding ingredients that are impure or of lesser quality: *chicken salad adulterated by the addition of tuna fish.*—**a·dul′ter·a′tion** *n.*

ad·ver·sar·y (ad′vər·ser′ē) *n.*, **ad·ver·sar·ies** *pl.*
A person who is actively hostile to another: *The boxer stared at his adversary across the ring.*
Syn. opponent, enemy, rival.
Ant. supporter, friend, confederate.

ad·verse (ad·vûrs′ or ad′vûrs) *adj.*
1 Acting against; opposing or opposed: *Adverse winds forced the little ship back to shore.* **2** Unfavorable or harmful: *The jury returned an adverse verdict.*—**ad·verse′ly** *adv.*
Ant. 1 helpful. **2** favorable, advantageous.

ad·ver·si·ty (ad·vûr′sə·tē) *n.*, **ad·ver·si·ties** *pl.*
A condition, circumstance, or occurrence of hardship, trouble, or misfortune: *Early settlers had to overcome many adversities.*
Syn. affliction, trial, calamity.

ad·ver·tise·ment (ad′vər·tīz′mənt or ad·vûr′tis·mənt) *n.*
A public notice, as in a newspaper or on a radio or TV program, about a product, service, etc.

ad·vis·er (ad·vī′zər) *n.*
A person who offers thoughtful suggestions, opinions, or counsel.
Spelling tip: Sometimes confusion arises in words like *adviser* about whether the final vowel is an *e* or an *o*. In this case there is no problem because the word can be spelled either way, *adviser* or *advisor.*

ad·vo·ca·cy (ad′və·kə·sē) *n.*
The act of supporting a position or person: *advocacy of free trade among the European nations.*
Syn. support, defense, backing.
Ant. opposition.

ad·vo·cate (ad′və·kāt *v.*, ad′və·kit *n.*) *v.* **ad·vo·cat·ed, ad·vo·cat·ing**; *n.*
v. To speak or write in favor of: *He advocates free speech.*
n. One who supports: *He is an advocate of a strong peacetime army.*
Syn. *v.* support, defend, favor. *n.* supporter, defender, backer.
Ant. *v.* oppose, resist. *n.* opponent, resister, antagonist.

aer·at·ed (âr′āt·id) *adj.*
Purified by exposure to air: *aerated water.*

aer·i·al (âr′ē·əl or ā·ir′ē·əl) *adj., n.*
adj. Of or in the air: *aerial vapor.*
n. A radio or television antenna.

aer·o·nau·tics (âr'ə·nô'tiks) *n.*
The science dealing with the design, construction, and operation of aircraft.

af·fect (ə·fekt') *v.*
To act upon or have an influence on: *Malnutrition adversely affects growth.*
Usage: The verbs *affect* and *effect* have totally different meanings and should be carefully used. *Effect* means to bring about, accomplish, cause, result in. To *effect* is to change the end result; to *affect* is to act upon. *A different climate may affect his health* (that is, may influence one way or another). *A sunnier climate may effect his recovery* (that is, may bring about his recovery). *Effect* is also a noun, meaning a result or influence: *the effect of smoking on health.*

af·fec·ta·tion (af'ek·tā'shon) *n.*
An artificial display or manner: *Grandfather's love of classical music was mere affectation.*
Syn. pretense, pose.

af·fi·ance (ə·fī'əns) *v.* **af·fi·anced, af·fi·anc·ing**
To promise in marriage: *affianced to the girl he had known since childhood.*
Syn. betroth, engage.

af·fi·da·vit (af'ə·dā'vit) *n.*
A written declaration sworn to be true before an official authority.

af·fil·i·ate (ə·fil'ē·āt *v.,* ə·fil'ē·it *n.*) *v.* **af·fil·i·at·ed, af·fil·i·at·ing; *n.***
v. To associate or unite: *The local club voted to affiliate with a national organization.*
n. An associated person, company, etc.: *My uncle is an affiliate of a large law firm.*
Syn. *v.* join, merge. *n.* associate, partner.

af·fil·i·a·tion (ə·fil'ē·ā'shon) *n.*
Association or connection: *He was suspected of having Communist affiliations.*
Syn. dealings, alliance.

af·fin·i·ty (ə·fin'ə·tē) *n.,* **af·fin·i·ties** *pl.*
A natural attraction or inclination: *He has an affinity for loud sport shirts.*
Syn. liking, enthusiasm, interest.
Ant. disinclination, repulsion.

af·fir·ma·tion (af'ər·mā'shən) *n.*
Something asserted to be true: *a solemn affirmation of the equal rights of all men.*
Syn. assertion.
Ant. denial, retraction.

af·flu·ence (af'lōō·əns) *n.*
Abundant wealth: *New cars and expensive homes attest to the affluence of the nation.*
Syn. opulence, abundance, riches.
Ant. poverty, destitution, deprivation.

a·gape (ə·gāp') *adv., adj.*
Gaping; wide open: *Mouth agape, he staggered with surprise.*

a·ged (ā'jid *for def. 1;* ājd *for def. 2*) *adj.*
1 Old: *An aged, bearded man sat silently on the park bench.* 2 At the age of: *a young man, aged twenty-three.*
Syn. 1 elderly, ancient.

a·gen·da (ə·jen'də) *n.*
A list, as of business to be acted upon at a meeting: *the agenda for the UN Security Council.*

Usage; *Agenda* was originally the plural of the Latin *agendum,* but is now usually considered as the singular form, with *agendas* as the plural.
Syn. calendar, schedule, program.

ag·gran·dize·ment (ə·gran'diz·mənt) *n.*
The accumulation of power, rank, or wealth: *He put the welfare of his country above personal aggrandizement.*

ag·gra·vate (ag'rə·vāt) *v.* **ag·gra·vat·ed, ag·gra·vat·ing**
1 To make worse: *the seasonal pollen that aggravated his allergies.* 2 *Informal* To arouse anger: *Don't keep aggravating me with your insinuations!*
Usage: The informal sense of *aggravate* illustrated by the second definition is best avoided in formal writing.
Syn. 1 worsen, intensify. 2 provoke, annoy, exasperate.
Ant. 1 improve, meliorate. 2 soothe, placate, mollify.

ag·gres·sive (ə·gres'iv) *adj.*
Disposed to act vigorously or boldly: *The fiercely aggressive man pursued his goals ruthlessly.*—**ag·gres·sive·ly** *adj.,* **ag·gres·sive·ness** *n.*
Syn. assertive, ambitious.
Ant. mild, meek, shy.

a·ghast (ə·gast') *adj.*
Speechless with horror; terrified: *aghast at the suffering of the war-torn nation.*
Syn. shocked, benumbed.

ag·ile (aj'əl *or* aj'īl) *adj.*
Able to move quickly and easily: *The agile athlete jumped over the hurdles effortlessly.*—**ag·ile·ly** *adv.*
Syn. nimble, spry.
Ant. clumsy, awkward, ungainly.

ag·i·tate (aj'ə·tāt) *v.* **ag·i·tat·ed, ag·i·tat·ing**
To stir up or disturb: *A storm agitated the ocean. He was extremely agitated by the illness of his daughter.*—**ag·i·ta·tion** *n.*
Syn. excite, perturb, upset.
Ant. calm, soothe, settle down.

a·grar·i·an (ə·grâr'ē·ən) *adj.*
Having to do with land, especially agricultural land, and its distribution and ownership: *The peasants received their own small farms under the agrarian reform program.*

ai·ler·on (ā'lə·ron) *n.*
A movable part near the trailing edge of an airplane wing, used to bank the plane.

air·foil (âr'foil') *n.*
A surface, such as a wing, aileron, etc., designed to provide lift or control for an airplane in flight.

aisle (īl) *n.*
A passageway between rows of seats: *The bride walked down the aisle.*
Syn. pathway, nave.

a·kim·bo (ə·kim'bō) *adj., adv.*
With the hands on the hips and the elbows extended outward: *He stood defiantly with arms akimbo, awaiting my reply.*

al·a·bas·ter (al'ə·bas'tər) *n.*
A fine-textured, white or tinted stone.

a·lac·ri·ty (ə·lak'rə·tē) *n.*
Willingness or readiness to respond or act
quickly: *The President responded with
alacrity to the danger by calling up the National Guard.*
Syn. quickness, promptness, speed, swiftness,
liveliness.
Ant. sluggishness, hesitation, reluctance.

al·be·it (ôl·bē'it) *conj.*
Even though: *I agreed to do it, albeit with
misgivings.*
Etymology: Albeit was derived from three
Middle English words, *al be it,* meaning
although it be.
Syn. notwithstanding, nevertheless, but.

al·bi·no (al·bī'nō) *n.*
A person or creature lacking normal pigmen-
tation and therefore white or very pale in
color.

al·bu·men (al·byōō'mən) *n.*
The white of an egg.

al·che·my (al'kə·mē) *n.*
Chemistry as practiced in the Middle Ages.
It was concerned chiefly with attempts to
change base metals into gold.—**al'che·mist** *n.*

al·fres·co (al·fre'skō) *adj., adv.*
In the open air; outdoors: *an alfresco exhibit.
We dined alfresco on the patio.*
Spelling tip: Also spelled *al fresco.*

al·ga (al'gə) *n.,* **al·gae** (al'jē) *pl.*
A primitive plant such as seaweed and
pond scum.—**al'gal** *adj.*
Etymology: *Alga* comes directly from the
Latin word for seaweed.

al·ge·bra (al'jə·brə) *n.*
The branch of mathematics dealing with
abstract quantities and the relations of
abstract numbers; calculations are done by
means of letters and symbols.

a·li·as (ā'lē·əs) *n., adv.;* **a·li·as·es** *n.pl.*
n. A false or assumed name: *The gangster was
known by several aliases.*
adv. Also called: *Jones, alias Smith.*
Syn. *n.* pseudonym.

al·i·bi (al'ə·bī) *n.,* **al·i·bis** *pl.;* *v.* **al·i·bied,
al·i·bi·ing**
n. 1 A legal defense by which an accused
person tries to show that he was somewhere
else when the crime was committed: *His alibi
was that he was in the hospital at the time of the
murder.* 2 *Informal* An excuse: *He used a
faulty alarm clock as his alibi for being late to
work.*

al·ien (āl'yən *or* ā'lē·ən) *adj., n.*
adj. 1 Of or related to another country:
refugees in alien territory. 2 Not natural;
strange: *an alien custom.*
n. A person who is not a citizen of the country
in which he lives: *The law requires that
aliens register with the government.*
Syn. *adj.* 1 foreign, strange. 2 outlandish,
peculiar. *n.* foreigner, stranger.
Ant. *adj.* 1 native, indigenous. 2 natural,
ordinary. *n.* native, citizen.

al·ien·ate (āl'yən·āt *or* ā'lē·ən·āt) *v.* **al·ien·
at·ed, al·ien·at·ing**
To make unfriendly or unable to communicate: *If you reveal your friend's secrets you will
alienate him.*—**al'ien·a'tion, al'ien·a'tor** *n.*
Syn. estrange, lose, put off.
Ant. hold, keep, win, conciliate.

a·lign (ə·līn') *v.*
1 To arrange into a line: *Align the books on
the shelf.* 2 To ally oneself with one side in a
controversy: *The U.S. was aligned with
England in World War II.*
Spelling tip: *Aline* is also acceptable, but
align is preferred.

al·i·mo·ny (al'ə·mō'nē) *n.*
The money that a court requires a man to
pay to his divorced or legally separated wife.

al·ka·li (al'kə·lī) *n.,* **al·ka·lis** *or* **al·ka·lies** *pl.*
A substance, such as soda or ammonia, that
neutralizes acids.

al·lay (ə·lā') *v.* **al·layed, al·lay·ing**
To calm, pacify, or diminish: *His calmness
allayed her anxiety.*
Syn. soothe, quiet, moderate.

al·lege (ə·lej') *v.* **al·leged, al·leg·ing**
1 To assert as true in the absence of proof:
*They alleged that he had been seen purchasing
the murder weapon.* 2 To plead as an excuse
or reason: *He alleged overwork as the cause of
his neglect.*—**al·leged** (ə·lejd' *or* ə·lej'id) *adj.,*
al·leg·ed·ly *adv.*
Syn. 1 claim, theorize.

al·le·giance (ə·lē'jəns) *n.*
Loyalty; faithful adherence: *allegiance to the
flag.*
Syn. dedication, devotion, fidelity.
Ant. hostility, enmity, antipathy.

al·le·go·ry (al'ə·gor'ē) *n.,* **al·le·go·ries** *pl.*
A story in which characters and images
represent abstract ideas: *an allegory in which
contentment was portrayed as a purring cat.*—
al'le·gor'i·cal *adj.*
Syn. parable, fable, apologue.

al·le·gro (ə·lā'grō *or* ə·leg'rō) *adj., adv., n.,*
al·le·gros *pl.*
adj., adv. In music Lively and fast.
n. A musical piece or passage in fast tempo.

al·le·vi·ate (ə·lē'vē·āt) *v.* **al·le·vi·at·ed, al·le·
vi·at·ing**
To make easier to bear: *Nurses alleviate
suffering.*—**al'le·vi·a'tion** *n.*
Syn. lessen, relieve, assuage.
Ant. worsen, aggravate.

al·lied (ə·līd' *or* al'īd) *adj.*
1 Joint; friendly; cooperating: *the allied
powers in Word War II.* 2 Closely related:
Biology and genetics are allied fields of science.
Syn. 1 united, joined. 2 interdependent.
Ant. 1 divided, hostile. 2 independent,
unrelated.

al·lit·er·a·tion (ə·lit'ə·rā'shən) *n.*
In a phrase or line, the presence of two or
more words with the same initial sound, as
the lovely lilt of Lily's laughter.—**al·lit'er·a·
tive** *adj.*

al·lo·cate (al′ə·kāt) v. **al·lo·cat·ed, al·lo·cat· ing**
1 To set aside for a specific purpose: *A budget allocates funds for various items.* 2 To distribute or divide into shares: *He allocated his time among several tasks.*
Syn. 1 earmark, tag. 2 allot, apportion.

al·lot (ə·lot′) v. **al·lot·ted, al·lot·ting**
To opportion or assign: *to allot committee assignments; to allot blame.*—**al·lot′ment** n.
Spelling tip: Note that the final *t* of *allot* is doubled in all forms of the word except in the noun *allotment.*

al·low·ance (ə·lou′əns) n.
1 A fixed amount that is given, permitted, or allotted, especially a sum of money paid at regular intervals for personal expenses: *His wife receives a weekly allowance. Forty pounds is the usual airplane luggage allowance.* 2 A taking into account of modifying circumstances: *The judge made allowance for the criminal's youth and ordered a reduced sentence.*
Syn. allotment, portion.

al·lude (ə·lōōd′) v. **al·lud·ed, al·lud·ing**
To make direct or casual mention (used with *to*): *In job hunting, she alluded to her father's influential friends.*

al·lu·sion (ə·lōō′zhən) n.
A brief or indirect reference: *His allusions to another job offer inspired a pay raise.*
Usage: Distinguish between this word and *illusion* (meaning fantasy) and the seldom-encountered *elusion* (meaning escape). An *allusion*, however brief, is based on reality; an *illusion* may have no basis whatsoever in reality.

al·ly (ə·lī′ *or* al′ī) n., **al·lies** *pl.*; v. **al·lied, al· ly·ing**
v. To affiliate in a common cause or defense: *Political bosses often ally themselves with the leading candidate.*
n. A person, nation, etc., associated with another for a specific purpose: *wartime allies.*
Syn. v. join, link, n. friend, backer, associate.
Ant. v. sever, dissociate, separate. n. enemy, foe, opponent.

al·ma ma·ter (al′mə ma′tər *or* äl′mə mä′tər) n.
1 The school or college one has attended. 2 The song or hymn of a school or college.
Etymology: *Alma mater* is from a Latin phrase that means *fostering mother.*

alms (ämz) n. *sing. and pl.*
A gift or gifts for the poor; charity.

a·loof (ə·loof′) adj., adv.
Cool or distant in manner; apart: *The aloof boss did not mingle with the workers.*
Syn. withdrawn, taciturn.
Ant. gregarious, friendly.

al·pac·a (al·pak′ə) n.
1 A domesticated mammal of South America, related to the llama. 2 The long silky wool of this animal, or cloth containing this wool.

al·read·y (ôl·red′ē) adv.
1 As of now or a special time: *We were al-*

ready asleep when you called. 2 So soon: *Are you dressed already?*
Usage: Don't confuse this word with the two-word phrase *all ready*, which means completely prepared or finished: *He is already all ready to go.*

all right (ôl rīt) adj., adv.
1 Correct; well; satisfactory: *His guesses were all right. I feel all right.* 2 Certainly: *I'll remember all right.*

al·ter (ôl′tər) v.
To make or become different; modify: *They altered their itinerary to include London.*—**al· ter·a′tion** n.
Syn. change, revise.
Ant. maintain, preserve.

al·ter·ca·tion (ôl′tər·kā′shən) n.
A heated dispute; wrangling (often accompanied by blows): *The union meeting remained free of any altercations.*
Syn. controversy, debate, quarrel.
Ant. agreement, cooperation.

al·ter·nate (ôl′tər·nāt v.; ôl′tər·nit adj., n.) v. **al·ter·nat·ed, al·ter·nat·ing;** adj., n.
v. 1 To follow or cause to follow one another by turns: *Good and bad times alternate.* 2 To take turns at: *Soldiers alternated sentry duty.*
adj. 1 Every other; every second: *The city museum is open on alternate weekends.* 2 Offering or expressing a choice: *an alternate route.*
n. A substitute: *An alternate is available if a delegate becomes ill.* —**al·ter·na′tion** n., **al′ter· nate·ly** adv.
Syn. v. interchange. adj. 2 additional, extra. n. deputy, replacement, proxy.

al·ter·na·tive (ôl·tûr′nə·tiv) n., adj.
n. One of two or more things to be chosen, or a choice between these things: *the alternative of death or dishonor.*
adj. Offering a choice of two or more things. —**al·ter′na·tive·ly** adv.
Syn. n. option, possibility.

al·though (ôl·thō′) conj.
Despite the fact that: *Although I was afraid, I did not panic.*
Spelling tip: *Altho* is still considered nonstandard by most authorities.

al·to·geth·er (ôl′tə·geth′ər) adv.
1 Thoroughly; completely: *an altogether worthless book.* 2 In all; all told: *Taken altogether, the returns are encouraging.*
Usage: Don't confuse this word with the two-word phrase *all together*, meaning as a group or in unison: *Let's sing this song all together.*
Syn. 1 wholly, entirely.

al·tru·ism (al′trōō·iz′əm) n.
Selfless devotion to the well-being of others: *The Peace Corps appeals to youthful altruism.* —**al′tru·ist** n., **al′tru·is′tic** adj.
Syn. unselfishness, idealism.
Ant. selfishness, greed.

a·lum·na (ə·lum′nə) n., **a·lum·nae** (ə·lum′nē) *pl.*
A female graduate or former student of a school or college.

a·lum·nus (ə·lum′nəs) *n.*, **a·lum·ni** (ə·lum′nī) *pl.*
A male graduate or former student of a school or college.
Usage: The plural *alumni* is often used to refer to graduates or students of coeducational institutions.

a·mal·gam (ə·mal′gəm) *n.*
A combination or mingling of two or more things: *Her confused feelings were an amalgam of love, hate, and fear.*
Syn. union, alloy, mixture.

a·mal·ga·mate (ə·mal′gə·māt) *v.* **a·mal·ga·mat·ed, a·mal·ga·mat·ing**
To unite or combine: *Various unions amalgamated to present a united front in wage negotiations.*—**a·mal·ga·ma′tion** *n.*
Syn. join, come together.
Ant. separate, part, split up.

a·mass (ə·mas′) *v.*
To heap up; accumulate: *He amassed great wealth.*
Syn. gather, collect, put together.
Ant. dwindle, evaporate, subside.

am·a·teur (am′ə·chŏŏr, am′ə·t(y)ŏŏr, *or* am′ə·tûr) *n.*, *adj.*
n. 1 A person who practices an art or activity for pleasure rather than as a profession: *Olympic game contestants must be amateurs.*
2 A person lacking skill in a particular activity: *Political amateurs can ruin a candidate's image.*
adj. Not expert or professional. Also **am′a·teur′ish** *adj.*
Syn. *n.* 1 *adj.* nonprofessional. *n.* 2 duffer, beginner.
Ant. professional, pro, expert.

am·a·to·ry (am′ə·tôr′ē *or* am′ə·tō′rē) *adj.*
Pertaining to or exciting love, especially sexual love: *an amatory poem.*
Syn. erotic, amorous.

am·a·zon (am′ə·zon) *n.*
A large, strong, or athletic woman.
Etymology: *Amazon* comes from Greek roots meaning *without a breast*, because of the fable that female Amazon warriors of Greek mythology cut off their right breasts so that they could more easily shoot with a bow.

am·bas·sa·dor (am·bas′ə·dər) *n.*
1 A diplomat of the highest rank who represents his government in a foreign country: *The new ambassador presented his credentials to the President.* 2 Any personal representative.—**am·bas′sa·do′ri·al** *adj.*
Syn. 2 agent, go-between, minister.

am·bi·dex·trous (am′bə·dek′strəs) *adj.*
Able to use both hands equally well.

am·bi·gu·i·ty (am′bə·gyŏŏ′ə·tē) *n.*, **am·bi·gu·i·ties** *pl.*
An expression, remark, etc. that can be variously interpreted.

am·big·u·ous (am·big′yŏŏ·əs) *adj.*
Capable of being variously understood: *"Yes and no," was his ambiguous response.*— **am·big′u·ous·ly** *adv.*

Syn. obscure, equivocal.
Ant. straightforward, direct.

am·bro·sia (am·brō′zhə *or* am·brō′zhē·ə) *n.*
1 In classical mythology, the food of the gods: *Nectar and ambrosia were the drink and food of the immortals.* 2 Any very delicious food or drink.

a·mel·io·rate (ə·mēl′yə·rāt) *v.* **a·mel·io·rat·ed, a·mel·io·rat·ing**
To make or become better: *Congress was urged to pass legislation to ameliorate the condition of the American Indian.*—**a·mel′io·ra′tion** *n.*
Syn. improve.
Ant. worsen, damage.

a·men (ā′men′ *or* ä′men′) *interj.*
So be it: used at the end of a prayer or statement to express agreement.
Etymology: *Amen* was originally a Hebrew word meaning *verily* or *truly.*

a·me·na·ble (ə·mē′nə·bəl *or* ə·men′ə·bəl) *adj.*
Willing to be persuaded or to submit to direction or authority: *The union was amenable to a proposal of a wage increase.*

a·mend (ə·mend′) *v.*
To change, especially so as to improve: *to amend the Constitution.*—**a·mend′ment** *n.*
Spelling tip: To *amend* is a way of *mending* something that is lacking in some respect.
Syn. Correct, rectify, revise.

am·i·ca·ble (am′i·kə·bəl) *adj.*
Characterized by good will or friendship: *Both parties reached an amicable settlement to the dispute.*—**am′i·ca·bil′i·ty** *n.*, **am′i·ca·bly** *adv.*
Usage: *Amicable* is normally used to describe an action, gesture, etc. *Amiable,* however, is usually used to describe a person.
Syn. peaceable, well-intentioned.
Ant. unfriendly, hostile.

am·mo·nia (ə·mōn′yə *or* ə·mō′nē·ə) *n.*
1 A colorless, suffocating gas formed from nitrogen and hydrogen. 2 Ammonia gas dissolved in water, used for cleaning.
Spelling tip: Don't get ammonia in your "i" —but remember the *i* in this word.

am·ne·sia (am·nē′zhə) *n.*
Partial or total loss or impairment of memory: *After the automobile crash, he suffered from partial amnesia for several days.* —**am·nes·ic** (am·nē′sik *or* am·nē′zik) *adj.*

am·nes·ty (am′nəs·tē) *n.*
An official, general pardon of offenders by a government: *After the Civil War ended, the U.S. granted an amnesty to most captured soldiers.*

a·mong (ə·mung′) *prep.*
1 In the midst of: *a house among the trees.* 2 Within or by the group of: *agreement among all the nations.*
Usage: *Among* is preferred when more than two objects are considered as a group; *between* is preferred when comparing only two things: *The trade between the Dodgers and Mets was the first stage of a deal among four clubs.*

a·mor·al (ā·môr'əl) *adj.*
Not concerned with, or lacking sense of, rightness and wrongness: *Some scientists regard the first atomic bomb project as an amoral effort—the development of the bomb rather than its potential use was the sole consideration.*—**a'mor·al'i·ty** *n.*, **a·mor'al·ly** *adv.*

am·or·tize (am'ər·tīz) *v.* **am·or·tized, am·or·tiz·ing**
To extinguish gradually, as a debt or liability: *to amortize a debt by making periodic installment payments.*—**am'or·ti·za'tion** *n.*

am·pere (am'pir *or* am·pir') *n.*
Electricity The unit for measuring the strength of current.
Etymology: *Ampere* was named after André Marie Ampère, 1775–1836, a French physicist.

am·per·sand (am'pər·sand) *n.*
The character "&," meaning *and.*
Usage: An ampersand should not be used in formal composition. It occurs most often in company names (Funk & Wagnalls, etc.).

am·phib·i·an (am'fib'ē·ən) *adj., n.*
adj. Pertaining to a class of cold-blooded organisms adapted for life both on land and in water: *Frogs and salamanders are amphibian creatures.*
n. Such an animal or plant.

am·phi·the·a·ter (am'fə·thē'ə·tər) *n.*
An oval structure with tiers of seats built around an open area: *Baseball stadiums are amphitheaters.*

am·ple (am'pəl) *adj.*
1 Large: *a matronly woman with an ample bosom.* **2** Adequate: *Many people consider $10,000 an ample yearly income.*—**am'ply** *adv.*
Syn. 1 full, big, abundant. 2 sufficient, enough.
Ant. 1 small, scanty, slight. 2 insufficient, lacking.

am·pli·fy (am'plə·fī) *v.* **am·pli·fied, am·pli·fy·ing**
1 To enlarge or add to: *After his brief speech, reporters asked the President to amplify his statements.* **2** *Electronics* To increase the strength of: *to amplify a signal.*—**am'pli·fi·ca'tion** *n.*
Syn. 1 increase, expand.
Ant. 1 diminish, lessen.

am·pu·tate (am'pyōō·tāt) *v.* **am·pu·tat·ed, am·pu·tat·ing**
To cut off by surgery: *They were forced to amputate the gangrenous toe.*

am·u·let (am'yə·lit) *n.*
An object worn by the superstitious as a supposed protection against sickness, accident, bad luck, etc. Amulets are most often worn around the neck, and are often engraved with magic figures or inscriptions.
Syn. charm, talisman, fetish.

an·a·gram (an'ə·gram) *n.*
A word or phrase formed by reordering the letters of another word or phrase: *"Tame" is an anagram of "mate." Anagrams* is a game based on such word play.

an·al·ge·sic (an'əl·jē'zik) *adj., n.*
adj. Promoting or pertaining to the alleviation of pain: *an analgesic drug.*
n. A drug that alleviates pain: *Aspirin is an analgesic.*
Syn. painkiller.

a·nal·o·gy (ə·nal'ə·jē) *n.*, **a·nal·o·gies** *pl.*
A similarity or resemblance in certain respects between things that are otherwise dissimilar: *The newspaper noted the analogy between one troublemaker in a group of twenty boys and one rotten apple in a barrel.*—**a·nal·o·gous** (ə·nal'ə·gəs) *adj.*
Spelling tip: Note the *o* in this word, and the *g* in the last syllable (pronounced as a *j*).
Syn. comparison, agreement, likeness.
Ant. difference, dissimilarity.

a·nal·y·sis (ə·nal'ə·sis) *n.*, **a·nal·y·ses** (ə·nal'ə·sēz) *pl.*
A way of determining or describing something by separating it into its component parts: *A thorough analysis of the nation's economic situation requires many statistics.*
Spelling tip: Remember the *y* in the middle of the word.

an·a·lyze (an'ə·līz) *v.* **an·a·lyzed, an·a·lyz·ing**
To separate into parts or elements, especially in order to determine the nature or form of something: *He carefully analyzed the candidate's proposals.*

an·ar·chy (an'ər·kē) *n.*
1 Absence of government: *Some radicals in the 1930s favored anarchy.* **2** Lawless confusion and disorder: *Rioting could lead to a state of anarchy.*
Syn. 2 chaos, turbulence, bedlam.
Ant. 2 order, peace, serenity.

an·cho·vy (an'chō·vē, an'chə·vē, *or* an·chō'vē) *n.*, **an·cho·vies** *pl.*
A small, herringlike fish that is cut into small strips and packed in brine. This delicacy is often used to garnish salads or is served as an appetizer.

an·dan·te (än·dän'tā *or* an·dan'tē) *adj., adv., n.*
adj., adv. In music Moderately slow: *an andante passage; played andante.*
n. A moderately slow movement or passage in a musical composition.
Etymology: *Andante* comes from an Italian word meaning *walking.*

and·i·ron (and'ī'ərn) *n.*
One of two metal supports for holding wood in an open fireplace.

an·ec·dote (an'ik·dōt) *n.*
A short narrative of an interesting or entertaining incident.

a·ne·mi·a (ə·nē'mē·ə) *n.*
A condition of the blood in which there is a deficiency in the number of red corpuscles or in the amount of hemoglobin. It results in pallor, loss of energy, and other symptoms.
—**a·ne'mic** *adj.*

an·es·the·sia (an'is·thē'zhə *or* an'is·thē'-zhē·ə) *n.*
Localized or general insensitivity to pain, with or without loss of consciousness, due to the use of a drug such as ether, novocaine, etc.

an·es·thet·ic (an'is·thet'ik) *n., adj.*
n. A substance that causes unconsciousness or deadens sensation in part of the body, used especially during surgery.
adj. Of or having to do with such a substance.

an·es·the·tist (ə·nes'thə·tist) *n.*
A person, especially a doctor, trained to administer anesthetics.

an·gle (ang'gəl) *n., v.* **an·gled, an·gling**
n. 1 A geometric figure formed by the divergence of two straight lines or surfaces from a common point. 2 The space between these lines or surfaces, measured in degrees. 3 A point of view or aspect from which something is regarded: *We looked at the situation from all angles.*
v. To move or turn at an angle or by angles: *The startled deer angled across the field.*

an·go·ra (ang·gôr'ə *or* ang·gō'rə) *n.*
1 A goat, originally from Ankara, Turkey, raised for its long, silky hair. 2 The long, silky hair of this goat, or cloth woven from it. 3 A variety of cat with long, silky hair.

an·i·mos·i·ty (an'ə·mos'ə·tē) *n.,* **an·i·mos·i·ties** *pl.*
Dislike or hatred; hostility.
Syn. enmity, antagonism.
Ant. love, friendship, amity.

an·ise (an'is) *n.*
A small South European and North African plant cultivated for its flavorful seeds, which are used in medicine and as a flavoring in cooking.

an·nals (an'əlz) *n.pl.*
1 A record of events in their chronological order, year by year: *the annals of aerospace.* 2 Historical records: *the annals of the early English kings.*
Etymology: *Annals* comes from the Latin word *annus*, meaning *year.*

an·nex (a·neks' *v.* an'eks *n.*) *v., n.*
v. To add, as an additional or minor part: *The powerful but small nation yearned to annex surrounding territories.*
n. An addition to a building, or a nearby building used in addition to the main one.
Syn. *v.* append, attach.
Ant. *v.* detach, separate.

an·ni·hi·late (ə·nī'ə·lāt) *v.* **an·ni·hi·lat·ed, an·ni·hi·lat·ing**
To destroy completely; do away with: *The platoon was annihilated during the vicious attack.*—**an·ni'hi·la'tion** *n.*
Spelling tip: Note this word has an *h*, as in H-bomb.
Syn. exterminate, eradicate, abolish.
Ant. preserve, protect, save.

an·ni·ver·sa·ry (an'ə·vûr'sər·ē) *n.,* **an·ni·ver·sa·ries** *pl.*
The day of the year on which some event

took place in a preceding year: *a wedding anniversary.*

an·no·tate (an'ō·tāt) *v.* **an·no·tat·ed, an·no·tat·ing**
To provide a text, etc. with explanatory or critical notes: *The Bible has been annotated by many scholars.*—**an'no·ta'tion** *n.*

an·nu·al (an'yōō·əl) *adj., n.*
adj. 1 Performing or occurring every year: *Independence Day is an annual holiday.* 2 Reckoned by the year: *He has an annual income of $5000.*
n. 1 A book or pamphlet issued once a year: *a photography annual.* 2 A plant that lives for only a single year or season.—**an'nu·al·ly** *adv.*

an·nu·i·ty (ə·n(y)ōō'ə·tē) *n.,* **an·nu·i·ties** *pl.*
1 Money paid yearly or at specified periods: *The widow receives an annuity from her husband's estate.* 2 The right to receive or the obligation to pay such money.

an·nul (ə·nul') *v.* **an·nulled, an·nul·ling**
1 To make null or declare invalid: *to annul a marriage.* 2 To put an end to something: *His mother annulled his fears.*—**an·nul'ment** *n.*
Syn. 1 nullify, cancel, void. 2 obliterate, abolish, annihilate.

a·nom·a·lous (ə·nom'ə·ləs) *adj.*
Deviating from the ordinary rule or condition or from what would normally be expected; unusual: *The incorruptible politician was an anomalous person in the graft-ridden city.*
Syn. abnormal, atypical, aberrant.
Ant. normal, usual, typical.

a·nom·a·ly (ə·nom'ə·lē) *n.,* **a·nom·a·lies** *pl.*
1 Deviation from the common rule, type, or form; irregularity. 2 Anything anomalous: *The platypus, an egg-laying mammal, is an anomaly.*
Syn. 1, 2 peculiarity, abnormality.

a·non·y·mous (ə·non'ə·məs) *adj.*
1 Having no acknowledged name; bearing no name: *the anonymous hordes of the poor.* 2 By or from someone whose name is unknown: *The famous poet wrote an anonymous poem.*—**a·non'y·mous·ly** *adv.*

an·te·bel·lum (an'tē·bel'əm) *adj.*
Before the war, especially before the Civil War in the U.S.: *There were many large cotton plantations in the ante-bellum South.*

an·te·date (an'ti·dāt') *v.* **an·te·dat·ed, an·te·dat·ing**
1 To be or occur earlier than: *The sword antedates the gun.* 2 To assign to a date earlier than the actual one: *to antedate a check.*
Syn. 1 precede, preexist. 2 predate.
Ant. 1 follow, come after. 2 postdate.

an·thro·poid (an'thrə·poid) *adj., n.*
adj. Like a human being in form or in other characteristics; manlike: *The gorilla is an anthropoid ape.*
n. A manlike ape, such as the chimpanzee.

an·thro·pol·o·gy (an'thrə·pol'ə·jē) *n.*
1 The science that deals with the physical, social, and cultural development of man, his origin, evolution, and geographic distribution. 2 The study of the customs, and folkways of an ethnic group.—**an'thro·pol'o·gist** *n.*

an·thro·po·mor·phic (an'thrə·pō·môr'fik) *adj.*
Described or thought of as having human form and human characteristics: used in referring to a deity or to any being that is not human.—**an'thro·po·mor'phism** *n.*

an·tic·i·pate (an·tis'ə·pāt) *v.* **an·tic·i·pat·ed, an·tic·i·pat·ing**
1 To look forward to or expect: *to anticipate a pleasant vacation.* 2 To foresee: *Science-fiction writers have long anticipated flights to the Moon.* 3 To act or arrive sooner than, especially so as to forestall: *to anticipate the enemy's next move.*—**an·tic'i·pa'tion** *n.*
Syn. 1 await, hope for.

an·ti·mo·ny (an'tə·mō'nē) *n.*
A silver-white, hard metallic element used in making alloys, and in medicine and the arts.

an·tip·a·thy (an·tip'ə·thē) *n.*, **an·tip·a·thies** *pl.*
1 A feeling of aversion or dislike: *an antipathy to greasy foods.* 2 A person or thing that causes such aversion or dislike.
Syn. 1 hatred, loathing.
Ant. 1 liking, preference.

an·ti·quar·y (an'ti·kwer'ē) *n.*, **an·ti·quar·ies** *pl.*
A person who collects, deals in, or studies antiques and very ancient relics.

an·ti·sep·tic (an'tə·sep'tik) *adj.*, *n.*
adj. Preventing or counteracting the growth of germs so that infection is stopped: *the antiseptic action of iodine.*
n. Any substance having antiseptic qualities: *Medical alcohol is a widely used antiseptic.*
Syn. *n.* disinfectant.

an·tith·e·sis (an·tith'ə·sis) *n.*, **an·tith·e·ses** *pl.*
1 The direct opposite; a strong contrast: *Pleasure is the antithesis of pain.* 2 Opposition, contrast: *the antithesis of cold and hot.*
Syn. 1, 2 reverse, converse.
Ant. 1, 2 agreement, accord.

anx·i·e·ty (ang·zī'ə·tē) *n.*, **anx·i·e·ties** *pl.*
1 An uneasy or fearful feeling: *He has great anxiety about his health.* 2 Great eagerness: *his anxiety to be successful.*
Spelling tip: Remember that this word is spelled with an *x* that is actually pronounced *gz.*

A·pach·e (ə·pach'ē) *n.*, **A·pach·es** or **A·pach·e** *pl.*
A member of a group of North American Indians living in southern and southwestern parts of the U.S. and famous as warriors.

ap·a·thet·ic (ap'ə·thet'ik) *adj.*
Lacking emotion; indifferent: *Many people are apathetic about current events.*—**ap'a·thet'i·cal·ly** *adv.*
Syn. uninterested, unconcerned, passive.
Ant. excited, interested, aware.

ap·a·thy (ap'ə·thē) *n.*
1 Lack of emotion: *the apathy of a depressed person.* 2 Lack of interest; indifference: *the apathy toward religion in modern times.*

Syn. 1 insensibility. 2 unconcern, coolness, neutrality.
Ant. 1 feeling, excitement, sensitivity. 2 interest, concern, involvement.

a·per·ture (ap'ər·chŏŏr *or* ap'ər·chər) *n.*
An opening or gap, as between sections of a solid object: *an aperture between her front teeth.*
Syn. space, hole.

a·pex (ā'peks) *n.*, **a·pex·es** or **ap·i·ces** (ap'ə·sēz) *pl.*
1 The highest point; top: *the apex of a pyramid.* 2 A climax: *His election to the Presidency was the apex of his career.*
Syn. 1 pinnacle, summit. 2 culmination, high point, acme.
Ant. 1 base, foot. 2 nadir.

a·pi·ar·y (ā'pē·er'ē) *n.*, **a·pi·ar·ies** *pl.*
A place where bees are kept.

a·plomb (ə·plom' *or* ə·plum') *n.*
Assurance, self-confidence: *She acted with aplomb in the most difficult social situations.*
Spelling tip: Watch the silent *b.*
Syn. poise, self-possession, calmness.
Ant. discomposure, confusion, embarrassment.

a·poc·a·lyp·tic (ə·pok'ə·lip'tik) *adj.*
Of, like, or having to do with a revelation: *a sermon with almost apocalyptic overtones.*
Syn. prophetic, revelatory.

a·poc·ry·phal (ə·pok'rə·fəl) *adj.*
Having little or no authenticity: *He told an apocryphal story about lassoing a grizzly bear.*
Etymology: This word is derived from *Apocrypha,* the name for a group of books included in some versions of the Old Testament. (The Apocrypha is not included in others because it is considered unauthenticated.)
Syn. questionable, spurious, dubious.
Ant. authentic, genuine, reliable.

ap·o·gee (ap'ə·jē) *n.*
1 The point in the orbit of a celestial body, such as the Moon or an artificial satellite, that is farthest from the Earth. 2 Figuratively, the highest or farthest point: *at the apogee of his career.*
Syn. 2 culmination, apex, climax.

a·pol·o·gy (ə·pol'ə·jē) *n.*, **a·pol·o·gies** *pl.*
1 A statement or explanation expressing regret for some error or offense. 2 A justification or defense, either written or spoken: *to offer an apology for one's philosophy of life.* 3 A poor substitute: *The snack was only an apology for a full meal.*

a·pos·ta·sy (ə·pos'tə·sē) *n.*, **a·pos·ta·sies** *pl.*
Desertion of one's faith, religion, party, principles, etc.

a·pos·tle (ə·pos'əl) *n.*
1 A preacher or missionary, as one of Christ's twelve disciples. 2 An early or important advocate of a cause: *one of the apostles of the ban-the-bomb movement.*
Syn. 1 evangelist, revivalist. 2 espouser, promoter, supporter.

a·pos·tro·phe (ə·pos′trə·fē) *n.*
1 A symbol (′) used to mark the omission of a letter or letters, or to indicate the possessive case, as in *Gene's house.* **2** A digression from a discourse, consisting of an address to an imaginary or absent person: *The speaker stirred us with an apostrophe to Lincoln.*

a·poth·e·car·y (ə·poth′ə·ker′ē) *n.,* **a·poth·e·car·ies** *pl.*
A person who sells drugs and fills prescriptions.
Syn. druggist, pharmacist.

ap·pal·ling (ə·pô′ling) *adj.*
Causing dismay, horror, or terror: *the appalling devastation of Hiroshima.*—**ap·pal′·ling·ly** *adv.*
Spelling tip: Remember that the root word, *appall,* has two *a*'s, two *p*'s, and two *l*'s.
Syn. frightful, shocking, horrifying.

ap·pa·ra·tus (ap′ə·rā′təs *or* ap′ə·rat′əs) *n.,* **ap·pa·ra·tus** (rarely) **ap·pa·ra·tus·es** *pl.*
A device or machine, or group of tools, appliances, instruments, etc., used for a particular purpose: *the complicated apparatus necessary to heat a large office building.*
Syn. appliance, equipment, mechanism.

ap·par·ent (ə·par′ənt *or* ə·pâr′ənt) *adj.*
1 Easily perceived by the mind or the eyes: *It was apparent that he was bluffing.* **2** Seeming, as opposed to real or true: *apparent optimism despite failure.*—**ap·par′ent·ly** *adv.*
Spelling tip: Watch the two *p*'s and the *e* in this word.
Syn. **1** obvious, self-evident. **2** ostensible.
Ant. **1** concealed, hidden. **2** actual, genuine.

ap·pa·ri·tion (ap′ə·rish′ən) *n.*
1 A visual appearance of a disembodied spirit: *periodic sightings of a weird apparition in the deserted castle.* **2** Anything that appears, especially if it is remarkable or startling: *Her talent was a glorious apparition in a child of such ordinary parents.*
Syn. **1** ghost, phantom. **2** phenomenon, marvel, wonder.

ap·pease (ə·pēz′) *v.* **ap·peased, ap·peas·ing**
1 To make calm or peaceful, especially by conceding something or giving into demands: *Conciliatory moves by management tend to appease strikers.* **2** To satisfy or cause to subside: *Appease your thirst with iced tea.*
Syn. **1** placate, soothe, pacify. **2** lessen, alleviate, ease.
Ant. **1** aggravate, worsen, irritate. **2** intensify, increase, magnify.

ap·pel·la·tion (ap′ə·lā′shən) *n.*
A name or title, especially an added or identifying name as a nickname, pseudonym, etc., that is separate and distinct from a proper name: *The appellation of King Richard I was Richard the Lion Hearted.*
Syn. designation, moniker, cognomen.

ap·pend (ə·pend′) *v.*
To add or attach, as something subordinate or supplemental: *to append a series of footnotes.*

ap·pen·dage (ə·pen′dij) *n.*
Anything that is added or attached to something larger or more important, as a leg to a torso or a leaf to a tree.
Syn. addition, accessory, supplement.

ap·pen·dix (ə·pen′diks) *n.,* **ap·pen·dix·es** or **ap·pen·di·ces** (ə·pen′də·sēz) *pl.*
1 An addition or appendage, as of supplementary matter at the end of a book. **2** A slender wormlike structure, three to six inches long, that protrudes from the large intestine in man and in certain other animals.
Usage: Both plurals are acceptable for this word, but *appendixes* is probably more common.
Syn. **1** addendum, postscript, supplement.

ap·pli·ca·tion (ap′li·kā′shən) *n.*
1 A substance that is placed on someone or something, or the act of putting it there: *the application of furniture polish.* **2** A written or formal request, especially for a job, or the act of making such a request: *Submit your application to the personnel manager.* **3** Employment for a special purpose or use: *the industrial applications of theoretical chemistry.* **4** Close attention to a task, etc.; diligence: *application to one's studies.*

ap·por·tion (ə·pôr′shən) *v.*
To divide and give out proportionally or in keeping with some rule: *to apportion your time between various tasks.*—**ap·por′tion·ment** *n.*
Syn. allot, prorate, allocate.

ap·prais·al (ə·prā′zəl) *n.*
1 An official valuation, as for sale, taxation, etc.: *appraisal of jewelry.* **2** An act of judging the amount, quality, or worth of something: *Because of his favorable appraisal of the secretary's skills, he hired her.*
Syn. **1, 2** evaluation, estimate, assessment.

ap·praise (ə·prāz′) *v.* **ap·praised, ap·prais·ing**
1 To make an official valuation of; set a price or value on: *to appraise a painting.* **2** To estimate the amount, quality, or worth of: *to appraise a current crop of novels in a newspaper review.*—**ap·prais′a·ble** *adj.,* **ap·prais′er** *n.*
Syn. **1** evaluate, value, assess. **2** judge.

ap·pre·ci·ate (ə·prē′shē·āt) *v.* **ap·pre·ci·at·ed, ap·pre·ci·at·ing**
1 To be fully aware of the value, importance, etc. of; understand or enjoy: *to appreciate classical music.* **2** To be keenly aware of or sensitive to: *to appreciate the gravity of another's problems.* **3** To feel gratitude for: *I appreciate your kindness.* **4** To become or make more valuable: *Real estate appreciates as a city grows.*—**ap·pre′ci·a′tion** *n.*
Syn. **1** esteem, cherish. **2** recognize, understand.
Ant. **4** depreciate, cheapen.

ap·pre·hend (ap′ri·hend′) *v.*
1 To capture or take into custody; arrest: *The FBI apprehended the kidnaper.* **2** To understand the meaning of; grasp: *to apprehend the difference between right and*

wrong. **3** To expect with anxiety; dread: *to apprehend the difficulties inherent in a new job.*

ap·pre·hen·sive (ap'rə·hen'siv) *adj.*
Fearful concerning the future: *apprehensive about his next day's appointment with the dentist.*—**ap'pre·hen'sive·ly** *adv.*, **ap'pre·hen'sive·ness** *n.*
Syn. anxious, worried, uneasy, afraid.
Ant. confident, composed, courageous, fearless.

ap·prise (ə·prīz') *v.* **ap·prised, ap·pris·ing**
To notify, as of some event: *to be apprised of a friend's enagement.*
Syn. inform, tell, advise.

ap·pro·pri·ate (ə·prō'prē·it *adj.*, ə·prō'prē·āt *v.*) *adj.; v.* **ap·pro·pri·ated, ap·pro·pri·at·ing**
adj. Suitable or belonging, as to some person, circumstance, or place: *Are miniskirts appropriate for women over fifty?*
v. **1** To set apart for a particular use: *Congress appropriated funds for disaster areas.* **2** To take for one's own use without permission: *Don't appropriate someone else's property—ask and you may receive.*—**ap·pro'pri·ate·ly** *adv.*, **ap·pro'pri·ate·ness** *n.*
Syn. *adj.* proper, relevant. *v.* **1** allot. **2** steal.
Ant. *adj.* unfit, improper.

ap·pro·pri·a·tion (ə·prō'prē·ā'shən) *n.*
1 A sum of money allotted, as by legislation, for a specified use, or the act of allotting: *an appropriation of millions for the space program.* **2** The act of taking possession, as of something belonging to someone else: *his daughter's appropriation of his white shirt.*

ap·prox·i·mate (ə·prok'sə·mit *adj.*, ə·prok'sə·māt *v.*) *adj.; v.* **ap·prox·i·mated, ap·prox·i·mat·ing**
adj. Nearly exact, accurate, or like: *The reporter wrote down the approximate wording of the speech.*
v. To come near to; approach: *His income approximates $10,000 annually.*—**ap·prox'i·mate·ly** *adv.*, **ap·prox'i·ma'tion** *n.*

ap·ro·pos (ap'rə·pō') *adj.*, *adv.*
adj. Suited to the time, place, or occasion: *Condolences are not apropos at a wedding.*
adv. At the proper time or in the proper way: *He spoke quite apropos.*
Usage: *Apropos of* is a phrase meaning *with reference to* or *in regard to: Apropos of our next meeting, remember to bring a present for an orphan.*
Syn. *adj.* pertinent, appropriate. *adv.* pertinently, appropriately.
Ant. *adj.* inopportune, irrelevant. *adv.* inopportunely, irrelevantly.

apt (apt) *adj.*
1 Having a natural or habitual tendency: *An idle person is apt to get into mischief.* **2** Quick to learn: *Your ability to read and remember will make you an apt student.* **3** Suitable, as to some specific purpose or occasion: *He made apt comments on the previous speaker's suggestions.*—**apt'ly** *adv.*, **apt'ness** *n.*
Syn. **1** liable, likely. **2** intelligent, bright. **3** pertinent, relevant.

Ant. **1** unlikely. **2** dull, incompetent. **3** impertinent, irrelevant.

ap·ti·tude (ap'tə·t(y)ōod) *n.*
Natural ability or capacity to learn or become proficient: *an aptitude for business.*
Syn. gift, genius, talent, faculty.

a·quar·i·um (ə·kwâr'ē·əm) *n.*, **a·quar·i·ums** or **a·quar·i·a** (ə·kwâr'ē·ə) *pl.*
1 A tank, pond, or the like, for the exhibition or study of aquatic animals or plants. **2** A public building containing such an exhibition.

a·quat·ic (ə·kwat'ik *or* ə·kwot'ik) *adj.*
1 Living or growing in or near water: *Sea gulls are aquatic birds.* **2** Performed on or in water: *Water-skiing is an aquatic sport.*
Spelling tip: Remember that whenever *q* appears in an English word it is always followed by *u.*
Syn. **1** marine.

aq·ui·line (ak'wə·līn *or* ak'wə·lin) *adj.*
1 Of or like an eagle. **2** Curving or hooked, like an eagle's beak: *an aquiline nose.*
Syn. **2** bent, beaklike.

ar·a·ble (ar'ə·bəl) *adj.*
Capable of being plowed or cultivated: *Rocky soil is usually not arable.*

ar·bi·ter (är'bə·tər) *n.*
1 A chosen or appointed judge or umpire, as between parties in a dispute. **2** A person or agency with absolute and final power of judgment or decision: *Which magazine do you consider the final arbiter of women's fashions?*—**ar'bi·tress** *n.fem.*
Syn. **1** referee, mediator. **2** authority, expert.

ar·bit·ra·ment (är·bit'rə·mənt) *n.*
1 The act of deciding or judging as an arbiter; arbitration: *submitting the labor dispute to arbitrament.* **2** The decision of an arbiter. Also **ar·bit're·ment** *n.*
Syn. **1** mediation, conciliation. **2** award, determination.

ar·bi·trar·y (är'bə·trer'ē) *adj.*
1 Based merely on one's own opinion, judgment, prejudice, etc.: *When he finally learned all the facts he regretted his arbitrary decision.* **2** Bound by no law or rules: *an arbitrary dictator.* —**ar'bi·trar'i·ly** *adv.*, **ar'bi·trar'i·ness** *n.*
Syn. **1** capricious. **2** absolute, despotic.
Ant. **1** reasonable. **2** restricted, limited.

ar·bi·trate (är'bə·trāt) *v.* **ar·bi·trat·ed, ar·bi·trat·ing**
1 To act or decide as an arbiter: *to arbitrate the dispute between two major world powers.* **2** To submit to or settle a dispute by arbitration.
Syn. **1** judge, umpire, referee.

arc (ärk) *n.*
1 A part of a curve, especially a part of a circle. **2** Something having the shape of an arch, bow, or similar curve: *the arc of the rainbow.*

ar·cade (är·kād') *n.*
1 A series of arches with supporting columns or piers. **2** A roofed passageway or street,

especially one having shops, etc., opening from it.

ar·cane (är·kān') *adj.*
Secret; hidden: *The origin of rain was arcane to early Indians.*
Syn. mysterious, obscure.
Ant. commonplace, familiar.

ar·cha·ic (är·kā'ik) *adj.*
1 Belonging to an earlier period and no longer in common use, as a word or phrase: *"Methinks" is an archaic word.* 2 Belonging to a former time; antiquated: *an exhibition of archaic pottery.*
Spelling tip: Remember the silent *h.*
Syn. 1 old-fashioned, obsolete. 2 primitive, ancient.
Ant. 1 current, new. 2 modern.

ar·che·ol·o·gy (är'kē·ol'ə·jē) *n.*
The study of history through examination of the remains of early human cultures as discovered chiefly in excavations.—**ar'che·ol'o·gist** *n.,* **ar'che·o·log'i·cal** *adj.*
Spelling tip: This word may also be spelled *archaeology.*

ar·che·type (är'kə·tīp) *n.*
A first model, form, or pattern from which others are derived or copied: *Daniel Boone was the archetype of American frontiersmen.*
Syn. ideal, prototype.

ar·chi·pel·a·go (är'kə·pel'ə·gō) *n.,* **ar·chi·pel·a·goes** or **ar·chi·pel·a·gos** *pl.*
1 A group of many islands: *The Aleutian Islands are an archipelago off the Alaskan coast.* 2 A sea with many islands in it: *The Aegean Sea is known as "the Archipelago."*

ar·chi·tect (är'kə·tekt) *n.*
A person who designs and draws up the plans for buildings.—**ar'chi·tec'ture** *n.*

ar·chives (är'kīvz) *n.pl.*
1 A place where public records and historical papers are kept: *Only authorized personnel are allowed in the archives.* 2 Such records and papers: *The Jefferson archives became the property of the university.*

arc·tic (ark'tik or är'tik) *n., adj.*
n. 1 (Usually capital *A*) The region around the North Pole. 2 *Usually pl.* Warm, waterproof overshoe.
adj. 1 (Usually capital *A*) Of or living in the North Pole region: *Polar bears are Arctic animals.* 2 Extremely cold; freezing: *The soldiers had to endure the arctic temperatures.*
Spelling tip: Remember the two *c*'s in this word.

ar·dor (är'dər) *n.*
Strong emotion or enthusiasm: *He spoke of his country with the ardor of a true patriot.*
Syn. passion, fervor, zeal.

ar·du·ous (är'jōō·es) *adj.*
Difficult to do or achieve: *Climbing a mountain is an arduous task.*
Syn. hard, strenuous, laborious.
Ant. easy, facile.

ar·id (ar'id) *adj.*
1 Without moisture; dry: *the arid wastelands of Nevada.* 2 Without interest; dull: *The*

campaign was a series of arid, uninformative speeches.
Syn. 1 barren, parched. 2 monotonous.

a·ris·to·crat (ə·ris'tə·krat or ar'is·tə·krat') *n.*
A person who has the opinions, manners, or appearance of a privileged or upper class: *There were few aristocrats among the early pioneers.*—**a·ris'to·crat'ic** *adj.,* **a·ris'to·crat'·i·cal·ly** *adv.,* **ar'is·toc'ra·cy** *n.*
Syn. noble.
Ant. peasant.

a·rith·me·tic (ə·rith'mə·tik) *n.*
The study or technique of working with numbers, mainly in addition, subtraction, division, and multiplication.

ar·ma·da (är·mä'də) *n.*
1 A fleet of warships; specifically, the Armada, the fleet sent by Spain to battle the English in 1588. 2 A large number of things, especially moving things such as vehicles: *An armada of tanks led the attack.*

ar·mi·stice (ar'mə·stis) *n.*
An agreement to stop fighting for a short time: *During the armistice the two sides held peace talks.*
Spelling tip: Note the *i* in the second syllable.
Syn. truce.

ar·o·mat·ic (ar'ə·mat'ik) *adj.*
Having a sweet or spicy smell: *an aromatic blend of tobacco.*

ar·raign (ə·rān') *v.*
To call into court to answer to a charge or accusation: *The prisoner will be arraigned tomorrow.*—**ar·raign'ment** *n.*
Spelling tip: Remember the silent *g.*

ar·rant (ar'ənt) *adj.*
Out-and-out; thorough (used in a negative sense): *arrant nonsense; arrant fool.*
Syn. downright, utter.

ar·riv·al (ə·rī'vəl) *n.*
1 The act of arriving: *We awaited his arrival.* 2 A person or thing that arrives: *Welcome the new arrivals in your community.*

ar·ro·gant (ar'ə·gənt) *adj.*
Excessively proud and overbearing, or characterized by such excessive pride: *The dictator was an arrogant man.*
Syn. insolent, presumptuous, disdainful.
Ant. diffident, humble, meek.

ar·ro·gate (ar'ə·gāt) *v.*
Take or claim unjustly: *The chairman arrogated power to himself from the start.*
Syn. assume, usurp, appropriate.
Ant. delegate.

ar·ti·cle (är'ti·kəl) *n.*
1 An individual item: *an article of clothing.* 2 A literary composition: *a good article on bridge.* 3 In the English language, the words *a, an,* and *the,* used to make a noun definite (*the* chair) or indefinite (*a* chair, *an* ottoman).
Spelling tip: Be sure to put an *i* in this word.
Syn. 1 piece, object.

ar·tic·u·late (är·tik'yə·lit *adj.,* är·tik'yə·lāt *v.*) *adj.; v.* **ar·tic·u·lat·ed, ar·tic·u·lat·ing**
adj. 1 Able to speak, especially having the power to express thoughts clearly: *Martin*

Luther King, Jr., was an articulate defender of human rights. **2** Using clear and distinct words or syllables: *too shocked for articulate speech.*
v. **1** To speak distinctly: *too frightened to articulate.* **2** To say or tell in words: *to articulate your feelings.*

ar·ti·fact (är′tə·fakt) *n.*
An object—usually a simple one such as a tool, ornament, or container—made by human work: *Archeologists discovered crude Indian shovels and other simple artifacts.*

ar·ti·fice (är′tə·fis) *n.*
A sly or clever trick: *He used every artifice to conceal his motive.*
Syn. device, wile, ruse.

ar·ti·san (är′tə·zən) *n.*
A trained or skilled workman: *Indian artisans produce lovely silver jewelry.*
Syn. craftsman.

as·bes·tos (as·bes′təs *or* az·bes′təs) *n., adj.*
n. A grayish-white mineral that will not burn.
adj. Woven of or containing this mineral: *asbestos shingles.*
Spelling tip: Put a different vowel in each syllable—*a, e, o.*

as·cent (ə·sent′) *n.*
The act of rising or climbing: *the ascent of the rocket as it left its launch pad.*

as·cer·tain (as′ər·tān′) *v.*
To find out for certain; make sure of: *an investigation to ascertain the facts.*
Syn. discover.

as·cet·ic (ə·set′ik) *n., adj.*
n. One who chooses to live without comfort and pleasure, usually for religious reasons.
adj. Severely simple: *He led a lonely, ascetic existence.*—**as·cet·i·cism** (ə·set′ə·siz′əm) *n.*
Syn. *adj.* austere, self-denying, rigid.
Ant. *n.* sybarite.

a·sep·tic (ə·sep′tik *or* ā·sep′tik) *adj.*
Free from infection-causing bacteria: *Sterilized instruments are aseptic.*
Syn. clean
Ant. dirty, polluted.

a·skance (ə·skans′) *adv.*
1 With distrust: *Farmers look askance at city slickers.* **2** With a side glance: *She looked askance at the mirror as she hurried by.*

as·per·sion (ə·spûr′zhən *or* ə·spûr′shən) *n.*
A false or damaging report or remark: *Do not cast aspersions on his good name.*
Syn. slander, defamation.
Ant. praise.

as·phalt (as′fôlt *or* as′falt) *n.*
A dark, tarlike substance mixed with rock or sand to make paving or roofing material.

as·phyx·i·ate (as·fik′sē·āt) *v.* **as·phyx·i·at·ed, as·phyx·i·at·ing**
Suffocate: *Two firemen were asphyxiated by the smoke.*—**as·phyx′i·a′tion** *n.*

as·pir·ant (ə·spīr′ənt *or* as′pər·ənt) *n.*
A person who tries to achieve honors, high position, etc.: *There are many aspirants for each West Point appointment.*
Syn. candidate.

as·pi·ra·tion (as′pə·rā′shən) *n.*
Great hope or high ambition: *His lifelong aspiration was to visit his homeland.*

as·sail (ə·sāl′) *v.*
1 To attack violently, as by words or blows: *The mayor was assailed with every form of ridicule and abuse.* **2** To approach a difficulty, task, etc., with the intent of mastering it: *She assailed the dirty windows.*
Syn. **1** assault, bombard. **2** tackle.
Ant. **1** aid, uphold.

as·sas·sin (ə·sas′in) *n.*
A murderer, especially a fanatic or a person hired to kill another: *Assassins have killed four U.S. Presidents.* **as·sas′si·na′tion** *n.*
Spelling tip: Remember to put four *s*'s in this word.
Syn. killer, slayer.

as·sem·bly (ə·sem′blē) *n.,* **as·sem·blies** *pl.*
1 A group of persons who have met together: *an assembly of the townspeople.* **2** The act of fitting together the individual parts of a machine, etc.: *the manufacture and assembly of automobiles.*
Spelling tip: Note the *s* in the first two syllables, and note how the spelling changes for the plural.
Syn. **1** meeting, gathering, assemblage, mustering.

as·sent (ə·sent′) *v., n.*
v. Agree or consent: *The committee assented to the request.*
n. Agreement or consent: *He indicated his assent to the proposal.*

as·sert (ə·sûrt′) *v.*
1 State positively: *The chairman asserted that the hearing would be held in March.* **2** Insist on; defend: *Teen-agers assert their independence in various ways.*

as·sess (ə·ses′) *v.*
1 To set a value on property for taxation purposes: *Their house is assessed at $12,000.* **2** To charge with a tax, fine, or other payment, as a person or property: *Each union member was assessed $10 per month.* **3** To set the amount of, as a tax, fine, etc. **4** To determine the importance, size, or value of: *Voters should assess each candidate's qualifications.*—**as·sess′ment** *n.*
Spelling tip: Notice that this word has four *s*'s.
Syn. **1** appraise, estimate.

as·set (as′et) *n.*
1 *Often pl.* An item of property, as of a person, corporation, etc. *His assets include a house and car.* **2** Any valuable quality or thing: *Brains and ambition are great assets in business.*
Syn. **2** advantage, benefit.

as·sev·er·ate (ə·sev′ə·rāt) *v.* **as·sev·er·at·ed, as·sev·er·at·ing**
To affirm or declare emphatically or solemn-

ly: *The lawyer asseverated that his client was innocent.*—**as·sev′er·a′tion** *n.*
Syn. allege, assert, aver, protest.
Ant. deny, doubt, demur, dispute.

as·sid·u·ous (ə·sij′o͞o·əs) *adj.*
Showing or marked by constant effort and attention: *an assiduous student; assiduous research.*—**as·sid′u·ous·ly** *adv.*, **as·sid′u·ous·ness** *n.*

as·sign (ə·sīn′) *v.*
1 To set apart; designate: *Monday is assigned as washday.* **2** To appoint to a post or duty: *The reporter was assigned to the story.* **3** To allot as a task: *The teacher assigned twenty pages of reading.* **4** To ascribe or attribute: *Jealousy was assigned as the murder motive.*—**as·sign′ment** *n.*

as·sim·i·late (ə·sim′ə·lāt) *v.* **as·sim·i·lat·ed, as·sim·i·lat·ing**
1 To take into and make part of the body: *Milk is easily assimilated.* **2** To receive into the mind and understand: *to assimilate the rules of grammar.* **3** To make or to become alike or similar: *to assimilate one's way of speaking to that of one's friends.*—**as·sim′i·la′tion** *n.*
Spelling tip: Remember that *assimilate* has two *s*'s.
Syn. 2 digest, master, learn.

as·so·ci·ate (ə·sō′s(h)ē·āt *v.;* ə·sō′s(h)ē·it *n., adj.*) *v.* **as·so·ci·at·ed, as·so·ci·at·ing;** *n., adj.*
v. **1** To bring into company with another or with others, as in friendship or partnership: *to associate with the neighbors.* **2** To connect mentally: *to associate the smell of baking bread with one's childhood.*
n. One who is frequently in the company of another: *They were associates in the same office for twenty years.*
adj. **1** Joined with another or others in a common pursuit or office: *associate directors of a hospital.* **2** Having lower status or privileges: *an associate professor.*
Spelling tip: Although the third syllable is pronounced *see* or *shee*, remember that it is spelled *ci.*
Syn. *v.* 1 fraternize, mix. *n.* companion, co-worker, friend, ally, partner.
Ant. *v.* 1 reject, snub, ignore. *n.* rival, stranger, enemy, antagonist.

as·so·ci·a·tion (ə·sō′s(h)ē·ā′shən) *n.*
1 The act of joining with others. **2** Fellowship: *We enjoyed our long association with the Browns.* **3** The connection or relation of ideas, feelings, etc.: *the association of June with weddings.* **4** A group of persons united for some common purpose: *an association of lawyers.*
Syn. 2 friendship, fellowship, company, alliance. 4 society, club, league.

as·suage (ə·swāj′) *v.,* **as·suaged, as·suag·ing**
1 To make less harsh or severe: *Time will assuage his grief.* **2** To satisfy: *The cold spring water assuaged his thirst.*

as·sume (ə·so͞om′) *v.* **as·sumed, as·sum·ing**
1 To take for granted; suppose to be a fact: *I assume that he will pay back the money.* **2** To

take on or adopt (an aspect or characteristic): *The stain on the wall assumed the shape of a dragon.* **3** To undertake, as an office or duty: *to assume responsibility for another person.* **4** To pretend, feign: *The culprit assumed an air of innocence.*
Syn. 1 imagine, believe. 3 shoulder, accept. 4 sham, counterfeit.

as·sump·tion (ə·sump′shən) *n.*
1 The act of taking over: *assumption of the duties by the mayor-elect.* **2** Something that is taken for granted: *The ancient assumption that the world was flat.*

as·ter·isk (as′tər·isk) *n.*
A starlike figure (*) used in printing or writing to indicate footnotes, references, or something that has been left out.

as·ter·oid (as′tə·roid) *n., adj.*
n. Any of several hundred small planets between Mars and Jupiter.
adj. Shaped like a star.

asth·ma (az′mə) *n.*
A chronic condition of the bronchial tubes that makes breathing difficult and brings on wheezing and coughing.—**asth·mat·ic** (az-mat′ik) *n., adj.*

as·trin·gent (ə·strin′jənt) *n., adj.*
n. A substance such as alum that draws body tissues together. It is sometimes used to stop bleeding and to tighten the skin.
adj. **1** Having the ability to draw body tissues together: *an astringent lotion for the skin.* **2** Harsh; stern: *His astringent personal criticisms alienated his friends.*—**as·trin′gen·cy** *n.,* **as·trin′gent·ly** *adv.*
Syn. *adj.* 2 strict, sharp, biting.
Ant. *adj.* 2 gentle, kindly.

as·tro·naut (as′trə·nôt) *n.*
A person who travels in space.
Etymology: *Astronaut* comes from two Greek roots, *nautes* meaning sailor and *astro* meaning (among the) stars.

as·tute (ə·st(y)o͞ot′) *adj.*
Having or coming from a shrewd, clever mind: *Psychiatrists are astute observers of people. The drama critic made astute comments.*—**as·tute′ly** *adv.,* **as·tute′ness** *n.*
Syn. sharp, keen.
Ant. stupid, unintelligent.

at·om (at′əm) *n.*
1 The smallest unit of an element that is capable of existing alone or in combination, and that cannot be changed or destroyed in any chemical reaction. **2** A very small quantity or particle; the least bit: *She doesn't have an atom of common sense.*
Syn. 2 bit, iota, fragment, modicum.

a·troc·i·ty (ə·tros′ə·tē) *n.,* **a·troc·i·ties** *pl.*
1 A very evil or horrible act: *atrocities committed against civilians in wartime.* **2** Cruelty or evil: *the jailer's atrocity in dealing with his prisoners.* **3** *Informal* Something in very bad taste: *Her feathered purple hat was an absolute atrocity.*
Syn. 1 crime, outrage. 2 infamy, villainy.
Ant. 2 kindness, mercy, humanity.

at·ro·phy (at′rə·fē) *v.* **at·ro·phied, at·ro·phy·ing;** *n.,* **at·ro·phies** *pl.*
v. To waste away or cause to waste away or decline: *Prolonged bed rest will cause the muscles to atrophy. Boredom will atrophy the mind.*
n. 1 A wasting away or withering of the body or any of its parts: *the atrophy of a paralyzed arm.* 2 A stoppage of any growth or development: *the atrophy of the ancient Roman Empire.*
Syn. *v.* weaken, shrink, wane, deteriorate. *n.* 1 weakening, deterioration. 2 decline, deterioration, decay, crumbling.

at·ta·ché (at′ə·shā′) *n.*
A person officially attached to a diplomatic mission or staff for a specific assignment: *a military attaché.*

at·ten·dant (ə·ten′dənt) *n., adj.*
n. One who serves or accompanies: *the queen's retinue of attendants.*
adj. Accompanying: *a war and its attendant destruction.*
Syn. *n.* follower, servant. *adj.* associated, connected.

at·tor·ney (ə·tûr′nē) *n.*
A person empowered by another to act in his stead; especially, a lawyer: *Consult an attorney about a libel suit.*
Syn. advocate, counsel.

at·trib·ute (ə·trib′yo͞ot *v.,* at′rə·byo͞ot *n.*) *v.* **at·trib·ut·ed, at·trib·ut·ing;** *n.*
v. To consider as belonging to, resulting from, or caused by: *to attribute wisdom to old age.*
n. 1 A quality or characteristic of a person or thing: *Energy is an attribute of childhood.* 2 *In art or mythology* A distinctive mark or symbol: *Winged heels are an attribute of the Roman god Mercury.*
Syn. *v.* ascribe, impute.

at·tri·tion (ə·trish′ən) *n.*
1 A gradual wearing down or weakening: *a war of attrition; the attrition of a nation's economy.* 2 A rubbing or grinding down, as by friction: *the attrition of rocks by glaciers.*

a·typ·i·cal (ā·tip′i·kəl) *adj.*
Not typical; differing from the usual type: *Hippies exhibit atypical behavior. He had an atypical case of chickenpox.*—**a·typ′i·cal·ly** *adv.*
Syn. unusual, irregular, anomalous.
Ant. usual, regular, typical.

au·dac·i·ty (ô·das′ə·tē) *n.*
1 Boldness; daring: *The Apaches were famous for their skill and audacity as warriors.* 2 Disregard of decency or courtesy: *She had the audacity to ask how much I had paid for my dress.*
Syn. 1 bravery. 2 impudence, brazenness, nerve.

au·di·ble (ô′də·bəl) *adj.*
Loud enough to be heard: *A microphone made her voice audible to the crowd.*
Spelling tip: Remember the *i* in this word.

au·dit (ô′dit) *v., n.*
v. To make an official examination of the accounts of a business or other organization

to establish correctness: *The accounting firm audited the financial statement.*
n. An examination of accounts, as of a business or other organization, to establish correctness: *a bank audit.*

au·ger (ô′gər) *n.*
A tool for boring into wood or into the ground.

aught (ôt) *n.*
The figure zero; naught; nothing.
Spelling tip: *Aught* may also be spelled *ought.*

aug·ment (ôg·ment′) *v.*
To make or become greater, as in size, number, or amount: *He augmented his small income by driving a taxi on weekends.*
Syn. increase, enlarge.
Ant. decrease, reduce.

au·gur (ô′gər *or* ô′gyər) *n., v.*
n. A person who foretells the future.
v. To be a sign or omen of: *Her good natuer augurs lifelong popularity.*
Syn. *n.* soothsayer, prophet.

au·gust (ô·gust′) *adj.*
1 Inspiring awe or reverence; imposing: *the august beauty of the old cathedral.* 2 Of high rank or birth: *an august justice of the Supreme Court.*—**au·gust′ly** *adv.,* **au·gust′ness** *n.*
Syn. 1 majestic, stately, awesome. 2 honored, eminent.

auld lang syne (ōld′ lang sīn′ *or* ōld′ lang zīn′)
Literally, old long since; long ago.
Etymology: *Auld lang syne* is a Scottish expression popularized by the well known song of the same name, which is often sung at reunions, New Year's Eve parties, etc.

au na·tu·rel (ō nà·tû·rel′)
1 Plainly cooked; ungarnished: *potatoes served au naturel.* 2 In the natural condition; especially, in the nude: *to go swimming au naturel.*
Etymology: *Au naturel* is a French expression that literally means "naturally" or "to the life."

au·ral (ôr′əl) *adj.*
Pertaining to the ear or to the sense of hearing: *Dogs have keen aural ability.*—**au′ral·ly** *adv.*
Usage: Do not confuse *aural* with *oral,* which means of or having to do with the mouth or with speech.

au·ri·cle (ôr′i·kəl) *n.*
1 One of the upper chambers of the heart. 2 The outside part of the ear.

aus·pi·ces (ôs′pə·sēz) *n.pl.*
A guiding or favoring influence; sponsorship: *The park was built under the auspices of the city government.*
Syn. patronage.

aus·ter·i·ty (ô·ster′ə·tē) *n.,* **aus·ter·i·ties** *pl.*
1 Sternness and severity, as of conduct and appearance: *the austerity of the Puritans.* 2 *Usually pl.* Acts or practices of self-denial: *During a war people must endure many austerities.*
Syn. 1 strictness, harshness. 2 rigor, hardship.
Ant. 2 indulgence, pleasure.

au·then·tic (ô·then'tik) *adj.*
1 Genuine; not counterfeit: *an authentic painting by Rembrandt.* 2 Trustworthy; reliable: *The scholar compiled an authentic book on American Indian lore.*—**au·then'ti·cal·ly** *adv.*
Syn. 1 real, true. 2 accurate, authoritative.

au·then·ti·cate (ô·then'ti·kāt) *v.* **au·then·ti·cat·ed, au·then·ti·cat·ing**
To show or prove to be true or genuine: *an authenticated tapestry of the twelfth century.*

au·thor·i·ta·tive (ə·thôr'ə·tā'tiv) *adj.*
1 Possessing or coming from proper authority; official: *an authoritative decision, an authoritative book.* 2 Exercising or showing authority: *The warden spoke in an authoritative voice.*—**au·thor'i·ta'tive·ly** *adv.*

au·to·bi·og·ra·phy (ô'tə·bī·og'rə·fē *or* ô'tə·bē·og'rə·fē) *n.,* **au·to·bi·og·ra·phies** *pl.*
A person's written account of his own life.

au·toc·ra·cy (ô·tok'rə·sē) *n.,* **au·toc·ra·cies** *pl.*
Absolute rule by one person, or a state so ruled: *Athens became an autocracy.*—**au·to·crat** (ô'tə·krat) *n.,* **au'to·crat'ic** *or* **au'to·crat'·i·cal** *adj.,* **au'to·crat'i·cal·ly** *adv.*
Syn. tyranny, dictatorship.

au·tom·a·ton (ô·tom'ə·ton *or* ô·tom'ə·tən) *n.*
1 A self-operating machine. 2 A living thing that is or appears to be mechanical in its actions: *He was an automaton when dealing cards.*

au·ton·o·mous (ô·ton'ə·məs) *adj.*
Independent; self-governing: *The former colony became an autonomous state.*
Syn. self-determining, free.

au·top·sy (ô'top·sē *or* ô'təp·sē) *n.,* **au·top·sies** *pl.*
Examination of a human body after death, especially when ordered by a coroner.

aux·il·ia·ry (ôg·zil'yər·ē *or* ôg·zil'ər·ē) *adj., n.;* **aux·il·ia·ries** *n.pl.*
adj. Furnishing aid; subsidiary; supplementary: *He kept an auxiliary set of keys in his briefcase.*
n. Someone or something that aids or helps; assistant.
Syn. *adj.* reserve, spare, extra.

a·vant-garde (ə·vänt'gärd'; *French* à·vän'gàrd') *n., adj.*
n. The group, especially in the arts, regarded as being the most experimental: *Op art and pop art were the rage among the avant-garde.*
adj. Having to do with the bold, new, or experimental: *New novels often exhibit avant-garde tendencies.*
Etymology: In French, this word literally means *advance guard.*
Syn. *adj.* innovative, radical, far-out, extreme.
Ant. *adj.* conservative, old-fashioned, routine, traditional.

av·a·rice (av'ə·ris) *n.*
Passion for accumulating riches; greed: *Some politicians are motivated by avarice.*
Syn. covetousness, acquisitiveness.

av·a·ri·cious (av'ə·rish'əs) *adj.*
Greedy of gain: *He was an avaricious collector of paintings.*—**av'a·ri'cious·ly** *adv.,* **av'a·ri'cious·ness** *n.*
Syn. acquisitive, covetous.
Ant. generous, liberal.

a·venge (ə·venj') *v.,* **a·venged, a·veng·ing**
To inflict punishment in retaliation for an injury or offense: *He avenged his brother's murder.*
Syn. pay back, revenge.
Ant. forbear, pardon, forgive.

a·vert (ə·vurt') *v.*
1 To turn away: *She averted her eyes.* 2 To ward off: *They averted the danger.*—**a·vert'ed·ly** *adv.,* **a·vert'i·ble** *or* **a·vert'a·ble** *adj.*
Syn. 2 prevent, avoid, escape.

a·vi·ar·y (ā'vē·er'ē) *n.,* **a·vi·ar·ies** *pl.*
A large cage or enclosure for live birds.

av·id (av'id) *adj.*
1 Eager; enthusiastic: *He was an avid football fan.* 2 Greedy: *The whole family was avid for success.*
Syn. 2 gluttonous, ambitious.
Ant. 1 indifferent, uninterested.

av·o·ca·do (av'ə·kä'dō *or* a'və·kä'dō) *n.,* **av·o·ca·dos** *pl.*
The pear-shaped fruit of a West Indian tree, having a green skin and fleshy, edible pulp enclosing a single large pit.
Syn. alligator pear.

av·o·ca·tion (av'ə·kā'shən) *n.*
A casual or occasional occupation: *Her avocation was collecting stamps.*
Syn. hobby, diversion, pastime.

av·oir·du·pois (av'ər·də·poiz') *n.*
1 The system of weights in the U.S. and Britain based on the pound of sixteen ounces. 2 *Informal* Weight; corpulence: *Her figure was padded with considerable avoirdupois.*
Syn. 2 fat, bulk, flesh, adiposity.
Ant. 2 leanness, thinness, trimness.

a·vow (ə·vou') *v.*
To assert openly as fact; admit: *He avowed his part in the crime.*—**a·vow'al** *n.*
Syn. declare, acknowledge, assert.
Ant. disavow, disown, deny.

aw·ful (ô'fəl) *adj.*
1 *Informal* Exceedingly bad or unpleasant: *an awful hairdo.* 2 Terrifying; dreadful: *the awful destruction of a tornado.*
Spelling tip: If you write *awe + full,* your spelling will be awful.
Syn. 2 appalling, horrible, terrible.

awk·ward (ôk'wərd) *adj.*
Ungraceful; embarrassing; difficult or inconvenient: *an awkward movement; an awkward situation; an awkward position.*—**awk'ward·ly** *adv.,* **awk'ward·ness** *n.*

a·wry (ə·rī') *adj., adv.*
1 Toward one side: *Your cap is awry.*
2 Wrong; out of the right course: *Our picnic plans went awry because of the rain.*

ax·i·om (ak′sē·əm) *n.*
A self-evident or universally recognized truth: *It is an axiom that nature abhors a vacuum.*
Syn. theorem, law, principle, truism.

ax·i·o·mat·ic (ak′sē·ə·mat′ik) *adj.*
1 Self-evident: *It is axiomatic that two things cannot occupy the same place at the same time.* 2 Full of axioms; aphoristic: *a collection of short, axiomatic sayings.*—**ax′i·o·mat′i·cal** *adj.,* **ax′i·o·mat′i·cal·ly** *adv.*

a·zal·ea (ə·zāl′yə) *n.*
A shrub having showy red or orange flowers.
Spelling tip: Each syllable has an *a* in it, but remember to put an *e* before the final *a.*

az·ure (azh′ər) *n., adj.*
Sky blue: *His favorite color was azure. Delphiniums have azure flowers.*

B

bab·ble (bab′əl) *v.* **bab·bled, bab·bling;** *n.*
v. 1 To make inarticulate sounds: *the baby babbling in its playpen.* 2 To talk foolishly: *She babbled on about her genteel upbringing.* 3 To murmur or ripple: *The stream babbled along.*
n. 1 Inarticulate sounds. 2 Foolish talk. 3 Murmuring or rippling sound.—**bab′bler** *n.*
Syn. *v., n.* 1, 2 prattle, chatter.

bac·ca·lau·re·ate (bak′ə·lôr′ē·it) *n.*
1 A bachelor's degree. 2 An address to a graduating class at commencement.

ba·cil·lus (bə·sil′əs) *n.,* **ba·cil·li** (bə·sil′ī) *pl.*
Any of a class of rod-shaped bacteria, some of which cause diseases such as tuberculosis or tetanus.

bac·te·ri·a (bak·tir′ē·ə) *n.pl.*
One-celled microorganisms that range in their effect on other life from beneficial to lethal.
Usage: *Bacterium,* the singular form of *bacteria,* is almost never used except possibly by biologists. *Bacteria* should take a plural verb, except to designate a class, in which case a singular verb is used: *Bacteria are everywhere—in the air we breathe and in the food we eat. This bacteria is a new type.*

badg·er (baj′ər) *n., v.*
n. A small, burrowing animal with short, claw-toed legs.
v. To nag at or harass: *He badgered me into going to a football game with him.*
Syn. *v.* pester, pressure, irritate, hound.

baf·fle (baf′əl) *v.* **baf·fled, baf·fling;** *n.*
v. To confuse, bewilder, or perplex: *The unsolved crime baffled the police.*
n. A screen or partition used to control or hinder a flow, as of fluids or sound waves.

bag·a·telle (bag′ə·tel′) *n.*
1 A trifle: *He would not accept thanks for what he called a mere bagatelle.* 2 A short musical composition, often for piano.

bai·li·wick (bā′lə·wik) *n.*
1 The jurisdiction of a bailiff. 2 A person's own field of concern or scope of knowledge: *Planning the food budget is my wife's bailiwick, not mine.*

baize (bāz) *n.*
A loosely woven cloth, usually finished to resemble green felt and used for table coverings, etc.

bal·ance (bal′əns) *n.; v.* **bal·anced, bal·anc·ing**
n. 1 An instrument for weighing; scale. 2 A state of equilibrium or poise: *She lost her balance.* 3 Remainder: *They ate some of the food and gave away the balance.*
v. To bring into or keep in equilibrium: *The juggler balanced the cane on his nose.*

balk (bôk) *v., n.*
v. 1 To stop short and refuse to proceed or take action: *The donkey balked when he saw the steep cliff.* 2 To render unsuccessful; thwart: *Quick police action balked the robbery attempt.*
n. 1 A hindrance, defeat, or disappointment: *Timidity is a balk to success.* 2 In baseball, an illegal motion made by the pitcher.
Spelling tip: Be sure to write the *l* in this word, but do not pronounce it.

bal·lis·tics (bə·lis′tiks) *n.pl.*
The science concerned with the motion of projectiles and missiles, such as bullets and rockets: *The police laboratory specializes in ballistics.*

bal·loon (bə·lōōn′) *n., v.*
n. 1 A large, airtight bag that rises and floats in the air when inflated with a gas lighter than air. 2 A small rubber bag that can be inflated and used as a toy.
v. To swell out so as to resemble a balloon: *The sail ballooned in the wind.*
Spelling tip: Double the *l* and the *o.*

bal·lot (bal′ət) *n., v.*
n. The piece of paper used in casting a secret vote, or the system of voting in this way: *Governments should be changed by the ballot, not the bullet.*
v. To vote or decide by ballot: *Citizens will begin balloting today.*

balm (bäm) *n.*
1 A salve or ointment made of aromatic resins exuded by certain trees. 2 Anything that heals or soothes: *Her words were a balm to his injured feelings.*
Spelling tip: Note that this word has a silent *l,* as in *calm* and *psalm.*

ba·nal (bā′nəl or bə·nal′) *adj.*
Meaningless from overuse; trite: *His speech on brotherly love, delivered at the peak of the riot, sounded banal and out of place.*—**ba·nal·i·ty** (bə·nal′ə·tē) *n.*

bank·rupt·cy (bangk′rupt·sē or bangk′rəp·sē) *n.,* **bank·rupt·cies** *pl.*
A state in which a person is declared unable to pay his debts, and his remaining assets are divided among his creditors; financial ruin.

ban·quet (bang′kwit) *n., v.*
n. A feast or ceremonial dinner, often including speeches.
v. To entertain at a banquet: *We banqueted our visitors.* 2 To eat well: *We banqueted on caviar.*—**ban′quet·er** *n.*

ban·ter (ban′tər) *n., v.*
n. Playful ridicule: *He was amused by their banter about his late arrival.*
v. To tease or exchange remarks in good humor: *The wits at the party were bantering with each other.*
Syn. *n.* badinage, raillery, repartee, riposte. *v.* josh, twit.

bap·tize (bap·tīz′ *or* bap′tīz) *v.* **bap·tized, bap·tiz·ing**
1 To immerse a person in or sprinkle with water as a symbol of admission to Christianity. 2 To give a first name to a person as part of the baptismal ceremony: *He was baptized Robert.*
Syn. 2 christen.

bar (bär) *v.* **barred, bar·ring**
1 To fasten or secure with or as with a piece of wood, metal, etc.: *Bar the door.* 2 To obstruct or hinder: *The police barred the way.* 3 To exclude or keep out: *Women are barred from entering the men's grill.*
Spelling tip: Before adding a suffix beginning with a vowel, double the final consonant of all one-syllable words ending in a single consonant preceded by a single vowel.
Syn. 1 bolt, lock. 2 barricade. 3 blackball.
Ant. 1 unlock, unbar, unfasten. 2 open. 3 permit, allow, welcome.

barb (bärb) *n.*
1 Any sharp point that sticks out and back from a main point, as on an arrow, fishhook, spear, etc. 2 Pointedness or sting, as of wit; also, a stinging remark: *attacking political candidates with personal barbs.*

bar·ba·rous (bär′bər·əs) *adj.*
Uncivilized; savagely cruel: *the barbarous treatment of the prisoners.*
Syn. savage, coarse, brutal.

bare (bâr) *adj.* **bar·er, bar·est;** *v.* **bared, bar·ing**
adj. 1 Without clothing or covering; naked. 2 Without the usual furnishings or equipment; empty: *a bare room.* 3 Unadorned, plain: *the bare truth.* 4 Just sufficient; mere: *the bare necessities.*
v. To make uncovered or lay open: *to bare one's head; to bare one's heart.*—**bare′ness** *n.*
Spelling tip: The silent *e* that ends this word is dropped before adding a suffix beginning with a vowel.
Syn. *adj.* 1 nude, undressed. 2 unfurnished. 3 unembellished. 4 absolute, stark, sheer.
Ant. *adj.* 1 dressed, clothed. 2 full, well-stocked. 3 embellished.

ba·roque (bə·rōk′) *adj.*
1 Of or characteristic of the art and architecture of the seventeenth century, which was elaborately ornate and had curved rather than straight lines: *The building's baroque style looked out of place in the midst of modern buildings.* 2 Irregular in shape (said of pearls).
Etymology: This word is derived from the Portuguese *barroco,* which means rough or imperfect pearl.

bar·rage (bə·räzh′) *n.*
1 A curtain of gunfire designed to protect troops by impeding the movement of the enemy. 2 Any overwhelming attack, as of words or blows: *a barrage of critical comments.*

bar·ris·ter (bar′is·tər) *n.*
The British word for a member of the legal profession who argues cases in court: distinguished from *solicitor.*

bar·ter (bär′tər) *v., n.*
v. To trade goods or services for something of equal value: *The trapper bartered furs for food and supplies.*
n. The act of bartering.
Syn. *v., n.* exchange, swap.

bas-re·lief (bä′ri·lēf′ *or* bas′ri·lēf′) *n.*
A type of sculpture in which the figures project only slightly from the background.

bass (bās) *adj., n.*
adj. Very low in pitch.
n. 1 The lowest-pitched male singing voice. 2 The lowest part in vocal or instrumental music. 3 One who sings or an instrument that plays such a part.

bas·tion (bas′chən *or* bas′tē·ən) *n.*
1 In fortifications, the part of a rampart that projects so as to give a wider firing range. 2 Any fortified or strongly defended place, position, thing, etc.: *a bastion of democracy.*
—**bas′tioned** *adj.*

bathe (bāth) *v.* **bathed, bath·ing**
1 To wash or give a bath to someone else or to oneself. 2 To go into or remain in water so as to swim or cool off. 3 To apply liquid for comfort or healing: *Bathe your bruised leg.* 4 To cover or suffuse: *The garden was bathed in moonlight.*—**bathe′a·ble** *adj.,* **bath′er** *n.*

bat·tal·ion (bə·tal′yən) *n.*
1 A military unit consisting of a headquarters and two or more companies, batteries, or comparable units. 2 A large group or number: *A battalion of strikers picketed the company.*

bat·tle (bat′l) *n.; v.* **bat·tled, bat·tling**
n. A fight or struggle between hostile groups or persons: *a Congressional battle over gun-control laws.*
v. To struggle against opposition: *battle for a cause.*
Syn. *n.* conflict. *v.* fight, contend.

bau·ble (bô′bəl) *n.*
A worthless, showy trinket.
Syn. gewgaw, gimcrack, knickknack.

bay·ou (bī′ōō) *n.*
A marshy inlet or outlet of a lake, river, etc.
Usage: This word is used principally in the southern U.S.

ba·zaar (bə·zär′) *n.*
1 An Oriental market or street of shops. 2 A shop selling various kinds of merchandise. 3 A fair at which miscellaneous articles are sold, especially to raise money for charity.

be·a·tif·ic (bē′ə·tif′ik) *adj.*
Giving or expressing blessedness or bliss: *the Madonna's beatific smile.*—**be′a·tif′i·cal·ly** *adv.*
Syn. angelic, seraphic.

be·com·ing (bi·kum′ing) *adj.*
Appropriate or attractive: *a very becoming dress.*
Spelling tip: This word is derived from the verb *become.* As in most words that end in a silent *e,* that *e* is dropped when a suffix such as *-ing* is added.

beg·gar (beg′ər) *n., v.*
n. 1 A person who asks or pleads. 2 A poor person; pauper.
v. 1 To reduce to a state of poverty: *beggared by the depression.* 2 To make seem useless or inadequate: *a tragedy so terrible that it beggared description.*—**beg′gar·ly** *adv.*
Syn. *v.* 1 impoverish, ruin, bankrupt.

be·guile (bi·gīl′) *v.* **be·guiled, be·guil·ing**
1 To deceive; fool: *The get-rich-quick scheme beguiled him into investing all his money.* 2 To pass or while away pleasantly: *to beguile a summer afternoon sitting under a shady tree.* 3 To charm; divert: *The child's attempts to dance on her toes beguiled me.*—**be·guile′ment** *n.,* **be·guil′er** *n.*
Syn. 1 delude, dupe, bamboozle, trick. 3 captivate, fascinate, enchant, delight.
Ant. 3 bore, weary, displease, annoy.

be·hav·ior (bi·hāv′yər) *n.*
1 The manner in which a person conducts himself: *on good behavior.* 2 The way something or someone acts under given circumstances: *Test the behavior of a new car under optimum road conditions.*
Syn. 1 deportment, demeanor, actions, manner. 2 reaction, response, performance.

be·he·moth (bi·hē′məth *or* bē′ə·məth) *n.*
1 In the Bible, a colossal beast, probably a hippopotamus. 2 Any large beast or thing.

be·hoove (bi·hōōv′) *v.* **be·hooved, be·hoov·ing**
To be necessary, fit, or proper (used impersonally): *It behooves me to leave before I overstay my welcome.*

be·la·bor (bi·lā′bər) *v.*
1 To be concerned with or place emphasis on in an overlong, nagging, repetitious way: *He made his point early in the speech and then belabored it for an hour.* 2 To attack, especially verbally; assail: *The novel belabored phony middle-class morality.*

be·lat·ed (bi·lā′tid) *adj.*
Late or too late: *a belated note of thanks.*
Syn. delayed, slow, overdue.
Ant. early, premature.

be·lea·guer (bi·lē′gər) *v.*
1 To surround or shut in with an armed force: *The town was beleaguered for two weeks before friendly troops arrived.* 2 To beset; harass: *The widow was beleaguered by the problems of raising five children.*—**be·lea′guered** *adj.*
Syn. 1 beset, besiege. 2 badger, worry.

be·lieve (bi·lēv′) *v.* **be·lieved, be·liev·ing**
1 To accept as true or real: *I do not believe his story.* 2 To credit (a person) with having told the truth: *I believe him.* 3 To think; to suppose: *I believe he is away for the day.* 4 To have confidence: *His colleagues believe*

in him. 5 To have religious faith.—**be·liev′a·ble** *adj.,* **be·liev′er** *n.*
Spelling tip: Remember *i* before *e* except after *c* (or when sounded like *a* as in *neighbor* and *weigh.*)

belles-let·tres (bel′let′rə) *n.pl.*
Literature that is beautiful and artistic rather than informative or moralistic: *Poetry, drama, and fiction are considered belles-lettres.*

bel·li·cose (bel′ə·kōs) *adj.*
Having a tendency to fight: *a bellicose young man.*—**bel′li·cose′ly** *adv.*
Syn. pugnacious, warlike, belligerent, hostile, quarrelsome.
Ant. friendly, peaceable, amicable, gentle, pacific.

bel·lig·er·ent (be·lij′ər·ənt) *adj., n.*
adj. 1 Having or showing a tendency to fight: *His belligerent attitude consistently gets him into trouble.* 2 Having to do with or engaged in war: *the belligerent powers of World War II.*
n. A person or nation engaged in warfare or fighting.—**bel·lig′er·ent·ly** *adv.*
Syn. 1 *adj.* pugnacious, quarrelsome, hostile.

bel·ly (bel′ē) *n.,* **bel·lies** *pl.*
1 The abdomen in man and in animals with backbones. 2 Any curved or protruding line or surface: *the belly of a sail.* 3 A deep interior cavity: *the belly of a ship.* 4 The curved front piece, containing the sound holes, of a violin, viola, etc.
Usage: *Definition 1* The word *abdomen* is the scientific, formal term for *belly; stomach* is actually the internal digestive organ. Many good writers have recently begun using *belly* rather than *stomach* or *abdomen,* and *belly* may soon return to its once leading position in common usage. However, *belly* is jarring to some people, and it often suggests a large, protruding abdomen.

ben·e·dic·tion (ben′ə·dik′shən) *n.*
1 An asking of God's blessing on someone or something, as at the end of a religious service. 2 The expression of a blessing or good wishes: *He received his father's benediction before he went overseas.*
Syn. 2 approval, encouragement, sanction.
Ant. 2 curse, malediction, denunciation.

ben·ef·i·cence (bə·nef′ə·səns) *n.*
1 Goodness or kindness: *Her beneficence was manifested every day of her life.* 2 An act that reflects goodness or kindness: *a beneficence that was not fully appreciated by the recipient.*
Syn. 1 charity, benevolence, generosity, graciousness.
Ant. 1 meanness, stinginess, economy, selfishness.

be·nef·i·cent (bə·nef′ə·sənt) *adj.*
Doing good: *He was a beneficent ruler, beloved by his people.*—**be·nef′i·cent·ly** *adv.*
Syn. benevolent, charitable, humane, generous, kind, altruistic.

ben·e·fi·cial (ben′ə·fish′əl) *adj.*
Helpful: *Country air is beneficial to health.*—**ben′e·fi′cial·ly** *adv.*
Spelling tip: There is no *fish* in *beneficial.*
Syn. advantageous, useful, good, salutary.
Ant. harmful, bad, injurious, detrimental.

be·nev·o·lence (bə·nev′ə·ləns) *n.*
Kindliness or charitableness: *the benevolence of nuns in caring for the homeless.*
Syn. kindness, humaneness, philanthropy.
Ant. cruelty, destructiveness.

be·nign (bi·nīn′) *adj.*
1 Favorable or mild: *a benign influence; a benign climate.* **2** Not dangerously harmful: *a benign tumor.*
Spelling tip: Don't forget the silent *g.*

ben·zine (ben′zēn *or* ben·zēn′) *n.*
A colorless, flammable liquid derived from crude petroleum and used as a solvent, cleaner, and motor fuel.

be·queath (bi·kwēth′ *or* bi·kwēth′) *v.*
To leave as an inheritance: *In his will he bequeathed his estate to his son. Moral concepts bequeathed to us by the Victorian era.*
Syn. will, devise, transmit.

be·rate (bi·rāt′) *v.* **be·rat·ed, be·rat·ing**
To scold severely: *She berated him for his cowardice.*
Syn. upbraid, chide, censure, rebuke, reprove.
Ant. praise, acclaim, extol, laud, commend.

be·reave·ment (bi·rēv′mənt) *n.*
Loss through death of a loved one: *The young widow bore her bereavement bravely.*
Spelling tip: Remember the *a* in this word.

ber·serk (bə(r)·sûrk′ *or* bə(r)·zûrk′) *adj.*
In a frenzy of wild rage; violently destructive: *The wounded beast was berserk.*
Syn. crazy, mad, frenzied, out of control.
Ant. calm, peaceful, placid, tranquil.

berth (bûrth) *n., v.*
n. **1** A bunk or bed in a ship or train: *to sleep in the upper berth.* **2** A space where a ship may dock or anchor.
v. To bring to or provide with a place to dock.

be·siege (bi·sēj′) *v.* **be·sieged, be·sieg·ing**
1 To surround with intent to capture: *The army besieged the enemy fort.* **2** To harass or overwhelm: *Fans besieged the star with requests for autographs.*
Syn. 1 siege, beleaguer, beset, storm. **2** flood, swamp, deluge.
Ant. 1 aid, uphold, protect, defend, guard.

bes·tial (bes′chəl *or* best′yəl) *adj.*
Savage, low, and brutish, like a beast: *the bestial appetites of a supposedly civilized man; a bestial orgy.*—**bes·ti·al·i·ty** (bes′chē·al′·ə·tē) *n.*
Syn. depraved, degenerate, animalistic, vicious, degraded, base, vile, brutal.
Ant. human, civilized, refined, cultured.

be·stow (bi·stō′) *v.*
To give as a gift: *to bestow honors on a poet.*
Syn. confer, present, award.
Ant. withhold, withdraw, deny.

be·trothed (bi·trōthd′ *or* bi·trôtht′) *adj., n.*
adj. Engaged to be married: *a betrothed couple.*
n. A fiancé or fiancée: *He promised to return to his betrothed.*
Syn. *adj.* affianced. *n.* sweetheart.

bev·el (bev′əl) *n.; v.* **bev·eled** or **bev·elled, bev·el·ing** or **bev·el·ling**
n. A slanting angle, edge, or surface: *to cut or shape the end of a timber to a bevel.*
v. To cut or bring to a bevel: *to bevel the edges of a plate of glass for a car window.*

bi·an·nu·al (bī·an′yōō·əl) *adj.*
Occurring twice a year: *The biannual board meetings are held in January and July.*
Syn. semiannual.

bi·as (bī·əs) *n.,* **bi·as·es** *pl.; v.* **bi·ased** or **bi·assed, bi·as·ing** or **bi·as·sing**
n. **1** A line running slantwise across a fabric: *to cut on the bias.* **2** A prejudice: *The union showed a bias for the children of members.*
v. To prejudice: *Her bad record biased the jury against her.*
Syn. *n.* **2** leaning, inclination, predisposition. *v.* influence.
Ant. *n.* **2** impartiality, objectivity, fairness.

bi·ased (bī′əsd) *adj.*
Prejudiced: *a biased jury; a biased story of the war.*
Syn. partial, unfair, one-sided, slanted.
Ant. impartial, objective, fair.

Bi·ble (bī′bəl) *n.*
The sacred writings of Christianity, Judaism, or any other religion.
Spelling tip: The first letter of this word is always capitalized when it means sacred religious writings. It is written *bible* only when used in the broad sense of any written authority: *That guidebook was his bible while he traveled.*
Syn. Scripture, the Scriptures, the Word, Holy Writ.

bib·li·og·ra·phy (bib′lē·og′rə·fē) *n.,* **bib·li·og·ra·phies** *pl.*
1 A list of the works by a particular author or on a particular subject: *a Frost bibliography; a bibliography of nineteenth-century novels.* **2** A list of the works mentioned or consulted by a writer, given at the end of his text. **3** The detailed, technical history, description, and classification of books and texts.
Etymology: *Bibliography* comes from two Greek words: *biblion* (book) + *graphein* (to write).

bi·cam·er·al (bī·kam′ər·əl) *adj.*
Consisting of two chambers or branches: *The U.S. Congress and British Parliament are bicameral legislatures, each having an upper and a lower house.*
Etymology: *Bicameral* comes from the Latin *bi-* (two) + *camera* (chamber).

bi·cen·te·nar·y (bī·sen′tə·ner′ē) *adj., n.*
adj. Of or concerning a 200th anniversary: *a bicentenary celebration.*
n. A 200th anniversary: *The town was celebrating its bicentenary.*
Syn. bicentennial.

bi·en·ni·al (bī·en′ē·əl) *adj., n.*
adj. **1** Happening every second year: *a biennial election.* **2** Lasting or living for two years: *Cabbage is a biennial plant.*
n. A plant that produces flowers and fruit in its second year and then dies.

bi·fo·cal (bī·fō′kəl) *adj.*
Having a dual focus: said about a lens ground for both near and far vision. Eyeglasses having such lenses are called *bifocals.*

big·ot·ry (big′ə·trē) *n.*, **big·ot·ries** *pl.*
Bitter, hostile prejudice, as against a group, race, religion, etc.: *the shameless bigotry of the employers who said that immigrants need not apply.*—**big′ot** *n.*
Syn. bias, intolerance, narrow-mindedness.
Ant. impartiality, tolerance, open-mindedness.

bil·ious (bil′yəs) *adj.*
1 Caused by or affected with liver trouble: *a bilious fever; a bilious patient.* 2 Peevish in temper: *a bilious old codger.*
Syn. 2 ill-tempered, choleric, cross, irritable.
Ant. 2 amiable, sweet-tempered, good-humored.

bil·let-doux (bil′ā·dōō′ *or* bē·yā·dōō′) *n.*, **billets-doux** (bil′ā·dōōz′ *or* bē·yā·dōō′) *pl.*
A love letter: *sweethearts exchanging billets-doux.*
Etymology: *Billet-doux* comes from two French words: *doux* (sweet) and *billet* (note).
Spelling tip: When writing more than one note, add the *s* to *billet.*

bil·liards (bil′yərdz) *n.pl.*
A game played with hard balls that are hit by cues on an oblong, cloth-covered table.
Usage: Use a singular verb with this word: *Billiards is often played with three balls.*

bin·oc·u·lar (bə·nok′yə·lər) *adj.*, *n.*
adj. Of, for, or used by both eyes at once: *a binocular telescope.*
n.pl. An optical instrument consisting of two short telescopes, one for each eye: *Binoculars are used for viewing things at a distance.*
Syn. *n.* field glasses, opera glasses.

bi·og·ra·phy (bī·og′rə·fē) *n.*, **bi·og·ra·phies** *pl.*
An account of a person's life: *Sandburg's biography of Abraham Lincoln.*—**bi·og′ra·pher** *n.*
Etymology: *Biography* comes from two Greek words: *bios* (life) + *graphein* (to write).

bis·cuit (bis′kit) *n.*
A kind of bread baked in small cakes.

bisque (bisk) *n.*
A thick, creamy soup: *lobster bisque.*

bis·tro (bis′trō) *n.*
A small bar or nightclub.
Syn. tavern.

biv·ou·ac (biv′ōō·ak *or* biv′wak) *n.*; *v.* **biv·ou·acked, biv·ou·ack·ing**
n. A temporary camp, usually without shelter, especially for soldiers.
v. To camp out in a bivouac.
Spelling tip: Words ending in *c* (*mimic, picnic, frolic,* etc.) usually have a *k* inserted when adding an ending such as *-ed* or *-ing.*

bi·zarre (bi·zär′) *adj.*
Very different from what is usual or normal: *bizarre styles; bizarre art forms.*
Syn. fantastic, odd, eccentric.
Ant. common, natural, ordinary.

blan·dish·ment (blan′dish·mənt) *n.*
Flattering speech or actions: *It was difficult to resist the blandishments of the salesman.*
Syn. coaxing.
Ant. abuse, contempt.

bla·sé (blä·zā′) *adj.*
Bored: *She pretended a blasé indifference.*
Syn. weary, exhausted, jaded.
Ant. enthusiastic, keen.

blas·phe·my (blas′fə·mē) *n.*, **blas·phe·mies** *pl.*
Words or actions that deliberately mock or show contempt for sacred things, especially for God: *His blasphemies against God and country made him an outcast.*—**blas′phe·mous** *adj.*, **blas·pheme** (blas·fēm′) *v.*

bla·tant (blā′tənt) *adj.*
1 Disagreeably loud: *a blatant jukebox.* 2 Completely or crassly obvious: *Some young people show a blatant contempt for tradition.*
Syn. 1 noisy, piercing, clamorous. 2 obtrusive, brazen.
Ant. 1 quiet, subdued.

bla·zon (blā′zən) *n.*, *v.*
n. A coat of arms.
v. To make public; proclaim; display: *Colorful posters blazoned the new product from every billboard.*

bleak (blēk) *adj.*, **bleak·er, bleak·est**
Cold; dismal; barren: *a bleak coast; The future looks pretty bleak.*
Syn. cheerless, gloomy, bare.

blithe (blīth *or* blīth) *adj.*
Joyous, gay: *a blithe spirit.*—**blithe′ly** *adv.*

bloc (blok) *n.*
A group of politicians, nations, etc., formed to promote certain interests: *the farm bloc.*
Usage: *Faction, wing,* and *bloc* refer to subgroups, especially within political parties. A *faction* is often a disruptive subgroup. A *wing* is one of two directly opposed groups: *the liberal and conservative wings of the Republican party.* A *bloc* is a coalition that cuts across party lines.

bludg·eon (bluj′ən) *n.*, *v.*
n. A short club used as a weapon.
v. To strike with a bludgeon: *He was found bludgeoned to death.*

board·er (bôr′dər) *n.*
A person who pays to eat and sleep at another's house.

bode (bōd) *v.* **bod·ed, bod·ing**
To be an omen or sign of: *A motorcycle gang bodes trouble for a town.*

bois·ter·ous (bois′tər·əs *or* bois′trəs) *adj.*
Noisy and wild: *a boisterous mob.*
Spelling tip: Pronounce this word with two or three syllables, but be sure to spell it with three.

bold·face (bōld′fās′) *n.*
A printing type with thick lines to make it stand out, like **this.**

boll (bōl) *n.*
The seed pod of certain plants, as cotton.

bor·der (bôr′dər) *n.*
A margin, edge, or boundary: *The towel had a pink border.*

bouil·lon (bŏŏl'yon *or* bōōl'yən) *n.*
A clear soup made from beef, chicken, or other meats.
Syn. consommé.

bound·a·ry (boun'drē *or* boun'də·rē) *n.*, **bound·a·ries** *pl.*
A limiting or dividing line or mark: *The Mississippi River is Tennessee's western boundary.*
Spelling tip: Whether you pronounce this word with two or three syllables, be sure to spell it with three.
Syn. limit, edge, bounds.

bou·quet (bōō·kā'; *also* bō·kā' *for def.* 1) *n.*
1 A bunch of flowers. 2 Delicate aroma, especially of wine.
Syn. 1 nosegay, spray. 2 odor, scent.

bowd·ler·ize (boud'lər·īz) *v.* **bowd·ler·ized, bowd·ler·iz·ing**
To prudishly remove supposedly objectionable matter from a manuscript, etc.: *The censor bowdlerized the avant-garde movie.*
Etymology: This word comes from Dr. Thomas *Bowdler*, an English editor who in 1818 published a "family" edition of Shakespeare in which he removed all possibly offensive passages.
Syn. censor, expurgate.

brag·ga·do·ci·o (brag'ə·dō'shē·ō) *n.*, **brag·ga·do·ci·os** *pl.*
Empty boasting, or a person who engages in such boasting: *the braggadocio of a teen-ager.*

bra·va·do (brə·vä'dō) *n.*, **bra·va·does** *or* **bra·va·dos** *pl.*
A pretense of bravery: *His attempt at resistance was sheer bravado.*

bra·zen (brā'zən) *adj.*
Impudent, shameless: *Brazen defiance of the law by the rioters.*

bra·zier (brā'zhər) *n.*
A pan for holding live coals: *She heated water for tea on an antique brazier.*

breach (brēch) *n., v.*
n. A break or violation: *a breach of contract; a breach of good manners.*
v. To break through: *The troops managed to breach the enemy's defenses.*
Syn. *n.* infraction. *v.* crack, fracture.

breadth (bredth *or* bretth) *n.*
Measure of distance from side to side: *The tailor had to allow for the breadth of the athlete's shoulders.*
Syn. width, wideness, span, broadness.

breath (breth) *n.*
Air inhaled and exhaled.

breathe (brēth) *v.* **breathed** (brēthd), **breath·ing**
To inhale and exhale.
Syn. respire.

bre·vi·ar·y (brē'vē·er'ē *or* brev'ē·er'ē) *n.*, **bre·vi·ar·ies** *pl.*
(Usually capital *B*) In the Roman Catholic and Eastern Orthodox churches, a book of prayers for the canonical hours: *The young priest read his Breviary as he walked in the garden.*

brev·i·ty (brev'ə·tē) *n.*
1 Brief time: *the brevity of life.* 2 Conciseness: *Brevity is said to be the soul of wit.*
Syn. 1 shortness, transience. 2 terseness, succinctness.
Ant. 1 lengthiness. 2 wordiness.

bric-a-brac (brik'ə·brak) *n.*
Objects of curiosity or decoration: *She collected china figurines and other bric-a-brac.*
Usage: *Bric-a-brac* is a collective noun and customarily takes a singular verb: *The bric-a-brac needs dusting.*
Syn. baubles, ornaments, knickknacks.

bri·dle (brī'dəl) *n.; v.* **bri·dled, bri·dling**
n. 1 The head harness, including the bit and reins, used to guide or restrain a horse. 2 A check; restraint: *Put a bridle on your tongue, young man!*
v. 1 To put a bridle on. 2 To control or check. 3 To show anger, pride, etc., by a movement of the head: *She bridled when her friend was criticized.*

brig·and (brig'ənd) *n.*
A bandit: *The brigands of Sicily were well-organized and fierce.*
Syn. outlaw, thug, robber, desperado.

brin·dled (brin'dəld) *adj.*
Tawny or grayish in color, with irregular streaks or spots: *a brindled cat.*

bris·tle (bris'əl) *n.; v.* **bris·tled, bris·tling**
n. 1 One of the coarse, stiff hairs from a hog, used in making brushes. 2 Any similar hair, real or artificial: *the bristles of a mustache; nylon bristles on a toothbrush.*
v. 1 To be thickly set, as if with bristles: *The crowd bristled with sightseers.* 2 To stand or become erect like bristles. 3 To stiffen the bristles in anger or fright: *All at once the cat bristled.* 4 To show anger or irritation: *He always bristles when asked for money.*

Brit·ain (brit'n) *n.*
The principal island of the United Kingdom, made up of England, Scotland, and Wales.
Usage: *Britain* is a shortened form of *Great Britain.*
Spelling tip: Be careful not to confuse *Britain* with *Briton*, another name for a *Britisher* or *Englishman.*

broach (brōch) *v.*
1 To mention or suggest for the first time: *He finally broached the subject of marriage.* 2 To pierce so as to withdraw a liquid: *to broach a cask of wine.*

broad·side (brôd'sīd') *n., adv.*
n. 1 A ship's side above the water line. 2 All of the guns on one side of a warship; also, the firing of all these guns at one time. 3 A single sheet of paper printed on one side: *a broadside advertising supermarket bargains.*
adv. With the side turned or exposed: *The truck went through a red light and struck the bus broadside.*

bro·cade (brō·kād') *n.; v.* **bro·cad·ed, bro·cad·ing**
n. A rich fabric interwoven with a raised

design, often in silk or gold thread: *an evening wrap of brocade.*
v. To weave (a cloth) with a raised design or figure.

broc·co·li (brok'ə·lē) *n.*
A green variety of cauliflower, of which the sprouts and tender stalks are eaten.
Etymology: *Broccoli* comes from the Italian word *broccolo*, meaning "cabbage sprout."

bro·chure (brō·shoor') *n.*
A booklet or similar publication, without a stiff cover: *a government brochure on how to raise bees.*
Etymology: *Brochure* comes from a French word meaning "a stitched book."
Syn. pamphlet.

brogue (brōg) *n.*
A speech characteristic common to a specific region, especially an Irish accent in the pronunciation of English.
Spelling tip: Note the silent *ue* in this word.

bron·chi·al (brong'kē·əl) *adj.*
Of or pertaining to the bronchi, or chief air passages of the lungs: *bronchial pneumonia.*
Spelling tip: Many people misspell and mispronounce this word as *bron'i·chal.*

bron·chi·tis (brong·kī'tis) *n.*
Inflammation of the bronchial tubes, marked by heavy coughing.

brooch (brōch *or* brooch) *n.*
An ornamental pin with a clasp for wearing at the neck or at the shoulder of a dress: *My grandmother always wore a pearl brooch.*

brusque (brusk) *adj.*
Rough and abrupt in manner; blunt: *The doctor is a kindly man but brusque.*—**brusque'ly** *adv.,* **brusque'ness** *n.*
Syn. curt, terse, laconic, uncivil.
Ant. expansive, talkative, warm, ingratiating.

buc·ca·neer (buk'ə·nir') *n.*
A pirate, especially one who robbed along the Spanish coasts of America in the seventeenth and eighteenth centuries.

buf·foon (bu·foon') *n.*
1 A clown. 2 A person given to jokes, pranks, etc.: *At parties he always acts the buffoon.*—**buf·foon'er·y** *n.,* **buf·foon'ish** *adj.*
Syn. 2 jokester, prankster, fool.

bul·le·tin (bool'ə·tən) *n.*
1 A brief account of the news, as in a newspaper or on the radio: *Stand by for a special bulletin.* 2 A periodical publication, especially one issued by a society or organization for its members: *the medical society bulletin.* 3 A brief official statement: *a police bulletin describing the kidnaper.*

bul·lion (bool'yən) *n.*
Gold and silver in bars, which may later be made into coins: *a billion in bullion.*

bul·rush (bool'rush') *n.*
A tall, rushlike plant, growing in damp ground or shallow water: *The baby Moses was found in the bulrushes.*

bul·wark (bool'wərk) *n.*
1 A defensive wall of stone, earth, etc., built as protection against an enemy: *The soldiers crouched behind the bulwark.* 2 Any safeguard or defense: *The law is the bulwark of civilization.* 3 *Usually pl.* The raised side of a ship, above the upper deck.

bun·combe (bung'kəm) *n.*
1 *Informal* Empty speechmaking for political effect or to please constituents: *What the candidate says is pure buncombe.* 2 Any empty, foolish talk.
Etymology and spelling tip: *Buncombe,* which is often spelled *bunkum* or shortened to the more familiar *bunk,* is derived from Buncombe County, N.C., which once had a congressman who made long, windy speeches.

bun·gle (bung'gəl) *v.* **bun·gled, bun·gling;** *n.*
v. To work, make, or do (something) clumsily and unskillfully: *The robber bungled the job.*
n. An awkward or badly done job or performance: *He made a bungle of trying to go into business for himself.*—**bun'gler** *n.*
Syn. *v.* botch, mess up, muff, fail at. *n.* botch, mess, failure, flop.

buoy (boi *or* boo'ē) *n., v.*
n. 1 A floating wood or metal object moored in a sea, river, etc.; to mark a channel or dangerous rocks and shoals. 2 A life preserver.
v. 1 To keep from sinking in a liquid; keep afloat: *The child was buoyed up by water wings.* 2 To raise the courage or spirits of (usually followed by *up*): *The new hat buoyed up her spirits.*
Syn. *n.* 1 float. 2 life buoy, life jacket. *v.* 1 sustain, hold up. 2 encourage, cheer, enliven, elevate.
Ant. *v.* 2 depress, discourage, deject.

buoy·an·cy (boi'ən·sē *or* boo'yən·sē) *n.*
1 The tendency or ability to keep afloat: *the buoyancy of cork.* 2 The power of a fluid to keep an object afloat. 3 Highness of spirits; cheerfulness: *his buoyancy at finding a new job.* Also **buoy'ance** *n.*
Syn. 3 vivacity, hopefulness, jubilation.
Ant. 3 dejection, depression, discouragement.

buoy·ant (boi'ənt *or* boo'yənt) *adj.*
1 Able to stay afloat or rise up, as in a liquid or air: *Balloons filled with helium are buoyant.* 2 Gay; lighthearted: *a buoyant welcome.*
buoy'ant·ly *adv.*
Syn. 2 cheerful, happy.
Ant. 2 dejected, depressed, sad, discouraged.

bu·reau·cra·cy (byoo·rok'rə·sē) *n.,* **bu·reauc·ra·cies** *pl.*
1 Government made up of many departments or bureaus, each following definite sets of rules; also, the officials making up such bureaus. 2 Any system in which there is too much red tape and delay because of the great number of rigid rules that must be followed.

bu·reau·crat (byoor'ə·krat) *n.*
1 A member of a bureaucracy. 2 An official who narrowly and rigidly follows the rules.
—**bu'reau·crat'ic** *adj.*

bur·glar (bur'glər) *n.*
A person who breaks into and enters a

building, especially with intent to steal.—
bur′gla·ry *n.*
Syn. thief, robber.

bur·lesque (bər·lesk′) *n.; v.* **bur·lesqued, bur·les·quing**
n. **1** A theatrical entertainment with dancing, low comedy, striptease, etc. **2** A literary or dramatic work that is a comic or satiric imitation, usually of a serious, dignified subject: *a burlesque of Shakespeare's works.*
v. To imitate in a laughable or satiric way: *The students burlesqued the mannerisms of their teachers.*

bur·nish (bûr′nish) *v., n.*
v. To polish by rubbing; make or become shiny or lustrous: *to burnish leather.*
n. A lustrous or polished surface: *to protect the burnish of a table top with a sheet of glass.*
Syn. *v.* shine, buff. *n.* gloss, luster, sheen.

bur·noose (bər·nōōs′ or bûr′nōōs) *n.*
A hooded cloak worn by Arab men: *The burnoose offered protection from the fierce desert sun.*
Spelling tip: Also spelled *burnous.*

burst (bûrst) *v.* **burst, burst·ing;** *n.*
v. **1** To break open or apart suddenly and violently: *The inner tube burst.* **2** To be full to the point of breaking open: *a suitcase bursting with clothes.* **3** To give sudden expression to an emotion: *She burst into tears.* **4** To appear or enter suddenly and violently: *She burst angrily into the room.*
n. **1** A sudden exploding or breaking forth: *a burst of thunder.* **2** A sudden spurt: *a burst of speed.* **3** A crack or break: *a burst in the side of a water tank.*
Usage: *Burst* is the correct past tense and past participle of *to burst:* *The dam burst during the heavy floods. Bust* (*busted*) is an incorrect usage in any tense, but is sometimes used humorously.
Syn. *v.* **1** explode, blow up, shatter. **2** bulge, swell. **4** rush, run. *n.* **1** explosion.

busi·ness (biz′nis) *n.*
1 Any occupation, trade, or profession. **2** Any of the various operations or details of trade or industry. **3** A commercial enterprise, such as a store or factory. **4** A matter or affair: *Driving on icy streets is a dangerous business.* **5** A proper interest or concern; duty: *none of your business.*
Spelling tip: Don't confuse *business* with *busyness,* which means *being busy.*

bus·tle (bus′əl) *v.* **bus·tled, bus·tling;** *n.*
v. To move about noisily or energetically: *She bustled about the room dusting and tidying things.*
n. Excited activity; noisy stir: *the bustle of a crowded playground.*
Spelling tip: Remember to write the *t* in this word, but don't pronounce it.
Syn. *v.* fuss, flutter. *n.* commotion, flurry, haste, energy.

but·tress (but′tris) *n., v.*
n. **1** A structure built against a wall to strengthen it: *a flying buttress on a cathedral.* **2** Something that strengthens, defends, or upholds: *a buttress of world peace.*

v. **1** To support with a buttress: *to buttress a wall.* **2** To prop up; sustain: *He buttressed his arguments with facts and figures.*
Syn. *v.* **2** reinforce, strengthen.

bux·om (buk′səm) *adj.*
Plump and healthy; especially, full-bosomed: *In the 1890s buxom women were in fashion.*—
bux′om·ness *n.*
Usage: *Buxom* refers only to women.

C

ca·bal (kə·bal′) *n.*
1 A number of persons secretly united in a plot or other plan, especially one to overthrow a ruler. **2** An intrigue or plot by such a group.
Syn. 1 junta, gang. **2** scheme, conspiracy, plan, machination.

ca·ca·o (kə·kā′ō or kə·kä′ō) *n.,* **ca·ca·os** *pl.*
1 A small evergreen tree of tropical America. **2** The large seeds of this tree, used in making cocoa and chocolate.

cache (kash) *v.* **cached, cach·ing;** *n.*
v. To conceal or store in a secret place: *My grandfather cached silver dollars in an old trunk.*
n. **1** A place for hiding provisions, equipment, etc.: *An abandoned mine served as an ammunition cache.* **2** Things that are stored or hidden in a cache.
Spelling tip: It's dangerous to *cache* your *cash.* Watch the spelling of these two words that are pronounced alike but have different meanings.

ca·coph·o·ny (kə·kof′ə·nē) *n.,* **ca·coph·o·nies** *pl.*
Disagreeable or discordant sound: *the cacophony of a flock of crows.*—**ca·coph′o·nous** *adj.,* **ca·coph′o·nous·ly** *adv.*
Syn. discord, dissonance, noise, clamor, hubbub, uproar.

ca·dav·er·ous (kə·dav′ər·əs) *adj.*
Resembling a corpse in appearance; pale and gaunt: *The cadaverous face of Boris Karloff appeared in many horror films.*
Syn. deathlike, deathly, macabre, ghastly.
Ant. ruddy, wholesome, robust, hale.

ca·dence (kād′ns) *n.*
1 Rhythmic or measured flow or beat: *When the sergeant gave the order for quick cadence, the troops increased their pace.* **2** Modulation, as of the voice; intonation. **3** The falling inflection of the voice, as at the end of a sentence. **4** A melodic, harmonic, or rhythmic formula ending part of a piece of music.

cae·su·ra (si·zhŏŏr′ə) *n.,* **cae·su·ras** or **cae·su·rae** (si·zhŏŏr′ē) *pl.*
A pause or break in a line of verse, indicated by two vertical lines (‖).
Etymology: The Latin word *caesura* means cutting.

cais·son (kā′sən or kā′son) *n.*
A large chamber within which work is done underwater, as in laying bridge supports.

ca·jole (kə·jōl′) *v.* **ca·joled, ca·jol·ing**
To coax with flattery: *She begged and cajoled*

her parents *until they consented to let her go to the party.*—**ca·jol'er·y** *n.*

ca·lam·i·ty (kə·lam'ə·tē) *n.,* **ca·lam·i·ties** *pl.*
A great misfortune; disaster: *The 1966 flooding in Florence, Italy, was a calamity to the world of art, since many precious paintings were damaged and destroyed.*
Syn. debacle, catastrophe.

cal·cu·late (kal'kyə·lāt) *v.* **cal·cu·lat·ed, cal·cu·lat·ing**
1 To determine by arithmetic: *to calculate the average grade.* 2 To estimate: *to calculate the chance of failure.* 3 *Informal* To think or expect: *I calculate he'll be here next Wednesday.*—**cal'cu·la'tion** *n.*

cal·cu·la·tor (kal'kyə·lā'tər) *n.*
1 A person who calculates. 2 A calculating machine or a set of tables for computing: *a calculator that can subtract, multiply, and divide as well as add.*

cal·i·ber (kal'ə·bər) *n.*
1 The internal diameter of a tube, as of the barrel of a gun. 2 The diameter of a bullet, shell, etc. 3 Degree of worth: *a man of the highest caliber.*
Spelling tip: *Caliber* is a common U.S. spelling, but *calibre,* the only form used in Britain, is also widely used in the U.S.

cal·is·then·ics (kal'is·then'iks) *n.pl.*
Physical exercises to promote health and agility: *His morning calisthenics consisted of knee bends and toe-touching.*

ca·lix (kā'liks *or* kal'iks) *n.,* **cal·i·ces** (kal'ə·sēz) *pl.*
A cup or a cup-shaped part, especially an ecclesiastical chalice.
Etymology: *Calix* is the Latin word for cup.

cal·lig·ra·phy (kə·lig'rə·fē) *n.*
Beautiful penmanship, or handwriting in general: *Chinese calligraphy has been developed into a fine art.*—**cal·lig'ra·pher** *n.*

cal·li·o·pe (kə·lī'ə·pē *or* kal'ē·ōp) *n.*
A keyboard instrument consisting of a series of steam whistles. Also called a **steam organ.**

cal·lous (kal'əs) *adj.*
Hardened in feelings: *Don't be callous to the suffering of others.*—**cal'lous·ness** *n.*
Usage: See CALLOW.

cal·low (kal'ō) *adj.*
Inexperienced; immature.—**cal'low·ness** *n.*
Usage: A *callow* youth is an immature or inexperienced one; a *callous* soldier is one so used to cruelty or suffering as to be insensitive to it. The two words are opposite in meaning.
Syn. green, juvenile, puerile, unsophisticated.
Ant. adult, experienced, mature, sophisticated.

calm (käm) *adj.*
Quiet; still; peaceful: *He remained calm in spite of the emergency.*—**calm'ly** *adv.,* **calm'ness** *n.*
Spelling tip: Remember the *l.*
Syn. serene, tranquil, placid.
Ant. agitated, upset, disturbed.

cam·e·o (kam'ē·ō) *n.,* **cam·e·os** *pl.*
A gem, stone, or shell having a design carved in relief on one layer, with the other layers serving as background.

cam·ou·flage (kam'ə·fläzh) *n.; v.* **cam·ou·flaged, cam·ou·flag·ing**
n. Means or material used to conceal or disguise military installations, personnel, etc.
v. To hide or obscure, as with disguises.

cam·paign (kam·pān') *n., v.*
n. An organized series of events, as a military operation or a political movement, designed to achieve some end.
v. To serve in or conduct such series of events: *to campaign for Congress.*

can·a·pé (kan'ə·pē *or* kan'ə·pā) *n.*
A thin piece of toasted or fried bread spread with cheese, caviar, etc.

can·cel (kan'səl) *v.* **can·celed** *or* **can·celled, can·cel·ing** *or* **can·cel·ling**
1 To mark out or off, as by drawing lines through: *The post office cancels stamps.* 2 To make null and void; delete or withdraw: *The show was canceled (cancelled).*

can·di·date (kan'də·dāt) *n.*
One who seeks an office or honor: *a candidate for governor.*—**can·di·da·cy** (kan'də·də·sē) *n.*
Etymology: This word is derived from a Latin word meaning white, because office seekers in Rome wore white togas.

can·dor (kan'dər) *n.*
Frankness; openness: *His candor in admitting his faults surprised me.*
Syn. bluntness, honesty, candidness.
Ant. deviousness, slyness.

can·ker (kang'kər) *n.*
1 An ulceration or sore, as of the mouth. 2 Anything causing corruption, decay, etc.: *The slums were a canker in the urban environment.*—**can'ker·ous** *adj.*

can·non (kan'ən) *n.,* **can·nons** *or* **can·non** *pl.*
A large tubelike weapon that discharges a projectile by means of an explosive charge.
Spelling tip: Note the double *n.* Do not confuse this word with *canon* (rule or law), which is pronounced the same but spelled without the double *n.*

can·o·py (kan'ə·pē) *n.,* **can·o·pies** *pl.*
1 A covering suspended over a throne, bed, shrine, etc.: *Colonial beds had canopies.* 2 Any overhead covering, as the sky.

cant (kant) *n.*
1 Insincere religious or moralistic talk: *the usual cant about the need to inspire youth.* 2 Words or talk characteristic of a particular group or class: *legal cant.* 3 Whining speech, especially of beggars; or the secret slang of beggars, thieves, etc.: *I can't understand the beggar's cant.*
Spelling tip: Do not confuse this word with *can't* (cannot).
Syn. 1 hypocrisy. 2 jargon, lingo.

can't (kant) *contraction*
Cannot: *I can't hear you.*
Spelling tip: The apostrophe indicates that certain letters—in this case the *n* and *o* of *cannot*—have been omitted.

can·ta·loupe (kan'tə·lōp) *n.*
A variety of muskmelon having a sweet, orange flesh.

can·ta·ta (kən·tä'tə) *n.*
A vocal composition in the style of a short drama, to be sung but not acted.

can·ter (kan'tər) *n., v.*
n. A moderate, easy gallop.
v. To ride or go at a canter: *We cantered for a mile and then broke into a full gallop.*
Etymology: *Canter* is short for *Canterbury gallop,* derived from the pace of pilgrims riding to Canterbury.

can·vas (kan'vəs) *n.*
A heavy, closely woven cloth used for sails, tents, material on which to paint, etc.

can·vass (kan'vəs) *v., n.*
v. To go about a region or among persons to solicit votes, opinions, orders for goods, etc.: *The pollsters canvassed three typical communities for opinions on the war.*
n. The act of canvassing.—**can'vass·er** *n.*

cap·il·lar·y (kap'ə·ler'ē) *n.*, **cap·il·lar·ies** *pl.; adj.*
n. A very small blood vessel, as those connecting arteries and veins.
adj. Pertaining to or like a hair; slender or fine: *a capillary tube.*

cap·i·tal (kap'ə·təl) *n., adj.*
1 The city or town in a country, state, etc. that is the seat of government: *Washington, D.C., is the capital of the U.S. Lansing is the capital of Michigan.* **2** Wealth used to produce more wealth: *The business needs more capital to expand.* **3** The top part of a column. **4** An upper-case letter (*A* rather than *a,* etc.).
adj. **1** Chief: *the capital city.* **2** Of excellent quality: *a capital idea.* **3** Punishable by death: *a capital crime.* **4** Very injurious; grave: *a capital error.*
Spelling tip: *Capitol* (with an *o*) refers only to a legislative building—often with a dome. Thus the U.S. Congress meets in the *Capitol,* located in Washington, D.C., the nation's *capital.*

cap·i·tal·ism (kap'ə·təl·iz'əm) *n.*
An economic system depending primarily upon the private ownership of the means of production and distribution of goods.

cap·i·tol (kap'ə·təl) *n.*
1 The building in which a legislature convenes. **2** (Capital *C*) The official building of the U.S. Congress in Washington, D.C.
Spelling tip: See CAPITAL.

ca·pit·u·late (kə·pich'ŏŏ·lāt) *v.* **ca·pit·u·lat·ed, ca·pit·u·lat·ing**
To surrender, often on stipulated terms: *The enemy capitulated after being promised fair treatment.*—**ca·pit'u·la'tion** *n.*
Syn. yield, give up, give in.
Ant. hold out, resist.

ca·price (kə·prēs') *n.*
A sudden, fanciful change of mind, mood, or opinion; whim: *She bought a huge bear rug, merely out of caprice.*

ca·pri·cious (kə·prish'əs) *adj.*
Resulting from caprice: *The actions of*

diplomats must never be capricious.—**ca·pri'cious·ly** *adv.*
Syn. whimsical, fickle, fanciful.
Ant. thoughtful, reasoned, careful, deliberate.

cap·tion (kap'shən) *n.*
A heading, as of a chapter or newspaper article, or a description accompanying an illustration.

cap·tious (kap'shəs) *adj.*
Apt to find fault: *A captious critic, he would object to chapter titles if he could find nothing else to offend him.*—**cap'tious·ness** *n.*
Syn. faultfinding, nit-picking, hypercritical.
Ant. easygoing, uncritical.

car·at (kar'ət) *n.*
A unit of weight for a gem.
Usage: Be sure you don't confuse *carat, caret, carrot,* and *karat* (all pronounced the same). A *caret* (∧) is a mark that shows where additional words or letters should be inserted. A *carrot* is an edible root. A *karat* indicates the fineness or purity of gold (although sometimes *carat* is loosely used to refer to the fineness of gold). *Carat,* however, should not be confused with *karat: a one-carat diamond in a 14-karat gold setting.*

car·di·o·graph (kär'dē·ə·graf') *n.*
An instrument that records the force and character of heart movements. (The record itself is called a *cardiogram.*)

ca·ress (kə·res') *n., v.*
n. A tender, loving touch: *the caress of her hand.*
v. To touch, embrace, or fondle lovingly and gently: *The breeze caressed the trees.*

Car·ib·be·an (kar'ə·bē'ən or kə·rib'ē·ən) *n.*
A sea in the Atlantic Ocean that touches on the West Indies and on Central and South America.

car·i·ca·ture (kar'i·kə·chŏŏr) *n.; v.* **car·i·ca·tured, car·i·ca·tur·ing**
n. **1** A portrayal that uses exaggeration or distortion to ridicule or provoke wry amusement: *The cartoon caricature emphasized the candidate's double chin.* **2** An inept likeness or rendition: *The corrupt jury made a caricature of justice.*
v. To represent so as to make ridiculous: *He caricatured his opponent's views.*—**car'i·ca·tur'ist** *n.*

car·il·lon (kar'ə·lon or kə·ril'yən) *n.*
1 A set of bells on which melodies can be played, often by hammers connected to a keyboard. **2** An organ stop imitating bells.

car·nage (kär'nij) *n.*
A mass or wanton killing of people: *the carnage of battle.*
Syn. massacre, slaughter, butchery.

car·niv·o·rous (kär·niv'ə·rəs) *adj.*
Meat-eating: *Wolves are carnivorous animals.*

carp (kärp) *v.*
To find fault in a harsh, unreasonable, insistent way: *His wife kept carping about his low salary.*
Syn. nag, criticize, deplore.
Ant. praise, applaud, flatter.

car·riage (kar'ij) *n.*
1 A wheeled vehicle or frame for transporting people or things, often horse-drawn: *a ride through the park in their carriage.* 2 A moving machine part that supports or conveys something: *a typewriter carriage.*
Spelling tip: This word rhymes with and is spelled like *marriage.*

car·ri·er (kar'ē·ər) *n.*
Someone or something involved in carrying, conveying, or transporting people or things: *Interstate carriers include truckers, bus companies, railroads, and airlines.*

car·ri·on (kar'ē·ən) *n., adj.*
n. Dead and decaying flesh; meat unfit for human consumption: *Jackals live on carrion.*
adj. 1 Feeding on carrion: *a carrion crow.* 2 Resembling carrion.

car·ry (kar'ē) *v.* **car·ried, car·ry·ing**
To have, transport, support, or include: *The flag carries a motto. He carried a package. The bridge can carry a lot of weight.*
Spelling tip: Words ending in *y* preceded by a consonant usually change the *y* to *i* before any suffix except one beginning with *i*.

carte blanche (kärt' blänsh')
Unrestricted authority: *They gave him carte blanche to print controversial views in the newspaper.*

car·tog·ra·phy (kär·tog'rə·fē) *n.*
The art of creating maps and charts.—**car·tog'ra·pher** *n.*

car·tridge (kär'trij) *n.*
1 A casing containing the powder charge and usually the bullet or shot for a firearm. 2 Any container used for holding or mounting a piece of equipment, as a phonograph needle.

cas·se·role (kas'ə·rōl) *n.*
1 A dish, often covered, for baking and serving food. 2 Food prepared in such a dish.
Spelling tip: The ingredients in this word include a double *s* and two *e*'s.

cas·ti·gate (kas'tə·gāt) *v.* **cas·ti·gat·ed, cas·ti·gat·ing**
To censure severely or unremittingly: *She endlessly castigated her husband for every small failing.*

cas·tle (kas'əl) *n.*
1 In feudal times, the fortress or walled town where the nobility lived. 2 Any large house or stronghold. 3 A place of refuge: *His home is his castle.*
Spelling tip: Don't pronounce the silent *t*, but don't forget to write it.

cas·u·al·ty (kazh'ōō·əl·tē) *n.,* **cas·u·al·ties** *pl.*
1 An accident, or someone who is injured or killed in an accident: *an increase in automobile casualties.* 2 Someone who is injured, missing, or killed in battle: *Civilian casualties exceeded those of either army.*

cat·a·clysm (kat'ə·kliz'əm) *n.*
A violent disruption such as a flood, famine, or insurrection: *The eruption of Vesuvius was an unforgettable cataclysm.*
Syn. catastrophe, holocaust, disaster.

cat·a·falque (kat'ə·falk) *n.*
A structure on which a coffin rests during a funeral.

cat·a·logue (kat'ə·log) *n.; v.* **cat·a·logued, cat·a·logu·ing**
n. A book, pamphlet, card file, or list of names, titles, or objects, often including description and illustration, in some order convenient for reference: *a mail-order catalogue.*
v. To list or enter items in a catalogue.
Spelling tip: This word may also be spelled *catalog.*

cat·a·ract (kat'ə·rakt) *n.*
1 A great waterfall or heavy downpour of water: *The rain fell in cataracts.* 2 Cloudiness of the lens of the eye, causing partial or total blindness.
Spelling tip: Use no other vowel except *a* in *cataract.*

ca·tarrh (kə·tär') *n.*
Inflammation of the mucous membranes of the nose and throat.

cat·e·chism (kat'ə·kiz'əm) *n.*
1 A manual presenting religious principles in the form of questions and answers. 2 Any list of questions and answers like this used for teaching.

cat·e·gor·i·cal (kat'ə·gôr'i·kəl) *adj.*
1 Definite; without qualification: *his categorical denial of the charges.* 2 Pertaining to or included in a category: *a categorical list of the library books.*
Syn. 1 absolute, unequivocal, unreserved, positive, complete, total.
Ant. 1 partial, tentative, limited, qualified.

cat·e·go·ry (kat'ə·gôr'ē) *n.,* **cat·e·go·ries** *pl.*
A division of any classified system or branch of any subject: *Poetry is one category of literature.*
Syn. class, group, rank, subdivision.

ca·thar·sis (kə·thär'sis) *n.*
1 Purgation of the bowels. 2 The psychological release of buried emotions, as in psychotherapy. 3 A purifying or purging of pity, terror, or other emotions, through witnessing a work of art such as a tragic drama.

ca·thar·tic (kə·thär'tik) *n., adj.*
n. A medicine used as a laxative.
adj. Purifying; purgative: *Violence in drama can be cathartic.*
Syn. *adj.* cleansing, expiatory.

cath·ode (kath'ōd) *n.*
1 The negatively charged electrode of a battery. 2 The element of an electron tube that emits electrons.

cath·o·lic (kath'ə·lik or kath'lik) *adj.*
1 Broad-minded or liberal: *a catholic respect for different customs.* 2 Broad or universal in scope: *a grasp of human knowledge that is catholic.*
Syn. 1 tolerant, generous, cosmopolitan. 2 general, comprehensive, all-embracing.
Ant. 1 provincial, restricted. 2 narrow, limited.

cat·sup (kech′əp, kach′əp, *or* kat′səp) *n.*
A tomato sauce for meat, fish, etc., often spiced.
Spelling tip: Secondary spellings are *ketchup* and *catchup.*

Cau·ca·sian (kô·kā′zhən *or* kô·kash′ən) *n., adj.*
n. A member of the so-called white race.
adj. 1 Of or pertaining to this group. 2 Of the Caucasus region (in the southwest part of the Soviet Union).

cau·cus (kô′kəs) *n.; v.* **cau·cused** *or* **cau-cussed, cau·cus·ing** *or* **cau·cus·sing**
n. A meeting of a political group to determine policy: *a secret caucus of delegates supporting the dark-horse candidate.*
v. To hold a meeting or conference: *They caucused for an hour before deciding how to vote.*
Spelling tip: Both *k* sounds are spelled with a *c* and both syllables include a *u.*

cause cé·lè·bre (kōz sā·leb′r′) *n.,* **causes cé·lè·brés** *pl.*
French 1 Any famous law case. 2 Any well-known controversy or cause to which people have rallied: *The fiery death of the Czech student became a cause célèbre throughout the world.*

caus·tic (kôs′tik) *adj., n.*
adj. 1 Capable of corroding organic tissues, as lye. 2 Extremely hostile or biting: *Ignore the caustic slurs of your enemy.*
n. A caustic substance.
Syn. *adj.* 1 burning, corrosive. 2 sarcastic, acerbic, venomous, satirical.
Ant. *adj.* 2 admiring, flattering, approving.

cau·ter·ize (kô′tə·rīz) *v.* **cau·ter·ized, cau·ter·iz·ing**
To sear (living tissue) with a hot iron or caustic substance: *The doctor cauterized the wound.*

cav·al·cade (kav′əl·kād′ *or* kav′əl·kād) *n.*
1 A procession on horseback or in carriages.
2 Any parade or sequence of events: *the cavalcade of history.*

cav·al·ry (kav′əl·rē) *n.,* **cav·al·ries** *pl.*
Troops that fight on horseback or, more recently, in armored motor vehicles.
Spelling tip: Do not confuse this word and *Calvary* (the place where Christ was crucified).

cav·i·ar (kav′ē·är) *n.*
The salted eggs of sturgeon, often eaten as an appetizer.
Spelling tip: This word may also be spelled *caviare.*

cav·il (kav′əl) *v.* **cav·iled** *or* **cav·illed, cav·il·ing** *or* **cav·il·ling;** *n.*
v. To find fault with or raise trivial objections to: *He caviled about every departure from the letter of the law.*
n. A severe objection to minor failings: *His cavils over procedure prevented them from coping with the emergency.*

ceil·ing (sē′ling) *n.*
1 The top side of a room. 2 The height of the bottom layer of clouds. 3 The upper limit set on something: *a wage ceiling.*
Spelling tip: Remember *i* before *e* except after *c.*

cel·er·y (sel′ər·ē *or* sel′rē) *n.*
A biennial herb whose stalks are used as a vegetable or in a salad.

ce·les·tial (sə·les′chəl) *adj.*
1 Of or having to do with heaven, the heavens, or the sky: *a celestial map.* 2 Having qualities worthy of a divine origin (extremely beautiful, benevolent, virtuous, etc.): *Bach's celestial music.*—**ce·les′tial·ly** *adv.*
Syn. 1 heavenly, astral, supernal. 2 exquisite, sublime, perfect, divine.

cel·lo (chel′ō) *n.,* **cel·los** *pl.*
A large bass instrument of the violin family, held between the performer's knees when played.
Spelling tip: This word, short for *violoncello,* may also be spelled *'cello.*

cen·sor (sen′sər) *v., n.*
v. To examine, review, suppress, delete, or change objectionable or forbidden matter in literature, motion pictures, etc.: *Parts of the letter from Russia had been censored. The film was censored before it was released.*
n. A person who censors.

cen·sure (sen′shər) *v.* **cen·sured, cen·sur·ing;** *n.*
v. To express disapproval of; condemn; blame: *The senator was censured by his colleagues for misusing government funds.*
n. The expression of disapproval or blame; reprimand.

cen·taur (sen′tôr) *n.*
In Greek mythology One of a race of monsters having the head, arms, and torso of a man united to the body and legs of a horse.

cen·trif·u·gal (sen·trif′(y)ə·gəl) *adj.*
1 Moving or tending to move away from a center: *centrifugal rays.* 2 Using centrifugal force, which is the force that tends to move a body away from a center about which it is revolving: *a centrifugal pump.*
Ant. centripetal.

ce·ram·ics (sə·ram′iks) *n.pl.*
1 The art of molding, modeling, and baking clay. 2 Objects made of fired and baked clay.
Usage: In definition 1, this word is construed as singular and therefore takes a singular verb: *Ceramics is an interesting hobby. The ceramics we produced are now on display.*

cer·e·bral (ser′ə·brəl *or* sə·rē′brəl) *adj.*
1 Of or having to do with the cerebrum (the part of the brain controlling conscious processes) or the brain itself: *a cerebral hemorrhage.* 2 Having, involving, requiring, or appealing to the intellect; intellectual: *a drama that was more cerebral than emotional.*

cer·e·brum (ser′ə·brəm *or* sə·rē′brəm) *n.,* **cer·e·brums** *or* **cer·e·bra** (ser′ə·brə *or* sə·rē′brə) *pl.*
The upper part of the brain, constituting its chief bulk. The cerebrum is assumed to be the seat of conscious and voluntary processes.

cer·ti·fied check (sûr′tə·fīd chek)
A check issued by a bank that guarantees
that it is drawn on an account having sufficient funds.

ce·ru·le·an (sə·roō′lē·ən *or* sə·roō′lyən) *n.*, *adj.*
Sky blue.

ces·sa·tion (se·sā′shən) *n.*
A ceasing, either temporary or final: *a cessa-
tion of the war for the Christmas holidays.*
Syn. stopping, pause, interruption, suspen-
sion, halt.
Ant. continuation, resumption, renewal.

chafe (chāf) *v.* **chafed, chaf·ing**
1 To rub so as to wear away: *The tight collar
was chafing his skin.* 2 To irritate or be
irritated: *The long delay chafed her.*

cha·grin (shə·grin′) *n.*, *v.*
n. A feeling of annoyance or embarrassment
caused by failure, disappointment, etc.: *the
chagrin she felt when publicly insulted by her
husband.*
v. To annoy or embarrass: *The student was
chagrined at failing the exam.*
Syn. *n.* distress, humiliation, mortification.
v. distress, humiliate, mortify.

chaise longue (shāz′ lông′, *French* shez lông′)
n., **chaise longues** *or* **chaises longues** *pl.*
A couchlike chair that has a long seat on
which the sitter can stretch his legs. The
term literally means long chair.

cha·let (sha·lā′ *or* shal′ā) *n.*
1 A Swiss cottage with a gently sloping,
projecting roof. 2 Any cottage built in this
style.

chal·ice (chal′is) *n.*
1 A drinking cup or goblet, especially a cup
in which the wine is consecrated in a Communion service. 2 The consecrated wine.

chal·lis (shal′ē) *n.*
A light fabric, as of wool, cotton, or a
synthetic, sometimes in a solid color but more
often in a small print.

cha·me·le·on (kə·mē′lē·ən *or* kə·mēl′yən) *n.*
1 Any of a number of different lizards that
have the ability to change color. 2 A person
who frequently changes his mind, habits, or
disposition: *such a chameleon that she would
change her mind three times before deciding on
a luncheon spot.*

cham·ois (sham′ē, *French* sha·mwä′) *n.*,
cham·ois *pl.*
1 An antelope found in the mountains of
Europe, the Caucasus, and western Asia.
2 A soft leather originally prepared from the
skin of chamois, but now made from the skin
of sheep, goats, deer, etc.
Spelling tip: This word may also be spelled
chammy for definition 2.

cham·pagne (sham·pān′) *n.*
1 A sparkling white wine made in the area of
Champagne, France; also, any wine made in
imitation of this. 2 The color of champagne
(pale or tawny yellow).

change·a·ble (chān′jə·bəl) *adj.*
1 Likely to change or vary: *a woman of very
changeable moods.* 2 Reflecting light so as
to appear of different color from different
points of view: *changeable taffeta.*—**change′-
a·ble·ness** *n.*
Spelling tip: Words ending in *ge* retain the *e*
when adding *-able.*
Syn. 1 inconstant, fluctuating, mercurial.
Ant. constant, unchanging, fixed.

chan·nel (chan′əl) *n.*; *v.* **chan·neled** *or* **chan·
nelled, chan·nel·ing** *or* **chan·nel·ling**
n. 1 A wide strait: *the English Channel.* 2 The
deep or navigable part of a river, harbor, etc.
3 Any course or passage through which
something moves: *a channel for breathing.*
4 *pl.* The official routes of communication:
*In a large company you must go through
proper channels.*
v. To direct, as along or through a channel:
to channel your efforts toward a specific goal.
Spelling tip: There are two syllables in this
word and an *n* in each syllable.

chan·son (shan′sən, *French* shän·sôn′) *n.*
A song. This word is taken directly from the
French.

cha·os (kā′os) *n.*
Total disorder or confusion: *The room was in
chaos after the wild party.*
Syn. disarray, turmoil.
Ant. order, calm, harmony.

chap·ar·ral (chap′ə·ral′) *n.*
A thick, dense growth, as of dwarf oak, low
thorny shrubs, etc.

cha·peau (sha·pō′, *French* shȧ·pō′) *n.*, **cha·
peaux** *or* **cha·peaus** (sha·pōz′, *French* shȧ·
pō′) *pl.*
A hat. This word is taken directly from the
French.

chap·er·on (shap′ə·rōn) *n.*, *v.*
n. 1 An older woman who, in certain societies,
accompanies a young unmarried woman in
public. 2 An older person who supervises a
group of young people, as at a party, dance,
etc.
v. To act as a chaperon to or for: *to chaperon
a fraternity party.*
Etymology: This word is derived from the
French *chape,* meaning "cape," because a
chaperon acts as a protector. It may also be
spelled *chaperone.*

char·ac·ter·is·tic (kar′ik·tə·ris′tik) *n.*, *adj.*
n. A distinctive quality, trait, or feature: *A
characteristic of cats is independence.*
adj. Making up or showing a special quality,
character, or disposition: *a remark characteristic of someone with her particular prejudices.*—**char′ac·ter·is′ti·cal·ly** *adv.*
Syn. *n.* peculiarity, property, idiosyncrasy.
adj. typical, particular, idiosyncratic.

cha·riv·a·ri (shə·riv′ə·rē′, shiv′ə·rē′, *or* shä′-
rē·vä′rē) *n.*, **cha·riv·a·ris** *pl.*
A mock serenade, as to newlyweds, performed with tin pans, horns, kettles, etc.

char·la·tan (shär′lə·tən) *n.*
A person who claims to have skill and
knowledge he does not possess: *A medical
charlatan can endanger your life.*
Syn. fake, quack, imposter, fraud.

char·treuse (shär·trōōz′) *n., adj.*
n. 1 A yellow, pale green, or white liqueur made by Carthusian monks. 2 Yellowish green.
adj. Yellow-green in color.
Etymology: This word is derived from *La Grande Chartreuse,* the chief Carthusian monastery in France.

char·y (châr′ē) *adj.* **char·i·er, char·i·est**
1 Cautious; careful; wary: *chary of strangers.* 2 Ungenerous; stingy: *chary of praise.*
Syn. 1 guarded, circumspect, suspicious, leery, watchful. 2 thrifty, frugal, sparing, miserly.
Ant. 1 careless, incautious, unwary, reckless. 2 generous, liberal, lavish, extravagant.

chasm (kaz′əm) *n.*
1 A deep crack in the Earth's surface: *The earthquake opened a steep, gaping chasm.* 2 A divisive difference of opinion: *the chasm between North and South in the Civil War.*
Syn. 1 gorge, ravine, abyss, gap. 2 division, rift, estrangement.
Ant. 2 union, reconciliation.

chas·sis (shas′ē *or* chas′ē) *n.,* **chas·sis** (shas′ēz *or* chas′ēz) *pl.*
A framework to which working parts are attached, as the frame that supports the body of a motor vehicle and includes the wheels, springs, motor, etc.
Spelling tip: Remember the three *s*'s in this word.

chas·ten (chā′sən) *v.*
1 To correct or discipline through punishment: *She chastened her son for striking the younger boy.* 2 To moderate; soften: *Her anger toward him was chastened by news of his illness.*
Syn. punish, chastise, castigate.
Ant. reward, praise, applaud, commend.

chas·tise (chas·tīz′) *v.* **chas·tised, chas·tis·ing**
To punish, especially by beating: *A leather strap was used to chastise the disobedient boys.*
—**chas·tise·ment** (chas′tiz·mənt *or* chas·tīz′-mənt) *n.*
Syn. whip, beat, flog, scourge.

cha·teau (sha·tō′) *n.,* **cha·teaux** (sha·tōz′) *pl.*
1 A French castle or manor house. 2 A country mansion.
Spelling tip: French spelling is *château.*

chat·tel (chat′l) *n.*
A piece of personal property that is not a house or piece of land: *They auctioned off the furniture and other chattels.*

chauf·feur (shō′fər *or* shō·fûr′) *n., v.*
n. A person employed as the driver of a car: *a chauffeur waiting in a Rolls-Royce.*
v. To serve as driver for: *She chauffeured an invalid friend to the doctor's office.*
Etymology: *Chauffeur* goes back to the French word *chauffer,* to heat. It originally meant *stoker,* a humorous term for a driver in the days of steam-propelled automobiles.
Syn. *v.* drive, ride.

che·mise (shə·mēz′) *n.*
1 A woman's loose undergarment resembling a short slip. 2 A dress hanging straight from the shoulders.
Syn. 2 shift.

che·nille (shə·nēl′) *n.*
1 A soft, fuzzy yarn of silk, rayon, cotton, or worsted, used for embroidery, fringes, etc. 2 A fabric made with filling of this yarn, used for bedspreads, rugs, etc.
Etymology: *Chenille* is the French word for caterpillar.

che·root (shə·rōōt′) *n.*
A cigar cut square at both ends.

chev·a·lier (shev′ə·lir′) *n.*
1 A member of certain orders of knighthood or honor, as the French Legion of Honor. 2 A knight; gallant: *a chevalier mounted on a spirited steed.*
Syn. 2 cavalier.

chic (shēk) *adj.*
Smart and stylish: *The Duchess of Windsor always looks chic.*
Syn. fashionable, voguish, elegant, modish.
Ant. dowdy, frowzy, tacky.

chi·can·er·y (shi·kā′nər·ē) *n.*
Petty trickery and cunning involving misrepresentation: *The gullible jury was deceived by the chicanery of a shyster lawyer.*
Syn. deceit, deception, quibbling, subterfuge.
Ant. honesty, veracity, candor.

chide (chīd) *v.* **chid·ed** *or* **chid** (chid), **chid·ed** *or* **chid** *or* **chid·den** (chid′n), **chid·ing**
To scold: *to chide a child for being lazy.*
Syn. rebuke, reprimand, criticize, upbraid.
Ant. praise, commend, compliment, applaud.

chief (chēf) *n., adj.*
n. The leader of a group or organization: *an Indian chief; the chief of police.*
adj. First in rank or importance: *the chief justice; their chief purpose.*
Spelling tip: Remember *i* before *e.*

chif·fon (shi·fon′) *n., adj.*
n. A sheer silk or rayon fabric.
adj. In cooking Having a light, fluffy texture: *a lemon chiffon pie.*

chif·fo·nier (shif′ə·nir′) *n.*
A high chest of drawers, often with a mirror at the top.
Spelling tip: Also spelled *chiffonnier.*

chim·ney (chim′nē) *n.*
1 A hollow structure rising above a roof, serving to carry off fumes, as from a fireplace. 2 A glass tube for enclosing the flame of a lamp.
Spelling tip: Common nouns ending in *y* preceded by a vowel form the plural by adding *s: boys, days, chimneys.*

chim·pan·zee (chim′pan·zē′ *or* chim·pan′zē) *n.*
A tree-dwelling anthropoid ape of Africa, smaller and more intelligent than a gorilla.
Syn. monkey.

chi·rop·o·dist (kə·rop′ə·dist *or* shə·rop′ə·dist) *n.*
A foot doctor.—**chi·rop′o·dy** *n.*
Etymology: This word is from the Greek *chir-* (hand) + *pod* (foot), because such practitioners originally treated both extremities.

Spelling tip: Remember to include two *o*'s, as in f*oo*t.
Syn. podiatrist.

chiv·al·rous (shiv'əl·rəs) *adj.*
Gallant and valiant, as the ideal knight: *a chivalrous gentleman.* Also **chi·val·ric** (shiv'-əl·rik *or* shi·val'rik) *adj.*—**chiv'al·ry** *n.*
Syn. courteous, knightly.
Ant. boorish, rude, vulgar, cowardly.

chlo·rine (klôr'ēn) *n.*
A greenish yellow, poisonous gaseous element with a suffocating odor, obtained principally from common salt, and readily liquefied.

choc·o·late (chok'lit *or* chok'ə·lit) *n.*
1 A preparation of cacao nuts roasted and ground and usually sweetened and flavored- **2** A candy or drink made from this. **3** A deep reddish brown color.

choose (chōoz) *v.* **chose** (chōz), **cho·sen** (chō'-zən), **choos·ing** (chōoz'ing)
To select or prefer among alternatives: *to choose a gift; free to pick and choose.*
Syn. pick, decide (on), elect.
Ant. refuse, decline, reject.

chord (kôrd) *n.*
1 A combination of three or more musical tones sounded together. **2** A string of a musical instrument. **3** An emotional response· *His plea struck a responsive chord in the congregation.* **4** *In geometry* A straight line connecting the extremities of an arc.

chris·ten (kris'ən) *v.*
To name in a formal ceremony: *The priest christened the child Irene; to christen a ship by breaking a bottle of champagne over the prow.*

chron·ic (kron'ik) *adj.*
1 Prolonged or recurrent: *chronic unrest; a chronic disease.* **2** Habitual: *a chronic alcoholic.* —**chron'i·cal·ly** *adv.*
Usage: A *chronic* illness continues year in, year out. An *acute* illness comes to a crisis quickly: *chronic indigestion; acute appendicitis.*
Syn. 1 persistent, lingering, constant. **2** confirmed, inveterate.
Ant. 1 occasional, temporary.

chron·i·cle (kron'i·kəl) *n.; v.* **chron·i·cled, chron·i·cling**
n. A detailed historical account of events in their order of occurrence: *A chronicle of the President's term of office.*
v. To record in, or in the manner of, such an account: *He chronicled the events leading to the war.*
Syn. *n.* history, annals. *v.* report, list.

churl·ish (chûr'lish) *adj.*
Rude and ill-tempered: *a churlish brute who muttered menacingly when asked to move.*—**churl'ish·ly** *adv.*, **churl'ish·ness** *n.*
Syn. surly, boorish, sullen, insolent.
Ant. polite, civil, courteous, well-mannered.

chute (shōot) *n.*
1 An inclined trough or vertical passage down which water, coal, trash, etc., may pass: *an incinerator chute; a laundry chute.* **2** A slide, as for toboggans. **3** A steep, narrow watercourse. **4** *Informal* A parachute: *His chute failed to open.*
Syn. 1 shoot, slide. **3** rapids, flume.

ci·ca·da (si·kā'də *or* si·kä'də) *n.*, **ci·ca·das** *or* **ci·ca·dae** (si·kā'dē *or* si·kä'dē) *pl.*
A large, four-winged insect, the male having vibrating membranes that produce a loud, shrill sound when rubbed with the legs.
Syn. locust.

ci·gar (si·gär') *n.*
A roll of tobacco leaves prepared and shaped for smoking.

cig·a·rette (sig'ə·ret' *or* sig'ə·ret) *n.*
A tube of thin paper filled with a small roll of finely cut tobacco for smoking.
Spelling tip: The suffix *-ette* means "little." A *cigarette* is a little cigar, just as *kitchenette* is a little kitchen. The word is sometimes spelled *cigaret.*

cinch (sinch) *n.*
1 A band or strap used to fasten a saddle or pack onto an animal. **2** *Slang* An easy or sure thing: *That job's a cinch.*
Syn. 1 girth, surcingle. **2** snap, certainty.

cin·e·ma (sin'ə·mə) *n.*
Chiefly British A motion picture or motion-picture theater: *the neighborhood cinema.*
Etymology: *Cinema* comes from the Greek word *kinēma,* meaning movement.

cin·e·mat·o·graph (sin'ə·mat'ə·graf) *n., v.*
n. A motion-picture camera or projector.
v. To film with a motion-picture camera.
Spelling tip: Also spelled *kinematograph.*

cin·e·ma·tog·ra·phy (sin'ə·mə·tog'rə·fē) *n.*
The art and process of making motion pictures.—**cin'e·ma·tog'ra·pher** *n.*

cir·cu·i·tous (sər·kyōo'ə·təs) *adj.*
Roundabout or indirect: *He followed a circuitous route to escape detection.*
Spelling tip: *Circuit* (a circular course) + *-ous* (meaning *like*).
Syn. meandering, devious, zigzag, tortuous.
Ant. straight, direct, unswerving.

cir·cum·lo·cu·tion (sûr'kəm·lō·kyōo'shən) *n.*
Indirect or roundabout expression involving the use of more words than necessary: *"Refrain from perambulating on the green growing carpet"* is a *circumlocution* for *"Don't walk on the grass."*
Etymology: *Circum-* (around) + *locutio* (speaking).
Syn. wordiness, verbosity, pleonasm, tautology.
Ant. brevity, conciseness, terseness.

cir·cum·scribe (sûr'kəm·skrīb') *v.* **cir·cum·scribed, cir·cum·scrib·ing**
1 To set bounds to; limit: *His practical working experience is circumscribed by his extreme youth.* **2** To mark the boundaries of: *a field circumscribed by a wire fence.*
Etymology: *Circum-* (around) + *scribere* (to write).
Syn. 1 restrict, curtail. **2** encompass, enclose, surround.

cir·cum·spect (sûr'kəm·spekt) *adj.*
Carefully attentive to all circumstances and

possible consequences, usually involving prudence and discretion: *The circumspect investor put his money in blue-chip stocks. A lady always acts in a circumspect manner.*
Etymology: *Circum-* (around) + *specere* (to look).
Syn. cautious, careful, judicious.
Ant. careless, heedless, reckless.

cit·a·del (sit′ə·dəl *or* sit′ə·del) *n.*
A fortress or stronghold, especially one overlooking a town.
Syn. fort.

cite (sīt) *v.* **cit·ed, cit·ing**
1 To quote as authority or illustration: *He cited many references to ghosts in Shakespeare's plays.* **2** To mention in a report, etc., especially for bravery: *The sergeant was cited for exceptional valor.* **3** To summon to appear in court.—**ci·ta′tion** *n.*

civ·il (siv′əl) *adj.*
1 Of or relating to citizens or their government: *civil affairs; civil service; civil war.* **2** Not military or ecclesiastical: *civil marriage; civil law.* **3** Relating to private rights and to legal proceedings involving those rights: *Divorce proceedings are a civil court action.* **4** Polite; proper: *Keep a civil tongue.*
Syn. 4 courteous, amenable, decent.
Ant. 4 rude, surly, gruff, curt.

civ·i·li·za·tion (siv′ə·lə·zā′shən *or* siv′ə·lī·zā′-shən) *n.*
1 A state of human society characterized by a high level of intellectual, social, and cultural development: *the advanced civilization of the ancient Egyptians.* **2** The countries and peoples thought of as having reached this stage: *European civilization.* **3** The cultural development of a particular people, country, or region: *the Aztec civilization.*
Spelling tip: The spelling of the suffix *-ization* varies in British and American usage; *isation* is preferred in England, but not in the U.S.

clair·voy·ant (klar·voi′ənt) *adj., n.*
adj. Having alleged unnatural powers to see or know things not present to the senses: *The medium was clairvoyant about the future.*
n. A person who has clairvoyant powers.—**clair·voy′ance** *n.*
Etymology: *Clairvoyant* comes from French words meaning *seeing clearly.*
Syn. *adj.* psychic, telepathic. *n.* medium, spiritualist.

clan·des·tine (klan·des′tin) *adj.*
Kept secret for a purpose, often for something illicit or evil: *clandestine meetings between lovers.*—**clan·des′tine·ly** *adv.*
Syn. secret, furtive, stealthy, surreptitious, underhand.
Ant. aboveboard, open, candid.

clar·i·fy (klar′ə·fī) *v.* **clar·i·fied, clar·i·fy·ing**
1 To make or become clear or understandable: *The speaker clarified his previous remarks.* **2** To make or become clear or pure; free from impurities: *to clarify melted butter.*
—**clar′i·fi·ca′tion** *n.*

Syn. 1 elucidate, explain, expound. **2** purify, refine.
Ant. 1 confuse, obfuscate.

claus·tro·pho·bi·a (klôs′trə·fō′bē·ə) *n.*
A fear of enclosed or small spaces: *An elevator gives me claustrophobia.*—**claus′tro·pho′bic** *adj.*
Etymology: *Claustrophobia* comes from the Latin *claustrum* (a closed place) and the Greek root *-phobia* (fear).

cleft (kleft) *adj., n.*
adj. Divided partially or completely: *He was born with a cleft palate.*
n. **1** A division or indentation between two parts, as of a hoof, chin, etc. **2** A fissure or crack: *He dropped his watch in a cleft between two rocks.*
Syn. *adj.* bisected, split. *n.* **1** notch, split. **2** crevice, gap, split, cranny.

clem·a·tis (klem′ə·tis *or* kli·ma′təs) *n.*
One of a large group of climbing, ornamental plants, often having purple or white flowers.

clem·en·cy (klem′ən·sē) *n.*, **clem·en·cies** *pl.*
1 Gentleness and leniency, especially toward offenders: *The judge exercised clemency.* **2** An act of mercy or leniency. **3** Mildness of weather: *the clemency of a June day.*
Syn. 1 mercy, forbearance. **3** fairness.

cli·ché (klē·shā′) *n.*
An expression that has been used so often that it has become dull and ordinary: *"Happy as a lark" is a familiar cliché.*
Syn. banality, platitude.

cli·en·tele (klī′ən·tel′) *n.*
The clients of a doctor, lawyer, etc., or the usual customers of a store, hotel, etc.: *The store catered to a wealthy clientele.*

cli·mac·tic (klī·mak′tik) *adj.*
Having to do with or constituting a climax: *The murder is the play's climactic moment.*
Spelling tip: Don't confuse *climactic* with *climatic,* which refers to climate.

clois·ter (klois′tər) *n., v.*
n. **1** A covered walk along the inside walls of a building or around a courtyard, as in a college or monastery. **2** A building used for religious seclusion; a monastery or convent.
v. To seclude or confine, as in a cloister.
Syn. *n.* **1** gallery, passage, arcade, colonnade. **2** priory, friary, nunnery, abbey.

clothes (klōz, klōthz) *n.pl.*
1 Articles of dress such as coats, suits, dresses, etc. **2** Bedclothes.
Spelling tip: See CLOTH.
Syn. 1 raiment, garments, clothing, array. **2** linens.

cloth·i·er (klōth′yər) *n.*
A retailer of clothing, especially men's clothing.
Spelling tip: Pronounce this word with two syllables, but spell it with three.
Syn. haberdasher, tailor.

co·a·lesce (kō′ə·les′) *v.* **co·a·lesced, co·a·lescing**
To grow or come together into one: *A number of small businesses coalesced into a large*

corporation.—**co'a·les'cence** *n.*, **co'a·les'cent**
adj.
Syn. fuse, blend, unite.

co·a·li·tion (kō'ə·lish'ən) *n.*
1 A temporary alliance of persons, parties, or
states: *The farmers formed a coalition to raise
farm prices.* 2 The uniting of separate things
into a single body or group: *The coalition of
water and oil is impossible.*

coarse (kôrs) *adj.*
1 Lacking refinement or delicacy: *Gangsters
often speak in a coarse manner.* 2 Composed
of large parts or particles; not fine in texture:
coarse gravel; coarse salt.
Spelling tip: Don't confuse *coarse* with *course*
(a program of study).
Syn. 1 gross, vulgar, earthy, crude, indecent.
Ant. 1 civilized, decorous, gentle. 2 fine,
refined.

co·coa (kō'kō) *n.*
1 A powder made from the roasted, husked
seed kernels of the cacao; chocolate. 2 A
beverage made from this.

co·co·nut (kō'kə nut' *or* kō'kə·nət) *n.*
The fruit of the coconut palm, a large nut
with white meat enclosed in a hard shell and
containing a drinkable milky liquid.
Spelling tip: This word may also be spelled
cocoanut.

co·coon (kə·kōōn') *n.*
The protective envelope spun by the larvae
of certain insects, as moths, silkworms, etc.,
in which they remain while undergoing the
stages of development into adulthood.

cod·i·cil (kod'ə·səl) *n.*
1 An addition to a will, changing or explaining something in it: *When Louis' grandson
was born he added a codicil to his will be-
queathing the child money for a college education.* 2 An appendix or addition, as to a piece
of writing in order to correct errors, provide
additional information, etc.
Syn. 1 addendum, clause. 2 supplement.

co·erce (kō·ûrs') *v.* **co·erced, co·erc·ing**
To compel (a person) by use of authority,
force, or threats to act in a certain way: *The
witness was coerced into silence through fear of
personal harm.*—**co·er·cion** (kō·ûr'shən) *n.*

co·gent (kō'jənt) *adj.*
Appealing to the mind so as to influence it
powerfully: *a cogent argument for calling a
cease-fire.*—**co'gen·cy** *n.*, **co'gent·ly** *adv.*
Syn. forceful, convincing, persuasive.
Ant. weak, ineffectual, ineffective.

cog·i·tate (koj'ə·tāt) *v.* **cog·i·tat·ed, cog·i·tat·
ing**
To give careful thought to something;
ponder; meditate: *He was cogitating on the
errors he made in the exam.*
Syn. reflect, contemplate.

co·gnac (kōn'yak *or* kon'yak) *n.*
Brandy, especially a type produced in the
Cognac region of western France.

cog·ni·zant (kog'nə·zənt) *adj.*
Having knowledge, especially special or
certain knowledge as from first-hand

sources (used with *of*): *Although cognizant of
his own weaknesses, he was sure he could do
the job.*—**cog'ni·zance** *n.*
Syn. aware, informed.
Ant. unaware, ignorant.

co·here (kō·hir') *v.* **co·hered, co·her·ing**
1 To stick or hold firmly together: *The grains
of damp salt cohered.* 2 To be logically connected; be consistent, as the parts of a story.
—**co·her'ent** *adj.*, **co·her'ent·ly** *adv.*
Syn. 1 cling, adhere.

co·her·ence (kō·hir'əns) *n.*
A sticking together; logical connection: *The
essay lacked coherence of thought, dwelling on
too many different and unrelated subjects.*
Syn. cohesion, conjunction, congruity, consistency.
Ant. haphazardness, disconnectedness, loose-
ness, inconsistency.

co·he·sion (kō·hē'zhən) *n.*
1 The act or state of sticking together: *The
cohesion of the free world is based on mutual
trust and needs.* 2 *In physics* The force by
which molecules of the same kind or of the
same body are held together.

coif·fure (kwä·fyoor') *n.; v.* **coif·fured, coif·fur·
ing**
n. 1 A style of arranging or dressing the hair:
Marie Antoinette's elaborate coiffure. 2 A
headdress.
v. To dress the hair: *coiffured for a Saturday
night date.*
Syn. *n.* 1 hairdo. *v.* coif.

co·in·ci·dent (kō·in'sə·dənt) *adj.*
1 Occurring at exactly the same time: *His
arrival at the house was coincident with mine.*
2 In exact agreement; harmonious: *Her
tastes were coincident with her husband's.*—**co·
in'ci·dent·ly** *adv.*
Syn. 1 simultaneous. 2 coinciding, corresponding, indistinguishable, like.

col·an·der (kul'ən·dər *or* kol'ən·dər) *n.*
A bowl-shaped perforated kitchen utensil
used as a strainer.

col·lab·o·rate (kə·lab'ə·rāt) *v.* **col·lab·o·rat·ed,
col·lab·o·rat·ing**
1 To cooperate or work together, as on a
literary or scientific project: *They collaborated on researching the book.* 2 To conspire or
work traitorously with the enemy: *The French
underground retaliated against those who
collaborated with the Nazis.*—**col·lab'o·ra'-
tion, col·lab'o·ra'tor** *n.; * **col·lab'o·ra'tive**
adj.

col·late (kə·lāt' *or* kol'āt) *v.* **col·lated, col·lat·
ing**
1 To assemble pages of a manuscript, etc., in
proper order: *The secretary collated the loose
sheets of the report and stapled each complete
set.* 2 To compare critically, as writings or
facts: *Scholars collated all existing copies of
the Shakespeare Folio.*—**col·la·tor** (kə·lā'tər
or kol'ā·tər) *n.*

col·lat·er·al (kə·lat'ər·əl) *adj., n.*
adj. Secondary, parallel, or additional: *The*

danger of plague was a collateral factor in causing the besieged town to surrender.
n. Money or valuables put up as security for a loan: *A deed to the land was accepted as collateral by the bank.*
Syn. *adj.* subordinate, supporting, corroborative, concomitant.

col·la·tion (kə·lā'shən) *n.*
1 The act of collating. 2 A light, informal meal.

col·lo·qui·al (kə·lō'kwē·əl) *adj.*
Characteristic of familiar conversation; informal.—**col·lo'qui·al·ism'** *n.*

col·lo·quy (kol'ə·kwē) *n.*, **col·lo·quies** *pl.*
1 Conversation, especially a formal conference: *Several nations engaged in a colloquy on disarmament.* 2 A literary piece written in dialogue form.
Syn. 1 discussion, talk, symposium.

col·lu·sion (kə·lōō'zhen) *n.*
A secret agreement to achieve improper or illegal ends: *the collusion of enemies.*

co·logne (kə·lōn') *n.*
A fragrant liquid consisting of alcohol and aromatic oils, used like perfume.
Spelling tip: Remember the silent *g.*

colo·nel (kûr'nəl) *n.*
In the U.S. Army, a commissioned officer who ranks above a lieutenant colonel and below a brigadier general.

co·los·sal (kə·los'əl) *adj.*
1 Of immense size: *a colossal skyscraper.* 2 *Informal* Beyond comprehension or credibility: *colossal pride.*
Syn. 1 huge, gigantic, tremendous, titanic, vast, mammoth.
Ant. 1 tiny, minuscule, miniature, small, miniaturized, infinitesimal.

col·umn (kol'əm) *n.*
1 A pillar: *the columns of the Parthenon.* 2 Something that suggests or is shaped like a column: *to add a column of figures; a spinal column.* 3 Printed matter arranged in lines of narrow width, as in a newspaper.
Spelling tip: The *u* and the silent *n* are the troublemakers here.

co·ma (kō'mə) *n.*
A condition of stupor or pathological unconsciousness: *The accident left him in a coma.*
Spelling tip: Don't confuse this word with *comma,* the punctuation mark.

co·ma·tose (kō'mə·tōs *or* kom'ə·tōs) *adj.*
1 Having to do with coma or unconsciousness: *The concussion left him in a comatose state.* 2 Torpid; lethargic: *The hot weather made him feel comatose.*
Syn. 2 lazy, sleepy, dormant.

comb (kōm) *n., v.*
n. 1 A toothed instrument for grooming or fastening hair: *Jeweled combs held her hair in place.* 2 The fleshy crest on the head of a fowl.
v. 1 To groom hair with or as with a comb.
2 To search carefully and exhaustively: *They combed the haystack for the missing needle.*

Spelling tip: "B" wary of words that end in a silent *b—comb, lamb, bomb, climb, limb,* etc.

com·bus·ti·ble (kəm·bus'tə·bəl) *adj., n.*
adj. Readily ignited; flammable: *Oily rags are highly combustible.*
n. Anything easily burned.

come·ly (kum'lē) *adj.* **come·li·er, come·li·est**
Of pleasing appearance; handsome; graceful: *Barbara and Joe were a comely young couple.*
Syn. attractive, pleasant.
Ant. plain, awkward, homely.

com·i·cal (kom'i·kəl) *adj.*
Funny; ludicrous: *a comical cartoon.*
Syn. humorous, laughable, silly.
Ant. sober, serious, solemn, dour.

com·ma (kom'ə) *n.*
A punctuation mark (,) indicating a slight separation in ideas or in grammatical construction within a sentence.

com·man·dant (kom'ən·dant' *or* kom'ən·dänt') *n.*
A commanding officer, as of an installation, school, or military district.

com·man·deer (kom'ən·dir') *v.*
1 To force into military service or seize for public use: *A policeman may commandeer a passing taxicab in an emergency.* 2 *Informal* To seize by force or compulsion.
Syn. appropriate, confiscate.

com·mence (kə·mens') *v.* **com·menced, com·menc·ing**
To start or begin: *Commence firing!*
Spelling tip: Note the two *m*'s.
Ant. end, finish, complete.

com·men·su·rate (kə·men'shə·rit *or* kə·men'sə·rit) *adj.*
1 The same in scope or size: *Our actions are seldom commensurate with our ideals.* 2 In proportion: *The quality is commensurate with the cost.*—**com·men'su·rate·ly** *adv.*; **com·men'su·rate·ness, com·men'su·ra'tion** *n.*

com·merce (kom'ərs) *n.*
The exchange of materials and goods; trade: *High tariffs restrict commerce.*
Spelling tip: Don't forget the two *m*'s or the two *c*'s.

com·mis·er·ate (kə·miz'ə·rāt) *v.* **com·mis·er·at·ed, com·mis·er·at·ing**
1 To feel or express pity for: *Don't just commiserate; help the survivors.* 2 To sympathize: *He commiserated with the injured strikers.*—**com·mis'er·a·'tion** *n.*
Spelling tip: As an aid to remembering the double *m,* note that this word is from the Latin *com-* (with) + *miserari* (to feel pity).

com·mis·sar·i·at (kom'ə·sâr'ē·ət) *n.*
A military agency responsible for food and daily necessities.

com·mis·sion (kə·mish'ən) *n., v.*
n. 1 The act of entrusting something to another, the thing entrusted, or the fee given to an agent for such action. 2 A document conferring military rank, or the rank itself. 3 A body of persons authorized to perform duties, or the authorization conferring or commanding such powers. 4 The act of doing

or perpetrating (opposed to *omission*): *His attempts at bribery were a patent sin of commission.*
v. To give rank; appoint; empower; delegate: *A panel was commissioned to study air pollution.*—**com·mis′sion·er** *n.*
Spelling tip: Double both the *m* and the *s*.

com·mit (kə·mit′) *v.* **com·mit·ted, com·mit·ting**
1 To do; perform: *to commit an evil act.* 2 To entrust, pledge, or refer for consideration: *He committed himself to helping others.*
Spelling tip: Words ending in a consonant preceded by a single vowel, with an accent on the last syllable, double the final consonant before adding a suffix beginning with a vowel—commit*ted*, forget*ting*, occur*red*, control*ling.*

com·mit·tee (kə·mit′ē) *n.*
A group of people chosen to perform certain tasks: *the Senate committee.*
Spelling tip: *Committee* is the only word in the following troublesome series to contain three doubled letters: *commit, commitment, committed, committal, committee.*

com·mo·di·ous (kə·mō′dē·əs) *adj.*
Having a great deal of room; spacious: *They have a commodious seven-room apartment.*
Syn. ample, capacious, vast, roomy.
Ant. confined, small, crowded, close.

com·mu·nal (kom′yə·nəl or kə·myōō′nəl) *adj.*
Having to do with or belonging to a community: *a communal July 4 celebration.*

com·mu·ni·cate (kə·myōō′nə·kāt′) *v.* **com·mu·ni·cat·ed, com·mu·ni·cat·ing**
To cause another to understand or share in; convey knowledge of: *It is possible to talk with someone and still not communicate.*—**com·mu′ni·ca′tion** *n.*
Spelling tip: Double the *m* and include every vowel.
Syn. impart, convey, transmit.

com·mu·ni·qué (kə·myōō′nə·kā′ or kə·myōō′-nə·ka′) *n.*
An official bulletin: *The President sent a communiqué to all foreign embassies.*

com·mu·ni·ty (kə·myōō′nə·tē) *n.,* **com·mu·ni·ties** *pl.*
1 A group of people living in the same local area and sharing common interests, customs, etc.: *a community of hippies.* 2 The district or area in which these people live: *a suburban community.*

com·mu·ter (kə·myōō′tər) *n.*
One who regularly travels some distance between his home and place of work.

com·pa·ra·ble (kom′pər·ə·bəl) *adj.*
Capable or worthy of comparison: *Are American League baseball teams comparable to National League teams?*—**com′pa·ra·bil′i·ty** *n.,* **com′pa·ra·bly** *adv.*

com·par·a·tive (kəm·par′ə·tiv) *adj.*
1 Having to do with the noting of likenesses and differences: *A shrewd buyer has the comparative instinct.* 2 Relative: *A true blond is a comparative rarity.*—**com·par′a·tive·ly** *adv.*

com·pat·i·ble (kəm·pat′ə·bəl) *adj.*
Capable of getting along together or fitting in: *Despite differences, Jack Spratt and his wife were compatible.*—**com·pat′i·bil′i·ty** *n.*
Syn. congenial, agreeable, complementary.
Ant. incompatible, at odds, discordant.

com·pel (kəm·pel′) *v.* **com·pelled, com·pel·ling**
To urge irresistibly; force: *He was compelled to admit his bankruptcy.*
Spelling tip: Apply the same rule as for *commit:* Words ending in an accented vowel-consonant double the consonant before suffixes beginning with a vowel (compel*led,* compel*ling*).
Syn. make, constrain, enjoin.

com·pen·di·um (kəm·pen′dē·əm) *n., pl.* **com·pen·di·ums** or **com·pen·di·a** *pl.*
A brief, comprehensive abridgment: *The opening chapter is a compendium of the whole book.*
Syn. summary, digest, précis, abstract, synopsis.

com·pe·tence (kom′pə·təns) *n.*
The state of being competent; ability: *the doctor's professional competence.*
Syn. expertise, capability, knowledge.
Ant. incompetence, ignorance, ineptitude.

com·pe·tent (kom′pə·tənt) *adj.*
Capable or adequate: *a competent but uninspiring pianist.*—**com′pe·tent·ly** *adv.*
Spelling tip: Remember the *e*'s in this word.
Syn. skilled, able, efficient, trained.
Ant. inept, blundering, amateurish.

com·pe·ti·tion (kom′pə·tish′ən) *n.*
1 An attempt to excel others or to vie with others for the attainment of a goal: *Two supermarkets were in competition for business.* 2 A contest: *an athletic competition.*
Spelling tip: Note the *e,* as in *compete.*

com·pile (kəm·pīl′) *v.* **com·piled, com·pil·ing**
To assemble or compose from various sources: *The Census Bureau constantly compiles new population estimates.*—**com·pil′er, com′pi·la′tion** *n.*
Syn. gather, accumulate, list.

com·pla·cent (kəm·plā′sənt) *adj.*
Satisfied with oneself; smug: *Early success made him complacent, and from then on he never tried to improve.*—**com·pla′cent·ly** *adv.,* **com·pla′·cen·cy** *n.*

com·plai·sant (kəm·plā′zənt) *adj.*
Willing to please: *He was lucky to find a complaisant housekeeper.*—**com·plai′sance** *n.*
Syn. agreeable, good-humored, yielding, compliant, obedient.
Ant. intransigent, stubborn, inflexible.

com·ple·ment (kom′plə·mənt *n.,* kom′plə·ment *v.*) *n., v.*
n. Something that completes, fills up, or makes perfect: *lyrics that were a marvelous complement to the music.*
v. To make complete, fit in with, or supply a lack in: *Red wine complements meat.*
Etymology: *Complement* and *complete* come from the same Latin word, *complere* (to fill thoroughly).

com·plex·ion (kəm·plek'shən) *n.*
1 Skin color: *a fair complexion*. **2** Character or quality: *the serious complexion of the world situation.*—**com·plex'ion·al, com·plex'-ioned** *adj.*
Spelling tip: Be *x*-tra careful spelling this word.

com·pli·ance (kəm·plī'əns) *n.*
The act of complying or yielding: *Courts enforce compliance with their directives.*
Syn. obedience, acquiescence.
Ant. defiance.

com·pli·ant (kəm·plī'ənt) *adj.*
Submissive or yielding, as to the wishes or pressure of another person: *The compliant secretary agreed to take work home.*
Syn. docile, flexible, pliable, complying.
Ant. intractable, stubborn, resistant.

com·pli·ment (kom'plə·mənt *n.,* kom'plə·ment *v.*) *n., v.*
n. **1** An expression of praise, congratulation, or flattery: *She loved his compliments.* **2** *Usually pl.* A formal greeting or remembrance: *Send my compliments to your father.*
v. To praise: *She complimented him on his good taste.*

com·po·nent (kəm·pō'nənt) *n.*
An element or part: *the audio component of a television set.*
Syn. constituent, unit, ingredient.

com·pro·mise (kom'prə·mīz) *n.; v.* **com·pro·mised, com·pro·mis·ing**
n. An adjustment or settlement by mutual concession.
v. **1** To make a mutual adjustment or settlement: *We compromised on my salary demands.*
2 To expose to risk, suspicion, or disrepute: *Staying out all night on a date may compromise your reputation.*

comp·trol·ler (kən·trō'lər) *n.*
An administrator responsible for fiscal planning and control, as of budgeting, accounting, and tax procedures.
Spelling tip: Also spelled *controller.*

com·pul·sion (kəm·pul'shən) *n.*
1 The act of compelling, or the state of being compelled: *The police used physical compulsion to disperse the crowd.* **2** *In psychology* An irresistible impulse to perform an irrational act: *a compulsion to make obscene telephone calls.*
Syn. **1** force, constraint.

com·pul·so·ry (kəm·pul'sər·ē) *adj.*
Required; obligatory: *compulsory military service.*
Spelling tip: Two *o*'s are compulsory in this word.
Syn. mandatory.
Ant. optional, elective.

com·punc·tion (kəm·pungk'shən) *n.*
1 Uneasiness stemming from a sense of guilt: *He felt no compunction about wiping out his business competitors.* **2** A slight regret: *He felt some compunction about leaving the party early, but he had no choice.*

com·pute (kəm·pyo͞ot') *v.* **com·put·ed, com·put·ing**
To find out (a number or amount) by calculating: *Compute the area by multiplying length by width.*—**com'pu·ta'tion** *n.*
Syn. figure out, reckon.

con·cave (kon·kāv') *adj.*
Hollow and curving inward, as the interior of a bowl.—**con·cav·i·ty** (kən·kav'ə·tē) *n.*
Ant. convex.

con·cede (kən·sēd') *v.* **con·ced·ed, con·ced·ing**
To acknowledge as true, correct, or proper; admit: *The eyewitness conceded under questioning that he might have been mistaken.*
Syn. grant, confess, allow.
Ant. deny.

con·ceiv·a·ble (kən·sēv'ə·bəl) *adj.*
Possible to believe: *It is hardly conceivable that he failed the exam.*—**con·ceiv'a·bly** *adv.*
Spelling tip: *E* before *i* when a *c* you spy.
Syn. believable, credible.
Ant. inconceivable, incredible, unbelievable.

con·ceive (kən·sēv') *v.* **con·ceived, con·ceiv·ing**
1 To become pregnant. **2** To form a notion of; understand or imagine: *to conceive of a world in which all men are treated equally.*
Spelling tip: See CONCEIVABLE.

con·cen·trate (kon'sən·trāt) *v.* **con·cen·trat·ed, con·cen·trat·ing**
1 To draw or direct to a common point: *to concentrate troops.* **2** To direct one's attention: *to concentrate on learning Italian.*—**con'cen·tra'tion** *n.*
Spelling tip: Concentrate on the two *c*'s.
Syn. focus.
Ant. **1** disperse, diffuse, spread out.

con·cen·tric (kən·sen'trik) *adj.*
Having a common center, as a circle within a circle: *Targets often consist of concentric circles.*

con·cep·tion (kən·sep'shən) *n.*
1 The act of conceiving; the onset of pregnancy. **2** The forming of an idea, or that which is conceived mentally: *a noble conception of the role of the U.S. in maintaining freedom.*

con·cern (kən·sûrn') *v. n.*
v. **1** To relate or pertain to: *How does that concern me?* **2** To affect with anxiety: *His illness concerned me deeply.* **3** To occupy the attention or mind of (reflexive or passive word often followed by *with* or *in*): *He concerns himself with petty details.*
n. **1** That which relates or pertains to a person: *His salary is no concern of mine.* **2** Anxiety or interest: *my concern for her in this difficult time.* **3** A business enterprise: *an electronics concern.*

con·cer·to (kən·cher'tō) *n.,* **con·cer·tos** or **con·cer·ti** (kən·cher'ē) *pl.*
A musical composition performed by a solo instrument or instruments accompanied by an orchestra.
Spelling tip: *Concerto,* an Italian word, takes an Italian *i* plural. An English plural, conventionally formed by adding *s,* is also acceptable.

con·ces·sion (kən·sesh′ən) *n.*
1 The act of conceding or yielding, as to a demand, point of argument, etc. 2 Anything so yielded.

con·cil·i·ate (kən·sil′ē·āt) *v.* **con·cil·i·at·ed, con·cil·i·at·ing**
1 To overcome the hostility or mistrust of: *The mediator was able to conciliate both sides.* 2 To make compatible or consistent: *It is impossible to conciliate my salary demands and his offer.*—**con·cil′i·a′tion, con·cil′i·a′tor** *n.*

con·cise (kən·sīs′) *adj.*
Expressing much in brief form: *Dictionary definitions must be concise.*—**con·cise′ly** *adv.*, **con·cise′ness** *n.*
Syn. compact, terse, succinct.
Ant. lengthy, voluminous, expanded.

con·com·i·tant (kon·kom′ə·tənt) *adj.*
Existing or occurring together: *A tax increase was a concomitant effect of the expanded war effort.*—**con·com′i·tant·ly** *adv.*
Syn. attendant, concurrent.
Ant. unrelated, unconnected.

con·cord (kon′kôrd) *n.*
Unity of feeling; agreement: *The U.N. strives to achieve concord among nations.*—**con·cor′dance** *n.*
Syn. accord, peace, harmony.
Ant. discord, disharmony.

con·crete (kon′krēt *or* kon·krēt′) *adj., n.*
adj. Specific or actual: *Foster Parents' Plan is a concrete way to help needy children.*
n. A building material consisting of sand and gravel or broken rock, held together by cement.—**con·crete′ly** *adv.*, **con·crete′ness** *n.*
Syn. *adj.* particular, real.
Ant. *adj.* general, imaginary.

con·cur·rence (kən·kûr′əns) *n.*
Cooperation or agreement to bring about some result: *Congressional concurrence was necessary before the trade agreement could be ratified.*

con·cur·rent (kən·kûr′ənt) *adj.*
Occurring together or at the same time or place: *Two concurrent events, expanding world population and increased technology, have urged men to the Moon.* **con·cur′rent·ly** *adv.*

con·cur·ring (kən·kûr′ing) *adj.*
Agreeing or approving: *a concurring judicial opinion.*
Ant. disagreeing, contrary.

con·de·scend (kon′di·send′) *v.*
1 To come down voluntarily to equal terms with inferiors: *The prince often condescended to chat with his subjects.* 2 To lower oneself to do something: *Her boss would not even condescend to get his own coffee.* 3 To act in a superior or patronizing way: *a social worker condescending to a prison inmate.*—**con′de·scend′ing·ly** *adv.*, **con′de·scen′sion** *n.*
Syn. 2 deign. 3 patronize, look down on.

con·di·ment (kon′də·mənt) *n.*
A sauce, relish, spice, etc., used to season food.

con·do·lence (kən·dō′ləns) *n.*
Sympathy, as expressed to a person suffering from grief, sorrow, etc.: *Please extend my condolence to the widow.*

con·done (kən·dōn′) *v.* **con·doned, con·don·ing**
To overlook an offense or treat it as if it had not happened: *This government will not condone actions that trample the rights of others.*
Syn. forgive, pardon, excuse.

con·duit (kon′dit *or* kon′dōō·it) *n.*
1 A channel or pipe for conveying water or other liquid. 2 A passage or tube for electric wires.
Syn. 1 aqueduct, canal.

con·fer·ence (kon′fər·əns *or* kon′frəns) *n.*
A discussion on some important matter, or a meeting at which such a discussion takes place: *a conference on nuclear disarmament.*
Spelling tip: No matter how you pronounce this word, remember to write all three syllables.

con·fi·dant (kon′fə·dant′, kon′fə·dänt′, kon′-fə·dant, *or* kon′fə·dänt) *n.*
A person to whom one confides secrets or personal confidences: *my dearest friend and long-time confidant.*
Spelling tip: A *confidante* (pronounced the same as *confidant*) is a female *confidant*. Do not confuse these two words with *confident* (assured).

con·fi·dent (kon′fə·dənt) *adj.*
Having confidence; sure of oneself: *He was confident that he could do the job.*—**con′fi·dence** *n.*, **con′fi·dent·ly** *adv.*
Syn. assured, certain, self-assured.
Ant. doubtful, dubious, uncertain.

con·fi·den·tial (kon′fə·den′shəl) *adj.*
1 Given in confidence; meant to be secret: *confidential information.* 2 Intimate: *a confidential tone.*—**con′fi·den′tial·ly** *adj.*
Syn. 1 private, secret. 2 friendly.
Ant. 1 public, general. 2 distant, reserved.

con·fir·ma·tion (kon′fər·mā′shēn) *n.*
1 That which confirms; proof: *The fact that he did not try to flee was confirmation of his innocence.* 2 Formal approval and acceptance: *We awaited Senate confirmation of the President's nominee.* 3 A religious ceremony in which a person is admitted to all the privileges of the church.

con·fis·cate (kon′fis·kāt) *v.* **con·fis·cat·ed, con·fis·cat·ing**
To seize or appropriate as for public use or in payment of some obligation: *Mexican farm holdings were confiscated and redistributed to the peasants.*—**con′fis·ca′tion** *n.*

con·fis·ca·to·ry (kən·fis′kə·tôr′ē) *adj.*
Of the nature of or resulting from confiscation: *a confiscatory action involving millions of dollars.*

con·fla·gra·tion (kon′flə·grā′shən) *n.*
A great and widely destructive fire: *The saturation bombing of Dresden in World War II caused a conflagration that leveled the city.*

565

con·form·i·ty (kən·fôr′mə·tē) *n.*
1 Correspondence in form, manner, etc.:
Conformity of like parts is essential in mass-producing goods. 2 The habit of conforming:
Hippies reject conformity to middle-class conventions.
Syn. 1 agreement, congruity.
Ant. 1 disagreement, difference.

con·geal (kən·jēl′) *v.*
To change from a fluid to a solid condition:
The custard congealed after being refrigerated.
Syn. harden, solidify.
Ant. melt, soften, liquefy.

con·gen·ial (kən·jēn′yəl) *adj.*
1 Having similar character, nature, or tastes:
a congenial group of friends. 2 Suited to one's needs or disposition: *She enjoyed her job because of the congenial surroundings.*
Syn. 1 kindred, sympathetic. 2 agreeable, likable.
Ant. dissimilar, unsympathetic. 2 disagreeable, repugnant, undesirable.

con·gen·i·tal (kən·jen′ə·təl) *adj.*
Existing prior to or at birth, but not inherited: *a congenital defect resulting from a temporary lack of oxygen during birth.*

con·ger (kong′gər) *n.*
A marine eel from four to ten feet long, used as a food fish.

con·glom·er·a·tion (kən·glom′ə·rā′shən) *n.*
A mixed collection of things: *a wild conglomeration of opinions and facts.*

con·grat·u·la·to·ry (kən·grach′ōō·lə·tôr′ē) *adj.*
Expressing congratulations: *a congratulatory telegram.*

con·gru·ent (kong′grōō·ənt) *adj.*
1 *In geometry* Coinciding exactly when superimposed: *Congruent triangles are identical in shape and size.* 2 In agreement or conformity:
He kept his stories congruent with the logic of real life.—**con′gru·ence** *n.,* **con′gru·ous** *adj.*
Syn. 1 identical, duplicate. 2 consistent, compatible, harmonious, concordant.
Ant. 1 different, dissimilar, unlike. 2 incompatible, inconsistent, discordant.

con·ic (kon′ik) *adj.*
Of or like a cone: *the conic root of a carrot.*
Also **con′i·cal** *adj.*—**con′i·cal·ly** *adv.*

con·i·fer (kon′ə·fər *or* kō′nə·fər) *n.*
Any evergreen shrub or tree bearing cones and needles and having resinous wood: *Pines, spruces, and firs are conifers.*—**co·nif·er·ous** (kō·nif′ər·əs) *adj.*
Etymology: *Conifer* comes from two Latin words: *conus* (cone) + *ferre* (to bear).

con·jec·ture (kən·jek′chər) *n.; v.* **con·jec·tured, con·jec·tur·ing**
n. 1 A guess made when there are not enough facts to be certain: *a detective's shrewd conjecture about the murderer.* 2 Guessing or guesswork: *Without concrete evidence, your theory is mere conjecture.*
v. To guess: *He conjectured that the other side would stall for time.*—**con·jec′tur·al** *adj.*
Syn. *n.* 1 theory, surmise, hypothesis, notion.

2 supposition, inference, speculation. *v.* surmise, speculate, suppose, think.
Ant. *n.* 1 certainty, knowledge, proof. 2 fact.

con·ju·gal (kon′jōō·gəl) *adj.*
Of or concerning marriage or the married: *a conjugal relationship; conjugal contentment.*
Syn. matrimonial, marital.

con·nois·seur (kon′ə·sûr′) *n.*
A discriminating judge in matters of art or taste: *The connoisseur of fine foods knew exactly what condiments to use.*
Syn. expert, critic, cognoscente.
Ant. amateur, novice.

con·no·ta·tion (kon′ə·tā′shən) *n.*
What a word or phrase suggests or implies, as distinguished from what it means.
Usage: The *denotation* of a word is its actual, literal meaning. The *connotation* is the feeling it calls up or the associations that cluster around it. "Swarthy" and "dusky" are similar in *denotation,* both meaning dark-complexioned. But they are radically different in *connotation:* "Swarthy" has vaguely sinister overtones, while the exotic "dusky" carries an air of mystery rather than menace.
Syn. implication, overtone, suggestion.

con·quer (kong′kər) *v.*
1 To defeat or take by force of arms: *to conquer enemy territory.* 2 To overcome by force of will: *to conquer fear.* 3 To be victorious.
—**con·quest** (kon′kwest) *n.*

con·science (kon′shəns) *n.*
A personal, inner sense of right and wrong:
His guilty conscience deprived him of peace of mind.
Spelling tip: Don't confuse this word with *conscious.*

con·sci·en·tious (kon′shē·en′shəs) *adj.*
1 Governed by conscience in trying to do right: *a conscientious welfare worker.* 2 Careful and thorough: *a conscientious report covering all sides of the issue.*
Syn. 1 scrupulous, honorable, ethical. 2 painstaking, exact, precise.
Ant. 1 unscrupulous, dishonorable, unethical. 2 sloppy, careless, inexact.

con·scious (kon′shəs) *adj.*
1 Mentally awake: *Although hit on the head, he was still conscious.* 2 Aware: *conscious of my shortcomings.* 3 Deliberate: *a conscious slight.*—**con′scious·ness** *n.*
Spelling tip: Don't confuse this word with *conscience.*
Syn. 1 sentient. 2 cognizant. 3 intentional.
Ant. unconscious.

con·se·crate (kon′sə·krāt) *v.* **con·se·crat·ed, con·se·crat·ing**
1 To dedicate to sacred use: *The bishop will consecrate a chapel.* 2 To devote to a cause: *He consecrated his life to service.*
Syn. 1 sanctify, hallow. 2 dedicate, give.

con·se·quent·ly (kon′sə·kwent′lē) *adv.*
As a result: *It was raining; consequently, the picnic was postponed.*
Syn. therefore, so, hence, accordingly.

con·sid·er·a·ble (kən·sid′ər·ə·bəl) *adj.*
Great enough to be noticed: *a considerable fortune.*—**con·sid′er·a·bly** *adv.*
Spelling tip: Use *-able*, not *-ible*.
Syn. substantial, noteworthy, significant.
Ant. inconsiderable, insignificant, trivial.

con·sid·er·ate (kən·sid′ər·it) *adj.*
Thoughtful of others: *Be considerate of older people.*
Syn. kind, solicitous, obliging.
Ant. unkind, rude, neglectful.

con·sis·ten·cy (kən·sis′tən·sē) *n.*, **con·sis·ten·cies** *pl.*
1 Degree of firmness, thickness, or density: *liquid gelatin cooled to the consistency of jelly.*
2 A holding to the same line of thought or action: *his consistency in opposing censorship throughout his career.* 3 Agreement or uniformity: *the consistency of his testimony.* Also **con·sis′tence** *n.*—**con·sis′tent** *adj.*
Syn. 3 correspondence, compatibility, harmony.
Ant. 3 inconsistency, contradiction.

con·som·mé (kon′sə·mā′) *n.*
A clear soup made of meat or meat stock boiled in water: *beef or chicken consommé.*

con·so·nant (kon′sə·nənt) *adj.*, *n.*
adj. In agreement or harmony: *a decision consonant with his views of the situation.*
n. A letter or speech sound other than a vowel, as *b*, *f*, *s*, and *k*. Consonants are pronounced by blocking the breath stream with the lips, teeth, or tongue.
Syn. *adj.* consistent, accordant, compatible.
Ant. *adj.* inconsistent, discordant, incompatible.

con·sort (kon′sôrt *n.*, kən·sôrt′ *v.*) *n.*, *v.*
n. A spouse, companion, or escort: *Prince Albert was Queen Victoria's consort.*
v. To keep company: *He was accused of consorting with known criminals.*
Syn. *v.* associate, fraternize.
Ant. *v.* part company, avoid.

con·spir·a·cy (kən·spir′ə·sē) *n.*, **con·spir·a·cies** *pl.*
1 A plot involving two or more persons who plan to commit an evil or unlawful act: *a price-fixing conspiracy.* 2 An acting together: *They were unavoidably delayed by a conspiracy of the elements.*—**con·spir′a·tor** *n.*, **con·spire** (kən·spīr′) *v.*
Syn. 1 scheme, intrigue, collusion. 2 concurrence, conjunction.

con·stel·la·tion (kon′stə·lā′shən) *n.*
1 A group of stars imagined to represent the outline of a being or thing, and named accordingly, as Orion, the Big Dipper (Ursa Major), etc. 2 *In astrology* The position of the stars at a particular time, especially at one's birth.

con·stit·u·ent (kən·stich′ōō·ənt) *n.*
1 A necessary part or element: *Nitrogen is a constituent of TNT.* 2 A voter represented by an elective official: *The congressman sent a quarterly report to his constituents.*—**con·stit′u·en·cy** *n.*
Syn. 1 component, ingredient. 2 elector.

con·strue (kən·strōō′) *v.*
1 To interpret: *They construed his silence as consent.* 2 To analyze the grammatical structure of a clause or sentence. 3 To use grammatically: *"Mathematics" is construed as a singular word.*
Syn. 1 understand, explain. 2 parse.

con·sul (kon′səl) *n.*
An official representative of one country living in a foreign city to protect his country's commercial interests and ensure the welfare of its citizens.—**con′sul·ar** *adj.*
Usage: Don't confuse *consul, counsel,* and *council,* all of which sound quite alike. *Counsel* means advice, or denotes one or more lawyers who give a client advice. *Council* denotes a group that meets to discuss issues or to make decisions: *The U.S. consul in Istanbul wrote for counsel to the Milwaukee city council.*

con·sum·mate (kon′sə·māt *v.*, kən·sum′it *adj.*) *v.* **con·sum·mat·ed, con·sum·mat·ing;** *adj.*
v. To complete, perfect, or fulfill: *The Constitution consummated the union between the states.*—**con′sum·ma′tion** *n.*
adj. Of or in the highest degree: *a consummate artist.*
Syn. *v.* finish, crown, cap. *adj.* perfect, complete, matchless, flawless.
Ant. *adj.* poor, inadequate, flawed, imperfect.

con·tam·i·nate (kən·tam′ə·nāt) *v.* **con·tam·i·nat·ed, con·tam·i·nat·ing**
To make dirty or impure: *a stream contaminated by industrial waste.*—**con·tam′i·na′tion** *n.*
Syn. pollute, defile, taint.
Ant. purify, sterilize, disinfect.

con·tem·plate (kon′təm·plāt) *v.* **con·tem·plat·ed, con·tem·plat·ing**
1 To gaze at thoughtfully: *He stood contemplating the Parthenon by moonlight.* 2 To consider, anticipate, or plan: *She is contemplating a trip to Europe. Do you contemplate changing your job?* 3 To meditate: *a scholar contemplating in his study.*—**con′tem·pla′tion** *n.*
Syn. 1 regard, behold. 2 intend, propose, envision. 3 ponder, think, muse, reflect.

con·tem·pla·tive (kən·tem′plə·tiv or kən·tem′plə·tiv) *adj.*
Given to unhurried thought: *the contemplative life of a hermit or monk.*
Syn. thoughtful, meditative, reflective.

con·test·ant (kən·tes′tənt) *n.*
A person who enters a competition or who challenges something: *A local contestant won the prize. Contestants broke the disputed will.*

con·text (kon′tekst) *n.*
The passage or frame of reference in which a word or group of words is used: *The meaning of the word "sore" depends upon the context. Taken out of context, his statement was misleading.*

con·tig·u·ous (kən·tig′yōō·əs) *adj.*
1 Touching at the edge or along a boundary: *Virginia and North Carolina are contiguous.* 2 Close, but not touching: *Two contiguous roadside stands competed for business.*

con·tin·gen·cy (kən·tin′jən·sē) *n.*, **con·tin·gen·cies** *pl.*
1 An unforeseen but possible event: *The expedition was prepared for any contingency.* 2 The condition of being dependent on chance or circumstance: *the contingency of their tentative plans.*
Syn. 2 uncertainty, fortuitousness.
Ant. 2 certainty, firmness.

con·tin·gent (kən·tin′jənt) *adj.*, *n.*
adj. 1 Dependent upon an uncertain event, condition, or outcome: *An increase in your allowance is contingent upon your grades.* 2 Liable but not certain to happen: *a contingent outcome.* 3 Occurring by chance: *contingent catastrophes.*
n. A representative group or proportional part: *the liberal contingent at the meeting; the California contingent of troops.*

con·tin·u·ous (kən·tin′yo͞o·əs) *adj.*
Going on or extending without a break or letup: *a continuous expanse of ocean.*—**con·tin′u·ous·ly** *adv.*
Syn. uninterrupted, unbroken, prolonged.

con·tor·tion (kən·tôr′shən) *n.*
1 A twisting or being twisted: *the contortion of his features in anger and hate.* 2 An unnaturally twisted position or shape: *the contortions of a circus acrobat.*—**con·tor′tion·ist** *n.*

con·tour (kon′to͞or) *n.*, *adj.*
n. The shape or outline of an object: *the cylindrical contour of a cigarette.*
adj. Shaped to fit the outline of something: *contour sheets.*

con·tra·band (kon′trə·band) *n.*, *adj.*
n. Goods that are illegal to import or export: *The border guards searched for contraband.*
adj. Illegal to import or export: *The rebels used contraband weapons.*
Usage: The phrase *contraband of war* denotes goods that a neutral nation may not furnish to a belligerent nation in time of war.

con·tral·to (kən·tral′tō) *n.*
The lowest female singing voice, or a singer with such a voice: *Her voice developed into a deep, husky contralto.*

con·tra·vene (kon′trə·vēn′) *v.* **con·tra·vened, con·tra·ven·ing**
To come into conflict with; oppose, or contradict: *to contravene a law; contravening an orthodox theory.*

con·trib·ute (kən·trib′yo͞ot) *v.* **con·trib·ut·ed, con·trib·ut·ing**
1 To give or provide jointly with others: *Contribute your time to charitable groups.* 2 To help cause: *Popular discontent contributed to the king's downfall.*
Syn. 1 donate, subscribe. 2 influence, affect.
Ant. 1 take, receive. 2 prevent, impede.

con·trite (kən·trīt′ or kon′trīt) *adj.*
Deeply and humbly sorry for one's sin or sins; penitent: *Reformed and contrite, he begged forgiveness.*—**con·tri′tion** (kən·trish′-ən) *n.*

Syn. remorseful, repentant.
Ant. impenitent, uncontrite, unashamed.

con·trol (kən·trōl′) *v.* **con·trolled, con·trol·ling**
1 To exercise a directing, regulatory, or governing influence over: *Parents should control their children.* 2 To regulate or verify, as an experiment.
Spelling tip: For words ending in a vowel and a consonant, with the accent on the last syllable, double the final consonant before a suffix beginning with a vowel.

con·trol·ler (kən·trō′lər) *n.*
1 An administrator responsible for fiscal planning and control, as of budgeting, accounting, and tax procedures. 2 A person who regulates or controls something.
Spelling tip: *Controller*, definition 1, may also be spelled *comptroller.*

con·tro·ver·sial (kon′trə·vûr′shəl) *adj.*
Characterized by or subject to disagreement and debate: *the controversial Vietnam policy.* —**con′tro·ver′sy** *n.*
Syn. contested, disputed, arguable.
Ant. unchallenged, undisputed.

con·tro·vert (kon′trə·vûrt or kon′trə·vûrt′) *v.*
To dispute by evidence or by reasoning: *The defendant tried to controvert the plantiff's story.*
Usage: *Controvert* is a rather formal word with standard legal usage.
Syn. contradict, challenge, refute.
Ant. confirm, support, prove, verify.

con·tu·sion (kən·t(y)o͞o′zhən) *n.*
A bruise: *Thanks to the safety belt, he suffered only contusions and other minor injuries.*

con·va·les·cence (kon′və·les′əns) *n.*
A gradual recovery after the termination of an illness or after surgery, or the period of such a recovery: *The heart operation was successful, but complications prolonged his convalescence.*—**con′va·lesce′** *v.*
Syn. recuperation.

con·vene (kən·vēn′) *v.* **con·vened, con·ven·ing**
To assemble. *The delegates convened at 3:30 and dispersed at 5:30.*
Syn. gather, collect.
Ant. adjourn, disperse, break up.

con·ven·ience (kən·vēn′yəns) *n.*
1 Anything that increases comfort or saves work: *dishwashing machines and other domestic conveniences.* 2 Suitability: *the convenience of using French as an international language.* 3 Personal comfort; ease: *a hotel beauty shop for the convenience of guests.*
Usage: The phrase *at one's convenience* means at a time or occasion suiting a person's needs or preference: *I will be glad to meet him at his convenience.*
Spelling tip: Watch the spelling (and pronunciation) of the last syllable.

con·ver·sant (kon′vər·sənt or kən·vûr′sənt) *adj.*
Familiar, as by extensive study: *Professor Smith is conversant with the history of Iceland.*
Syn. knowledgeable, informed.
Ant. ignorant, unfamiliar.

con·vex (kon′veks *or* kon·veks′) *adj.*
Curving outward, as the surface of a globe.
Ant. concave.

con·vey·ance (kən·vā′əns) *n.*
1 A vehicle or other means of transport: *planes and other modern conveyances.* 2 The act of transporting: *conveyance of secret documents by diplomatic couriers.*
Syn. 1 carrier. 2 transport, transmittal.

con·vey·er (kən·vā′ər) *n.*
Something or someone that transports, as an endless belt.
Spelling tip: This word may also be spelled *conveyor.*

con·viv·i·al (kən·viv′ē·əl) *adj.*
Characterized by good fellowship: *a convivial college reunion.*—**con·viv′i·al′i·ty** (kən·viv′ē·al′ə·tē) *n.*
Syn. jovial, sociable, companionable, merry.
Ant. unfriendly, cold, stiff, gloomy.

con·voke (kən·vōk′) *v.* **con·voked, con·vok·ing**
To summon for a meeting: *The President convoked the regional council.*
Syn. convene, call, assemble.
Ant. adjourn.

coo·lie (kōō′lē) *n.*
In the Orient, an unskilled, very low-paid laborer: *He hired a coolie to carry the trunk.*
Spelling tip: This word may also be spelled *cooly.*

co·op·er·ate (kō·op′ə·rāt) *v.* **co·op·er·at·ed, co·op·er·at·ing**
To work together for a common end: *Teachers and students cooperated in producing the play.*—**co·op′er·a′tion** *n.*
Spelling tip: *Cooperate* is the most common spelling, but *co-operate* and *coöperate* are also acceptable. However, the use of a dieresis (¨) is considered quite old-fashioned.

co·pi·ous (kō′pē·əs) *adj.*
Plentiful; consisting of a large quantity or rich assortment.
Syn. abundant, bountiful, lavish.
Ant. meager, insufficient, minimal, spare.

co·quet·ry (kō′kə·trē *or* kō·ket′rē) *n.*
Female flirting: *Her come-hither glances are only coquetry.*
Syn. flirtatiousness, vamping, dalliance.

co·quette (kō·ket′) *n.*
A flirtatious woman: *a pretty coquette, smiling suggestively.*
Syn. flirt.

cor·al (kôr′əl *or* kor′əl) *n.*
1 A substance formed from the external skeletons of certain primitive marine organisms; also, the individual skeleton. 2 A color ranging from delicate pink-red to orange-red.
Spelling tip: Do not confuse *coral* with *corral.*

cor·dial (kôr′jəl) *adj.*
adj. Friendly; warm: *a cordial meeting of old friends.*
Syn. *adj.* affable, genial.
Ant. *adj.* formal, hostile, surly.

cor·dial·i·ty (kôr·jal′ə·tē *or* kôr·jē·al′ə·tē) *n.*

Sincerity of feeling; warmth: *He greeted his friend with much cordiality.*
Syn. geniality, friendliness, heartiness.
Ant. aloofness, coldness.

cor·dial·ly (kôr′jəl·ē) *adv.*
In a warm, friendly manner: *cordially welcomed.*
Syn. warmly, heartily, genially, sincerely.
Ant. formally, coldly, gruffly, belligerently.

cor·du·roy (kôr′də·roi) *n.*
A durable, heavy fabric, usually of cotton, with vertical ribs.

cor·nice (kôr′nis) *n.*
1 A horizontal molding projecting from the top of a wall, building, etc., for ornamentation.
2 A decorative frame of wood or metal to cover curtain fixtures.

cor·nu·co·pi·a (kôr′nə·kō′pē·ə) *n.*
A symbol of abundance, represented as a curved horn overflowing with fruits, vegetables, grains, etc.
Syn. horn of plenty.

cor·o·ner (kôr′ə·nər *or* kor′ə·ner) *n.*
A local official who presides over inquests: *The verdict of the coroner's jury was murder by persons unknown.*

cor·po·rate (kôr′pər·it) *adj.*
Pertaining to a business corporation: *the corporate charter.*

cor·po·re·al (kôr·pôr′ē·əl *or* kôr·pō′rē·əl) *adj.*
Material; tangible: *corporeal things such as typewriters, as opposed to ghosts or to such intangibles as happiness.*
Syn. physical, concrete.
Ant. incorporeal, spiritual, intangible, abstract.

corps (kôr *or* kōr) *n.,* **corps** *pl.*
1 A military unit or special department: *the Third Corps; the Transport Corps.* 2 A group of persons acting or working together.

cor·pu·lent (kôr′pyə·lənt) *adj.*
Fat: *A corpulent man should diet.*
Syn. obese, fleshy, portly.
Ant. lean, skinny, thin, gaunt.

cor·pus de·lic·ti (kôr′pəs di·lik′tī) *n.*
In law Literally, "the body of the crime," the basic piece of evidence that proves a crime has been committed: *A dead body is the corpus delicti in a murder, and a slashed painting is the corpus delicti in a vandalism.*

cor·ral (kə·ral′) *n.; v.* **cor·ralled, cor·ral·ling** *n.* An enclosed space or pen for livestock: *Drive the horses into the corral.*
v. To drive into and enclose in a corral: *He corralled the steer.*
Syn. *n.* pen, enclosure, fold. *v.* pen, coop, round up.
Ant. *v.* free.

cor·re·late (kôr′ə·lāt *or* kor′ə·lāt) *v.* **cor·re·lat·ed, cor·re·lat·ing**
v. To demonstrate a relationship between: *Scientists have correlated cancer and cigarette smoking.*
Syn. *v.* relate, connect, link.

cor·re·spon·dence (kôr′ə·spon′dəns *or* kor′ə·spon′dəns) *n.*

1 An exchange of letters; also, the letters written. 2 A resemblance or analogy: *the correspondence between the Greek and Roman gods.*
Syn. 1 notes, epistles. 2 congruity, similarity, likeness.
Ant. 2 incongruity, discrepancy, contrast, difference.

cor·rob·o·rate (kə·rob'ə·rāt) *v.* **cor·rob·o·rat·ed, cor·rob·o·rat·ing**
To confirm: *Eyewitness testimony corroborated the circumstantial evidence.*
Syn. confirm, verify, substantiate, support.
Ant. disprove, contradict, controvert.

cor·rode (kə·rōd') *v.* **cor·rod·ed, cor·rod·ing**
To eat away, as by chemical action: *an old tin box, badly corroded.*
Syn. erode.

cor·ro·sive (kə·rō'siv) *adj.*
1 Having the power to eat away, as by chemical action: *a highly corrosive acid.* 2 Tending to destroy or to hurt feelings: *a corrosive wit.*

cor·ru·gat·ed (kôr'ə·gāt'əd *or* kor'ə·gāt'əd) *adj.*
Shaped in alternate parallel ridges and furrows: *corrugated cardboard.*
Syn. ridged, furrowed, grooved.
Ant. smooth, flattened.

cor·tege (kôr·tezh' *or* kôr·tāzh') *n.*
A group of attendants: *the queen and her cortege.*
Syn. retinue, entourage, escort.

cos·mic (koz'mik) *adj.*
Pertaining to the universe or cosmos.
Syn. macrocosmic, universal.

cos·mos (koz'məs *or* koz'mos) *n.*
The universe.
Syn. macrocosm.

co·te·rie (kō'tə·rē) *n.*
A small, exclusive group of persons who share certain interests or pursuits: *an artistic and literary coterie.*
Syn. clique, circle.

co·til·lion (kō·til'yən *or* kə·til'yən) *n.*
A kind of dance or ball: *the spring cotillion.*
Spelling tip: This word is also spelled *cotillon.*

coun·cil (koun'səl) *n.*
1 A meeting of persons for discussion or consultation: *a council of physicians.* 2 A group of people elected or appointed to make laws and administer the affairs of a territory, colony, city, etc.
Usage: See CONSUL.

coun·cil·or (koun'səl·ər) *n.*
A member of a council: *a councilor of a city government.*
Spelling tip: Do not confuse *councilor* with *counselor.*

coun·sel (koun'səl) *n.; v.* **coun·seled** *or* **coun·selled, coun·sel·ing** *or* **coun·sel·ling**
n. 1 Exchange of opinions and ideas; discussion. 2 Advice: *He followed the counsel of his wise old professor.* 3 A lawyer or group of

lawyers engaged to give advice in legal matters or to conduct a case in court.
v. 1 To give advice; advise: *He was counseled to sell his stocks.* 2 To advise in favor of; recommend: *to counsel prudence in making decisions.*
Usage: See CONSUL.

coun·sel·or (koun'sə·lər *or* koun'slər) *n.*
1 One who gives counsel; an adviser. 2 An attorney at law. 3 A member of the supervisory staff at a children's camp: *a swimming counselor.*

coun·ter·feit (koun'tər·fit) *adj., n., v.*
adj. Made to resemble some genuine thing with the intent to deceive: *counterfeit money.*
n. Something made fraudulently to resemble something else: *The large diamond she wore proved to be a counterfeit.*
v. 1 To make an imitation with the intent to defraud: *to counterfeit fifty-dollar bills.* 2 To feign or sham: *to counterfeit remorse.*
Syn. *adj.* false, phony, sham. *n.* forgery, sham. *v.* 2 pretend, affect.

coun·ter·mand (koun'tər·mand') *v.*
To cancel (a previous command or order), often by giving an opposite one: *After instructing his men to attack, he countermanded the order and called for a retreat.*
Syn. rescind, revoke.

coun·ter·part (koun'tər·pärt') *n.*
1 A person or thing precisely or closely resembling another. 2 A person or thing that supplements or completes another: *Here's my left shoe, but where is its counterpart?*
Syn. 1 duplicate, copy. 2 complement.
Ant. 1 antithesis, opposite.

coup (kōō) *n.,* **coups** (kōōz) *pl.*
A sudden and brilliant move; masterstroke: *He made a coup when he submitted the lowest bid and was awarded the contract.*
Etymology: *Coup,* adopted from a French word, literally means "a stroke or blow."

coup de grâce (kōō' də gräs'), **coups de grâce** *pl.*
1 A death blow or shot given to a wounded enemy or to an animal to end suffering. 2 Any act or event putting an end to something: *The large-scale production of the Model-T Ford gave the* coup de grâce *to the horse and buggy.*
Etymology: *Coup de grâce* is a French term that literally means "a stroke of mercy."

coup d'é·tat (kōō' dā·tà'), **coups d'état** *pl.*
An unexpected stroke of political policy, especially a sudden seizure of a government often involving force and violence: *On Dec. 2, 1851, Louis Napoleon by a coup d'état made himself emperor of France.*
Etymology: *Coup d'état* is a French phrase that literally means "a stroke of state."

coup·ling (kup'ling) *n.*
1 A linking device, especially one for joining railroad cars. 2 The act of joining or linking one thing to another: *a coupling of great charm and keen intellect.*
Syn. 2 union, uniting, pairing.

cou·ra·geous (kə·rā′jəs) *adj.*
Possessing or characterized by courage: *a courageous soldier.*—**cou·ra′geous·ly** *adv.*, **cou·ra′geous·ness** *n.*
Syn. daring, brave, fearless, valorous.
Ant. cowardly, timid, fearful.

cour·te·ous (kûr′tē·əs) *adj.*
Showing courtesy to others.—**cour′te·ous·ly** *adv.*, **cour′te·ous·ness** *n.*
Syn. polite, courtly, obliging, gracious.
Ant. unmannerly, boorish, rude, impolite, discourteous.

cour·te·san (kôr′tə·zən *or* kōr′tə·zen) *n.*
A woman who prostitutes herself to men of wealth and high rank; a kept woman: *Nell Gwyn was a famous courtesan in the court of Charles II of England.*

cour·te·sy (kûr′tə·sē) *n.*, **cour·te·sies** *pl.*
1 Politeness, kindness, and thoughtfulness to others. 2 A polite, kind, or thoughtful act: *the courtesy of breaking a date well in advance.*
Spelling tip: It is an old-fashioned *courtesy* for a woman to *curtsy*—but don't confuse these two words.
Syn. 1 manners, affability, civility.
Ant. 1 rudeness, incivility, impoliteness.

cour·ti·er (kôr′tē·ər) *n.*
1 A member of a sovereign's court. 2 A person who seeks favor of those in a higher position by flattery and a desire to please.

cov·e·nant (kuv′ə·nənt) *n.*, *v.*
n. An agreement entered into by two or more persons or parties: *a covenant among neighboring powers to keep peace.*
v. To promise by or in a covenant.
Syn. *n.* pact, treaty, concordat. *v.* agree, contract.

cov·et (kuv′it) *v.*
1 To desire eagerly; long for: *Many people coveted invitations to the party.* 2 To desire something belonging to someone else: *Early settlers coveted land belonging to the Indians.*

cov·et·ous (kuv′ə·təs) *adj.*
Excessively desirous of something, especially something belonging to another: *covetous of his neighbor's wife.*—**cov′et·ous·ly** *adv.*, **cov′et·ous·ness** *n.*

cov·ey (kuv′ē) *n.*, **cov·eys** *pl.*
1 A flock of quails or partridges. 2 A group: *A covey of autograph-seekers surrounded the screen idol.*
Syn. 2 bevy, flock, herd, crowd.

cow·er (kou′ər) *v.*
To crouch or cringe, as in fear or shame: *When the cat was nearby, the mice cowered in their holes.*
Syn. quail, tremble, shrink, flinch.

cox·swain (kok′sən *or* kok′swān′) *n.*
A person who steers or has charge of a small boat or racing shell.

coy·o·te (kī·ō′tē) *n.*, **coy·o·tes** *or* **coy·o·te** *pl.*
A small wolf with a piercing howl, common to the prairies of the western United States.

crass (kras) *adj.*
Grossly vulgar or stupid: *She always makes crass remarks about the cost of things.*—**crass′ly** *adv.*, **crass′ness** *n.*
Syn. crude, ignorant, unmannerly.

cra·vat (krə·vat′) *n.*
1 A man's scarf, often worn in the open neck of a shirt in place of a necktie. 2 Formerly, any necktie.

crea·ture (krē′chər) *n.*
1 A living being, especially an animal: *Rabbits and deer are shy woodland creatures.* 2 A person, especially when regarded with pity, scorn, etc.: *The poor creature could scarcely read or write.* 3 A person who is dependent upon, influenced by, or dominated by another: *The king was a mere creature of the prime minister.*
Syn. 3 puppet, tool.

cre·dence (krēd′(ə)ns) *n.*
Belief, especially as based upon the evidence or reports of others: *He does not give credence to rumors.*
Syn. trust, faith, acceptance, confidence, reliance.
Ant. disbelief, denial, distrust, doubt, skepticism.

cre·den·tials (kri·den′shəlz) *n.pl.*
A certificate giving evidence of one's authority, identity, or claim to trustworthiness: *A convention delegate must present his credentials.*

cred·i·ble (kred′ə·bəl) *adj.*
1 Capable of being believed: *He told a credible story to explain his delay.* 2 Worthy of confidence; reliable: *a credible witness.*—**cred·i·bil·i·ty** (kred′ə·bil′ə·tē) *n.*, **cred′i·bly** *adv.*
Usage: Be careful not to confuse *credible* with *creditable* and *credulous. Creditable* means deserving credit or esteem; *credulous* means apt to believe anything without question. Both *credible* and *creditable* apply to people and statements, but *credulous* applies only to people.

cre·do (krē′dō *or* krā′dō) *n.*, **cre·dos** *pl.*
1 A set of beliefs; creed: *the credo of a socialist.* 2 (Often capital *C*) In some Christian churches, a confession of faith, either sung or recited; also, a musical setting for this.
Syn. 1 doctrine, tenets, principles.

cre·du·li·ty (kre·d(y)ōō′lə·tē) *n.*
Readiness to believe anything on very slight evidence; foolish, unjustified trustfulness: *Advertisers depend upon the credulity of the public to sell many of their products.*
Syn. gullibility, naiveté, unsophistication.
Ant. skepticism, shrewdness, suspiciousness.

cred·u·lous (krej′ōō·ləs) *adj.*
Apt to believe anything without question; easy to mislead: *a credulous young man from the country.*—**cred′u·lous·ly** *adv.*, **cred′u·lous·ness** *n.*
Usage: See CREDIBLE.
Syn. gullible, naive, trusting.
Ant. skeptical, shrewd, suspicious, cautious.

creel (krēl) *n.*
1 An angler's wicker basket for carrying fish. 2 A frame in a spinning machine that holds the bobbins.

cre·ma·to·ry (krē'mə·tôr'ē) *n.*, **cre·ma·to·ries** *pl.*
A furnace for reducing dead bodies to ashes; also, the building containing such a furnace.

cre·ole (krē'ōl) *adj.*
Cooked with a savory sauce containing peppers, okra, tomatoes, onions, etc.: *shrimp creole.*
Etymology: *Creole* as a cooking term means cooked in the style of the *Creoles,* descendants of the original French settlers in and about New Orleans.

cre·scen·do (krə·shen'dō) *n.*, **cre·scen·dos** *pl.*
A gradual increase in the volume of sound or in emotional intensity, usually used in connection with singing or instrumental playing: *The sonata ended in a crescendo.*
Etymology: *Crescendo* comes from the Italian word *crescere,* to grow or to increase.

cres·cent (kres'ənt) *n., adj.*
n. **1** The curved shape that is the visible part of the moon in its first or last quarter. **2** Anything so shaped: *crescents of beautifully browned, crisp pastry.*
adj. Having such a shape: *a crescent moon.*

cre·vasse (krə·vas') *n.*
1 A deep crack or chasm, as in a glacier. **2** A break in the levee of a river.

crev·ice (krev'is) *n.*
An opening or crack on or through the surface of a wall, rock, etc.
Syn. split, fissure, cleft, chink.

crin·o·line (krin'ə·lin) *n.*
1 A very stiff material used in puffed sleeves, hems, interlinings, etc. **2** A petticoat of this fabric. **3** A hoop skirt.

cri·te·ri·on (krī·tir'ē·ən) *n.*, **cri·te·ri·a** (krī·tir'ē·ə) or **cri·te·ri·ons** *pl.*
A standard or rule by which a judgment can be made.
Usage: Note that there are two acceptable plurals for *criterion,* and be careful not to mistake *criteria* for a singular noun taking a singular verb: *Each college-admission criterion is being reviewed, and new criteria are expected soon.*

crit·i·cize (krit'ə·sīz) *v.* **crit·i·cized, crit·i·ciz·ing**
1 To judge severely; find fault with. **2** To examine critically: *to criticize a new novel.*
Spelling tip: American and British spelling differ on words ending in an *-iz* sound. American spelling calls for a *z,* while British spelling is with an *s* (criticize, criticise; organize, organise; etc.).
Syn. 1 censure, reprove, castigate. **2** appraise, review, analyze.
Ant. 1 praise, commend, acclaim.

cro·chet (krō·shā') *v.* **cro·cheted** (krō·shād'), **cro·chet·ing** (krō·shā'ing)
To form or decorate a fabric by interlacing thread with a hooked needle.
Spelling tip: The final *-et* of French-derived words is pronounced *ā:* crochet, beret, sachet, filet mignon—and Robert Goulet.

crone (krōn) *n.*
A withered old woman.

cro·quet (krō·kā') *n.*
An outdoor game in which the players use long-handled mallets to drive wooden balls through a series of wire arches.
Spelling tip: Note the *ā*-sounding *-et.* Also, do not confuse this word with *croquette* (a cake of minced food).

cro·quette (krō·ket') *n.*
A ball or cake of minced food, such as meat, fowl, or fish, fried in deep fat.

crotch·et (kroch'it) *n.*
An odd or perverse notion or whim: *One of the old man's crotchets was going to bed with all his clothes on.*
Syn. eccentricity, quirk, vagary, caprice.

crotch·et·y (kroch'ə·tē) *adj.*
1 Given to whimsical or cranky behavior: *a crotchety old crone.* **2** Like a crotchet: *crotchety mannerisms.*
Syn. eccentric, whimsical, capricious.

cru·cial (krōō'shəl) *adj.*
1 Important because of its critical or decisive nature: *This crucial game will determine the section winner.* **2** Involving trials and difficulties; severe: *a crucial moment in her life.*
Syn. 1 pivotal, deciding, definitive. **2** grave, trying, acute, momentous.

cru·et (krōō'it) *n.*
1 A small glass bottle for vinegar, oil, etc., used at the dining table. **2** A similar vessel used to hold wine or water at an ecclesiastical service.

crux (kruks) *n.*, **crux·es** or **cru·ces** (krōō'sēz) *pl.*
A main, central, pivotal, or vital point: *Many consider lack of education the crux of the poverty cycle.*

cryp·tic (krip'tik) *adj.*
Not plainly evident or easily understandable: *a cryptic message hidden in a maze of undecipherable prose.*
Syn. hidden, secret, mysterious, occult.
Ant. clear, understandable, explicit.

crys·tal·line (kris'tə·line) *adj.*
1 Of, having to do with, or like crystal or crystals: *a crystalline compound.* **2** Resembling crystal in appearance: *a crystalline sky.* **3** Composed or made of crystal or crystals: *Granite is crystalline.*
Syn. 2 clear, transparent, pure, pellucid.

cuck·oo (kōōk'ōō; *also* kōō'kōō *for adj.*) *n.*, **cuck·oos** *pl.; adj.*
n. Any of a number of birds whose call sounds like the word "cuckoo."
adj. Slang Crazy, silly, stupid.

cu·cum·ber (kyōō'kum·bər) *n.*
1 A long, cylindrical fruit that has a hard, green rind and a crisp, white flesh. **2** The creeping plant on which this fruit grows.

cui·sine (kwi·zēn') *n.*
A type, method, or quality of cooking: *Chinese cuisine; the excellent cuisine of our neighborhood restaurant.*

cul-de-sac (kul'də·sak' or kōōl'də·sak') *n.*, **cul-de-sacs** *pl.*
1 A passage open only at one end. **2** A place,

position, or situation in which one is trapped: *His illogical arguments led him into a cul-de-sac where he was bested by his opponent's consistent reasoning.*

cu·li·nar·y (kyōō'lə·ner'ē *or* kul'ə·ner'ē) *adj.*
Of or having to do with cooking or the kitchen: *Julia Child is a master of culinary techniques.*

cul·mi·nate (kul'min·āt) *v.* **cul·mi·nat·ed, cul·mi·nat·ing**
To reach the highest point or degree; come to a final result or effect: *The long strike culminated in a settlement.*—**cul'mi·na'tion** *n.*
Syn. climax, end.

cul·pa·ble (kul'pə·bəl) *adj.*
Deserving blame or censure: *a nurse guilty of culpable neglect.*—**cul·pa·bil·i·ty** (kul'pə·bil'-ə·tē) *n.,* **cul'pa·bly** *adv.*
Syn. blameworthy, reproachable, censurable, reprehensible.
Ant. blameless, guiltless, innocent, faultless.

cul·vert (kul'vərt) *n.*
An artificial, covered channel for water, as under a road.

cu·ne·i·form (kyōō·nē'ə·fôrm *or* kyōō'nē·ə·fôrm') *adj., n.*
adj. Wedge-shaped, as the characters in some ancient Sumerian, Assyrian, Babylonian, and Persian inscriptions.
n. The writing done in cuneiform characters.

cu·pid·i·ty (kyōō·pid'ə·tē) *n.*
Eager desire for possession, especially of wealth.
Syn. avarice, greed, covetousness.
Ant. liberality, generosity, unselfishness.

cu·po·la (kyōō'pə·lə) *n.*
1 A rounded roof; dome. 2 A small, towerlike structure with a dome-shaped top, rising above the roof of a building.

cu·ri·os·i·ty (kyoor'ē·os'ə·tē) *n.,* **cu·ri·os·i·ties** *pl.*
1 Eager desire for knowledge of something, especially of something novel or unusual. 2 Interest in the private affairs of others. 3 Something that is interesting because of its strangeness or rarity.
Syn. 1 inquisitiveness, interest. 2 meddlesomeness, nosiness. 3 oddity, marvel, phenomenon.
Ant. 1 disinterest, indifference, apathy.

cur·mudg·eon (kər·muj'ən) *n.*
A gruff or irritable person, especially an elderly man.—**cur·mudg'eon·ly** *adj.*
Syn. codger, churl.

cur·ric·u·lum (kə·rik'yə·ləm) *n.,* **cur·ric·u·lums** or **cur·ric·u·la** (kə·rik'yə·lə) *pl.*
All the courses of study offered at a school or for any particular grade in a school.

cur·ry (kûr'ē) *v.* **cur·ried, cur·ry·ing;** *n.*
v. To rub down and clean with a currycomb; groom (a horse, etc.).
n. A pungent sauce of East Indian origin, used as a relish for meats, rice, etc.
Usage: This word is often used in the expression *to curry favor,* which means to seek favor by flattery, etc.

cur·so·ry (kûr'sər·ē) *adj.*
Not thorough; too fast: *A cursory reading of the manuscript failed to reveal its true worth.*—**cur'so·ri·ly** *adv.,* **cur'so·ri·ness** *n.*
Syn. superficial, careless, slapdash, perfunctory.
Ant. thorough, careful, painstaking.

cur·tail (kər·tāl') *v.*
To cut off or cut short: *to curtail expenditures.*—**cur·tail'er, cur·tail'ment** *n.*
Syn. reduce, abbreviate, lessen, diminish.
Ant. extend, expand, enlarge, increase.

cur·tain (kûr'tən) *n., v.*
n. 1 A piece or pieces of cloth, etc., hanging in a window or other opening. 2 Something that conceals or separates like a curtain: *the curtain of darkness.*
v. To provide, shut off, or conceal with or as if with a curtain: *to curtain off the pantry.*
Spelling tip: Be *certain* to spell *curtain* with an *ain.*
Syn. *n.* 1 drapery, tapestry, hanging, portière.
v. cover, conceal, screen, hide.

cy·a·nide (sī'ə·nīd) *n.*
Any one of a number of highly poisonous chemical compounds.

cyc·la·men (sik'lə·mən *or* sī'klə·mən) *n.*
A plant of the primrose family, with large white, pink, or crimson flowers.

cy·clo·tron (sī'klə·tron) *n.*
An accelerator in which electrified particles are whirled at very high speeds in a strong magnetic field.

cyl·in·der (sil'in·dər) *n.*
1 A solid figure described by the circumference of a circle whose center moves along a straight line: *A cylinder resembles a section of pipe.* 2 Any shape similar to this.—**cy·lin'dri·cal** *adj.*

cym·bal (sim'bəl) *n.*
A concave metal plate that is beaten or is clashed in pairs to produce a musical, ringing sound.—**cym'bal·ist** *n.*
Spelling tip: Don't confuse this word with *symbol* (something that stands for something else).

cyn·ic (sin'ik) *n.*
A sneering, faultfinding person, especially one who believes that all men are motivated by selfishness or insincerity.—**cyn'i·cal** *adj.,* **cyn'i·cal·ly** *adv.*
Syn. skeptic, sneerer, misanthrope, pessimist.

cyst (sist) *n.*
Any abnormal sac or vesicle in the body in which matter may collect and be retained.

czar (zär) *n.*
1 An emperor or king, especially one of the former emperors of Russia. 2 A person who has great power or authority: *a czar of industry.*—**cza·ri'na** *n.fem.*
Etymology: This word derives from Gaius Julius *Caesar,* the Roman general and statesman who died in 44 B.C.
Spelling tip: Although *czar* is the most common spelling, *tsar* and *tzar* are acceptable variations.
Syn. 2 boss, chief, dictator, captain, arbiter.

D

dachs·hund (däks'hoŏnt' *or* daks'hoŏnd') *n.*
A breed of dog native to Germany, having a long body, short legs, and a short coat.
Spelling tip: Heed the two *h*'s in *dachshund.*

dahl·ia (dal'yə) *n.*
A perennial plant having showy red, purple, yellow, or white flowers.
Etymology: Named after Anders Dahl, an eighteenth-century Swedish botanist.

dair·y (dâr'ē) *n.*, **dair·ies** *pl.*
1 A farm for producing milk. 2 A place where milk and milk products are kept, processed, or sold.

da·is (dā'is, dī'əs, *or* dās) *n.*
A raised platform in a room or hall on which a speaker, eminent guests, etc. may sit or stand: *He had a seat on the dais.*
Syn. stage, rostrum, podium.

dal·ly (dal'ē) *v.* **dal·lied, dal·ly·ing**
1 To treat lightly or mockingly: *the danger of dallying with temptation.* 2 To waste time: *We're already late, so stop dallying.*—**dal'li·ance** *n.*
Syn. 1 play, trifle, sport, tamper, toy. 2 dawdle, delay, linger, tarry.
Ant. 2 hurry, hasten, rush.

dan·ger·ous (dān'jər·əs) *adj.*
Involving risk or threatening peril: *a dangerous mission.*
Syn. perilous, hazardous, risky.
Ant. safe, secure, harmless.

da·ta (dā'tə *or* dat'ə) *n.pl.*
Facts or figures from which conclusions may be drawn: *data processing.*
Usage: *Data* is the Latin plural of *datum,* and some still treat it as a plural in English: *These data have been studied.* But the word is now widely used with a singular verb: *No data is available.*
Syn. information, intelligence, evidence.

daub (dôb) *v., n.*
v. 1 To smear or coat with something sticky or oily: *She daubed her face with cold cream.* 2 To apply paint or color in a crude or careless way: *an unskilled amateur daubing on splashes of paint.*
n. Any sticky application, smear, or spot.
Syn. *v.* 1 cover, plaster. 2 splash, dash. *n.* splash, smirch, stain.

daunt (dônt *or* dänt) *v.*
To dishearten, frighten, or discourage: *Failure did not daunt him.*
Syn. intimidate, cow, dismay, abash.
Ant. encourage, hearten, embolden.

daunt·less (dônt'lis *or* dänt'lis) *adj.*
Not shaken or discouraged by fear: *He pressed on with dauntless determination.*
Syn. fearless, intrepid, valiant.
Ant. intimidated, timid, fainthearted.

dau·phin (dô'fin; *French* dō·faṅ') *n.*
The eldest son of a king of France, a title used from 1349 to 1830.
Spelling tip: Don't confuse *dauphin* (a prince) with *dolphin* (a porpoise).

daw·dle (dôd'l) *v.* **daw·dled, daw·dling**
To waste time in slow trifling: *Hurry up—don't dawdle.*
Syn. idle, dally, loiter, fiddle.
Ant. hurry, rush, hasten.

dearth (dûrth) *n.*
A lack or scarcity: *a dearth of fresh ideas.*
Syn. absence, shortage, deficiency.
Ant. abundance, plenitude, sufficiency.

de·base (di·bās') *v.* **de·based, de·bas·ing**
To lower in quality, character, or worth: *Inflation debases the currency.*
Syn. degrade, demean, depreciate.
Ant. raise, exalt, uplift, ennoble.

de·bauch (di·bôch') *v., n.*
v. 1 To corrupt in morals or principles: *debauched by evil associates.* 2 To overindulge one's sensual appetites.
n. An act or period of gross sensual indulgence or riotous living: *a week's debauch.* Also **de·bauch·er·y** (di·bô'chər·ē) *n.*
Syn. *v.* 1 seduce, degrade. 2 dissipate, carouse. *n.* orgy, carousal.
Ant. *v.* 1 purify, uplift. 2 abstain. *n.* self-denial, continence, temperance.

de·ben·ture (di·ben'chər) *n.*
1 A certificate given as acknowledgment of debt. 2 A bond, usually without security, issued by a corporation and often convertible into common stock.
Etymology: *Debenture* goes back to the Latin verb *debere,* to owe.

de·bil·i·tate (di·bil'ə·tāt) *v.* **de·bil·i·tat·ed, de·bil·i·tat·ing**
To make feeble or languid: *a body debilitated by a lingering illness; a hot, humid, debilitating climate.*
Syn. weaken, enfeeble, enervate.
Ant. strengthen, invigorate, enliven.

deb·o·nair (deb'ə·nâr') *adj.*
Cheerful, pleasant, and assured, with carefree good spirits or a worldly-wise air of elegance: *a lighthearted, debonair fellow with a flower in his buttonhole.*
Syn. urbane, jaunty, suave, nonchalant.
Ant. sedate, staid, gauche, clumsy.

de·but (di·byoō', dā·byoō', *or* dā'byoō) *n.*
1 A first public appearance, as on the stage: *an actor's Broadway debut.* 2 The formal entrance of a girl into fashionable society: *She made her debut at the ball.*
Syn. 1 bow. 2 coming-out.

deb·u·tante (deb'yoō·tänt) *n.*
A young woman making a debut in society.

dec·ade (dek'ād) *n.*
A period of ten years: *the decade of the 1950s.*
Etymology: *Decade* goes back to the Greek word *deka,* meaning ten. A *decagon* has ten sides; the *decathlon* is a ten-event contest.

dec·a·dence (dek'ə·dəns *or* di·kād'ns) *n.*
A process or period of deterioration or decline, as in art or morals: *the decadence of the Roman Empire in its last years.*
Syn. decay, degeneration, wane, retrogression.
Ant. rise, flowering, blossoming, progress.

de·ceive (di·sēv′) *v.* **de·ceived, de·ceiv·ing**
To trick or mislead by deliberately giving a false impression: *I thought him honest, but he deceived me about his past.*
Spelling tip: Don't let this word deceive you —remember the *c*, and the old rule "*i* before *e* except after *c*."
Syn. fool, delude, dupe, hoodwink.

de·cent (dē′sənt) *adj.*
1 Proper or respectable: *decent behavior.* 2 Fairly good: *a decent place to live, but no palace.* 3 Generous or kind: *He was very decent in his treatment of us.*—**de′cen·cy** *n.*, **de′cent·ly** *adv.*
Spelling tip: Don't confuse *decent* with *descent′* (a going down) or with *dis·sent′* (disagreement or to disagree). *A decent man expresses dissent without a descent to indecency.*
Syn. 1 appropriate, seemly, suitable. 2 satisfactory, adequate, passable. 3 honorable, fair, reasonable.
Ant. 1 indecent, unseemly. 2 poor, inadequate. 3 unfair, harsh.

de·cid·u·ous (di·sij′ōō·əs) *adj.*
1 Falling off when mature or at certain seasons: *deciduous fruit. An antler is a deciduous outgrowth that a deer sheds annually.* 2 Annually shedding leaves or foliage: *deciduous trees.*
Ant. 2 evergreen.

dec·i·mate (des′ə·māt) *v.* **dec·i·mat·ed, dec·i·mat·ing**
To destroy or kill a large proportion of: *Disease decimated their ranks.*—**dec′i·ma′-tion** *n.*
Etymology: *Decimate* derives from the Latin *decimare*, meaning to take a tenth part from. Hence *decimate* came to indicate the killing of one out of every ten of a given group. Now it points to an even more disastrous reduction.
Syn. massacre, slaughter.

de·ci·sion (di·sizh′ən) *n.*
1 The act of deciding: *a difficult decision.* 2 A conclusion or judgment: *a court decision.* 3 Firmness in judgment, action, or character: *She acted with decision.*
Syn. 1 choice, determination. 2 settlement, verdict, finding. 3 determination, resolution, resolve.
Ant. 3 doubt, hesitation, indecision.

de·ci·sive (di·sī′siv) *adj.*
1 Settling a matter definitely: *a decisive defeat.* 2 Firm and definite: *a decisive executive.* 3 Unquestionable: *They had a decisive edge on their competitors.*—**de·ci′sive·ly** *adv.*, **de·ci′sive·ness** *n.*
Syn. 1 conclusive, definitive, positive. 2 determined, resolute. 3 unmistakable, undoubtable.
Ant. 1 inconclusive, disputable, debatable. 2 indecisive, irresolute, vacillating. 3 dubious.

de·cliv·i·ty (di·kliv′ə·tē) *n.*, **de·cliv·i·ties** *pl.*
A downward slope or descending surface: *They looked down to the bottom of the immense declivity from their upland vantage point.*—**de·cli·vous** (di·klī′vəs) *adj.*

Syn. downgrade, incline, descent.
Ant. acclivity, upgrade, rise, ascent.

de·cor (dā′kôr *or* dā·kôr′) *n.*
1 The scheme or style of decoration in a room, home, club, etc.: *The guest house has French Provincial decor.* 2 Stage scenery.
Spelling tip: Also written *décor.*
Syn. 2 sets, *mise en scène.*

dec·o·ra·tive (dek′(ə)rə·tiv *or* dek′ə·rā′tiv) *adj.*
Serving to make more fancy or attractive: *a decorative pin on her blouse.*
Syn. ornamental, dressy.

dec·o·rous (dek′ər·əs *or* di·kôr′əs) *adj.*
Proper and correct in a restrained or formal way: *the decorous behavior of Sunday church-goers.*—**dec′o·rous·ly** *adv.*
Syn. seemly, conventional, demure.
Ant. unconventional, unorthodox.

de·co·rum (di·kôr′əm) *n.*
Conformity to set requirements of taste or social convention: *the governess's perpetual insistence on dignity and decorum.*
Syn. propriety, seemliness, etiquette.
Ant. impropriety, indecorum, nonconformity.

de·coy (di·koi′ *or* dē′koi *n.*; di·koi′ *v.*) *n., v.*
n. A person, animal, or thing used to lure an unsuspecting victim into a trap.
v. To lure or be lured: *A lone runner decoyed them away from the real escape route.*
Syn. *n.* lure, bait, enticement. *v.* entice.

de·cry (di·krī′) *v.* **de·cried, de·cry·ing**
To denounce or condemn: *The newspaper decried the cowardice of the legislature.*
Syn. deplore, censure.
Ant. praise, extol, laud, commend.

de fac·to (dē fak′tō)
Existing in fact, with or without legal sanction: *de facto segregation in neighborhood schools; a de facto government after the coup d'état.*

def·a·ma·tion (def′ə·mā′shən) *n.*
Slanderous abuse of the character or reputation of an individual or group: *The politician sued the magazine for defamation of character; the Anti-Defamation League of B'nai B'rith.*—**de·fame** (di·fām′) *v.*, **de·fam·a·to·ry** (di·fam′ə·tôr′ē) *adj.*
Syn. slander, libel, vilification, disparagement, aspersion, calumny.

de·fault (di·fôlt′) *n., v.*
n. A failure to fulfill an obligation or requirement, as to pay money due, to appear in court, or to appear for or finish a contest: *to lose by default; judgment by default.*
v. To fail to perform or pay: *to default a payment.*

de·feat·ist (di·fē′tist) *n., adj.*
n. A person who expects to lose or fail and therefore does not really try: *A true defeatist is convinced he will never win.*
adj. Typical of a defeatist: *a defeatist attitude.*—**de·feat′ism** *n.*
Syn. *n.* pessimist. *adj.* pessimistic, negative.
Ant. *n.* optimist. *adj.* optimistic, positive.

de·fec·tion (di·fek'shən) *n.*
The act of deserting one's own side and going over to the opponents: *the defection of a Communist to the West.*—**de·fect'** *v.*, **de·fec'tor** *n.*

de·fense (di·fens') *n.*
1 A guarding against danger or attack, or something that gives protection: *national defense.* 2 A justifying argument or answer to charges: *A plea of insanity was the basis of his defense.*

de·fer (di·fûr') *v.* **de·ferred, de·fer·ring**
1 To put off or postpone: *to defer payment.*
2 To yield out of respect: *Defer to the wishes of your elders.*
Spelling tip: Words that end in a single vowel and consonant, and are accented on the last syllable, double the final consonant before a suffix beginning with a vowel.
Syn. 1 delay, procrastinate. 2 submit, give in, accede.
Ant. 1 rush, expedite. 2 defy, resist.

def·er·ence (def'ər·əns) *n.*
Respect for or obedience to another's opinions or wishes: *In deference to the wishes of the widow, charitable contributions should be made in lieu of flowers.*
Syn. consideration, submission.
Ant. disregard, defiance, scorn.

de·fi·cient (di·fish'ənt) *adj.*
Not complete: *a diet deficient in protein.*

def·i·cit (def'ə·sit) *n.*
The amount by which an expected or required sum falls short, or an excess of debits over credits: *the national deficit.*
Syn. shortage.
Ant. surplus, excess.

de·file (di·fīl') *v.* **de·filed, de·fil'ing**
To make foul or dirty; to pollute something previously pure or holy: *Unsubstantiated charges of corruption defiled his reputation.*
Syn. sully, besmirch.
Ant. cleanse, purify.

de·fin·i·tive (di·fin'ə·tiv) *adj.*
1 Sharply defined; explicit: *a definitive program for reform.* 2 Conclusive or final: *a definitive victory.*
Syn. 1 categorical, exact. 2 decisive, ultimate.
Ant. 1 vague, ill-defined. 2 equivocal, tentative, preliminary.

de·flect (di·flekt') *v.*
To turn aside; to cause to swerve from a straight course: *The net deflected the tennis ball.*
Syn. divert, refract.

de·funct (di·fungkt') *adj.*
Dead; extinct: *Many once-prosperous newspapers have gone bankrupt and are now defunct.*

de·i·fy (dē'ə·fī) *v.* **de·i·fied, de·i·fy·ing**
To make a god of: *The Roman emperor Augustus was deified and worshiped after his death.*
Spelling tip: Remember the *i* in this word, which is pronounced ə.

deign (dān) *v.*
To condescend to do something: *The queen deigned to speak to the commoner.*

de jure (dē jŏŏr'ē) *adj.*
By right; according to law: *The government-in-exile is recognized as the de jure government.*
Syn. rightful, legitimate, legal.

del·e·gate (del'ə·gāt *n.*, *v.*; *also* del'ə·git *for n.*) *n.*; *v.* **del·e·gated, del·e·gat·ing**
n. A person with authority to speak for or act for others; a representative: *congressional delegates.*
v. 1 To send as a representative: *He delegated his assistant to work out the details.* 2 To turn over to an agent or representative: *He delegated his authority to his assistant.*
Syn. *n.* deputy, envoy, emissary. *v.* 1 deputize, commission, authorize. 2 assign, entrust.

de·lete (di·lēt') *v.* **de·let·ed, de·let·ing**
To take out written or printed matter: *He deleted the last paragraph of the article.*
Syn. strike out, excise, expunge, cancel.
Ant. insert, add.

de·lin·e·a·tion (di·lin'ē·ā'shən) *n.*
Pictorial or verbal portrayal: *delineation of a face; delineation of character.*
Syn. depiction, representation.

de·lin·quent (di·ling'kwənt) *n.*, *adj.*
n. A person guilty of negligence, wrongdoing, or lawbreaking: *juvenile delinquents.*
adj. 1 Late or neglectful: *He is always delinquent in paying the rent.* 2 Due but unpaid: *delinquent taxes.*—**de·lin'quen·cy** *n.*

de·lir·i·um (di·lir'ē·əm) *n.*
A temporary mental disturbance characterized by hallucination and excitement, and caused by fever, injury, or intoxication.

de·liv·er·ance (di·liv'ər·əns) *n.*
Release or rescue: *deliverance from her captors.*

de·lude (di·lōōd') *v.* **de·lud·ed, de·lud·ing**
To deceive, mislead: *They thought the war would end by Christmas, but they were deluded.*
Syn. fool, dupe.
Ant. enlighten.

del·uge (del'yōōj) *n.*; *v.* **del·uged, del·ug·ing**
n. 1 A great flood or downpour of water.
2 Something that overwhelms or engulfs: *a deluge of Christmas mail.*
v. 1 To flood with water: *The rains deluged the land.* 2 To overwhelm or engulf: *The stock market is deluged with orders.*
Syn. *n.* 1 cloudburst, inundation. 2 mass, heap. *v.* 1 inundate, drown. 2 swamp.

de·lu·sion (di·lōō'zhən) *n.*
A false belief, or a persistent false belief held in spite of evidence to the contrary: *delusions of grandeur.*
Syn. illusion, hallucination.

de·luxe (di·lōōks' *or* di·luks') *adj.*
Of extra-fine quality; elegant and expensive: *the deluxe suite at the very best hotel in New York City.*
Syn. luxurious, sumptuous, princely.
Ant. cheap, second-rate.

dem·a·gogue (dem'ə·gôg *or* dem'ə·gog) *n.*
A leader who influences the populace by appealing to prejudices and passion: *Hitler was a demagogue.*
Syn. rabble-rouser, agitator, haranguer.

de·mean·or (di·mē'nər) *n.*
The manner in which a person behaves: *The judge's dignified demeanor.*
Syn. bearing, deportment, presence.

de·mise (di·mīz') *n.*
Death: *his untimely demise.*
Syn. decease.
Ant. birth.

dem·i·tasse (dem'ē·tas' *or* dem'ē·täs') *n.*
A small cup of black coffee, or the cup itself: *sipping a demitasse after dinner.*
Etymology: This is a French word meaning a half (*demi*) cup (*tasse*).

de·mol·ish (di·mol'ish) *v.*
To tear down; raze, as a building; destroy; ruin.—**dem·o·li·tion** (dem'ə·lish'ən) *n.*
Syn. wreck.
Ant. build, erect, preserve.

de·mon·stra·ble (di·mon'strə·bəl *or* dem'ən·strə·bel) *adj.*
Capable of being demonstrated or proved; provable: *the demonstrable fact that the earth is round.*
Syn. confirmable, verifiable.
Ant. unverifiable.

dem·on·strate (dem'ən·strāt) *v.* **dem·on·strat·ed, dem·on·strat·ing**
1 To make clear by means of illustration or by reasoning: *He demonstrated how the can opener worked.* 2 To take part in a public meeting, parade, etc.: *The peace marchers demonstrated last Tuesday.*
Syn. 1 explain, show, illustrate.

de·mur (di·mûr') *v.* **de·murred, de·mur·ring**
To offer objections; to take exception: *The others agreed, but Jim demurred.*
Spelling tip: Do not confuse this word with *demure* (di·myŏŏr'), meaning prim or sedate.
Syn. dissent, object, hedge.
Ant. agree, consent, comply, concur.

de·mur·rage (di·mûr'ij) *n.*
1 The detention of a freighter, freight car, or other commercial conveyance beyond the scheduled departure time as a result of delay in loading or unloading: *a two-day demurrage because of the strike.* 2 Compensation for such a delay: *fifty dollars demurrage.*

den·i·grate (den'ə·grāt) *v.* **den·i·grat·ed, den·i·grat·ing**
To slander or defame: *Journalists denigrated the great man.*
Syn. asperse, disparage, malign.
Ant. praise, acclaim, laud, extol.

den·im (den'əm) *n.*
A strong, twilled cotton used for such garments as overalls: *blue denim dungarees.*

den·i·zen (den'ə·zen) *n.*
An inhabitant or occupant: *rabbits, chipmunks, and other denizens of the woods.*
Syn. resident, native, habitué.

de·no·ta·tion (dē'nō·tā'shən) *n.*
The literal meaning of a word, as distinguished from its *connotation* (what it suggests): *The denotation of "a blonde" is "a girl with golden hair."*
Usage: See CONNOTATION.
Syn. meaning, designation.

de·pict (di·pikt') *v.*
To portray, either pictorially or verbally: *to depict the scene.*
Syn. represent, describe, delineate.

de·plete (di·plēt') *v.* **de·plet·ed, de·plet·ing**
To reduce, as by using up: *Illness depleted his strength.*
Syn. lessen, exhaust, drain.
Ant. supplement, increase, augment.

dep·o·si·tion (dep'ə·zish'ən *or* dē'pə·zish'ən) *n.*
Law A written testimony given under oath: *His deposition was introduced as evidence during the trial.*

de·prav·i·ty (di·prav'ə·tē) *n.*
Wickedness or sexual immorality: *Nero's depravity.*
Syn. sinfulness, vice.
Ant. purity, chastity, virtue.

dep·re·cate (dep'rə·kāt) *v.* **dep·re·cat·ed, dep·re·cat·ing**
To express disapproval of: *He deprecated the proposal to build a new highway.*—**dep·re·ca·to·ry** (dep'rə·kə·tôr'ē *or* dep'rə·kə·tō'rē) *adj.*
Etymology: *Deprecate* derives from the Latin word *deprecari*, which means to pray away.
Usage: See DEPRECIATE.
Syn. criticize, disparage, deplore.
Ant. praise, compliment, acclaim.

de·pre·ci·ate (di·prē'shē·āt) *v.* **de·pre·ci·at·ed, de·pre·ci·at·ing**
1 To make or become less valuable. 2 To belittle; to minimize the importance of: *The tobacco-industry spokesman depreciated the medical findings.*—**de·pre'ci·a'tion** *n.*
Usage: *Deprecate* means to express disapproval of or regret for. However, in recent years *deprecate* has often been used in place of *depreciate* to mean belittle: *to deprecate another's accomplishments; a self-deprecating smile.*
Syn. 1 devalue, lower. 2 disparage, underrate.
Ant. 1 inflate. 2 exaggerate, overrate.

dep·re·da·tion (dep'rə·dā'shən) *n.*
The act of plundering or robbing: *Wartime depredations left the country in a state of lawlessness and disorder.*
Syn. sacking, thievery, rapacity.

depth (depth) *n.*
1 Extent or distance downward, inward, or backward: *the depth of the ocean.* 2 Deepness of thought or feeling: *a play with great depth.*
Syn. 2 profundity, intensity.
Ant. 2 superficiality, shallowness.

der·e·lict (der'ə·likt) *adj., n.*
adj. Neglectful; remiss: *The filthy house proved she was derelict in performing household chores.*
n. A social outcast, as a tramp or vagrant.—**der'e·lic'tion** *n.*
Syn. *adj.* negligent. *n.* bum, wastrel, panhandler, wino.
Ant. *adj.* responsible, dutiful. *n.* solid citizen.

de·ride (di·rīd') *v.* **de·rid·ed, de·rid·ing**
To treat scornfully; ridicule: *He derided the idea that poverty could be eliminated simply by handing out money to the poor.*
Syn. make fun of, scorn, mock.

de·ri·sion (di·rizh'ən) *n.*
Ridicule, mockery: *The politician's claim that his visit was "nonpolitical" was the subject of some derision.*

der·ma·ti·tis (dûr'mə·tī'tis) *n.*
Inflammation of the skin.
Spelling tip: The suffix that means "inflammation of" is *-itis,* as in *appendicitis* and *neuritis.*

der·ma·tol·o·gist (dûr'mə·tol'ə·jist) *n.*
A doctor who specializes in dermatology, the branch of medicine relating to the skin and its diseases.

de·rog·a·to·ry (di·rog'ə·tôr'ē) *adj.*
Belittling, disparaging: *Her grandmother made derogatory remarks about her short skirt.*
Syn. critical.
Ant. complimentary, laudatory.

de·scend (di·send') *v.*
1 To go from a higher level to a lower one: *She descended the stairway.* 2 To lower oneself: *She descended to tattling.* 3 To be derived by heredity: *Most Americans are descended from immigrants.* 4 To attack suddenly in great numbers, so as to overwhelm: *The Nazis descended on Paris.*

de·scen·dant (di·sen'dənt) *n.*
One who is descended from another; offspring: *a descendant of early Irish immigrants.*

de·scent (di·sent') *n.*
The act of moving downward: *The descent from the mountain was more dangerous than the ascent.*
Spelling tip: Do not confuse *descent* (from descend), *dissent,* and *decent.* *Dissent* (di-sent') refers to differences of opinion: *Dissent must be tolerated in a democracy. Decent* (dē'-sənt) means proper or respectable: *decent manners.*
Syn. coming down.
Ant. going up, climbing.

de·scry (di·skrī') *v.* **de·scried, de·scry·ing**
To discover or discern visually: *to descry a man on horseback far up the road.*
Syn. detect, perceive, spot.

des·e·crate (des'ə·krāt) *v.* **des·e·crat·ed, des·e·crat·ing**
To treat sacrilegiously something held sacred: *to desecrate the shrine by herding goats into it.*
Syn. profane, defile, sully.
Ant. revere, consecrate, hallow.

des·ic·cate (des'ə·kāt) *v.* **des·ic·cat·ed, des·ic·cat·ing**
To remove the moisture from food in order to preserve it; also, to dry thoroughly: *to desiccate apricots.*—**des'ic·ca'tion** *n.*

des·o·late (des'ə·lit *adj.,* des'ə·lāt *v.*) *adj.; v.* **des·o·lat·ed, des·o·lat·ing**
adj. 1 Destitute of inhabitants or dwellings; abandoned: *towns made desolate by the war.* 2 Without friends; forlorn: *the desolate immigrant alone in the big city.* 3 Gloomy, dreary: *the desolate, dark days of November.*
v. 1 To lay waste or empty of inhabitants: *The plague desolated the city.* 2 To leave grief-

stricken and wretched: *His sudden death desolated his family.*—**des'o·la'tion** *n.*
Syn. *adj.* 1 deserted, barren. 2 lonely, isolated. 3 cheerless. *v.* 1 ravage. 2 depress.
Ant. *adj.* 1 populated, lively. 3 cheerful. *v.* 2 cheer, enliven.

de·spair (di·spâr') *n., v.*
n. Utter hopelessness and discouragement: *In despair he watched his burning house.*
v. To lose or abandon hope: *He despaired of ever recapturing his youthful enthusiasm.*
Syn. *n.* gloom, despondency, desperation.
Ant. *n.* hopefulness, cheer.
v. hope.

des·per·a·do (des'pə·rä'dō *or* des'pə·rā'dō) *n.,* **des·per·a·does** *or* **des·per·a·dos** *pl.*
A desperate or violent criminal.
Etymology: *Desperado* is an Old Spanish word related to *despair* and *desperate.*
Syn. ruffian, brigand, gangster.

des·pi·ca·ble (des'pi·kə·bəl *or* di·spik'ə·bəl) *adj.*
Contemptible, vile: *despicable men who profit by human suffering.*
Syn. mean, wicked, awful.
Ant. admirable, wonderful.

de·spoil (di·spoil') *v.*
To strip of possessions; rob: *The conquering tribes despoiled the land.*
Syn. plunder, pillage.

de·spon·den·cy (di·spon'dən·sē) *n.*
A feeling of depression or hopelessness: *despondency over his father's death.* Also **de·spon'dence** *n.*
Syn. dejection, despair, demoralization.
Ant. cheerfulness, joy, exuberance.

de·spon·dent (di·spon'dənt) *adj.*
Depressed because of a sense of hopelessness or loss of courage: *The prolonged illness made him despondent.*—**de·spon'dent·ly** *adv.*
Syn. discouraged, dejected.
Ant. cheerful, hopeful, optimistic.

des·pot·ism (des'pə·tiz'əm) *n.*
Unlimited authority; tyrannical control: *Some adolescents regard parental control as a form of despotism.*
Syn. authoritarianism, absolutism, totalitarianism.

des·sert (di·zûrt') *n.*
A serving of pastry, ice cream, fruit, etc. at the end of lunch or dinner.

des·ti·tute (des'tə·tōōt) *adj.*
1 Entirely lacking: *destitute of hope.* 2 Extremely poor: *destitute people who suffer from malnutrition.*—**des'ti·tu'tion** *n.*
Syn. 1 bereft. 2 poverty-stricken.

de·struc·tion (di·struk'shən) *n.*
The act of destroying, or the state of being destroyed: *the destruction of the city by air attack.*
Syn. devastation, demolition, ruin.
Ant. renewal, creation, birth.

des·ul·to·ry (des'əl·tôr'ē *or* des'əl·tō'rē) *adj.*
Passing abruptly from one thing to another; disconnected: *a desultory conversation.*
Syn. unmethodical, casual, discontinuous.

de·tached (di·tacht′) *adj.*
1 Separate from others; disconnected: *a detached garage.* 2 Free from intellectual or emotional involvement: *A good judge is capable of taking a detached view of a case.*
Syn. 1 distinct, individual. 2 unconcerned, impartial.
Ant. 1 joined, connected. 2 involved, concerned, biased.

de·tail (*n.* di·tāl′, dē′tāl; *v.* di·tāl′; *Mil.* dē′tāl) *n., v.*
n. 1 A separately considered part: *the details of the plan.* 2 *Military* A small detachment picked to do a particular job: *a detail assigned to KP.*
v. 1 To report minutely: *to detail our government's position in the peace talks.* 2 *Military* To pick and send off for a special duty: *to detail ten men for reconnaissance.*
Syn. *n.* 1 item. *v.* 1 spell out, specify.

de·ter·gent (di·tûr′jənt) *adj., n.*
adj. Having cleansing qualities: *a detergent solution.*
n. A cleansing agent: *a liquid detergent for cleaning dishes.*

de·te·ri·o·rate (di·tir′ē·ə·rāt′) *v.* **de·te·ri·or·at·ed, de·te·ri·or·at·ing**
To make or become worse: *The quality of workmanship has deteriorated since the turn of the century.*—**de·te′ri·or·a′tion** *n.*
Syn. depreciate, worsen, decay.
Ant. improve, meliorate, better.

de·ter·rent (di·tûr′ənt) *adj., n.*
adj. Tending to prevent or discourage some action: *the deterrent effect of a tax increase on consumer spending.*
n. That which prevents or discourages some action: *Military strength serves as a deterrent to would-be aggressors.*
Spelling tip: The need to remember three *e*'s and two *r*'s is a *deterrent* to writing this word.

det·o·na·tion (det′ə·nā′shən) *n.*
1 The act of exploding something: *the detonation of a bomb.* 2 A sudden explosion: *a violent detonation shattered many windows.*

de·trac·tion (di·trak′shən) *n.*
The act of diminishing a person's reputation: *All public figures suffer the detractions of petty, jealous people.*
Syn. disparagement, slander, defamation
Ant. flattery, praise.

dev·as·tate (dev′əs·tāt) *v.* **dev·as·tat·ed, dev·as·tat·ing**
To lay waste, as by war, fire, or flood; ravage: *Large parts of London were devastated by the Nazi blitz.*
Syn. desolate, destroy, ruin.
Ant. build, create.

de·vel·op (di·vel′əp) *v.*
1 To expand or work out: *to develop an idea.* 2 *In photography* To subject exposed photograph material to a chemical treatment so as to produce a visual image: *to develop film.*—**de·vel′op·ment** *n.*, **de·vel′oped** *adj.*

de·vice (di·vīs′) *n*
1 Something devised or constructed for a specific purpose: *A barometer is a device for*

measuring atmospheric pressure. 2 A scheme, plan, etc., especially a crafty or evil one: *Is alcohol a device of the devil?*
Syn. 1 instrument, tool. 2 stratagem, plot.

de·vi·ous (dē′vē·əs) *adj.*
1 Winding or leading away from the regular, straight, or direct course: *a devious country lane that led nowhere.* 2 Straying from the proper or accepted way: *devious behavior.*—**de′vi·ous·ly** *adv.*, **de′vi·ous·ness** *n.*
Syn. 1 roundabout, rambling, indirect. 2 untrustworthy, dishonest, erring.
Ant. 1 straight, direct, simple. 2 honest, trustworthy, correct.

de·vise (di·vīz′) *v.* **de·vised, de·vis·ing**
To plan or form a plan: *He devised a scheme for escaping from prison.*—**de·vis′er** *n.*
Syn. invent, contrive, fabricate.

de·void (di·void′) *adj.*
Not possessing; without: *a personality entirely devoid of humor.*
Syn. destitute, empty, lacking.
Ant. replete, filled, abounding.

de·vout (di·vout′) *adj.*
1 Earnestly religious: *a devout old woman.* 2 Sincere, heartfelt: *devout hope for his continued success.*—**de·vout′ly** *adv.*, **de·vout′ness** *n.*
Syn. 1 pious, reverent, holy. 2 earnest, fervent.
Ant. irreligious, impious, ungodly. 2 insincere, hypocritical, deceitful.

dex·ter·ous (dek′st(ə)rəs) *adj.*
1 Possessing skill and ease in the use of the hands or body: *a dexterous magician.* 2 Possessing a quick, clever mind: *a dexterous lawyer.* 3 Done with skill and ease: *his dexterous handling of the dispute.*—**dex′ter·ous·ly** *adv.*, **dex′ter·ous·ness** *n.*
Spelling tip: This word may also be spelled *dextrous.*

di·a·be·tes (dī·ə·bē′tis *or* dī·ə·bē′tēz) *n.*
A disease associated with deficient insulin secretion, leading to an excess of sugar in the blood and urine and characterized by progressive emaciation, extreme hunger and thirst, and metabolic failure.—**di·a·bet·ic** (dī′ə·bet′ik *or* dī′ə·bē′tik) *adj., n.*

di·a·bol·ic (dī′ə·bol′ik) *adj.*
Of, belonging to, coming from, or like the devil: *a diabolic crime.* Also **di·a·bol′i·cal** *adj.*—**di′a·bol′i·cal·ly** *adv.*
Syn. satanic, wicked, fiendish.

di·a·logue (dī′ə·lôg *or* dī′ə·log) *n.*
1 A conversation in which two or more persons take part: *Did you hear the dialogue at the table next to ours?* 2 The conversation in a play, novel, etc.
Spelling tip: Although *dialog* is an acceptable spelling of this word, *dialogue* is preferred.
Syn. 1 talk, chat, discussion.

di·aph·a·nous (dī·af′ə·nəs) *adj.*
So thin in substance that light shows through: *a diaphanous nightgown.*
Syn. translucent, transparent, sheer, gauzy, gossamer.

di·a·phragm (dī′ə·fram) *n.*
1 The muscular wall that separates the chest and abdominal cavities in mammals. **2** Any membrane or partition that separates or divides; also, any device that resembles such a partition in appearance or function: *A diaphragm is a birth-control device.* **3** A disk with an adjustable opening that can control the amount of light passing through the lens of a camera, telescope, etc.
Spelling tip: Watch the silent *g* and the *ph* (pronounced *f*, as in *phone*).

di·ar·rhe·a (dī·ə·rē′ə) *n.*
A bodily disorder in which the bowels move too frequently and too loosely.

di·a·ry (dī′(ə)rē) *n.,* **di·a·ries** *pl.*
1 A record of daily events, especially a personal record of a person's activities, experiences, or observations. **2** A book for keeping such a record.

di·a·ther·my (dī′ə·thûr′mē) *n.,* **di·a·ther·mies** *pl.*
A treatment used for medical or surgical purposes, in which heat is generated in the body tissues through their resistance to the passage of high-frequency electric currents.

di·a·tribe (dī′ə·trīb) *n.*
A bitter or malicious speech or piece of writing, usually critical and often long: *Castro's frequent diatribes against the U.S.*
Syn. harangue, tirade, vilification.

dic·ta·tor (dik′tā·tər *or* dik·tā′tər) *n.*
1 A person who has absolute powers of government in a state. **2** A person who rules, prescribes, or suggests authoritatively: *Dior is a dictator of fashion.* **3** A person who speaks words that are to be recorded or written.—**dic′ta·to′ri·al** *adj.,* **dic′ta·to′ri·al·ly** *adv.,* **dic·ta′tor·ship′** *n.*
Syn. 1 tyrant, despot, autocrat. 2 arbiter, czar.

dic·tum (dik′təm) *n.,* **dic·tums** *or* **dic·ta** (dik′tə) *pl.*
An authoritative statement, usually made in a formal way: *the first dictum of the junta after their overthrow of the monarchy.*
Syn. pronouncement, dictate.

di·dac·tic (dī·dak′tik *or* di·dak′tik) *adj.*
1 Intended to instruct or guide: *a didactic essay.* **2** Inclined to teach or moralize: *a very stuffy person whose most casual conversation revealed his didactic nature.*—**di·dac′ti·cal·ly** *adv.*
Syn. 1 instructive, expository, informative. 2 pedantic, moralistic, pedagogic.

die (dī) *n.,* **dice** *pl. for def. 1,* **dies** *pl. for def. 2; n.* **1** A small marked cube. Note that the irregular plural form of this word, *dice,* not only designates more than one *die* but also is the name of the game of chance played with these cubes. **2** Any of various tools or devices for shaping, stamping, or cutting out some object, as the engraved stamp used to press a design on metal in coining money.

di·er·e·sis (dī·er′ə·sis) *n.,* **di·er·e·ses** (dī·er′ə·sēz) *pl.*
Two dots (¨) placed over the second of two adjacent vowels to indicate that two separate vowel sounds are to be pronounced, as sometimes in *naïve.*
Spelling tip: Also spelled *diaeresis.*

dif·fer·en·tial (dif′ə·ren′shəl) *adj., n.*
adj. Having to do with, indicating, or based on a difference or differences: *a differential pay scale for union and nonunion employees.*
n. An arrangement of gears used to connect two or more shafts, as in the driving axle of an automobile, so that the wheels can move at different speeds on curves.
Spelling tip: *Different* + *-ial*—watch the last syllable!

dif·fi·dence (dif′ə·dəns) *n.*
Lack of confidence in oneself; timidity or shyness: *the diffidence of the trainee in addressing the company president.*—**dif′fi·dent** *adj.,* **dif′fi·dent·ly** *adv.*
Syn. bashfulness, modesty.
Ant. self-confidence, self-assurance, boldness, forwardness.

dif·fuse (di·fyo͞oz′ *v.,* di·fyo͞os′ *adj.*) *v.* **dif·fused, dif·fus·ing;** *adj.*
v. To spread about in all directions: *Heat from the fireplace diffused throughout the room.*
adj. **1** Widely spread out: *diffuse inflammation of the tissues.* **2** Characterized by the excessive use of words: *a diffuse prose style.* —**dif·fu′sion** *n.*
Syn. *v.* circulate, permeate. *adj.* 1 dispersed, scattered, widespread. 2 verbose, wordy, long-winded.

di·gest (di·jest′ *or* dī·jest′ *v.;* dī′jest *n.*) *v., n.*
v. **1** To change food chemically in the alimentary canal into a form that can be assimilated by the body: *Some people find it difficult to digest nuts.* **2** To take in mentally: *The student scratched his head as he tried to digest what the teacher was saying.*
n. A collection or summary of literary, scientific, or other material: *a digest of articles from leading magazines.*—**di·ges′tion** *n.*
Syn. *v.* 2 comprehend, understand.

dig·i·tal (dij′ə·təl) *adj.*
1 Of or relating to the fingers or toes: *a baby with poor digital grasp.* **2** Of or relating to calculation by numerical methods: *a digital computer.*

di·gres·sive (di·gres′iv *or* dī·gres′iv) *adj.*
Given to or marked by a turning aside from the main subject: *a digressive speech that overlooked essentials for incidentals.*—**di·gres′·sion** *n.,* **di·gress′** *v.*
Syn. discursive, excursive, rambling, wandering.
Ant. direct, pointed, succinct, terse.

di·lap·i·dat·ed (di·lap′ə·dā′tid) *adj.*
Fallen into decay or partial ruin: *a dilapidated 1950 Ford.*
Spelling tip: Note the two *i*'s in this word.
Syn. neglected, ramshackle, decayed, rickety.

di·late (dī·lāt′ *or* di·lāt′) *v.* **di·lat·ed, di·lat·ing**
1 To make or become larger or wider: *The pupil of the eye dilates in the dark.* **2** To speak or write diffusely: *to dilate on a subject that required simplicity and directness.*—**di·lat′a·**

ble *adj.*, **di·lat′a·bil′i·ty, di·lat′a·ble·ness** *n.*,
di·lat′a·bly *adv.*
Syn. 1 enlarge, widen, distend. 2 enlarge,
expatiate, descant.
Ant. 1 contract, shrink, lessen. 2 shorten,
condense, abridge.

dil·a·to·ry (dil′ə·tôr′ē *or* dil′ə·tō′rē) *adj.*
1 Given to or characterized by delay:
dilatory in paying bills. 2 Tending to cause
delay: *dilatory tactics that hindered passage of
the tax reforms.*—**dil′a·to′ri·ly** *adv.*, **dil′a·to′·
ri·ness** *n.*
Syn. 1 tardy, slow, sluggish. 2 obstructive,
impeding, retarding.
Ant. 1 prompt, punctual.

di·lem·ma (di·lem′ə) *n.*
A situation requiring a choice between two
alternatives that are equally bad, unpleasant,
or undesirable.
Syn. predicament, quandary, plight, impasse.

dil·et·tan·te (dil′ə·tänt′ *or* dil′ə·tan′tē) *n.*,
dil·et·tan·tes *or* **dil·et·tan·ti** (dil′ə·tan′tē) *pl.*
A person who interests himself superficially
or merely for amusement in art, science, or
another subject.
Syn. dabbler, amateur.

dil·i·gent (dil′ə·jənt) *adj.*
1 Showing perseverance and application in
whatever is undertaken: *a diligent employee.*
2 Pursued with painstaking effort: *a diligent
search.*—**dil′i·gent·ly** *adv.*
Syn. 1 industrious, hard-working, assiduous.
2 careful, precise, scrupulous.
Ant. 1 lazy, remiss. 2 careless, slipshod,
perfunctory.

di·min·ish (di·min′ish) *v.*
To make or grow smaller or less, as in size,
amount, or degree: *Lack of rainfall diminished
the water supply.*
Syn. decrease, lessen, reduce.
Ant. enlarge, augment, increase.

dine (dīn) *v.* **dined, din·ing**
1 To eat a meal, especially the principal meal
of the day: *We dine at nine.* 2 To entertain at
dinner: *Wine and dine the visiting celebrity.*
3 To eat; feed upon: *to dine on food that is too
rich.*

din·ghy (ding′gē *or* ding′ē) *n.*, **din·ghies** *pl.*
Any of various kinds of small rowing boats,
as the tenders used by large vessels.
Spelling tip: Beware of the silent *h.*

din·gy (din′jē) *adj.* **din·gi·er, din·gi·est**
Darkened or discolored as if soiled; grimy:
a dingy office in the old factory building.—**din′·
gi·ly** *adv.*, **din′gi·ness** *n.*
Syn. dull, shabby, seedy, tacky.
Ant. sparkling, clean, attractive.

dint (dint) *n.*, *v.*
n. 1 Force, effort, means (usually used in the
phrase *by dint of*): *successful by dint of hard
work.* 2 A dent: *a dint in a car fender.*
v. To make a dent in: *old cooking pots dinted
by years of use.*
Syn. *n.* 2 depression, indentation.

di·o·cese (dī′ə·sēs *or* dī′ə·sis) *n.*
The territory and churches under the

jurisdiction of a bishop: *the diocese of New
York.*—**di·oc·e·san** (dī·os′ə·sən *or* dī′ə·sē′sən)
adj., *n.*

diph·the·ri·a (dif·thir′ē·ə *or* dip·thir′ē·ə) *n.*
A highly contagious disease, usually contracted by children, characterized by fever,
great weakness, and the formation of a false
membrane in the air passages which impedes
breathing.
Spelling tip: Beware of the *ph*, which may be
pronounced *f* (as in *phone*) or *p.*

diph·thong (dif′thông *or* dip′thông) *n.*
A blend of two vowel sounds in one syllable,
whether written with two letters (*oi* in *coil*)
or one letter (*i* in *fine*).
Spelling tip: See DIPHTHERIA.

di·plo·ma (di·plō′mə) *n.*
A certificate given by a school, college, or
university testifying that a student has
earned a degree or completed a course of
study.
Etymology: *Diploma* comes from an ancient
Greek word that literally means *a paper
folded twice.*

di·plo·mat (dip′lə·mat) *n.*
1 A person engaged in conducting negotiations between countries. 2 Any person having
skill and tact in dealing with others: *an office
diplomat.*—**dip′lo·mat′ic** *adj.*, **dip′lo·mat′i·
cal·ly** *adv.*
Syn. 1 emissary, envoy, ambassador, legate,
consul. 2 strategist, negotiator, politician.
Ant. 2 bungler, blunderer.

dip·so·ma·ni·ac (dip′sə·mā′nē·ak) *n.*, *adj.*
n. A person who has an uncontrollable
craving for alcoholic drink.
adj. Having to do with or affected by an
uncontrollable craving for alcoholic drink.—
dip′so·ma′ni·a *n.*
Syn. *n.* alcoholic, drunkard, inebriate. *adj.*
alcoholic, drunk, intemperate.
Ant. *n.* teetotaler, abstainer. *v.* sober,
temperate, abstinent.

dire (dīr) *adj.* **dir·er, dir·est**
Dreadful; terrible: *The lengthy illness left
them in dire financial straits.*—**dire′ly** *adv.*,
dire′ness *n.*
Syn. grim, harrowing, woeful.

dis·ap·point (dis′ə·point′) *v.*
To fail to fulfill the hopes of; frustrate: *His
vacation disappointed him.*—**dis′ap·point′·
ment** *n.*

dis·ap·prove (dis′ə·prōōv′) *v.* **dis·ap·proved,
dis·ap·prov·ing**
To reject or look upon with disfavor: *They
disapproved of her fiancé.*—**dis′ap·prov′ing·ly**
adv., **dis′ap·prov′al** *n.*
Syn. condemn, censure, criticize.
Ant. praise, admire, like, accept.

dis·a·vow·al (dis′ə·vou′əl) *n.*
Refusal to claim knowledge of or responsi-
bility for something: *his disavowal of his own
shortcomings.*
Syn. denial, abnegation, forswearing.
Ant. admission, acknowledgment, avowal.

dis·cern (di·sûrn′ *or* di·zûrn′) *v.*
1 To perceive, as with the sight or the mind: *to discern new buds on an apple tree; to discern that the child was lying.* 2 To recognize as separate or different: *to discern right from wrong.*—**dis·cern′i·ble** *adj.*, **dis·cern′i·bly** *adv.*
Spelling tip: Watch the *sc.*
Syn. 1 see, recognize. 2 distinguish, differentiate, discriminate.

dis·cern·ing (di·sûr′ning *or* di·zûr′ning) *adj.*
Quick to discern; discriminating: *Many people follow the advice of a discerning movie critic.*—**dis·cern′ing·ly** *adv.*
Syn. knowing, sensitive, observant.

dis·ci·ple (di·sī′pəl) *n.*
1 One who accepts or follows a teacher or a doctrine: *a disciple of Freud.* 2 (*Often capital D*) One of the twelve chosen companions of Christ.
Syn. 1 follower, pupil, adherent, supporter. 2 apostle.

dis·ci·pline (dis′ə·plin) *n.; v.* **dis·ci·plined, dis·ci·plin·ing**
n. 1 Systematic training in obedience to rules and authority: *army discipline.* 2 Orderliness of behavior and self-control resulting from such training. 3 A branch of knowledge or instruction. 4 Punishment for the sake of training or correction: *discipline for failing to do homework.*
v. 1 To train to obedience: *Discipline your dog.* 2 To punish: *Latecomers will be disciplined.*—**dis′ci·pli·nar′y** *adj.*

dis·claim (dis·klām′) *v.*
1 To deny any claim to, connection with, or knowledge of: *He disclaimed any responsibility for the firm's loss.* 2 To reject or deny: *Protestants disclaim the authority of the Pope.* 3 *In law* To renounce a right or claim to: *to disclaim a share in an inheritance.*
Syn. 1 disavow, disown. 2 repudiate. 3 give up, abandon.
Ant. 1 admit, acknowledge. 2 accept. 3 claim, demand.

dis·con·cert (dis′kən·sûrt′) *v.*
To disturb the self-possession or composure of; upset: *disconcerted at having to make a speech to a large audience.*
Syn. embarrass, rattle, confuse, abash.

dis·con·so·late (dis·kon′sə·lit) *adj.*
1 Full of grief and sadness; unhappy: *a disconsolate widow.* 2 Cheerless, gloomy: *a disconsolate hospital ward.*—**dis·con′so·late·ly** *adv.*, **dis·con′so·late·ness** *n.*
Syn. 1 inconsolable, forlorn, grief-stricken. 2 dismal, dreary, depressing.
Ant. 1 happy, gay, hopeful. 2 cheerful, bright, radiant.

dis·cor·dant (dis·kôr′dənt) *adj.*
1 Lacking agreement or unity; clashing: *a couple with discordant viewpoints on raising children.* 2 Harsh or disagreeable in sound: *discordant voices.*—**dis·cor′dant·y** *adv.*
Syn. 1 differing, divergent, contradictory. 2 inharmonious, unmelodic, grating.

dis·course (dis·kôrs′; *also* dis′kôrs for *n.*) *n.; v.* **dis·coursed, dis·cours·ing**
n. 1 Conversation, talk: *intellectual discourse.* 2 A formal written or oral treatment of a subject: *a discourse on world population.*
v. To set forth one's ideas concerning a subject: *The minister discoursed upon brotherly love.*
Syn. *n.* 1 speech, chat, palaver. 2 dissertation, lecture, sermon, speech. *v.* discuss, orate, declaim.

dis·cov·er (dis·kuv′ər) *v.*
1 To get knowledge of or come upon, especially for the first time. 2 To find out; detect: *He discovered that his wallet was missing.*
Usage: To come across something that was always there but not previously known, recognized, or understood is to *discover* it. But to take things already at hand or available and put them together in ways that will serve some special purpose is to invent something: *Newton discovered the law of gravitation. Alexander Bell invented the telephone.*

dis·creet (dis·krēt′) *adj.*
Tactful in dealing with others; careful not to do or say the wrong thing: *He is so discreet that you can confide in him without uneasiness.*—**dis·creet′ly** *adv.*, **dis·creet′ness** *n.*
Spelling tip: Be careful not to confuse *discreet* and *discrete*, which are pronounced alike. *Discrete* means distinct or separate.
Syn. prudent, circumspect, cautious.
Ant. careless, imprudent, indiscreet.

dis·crep·an·cy (dis·krep′ən·sē) *n.*, **dis·crep·an·cies** *pl.*
Lack of agreement or consistency, as between facts: *There were some discrepancies in the accounts given by the two witnesses.*
Syn. disparity, disagreement, inconsistency, difference.
Ant. similarity, congruity, accord, agreement.

dis·crete (dis·krēt′) *adj.*
Disconnected from others; distinct or separate: *A molecule is composed of discrete atoms.*—**dis·crete′ly** *adv.*, **dis·crete′ness** *n.*

dis·cre·tion (dis·kresh′ən) *n.*
1 The quality of being discreet; tactfulness: *A doctor must use discretion in dealing with patients.* 2 Freedom or power to make one's own judgments and to act as one sees fit: *Use your own discretion in choosing a career.*
Syn. 1 prudence, circumspection, restraint, delicacy.
Ant. 1 heedlessness, recklessness, imprudence.

dis·crim·i·nate (dis·krim′ə·nāt) *v.* **dis·crim·i·nat·ed, dis·crim·i·nat·ing**
1 To draw a clear distinction; differentiate: *to discriminate between good and evil.* 2 To act toward a person or thing with prejudice or partiality: *to discriminate against a minority group.*—**dis·crim′i·na′tion** *n.*, **dis·crim·i·na·to·ry** (dis·krim′ə·nə·tor′ē) *adj.*

dis·crim·i·nat·ing (dis·krim′ə·nā′ting) *adj.*
1 Able to make precise distinctions or perceptive choices: *a discriminating critic who could sort the good from the bad.* 2 Serving to

identify or particularize: *a discriminating mole on his forehead.*
Spelling tip: There are four *i*'s.
Syn. 1 fastidious, choosy, discerning, particular. 2 distinguishing, unique.

dis·cur·sive (dis-kûr′siv) *adj.*
Passing quickly from one subject to another; wandering from the main point: *The old professor's lectures tended to be discursive.*— **dis·cur′sive·ly** *adv.*, **dis·cur′sive·ness** *n.*
Syn. digressive, long-winded, diffuse, rambling.
Ant. orderly, coherent, logical.

dis·ease (di-zēz′) *n.*
1 A condition of ill health in a person, plant, or animal, especially a disordered physical condition having particular symptoms: *Diphtheria has become a rare disease.* 2 Any disordered or unwholesome condition: *Poverty is a disease of our cities.*
Syn. 1 malady, illness, ailment, sickness. 2 blight, scourge, plague.

dis·eased (di-zēzd′) *adj.*
1 Affected with an illness: *Robert Louis Stevenson had diseased lungs.* 2 Disordered or disturbed: *a diseased mind; a society diseased by greed and fear.*
Spelling tip: Be careful not to confuse *diseased* with *deceased* (di-sēst′), which means dead.
Syn. 1 sickly, unhealthy. 2 unbalanced, demented, unwholesome.
Ant. 1 hearty, healthy, well. 2 sane, sensible, wholesome.

dis·ha·bille (dis′ə-bēl′) *n.*
The state of being partially or negligently dressed: *the dishabille of the hotel guests rescued from the fire.*
Etymology: *Dishabille* comes from a French word, *déshabillé,* meaning undressed.

di·shev·eled (di-shev′əld) *adj.*
Untidy or unkempt: *After traveling by train for three days, he looked somewhat disheveled.*— **di·shev′el·ment** *n.*
Spelling tip: This word may also be spelled *dishevelled.* Most words that end in *-vel* offer this alternate spelling: travelled, marvelled, levelled.
Syn. tousled, rumpled, slovenly, sloppy.
Ant. neat, tidy, spruce, well-groomed.

dis·in·gen·u·ous (dis′in-jen′yōō-əs) *adj.*
Lacking sincerity, frankness, or simplicity; not straightforward: *The candidate's disingenuous speech promising reforms failed to convince his audience.*— **dis′in·gen′u·ous·ly** *adv.*, **dis′in·gen′u·ous·ness** *n.*
Syn. insincere, underhanded, deceitful.
Ant. honest, frank, candid.

dis·in·ter·est·ed (dis·in′tris-tid *or* dis·in′tə-res′tid) *adj.*
Impartial and objective; without selfish motives: *Judges must make disinterested decisions.*— **dis·in′ter·est·ed·ly** *adv.*, **dis·in′ter·est·ed·ness** *n.*
Usage: *Disinterested* is often used as a synonym for *uninterested,* but careful speakers will use it more precisely to mean *impartial* and *unbiased.* A person is *disinter-*

ested if he does not stand to gain by his actions in a particular situation. An *uninterested* person is one without interest in something, either through boredom or indifference.
Syn. unprejudiced, unbiased, detached, aloof.
Ant. prejudiced, biased, self-seeking.

dis·joint·ed (dis-join′tid) *adj.*
1 Taken apart at the joints: *a disjointed fowl.* 2 Dislocated: *a disjointed knee.* 3 Lacking in coherence; rambling: *a disjointed conversation between two mothers, both trying to watch their children, cook dinner, and talk on the telephone.*—**dis·joint′ed·ly** *adv.*, **dis·joint·ed·ness** *n.*
Syn. 3 incoherent, wandering, desultory.
Ant. 3 coherent, logical, consistent.

dis·o·be·di·ent (dis′ə-bē′dē-ənt) *adj.*
Refusing or failing to follow orders or rules: *Disobedient students assembled unlawfully.*— **dis′o·be′di·ence** *n.*, **dis′o·be′di·ent·ly** *adv.*
Syn. insubordinate, refractory, defiant.
Ant. compliant, submissive, tractable.

dis·par·age (dis-par′ij) *v.* **dis·par·aged, dis·par·ag·ing**
To treat or speak of with disrespect or contempt; belittle: *A good teacher does not disparage the efforts of students.*—**dis·par′age·ment** *n.*
Syn. run down, undervalue, underrate, discredit.
Ant. praise, extol.

dis·par·i·ty (dis-par′ə-tē) *n.*, **dis·par·i·ties** *pl.*
An obvious difference or inequality: *the great disparity between the rich old man and the penniless girl he married; the painful disparity between human expectations and achievements.*
Syn. unlikeness, dissimilarity, discrepancy.
Ant. likeness, similarity, equality.

dis·pel (dis-pel′) *v.* **dis·pelled, dis·pel·ling**
To drive away by or as if by scattering: *Education dispels superstitions.*
Syn. disperse, dissipate, dissolve.

dis·pen·sa·ry (dis-pen′sər-ē) *n.*, **dis·pen·sa·ries** *pl.*
A place where medicines and medical advice are given out free or at a nominal fee: *first aid at the school dispensary.*

dis·perse (dis-pûrs′) *v.* **dis·persed, dis·pers·ing**
To break up and scatter in different directions: *The sun dispersed the morning mists. Police ordered the crowd to disperse.*—**dis·per′sal, dis·per·sion** (dis-pûr′zhən) *n.*
Syn. dispel, collect, concentrate.
Ant. gather, collect, concentrate.

dis·pir·it·ed (dis-pir′it-id) *adj.*
Depressed or dejected: *They were a thoroughly dispirited team after their defeat.*
Syn. discouraged, downcast, disheartened.
Ant. encouraged, elated, heartened.

dis·put·a·ble (dis-pyōō′tə-bəl *or* dis′pyōō-tə-bəl) *adj.*
Open to question or challenge: *Whether the National Football League or the American is stronger is a disputable point.*
Syn. arguable, debatable, questionable.
Ant. indisputable, incontestable, undeniable.

dis·rep·u·ta·ble (dis·rep'yə·tə·bəl) *adj.*
Having a bad reputation: *a disreputable bar frequented by undesirables.*
Syn. notorious, unsavory, shady, infamous.
Ant. respectable, reputable.

dis·sect (di·sekt' *or* dī·sekt') *v.*
1 To cut apart in order to study the structure: *to dissect a frog.* 2 To analyze critically: *to dissect a poem line by line.*—**dis·sec'tion** *n.*
Spelling tip: Remember to write two *s*'s, but pronounce just one.
Syn. 1 anatomize, dismember, vivisect. 2 study, examine.

dis·sem·ble (di·sem'bəl) *v.* **dis·sem·bled, dis·sem·bling**
1 To cover up one's true feelings or intentions by pretending: *She dissembled her jealousy with a bright smile.* 2 To pretend: *Hamlet dissembled madness to deceive the king.*
—**dis·sem'bler** *n.*
Syn. 1 camouflage, conceal, disguise. 2 feign, counterfeit, simulate.
Ant. 1 reveal, expose, show, manifest.

dis·sem·i·nate (di·sem'ə·nāt) *v.* **dis·sem·i·nat·ed, dis·sem·i·nat·ing**
To spread far and wide, as if sowing seeds: *Television and radio disseminate ideas and information.*—**dis·sem'i·na'tion** *n.*
Etymology: *Disseminate* derives from Latin roots meaning to scatter seed, or sow.
Syn. broadcast, circulate, propagate.

dis·sent (di·sent') *v., n.*
v. To differ in thought, opinion, or belief: *Three Supreme Court justices dissented from the majority opinion.*
n. Difference of opinion: *Seventeenth-century religious dissent led to the Reformation.*—**dis·sent'er** *n.*
Syn. *v.* disagree, demur, dispute. *n.* disagreement, discord.
Ant. *v.* agree, assent, concur. *n.* agreement, concurrence.

dis·ser·ta·tion (dis'ər·tā'shən) *n.*
1 An extended, formal, oral or written treatment of a subject: *The professor launched into a dissertation on the habits of kangaroos.* 2 A long, written treatise required of a candidate for a doctoral degree.
Syn. 1 treatise, discourse. 2 thesis.

dis·si·dent (dis'ə·dənt) *adj., n.*
adj. Expressing disagreement: *a dissident faction within the university.*
n. A person who actively disagrees: *conscientious objectors and other peaceful dissidents.*
Syn. *adj.* dissenting. *n.* dissenter, nonconformist.
Ant. *adj.* concordant, harmonious. *n.* conformist.

dis·si·pate (dis'ə·pāt) *v.* **dis·si·pat·ed, dis·si·pat·ing**
1 To break up and scatter away: *With daylight, their fears dissipated.* 2 To spend wastefully: *Don't dissipate your strength on useless projects.* 3 To overindulge in destructive pleasures: *dissipating recklessly until he became an alcoholic.*—**dis'si·pa'tion** *n.*
Syn. 1 disperse, dispel. 2 squander.

Ant. 1 consolidate, crystallize. 2 save, preserve, conserve.

dis·so·lu·tion (dis'ə·lōō'shən) *n.*
1 A breaking up or breaking down: *the dissolution of a marriage because of extreme cruelty.* 2 Separation into parts or components: *the dissolution of a nation during civil war.* 3 Dismissal of a meeting or assembly.
Syn. 1 termination, destruction. 2 disintegration. 3 adjournment.
Ant. 1 building, creation. 2 integration, uniting. 3 convocation.

dis·so·nance (dis'ə·nəns) *n.*
1 A mingling or combination of clashing sounds: *Some modern music has jarring dissonances.* 2 Natural hostility: *the dissonance between in-laws.*—**dis'so·nant** *adj.*
Syn. 1 discord, cacophony. 2 disagreement, antagonism, conflict.
Ant. 1 harmony, concord. 2 agreement, accord, affinity.

dis·suade (di·swād') *v.* **dis·suad·ed, dis·suad·ing**
To discourage from some intention by persuasion: *The policeman tried to dissuade him from jumping off the bridge.*
Syn. deter, prevent, divert.
Ant. encourage, persuade, induce.

dis·taff (dis'taf) *n.*
A rotating vertical staff that holds flax or wool for use in spinning by hand.
Usage: The *distaff side* refers to the maternal branch or female line of a family, as opposed to the *spear side*, or male branch. In olden times, spinning was considered woman's work and *distaff* came to mean women in general.

dis·tin·guished (dis·ting'gwisht) *adj.*
Outstanding because of excellence: *a distinguished professor.*
Syn. celebrated, eminent, illustrious.

dis·trib·ute (dis·trib'yōōt) *v.* **dis·trib·ut·ed, dis·trib·ut·ing**
1 To divide and give out: *Distribute the books to the students.* 2 To scatter or spread out: *Dandelions are widely distributed over the U.S.* 3 To divide and classify: *Distribute the new file records alphabetically.*—**dis·tri·bu·tion** (dis'trə·byōō'shən) *n.*
Syn. 1 apportion, allot. 2 diffuse, disperse. 3 arrange, categorize.

dis·tur·bance (dis·tûr'bəns) *n.*
1 The act of interrupting, bothering, or upsetting someone or something: *his disturbance of the library silence.* 2 The state of being annoyed, troubled, or restive: *mental disturbance.* 3 Tumult or disruptive disorder: *ghetto disturbances that lead to riots.*
Spelling tip: Watch the *u* and the *a.*
Syn. 2 uneasiness, agitation. 3 commotion, unrest.
Ant. 2 calm, stability. 3 peace, amity.

di·va (dē'və) *n.,* **di·vas** *or* **di·ve** (dē'vā) *pl.*
A famous female opera singer: *Maria Callas and Joan Sutherland are divas.*
Etymology: *Diva* is an Italian word that means divine.
Syn. prima donna.

di·verge (di·vûrj′ *or* dī·vûrj′) *v.* **di·verged, di·verg·ing**
1 To branch off in different directions from a common point: *Two roads diverged at a fork.* 2 To turn aside from a given course: *She diverged from her usual route because of a traffic jam.* 3 To differ, as in opinion: *There are many diverging viewpoints on nuclear protection.*—**di·ver·gence** (di·vûr′jəns *or* dī·vûr′jəns) *n.*, **di·ver′gent** *adj.*
Syn. 1 radiate, fork. 2 deviate. 3 disagree, dissent.

di·verse (di·vûrs′ *or* dī′vûrs) *adj.*
1 Marked by distinct differences: *diverse viewpoints on birth control.* 2 Varied: *The U.S. has a diverse population, embracing many ethnic groups.*
Syn. 1 different, various. 2 heterogeneous.
Ant. 1 similar. 2 homogeneous.

di·ver·sion (di·vûr′zhən) *n.*
1 Entertainment that draws the mind away from work or worry: *The movie was a pleasant diversion.* 2 A turning aside, as from a course: *the diversion of his youthful energy into a safe channel.* 3 An attack or disturbance meant to draw the enemy's attention away from the principal point of operation.
Syn. 1 amusement, pastime. 2 deflection, divergence. 3 ruse, blind.

di·vest (di·vest′ *or* dī·vest′) *v.*
1 To strip, as of clothes: *He divested himself of his overcoat.* 2 To deprive, as of rights or possessions: *To avoid conflict-of-interest charges, the political candidate divested himself of his stock in the company.*

div·i·dend (div′ə·dend) *n.*
1 A sum of money that is to be proportionally divided, as profits from a corporation to be distributed among its stockholders. 2 An individual share of such a sum: *a quarterly dividend on stock.*

div·i·na·tion (div′ə·nā′shən) *n.*
1 The art of foretelling the future or of discovering hidden things, as by reading omens or using supernatural insight: *Jeanne Dixon is famed for her powers of divination.* 2 A prophecy: *a divination of the death of Caesar.* 3 A successful or clever guess: *her divination of the truth.*
Syn. 1 augury, soothsaying. 2 prediction, forecast. 3 surmise.

di·vine (di·vīn′) *adj., n., v.* **di·vined, di·vin·ing**
adj. 1 Of, like, from, or devoted to God: *divine wisdom.* 2 So excellent as to seem heavenly: *That perfume is divine.*
n. A clergyman or theologian: *the Dean of St. Paul's, and other noted divines.*
v. To find out hidden or future things through divination or insight: *Despite his evasions, she divined the truth.*
Spelling tip: *Divine,* like *religious,* has two *i*'s.

di·vorce (di·vôrs′) *n.; v.* **di·vorced, di·vorc·ing**
n. 1 The legal process by which a marriage is dissolved. 2 Any radical or complete separation: *the divorce of sound and sense in her poetry.*

v. 1 To free from the legal ties of marriage. 2 To separate forcibly: *It is essential to divorce reason from emotion.*

di·vor·cee (di·vôr′sē′ *or* di·vôr′sā′) *n.*
A divorced person.
Usage: When spelled *divorcée,* with an accent, this word is applied only to women and should be pronounced di·vôr′sā′.

di·vulge (di·vulj′) *v.* **di·vulged, di·vulg·ing**
To tell, as a secret: *He was accused of divulging confidential information.*
Syn. disclose, reveal, expose.
Ant. conceal, hide, withhold.

doc·ile (dos′əl) *adj.*
Easy to teach, train, or manage: *a child as docile as a lamb.*—**do·cil·i·ty** (do·sil′ə·tē) *n.*
Spelling tip: Remember to write a *c* in this word, but pronounce it as an *s.*
Syn. obedient, submissive, compliant.
Ant. willful, obstinate, intractable.

dock·et (dok′it) *n., v.*
n. 1 A court calendar of the cases still awaiting trial. 2 Any schedule or list of things to be done: *a piece of business put on the legislative docket.*
v. To enter in a docket: *The case of Smith vs. Jones was docketed.*
Syn. *n.* 1, 2 agenda. *v.* schedule.

doc·trine (dok′trin) *n.*
One or more principles or tenets that are taught and believed, as by a religious or political group: *the doctrine of the Trinity; Marxist doctrine.*—**doc′tri·nal** *adj.*
Syn. theory, dogma, philosophy, teaching.

doff (dof *or* dôf) *v.*
To take off, as clothing or a hat: *He doffed his cap.*
Syn. remove.
Ant. don.

dog·ger·el (dog′ər·əl *or* dôg′ər·el) *n.*
Trivial, badly written verse: *His poetry is nothing but doggerel.*

dog·ma (dôg′mə *or* dog′mə) *n.,* **dog·mas** *or* **dog·ma·ta** *pl.*
A religious or other doctrine officially proclaimed as axiomatic, or a body of such doctrines: *The Immaculate Conception is part of Catholic dogma.*
Ant. heresy, heterodoxy.

do·lor·ous (dō′lər·əs *or* dol′ər·əs) *adj.*
Mournful; sad: *the dolorous expression of a basset hound.*
Syn. melancholy, gloomy, woebegone.
Ant. happy, cheerful, merry.

dom·i·cile (dom′ə·səl *or* dom′ə·sīl) *n.*
A person's dwelling; home: *His domicile is 320 Main Street.*
Syn. house, residence, abode.

dom·i·nant (dom′ə·nənt) *adj.*
1 Exercising the most authority: *During the Depression, Franklin D. Roosevelt was the dominant figure in the U.S.* 2 Most noticeable: *The Empire State Building is the dominant feature of the New York skyline.*
Spelling tip: Remember the *i* in this word.

Syn. predominant, paramount, controlling.
Ant. subordinate, weak, unimportant.

dom·i·neer·ing (dom'ə·nir'ing) *adj.*
Overbearing; tyrannical: *Timid men often have domineering wives.*
Syn. bullying, strict, despotic, autocratic.
Ant. submissive, obedient, compliant, servile.

Don Juan (don wän') *n.*
1 A legendary Spanish nobleman and seducer of women, who was the hero of many poems, operas, plays, etc. 2 Any fickle seducer: *He daydreamed about being a Don Juan.*
Syn. 2 philanderer, Casanova, Lothario, libertine.

do·nor (dō'nər) *n.*
One who gives: *a blood donor.*
Syn. contributor, giver, almsgiver.
Ant. recipient, taker.

don't dōnt) *contraction*
Do not: *Don't forget your appointment.*

dor·sal (dôr'səl) *adj.*
Situated on or near, or pertaining to, the rear part of an animal or the human body: *the front fins and the dorsal fins.*
Syn. back, posterior, tail.
Ant. front.

dose (dōs) *n.*
A specific quantity of medicine prescribed to be taken at one time: *a dose of cough syrup.*

do·tage (dō'tij) *n.*
Feebleness of mind as a result of old age; senility.

dote (dōt) *v.* **dot·ed, dot·ing**
To lavish love; to adore: *He doted on his youngest child.*
Syn. love, cherish, treasure.
Ant. hate, dislike, neglect, ignore.

dou·ble-en·ten·dre (dōō·blän·tän'dr') *n.*
A statement or phrase that can be interpreted in two ways with the less obvious meaning often improper: *the double-entendres of a nightclub entertainer.*

douche (dōōsh) *n.; v.* **douched, douch·ing**
n. A jet of water or other fluid directed into or onto some part of the body for medicinal or cleansing purposes: *The doctor prescribed warm douches.*
v. To administer a douche.

dough·ty (dou'tē) *adj.* **dough·ti·er, dough·ti·est**
Valiant; brave: *Doughty Paul Bunyan wielded his seven-foot ax.*
Usage: This word is used chiefly in humorous contexts.
Syn. bold, dauntless, fearless.
Ant. pusillanimous, craven, cowardly.

dour (dŏŏr *or* dour) *adj.*
Morose and grim; surly: *The residents of the dreary little town were a dour lot.*
Syn. forbidding, ill-tempered.
Ant. pleasant, agreeable, amiable.

dox·ol·o·gy (dok·sol'ə·jē) *n.,* **dox·ol·o·gies** *pl.*
A hymn of praise to God, specifically applied to a stanza beginning, "Praise God,

from whom all blessings flow"; or an expression of such praise used as the closing words of a sermon: *The minister pronounced the doxology.*

dregs (dregz) *n.pl.*
1 The sediment of liquids, especially of beverages: *the dregs left in a glass of wine.* 2 The poorest or least desirable part: *the dregs of society.*
Syn. 2 scum, scrapings, rejects.

droll (drōl) *adj.*
Odd and amusing in a charming sort of way: *a droll man; a droll story.*
Syn. comical, fantastical.
Ant. commonplace, ordinary, dull.

drom·e·dar·y (drom'ə·der'ē *or* drum'ə·der'ē) *n.,* **drom·e·dar·ies** *pl.*
The swift, one-humped Arabian camel.

drown (droun) *v.*
1 To die or to kill by suffocation in water or other liquid: *They drowned a short distance from shore.* 2 To become inundated or overwhelmed: *drowning in self-pity.*

drudg·er·y (druj'ər·ē) *n.* **drudg·er·ies** *pl.*
Hard and boring work: *the drudgery of scrubbing floors.*
Syn. toil, grind.

du·al (d(y)ōō·əl) *adj.*
Consisting of two things; double: *The book fills the dual need for education and for entertainment.*
Spelling tip: Don't confuse this word with *duel.*
Syn. twofold, twin.
Ant. single.

du·bi·ous (d(y)ōō'bē·əs) *adj.*
1 Not sure; doubtful: *Her husband was dubious about her need for two mink coats.* 2 Open to question or to criticism: *of dubious quality.*
Syn. 1 skeptical, unconvinced. 2 questionable, debatable.
Ant. 1 confident, positive. 2 indisputable, unassailable.

duc·at (duk'ət) *n.*
Any of several gold or silver coins formerly used in Europe and ranging in value from about $2.34 to 83¢; especially, the Dutch or Venetian gold coin.

duc·tile (duk'təl *or* duk'til) *adj.*
1 Moldable into many shapes, as certain materials: *Plastics are more ductile than any metal, even soft gold.* 2 Easily influenced, as a person: *an obedient, ductile child.*
Syn. 1, 2 pliable, malleable, plastic, yielding.
Ant. 1, 2 rigid, inelastic, unmalleable.

due (d(y)ōō) *adj., n.*
adj. Owing, expected, appropriate, or ascribable: *the moneys due; a bus due at six o'clock; with due appreciation; a delay due to rain.*
n. 1 That which is owed or appropriate: *the honor that is his due.* 2 *pl.* Charge or fee: *club dues.*

du·el (d(y)ōō'əl) *n.; v.* **du·eled** *or* **du·elled, du·el·ing** *or* **du·el·ling**

n. **1** A prearranged combat between two persons, usually fought with deadly weapons and in the presence of witnesses or seconds. **2** By extension, any struggle: *a duel of words.*
v. To fight in a duel.

du·et (d(y)ŏŏ·et′) *n.*
Musical composition for or performance by two voices or instruments: *The tenor and soprano sing a duet.*
Syn. duo.

duke (d(y)ŏŏk) *n.*
1 In England and some other European countries, a nobleman having a hereditary rank below that of a prince and above that of a marquis. **2** A European prince ruling over a duchy.

du·ly (d(y)ŏŏ′lē) *adv.*
Appropriately or to an adequate degree; fitly: *thanks duly rendered.*
Syn. suitably, properly, adequately.
Ant. inappropriately, improperly.

du·o·de·num (d(y)ŏŏ′ə·dē′nəm *or* dŏŏ·od′ə·nəm) *n.,* **du·o·de·na** *pl.*
The part of the small intestine extending from the stomach to the jejunum: *In digestion, food passes through the stomach and then enters the duodenum.*

dupe (d(y)ŏŏp) *v.* **duped, dup·ing;** *n.*
v. To trick; to deceive deliberately: *The con man used realistic-looking stock certificates to dupe his victims.*
n. One who is easily tricked: *an unsuspecting dupe.*

du·pli·cate (d(y)ŏŏ′plə·kāt *v.;* d(y)ŏŏ′plə·kit *n., adj.*) *v.* **du·pli·cat·ed, du·pli·cat·ing;** *n., adj.*
v. To copy exactly or do a second time.
n. An exact copy: *a duplicate of the memo.*
adj. In pairs, or corresponding exactly to an original: *a duplicate key.*—**du′pli·ca′tor** *n.*
Spelling tip: Use every vowel except an *o.*
Syn. *n.* facsimile, replica, likeness.

du·plic·i·ty (d(y)ŏŏ·plis′ə·tē) *n.,* **du·plic·i·ties** *pl.*
Tricky deceitfulness; double-dealing: *the con man's duplicity.*
Syn. trickery, dishonesty, misrepresentation.
Ant. honesty, candor, good faith.

du·ra·ble (d(y)ŏŏr′ə·bel) *adj.*
Able to withstand decay or wear; hardy and lasting: *Denim is a strong, durable fabric.*
Syn. enduring, tough.
Ant. fragile, frail.

du·ress (d(y)ŏŏ·res′ *or* d(y)ŏŏr′is) *n.*
Coercion or compulsion by means of force or threats: *a confession extracted under duress.*
Syn. constraint, pressure.

dy·nam·ic (dī·nam′ik) *adj.*
1 Of or having to do with physical force or energy as the result of force. **2** Having to do with or causing change or action: *the most dynamic period in our country's development.* **3** Characterized by energy or forcefulness: *a dynamic personality.*—**dy·nam′i·cal·ly** *adv.*
Syn. **1** kinetic, active, propulsive. **2** active,

eventful, momentous. **3** vigorous, high-powered.
Ant. **1** static, inactive. **2** unimportant, uneventful. **3** impotent, powerless, weak.

dy·nam·ics (dī·nam′iks) *n.pl.*
1 The branch of physics that treats of the motion of bodies and the effects of forces in producing motion. **2** The forces producing or governing activity or movement of any kind: *spiritual dynamics.*
Usage: This plural noun is construed as singular and uses a singular verb.

dy·na·mite (dī′nə·mīt) *n.; v.* **dy·na·mit·ed, dy·na·mit·ing**
n. **1** An explosive composed of nitroglycerin held in some absorbent substance. **2** Anything or anybody characterized by great potential or effectiveness: *Doris Day and Rock Hudson were dynamite at the box office.*
v. To charge, blow up, or shatter with or as if with dynamite.—**dy′na·mit′er** *n.*

dy·nast (dī′nast *or* dī′nəst) *n.*
A ruler, especially a hereditary one.

dy·nas·ty (dī′nas·tē) *n., pl.* **dy·nas·ties**
1 A group of rulers who belong to one family and who succeed each other as rulers over a long period of time. **2** The length of time during which such a family is in power. **3** A group or family whose power or prominence extends over a period of time as though inherited from one generation to the next: *a political dynasty.*

dys·en·ter·y (dis′ən·ter′ē) *n.*
A severe inflammation of the mucous membrane of the large intestine, marked by the passage of blood, griping pains, and some fever.

dys·pep·sia (dis·pep′shə *or* dis·pep′sē·ə) *n.*
Difficult or painful digestion, usually chronic.

E

ear·nest (ûr′nist) *adj., n.*
adj. Characterized by seriousness, sincerity, or determination: *an earnest plea for peace.*
n. An assurance or token of something to come, as money paid in advance to bind a contract. —**ear′nest·ly** *adv.,* **ear′nest·ness** *n.*
Syn. *adj.* ardent, fervent, zealous.
Ant. *adj.* frivolous, insincere.

earth·y (ûr′thē) *adj.* **earth·i·er, earth·i·est**
1 Composed of or suggesting the qualities of earth: *the earthy flavor of some wines.* **2** Having qualities that pertain to the world: *the earthy dialogue in present-day films.*
Syn. **2** worldly, robust, lusty.
Ant. **2** unworldly, spiritual, ethereal.

ea·sel (ē′zəl) *n.*
A folding frame or tripod used to support an artist's canvas, a painting being displayed, etc.
Etymology: This word comes from the Dutch *ezel,* which originally meant beast of burden (ass).

e·bul·lient (i·bul′yənt) *adj.*
Bubbling over with enthusiasm or excite-
ment: *the ebullient performance of Carol Chan-
ning.*—**e·bul′lient·ly** *adv.*
Syn. exuberant, high-spirited, vivacious.
Ant. unenthusiastic, blasé, bored.

ec·cen·tric (ek·sen′trik) *adj., n.*
adj. Differing greatly from conventional behavior, appearance, or opinions: *The eccentric old man always wore his shoes to bed.*
n. 1 A person or thing that behaves in an
eccentric fashion. 2 A disk attached off center
to a driving shaft and able to revolve freely
within a ring or collar, used to change rotary
motion into up-and-down motion.—**ec·cen′-
tri·cal·ly** *adv.*
Spelling tip: Watch the three *c*'s.
Syn. *adj.* strange, unorthodox, unusual.
n. 1 crackpot, character.
Ant. *adj.* orthodox, conventional.

ec·cle·si·as·ti·cal (i·klē′zē·as′ti·kəl) *adj.*
Of or having to do with the church, especially
as an organized and governing power. Also
ec·cle′si·as′tic *adj.*—**ec·cle′si·as′ti·cal·ly** *adv.*

ech·o (ek′ō) *n.,* **echoes** *pl.; v.* **ech·oed, ech·o·
ing**
n. The repetition of a sound by the reflection
of sound waves from an opposing surface.
v. 1 To repeat or send back sound by echo:
The walls echoed the shot. 2 To be repeated or
given back: *His shouts echoed throughout the
valley.* 3 To repeat the words, opinions, etc.
of someone: *to echo leaders of the past.*
Spelling tip: Remember that the *k* sound in
this word is spelled *ch* and that the plural is
formed with *es*, not just *s*.

é·clair (ā·klâr′ *or* i·klâr′ *or* ā′klâr) *n.*
A small, oblong pastry shell filled with custard or whipped cream and usually iced with
chocolate.

ec·lec·tic (ek·lek′tik) *adj.*
Composed of elements selected from various
sources: *an eclectic musical program.*
Spelling tip: Remember that this word has
three *c*'s, not three *k*'s (it just sounds that
way).

ec·sta·sy (ek′stə·sē) *n.,* **ec·sta·sies** *pl.*
A feeling of intense delight or great happiness: *the ecstasy of a young actress who received rave opening-night notices.*
Syn. rapture, bliss, exultation.

ec·stat·ic (ek·stat′ik) *adj.*
Filled with or exhibiting great joy or rap-
ture: *the ecstatic bride.*—**ec·stat′i·cal·ly** *adv.*
Syn. joyous, rapturous, sublime.
Ant. downcast, depressed, apathetic.

ec·u·men·i·cal (ek′yŏŏ·men′i·kəl) *adj.*
1 Belonging to, representing, or accepted by
the Christian church throughout the world:
an ecumenical council. 2 Of, desiring, or promoting worldwide Christian unity: *an ecumenical movement.*

ec·ze·ma (ek′sə·mə, eg′zə·mə, *or* eg·zē′mə) *n.*
An inflammatory disease of the skin, marked
by itching, watery discharge, and the appearance of red, scaly pimples.

e·del·weiss (ā′dəl·vīs) *n.*
A small, perennial herb growing chiefly in
the Alps, with white, woolly leaves that suggest a flower.

ed·i·ble (ed′ə·bəl) *adj., n.*
adj. Suitable for eating: *edible berries.*
n. Usually pl. Something that can be eaten:
a stockpile of emergency edibles.

ed·i·fice (ed′ə·fis) *n.*
A building or other structure, especially one
that is large and impressive.

ed·i·fy (ed′ə·fī) *v.* **ed·i·fied, ed·i·fy·ing**
To instruct, benefit, or uplift, especially
spiritually or morally: *The speaker entertained as well as edified his audience.*—**ed′i·
fi·ca′tion** *n.*
Syn. teach, guide, direct, educate.

e·di·tion (i·dish′ən) *n.*
1 The particular form in which a book, magazine, or other literary work is published: *a
three-volume edition.* 2 The total number of
copies of a publication issued at any one
time and printed from the same plates: *the
morning edition.* 3 A copy belonging to such
a printing: *a first edition.*

ed·u·cate (ej′ŏŏ·kāt) *v.* **ed·u·cat·ed, ed·u·cat·
ing**
1 To teach or provide schooling for: *to educate children in private schools.* 2 To develop
or train taste, special ability, etc.: *to educate
the eyes to appreciate the beauty of art.*—**ed′u·
ca′tion** *n.,* **ed′u·ca′tion·al** *adj.*

ee·rie (ir′ē *or* ē′rē) *adj.* **ee·ri·er, ee·ri·est**
Causing a feeling of fear and mystery: *eerie
noises in the deserted house.*—**ee′ri·ly** *adv.,*
ee′ri·ness *n.*
Spelling tip: This word is also spelled *eery.*
Syn. weird, ghostly, frightening.

ef·face (i·fās′) *v.* **ef·faced, ef·fac·ing**
1 To rub out, as written characters: *a tombstone inscription effaced by time.* 2 To destroy
or get rid of, as a memory. 3 To make oneself
inconspicuous or insignificant: *trying to efface herself after making a disastrous social
blunder.*
Syn. 1 erase, cancel, delete. 2 blot out, obliterate.

ef·fect (i·fekt′) *n., v.*
n. 1 Something brought about by some cause
or action: *Fire was one effect of the explosion.*
2 The power or capacity to produce some
result: *a statement of little effect.* 3 The overall
reaction or impression made on the mind or
body by something seen, heard, eaten, etc.:
the effect of morphine; the effect of a work of art.
4 *pl.* Personal or movable goods; belongings.
v. To bring about or accomplish: *to effect an
escape.*
Usage: *Effect* as a verb should be carefully
distinguished from *affect,* meaning to act
upon or influence: *Treatment effected an early
cure, but the long illness had affected his mind.*
Syn. *n.* 1 result, consequence. 2 force, influence. 4 possessions, goods. *v.* cause, create,
produce, achieve.

ef·fem·i·nate (i·fem′ə·nit) *adj.*
Having traits, qualities, or mannerisms more usually found in a woman than in a man: *He has an effeminate voice.*—**ef·fem′i·na·cy** *n.*, **ef·fem′i·nate·ly** *adv.*
Syn. womanish, unmanly, feminine.
Ant. masculine, virile, mannish.

ef·fer·vesce (ef′ər·ves′) *v.* **ef·fer·vesced, ef·fer·vesc·ing**
1 To give off or come forth in bubbles: *Soda water effervesces.* 2 To show enthusiasm or lively spirits: *children effervescing at a birthday party.*—**ef′fer·ves′cence** *n.*, **ef′fer·ves′cent** *adj.*
Spelling tip: Remember that although this word has two *f*'s it has only one *s*.
Syn. 1 bubble, foam, froth, fizz.

ef·fete (i·fēt′) *adj.*
1 Having lost strength, vitality, creativity, etc.: *effete noblemen unable to perform any useful functions in society.* 2 Incapable of further production; barren, as an animal, plant, or the soil.—**ef·fete′ly** *adv.*, **ef·fete′ness** *n.*
Syn. 1 worn out, exhausted, spent. 2 unfruitful, sterile, unprolific.

ef·fi·ca·cy (ef′ə·kə·sē) *n.*
Power to produce a desired or intended result: *He questioned the efficacy of the sedative prescribed by his doctor.*
Syn. effectiveness, capability, value.

ef·fi·gy (ef′ə·jē) *n.*, **ef·fi·gies** *pl.*
1 A likeness or representation, especially, a sculptured portrait. 2 A crude image of a disliked person: *The coach was hung in effigy after the team lost.*

ef·front·er·y (i·frun′tər·ē) *n.*
Shameless or insolent boldness: *The dinner guest had the effrontery to criticize everything about the meal.*
Syn. audacity, impudence, nerve, gall.

ef·ful·gent (i·ful′jənt) *adj.*
Shining brilliantly: *the effulgent beauty of her smile.*—**ef·ful′gent·ly** *adv.*
Syn. radiant, glowing, dazzling.

ef·fu·sive (i·fyōō′siv) *adj.*
Overflowing with sentiment or enthusiasm: *He was embarrassed by her effusive introduction.*—**ef·fu′sive·ly** *adv.*, **ef·fu′sive·ness** *n.*
Syn. gushing, profuse, exuberant.
Ant. restrained, cold, reserved.

e·go (ē′gō) *n.*
1 The part of a person's consciousness that is aware of itself and also of its difference from the selves of others and from the objects of its thought and other operations.
2 Egotism.
Etymology: *Ego* comes from the Latin word meaning *I*.

e·go·ism (ē′gō·iz′əm) *n.*
1 Great concern for one's own welfare and interests; selfishness: *the egoism of a person who demands the largest share for himself.* 2 Self-conceit; egotism.—**e′go·ist** *n.*, **e′go·is′tic** *adj.*
Usage: Although *egoism* and *egotism* are sometimes used interchangeably, *egoism*

usually refers to a person's tendency to view things as they bear upon himself. *Egotism* points to the practice of talking or writing about oneself excessively. *Egotism* is the more commonly used of these two words, as *egoism* is now largely a philosophical term.
Syn. 1 self-absorption, self-regard.
Ant. 1 altruism, self-abnegation, humility.

e·go·tism (ē′gə·tiz′əm) *n.*
1 Excessive reference to oneself in speech or writing; boastfulness; conceit: *Her egotism made her a boring conversationalist.* 2 Selfishness, egoism.—**e′go·tist** *n.*, **e′go·tis′tic** *adj.*
Usage: See EGOISM.
Syn. 1 vanity, self-esteem, self-aggrandizement.
Ant. 1 humility, self-effacement, modesty.

e·gre·gious (i·grē′jəs *or* i·grē′jē·əs) *adj.*
Conspicuously bad, as in taste or quality: *Failing to greet one's guests is an egregious social blunder.*—**e·gre′gious·ly** *adv.*, **e·gre′gious·ness** *n.*
Etymology: *Egregious* comes from the Latin words *e* (out) and *grex, gregis* (herd), meaning out of the herd or outstanding.
Syn. flagrant, glaring, intolerable, shocking.

ei·ther (ē′thər *or* ī′thər) *adj., pron., conj., adv.*
adj. 1 One or the other of two: *Hold out either hand.* 2 One and the other: *They sat on either side of him.*
pron. One or the other: *Choose either.*
conj. In one of two or more cases (used before two or more alternatives joined by *or*): *Either I shall go there or he will come here.*
adv. Any more so: *He cannot sing and I cannot either.*
Usage: This word is singular and takes a singular verb in formal writing: *Either of them is suitable.* However, in informal writing or speech, a plural verb is frequently used: *Are either of you leaving?* When there are two subjects, one singular and one plural, the verb agrees with the nearer subject: *Either the boss or his assistants are responsible. Either they or the boss is responsible.*
Spelling tip: Note that this word is an exception to the *i* before *e* rule.

é·lan (ā·län′) *n.*
Enthusiasm or vigor as shown by a person's manner, beauty of performance, or keenness of imagination: *a young pianist of great charm and élan.*
Syn. vivacity, zest, liveliness.

e·la·tion (i·lā′shən) *n.*
Exalted feeling, as from success or triumph: *his elation at having been selected.*
Syn. exhilaration, excitement, joy, happiness.
Ant. dejection, depression, discouragement.

el·ee·mos·y·nar·y (el′ə·mos′ə·ner′ē *or* el′ē·ə·mos′ə·ner′ē) *adj.*
Of, having to do with, or supported by charity: *an eleemosynary organization; a wealthy man famed for his eleemosynary activities.*

el·e·gi·ac (el′ə·jī′ək *or* i·lē′jē·ak) *adj.*
1 Of or having to do with meditative poems or musical works of lamentation: *elegiac*

verse. 2 Expressing sorrow or regret, especially for something in the past: *elegiac laments about one's lost, idyllic childhood.*
Syn. 2 nostalgic, poignant, melancholy.
Ant. 2 joyful, happy, jubilant.

e·lic·it (i·lis'it) *v.*
To draw out or bring forth: *to elicit the truth.*
—**e·lic'i·ta'tion** *n.*
Usage: Although they are pronounced alike, *elicit* and *illicit* have completely different meanings. *Illicit* is an adjective meaning *unlawful* or *not permitted: The district attorney elicited information about the illicit selling of narcotics.*
Syn. extract, obtain, wrest, wring.

el·i·gi·ble (el'ə·jə·bəl) *adj.*
Qualified or suitable: *eligible to vote; an eligible young man.*—**el'i·gi·bil'i·ty** *n.*
Syn. capable, fit, desirable.

e·lim·i·nate (i·lim'ə·nāt) *v.* **e·lim·i·nat·ed, e·lim·i·nat·ing**
1 To get rid of; exclude: *Some people must eliminate salt from their diets.* 2 To discard as irrelevant; ignore: *In his argument he eliminated several major points.* 3 To remove by defeating, as a contestant, team, etc: *His second defeat eliminated him from the tournament.*—**e·lim'i·na'tion** *n.*
Syn. 1 leave out, give up. 2 omit, overlook.
Ant. 1 add. 2 include.

el·lip·sis (i·lip'sis) *n.*, **el·lip·ses** (i·lip'sēz) *pl.*
1 *In grammar* The omission of a word or words necessary for the complete grammatical construction of a sentence, but not required for the understanding of it. 2 The marks (. . . or * * *) used to indicate such omissions on a written or printed page.

e·lon·gate (i·lông'gāt) *v.* **e·lon·gat·ed, e·lon·gat·ing;** *adj.*
v. To increase in length; stretch: *His face became elongated when he heard the bad news.*
adj. Drawn out; lengthened: *A dachshund has short legs and an elongate body.*—**e'lon·ga'tion** *n.*
Syn. *v.* extend, lengthen. *adj.* long.
Ant. *v.* shorten, compress. *adj.* short.

e·lu·ci·date (i·lōō'sə·dāt)*v.* **e·lu·ci·dat·ed, e·lu·ci·dat·ing**
To make clear; explain: *Footnotes elucidate the text.*—**e·lu'ci·da'tion** *n.*
Syn. clarify, illuminate, make plain.

e·lude (i·lōōd') *v.* **e·lud·ed, e·lud·ing**
1 To avoid or escape from by trickery: *The fleeing thief eluded his pursuers.* 2 To escape the notice or understanding of: *The meaning of his remarks eluded me.*

e·lu·sive (i·lōō'siv) *adj.*
1 Tending to flee or avoid capture: *Wild rabbits are elusive creatures.* 2 Hard to grasp, perceive, or remember: *an elusive fragrance.*
—**e·lu'sive·ly** *adv.*, **e·lu'sive·ness** *n.*
Syn. 2 intangible, shadowy, insubstantial.

e·ma·ci·a·ted (i·mā'shē·ā'tid) *adj.*
Very thin or wasted away, as from illness or poor nutrition: *emaciated beggars in the streets of Bombay.*

Syn. gaunt, skinny, skeletal.
Ant. plump, fat, obese.

e·man·ci·pate (i·man'sə·pāt) *v.* **e·man·ci·pat·ed, e·man·ci·pat·ing**
To set free from slavery, oppression, or authority: *to emancipate the prisoners of a concentration camp.*—**e·man'ci·pa'tion** *n.*
Syn. release, liberate.
Ant. subjugate, enslave.

em·bark (im·bärk') *v.*
1 To put on or go aboard a ship before a voyage: *In August we embarked for South Africa.* 2 To begin a venture or undertaking: *At the age of sixty he embarked on a career as a painter.*—**em'bar·ka'tion** *n.*
Syn. 2 enter upon, start, launch.
Ant. 1 land, arrive, disembark.

em·bar·rass (im·bar'əs) *v.*
1 To make self-conscious and uncomfortable: *He was embarrassed by the compliment.* 2 To hinder, hamper: *She was embarrassed by a lack of funds.*
Syn. 1 disconcert, discomfit. 2 impede.

em·bel·lish (im·bel'ish) *v.*
1 To beautify by adding ornamental features; decorate: *to embellish a room with fine paintings.* 2 To heighten the interest of a story by adding extra or fanciful details: *He embellished the description of the party by relating antics of the guests.*—**em·bel'lish·ment** *n.*
Syn. 1 adorn, garnish. 2 enliven.

em·bez·zle (im·bez'əl) *v.* **em·bez·zled, em·bez·zling**
To take illegally for one's own use another person's money, securities, etc.: *It was discovered that the bank clerk had embezzled thousands of dollars.*—**em·bez'zle·ment, em·bez'zler** *n.*
Syn. steal, appropriate.

em·broi·der·y (im·broi'dər·ē) *n.*, **em·broi·der·ies** *pl.*
1 Ornamental needlework, or the art of producing such work: *Every young lady should do embroidery.* 2 Any elaborate ornamentation, as of facts or details: *The witness told what he had observed without embroidery.*
Syn. 2 elaboration, embellishment.

em·broil (em·broil') *v.*
To involve in disturbances, conflicts, etc.: *The whole neighborhood became embroiled in the dispute.*—**em·broil'ment** *n.*
Syn. implicate.

em·bry·o (em'brē·ō) *n.*, **em·bry·os** *pl.*
1 *In biology* The earliest stage in the development of a plant or animal before it has taken on its distinctive form. In the human, the developing child is an embryo for seven weeks; after that and until birth it is called a fetus. 2 Any early, undeveloped stage: *His plans for the future are still in embryo.*

e·mend (i·mend') *v.*
To make corrections or changes, as in a literary work, especially after scholarly study: *In his novel about the Civil War, he emended several chapters dealing with battle scenes.*—**e·men·da·tion** (e'men·dā'shən) *n.*
Syn. revise, edit, rewrite.

e·mer·i·tus (i·mer′ə·təs) *adj.*
Retired from active service, usually because of age, but retained in an honorary position: *a professor emeritus.*

e·met·ic (i·met′ik) *adj., n.*
adj. Causing vomiting, as when deliberately given after a person has swallowed poison, a foreign object, etc.
n. A substance that induces vomiting: *A teaspoonful of mustard in warm water is an effective emetic.*

em·i·grate (em′ə·grāt) *v.* **em·i·grat·ed, em·i·grat·ing**
To move from one country or one section of a country to settle in another: *His ancestors emigrated from Ireland before the Civil War.*—**em′i·gra′tion, em′i·grant** *n.*
Usage: To *emigrate* is to move from one's own country in order to settle in another place. To *immigrate* is to come into a country of which one is not a native in order to live there permanently.

em·i·nent (em′ə·nənt) *adj.*
Esteemed or looked up to because of great merit or high rank: *Bernard Baruch was an eminent statesman.*—**em′i·nent·ly** *adv.*
Syn. outstanding, distinguished, prominent, celebrated, illustrious.
Ant. mediocre, worthless, infamous, notorious.
Usage: *Eminent* should not be confused with *imminent*, although their spellings and pronunciations are similar. *Imminent* means about to happen, and is used especially of danger or catastrophe: *We knew that a collision with the oncoming truck was imminent.*

em·is·sar·y (em′ə·ser′ē) *n.,* **em·is·sar·ies** *pl.*
A person sent on a mission: *an emissary hastily dispatched to the Middle East to attempt to arrange a cease-fire.*
Syn. representative, agent, envoy.

e·mol·lient (i·mol′yənt) *adj., n.*
adj. Soothing, especially to the skin: *an emollient ointment.*
n. In medicine A softening or soothing medicinal preparation.
Syn. *adj.* softening, relaxing, easing. *n.* salve, unguent, ointment.

em·pha·sis (em′fə·sis) *n.,* **em·pha·ses** (em′-fə·sēz) *pl.*
1 Special significance or importance given to something: *The diplomatic note put great emphasis on the choice of a neutral meeting place.* 2 Stress given by voice or gesture: *The strong emphasis he gave the word "you" suggested that he meant his remark sarcastically.*

em·pha·size (em′fə·sīz) *v.* **em·pha·sized, em·pha·siz·ing**
To give emphasis to; stress: *He emphasized that he was issuing no ultimatums, only making a suggestion.*

em·phat·i·cal·ly (em·fat′ik·lē) *adv.*
With emphasis; strongly or forcefully: *He emphatically rejected the idea that he resign.*—**em·phat′ic** *adj.*
Syn. firmly, vigorously, forcibly.
Ant. timidly, mildly, weakly.

em·pir·i·cal (em·pir′i·kəl) *adj.*
Based solely upon direct experience or observation: *Empirical evidence confirmed the speed of light.*—**em·pir′i·cal·ly** *adv.*
Syn. experiential, observational, inductive, a posteriori.
Ant. deductive, theoretical, a priori.

em·ploy·ee (im·ploi′ē *or* em′ploi·ē′) *n.*
A person who works for another for salary, wages, or other return: *a bakery with five employees.*
Spelling tip: *Employe* is an acceptable variant spelling.
Syn. worker; *plural* help, personnel.

em·u·late (em′yə·lāt) *v.* **em·u·lat·ed, em·u·lat·ing**
1 To try to equal or surpass: *Emulate the achievements of your father.* 2 To rival: *The reproduction could not emulate the original painting.*

en·am·ored (in·am′ərd) *adj.*
In love, especially in the phrase *enamored of,* in love with: *He has always been enamored of Venice.*
Syn. charmed, fascinated, infatuated.

en·clave (en′klāv *or* än′klāv) *n.*
A territory completely or partially enclosed within the territory of a nation to which it is not politically subject, as the Vatican in Italy.

en·co·mi·um (en·kō′mē·əm) *n.,* **en·co·mi·ums** *or* **en·co·mi·a** (en·kō′mē·ə) *pl.*
A formal expression of praise: *political encomiums exchanged by members of the same party during an election year.*
Syn. eulogy, panegyric.
Ant. vilification, attack, disparagement.

en·com·pass (in·kum′pəs) *v.*
To enclose or contain: *The study encompasses a number of different subjects.*
Syn. include, relate to, deal with.

en·croach·ment (in·krōch′mənt) *n.*
The act of stealthily intruding: *The nation vigorously protested its neighbor's encroachment upon its territory.*
Syn. intrusion, trespassing, invasion.

en·cy·clo·pe·di·a (en·sī′klə·pē′dē·ə) *n.*
A book or set of books with information arranged alphabetically according to subject.
Spelling tip: This word may also be spelled encyclopædia.

en·dear·ment (in·dir′mənt) *n.*
A loving word, act, etc.: *He suspected that her endearments were meant to distract him from the extravagance of her shopping spree.*
Syn. blandishment, allurement, caress.

en·deav·or (in·dev′ər) *n., v.*
n. An attempt or effort to do or attain something: *an earnest endeavor to end the strike.*
v. To try: *The Red Cross endeavors to alleviate the suffering of mankind.*
Syn. *n.* try, exertion, undertaking.
v. attempt, undertake.

en·dive (en′dīv *or* än′dēv) *n.*
An herb related to chicory, or its leaves, used in a salad.

en·er·gize (en'ər·jīz) *v.* **en·er·gized, en·er·giz·**
ing
To give energy, force, or strength to: *A big*
contribution energized plans to reconstruct the
church.
Syn. activate, invigorate, excite.
Ant. impede, obstruct, retard, weaken.

en·er·vate (en'ər·vāt) *v.* **en·er·vat·ed, en·er·**
vat·ing
To sap the strength or vitality of: *The long*
walk in the hot sun enervated him.
Syn. enfeeble, weaken, drain.
Ant. energize, invigorate, strengthen.

en·gen·der (in·jen'dər) *v.*
To give rise to; produce: *The highhanded*
methods of the captain engendered a sense of
insecurity in his men.

en·gross (in·grōs') *v.*
To occupy completely; absorb: *I was so en-*
grossed in a mystery story that I did not hear
the phone ring.—**en·gross'ing** *adj.*

en·hance (in·hans') *v.* **en·hanced, en·hanc·ing**
To heighten or increase: *His reputation was*
greatly enhanced by the success of his new play.
Syn. strengthen, contribute to, improve.
Ant. diminish, lessen, weaken.

e·nig·ma (i·nig'mə) *n.*
A baffling or ambiguous saying; also, anything that puzzles or baffles: *The Delphic*
oracle spoke in enigmas; Teen-agers are
enigmas to many parents.

en·ig·mat·ic (en'ig·mat'ik) *adj.*
Puzzling or baffling: *Her enigmatic shrug was*
impossible to understand.
Syn. ambiguous, inexplicable, mysterious.
Ant. clear, obvious, understandable.

en·join (in·join') *v.*
1 To forbid or prohibit: *The judge enjoined*
him from operating a motor vehicle for three
months as punishment for speeding. **2** To
order authoritatively: *The doctor enjoined his*
patients to stop smoking.
Syn. 2 command, direct.

en·mi·ty (en'mə·tē) *n.,* **en·mi·ties** *pl.*
Deep-seated unfriendliness or hostility: *Al-*
though the two candidates disagreed on many
issues, there was no enmity between them.
Syn. antagonism, hatred, ill will.
Ant. affection, fondness, good will.

en·nui (än'wē *or* än·wē') *n.*
Weary listlessness or discontent; boredom:
Retired people without outside interests may
suffer ennui.
Syn. weariness, indifference, lethargy.
Ant. enthusiasm, activity, interest.

e·nough (i·nuf') *adj.*
Adequate for any need: *enough water to last*
through the drought.
Spelling tip: Beware of the *f* sound of *-ough:*
rough, tough, cough.
Syn. sufficient, ample.
Ant. insufficient, inadequate.

en·rap·ture (in·rap'chər) *v.* **en·rap·tured, en·**
rap·tur·ing
To bring into a state of rapture or delight:

He was enraptured by her warm smile and
charming manner.
Syn. charm, entrance, delight.
Ant. put off, repel.

en route (än rōōt')
On the road; on the way: *En route to Boston*
he met an old friend; we'll have lunch en route.

en·sconce (en·skons') *v.* **en·sconced, en·sconc·**
ing
To settle or place snugly: *The cat was happily*
ensconced on the sofa.

en·sem·ble (än·säm'bəl) *n.*
1 The parts of something viewed together as
a unit. **2** The entire cast of a play, ballet,
etc.; also, the cast's appearance together in a
particular scene.

en·sign (en'sən; *also* en'sīn *for def.* 2) *n.*
1 In the U.S. Navy or Coast Guard, a commissioned officer of the lowest grade. **2** A
flag or banner, especially a national standard
or naval flag.

en·tente (än·tänt') *n.*
A mutual agreement: *Representatives of the*
two nations finally reached an entente on the
disposition of the disputed territory.

en·thrall (in·thrôl') *v.*
To keep spellbound; fascinate: *The children*
were enthralled by the puppet show.
Syn. charm, entrance, enrapture.

en·thu·si·asm (in·thōō'zē·az'əm) *n.*
Keen interest in something: *an active en-*
thusiasm for sports.—**en·thu'si·as'tic** *adj.*
Syn. zeal, ardor, fondness, devotion.
Ant. boredom, ennui, lethargy.

en·tour·age (än'tŏŏ·räzh') *n.*
A group of followers or attendants: *The*
candidate's entourage consisted of his press
secretary, party leaders, several bodyguards,
and a dozen reporters.
Syn. following, retinue.

en·trails (en'trālz) *n.pl.*
The intestines; bowels.
Syn. guts, innards.

en·trée (än'trā) *n.*
1 The act or privilege of entering: *to gain*
entrée to an exclusive circle of prominent peo-
ple. **2** The principal course of a meal: *The*
entrée was roast beef and mashed potatoes.
Spelling tip: This word may also be written
without the accent: *entree.*

en·tre·pre·neur (än'trə·prə·nûr') *n.*
A person who starts and runs his own enterprise or business.

en·vel·op (in·vel'əp) *v.* **en·vel·oped, en·vel·**
op·ing
To enclose or cover, as by wrapping around:
The folds of the cloak enveloped him.
Etymology: See ENVELOPE.
Syn. encompass, surround, swathe.
Ant. uncover, expose.

en·ve·lope (en'və·lōp *or* än'və·lōp) *n.*
A paper case or wrapper for enclosing a letter,
or any enveloping cover or wrapper: *He*
placed the letter in the envelope.

Etymology: The words *envelope* and *envelop* both derive from the Old French word *enveloper*, which means "to wrap in."

en·vi·ron (in·vī'rən) *v.*
To extend around; encircle; surround: *The suburbs environ the city.*
Syn. ring, girdle, enclose, encompass.

en·vi·ron·ment (in·vī'rən·mənt *or* in·vī'ərn·mənt) *n.*
The aggregate of external circumstances, conditions, and things that affect an individual, organism, or group: *the unstable environment of wartime London.*
Syn. surroundings, milieu.

en·vi·rons (in·vī'rənz) *n.pl.*
A surrounding, outlying area, as around a city; outskirts: *The train passed through the environs and then entered the central city.*

e·phem·er·al (i·fem'ər·əl) *adj.*
Lasting but a short time; transitory: *Ephemeral summer flowers wilt a few hours after blooming.*
Syn. fleeting, evanescent, short-lived.
Ant. permanent, enduring, imperishable.

ep·i·cure (ep'ə·kyŏŏr) *n.*
A person given to luxurious living and discriminating gratification of the senses; especially, a fastidious devotee of good food and drink: *The French chef prepared a meal good enough for an epicure.*—**ep'i·cu·re'an** *adj.*
Syn. gourmet, sybarite, gastronome.

ep·i·logue (ep'ə·lôg *or* ep'ə·log) *n.*
A short section appended to a novel or poem, or a short speech appended to a play, to give amplification or commentary.

e·pis·tle (i·pis'əl) *n.*
1 A letter, especially when long or formal: *the ambassador delivered his king's epistle.*
2 (Usually capital *E*). One of the letters written by an apostle of Christ, or a selection from one of the apostles' letters read as part of a religious service: *St. Paul's Epistle to the Romans.*
Syn. 1 missive.

ep·i·thet (ep'ə·thet) *n.*
1 A descriptive word or phrase used with or in place of the usual name of a person or thing: *In the phrase "rosy-fingered dawn," the term "rosy-fingered" is an epithet. The term "Little Father" used to be an epithet for the Russian czar.* 2 Loosely, any disparaging name, especially for a person.

e·pit·o·me (i·pit'ə·mē) *n.*
1 A person or thing that is a perfect example of something: *The works of Plato are an epitome of logical reasoning.* 2 A condensed account of a theory, speech, etc.: *an epitome of the debate.*
Syn. 2 synopsis, summary, précis, abstract.

e·qua·nim·i·ty (ē'kwə·nim'ə·tē *or* ek'wə·nim'ə·tē) *n.*
Evenness of mind or temper; composure: *He accepted the bad news with equanimity.*
Syn. calmness, equability.

Ant. excitability, nervousness, agitation, passion.

e·ques·tri·an (i·kwes'trē·ən) *adj., n.*
adj. 1 Pertaining to the riding of horses: *The rodeo included a display of equestrian skill.* 2 Representing a person on horseback: *an equestrian statue.*
n. A rider on horseback, especially a performer on horseback: *The circus featured an equestrian who rode standing up.*

e·qui·lib·ri·um (ē'kwə·lib'rē·əm) *n.*
1 Any state of balance or adjustment between opposing forces: *the uneasy equilibrium between the two major nations.* 2 A state of balance in the mind or feelings: *He was no longer driven by conflicting passions, but achieved a sort of equilibrium.*
Syn. 2 stability, equanimity, calm.
Ant. 2 agitation, perturbation.

e·quine (ē'kwīn) *adj., n.*
adj. Of, pertaining to, or like a horse: *an equine stable; a long, equine face.*
n. A horse: *The equine began to gallop.*

e·quip (i·kwip') *v.* **e·quipped, e·quip·ping**
1 To furnish, endow, or fit out with whatever is needed for any purpose or undertaking. 2 To dress or attire: *The king was equipped in regal robes.*
Spelling tip: Note the double *p* in *equipped* and *equipping* (but not in *equipment*). Words ending in a single consonant with the accent on the last syllable, double the final consonant before a suffix beginning with a *vowel*.
Syn. 1 outfit, rig. 2 array, garb, accouter.

eq·ui·ta·ble (ek'wə·tə·bəl) *adj.*
Fair: *an equitable decision.*
Syn. just, impartial, unbiased.
Ant. unfair, unjust, biased.

eq·ui·ty (ek'wə·tē) *n.* **eq·ui·ties** *pl.*
Fairness or impartiality, or something that is fair or just: *the equity of an even division of property between the two sons.*
Syn. justice, equitableness.
Ant. unfairness, injustice, discrimination.

e·quiv·a·lent (i·kwiv'ə·lənt) *adj., n.*
adj. Equal in value, amount, force, effect, meaning, etc.
n. Something equal in some way to something else: *a dollar bill or its equivalent in coins.*—**e·quiv'a·lence** *n*
Syn. *adj.* comparable, similar, alike, parallel.
Ant. *adj.* different, unrelated.

e·quiv·o·cal (i·kwiv'ə·kəl) *adj.*
Having more than one possible interpretation; ambiguous or indeterminate: *"Oh, a dress you sewed yourself" may be an equivocal compliment.*

e·quiv·o·cate (i·kwiv'ə·kāt) *v.* **e·quiv·o·cat·ed, e·quiv·o·cat·ing**
To use double meanings in order to mislead or deceive: *The bigamist equivocated by referring to "my first wife" and letting his bride assume he meant a former wife.*—**e·quiv'o·ca'tion** *n.*

e·rad·i·cate (i·rad′ə·kāt) *v.* **e·rad·i·cat·ed, e·rad·i·cat·ing**
To destroy utterly; to wipe out: *During the African civil war, a whole tribe was eradicated.*
Syn. root out, extirpate, annihilate.

e·rode (i·rōd′) *v.* **e·rod·ed, e·rod·ing**
1 To wear away or wear down gradually by constant friction: *rocks eroded by the sea.* **2** To eat into; to corrode: *The acid eroded the metal.* **3** To become worn down: *Over the years, the cliffs eroded.*
Syn. 1 abrade, grind down.

er·rant (er′rənt) *adj.*
1 Roving or wandering, especially in search of adventure: *a knight errant.* **2** Straying from the proper course of conduct: *an errant son who tried hard to reform.*
Syn. 1 roaming, traveling. **2** wayward, erring.

er·rat·ic (i·rat′ik) *adj.*
Having no fixed course, or deviating from the conventional, expected course; irregular, eccentric, or both: *He is so erratic that he may suddenly decide to eat his dinner at midnight.*
Syn. unpredictable, outlandish, odd.
Ant. regular, patterned, usual, conventional.

er·ro·ne·ous (ə·rō′nē·əs *or* e·rō′nē·əs) *adj.*
Wrong: *the erroneous belief that the world is flat.*
Syn. mistaken, incorrect.
Ant. right, correct, accurate.

er·satz (er·zäts′ *or* er′zäts) *adj.*
Substitute, and usually inferior: *Bitter ersatz coffee was all we had during World War II.*
Ant. real, genuine.

er·u·dite (er′yŏŏ·dīt) *adj.*
Very learned; scholarly: *an erudite professor.*
Syn. cultured.
Ant. illiterate, unlettered.

er·u·di·tion (er′yŏŏ·dish′ən) *n.*
Great learning acquired by reading and study: *His erudition enabled him to write scholarly articles on many different subjects.*

es·ca·pade (es′kə·pād) *n.*
A brief incident of reckless behavior or prankishly unconventional behavior: *After his escapade, he resumed his conventional life.*
Syn. spree, fling, adventure, lark.

es·cape (ə·skāp′) *v.* **es·caped, es·cap·ing;** *n.*
v. **1** To get away, get loose, or break free: *to escape from prison.* **2** To get or slip away from, as by forgetfulness, evasion, or inattention: *His name escapes me.* **3** To avoid: *The spy escaped detection.* **4** To leak out gradually: *Gas was escaping from the pipe.*
n. An act or means of escaping: *Drinking was an escape for him.*
Spelling tip: Watch the *sc.*

es·chew (es·chōŏ′) *v.*
To shun, as something unworthy or injurious: *The minister told him to eschew going to bars.*
Syn. avoid.
Ant. embrace, seek out.

es·o·ter·ic (es′ə·ter′ik) *adj.*
Understood by only a few specially instructed or initiated persons, or lying beyond ordinary comprehension: *an esoteric treatise on nuclear propulsion.*
Syn. abstruse, arcane, recondite.
Ant. exoteric, simple, comprehensible.

es·pi·o·nage (es′pē·ə·nij′ *or* es′pē·ə·näzh′) *n.*
Spying, especially the securing of one country's secret information by agents of another country: *Effective espionage requires skilled spies.*

es·pou·sal (es·pou′zəl) *n.*
1 Adoption or support, as of a cause: *their enthusiastic espousal of civil rights.* **2** An engagement: *the espousal of his sister to his friend.*—**es·pouse′** *v.*
Syn. 1 championing, advocacy, defense. **2** betrothal.

es·prit de corps (es·prē′ də kôr′)
Deep loyalty and enthusiastic devotion on the part of members to their group and to its goals: *an enviable esprit de corps that united the team against all challengers.*
Etymology: *Esprit de corps* is a French phrase and literally means corps spirit.
Syn. spirit, morale, solidarity.

es·say (es′ā *for n. def. 1;* es′ā *or* e·sā′ *for n. def. 2;* e·sā′ *for v.*) *n., v.*
n. **1** A short composition presenting the writer's ideas on a given topic: *the essays of Addison and Steele.* **2** An attempt: *a crawling child about to make his first essay at walking.*
v. To attempt or try: *He essayed a comic little dance step to reduce the tension in the waiting room.*
Usage: Do not confuse the verb *essay* with *assay,* which means to analyze or test: *to assay an ore or to determine its gold content.*
Syn. *n.* **1** theme, commentary. **2** trial, endeavor. *v.* undertake, venture.

es·tu·ar·y (es′chōŏ·er′ē) *n.,* **es·tu·ar·ies** *pl.*
1 A wide mouth of a river where its current meets the sea and is influenced by the tides. **2** An inlet or arm of the sea.
Syn. 2 bay, cove, fiord.

etc. *abbreviation*
And so forth (et cetera).
Usage: Because the Latin phrase *et cetera* means *and so forth,* saying *and etc.* is repetitious. When used to shorten a list, *etc.* should follow at least two concrete examples: *They award degrees in art, music, drama, etc.*

eth·i·cal (eth′i·kəl) *adj.*
Conforming to certain standards of morality or conduct: *It is not ethical for a public servant to take a bribe.*
Syn. moral.
Ant. unethical, immoral.

eth·nic (eth′nik) *adj.*
Of or belonging to a segment of mankind united by heredity, culture, language, or customs: *a political candidate with a broad appeal to Negroes, Italians, Puerto Ricans, Irish, and other ethnic groups.*

et·i·quette (et′ə·ket) *n.*
The rules established by convention to govern behavior in polite society or in official or professional life: *Emily Post's famous books on etiquette.*

Eu·char·ist (yōō'kə·rist) *n.*
1 A Christian sacrament in which bread and wine are consecrated and partaken of in remembrance of the suffering and death of Christ. 2 The consecrated bread and wine.
Etymology: *Eucharist* comes from a Latin word meaning thanksgiving.
Syn. 1 Communion, Holy Communion.

eu·lo·gize (yōō'lə·jīz) *v.* **eu·lo·gized, eu·lo·giz·ing**
To praise highly in a formal way, as in a public speech or written tribute: *The bishop eulogized the dead hero in an eloquent funeral oration.*
Syn. extol, laud, acclaim, celebrate.

eu·lo·gy (yōō'lə·jē) *n.,* **eu·lo·gies** *pl.*
A spoken or written piece of high praise, especially when formal and delivered publicly: *a eulogy of the former President, delivered in the Senate.*—**eu'lo·gis'tic** *adj.*
Syn. encomium, panegyric, laudation.

eu·nuch (yōō'nək) *n.*
A castrated man or youth, especially one employed as an attendant in a harem or as an Oriental palace chamberlain.

eu·phe·mism (yōō'fə·miz'əm) *n.*
A mild word or roundabout expression substituted for another that is felt to be blunt or distasteful: *"Pass away" is a euphemism for "die."*—**eu'phe·mis'tic** *adj.*

eu·pho·ni·ous (yōō·fō'nē·əs) *adj.*
Agreeable, pleasant, or sweet in sound: *the euphonious speech of a Southern belle.*—**eu·pho·ny** (yōō'fə·nē) *n.*
Etymology: *Euphonious* goes back to Greek roots: *eu-* (good) + *phōnē* (sound).
Syn. melodious, mellifluous, dulcet.
Ant. cacophonous, discordant, harsh.

eu·re·ka (yōō·rē'kə) *interj.*
I have found it!
Usage: *Eureka* is used as an exclamation of triumph upon suddenly discovering or figuring out something: *"Eureka!" shouted the inventor, "I've got it!"*

eu·tha·na·si·a (yōō'thə·nā'zhə) *n.*
The deliberate putting to death, in an easy, painless way, of a person suffering from an incurable and agonizing disease.
Syn. mercy killing.

ev·i·dent (ev'ə·dənt) *adj.*
Obvious or apparent: *Because he did not call, it is evident that he is not interested.*
Syn. clear, plain, unmistakable.

e·vince (i·vins') *v.* **e·vinced, e·vinc·ing**
To show openly or clearly: *Her flair for color and form first evinced itself in grade-school drawings.*
Syn. display, manifest, reveal.
Ant. conceal, hide, camouflage.

e·vis·cer·ate (i·vis'ə·rāt) *v.* **e·vis·cer·at·ed, e·vis·cer·at·ing**
1 To take out the bowels or entrails of: *to eviscerate a chicken.* 2 To remove the essential or vital part of: *The gun-control bill was so eviscerated by exceptions that it was practically worthless.*—**e·vis'cer·a'tion** *n.*

Syn. 1 disembowel, gut. 2 weaken, devitalize.
Ant. 2 strengthen, toughen.

e·voke (i·vōk') *v.* **e·voked, e·vok·ing**
To call up or summon forth: *The writer vividly evoked the memory of childhood summers.*
Syn. conjure up, invoke, arouse.

ev·o·lu·tion (ev'ə·lōō'shən) *n.*
1 The gradual process of change from an earlier or simpler form to a later, more advanced, or more complex form: *the evolution of a tadpole into a frog.* 2 The biological theory that all existent forms of life are descended from earlier forms through gradual changes or abrupt mutations: *Darwin's theory of evolution.*

ewe (yōō) *n.*
A female sheep.

ex·ag·ger·ate (ig·zaj'ə·rāt) *v.* **ex·ag·ger·at·ed, ex·ag·ger·at·ing**
1 To represent or look upon as greater than is really the case: *She tends to exaggerate her troubles.* 2 To overstate things: *Don't exaggerate.* 3 To enlarge or heighten to an unnatural size or intensity: *She exaggerates her eyes by using mascara and false eyelashes.*—**ex·ag'ger·a'tion** *n.*
Syn. 1 overstate, magnify. 3 enhance.

ex·alt (ig·zôlt') *v.*
1 To glorify or praise: *a psalm exalting the Lord.* 2 To raise in rank, honor, or esteem: *The Queen exalted him to a high office.* 3 To fill with joy or rapture: *They were exalted by their victory.*—**ex·al·ta·tion** (eg'zôl·tā'shən) *n.,* **ex·alt'ed** *adj.*
Spelling tip: There is no *z* in *exalt.* This word comes from Latin roots: *ex-* (out) + *altus* (high).
Syn. 2 promote, elevate, uplift. 3 elate, delight, enrapture.
Ant. 2 degrade, debase. 3 depress, dishearten.

ex·as·per·ate (ig·zas'pə·rāt) *v.* **ex·as·per·at·ed, ex·as·per·at·ing**
To annoy or irritate to the point of losing patience: *Her constant whining and complaining finally exasperated everyone.*—**ex·as'per·a'tion** *n.*
Syn. aggravate, infuriate, provoke, outrage.
Ant. please, soothe, mollify.

ex ca·the·dra (eks kə·thē'drə) *adv., adj.*
adv. With the authority of one's official position: *The Pope spoke ex cathedra.*
adj. Official and authoritative: *an ex cathedra proclamation.*
Etymology: *Ex cathedra* is a Latin phrase that literally means from the chair.
Syn. *adv.* authoritatively, officially.
Ant. *adv.* unofficially, off the record.

ex·ceed (ik·sēd') *v.*
1 To go beyond the limits of: *Don't exceed the speed limit.* 2 To be greater than: *Their margin of victory exceeded expectations.*—**ex·ceed'ing** *adj., adv.*
Syn. 1 overstep. 2 surpass, outstrip.
Ant. 1 stay within. 2 fall below.

ex·ceed·ing·ly (ik·sē'ding·lē) *adv.*
Extremely: *He is exceedingly angry.*

Syn. very, greatly, enormously.
Ant. slightly, moderately.

ex·cel·lent (ek'sə·lənt) *adj.*
Of the highest quality; extremely good: *excellent work.*—**ex'cel·lence** *n.*
Syn. superior, first-rate, fine.
Ant. poor, inferior, bad, worthless.

ex·cept (ik·sept') *prep., v., conj.*
prep. But: *Everyone agreed except Sue.*
v. To leave out: *The boss excepted John, a lazy worker, when giving raises.*
conj. Only: *She could have come, except she did not want to.*—**ex·cep'tion** *n.*
Spelling tip: Don't confuse the verb *except* with *accept*, which means to take.
Syn. *v.* exclude, omit. *conj.* but, however.
Ant. *v.* include.

ex·cep·tion·al (ik·sep'shən·əl) *adj.*
Out of the ordinary: *The Medal of Honor winner showed exceptional courage.*—**ex·cep'tion·al·ly** *adv.*
Syn. remarkable, extraordinary, rare.
Ant. ordinary, normal, common.

ex·cerpt (ek'sûrpt *n.,* ik·sûrpt' *v.*) *n., v.*
n. A passage selected from a book, article, speech, etc. and quoted separately: *The newspaper published excerpts from his speech.*
v. To select and quote a passage from a piece of writing: *a collection of memorable quotations excerpted from Shakespeare's plays.*
Syn. *n.* extract, citation, quotation. *v.* cite, cull, extract.

ex·cess (ik·ses' or ek'ses) *n., adj.*
n. 1 An amount above what is used, necessary, or desirable: *explorers weighted down with an excess of equipment.* 2 Going beyond what is necessary: *Avoid excess in all things.*
adj. Over the necessary, desirable, or allotted amount: *Airlines charge for excess luggage.*
Spelling tip: Don't confuse this word with *access*, which means right or chance of entry.
Syn. *n.* 1 surplus, plethora. 2 overindulgence. *adj.* surplus.
Ant. *n.* 1 shortage, deficiency. 2 temperance, restraint. *adj.* insufficient.

ex·cru·ci·at·ing (iks·krōō'shē·ā'ting) *adj.*
Causing or inflicting intense pain: *an excruciating toothache.*
Syn. agonizing, tormenting.
Ant. painless.

ex·em·pla·ry (ig·zem'plər·ē) *adj.*
1 Serving as an example worthy of imitation: *exemplary conduct.* 2 Serving as a warning: *exemplary punishment.*
Syn. 1 commendable, model, laudable. 2 admonitory.
Ant. 1 blameworthy, objectionable.

ex·em·pli·fy (ig·zem'plə·fī) *v.* **ex·em·pli·fied, ex·em·pli·fy·ing**
To show by example; illustrate: *Lindbergh exemplified the young hero of the 1920s.*—**ex·em'pli·fi·ca'tion** *n.*
Syn. represent, embody.

ex·er·cise (ek'sər·sīz) *v.* **ex·er·cised, ex·er·cis·ing;** *n.*
v. 1 To subject to mental or physical drills,

so as to train or develop: *Swimming exercises the entire body.* 2 To make use of: *to exercise the right to vote.* 3 To perform exercises: *He exercises by jogging before breakfast.*
n. 1 Activity of the body performed for training or physical conditioning: *strenuous exercises.* 2 A putting into use, action, or practice: *an exercise of patience.* 3 A lesson, problem, etc. to train some particular skill: *to play exercises on the violin.* 4 Usually *pl.* A ceremony, program of speeches, etc., as at a graduation: *commencement exercises.*—**ex'er·cis'er** *n.*
Spelling tip: Distinguish between *exercise* and *exorcise*, which means to cast out an evil spirit by prayers or magic words.

ex·hale (eks·hāl') *v.* **ex·haled, ex·hal·ing**
1 To breathe out: *Inhale and exhale.* 2 To give off or emanate, as a vapor or odor: *The barn exhaled the odors of hay and milk.*—**ex·hal·a·tion** (eks'hə·lā'shən) *n.*
Syn. 2 emit, exude.

ex·haust (ig·zôst') *v., n.*
v. 1 To make extremely tired: *The long journey exhausted her.* 2 To use up completely: *We have exhausted our food supply.* 3 To empty a container of its contents; drain: *to exhaust a well of its water.* 4 To study or develop thoroughly or completely: *After twelve hours of conversation we have exhausted this subject.*
n. 1 The escape of waste gases, as from an engine; also, the gases or fumes that escape. 2 A pipe or other engine part through which waste gases and fumes escape.
Syn. *v.* 1 weary, fatigue, wear out.
Ant. *v.* 1 refresh, invigorate, enliven.

ex·haus·tion (ig·zôs'chən) *n.*
1 Extreme fatigue: *The soldiers suffered from hunger and exhaustion.* 2 The condition of being completely used up: *exhaustion of a water supply.* 3 The condition of being deprived of valuable or useful elements: *Crop rotation prevents soil exhaustion.*
Syn. 1 weariness, tiredness, faintness.
Ant. 1 vigor, verve, liveliness.

ex·hil·a·rate (ig·zil'ə·rāt) *v.* **ex·hil·a·rat·ed, ex·hil·a·rat·ing**
To make buoyantly cheerful or invigorated; pep up: *The young couple were exhilarated over the birth of a son.*—**ex·hil'a·ra'tion** *n.*
Syn. gladden, delight, elate.
Ant. grieve, disappoint, depress.

ex·hume (ig·zyōōm' or iks·hyōōm') *v.* **ex·humed, ex·hum·ing**
1 To dig up a corpse or other buried thing: *The coroner's office was ordered to exhume the body of the supposed suicide.* 2 To bring something hidden or uncertain to light: *Reporters exhumed some damaging facts about the candidate's past.*—**ex'hu·ma'tion** *n.*
Etymology: *Exhume* comes from two Latin words: *ex* (out) + *humus* (earth).
Syn. 1 disinter. 2 reveal, expose.
Ant. 1 bury. 2 hide, conceal.

ex·ile (eg'zīl or ek'sīl) *v.* **ex·iled, ex·il·ing;** *n.*
v. To banish a person from his native land

or home and forbid him to return: *He was exiled for plotting against the government.*
n. 1 Separation from one's native country, especially as a punishment: *Napoleon's exile to St. Helena.* 2 A person who has been exiled: *Paris used to be full of White Russian exiles.*
Syn. *v.* expatriate. *n.* 1 banishment, expatriation. 2 expatriate.

ex·o·dus (ek′sə·dəs) *n.*, **ex·o·dus·es** *pl.*
1 A going forth, as of many people, from a place or country: *the summer exodus from the city to the mountains and the beaches.* 2 (Capital *E*) The second book of the Old Testament, in which the departure of Moses and the Israelites from Egypt is described.

ex of·fi·ci·o (eks ə·fish′ē·ō)
A Latin phrase meaning by virtue of or because of one's office or position: *The President is ex officio commander in chief of the armed services.*

ex·on·er·ate (ig·zon′ə·rāt) *v.* **ex·on·er·at·ed, ex·on·er·at·ing**
To free from blame or accusation: *The accused was exonerated from any connection with the crime.*—**ex·on′er·a′tion** *n.*, **ex·on′er·a′tive** *adj.*
Syn. absolve, acquit, vindicate.

ex·or·bi·tant (ig·zôr′bə·tənt) *adj.*
Going beyond usual or proper limits; excessive: *exorbitant taxes; exorbitant demands upon one's time and energy.*—**ex·or′bi·tance** *n.*, **ex·or′bi·tant·ly** *adv.*
Syn. immoderate, high, great.
Ant. scant, little, modest.

ex·or·cise (ek′sôr·sīz) *v.* **ex·or·cised, ex·or·cis·ing**
1 To cast out an evil spirit by prayers or incantations: *to exorcise the devil.* 2 To free a person or place from an evil spirit.

ex·ot·ic (ig·zot′ik) *adj.*, *n.*
adj. 1 Belonging by nature or origin to another part of the world; not native: *an exotic plant.* 2 Strangely different and fascinating: *an exotic custom; an exotic woman.*
n. Something that is exotic.—**ex·ot′i·cal·ly** *adv.*
Ant. *adj.* 1 native, indigenous. 2 commonplace, ordinary, plain.

ex·pa·tri·ate (eks·pā′trē·āt *v.*, eks·pā′tre·it *n.*) *v.* **ex·pa·tri·at·ed, ex·pa·tri·at·ing;** *n.*
v. 1 To drive a person from his native land: *to expatriate political suspects.* 2 To withdraw oneself from one's native land to live elsewhere: *Many artists expatriate themselves to Paris.*
n. An expatriated person: *For years Hemingway was an expatriate.*—**ex·pa′tri·a′tion** *n.*
Syn. *v.* 1 exile, deport, banish. *n.* exile.

ex·pe·di·ent (ik·spē′dē·ənt) *adj.*, *n.*
adj. 1 Serving to promote a desired end: *Examination by a doctor is expedient for those involved in an automobile accident.* 2 Prompted by self-interest rather than by what is proper; easy or selfish rather than right: *It was expedient to conceal his past from his wife.*
n. 1 Something expedient; a means to an end: *the expedient of cutting costs by giving inferior service.* 2 A means employed in an emergency: *the expedient of living on plants and berries when lost in the wilderness.*—**ex·pe′di·ent·ly** *adv.*
Syn. *adj.* 1 fitting, proper, desirable.
Ant. *adj.* 1 detrimental, incorrect.

ex·pe·dite (ek′spə·dīt) *v.* **ex·pe·dit·ed, ex·pe·dit·ing**
To speed up the process or progress of; facilitate: *to expedite an application for a government job.*
Syn. quicken, hurry, further, advance.
Ant. delay, hold up, procrastinate.

ex·pe·di·tious (ek′spə·dish′əs) *adj.*
Marked by or done with energy and efficiency: *The hotel had courteous and expeditious service.*—**ex′pe·di′tious·ly** *adv.*
Syn. rapid, fast, prompt, quick, punctual.
Ant. slow, inefficient, lagging.

ex·pe·ri·ence (ik·spir′ē·əns) *n.*; *v.* **ex·pe·ri·enced, ex·pe·ri·enc·ing**
n. 1 Actual participation in or direct contact with something: *experience in business.* 2 An activity or occurrence in which one has participated: *Flying for the first time is quite an experience; an interesting experience.* 3 Knowledge or skill derived from doing something: *This job requires several years of experience.*
v. To have an experience of: *to experience war.*
Syn. *n.* 1 involvement, practice. 2 event, episode, adventure, happening. *v.* undergo, meet with.

ex·pe·ri·enced (ik·spir′ē·ənst) *adj.*
Having had first-hand involvement or possessing abilities developed by use or practice: *an experienced soldier; an experienced pianist.*

ex·per·i·ment (ik·sper′ə·mənt *n.*, ik·sper′ə·ment *v.*) *n.*, *v.*
n. A test or trial carried out under certain conditions in order to find out something or to put a theory into practice: *an experiment in chemistry.*
v. To make experiments: *to experiment with guinea pigs to find a new vaccine.*

ex·pi·ate (ek′spē·āt) *v.* **ex·pi·at·ed, ex·pi·at·ing**
To make amends for, as an offense, failure, sin, etc.—**ex′pi·a′tion** *n.*
Syn. atone for, do penance for, absolve.

ex·pi·ra·tion (ek′spə·rā′shən) *n.*
1 Completion or running out of something: *the expiration of a lease.* 2 The act of breathing out air from the lungs.
Syn. 1 termination, conclusion, end, finish. 2 exhalation.
Ant. 1 beginning, start, commencement, initiation. 2 inspiration, breathing in.

ex·plan·a·to·ry (ek·splan′ə·tôr′ē) *adj.*
Clarifying, interpretive, or justifying: *explanatory footnotes for difficult terms.*
Spelling tip: Put an *a* on either side of the *n*.

ex·ploit (eks′ploit *n.*, ik·sploit′ *v.*) *n.*, *v.*
n. A deed or act, especially one that is heroic or daring: *the exploits of Daniel Boone.*
v. 1 To use unfairly or meanly for one's own advantage: *shopkeepers in the slums who exploit the poor.* 2 To put to practical use: *to exploit waterpower.*
Syn. *n.* feat, adventure. *v.* 2 utilize.

ex·ploi·ta·tion (eks'ploi·tā'shən) *n.*
1 The act of using or utilizing something: *the exploitation of natural resources.* **2** The using of someone or something for purely selfish ends: *the exploitation of tenant farmers by landlords.*
Syn. 1 utilization.

ex·po·nent (ik·spō'nənt; *also* ek'spō·nənt *for def. 3*) *n.*
1 A person or thing that explains or expounds: *an exponent of modern music.* **2** A person or thing that represents or symbolizes something: *Byron was the exponent of romantic poetry.* **3** In mathematics, a symbol written above and to the right of another symbol to indicate to what power the latter is to be taken: *2 is the exponent in A^2.*
Syn. 1 explainer, interpreter, expounder. **2** symbol, exemplifier.

ex·po·si·tion (eks'pə·zish'ən) *n.*
1 A public display or show; especially, a large exhibition of arts, products, etc.: *the Panama-Pacific International Exposition.* **2** A detailed presentation of a process, idea, work, etc.: *an exposition of the principles of the steam engine.*
Syn. 1 exhibit, fair. **2** explanation, elucidation.

ex·punge (ik·spunj') *v.* **ex·punged, ex·pung·ing**
To strike out something written; delete; erase: *to expunge a word from a sentence.* —**ex·pung'er** *n.*

ex·pur·gate (eks'pər·gāt) *v.* **ex·pur·gat·ed, ex·pur·gat·ing**
1 To take out obscene or otherwise objectionable material from: *Censors expurgated the novel.* **2** To remove or omit objectionable words, lines, etc.: *to reprint a book after expurgating several chapters.*—**ex'pur·ga'tion, ex'pur·ga'tor** *n.*

ex·qui·site (eks'kwi·zit *or* ik·skwiz'it) *adj.*
1 Showing great care and delicacy of craftsmanship: *an exquisite lace tablecloth.* **2** Very beautiful: *exquisite gardens.* **3** Extremely refined; fastidious: *exquisite taste.* **4** Intensely keen or acute: *exquisite pleasure.*—**ex'qui·site·ly** *adv.,* **ex'qui·site·ness** *n.*
Syn. 2 lovely, magnificent. **4** sharp.
Ant. 4 dull, slight.

ex·tant (ek'stənt *or* ik·stant') *adj.*
Still existing; not lost or destroyed: *the extant first folios of Shakespeare's plays.*
Syn. surviving, existent.

ex·tem·po·ra·ne·ous (ik·stem'pə·rā'nē·əs) *adj.*
Spoken, performed, or composed with little or no advance preparation: *an extemporaneous speech.*—**ex·tem'po·ra'ne·ous·ly** *adv.,* **ex·tem'po·ra'ne·ous·ness** *n.*
Syn. impromptu, improvised, offhand.
Ant. prepared, planned.

ex·ten·sion (ik·sten'shən) *n.*
1 The act of opening or stretching to full length: *the arm extension necessary to swim the Australian crawl.* **2** That which extends something. **3** An agreement by which a creditor allows a debtor further time in which to pay a debt: *an extension of thirty days.*

ex·ten·u·a·ting (ik·sten'yōō·ā'ting) *adj.*
Serving to excuse or lessen guilt, especially in a crime: *the extenuating circumstances that surrounded the murder.*

ex·tol (ik·stōl' *or* ik·stol') *v.* **ex·tolled, ex·tol·ling**
To praise in the highest terms: *to extol the virtues of your children.*—**ex·tol'ler, ex·tol'ment** *or* **ex·toll'ment** *n.*
Spelling tip: This word is also spelled *extoll.*
Syn. exalt, glorify.
Ant. disparage, condemn, discredit.

ex·tra·dite (eks'trə·dīt) *v.* **ex·tra·dit·ed, ex·tra·dit·ing**
1 To deliver a suspect, prisoner, or fugitive to the authority of some other state, country, etc.: *Britain will extradite the suspected assassin to the U.S.* **2** To effect the return of a suspect, fugitive, etc., from another state or country: *New Jersey extradited the murderer from Massachusetts.*—**ex·tra·di·tion** (eks'trə·dish'ən) *n.*

ex·traor·di·nar·y (ik·strôr'də·ner'ē *or* eks'trə·ôr'də·ner'ē) *adj.*
1 Far exceeding the ordinary or usual: *an extraordinary talent.* **2** Employed for a special purpose or on an exceptional occasion: *an envoy extraordinary.*—**ex·traor'di·nar'i·ly** *adv.*
Spelling tip: *Extra* + *ordinary,* as in the second pronunciation. Note, however, that the first pronunciation is more common. The second is used most often with the second meaning of the word.
Syn. 1 remarkable, unusual, surprising, exceptional. **2** special.
Ant. 1 commonplace, usual, ordinary, customary.

ex·trav·a·gan·za (ik·strav'ə·gan'zə) *n.*
An elaborate musical or dramatic composition, especially a lavish, spectacular theatrical production.

ex·treme·ly (ik·strēm'lē) *adv.*
Much more than usually: *an extremely cautious driver.*
Syn. exceedingly, excessively.

ex·tri·cate (eks'trə·kāt) *v.* **ex·tri·cat·ed, ex·tri·cat·ing**
To free from something that entangles, hinders, or causes difficulties: *The lion extricated itself from the net.*
Syn. disentangle, liberate, loose.
Ant. entangle, enmesh, entrap.

ex·tro·vert (eks'trə·vûrt) *n.*
A person whose interest is toward objects and actions outside himself rather than toward his own thoughts or feelings.
Spelling tip: This word is also spelled *extravert.*
Ant. introvert.

ex·u·ber·ant (ig·zōō'bər·ənt) *adj.*
1 Full of vitality, high spirits, joy, etc.: *exuberant youth.* **2** Characterized by abundance or overabundance: *the beauty of the exuberant foliage.*—**ex·u'ber·ant·ly** *adv.*
Syn. 1 joyful, enthusiastic. **2** lavish, ample, luxuriant.

ex·ude (ig·z(y)o͞od' *or* ik·s(y)o͞od') *v.* **ex·ud·ed, ex·ud·ing**
To discharge something through or as if through pores, gashes, etc.: *sweat exuding from his face; a young man who exuded confidence.*
Syn. excrete, emit, give off, radiate.

F

fab·ri·cate (fab'rə·kāt) *v.* **fab·ri·cat·ed, fab·ri·cat·ing**
1 To make or manufacture, as by combining parts: *to fabricate a bridge.* 2 To make up or invent, as a lie or story: *He fabricated a story about heavy traffic to cover up for oversleeping.* —**fab'ri·ca'tion** *n.*
Syn. 1 assemble, build, construct. 2 trump up, concoct, devise.

fab·u·lous (fab'yə·ləs) *adj.*
1 Passing the limits of belief: *a fabulous story that made us gasp in astonishment.* 2 Of, like, or recorded in fables: *the griffin, the unicorn, and other fabulous beasts.*—**fab'u·lous·ly** *adv.*
Syn. 1 incredible, astounding, amazing. 2 mythical, imaginary, legendary.

fac·et (fas'it) *n.*
1 One of the small plane surfaces cut upon a gem: *Each facet of the emerald sparkled in the sunlight.* 2 One of a number of aspects of a subject or person: *the many facets of his personality.*
Syn. 2 side, phase.

fa·ce·tious (fə·sē'shəs) *adj.*
Given to or marked by humor, especially humor that is flippant or ill-timed: *a facetious young hippie.*—**fa·ce'tious·ly** *adv.*, **fa·ce'tious·ness** *n.*
Syn. flippant, frivolous, tongue-in-cheek.

fac·ile (fas'(ə)l) *adj.*
1 Requiring little effort; easily achieved or performed: *a facile victory.* 2 Showing so little expenditure of effort as to be superficial: *a facile solution to a difficult problem.* 3 Ready or quick in performance: *a facile speaker.*—**fac'ile·ly** *adv.*, **fac'ile·ness** *n.*

fa·cil·i·tate (fə·sil'ə·tāt) *v.* **fa·cil·i·tat·ed, fa·cil·i·tat·ing**
To make easier or more convenient: *to facilitate the operation of a large corporation by the use of computers.*—**fa·cil'i·ta'tion** *n.*
Syn. expedite, assist, smooth.
Ant. hinder, complicate, handicap.

fa·cil·i·ty (fə·sil'ə·tē) *n.*, **fa·cil·i·ties** *pl.*
1 Ease or skill in performance or action: *facility of movement.* 2 *Usually pl.* A building, room, area, equipment, etc., that makes an action or operation easier or serves a special purpose: *a university with excellent facilities for scientific research.*
Syn. 1 quickness, readiness, dexterity, adroitness.

fac·sim·i·le (fak·sim'ə·lē) *n.*
An exact copy or reproduction: *a carbon copy is a facsimile.*

fac·tion (fak'shən) *n.*
1 A group of people operating within, and often in opposition to, a larger group, to gain its own ends. 2 Strife or disagreement within a group: *Faction within the political party caused a loss of strength at the polls.*—**fac'tion·al** *adj.*
Syn. 1 clique, splinter party, bloc, wing. 2 dissension, contention, discord, feud.

fac·to·tum (fak·tō'təm) *n.*
A person who has tasks or responsibilities of all kinds.
Syn. handyman, jack-of-all-trades.

fait ac·com·pli (fe·tà·kôṅ·plē')
A French phrase meaning a thing done beyond recall or opposition; literally, an accomplished fact: *Why ask the committee members to give their approval to a fait accompli?*

fa·kir (fə·kir' *or* fā'kər) *n.*
A Moslem or Hindu religious devotee, especially a Moslem holy man who is a beggar.

fal·la·cious (fə·lā'shəs) *adj.*
1 Deceptive or misleading: *fallacious documents.* 2 Containing or involving reasoning contrary to logic: *a fallacious conclusion.*—**fal·la'cious·ly** *adv.*, **fal·la'cious·ness** *n.*
Syn. 1 erroneous, false. 2 unfounded, illogical, inconsistent.
Ant. 1 correct, truthful, factual. 2 logical, consistent, sound.

fal·la·cy (fal'ə·sē) *n.*, **fal·la·cies** *pl.*
1 An erroneous or misleading notion: *the fallacy that money brings happiness.* 2 Any reasoning, argument, etc., contrary to the rules of logic.

fal·li·ble (fal'ə·bəl) *adj.*
Liable to err, to be misled, or to be wrong: *Humans are fallible.*—**fal'li·bil'i·ty** *n.*, **fal'li·bly** *adv.*

fal·low (fal'ō) *adj.*, *n.*
adj. Left unseeded after being plowed: *a fallow field.*
n. Land left unseeded after plowing so as to make it more fertile.

fa·mil·iar (fə·mil'yər) *adj.*, *n.*
adj. 1 Having a thorough knowledge, as through study or experience: *familiar with electronic music.* 2 Well-known because often seen, heard, etc.: *Snow is a familiar sight in Alaska.* 3 Friendly, sometimes overly or improperly so: *to be on familiar terms.*
n. 1 A friend or close associate. 2 A spirit supposed to attend and serve a witch, usually in animal form.—**fa·mil'iar·ly** *adv.*
Syn. *adj.* 1 informed, aware, conversant. 2 frequent, accustomed. 3 intimate, close, impudent. *n.* 1 pal, confidant.
Ant. *adj.* 1 unfamiliar, uninformed, unaware. 2 infrequent, unaccustomed.

fa·mil·i·ar·i·ty (fə·mil'ē·ar'ətē *or* fə·mil'yar'ə·tē) *n.*, **fa·mil·i·ar·i·ties** *pl.*
1 Thorough acquaintance: *his familiarity with French slang.* 2 Informality, friendliness, or impertinent intimacy: *She found his familiarities to be offensive.*
Spelling tip: Put an *i* on either side of the single *l.*

fa·nat·ic (fə·nat′ik) *n.*
A person moved by exaggerated enthusiasm or zeal to beliefs that go beyond the bounds of reason: *a speech that appealed to the prejudice of religious fanatics.*
Syn. zealot, extremist.

fa·nat·i·cism (fə·nat′ə·siz′əm) *n.*
The spirit or conduct of a fanatic; beliefs or actions that are not in accord with reason.

fan·ci·ful (fan′si·fəl) *adj.*
1 Produced by or existing only in the imagination: *fanciful schemes.* **2** Pleasantly odd in appearance: *a fanciful costume.* **3** Indulging in imaginative ideas: *a fanciful mind.*— **fan′ci·ful·ly** *adv.,* **fan′ci·ful·ness** *n.*
Syn. 1 unreal, unsubstantial, imaginative, visionary. **2** quaint, strange, queer. **3** inventive, whimsical, creative, romantic.

fan·fare (fan′fâr′) *n.*
1 A short, lively musical call or passage, as of trumpets. **2** Any display that is noisy or showy: *Because of security difficulties, the President slipped into the city with a minimum of fanfare.*
Syn. 2 flourish, demonstration.

fan·tas·tic (fan·tas′tik) *adj.*
1 Odd, grotesque, or whimsical in appearance, form, construction, etc.: *a fantastic room.* **2** Fanciful, capricious, or impulsive, as ideas, moods, actions, etc.
Syn. 1 strange, unreal, bizarre. **2** romantic, eccentric, erratic.

fan·ta·sy (fan′tə·sē) *n.,* **fan·ta·sies** *pl.*
1 Unrestrained imagination; wild fancy: *She lived a life of fantasy.* **2** A mental image or a sequence of mental images, usually pleasant in nature, often serving to fulfill a need not gratified in the real world: *In his fantasies he always saw himself as a captain of industry.*
Spelling tip: This word is also spelled *phantasy.*

far·ther (fär′thər) comparative of **far** *adv., adj.*
adv. To or at a more advanced point in space, or, less often, time: *I shall walk no farther.* *adj.* **1** More distant or remote: *the farther shore.* **2** Additional; more.
Usage: When referring to distance in space, *farther* is preferred: *We have to drive ten miles farther.* When referring to time, degree, or quantity, *further* is preferred: *further in the future; getting further information.*

fas·cism (fash′iz·əm) *n.*
1 A one-party system of government (or the principles behind it) that is autocratic or dictatorial in nature, and under which the government strictly controls industry and labor and subordinates individualism by military and police force and rigid censorship. **2** Any kind of control that is autocratic or dictatorial in nature.

fas·cist (fash′ist) *n., adj.*
n. **1** An advocate of the principles of fascism. **2** A member of a party that advocates or practices fascism. **3** A person who is extremely autocratic or dictatorial in nature.

adj. Of, advocating, or practicing fascism: *a fascist state.*

fas·tid·i·ous (fas·tid′ē·əs) *adj.*
Hard to please in matters of taste: *a fastidious diner.*— **fas·tid′i·ous·ly** *adv.,* **fas·tid′i·ous·ness** *n.*
Syn. refined, particular.
Ant. uncritical, easygoing.

fa·tal·ism (fāt′(ə)l·iz′əm) *n.*
1 The philosophical doctrine that all things and events are predetermined and therefore not alterable. **2** A disposition to accept every event or condition as being inevitable.

fa·ther-in-law (fä′thər·in·lô′) *n.,* **fa·thers-in-law** *pl.*
The father of one's spouse.

fat·u·ous (fach′oo·əs) *adj.*
Foolish or idiotic in a self-satisfied way: *the fatuous grins of the audience in a burlesque house.*—**fat′u·ous·ly** *adv.,* **fat′u·ous·ness** *n.*
Syn. silly, inane, vacant, stupid.

fau·na (fô′nə) *n.*
The animals living within a given area or environment, or during a stated period.

faux pas (fō pä′), **faux pas** (fō päz′) *pl.*
A French phrase that literally means a false step; a mistake or error, especially a breach of etiquette: *He committed a faux pas at the dinner party by drinking from his finger bowl.*

faze (fāz) *v.* **fazed, faz·ing**
To bother, upset, or embarrass: *Their catcalls did not faze him.*
Etymology: *Faze* comes from the Old English word *fēsian,* to frighten.
Syn. worry, disturb, disconcert, intimidate.
Ant. encourage, embolden, reassure, calm.

fea·si·ble (fē′zə·bəl) *adj.*
1 Capable of being accomplished or put into effect: *His utopian plans are not feasible, given the present conditions.* **2** Fairly probable: *a feasible explanation.*
Syn. 1 practicable, possible, achievable, attainable. **2** likely, reasonable.
Ant. 1 impracticable, unattainable. **2** unlikely, improbable.

fe·brile (fē′brəl or feb′rəl) *adj.*
Feverish: *febrile delirium; the febrile, frantic pace of modern life.*
Syn. delirious, frenzied, hysterical.
Ant. calm, cool.

Feb·ru·ar·y (feb′roo·er·ē or feb′yoo·er·ē) *n.*
The second month of the year.
Spelling tip: The second month has two *r*'s.

fe·cund (fē′kənd or fek′ənd) *adj.*
Fruitful or fertile: *the fecund mother of twelve; the fecund brain of Benjamin Franklin.*— **fe·cun·di·ty** (fi·kun′də·tē) *n.*
Syn. prolific, productive, creative.
Ant. sterile, barren, unproductive.

feign (fān) *v.*
To pretend: *The child feigned sleep to fool her mother.*
Spelling tip: Remember *i* before *e* except after *c,* or when sounded as *a* as in *neighbor* and *weigh.* The *ei* in *feign* is sounded as *a.*
Syn. sham, simulate, dissemble, counterfeit.

feigned (fānd) *adj.*
Imaginary, pretended, or meant to deceive: *Hamlet's feigned madness.*
Spelling tip: See FEIGN, and don't give up the silent *g.*
Syn. sham, false, counterfeit, make-believe.
Ant. genuine, real, true, authentic.

feint (fānt) *n., v.*
n. **1** An apparent or pretended blow or attack meant to divert attention from an attack to be made elsewhere: *a skillful feint in fencing.* **2** A deceptive appearance or movement: *to make a feint of withdrawing in order to regroup the forces.*
v. To make a feint: *The boxer was fast on his feet and good at parrying and feinting.*
Spelling tip: The *ei* in *feint* is sounded as *a,* as in *neighbor* and *weigh.* See FEIGN.
Syn. *n.* **1** diversion. **2** pretense, show, ruse, trick, stratagem.

fe·lic·i·tous (fə·lis′ə·təs) *adj.*
Especially well chosen: *a felicitous phrase quoted by many reviewers.*—**fe·lic′i·ty** *n.*
Syn. apt, appropriate, pertinent, effective.
Ant. unfortunate, inept, awkward.

fel·on (fel′ən) *n.*
A person who has committed a serious crime such as murder, rape, arson, or burglary, for which the punishment is more severe than for a misdemeanor.—**fe·lo·ni·ous** (fə·lō′nē·əs) *adj.,* **fel′o·ny** *n.*

fem·i·nine (fem′ə·nin) *adj.*
Having to do with the female sex or with what is like, typical of, or appropriate to women: *feminine intuition.*—**fem′i·nin′i·ty** *n.*

fe·mur (fē′mər) *n.*
The long leg bone extending from the pelvis to the knee.—**fem′o·ral** *adj.*
Syn. thighbone.

fer·ment (fûr′mənt *n.,* fər·ment′ *v.*) *n., v.*
n. **1** Fermentation, the gradual decomposition of organic compounds induced by the action of enzymes, yeast, bacteria, etc. **2** Any substance or agent producing such decomposition: *The enzyme zymase is a ferment.* **3** Excitement or agitation: *a mind in creative ferment.*
v. **1** To undergo fermentation or produce fermentation in: *apple cider that ferments and turns into vinegar.* **2** To make or become mentally or emotionally agitated.—**fer′men·ta′tion** *n.*
Usage: The verb *ferment* indicates activity within. The verb *foment* points to an outward stirring up of discontent or discord: *anarchists working to foment a rebellion.*
Syn. *n.* **3** commotion, turmoil, restlessness. *v.* **1** work. **2** seethe.

fer·ret (fer′it) *n., v.*
n. A small, weasellike polecat, often tamed and used in hunting rats and rabbits.
v. To search out and uncover by careful investigation: *Despite the lack of clues, the detective managed to ferret out the facts.*
Usage: Treat *ferret out* as a verb phrase.

fer·tile (fûr′təl) *adj.*
1 Capable of bearing crops, vegetation, fruit, or young: *fertile soil; a fertile woman.* **2** Capable of growth, development, or invention: *a fertile imagination.*—**fer·til·i·ty** (fər·til′ə·tē) *n.,* **fer′til·ize** *v.*

fer·vent (fûr′vənt) *adj.*
Very earnest and intense: *a fervent prayer; a candidate's fervent supporters.*—**fer′ven·cy** *n.*
Etymology: *Fervent, fervid,* and *fervor* come from the Latin word *fervere,* to boil, and imply the heat of strong feelings that are deeply stirred.
Syn. ardent, fervid, impassioned, passionate.

fer·vid (fûr′vid) *adj.*
Highly impassioned: *a fervid plea for help.*—**fer′vid·ly** *n.*
Etymology: See FERVENT.
Usage: *Fervid* is an intensification of *fervent.*
Syn. vehement, fiery, passionate, zealous.

fer·vor (fûr′vər) *n.*
Great earnestness, enthusiasm, or intensity of feeling or expression: *an evangelist's fervor at a revival meeting.*
Etymology: See FERVENT.
Syn. zeal, ardor, passion, fervency.
Ant. coolness, indifference, impassiveness.

fes·ter (fes′tər) *v.*
1 To develop pus: *An untreated sore or wound may fester.* **2** To be a constant source of smoldering rage, vexation, or irritation: *Envy of his brother festered within him.*

fet·id (fet′id) *adj.*
Having a foul odor, as of rot or decay: *the fetid stagnant water.*
Syn. stinking, rank, putrid, malodorous.
Ant. fragrant, sweet, aromatic.

fet·ish (fet′ish *or* fē′tish) *n.*
1 A natural object worshiped in some primitive religions as the dwelling place of a supernatural spirit and the possessor of magic powers: *Stones, teeth, and carved bits of wood are sometimes used as fetishes.* **2** Anything to which a person is excessively or irrationally devoted: *She made a fetish of cleanliness.*
Syn. **1** talisman, amulet, charm.

fet·ter (fet′ər) *n., v.*
n. **1** A chain or other bond put about the ankles to restrain movement: *a prisoner in fetters.* **2** *Usually plural* Anything checking freedom of movement or expression: *the fetters of slavery.*
v. To restrain with or as if with fetters: *a dictatorship that fettered the press.*
Syn. *n.* **1** shackle. **2** restraint. *v.* shackle, chain, bind, confine, hobble.
Ant. *v.* free, liberate, unchain.

fe·tus (fē′təs) *n.,* **fe·tus·es** *pl.*
In biology The unborn human being or animal carried in the uterus in the later stages of its development; especially, the unborn human child from the end of the second month until birth.—**fe′tal** *adj.*
Spelling tip: This word is also spelled *foetus.*

fi·an·cé (fē′än·sā′ *or* fē·än′sā) *n.*
A man to whom a woman is engaged to be married.
Syn. betrothed, intended.

fi·an·cée (fē'än·sā' *or* fē·än'sā) *n.*
A woman to whom a man is engaged to be married.
Syn. betrothed, intended.

fi·as·co (fē·as'kō) *n.,* **fi·as·coes** *or* **fi·as·cos** *pl.*
A complete or humiliating failure: *The new Broadway play was a fiasco.*
Syn. flop, bust, disaster.
Ant. success, winner, hit.

fic·ti·tious (fik·tish'əs) *adj.*
Made up, rather than real: *An alias is a fictitious name.*
Spelling tip: *Fictitious* has two *ti*'s.
Syn. invented, assumed, false, fake, phony.
Ant. real, genuine, actual, true.

fi·del·i·ty (fə·del'ə·tē *or* fī·del'ə·tē) *n.*
1 Faithfulness; loyalty: *a husband's fidelity.*
2 Truthfulness; accuracy: *the fidelity of sound reproduction on a recording.*
Syn. 1 trustworthiness, constancy, devotion.
2 exactness, precision, reliability.
Ant. 1 disloyalty, infidelity. **2** inaccuracy, unreliability, distortion.

fi·du·ci·ar·y (fi·dōō'shē·er'ē) *n., adj.*
n. One who is entrusted with property or authority to be used for another's benefit, as a trustee: *A bank, acting as fiduciary, handled the trust funds set up for the heirs.*
adj. Of or involving the kind of trust and confidence placed in a trustee: *the fiduciary relation between a guardian and his ward.*

fiend (fēnd) *n.*
1 An evil spirit: *the fiends of hell.* **2** An intensely wicked or cruel person: *The torturer was a fiend.* **3** An enthusiast or addict: *a bridge fiend; a dope fiend.*—**fiend'ish** *adj.,* **fiend'ish·ly** *adv.*
Syn. 1 devil, demon. **2** brute, savage, barbarian. **3** devotee, fanatic.

fierce (firs) *adj.* **fierc·er, fierc·est**
Violent, vehement, or intense: *fierce warriors; a fierce argument; a fierce explosion.*—**fierce'ly** *adv.,* **fierce'ness** *n.*

fig·ment (fig'mənt) *n.*
An unreal invention of the mind: *The dagger in the air was a figment of his imagination.*
Syn. fabrication, fiction, fancy.
Ant. fact, reality, actuality.

fil·a·ment (fil'ə·mənt) *n.*
1 A fine thread, fiber, strand, or threadlike structure: *the filaments of a spider's web.* **2** The slender wire in an electric bulb, which produces light when an electric current is passed through it in a vacuum.

filch (filch) *v.*
To steal slyly and in small amounts: *to filch apples from a fruit stand.*
Syn. snitch, swipe, pilfer, purloin.

fil·i·al (fil'ē·əl) *adj.*
Of or befitting a son or daughter: *filial loyalty and devotion.*
Etymology: *Filial* comes from *filius,* the Latin word for son.
Syn. dutiful, respectful.

fil·i·bus·ter (fil'ə·bus'tər) *n., v.*
n. The use of time-consuming legislative tactics, especially long and irrelevant speeches, to delay debate and prevent passage of a bill: *A filibuster in the U.S. Senate stalled the reform legislation.*
v. To block passage of legislation by long speeches and other delaying tactics: *The Senator filibustered for a full twenty-four hours.*

fi·na·le (fə·nal'ē *or* fə·nä'lē) *n.*
The last part of a sequence or performance, as the concluding section of a musical composition: *the dazzling finale of a Broadway musical, with the entire cast on stage.*
Syn. end, close, climax, conclusion.
Ant. opening, prelude, overture.

fi·nal·i·ty (fī·nal'ə·tē) *n.,* **fi·nal·i·ties** *pl.*
Conclusiveness or decisiveness, or something possessing these qualities: *He spoke with an air of finality.*

fi·nal·ly (fī'nəl·ē) *adv.*
1 At or in the end: *He finally won the girl.*
2 Conclusively and decisively: *The Supreme Court decided the issue finally.*
Usage: Don't confuse *finally* with *finely*: *He finally cut his hair; a finely cut diamond.* "Finely trained" means very well trained. "Finally trained" means trained at last.
Syn. 1 at last, in conclusion. **2** definitively, irrevocably.
Ant. 1 immediately, initially, first.

fi·nance (fi·nans' *or* fī'nans) *n.; v.* **fi·nanced, fi·nanc·ing**
n. **1** *pl.* Available funds, income, or revenue: *sound personal finances.* **2** The management of money, income, or revenue: *an approved system of national finance.*
v. To supply or obtain the necessary money for: *a mortgage loan to finance a house.*
Syn. *n.* **1** resources, assets.

fin·an·cier (fin'ən·sir') *n.*
A financial expert, or a person engaged in financial affairs on a large scale.
Spelling tip: When writing the word *financier,* break the rule and put *i* before *e* after *c.*
Syn. banker, broker, capitalist.

fi·nesse (fi·nes') *n.*
1 Highly refined skill or technique: *The pianist negotiated the tricky passage with finesse.*
2 Artful strategy or tact: *a skilled mediator who handled the negotiations with finesse.*
Syn. 1 adroitness, deftness, flair. **2** craft, cunning, diplomacy.
Ant. 1 clumsiness, incompetence, ineptitude.
2 maladroitness, tactlessness.

fin·ick·y (fin'i·kē) *adj.*
Overly fastidious or fussy; exacting: *finicky about her appearance.*
Syn. particular, overnice, meticulous.

fin·is (fin'is *or* fī'nis) *n.,* **fin·is·es** *pl.*
The end; conclusion: *Marriage marks the finis of a man's carefree, bachelor existence.*
Syn. termination, finish, ending.
Ant. beginning, onset, start.

fi·nite (fī'nīt) *adj.*
Having bounds or limits; not infinite: *the*

finite human mind.—**fi'nite·ly** *adv.*, **fi'nite·ness** *n.*
Syn. measurable, terminable, restricted.
Ant. measureless, unlimited, unbounded.

fiord (fyôrd *or* fyōrd) *n.*
A long and narrow arm of the sea running between high rocky cliffs or banks, especially in Norway and Alaska.
Spelling tip: This Norwegian word may also be spelled *fjord*. Notice that the word is always pronounced as one syllable.

fis·cal (fis'kəl) *adj.*
1 Of or having to do with the treasury or finances of a government. 2 Having to do with financial matters in general: *fiscal records.*

fis·sion (fish'ən) *n.*
1 The act of splitting or breaking apart: *a fission of loyalties within a political party.* 2 *In biology* The division of a cell or organism into new cells or organisms: *The ameba reproduces itself by fission.* 3 *In physics* The breakdown of the nucleus of a heavy atom, leading to the formation of nuclei of lighter atoms with the release of great energy.
Syn. 1 cleaving, parting, rupture, break.

fis·sure (fish'ər) *n.; v.* **fis·sured, fis·sur·ing**
n. A narrow crevice or crack: *a fissure in a rock.*
v. To crack or split: *During the drought, the parched earth became fissured.*
Syn. *n.* split, cleft. *v.* cleave.

fis·tu·la (fis'chŏŏ·lə) *n.,* **fis·tu·las** *or* **fis·tu·lae** (fis'chŏŏ·le) *pl.*
In medicine A duct or canal formed by the imperfect closing of a wound, abscess, etc., and leading to the outside of the body or from one cavity or hollow organ to another.

flac·cid (flak'sid *or* flas'əd) *adj.*
Lacking firmness or elasticity; limp or flabby: *flaccid muscles; His leadership of the party is ineffective and flaccid.*—**flac'cid·ly** *adv.,* **flac·cid'i·ty** *or* **flac'cid·ness** *n.*
Syn. weak, lax, drooping, incompetent.
Ant. firm, effective, strong.

flag·el·late (flaj'ə·lāt) *v.,* **flag·el·lat·ed, flag·el·lat·ing;** *adj.*
v. To whip or flog: *Some members of religious orders flagellate themselves as a form of discipline.*
adj. In biology Shaped like a whip or lashlike part, as of a protozoan.—**flag'el·la'tion** *n.*
Syn. *v.* beat, scourge.

fla·grant (flā'grənt) *adj.*
Openly disgraceful; shockingly bad: *a flagrant breaking of the law.*—**fla'grance, fla'gran·cy** *n.;* **fla'grant·ly** *adv.*
Syn. glaring, gross, notorious, heinous, rank.
Ant. mild, slight, venial.

flair (flâr) *n.*
1 A talent or natural aptitude: *a flair for acting.* 2 Instinctive perceptiveness; discernment.

flam·boy·ant (flam·boi'ənt) *adj.*
1 Extravagantly ornate; showy: *Flamboyant hair styles prevailed during the reign of Louis XIV.* 2 Brilliant in color; resplendent: *a*

garden of flamboyant flowers.—**flam·boy'ance** *n.,* **flam·boy'ant·ly** *adv.*
Syn. 1 overelaborate, ostentatious, florid, rococo. 2 showy, gorgeous, flaming.
Ant. 1 plain, simple, bare. 2 dull, dreary.

flange (flanj) *n.; v.* **flanged, flang·ing**
n. 1 A projecting rim or collar on a wheel, designed to keep it on a fixed track: *the flange on a boxcar wheel.* 2 A similar projecting part of a beam, pipe, etc., designed to aid attachment or to increase stiffness.
v. To provide with a flange: *to flange a pipe.*

flaunt (flônt) *v.*
1 To wave or flutter freely: *banners flaunting in the breeze.* 2 To display in an impudent or brazen manner: *He loves to flaunt his knowledge of art.*—**flaunt'er** *n.,* **flaunt'ing·ly** *adv.*
Usage: *Flaunt* and *flout* are frequently confused, especially in the misuse of *flaunt* for *flout.* The word *flout* means to express scorn or contempt for something. Note the difference between the two words in this sentence: *Teen-agers flaunt their youthful independence by flouting the authority of their parents.*

flay (flā) *v.*
1 To remove all or part of the skin, hide, or bark: *to flay a lion carcass.* 2 To criticize harshly: *His boss flayed him for taking long lunch hours.* 3 To get money or goods by extortion or swindling: *to flay gullible customers.*—**flay'er** *n.*
Syn. 1 skin, strip. 2 scold, castigate, rebuke. 3 cheat, fleece.

fledg·ling (flej'ling) *n.*
1 A young bird with enough feathers to enable it to learn to fly. 2 A young inexperienced person; beginner: *nine-year-old fledglings with their own baseball team.*
Syn. 2 novice, tyro, apprentice, neophyte.
Ant. 2 expert, professional, old hand.

flick (flik) *n., v.*
n. 1 A quick, light, snapping movement or blow: *the flick of a horse's tail.* 2 A slight, crackling sound made by such a movement or blow: *the flick of a whip.*
v. 1 To cause to move or snap with a quick, light movement: *flicking a powder puff all over her face.* 2 To strike and remove with a quick, light movement: *to flick crumbs from a tablecloth.*

flip·pan·cy (flip'ən·sē) *n.,* **flip·pan·cies** *pl.*
1 A lack of respect or seriousness: *treating his religious background with flippancy.* 2 An impertinent or frivolous act or remark: *the unpardonable flippancy of thumbing one's nose.*—**flip'pant** *adj.,* **flip'pant·ly** *adv.*
Syn. 1 irreverence, levity, cheek, pertness, impudence, impertinence.

floe (flō) *n.*
A large, comparatively level field of floating ice on a sea or other body of water; also, a detached section of such a field: *Polar bears are often seen on ice floes.*

flor·id (flôr'id *or* flor'id) *adj.*
1 Having a ruddy color; flushed: *a large, stout man with a florid face.* 2 Ornate, especially to an excessive degree: *prose written*

in a wordy and florid style.—**flor′id·ly** *adv.;* **flor′id·ness, flo·rid·i·ty** (flə·rid′ə·tē) *n.*
Syn. 1 high-colored, rubicund, red. 2 flowery, embellished, flamboyant, fancy, elaborate.
Ant. 1 pale, ashen, pallid, anemic, bloodless. 2 plain, unadorned, simple, classic.

flo·til·la (flō·til′ə) *n.*
1 A fleet of small vessels: *a flotilla of fishing boats.* 2 *U.S. Navy* A small fleet of ships of the same or related types.

flot·sam (flot′səm) *n.*
1 Goods from or parts of a wrecked ship that are found floating on the sea or are swept ashore. 2 Homeless, very poor, or unattached persons: *the flotsam sleeping on park benches in a big city.*

flour·ish (flûr′ish) *v., n.*
v. 1 To grow or fare well or prosperously; thrive: *Our tomato plants are flourishing.* 2 To move with sweeping motions; wave about: *The orchestra conductor flourished his baton.*
n. 1 The act of waving about or brandishing: *a flourish of a fencing foil.* 2 A curved or decorative stroke in penmanship: *She signed her name with a flourish.* 3 Something done primarily for effect or display: *He recited the poem with a flourish.* 4 A lively, decorative passage of music: *a flourish of trumpets.*

flout (flout) *v.*
To express scorn or contempt for; defy with open contempt: *to flout convention.*—**flout′er** *n.,* **flout′ing·ly** *adv.*
Usage: See FLAUNT.
Syn. scoff, jeer, mock.
Ant. approve, respect, esteem.

fluc·tu·ate (fluk′chōō·āt) *v.* **fluc·tu·at·ed, fluc·tu·at·ing**
To change or vary often and in an irregular manner; be unsteady or move up and down: *His moods fluctuated from great friendliness to sullen anger.*—**fluc′tu·a′tion** *n.*
Syn. shift, swing, sway, waver.
Ant. abide, remain steady, hold fast.

flu·en·cy (flōō′ən·sē) *n.*
Smoothness and readiness in speech and writing: *a fluency in French.*
Syn. ease, eloquence, mellifluousness.

flu·o·res·cent (flōō′ə·res′ənt or flôr·es′ent) *adj.*
Absorbing radiation of a certain wavelength and giving it off as light: *a fluorescent lamp.*
—**flu′o·res′cence** *n.*

fluor·o·scope (flōōr′ə·skōp) *n.*
A device for looking at the shadows projected upon a fluorescent screen by objects put between it and a direct beam of X rays or other radiation. Doctors often use fluoroscopes to study the inner organs of the body.—**fluor′o·scop′ic** *adj.,* **fluor·os·co·py** (flōōr·os′kə·pē) *n.*

flux (fluks) *n.*
1 A continuous flowing out: *a flux of new publications to the newstands.* 2 Constant movement or change: *The stock market is always in a state of flux.* 3 *In medicine* An abnormal and excessive discharge of fluid matter from the body, especially in dysentery.
Syn. 1 flood, stream.

foi·ble (foi′bəl) *n.*
A personal weakness or failing; slight fault of character: *Dwelling on the past is a foible of many older people.*
Syn. frailty, defect, imperfection, shortcoming.

fo·ment (fō·ment′) *v.*
To stir up or instigate rebellion, discord, etc.: *Communists fomented a riot.*—**fo′men·ta′tion, fo·ment′er** *n.*
Usage: See FERMENT.
Syn. promote, encourage, stimulate.
Ant. quench, quell, discourage.

fool·har·dy (fōōl′här′dē) *adj.* **fool·har·di·er, fool·har·di·est**
Bold and daring in a foolish and reckless way: *Climbing a mountain without the proper equipment is a foolhardy venture.*—**fool′har′di·ness** *n.*
Syn. rash, imprudent, careless, impulsive.
Ant. sensible, careful, prudent.

for·age (fôr′ij or for′ij) *n.; v.* **for·aged, for·ag·ing**
n. 1 Food suitable for horses, cattle, and other farm animals: *Hay and grain are types of forage.* 2 A searching about for food or supplies, or a raid to capture such provisions: *After the battle the soldiers went on a forage.*
v. 1 To search about or rummage around for something, as for food or supplies: *to forage in the woods for grass and berries; foraging in the closet for his other rubber.* 2 To strip of provisions by plundering and seizing: *Retreating armies foraged the entire countryside.*
Syn. *n.* 1 feed, fodder, provender. 2 foray. *v.* 1 hunt. 2 loot, ravage, despoil, maraud.

for·ay (fôr′ā or for′ā) *n., v.*
n. An expedition or raid, as for plunder: *The college students went on forays in the town.*
v. To make a foray; plunder: *A group of soldiers forayed behind enemy lines.*
Syn. *n.* incursion, invasion. *v.* pillage, loot, despoil, strip, sack, raid.

for·bear (fôr·bâr′) *v.* **for·bore, for·borne, for·bear·ing**
1 To refrain from or cease some action, etc.: *to forbear entering into an argument.* 2 To act with patience: *to forbear from punishing him for his fits of bad temper.*—**for·bear′ance** *n.*

for·bid (fər·bid′ or fôr·bid′) *v.* **for·bade** (fər·bad′) or **for·bad, for·bid·den, for·bid·ding**
1 To command a person not to do something: *The policeman forbade me to jaywalk.* 2 To have the effect of preventing; make impossible: *The storm forbids our driving to the beach.*—**for·bid′dance** *n.*
Syn. 1 prohibit. 2 hinder, hamper.
Ant. 1 allow, permit. 2 facilitate, expedite.

for·ceps (fôr′səps) *n.,* **for·ceps** *pl.*
A pair of pincers for grasping and manipulating small or delicate objects, used by doctors, surgeons, dentists, etc.

for·ci·ble (fôr′sə·bəl) *adj.*
1 Brought about by strength: *the forcible ejection of the intruders.* 2 Having strength; powerful: *a forcible argument; a forcible blow.*
Syn. 1 forced, violent. 2 forceful, strong, vigorous, mighty.

Ant. 1 nonviolent. **2** weak, ineffective, impotent.

fore·bear (fôr′bâr) *n.*
An ancestor.
Spelling tip: Also spelled *forbear.*
Syn. progenitor, forefather.

fore·bode (fôr·bōd′ *or* fōr·bōd′) *v.* **fore·bod·ed, fore·bod·ing**
1 To indicate in advance; to be an omen of: *Shooting stars were once thought to forebode disaster.* **2** To have a premonition of something evil or harmful: *He foreboded a disaster, but did not divulge his fear to anyone.*
Syn. 1 augur, bode, portend. **2** foresee.

fore·bod·ing (fôr·bō′ding *or* fōr·bō′ding) *n.*
A feeling that something bad is going to happen: *to awaken with a foreboding of imminent disaster.*
Syn. premonition, presentiment, apprehension.

fore·cast (fôr′kast′ *or* fōr′kast′) *n,; v.* **fore·cast** *or* **fore·cast·ed, fore·cast·ing**
n. A prediction or prophecy: *the weather forecast.*
v. **1** To predict by means of observation and study: *to forecast rain; to forecast a stock-market boom.* **2** To be an advance indication of: *The sudden drop in the barometer forecast a hurricane.*
Syn. *n.* projection, prognostication. *v.* **2** augur, presage, foreshadow.

fore·cas·tle (fōk′səl) *n.*
The part of the upper deck of a ship located forward of the mast nearest the bow, or a section of a merchant ship near the bow in which the sailors' living quarters are located.

fo·ren·sic (fə·ren′sik) *adj.*
1 Pertaining to, characteristic of, or used in courts of justice or public debate. **2** Pertaining to forensics (the art or study of argumentation): *His forensic ability made him a famous debater.*
Syn. 1 legal. **2** dialectical.

fore·see (fôr·sē′ *or* fōr·sē′) *v.* **fore·saw, fore·seen, fore·see·ing**
To know about an event before it happens: *The soothsayer foresaw Julius Caesar's assassination.*
Syn. foreknow.

for·feit (fôr′fit) *n., v., adj.*
n. Something taken away or given up as a penalty, or the giving up or loss of something as a penalty: *the forfeit of his good name.*
v. To lose or give up as a penalty: *The team did not appear and therefore forfeited the game.*
adj. Taken away or liable to be taken away as a penalty: *Their lives will be forfeit.*
Syn. *n.* forfeiture, loss. *adj.* lost, forfeited.

for·mat (fôr′mat) *n.*
The overall arrangement of something, as the form, size, margins, and graphic and typographical style of a book or other publication: *the format of the brochure; the format of the television show.*
Syn. form, design.

form·a·tive (fôr′mə·tiv) *adj.*
1 Having power to shape or mold: *Parents are a formative influence.* **2** Pertaining to formation or development: *The formative years occur in early childhood.*

for·mi·da·ble (fôr′mi·də·bəl) *adj.*
1 Exciting fear or dread by reason of great size or strength: *a formidable opponent.* **2** Extremely difficult because of great size, etc.: *a formidable task.*
Syn. 1 fierce, fearsome. **2** overpowering, massive, Herculean.
Ant. 1 weak, inferior, negligible. **2** easy, simple, trifling.

for·mu·la (fôr′myə·lə) *n.,* **for·mu·las** *or* **for·mu·lae** (fôr′myə·lē) *pl.*
1 A prescription or recipe, or the mixture prepared according to a prescription or recipe: *a formula for a cough medicine. We changed the baby's formula.* **2** A set of words fixed by convention or tradition, especially one which has become a meaningless formality. **3** A rule or combination represented in mathematical symbols.

for·syth·i·a (fôr·sith′ē·ə, fôr·sī′thē·ə *or* fər·sith′ē·ə) *n.*
A shrub of the olive family that bears bright yellow flowers: *Forsythia flowers appear in early spring.*
Etymology: This shrub was named after William Forsyth (1737–1804), a British botanist who brought it to England.

forth (fôrth *or* fōrth) *adv.*
1 Forward in place or time: *from this day forth.* **2** Out, as from hiding or place of origin: *Come forth! Put forth some effort!*
Spelling tip: Do not confuse *forth* and *fourth* (4th).
Syn. 1 on, onward.

fort·night (fôrt′nīt′ *or* fôrt′nit′) *n.*
Two weeks: *to get paid once a fortnight.*

for·tu·i·tous (fôr·t(y)ōō′ə·təs) *adj.*
Occurring by chance rather than by design; accidental: *an unexpected, fortuitous encounter.*
Syn. chance, adventitious.

for·ward (fôr′wərd) *adv., adj., n., v.*
adv. Toward the front or toward the future: *to move forward; to look forward to retirement.*
adj. **1** At or in the front part: *the forward cars of the train.* **2** Overly aggressive; bold or rude: *The young man had a distressingly forward manner, and was not very popular.*
n. A player in the front line, or one who leads the offensive: *the two forwards on the basketball team.*
v. **1** To help to advance: *An advanced degree forwarded his career.* **2** To send on, as to a new address: *to forward mail.*
Spelling tip: Do not confuse *forward* with *foreword*, meaning the preface of a book (pronounced the same as *forward*).

fos·ter (fôs′tər *or* fos′tər) *v., adj.*
v. **1** To bring up a child: *She lovingly fostered both children.* **2** To promote the development or growth of, or to keep alive: *Tutoring fos-*

tered his genius. The interview fostered his hopes of getting the job.
adj. Having a given relationship as a result of rearing only, not by birth: *a foster child or foster parent.*
Syn. *v.* 1 rear, raise, nurture. 2 advance, promote, sustain.
Ant. *v.* 2 discourage, destroy, ruin, kill.

foy·er (foi′ər *or* foi′ā) *n.*
1 A public lobby in a hotel, theater, etc.: *to smoke in the foyer during intermission.* 2 An entrance hall in a house or apartment: *through the front door into the foyer.*
Syn. 1 lobby, hall. 2 vestibule, entranceway.

fra·cas (frā′kəs *or* frak′əs) *n.*
A noisy disturbance or fight; brawl: *Their fight attracted a mob and turned into a real fracas.*
Syn. row, melee, ruckus.

frac·tious (frak′shəs) *adj.*
1 Apt to be unruly or rebellious: *a fractious, spoiled child.* 2 Easily annoyed or angered; cranky: *a fractious old man.*
Syn. 1 wayward, disorderly. 2 irritable, peevish, querulous, bad-tempered.
Ant. 1 obedient, docile. 2 good-natured, amiable.

frag·ile (fraj′əl) *adj.*
Easily broken: *a fragile porcelain teacup.*
Syn. frail, delicate, brittle, breakable.
Ant. tough, sturdy.

frail·ty (frāl′tē) *n.,* **frail·ties** *pl.*
1 The state or quality of being delicate and weak: *the frailty of a porcelain vase; the frailty of an emaciated, tubercular old man.* 2 A fault or moral weakness: *Drinking too much is his great frailty.*
Syn. 1 delicacy, fragility, weakness. 2 flaw, failing.
Ant. 1 strength, toughness, sturdiness, resilience.

fran·chise (fran′chīz) *n.*
1 The right to vote; suffrage: *The franchise was extended to all citizens.* 2 A special privilege granted by a government: *a franchise to operate a bus line.* 3 Permission given to a dealer to market a certain company's goods or services using the name of the parent company: *The famous restaurant granted a franchise to two individuals.* 4 The territory over which such special permissions extend: *the Eastern States franchise.*

fra·ter·ni·ty (frə·tûr′nə·tē) *n.,* **fra·ter·ni·ties** *pl.*
1 The state or spirit of being brothers: *the fraternity among all who had been through the revolution together.* 2 *In U.S. colleges* A society of male students, usually having a Greek-letter name: *the Sigma Chi fraternity.* 3 A body of people sharing the same interests, profession, etc.: *the medical fraternity.*
Syn. 1 brotherhood, camaraderie, fraternalism. 3 brotherhood, fellowship.

fraud·u·lent (frô′jə·lənt) *adj.*
Characterized by deception and trickery: *a fraudulent stock manipulation.*
Syn. dishonest, deceitful.
Ant. honest, legal, aboveboard.

fraught (frôt) *adj.*
Filled with: *a journey fraught with danger.*
Syn. laden, loaded.

fray (frā) *v.*
1 To cause cloth, rope, etc., to separate into loose threads at the edges by friction or wear: *Long wear had frayed the collar of his shirt.* 2 To become frayed: *The collar frayed after a few months of wear.*
Syn. 1, 2 frazzle, tatter.

freeze (frēz) *v.* **froze, fro·zen, freez·ing**
1 To change into ice by the action of cold: *to freeze water into ice cubes.* 2 To become or cause to be covered or filled with ice: *The pond froze over.* 3 To damage or kill, or be damaged or killed, by great cold: *The crop froze during the night.* 4 To hold prices, wages, etc., at a fixed level: *to freeze wages during wartime.* 5 To become motionless, as through fear or shock: *They had frozen with terror.* 6 To become icily aloof, formal, or unfriendly in manner: *He wanted to be a genial host but he froze up as the first guest arrived.*

fren·zied (fren′zēd) *adj.*
Wildly, almost insanely, excited: *A frenzied mob attacked the hated tyrant.*
Syn. wild, frantic, hysterical.

fres·co (fres′kō) *n.,* **fres·coes** *or* **fres·cos** *pl.*
The art of painting on a plaster surface, especially while the plaster is still moist; also, a picture so painted.

fric·as·see (frik′ə·sē′) *n.; v.* **fric·as·seed, fric·as·see·ing**
n. Meat that is cut small, stewed, and served in gravy: *chicken fricassee.*
v. To make into such a dish: *She fricasseed the chicken.*

friend (frend) *n.*
1 A person one knows very well and for whom one has warm regard or affection. 2 A patron or supporter: *a friend of the arts.* 3 A person who belongs to the same nation, party, etc. as oneself or with whom one is united in some purpose: *Friend or foe?* 4 (Capital *F*) A member of the Society of Friends; Quaker.
Syn. 1 intimate, buddy. 2 advocate, benefactor. 3 associate, comrade, ally.
Ant. 3 enemy, opponent, foe.

frieze (frēz) *n.*
A decorative horizontal strip, as along the top of a wall in a room.

frig·id (frij′id) *adj.*
1 Bitterly cold: *a frigid winter day.* 2 Lacking warmth of feeling: *a frigid response to my invitation.* 3 Habitually lacking sexual feeling or reaction (said of women).—**frig′id·ly** *adv.,* **fri·gid′i·ty** *n.*
Syn. 1 freezing, wintry, icy. 2 indifferent, unenthusiastic, reserved.
Ant. 1 hot, torrid, sultry. 2 warm, enthusiastic.

frit·ter (frit′ər) *v., n.*
v. To waste or squander little by little: *to fritter away an inheritance.*
n. A small cake made of plain batter or of corn, meat, fruit, etc.

frol·ic·some (frol'ik·səm) *adj.*
Gay and lighthearted: *a frolicsome colt.*
Syn. playful, prankish.

frond (frond) *n.*
A large leaf, or a leaflike expansion, as of a palm tree or fern.

fron·tal (frun'təl) *adj.*
1 Of, in, on, or having to do with the front: *a massive frontal attack on the enemy forces.*
2 Of, for, or having to do with the forehead or frontal bone.

frow·zy (frou'zē) *adj.* **frow·zi·er, frow·zi·est**
1 Slovenly in appearance: *a frowzy housewife in front of her TV set.* 2 Having a disagreeable smell: *a room filled with the frowzy odor of stale cigarette smoke and dirty laundry.*— **frow'zi·ness** *n.*
Spelling tip: This word is also spelled *frowsy.*
Syn. 1 messy, slatternly, unkempt. 2 musty, stuffy, offensive.
Ant. 1 neat, attractive. 2 agreeable, pleasing.

fru·gal·i·ty (frōō·gal'ə·tē) *n.*
The quality of being economical; carefulness in using and spending.
Syn. thrift, economy.
Ant. extravagance, wastefulness.

fuch·sia (fyōō'shə) *n., adj.*
n. 1 Any of various plants with drooping, four-petaled flowers. 2 A bright bluish red, the typical color of the fuchsia.
adj. Bright bluish red: *fuchsia draperies.*

ful·crum (fōōl'krəm) *n.,* **ful·crums** or **ful·cra** (fōōl'krə) *pl.*
The support on which a lever rests, or about which it turns.

ful·fill (fōōl·fil') *v.* **ful·filled, ful·fill·ing**
1 To make real something promised, hoped for, etc.: *fulfilling the high hopes his parents had for him.* 2 To do or perform something commanded or requested: *failing to fulfill a direct order.* 3 To come up to or satisfy: *fulfilling the requirements for university admission.* 4 To get through to the end of: *fulfilling her assigned tasks for the day.*—**ful·fill'ment** *n.*
Spelling tip: *Fulfil* is an alternate spelling for this word. However, *fulfill* is preferred in the U.S.

ful·mi·nate (ful'mə·nāt) *v.* **ful·mi·nat·ed, ful·mi·nat·ing**
1 To make loud or violent verbal attacks: *to fulminate against taxes.* 2 To explode suddenly and violently, as a chemical.—**ful'mi·na'tor** *n.*
Syn. 1 denounce, inveigh.

ful·some (fōōl'səm) *adj.*
Excessive in such an insincere way as to be distasteful: *a fulsome compliment.*—**ful'some·ly** *adv.,* **ful'some·ness** *n.*
Etymology: *Fulsome* once meant plentiful, abundant, or full. In time, however, the word began to mean too full or full in a false way, and this is the only sense in which it is used today.
Syn. immoderate, gross, exaggerated.

func·tion·ar·y (fungk'shən·er'ē) *n.,* **func·tion·ar·ies** *pl.*
A person who serves in some specific capacity, especially in a governmental or political position: *one of the many useless functionaries in city hall.*
Syn. official, civil servant, bureaucrat.

fu·ne·re·al (fyōō·nir'ē·əl) *adj.*
Depressingly sad or gloomy: *A basset hound has a funereal expression.*
Syn. melancholy, doleful.
Ant. cheerful, joyous.

fun·gus (fung'gəs) *n.,* **fun·gi** (fun'jī) or **fun·gus·es** *pl.*
Any of a group of plants that are nonflowering and have no chlorophyll: *Mushrooms, molds, and mildews are fungi.*

fu·nic·u·lar (fyōō·nik'yə·lər) *adj., n.*
adj. Moved by the pull of a cable, rope, etc., as a streetcar in a hilly section.
n. A railway along which cable cars are drawn.

fur·be·low (fûr'bə·lō) *n., v.*
n. A ruffle, frill, or similar piece of trimming: *an attractively simple dress with no fussy furbelows.*
v. To trim with furbelows.

fu·ror (fyōōr'ôr) *n.*
1 A fit of great rage; maniacal fury: *The mob's furor was terrifying.* 2 Intense, usually widespread excitement or enthusiasm: *the great furor caused by his new play.*
Spelling tip: Also spelled *furore.*
Syn. 1 madness, frenzy. 2 admiration, stir.

fur·ther (fûr'thər) comparative of **far;** *adv., adj., v.*
adv. 1 At or to a more distant or remote point: *further back in history.* 2 To a greater degree: *In a little while we will question him further.*
adj. 1 More distant: *the further side of the village.* 2 Additional: *Make no further remarks.*
v. To help forward; promote: *to further the project with a financial contribution.*
Usage: See FARTHER.

fur·tive (fûr'tiv) *adj.*
1 Done in secret: *She stole a furtive glance.*
2 Sly: *There was a furtive look about him that made me immediately suspicious.*—**fur'tive·ly** *adv.,* **fur'tive·ness** *n.*
Syn. 1 stealthy, surreptitious, concealed. 2 evasive, shifty.
Ant. 1 open, apparent. 2 honest, forthright.

fu·se·lage (fyōō'sə·lij or fyōō'sə·läzh) *n.*
The body of an airplane, containing the cockpit, cabin, etc., but excluding the wings and tail.

fu·sil·lade (fyōō'sə·lād', fyōō'sə·läd', fyōō'sə·lād', or fyōō'sə·läd') *n.*
1 The simultaneous or rapidly repeated discharge of many firearms. 2 Anything that is like such a discharge: *a fusillade of hailstones.*
Syn. volley, salvo, broadside.

fu·sion (fyōō'zhən) *n.*
1 A melting or blending together: *a metallic component, susceptible to fusion.* 2 The state

or condition of being melted or blended together, or something formed in this way: *the fusion that resulted from the reconciliation of two dissident factions.* **3** A thermonuclear reaction in which the nuclei of a light element undergo transformation into those of a heavier element, with the release of great energy. **Usage:** See FISSION.

fus·tian (fus'chən) *n.*
1 A coarse, twilled cotton fabric, as corduroy. **2** Pretentious speech or writing: *a political rally filled with fustian.*
Syn. 2 bombast, rhetoric.

fu·tile (fyōō'təl) *adj.*
1 Being of no avail; done in vain: *futile attempts to change her husband.* **2** Of no importance: *futile chatter.*—**fu'tile·ly** *adv.*, **fu'tile·ness** *n.*
Syn. 1 ineffectual, fruitless. **2** frivolous, trivial, unimportant.

G

gad·fly (gad'flī') *n.*, **gad·flies** *pl.*
1 One of various large flies, as the horsefly, that bite cattle, horses, etc. **2** An irritating, persistent person; especially, one who tries to stimulate others to activity: *The newspaper columnist is a gadfly about improper government spending.*
Syn. 2 nuisance, annoyance, scourge.

gaff (gaf) *n.*, *v.*
n. A sharp iron hook at the end of a pole, for landing a large fish. **2** A spar for extending the upper edge of a fore-and-aft sail.
v. To strike or land with a gaff: *to gaff a blue marlin.*
Usage: *Gaff* is often used in the informal idiom *to stand the gaff*, which means to patiently endure hardship, ridicule, etc.: *Why don't you come to my little boy's birthday party, if you can stand the gaff?*

gai·e·ty (gā'ə·tē) *n.*, **gai·e·ties** *pl.*
1 Gay, merry spirits: *the children's gaiety.* **2** Fun and frolic: *the gaiety of the festival.* **3** Bright colorfulness: *the gaiety of their costumes.*—**gay'ness** *n.*

gain·say (gān·sā') *v.* **gain·said, gain·say·ing**
1 To deny: *That health is the greatest wealth cannot be gainsaid.* **2** To contradict: *I will not gainsay his statement, although I do not believe it is true.*

ga·la (gā'lə *or* gal'ə) *adj.*, *n.*
adj. Having to do with or fitting for a festive occasion; gay: *a gala night on the town.*
n. A joyous or festive occasion or celebration.
Syn. *adj.* festal, colorful, splendid. *n.* holiday, festival, feast, fete.

gal·ax·y (gal'ək·sē) *n.*, **gal·ax·ies** *pl.*
1 *In astronomy* Any large system of stars or other heavenly bodies. **2** (Usually capital *G*) The Milky Way. **3** Any brilliant group, as of persons: *a galaxy of well-known actors.*

gam·ut (gam'ət) *n.*
1 The whole range of anything from one extreme to the other: *His crimes ran the gamut from petty thievery to murder.* **2** The entire range or compass of tones used in modern music.

gant·let (gônt'lit *or* gant'lit) *n.*
1 A former military punishment in which the offender ran between two lines of men armed with clubs, whips, etc., who struck him as he passed. **2** A series of difficulties of any kind.
Usage: *Gantlet* is usually used only in the phrase *to run the gantlet: Military prisoners often had to run the gantlet as part of their punishment. The new star had to run the gantlet of unfavorable critical reviews.*
Spelling tip: See GAUNTLET.
Syn. 2 ordeal, test, trial.

gape (gāp) *v.* **gaped, gap·ing;** *n.*
v. **1** To stare with the mouth open, as in wonder or surprise: *The crowd gaped at the accident.* **2** To open the mouth wide, as in yawning: *Baby birds gape to receive food.* **3** To be or become open wide: *a gaping hole in the ground.*
n. **1** The act of gaping. **2** A wide opening or gap: *the huge gape of an extinct volcano.*
Syn. *v.* **1** goggle, gawk, rubberneck.

Gar·gan·tu·an (gär·gan'chōō·ən) *adj.*
Very large; having tremendous size or capacity: *the Gargantuan stretches of Antarctica; a Gargantuan appetite.*
Etymology: *Gargantuan* comes from *Gargantua*, the peace-loving giant prince of the French writer Rabelais' book of the same name (1534). This giant was known especially for his enormous appetite.
Syn. huge, colossal, enormous.
Ant. average, small, scant.

gar·ish (gâr'ish) *adj.*
Too showy or gaudy: *a woman in a garish red dress; a garish electric sign.*—**gar'ish·ly** *adv.*, **gar'ish·ness** *n.*
Syn. flashy, tawdry, ornate.
Ant. plain, simple, subdued.

gar·nish (gär'nish) *v.*, *n.*
v. **1** *In cooking* To decorate a dish with flavorsome or colorful trimmings: *Boiled potatoes garnished with parsley.* **2** To embellish.
n. **1** Something added to food ready for serving to decorate it or improve its flavor: *fish with a garnish of lemon wedges.* **2** Any added decoration or embellishment: *The lectures often had a garnish of humor.*

gar·nish·ee (gär'nish·ē') *v.* **gar·nish·eed, gar·nish·ee·ing;** *n.*
v. *In law* To take a certain percentage of a person's salary, wages, etc., by legal means in order to settle a debt.
n. A person whose salary, etc., has been so taken.—**gar·nish·ment** (gär'nish·mənt) *n.*
Syn. *v.* attach.

gar·ru·li·ty (gə·rōō'lə·tē) *n.*
Glib, empty, or excessive talkativeness: *The garrulity of a lonely housewife is often irritating.*

gar·ru·lous (gar'ə·ləs *or* gar'yə·ləs) *adj.*
1 Talking a great deal, especially about unimportant or boring things: *a lonely, garrulous old man.* **2** Rambling and wordy: *a garru-*

lous account of his vacation.—**gar′ru·lous·ly** *adv.*, **gar′ru·lous·ness** *n.*
Syn. 1 talkative, loquacious, chatty. 2 verbose, long-winded.
Ant. 1 quiet, laconic, unresponsive. 2 terse, concise, succinct.

gas·e·ous (gas′ē·əs, gas′yəs, *or* gash′əs) *adj.*
Being, having to do with, or like gas: *a gaseous substance.*

gas·tri·tis (gas·trī′tis) *n.*
Inflammation of the lining of the stomach, especially of the mucous membranes.

gas·tro·nome (gas′trə·nōm) *n.*
A person who delights in fine food and drink.—**gas·tro·nom·ic** (gas′trə·nom′ik) *adj.*, **gas·tron·o·my** (gas·tron′ə·mē) *n.*
Syn. gourmet, epicure.

gauche (gōsh′) *adj.*
Awkward, clumsy, or inept, especially in social behavior: *She was frequently embarrassed by the gauche actions of her roommate.*
Etymology: *Gauche* has been borrowed from the French word for left-handed.
Syn. maladroit, boorish.
Ant. adroit.

gaunt·let (gônt′lit *or* gänt′lit) *n.*
1 *In medieval armor* A glove covered with metal plates to protect the hand. 2 A modern type of glove with a long, often flaring extension over the wrist.
Spelling tip: Be careful not to confuse *gauntlet*, the glove, with *gantlet*, the punishment. Although both words may be spelled either way, *gauntlet* is preferred for the glove and *gantlet* for the punishment or ordeal.

ga·zette (gə·zet′) *n.; v.* **ga·zet·ted, ga·zet·ting**
n. 1 A newspaper or similar regular publication (now usually used in the titles of some publications). 2 An official publication, as of a government or society; especially one issued by the British government listing official appointments, bankruptcies, etc.
v. To publish or announce in a gazette.
Etymology: *Gazette* comes from the Italian (Venetian) dialect word *gazeta*, a small coin that was originally the price of such a publication.

gaz·et·teer (gaz′ə·tir′) *n.*
A work or section of a work, such as a dictionary, listing countries, cities, rivers, etc., together with such statistics as their location, size, and population.

gei·sha (gā′shə *or* gē′shə) *n.*, **gei·sha** *or* **gei·shas** *pl.*
A Japanese girl who has been trained to furnish entertainment by singing, dancing, conversing, and serving tea.

gen·darme (zhän′därm) *n.*
1 *In France* A member of a corps of armed police. 2 Any policeman (a humorous usage).
Etymology: *Gendarme* has been borrowed directly from the French, where it was once written as a plural, *gens d'armes*, literally meaning men-at-arms.

ge·ne·al·o·gy (jē′nē·ol′ə·jē *or* jē′nē·al′ə·jē) *n.*, **ge·ne·al·o·gies** *pl.*

1 A record or table showing the descent of a person or a family from a certain ancestor: *the genealogy of the Adams family.* 2 Descent in a direct line from a specific ancestor: *proud of his illustrious genealogy.* 3 The study of family descent: *an expert in genealogy.*—**ge·ne·a·log·ic** (jē′nē·ə·loj′ik) *or* **ge′ne·a·log′i·cal** *adj.*, **ge′ne·a·log′i·cal·ly** *adv.*
Spelling tip: Many of our words ending in *-logy* have an *o* before the ending, as *biology, philology, embryology. Genealogy,* however, has an *a* preceding *-logy,* although the word is pronounced (jē′nē·ol′ə·jē).
Syn. 1 lineage, ancestry, pedigree.

gen·er·al·i·ty (jen′ə·ral′ə·tē) *n.*, **gen·er·al·i·ties** *pl.*
1 The state or quality of affecting, pertaining to, or including all or the whole. 2 A statement or idea lacking in detail and preciseness: *a speech full of meaningless generalities.* 3 The greater number of a group: *The generality of voters selected a straight ticket.*

ge·ner·ic (ji·ner′ik) *adj.*
1 Of or having to do with a genus, group, or class of related things: *Homo is the generic name of various species of erect, large-brained primates.* 2 Having a wide, general application; not specific: *mental illnesses grouped under the generic heading of "psychoses."*—**ge·ner′i·cal·ly** *adv.*
Syn. 2 collective, comprehensive.
Ant. 2 particular, definite, explicit.

ge·nie (jē′nē) *n.*, **ge·ni·i** (jē′nē·ī) *pl.*
In Moslem mythology A supernatural being who has great powers and is often at the call and service of men.
Spelling tip: *Genie* is also spelled *djinni* (ji·nē′), *jinnee* (jin·nē′), *or jinni* (jin′ē *or* ji·nē′), but *genie* is usually preferred.

gen·ius (jēn′yəs) *n.*, **gen·ius·es** *for defs. 1, 2, 4, 5, 6* and **ge·ni·i** (jē·nē·ī) *for def. 3.*
1 A very high degree of intelligence or talent, or a person who possesses this: *the genius of Einstein.* 2 An aptitude for doing some specific thing: *She has a genius for making tactless remarks.* 3 *In ancient mythology* A supernatural being appointed to guide a person throughout life; guardian spirit. 4 The spirit or distinguishing characteristic of a particular person, people, place, time in history, etc.: *the genius of Renaissance art and letters.* 5 A person who exerts a strong influence over another for good or evil: *Rasputin was the evil genius of the Empress of Russia.*

gen·re (zhän′rə) *n., adj.*
n. 1 A particular sort, kind, or category, especially a category of art or literature characterized by a certain form, style, or subject matter: *Hindu music sounds odd to many Westerners not familiar with the genre.* 2 A type of painting that deals with everyday life: *the genre produced by the Dutch masters.*
adj. Of or having to do with painting dealing with everyday life: *Rembrandt is a genre painter.*

gen·tian (jen′shən) *n.*
1 Any of a large group of European and

American plants with showy, usually blue or yellow flowers. 2 The root of this plant from which is made a medicine for soothing the stomach.

gen·try (jen′trē) *n.*
1 People of good family or social background: *a member of the New England gentry.* 2 People of a particular area, occupation, or kind (now used chiefly in a patronizing or humorous way): *the local gentry; the gambling gentry.*
Syn. 1 aristocracy. 2 folks.
Ant. 1 masses, hoi polloi.

gen·u·flect (jen′yə·flekt) *v.*
To bend the knee, as in worship: *The priest genuflected before the altar.*—**gen′u·flec′tion** *n.*
Etymology: *Genuflect* comes from two Latin words, *genu* (knee) and *flectere* (to bend).

ge·nus (jē′nəs) *n.,* **gen·e·ra** (jen′ər·ə) or **ge·nus·es** *pl.*
In biology A closely related group or category of plants or animals made up of one or more species: *Both horses and donkeys belong to the genus "Equus."*

ger·mane (jər·mān′) *adj.*
Related to what is being discussed or considered; relevant: *His comments are not germane to this argument.*
Syn. pertinent, appropriate, relative, fitting, suitable, proper.
Ant. irrelevant, alien, unsuitable, unrelated.

ger·mi·nate (jûr′mə·nāt) *v.* **ger·mi·nat·ed, ger·mi·nat·ing**
1 To begin or cause to grow or develop; sprout: *Seeds germinate in the spring.* 2 To evolve or cause to evolve: *Teen-agers today germinate new trends of thought.*—**ger′mi·na′tion, ger′mi·na′tor** *n.*
Syn. 1 bud, shoot, burgeon. 2 develop, unfold, produce.

ger·ry·man·der (jer′i·man′dər) *v., n.*
v. To alter a voting area so as to advance unfairly the interests of one political party. *n.* The act or result of gerrymandering.
Etymology: *Gerrymander* was formed from the name *Gerry* + (*sala*)*mander*, from the salamander shape of a voting district in Massachusetts carved out for political advantage while Elbridge Gerry (1744–1814) was governor.

ges·tate (jes′tāt) *v.* **ges·tat·ed, ges·tat·ing**
1 To carry unborn young in the uterus until birth: *A mouse gestates its young for only nineteen days.* 2 To develop gradually in the mind: *to gestate new ways of solving a problem.*—**ges·ta′tion** *n.*
Syn. 2 ponder, consider, speculate.

ges·tic·u·late (jes·tik′yə·lāt) *v.* **ges·tic·u·lat·ed, ges·tic·u·lat·ing**
To make emphatic or expressive gestures: *He was unable to say the simplest thing without gesticulating.*—**ges·tic′u·la′tion** *n.*
Syn. gesture, signal, pantomime.

ges·ture (jes′chər) *n.; v.* **ges·tured, ges·tur·ing**
n. 1 A bodily motion, as of the hands, head, etc., made while speaking in order to emphasize or express some idea or emotion: *A nod is*

a gesture meaning "yes." 2 Something done or said as a mere formality or for an effect: *Because he was broke, everyone knew his offer to pay the tab was a mere gesture.*
v. 1 To make gestures: *gesturing that his mouth was full and that he could not answer.* 2 To express by gestures: *He gestured to me to sit down.*

gew·gaw (gyo͞o′gô) *n.*
A small, ornamental article of little value; trinket: *gewgaws from the ten-cent store.*
Syn. bauble, trifle, knickknack.

gey·ser (gī′zər or gī′sər) *n.*
A natural hot spring from which jets of steam, hot water, or mud are ejected at intervals in a fountainlike column: *the geysers at Yellowstone National Park.*

ghast·ly (gast′lē or gäst′lē) *adj.* **ghast·li·er, ghast·li·est**
1 Horrible; terrifying: *the ghastly sight of a battlefield strewn with corpses.* 2 Deathlike in appearance; pale: *The unconscious man looked ghastly.* 3 *Informal* Very bad or unpleasant: *a ghastly, overly sentimental painting.*—**ghast′li·ness** *n.*
Syn. 1 fearful, gruesome, appalling. 2 wan, blanched, ashen. 3 tasteless, insipid, tawdry.

ghet·to (get′ō) *n.,* **ghet·tos** *pl.*
1 A section of a city or town in which Jews were made to live in former times. 2 Any section of a city or town inhabited by members of some minority group or by very poor people: *Harlem is a ghetto of New York.*

ghoul (go͞ol) *n.*
1 A person who robs graves. 2 *In Moslem legend* An evil spirit who robs graves and preys on corpses. 3 A person who takes pleasure in revolting things or practices.—**ghoul′ish** *adj.,* **ghoul′ish·ness** *n.*

gib·ber (jib′ər or gib′ər) *v., n.*
v. To talk rapidly and incoherently; jabber: *The streets seemed full of mad people clucking and gibbering to themselves.*
n. Rapid or unintelligible talk: *the gibber of a toothless old man.*
Syn. *v.* babble, prattle, chatter, gabble. *n.* gabble, palaver, babble, twaddle, nonsense.

gib·ber·ish (jib′ər·ish or gib′ər·ish) *n.*
1 Rapid, inarticulate, or foolish talk: *the gibberish of an idiot.* 2 Needlessly difficult or obscure language: *the gibberish in which certain social scientists communicate with one another.*
Syn. 1 chatter, gabble, gibber, prattle. 2 jargon, argot, gobbledygook.

gib·bet (jib′it) *n.; v.* **gib·bet·ed** or **gib·bet·ted, gib·bet·ing** or **gib·bet·ting**
n. An upright timber with a crosspiece projecting from its top, upon which criminals were formerly hanged or their corpses displayed to the public.
v. 1 To execute on a gibbet. 2 To expose to public scorn: *The innocent wife and children of the murderer were slandered and gibbeted by the townspeople.*
Syn. *n.* gallows, scaffold. *v.* 1 hang. 2 pillory, persecute.

gib·bon (gib′ən) *n.*
A slender, long-armed anthropoid ape that lives in trees and is found in Asia and the East Indies.

gibe (jīb) *v.* **gibed, gib·ing;** *n.*
v. To utter jeers or make derisive remarks; taunt: *gibing at him for his laziness.*
n. A derisive remark; jeer: *The child tried to ignore the gibes of the older boys.*
Spelling tip: This word may also be spelled *jibe*, but *gibe* is preferred.
Syn. *v.* mock, ridicule, laugh at. *n.* taunt, derision, sarcasm.

gib·let (jib′lit) *n.*
Usually pl. Any of the parts of a fowl that are usually cooked separately, as the heart, liver, and gizzard: *gravy made with chopped giblets.*

gill (gil *for def. 1*, jil *for def. 2*) *n.*
1 The organ used by fishes and some other animals for breathing under water: *Gills absorb oxygen from the surrounding water and give out carbon dioxide as waste.* **2** A liquid measure equal to one-fourth pint: *Four gills make a pint, and eight gills make a quart.*

gil·ly·flow·er (jil′ē·flou′ər) *n.*
1 One of various plants of the mustard family. **2** A plant of the pink family, as the clove pink. **3** A variety of apple.
Spelling tip: This word is also spelled *gilliflower.*

gim·crack (jim′krak) *n., adj.*
n. A cheap, showy knickknack: *a souvenir stand selling useless gimcracks.*
adj. Cheap and flimsy or gaudy: *gimcrack souvenirs.*
Syn. *n.* trinket, trifle, bauble, gewgaw. *adj.* showy, worthless, trashy, sleazy.
Ant. *adj.* substantial, well-made, valuable.

gim·let (gim′lit) *n.*
A small, sharp tool with a cross handle and a pointed, spiral tip for boring holes.
Syn. auger.

gin·gi·vi·tis (jin′jə·vī′tis) *n.*
Inflammation of the gums.

gist (jist) *n.*
The main idea or essential part: *You may not grasp every detail, but do you understand the gist of my argument?*
Syn. essence, substance, pith.

gla·cial (glā′shəl) *adj.*
1 Of, pertaining to, or marked by the presence of glaciers: *a glacial formation.* **2** Freezingly cold or chillingly unfriendly: *a glacial wind; a glacial stare.*—**gla′cial·ly** *adv.*
Syn. 2 icy, frigid, frosty, wintry.

gla·cier (glā′shər) *n.*
A great field of ice or packed snow that slowly moves down through valleys or spreads across land until it melts in warmer regions or breaks off in the sea to form icebergs.

glad·i·o·lus (glad′ē·ō′ləs) *n.*, **glad·i·o·lus·es** or **glad·i·o·li** (glad′ē·ō′lī) *pl.*
A plant of the iris family, having sword-shaped leaves and spikes of colored flowers.

Etymology: Both *gladiolus* and *gladiator* go back to the Latin word *gladius*, meaning sword.

glaze (glāz) *v.* **glazed, glaz·ing;** *n.*
v. **1** To cover with a glossy, glasslike coating: *a glazed doughnut.* **2** To overspread with a thin, glassy film: *The alcoholic's eyes were glazed.* **3** To fit with glass panes: *to glaze a window.*
n. **1** A thin, smooth, glossy or glasslike coating: *an icy glaze on the sidewalk.* **2** A substance used for coating something: *Egg white is a glaze for foods.*

gla·zier (glā′zhər) *n.*
1 A person who fits windows, doors, etc., with panes of glass. **2** A person who applies glaze to pottery.

glean (glēn) *v.*
1 To gather the leavings from a field after the crop has been reaped: *to glean wheat.* **2** To collect facts, etc., by patient effort: *He combed the files and gleaned some useful information.*
—**glean′er, glean′ing** *n.*
Syn. 1 harvest, pick, reap. 2 collect, cull, gather, accumulate.

glib (glib) *adj.* **glib·ber, glib·best**
Smooth-tongued but shallow or insincere: *a glib politician, full of simplistic solutions for complex problems.*—**glib′ly** *adv.*, **glib′ness** *n.*

gloat (glōt) *v.*
To experience a strong, selfish, and often malicious or evil delight: *He gloated over his rival's bad luck.*
Etymology: From an Old Norse word *glotta* meaning to grin.

glob·u·lar (glob′yə·lər) *adj.*
1 Round like a sphere: *a globular drop of liquid.* **2** Worldwide: *globular conflict.*
Etymology: *Globular* goes back to the Latin word for ball, *globus.*
Syn. 1 spherical. 2 global.

glos·sa·ry (glos′ə·rē) *n.*, **glos·sa·ries** *pl.*
A list of technical, obscure, or foreign words used in a book or field, along with their definitions: *The English textbook contained a glossary of literary terms.*
Syn. lexicon, vocabulary.

glut (glut) *v.* **glut·ted, glut·ting;** *n.*
v. **1** To stuff full of food: *She glutted herself with pie.* **2** To supply with an excess of anything: *to glut the market with glamour stocks.*
n. An excessive supply: *a glut of tomatoes at the end of summer.*
Syn. *v.* 1 gorge, satiate. 2 flood, deluge, swamp. *n.* oversupply, plethora, super-abundance.
Ant. *v.* 1 starve. *n.* shortage, scarcity.

glut·ton·ous (glut′n·əs) *adj.*
Greedy, especially in eating: *a gluttonous appetite.*—**glut′ton, glut′ton·y** *n.*
Syn. voracious, rapacious, ravenous.
Ant. sparing, temperate, abstemious.

gnarled (närld) *adj.*
Knotty and twisted: *a nightmare landscape of stunted and gnarled trees; the gnarled, work-hardened hands of an old farmer.*
Spelling tip: Remember the silent *g.*

gnaw (nô) *v.* **gnawed, gnawed** o'r **gnawn** (nôn), **gnaw·ing**
1 To bite or eat away little by little: *a dog gnawing a bone.* 2 To make something by gnawing with sharp teeth: *The rat gnawed a hole in the wall.* 3 To torment constantly: *Guilt was gnawing at his conscience.*

gnome (nōm) *n.*
In folklore A dwarf resembling a little old man, who lives in a cave guarding hidden treasure.
Spelling tip: The silent *g* should be in plain view, although the sound is hidden.

gnu (nōō *or* nyōō) *n.,* **gnus** *or* **gnu** *pl.*
A South African antelope with an oxlike head, curved horns, a mane, and a long tail.
Spelling tip: *Gnu* looks strange, while *who* is perfectly familiar. Yet both of these rhyming words start with a silent letter.
Syn. wildebeest.

goad (gōd) *n., v.*
n. 1 A pointed stick used to drive animals forward: *a goad for oxen.* 2 Anything that acts as a spur or motive force: *Fear was the goad that drove him to greater efforts.*
v. To prick or drive with or as with a goad: *Repressive measures goaded the captives into open rebellion.*
Syn. *n.* 1 prod. 2 stimulus, incentive.

god·dess (god'is) *n.*
1 A female deity: *Athena was the Greek goddess of wisdom.* 2 A woman or girl of extraordinary beauty: *a film goddess.*

gon·do·la (gon'də·lə) *n.*
A long, narrow, flat-bottomed boat with high points at either end, used on the canals of Venice. It is propelled with a single oar by the gondolier, who stands in the stern.—**gon·do·lier** (gon'də·lir') *n.*

gorge (gôrj) *n.; v.* **gorged, gorg·ing**
n. A narrow, deep ravine, especially one with a stream flowing through it.
v. To stuff oneself greedily with food: *He gorged himself with rich desserts.*
Syn. *n.* canyon, gully, pass. *v.* cram, glut, sate.

gor·geous (gôr'jəs) *adj.*
1 Dazzlingly colorful: *gorgeous displays of the northern lights.* 2 *Informal* Perfectly beautiful: *gorgeous girls.*—**gor'geous·ly** *adv.*
Syn. 1 brilliant, splendid, magnificent. 2 lovely.
Ant. 1 colorless, faded, drab. 2 ugly, awful.

go·ril·la (gə·ril'ə) *n.*
The largest and most powerful of the manlike apes, native to central Africa.

go·ry (gôr'ē) *adj.* **go·ri·er, go·ri·est**
1 Covered or stained with thick, clotted blood: *a gory ax.* 2 Characterized by bloodshed or violence: *all the gory details of the crime.*—**gore** *n.*
Syn. 1 bloody, bloodstained. 2 sanguinary.

gos·ling (goz'ling) *n.*
A young goose.

gos·sa·mer (gos'ə·mər) *n., adj.*
n. 1 Fine strands of spider's silk. 2 Any flimsy,

delicate material or substance. *The costumes for the prima ballerina were sheer gossamer.*
adj. Filmy and delicate: *Her gossamer gown seemed to float behind her.*
Etymology: *Gossamer* comes from an English word meaning "goose summer," or Indian summer. That was the time of year for plucking geese, when gauzy cobwebs, like fine goose down, floated in the air.
Syn. *n.* 1 cobwebs. 2 gauze, chiffon. *adj.* light, gauzy, silken, diaphanous.

gouge (gouj) *n.; v.* **gouged, goug·ing**
n. 1 A chisel with a scoop-shaped blade, used for cutting or carving wood. 2 A groove such as is made by a gouge.
v. 1 To cut or carve with a gouge. 2 To scoop, force, or tear out: *to gouge out an eye with the thumb.* 3 *Informal* To cheat by overcharging: *He gouged the public by scalping tickets to hit plays.*
Syn. *v.* 3 swindle, victimize, exploit.

gou·lash (gōō'läsh) *n.*
A stew made with beef or veal and with vegetables.
Etymology: *Goulash* comes from a Hungarian word that literally means shepherd's meat.

gourd (gôrd *or* gōōrd) *n.*
1 The hard-shelled, inedible fruit of a plant of the gourd family, which also includes the squash, pumpkin, watermelon, and cucumber. 2 A utensil, as a ladle or dipper, made from the dried shell of a gourd.

gour·mand (gōōr'mənd *or* gōōr·män') *n.*
One who finds hearty enjoyment in eating.

gour·met (gōōr·mā') *n.*
A connoisseur of food and drink who has highly refined, discriminating tastes: *a true gourmet, concerned with all aspects of the ritual of dining.*
Etymology: *Gourmet* was originally an Old French word meaning winetaster.
Syn. gastronome, epicure.

gov·er·nor (guv'ər·nər) *n.*
1 The elected chief executive of a state: *the Governor of Michigan.* 2 An official who administers the affairs of a province, territory, organization, etc.: *a board of governors.* 3 A device for controlling the speed of an engine, motor, etc.: *the governor of a steam engine.*
Usage: *Governor* is capitalized when used as the title of a high-ranking government official: *Governor Rockefeller, the Governor of New York.* However, when not accompanied by the name of the official, *governor* is often spelled with a small letter: *the governor's news conference.*

gra·di·ent (grā'dē·ənt) *n.*
1 Degree of upward or downward slope: *the gradient of a road.* 2 An incline or ramp. 3 *In physics* A rate of change in certain variable factors: *a pressure gradient.*
Syn. 1 grade, inclination. 2 slope.

grad·u·a·tion (graj'ōō·ā'shən) *n.*
1 The act of receiving a diploma or degree

upon completion of a course of study: *high school graduation.* 2 The ceremony of presenting diplomas or degrees: *to wear a cap and gown for graduation.* 3 A mark on a measured scale: *the graduations on a yard-stick.*—**grad′u·ate** *v.*
Syn. 1 promotion. 2 commencement. 3 division.

gram·mat·i·cal·ly (grə·mat′i·kə·lē) *adv.*
According to the rules of grammar: *This sentence is grammatically correct.*—**gram·mat′i·cal** *adj.,* **gram·mat′i·cal·ness** *n.*

gran·a·ry (grā′nər·ē *or* gran′ər·ē) *n.,* **gran·a·ries** *pl.*
A storehouse for threshed grain.

gran·di·ose (gran′dē·ōs *or* gran′dē·ōs′) *adj.*
1 Impressively grand: *grandiose plans for the world's fair.* 2 Pretentiously grand: *a grandiose oration full of empty rhetoric.*
Syn. 1 magnificent, imposing, majestic. 2 pompous, inflated, high-flown.

gran·u·late (gran′yə·lāt) *v.* **gran·u·lat·ed, gran·u·lat·ing**
To form into grains; make or become granular: *granulated sugar.*—**gran′u·la′tion** *n.*

graph·ic (graf′ik) *adj.*
1 Giving an exact picture; describing in full detail: *a graphic report of the crime.* 2 Of, having to do with, or illustrated by graphs or diagrams. 3 Having to do with, made up of, or expressed by writing: *graphic signs.* 4 Of, having to do with, or like painting, drawing, engraving, etc.: *making his living in the graphic arts.*—**graph′i·cal·ly** *adv.*
Syn. 1 vivid, pictorial, picturesque.

grate·ful (grāt′fəl) *adj.*
1 Feeling or expressing gratitude: *a grateful look.* 2 Giving pleasure: *the grateful relief of an air-conditioned room on a hot summer day.*
Syn. 1 thankful, appreciative. 2 agreeable, welcome, pleasing.
Ant. 1 ungrateful, unthankful, unapprecia-tive. 2 disagreeable, unwelcome, unpleasant.

gra·tis (grā′tis *or* grat′is) *adv., adj.*
adv. Without payment: *The orphans were allowed into the theater gratis.*
adj. Free of charge: *The gratis meal served by the Salvation Army.*

gra·tu·i·tous (grə·t(y)ōō′ə·təs) *adj.*
1 Given or accepted without requirement of payment or return; gratis; free: *a gratuitous ticket to a Broadway show.* 2 Lacking cause or justification: *a gratuitous snub.*— **gra·tu′i·tous·ly** *adv.,* **gra·tu′i·tous·ness** *n.*
Syn. 2 uncalled-for, unwarranted, needless.

greas·y (grē′sē *or* grē′zē) *adj.* **greas·i·er, greas·i·est**
1 Smeared or spotted with grease: *a greasy apron.* 2 Containing much grease or fat: *applying a greasy ointment.* 3 Appearing or feeling like grease: *the greasy surface of the wet rocks.*
Syn 1 stained, grimy, dirty. 2 oily, fatty. 3 slippery, slick.

gre·gar·i·ous (gri·gâr′ē·əs) *adj.*
1 Always associating with others, as in flocks, herds, or groups. 2 Enjoying or seeking the company of others: *gregarious teen-agers always with their friends.*
Syn. 2 sociable, friendly, chummy.

gren·a·dier (gren′ə·dir′) *n.*
1 In former times, a soldier assigned to throw grenades. 2 A member of a specially consti-tuted corps or regiment, as the British Grenadier Guards.

grief (grēf) *n.*
1 Deep sorrow or mental distress: *his grief over the loss of his wife.* 2 A cause of acute sorrow.
Usage: The idiom *to come to grief* means to meet with disaster or end badly: *star-crossed lovers, doomed to come to grief.*
Spelling tip: Remember *i* before *e.*
Syn. 1 anguish, woe, heartache. 2 affliction, trial, tribulation.
Ant. 1 happiness, gladness.

griev·ance (grē′vəns) *n.*
A real or imaginary wrong regarded as a cause for complaint or resentment: *The strikers submitted a long list of grievances.*
Syn. dissatisfaction, injustice.
Ant. satisfaction.

grieve (grēv) *v.* **grieved, griev·ing**
1 To feel or suffer grief: *The widower grieved for his wife.* 2 To cause sorrow: *Her ingrati-tude grieves me.*
Syn. 1 mourn, sorrow, lament. 2 sadden, hurt, wound, trouble.
Ant. 1 rejoice, exult. 2 comfort, gladden.

griev·ous (grē′vəs) *adj.*
1 Causing grief, sorrow, or misfortune: *a grievous situation.* 2 Deserving severe punish-ment or censure: *a grievous offense.* 3 Ex-pressing grief or sorrow: *a grievous cry.* 4 Causing pain or physical suffering: *a grievous wound.*—**griev′ous·ly** *adv.,* **griev′ous·ness** *n.*
Syn. 1 distressing, oppressive. 2 serious, grave. 3 anguished, tortured. 4 severe, acute.
Ant. 1 happy, cheering. 2 trivial, minor. 3 joyful, exultant.

gri·mace (gri·mās′ *or* grim′əs) *n.; v.* **gri·maced, gri·mac·ing**
n. A distorted facial expression, usually, indicative of pain, annoyance, disgust, etc.
v. To distort the features; make faces.

gris·ly (griz′lē) *adj.* **gris·li·er, gris·li·est**
Inspiring fear or horror; macabre; grue-some.
Usage: Don't confuse *grisly* with *grizzly* or *gristly.* Something *grisly* makes one afraid: *a grisly ghost story.* That which is *grizzly* is gray or streaked with gray, as hair or beards. *Gristly* (gris′lē) pertains to *gristle,* the inedible cartilage in meat.

gris·tle (gris′əl) *n.*
A tough, elastic tissue found in meat; cartilage.—**gris′tly** *adj.*

griz·zly (griz′lē) *adj.,* **griz·zli·er, griz·zli′est;** *n*
adj. Grayish.
n. A large, brownish or grayish bear.

gro·tesque (grō·tesk′) *adj.*
Distorted, ugly, or made up of elements that

do not properly belong together: *the grotesque makeup of Boris Karloff.*—**gro·tesque′ly** *adv.*, **gro·tesque′ness** *n.*
Syn. fantastic, unnatural, misshapen, deformed.

grot·to (grot′ō) *n.*, **grot·toes** or **grot·tos** *pl.*
1 A cave. 2 An artificial cavelike structure, as for a recreational retreat, shrine, etc.

grov·el (gruv′əl *or* grov′əl) *v.* **grov·eled** or **grov·elled, grov·el·ing** or **grov·el·ling**
1 To lie prostrate or crawl face downward, as in humility or fear. 2 To behave in an excessively humble or submissive way, usually out of fear or to curry favor: *a terrified recruit groveling before the sergeant.*
Syn. 2 truckle, fawn, toady.

gru·el (grōō′əl) *n.*
A semiliquid food made by boiling cereal in water or milk.

gru·el·ing or **gru·el·ling** (grōō′əl·ing) *adj.*
So trying or tiring as to cause strain or exhaustion: *a grueling march in mountainous terrain.*
Syn. taxing, severe, arduous.

grue·some (grōō′səm) *adj.*
Causing disgust or fright: *a graphic war movie with gruesome scenes.*—**gru′some·ness** *n.*
Syn. repulsive, frightful, disgusting.

guar·an·tee (gar′ən·tē′) *n.; v.* **guar·an·teed, guar·an·tee·ing**
n. 1 A pledge or promise that something will meet stated specifications or that a specified act will be performed or continued. 2 Something that assures or seems to assure a specified condition or outcome: *Dedication is no guarantee of success in a teaching career.*
v. To assume or accept responsibility for: *to guarantee payment of a debt.*

guar·an·ty (gar′ən·tē) *n.*, **guar·an·ties** *pl.*
1 A pledge or promise to be responsible for the contract, debt, or duty of another in case of his default or miscarriage. 2 Something given or taken as security to insure that such a pledge or promise will be carried out.

guard·i·an (gär′dē·ən) *n.*, *adj.*
n. 1 A person who guards or watches over for safekeeping, preservation, confinement, etc.: *the guardians of justice.* 2 A person who is legally assigned to care for someone who is young or incompetent to care for himself.
adj. Keeping guard; protecting: *a guardian angel.*
Syn. 1 guard, custodian, trustee.

gu·ber·na·to·ri·al (gōō′bər·nə·tôr′ē·əl) *adj.*
Of or having to do with a governor or the office of governor: *the gubernatorial candidates.*

guer·ril·la (gə·ril′ə) *n.*, *adj.*
n. One of a band of fighters that is not part of a regular army. Guerrillas engage in sabotage and surprise raids, often in the rear of the enemy; partisan.
adj. Of or having to do with guerrillas or their kind of warfare: *takeover of the village by a guerrilla band.*
Spelling tip: Also spelled *guerilla.*

guess (ges) *v., n.*
v. 1 To form a judgment or opinion on uncertain or incomplete knowledge: *to guess someone's weight.* 2 To arrive at a correct answer in this way: *to guess the number of marbles in a jar.* 3 To suppose: *I guess we'll get there on time.*
n. An opinion, answer, etc., arrived at by guessing.

guf·faw (gə·fô′) *n., v.*
n. A loud burst of boisterous laughter.
v. To utter such laughter.

guile (gīl) *n.*
Treacherous cunning or craft: *a person who seemed honest but was really full of guile.*
Syn. deceit, slyness, trickery.
Ant. honesty, guilelessness, naiveté.

guile·less (gīl′lis) *adj.*
Free from treacherous cunning or craft.—**guile′less·ly** *adv.*, **guile′less·ness** *n.*
Syn. innocent, sincere, candid.
Ant. insincere, crafty, cunning.

guil·lo·tine (gil′ə·tēn or gē′ə·tēn *n.*; gil′ə·tēn′ or gil′ə·tēn *v.*) *n.; v.* **guil·lo·tined, guil·lo·tin·ing**
n. The instrument of capital punishment in France, consisting of a weighted blade that slides down between two vertical guides and beheads the victim.
v. To behead with the guillotine.

guise (gīz) *n.*
1 Style or form of dress; garb: *He appeared in the guise of a pirate.* 2 Misleading appearance; pretense: *We never expected that such betrayal would take the guise of friendship.*
Syn. 1 costume. 2 semblance, aspect.

gul·li·ble (gul′ə·bəl) *adj.*
Easily cheated or fooled: *a gullible newcomer to the city.*
Syn. unsophisticated, inexperienced, trusting.
Ant. disbelieving, distrustful, sophisticated.

gun·wale (gun′əl) *n.*
The upper edge of the side of a boat or ship.

gus·ta·to·ry (gus′tə·tôr′ē) *adj.*
Of or having to do with the sense of taste or the act of tasting: *the gustatory delights in a bakery.*

gus·to (gus′tō) *n.*
Keen enjoyment or enthusiasm: *He drank with gusto.*
Syn. zest, relish, delight.

gut·tur·al (gut′ər·əl) *adj.*
1 Having a harsh or muffled grating quality, as sounds produced in the throat: *German is considered a gutteral language.* 2 Formed with the back of the tongue touching or near the soft palate: *The "g" in "go" is a gutteral sound.*

gym·na·si·um (jim·nā′zē·əm)*n.*, **gym·na·si·ums** or **gym·na·si·a** (jim·nā′zē·ə) *pl.*
A building or room equipped for certain athletic activities or contests.

gyp·sum (jip′səm) *n.*
A mineral found in massive or granular form, used to make plaster of Paris, as a fertilizer, etc.

gy·rate (jī′rāt) *v.* **gy·rat·ed, gy·rat·ing**
To turn in a spiral or circular motion: *Elvis Presley used to gyrate when he sang.*—**gy′ra′-tor, gy·ra′tion** *n.*
Syn. rotate, revolve, swirl, whirl.

gy·ro·scope (jī′rə·skōp) *n.*
A heavy wheel, so mounted that when set to rotate at high speeds it resists all forces tending to change the angular position of its axis of rotation. Gyroscopes are used in stabilizing and navigational devices, as toys, etc.

H

ha·bil·i·ment (hə·bil′ə·mənt) *n.*
Usually pl. Clothing or attire: *to be dressed in priestly habiliments.*
Syn. garb, dress, garments, apparel, costume, clothes.

ha·bit·u·é (hə·bich′ōō·ā *or* hə·bich′ōō·ā′) *n.*
A person who often goes to a specific restaurant, club, place of amusement, etc.: *the habitués of the neighborhood tavern.*

hack·le (hak′əl) *n.*
1 One of the long, narrow feathers on the neck of a rooster, pigeon, etc. 2 *pl.* The hairs on the neck of a dog, cat, etc., that rise in anger or fear: *As we approached, the watchdog's hackles rose and he growled.*
Usage: *Hackle* is often used figuratively of people, especially in the idiom *to make someone's hackles rise* (meaning to make someone very angry): *Teasing always makes his hackles rise.*

hack·neyed (hak′nēd) *adj.*
Made commonplace and dull by too frequent use: *a hackneyed story of boy meets girl. "Haste makes waste" is a hackneyed expression.*
Syn. trite, stereotyped, common.
Ant. original, fresh, vivid.

Ha·des (hā′dēz) *n.*
1 *In Greek mythology* The underground kingdom of the dead, ruled over by the god Pluto. 2 *Informal* Hell.
Syn. 1 underworld, inferno, hell.
Ant. heaven, paradise.

hag·gard (hag′ərd) *adj.*
Having a worn or gaunt look, as from fatigue, worry, illness, hunger, etc.: *haggard from anxiety and loss of sleep.*—**hag′gard·ly** *adv.,* **hag′gard·ness** *n.*
Syn. tired, weary, exhausted.
Ant. fresh, rested.

hag·gle (hag′əl) *v.* **hag·gled, hag·gling;** *n.*
v. To argue or bargain in a petty, mean way, especially about money or terms: *to haggle over unimportant details.*
n. The act of haggling: *They became involved in a haggle over who was to pay the luncheon check.*—**hag′gler** *n.*

hal·berd (hal′bərd) *n.*
A weapon used in the fifteenth and sixteenth centuries that consisted of an ax and a spear point combined, mounted on a long pole.

half (haf *or* häf) *n.,* **halves** (havz *or* hävz) *pl. adj., adv.*
n. 1 Either of two equal or almost equal parts; also a quantity equal to such a part: *He handed me half his sandwich.* 2 *In some sports* Either of two equal periods into which a game is divided: *We left before the second half of the football game.*
adj. 1 Being half of a standard measurement: *a half gallon.* 2 Not complete; partial: *half rhyme.*
adv. 1 To the extent of a half or approximately half: *The bottle was half full.* 2 Very nearly: *He sat there half asleep.* 3 *Informal* To any extent; at all (used with *not*): *Your efforts are not half good enough.*

hal·le·lu·jah (hal′ə·lōō′yə) *interj., n.*
interj. Praise ye the Lord!
n. A musical composition whose theme is one of praise based on the word *hallelujah.*
Etymology: *Hallelujah* comes from two Hebrew words, *hallelū,* praise (imperative) and *yāh,* Jehovah.

hal·lowed (hal′ōd; *in liturgical use,* hal′ō·id) *adj.*
1 Made holy; consecrated: *to be buried in hallowed ground.* 2 Honored or regarded as holy: *hallowed saints.*—**hal′lowed·ness** *n.*
Syn. 1 sacred, sanctified, blessed. 2 venerated, revered, worshiped, holy.

ha·lo (hā′lō) *n.,* **ha·los** *or* **ha·loes** *pl.*
1 *In art* A disk or ring of light surrounding the head of a deity or holy person: *Angels are generally depicted with halos.* 2 A splendor or glory surrounding a person or thing held in reverence or great esteem: *the halo that surrounds the present-day nuclear physicist.* 3 A luminous circle around the sun or moon.
Syn. 1 nimbus, aureole.

halve (hav *or* häv) *v.* **halved, halv·ing**
1 To divide into two equal parts: *to halve an apple.* 2 To lessen by half; take away half of: *During the Depression our income was halved.*

hal·yard (hal′yərd) *n.*
Nautical A rope for hoisting or lowering a sail, a yard, or a flag.

hand·ker·chief (hang′kər·chif) *n.*
A piece of cloth, usually square, used for wiping the nose or face, or worn or carried as an ornamental accessory: *She uses tissues instead of handkerchiefs.*

han·dle (han′dəl) *v.* **han·dled, han·dling;** *n.*
v. 1 To touch, move, or hold with the hand or hands: *She handled the delicate china with care.* 2 To use the hands upon or in the operation of: *to handle clay; to handle a sailboat.* 3 To have control over; direct: *to handle one's financial affairs.* 4 To treat of or discuss: *to handle a difficult subject well.* 5 To trade or deal in: *Nowadays drugstores handle many items besides drugs.* 6 To respond to manipulation or control: *This car handles well.*
n. The part of an object to be grasped by the hand: *the handle of a frying pan.*—**hand′ler** *n.*

hand·some (han′səm) *adj.* **hand·som·er, hand·som·est**
1 Pleasing or well-proportioned in appear-

ance, especially in a manly or stately way: *a handsome man; a handsome dowager queen.* **2** Considerable in quantity: *a handsome donation to charity.* **3** Gracious; generous: *a handsome gesture.*—**hand'some·ly** *adv.,* **hand'some·ness** *n.*
Syn. 1 good-looking, attractive. **2** generous, liberal. **3** kindly, courteous.
Ant. 1 ugly, unattractive. **2** stingy, skimpy. **3** ignoble, selfish.

hang (hang) *v.* **hung** or **hanged, hanging**; *n.*
v. **1** To fasten or be supported from above: *Hang up your coat.* **2** To droop: *Hang your head in shame.* **3** To put to death or to die by suspending with a noose around the neck: *The murderer is to hang next week.* **4** To cause a jury to be unable to reach a decision. **5** To pay close attention: *The audience hung on the speaker's words.* **6** To depend: *His promotion hangs on his boss's recommendation.*
n. **1** The way in which a thing hangs; drape: *the hang of a coat.* **2** *Informal* A knack or way of doing something: *The boy finally got the hang of riding a bicycle.*

han·gar (hang'ər) *n.*
A shelter or workshop for aircraft: *Many jet planes are too large to enter a hangar.*

hap·less (hap'lis) *adj.*
Having no luck; unfortunate: *a hapless child deserted by his parents.*—**hap'less·ly** *adv.,* **hap'less·ness** *n.*
Syn. unlucky, miserable, wretched.
Ant. lucky, favored, fortunate.

hap·pen (hap'ən) *v.*
1 To take place or occur: *The battle happened in 1943.* **2** To occur by chance rather than by plan: *We happened to meet.* **3** To become of: *What happened to him?*—**hap'pen·ing** *n.*

har·ass (har'əs or hə·ras') *v.*
1 To trouble with cares, annoyances, etc.: *harassed by too many demands upon his time.* **2** To worry or annoy an enemy by constant raids and attacks: *Indian tribes harassed the homesteaders in the early West.*—**har'ass·er,** **har'ass·ment** *n.*
Syn. 1 bother, plague, fatigue. **2** besiege, harry, terrorize.
Ant. 1 refresh, comfort, solace, soothe.

har·bin·ger (här'bin·jər) *n., v.*
n. A person or thing that goes before and announces the coming of something: *The crocus is a harbinger of spring.*
v. To act as a harbinger; presage: *The collapse of the stock market harbingered the Great Depression of the 1930s.*
Syn. *n.* herald, precursor, forerunner. *v.* herald, foretell, predict, foreshadow.

har·le·quin (här'lə·kwin) *n., adj.*
n. **1** (Capital *H*) A pantomime character traditionally dressed in parti-colored tights and a mask, and having a shaved head. **2** A clown or buffoon.
adj. Parti-colored or motley, like the costume of a Harlequin: *a harlequin sweater.*
Syn. *n.* **2** jester, entertainer, fool, comedian.

har·mo·ni·ous (här·mō'nē·əs) *adj.*
1 Made up of sounds, colors, or other

elements that combine agreeably: *the harmonious décor of a room.* **2** Agreeing in points of view, attitudes, feelings, etc.: *a harmonious family group in which there was little dissension.* **3** Pleasing to the ear: *harmonious voices.*—**har·mo'ni·ous·ly** *adv.,* **har·mo'ni·ous·ness** *n.*
Syn. 1 tasteful, artistic, attractive. **2** congenial, compatible. **3** melodious, euphonious, tuneful.
Ant. 1 garish, harsh, clashing. **2** quarrelsome, hostile. **3** discordant, grating.

har·row (har'ō) *n., v.*
n. A farm implement set with spikes or disks for leveling plowed ground, breaking up clods of earth, etc.
v. **1** To use a harrow upon: *to harrow a corn field.* **2** To upset the mind or feelings of someone; distress: *harrowed by lack of money and mounting debts.*—**har'row·er** *n.,* **har'row·ing** *adj.,* **har'row·ing·ly** *adv.*
Syn. *v.* **2** afflict, burden, agonize, torment.

har·ry (har'ē) *v.* **har·ried, har·ry·ing**
1 To lay waste, as in war or invasion; sack: *The Danes harried many parts of England in the Dark Ages.* **2** To harass or persecute a person: *The big boys always harry the smaller ones.*
Syn. 1 pillage, plunder, ravage, devastate. **2** annoy, torment, tease.

haunch (hônch or hänch) *n.*
1 In man and animals, the part of the body consisting of the upper thigh including the hip and buttock: *Cats and dogs sit on their haunches.* **2** The back leg and loin of an animal considered as meat: *a haunch of beef.*—**haunched** *adj.*

haut·boy (hō'boi or ō'boi) *n.*
An oboe.
Etymology: *Hautboy* comes from two French words, *haut* meaning high (in tone) and *bois,* wood.

hau·teur (hō·tûr') *n.*
A haughty manner or attitude; arrogance: *the hauteur of the newly rich.*
Syn. snobbishness, haughtiness.
Ant. meekness, modesty.

have·n't (hav'ənt) *contraction*
Have not: *We haven't heard from him.*
Spelling tip: In contractions, the apostrophe takes the place of the missing letter or letters: *does not* becomes *doesn't, cannot* changes to *can't,* and *I will* is written *I'll.*

haz·ard·ous (haz'ər·dəs) *adj.*
Full of or involving danger, risk, loss, etc.: *A test pilot has a hazardous job. Gambling is a hazardous way to make a living.*—**haz'ard·ous·ly** *adv.,* **haz'ard·ous·ness** *n.*
Syn. dangerous, perilous, unsafe.
Ant. safe, secure, prudent.

hec·tic (hek'tik) *adj.*
Characterized by haste, helter-skelter, excitement, or turmoil: *a hectic day at the office trying to meet last-minute deadlines.*—**hec'ti·cal·ly** *adv.*
Syn. feverish, frantic, frenzied.
Ant. slow, calm, tranquil, relaxed.

he·don·ism (hēd'n·iz'əm) *n.*
1 The philosophical doctrine that pleasure is the only good and proper goal of moral endeavor. 2 The self-indulgent pursuit of pleasure: *the hedonism of the idle rich.*—**he'·don·ist** *n.*, **he'don·is'tic** *adj.*, **he'don·is'ti·cal·ly** *adv.*
Syn. 2 epicureanism, sensualism, debauchery.
Ant. 2 temperance, abstemiousness, self-restraint.

heed·less (hēd'lis) *adj.*
Not showing any attention; careless or reckless: *The driver was heedless of local speed limits.*—**heed'less·ly** *adv.*, **heed'less·ness** *n.*
Syn. thoughtless, unmindful, negligent.
Ant. careful, cautious, attentive.

heif·er (hef'ər) *n.*
A young cow that has not yet produced a calf.
Spelling tip: This is another exception to the rule *i* before *e* except after *c*, or when sounded as *a*.

height (hīt) *n.*
1 The state or quality of being high or relatively high: *a tree of great height.* 2 The distance from the bottom to the top: *What is the height of the Washington Monument?* 3 *Often pl.* A lofty or high place: *They went up into the heights to ski.* 4 The distance above a given level, as the ground or sea level; altitude: *a plane flying at a height of 30,000 feet.* 5 The highest part of anything; summit or apex: *the height of the social season.* 6 The highest degree: *the height of quality.*

hei·nous (hā'nəs) *adj.*
Extremely wicked or evil; atrocious: *a heinous murder.*—**hei'nous·ly** *adv.*, **hei'nous·ness** *n.*
Syn. odious, infamous, villainous.

heir (âr) *n.*
A person who inherits rank or property from someone who has died; also, any person likely to inherit such rank or property.

hel·i·cop·ter (hel'ə·kop'tər) *n.*
A type of aircraft with engine-driven horizontal blades that rotate around a vertical axis. Helicopters can rise and descend vertically, hover, and fly in any direction.

he·li·o·trope (hē'lē·ə·trōp') *n., adj.*
n. 1 A plant with white or purplish fragrant flowers. 2 A soft, rosy purple color.
adj. Soft, rosy purple: *heliotrope draperies.*

he·li·um (hē'lē·əm) *n.*
An odorless, nonflammable, gaseous element that is found chiefly in certain natural gas deposits, used to inflate balloons, dirigibles, etc.

helm (helm) *n., v.*
n. 1 The steering apparatus of a vessel, especially the tiller or wheel. 2 Any place of control or responsibility: *a small company with a brilliant administrator at the helm.*
v. To manage the helm of; steer or direct.

hem·or·rhage (hem'ər·ij) *n., v.*
n. A heavy flow of blood from a blood vessel, especially one that has ruptured.
v. To bleed copiously.

her·ald (her'əld) *n., v.*
n. 1 Any bearer of important news: *A herald brought word of the king's death.* 2 Someone or something that announces or indicates what is to follow: *The first crocus is a herald of spring.*
v. To announce, foretell, or usher in: *Faraway thunder heralded the approaching storm.*
Syn. *n.* 1 messenger, announcer, courier. 2 harbinger, forerunner, precursor. *v.* proclaim, inform, foreshadow.

her·ald·ry (her'əl·drē) *n.*, **her·ald·ries** *pl.*
1 The art or occupation that has to do with coats of arms, including their design and execution and the tracing of family genealogies that bear upon the right to use a coat of arms. 2 A coat of arms or a collection of such ensigns. 3 Formal ceremony and pageantry, especially with a display of heraldic devices.

herb·age (ûr'bij *or* hûr'bij) *n.*
Grass or other green field plants used for grazing animals.

her·bar·i·um (hûr·bâr'ē·əm) *n.*, **her·bar·i·ums** *or* **her·bar·i·a** (hûr·bâr'ē·ə) *pl.*
1 A collection of dried plants scientifically arranged. 2 A room or building containing such a collection.

her·cu·le·an (hûr·kyōō'lē·ən *or* hûr'kyə·lē'ən) *adj.*
1 Possessing great strength, daring, perseverance, etc.: *a herculean laborer.* 2 Requiring great strength, daring, perseverance, etc.: *Rebuilding London after World War II was a herculean task.* 3 (Capital *H*) Having to do with Hercules: *Herculean myths.*
Etymology: This word comes from Hercules, a hero of classical mythology noted for his great strength and endurance.
Syn. 1 rugged, enduring, steadfast. 2 arduous, rigorous.

her·e·sy (her'ə·sē) *n.*, **her·e·sies** *pl.*
1 A belief or opinion contrary to the accepted doctrine of a church, political organization, professional group, etc.: *The liberal's ideas were heresy to the conservative wing of his party.* 2 The holding of such a belief or opinion: *to be guilty of heresy.*
Syn. 2 dissent, nonconformity, schism, apostasy, disbelief.

her·e·tic (her'ə·tik) *n.*
A person who holds beliefs or opinions contrary to the established doctrines of his religion, political party, profession, etc.
Syn. schismatic, dissenter, nonconformist, apostate, separatist, deserter.

her·met·ic (hûr·met'ik) *adj.*
Impervious to gases or liquids; airtight: *a hermetic seal.*—**her·met'i·cal·ly** *adv.*

her·mit·age (hûr'mə·tij) *n.*
1 The retreat or dwelling place of a hermit. 2 Any secluded dwelling place.
Syn. 2 cloister, hideaway, haven.

he·ro·ic (hi·rō'ik) *adj.*
1 Of, having to do with, like, or suitable to a hero: *a heroic warrior.* 2 Relating to or

describing a hero or heroic deeds; epic: *heroic poetry.*—**he·ro'i·cal·ly** *adv.*
Syn. 1 brave, fearless, dauntless.
Ant. cowardly.

her·o·ine (her'ō·in) *n.*
1 A girl or woman of heroic character; the female counterpart of a hero. 2 The principal female character of a drama, fictional work, etc.

her·on (her'ən) *n.*
Any of several wading birds, having a long neck, a long slender bill, and long legs.

het·er·o·ge·ne·ous (het'ər·ə·jē'nē·əs) *adj.*
Made up of parts or elements that are not alike, not unified, not compatible, or not in proportion: *a heterogeneous society.*—**het'er·o·ge'ne·ous·ly** *adv.,* **het'er·o·ge'ne·ous·ness** *n.*
Syn. dissimilar, incongruous, various, mixed.
Ant. homogeneous, uniform, similar, compatible.

hi·a·tus (hī·ā'təs) *n.,* **hi·a·tus·es** or **hi·a·tus** *pl.*
1 A gap or space from which something is missing, as in a manuscript. 2 Any break or interruption of continuity: *During the summer hiatus on TV, reruns are often shown.*

hi·ber·nal (hī·bûr'nəl) *adj.*
Of or having to do with winter; wintry.

hi·ber·nate (hī'bər·nāt) *v.* **hi·ber·nat·ed, hi·ber·nat·ing**
To pass the winter in a dormant state, as certain animals do.—**hi'ber·na'tion** *n.*

hic·cup (hik'əp) *n.; v.* **hic·cuped** or **hic·cupped, hic·cup·ing** or **hic·cup·ping**
n. 1 An involuntary contraction of the diaphragm, causing a sudden gasp of breath that is immediately checked by a spasm in the throat. 2 *pl.* A condition in which such spasms are repeated.
v. To undergo such a spasm or spasms.
Spelling tip: This word is also spelled *hiccough.*

hi·er·ar·chy (hī'ə·rär'kē) *n.,* **hi·er·ar·chies** *pl.*
1 Any group of persons or things arranged in successive orders or classes, each of which is subject to or dependent on the one above it. 2 A group of clergymen arranged in this way.

hi·er·o·glyph·ic (hī'ər·ə·glif'ik or hī'rə·glif'ik) *n.*
1 A picture or symbol representing an object, idea, or sound, as in the writing system of the ancient Egyptians. 2 *pl.* A system of writing using such pictures or symbols. 3 *pl.* Writing that for some reason is difficult to read: *a druggist trying to decipher the hieroglyphics of a doctor.*

hi·lar·i·ous (hi·lâr'ē·əs or hī·lâr'ē·əs) *adj.*
Characterized by or providing exuberant, noisy merriment: *a hilarious play.*—**hi·lar'i·ous·ly** *adv.,* **hi·lar'i·ous·ness** *n.*
Syn. boisterous, mirthful, jolly.

hi·lar·i·ty (hi·lar'ə·tē or hī·lar'ə·tē) *n.,* **hi·lar·i·ties** *pl.*
Very exuberant and noisy merriment: *The hilarity of the party was contagious, and each new guest was suddenly dissolved in laughter.*

hind·most (hīnd'mōst') *adj.*
Farthest from the front; most to the rear.

hin·drance (hin'drəns) *n.*
1 The act of delaying or thwarting. 2 Someone or something that delays or thwarts: *Lack of education is a hindrance to advancement.*
Syn. 1 retardation, restriction, restraint, prohibition. 2 obstacle, impediment, encumbrance, obstruction.
Ant. 1 cooperation, assistance, collaboration, support. 2 aid, help, asset, contribution.

hip·po·pot·a·mus (hip'ə·pot'ə·məs) *n.,* **hip·po·pot·a·mus·es** or **hip·po·pot·a·mi** (hip'ə·pot'ə·mī) *pl.*
A large, plant-eating mammal having four short legs and a thick-skinned, hairless body, found in and near African rivers.
Etymology: A *hippopotamus* is literally a river horse, from the Greek *hippos* (horse) and *potamos* (river).

hire·ling (hīr'ling) *n.*
A person who works for wages; especially, one who does something unpleasant or reprehensible for no reason except the wages he receives.
Syn. flunky, hack, mercenary.

hir·sute (hûr'sōōt or hûr·sōōt') *adj.*
Covered with hair or bristles; hairy; shaggy: —**hir'sute·ness** *n.*

his·tri·on·ic (his'trē·on'ik) *adj.*
1 Of or having to do with actors or acting: *histrionic ability that was more at home on stage than before the camera.* 2 Overly dramatic; affectedly emotional: *her embarrassing histrionic display at the wedding.*
Syn. 1 dramatic, theatrical. 2 flamboyant, melodramatic.

hoarse (hôrs) *adj.*
Deep, harsh, and grating in sound, as the voice of a person with a cold, the croaking of frogs, etc.—**hoarse'ly** *adv.,* **hoarse'ness** *n.*
Syn. husky, gruff, throaty, raucous, guttural.

hoar·y (hôr'ē) *adj.* **hoar·i·er, hoar·i·est**
1 White or whitish gray, as from age: *tired old men with hoary locks.* 2 White or whitish in color: *hoary foam.* 3 Very old, and usually impressive or venerable: *a hoary Roman wall.* 4 So old, familiar, or used as to be hackneyed: *a hoary joke.*—**hoar'i·ness** *n.*
Syn. 3 ancient, aged, antique. 4 trite, stale, clichéd.

hoi pol·loi (hoi' pə·loi')
An expression taken from the Greek, meaning the common people. It is usually used in a contemptuous way, and it is preceded by a redundant *the: a politician who, in private, always referred to voters as "the hoi polloi."*
Syn. masses, herd, crowd, riffraff.
Ant. elite, society.

hol·o·caust (hol'ə·kôst) *n.*
Vast destruction, especially by fire, and usually accompanied by great loss of life: *preoccupation with the threat of nuclear holocaust.*
Syn. conflagration, devastation, ruin.

home·spun (hōm'spun') *adj.*
Plain and simple: *homespun humor.*
Syn. unsophisticated, humble.
Ant. pretentious, sophisticated, fancy.

hom·i·ly (hom'ə·lē) *n.*, **hom·i·lies** *pl.*
1 A sermon based on a Biblical text. 2 A
solemn discourse or reproof, especially on
morals or conduct: *a homily on the subject of
modesty of dress.*
Syn. 2 lecture, talk.

ho·mo·ge·ne·ous (hō'mə·jē'nē·əs *or* hom'ə·
jē'nē·əs) *adj.*
Having the same composition, structure, or
character throughout: *a homogeneous society.*
Syn. uniform, consistent, harmonious, regular.
Ant. heterogeneous, mixed.

hon·or·ar·i·um (on'ə·râr'ē·əm) *n.*, **hon·or·ar·i·
ums** or **hon·or·ar·i·a** *pl.*
A payment given, as to a professional man,
for services rendered when law, custom, or
propriety forbid a set fee: *an honorarium for
the physicist's lengthy book review in the
professional journal.*

hoof (hŏof *or* hōof) *n.*, **hoofs** or **hooves** (hŏovz
or hōovz) *pl.*
1 The horny sheath encasing the foot of
certain mammals, as horses and cattle. 2 The
entire foot of such an animal.

hors d'oeuvre (ôr dûrv'; *French* ôr dœ'vr')
An appetizer, as olives, celery, etc., generally
served before a meal.

ho·sier·y (hō'zhər·ē) *n.*
Stockings and socks: *a store specializing in
women's hosiery.*

hos·pi·ta·ble (hos'pi·tə·bəl *or* hos·pit'ə·bəl)
adj.
1 Acting in a kind and generous manner toward guests. 2 Expressing such a manner: *a
hospitable welcome.*
Syn. gracious, warm, friendly, welcoming.
Ant. cold, reserved, aloof, standoffish.

hos·tile (hos'təl; *esp. British* hos'tīl) *adj.*
Expressing enmity or characteristic of an
enemy; antagonistic: *The blockade was viewed
as a hostile act.*—**hos·til'i·ty** *n.*

hour (our) *n.*
1 A span of time equal to 1/24 of a day;
sixty minutes. 2 A definite time of day: *The
hour is 6:15.* 3 *pl.* A set period of time, as for
work: *office hours.*
Spelling tip: Remember the *h* in *hour.*

hov·el (huv'əl *or* hov'əl) *n.*
A small, wretched dwelling: *The poverty-
striken tenant farmers lived in hovels.*
Syn. shack, hut, shanty.
Ant. palace, mansion.

how·it·zer (hou'it·sər) *n.*
A cannon with a barrel of medium length
that operates at a relatively high angle of
fire.
Etymology: *Howitzer* comes from a Dutch
word that goes back ultimately to the
Czechoslovakian *houfnice*, which means
"catapult."

hoy·den (hoid'n) *n.*
A boisterous or ill-mannered girl; tomboy:
*As soon as the teacher left the room, the girls
began to act like blue-jeaned hoydens.*

hub·bub (hub'ub) *n.*
A loud, confused uproar, as of many voices:
*We could barely hear the speaker over the
hubbub of shouted questions.*
Syn. clatter, clamor, to-do, racket.
Ant. quiet, serenity, stillness, silence.

hu·mane (hyōō·mān') *adj.*
Having or characterized by kindness,
sympathy, tenderness, etc.: *a humane social
worker who cared about each individual client.*
Syn. compassionate, benevolent, good.
Ant. cruel, callous, heartless.

hum·drum (hum'drum') *adj.*
Tedious and dull: *a humdrum existence that
nearly drove him mad.*
Syn. uninteresting, boring, monotonous.
Ant. exciting, interesting, challenging.

hu·mor (hyōō'mər) *n.*, *v.*
n. 1 The quality of anything that seems
funny or comical: *devoid of humor.* 2 The
ability to appreciate this quality. 3 A
temporary state of mind or feeling: *to be in
good humor.*
v. To go along with the moods or desires of
someone; indulge: *We humored the child and
said he was indeed very, very strong, since it
pleased him to think so.*—**hum'or·ous** *adj.*
Syn. *n.* 3 mood, temperament, disposition.

hu·mus (hyōō'məs) *n.*
The black or brown substance of the soil,
formed by the decay of animal and vegetable
matter, and providing nutrition for plant life.

hun·gry (hung'grē) *adj.* **hung·ri·er, hung·ri·est**
1 Desiring or in need of food. 2 Showing or
characterized by hunger or craving: *a lean
and hungry look.*
Syn. 1 starved, famished. 2 yearning,
desirous.
Ant. 1 satiated, sated, full, stuffed.

hur·ri·cane (hûr'ə·kān) *n.*
A tropical cyclone, especially one originating
in the West Indies, having a wind velocity of
over 75 miles per hour.

hur·ried·ly (hûr'ēd·lē) *adv.*
In a rushed manner; hastily: *He spoke so
hurriedly, in his rush to be off, that we could
scarcely understand him.*
Syn. quickly, rapidly, fast.
Ant. leisurely, unhurriedly, slow.

hus·band·ry (huz'bən·drē) *n.*
The occupation or business of farming:
hundreds of acres devoted to husbandry.
Syn. agriculture.

hus·tle (hus'əl) *v.* **hus·tled, hus·tling;** *n.*
v. 1 To push or force: *to hustle an intruder
outside.* 2 *Informal* To move or work with
great energy: *The manager implored his team
to hustle.*
n. Informal Energetic activity: *The team
showed a lot of hustle but not much skill.*
Syn. *v.* 1 thrust, jostle, crowd. *n.* get-up-and-
go, vigor, vim, effort.
Ant. *v.* 2 take it easy, malinger. *n.* laziness,
lethargy, lassitude.

hy·brid (hī'brid) *n.*
An animal or plant produced by a male and female of different species, varieties, or breeds: *hybrid corn.*—**hy'brid·ism, hy·brid'i·ty** *n.*

hy·dran·ge·a (hī·drān'jē·ə *or* hī·drān'jə) *n.*
A tree or shrub having opposite leaves and large clusters of white, blue, or pink flowers.

hy·drant (hī'drənt) *n.*
A large, upright pipe connected to a water main, used for firefighting.
Syn. fireplug.

hy·dro·gen (hī'drə·jən) *n.*
The lightest of the elements (symbol: H), an odorless, colorless, flammable gas, occurring in water and uniting chemically with many elements.

hy·giene (hī'jēn) *n.*
The science dealing with the preservation of health.

hymn (him) *n., v.*
n. A song of praise, adoration, thanksgiving, etc., especially one sung at a religious service.
v. To sing hymns or praise with hymns.

hy·per·crit·i·cal (hī'pər·krit'i·kəl) *adj.*
Overly critical: *An astute judge of movies, he tended however to be hypercritical.*
Syn. carping, faultfinding, captious.

hy·po·chon·dri·a (hī'pə·kon'drē·ə) *n.*
A persistent anxiety about one's health, usually involving imagined symptoms of illness.

hy·po·chon·dri·ac (hī'pə·kon'drē·ak) *n., adj.*
n. A person subject to hypochondria.
adj. Pertaining to or affected with hypochondria: *a hypochondriac patient.*

hy·poc·ri·sy (hi·pok'rə·sē) *n.,* **hy·poc·ri·sies** *pl.*
The pretense of having feelings or qualities that one really does not have: *It was sheer hypocrisy to act surprised when she knew very well it was going to happen.*
Syn. dissembling, insincerity, deceit, falseness.
Ant. honesty, straightforwardness, integrity.

hyp·o·crite (hip'ə·krit) *n.*
One who practices hypocrisy: *No hypocrite, he practiced what he preached.*
Syn. deceiver, dissembler.

hyp·o·crit·i·cal (hip'ə·krit'ə·kəl) *adj.*
Pertaining to or characterized by hypocrisy: *a hypocritical attitude.*
Syn. two-faced, insincere, deceitful.
Ant. honest, straightforward.

hy·poth·e·sis (hī·poth'ə·sis *or* hi·poth'ə·sis) *n.,* **hy·poth·e·ses** *pl.*
An idea tentatively assumed to be true for the sake of argument or of further study: *the hypothesis that racial prejudice is increased by segregated housing.*

hy·po·thet·i·cal (hī'pə·thet'i·kəl) *adj.*
Based on hypothesis or on supposition; theoretical or imaginary: *the hypothetical situation of winning the sweepstakes.*
Syn. conjectural, suppositive, academic.
Ant. actual.

I

i·bis (ī'bis) *n.,* **i·bis·es** or **i·bis** *pl.*
One of various wading birds that are related to the heron, especially the sacred ibis venerated by the ancient Egyptians: *The ibis has a long bill that curves downward.*

i·ci·cle (ī'si·kəl) *n.*
A hanging, tapering rod of ice formed by the freezing of drops of dripping water.

ic·ing (ī'sing) *n.*
A smooth glaze of sugar, butter, egg whites, etc., used as a coating for cakes.
Syn. frosting.

i·con (ī'kon) *n.*
1 In the Eastern Orthodox Church, a pictorial representation of Jesus Christ, the Virgin Mary, or some other sacred figure, to which veneration is offered: *an icon of a saint.*
2 A picture or other image of someone or something: *a painted icon.*
Spelling tip: This word is also spelled *ikon* and *eikon.*
Syn. 2 representation.

i·con·o·clast (ī·kon'ə·klast) *n.*
One who attacks or ridicules conventional or cherished beliefs or institutions as being false or harmful: *an iconoclast who made fun of patriotism.*

i·con·o·clas·tic (ī·kon'ə·klas'tik) *adj.*
Characterized by overt contempt for conventional or cherished ideas, institutions, etc.: *an iconoclastic writer who ridicules patriotism.*

i·de·al (ī·dē'əl *or* ī·dēl') *n., adj.*
n. 1 A concept of what something would be like if it were perfect: *The ideal of completeness is often symbolized by a snake with its tail in its mouth.* 2 An ethical standard or principle: *to live up to one's ideals.* 3 A perfect model; an exemplar: *His teacher is his ideal.* 4 Something that exists only in the mind as a concept: *the ideal of a peaceful world.*
adj. 1 Embodying a standard of absolute perfection, or existing only in the mind as a concept of absolute perfection: *the ideal society.* 2 Representing the best of its kind; completely desirable: *an ideal husband.*
Syn. *adj.* 1 model, perfect, utopian. 2 perfect, excellent, best.

i·dée fixe (ē·dā' fēks') *n.,* **i·dées fixes** *pl.*
A fixed idea, as a delusion or obsession: *an idée fixe that he was of royal blood.*

i·den·ti·ty (ī·den'ti·tē) *n.,* **i·den·ti·ties** *pl.*
1 The fact of being a specific person or thing and no other: *His passport established his identity.* 2 The state of being the same thing; complete similarity or complete union: *the identity of the handwriting in two letters.* 3 The unity and self-awareness of the personality: *his sense of identity.*
Syn. 2 unity, sameness, oneness, correspondence.
Ant. 2 difference, separateness.

ides (īdz) *n., pl.*
In the ancient Roman calendar, the fifteenth day of March, May, July, and October and

the thirteenth day of the other eight months: *Beware the ides of March.*

id·i·o·syn·cra·sy (id'ē·ō·sing'krə·sē) *n.*, **id·i·o·syn·cra·sies** *pl.*
A habit, mannerism, reaction, etc., that is peculiar to an individual; especially, an odd, atypical, or eccentric trait: *an idiosyncrasy such as using a sundial instead of a clock.*
Syn. quirk, peculiarity, eccentricity, abnormality.

i·dle (īd'l) *adj.* **i·dler, i·dlest;** *v.* **i·dled, i·dling** *adj.* **1** Not active or in operation: *machinery idle during a strike.* **2** Lazy; avoiding work: *an idle rogue.* **3** Having no value; ineffectual, of no importance, or ungrounded: *an idle threat; idle chatter.*
v. **1** To spend time doing nothing or engaged in pointless, trivial activities: *to spend a morning idling.* **2** To wander or loiter lazily and aimlessly: *to idle along the riverbank.* **3** To operate without power at reduced speed: *to idle a motor.*
Spelling tip: Be careful to differentiate between *idle, idyl,* and *idol* (all pronounced the same).

i·dol (īd'l) *n.*
1 An image or object representing or considered to be a god and worshiped as having divine powers: *to pay homage to a huge golden idol representing the sun god.* **2** Someone who is loved or admired to an excessive degree; an object of infatuation: *She is his idol.*
Syn. 1 fetish. **2** goddess, god.

i·dol·a·try (ī·dol'ə·trē) *n.*, **i·dol·a·tries** *pl.*
1 The worship of idols: *the idolatry of primitive people who pray to a carved statue.* **2** Excessive or undiscerning admiration or reverence; blind infatuation: *She adores him to the point of idolatry.*
Syn. 1 idolism. **2** hero worship, infatuation.

i·dyl (īd'l) *n.*
1 A short poem or prose piece depicting simple and pleasant scenes of pastoral, country, or domestic life. **2** Any scene or event whose simple charm might inspire an idyl.—**i·dyl'ic** *adj.*
Spelling tip: This word may also be spelled *idyll.*

i.e. (ī'ē')
The abbreviation for the Latin term *id est,* meaning "that is": *His nationality is American, i.e., he is a citizen of the U.S.*

ig·no·ble (ig·nō'bəl) *adj.*
Dishonorable and contemptible; base: *an ignoble betrayal of his best friend.*
Syn. mean, shameful, vile, despicable.
Ant. noble, honorable, high-minded.

ig·no·min·i·ous (ig'nə·min'ē·əs) *adj.*
Involving dishonor or disgrace; dishonorable, despicable, or humiliating: *an ignominious defeat.*
Syn. shameful, degrading.
Ant. honorable, dignified, illustrious.

ig·no·min·y (ig'nə·min'ē) *n.*, **ig·no·min·ies** *pl.*
Public disgrace and dishonor: *the ignominy of losing a war to a tiny, ill-equipped army.*

Syn. shame, humiliation, stigma.
Ant. honor, glory, distinction.

ig·no·ra·mus (ig'nə·rā'məs *or* ig'nə·ram'əs) *n.*, **ig·no·ra·mus·es** *pl.*
An ignorant person: *He's such an ignoramus he doesn't even know that China's in Asia.*
Syn. dolt, dunce, dope.
Ant. genius, prodigy, scholar.

ig·no·rant (ig'nər·ənt) *adj.*
1 Having little or no learning or knowledge; uneducated: *an ignorant man who had left school after the fourth grade.* **2** Lacking information about; unaware of: *to be ignorant of a fact.* **3** Indicating a lack of information: *an ignorant superstition.*
Syn. 1 unlettered, unschooled, illiterate. **2** uninformed, unaware. **3** naive.
Ant. 1 learned, educated. **2** informed, aware.

i·gua·na (i·gwä'nə) *n.*
Any of several tropical American lizards that sometimes attain a length of six feet.

il·leg·i·ble (i·lej'ə·bəl) *adj.*
Not capable of being read: *an illegible scrawl.*
—**il·leg'i·bly** *adv.*
Spelling tip: Be careful and don't confuse *illegible* (not legible) with *ineligible* (not eligible) and *unintelligible* (not intelligible).
Syn. indecipherable, unreadable.
Ant. legible, readable, decipherable.

il·lic·it (i·lis'it) *adj.*
Not permitted by law, rule, or custom: *illicit traffic in drugs; an illicit love affair.*—**il·lic'it·ly** *adv.*
Spelling tip: Be careful and don't confuse the adjective *illicit* (not lawful) with the verb *elicit* (to draw or call forth).
Syn. illegal, unauthorized, forbidden, improper.
Ant. legal, proper, licit.

il·lit·er·a·cy (i·lit'ər·ə·sē) *n.*, **il·lit·er·a·cies** *pl.*
Lack of education, especially inability to read and write: *the widespread illiteracy in Asia.*
Ant. literacy.

il·lu·sion (i·lōō'zhən) *n.*
1 A false, misleading, or overly optimistic idea: *to lose one's youthful illusions.* **2** A deceiving appearance or the false impression it gives: *an optical illusion.*
Etymology: *Illusion* is derived from the Latin verb *ludere,* meaning to play, mock, or jeer.
Syn. 1 misconception, delusion. **2** mirage, chimera.
Ant. 1 truth, verity.

il·lus·tra·tive (i·lus'trə·tiv *or* il'ə·strā'tiv) *adj.*
Serving to illustrate: *an illustrative diagram.*

il·lus·tra·tor (il'ə·strā'tər) *n.*
An artist who does illustrations for books.

il·lus·tri·ous (i·lus'trē·əs) *adj.*
1 Very famous and highly distinguished: *an illustrious statesman.* **2** Bringing greatness or glory: *The poet sang of illustrious deeds.*
Syn. 1 great, eminent, notable, renowned. **2** glorious, noble, brilliant, splendid.
Ant. 1 ordinary, undistinguished, obscure.

im·age·ry (im'ij·rē) *n.*, **im·age·ries** *pl.*
Images, especially word pictures or figures of speech in poetry: *the rich imagery of his poetry.*

im·ag·i·nar·y (i·maj'ə·ner'ē) *adj.*
Existing only in the imagination; unreal: *an imaginary creature such as a leprechaun.*
Syn. fancied, fantastic, fictional.
Ant. real, actual.

im·ag·ine (i·maj'in) *v.* **im·ag·ined, im·ag·in·ing**
1 To form a mental picture or idea of: *Try to imagine how a cave man must have lived.* **2** To suppose, guess, or conjecture: *I imagine I'll be able to go.*
Syn. 1 picture, visualize, conceive. **2** think, believe.
Ant. 2 doubt.

im·bibe (im·bīb') *v.* **im·bibed, im·bib·ing**
1 To drink, especially to drink an alcoholic beverage: *He imbibed too much whiskey.* **2** To suck up as if drinking: *The soil was imbibing the rain.* **3** To absorb mentally: *Scholars imbibe learning.*
Syn. 1 quaff, swig. **2, 3** drink in, absorb, ingest, soak up.

im·bue (im·byoo') *v.* **im·bued, im·bu·ing**
1 To pervade or permeate, as with ideals, emotions, etc.: *to be imbued with the spirit of democracy.* **2** To saturate, as with color or moisture: *to soak cloth in a dye until it is imbued with color.*

im·i·ta·tion (im'ə·tā'shən) *n., adj.*
n. **1** The act of copying or mimicking: *his imitation of an orchestra conductor.* **2** A copy: *The imitation was almost identical to the original.*
adj. Resembling or made to resemble something superior: *an imitation diamond.*
Syn. *n.* **1** mimicry, simulation, emulation. **2** duplicate, facsimile, counterfeit. *adj.* mock, pseudo, sham, counterfeit, ersatz.
Ant. *n.* **2** original, model. *adj.* real, genuine, original.

im·mac·u·late (i·mak'yə·lit) *adj.*
1 Completely clean: *With two maids, her house was always immaculate.* **2** Completely unsullied; without sin or blemish: *an immaculate life.*
Syn. 1 spotless, spick-and-span. **2** stainless, pure, untainted.
Ant. 1 dirty, filthy. **2** stained, tainted, defiled.

im·me·di·ate·ly (i·mē'dē·it·lē) *adv.*
1 Without delay; instantly: *Come home immediately.* **2** In close relation; with nothing between: *Immediately beyond our yard is a parking lot.*
Syn. 1 instantaneously, at once. **2** directly, proximately.
Ant. 1 later, belatedly. **2** far.

im·mense (i·mens') *adj.*
Extremely large; huge: *an immense boulder.*
Syn. mammoth, gigantic, enormous.
Ant. small, tiny, diminutive.

im·mi·grate (im'ə·grāt) *v.* **im·mi·grat·ed, im·mi·grat·ing**

To come into a country or region of which one is not a native in order to settle there; migrate.—**im'mi·gra'tion, im'mi·grant** *n.*

im·mi·nence (im'ə·nəns) *n.*
The state or quality of being imminent; nearness: *a driver unaware of the imminence of danger on the icy road.*
Ant. distance, remoteness.

im·mi·nent (im'ə·nənt) *adj.*
About to happen: said especially of danger or catastrophe: *safety preparations against the imminent hurricane.*—**im'mi·nent·ly** *adv.*
Syn. threatening, impending, coming, approaching.
Ant. remote, distant, far-off.

im·mo·late (im'ə·lāt) *v.* **im·mo·lat·ed, im·mo·lat·ing**
1 To sacrifice, especially to kill as a sacrificial victim: *In protest against the war, the Vietnamese monk immolated himself.* **2** To give up: *to immolate one's ambitions because of a sense of duty.*—**im'mo·la'tion** *n.*
Syn. 2 relinquish, renounce, forgo, abandon.

im·mor·tal·ize (i·môr'təl·īz) *v.* **im·mor·tal·ized, im·mor·tal·iz·ing**
To give unending life or fame to: *a rapturous poem that immortalized his beloved.*—**im·mor'tal·i·za'tion** *n.*

im·mune (i·myoon') *adj.*
1 Protected against a disease, poison, or the like, as by inoculation: *immune to typhoid fever.* **2** Not subject to, susceptible to, or responsive to: *immune to the criticisms of his administration.*

im·mu·ta·ble (i·myoo'tə·bəl) *adj.*
Not capable of changing or being changed: *the immutable laws of the universe.*—**im·mu'ta·bil'i·ty, im·mu'ta·ble·ness** *n.*; **im·mu'ta·bly** *adv.*
Syn. unchanging, unalterable, invariable, permanent.
Ant. changeable, impermanent, variable, alterable.

im·passe (im'pas *or* im·pas') *n.*
A location or situation from which there is or seems to be no way out: *Discussions between management and labor reached an impasse and a strike was inevitable.*
Syn. blind alley, deadlock, stalemate, dead end, cul-de-sac.

im·pas·sive (im·pas'iv) *adj.*
Not feeling or showing emotion: *De Gaulle remained impassive in the midst of nationwide strikes.*—**im·pas'sive·ly** *adv.*; **im·pas'sive·ness, im·pas·siv'i·ty** *n.*
Syn. unmoved, calm, dispassionate, unconcerned, insensitive.
Ant. emotional, demonstrative, excitable, sensitive, overwrought.

im·pa·tient (im·pā'shənt) *adj.*
1 Easily annoyed at delay, discomfort, etc.: *impatient drivers in a traffic jam, blowing their horns.* **2** Showing a lack of patience: *He dismissed their petition with an impatient gesture.* **3** Restlessly eager: *impatient for results.* **4** Unwilling to tolerate: *impatient of delay.*—**im·pa'tient·ly** *adv.*

Syn. 1 irritable, fretful. 2 curt, abrupt. 3 avid, anxious. 4 intolerant.
Ant. 1 calm, resigned. 2 courteous, polite. 3 apathetic, unconcerned. 4 tolerant, understanding.

im·peach (im·pēch′) *v.*
1 To accuse of doing wrong, especially to formally charge a high public official with crime or misdemeanor in office: *President Andrew Johnson was impeached but not convicted.* 2 To challenge or bring discredit on, as for dishonesty, validity, etc.: *to impeach a witness.*—**im·peach′ment** *n.*

im·pec·ca·ble (im·pek′ə·bəl) *adj.*
Free from error, fault, or flaw: *an impeccable dresser.*—**im·pec′ca·bly** *adv.*
Syn. perfect, flawless, irreproachable, faultless.
Ant. imperfect, defective, marred.

im·pend·ing (im·pen′ding) *adj.*
1 About to occur: *Dark clouds warned of the impending snowstorm.* 2 Overhanging: *impending cliffs.*
Syn. 1 imminent, threatening, coming, approaching.
Ant. 1 remote, distant, far-off.

im·per·cep·ti·ble (im′pər·sep′tə·bəl) *adj.*
So small, slight, subtle, or gradual as to escape notice: *a change imperceptible to the naked eye.*—**im′per·cep′ti·bly** *adv.*
Spelling tip: The prefix *in-*, meaning "not," changes to *im-* before a *p.* Hence anything "not perceptible" is *imperceptible.*
Syn. invisible, undiscernible, unnoticeable.
Ant. perceptible, apparent, discernible.

im·pe·ri·ous (im·pir′ē·əs) *adj.*
1 Characterized by arrogance and command: *a petty official who tried to compensate for his lack of talent by an imperious manner.* 2 Urgent, imperative: *an imperious need.*
Syn. 1 dictatorial, overbearing, haughty, despotic. 2 necessary, critical.
Ant. 1 submissive, yielding, humble. 2 unnecessary, insignificant.

im·per·me·a·ble (im·pûr′mē·ə·bəl) *adj.*
Not capable of being passed through or penetrated, as by a liquid: *an impermeable fabric.*—**im·per′me·a·bil′i·ty** *n.*
Syn. impervious, impenetrable, impassable.
Ant. permeable, porous.

im·per·ti·nent (im·pûr′tə·nənt) *adj.*
1 Deliberately disrespectful or unmannerly: *an impertinent waitress.* 2 Not pertinent: *a remark that was impertinent to the conversation.*—**im·per′ti·nent·ly** *adv.*
Syn. 1 uncivil, impudent, fresh. 2 irrelevant, inapplicable, inappropriate.
Ant. 1 civil, polite, mannerly. 2 relevant, applicable, appropriate.

im·per·turb·a·ble (im′pər·tûr′bə·bəl) *adj.*
Incapable of being disturbed or agitated: *She remained imperturbable even in the face of disaster.*—**im′per·turb′a·bil′i·ty, im′per·turb′-a·ble·ness** *n.;* **im′per·turb′a·bly** *adv.*
Syn. calm, unshaken.
Ant. emotional, hysterical.

im·per·vi·ous (im·pûr′vē·əs) *adj.*
1 Incapable of being passed through, as by moisture or light rays: *a coat impervious to rain.* 2 Not open or receptive:. *a mind impervious to reason.*—**im·per′vi·ous·ness** *n.*
Syn. 1 impenetrable, impermeable, impassable. 2 unreceptive, unresponsive, unmovable.
Ant. 1 pervious, permeable, porous, penetrable. 2 receptive, responsive.

im·pet·u·ous (im·pech′ōō·əs) *adj.*
1 Tending to act on sudden impulse and without forethought: *an impetuous young man.* 2 Resulting from sudden impulse: *an impetuous decision.* 3 Moving with violent force: *an impetuous wind.*—**im·pet′u·ous·ly** *adv.;* **im·pet′-u·ous·ness, im·pet′u·os′i·ty** *n.*
Syn. 1 impulsive, reckless, rash, careless. 2 sudden, spontaneous, precipitate, headlong. 3 furious, rushing, wild, intense.
Ant. 1, 2 cautious, wary, timid, deliberate.

im·pe·tus (im′pə·təs) *n.*
1 The force that sets a body in motion, or the energy with which a body moves. 2 Any moving force: *Are raises an impetus to better working habits?*
Syn. 2 stimulus, incentive, influence, encouragement.

im·pi·e·ty (im·pī′ə·tē) *n.,* **im·pi·e·ties** *pl.*
1 Lack of respect and reverence for those to whom it is due or expected, especially for God or sacred things. 2 An impious act: *shocked at what she considered the unforgivable impieties of the hippies.*
Syn. 1 irreverence, ungodliness, undutifulness, disrespect. 2 sin, offense, wrongdoing, transgression.
Ant. 1 reverence, godliness, dutifulness, respect.

im·pi·ous (im′pē·əs) *adj.*
Lacking in reverence or respect, as for God or one's parents: *Given his total disinterest in religion, his behavior in the church was not so much impious as just plain boorish.*—**im′pi·ous·ly** *adv.,* **im′pi·ous·ness** *n.*
Syn. irreverent, ungodly, undutiful, disrespectful.
Ant. reverent, godly, dutiful, respectful.

im·pla·ca·ble (im·plā′kə·bəl *or* im·plak′ə·bəl) *adj.*
That cannot be appeased or pacified: *an implacable enemy.*—**im·pla′ca·bil′i·ty, im·pla′-ca·ble·ness** *n.;* **im·pla′ca·bly** *adv.*
Syn. unrelenting, unforgiving, unappeasable, relentless.
Ant. placable, lenient, clement, yielding, forgiving.

im·ple·ment (im′plə·mənt *n.,* im′plə·ment *v.*) *n., v.*
n. A piece of equipment used in some form of work or activity: *A hoe is an implement for removing weeds.*
v. 1 To provide with such equipment. 2 To provide whatever is necessary to accomplish or carry something into effect: *to implement a relief program.*—**im′ple·men·ta′tion** *n.*
Syn. *n.* tool, instrument, utensil, device, contrivance.

im·pli·cate (im'plə·kāt) *v.* **im·pli·cat·ed, im·pli·cat·ing**
To show or prove to be involved or concerned: *evidence implicating him in the bank robbery.*
Syn. connect, associate, entangle.

im·pli·ca·tion (im'plə·kā'shən) *n.*
1 The act of involving: *the mayor's implication of two top police officials in a narcotics scandal.* **2** The condition of being involved: *The police officers' implication in the scandal brought an end to their careers.* **3** The act of implying: *Implication rather than accusation brought the witness to the point of hysteria.* **4** Something that is implied: *The implication was that the witness was guilty of perjury.*
Syn. 1, 2 involvement, entanglement, connection. **3, 4** allusion, suggestion, inference.

im·plic·it (im·plis'it) *adj.*
1 Unreserved, absolute: *implicit confidence.* **2** Implied or understood, but not specifically expressed: *implicit agreement.*—**im·plic'it·ly** *adv.,* **im·plic'it·ness** *n.*
Syn. 1 complete, unquestioning, positive. **2** tacit, inferred.
Ant. 1 limited, partial, moderate. **2** expressed, spoken, written, formal.

im·ply (im·plī') *v.* **im·plied, im·ply·ing**
1 To involve necessarily as a conclusion, circumstance, condition, effect, etc.: *An action implies an agent.* **2** To indicate or suggest without stating: *He implied that his employer was dishonest.*
Usage: *Imply* and *infer* both mean to involve as a necessary conclusion, and in this sense they are often used interchangeably: *An effect implies a cause; an effect infers a cause.* Loosely, *infer* means to indicate or suggest without stating, but in this sense *imply* has far better standing.
Syn. 1 infer, assume, presume. **2** hint, intimate, insinuate, suggest.

im·por·tance (im·pôr'təns) *n.*
1 Significance: *the importance of the issue.* **2** Prestige, authority, or standing: *a man of some importance in the business world.*
Syn. 1 consequence, momentousness, weightiness. **2** influence, rank, distinction.
Ant. 1, 2 unimportance, insignificance.

im·po·tent (im'pə·tent) *adj.*
1 Without power, strength, or authority: *The deposed king was an impotent figurehead.* **2** Sexually incapable (said of males): *an impotent old man.*—**im'po·tence** *n.,* **im'po·tent·ly** *adv.*
Syn. 1 powerless, weak, helpless. **2** sterile.
Ant. 1 potent, powerful, strong. **2** potent.

im·preg·na·ble (im·preg'nə·bəl) *adj.*
1 Too strong to be conquered or overcome when placed under attack: *an impregnable fortress; impregnable moral strength.* **2** Capable of being fertilized or filled (impregnated): *an impregnable egg.*
Syn. 1 invincible, unconquerable, invulnerable.
Ant. 1 vulnerable, weak, insecure.

im·preg·nate (im·preg'nāt) *v.* **im·preg·nat·ed, im·preg·nat·ing**
1 To make pregnant or fertile: *to impregnate*

an ovum. **2** To fill, spreading through every part: *air impregnated with poisonous gas.*
Syn. 1 fertilize, fecundate. **2** permeate, saturate, imbue.

im·pre·sa·ri·o (im'prə·sä'rē·ō) *n.,* **im·pre·sa·ri·os** *pl.*
A person who manages performers or puts on performances, as the manager, director, or sponsor of an opera, ballet, or concert company: *Rudolf Bing and S. Hurok are well-known impresarios.*
Etymology: *Impresario* goes back to the Italian word for enterprise, *impresa.*
Syn. entrepreneur, producer.

im·pri·ma·tur (im'pri·mä'tər *or* im'pri·mā'-tər) *n.*
License to print or approval for publication, granted by an official censor, especially in the Roman Catholic Church: *The Douay Bible bears a bishop's imprimatur.*
Etymology: In Latin *imprimatur* means let it be printed.

im·promp·tu (im·promp'tōō) *adj., adv.*
adj. Not planned ahead of time: *Unexpectedly besieged by reporters, he made an impromptu speech.*
adv. Without preparation: *an entertainer always able to perform impromptu.*
Etymology: The Latin phrase *in promptu* means in readiness.
Syn. *adj.* extemporaneous, spontaneous, off-the-cuff. *adv.* extemporaneously, extempore.
Ant. *adj.* planned, scheduled, prepared, rehearsed.

im·pro·vi·sa·tion (im'prov·ə·zā'shən *or* im'-prə·vī·zā'shən) *n.*
1 The act of producing without previous planning: *the improvisation of jazz.* **2** Something produced without previous planning, as a dramatic sketch: *a comedian who could do a series of improvisations around any prop he was handed.*—**im'pro·vi·sa'tion·al** *adj.*
Syn. 1 extemporization.

im·pro·vise (im'prə·vīz) *v.* **im·pro·vised, im·pro·vis·ing**
1 To make up music, drama, etc. on the spur of the moment, without previous planning: *a pianist good at improvising.* **2** To make from whatever is at hand: *to improvise a playhouse out of a card table and a sheet.*
Syn. 1 invent, extemporize. **2** fashion, fabricate.

in·ad·e·quate (in·ad'ə·kwit) *adj.*
Not enough or not good enough to meet requirements: *an inadequate water supply.*—**in·ad·e·qua·cy** (in·ad'ə·kwə·sē) *n.*
Syn. insufficient, deficient, unsatisfactory.
Ant. adequate, sufficient, satisfactory.

in·ad·ver·tence (in'əd·vûr'təns) *n.*
1 Lack of due care or attention: *Babe Ruth's name was omitted from the Baseball Hall of Fame list by inadvertence.* **2** A result of inattention, as an oversight, slip of the tongue, boner, or other blunder.—**in'ad·ver'tent** *adj.,* **in'ad·ver'tent·ly** *adv.*
Syn. 1 negligence, carelessness, inattention.

in·al·ien·a·ble (in·āl'yən·ə·bəl) *adj.*
That cannot rightfully be taken away or transferred: *man's inalienable rights to life, liberty, and the pursuit of happiness.*
Syn. undeniable, inviolable, irrevocable.
Ant. disputable, repealable, alienable.

in·am·o·ra·ta (in·am'ə·rä'tə) *n.*, **in·am·o·ra·tas** *pl.*
A woman with whom a man is in love.
Syn. beloved, mistress, love.

in·ane (in·ān') *adj.*
Stupid, silly, or pointless: *an inane remark.*
Syn. senseless, foolish.
Ant. sensible, meaningful.

in·an·i·mate (in·an'ə·mit) *adj.*
1 Not possessing animal life: *sticks, stones, and other inanimate objects.* **2** No longer conscious or alive: *an inanimate body.* **3** Lacking spirit or liveliness: *a listless, inanimate acquiescence.*
Syn. 1 lifeless, inert. **2** unconscious, dead.
Ant. 1 animate, sentient, living. **2** conscious, alive. **3** lively, active.

in·ar·tic·u·late (in'är·tik'yə·lit) *adj.*
1 Uttered without the distinct sounds of spoken language: *inarticulate cries.* **2** Incapable of speech: *inarticulate beasts.* **3** Unable to express oneself fully or well: *tongue-tied and inarticulate.*
Syn. 1 indistinct, muffled. **2** mute, speechless. **3** silent.

in·au·gu·rate (in·ô'gyə·rāt) *v.* **in·au·gu·rat·ed, in·au·gu·rat·ing**
1 To induct into office with formal ceremony: *to inaugurate a President.* **2** To begin or commence formally: *to inaugurate a new postal system.* **3** To celebrate the public opening or first use of: *to inaugurate a bridge.*—**in·au'gu·ra'tion** *n.*
Syn. 1 install, invest. **2** initiate. **3** open.

in·cal·cu·la·ble (in·kal'kyə·lə·bəl) *adj.*
1 Too great or numerous to be determined: *His blunder did incalculable harm.* **2** Not predictable: *her incalculable reactions.*
Syn. 1 immeasurable, inestimable, untold. **2** unpredictable, uncertain.
Ant. 1 little, limited. **2** predictable, reliable, dependable.

in·can·ta·tion (in'kan·tā'shən) *n.*
1 The uttering or intoning of words or syllables supposed to produce magical results: *to cast out an evil spirit by incantation.* **2** The magic words or formula intoned: *a book of occult incantations.*
Syn. 2 spell, charm.

in·ca·pac·i·tate (in'kə·pas'ə·tāt) *v.* **in·ca·pac·i·tat·ed, in·ca·pac·i·tat·ing**
To render incapable, especially for normal physical activity: *A stroke totally incapacitated the formerly active man.*
Syn. disable, cripple.

in·car·cer·ate (in·kär'sə·rāt) *v.* **in·car·cer·at·ed, in·car·cer·at·ing**
To put in prison: *to incarcerate a felon in a maximum-security cell.*
Syn. imprison, confine, jail.
Ant. release, free.

in·car·nate (in·kär'nit *adj.*, in·kär'nāt *v.*) *adj.; v.* **in·car·nat·ed, in·car·nat·ing**
adj. **1** Embodied in human form: *the belief that Jesus was God incarnate.* **2** Represented in a perfect example: *Hitler and Göring were cruelty incarnate.*
v. To represent in living or concrete form: *The child incarnated all their hopes.*
Syn. *adj.* **2** personified, exemplified, typified.
v. embody.

in·car·na·tion (in'kär·nā'shən) *n.*
1 The assumption of bodily form: *an angel's miraculous incarnation.* **2** (Written **the Incarnation**) The assumption of human form by Jesus Christ. **3** A person or thing that perfectly typifies some abstract quality or idea: *a mother who was the very incarnation of kindness.*
Syn. 3 embodiment, personification, exemplification.

in·cen·di·ar·y (in·sen'dē·er'ē) *adj.; n.*, **in·cen·di·ar·ies** *pl.*
adj. **1** Of or involving the malicious burning of property: *an incendiary holocaust.* **2** Designed to start a fire: *an incendiary bomb.* **3** Tending to inflame mob passions: *a demagogue's incendiary speeches.*
n. **1** A person who maliciously sets fire to property: *an incendiary who burned barns.* **2** A person who stirs up strife and violence: *youthful incendiaries who incited a riot.*
Syn. *adj.* **3** inflammatory, seditious, fiery. *n.* **1** arsonist. **2** agitator, firebrand.

in·cep·tion (in·sep'shən) *n.*
Beginning, as of an undertaking: *The business was a success from the time of its inception.*
Syn. start, commencement, inauguration.
Ant. end, close, finish, termination.

in·ci·dence (in'sə·dəns) *n.*
The degree, amount, or range of occurrence or effect: *The high incidence of illiteracy in some remote mountain regions.*
Syn. rate.

in·ci·den·tal·ly (in'sə·den'tə·lē) *adv.*
1 As a subordinate, casual, or chance occurrence along with something else: *This mystery novel incidentally contains some intriguing descriptions of Morocco.* **2** By the way: *Incidentally, I happened to run into Otto yesterday.*—**in'ci·den'tal** *adj.*
Spelling tip: Tally up two *l*'s when you spell *incidentally.*

in·cin·er·a·tor (in·sin'ə·rā'tər) *n.*
A furnace for burning trash, garbage, and other refuse.

in·cip·i·ent (in·sip'ē·ənt) *adj.*
Just beginning, and still in an early stage: *an incipient rebellion; an incipient ulcer.*—**in·cip'i·ence** *n.*
Syn. starting, embryonic.
Ant. full-fledged, full-scale.

in·ci·sive (in·sī'siv) *adj.*
Sharp and penetrating or cutting: *an incisive critical commentary; incisive wit.*
Syn. keen, trenchant, biting, piercing.
Ant. bland, blunt, gentle.

in·cite (in·sīt′) *v.* **in·cit·ed, in·cit·ing**
To stir up or spur on to action: *He incited a riot by making inflammatory speeches.*
Etymology: *Incite* goes back to Latin roots: *in-* (thoroughly) and *citare* (to rouse).
Usage: Don't confuse the verb *incite* (in·sīt′) with the noun *insight* (in′sīt′), which means perception into the heart of something.
Syn. provoke, rouse, stimulate.
Ant. calm, discourage.

in·clem·ent (in·klem′ənt) *adj.*
1 Bad, rough, or stormy (said of the weather): *The outing was canceled because of inclement weather.* **2** Without mercy: *a stiff sentence imposed by an inclement judge.*
Syn. 1 severe, rigorous. **2** harsh, merciless.
Ant. 1 mild, fair. **2** merciful, lenient.

in·cog·ni·to (in·kog′nə·tō *or* in′kog·nē′tō) *adv.; adj.; n.*, **in·cog·ni·tos** *pl.*
adv., adj. Under an assumed name or identity, especially so as to avoid recognition: *The star traveled incognito, using an alias.*
n. **1** A person who takes on an assumed name or identity. **2** An assumed name or disguise. **3** The state of being in disguise.

in·com·pat·i·ble (in′kəm·pat′ə·bəl) *adj.*
1 Unable to live together or to get along easily with each other: *an incompatible couple, filing for divorce.* **2** Unable to be reconciled because of a basic difference in nature: *incompatible beliefs or theories.*—**in·com·pat·i·bil·i·ty** (in′kəm·pat′ə·bil′ə·tē) *n.*
Syn. clashing, conflicting, irreconcilable, discordant.
Ant. congenial, harmonious, concordant.

in·com·pre·hen·si·ble (in′kom·pri·hen′sə·bəl) *adj.*
Impossible to understand: *To him, nuclear physics was incomprehensible.*
Usage: See INCOMPREHENSIVE.
Syn. unintelligible, unfathomable.
Ant. comprehensible, understandable.

in·com·pre·hen·sive (in′kom·pri·hen′siv) *adj.*
1 Limited in scope: *an incomprehensive course that concentrated on a specialized aspect of the subject.* **2** Not able to understand much: *incomprehensive retarded children.*
Usage: Don't confuse *incomprehensive* with *incomprehensible: An incomprehensive child might find even simple subjects incomprehensible.*
Syn. 1 narrow, restricted. **2** dull, slow-witted.
Ant. 1 broad, comprehensive. **2** intelligent, bright, quick-witted.

in·con·ceiv·a·ble (in′kən·sē′və·bəl) *adj.*
Impossible to conceive of or imagine: *It is inconceivable that man should utterly destroy the human race.*—**in′con·ceiv′a·bly** *adv.*
Spelling tip: Remember *i* before *e* except after *c.*
Syn. unthinkable, unimaginable, unbelievable.
Ant. expectable, predictable.

in·con·gru·ous (in·kong′grōō·əs) *adj.*
1 Not suitable, proper, or appropriate: *He appeared at the formal dinner in an absurdly incongruous cowboy outfit.* **2** Composed of

elements or parts not properly belonging together: *the incongruous combination of a formal gown and tennis shoes.*—**in′con·gru′i·ty** *n.*
Syn. 1 inappropriate, improper. **2** inharmonious, incompatible, contradictory.
Ant. 1 apt, reasonable. **2** harmonious, consistent.

in·con·se·quen·tial (in′kon·sə·kwen′shəl) *adj.*
Having little or no importance: *an inconsequential decision.*—**in′con·se·quen′tial·ly** *adv.*
Syn. unimportant, trivial.
Ant. important, significant.

in·con·ven·ience (in′kən·vēn′yəns) *n.; v.* **in·con·ven·ienced, in·con·ven·ienc·ing**
n. **1** Trouble, annoyance, difficulty, or discomfort: *the inconvenience of a long delay.* **2** A source of trouble or annoyance: *Having no hot water is an inconvenience.*
v. To trouble or annoy: *We are sorry to inconvenience you, but we must make repairs.*
Syn. *n.* vexation, bother, nuisance. *v.* bother, vex, disturb.
Ant. *n.* convenience, advantage. *v.* accommodate, oblige.

in·cor·ri·gi·ble (in·kôr′ə·jə·bəl) *adj., n.*
adj. Not capable of being improved, corrected, or reformed: *an incorrigible criminal.*
n. A person who is incorrigible: *The young boy was considered an incorrigible by his teachers.*—**in·cor′ri·gi·bly** *adv.*
Syn. *adj.* unmanageable, incurable, uncorrectable, unregenerate.
Ant. *adj.* corrigible, correctable, improvable, manageable.

in·crease (in·krēs′ *v.*, in′krēs *n.*) *v.* **in·creased, in·creas·ing;** *n.*
v. To make or become greater, as in number, size, degree, etc.: *increasing his wealth.*
n. **1** A growing or becoming greater: *a gradual increase in temperature.* **2** The amount added by such an increase: *His salary increase amounted to $20 a week.*—**in·creas′ing·ly** *adv.*

in·cre·du·li·ty (in′krə·d(y)ōō′lə·tē) *n.*
The quality or state of being incredulous; doubt: *A look of incredulity covered the supervisor's face when his assistant explained his late arrival at work.*—**in·cred·u·lous·ness** (in·krej′ə·ləs·nis) *n.*
Syn. uncertainty, indecision, skepticism, disbelief.
Ant. credulity, belief, conviction, certainty.

in·cre·ment (in′krə·mənt) *n.*
1 The act or process of increasing; addition: *an annual increment in salary.* **2** The amount of an added quantity: *an increment of $1000.*
Syn. 1 increase, addition, augmentation. **2** increase, raise.
Ant. 1 decrease, lessening, reduction, loss.

in·cul·cate (in·kul′kāt *or* in′kul·kāt) *v.* **in·cul·cat·ed, in·cul·cat·ing**
To impress upon the mind by frequent repetition or forceful persuasion: *to inculcate acceptable behavior patterns in children.*—**in′cul·ca′tion** *n.*
Syn. teach, instill.

in·cum·bent (in·kum′bənt) *adj., n.*
adj. 1 Resting upon a person as a moral obligation, or as necessary under the circumstances: *It is incumbent upon all of us to love our neighbors.* 2 Being in the position of an officeholder: *an incumbent governor who is a possible Presidential candidate.*
n. A person who holds an office or performs official duties: *the present incumbent in the White House.*—**in·cum′ben·cy** *n.*

in·cur·sion (in·kûr′zhən *or* in·kûr′shən) *n.*
A hostile, often sudden, invasion or raid: *an incursion into the enemy's fortress.*—**in·cur′sive** *adj.*
Syn. attack, assault, sortie, foray.

in·de·cent (in·dē′sənt) *adj.*
1 Vulgar, immodest, or obscene: *arrested for indecent exposure.* 2 Not proper or respectable: *After King Hamlet died, the queen remarried with indecent haste.*—**in·de′cen·cy** *n.*
Syn. 1 lewd, shameless, wanton. 2 unseemly, improper, indecorous.
Ant. 1 decent, modest, chaste. 2 seemly, proper, decorous.

in·dec·or·ous (in·dek′ər·əs) *adj.*
Not fitting or proper; unseemly; unbecoming: *It is considered indecorous to comb one's hair at the dinner table.*—**in·dec′or·ous·ly** *adv.,* **in·dec′or·ous·ness** *n.*
Syn. ill-mannered, rude, crude.
Ant. polite, proper, refined.

in·de·fat·i·ga·ble (in′də·fat′ə·gə·bəl) *adj.*
Never tiring or weakening: *indefatigable efforts to pass a strong gun-control law.*
Syn. tireless, untiring, unflagging.
Ant. tired, flagging, halfhearted.

in·de·fen·si·ble (in′di·fen′sə·bəl) *adj.*
1 Incapable of being justified or excused: *an indefensible error.* 2 Incapable of being defended against attack: *an indefensible position, exposed on all sides.*
Syn. 1 unjustifiable, inexcusable, unpardonable. 2 vulnerable, untenable.
Ant. 1 justifiable, excusable, pardonable. 2 invulnerable, impregnable, defensible.

in·del·i·ble (in·del′ə·bəl) *adj.*
1 Incapable of being blotted out or erased: *His teacher made an indelible impression on him.* 2 Leaving a mark or stain not easily erased: *indelible ink.*—**in·del′i·bly** *adv.*
Etymology: *Indelible* comes from Latin roots: *in-* (not) + *delibilis* (perishable).
Syn. 1 permanent, lasting, ineradicable.
Ant. 1 temporary, passing, momentary.

in·dem·ni·fy (in·dem′nə·fī) *v.* **in·dem·ni·fied, in·dem·ni·fy·ing**
1 To compensate a person, etc., for loss or damage: *The insurance company indemnified him for the loss of his car.* 2 To give security against future loss or damage: *a proposal to indemnify merchants for property damage during riots.*—**in·dem′ni·fi·ca′tion** *n.*
Syn. 1 recompense, pay, reimburse. 2 insure, secure.

in·dem·ni·ty (in·dem′nə·tē) *n.,* **in·dem·ni·ties** *pl.*
1 Payment given as compensation for loss or

damage: *The insurance company had to pay a large indemnity for his injuries.* 2 An agreement to insure another against loss or damage: *a plan that included indemnity against financial loss during illness.*
Syn. 1 recompense, remuneration.

in·den·ture (in·den′chər) *n.; v.* **in·den·tured, in·den·tur·ing**
n. In law A deed or contract made between two or more parties, especially one between master and apprentice.
v. To bind a person by indenture: *He was indentured to the farmer for six years.*
Syn. *v.* apprentice.

in·de·pen·dent (in′di·pen′dənt) *adj., n.*
adj. 1 Not subject to the authority of another; free: *an independent country.* 2 Acting so as to manage one's own affairs: *Women have become very independent in the last fifty years.* 3 Not part of some larger group, system, etc.: *an independent neighborhood grocer.* 4 Not needing financial support or help from others: *to find a job and become independent.* 5 Not belonging to a particular political party or faction: *an independent voter.* 6 Not influenced or guided by others: *an independent opinion.* 7 Sufficient to live on without being employed: *an independent income.* 8 *In grammar* Able to be a complete sentence: *an independent clause.*
n. A person who is independent, especially a voter who belongs to no party or faction.

in·dex (in′deks) *n.,* **in·dex·es** *or* **in·di·ces** (in′-də·sēz) *pl.; v.*
n. 1 An alphabetical list, as at the end of a book, etc., of topics and names and the numbers of the pages where they occur in the text: *the index of a cookbook.* 2 Anything that indicates or gives evidence of something: *Alertness is an index of intelligence.* 3 Anything that serves as an indicator, as a needle on a dial. 4 The finger next to the thumb; *index finger.*
v. 1 To provide with an index, as a book: *Books of fiction are not indexed.* 2 To enter a name or topic in an index: *to index references to Roosevelt.*
Usage: *Indices* is the Latin plural of *index,* which is also a Latin word. Some purists feel that *indices* is the proper form, but *indexes* has been used by most people for many years and is quite correct.

in·dict (in·dīt′) *v.*
1 To charge with a wrong, offense, or shortcoming: *The mayor indicted citizens who remained indifferent to the city's problems.* 2 *In law* To bring a formal accusation against as a basis for a trial (said of a prosecuting authority): *The grand jury indicted him for murder.*—**in·dict′ment** *n.*
Spelling tip: Remember to include the silent *c.*
Syn. 1 accuse, incriminate.

in·dig·e·nous (in·dij′ə·nəs) *adj.*
Originating or occurring naturally in the place or country where found: *Koala bears are indigenous to Australia.*—**in·dig′e·nous·ly** *adv.,* **in·dig′e·nous·ness** *n.*

Syn. native, aboriginal.
Ant. alien, foreign, immigrant.

in·di·gent (in′də·jənt) *adj.*
Having little or no money; poor: *indigent families forced to go on relief.*—**in′di·gence** *n.*, **in′di·gent·ly** *adv.*
Syn. needy, penniless, destitute.
Ant. rich, wealthy, prosperous.

in·dis·pen·sa·ble (in′dis·pen′sə·bəl) *adj.*
Absolutely essential; necessary: *He is indispensable to his boss.*—**in′dis·pen′sa·bil′i·ty, in′dis·pen′sa·ble·ness** *n.*; **in′dis·pen′sa·bly** *adv.*
Spelling tip: Notice that *indispensable* ends in *-able*, not *-ible*. Since the choice of *-able* and *-ible*, in the case of words derived from Latin, depends upon the conjugation of the original Latin verb to which the suffix is added, it is easier for most people to learn the spelling of the individual words. However, *-able* is always the suffix used to form adjectives from English verbs, such as *answerable, plowable, understandable.*

in·dis·put·a·ble (in′dis·pyo͞o′tə·bəl) *adj.*
Not to be disputed; unquestionable: *His canceled check was indisputable proof that he had paid.*—**in′dis·put′a·bil′i·ty, in′dis·put′a·ble·ness** *n.*; **in′dis·put′a·bly** *adv.*
Syn. incontestable, undeniable, indubitable, incontrovertible.
Ant. dubious, doubtful, questionable, uncertain.

in·do·lent (in′də·lənt) *adj.*
Averse to exertion or work; lazy: *an indolent boy who lounged on the porch all day.*—**in′do·lence** *n.*, **in′do·lent·ly** *adv.*
Syn. idle, inactive, sluggish.
Ant. active, busy, energetic.

in·dom·i·ta·ble (in·dom′i·tə·bəl) *adj.*
Not easily defeated; persevering; stubborn: *an indomitable urge to succeed.*—**in·dom′i·ta·bly** *adv.*
Syn. unyielding, unconquerable, invincible.
Ant. feeble, languid, weak.

in·du·bi·ta·ble (in·d(y)o͞o′bə·tə·bəl) *adj.*
Not to be doubted; unquestionable: *A birth certificate is indubitable proof of age.*—**in·du′bi·ta·bly** *adv.*
Syn. indisputable, undeniable, positive.
Ant. dubious, doubtful, uncertain.

in·duce·ment (in·d(y)o͞os′mənt) *n.*
1 The act of inducing or persuading. 2 Something that serves to persuade a person to do something: *Is the piecework system an inducement to produce more per hour?*
Syn. 2 incentive, spur, stimulus.
Ant. 2 deterrent, hindrance.

in·e·bri·at·ed (in·ē′brē·ā′tid) *adj.*
Intoxicated; drunk: *The policeman stated that his prisoner was in an inebriated condition at the time of the arrest.*—**in·e′bri·a′tion** *n.*
Syn. tipsy, high.
Ant. sober.

in·ed·i·ble (in·ed′ə·bəl) *adj.*
Not fit to eat: *Squash and pumpkins are edible, but gourds are inedible.*
Syn. uneatable, unpalatable.
Ant. edible, eatable, palatable.

in·ef·fa·ble (in·ef′ə·bəl) *adj.*
Too overpowering to be expressed in words; indescribable: *When he saw the brilliant sunset he experienced ineffable peace.*—**in·ef′fa·bil′ity, in·ef′fa·ble·ness** *n.*; **in·ef′fa·bly** *adv.*
Syn. unutterable, inexpressible, mysterious.

in·el·i·gi·ble (in·el′ə·jə·bəl) *adj.*
Not eligible, qualified, or suitable: *Low grades made him ineligible for a scholarship.*—**in·el′i·gi·bil′i·ty** *n.*
Syn. unqualified, disqualified, unfit.
Ant. eligible, qualified, fit.

in·ept (in·ept′) *n.*
1 Not suitable or appropriate; out of place: *an inept and highly tactless remark.* 2 Clumsy; incompetent: *an inept cook.*—**in·ept′ness** *n.*, **in·ept′ly** *adv.*
Syn. 1 ill-timed, inopportune. 2 inefficient.
Ant. 1 proper, appropriate. 2 capable, efficient, competent.

in·eq·ui·ty (in·ek′wə·tē) *n.*, **in·eq·ui·ties** *pl.*
1 A lack of justice or fairness: *the inequity of a rigid caste system.* 2 An unfair act or course of action; an instance of injustice.
Usage: Do not confuse *inequity* with *iniquity*. *Inequity* is formed from *equity* (meaning fairness or something that is fair) plus the prefix *in-* (meaning *not*). Consequently it means unfairness or an unfair thing. *Iniquity*, which is not the negative form of any other word, means wickedness or a wicked deed: *He will be punished for his iniquities.*

in·er·tia (in·ûr′shə) *n.*
1 A disinclination to move or act; sluggishness: *the inertia produced by a hot, muggy day.* 2 *In physics* A property of matter by which a physical body persists in its state of rest or of uniform motion until acted upon by some external force.—**in·er′tial** *adj.*
Syn. 1 laziness, inactivity, indolence.
Ant. 1 alertness, energy, vigor.

in·ev·i·ta·ble (in·ev′ə·tə·bəl) *adj.*, *n.*
adj. Unable to be avoided or prevented from happening; unavoidable; certain: *To grow old is inevitable.*
n. Something that is unavoidable: *The mature person learns to accept the inevitables of life.*
Syn. *adj.* inescapable, destined, unpreventable. *n.* certainty.
Ant. *adj.* uncertain, avoidable, preventable. *n.* uncertainty.

in·ex·pli·ca·ble (in·eks′pli·kə·bəl *or* in′iks·plik′-ə·bəl) *adj.*
Impossible to explain; unexplainable: *Their sudden deaths are an inexplicable mystery.*—**in·ex′pli·ca·bil′i·ty, in·ex′pli·ca·ble·ness** *n.*; **in·ex′pli·ca·bly** *adv.*
Syn. unaccountable, mysterious.
Ant. clear, obvious.

in·fal·li·ble (in·fal′ə·bəl) *adj.*
1 Incapable of error in thought or action; never mistaken; *No human being] is infallible —although lots of people would argue the point.* 2 Not liable to fail; unerring: *an encyclopedia that is an infallible source of information.*—**in·fal′li·bil′i·ty, in·fal′li·ble·ness** *n.*; **in·fal′li·bly** *adv.*

Syn. 1 unfailing, inerrable. **2** certain, trustworthy, dependable.
Ant. 1 fallible, uncertain, unreliable. **2** inaccurate, unsure, uncertain.

in·fa·mous (in'fə·məs) *adj.*
1 Having a bad reputation; notoriously bad: *Benedict Arnold, an infamous traitor.* **2** Extremely evil; shameful; odious: *the infamous crimes of Jack the Ripper.*—**in'fa·mous·ly** *adv.*, **in'fa·mous·ness** *n.*
Syn. 1 evil, scandalous. **2** heinous, shocking, vile.
Ant. 1 noble, honorable, reputable. **2** laudable, excellent, meritorious.

in·fa·my (in'fə·mē) *n.*, **in·fa·mies** *pl.*
1 Lack of honor or good reputation; evil notoriety: *the infamy of the gangsters of the 1920s.* **2** The state or quality of being infamous: *the infamy of infanticide.* **3** An infamous act: *He included the killing of his wife among his infamies.*
Syn. 1 ill-repute, disgrace, disrepute. **3** crime, offense, felony, wrongdoing.

in·fan·tile (in'fən·tīl *or* in'fən·til) *adj.*
1 Of or having to do with infancy or infants: *an infantile disease.* **2** Like or characteristic of infancy or infants; babyish: *television programs geared to an infantile audience.*
Syn. 2 immature, childish.
Ant. 2 grown-up, adult, mature.

in·fer (in·fûr') *v.* **in·ferred, in·fer·ring**
1 To arrive at by reasoning; conclude or deduce from evidence or premises: *From his silence at the party we inferred that he was not enjoying himself.* **2** To involve or imply as a conclusion; give evidence of: *A happy family life infers contentment.* **3** Loosely, to indicate without actually stating; suggest; imply: *He inferred that others were involved in the plot.*
Usage: See IMPLY.

in·fer·ence (in'fər·əns) *n.*
1 That which is inferred; deduction: *Certain inferences may be drawn from even a casual study of the data.* **2** The act or process of inferring. **3** Loosely, a guess or surmise: *Scientific conclusions must be based on facts, not on inferences.*
Syn. 1 conclusion. **3** conjecture, supposition.

in·fin·ite (in'fə·nit) *adj.*
1 Having no boundaries or limits: *infinite space.* **2** Very numerous or great: *an infinite supply.* **3** All-embracing: *infinite wisdom.*—**in'fi·nite·ly** *adv.*, **in'fi·nite·ness** *n.*
Syn. 1 limitless, boundless. **2** vast, countless. **3** absolute, perfect.
Ant. 1 limited, definable. **2** measurable, insignificant. **3** circumscribed, restricted.

in·fin·i·tes·i·mal (in'fin·ə·tes'ə·məl) *adj.*
So small in size, significance, etc., as to amount to practically nothing: *A grain of sand is an infinitesimal part of the desert.*—**in'fin·i·tes'i·mal·ly** *adv.*
Syn. inappreciable, imperceptible.
Ant. huge, enormous, great.

in·fir·mi·ty (in·fûr'mə·tē) *n.*, **in·fir·mi·ties** *pl.*

A physical or mental defect or ailment: *the infirmities of old age.*
Syn. debility, weakness, illness.

in·flam·ma·ble (in·flam'ə·bəl) *adj.*
1 Capable of catching fire easily: *a dangerously inflammable gas.* **2** Easily excited or aroused: *an inflammable temper.*
Usage: *Inflammable* does *not* mean "not flammable"; it means *flammable*, coming from the same Latin source as the word *inflame*. *Flammable* is preferred in technical contexts because it is not confusing: *Gasoline is a flammable liquid.*

in·flam·ma·to·ry (in·flam'ə·tôr'ē) *adj.*
Tending to produce or arouse excitement, violence, anger, etc.: *a politician given to inflammatory speeches.*
Syn. incendiary, rabble-rousing.

in·flex·i·ble (in·flek'sə·bəl) *adj.*
Incapable of being bent, swayed, or changed: *an inflexible disciplinarian.*—**in·flex'i·bil'i·ty** *n.*
Syn. rigid, unbending, unyielding.
Ant. flexible, elastic, pliable.

in·flu·ence (in'floo·əns) *n.; v.* **in·flu·enced, in·flu·enc·ing**
n. **1** The power of persons or things to produce effects on others: *the influence of a bad environment.* **2** The kind of power that is indirect or nonforceful: *Use your influence to help me get a job.* **3** A person or thing that possesses such power: *a teacher who was a strong influence for better education.*
v. To have or produce an effect on: *The moon influences the tides.*

in·flux (in'fluks) *n.*
A flowing or coming in: *an influx of people into the auditorium.*
Syn. inflow, ingress, inrush.
Ant. outflow, efflux, emanation.

in·frac·tion (in·frak'shən) *n.*
The act of breaking or violating a pledge, law, etc.: *an infraction of the city's parking regulations.*
Syn. violation, infringement.

in·fringe (in·frinj') *v.* **in·fringed, in·fring·ing**
1 To break or disregard the terms or requirements of, as an oath or law: *causing an international dispute by infringing a treaty.* **2** To trespass or encroach: *to infringe on a patent right.* **in·fringe'ment** *n.*

in·gen·ious (in·jēn'yəs) *adj.*
1 Showing originality in its conception or execution: *an ingenious plan.* **2** Having inventiveness and skill: *an ingenious designer.*—**in·gen'ious·ly** *adv.*, **in·gen'ious·ness** *n.*
Syn. 1, 2 clever, inventive, original.
Ant. 1, 2 unoriginal, inept, uninventive.

in·gé·nue (an'zhə·noo' *or* än'zhə·noo') *n.*
1 The role of a girl or young woman in a play, film, etc. **2** An actress who plays such a role. **3** A girl or young woman of guileless simplicity and innocence.
Spelling tip: This word may also be spelled without the accent on the *e.*

in·ge·nu·i·ty (in'jə·n(y)ōō'ə·tē) *n.*, **in·ge·nu·i·ties** *pl.*
1 Cleverness or skill, as in invention, designing, problem-solving, etc.: *the ingenuity he displayed in building his own home.* 2 A clever plan, act, device, etc.: *the numberless ingenuities of the modern American kitchen.*
Syn. 1 resourcefulness, ability, aptitude.
Ant. 1 unskillfulness, inexpertness, inaptitude.

in·gen·u·ous (in·jen'yōō·əs) *adj.*
Characterized by sincerity, openness, or innocent candor: *the young girl's ingenuous remark.*—**in·gen'u·ous·ly** *adv.*, **in·gen'u·ous·ness** *n.*
Syn. simple, guileless, naive.
Ant. disingenuous, insincere, sly.

in·gra·ti·ate (in·grā'shē·āt) *v.* **in·gra·ti·at·ed, in·gra·ti·at·ing**
To bring oneself deliberately into the favor or confidence of others: *a boss who resented his employees' efforts to ingratiate themselves with him.*

in·her·ent (in·hir'ənt *or* in·her'ənt) *adj.*
Being a permanent and essential element or quality of something: *a person's inherent will to live.*—**in·her'ent·ly** *adv.*
Syn. intrinsic, innate, natural.
Ant. extrinsic, extraneous.

in·her·i·tance (in·her'ə·təns) *n.*
1 The act or fact of receiving something from an ancestor at death: *She is an heiress, rich by inheritance.* 2 Hereditary right: *an earl by inheritance.* 3 Anything inherited, as a sum of money or a family trait: *He squandered his inheritance and was soon penniless.*
Syn. 3 patrimony, bequest, legacy.

in·hib·it (in·hib'it) *v.*
To hold back or check an impulse, action, process, etc.: *Lack of self-confidence inhibited the young man's efforts to get ahead.*
Syn. restrain, repress, suppress.
Ant. support, encourage, promote.

in·im·i·cal (in·im'i·kəl) *adj.*
1 Showing harmful opposition: *a conservative trend inimical to the advancement of the civil rights movement.* 2 Behaving in an unfriendly or hostile way: *inimical neighbors.*—**in·im'i·cal·ly** *adv.*
Syn. 1 antagonistic, opposed, adverse. 2 unsociable, contentious, bellicose.
Ant. 1 favorable, helpful. 2 friendly, peaceable.

in·im·i·ta·ble (in·im'ə·tə·bəl) *adj.*
Impossible to copy or imitate: *his inimitable musical style.*—**in·im'i·ta·bly** *adv.*

in·iq·ui·tous (in·ik'wə·təs) *adj.*
Very wicked or unjust: *iniquitous behavior.*—**in·iq'ui·tous·ly** *adv.*
Syn. sinful, villainous.

in·iq·ui·ty (in·ik'wə·tē) *n.*, **in·iq·ui·ties** *pl.*
1 Serious violation of right or justice: *the iniquity of segregation.* 2 A wrong or unjust action: *the uncountable iniquities of the Hitler regime.*
Usage: See INEQUITY.
Syn. 1 wickedness, sinfulness, injustice. 2 sin, crime, outrage.

in·i·ti·a·tion (in·ish'ē·ā'shən) *n.*
1 The act of starting: *At the initiation of the project we had no confidence in the ability of its director.* 2 The special instruction or ceremony that admits a person to some position, society, knowledge, etc.: *His initiation into the fraternity was a solemn affair.*
Syn. 1 beginning, commencement.
Ant. 1 conclusion, finish.

ink·ling (ingk'ling) *n.*
A slight suggestion or notion: *I had no inkling of his plans.*
Syn. hint, intimation, idea.

in·nate (i·nāt' *or* in'āt) *adj.*
Springing from a person's nature: *an innate love of music.*—**in·nate'ly** *adv.*
Syn. inborn, natural, intrinsic, inherent.
Ant. extrinsic, acquired, learned.

in·no·cent (in'ə·sənt) *adj.*, *n.*
adj. 1 Free from guilt, sin, or blame: *an innocent bystander.* 2 Simple, unworldly, and unspoiled: *an innocent idea.* 3 Harmless: *innocent pastimes.*
n. An innocent person, especially a young child: *the slaughter of the innocents.*
Spelling tip: Don't confuse *innocents* (innocent persons) with *innocence* (the quality or fact of being innocent).
Syn. *adj.* 1 guiltless, blameless. 2 naive, ingenuous. 3 innocuous, inoffensive.
Ant. *adj.* 1 guilty, culpable. 2 worldly, sophisticated. 3 harmful, evil.

in·noc·u·ous (i·nok'yōō·əs) *adj.*
1 Having no harmful qualities or effects: *an innocuous garter snake.* 2 Not likely to offend or arouse strong feelings: *an innocuous speech.*—**in·noc'u·ous·ly** *adv.*, **in·noc'u·ous·ness** *n.*
Syn. 1 harmless, safe. 2 inoffensive, bland.
Ant. 1 harmful, dangerous. 2 inflammatory, offensive.

in·no·va·tion (in'ə·vā'shən) *n.*
1 The introduction of a change or of something new: *a dull office routine that was markedly improved by creative innovation.* 2 Something newly introduced: *the innovations of the last city administration.*

in·nu·en·do (in'yōō·en'dō) *n.*, **in·nu·en·does** *pl.*
An indirect hint, comment, or suggestion, especially one that is derogatory: *The woman's reputation was ruined by innuendoes concerning her personal life.*
Syn. allusion, insinuation, intimation.

in·nu·mer·a·ble (i·n(y)ōō'mər·ə·bəl) *adj.*
Too many to be counted or numbered.
Syn. countless, measureless, numberless.

in·oc·u·late (in·ok'yə·lāt) *v.* **in·oc·u·lat·ed, in·oc·u·lat·ing**
1 To give a mild form of a disease to a person, animal, etc., by implanting its bacteria or virus, usually as a means of producing immunity: *to inoculate a child with smallpox virus.* 2 To implant ideas, opinions, etc., in the mind of someone: *to inoculate a child with racial prejudice.*
Syn. 2 instill, inculcate.

in·or·di·nate (in·ôr′də·nit) *adj.*
Exceeding usual or proper limits: *an inordinate devotion to her job that resulted in a physical breakdown.*—**in·or′di·nate·ly** *adv.*
Syn. immoderate, excessive.
Ant. moderate, restrained.

in·quir·y (in·kwīr′ē *or* in′kwər·ē) *n.*, **in·quir·ies** *pl.*
1 The act of seeking answers, facts, truth, etc., especially in relation to some matter of public interest: *an inquiry into the charges of brutality brought against the police.* 2 A question: *a girl hired to answer telephone inquiries.*
Spelling tip: A less common spelling of this word is *enquiry.*
Syn. 1 investigation, examination. 2 query.

in·sa·tia·ble (in·sā′shə·bəl *or* in·sā′shē·ə·bəl) *adj.*
Incapable of being satisfied; never getting enough: *insatiable ambition.*—**in·sa′tia·bly** *adv.*
Syn. unappeasable, unquenchable.

in·scru·ta·ble (in·skrōō′tə·bəl) *adj.*
That cannot be understood or searched into: *an inscrutable glance.*—**in·scru′ta·bil′i·ty** *n.*, **in·scru′ta·bly** *adv.*
Syn. mysterious, incomprehensible.
Ant. clear, understandable.

in·sen·sate (in·sen′sāt) *adj.*
1 Showing a lack of human feeling: *insensate cruelty.* 2 Without sense or reason: *his insensate anger.* 3 Lacking physical sensation: *insensate stone.*
Syn. 1 unmoved, pitiless. 2 stupid, foolish. 3 inanimate.
Ant. 1 humane, compassionate, kindly, sympathetic. 2 reasonable, sensible, thoughtful, rational. 3 animate, sentient, sensible.

in·sep·a·ra·ble (in·sep′ər·ə·bəl) *adj.*
Incapable of being separated: *lifelong, inseparable friends.*—**in·sep′a·ra·bly** *adv.*

in·sid·i·ous (in·sid′ē·əs) *adj.*
1 Slyly cunning or deceitful: *an insidious plot to overthrow the government.* 2 Acting or developing gradually and usually harmfully: *an insidious disease.*—**in·sid′i·ous·ly** *adv.*, **in·sid′i·ous·ness** *n.*
Syn. 1 treacherous, wily, crafty. 2 undetected.
Ant. 1 overt, manifest, obvious.

in·sin·u·ate (in·sin′yōō·āt) *v.* **in·sin·u·at·ed, in·sin·u·at·ing**
1 To suggest slyly or indirectly: *insinuating that her behavior was in bad taste.* 2 To introduce or work gradually in a subtle or indirect way: *insinuating himself into his employer's favor.*—**in·sin′u·at′ing·ly** *adv.*, **in·sin′u·a′tion** *n.*
Syn. 1 hint, imply, infer. 2 instill, implant.

in·sip·id (in·sip′id) *adj.*
1 Lacking spirit, vivacity, and interest: *an insipid recital.* 2 Lacking flavor or savor: *an insipid meal.*—**in·sip′id·ly** *adv.*, **in·sip′id·ness** *n.*
Syn. 1 dull, spiritless, uninteresting. 2 tasteless, bland, flat.

Ant. 1 spirited, vivacious, exciting. 2 tasty, appetizing.

in·sis·tent (in·sis′tənt) *adj.*
Persistent or demanding: *insistent phone calls.*
—**in·sis′tence** *n.*, **in·sis′tent·ly** *adv.*

in·sol·vent (in·sol′vənt) *adj.*
Not able to pay debts as they become due; bankrupt.—**in·sol′ven·cy** *n.*

in·som·ni·a (in·som′nē·ə) *n.*
Chronic inability to get enough sleep.

in·spire (in·spīr′) *v.* **in·spired, in·spir·ing**
1 To stir deeply; arouse to action: *His speech inspired me to try harder.* 2 To arouse (a feeling, idea, etc.) in someone: *He inspired fear in his followers.* 3 To inhale.—**in′spi·ra′tion** *n.*, **in′spir·a′tion·al** *adj.*

in·stal·la·tion (in′stə·lā′shən) *n.*
1 The act of placing or positioning for use: *Workmen are required for the installation of traffic lights.* 2 A large complex of buildings in which personnel work and, possibly, are housed, as an army base or fort: *military installations in Germany.*

in·stant (in·stənt) *n.*, *adj.*
n. A very short time.
adj. Happening with no delay; immediate.

in·sti·gate (in′stə·gāt) *v.* **in·sti·gat·ed, in·sti·gat·ing**
To bring about by inciting; to goad or spur on to some drastic course or deed: *to instigate a nationwide revolt among car buyers.*
Syn. incite, provoke, foment.
Ant. prevent, discourage.

in·sti·tute (in′stə·t(y)ōōt) *v.* **in·sti·tut·ed, in·sti·tut·ing**; *n.*
v. To set up; to found or get going: *The Justice Department instituted an investigation.*
n. An organization or school devoted to a special study or cause: *an art institute.*
Syn. *v.* establish, start, organize, initiate.

in·sti·tu·tion (in′stə·t(y)ōō′shən) *n.*
1 An established organization: *hospitals, universities, and other institutions.* 2 An accepted practice, belief, custom, etc.: *the institution of marriage.* 3 The initiation of something: *the institution of a guaranteed annual wage.*

in·su·la·tion (in′s(y)ə·lā′shən) *n.*
Nonconducting material used to surround something in order to prevent the leakage of electricity, heat, sound, etc.: *a gas leak caused by inadequate insulation.*

in·su·per·a·ble (in·sōō′pər·ə·bəl) *adj.*
Not possible to surmount or overcome: *an insuperable obstacle.*
Syn. insurmountable, unconquerable.
Ant. surmountable, defeatable.

in·sur·gent (in·sûr′jənt) *adj.*, *n.*
adj. Rising in revolt against authority: *The insurgent forces defeated the dictator's army.*
n. A rebel: *Castro's insurgents were victorious.*

in·te·grate (in′tə·grāt) *v.* **in·te·grat·ed, in·te·grat·ing**
1 To bring together or fit together into a whole; to unify: *He integrated the various*

631

episodes into a narrative. **2** To cause to be used or occupied (as a school, park, neighborhood, etc.) by both blacks and whites: *America's continued attempt to integrate public schools.*—**in'te·gra'tion** *n.*
Syn. 1 unite, consolidate, fuse.

in·teg·ri·ty (in·teg'rə·tē) *n.*
1 The quality or state of being honorable, principled, and sincere: *a man of integrity who would never sell out.* **2** The quality or state of being whole and undivided: *the lost integrity of Germany.*
Syn. 1 character, honor. **2** unity, completeness.
Ant. 1 unscrupulousness, immorality. **2** division, fragmentation.

in·tel·li·gent (in·tel'ə·gənt) *adj.*
1 Having an active, discerning mind with the power to reason: *an intelligent child who grew up to be a famous scholar.* **2** Characterized by good reasoning: *an intelligent remark.* **3** Endowed with intellect or understanding: *Is there intelligent life on Mars?*
Syn. 1, 2 bright, brainy, smart. **3** thinking, reasoning.

in·ter (in·tûr') *v.* **in·terred, in·ter·ring**
To place in a grave; bury: *The war hero was interred in Arlington.*—**in·ter'ment** *n.*
Syn. entomb.
Ant. exhume, disinter, disentomb.

in·ter·cept (in'tər·sept') *v.*
To prevent from reaching a destination, as by seizing or destroying: *His uncle intercepted all love letters addressed to him.*

in·ter·cep·tor (in'tər·sep'tər) *n.*
A person or thing that intercepts, especially a fighter plane: *a formation of interceptors.*

in·ter·fer·ence (in'tər·fir'əns) *n.*
1 Obstructing, meddling, or conflicting: *the interference of an electrical storm with television reception.* **2** *In sports* Illegal obstruction of an opponent.

in·ter·im (in'tər·im) *n., adj.*
n. A time between periods or events; an intervening time: *The interim of peace between World Wars I and II.*
adj. Temporary; existing only in the time between periods or events: *an interim appointment.*
Syn. *n.* intermission, interlude.

in·ter·loc·u·to·ry (in'tər·lok'yə·tôr'ē *or* in'tər·lok'yə·tō'rē) *adj.*
Pertaining to or being like a dialogue: *the interlocutory format of TV panel shows.*
Syn. conversational, chatty.

in·ter·mi·na·ble (in·tûr'mə·nə·bəl) *adj.*
Unending or continuing for an unduly long time: *an evening so dull it seemed interminable.*

in·ter·mit·tent (in'tər·mit'ənt) *adj.*
Not continuous; stopping and then starting again at intervals: *intermittent attacks of hay fever.*
Syn. sporadic, discontinuous, interrupted.
Ant. continuous, unbroken, unremitting.

in·ter·pret (in·tûr'prit) *v.* **in·ter·pret·ed, in·ter·pret·ing**

1 To explain the meaning of or to make clear: *to interpret a friend's nail-biting as a sign of nervousness.* **2** To translate out loud: *He interprets Russian speeches for the U.N.*—**in·ter'pret·er** *n.*

in·ter·rupt (in'tə·rupt') *v.*
1 To hinder or stop someone who is talking, working, etc. by speaking or otherwise distracting attention: *to interrupt a conversation.* **2** To break the continuity of; to bring to a temporary halt: *The seamen's strike interrupted the activity of most passenger ships.*

in·ter·sperse (in'tər·spûrs') *v.* **in·ter·spersed, in·ter·spers·ing**
To scatter among other things or to diversify or adorn with other things scattered here and there: *to intersperse the lights with candy canes.*

in·ter·state (in'tər·stāt') *adj.*
Involving two or more states of the United States: *interstate commerce between New York and New Jersey.*

in·ter·stel·lar (in'tər·stel'ər) *adj.*
Between or among the stars: *the vastness of interstellar space.*

in·tes·tate (in·tes'tāt *or* in·tes'tit) *adj.*
Not having made a will before death.

in·tes·ti·nal (in·tes'tə·nəl) *adj.*
Part of or affecting the intestines (the portion of the digestive system extending from the stomach to the anus): *an intestinal virus.*

in·tim·i·date (in·tim'ə·dāt) *v.* **in·tim·i·dat·ed, in·tim·i·dat·ing**
To arouse fear in or to frighten deliberately in order to make compliant: *His deep voice intimidated the child.*—**in·tim'i·da'tion** *n.*
Syn. frighten, scare, terrify.

in to·to (in tō'tō) *adv.*
Latin for completely; with nothing omitted: *to publish the statesman's correspondence in toto.*
Syn. totally, entirely.

in·trac·ta·ble (in·trak'tə·bəl) *adj.*
Stubborn and uncooperative; difficult to control: *an intractable child who responds to every request by howling "No!"*
Syn. unmalleable, disobedient, strong-willed, unruly.
Ant. tractable, docile, submissive.

in·tran·si·gence (in·tran'sə·jəns) *n.*
The act or quality of refusing to compromise: *The intransigence of both management and labor resulted in a ten-month strike.*
Syn. stubbornness, inflexibility, resoluteness.
Ant. cooperativeness, reasonableness.

in·tran·si·gent (in·tran'sə·jənt) *adj., n.*
adj. Refusing to compromise: *The intransigent candidate refused to deviate from his policy even though no one else agreed with him.*
n. One who refuses to compromise: *The convention ended in a deadlock because rightist and leftist intransigents refused to release their delegates to any other candidate.*
Syn. *adj.* uncompromising, unbending, adamant. *n.* irreconcilable, holdout, die-hard.
Ant. *adj.* reasonable, cooperative, flexible.

in·tra·state (in'trə·stāt') *adj.*
Confined within or pertaining to a single state, especially one of the United States: *Certain Federal laws do not apply to intrastate commerce.*

in·trep·id (in·trep'id) *adj.*
Unusually brave; fearless: *an intrepid mountain climber attempting a peak that no one else had dared to climb.*
Syn. dauntless, heroic.
Ant. cowardly, craven, yellow.

in·tri·ca·cy (in'tri·kə·sē) *n.*
1 The condition of being difficult to follow or understand: *We were amazed at the intricacy of his ideas.* 2 Something difficult to follow or understand: *the intricacies of the subway system.*
Syn. complexity.
Ant. simplicity.

in·tri·cate (in'tri·kit) *adj.*
Difficult to follow or understand: *an intricate design.*
Syn. puzzling, complicated, involved.
Ant. simple.

in·trigue (in·trēg' *or* in'trēg) *n.; v.* **in·trigued, in·tri·guing**
n. A plot or scheme: *They arrested the insurgents involved in the political intrigue.*
v. To plot: *to intrigue against those in command.*
Syn. *n.* conspiracy. *v.* conspire.

in·trin·sic (in·trin'sik) *adj.*
Belonging to the true or inner nature of a thing: *First editions are collected for their rarity, not for their intrinsic value.*
Syn. inherent, essential, real, actual.

in·tro·vert (in'trə·vûrt) *n.*
A person whose interest is directed toward himself and his thoughts: *He was too much of an introvert to be a press agent.*
Ant. exhibitionist.

in·tu·i·tion (in'tōō·ish'ən) *n.*
Direct knowledge based on an inner feeling rather than conscious reasoning: *Woman's intuition is often accurate.*
Syn. instinct, hunch.

in·tu·i·tive (in·tōō'ə·tiv) *adj.*
Resulting from intuition: *Her intuitive understanding of his unhappiness surprised him.*

in·un·date (in'un·dāt) *v.* **in·un·dat·ed, in·un·dat·ing**
1 To cover by overflowing: *The swollen river completely inundated the small farm.* 2 To overwhelm with abundance or excess: *The switchboard was inundated with calls.*
Syn. 1 flood, submerge.

in·val·i·date (in·val'ə·dāt) *v.* **in·val·i·dat·ed, in·val·i·dat·ing**
To make worthless or invalid: *His passport was invalidated because he traveled to Cuba.*
Syn. annul, discredit, nullify.
Ant. ratify, confirm, legalize.

in·veigh (in·vā') *v.*
To make a bitter attack in words: *The tenement dwellers inveighed against exorbitant rent increases.*

in·vei·gle (in·vē'gəl *or* in·vā'gəl) *v.* **in·vei·gled, in·vei·gling**
To coax or entice by guile or flattery: *If we try hard, we might inveigle mother into baking us a cake.*
Syn. cajole, beguile.
Ant. discourage.

in·ven·to·ry (in'vən·tôr'ē) *n.*, **in·ven·to·ries** *pl.*,
A complete list of articles, with description, quantity, and value of each: *The owner of the shop submitted an inventory and the price he wanted for the property.*
Syn. stock, supply.

in·verse (in·vûrs' *or* in'vûrs) *adj., n.*
adj. Opposite or reversed in order, effect, etc.: *Subtraction is the inverse operation of addition.*
n. The direct opposite: *Subtraction is the inverse of addition.*
Syn. contrary.

in·vet·er·ate (in·vet'ər·it) *adj.*
Firmly established by long habit or usage: *an inveterate smoker; an inveterate gambler.*
Syn. confirmed, habitual, persistent.

in·vid·i·ous (in·vid'ē·əs) *adj.*
Likely to cause ill will, resentment, or hatred: *invidious remarks attributed to a disgruntled employee.*

in·vin·ci·ble (in·vin'sə·bəl) *adj.*
Not to be overcome or defeated: *invincible guerrillas.*
Spelling tip: The first three vowels are *i*'s; there is no *able* in this word.
Syn. unconquerable, indomitable, irresistible.
Ant. vulnerable, weak, submissive.

in·vis·i·ble (in·viz'ə·bəl) *adj.*
Not capable of being seen: *The bridge was invisible in the fog.*

in·voice (in'vois) *n.; v.* **in·voiced, in·voic·ing**
n. A list sent to a customer describing merchandise shipped, including prices: *There is an error in the invoice.*
v. To list on an invoice: *The dishes were packed and invoiced.*

in·volve (in·volv') *v.* **in·volved, in·volv·ing**
To include or draw in: *They were involved in his business ventures.*

in·vul·ner·a·ble (in·vul'nər·ə·bəl) *adj.*
Incapable of being hurt or damaged: *The fortress was thought to be invulnerable.*
Syn. invincible, secure, impregnable.

i·o·dine (ī'ə·dīn *or* ī'ə·dīn) *n.*
1 A nonmetallic element. 2 An antiseptic.
Spelling tip: This word may also be spelled *iodin.*

i·o·ta (ī·ō'tə) *n.*
1 The ninth letter of the Greek alphabet. 2 A very small amount: *It doesn't make an iota of difference whether you come or not.*
Syn. 2 jot, bit.

i·ras·ci·ble (i·ras'ə·bəl) *adj.*
Easily provoked to anger: *The nurse complained about her irascible and uncooperative patients.*—**i·ras'ci·bil'i·ty** *n.*
Syn. irritable, quick-tempered.

i·rate (ī'rāt) *adj.*
Angry: *The manager listened to the irate customer.*
Syn. enraged.

ir·i·des·cent (ir'ə·des'ənt) *adj.*
Displaying the colors of the rainbow in shifting hues and patterns: *the iridescent glow of soap bubbles.*—**ir'i·des'cence** *n.*

i·ris (ī'ris) *n.*
1 The colored part of the eye around the pupil. **2** A plant with long leaves and colorful flowers. **3** The rainbow.
Etymology: *Iris* is the Greek word for rainbow.

i·ro·ny (ī'rə·nē) *n.*, **i·ro·nies** *pl.*
1 A sarcastic or humorous way of talking in which a person means the opposite of what is said, as "You're welcome" after something has been taken away by force. **2** Such an utterance.—**i·ron'ic** *adj.*
Syn. sarcasm.

ir·rec·on·cil·a·ble (i·rek'ən·sī'lə·bəl) *adj.*
Not able or willing to be reconciled: *irreconcilable factions.*

ir·re·cov·er·a·ble (ir'i·kuv'ər·ə·bəl) *adj.*
Incapable of being recovered or regained: *Youth is irrecoverable.*

ir·re·duc·i·ble (ir'i·dōō'sə·bəl) *adj.*
Not capable of being reduced or made simpler: *an irreducible formula.*

ir·rel·e·vant (i·rel'ə·vənt) *adj.*
Not related to the subject or topic: *She interrupted with a completely irrelevant comment.*

ir·re·me·di·a·ble (ir'i·mē'dē·ə·bəl) *adj.*
Incapable of being remedied, cured, or corrected: *an irremediable mistake.*
Syn. incurable, irreparable, uncorrectable.
Ant. remediable, curable, reparable, correctable.

ir·rep·a·ra·ble (i·rep'ər·ə·bəl) *adj.*
Incapable of being repaired, rectified, remedied, or made good: *irreparable loss of valued antiques destroyed by fire.*—**ir·rep'a·ra·bly** *adv.*
Syn. irremediable, irretrievable, irredeemable, irrecoverable.
Ant. remediable, retrievable, redeemable, recoverable.

ir·re·sis·ti·ble (ir'i·zis'tə·bəl) *adj.*
Incapable of being resisted or opposed: *irresistible charm.*—**ir're·sis'ti·bly** *adv.*
Syn. overwhelming, overpowering, seductive, alluring.

ir·re·spec·tive (ir'i·spek'tiv) *adj.*
Existing without regard or relationship to something else.
Usage: *Irrespective* is used in the adverbial phrase *irrespective of*, which means regardless of; independent of.

ir·re·triev·a·ble (ir'i·trē'və·bəl) *adj.*
Not capable of being retrieved, repaired, or overcome: *an irretrievable loss.*—**ir're·triev'-a·bly** *adv.*
Syn. irreparable, irrecoverable, irremediable, incurable.

Ant. retrievable, recoverable, reparable, remediable, curable.

ir·rev·er·ent (i·rev'ər·ənt) *adj.*
Characterized by or showing a lack of awe, veneration, or respect: *irreverent behavior in church.*—**ir·rev'er·ence** *n.*, **ir·rev'er·ent·ly** *adv.*
Syn. disrespectful, irreligious, blasphemous.
Ant. respectful, pious, religious.

ir·rev·o·ca·ble (i·rev'ə·kə·bəl) *adj.*
Incapable of being revoked, repealed, or brought back: *the irrevocable past.*—**ir·rev'o·ca·bly** *adv.*
Syn. irretrievable, irrecoverable, irreversible, unalterable.
Ant. retrievable, recoverable, reversible, alterable.

ir·ri·ta·ble (ir'ə·tə·bəl) *adj.*
1 Easily aroused, annoyed, or angered: *He was unusually irritable because of a bad night's sleep.* **2** Responding readily or to an abnormal degree to stimuli or the environment: *an irritable muscle.*—**ir'ri·ta·ble·ness** *n.*, **ir'ri·ta·bly** *adv.*
Syn. **1** peevish, snappish, petulant. **2** sensitive, susceptible.
Ant. **1** indifferent, calm, apathetic. **2** insensitive, unsusceptible, insensible.

i·sin·glass (ī'zing·glas' *or* ī'zən·glas') *n.*
1 A preparation of nearly pure gelatin made from the bladders of certain fishes. **2** Another name for mica, a mineral that forms thin, easily separated layers that are tough, flexible, and often transparent.

isle (īl) *n.*
An island, especially one of comparatively small size.

is·n't (iz'ənt) *contraction*
Is not: *Isn't he going?*
Spelling tip: The apostrophe stands for the omitted *o*, so it must be placed between the *n* and the *t*.

i·so·late (ī'sə·lāt) *v.* **i·so·lat·ed, i·so·lat·ing**
To set apart, as from a mass, group, or situation; cause to be alone: *to isolate a person who has a communicable disease.*—**i'so·la'tion** *n.*, **i'so·lat'ed** *adj.*
Syn. separate, segregate, quarantine, exclude.
Ant. join, connect, integrate, include.

i·sos·ce·les (ī·sos'ə·lēz) *adj.*
In geometry A word used to describe a triangle having two sides of equal length.

i·so·tope (ī'sə·tōp) *n.*
Any of two or more forms of an element that have the same atomic number and similar chemical properties but differ in mass number and radioactive behavior.

isth·mus (is'məs) *n.*
A narrow piece of land extending into a body of water and connecting two larger land masses: *the Isthmus of Panama.*

i·tal·ic (i·tal'ik) *n.*, *adj.*
n. Usually pl. A style of type in which the letters slant upward to the right: *These words are printed in italics.*
adj. Designating or printed in such a style of type: *an italic passage.*

i·tin·er·ant (ī·tin'ər·ənt) *adj., n.*
adj. Wandering or traveling from place to place, as in search of employment or to fulfill official duties: *an itinerant preacher.*
n. A person who wanders or travels from place to place.
Syn. *adj.* roving, nomadic. *n.* nomad, migrant.

i·tin·er·ar·y (ī·tin'ə·rer'ē) *n.*, **i·tin·er·ar·ies** *pl.*
1 A plan for or the route to be followed on a journey. 2 A detailed account or record of a journey. 3 A guidebook for travelers.

its (its) *pron.*
The possessive form of *it: The tree has lost its leaves.*
Spelling tip: Don't confuse *its* with the contraction *it's* (meaning *it is* or *it has*).

it's (its) *contraction*
1 It is: *It's two o'clock.* 2 It has: *It's been two years since I last saw her.*

J

jack·al (jak'əl) *n.*
A doglike mammal of Africa or Asia that hunts in packs and feeds on small animals and carrion.

jad·ed (jā'did) *adj.*
Dulled or wearied, as from having too much, eating too much, drinking too much, etc.
Syn. satiated, bored, surfeited.
Ant. excited, keen, titillated.

jag·uar (jag'wär) *n.*
A large, tawny, spotted cat of Central and South America.

jar·gon (jär'gən) *n.*
1 Confused, unintelligible speech. 2 A mixture of two or more dissimilar languages, as Pidgin English. 3 The technical or specialized vocabulary used by the members of a particular profession, sect, etc., when communicating among themselves: *legal jargon.*

jas·mine (jaz'min *or* jas'min) *n.*
Any of various shrubs having very fragrant white, red, or yellow flowers.

jaunt (jônt) *n., v.*
n. A short journey, especially for pleasure: *a jaunt to the country.*
v. To make such a journey: *to jaunt to the seashore for a day of swimming.*

jave·lin (jav'(ə)lin) *n.*
1 A light spear thrown as a weapon. 2 A long spear with a wooden shaft, thrown for distance in an athletic contest.

jeal·ous (jel'əs) *adj.*
1 Fearful or suspicious of being displaced by a rival in affection or favor: *jealous every time his girl friend even looked at another man.* 2 Hostile toward someone because of what he is, has, etc.; envious: *jealous of his brother's wealth.* 3 Careful in guarding or watching: *to be jealous of one's reputation.*—**jeal'ous·y** *n.*, **jeal'ous·ly** *adv.*

Je·ho·vah (ji·hō'və) *n.*
In the Old Testament, a name for God.

jeop·ard·ize (jep'ər·dīz) *v.* **jeop·ard·ized, jeop·ard·iz·ing**
To expose to injury, loss, or failure: *He jeopardized his chances of being elected by speaking too frankly.*
Syn. imperil, risk, endanger.
Ant. safeguard, protect, guard.

jeop·ar·dy (jep'ər·dē) *n.*
Danger of death, loss, injury, failure, etc.: *to put one's life in jeopardy by an act of bravado.*
Syn. peril, risk, hazard.
Ant. safety, security, sanctuary.

jest (jest) *n., v.*
n. 1 Something said or done to provoke laughter: *His constant jests kept the party alive.* 2 A spirit of playfulness; a frivolous mood: *Many serious things are said in jest.*
v. To speak or act in a joking, playful, or frivolous way: *jesting about his own failures.*
Syn. *n.* 1 joke, quip, prank, antic. *v.* joke, quip, caper, frolic.

jet·ti·son (jet'ə·sən) *v.*
1 To drop or throw overboard auxiliary equipment, cargo, etc.: *The airplane jettisoned its auxiliary fuel before making an emergency landing.* 2 To throw away or get rid of anything that hinders or burdens: *The inhumane boss jettisoned his employees as soon as they neared retirement age.*
Syn. 2 eliminate, abandon, forsake.

jew·el·ry (jōo'əl·rē) *n.*
Articles of personal adornment, as rings, necklaces, brooches, etc.

jin·go (jing'gō) *n.*, **jin·goes** *pl.*
A person who boasts of his patriotism and favors an aggressive foreign policy.

jin·go·ism (jing'gō·iz'əm) *n.*
Loud, boastful patriotism or chauvinism, especially when accompanied by demands for an aggressive foreign policy.

jo·cose (jō·kōs') *adj.*
Characterized by, like, or disposed to jesting or joking: *a jocose personality.*—**jo·cose'ly** *adv.*
Syn. jocular, playful.
Ant. serious, solemn.

joc·u·lar (jok'yə·lər) *adj.*
1 Given to joking: *The jocular newcomer was the life of the party.* 2 Having the nature of a joke: *A jocular remark destroyed the serious tone of the conversation.*—**joc'u·lar'i·ty** *n.*, **joc'u·lar·ly** *adv.*
Syn. 1 jesting, waggish. 2 humorous, witty.

joie de vi·vre (zhwà də vēv'r')
A French phrase meaning joy of living: *The old man's joie de vivre was the envy of many younger associates.*

jour·ney·man (jûr'nē·mən) *n.*, **jour·ney·men** *pl.*
A worker who has completed his apprenticeship in a skilled trade or craft.

joust (joust *or* just) *n., v.*
n. A formal combat between two mounted knights armed with lances.
v. To engage in such combat.
Syn. *n., v.* tourney, tilt.

jowl (joul) *n.*
The fleshy part under the lower jaw, especially when it is fat and pendulous.

ju·bi·la·tion (jōō′bə·lā′shən) *n.*
Rejoicing; exultation: *the jubilation of a candidate's supporters after he was elected.*
Syn. delight, elation.
Ant. unhappiness, depression.

judg·ment (juj′mənt) *n.*
1 The act or result of hearing and deciding cases, as by a judge in a court of law. 2 The ability to make wise decisions: *a man with vision and judgment.* 3 A disaster or misfortune regarded as a punishment for sin.
Spelling tip: Words ending in a silent *e* usually retain the *e* before adding *-ment* (as in management or movement). However, there are four notable exceptions in American usage: abridgment, acknowledgment, argument, and judgment.

ju·di·ci·ar·y (jōō·dish′ē·er′ē *or* jōō·dish′ə·rē) *n.*, **ju·di·ci·ar·ies** *pl.; adj.*
n. 1 The department of government that administers the law. 2 The system of courts set up to carry out this function. 3 Judges as a group.
adj. Of or having to do with courts, judges, or the judgments made in courts of law: *judiciary protocol.*

ju·di·cious (jōō·dish′əs) *adj.*
1 Having, showing, or exercising good judgment: *a judicious executive.* 2 Proceeding from or done with good judgment: *a judicious decision.*—**ju·di′cious·ly** *adv.*, **ju·di′cious·ness** *n.*
Syn. 1, 2 wise, sensible.
Ant. 1, 2 unwise.

jug·u·lar (jug′yə·lər) *n., adj.*
n. One of the large veins on either side of the neck that returns blood from the brain, neck, and face to the heart.
adj. Of or having to do with the throat or a jugular vein.

ju·jit·su (jōō·jit′sōō) *n.*
A Japanese system of hand-to-hand fighting in which surprise and a knowledge of anatomy and leverage are used to overcome the weight and strength of one's opponent.
Spelling tip: This word is also spelled *jiujitsu* and *jiujutsu.*

junc·ture (jungk′chər) *n.*
1 A point or line where things are joined; a joint or seam: *the juncture of the finger and the palm.* 2 A point in time, especially one at which a critical decision must be made: *At this juncture, the U.N. must attempt to resolve the Mideast problem.*

jun·ket (jung′kit) *n., v.*
n. 1 A mild-flavored puddinglike dessert made with milk and sugar and coagulated with rennet. 2 A feast, banquet, party, pleasure trip, outing, etc.: *a weekend junket to the country.* 3 An excursion for which all expenses are paid, especially one made by a public official at public expense: *a press junket made in connection with the opening of an important new motion picture.*

v. To go on or take part in a junket.
Syn. *n.* 3 tour. *v.* travel.

jun·ta (jun′tə; *Spanish* hōōn′tä) *n.*
A group of persons who band together for some secret purpose, especially for political intrigue.
Spelling tip: This word may also be spelled *junto* (jun′tō).
Syn. cabal, faction.

ju·ris·dic·tion (jōōr′is·dik′shən) *n.*
1 The legal right to exercise official authority. 2 The extent of such authority, or the territory within which it may be lawfully exercised. 3 The power of those persons who exercise such authority.

ju·ris·pru·dence (jōōr′is·prōōd′ns) *n.*
1 The philosophy or science of law and its administration. 2 A system of laws.

ju·ve·nile (jōō′və·nəl *or* jōō′və·nīl) *adj., n.*
adj. 1 Youthful, young, or immature: *He is constantly criticized for his juvenile approach to life.* 2 Designed or proper for a young person: *juvenile books.*
n. 1 A young person; youth. 2 A book for young persons.

jux·ta·pose (juks′tə·pōz′) *v.* **jux·ta·posed, jux·ta·pos·ing**
To place close together; put side by side: *The designer juxtaposed clashing colors to attain a dramatic effect.*—**jux′ta·po·si′tion** *n.*

K

kai·ser (kī′zər) *n.*
An emperor: *the German Kaiser.*
Etymology: *Kaiser,* as well as *czar,* is derived from the Latin word *Caesar,* the name given to many Roman emperors following Gaius Julius Caesar.

ka·lei·do·scope (kə·lī′də·skōp) *n.*
1 A tube-shaped optical toy that shows constantly changing symmetrical patterns as loose bits of colored glass are moved about under a set of mirrors. 2 A swiftly changing scene, pattern, etc.: *As we flew cross-country we saw a kaleidoscope of land formations.*

ka·lei·do·scop·ic (kə·lī′də·skop′ik) *adj.*
Constantly and swiftly changing like the patterns in a kaleidoscope: *her kaleidoscopic moods.*
Syn. shifting, fluid.
Ant. steady, constant.

kan·ga·roo (kang′gə·rōō′) *n.*
A plant-eating animal native to Australia that has short, weak forelegs, strong hind legs used for leaping, and a long, thick tail: *Female kangaroos carry their young in pouches.*
Syn. wallaby.

ker·o·sene (ker′ə·sēn *or* ker′ə·sēn′) *n.*
An oil distilled from petroleum and used as a fuel in lamps, stoves, and some engines.

key·note (kē′nōt′) *n.*
The basic idea of a philosophy, political platform, literary work, etc.: *Personal liberty is the keynote of American democracy.*
Syn. theme, nub.

khak·i (kak′ē or kä′kē) n., adj.
n. **1** A color ranging from light sand to medium brown. **2** A sturdy cotton cloth of this color, usually used for uniforms: *work pants of khaki.* **3** pl. A uniform made of khaki cloth: *a soldier wearing his khakis.*
adj. Of the color khaki: *a khaki shirt.*

kid·nap (kid′nap) v. **kid·naped** or **kid·napped, kid·nap·ing** or **kid·nap·ping**
To abduct forcefully or fraudulently, often for ransom.—**kid′nap·er** or **kid′nap·per** n.

kiln (kil or kiln) n.
An oven or furnace used for baking pottery, bricks, etc.: *to fire a vase in a kiln.*

kil·o·me·ter (kil′ə·mē′tər or ki·lom′ə·tər) n.
In the metric system, 1000 meters.

ki·mo·no (kə·mō′nə or ki·mō′nō) n.
1 A loose robe fastened with a wide sash, worn in Japan as an outer garment by both men and women. **2** A woman's robe that resembles such a garment.
Syn. 2 dressing gown, housecoat.

kin·der·gar·ten (kin′dər·gär′tən) n.
A school or class for young children, usually between the ages of four and six, in which activities include games, singing, handicrafts, group play, etc.

ki·net·ic (ki·net′ik) adj.
Pertaining to or involving motion: *kinetic energy.*
Ant. static.

kins·man (kinz′mən) n., **kins·men** pl.
A male relative: *his cousins and other kinsmen and kinswomen.*

ki·osk (kē·osk′, kē′osk, or kī′osk) n.
A lightly constructed open booth generally used as a newsstand.

kis·met (kiz′met or kis′met) n.
Fate: *People who believe in kismet think they cannot escape their destinies.*
Etymology: *Kismet* is the English transliteration of *qismet,* the Turkish word meaning fate.
Syn. destiny, predestination.
Ant. chance, accident, luck.

klep·to·ma·ni·a (klep′tə·mā′nē·ə) n.
The compulsion to steal.

klep·to·ma·ni·ac (klep′tə·mā′nē·ak) n.
A person with an irresistible and persistent desire to steal.

knack (nak) n.
The ability to learn something effortlessly and do it skillfully: *a knack for carpentry.*
Syn. talent, aptitude.

knap·sack (nap′sak′) n.
A case or bag worn strapped across the shoulders and used for carrying equipment and supplies.
Syn. rucksack, haversack.

knave (nāv) n.
1 A dishonest or dishonorable man; a scoundrel: *Don't trust him—he's a knave.* **2** A playing card (the jack).
Syn. 1 rogue, rascal.

knead (nēd) v.
1 To mix and work dough, clay, etc., into a mass of uniform consistency by pressing, turning, and pulling with the hands: *She kneaded the dough.* **2** To massage by thumps and squeezes with the hands: *The masseur kneaded the soft flesh.*

knick·er·bock·ers (nik′ər·bok′erz) n.pl.
Wide, short breeches gathered below the knee.
Etymology: This word came from Diedrich *Knickerbocker,* the fictitious Dutch author of Washington Irving's *History of New York,* because knickerbockers resemble Dutch breeches.

knick·knack (nik′nak) n.
A trifling article; a trinket: *to arrange china dogs and other knickknacks on a shelf.*
Syn. trifle, gewgaw, bagatelle.

knit (nit) v. **knit** or **knit·ted, knit·ting;** n.
v. **1** To form a fabric or garment by interlocking loops of a single yarn: *to knit a sweater.* **2** To fasten or unite closely and firmly, or to reunite or mend: *His broken bone knitted well.* **3** To draw the brow together into wrinkles: *to knit one's brows in thought.*
n. The fabric or garment made by knitting: *a wool knit.*
Syn. v. 3 furrow, contract, pucker.

knob (nob) n.
1 A rounded handle, as for opening a door. **2** Any rounded protuberance; a lump: *a knob on the tree trunk.*
Syn. 2 swelling, knurl.

knock (nok) n., v.
n. A sharp rapping sound: *a knock at the door.*
v. **1** To make a sharp rapping noise, as by striking with the knuckles: *to knock on a door.* **2** To make a pounding or clanking noise, as an engine with faulty transmission: *the car is old and the engine knocks.* **3** To bump or strike: *to knock a man down.* **4** *Informal* To disparage, criticize, or belittle: *Don't knock her efforts at self-improvement.*

knoll (nōl) n.
A small, round hill: *a grassy knoll.*
Syn. mound, hillock, hummock.

know (nō) v. **knew, known, know·ing**
1 To be aware of or to have the facts about: *Do you know what happened?* **2** To be familiar with or acquainted with: *I have known her for years.* **3** To be certain of: *I know the sun will rise tomorrow.* **4** To be able to identify or to be able to distinguish between: *to know the difference between right and wrong.*

knowl·edge (nol′ij) n.
1 Awareness or recognition of: *A baby has no knowledge of right and wrong.* **2** What someone knows: *His knowledge is limited.*

kum·quat (kum′kwot) n. or **cum·quat**
A small orangelike fruit with a sour pulp and edible rind, or the tree that bears this fruit.

L

lab·o·ra·to·ry (lab′rə·tôr′ē or lab′rə·tō′rē) n.
lab·o·ra·to·ries pl.
A building or room equipped for scientific experiments, analyses, tissue and blood

examinations, etc.: *to conduct an experiment in a laboratory.*

la·bo·ri·ous (lə·bôr′ē·əs *or* lə·bō′rē·əs) *adj.*
1 Requiring much hard work: *Digging a trench is a laborious task.* **2** Hard-working; industrious: *A laborious worker earns quick promotions.*
Syn. 1 strenuous, difficult. **2** diligent, assiduous.
Ant. 1 easy, effortless. **2** lazy, feckless.

lab·y·rinth (lab′ə·rinth) *n.*
1 An arrangement of winding, intricate passages or paths designed to confuse whoever tries to go through and find the exit. **2** By extension, any intricate, perplexing, hard-to-solve problem, condition, etc.: *The three-page labyrinth of instructions was utterly confusing.*
Syn. maze.

lab·y·rin·thine (lab′ə·rin′thin *or* lab′ə·rin′-thēn) *adj.*
Pertaining to a maze, or as intricate and perplexing as a maze: *a labyrinthine geometry problem.*
Syn. baffling, complicated.
Ant. simple, uncomplicated.

lack·a·dai·si·cal (lak′ə·dā′zi·kəl) *adj.*
Languid; listless: *Everyone moves in a lackadaisical manner in very hot weather.*
Syn. enervated, sluggish, half-hearted.
Ant. energetic, peppy, animated.

la·con·ic (lə·kon′ik) *adj.*
Brief and concise: *a laconic summary.*
Syn. terse, pithy.
Ant. wordy, verbose, redundant.

la·ger (lä′gər) *n.*
A beer stored for sedimentation before use: *Drink lager from a stein.*

lag·gard (lag′ərd) *n., adj.*
n. One who is slow and usually falls behind; a straggler: *Everyone except a few laggards finished the task in twenty minutes.*
adj. Falling behind; slow or delayed: *The laggard postman never delivered our mail until late afternoon.*
Syn. *n.* slowpoke, dawdler. *adj.* tardy.
Ant. *adj.* fast, prompt, punctual.

la·gniappe (lan′yap *or* lan·yap′) *n.*
A small gift given to a customer by a merchant: *The grocer gave small boxes of candy as lagniappes.*
Syn. gratuity, bonus, tip.

lais·sez faire (les′ā fâr′)
A doctrine opposing government control or interference in economic affairs.

la·i·ty (lā′ə·tē) *n.*
The people who are not members of the clergy or of a specific profession: *Such problems must be decided by medical men and not the laity.*
Syn. laymen.

lamb (lam) *n.*
A young sheep.
Spelling tip: Watch the silent *b* in words such as lam*b*, bom*b*, com*b*, and dum*b*.

la·men·ta·ble (lam′ən·tə·bəl *or* lə·ment′ə·bəl) *adj.*
Bad or unfortunate enough to warrant regret or pity: *a shocking and lamentable failure.*
Syn. deplorable, distressing, sorrowful.

lam·poon (lam·poon′) *n., v.*
n. A written attack using humor to provoke contempt: *The losing coach was the object of a lampoon in the college paper.*
v. To attack in a lampoon.
Syn. *n.* satire, mockery. *v.* satirize, ridicule.

lan·guid (lang′gwid) *adj.*
Lacking energy or spirit: *She extended her hand in a languid gesture of welcome.*
Syn. weak, listless.
Ant. energetic.

lan·guor (lang′gər) *n.*
A lack of energy or enthusiasm: *the languor of patients convalescing from serious illnesses.*—**lan′guor·ous** *adj.*
Syn. listlessness, lassitude.
Ant. vivacity, liveliness.

lap·i·dar·y (lap′ə·der′ē) *n.*
A workman who cuts, engraves, or polishes precious stones.

lapse (laps) *n.; v.* **lapsed, laps·ing**
n. **1** An error or slip: *a lapse of taste.* **2** An interval; pause: *a lapse of time.*
v. **1** To pass gradually: *to lapse into a coma.* **2** To become void: *His insurance policy lapsed when he did not pay the premium.*

lar·ce·ny (lär′sə·nē) *n.,* **lar·ce·nies** *pl.*
The unlawful taking of another person's property: *He was charged with grand larceny.*—**lar′ce·nous** *adj.,* **lar′ce·nous·ly** *adv.*
Syn. theft.

lar·gess (lär·jes′) *n.*
Liberal giving: *The poor used to depend on the largess of the wealthy for food and clothing.*

lar·i·at (lar′ē·ət) *n.*
1 A rope used to tie an animal to a stake while grazing. **2** A lasso.

lar·va (lär′və) *n.,* **lar·vae** (lär′vē) *pl.*
An insect in its early stage of development.

lar·yn·gi·tis (lar′ən·jī′tis) *n.*
Inflammation of the larynx: *The singer had laryngitis, so the performance was canceled.*

lar·ynx (lar′ingks) *n.,* **la·ryn·ges** *or* **lar·ynx·es** *pl.*
The upper part of the respiratory tract containing the vocal cords.

las·civ·i·ous (lə·siv′ē·əs) *adj.*
Having or arousing sexual desires: *The play was denounced as being lewd and lascivious.*
Syn. lustful.
Ant. chaste, innocent.

las·si·tude (las′ə·t(y)ood) *n.*
A state of weariness or fatigue: *A deep lassitude overcame her, and she slept.*

la·tent (lā′tənt) *adj.*
Present but not visible or active: *the latent force of an atomic bomb.*
Syn. dormant, potential, abeyant.

lat·er·al (lat′ər·əl) *adj.*
Situated at, occurring, or coming from the side: *a lateral pass.*

lathe (lāth) *n.*
A machine used to hold and turn an article against a cutting tool so as to shape it.

lat·i·tude (lat'ə·t(y)ōōd) *n.*
1 Distance north and south of the Equator.
2 Freedom from restriction: *Seniors are allowed a certain latitude by the faculty.*

lat·ter (lat'ər) *adj.*
1 Nearer to the end: *reading the latter part of the book.* 2 Being the second of two things referred to: *Chocolate and vanilla ice cream are equally popular, but do you prefer the latter?*
Ant. former, first.

laud·a·ble (lôd'ə·bəl) *adj.*
Deserving praise: *Caring for foster children is a laudable occupation.*
Syn. commendable, admirable.

laud·a·tory (lô'də·tôr'ē) *adj.*
Expressing or containing praise: *a laudatory speech commending the astronauts.*
Syn. complimentary.
Ant. derogatory.

launch (lônch) *v., n.*
v. 1 To move or push a vessel into the water, especially for the first time: *The battleship was launched on Saturday.* 2 To start off; begin: *to launch an attack on crime.* 3 To set forcibly in motion: *They plan to launch the rocket at noon.*
n. A motor-driven pleasure boat.

lau·rel (lôr'əl) *n.*
An honor or distinction gained by outstanding achievement: *His promotion added another laurel to his career.*
Syn. decoration, prize, trophy.

lav·ish (lav'ish) *adj., v.*
adj. Generous to the point of being excessive: *Such lavish hospitality shocked the neighbors.*
v. To give generously: *She lavished affection on her family and friends.*
Syn. *adj.* profuse, bounteous. *v.* shower.
Ant. *adj.* limited. *v.* withhold.

lay (lā) *v.* laid, lay·ing; *adj.*
v. 1 To put or place: *Lay your keys on the table.* 2 To construct, produce, or establish as a basis or support: *to lay the groundwork.* 3 To settle: *Water helped lay the dust.* 4 To set; prepare: *Lay the table for dinner.*
adj. 1 Having to do with the laity as opposed to the clergy: *a lay preacher.* 2 Not belonging to or endorsed by a learned profession: *Solicit both expert and lay opinions.*

lead (lēd) *v.* led, lead·ing; *n.*
v. 1 To go with or ahead of in order to show the way: *The guide led the tourists.* 2 To control the actions of, or to command or influence greatly: *to lead a child by the hand; to lead a country.* 3 To be first: *The Yankees are leading in the pennant race.* 4 To be a way or a cause: *Idleness leads to boredom.*
n. 1 The act of commanding or guiding: *Follow his lead.* 2 A starring role, or the performer playing it: *Cary Grant played the male lead.* 3 The distance or amount by which one is ahead or winning: *The home run increased their lead.* 4 Indication; clue: *The detectives searched for some lead.*

league (lēg) *n.*
An association of persons, organizations, or states, formed for some common purpose: *the League of Nations.*
Syn. alliance.

lech·er·y (lech'ə·rē) *n.,* **lech·er·ies** *pl.*
Unrestrained and excessive sexual indulgence.
Syn. lasciviousness, debauchery.
Ant. celibacy, chastity.

lec·tern (lek'tərn) *n.*
A stand having a sloping, shelflike surface on which a lecturer standing behind it can place books, papers, etc.: *The speaker stood behind the lectern.*

leg·end (lej'ənd) *n.*
1 An unauthenticated story from very early times preserved by tradition and popularly thought to be historical: *the legends about Charlemagne.* 2 A title or caption, as accompanying an illustration, diagram, etc.: *The legend under the map explains the symbols.*
Syn. 1 saga, myth.

leg·en·dar·y (lej'ən·der'ē) *adj.*
Pertaining to, of the nature of, or famous in a legend: *the legendary adventures of Robin Hood.*
Syn. mythical, fabled.

leg·i·ble (lej'ə·bəl) *adj.*
Clearly written or printed; easy to read: *large, very legible type.* —**leg'i·bil'i·ty** *n.,* **leg'i·bly** *adv.*
Syn. readable, distinct, bold.
Ant. blurred, faint, unclear.

le·gion·naire (lē'jən·âr') *n.*
A member of any military or honorary organization called a legion.

leg·is·late (lej'is·lāt) *v.* **leg·is·lat·ed, leg·is·lat·ing**
To make a law or laws: *Congress is the branch of government that legislates.*

leg·is·la·ture (lej'is·lā'chər) *n.*
The lawmaking body of a nation or state.

lei·sure (lē'zhər *or* lezh'ər) *n.*
Time available for recreation and relaxation: *After he retired he did not know what to do with so much leisure.*

leit·mo·tif (līt'mō·tēf') *n.*
In music A theme that represents a certain person, event, emotion, or idea throughout an opera, etc.: *the leitmotif of a character in a Wagnerian opera.*
Spelling tip: This word may also be spelled *leitmotiv.*

length (lengkth *or* lenth) *n.*
1 Linear extent from end to end, as distinguished from width and thickness: *The length of the string is two inches.* 2 Extent or duration from beginning to end: *the length of a book.*

le·ni·ent (lē'nē·ənt *or* lēn'yənt) *adj.*
Gentle or merciful; mild: *The lenient judge gave him a suspended sentence.*
Syn. easygoing, tolerant.
Ant. severe, harsh.

lens (lenz) *n.*
1 A piece of glass or other transparent

substance that makes rays of light converge or diverge, or two or more such pieces in combination: *a microscope lens.* 2 The part behind the iris of the eye that focuses images on the retina.

leop·ard (lep′ərd) *n.*
A carnivorous mammal of the cat family, which has a tawny coat with clusters of dark brown or black spots.

le·sion (lē′zhən) *n.*
Any abnormal or harmful change in the structure of an organ or tissue: *a lesion of the kidney.*

less·en (les′ən) *v.*
To decrease: *The drug lessened his pain.*
Syn. reduce, diminish.
Ant. increase, augment.

le·thal (lē′thəl) *adj.*
Causing death: *a lethal blow.*
Syn. fatal, deadly, mortal.

le·thar·gic (li·thär′jik) *adj.*
Apathetic and drowsy; sluggish: *On hot, humid days people feel lethargic.*—**leth·ar·gy** (leth′ər·jē) *n.*
Syn. languid, listless..
Ant. energetic, peppy.

let·tuce (let′is) *n.*
A cultivated herb having crisp, edible leaves, or the leaves of such a plant.

leu·ke·mi·a (lōō·kē′mē·ə) *n.*
Cancer of the blood.

lev·ee (lev′ē) *n.*
1 An embankment, especially along the shore of a river, built for protection against floods. 2 An official reception given by a person of high rank early in the day; formerly, an official audience held by a person of high rank before or upon rising from bed: *the king's levee.*

lev·er (lev′ər *or* lē′vər) *n.*
1 A device consisting of a rigid bar pivoting on a fixed support and used to pry up heavier objects: *Use the lever to lift the heavy mass of iron.* 2 A bar that operates on this principle: *A crowbar is a type of lever.* 3 Any means of exerting effective power: *Lobbyists use money as a lever.*

lev·er·age (lev′ər·ij *or* lē′vər·ij) *n.*
The use of a lever, or the power exerted by using a lever: *enough leverage to move a rock.*

le·vi·a·than (lə·vī′ə·thən) *n., adj.*
n. 1 A gigantic water beast mentioned several times in the Bible. 2 Any enormous creature or thing: *a leviathan of a ship.*
adj. Gigantic: *Compiling a dictionary is a leviathan job.*

lewd (lōōd) *adj.*
1 Characterized by lust or debauchery: *a lewd, evil-minded man.* 2 Obscene: *a lewd joke.*
Syn. 1 lustful, lecherous, lascivious. 2 indecent, bawdy.
Ant. 1 pure, strait-laced. 2 decent, refined.

lex·i·con (lek′sə·kon) *n.*
1 A dictionary, especially a dictionary of

Greek, Latin, or Hebrew. 2 A list of words relating to a particular subject: *an engineering lexicon.*

li·a·bil·i·ty (lī′ə·bil′ə·tē) *n.,* **li·a·bil·i·ties** *pl.*
1 The state or condition of being legally responsible, as for debts or damages: *Each member of a corporation has limited financial liability.* 2 An obstacle in the way of success: *Lack of confidence is a liability to an actor.* 3 *pl.* Entries on a balance sheet showing debts.
Syn. 1 responsibility, accountability. 2 disadvantage, handicap.

li·ai·son (lē′ā·zon′, lē·ā′zon, *or* lē′ə·zon) *n.*
1 A means for maintaining communication, or the act or state of such communication: *An ambassador is the official liaison between two governments.* 2 A love affair: *a liaison lasting twenty-five years.*
Syn. 1 contact, link.

li·bel (lī′bəl) *n.; v.* **li·beled** *or* **li·belled, li·bel·ing** *or* **li·bel·ling**
n. 1 A false or malicious written statement or drawing, especially a published one, that damages a person's reputation or exposes him to public ridicule. 2 The act of making or having made such a statement.
v. To make such a statement or drawing about: *The jury ruled that the author had libeled Mr. X.*—**li′bel·ous** *adj.*
Usage: *Libel* denotes written defamation of character. Defamatory remarks made orally are *slander.*

li·bid·i·nous (li·bid′ə·nəs) *adj.*
Characterized by excessive sexual desire: *a man so libidinous that any woman excited him.*
Syn. lustful, lecherous.
Ant. pure, chaste, ascetic.

li·bi·do (li·bē′dō *or* li·bī′dō) *n.*
1 *In psychoanalysis* The instinctual craving or drive behind all human activities. 2 Sexual desire or impulse.

li·cense (lī′sens) *n.; v.* **li·censed, li·cens·ing**
n. 1 An official document giving permission to engage in some activity, own something, etc.: *Renew your driver's license.* 2 Excessive, unrestrained freedom that constitutes an abuse of liberty: *Freedom to murder with impunity is not liberty but license.* 3 Relaxation of the usual rules or restraints, especially for artistic effect: *poetic license.*
v. To grant a license to or for: *Each state licenses automobiles.*

li·chen (lī′kən) *n.*
Any of various flowerless plants composed of algae and fungi growing in flat, greenish gray, brown, yellow, or black patches on rocks, trees, etc.

lic·o·rice (lik′ə·ris *or* lik′rish) *n.*
A perennial herb, the dried root or extract of this plant, or a candy made from it.

lied (lēd; German lēt) *n.,* **lied·er** *pl.*
A German song, especially a ballad or love poem set to music.

lien (lēn) *n.*
A legal right to claim or dispose of property

in payment of or as security for a debt: *The bank has a lien on his estate.*
Syn. claim.

lieu (lōō) *n.*
Stead; place (now used only in the phrase *in lieu of*): *I'll take time off in lieu of overtime pay.*

lieu·ten·ant (lōō·ten'ənt) *n.*
1 A military rank. **2** A person able to perform the duties of his superior, either in the latter's absence or under his direction.
Etymology: This word comes from *lieu* (place) + *tenant* (to hold): someone who holds the place of someone else.

light·ning (līt'ning) *n.*
A sudden flash of light caused by a discharge of electricity between two clouds or between a cloud and the Earth.
Spelling note: There is no *e* in this word and there are only two syllables.

like·ly (līk'lē) *adj.* **like·li·er, like·li·est;** *adv.*
adj. **1** Having or showing a tendency (to); apt (to): *He is likely to forget our date.* **2** Plausible: *a likely explanation.* **3** Imminent; probable: *His promotion is likely.*
adv. Probably: *She will likely be early.*

li·lac (lī'lak) *n., adj.*
n. A shrub bearing fragrant purplish or white flowers.
adj. Having the purple color of lilac blossoms.

lim·pid (lim'pid) *adj.*
1 Not cloudy: *a limpid pool of water.* **2** Clear and simple, as in style: *a writer of limpid verse.*
Syn. 1 transparent. **2** lucid, logical.
Ant. 1 foggy. **2** vague.

lin·e·age (lin'ē·ij) *n.*
Line of descent: *He was of royal lineage.*
Spelling tip: Do not confuse *lineage* with *linage. Linage,* which can also be spelled *lineage,* refers to the number of lines in written or printed matter and is pronounced (lin'ij).
Syn. ancestry, family, stock.

lin·e·a·ment (lin'ē·ə·mənt) *n.*
A facial feature or contour: *The deep lineaments of his face evidenced a hard life.*
Spelling tip: Do not confuse this word with *liniment,* a liquid preparation to relieve pain and stiffness.

lin·ger·ie (lan'zhə·rē or län'zhə·rā) *n.*
Women's underwear or nightwear: *That shop specializes in stockings and lingerie.*

lin·guist (ling'gwist) *n.*
1 A person who speaks several languages. **2** An expert or student of linguistics.

lin·guis·tics (ling·gwis'tiks) *n.*
The scientific study of language.
Syn. philology.

li·queur (li·kûr') *n.*
A sweet alcoholic liquor: *cherry liqueur.*
Spelling tip: Do not confuse this word with *liquor,* meaning any alcoholic beverage.
Syn. cordial.

liq·ui·date (lik'wə·dāt) *v.* **liq·ui·dat·ed, liq·ui·dat·ing**
1 To pay off or settle, as a debt: *After twenty years the mortgage was finally liquidated.* **2** To convert into cash, as securities: *He liquidated his stock and put the money in his checking account.*—**liq'ui·da'tion** *n.*

liq·uor (lik'ər) *n.*
1 An alcoholic beverage, as whiskey, rum, etc. **2** Any liquid, as broth, juice, etc.

lisle (līl) *n.*
A fine twisted cotton thread, or a fabric made from it.

lis·some (lis'əm) *adj.*
Moving with ease and grace: *the lissome body of the Swedish starlet.*
Syn. lithe, supple, agile.

lit·a·ny (lit'ə·nē) *n.,* **lit·a·nies** *pl.*
A form of prayer consisting of a series of supplications by the minister with responses by the congregation: *the litany for the dead.*

li·ter (lē'tər) *n.*
In the metric system, a measure of capacity equal to the volume of one kilogram of water or of 1.0567 quarts liquid measure.

lit·e·ra·ti (lit'ə·rä'tē or lit'ə·rā'tē) *n.pl.*
Literate or educated persons collectively: *He was highly esteemed by the literati of Paris.*
Syn. intelligentsia, scholars, avant-garde.

lithe (līth) *adj.*
Bending easily or gracefully: *the lithe body of a trained dancer.*—**lithe'ly** *adv.,* **lithe'ness** *n.*
Syn. supple, pliant, limber.

lit·i·ga·tion (lit'ə·gā'shən) *n.*
The act or process of bringing or carrying on a lawsuit: *The estate was in litigation for years.*

lit·ur·gy (lit'ər·jē) *n.,* **lit·ur·gies** *pl.*
In various religions, the prescribed forms or rituals for public worship.

live·li·hood (līv'lē·hood) *n.*
Means of supporting oneself: *Do you earn your own livelihood?*
Syn. living, maintenance, support.

live·li·ness (līv'lē·nəs) *n.*
The quality of being full of energy or motion: *the liveliness of a fast dance.*
Syn. animation, bounce, vivacity.
Ant. quietness, lethargy.

loan (lōn) *n., v.*
n. Something lent, especially a sum of money lent at interest, or the act of lending.
v. To lend: *Don't loan money to a friend.*
Ant. *v.* borrow.

loath (lōth) *adj.*
Very reluctant; unwilling: *Many people are loath to get up in the morning.*
Syn. averse, disinclined.
Ant. willing, eager.

loathe (lōth) *v.* **loathed, loath·ing**
To feel great hatred or disgust for: *I loathe slimy snakes!*
Syn. detest, abhor, abominate.
Ant. like, love, admire.

loath·some (lōth′səm) *adj.*
Repulsive; arousing disgust: *the loathsome stench of rotting garbage.*
Syn. disgusting, revolting.
Ant. agreeable, pleasant.

lo·cale (lō·kal′) *n.*
A place or location: *The play is set in a rustic locale.*
Syn. locality, setting.

lode (lōd) *n.*
A large deposit of ore: *the mother lode of iron ore.*

loge (lōj) *n.*
A box or upper section in a theater.

lon·gev·i·ty (lon·jev′ə·tē) *n.*
Great age, or the tendency to live long: *The hundred-year-old man attributed his longevity to clean living.*

lon·gi·tude (lon′jə·t(y)ōod *or* long′gə·t(y)ōod) *n.*
Distance east or west from the Earth's center: *Longitude can be expressed either in time or in arc.*—**lon′gi·tu′di·nal** *adj.*
Ant. latitude.

lo·qua·cious (lō·kwā′shəs) *adj.*
Very talkative: *a loquacious woman who chatters almost constantly.*
Syn. garrulous, gabby.
Ant. silent, taciturn.

lor·gnette (lôr·nyet′) *n.*
1 Eyeglasses with an ornamental handle into which they may be folded when not in use. 2 Opera glasses with a long handle.

lo·thar·i·o (lō·thâr′ē·ō) *n.*, **lo·thar·i·os** *pl.*
(Often capital *L*) A fickle seducer: *a Lothario who had seduced at least a hundred women.*
Etymology: *Lothario* was a rake in Nicholas Rowe's play *The Fair Penitent.*
Syn. Don Juan, Casanova, rake.

lout (lout) *n.*
An awkward, boorish fellow: *The lout stepped all over my feet when we waltzed.*
Syn. boor, clod, oaf.

lu·cid (lōo′sid) *adj.*
1 Easily understood; clearly explained: *a lucid explanation.* 2 Rational; sane: *a lucid interval between spells of delirium.*
Syn. 1 clear, intelligible. 2 balanced.
Ant. 1 muddy, incomprehensible. 2 mad, deranged, irrational.

lu·cra·tive (lōo′krə·tiv) *adj.*
Producing or yielding money or other gain; profitable: *a lucrative business.*
Syn. money-making, remunerative.
Ant. unprofitable.

lu·di·crous (lōo′də·krəs) *adj.*
Ridiculous: *the ludicrous suggestion that Lassie run for President.*
Syn. absurd, laughable, preposterous.

lu·gu·bri·ous (lōo·g(y)ōo′brē·əs) *adj.*
Very sad or mournful, especially in a ludicrous manner: *the lugubrious expression of a clown who has just taken a pratfall.*

lu·mi·nar·y (lōo′mə·ner′ē) *n.*, **lu·mi·nar·ies** *pl.*
1 Any body that gives light, especially the sun or the moon: *the luminaries of the night sky.* 2 A very famous person: *Hollywood luminaries.*
Syn. 2 celebrity, star.

lu·mi·nous (lōo′mə·nəs) *adj.*
Full of light or giving off light; glowing or shining: *her luminous eyes; the luminous stars.*

lu·nar (lōo′nər) *adj.*
Pertaining to the moon: *the lunar landscape.*

lu·rid (l(y)ōor′id) *adj.*
Shocking, vivid, or sensational: *a magazine with lurid reports of sex and murder.*

lus·ter (lus′tər) *n.*
1 Soft, reflected light; sheen: *the luster of gold.* 2 Brightness or brilliance of light: *the matchless luster of the sun.* 3 Splendor or glory, as of achievement, renown, beauty, etc.: *the luster of the golden age of Greece.*
Syn. 1 gloss, shimmer. 2 radiance. 3 brilliance.
Ant. 1, 2 dullness, darkness, tarnish. 3 mediocrity, insignificance.

lus·trous (lus′trəs) *adj.*
Glossy or shining: *Gold is a lustrous metal.*
Syn. bright, gleaming, sparkling.
Ant. dark, dull.

lux·u·ri·ant (lug·zhŏŏr′ē·ənt *or* luk·shŏŏr′ē·ənt) *adj.*
Growing lushly and profusely, as vegetation, or abundant and ornate, as a design: *the luxuriant vegetation of a tropical rain forest; a luxuriant, noveau-art painting.*

lux·u·ri·ous (lug·zhŏŏr′ē·əs *or* luk·shŏŏr′ē·əs) *adj.*
Characterized by or conducive to opulence or extreme comfort: *a luxurious house complete with two Olympic-size swimming pools.*
Syn. sumptuous, plush, palatial.
Ant. poor, shabby, seedy.

ly·ce·um (lī·sē′əm) *n.*, **ly·ce·ums** *or* **ly·ce·a** (lī·sē′ə) *pl.*
1 An organization providing lectures, concerts, etc., for the public. 2 The building in which such an organization is housed.

lye (lī) *n.*
An acid solution usually leached from ashes or derived from an alkaline substance: *Lye is used in making soap.*

lyre (līr) *n.*
A harplike stringed instrument with four to ten strings and a sounding board: *The ancient Greeks played lyres.*

M

ma·ca·bre (mə·kä′brə *or* mə·kä′bər) *adj.*
Suggesting death and decay; gruesome: *a macabre movie about vampires and ghouls.*
Syn. bloodcurdling, horrible, creepy.

mac·ad·am (mə·kad′əm) *n.*
1 A road paved by spreading and fusing small pieces of stone. 2 The broken stone used to build such a road.
Etymology: John L. McAdam (1756–1836), a Scottish engineer, invented the process.
Ant. unpaved, dirt.

mac·er·ate (mas'ə·rāt) *v.* **mac·er·at·ed, mac·er·ating**
To reduce a solid substance to pulp by soaking in liquid: *Food is macerated as it passes through the digestive system.*

Mach·i·a·vel·li·an (mak'ē·ə·vel'ē·ən) *adj., n.*
adj. 1 Based on or resembling the amoral, practical principles for getting and keeping political power that were described in Niccolò Machiavelli's book *The Prince: Stalin maintained power through Machiavellian acts of persecution.* 2 By extension, any behavior involving scheming and deceitfulness: *his Machiavellian schemes to disgrace his boss.*
n. A follower of Machiavelli's principles.

mach·i·na·tion (mak'ə·nā'shən) *n.*
An act that is part of a scheme or plot: *His devious machinations were never publicized.*

mad·am (mad'əm) *n.,* **mes·dames** (mā·däm') *pl.*
A title meaning "my lady," formerly used to address noblewomen but now used to any woman: *"Yes, madam," said the maid.*

mad·ame (mad'əm, *French* mà·däm') *n.,* **mesdames** (mā·däm', *French* mā·däm') *pl.*
The French title of courtesy for a married woman, equivalent to the English *Mrs.*

mad·e·moi·selle (mad'ə·mə·zel', *French* màd·mwà·zel') *n.,* **mad·e·moi·selles** or *French* **mes·de·moi·selles** (mād·mwà·zel') *pl.*
The title of an unmarried Frenchwoman, equivalent to the English *Miss.*

mad·ri·gal (mad'rə·gəl) *n.*
An unaccompanied song with parts for several singers.

mael·strom (māl'strəm) *n.*
A whirlpool or any turbulent, dangerous, and irresistible force: *the maelstrom of passion.*

ma·es·tro (mä·es'trō or mīs'trō) *n.,* **ma·es·tros** *pl.*
An eminent conductor, composer, or performer of music, or a master in any other art.

mag·a·zine (mag'ə·zēn' or mag'ə·zēn) *n.*
1 A periodical publication, usually with a paper cover and illustrations, containing stories, articles, etc. 2 A part of a gun holding ammunition: *the magazine of the rifle.* 3 A building or room for storing explosives and ammunition, or a warehouse for storing military supplies.

mag·is·te·ri·al (maj'is·tir'ē·əl) *adj.*
1 Pertaining to or like a public official who administers and enforces the law: *the dean's magisterial duties.* 2 Dictatorial; domineering: *He barked out orders in a magisterial manner.*
Syn. 2 bossy, imperious.
Ant. 2 meek, deferential.

mag·na·nim·i·ty (mag'nə·nim'ə·tē) *n.*
The quality of generosity, as in forgiving insults or injuries: *the magnanimity of a man who goes out of his way to do a favor for a former enemy.*
Syn. nobility, high-mindedness.
Ant. pettiness, meanness.

mag·nan·i·mous (mag·nan'ə·məs) *adj.*
Manifesting or characterized by generosity in forgiving insults or injuries: *a magnanimous gesture.*
Syn. generous.
Ant. petty.

mag·nate (mag'nāt) *n.*
A famous or influential person, especially within some industry: *Hearst was a newspaper magnate.*
Syn. tycoon, mogul, VIP.

mag·ni·tude (mag'nə·t(y)ōōd) *n.*
1 Size; importance: *the magnitude of the problem.* 2 The relative brightness of a star: *The brightest stars have a magnitude of 1 and the weakest have a magnitude of 6.*
Syn. 1 extent, greatness.

main·tain (mān·tān') *v.*
1 To carry on or to preserve; to keep in existence: *to maintain friendly relations.* 2 To assert or to claim to be true: *He maintains his innocence.*
Syn. 1 sustain, continue. 2 uphold.
Ant. 1 discontinue, terminate, end. 2 deny.

main·te·nance (mān'tə·nəns) *n.*
1 The act of keeping or continuing, or the state of being kept or continued: *the maintenance of a standing army.* 2 Means of support. 3 The work of keeping roads, buildings, etc., in good condition: *the maintenance of highways.*

maitre d'hô·tel (me'tr' dō·tel') *n.*
A headwaiter or steward: *The maître d'hôtel led them to a table.*
Usage: In informal American usage this noun is often shortened to *maitre d'* (mā'trə dē').

ma·jor·i·ty (mə·jôr'ə·tē or mə·jor'ə·tē) *n.,* **ma·jor·i·ties** *pl.*
1 More than half of a given number or group: *the majority of the voters.* 2 The number of votes cast for a candidate, bill, etc. over and above the total number of remaining votes. 3 The time or fact of reaching legal age: *He will inherit the money on his majority.*

mal·a·prop·ism (mal'ə·prop·iz'əm) *n.*
1 A phrase or sentence that is comical or nonsensical because the speaker used a wrong word that sounded something like the word he really meant. 2 The act of misusing word(s) in this way.
Etymology: The word *malapropism* derives from the name of Mrs. Malaprop, a character who ludicrously misused words in the 1775 comedy *The Rivals* by Richard B. Sheridan.

mal·con·tent (mal'kən·tent) *adj., n.*
n. A person who is dissatisfied.
adj. Discontented; dissatisfied: *restless and malcontent youth.*
Syn. *n.* dissident, complainer. *adj.* unsatisfied, disgruntled.

mal·e·dic·tion (mal'ə·dik'shən) *n.*
The pronouncing of a curse against someone: *his maledictions against his enemies.*
Syn. execration, imprecation.
Ant. benediction, blessing.

ma·lev·o·lent (mə·lev′ə·lənt) *adj.*
Wishing evil toward others: *He is so malevolent that he hopes his enemies will die.*
Syn. malign, malignant, malicious.
Ant. benign, friendly.

ma·li·cious (mə·lish′əs) *adj.*
Revealing or characterized by the desire to injure another; spiteful: *her malicious gossiping.*
Syn. malevolent, vicious.
Ant. good-natured, helpful.

ma·lign (mə·līn′) *v.* **ma·ligned, ma·lign·ing;** *adj.*
v. To spread false charges about someone: *His enemies maligned him by saying he practiced black magic.*
adj. **1** Wishing or trying to do evil to others: *a malign man.* **2** Tending to do harm: *a malign infection.*
Syn. *v.* defame, villify. *adj.* **1** malevolent, malicious.
Ant. *v.* praise, extol. *adj.*

ma·lig·nant (mə·lig′nənt) *adj.*
1 Becoming progressively worse: *a malignant tumor.* **2** Tending to do great harm: *the malignant power of prejudice.* **3** Having an evil disposition toward others: *The malignant old man liked to make other people suffer.*
Syn. 1 virulent, cancerous. **2** pernicious, destructive. **3** evil, malevolent.
Ant. 1 benign, self-limited. **2** beneficial, innocuous. **3** kind, good-natured.

mall (môl, mal, *or* mel) *n.*
A promenade or walk, usually public and having trees, or a street of shops closed off to vehicles and enhanced with trees, benches, etc.

mal·le·a·ble (mal′ē·ə·bəl) *adj.*
1 Capable of being hammered or rolled out without breaking, as a metal: *Soft gold is very malleable.* **2** Easy to shape and mold: *a docile, malleable child.*
Syn. 1 ductile, pliable, flexible. **2** tractable.
Ant. 1 brittle, rigid, hard. **2** intractable, independent.

mam·mon (mam′ən) *n.*
Riches regarded as an evil influence and ignoble goal: *He who worships mammon does not worship God.*

mam·moth (mam′əth) *n., adj.*
n. **1** A large, once very abundant but now extinct elephant. **2** By extension, anything characterized by immense size, weight, etc.: *the ship was a mammoth.*
adj. Huge: *a mammoth factory covering forty acres.*
Syn. *n.* **2** colossus, giant. *adj.* immense, gigantic, enormous.
Ant. *n. adj.* tiny, diminutive, miniature.

man·date (man′dāt *or* man′dit) *n.*
1 An instruction from an electorate to its representative, expressed by the results of an election: *the people's mandate.* **2** An authoritative command, as of a sovereign: *the mandate of the king.* **3** Formerly, a charge to a nation by the League of Nations authorizing the administration and development of a territory, colony, etc.

man·da·to·ry (man′də·tôr′ē *or* man′də·tōr′ē) *adj.*
Required by or as if required by an authoritative command; compulsory: *soldiers wearing the mandatory khaki uniform.*
Syn. obligatory.
Ant. optional.

ma·neu·ver (mə·n(y)oo′vər) *n., v.*
n. **1** A planned movement, as of troops, warships, etc.: *to carry out military maneuvers.* **2** Any adroit move or instance of clever management: *a wily maneuver helped her get introduced to the prince.*
v. To manage or conduct skillfully; handle; manipulate.

mange (mānj) *n.*
An itching skin disease of dogs and other domestic animals caused by parasitic mites.

man·ger (mān′jər) *n.*
A trough or box for feeding horses and cattle: *the oats in the manger.*

man·gy (mān′jē) *adj.* **man·gi·er, man·gi·est**
1 Affected with or resembling mange (an animal skin disease): *a mangy dog.* **2** Shabby: *a mangy old rug.*

man·i·fest (man′ə·fest) *adj. v.*
adj. Plainly apparent or self-evident; obvious: *a manifest truth.*
v. To reveal or make apparent.
Syn. *adj.* evident, clear. *v.* show, display.
Ant. *adj.* doubtful, improbable. *v.* conceal, mask.

man·i·fes·to (man′ə·fes′tō) *n.,* **man·i·fes·toes** *or* **man·i·fes·tos** *pl.*
A public and formal declaration of principles, intentions, etc., as by a political faction or other movement: *the Dadaist manifesto.*
Syn. proclamation.

man·i·fold (man′ə·fōld) *adj.*
Having many and varied forms, types, elements, features, etc.: *the manifold joys of Man.*
Syn. multiple, many-faceted.

ma·nip·u·late (mə·nip′yə·lāt) *v.* **ma·nip·u·lat·ed, ma·nip·u·lat·ing**
1 To manage people, figures, stocks, etc., shrewdly and deviously, especially for one's own profit: *to manipulate people by using flattery.* **2** To control, move, etc., with the hands, especially to move skillfully: *a watchmaker manipulating all the minute parts.*

man·ne·quin (man′ə·kin) *n.*
1 A full-size model of a complete or partial human figure, especially a model with movable joints, used by tailors, artists, etc.: *Drape the clothes on the mannequin.* **2** A fashion model: *The mannequins paraded down the runway.*
Syn. 1 dummy.

man·u·fac·tur·er (man′yə·fak′chär·ər) *n.*
One who makes or produces some product, especially with machinery: *a radio manufacturer.*
Syn. maker, producer.

ma·raud·er (mə·rôd′ər) *n.*
A person who roves and raids in search of

plunder: *The marauders stripped twenty farm-houses.*
Syn. raider, plunderer, pillager.

mar·ga·rine (mär′jə·rin *or* mär′jə·rēn) *n.*
A butter substitute made from vegetable oils, milk, and seasoning.

mar·i·nate (mar′ə·nāt) *v.* **mar·i·nat·ed, mar·i·nat·ing**
To soak a food in a liquid before cooking or serving: *He marinated the beef in wine.*

mar·i·tal (mar′ə·təl) *adj.*
Pertaining to marriage: *He liked marital life better than life as a bachelor.*
Syn. matrimonial, conjugal.
Ant. unmarried, single.

mar·i·time (mar′ə·tīm) *adj.*
Situated on or near the sea or pertaining to ocean shipping, navigation, etc.: *Newfoundland is a maritime province. Maritime commerce is faster than overland commerce.*
Syn. sea, marine.

mar·mo·set (mär′mə·zet) *n.*
A small, squirrellike monkey having soft, woolly hair and a long, hairy tail: *Marmosets live in Central and South America.*

mar·quee (mär·kē′) *n.*
A canopy, usually of metal, used as a signboard and shelter over the sidewalk in front of a theater, hotel, etc.: *the neon-lit marquee of a movie theater.*

mar·quis (mär′kwis, *French* màr·kē′) *n.*
An aristocrat ranking below a duke but above a count or earl: *The title of marquis is hereditary.*

mar·quise (mär·kēz′) *n.*
1 The wife or widow of a French marquis.
2 In gem cutting, a pointed oval form, especially for diamonds.

mar·row (mar′ō) *n.*
1 A soft tissue in the cavities of most bones.
2 The essence, innermost part, or most important part of something: *the marrow of the problem.*
Syn. 2 pith, core, quintessence.
Ant. 2 surface, periphery.

mar·tial (mär′shəl) *adj.*
Characteristic of, suggesting, or suitable for war or warriors: *the martial music of John Philip Sousa.*
Etymology: The word *martial* derives from *Mars,* the Roman god of war.
Syn. warlike, military, militant.

mar·ti·net (mär′tə·net′) *n.*
Someone who demands rigid adherence to rules, etc.; one who imposes military or equally strict discipline: *a martinet who insisted that the cadets eat square meals while sitting at attention.*
Etymology: The word *martinet* derives from General Jean Martinet, a seventeenth-century French drillmaster.
Syn. disciplinarian, autocrat.

mar·tyr (mär′tər) *n., v.*
n. 1 A person who submits to death rather

than renounce his religion: *the early Christian martyrs.* 2 A person who dies, suffers, or sacrifices everything for a principle, cause, etc.: *a martyr who endured torture rather than betray his comrades.*
v. To make a martyr of someone by persecuting or killing him: *Joan of Arc was martyred.*

mar·vel·ous (mär′vəl·əs) *adj.*
1 Causing astonishment: *a marvelous juggler.*
2 *Informal* Very good: *a marvelous time—*
mar′vel·ous·ly *or* **mar′vel·lous·ly** *adv.*
Spelling tip: This word may also be spelled with two *l*'s: *marvellous.* Be sure to end the word with *-ous.*
Syn. 1 wondrous, amazing, awe-inspiring.

mas·quer·ade (mas′kə·rād′ *or* mäs′kə·rād′) *n.; v.* **mas·quer·ad·ed, mas·quer·ad·ing**
n. 1 A social gathering at which the guests are masked and dressed in costumes: *She wore a shepherdess costume to the masquerade.*
2 A pretense or disguise: *a masquerade of piety.*
v. 1 To take part in a masquerade; to wear a mask or disguise: *masquerading guests at the Halloween ball.* 2 To disguise one's true identity or character: *a Russian spy who masqueraded as a British newsman.*
Syn. *n.* 1 costume ball. 2 simulation, pose, sham. *v.* 2 pose.

mas·sa·cre (mas′ə·kər) *n.; v.* **mas·sa·cred, mas·sa·cring**
n. A savage and indiscriminate killing of human beings, as in warfare, persecutions, etc.: *the massacre of civilian populations.*
v. 1 To kill indiscriminately or in great numbers: *Nazis massacred the Jews.* 2 To defeat severly, as in sports: *The visitors massacred our home team.*
Syn. *n.* slaughter, butchery, bloodbath. *v.* slaughter, butcher, murder.

mas·sage (mə·säzh′) *n.; v.* **mas·saged, mas·sag·ing**
n. A mechanical or manual manipulation of parts of the body, as by rubbing, kneading, etc.: *A good massage relaxes the muscles.*
v. To rub and knead someone's body: *The masseuse massaged his back.*

mas·ti·cate (mas′tə·kāt) *v.* **mas·ti·cat·ed, mas·ti·cat·ing**
To grind to a pulp before swallowing: *Humans masticate solid food, but dogs swallow it in chunks.*
Syn. chew.

ma·te·ri·al (mə·tir′ē·əl) *n., adj.*
n. 1 The substance of which anything is made: *building material such as brick, concrete, and wood.* 2 Cloth: *Is that material cotton or rayon?* 3 Anything used for creating or developing something: *fresh material for his novel.*
adj. 1 Pertaining to the body (as opposed to the mind) or to tangible objects (as opposed to ideas, spirits, etc.): *their material well-being.* 2 Important or relevant: *The health of the President was a material issue in the campaign.*

ma·ter·nal (mə·tûr′nəl) *adj.*
Pertaining to, resembling, or inherited from
a mother: *maternal love.*
Syn. motherly, matriarchal.
Ant. paternal, fatherly.

mat·i·nee (mat′ə·nā′) *n.*
A performance of a play, movie, concert, etc.,
during the daytime, usually the afternoon.
Etymology: This word goes back to *Matuta*,
Roman goddess of morning.
Spelling tip: *Matinée* (same pronunciation)
is an alternate spelling.

mat·ri·cide (mat′rə·sīd) *n.*
1 The killing of one's mother: *Orestes committed matricide—he murdered his mother.*
2 One who kills his mother: *Orestes was a
matricide.*

ma·trix (mā′triks) *n.*, **ma·trix·es** or **ma·tri·ces**
(mā′trə·sēz *or* mat′rə·sēz) *pl.*
That in which something is created, shaped,
or contained: *to cast a printing plate in a
metal matrix.*
Syn. mold, womb, source.

ma·ture (mə·t(y)o͝or′ *or* mə·cho͝or′) *adj.; v.*
ma·tured, ma·tur·ing
adj. Fully grown or developed: *a puppy and
a mature dog; a mature, well-developed plan.*
v. **1** To grow to adulthood or to full development. **2** To come due: *The promissory note
had matured.*—**ma·tur′i·ty** *n.*
Ant. *adj.* immature, undeveloped.

maud·lin (môd′lin) *adj.*
Excessively and tearfully emotional or senti-
mental: *a maudlin drunk.*
Etymology: The word *maudlin* derives from
Madeleine, the Old French spelling of (Mary)
Magdalen, who is often depicted with eyes
swollen from weeping.
Syn. self-pitying, bathetic, weepy.
Ant. cheerful, gay.

mau·so·le·um (mô′sə·lē′əm) *n.*, **mau·so·le·ums**
or **mau·so·le·a** (mô′sə·lē′ə) *pl.*
1 A large, stately tomb: *The ancient ruler was
interred in a magnificent mausoleum.* **2** By
extension, a large and very gloomy house:
*The house he inherited was an ornate mauso-
leum without sunlight or cheer.*

mauve (mōv *or* mawv) *n.*
n. **1** A coal-tar violet dyestuff: *Mauve is
made by oxidizing aniline.* **2** Any of various
purplish-rose shades: *Mauve is brighter than
lavender but lighter than purple.*

mav·er·ick (mav′ər·ik) *n.*
1 An unbranded or orphaned calf or other
animal: *The first person to claim and brand a
maverick becomes its owner.* **2** One who is unorthodox in his ideas, attitudes, etc.: *the
unconventional, odd-sounding opinions of a
maverick.*
Etymology: This word derives from the
name of Samuel A. Maverick, a nineteenth-
century Texas lawyer who did not brand
his cattle.
Syn. 2 nonconformist.
Ant. 2 conformist, organization man.

max·im (mak′sim) *n.*
A proverb; a brief statement of a general
principle or rule of conduct: *The saying
"Don't throw good money after bad" is a
maxim.*
Syn. precept, adage.

may·hem (mā′hem) *n.*
1 *In law* The crime of violently injuring or
maiming someone's body: *He was convicted
of assault with the intent to commit mayhem.*
2 Any situation of violence, noise, confusion,
etc.: *the mayhem that resulted when five tigers
ran amok through the city.*

may·on·naise (mā′ə·nāz′) *n.*
A salad dressing made from egg yolks, butter
or olive oil, lemon juice or vinegar, and spices.

mean (mēn) *v.* **meant, mean·ing;** *adj.*
v. **1** To intend; to be planning or trying to do
something: *Did you mean to hurt her feelings?*
2 To intend to express: *That's not what I
meant.*
adj. Disagreeable or malicious, of inferior
quality, or ignoble and contemptible: *a mean,
sometimes vicious dog.*
Syn. *v.* 1 plan, desire. 2 denote, signify.

me·an·der (mē·an′dər) *v.*
To wander aimlessly or to follow a winding,
twisting path: *meandering along the river-
bank.*
Etymology: This word derives from the Greek
name of the extraordinarily winding Meander
River.
Syn. ramble, wind.

mec·ca (mek′ə) *n.*
A place or attraction visited by many people,
or the thing to which one aspires: *The Riviera
is a vacationer's mecca.*
Etymology: This word derives from the holy
city of Mecca, where Moslems make pilgrimages.

mech·a·nism (mek′ə·niz′əm) *n.*
1 The parts or arrangement of parts of a
machine, or something similar to a machine
in the working of its parts: *the mechanism of a
watch; the wonderful mechanism of the human
body.* **2** The process or technique by which
something works: *the mechanism of democracy.*

med·dle·some (med′l·səm) *adj.*
Interfering: *a meddlesome busybody.*
Syn. officious.

me·di·an (mē′dē·ən) *n.*
The point in a series in which there are as
many instances above as below.
Usage: *Mean* and *median* are both terms for
an arithmetic average. The *mean* is the average computed by adding the values and
dividing by the number of values; the *median*
is the midpoint. Thus in the series 1, 2, 3, 4,
10, the *arithmetic mean* is 4 (1 + 2 + 3 + 4
+ 10 ÷ 5, the total number of values) and
the *median* is 3 (two values are below the 3
and two are above it).
Syn. middle, midpoint.

med·i·cal (med′i·kəl) *adj.*
Pertaining to medicine: *a medical school for
future doctors.*

me·dic·i·nal (mə·dis′ə·nəl) *adj.*
Having the properties of a medicine; curative: *medicinal herbs.*

med·i·cine (med′ə·sən) *n.*
1 Any substance used in the treatment of disease or relief of pain: *Aspirin is a medicine.*
2 The science of the preservation of health and curing of disease: *Medicine is practiced by doctors.*
Syn. 1 drug, medicament.

me·di·e·val (mē′dē·ē′vəl *or* med′ē·ē′vəl) *adj.*
Pertaining to the Middle Ages (about A.D. 476 to about 1450): *Knights jousted in medieval times.*
Spelling tip: This word may also be spelled *mediæval.*

me·di·o·cre (mē′dē·ō′kər *or* mē′dē·ō′kər) *adj.*
Of only average quality; not of high quality: *a mediocre performance with nothing particular to recommend it.*—**me′di·oc′ri·ty** *n.*
Usage: Although *mediocre* means "average," it is a much more derogatory word.
Syn. commonplace, ordinary, run-of-the-mill.
Ant. excellent, fine, superior.

med·i·ta·tion (med′ə·tā′shon) *n.*
The act of musing or reflecting upon a subject; continuous and contemplative thinking: *to reach a conclusion after several hours of meditation.*
Syn. contemplation, pondering.

me·di·um (mē′dē·əm) *n.*, **me·di·ums** for def. 1, **me·di·ums** *or* **me·di·a** (mē′dē·ə) *for defs. 2, 3, pl.; adj.*
n. **1** A person who can communicate with supernatural forces, especially one who transmits messages from the spirits of the dead. **2** The form or materials used by an artist: *Sculptors' media include bronze, marble, and clay. His medium is poetry, not prose.* **3** A substance in which something lives or is transmitted: *Salt water is a fish's medium. News media are papers, magazines, radio, and television.*
adj. Intermediate in quantity, quality, size, degree, etc.: *Do you like rare or medium rare steak?*
Syn. *n.* **1** spiritualist, clairvoyant.

med·ley (med′lē) *n.*
1 A mingled and confused group of separate parts: *Her sewing basket is a medley of pins, needles, buttons, and thread.* **2** A musical composition made up of different airs or parts of songs arranged as a continuous whole: *a medley consisting of snatches of songs from "Oklahoma!"*

meer·schaum (mir′shəm, mir′shôm, *or* mir′shoum) *n.*
A soft, light, and heat-resistant material, or a pipe made from this material: *Does he smoke a corncob pipe or a meerschaum?*

mel·an·chol·y (mel′ən·kol′ē) *adj., n.*
adj. Very sad or gloomy: *a rainy, melancholy day.*
n. A mood of great sadness; low spirits: *He endured deep melancholy after his wife died.*

Syn. depression, despondency.
Ant. gaiety, happiness.

mé·lange (mā·länzh′) *n.*
A mixture of many different elements: *The furniture was a mélange of Victorian, Early American, and modern styles.*

me·lee mā·lā′ *or* mā′lā) *n.*
A confused, general fight involving many people and hand-to-hand fighting: *What started off as a fistfight between two men became a melee when many passers-by joined in.*
Syn. brawl, affray, fracas.

mel·lif·lu·ous (mə·lif′loo·əs) *adj.*
Sweetly or smoothly flowing: *the soothing, unbroken rhythm of a mellifluous religious chant.*—**mel·lif′lu·ous·ly** *adv.*, **mel·lif′lu·ous·ness** *n.*
Syn. dulcet, melodious.
Ant. harsh, discordant.

me·men·to (mə·men′tō) *n.*, **me·men·tos** or **me·men·toes** *pl.*
Anything that is a reminder of the past: *a scrapbook with mementos of school days.*
Syn. souvenir, remembrance.

mem·oir (mem′wär) *n.*
Usually pl, Personal reminiscences, especially a narrative of events that the writer participated in or observed: *the general's memoirs about World War II.*

mem·o·ran·dum (mem′ə·ran′dəm) *n.*, **mem·o·ran·dums** *or* **mem·o·ran·da** (mem′ə·ran′də) *pl.*
1 A brief note of something to be remembered, or an informal record of observations, transactions, etc.: *The businessman jotted down a memorandum of his telephone conversation.* **2** An informal letter, usually sent between departments in a firm: *an interoffice memorandum.* **3** *In diplomacy* An informal statement or summary of an issue, decision, etc.: *The ambassador sent the foreign minister a memorandum defining his government's position.*

mé·nage (mā·näzh′) *n.*
The members of a household; a domestic establishment.
Spelling tip: This word may also be written without the accent mark.

men·da·cious (men·dā′shəs) *adj.*
Lying; deceitful or false: *Don't believe anything he says for he is a mendacious man.*—**men·da′cious·ly** *adv.*
Ant. honest, trustworthy.

men·di·cant (men′də·kənt) *n., adj.*
n. **1** A beggar: *a mendicant beseeching passers-by for money.* **2** A member of an order of monks who beg: *Not all friars are mendicants.*
adj. Begging: *the mendicant children of war-torn lands.*
Syn. *n.* **1** panhandler.
Ant. *n.* **1** philanthropist, benefactor. *adj.* philanthropic.

men·in·gi·tis (men′ən·jī′tis) *n.*
A serious disease characterized by inflammation of the meninges (three membranes that envelop the brain and spinal cord).
—**men′in·git′ic** *adj.*

men·thol (men′thôl, men′thōl, *or* men′thol) *n.*
A white, waxy-textured crystalline alcohol obtained from (and smelling like) oil of peppermint: *Menthol is used as a flavoring agent in perfumes, medicines, and cigarettes.*—**men′-tho·lat′ed** *adj.*

men·tor (men′tər *or* men′tôr) *n.*
A wise and trusted teacher and guide: *The boy's uncle was his mentor, guiding him and molding his character.*—**men·to′ri·al** *adj.*
Etymology: This word derives from Mentor who, according to the *Odyssey*, was the wise guardian of Ulysses' son Telemachus.

men·u (men′yo͞o) *n.*
1 A list of the dishes being served at a meal, or a list of the dishes available in a restaurant and (usually) the price of each dish: *He read the menu and then ordered his dinner.* 2 The dishes that constitute a meal: *She planned the week's menus.*
Syn. 1 bill of fare.

mer·cu·ri·al (mər·kyo͞or′ē·əl) *adj.*
Lively, quick-witted, and characterized by rapid, unpredictable changes of mood or activity: *the prima donna's mercurial temperament.*
Etymology: *Mercurial* derives from Mercury, the Roman messenger of the gods who was depicted as fleet-footed, quick-witted, eloquent, and thievish.
Syn. volatile, changeable.

mere·ly (mir′lē) *adv.*
Nothing more than; only: *Don't worry about my illness—it's merely a cold.*
Syn. solely, simply.

mer·e·tri·cious (mer′ə·trish′əs) *adj.*
Flashy, attractive, or impressive but worthless or phony: *the meretricious kindliness of a political candidate kissing a baby.*—**mer′e·tri′-cious·ly** *adv.*, **mer′e·tri′cious·ness** *n.*

me·ringue (mə·rang′) *n.*
A cake, tart crust, or topping consisting of stiffly beaten whites of eggs mixed with sugar and baked.

mer·it (mer′it) *n.*
1 Excellence: *a man of merit; a book's literary merit.* 2 Something admirable, of high quality, or valuable: *Intelligence and unselfishness are his greatest merits.*
Syn. 1 worth, value. 2 virtue.
Ant. 1 worthlessness, trashiness. 2 failing, drawback, fault.

me·sa (mā′sə) *n.*
A high, broad, flat plateau with steep, rocky sides, common in the southwestern United States.

mes·mer·ize (mes′mə·rīz *or* mez′mə·rīz) *v.* **mes·mer·ized, mes·mer·iz·ing**
To hypnotize: *He mesmerized the subject, putting him into a deep trance and then having him obey orders.*—**mes′mer·ist** *n.*

mes·quite (mes·kēt′ *or* mes′kēt) *n.*
1 A spiny shrub that yields sweet pods used for cattle fodder, found in the southwestern U.S. and southward to Peru. 2 The screw bean (a shrub of the mimosa family).
Spelling tip: This word is also spelled *mesquit.*

met·al·lur·gy (met′ə·lûr′jē) *n.*
The science of extracting metals from ores and processing them into various raw materials.—**met′al·lur′gist** *n.*

met·a·mor·pho·sis (met′ə·môr′fə·sis) *n.*, **met·a·mor·pho·ses** (met′ə·môr′fə·sēz) *pl.*
1 A great change in the form and structure of an animal during its development from embryo to adult: *the metamorphosis of a tadpole into a frog.* 2 Any drastic change of appearance, basic characteristics, etc.: *her metamorphosis from a tomboy into a flirt.*
Syn. 2 transformation, transfiguration, transmutation.

met·a·phor (met·ə·fôr *or* met′ə·fər) *n.*
A phrase or sentence that expresses a likeness between two things but does not contain the word *like* or *as.*
Usage: A *simile* is the same as a *metaphor* except that it does contain the word *like* or *as: "He was a lion in battle" is a metaphor, but "He was like a lion in battle" is a simile.*

mete (mēt) *v.* **met·ed, met·ing**
To allot or distribute by or as by measure.
Spelling tip: Be careful not to confuse this word with *meet* or *meat.*
Syn. dole, measure.

me·te·or·ol·o·gy (mē′tē·ə·rol′ə·jē) *n.*
The scientific study of weather.—**me′te·or·ol′o·gist** *n.*

me·tic·u·lous (mə·tik′yə·ləs) *adj.*
Very or excessively careful about details, including tiny and unimportant details.—**me·tic′u·lous·ly** *adv.*, **me·tic′u·lous·ness** *n.*
Syn. painstaking, finicky.
Ant. careless, sloppy.

me·trop·o·lis (mə·trop′ə·lis) *n.*, **me·trop·o·lis·es** *pl.*
A large city that is a center of culture, trade etc., or the principal city of a region: *Omaha is a thriving metropolis in Nebraska.*

mien (mēn) *n.*
Bearing or appearance: *an old general with a soldierly mien.*
Spelling tip: A nasty man with a *mean mien*—watch the spelling of these two words, which are pronounced alike.

mi·grant (mī′grənt) *n.*, *adj.*
n. One who moves from one region to another regularly or often, as an itinerant worker: *grape-pickers and other migrants.*
adj. Moving from one region to another regularly or often: *migrant workers.*
Syn. *adj.* itinerant, migratory.

mile·age (mī′lij) *n.*
1 The total length (in miles) of a road, journey, etc. 2 The average number of miles traveled by a car per one gallon of fuel.

mi·lieu (mē·lyœ′) *n.*
An environment; surroundings: *Children of the jet set grow up in a high-society milieu.*
Syn. background, atmosphere.

mil·i·tant (mil′ə·tənt) *adj.*
adj. Aggressive, warlike, or actively engaged in conflict or fighting: *Was it a nonviolent or militant demonstration?*

n. One who believes in or practices militant political actions rather than peaceful ones: *Militants believe in massive civil disobedience.* **Syn.** *adj.* activist, revolutionary, aggressive, violent. *n.* activist. **Ant.** *adj.* nonviolent, peaceful, orderly, gradual.

mi·li·tia (mə·lish′ə) *n.*
A group of citizens enrolled in military units separate from the national army and navy and called out only in emergencies: *He isn't in the armed forces but he's in the militia.*—**mi·li′tia·man** *n.*

mil·len·ni·um (mi·len′ē·əm) *n.*, **mil·len·ni·a** (mi·len′nē·ə) or **mil·len·ni·ums** *pl.*
1 One thousand years: *Nearly two millennia have passed since* A.D. *1.* **2** According to the New Testament, a thousand years during which Christ will someday rule the world. **3** By extension, a hypothetical time of virtue, happiness, human perfection, etc.: *the Marxist millennium of economic equality.*—**mil·len′ni·al** *adj.*
Syn. 3 utopia, paradise, golden age.

mil·li·ner·y (mil′ə·ner′ē) *n.*
Women's hats, or the trade of making women's hats: *a shop selling berets, bonnets, cloches, and other millinery.*

mim·e·o·graph (mim′ē·ə·graf′ or mim′ē·ə·gräf′) *n.*, *v.*
n. A machine that reproduces copies of typewritten pages, tracings, etc., by means of a stencil wrapped around a rotary drum.
v. To produce with a mimeograph machine: *Mimeograph twelve more copies.*

mim·ic (mim′ik) *v.* **mim·icked, mim·ick·ing;** *n.*, *adj.*
v. **1** To imitate by copying: *a small boy mimicking his father shaving.* **2** To ridicule someone by imitating: *He cruelly mimicked her lisp.*
n. One who imitates, especially one clever at comic imitations: *mimics, comedians, and other nightclub entertainers.*
adj. Imitative: *the playful kitten's mimic ferocity.*
Syn. *v.* **1** ape, simulate, feign. **2** parody, caricature. *adj.* make-believe, mock. **Ant.** *adj.* natural, genuine.

min·a·ret (min′ə·ret′) *n.*
A high, slender, balconied tower attached to an Islamic mosque (temple) or any similar tower.

mince (mins) *v.* **minced, minc·ing**
1 To walk or behave in an excessively affected way: *The six-footer minced along with ridiculously tiny steps.* **2** To cut or chop into tiny pieces: *to mince an onion.*
Syn. 2 hash, dice.

min·er (mīn′ər) *n.*
One who digs for coal, metallic ores, etc.: *a coal miner.*
Spelling tip: Do not confuse miner and minor.

min·i·a·ture (min′ē·ə·cher or min′ə·chər) *n.*, *adj.*
n. A very small portrait or replica: *A ship in a bottle is a miniature of an actual ship.*

adj. Very small; tiny: *a miniature camera about the size of a matchbox.*
Syn. *adj.* minute, wee, Lilliputian.
Ant. *adj.* big, large.

min·ion (min′yən) *n.*
A despicably servile favorite or follower: *The prince's minions flattered him extravagantly.*
Syn. lackey, flunkey, toady.

min·is·ter (min′is·tər) *n.*, *v.*
n. **1** A clergyman: *the minister's Sunday sermon.* **2** An official appointed to head a department of a government: *the minister of finance.* **3** An official diplomatic representative ranking just below an ambassador: *a minister accredited to the French government.*
v. To give help or care: *Nurses minister to the sick.*
Syn. *n.* **1** pastor, cleric. *v.* tend, care for.

min·u·et (min′yōō·et′) *n.*
A stately dance for couples, or the music for such a dance: *The minuet originated in seventeenth-century France.*

min·utes (min′its) *n.pl.*
A formal record of the business discussed and transacted at a meeting: *The secretary of the club read the minutes of the last meeting.*

mi·nu·ti·a (mi·n(y)ōō′shi·ə or mi·n(y)ōō′shə) *n.*, **mi·nu·ti·ae** (mi·n(y)ōō′shi·ē) *pl.*
Usually pl. Small, unimportant details: *Concentrate on important things and not on minutiae.*
Syn. trivia, trifles.
Ant. essentials, basics.

mir·a·cle (mir′ə·kəl) *n.*
1 A supernatural happening or act: *the miracle of Lourdes.* **2** Any wonderful or amazing thing; marvel: *This secretary is a miracle of efficiency.*—**mi·rac′u·lous** *adj.*

mis·ad·ven·ture (mis′ad·ven′chər) *n.*
An unlucky happening or accident; misfortune: *Barring misadventure, we'll arrive before noon.*
Syn. mischance, mishap.

mis·al·li·ance (mis′ə·lī′əns) *n.*
An undesirable alliance or marriage: *With such different backgrounds their marriage would be a misalliance.*

mis·an·thrope (mis′ən·thrōp) *n.*
A person who hates his fellow men.

mis·ap·pre·hen·sion (mis′ap·ri·hen′shən) *n.*
A failure to understand or interpret correctly: *My misapprehensions about the candidate's qualifications vanished when I read his platform.*

mis·ce·ge·na·tion (mis′i·jə·nā′shən) *n.*
Marriage between persons of different races.

mis·chance (mis·chans′) *n.*
Bad luck: *If by some mischance you lose the directions, call me.*
Syn. mishap, misfortune, misadventure.

mis·con·strue (mis′kən·strōō′) *v.* **mis·con·strued, mis·con·stru·ing**
To interpret wrongly: *He misconstrued my intentions and thought I wanted to rob him instead of help him.*
Syn. misunderstand, misinterpret.

mis·cre·ant (mis′krē·ənt) *n., adj.*
n. An evildoer: *vicious crimes perpetrated by miscreants.*
adj. Villainous: *a miscreant gang of hoodlums.*

mis·de·mean·or (mis′di·mē′nər) *n.*
Any legal offense less serious than a felony.

mis·giv·ing (mis·giv′ing) *n.*
A feeling of doubt or mistrust: *He found college work very difficult and had misgivings about his ability to learn.*

mis·hap (mis′hap or mis·hap′) *n.*
An unfortunate accident: *She tripped on the stair, and as a result of this mishap she was on crutches for two weeks.*
Syn. misfortune.

mis·no·mer (mis·nō′mər) *n.*
An incorrect name: *"Fun City" would be a misnomer for a troubled town.*

mis·og·a·mist (mis·og′ə·mist) *n.*
A person who hates marriage.

mis·og·y·ny (mis·oj′ə·nē) *n.*
Hatred of women.—**mis·og′y·nist** *n.*, **mis·og′y·nous** *adj.*

mis·sal (mis′əl) *n.*
A book containing material used in celebrating Mass.
Spelling tip: Don't confuse *missal* and *missile.*

mis·shap·en (mis·shā′pən) *adj.*
Poorly shaped; deformed: *The pitcher had a misshapen spout.*

mis·sile (mis′əl) *n.*
An object, especially a weapon, intended to be thrown or projected: *The mob threw rocks and other missiles at the police.*

mis·spell (mis·spel′) *v.* **mis·spelled** or **mis·spelt, mis·spell·ing**
To spell incorrectly: *List the words you misspelled in this essay.*

mis·tle·toe (mis′əl·tō) *n.*
A small evergreen plant having white, waxy berries, often used as a Christmas decoration.

mit·i·gate (mit′ə·gāt) *v.* **mit·i·gat·ed, mit·i·gat·ing**
To make or become less severe or rigorous: *Morphine mitigates pain. The governor mitigated the prison sentence.*
Syn. alleviate, soften, lessen.

mo·bile (mo′bəl or mō′bēl *adj.*, mō′bēl *n.*) *adj., n.*
adj. 1 Easily moved: *a mobile army field hospital.* 2 Capable of changing or responding easily, as to emotions: *He had the mobile face of a well-trained actor.*
n. A type of sculpture made of movable parts: *She enjoyed making mobiles.*

mo·bi·lize (mō′bə·līz) *v.* **mo·bi·lized, mo·bi·liz·ing.**
1 To prepare for war: *to mobilize troops.* 2 To assemble and make ready for use: *to mobilize a nation's resources.*—**mo′bi·li·za′tion** *n.*

mode (mōd) *n.*
1 A way; method: *Flying is a swift mode of travel.* 2 Prevailing or current style or fashion, as of dress.

mod·er·ate (mod′ər·it *adj., n.*; mod′ə·rāt *v.*) *adj.; n.; v.* **mod·er·at·ed, mod·er·at·ing**
adj. Not extreme or excessive: *A moderate amount of rain is needed for gardens.*
n. A person whose ideas or opinions are not extreme or excessive: *a political moderate.*
v. To make or become less extreme or excessive: *The labor union moderated its demands.*—**mod′er·a′tion** *n.*

mod·i·cum (mod′ə·kəm or mōd′ə·kəm) *n.*
A small amount: *Does that fool have even a modicum of common sense?*

mod·u·late (moj′ōō·lāt) *v.* **mod·u·lat·ed, mod·u·lat·ing**
1 To vary the sound of: *to modulate one's voice.* 2 To adjust: *to modulate air pressure.*—**mod′u·la′tion** *n.*

mo·dus op·er·an·di (mō′dəs op′ə·ran′dī)
A Latin phrase meaning a manner of operating or proceeding: *The police were interested in the criminal's modus operandi.*

mol·li·fy (mol′ə·fī) *v.* **mol·li·fied, mol·li·fy·ing**
To soothe or calm: *The candidate tried to mollify his angry campaign manager.*
Syn. conciliate, pacify, assuage.

mo·men·tous (mō·men′təs) *adj.*
Very important: *Deciding to drop the first atom bomb was a momentous decision.*—**mo·men′tous·ly** *adv.*, **mo·men′tous·ness** *n.*

mon·as·ter·y (mon′əs·ter′ē) *n.*, **mon·as·te·ries** *pl.*
A place where monks live in seclusion.

mon·e·tar·y (mon′ə·ter′ē) *adj.*
Of or having to do with money: *a monetary system based on gold.*
Syn. financial, fiscal.

mon·grel (mung′grəl or mong′grəl) *n., adj.*
n. An animal or plant of mixed breed: *My dog is only a mongrel, not a purebred.*
adj. Of a mixed breed or kind: *a mongrel language.*—**mon′grel·ize** *v.*

mon·i·to·ry (mon′ə·tô′rē or mon′ə·tōr′ē) *adj.*
Giving a warning or admonition: *The teacher shook her finger in a monitory gesture.*

mon·o·logue (mon′ə·lôg) *n.*
A long speech by one person, or a dramatic speech or scene performed by one actor: *The meeting became a monologue when the manager got the microphone.*

mo·nop·o·lize (mə·nop′ə·līz) *v.* **mo·nop·o·lized, mo·nop·o·liz·ing**
To assume exclusive possession or control of: *She monopolized the conversation.*—**mo·nop′o·ly** *n.*, **mo·nop′o·lis′tic** *adj.*

mon·o·the·ism (mon′ə·thē·iz′əm) *n.*
The doctrine or belief that there is only one God.

mo·not·o·nous (mə·not′ə·nəs) *adj.*
Lacking change or variety: *monotonous desert landscape.*—**mo·not′o·ny** *n.*
Syn. repetitious.

mon·sieur (mə·syûr′, *French* mə·syœ′) *n.*, **mes·sieurs** (mes′ərz, *French* me·syœ′) *pl.*
The French equivalent of *Mr.* and *sir.*

mood·i·ness (mōod'ē·nəs) *n.*
A depressed or nervous state of mind: *On Mondays his moodiness became unbearable.*
Syn. melancholy, moroseness.
Ant. gaiety, serenity.

moor (mōor) *v.*
v. To secure or fasten a boat to the shore or to an anchorage by ropes: *We moored the boat for the night.*

mo·rass (mə·ras') *n.*, **mo·ras·ses** *pl.*
1 A marsh or bog. 2 Anything that perplexes or slows things up, as a difficult situation: *He was trapped in a morass of paperwork.*

mor·bid (môr'bid) *adj.*
1 Unhealthily concerned with death or gruesome topics: *He got morbid when depressed.*
2 Grisly; unwholesome: *a morbid fantasy.*—**mor'bid·ly** *adv.*

mo·res (môr'āz *or* môr'ēz) *n.pl.*
The customs and accepted conventions of a group or community: *The town's mores include regular churchgoing.*

mor·i·bund (môr'ə·bund) *adj.*
At the point of death; dying.

mo·rose (mə·rōs') *adj.*
Sullen or gloomy; ill-humored: *He became morose when he did not get his way.*
Ant. happy, bright.

mor·phine (môr'fēn) *n.*
An addictive opiate used to induce sleep or lessen pain.
Spelling tip: The trouble spot here is *phi.*

mor·tal (môr'təl) *adj., n.*
adj. 1 Subject to or related to death: *Humans are mortal.* 2 Lasting until or causing death: *He suffered a mortal wound.*
n. A human being: *laws that apply to every mortal.*—**mor'tal·ly** *adv.*

mor·ti·cian (môr·tish'ən) *n.*
A funeral director: *The mortician showed them a lined casket.*
Syn. undertaker.

mor·ti·fy (môr'tə·fī) *v.* **mor·ti·fied, mor·ti·fy·ing**
1 To humiliate; shame: *Her child's unruly behavior mortified her.* 2 To discipline the body by fasting, etc.: *The monk mortified himself by daily flagellation.*

mo·sa·ic (mō·zā'ik) *n.*
1 Inlaid work in which a pattern or picture is formed by small pieces of tile, glass, etc.
2 Anything resembling such work: *The light through the stained-glass windows made a mosaic on the floor.*

mo·tif (mō·tēf') *n.*
1 A series of notes making up a theme or part of a theme in a musical composition: *the Siegfried motif in "Walküre."* 2 An underlying theme, or the main element of any work of art.

mo·ti·vate (mō'tə·vāt) *v.* **mo·ti·vat·ed, mo·ti·vat·ing**
To provide with an incentive or goal: *He was motivated by a desire to make money.*
Syn. incite, encourage.

mot·ley (mot'lē) *adj.*
Made up of different colors, diverse elements, or unrelated persons: *The motley crowd included hippies and crew-cut students.*

moun·tain·ous (moun'tə·nəs) *adj.*
Full of mountains: *Switzerland is a mountainous country.*
Syn. hilly, rugged.
Ant. flat, plain.

mourn·ful (môrn'fəl) *adj.*
Showing or causing grief; sad: *the mournful whine of the wind.*
Syn. sad, doleful.
Ant. gay, happy.

mud·dle (mud'l) *n.; v.* **mud·dled, mud·dling**
n. A state of confusion, disorder, or uncertainty; a jumble: *He was in a muddle after drinking too much.*
v. To confuse, bewilder, or confound: *The complicated figures muddled him.*

mug·gy (mug'ē) *adj.*
Warm and humid: *a muggy June day.*—**mug'gi·ness** *n.*

mug·wump (mug'wump') *n.*
A person who is independent, as in politics: *sitting on the fence with the other mugwumps.*
Etymology: *Mugwump* is from the Algonquin Indian word for "big chief." The word was applied to the Republicans who bolted the party when James G. Blaine was Republican Presidential candidate in 1884.

mulch (mulch) *n.*
Loose material such as straw, leaves, or manure laid around plants to protect their roots from cold and drying out and to prevent the growth of weeds.

mulct (mulkt) *v.*
v. 1 To punish by a fine: *The judge mulcted the corporation for improper trading practices.*
2 To defraud; cheat; swindle.

mul·ti·pli·ca·tion (mul'tə·plə·kā'shən) *n.*
1 A mathematical operation to find the sum of a number that is repeated a certain number of times: *Multiplication of 3 times 2 gives 6.* 2 A great or rapid increase: *the multiplication of cars in cities.*
Syn. 2 proliferation.
Ant. 1 division. 2 decrease.

mul·ti·plic·i·ty (mul'tə·plis'ə·tē) *n.*
A large number: *A multiplicity of topics was discussed at the meeting.*

mun·dane (mun'dān) *adj.*
Concerning earthly things, especially ordinary, day-to-day concerns: *He was above the mundane task of earning a living.*
Syn. ordinary, common.

mu·nic·i·pal (myōō·nis'ə·pəl) *adj.*
Concerning a town or city or its government: *The councilman was a leader in municipal politics.*

mu·nif·i·cent (myōō·nif'ə·sənt) *adj.*
Extraordinarily generous (said of both gift and giver): *The private school received a munificent bequest of $1 million.*
Syn. generous, liberal.
Ant. mean, stingy.

mus·cle (mus'əl) *n.*
1 One of the bands of contractile tissue that produce bodily movement, or an organ comprised of these bands: *shoulder muscles.* 2 Power or brawn: *Weight lifters have muscle. The administration has enough muscle to get the job done.*
Spelling tip: Watch the *-cle* ending.

muse (myōōz) *n.; v.* **mused, mus·ing**
n. One of the nine demigoddesses believed to inspire artists: *Terpsichore is the muse of the dance.*
v. To consider thoughtfully: *He sat musing before the fire for an entire afternoon.*
Syn. *v.* ponder, meditate.

mu·si·cian (myōō·zish'ən) *n.*
A performer or composer of music.—**mu·si'cian·ly** *adj.*

mus·lin (muz'lin) *n.*
A plain-weave cotton fabric, especially a sturdy variety often used for sheets.

mus·tache (məs·tash' *or* mus'tash) *n.*
1 A growth of hair on the upper lip, especially when cultivated or groomed. 2 The hair or bristles growing near the mouth of an animal: *the cat's mustache.*—**mus·tached'** *adj.*

mu·ti·late (myōō'tə·lāt) *v.* **mu·ti·lat·ed, mu·ti·lat·ing**
1 To deprive a living being of a limb or essential part: *He was mutilated in the war.* 2 To damage or injure by the removal of an important part: *Narrow-minded censorship mutilated the movie.*—**mu'ti·la'tion, mu'ti·la'tor** *n.*

mu·ti·nous (myōō'tə·nəs) *adj.*
Disposed to or involved in mutiny: *The mutinous crew hanged the captain of the ship.*
Syn. seditious, rebellious.
Ant. loyal, obedient.

mu·tu·al (myōō'chōō·əl) *adj.*
1 Felt, expressed, or performed for or toward each other by the persons or parties concerned: *Their mutual hate destroyed their lives.* 2 Having the same attitude toward or relationship with each other or others: *mutual friends.* 3 Possessed or held in common: *Their friendship is based on mutual interests.*—**mu'tu·al·ly** *adv.*

myr·i·ad (mir'ē·əd) *adj., n.*
adj. Consisting of a very large, indefinite number: *the myriad stars in the firmament.*
n. 1 Ten thousand. 2 A vast number of persons or things: *A myriad of minor difficulties caused his nervous breakdown.*
Syn. *adj.* innumerable, countless.
Ant. *adj.* determinate, limited.

myrrh (mûr) *n.*
An aromatic gum resin exuding from certain small Arabian and African trees, used as incense, perfume, and in medicine.

N

na·bob (nā'bob) *n.*
1 A European who has become rich in India. 2 Any very rich or powerful man: *The president of General Motors is a nabob of industry.*

na·dir (nā'dər *or* nā'dir) *n.*
The lowest possible point: *After ten parole rejections the prisoner's faith had reached its nadir.*
Ant. zenith, summit, pinnacle.

na·ive (nä·ēv') *adj.*
1 Having an unaffected or simple nature; artless: *a naive young country girl.* 2 Lacking deliberate or careful analysis: *Those ideas are naive.*—**na·ive'ly** *adv.,* **na·ive'ness** *n.*
Spelling tip: This word is also spelled *naïve.*
Syn. 1 childlike, ingenuous, unsophisticated.
Ant. 1 artful, sophisticated.

nape (nāp) *n.*
The back of the neck.

naph·tha (naf'thə *or* nap'thə) *n.*
A volatile petroleum distillate used as a solvent, cleaning fluid, fuel, etc.

nar·cis·sism (när'sis·iz·əm *or* när·sis'iz·əm) *n.*
Excessive admiration for or fascination with oneself; self-love.—**nar'cis·sist** *n.,* **nar'cis·sis'tic** *adj.*

nar·rate (na·rāt' *or* nar'āt) *v.* **nar·rat·ed, nar·rat·ing**
1 To tell or relate: *to narrate a story.* 2 To speak in accompaniment and explanation of: *He narrated movies of their trip.*—**nar·ra'tor** *n.*
Syn. 1 recount, state, recite.

nas·cent (nā'sənt *or* nas'ənt) *adj.*
Beginning to exist or develop; newly conceived: *the nascent science of sociology.*—**nas'cence, nas'cen·cy** *n.*
Syn. youthful, rising, budding.
Ant. mature, developed, grown.

na·tal (nāt'l) *adj.*
Of or pertaining to a person's birth.

nau·ti·cal (nô'ti·kəl) *adj.*
Pertaining to or involving ships, seamen, or navigation: *Columbus' nautical charts were quite primitive.*—**nau'ti·cal·ly** *adv.*

na·val (nā'vəl) *adj.*
1 Of, involving, or having a navy: *England became a naval power in the sixteenth century.* 2 Of or pertaining to ships: *a naval officer.*

nave (nāv) *n.*
The main body of a church, situated between the side aisles: *Gothic churches usually have huge naves.*

na·vel (nā'vəl) *n.*
The depression on the abdomen where the umbilical cord was attached.
Syn. umbilicus, bellybutton.

neb·u·la (neb'yə·lə) *n.,* **neb·u·lae** (neb'yə·lē) *or* **neb·u·las** *pl.*
Any interstellar mass of cloudlike appearance and vast extent, often luminous, and composed of gaseous matter in various degrees of density.

neb·u·lous (neb'yə·ləs) *adj.*
1 Of, pertaining to, or like a nebula. 2 Cloudy; misty: *a nebulous day.* 3 Vague or confused; unclear: *He seemed to have a nebulous idea of his rights.*—**neb'u·lous·ly** *adv.,* **neb'u·lous·ness** *n.*

nec·es·sar·y (nes'ə·ser'ē) *adj.*
1 Absolutely needed; essential and indispensable: *Hard work is necessary for success.*
2 Being of such a nature that it must exist or occur; inevitable: *The cancellation of the program was a necessary consequence of the lack of funds to finance it.*

ne·ces·si·tate (nə·ses'ə·tāt) *v.* **ne·ces·si·tat·ed, ne·ces·si·tat·ing**
To make necessary: *The rain necessitated a postponement of the game.*—**ne·ces·si·ta'tion** *n.*, **ne·ces'si·ta'tive** *adj.*
Syn. force, oblige.

née (nā) *adj.*
Born with the name of (used chiefly to note the maiden name of a married woman): *Mrs. Jane Jones, née Jane Smith.*
Spelling tip: This word is also spelled *nee.*

ne·far·i·ous (ni·fâr'ē·əs) *adj.*
Extremely wicked; vile: *a nefarious plot to overthrow the President.*—**ne·far'i·ous·ly** *adv.*, **ne·far'i·ous·ness** *n.*
Syn. villainous, infamous, evil.

ne·ga·tion (ni·gā'shən) *n.*
1 The absence or opposite of something considered affirmative or existent: *Sleep is the negation of consciousness.* 2 The act of denying or contradicting: *Her negation of his statement was based on feminine intuition.*
Syn. 2 denial, contradiction, disavowal.
Ant. affirmation, assertion, declaration.

neg·li·gent (neg'lə·jənt) *adj.*
Irresponsible or incautious: *She was negligent about watching the baby, and that is why he fell.*
Syn. careless, reckless.
Ant. reliable, careful, cautious.

nei·ther (nē'thər *or* nī'thər) *adj., pron., conj.*
adj. Not either: *Neither eye has perfect vision.*
pron. Not the one nor the other: *Neither of the hats is becoming .*
conj. 1 Not either: *He neither reads nor writes.* 2 Nor yet: *He cannot write; neither can he read.*
Spelling tip: Note that this word is an exception to the *i* before *e* rule.

nem·e·sis (nem'ə·sis) *n.*, **nem·e·ses** (nem'ə·sēz) *pl.*
1 An unusually tenacious or fearsome opponent: *Wellington was Napoleon's nemesis.* 2 An instrument of just retribution or vengeance: *He will meet his nemesis sooner or later.*
Etymology: In Greek mythology, Nemesis was the goddess of retributive justice or vengeance.

ne·o·phyte (nē'ə·fīt) *n.*
Any novice or beginner; especially, one who is newly ordained or admitted into a religious or mystic order: *The actress was such a neophyte that her knees shook when she was on stage.*

neph·ew (nef'yōō) *n.*
The son of a brother or brother-in-law or of a sister or sister-in-law.

nep·o·tism (nep'ə·tiz'əm) *n.*
Favoritism; especially, governmental pa-

tronage extended toward relatives: *He denied that nepotism was a factor in the appointment of his brother-in-law to the high-paying job.*

nes·tle (nes'əl) *v.* **nes·tled nes·tling**
1 To lie or press closely and snugly; cuddle; snuggle: *The kittens nestled up to their mother.* 2 To settle down in comfort and pleasure: *to nestle among the pillows.* 3 To lie or be embedded, sheltered, or half-hidden: *The cottage nestled in a quiet valley.*

net·tle (net'l) *n.; v.* **net·tled, net·tling**
n. A plant having leaves with minute hairs that sting when touched.
v. To annoy or irritate: *Her insistence nettled him.*
Syn. *v.* provoke, pique, exasperate.

neu·rol·o·gy (n(y)ŏŏ·rol'ə·jē) *n.*
The branch of medicine that deals with the nervous system and its disorders.—**neu'ro·log'i·cal** *adj.*, **neu·rol'o·gist** *n.*

new·el (n(y)ōō'əl) *n.*
The post that terminates the handrail of a staircase. It is also called a *newel post.*

nib (nib) *n.*
1 The point of a pen. 2 The projecting, pointed part of anything; tip. 3 The beak or bill of a bird.

ni·ce·ty (nī'sə·tē) *n.*, **ni·ce·ties** *pl.*
1 *Usually pl.* A minute or subtle point, detail, or distinction: *The niceties of science elude the untrained mind.* 2 *Usually pl.* Delicacy or refinement: *Niceties at dinnertime include candlelight and linen napkins.*

niche (nich) *n.*
1 A recessed space or hollow, usually in a wall, for a statue or the like. 2 Any position specially adapted to its occupant: *The graduates must find their own niches in society.*
Syn. 1 nook, cavity. 2 spot, place.

nick·el (nik'əl) *n.*
1 A hard, silver-white metallic element. 2 A five-cent U.S. coin containing nickel.

nig·gard·ly (nig'ərd·lē) *adj., adv.*
adj. Stingy or scanty: *She got a niggardly portion of spaghetti.*
adv. In a stingy manner: *The governor acted niggardly in authorizing money for the needy university.*

nir·va·na (nir·vä'nə *or* nər·van'ə) *n.*
1 *In Buddhism* The state of absolute felicity, characterized by freedom from passion, desire, suffering, etc.: *Nirvana is attained through annihilation of the self.* 2 Any state of complete happiness: *Nice clothes and handsome friends are her idea of nirvana.*

no·bless o·blige (nō·bles' ō·blēzh')
A French phrase meaning that those of high birth, wealth, or social position must behave generously or nobly toward others (literally, "nobility obligates").

noc·tur·nal (nok·tûr'nal) *adj.*
1 Of, pertaining to, or occurring at night: *The Army scout made a nocturnal journey behind enemy lines.* 2 Active, blooming, etc., by night: *Owls are nocturnal birds.*—**noc·tur'nal·ly** *adv.*

noc·turne (nok'tûrn) *n.*
In music A composition of a pensive or romantic nature.

no·mad (nō'mad *or* nom'ad) *n.*
n. **1** One of a group of people that habitually shifts its abode to find food, avoid drought, etc.: *Sheepherders are often nomads, constantly seeking better grazing lands.* **2** A person who constantly moves about, usually without purpose.—**no·mad'ic** *adj.*

nom de plume (nom' də plo͞om')
A writer's assumed name: *O. Henry was the nom de plume of William Sydney Porter.*
Etymology: This French expression comes from *nom* (name) + *de* (of) + *plume* (pen).
Syn. pen name.

no·men·cla·ture (nō'mən·klā'chər *or* nō·men'·klə·chər) *n.*
The system of names used to describe everything discussed in a particular science: *The nomenclature of botany includes Latin names for every plant.*
Syn. terminology.

nom·i·nal (nom'ə·nəl) *adj.*
1 Existing in name rather than in fact: *The king was nominal ruler of the country, but the army had real control.* **2** Trifling or inconsiderable; token: *The entrance fee was a nominal sum of ten cents.*—**nom'i·nal·ly** *adv.*
Syn. 1 so-called. 2 insignificant.
Ant. 1 actual, virtual. 2 significant, substantial.

non·cha·lant (non'shə·lənt *or* non'shə·länt') *adj.*
Marked by or acting with a lack of interest or excitement: *He was nonchalant about his victory, and did not even appear at the award ceremony.*—**non'cha·lance** *n.,* **non'cha·lant·ly** *adv.*
Syn. casual, unconcerned.
Ant. excited, keen.

non·com·mit·tal (non'kə·mit'l) *adj.*
Avoiding committing oneself to an opinion, attitude, etc.: *He was noncommittal about running for office.*
Ant. forthright, outspoken.

non·de·script (non'də·skript) *adj.*
Lacking individual character: *She described the thief as a nondescript man of about forty.*

non·en·ti·ty (non·en'tə·tē) *n.*
One who or that which is of little or no account: *Recent U.S. Presidents have given specific responsibilities to the Vice President so that he will not be a nonentity.*
Syn. nobody.
Ant. somebody, personage.

non·pa·reil (non'pə·rel') *adj., n.*
adj. Having no equal; matchless: *a nonpareil performance by the great actor.*
n. One who has no equal: *A Stradivarius is a nonpareil among violins.*
Spelling tip: Note that nonpareil is one of the *i* before *e* exceptions.
Syn. *adj.* unrivaled, peerless. *n.* paragon.

non se·qui·tur (non sek'wə·tər)
A remark or conclusion that is irrelevant to, or does not follow from, what has been said before: *It would be a non sequitur to relate the whiteness of polar bears to the absence of honey in the Arctic.*
Etymology: This Latin phrase literally means "it does not follow."

nose·gay (nōz'gā') *n.*
A small bunch of flowers: *The flowergirl carried a nosegay of violets.*
Syn. posy, bouquet.

nos·tal·gi·a (nos·tal'jə) *n.*
A longing for things and places that are far away or gone forever: *The old man looked back with nostalgia on the days of his youth.*—**nos·tal'gic** *adj.*

no·ta·rize (nō'tə·rīz) *v.* **no·ta·rized, no·ta·riz·ing**
To attest to or authenticate as a notary: *The document was notarized.*

no·tice·a·ble (nō'tis·ə·bəl) *adj.*
Easily seen or worthy of attention: *The veteran has a noticeable limp. An actress noticeable for her diction.*—**no'tice·a·bly** *adv.*

no·to·ri·ous (nō·tôr'ē·əs) *adj.*
Widely known and generally disapproved of: *He is notorious for his extravagance.*—**no'to·ri'e·ty** *n.*
Syn. infamous.

nou·veau riche (no͞o'vō' rēsh') **nou·veaux riches** (no͞o'vō' rēsh') *pl.*
Someone who has recently become rich (usually employed as a term of abuse): *The nouveaux riches next door have built two swimming pools.*

nov·ice (nov'is) *n.*
1 A beginner in any occupation: *He was a novice at bridge.* **2** A member of a religious order who has not taken vows.
Syn. 1 tyro, beginner, recruit.
Ant. 1 veteran, expert.

nox·ious (nok'shəs) *adj.*
Causing harm to health or morals: *noxious factory fumes.*
Syn. harmful, injurious.
Ant. beneficial, healthy.

nu·ga·to·ry (no͞o'gə·tôr'ē) *adj.*
Having no worth or meaning.

nui·sance (n(y)o͞o'səns) *n.*
Anything or anyone that annoys or causes trouble: *That insistent panhandler is a real nuisance.*
Syn. trouble, annoyance, pest.

numb (num) *adj.*
Without feeling: *Her fingers were numb from the cold.*
Syn. senseless, unfeeling.

nup·tial (nup'shəl) *adj., n.*
adj. Of or pertaining to marriage or the marriage ceremony: *the nuptial rites.*
n. Usually *pl.* Wedding: *Their nuptials were celebrated on Thursday.*

nu·tri·ent (no͞o'trē·ənt) *adj., n.*
adj. Giving nourishment; nutritious: *a nutrient solution for intravenous feeding.*
n. Something that nourishes; food: *Plants require chemical nutrients.*

O

o·a·sis (ō·ā′sis) *n.*, **o·a·ses** (ō·ā′sēz) *pl.*
1 An area in a desert made fertile by natural springs or irrigation. 2 Figuratively, a place of relief or pleasure in otherwise unpleasant surroundings: *Her house was a musical oasis in a cultural desert.*

oath (ōth) *n.*
1 A formal declaration in support of a pledge or statement, usually based on an appeal to God: *He swore an oath to protect his country.* 2 A blasphemous imprecation: *With an oath, Blackbeard sprang aboard.*

ob·du·rate (ob′dyə·rit *or* ob′dyə·rāt) *adj.*
Hardened against the influence or arguments of others: *He was obdurate in his determination to punish his son.*
Syn. inflexible, hardhearted.
Ant. soft, compassionate.

o·be·di·ence (ō·bē′dē·əns) *n.*
The act or habit of submitting to authority: *The Nuremberg trials condemned obedience to unjust laws.*
Syn. submissiveness, conformity.
Ant. rebellion, defiance.

o·be·di·ent (ō·bē′dē·ənt) *adj.*
Following or submitting to orders: *an obedient wife.*—**o·be′di·ent·ly** *adv.*
Syn. compliant, docile.
Ant. unruly, defiant.

o·bei·sance (ō·bā′səns *or* ō·bē′səns) *n.*
An act of homage, such as a bow or curtsy: *He made his obeisances to his sovereign.*
Spelling tip: Remember *i* before *e* except after *c*, or when sounded like *a*—as in one pronunciation of *obeisance*.

ob·e·lisk (ob′ə·lisk) *n.*
A square shaft of stone tapering to a point, used as a monument: *The Washington Monument is an obelisk.*

o·bese (ō·bēs′) *adj.*
Exceedingly fat: *He was so obese he could not move himself.*—**o·bes′i·ty** *n.*

o·bit·u·a·ry (ō·bich′ōō·er′ē) *n.*, **o·bit·u·a·ries** *pl.*
A published notice of a death, especially in a newspaper: *The obituary included a brief biographical sketch of the dead mayor.*

ob·lig·a·to·ry (ə·blig′ə·tôr′ē *or* ob′lə·gə·tôr′ē) *adj.*
Being a duty or obligation: *It is obligatory to write thank-you notes for wedding presents.*
Syn. required, expected.
Ant. unnecessary, optional.

o·blige (ə·blīj′) *v.* **o·bliged, o·blig·ing**
1 To make indebted, as by a favor: *I'm obliged to you for your kindness.* 2 To do a favor: *He obliged them by answering their questions.* 3 To require or coerce: *Students are obliged to take examinations.*
Syn. 2 help, assist. 3 compel, force.
Ant. 2 hinder, resist.

ob·lique (ə·blēk′) *adj.*
1 Slanting: *Draw an oblique line from the top right-hand corner to the bottom left-hand corner.* 2 Indirect: *"When we met I didn't realize you were nice!" is an oblique compliment.*—**ob·lique′ly** *adv.*, **ob·lique′ness** *n.*
Syn. 1 sloping, diagonal. 2 devious, roundabout.
Ant. 2 straightforward, direct.

ob·lit·er·ate (ə·blit′ə·rāt) *v.* **ob·lit·er·at·ed, ob·lit·er·at·ing**
To destroy utterly, leaving no trace; completely exterminate or erase: *The nuclear bomb obliterated an entire city.*
Syn. wipe out, eradicate, raze.
Ant. create, preserve, build.

ob·liv·i·on (ə·bliv′ē·ən) *n.*
1 Total forgetfulness or unawareness: *the oblivion of a man in a drunken stupor.* 2 The condition of being totally forgotten: *the eventual oblivion of many once-famous men.*
Syn. 2 obscurity.
Ant. 1 awareness, realization. 2 fame, immortality.

ob·nox·ious (əb·nok′shəs) *adj.*
Very unpleasant (as a taste or smell) or very disagreeable or vulgar (as a person); revolting or objectionable: *a foul, obnoxious odor; a vulgar, obnoxious businessman.*

ob·se·qui·ous (əb·sē′kwē·əs) *adj.*
Submissive and flattering in a cringing way: *an obsequious courtier flattering the king.*—**ob·se′qui·ous·ly** *adv.*, **ob·se′qui·ous·ness** *n.*
Syn. servile, toadying, sycophantic.
Ant. proud, independent, rebellious.

ob·so·les·cence (ob′sə·les′əns) *n.*
The process of becoming out-of-date and going out of use.
Syn. decline, displacement.

ob·so·lete (ob′sə·lēt *or* ob′sə·lēt′) *adj.*
Outdated or no longer used.

ob·sta·cle (ob′stə·kəl) *n.*
A hindrance or obstruction: *A stammer is an obstacle to a public-speaking career.*
Syn. handicap, barrier, impediment.
Ant. asset, advantage.

ob·sti·nate (ob′stə·nit) *adj.*
1 Insistently maintaining one's position: *He was fired because of his obstinate refusal to follow orders.* 2 Difficult to overcome: *an obstinate cold.*
Syn. 1 stubborn, inflexible. 2 persistent, tenacious.
Ant. 1 willing, reasonable.

ob·strep·er·ous (əb·strep′ər·əs) *adj.*
Noisy or boisterous, especially in defiance of instructions or requests: *The teacher could not force the obstreperous children to sit quietly.*—**ob·strep′er·ous·ly** *adv.*, **ob·strep′er·ous·ness** *n.*
Syn. unruly, unmanageable, wild.
Ant. quiet, obedient, docile.

ob·tuse (əb·t(y)ōōs′) *adj.*
1 Dull-witted or insensitive; very slow or unable to perceive or understand: *He is too obtuse to understand a complex problem.* 2 Blunt or rounded, as opposed to sharp or angular: *an obtuse object with no pointed corners.*—**ob·tuse′ly** *adv.*, **ob·tuse′ness** *n.*
Syn. 1 dull, stupid. 2 dull.
Ant. 1 bright, sharp. 2 sharp, pointed.

ob·vi·ate (ob'vē·āt) *v.* **ob·vi·at·ed, ob·vi·at·ing**
To prevent or remove a difficulty, drawback, etc.: *Tinted light bulbs obviate the problem of glare.*—**ob'vi·a'tion** *n.*
Syn. eliminate, avoid.
Ant. create, aggravate.

oc·ca·sion (ə·kā'zhən) *n., v.*
n. **1** An event, the time of an event, the cause of something, or an opportunity to do something: *I saw her on three occasions. Your birthday is a good occasion for a party.* **2** A large, formal social event: *The inaugural ball was quite an occasion!*
v. To cause: *What occasioned their quarrel?*

oc·ca·sion·al (ə·kā'zhən·əl) *adj.*
Occurring now and then: *an occasional visit to your in-laws.*—**oc·ca'sion·al·ly** *adv.*
Syn. sporadic, infrequent.

Oc·ci·dent (ok'sə·dent) *n.*
The area of the world west of Asia: *the Asian culture of the Orient and the European culture of the Occident.*
Syn. West.
Ant. Orient, East, Asia.

oc·cu·py (ok'yə·pī) *v.* **oc·cu·pied, oc·cu·py·ing**
1 To fill up a piece of ground or span of time: *The factory occupies two acres.* **2** To live in a house: *Who occupies the cottage?* **3** To keep a person busy or interested: *He occupies himself with stamp collecting.* **4** To take and hold possession of by, or as if by, conquest or settlement. *Soviet troops occupied Czechoslovakia.*
Syn. 1 cover, span. **2** inhabit. **3** concern, interest. **4** overrun, garrison.
Ant. 4 liberate.

oc·cur (ə·kûr') *v.* **oc·curred, oc·cur·ring**
1 To happen: *The hurricane occurred on May 7.* **2** To be thought of; to enter the mind: *It never occurred to me!*—**oc·cur'rence** *n.*
Spelling tip: Note there is one *r* in the base word *occur*. However, occurred, occurring, and occurrence double the *r*.

o·ce·an·ic (ō'shē·an'ik) *adj.*
Living in or pertaining to the ocean: *whales, sharks, and other oceanic life.*

oc·u·lar (ok'yə·lər) *adj.*
Pertaining to, like, or part of the eye: *Glaucoma is an ocular disease.*
Syn. optical, optic, visual.

oc·u·list (ok'yə·list) *n.*
One skilled in treating diseases of the eye; ophthalmologist.

o·di·ous (ō'dē·əs) *adj.*
Hateful or disgusting: *an odious person.*
Syn. loathsome, abominable.
Ant. commendable, delightful.

o·dor·if·er·ous (ō'də·rif'ər·əs) *adj.*
Having or giving off an odor, especially an agreeable odor: *odoriferous lilacs.*
Syn. fragrant, aromatic.

o·dor·ous (ō'dər·əs) *adj.*
Having an odor.—**o'dor·ous·ly** *adv.*, **o'dor·ous·ness** *n.*

od·ys·sey (od'ə·sē) *n.*
A long, wandering trip: *a seven-year round-the-world odyssey.*
Etymology: This word derives from the *Odyssey*, a long poem by the ancient Greek poet Homer. The poem describes travels of Odysseus (or Ulysses), king of Ithaca, for ten years after the Trojan War.
Syn. travels, journey.

of·fal (ô'fəl) *n.*
1 The parts of a butchered animal that are worthless: *The offal is burned in an incinerator.* **2** Rubbish or refuse of any kind: *a garbage can filled with offal.*
Syn. 2 waste, garbage.

of·fen·sive (ə·fen'siv) *adj.*
Rude or unpleasant: *an offensive remark; an offensive smell.*—**of·fen'sive·ly** *adv.*, **of·fen'sive·ness** *n.*
Syn. disagreeable, foul.
Ant. nice, appealing.

of·fer·to·ry (ô'fər·tôr'ē, ô'fər·tō'rē, or of'ər·tôr'ē) *n.*, **of·fer·to·ries** *pl.*
1 The portion of a church service during which the bread and wine to be consecrated are offered and alms are collected: *The offertory usually follows the saying of the Creed.* **2** A collection taken, hymn sung, or prayer recited at such time.

of·fi·cial (ə·fish'əl) *n., adj.*
n. The holder of a public office: *a minor government official.*
adj. Coming from or supported by authority: *official approval from the mayor's office.*
Syn. *n.* officeholder. *adj.* authorized, authoritative, formal.
Ant. *adj.* unofficial, informal.

of·fi·cious (ə·fish'əs) *adj.*
Meddlesome; interfering in what is not one's concern: *an officious busybody offering unneeded and unwelcome advice.*—**of·fi'cious·ly** *adv.*, **of·fi'cious·ness** *n.*
Syn. interfering, obtrusive.

oft·en (ôf'ən *or* of'ən) *adv.*
Frequently: *He often visits his mother.*
Syn. repeatedly, recurrently.
Ant. seldom, rarely.

o·gle (ō'gəl) *v.* **o·gled, o·gling**
To look at admiringly in an amorous and impertinent manner: *a man ogling a pretty girl.*

o·le·o·mar·ga·rine (ō'lē·ō·mär'jə·rin) *n.*
A butter substitute containing more animal fat than does margarine.
Syn. oleo.

ol·fac·to·ry (ol·fak'tər·ē *or* ol·fak'trē) *adj.*
Pertaining to the sense of smell: *fine perfumes and other olfactory pleasures.*

ol·i·gar·chy (ol'ə·gär'kē) *n.*, **ol·i·gar·chies** *pl.*
A form of government in which power is restricted to a few: *an oligarchy ruled by the members of a small sect.*

om·e·let (om'ə·lit *or* om'lit) *n.*
A dish of eggs beaten together with water or milk and cooked in a frying pan.
Spelling tip: Note that this word is also spelled *omelette.*

om·i·nous (om'ə·nəs) *adj.*
Threatening: *an ominous silence.*—**om'i·nous·ly** *adv.*
Syn. menacing, sinister.
Ant. encouraging, auspicious.

o·mis·sion (ō·mish'ən) *n.*
The act of omitting or the state of being omitted: *The omission of a word in the sentence made it unintelligible.*

om·nip·o·tent (om·nip'ə·tənt) *adj.*
Almighty; not limited in authority or power.

om·ni·pres·ent (om'nə·prez'ənt) *adj.*
Being everywhere at the same time: *The President must accept the omnipresent Secret Service men.*
Syn. ubiquitous.

om·nis·cience (om·nish'əns) *n.*
1 Infinite knowledge: *Since no human has omniscience, each must accept advice.* 2 (Usually capital *O*) God.—**om·nis'cient·ly** *adv.*

once (wuns) *adv.*
1 One time: *I went there once.* 2 At or during some past time: *a once famous writer.*

on·er·ous (on'ər·əs) *adj.*
Burdensome or oppressive: *the onerous work of carrying bricks.*—**on'er·ous·ly** *adv.*

on·o·mat·o·poe·ia (on'ə·mat'ə·pē'ə) *n.*
The formation of words in imitation of natural sounds, or the words so formed, as *crack, splash,* etc.

on·slaught (on'slôt' *or* ôn'slôt') *n.*
A violent, often hostile assault: *a verbal onslaught by militants on conservative college students.*

on·yx (on'iks) *n.*
A semiprecious variety of quartz having layers of different colors.

o·pal·es·cent (ō'pəl·es'ənt) *adj.*
Having an iridescent play of brilliant or milky colors.

o·paque (ō·pāk') *adj.*
1 Impervious to light; not translucent or transparent: *The auditorium has opaque shades to keep out the light when movies are shown.* 2 Impervious to radiant heat, electric radiation, etc.—**o·paque'ly** *adv.*, **o·paque'ness** *n.*

op·er·ate (op'ə·rāt) *v.* **op·er·at·ed, op·er·at·ing**
1 To act or function; work: *The clock operates by batteries.* 2 To bring about an effect: *The medicine operated quickly.* 3 To perform an operation on the body: *The doctor operated on the little girl.* 4 To control the working of, as a machine: *He operates a lathe.*—**op'er·a'tion** *n.*
Syn. perform, function, work.

op·er·a·tor (op'ə·rā'tər) *n.*
A person who works a mechanism or who runs a business, factory, etc.: *a telephone operator; the operator of a coal mine.*

oph·thal·mol·o·gist (of'thal·mol'ə·jist) *n.*
A physician specializing in the study of the structure, functions, and diseases of the eye.

o·pi·ate (ō'pē·it *or* ō'pē·āt) *n., adj.*
n. 1 A medicine containing opium and therefore inducing relaxation or sleep. 2 Anything bringing relaxation or sleep: *Listening to lightly falling rain was her opiate.*
adj. 1 Consisting of opium. 2 Tending to induce sleep.

op·po·nent (ə·pō'nənt) *n.*
One who opposes another, as in battle, debate, sports etc.: *football opponents.*
Syn. adversary, antagonist.
Ant. supporter.

op·por·tune (op'ər·t(y)ōon') *adj.*
1 Especially right or fit: *A patio is an opportune place for a barbecue.* 2 Occurring at the right moment: *The opportune time to request a raise is when the boss is in a good mood.*
Syn. 1 appropriate, suitable. 2 timely.
Ant. 1 inappropriate, unsuitable. 2 untimely.

op·por·tu·nist (op'ər·t(y)ōo'nist) *n.*
A person who uses every opportunity to achieve some end, paying little attention to moral principles or sentiment.—**op'por·tu·nis'tic** *adj.*, **op'por·tu'nism** *n.*

op·por·tu·ni·ty (op'ər·t(y)ōo'nə·tē) *n.*, **op·por·tu·ni·ties** *pl.*
A fit or convenient time; favorable occasion or circumstance: *an opportunity to buy a car.*
Syn. chance, opening, break.

op·pose (ə·pōz') *v.* **op·posed, op·pos·ing**
1 To act or be against; resist or fight: *Democrats oppose Republicans.* 2 To set up against or contrast: *love as opposed to hate.*—**op·pos'er** *n.*

op·po·site (op'ə·zit) *adj., n., prep.*
adj. 1 On the other side, or on each side, of an intervening space or thing: *opposite ends of the room.* 2 Contrary: *opposite directions.*
n. Something or someone that is opposed or contrary: *That weakling is just the opposite of his burly father.*
prep. Across from; facing: *He sat opposite me.*—**op·po·site·ly** *adv.*
Usage: *Opposite* refers to things totally contrary to each other. *Apposite,* frequently mistaken for *opposite,* means apt or appropriate: *Although his political beliefs were totally opposite to mine, I found his remarks quite apposite to the subject of the debate.*

op·pro·bri·um (ə·prō'brē·əm) *n.*
The reproach brought about by shameful conduct; ignominy: *Her wild behavior has brought great opprobrium on her family.*
Syn. infamy, disgrace.

op·ti·cian (op·tish'ən) *n.*
One who makes or deals in optical goods.

op·ti·mism (op'tə·miz'm) *n.*
A disposition to look on the bright side of things.—**op'ti·mist** *n.*, **op'ti·mis'tic** *adj.*
Ant. pessimism.

op·tion (op'shən) *n.*
1 The right, power, or liberty of choosing; discretion: *They rearranged his office while he was away and did not give him any option in the matter.* 2 The purchased privilege of either buying or selling something at a specific price within a specified time: *an option to buy*

a house. **3** A thing that is or can be chosen: *He selected the first of the two options open to him.* —**op'tion·al** *adj.,* **op'tion·al·ly** *adv.*

op·tom·e·trist (op·tom'ə·trist) *n.*
A person trained to measure visual ability and to prescribe corrective lenses.

op·u·lence (op'yə·lens) *n.*
1 Wealth; affluence: *the opulence of the palace.* **2** Luxuriance; abundance: *the opulence of the Amazon vegetation.* Also **op·u·len·cy** (op'yə·lən·sē) *n.*—**op'u·lent** *adj.*

o·pus (ō'pəs) *n.,* **op·er·a** (op'ər·ə *or* op'rə) *pl.*
A literary or musical work or composition.

o·ral (ôr'əl *or* ō'rəl) *adj., n.*
adj. **1** Consisting of spoken words: *oral testimony.* **2** Of or pertaining to the mouth; situated at or near the mouth: *oral surgery.*
n. Usually pl. An academic examination in which the student speaks his answers aloud: *He passed his orals yesterday.*
Usage: Although *aural* and *oral* sound alike to most speakers, the former refers to the ear or the sense of hearing, not to the mouth: *an aural acuity test.*

o·rang·u·tan (ō·rang'ə·tan *or* ō·rang'ŏŏ·tan) *n.,* **o·rang·u·tans** *or* **o·rang·u·tan** *pl.*
A large ape of Borneo and Sumatra, having brownish red hair and extremely long arms.

or·a·to·ri·o (ôr'ə·tôr'ē·ō *or* ôr'ə·tō'rē·ō) *n.,* **or·a·to·ri·os** *pl.*
A musical composition for solo voices, chorus, and orchestra, usually dramatizing a sacred story, but without scenery or acting.

or·bit (ôr'bit) *n., v.*
n. The path followed by a heavenly body or artificial satellite about its center of attraction: *the orbit of the earth around the sun.*
v. To move or cause to move in an orbit: *The moon orbits around the earth.*—**or'bi·tal** *adj.*

or·deal (ôr·dēl' *or* ôr'dēl) *n.*
A severe test of character or endurance: *He survived the ordeal of two weeks alone in the jungle.*

or·di·nance (ôr'də·nəns) *n.*
An authoritative rule; an order, decree, or law of a municipal body: *a traffic ordinance.*

or·di·nar·y (ôr'də·ner'ē) *adj.*
1 Of common or everyday occurrence; customary: *an ordinary problem.* **2** Of average merit or consequence; commonplace: *an ordinary concert.*

ord·nance (ôrd'nəns) *n.*
Military weapons, ammunition, combat vehicles, etc.
Spelling tip: Do not confuse or*dinance* and *ordnance.*

or·gan·i·za·tion (ôr·gən·ə·zā'shən) *n.*
1 The act or state of arranging systematically: *Careful organization made the meeting run smoothly.* **2** A group working together with the same or similar aims: *the Organization of American States.*

or·gan·iz·er (ôr'gən·īz'ər) *n.*
A person who puts things in good order, works methodically, or brings people together and motivates them in a common cause: *File clerks should be good organizers of detail. A union organizer recruited members.*
Spelling tip: Remember the final *-er* by starting with *organize* and then adding *r.*

or·gy (ôr'jē) *n.,* **or·gies** *pl.*
1 A debauched or drunken party: *The decline of Rome was marked by a prevalence of orgies.* **2** Any uncontrolled excess: *He indulged in an orgy of self-abasement.*—**or'gi·as'tic** *adj.*

or·i·fice (ôr'ə·fis) *n.*
An opening into a hole or cavity: *Nostrils and mouths are facial orifices.*

or·i·gin (ôr'ə·jin) *n.*
The beginning of anything; the primary cause of something: *The origins of man are lost in obscurity.*
Syn. source, rising, cause.

or·nate (ôr·nāt') *adj.*
Elaborately ornamented; florid or showy: *The gold, jewel-encrusted walls were too ornate for her taste.*
Syn. elaborate, flamboyant.
Ant. plain, simple.

or·ni·thol·o·gy (ôr'nə·thol'ə·jē) *n.*
The study of birds.—**or'ni·thol'o·gist** *n.*

o·ro·tund (ôr'ə·tund) *adj.*
1 With a well-rounded, resonant voice: *Baritones should be orotund.* **2** Pompous; inflated: *The senator made an orotund speech.*
Etymology: *Orotund* comes from the Latin phrase *ore rotundo,* meaning with a round mouth.

or·phan (ôr'fən) *n., v.*
n. A child whose parents are dead.
v. To make an orphan: *He was orphaned by the death of his parents in an accident.*

or·tho·don·tist (ôr'thə·don'tist) *n.*
A dentist specializing in correcting irregularities in the set of the teeth: *The orthodontist advised braces for the child's teeth.*

os·cil·late (os'ə·lāt) *v.* **os·cil·lat·ed, os·cil·lat·ing**
To swing back and forth, as a pendulum: *He oscillated between two courses of action.*—**os'cil·la'tion** *n.*
Syn. vacillate, vibrate.

os·ten·si·ble (os·ten'sə·bəl) *adj.*
Offered as real or genuine: *The ostensible reason for the trip was to attend a convention, but actually he wanted a vacation.*—**os·ten'si·bly** *adv.*
Syn. apparent, professed.

os·ten·ta·tious (os'tən·tā'shəs) *adj.*
Intended to attract notice: *His gold-plated Rolls-Royce seemed unduly ostentatious.*
Syn. showy, conspicuous.
Ant. subdued, modest.

os·te·o·path (os'tē·ə·path') *n.*
A person who attempts to heal diseases by manipulation of affected parts of the body.—**os'te·op'a·thy** *n.*
Syn. chiropractor.

os·tra·cize (os'trə·sīz) *v.* **os·tra·cized, os·tra·ciz·ing**

To exclude from a particular society or group: *He was socially ostracized after his scandalous divorce.*

ought (ôt) *v.*
To be obliged by duty or common sense, or to be expected: *You ought to tell the truth. The train ought to be here any minute.*
Spelling tip: Do not confuse *ought* with *aught* (meaning zero).

oust (oust) *v.*
To force out from a place or position: *The incompetent man was ousted from his job.*
Syn. eject, expel.

out·ra·geous (out·rā'jəs) *adj.*
Extremely wrong, insulting, or fantastic: *outrageous behavior; an outrageous alibi.*
Syn. flagrant, scandalous, reprehensible.

o·vert (ō·vûrt') *adj.*
Open to view: *an overt movement of the hand.*
Ant. hidden, secret, covert.

o·ver·ween·ing (ō·vər·wē'ning) *adj.*
Characterized by disdain for others; arrogant: *a dictator's overweening exercise of power.*
Syn. presumptuous.
Ant. humble, subtle.

o·vip·a·rous (ō·vip'ər·əs) *adj.*
Producing eggs or ova that mature and are hatched outside the body: *Birds are oviparous.*

ox·i·da·tion (ok'sə·dā'shən) *n.*
The chemical process in which a substance combines with oxygen: *The oxidation of iron produces rust.*

P

pach·y·derm (pak'ə·dûrm) *n.*
Any of a group of animals with thick skins, including the elephant, rhinoceros, and hippopotamus.

pac·i·fist (pas'ə·fist) *n.*
One who opposes war as a means of settling disputes: *The pacifist served as an ambulance driver.*—**pac'i·fism** *n.*

pad·dock (pad'ək) *n.*
A field or enclosure in which horses are exercised: *The colt was being saddled in the paddock.*

pae·an (pē'ən) *n.*
A hymn of praise: used figuratively for any lavish praise: *a paean for the superb performance.*

pag·eant (paj'ənt) *n.*
A spectacular play or exhibition: *a pageant of American history.*

pag·eant·ry (paj'ən·trē) *n.*
Ceremonial splendor or display: *the pageantry accompanying the queen's coronation.*

pal·at·a·ble (pal'it·ə·bəl) *adj.*
1 Agreeable to the taste or palate: *That dinner was certainly palatable!* 2 Acceptable: *a palatable demand.*—**pal'at·a·ble·ness** *n.*, **pal'at·a·bly** *adv.*
Syn. 1 savory, tasteful.

pa·la·tial (pə·lā'shəl) *adj.*
Of, like, or befitting a palace; magnificent: *a palatial residence.*

pa·lav·er (pə·lav'ər) *n.*, *v.*
n. 1 Empty talk. 2 A public discussion or conference.
v. To flatter or talk idly and at length.—**pa·lav'er·er** *n.*

pal·ette (pal'it) *n.*
1 A thin board with a hole for the thumb, used by artists to mix their colors. 2 The colors characteristic of an artist, painting, etc.: *He used a wide palette.*
Spelling tip: This word is also spelled *pallet.*

pal·lid (pal'id) *adj.*
Pale; weak; lacking in color: *a very pallid complexion.*—**pal'lid·ly** *adv.*, **pal'lid·ness** *n.*
Syn. wan, faint, cadaverous.
Ant. ruddy.

palm (päm) *n.*, *v.*
n. 1 The inner surface of the hand between the wrist and the base of the fingers. 2 That which covers the inner surface of the hand, as part of a glove or mitten.
v. To hide something in or about the hand: *to palm a coin.*
Spelling tip: Remember the silent *l*, as in *calm* and *qualm.*

pal·pa·ble (pal'pə·bəl) *adj.*
1 Capable of being touched or felt. 2 Readily perceived: *There is a palpable difference between chocolate and vanilla.*—**pal'pa·bil'i·ty** *n.*
Syn. 2 obvious, evident.
Ant. 2 concealed, hidden.

pal·pi·tate (pal'pə·tāt) *v.* **pal·pi·tat·ed, pal·pi·tat·ing**
1 To quiver; tremble. 2 To flutter or beat more rapidly than normal (said of the heart): *His heart palpitated with fear.*—**pal'pi·ta'tion** *n.*

pal·sy (pôl'zē) *n.*, **pal·sies** *pl.*; *v.* **pal·sied, pal·sy·ing**
n. 1 Paralysis. 2 Any impairment or loss of ability to control movement.
v. 1 To paralyze. 2 To cause to tremble or become helpless: *She was palsied with rage.*

pal·try (pôl'trē) *adj.* **pal·tri·er, pal·tri·est**
1 Having little or no worth; trivial: *One dollar is a paltry contribution from a millionaire.* 2 Contemptible; petty: *The paltry trick of stealing candy from babies.*
Syn. 1 insignificant, trifling. 2 mean.
Ant. 1 worthy, estimable. 2 admirable.

pan·a·ce·a (pan'ə·sē'ə) *n.*
A remedy for all diseases or ills; a cure-all: *Some people use aspirin as if it were a panacea.*

pan·cre·as (pan'krē·os *or* pang'krē·əs) *n.*
A gland situated behind the stomach that produces a digestive juice and the hormone insulin.—**pan'cre·at'ic** *adj.*

pan·de·mo·ni·um (pan'də·mō'nē·əm) *n.*
Wild disorder and uproar: *The party ended in absolute pandemonium.*
Syn. chaos, riot, bedlam.

pan·e·gyr·ic (pan'ə·jir'ik) *n.*
1 A speech or writing praising a person or thing. 2 Elaborate praise; laudation.—**pan'-**

e·gyr'ist *n.*, pan'e·gyr'i·cal *adj.*, pan'e·gyr'-
i·cal·ly *adv.*
Syn. 1 eulogy, encomium.
Ant. 2 satire, lampoon.

pan·ic (pan'ik) *n.; v.* **pan·icked, pan·ick·ing**
n. A sudden, unreasonable, overpowering
fear, or an instance of such fear.
v. To affect with such a fear: *The crowd
panicked.*
Spelling tip: Words ending in *c* usually add a
k before an ending beginning with *e, i,* or *y:
mimic—mimicking; picnic—picnicked; shellac
—shellacked; panic—panicky.*

pan·o·ply (pan'ə·plē) *n.*, **pan·o·plies** *pl.*
1 The complete equipment of a warrior. 2 By
extension, any complete covering: *vaguely
seen through a panoply of smoke.* 3 A magnificent array: *Fall presents a panoply of magnificent color.*

pan·o·ram·a (pan'ə·ram'ə *or* pan'ə·rä'mə) *n.*
1 A series of pictures representing a continuous scene, arranged to unroll and pass
before the spectator. 2 A complete view in
every direction. 3 A complete or comprehensive view of a subject or of passing
events: *The movie gives a good panorama of the
Civil War.*

pan·to·mime (pan'tə·mīm) *n., v.* **pan·to·
mimed, pan·to·mim·ing**
n. 1 Any play in which the actors express
themselves by action and gestures only.
2 Gestures without speech.
v. To act or express in pantomime: *He
pantomimed his fear.*

pa·pier-mâ·ché (pā'pər·mə·shā') *n., adj.*
n. Paper pulp mixed with oil, resin, etc., that
can be molded into various shapes when wet
and becomes hard and tough when dry.
adj. Made of papier-mâché: *a papier-mâché
soldier.*

pa·py·rus (pə·pī'rəs) *n.*, **pa·py·ri** (pə·pī'rī) *pl.*
1 A tall water plant found in Israel, Ethiopia,
etc., and formerly common in Egypt. 2 A
type of writing paper made from this plant
by the ancient Egyptians. 3 A manuscript
written on this material.

par·a·dox (par'ə·doks) *n.*
1 A statement that seems absurd or contradictory, but is in fact true. 2 A self-contra-
dictory, false, or absurd statement, as
"Nothing is true."

par·af·fin (par'ə·fin) *n.*
A translucent, waxy substance obtained
principally from petroleum and widely used
for waterproofing, making candles, etc.

par·a·gon (par'ə·gon) *n.*
A model of excellence: *The Medal of Honor
winner was a paragon of courage.*

par·al·lel (par'ə·lel) *adj.; n.; v.* **par·al·leled** or
par·al·lelled, par·a·lel·ing or **par·a·lel·ling**
adj. 1 Not meeting, however far extended:
Opposite walls are parallel. 2 Having a close
resemblance or similar course: *parallel
tendencies in two brothers.*
n. 1 A parallel line or surface. 2 Comparison:
a parallel between two professions. 3 Any of the

imaginary circles on the earth's surface,
parallel to the equator, connecting points
with the same latitude.
v. To be, go, or extend parallel to: *Fifth
Avenue parallels Sixth Avenue.*

pa·ral·y·sis (pə·ral'ə·sis) *n.*, **pa·ral·y·ses** (pə·
ral'ə·sēz) *pl.*
1 The partial or complete loss of the power
of motion or sensation in any part of the
body. 2 A ceasing or crippling of normal
activities: *The pilots' strike brought about a
paralysis of transportation by air.*

par·a·lyze (par'ə·līz) *v.* **par·a·lyzed, par·a·lyz·
ing**
1 To cripple: *The accident paralyzed his legs.*
2 To render powerless, ineffective, or inactive:
Fear paralyzed his tongue.—**par'a·lyz'er, par'-
a·ly·za'tion** *n.*

par·a·mour (par'ə·mŏŏr) *n.*
A lover, especially one who unlawfully takes
the place of a husband or wife.

par·a·noi·a (par'ə·noi'ə) *n.*
A psychosis characterized by an elaborate
system of delusions of persecution or
grandeur.—**par'a·noi'ac** or **par'a·noid** *adj.*

par·a·pet (par'ə·pit *or* par'ə·pet) *n.*
A low wall around the edge of a roof, terrace,
bridge, etc.: *to build a parapet around a
balcony so that no one will fall off.*
Syn. rampart, breastwork, rail.

par·a·pher·na·li·a (par'ə·fər·nā'lē·a *or* par'ə·
fər·nāl'yə) *n.pl.*
1 Personal effects: *an old trunk filled with
Grandmother's trinkets, monogrammed towels,
and other paraphernalia.* 2 A group of articles
used for a special purpose: *a fireman's paraphernalia.*
Syn. 1 belongings, possessions. 2 equipment,
gear, apparatus.

par·a·phrase (par'ə·frāz) *v.* **par·a·phrased, par·
a·phras·ing; ** *n.*
v. To reword an essay, speech, poem, etc., as
for clarity: *to paraphrase a scientific article
using words that laymen can understand.*
n. A rewording of something: *a paraphrase of
the mayor's speech.*
Syn. *v.* restate, rephrase. *n.* recapitulation.
Ant. *v.* repeat, recite, quote. *n.* transcript,
excerpt.

par·a·site (par'ə·sīt) *n.*
1 A plant or animal that lives on or in
another organism from which it takes food
and shelter: *A tapeworm is a parasite.* 2 A
person who lives at someone else's expense
without giving anything in return: *The
courtiers were parasites, fed and clothed by the
king but doing no work.*
Syn. 2 sponger, sponge, leech, freeloader.
Ant. host.

par·cel (pär'səl) *n.; v.* **par·celed** or **par·celled,
par·cel·ing** or **par·cel·ling**
n. 1 A package: *She carried a gift-wrapped
parcel.* 2 A surveyed piece of land: *to stake out
and buy a parcel.*
v. To divide into shares: *They parceled out the
tasks among all the campers.*

par ex·cel·lence (pär ek′sə·läns)
Beyond comparison; superb: *Van Cliburn is a pianist par excellence.*
Syn. supreme, superlative.

pa·ri·ah (pə·rī′ə *or* par′ē·ə) *n.*
1 In India, a member of a former low caste (now officially abolished): *The pariahs were usually servants and laborers.* 2 A social outcast: *The scandal made him a pariah, shunned and scorned by everyone.*

par·i·mu·tu·el (par′i·myoo′choo·əl) *n.*
1 A system of racetrack betting in which those who have bet on the winners share in the total amount wagered. 2 A machine that records pari-mutuel bets: *The betting was registered by the pari-mutuel.*
Spelling tip: This word may also be spelled *parimutuel.*

pa·rish·ion·er (pə·rish′ən·ər) *n.*
A member of a parish: *The clergyman visited his parishioners.*

par·i·ty (par′ə·tē) *n.*, **par·i·ties** *pl.*
Equality, as of value, condition, rank, etc.: *parity between the American and Liberian dollars.*

par·lance (pär′ləns) *n.*
Manner of speech; special language: *lawyers conversing in legal parlance.*
Syn. terminology, jargon, talk.

par·lay (pär·lā′ *or* pär′lē) *v.*
To place winnings from a previous bet on a later race, contest, etc.: *At the casino last night I won $100 and then parlayed it into $500.*

par·ley (pär′lē) *v.*, *n.*
v. To hold a conference, especially with an enemy: *The Americans and North Vietnamese were parleying in Paris.*
n. A conference, as with an enemy: *A ceasefire was arranged at the parley.*
Syn. *v.* negotiate. *n.* negotiation, discussion, meeting.

par·lia·ment (pär′lə·mənt) *n.*
An assembly or national legislature: *the British Parliament.*
Syn. diet, senate, congress.

pa·ro·chi·al (pə·rō′kē·əl) *adj.*
Provincial; narrow-minded: *His parochial prejudices included the belief that women should not drink, or wear make-up.*—**pa·ro′chi·al·ly** *adv.*
Syn. narrow, limited, insular.
Ant. broad, cosmopolitan.

par·o·dy (par′ə·dē) *n.*, **par·o·dies** *pl.*; *v.* **par·o·died, par·o·dy·ing**
n. A humorous imitation of a serious literary work or of the style of a serious writer: *a parody of Hemingway.*
v. To make a parody of: *a humorous story that parodied Hemingway's style.*—**par′o·dist** *n.*
Syn. *n.*, *v.* caricature, burlesque.

pa·role (pə·rōl′) *n.*, *v.* **pa·roled, pa·rol·ing**
n. A release of a prisoner from jail before the end of his sentence on condition that he report regularly to penal authorities and not do anything illegal for the duration of the sentence: *He was sent back to jail for violating his parole.*
v. To release a prisoner on parole: *He was sentenced to five years but was paroled after two.*

par·ox·ysm (par′ək·siz′əm) *n.*
A sudden and violent outburst: *a paroxysm of coughing.*—**par′ox·ys′mal** *adj.*, **par′ox·ys′mal·ly** *adv.*
Syn. spasm, fit, convulsion.

par·quet (pär·kā′) *n.*
1 Inlaid mosaic wood flooring: *a parquet resembling a checkerboard.* 2 The main floor of a theater: *Did you sit in the parquet or the balcony?*

par·ry (par′ē) *v.* **par·ried, par·ry·ing**; *n.*, **par·ries** *pl.*
v. 1 To ward off a thrust or blow, as in fencing: *to parry a swordthrust.* 2 By extension, to dodge or to turn aside, as a question: *During the press conference he parried the reporter's questions.*
n. A warding-off, defensive movement: *That maneuver was a skillful parry in the fencing match. His answer was a good parry of his opponent's argument.*
Syn. *v.* 2 evade, sidestep, deflect.

par·si·mo·ni·ous (pär′sə·mō′nē·əs) *adj.*
Stingy with money: *a parsimonious old miser.*—**par′si·mo′ni·ous·ly** *adv.*, **par′si·mo′ni·ous·ness** *n.*
Syn. penurious, tight-fisted.
Ant. generous, philanthropic.

par·take (pär·tāk′) *v.* **par·took, par·tak·en, par·tak·ing**
1 To take, have, or receive a share in something: *The family gathered together to partake of the holiday meal.* 2 To be of the nature or have the quality of something: *His sassy answer partook of impertinence.*

par·tial (pär′shəl) *adj.*
1 Consisting of only a part; incomplete: *The colony was granted partial independence.* 2 Biased; prejudiced: *His best friend can't judge because he's partial.* 3 Having a special liking for something or someone (used with to): *He is partial to apple pie.*—**par′ti·al′i·ty** *n.*, **par′tial·ly** *adv.*
Syn. 1 fragmentary, limited. 2 partisan, slanted. 3 fond of.
Ant. 1 total, entire. 2 impartial, objective.

par·ti·cle (pär′ti·kəl) *n.*
1 A tiny piece: *a particle of sand.* 2 A tiny amount: *not a particle of truth!* 3 One of the elementary components of the atom, as an electron, neutron, etc.

par·tic·u·lar (pər·tik′yə·lər) *adj.*, *n.*
adj. 1 Pertaining to only one person, thing, place, etc.: *Golf is her particular hobby.* 2 Special: *of particular interest.* 3 Fussy about details: *Gourmets are very particular about food and wine.*
n. A single item, as a detail or as one example of a generalization, class of objects, etc.: *Tell me the particulars of your plan.*—**par·tic′u·lar·ly** *adv.*
Spelling tip: Watch the *u* in this word, and use *a*'s rather than *e*'s.

par·tu·ri·tion (pär′tyŏ͞o·rish′ən *or* pär′chŏ͞o·rish′ən) *n.*
The act or process of giving birth: *Parturition is the function of the female.*

par·ve·nu (par′və·n(y)ōō) *n., adj.*
n. A person who has risen above his class by attaining money or position: *Napoleon was not descended from royalty, but was a parvenu who made himself emperor.*
adj. Being a parvenu or characteristic of such a person: *the parvenu Bonaparte rulers.*
Syn. *adj.* upstart.

pas·sé (pa·sā′ *or* pas′ā) *adj.*
Out-of-date; old-fashioned: *Rumble seats are passé.*
Syn. outmoded, antiquated, obsolete.
Ant. contemporary, fashionable, avant-garde.

pas·sive (pas′iv) *adj.*
1 Not acting but being acted upon by something external: *a passive spectator who did not even cheer.* 2 Submitting or yielding without opposition: *The passive patient was too sick to care what happened.*—**pas′sive·ly** *adv.,* **pas′sive·ness** *n.*
Syn. 1 inactive, inert. 2 submissive, unresisting, limp.
Ant. 1 active, moving. 2 aggressive, assertive.

pas·teur·ize (pas′tə·rīz) *v.* **pas·teur·ized, pas·teur·iz·ing**
To sterilize a substance (as a liquid) by heating to a temperature (140°–155° F.) that kills bacteria, etc., without major chemical changes: *Milk should be pasteurized.*—**pas′teur·i·za′tion** *n.*
Etymology: This process was named after Louis Pasteur, the nineteenth-century French chemist who was the founder of modern bacteriology.

pas·tiche (pas·tēsh′ *or* päs·tēsh′) *n.*
A work of art, music, or literature composed of fragments from various sources, especially such a work imitating or satirizing the style of other artists.

pas·time (pas′tīm′ *or* päs′tīm′) *n.*
Something that makes time pass enjoyably, as a recreation: *reading, ping-pong, and other indoor pastimes.*
Syn. amusement, diversion.

pas·tor·al (pas′tər·əl *or* päs′tər·əl) *adj.*
Pertaining to the innocent, charming, idyllic life of shepherds or rural life: *flower-strewn meadows and other pastoral scenes.*
Syn. rural, rustic, bucolic.
Ant. urban, sophisticated.

pâ·té de foie gras (pä·tā′ də fwä grä′) *n.*
A French term for a paste made from fat goose livers: *Spread some pâté de foie gras on a cracker.*

pat·ent (pat′nt) *n., v., adj.*
n. A government protection to an inventor giving him for a specific time the exclusive right of manufacturing and selling his invention.
v. To obtain a patent on: *He patented his new process.*

adj. Self-evident; apparent to everyone: *a patent truth.*
Syn. *adj.* obvious, evident, plain.
Ant. *adj.* debatable, disputable.

pa·ter·nos·ter (pā′tər·nos′tər) *n.*
1 The Lord's Prayer, or a recitation of the Lord's Prayer: *The religious service opened with a paternoster.* 2 A large bead of a rosary, indicating that a paternoster is to be said.

pa·thet·ic (pə·thet′ik) *adj.*
Characterized by or arousing sadness, pity, and tenderness: *a pathetic little orphan.*
Syn. pitiful.

path·find·er (path′fin′dər *or* päth′fīn′dər) *n.*
A person who finds a new way in unknown regions, as one who opens new fields in philosophy, science, art, etc.: *Einstein and other pathfinders in nuclear physics.*
Syn. pioneer, leader.

pa·thol·o·gy (pə·thol′ə·jē) *n.*
1 The branch of medical science concerned with the origin, nature, and development of disease. 2 The abnormal condition caused by a specific disease: *the pathology of syphilis.*—**pa·thol′o·gist** *n.*

pa·thos (pā′thos) *n.*
The quality, especially in literature, that arouses feelings of sorrow, compassion, etc.: *the pathos of the tale about poor little foundlings.*

pa·tience (pā′shəns) *n.*
The state, quality, or fact of being longsuffering or tolerant: *the patience of a saint.*
Spelling tip: Do not confuse *patience* and *patients* (persons undergoing treatment).
Syn. resignation, submission.
Ant. resistance, impatience.

pat·ois (pat′wä) *n.,* **pat·ois** (pat′wäz) *pl.*
A local dialect, especially one that is rustic or illiterate: *the patois spoken by the natives of the island.*
Syn. lingo.

pat·ri·mo·ny (pat′rə·mō′nē) *n.*
An inheritance from a father or ancestor: *His patrimony consisted of a gold watch and three old suits.*

pa·tron (pā′trən) *n.*
1 One who supports and fosters an artist or enterprise: *The $1000-a-plate dinner was attended by the museum patrons.* 2 A regular customer: *the patrons of the bar.*
Syn. 1 protector. 2 client.

pau·ci·ty (pô′sə·tē) *n.*
Smallness of number or of quantity: *There was a paucity of seats in the small theater.*
Syn. dearth, scarcity.
Ant. abundance.

pau·per (pô′pər) *n.*
Any very poor person, especially one receiving public charity.

pa·vil·ion (pə·vil′yən) *n.*
1 A large tent or summerhouse: *Henry VIII received him in a sumptuous pavilion.* 2 An annex or building separated from the main structure: *The hospital had several pavilions for special diseases.*

peace·a·ble (pē'sə·bəl) *adj.*
Inclined toward peace: *Peaceable men cannot always avoid fighting.*
Spelling tip: *Peace* + *able* = *peaceable.*
Syn. amicable, pacific.

pec·ca·dil·lo (pek'ə·dil'ō) *n.*, **pec·ca·dil·los** or **pec·ca·dil·loes** *pl.*
A trifling fault: *Apart from some youthful peccadillos, his life had been blameless.*

pe·cul·iar (pi·kyōōl'yər) *adj.*
1 Having a character exclusively its own: *The cat is peculiar among domestic animals in being self-sufficient.* **2** Odd; strange: *He has a peculiar habit of wiggling his ears.*

pe·cu·ni·ar·y (pi·kyōō'nē·er'ē) *adj.*
Consisting of or relating to money: *The pecuniary rewards of the job were small compared to the job satisfaction.*
Syn. monetary.

ped·a·gog·i·cal (ped'ə·goj'i·kəl) *adj.*
Of or pertaining to the science and art of teaching.

ped·a·gogue (ped'ə·gog) *n.*
A schoolteacher; educator: *The pedagogue eschewed using a blackboard.*—**ped'a·gog'y** *n.*

ped·ant (ped'ənt) *n.*
One who makes a needless display of learning or insists on trifling points of scholarship: *The pedant condemned the book because it contained two split infinitives.*—**pe·dan'tic** *adj.*

ped·es·tal (ped'əs·təl) *n.*
The base or support of a statue, column, or vase.

pe·di·a·tri·cian (pē'dē·ə·trish'ən) *n.*
A doctor specializing in the diseases and hygienic care of children.

peen (pēn) *n.*
The end of a hammer head opposite the striking face, shaped for removing nails or for other specialized purposes.

peer (pir) *n.*
1 An equal, as in natural gifts or social rank: *He competed among his peers at the Olympics.* **2** A noble.

pe·nal (pē'nəl) *adj.*
Of or pertaining to punishment: *The penal code includes harsh punishment for kidnaping.*

pe·nal·ize (pē'nəl·īz) *v.* **pe·nal·ized, pe·nal·iz·ing**
To subject to a penalty, as for some violation of law or contract: *The referee penalized him for unnecessary roughness.*
Syn. punish, fine, handicap.
Ant. reward.

pen·chant (pen'chənt) *n.*
A strong liking or inclination for something or someone: *He has a penchant for chocolate.*

pen·dant (pen'dənt) *n.*
Anything hanging from something for ornament or use, as a jewel on a chain.

pen·dent (pen'dənt) *adj.*
Hanging down; suspended: *The blossoms were pendent from the branches.*
Spelling tip: Although *pendent* may be spelled *pendant*, an *e* is preferred when it is an adjective and an *a* when it is a noun.

pen·du·lous (pen'jōō·ləs) *adj.*
Hanging, especially so as to swing: *the bloodhound's pendulous jowls.*
Syn. pendent.

pen·i·cil·lin (pen'ə·sil'in) *n.*
A powerful antibiotic for the treatment of bacterial infections.
Spelling tip: Remember the two *l*'s, and watch the three *i*'s.

pen·i·tence (pen'ə·təns) *n.*
A feeling of sorrow for having done something wrong; repentance.
Syn. remorse, contrition.

pen·i·tent (pen'ə·tənt) *adj.*, *n.*
adj. Affected by a sense of guilt and resolved to do better: *He was penitent about his fit of bad temper.*
n. Someone who is penitent.
Syn. *adj.* sorry, regretful, contrite.
Ant. *adj.* impenitent.

pen·i·ten·tia·ry (pen'ə·ten'shər·ē) *n.*
A prison, especially a state or federal prison for those convicted of serious offenses: *Sing Sing is a state penitentiary.*
Spelling tip: Watch the *i* in the final syllable.

pen·nant (pen'ənt) *n.*
A long, narrow flag, usually triangular, used as a signal on naval vessels, as a school emblem, etc.

pen·ni·less (pen'i·lis) *adj.*
Poverty-stricken: *The fire left him penniless.*
Spelling tip: *Y* becomes *i* as in silliness.
Syn. poor, indigent, destitute.
Ant. rich, wealthy.

pe·nu·ri·ous (pə·noor'ē·əs) *adj.*
1 Excessively sparing in the use of money; stingy: *He was so penurious that he saved old socks.* **2** Very needy or scanty: *The sharecropper's penurious furnishings included a bare mattress and a box for a table.*—**pe·nu'ri·ous·ness** *n.*
Syn. 1 mean, parsimonious.

pen·u·ry (pen'yə·rē) *n.*
Extreme poverty and want: *The family was in a state of wretched penury.*
Syn. indigence, destitution.
Ant. wealth, riches.

per·cale (pər·kāl') *n.*
A closely woven cotton fabric.

per·ceive (pər·sēv') *v.* **per·ceived, per·ceiv·ing**
1 To become aware of something through the senses; see, hear, feel, taste, or smell: *He perceived movements in the next room.* **2** To come to understand: *He perceived the meaning of the cryptic message.*—**per·ceiv'a·ble** *adj.*
Spelling tip: *I* before *e* except after *c.*
Syn. 1 sense, apprehend. 2 comprehend.

per·cus·sion (pər·kush'ən) *n.*
1 The sharp striking of one object against another to cause a shock or sound, as a drumstick against a drum or a firing pin against a cartridge. **2** The group of musical instruments in an orchestra whose sound is produced by percussion: *The percussion drowned out the strings and wind instruments.*

per di·em (pər dē'əm)
A Latin phrase meaning by the day: *The consultant was paid ten dollars per diem.*

per·di·tion (pər·dish'ən) *n.*
Eternal damnation: *Hamlet would not kill his uncle unless he could be sure of the latter's perdition.*
Ant. salvation.

per·emp·to·ry (pə·remp'tər·ē) *adj.*
1 Not open to debate or appeal; decisive; absolute: *The court made a peremptory judgment.* 2 Intolerant of opposition; dictatorial: *He ordered her out of the house in a peremptory way.*—**per·emp'to·ri·ly** *adv.*, **per·emp'to·ri·ness** *n.*

per·en·ni·al (pə·ren'ē·əl) *adj., n.*
adj. Continuing or enduring through the year or through many years: *her perennial quarrels with her daughter-in-law.*
n. A plant with a life span of more than two years: *Roses are perennials.*

per·fid·i·ous (pər·fid'ē·əs) *adj.*
Guilty of breach of faith; treacherous: *a perfidious attack on an ally.*—**per'fi·dy** *n.*, **per·fid'i·ous·ly** *adj.*
Syn. faithless, disloyal.
Ant. loyal, trustworthy.

per·fo·rate (pûr'fə·rāt) *v.* **per·fo·rat·ed, per·fo·rat·ing**
To make a hole or rows of holes through: *a perforated appendix.*—**per'fo·ra'tion** *n.*
Syn. pierce, puncture.

per·force (pər·fôrs') *adv.*
By or of necessity; necessarily: *Since the bridge was down, he had perforce to use another route.*

per·func·to·ry (pər·fungk'tə·rē) *adj.*
Done or performed mechanically and merely for the sake of getting through; cursory: *His playing of the sonata was perfunctory and uninspired.*—**per·func'to·ri·ly** *adv.*

per·i·gee (per'ə·jē) *n.*
That point in the orbit of a satellite that is nearest to the earth.
Ant. apogee.

per·il (per'əl) *n.*
Exposure to the chance of destruction or injury; danger: *those in peril on the sea.*
Syn. risk, hazard.
Ant. safety.

per·i·pa·tet·ic (per'i·pə·tet'ik) *adj.*
Walking or moving about from place to place: *a peripatetic news reporter.*

per·ju·ry (pûr'jə·rē) *n.*
The deliberate telling of a lie under oath in judicial proceedings: *He committed perjury when he said that he had never been at the scene of the crime.*

per·me·able (pûr'mē·a·ble) *adj.*
Allowing the passage of fluids or gases: *Limestone is permeable to water.*
Syn. penetratable, pervious.

per·me·ate (pûr'mē·āt) *v.* **per·me·at·ed, per·me·at·ing**
To spread through thoroughly: *The smell of onions permeated the room.*
Syn. pervade, impregnate.

per·mis·si·ble (pər·mis'ə·bəl) *adj.*
That can be permitted; allowable: *Throwing stones is not permissible.*

per·ni·cious (pər·nish'əs) *adj.*
Having the power to destroy or injure; very injurious: *the pernicious business of selling heroin.*
Syn. deadly, baneful, harmful.

per·pet·u·al (pər·pech'ōō·əl) *adj.*
1 Continuing or lasting forever: *perpetual motion.* 2 Constant; continual: *a colicky baby's perpetual crying.*
Syn. 1 eternal, endless.
Ant. 2 spasmodic.

per·pet·u·ate (pər·pech'ōō·āt) *v.* **per·pet·u·at·ed, per·pet·u·at·ing**
To preserve from extinction or oblivion: *to perpetuate a myth.*

per·qui·site (pûr'kwə·zit) *n.*
Any profit, payment, etc., earned at a person's regular work in addition to salary or wages: *Perquisites of a salesman's job may include a car.*

per·se·cute (pûr'sə·kyōōt) *v.* **per·se·cut·ed, per·se·cut·ing**
1 To harass with cruel or oppressive treatment: *Jews have been persecuted throughout history.* 2 To annoy or harass persistently: *persecuted by mosquitoes.*—**per'se·cu'tion, per'se·cu'tor** *n.*
Spelling tip: *Persecute* should not be confused with *prosecute,* which means to press legal charges or conduct a trial against someone.

per·se·ver·ance (pûr'sə·vir'əns) *n.*
Persistence in an effort, purpose, or enterprise: *Perseverance is needed to attain your goals.*

per·se·vere (pûr'sə·vir') *v.* **per·se·vered, per·se·ver·ing**
To persist in any purpose or enterprise; continue striving in spite of difficulties.

per·si·flage (pûr'sə·fläzh) *n.*
A light, flippant style of conversation or writing: *The witty persiflage of two teen-agers.*

per·sis·tent (pər·sis'tənt or pər·zis'tənt) *adj.*
1 Persevering or stubborn in a course or resolve: *a persistent law violator.* 2 Enduring; permanent: *a persistent pain.*—**per·sis'tent·ly** *adv.*

per·so·na non gra·ta (pər·sō'nə non grä'tə or pər·sō'nə non grā'tə)
A Latin term meaning a person who is not welcome or acceptable: *The President declared the Soviet attaché persona non grata because he was accused of spying.*

per·son·nel (pur'sə·nel') *n.*
The persons employed in a business, engaged in military service, etc.

per·spi·ca·cious (pûr'spə·kā'shəs) *adj.*
Keenly discerning or understanding: *a perspicacious instructor.*—**per'spi·ca'cious·ly** *adv.*, **per'spi·ca'cious·ness** *n.*

Syn. astute, shrewd, sagacious.
Ant. undiscerning, shortsighted.

per·spi·ra·tion (pûr'spə·rā'shən) *n.*
Sweating or sweat: *Perspiration dripped from the athlete's brow.*

per·suade (pər·swād') *v.* **per·suad·ed, per·suad·ing**
1 To induce someone to do something: *I persuaded him to buy it.* 2 To induce to a belief; convince.—**per·suad'er** *n.*

per·sua·sive (pər·swā'siv) *adj.*
Having power or ability to induce someone to do something: *The candidate's persuasive speech earned him many votes.*—**per·sua'sive·ness** *n.*
Syn. moving, convincing.

pert (pûrt) *adj.*
Disrespectfully forward; impertinent; saucy: *a pert reply.*—**pert'ly** *adv.,* **pert'ness** *n.*
Syn. impudent, flippant.
Ant. modest, bashful, demure.

per·tain (pər·tān') *v.*
1 To have reference; relate: *That report pertains to the recent study.* 2 To belong as an adjunct, function, quality, etc.: *the loyalty pertaining to dogs.* 3 To be fitting or appropriate: *correct behavior pertaining to a girl.*

per·ti·nent (pûr'tə·nənt) *adj.*
Related to the matter at hand; to the point: *a pertinent question.* **per'ti·nence, per'ti·nen·cy** *n.*
Syn. relevant, connected.
Ant. alien, incongruous.

per·turb (pər·tûrb') *v.*
To disquiet or disturb greatly: *He was perturbed because she kept him wailing.*—**per·turb'a·ble** *adj.,* **per·tur·ba'tion** *n.*
Syn. agitate, excite, distress.
Ant. calm, soothe.

pe·ruse (pə·rōōz') *v.* **pe·rused, pe·rus·ing**
To read carefully: *to peruse a newspaper.*—**pe·rus'er, pe·rus'al** *n.*

per·vade (pər·vād') *v.* **per·vad·ed, per·vad·ing**
To spread through every part of something: *A pleasant odor pervaded the room.*
Syn. permeate, penetrate, impregnate.

per·vert·ed (pər·vûr'tid) *adj.*
Deviating widely from what is right or acceptable; distorted; twisted: *a perverted sense of humor.*

pes·si·mism (pes'ə·miz'əm) *n.*
1 A disposition to take a gloomy view of affairs. 2 The doctrine that the world and life are essentially evil.—**pes'si·mist** *n.*
Ant. optimism.

pes·tle (pes'əl) *n.; v.* **pes·tled, pes·tling**
n. An implement used for crushing, pulverizing, or mixing substances in a mortar.
v. To pound, grind, or mix with a pestle.

pe·tite (pə·tēt') *adj.*
Diminutive; little (said of women and girls).

pet·ri·fy (pet'rə·fī) *v.* **pet·ri·fied, pet·ri·fy·ing**
1 To turn into stone or like stone: *a petrified tree.* 2 To daze or paralyze with fear, sur-

prise, etc.: *She became petrified when she saw the intruder.*

pet·u·lant (pech'ōō·lənt) *adj.*
Expressing annoyance over trifles; peevish; bad-tempered: *The old woman became petulant if she did not get her way all the time.*—**pet'u·lant·ly** *adv.*

phan·tom (fan'təm) *n., adj.*
n. 1 Something that exists only in the mind but appears to be real: *the phantoms of delirium.* 2 An apparition; ghost.
adj. Illusive, ghostlike: *a phantom ship.*

phar·ma·ceu·ti·cal (far'mə·sōō'ti·kəl) *adj.*
Of or having to do with drugs: *pharmaceutical supplies.*

phase (fāz) *n.*
1 One of the appearances or forms presented periodically by the moon and planets. 2 Any of the distinctive stages of a development: *A phase of history was closed by the downfall of Rome.* 3 An aspect or part of something: *a phase of mathematics.*

phe·nom·e·non (fi·nom'ə·non) *n.,* **phe·nom·e·na** or **phe·nom·e·nons** *pl.*
1 Something visible or directly observable, as an appearance, action, change, etc.: *Motion is a mechanical phenomenon.* 2 An inexplicable or rare fact or event. 3 A person having some remarkable talents, power, or ability; prodigy: *Houdini was a phenomenon at extricating himself from chains.*—**phe·nom'e·nal** *adj.*

phi·lan·der·er (fi·lan'dər·ər) *n.*
A flirt or suitor.—Also **phi·lan·der** *n.*

phi·lol·o·gy (fi·lol'ə·jē) *n.*
1 The scientific study of language, especially the history of and relationships among languages. 2 The scientific study of literary works and other written records in order to establish accurate texts and determine their meaning.

phlegm (flem) *n.*
Mucus secreted in a person's air passages, especially when produced as a discharge through the mouth: *to cough up phlegm.*

phleg·mat·ic (fleg·mat'ik) *adj.*
Not easily moved or excited; sluggish: *a phlegmatic man who rarely displays emotion.*—**phleg·mat'i·cal·ly** *adv.*
Syn. apathetic, lethargic, indifferent.
Ant. emotional, excitable.

pho·bi·a (fō'bē·ə) *n.*
An exaggerated and compulsive dread of a certain object, situation, etc.: *fear of high places and other phobias.*

phra·se·ol·o·gy (frā'zē·ol'ə·jē) *n.,* **phra·se·ol·o·gies** *pl.*
The choice of words and phrases in expressing ideas: *The author's complicated phraseology made his book difficult to understand.*
Syn. wording, phrasing.

phy·si·cian (fi·zish'ən) *n.*
1 A doctor. 2 A doctor who practices medicine, not surgery: *Is he a physician or a surgeon?*

phys·i·cist (fiz'ə·sist) *n.*
A person who specializes in physics (the science dealing with matter, energy, motion, and their interrelations).

phys·i·og·no·my (fiz'ē·og'nə·mē) *n.*, **phys·i·og·no·mies** *pl.*
A person's face considered as revealing his character or disposition: *a weak-looking physiognomy.*

phy·sique (fi·zēk') *n.*
The structure, shape, or appearance of a person's body: *a muscular physique.*
Syn. body, figure, build.

pi·az·za (pē·az'ə; *Italian* pyät'tsä) *n.*
1 An open space or square in a town, especially in Italy: *The piazza was covered with pigeons.* 2 A veranda or porch: *The family was sitting on the piazza.*

pic·a·yune (pik'i·yōon') *n.*
1 Of little value or importance; practically worthless. 2 Petty: *It's picayune to criticize the color of a man's socks.*
Syn. 1 trivial, trifling, insignificant. 2 small.
Ant. 1 important, essential, momentous. 2 magnanimous, high-minded.

pie·bald (pī'bôld') *adj., n.*
adj. Having spots, especially of white and black: *a piebald hide.*
n. A spotted or mottled animal, especially a horse: *Is the horse a piebald?*

pièce de ré·sis·tance (pyes də rā·zē·stäns) *n.*, **pièces de résistance** *pl.*
A French phrase meaning the principal or most important piece, as the most important work in a collection of art, poems, etc., or the main dish of a dinner: *The pièce de résistance was the chocolate soufflé.*
Syn. showpiece.

pied-à-terre (pyā·då·târ') *n.*, **pieds-à-terre** *pl.*
A French word meaning a temporary or extra dwelling: *He lived in the country but maintained a pied-à-terre in the city.*

pil·lage (pil'ij) *n.; v.* **pil·laged, pil·lag·ing**
n. Looting, especially by soldiers in wartime: *Attila's Huns practiced pillage and rape.*
v. To loot: *The soldiers pillaged the conquered village.*—**pil'lag·er** *n.*
Syn. *n.* plunderage, ravage. *v.* plunder, despoil.

pince-nez (pans'nā' *or* pins'nā') *n.*, **pince-nez** *pl.*
Eyeglasses held upon the nose by a spring.

pincers (pin'sərz) *n.pl.*
1 An instrument with two handles and a pair of jaws working on a pivot, used to grasp objects: *The watchmaker picked up the tiny spring with a special pincers.* 2 The claw of a crab, lobster, etc.
Spelling tip: This word is also spelled *pinchers.*

pin·na·cle (pin'ə·kəl) *n.*
1 A tower rising above or from a roof: *The elaborate castle has many pinnacles.* 2 The highest point or place: *When he was elected*

President he knew he had reached the pinnacle of his political career.
Syn. 1 turret, spire. 2 peak, apex, summit.

pi·ous (pī'əs) *adj.*
Religious: *a pious Christian.*—**pi·ous·ly** *adv.*, **pi'ous·ness** *n.*
Syn. devout, reverential.
Ant. atheistic, irreligious.

pique (pēk) *n.; v.* **piqued, pi·quing**
n. A feeling of irritation or resentment: *She could sense his pique when she turned down the date.*
v. 1 To arouse a feeling of irritation or resentment in someone: *The bad reviews of his play piqued him.* 2 To arouse or stimulate: *Her air of mystery piqued his curiosity.*
Syn. *n.* annoyance, chagrin, *v.* 1 provoke, gall, roil.
Ant. *n.* pleasure, happiness. *v.* 1 please.

pith·y (pith'ē) *adj.* **pith·i·er, pith·i·est**
Terse, meaty, and forceful: *a pithy one-page summary of the complex issue.*—**pith'i·ly** *adv.*, **pith'i·ness** *n.*
Syn. pointed, succinct.
Ant. wordy, rambling.

plac·ard (plak'ärd) *n.*
A printed or written poster or proclamation that is displayed in a public place.
Syn. handbill, broadside.

pla·cate (plā'kāt, plak'āt, *or* plak'ət) *v.* **pla·cat·ed, pla·cat·ing**
To calm or appease the anger of: *The shopkeeper placated the irate customer by promising to replace the imperfect merchandise.*—**pla·ca'ter, pla·ca'tion** *n.*
Syn. pacify, soothe, mollify.
Ant. aggravate, antagonize.

plac·id (plas'id) *adj.*
Calm and undisturbed: *a placid lake.*
Syn. peaceful, tranquil.
Ant. churning, roiled, turbulent.

pla·gia·rize (plā'jə·rīz) *v.* **pla·gia·rized, pla·gia·riz·ing**
To pass off as one's own passages or ideas from someone else's writings: *Most of the student's term paper was plagiarized from a magazine article.*—**pla'gia·rism', pla'gia·rist', pla'gia·riz'er** *n.*
Syn. pirate, lift, crib.

plain (plān) *adj., n.*
adj. 1 Clear; understandable: *plain English.* 2 Straightforward; guileless: *a plain question.* 3 Lowly in condition or station; unlearned: *plain people.* 4 Not rich; simple: *plain food.*
n. An expanse of level, treeless land; a prairie.—**plain'ly** *adv.*, **plain'ness** *n.*
Spelling tip: Do not confuse *plain* and *plane.*

plain·tiff (plān'tif) *n.*
The complaining party in a lawsuit.
Ant. defendant.

plain·tive (plān'tiv) *adj.*
Expressing sadness; mournful: *a plaintive melody.*—**plain'tive·ly** *adv.*, **plain'tive·ness** *n.*
Syn. sorrowful, doleful, melancholy.
Ant. joyous, glad, cheerful.

plait (plat *or* plāt) *v.*, *n.*
v. 1 To braid: *She plaited her hair.* 2 To pleat.
n. 1 A braid, especially of hair. 2 A pleat.

plane (plān) *n.*, *adj.*
n. 1 Any flat surface. 2 A stage of development: *a plane of thought.* 3 An airplane.
adj. 1 Level; flat: *a plane figure.* 2 Dealing only with flat surfaces: *plane geometry.*

plaque (plak) *n.*
1 A plate, disk, or slab of metal, porcelain, or other material artistically ornamented and used as a wall decoration, etc. 2 A small disk or brooch worn as a badge of membership.

plat·i·tude (plat'ə·t(y)ōōd) *n.*
A flat, dull, or commonplace statement; a truism, such as "Hard work is the key to success."

pla·ton·ic (plə·ton'ik) *adj.*
Purely spiritual; lacking sensual feeling: *a platonic friendship.*

plau·si·ble (plô'zə·bəl) *adj.*
1 Seeming to be reasonable or probable, but open to doubt: *a plausible argument.* 2 Apparently trustworthy or believable: *a plausible salesman.*

play·wright (plā'rīt') *n.*
A writer of plays.
Spelling tip: A playwright is a *writer*.

pla·za (plaz'ə *or* plä'zə) *n.*
An open square or marketplace in a town or city.

pleas·ant (plez'ənt) *adj.*
1 Giving pleasure: *a pleasant trip.* 2 Agreeable in manner, appearance, etc.: *a pleasant smile.*
—**pleas'ant·ly** *adv.*, **pleas'ant·ness** *n.*

ple·be·ian (pli·bē'ən) *adj.*, *n.*
adj. 1 Of or pertaining to the common people, especially those of ancient Rome. 2 Common or vulgar: *a person with plebeian tastes.*
n. 1 One of the common people, especially of ancient Rome. 2 Anyone who is coarse or vulgar.

pleb·i·scite (pleb'ə·sīt *or* pleb'ə·sit) *n.*
An expression of the popular will concerning some important question, given by a direct vote of the whole people.
Spelling tip: Watch the *sc* in this word.

plen·i·po·ten·ti·ar·y (plen'i·pə·ten'shē·er'ē *or* plen'i·pə·ten'shə·rē) *n.*, **plen·i·po·ten·ti·ar·ies** *pl.*
A person with full powers to represent a government, as an ambassador, minister, or envoy.

pleth·o·ra (pleth'ər·ə) *n.*
A superabundance; excess: *a plethora of words.*

pleu·ri·sy (plōōr'ə·sē) *n.*
Inflammation of the thin membrane that envelops the lungs and lines the chest cavity.

plov·er (pluv'ər *or* plō'vər) *n.*
Any of various shore birds having long, pointed wings and a short tail.

plumb (plum) *n.*, *adj.*, *adv.*, *v.*
n. A lead weight on the end of a line used to find the exact perpendicular, to sound the depth of water, etc.
adj. Truly vertical: *a plumb pillar.*
adv. 1 Vertically: *It fell plumb.* 2 *Informal* Completely; entirely (also spelled *plum*): *plumb crazy.*
v. 1 To test the perpendicularity, depth, etc., with a plumb. 2 To get to the bottom of something: *to plumb the depths of despair.*
Spelling tip: Remember the silent *b*.

plu·ral·i·ty (plŏŏ·ral'ə·tē) *n.*, **plu·ral·i·ties** *pl.*
1 The number of votes that the winner of an election obtains over his nearest opponent. 2 The greater portion or number of anything. 3 The state or condition of being plural or numerous: *a plurality of viewpoints.*

pneu·mat·ic (n(y)ōō·mat'ik) *adj.*
1 Operated by compressed air: *a pneumatic pump.* 2 Containing air, especially compressed air: *a pneumatic tire.* 3 Having to do with air or gases: *pneumatic pressure.*

pneu·mo·nia (n(y)ōō·mōn'yə) *n.*
A disease of bacterial or viral origin causing inflammation of the lungs.

po·di·um (pō'dē·əm) *n.*, **po·di·a** *pl.*
A small platform for the conductor of an orchestra, a speaker, etc.

po·grom (pō'grəm *or* pō·grom') *n.*
An organized and often officially instigated local massacre, especially one directed against Jews.

poign·ant (poin'yənt·*or* poi'nənt) *adj.*
1 Painful: *poignant grief.* 2 Piercing, sharp, and cutting: *poignant sarcasm.* 3 Penetrating and apt: *poignant observations.*—**poign'an·cy** *n.*, **poign'ant·ly** *adv.*

poi·son (poi'zən) *n.*, *v.*
n. 1 A substance that harms or destroys the tissues of a living organism that absorbs it. 2 Anything that tends to harm, destroy, or corrupt.
v. 1 To administer poison to someone or something: *to poison a rat.* 2 To affect wrongfully; corrupt; pervert: *The brainwashing poisoned his mind.*—**poi'son·er** *n.*

pol·i·o·my·e·li·tis (pol'ē·ō·mī'ə·lī'tis *or* pō'lē·ō·mī'ə·lī'tis) *n.*
A virus disease characterized by inflammation of the gray matter of the spinal cord, followed by paralysis and atrophy of various muscle groups.
Syn. infantile paralysis, polio.

pol·i·ti·cian (pol'ə·tish'ən) *n.*
1 One who is actively engaged in politics, especially as a professional. 2 A person who engages in government for personal or partisan aims rather than for reasons of principle; a political opportunist.

pol·i·tics (pol'ə·tiks) *n.pl.*
1 The science or art of government. 2 The affairs or activities of those controlling or seeking to control a government: *He has made politics his career.*
Usage: This plural noun is usually construed as singular and therefore takes a singular verb: *Politics is a tough game.*

667

pol·i·ty (pol'ə·tē) *n.*, **pol·i·ties** *pl.*
1 The form or method of government of a nation, state, church, etc. 2 Any community living under some definite form of government.

pol·troon (pol·trōon') *n.*
A thorough coward; craven; dastard.

po·lyg·a·mist (pə·lig'ə·mist) *n.*
A person having more than one wife or husband at the same time.

pol·y·glot (pol'i·glot) *adj., n.*
adj. Expressed in several tongues or speaking several languages: *a polyglot dictionary.*
n. A person who speaks or writes several languages.

pom·mel (pum'əl *or* pom'əl) *n.*
1 A knob, as on the hilt of a sword, bayonet, etc. 2 A knob at the front and on the top of a saddle.

pon·tiff (pon'tif) *n.*
1 The Pope. 2 Any bishop.—**pon·tif'ic** *adj.*

pon·tif·i·cal (pon·tif'i·kəl) *adj.*
Of, pertaining to, or suitable for a Pope or bishop.

pope (pōp) *n.*
(Often capital *P*) The bishop of Rome and the head of the Roman Catholic Church.

porce·lain (pôrs'lin, pōrs'lin, pôr'sə·lin, *or* pōr'sə·lin) *n.*
A white, hard, translucent ceramic ware, usually glazed; china.

pore (pôr *or* pōr) *n.*; **pored, por·ing**
n. A minute opening, as in the skin or a leaf serving as an outlet for perspiration or as a means of absorption.
v. To study or read with care.

port·a·ble (pôr'tə·bəl *or* pōr'tə·bəl) *adj.*
That can be readily carried or moved: *a portable typewriter.*

port·age (pôr'tij *or* pōr'tij) *n.*
1 The act of transporting boats and goods from one navigable water to another. 2 The route over which and the place where such transportation is made. 3 The charge for transportation.

por·tend (pôr·tend' *or* pōr·tend') *v.*
To warn of as an omen; forebode: *Dark clouds portend rain.*
Syn. augur, presage.

por·tent (pôr'tent *or* pōr'tent) *n.*
An indication or sign of what is to happen; omen: *His words turned out to be a portent of the coming events.*

por·ten·tous (pôr·ten'təs *or* pōr·ten'təs) *adj.*
1 Ominous: *a portentous calm before a tempest.* 2 Causing astonishment; extraordinary: *The enemy offered a portentous resistance.*—**por·ten'tous·ly** *adv.*

por·tion (pôrshən *or* pōr'shən) *n.*
A part of a larger whole, as the amount of food given to one person: *Her portion of the estate amounted to $50,000.*

port·ly (pôrt'lē *or* pōrt'lē) *adj.* **port·li·er, port·li·est**
1 Somewhat corpulent; stout: *Older men are often portly.* 2 Stately in manner; impressive: *The portly butler unbent enough to smile at me.*
Syn. 1 plump. 2 dignified.

port·man·teau (pôrt·man'tō *or* pōrt·man'tō) *n.*
A large suitcase hinged to form two compartments.

por·trait (pôr'trit, pōr'trit, pôr'trāt, *or* pōr'trāt) *n.*
A likeness of a person created by an artist.

por·tray (pôr·trā' *or* pōr·trā') *v.*
To represent by drawing, painting, words, acting, etc.

pos·sess (pə·zes') *v.*
1 To own: *He possessed two cars.* 2 To enter and take control over: *The wild idea possessed him.*—**pos·ses'sion** *n.*

pos·ter·i·ty (pos·ter'ə·tē) *n.*.
1 Future generations taken collectively: *Today's medical research will benefit posterity.* 2 All of a particular person's descendants.

post·mor·tem (pōst·môr'təm) *adj., n.*
adj. Happening after death: *a post-mortem examination.*
n. An examination of a body after death.

pos·tu·lant (pos'chə·lənt) *n.*
An applicant for admission into a religious order.

pos·tu·late (pos'chə·lāt) *v.* **pos·tu·lat·ed, pos·tu·lat·ing**
To assume the truth or reality of something; to take for granted: *Early scientists postulated that the earth was the center of the universe.*
Syn. presume, posit.

po·ta·ble (pō'tə·bəl) *adj.*
Suitable for drinking: *The water is evil-tasting but potable.*
Syn. drinkable.

po·ten·tate (pōt'n·tāt) *n.*
A possessor of power or authority: *Hollywood potentates blackballed the actor.*
Syn. sovereign, monarch, mogul.

po·ten·tial (pə·ten'chəl) *adj., n.*
adj. Possible but not actual: *a potential source of aluminum.*
n. A possible source of development: *College graduates have much potential.*

po·tion (pō'shən) *n.*
A draft of liquid containing medicine or a drug: *The wizard gave her a magical potion.*
Spelling tip: Do not confuse *potion* and *portion.*

pot·pour·ri (pot·pŏŏr'ē *or* pō·pŏŏ·rē') *n.*
1 A mixture of dried flower petals kept in a jar and used to perfume a room. 2 A medley of different tunes, literary pieces, etc.: *a potpourri of Viennese waltzes.*

poul·tice (pōl'tis) *n.*
A moist, soft mass of flour, clay, mustard, etc., applied to a sore part of the body.
Syn. plaster, fomentation.

pour (pôr) *v.*
To flow or cause to flow in a continuous stream: *The crowd poured out of the stadium.*
Spelling tip: Do not confuse the verbs *pour* and *pore* (to study carefully).

prac·ti·cal·ly (prak'tik·lē) *adv.*
1 In a realistic manner: *He approached the problem practically.* **2** To all intents and purposes: *He was practically a pauper before he married an heiress.*

prac·tice (prak'tis) *v.* **prac·ticed, prac·tic·ing;** *n.*
v. **1** To use habitually: *He practiced economy.* **2** To apply in action: *Practice what you preach.* **3** To perform repeatedly in order to obtain greater skill: *He practiced at the piano six hours a day.*
n. Established custom or usage: *He made a practice of jogging two miles a day.*

prag·mat·ic (prag·mat'ik) *adj.*
Practical; matter-of-fact: *the pragmatic solution to a problem.*

prai·rie (prâr'ē) *n.*
A tract of grassland; especially the broad, grassy plain of central North America.

prat·tle (prat'l) *v.* **prat·tled, prat·tling;** *n.*
v. To talk foolishly or like a child: *The baby prattled happily to himself.*
n. Foolish talk: *the prattle of telephoning teen-agers.*
Syn. *v., n.* babble, chatter.

pre·am·ble (prē'am·bəl) *n.*
An introductory statement or fact: *the Pre-amble to the Constitution.*
Syn. introduction, preliminary.
Ant. postscript, afterthought.

pre·car·i·ous (pri·kâr'ē·əs) *adj.*
Subject to continued risk or danger: *his precarious position on the window sill.*
Syn. risky, hazardous, uncertain.

precede (pri·sēd') *v.* **pre·ced·ed, pre·ced·ing**
To go or be before: *Causes precede effects.*
Syn. antedate.
Ant. follow, succeed.

pre·ce·dence (pres'ə·dəns) *n.*
The act or right of preceding: priority in place, time, or rank: *A request by your boss takes precedence over less important work.*

prec·e·dent (pres'ə·dənt *n.*; pri·sēd'ənt *adj.*) *n., adj.*
n. An act or instance capable of being used as a guide or example in the future.
adj. Preceding; former.

pre·cept (prē'sept) *n.*
A rule of conduct or action: *the precept of doing unto others as you would have them do unto you.*

pre·cinct (prē'singkt) *n.*
1 An election district within a town, county, etc.: *the fifth precinct.* **2** A subdivision of a town or city under the supervision of a police unit, or the police station for the area: *He was arrested by detectives from the seventeenth precinct.*

pre·ci·os·i·ty (presh'ē·os'ə·tē) *n.*
Extreme refinements or affectation of style, speech, or taste: *Walter Pater's preciosity makes him unreadable to many.*
Syn. fastidiousness, purism.

pre·cious (presh'əs) *adj.*
1 Valuable: *precious metals.* **2** Beloved; cherished: *precious memories.*—**pre'cious·ly** *adv.*

pre·cip·i·tate (pri·sip'ə·tāt) *v.* **pre·cip·i·tat·ed, pre·cip·i·tat·ing**
v. To hasten the occurrence of something: *The verbal exchange precipitated a fistfight.*

pre·cip·i·tous (pri·sip'ə·təs) *adj.*
Steep; sheer: *a precipitous mountain peak.*

pré·cis (prā'sē) *n.*, **pré·cis** (prā'sēz) *pl.*
A concise summary, as of a book, article, document, or proceedings: *Because he was too busy to read the whole report, he read a précis of it.*
Syn. abstract, digest.

pre·clude (pri·klo͞od') *v.* **pre·clud·ed, pre·clud·ing**
To render impossible by necessary consequence or implication: *Our European trip precludes a visit to Canada this year.*
Syn. prevent, obviate.
Ant. allow.

pre·co·cious (pri·kō'shəs) *adj.*
Unusually developed or advanced, especially for one's age: *The precocious four-year-old could accurately multiply and divide.*
Syn. advanced.
Ant. backward.

pre·cur·sor (pri·kûr'sər) *n.*
A person who or a thing that precedes and suggests the course of future events: *Isaac Newton was the precursor of modern physicists.*
Syn. forerunner, predecessor.

pred·a·to·ry (pred'ə·tôr'ē) *adj.*
1 Of, related to, or characterized by plundering: *Predatory hordes of Huns invaded Europe.* **2** Living by preying upon others: *Falcons are predatory birds.*

pred·e·ces·sor (pred'ə·ses·ər) *n.*
One who has gone before another in point of time, as the previous holder of an office: *He inherited the mistakes of his predecessors.*
Syn. ancestor, precursor, forefather.
Ant. successor.

pred·i·cate (pred'i·kāt *v.*; pred'i·kit *n.*) *v.* **pred·i·cat·ed, pred·i·cat·ing;** *n.*
v. **1** To affirm as a quality of something: *He predicates the truth of his proposition.* **2** To imply or connote: *His buying of swampland in anticipation of a profit predicates advance information.* **3** To found or base an argument, etc., upon something: *He predicated his opinion on elaborate research.*
n. The verb in a sentence together with its object or complement and modifiers.

pre·dict (pri·dikt') *v.*
To make known beforehand; foretell: *He predicted the outcome of the race.*—**pre·dict'a·ble** *adj.*
Syn. prophesy, forecast.

669

pre·di·lec·tion (prē·də·lek′shən) *n.*
A preference or bias in favor of something: *a predilection for shrimps.*
Syn. inclination, liking.
Ant. antipathy, dislike.

pre·dom·i·nance (pri·dom′ə·nəns) *n.*
The state or quality of being superior in power, influence, effectiveness, number, or degree: *the predominance of elderly women over elderly men.*
Syn. ascendancy, preponderance, prevalence.

pre·em·i·nent (prē·em′ə·nənt) *adj.*
Distinguished above all others.
Syn. outstanding, conspicuous.

pre·empt (prē·empt′) *v.*
To acquire or appropriate beforehand: *The land speculator had preempted most of the mineral rights.*
Syn. acquire, appropriate.

pre·face (pref′is) *n.; v.* **pre·faced, pre·fac·ing** *n.* An introductory piece of writing or preliminary remarks, especially an essay to introduce a book.
v. To introduce with a preface: *He prefaced his remarks with a tribute to the chairman.*
Syn. *n.* introduction, foreword.
Ant. *n.* postscript, appendix.

pref·a·to·ry (pref′ə·tôr′ē) *adj.*
Introductory: *He explained his aims in a brief but important prefatory passage.*—**pref′a·to′ri·al** *adj.*
Syn. introductory.

pre·fer (pri·fûr′) *v.* **pre·ferred, pre·fer·ring**
1 To value more or to like better: *Do you prefer diamonds or sapphires?* 2 To give priority to someone or something.
Spelling tip: Beware of the doubled *r*'s in preferred and preferring.

pref·er·a·ble (pref′ər·ə·bəl) *adj.*
Desired or more desirable; worthy of choice: *Death is preferable to dishonor.*—**pref′er·a·bly** *adv.*

preg·nant (preg′nənt) *adj.*
1 Carrying a growing fetus in the uterus; being with child or with young. 2 Having considerable weight or significance; full of meaning: *a pregnant remark.* 3 Full or filled: *pregnant with meaning.*

prel·ate (prel′it) *n.*
An ecclesiastic of high rank, as a bishop, abbot, or patriarch.

prel·ude (prel′yōōd *or* prē′lōōd) *n.*
1 A musical piece or movement serving as an introduction to a larger work, or standing on its own as a comparatively short work: *Chopin's twenty-four preludes.* 2 Anything foreshadowing a greater event: *The occupation of Czechoslovakia was a prelude to World War II.*
Syn. 2 introduction, preface.
Ant. 2 aftermath.

pre·ma·ture (prē′mə·chŏŏr′) *adj.*
Existing, happening, or developing before the proper period; untimely: *The premature infant was placed in an incubator.*—**pre′ma·ture′ly** *adv.*

pre·mi·er (pri·mir′) *adj.*
First in rank or position: *the premier officer in the company.*

pre·miere (pri·mir′ *or* pri·myâr′) *n.*
1 The first performance of a play, movie, etc.: *Critics attended the premiere.* 2 The leading lady in a theatrical company: *The premiere's position was being challenged by her understudy.*
Spelling tip: This word is also spelled *première.*
Syn. 1 first night.

prem·ise (prem′is) *n.*
A statement accepted as true that serves as ground for argument, a conclusion, etc.: *If you accept his premise you must accept his conclusions.*
Syn. 1 assumption, presupposition.

pre·mi·um (prē′mē·əm) *n.*
1 Something offered free as an inducement to buy, rent, or contract for something else. *Free electricity was the premium for renting the apartment immediately.* 2 The amount payable for insurance: *The premium was raised after his second accident.* 3 High regard: *He put a premium on truth.*

pre·mo·ni·tion (prē′mə·nish′ən *or* prem′ə·nish′ən) *n.*
A feeling that something is going to happen, usually something bad: *She had a premonition that the business would fail.*
Syn. presentiment, foreboding.

pre·pare (pri·pâr′) *v.* **pre·pared, pre·par·ing**
1 To make ready: *We must prepare a place for our guests.* 2 To get ready: *We must prepare for a long campaign.*—**prep′a·ra′tion** *n.*

pre·pon·der·ance (pri·pon′dər·əns) *n.*
Superiority in weight, power, numbers, influence, etc.: *A preponderance of women attended the PTA meeting.*—**pre·pon′der·ant** *adj.*

pre·pos·ter·ous (pri·pos′tər·əs) *adj.*
Contrary to nature, reason, or common sense: *Three hundred dollars is a preposterous price for a hat.*—**pre·pos′ter·ous·ly** *adv.*
Syn. absurd, ridiculous.

pre·rog·a·tive (pri·rog′ə·tiv) *n.*
A special right or privilege: *The type of wedding is the bride's prerogative.*
Spelling tip: This word is often mistakenly pronounced per·og′ə·tiv, which makes it difficult to spell. Watch the pronunciation.

pre·sci·ence (prē′shē·əns *or* presh′ē·əns) *n.*
Knowledge of events before they happen.
—**pre′sci·ent** *adj.*

pre·scribe (pri·skrīb′) *v.* **pre·scribed, pre·scrib·ing**
1 To set down as a rule or direction to be followed. 2 To direct medically: *The doctor prescribed therapy for the patient.*

pre·scrip·tion (pri·skrip′shən) *n.*
A physician's formula for compounding a medicine, or the medicine itself.

pre·sen·ti·ment (pri·zen′tə·mənt) *n.*
A feeling that something is about to happen: *I have a strong presentiment that our plan will fail.*
Syn. premonition, apprehension, foreboding.

pres·i·den·cy (prez′ə·dən·sē) *n.*
The office, function, or term of office of a president.—**pres′i·den′tial** *adj.*

pres·i·dent (prez′ə·dent) *n.*
1 A person who presides over an organized body, as a business, college, etc.: *A college president is responsible for campus improvements.* 2 The chief executive of a republic: *the President of the United States.*
Spelling tip: When referring to the President of the United States, this word always should have a capital *P.*

pre·sume (pri·zo͞om′) *v.* **pre·sumed, pre·sum·ing**
To take for granted: *I presume you know what you are talking about.*—**pre·sump′tion** *n.*
Syn. suppose, assume.

pre·sump·tu·ous (pri·zump′cho͞o·əs) *adj.*
Too confident or bold: *It was presumptuous of you to say that I had recommended you for the job.*

pre·tense (pri·tens′ or prē′tens) *n.*
A false or hypocritical act, appearance, excuse, etc.: *He knew the children were coming, yet he made a great pretense of being surprised at seeing them.*

pre·text (prē′tekst) *n.*
A false reason or motive given to conceal the real one: *Use any pretext you can think of, but don't attend the party.*
Syn. excuse, pretense.

prev·a·lent (prev′ə·lənt) *adj.*
Widespread; common: *Illiteracy is prevalent in underdeveloped countries.*—**prev′a·lence** *n.*, **prev′a·lent·ly** *adv.*

pre·var·i·cate (pri·var′ə·kāt) *v.* **pre·var·i·cat·ed, pre·var·i·cat·ing**
To tell a lie: *Telling the truth is better than prevaricating.*—**pre·var′i·ca′tion** *n.*

prey (prā) *n., v.*
n. 1 Any animal seized by another for food. 2 A person or thing victimized by a harmful or hostile person or agent: *a prey to nerves.*
v. 1 To hunt and kill for food: *Foxes prey on poultry.* 2 To make someone a victim. 3 To exert a wearing or harmful influence: *His losses preyed on his mind.*

prim (prim) *adj.*
Stiffly proper and neat: *The librarian was a small, prim woman.*—**prim′ly** *adv.*, **prim′ness** *n.*

pri·ma don·na (prē′mə don′ə) *n.*, **pri·ma don·nas** *pl.*
1 A leading female singer: *Mary Garden was a famous prima donna.* 2 A temperamental person: *If she's going to be a prima donna, we'll avoid her.*

pri·ma·ri·ly (prī′mer·ə·lē or prī·mâr′ə·lē) *adv.*
In the first place: *Norsemen were primarily a seafaring people.*

prim·i·tive (prim′ə·tiv) *adj.*
Simple and crude: *primitive sanitary conditions in the camp.*—**prim′i·tive·ly** *adv.*
Syn. old-fashioned, rudimentary.

prin·ci·pal (prin′sə·pəl) *adj., n.*

adj. Most important: *Wheat is among the principal exports of the United States.*
n. A very important person or thing.

prin·ci·ple (prin′sə·pəl) *n.*
A basic truth or law: *the principles of democracy.*

pri·or·i·ty (prī·ôr′ə·tē) *n.*, **pri·or·i·ties** *pl.*
The right to be first in order, time, rank, etc.: *Slum clearance has priority in the new budget.*

pris·on·er (priz′ən·ər) *n.*
A person who is confined or restrained: *He was captured and remained a prisoner for five years.*
Spelling tip: Watch the *o* in this word.

pris·tine (pris′tēn) *adj.*
Extremely pure; untouched: *the pristine beauty of a snow-covered tree.*

pri·va·cy (prī′və·sē) *n.*, **pri·va·cies** *pl.*
Seclusion: *The wall was built to ensure complete privacy.*

priv·i·lege (priv′ə·lij) *n.*
A special advantage or benefit: *I hope to have the privilege of hearing you sing.*

priv·y (priv′ē) *adj.; n.*, **priv·ies** *pl.*
adj. Participating in the knowledge of something secret (used with *to*): *The queen's attendant was privy to the conspiracy.*
n. An outdoor toilet.

prob·a·bly (prob′ə·blē) *adv.*
So far as the evidence shows; presumably: *He'll probably call.*

pro·bos·cis (prō·bos′is) *n.*, **pro·bos·cis·es** or **pro·bos·ci·des** (prō·bos′ə·dēz) *pl.*
1 A long, flexible snout, as of a tapir or other animal. 2 The trunk of an elephant. 3 A feeding structure of certain insects, as of bees and mosquitoes. 4 A humorous term for a human nose, especially when unusually large or prominent.
Spelling tip: Watch the silent *c* in this word.

pro·ce·dure (prə·sē′jər) *n.*
1 A manner of acting or doing something: *a complicated procedure.* 2 The methods or forms of conducting a business, parliamentary affairs, etc.

pro·ceeds (prō′sēdz) *n.pl.*
The money obtained from a sale of goods, work, or the use of capital: *The proceeds from the auction were given to charity.*
Syn. return, yield, income.

proc·ess (pros′es or prō′ses) *n., v.*
n. 1 A course or method of operations in the production of something: *a metallurgical process.* 2 A series of actions, developments, etc., that bring about a particular result: *the process of growth.* 3 A writ issued to bring a defendant into court.
v. 1 To subject to a routine procedure: *Process his application.* 2 To treat or prepare by a special method: *to process meat.*—**proc′es·sor** *n.*

pro·ces·sion (prə·sesh′ən or prō·sesh′ən) *n.*
A group of persons, vehicles, etc., arranged in succession and moving in a formal way: *a funeral procession.*

pro·cliv·i·ty (prō·kliv′ə·tē) *n.*, **pro·cliv·i·ties** *pl.*
Natural disposition or tendency; propensity:
The old codger has a proclivity to grumble and grouse.
Syn. bias, disposition, inclination, bent.

pro·cras·ti·nate (prō·kras′tə·nāt) *v.* **pro·cras·ti·nat·ed, pro·cras·ti·nat·ing**
To put off taking action until a future time:
He procrastinated so long that he missed the opportunity.—**pro·cras′ti·na′tor** *n.*
Syn. defer, delay, postpone.
Ant. expedite, hasten, hurry.

pro·cure·ment (prō·kyŏŏr′mənt) *n.*
An obtaining or acquiring: *procurement of supplies.*

prod·i·gal (prod′ə·gəl) *adj., n.*
adj. **1** Wasteful, as of money, time, or strength; extravagant: *The young are prodigal of life.* **2** Lavish; profuse.
n. A person who is wasteful; a spendthrift.—**prod′i·gal·ly** *adv.*

pro·dig·ious (prə·dij′əs) *adj.*
Enormous or extraordinary in size, quantity, or degree: *There is a prodigious number of books in the library.*—**pro·dig′ious·ly** *adv.*
Syn. huge, vast.
Ant. small, moderate.

prod·i·gy (prod′ə·jē) *n.*, **prod·i·gies** *pl.*
A person having remarkable qualities or powers, especially a young child so gifted: *The pianist Van Cliburn was a child prodigy.*
Syn. wonder, marvel.

pro·fane (prə·fān′ *or* prō·fān′) *v.* **pro·faned, pro·fan·ing;** *adj.*
v. To treat something sacred with irreverence or abuse: *The church was profaned by a murder committed there.*
adj. Showing irreverence toward the sacred things: *When he got angry he used profane language.*—**pro·fan′er** *n.*, **pro·fane′ly** *adv.*
Syn. *v.* defile, desecrate. *adj.* blasphemous.

pro·fes·sion·al (prə·fesh′ən·əl) *adj.*
1 Connected with, engaged in, or preparing for a profession: *professional courtesy; professional organizations..* **2** Pertaining to an occupation pursued for gain: *A professional baseball player moved in next door to us.*

pro·fes·sor (prə·fes′ər) *n.*
1 A teacher of the highest rank in a university or college. **2** A person who openly declares his opinions, sentiments, or religious faith.

pro·fi·cient (prə·fish′ənt) *adj.*
Skilled; expert: *He was so proficient at his job that he got another promotion.*—**pro·fi′cient·ly** *adv.*

pro·file (prō′fīl) *n.*
1 A side view of something, or a drawing of such a side view. **2** A short biographical sketch: *a profile of each candidate.*

prof·it (prof′it) *n., v.*
n. **1** Any advantage or gain; benefit: *He used the information to his profit.* **2** Excess of returns over expenditures: *business profits.*
v. **1** To be of advantage or benefit: *The experience profited him greatly.* **2** To derive gain or benefit: *Few people profit by advice.*

prof·li·gate (prof′lə·git *or* prof′lə·gāt) *adj.*
1 Lost or insensible to principle, virtue, or decency: *orgies of profligate Roman emperors.* **2** Recklessly extravagant: *Because of her profligate use of the inheritance, she soon had nothing left.*—**prof′li·gate·ly** *adv.*
Syn. **1** immoral, dissolute. **2** wasteful.

pro·fu·sion (prə·fyōō′zhən *or* prō·fyōō′zhən) *n.*
A lavish supply or condition: *a profusion of buds on the rosebush.*
Syn. abundance, copiousness.
Ant. scarcity, pittance.

pro·gen·i·tor (prō·jen′ə·tər) *n.*
A forefather or parent.

prog·e·ny (proj′ə·nē) *n.*, **prog·e·nies** *pl.*
Offspring; children: *Most parents are proud of their progeny.*

prog·no·sis (prog·nō′sis) *n.*, **prog·no·ses** (prog·nō′sēz) *pl.*
A prediction or conclusion regarding the course of a disease and the probability of recovery.

prog·nos·ti·cate (prog·nos′tə·kāt) *v.* **prog·nos·ti·cat·ed, prog·nos·ti·cat·ing**
To foretell future events, etc., by present indications: *Churchill prognosticated World War II.*—**prog·nos′ti·ca′tion** *n.*
Syn. predict, forebode, augur.

pro·gram (prō′gram *or* prō′grəm) *n.; v.* **pro·gramed** *or* **pro·grammed, pro·gram·ing** *or* **pro·gram·ming**
n. **1** A performance or show. **2** A printed announcement or schedule of events: *a theater program.* **3** Any prearranged plan or course: *a school program.* **4** A sequence of instructions for an electronic computer.
v. **1** To arrange or include in a program. **2** To work out or make up a program for a radio station, computer, etc.

prog·ress (prog′res *or* prō′gres *n.*; prə·gres′ *v.*) *n., v.*
n. **1** A moving forward: *the progress of the disease.* **2** Gradual advancement toward maturity or completion; improvement: *the progress of civilization.*
v. **1** To move forward. **2** To advance; improve.

pro·hi·bi·tion (prō′ə·bish′ən) *n.*
The act of preventing or forbidding; also, a decree or order forbidding something.—**pro·hib′i·tive** *adj.*

pro·jec·tile (prə·jek′təl *or* prə·jek′tīl) *adj., n.*
adj. Projecting or impelling forward.
n. A body projected or thrown forth by force, as a missile fired from a gun, cannon, etc.

pro·le·tar·i·at (prō′lə·târ′ē·ət) *n.*
Wageworkers collectively; the working class.
—**pro′le·tar′i·an** *adj.*

pro·lif·ic (prō·lif′ik) *adj.*
Producing abundantly, as offspring, fruit, books, etc.: *The prolific writer finished fourteen books in one year.*—**pro·lif′i·cal·ly** *adv.*
Syn. fruitful, fecund, productive.

prom·e·nade (prom′ə·nād′ *or* prom′ə·näd′) *n.; v.* **prom·e·nad·ed, prom·e·nad·ing**
n. **1** A walk for amusement or exercise. **2** A

place for such walking, as a deck of a ship, etc.

v. To walk or stroll in public: *to promenade along the boardwalk.*—**prom′e·nad′er** *n.*

prom·i·nence (prom′ə·nəns) *n.*
1 The state or quality of being well-known.
2 A protuberance: *The surface was made up of many depressions and prominences.*

pro·mis·cu·ous (prə·mis′kyŏŏ·əs) *adj.*
1 Indiscriminate, especially in sexual relations. **2** Composed of individuals or things confusedly or indiscriminately mixed together: *a promiscuous pile of books.*—**pro·mis′cu·ous·ly** *adv.*, **pro·mis′cu·ous·ness** *n.*

prom·ise (prom′is) *n.; v.* **prom·ised, prom·is·ing**
n. **1** A positive assurance that one will or will not perform a specified act. **2** An indication of future excellence or satisfaction: *a new author with great promise.*
v. **1** To make a positive assurance: *MacArthur promised to return.* **2** To give reason for expecting something: *The dark sky promised rain.*—**prom′is·er** *n.*

prom·on·to·ry (prom′ən·tôr′ē *or* prom′ən·tō′-rō) *n.,* **prom·on·to·ries** *pl.*
A high point of land extending into the sea; headland.

pro·mul·gate (prō·mul′gāt *or* prom′əl·gāt) *v.* **pro·mul·gat·ed, pro·mul·gat·ing**
To make known or announce officially; put into effect by public proclamation: *to promulgate a new constitution.*—**pro′mul·ga′-tion** *n.*
Syn. proclaim, publish, declare.

prone (prōn) *adj.*
1 Lying flat with the face downward; prostrate: *After being knocked out he lay prone on the floor for ten minutes.* **2** Inclined or predisposed: *She is prone to crying because she is so sensitive.*
Syn. 2 given, subject.
Ant. 1 supine.

prop·a·gan·da (prop′ə·gan′də) *n.*
A systematic effort to persuade people to support or adopt a particular opinion, attitude, or course of action; also, the facts, opinions, ideas, etc., used in such an effort.

prop·a·gate (prop′ə·gāt) *v.* **prop·a·gat·ed, prop·a·gat·ing**
1 To cause animals or plants to multiply by natural reproduction; breed: *to propagate horses.* **2** To spread from person to person, as a doctrine or belief: *to propagate news.* **3** To transmit through a medium: *to propagate heat.*—**prop′a·ga′tor** *n.*

pro·pel·lant (prə·pel′ənt) *n.*
An explosive that propels a projectile from a gun, or a solid or liquid fuel that serves to propel a rocket, guided missile, etc.

pro·pen·si·ty (prə·pen′sə·tē) *n.,* **pro·pen·si·ties** *pl.*
A natural disposition or tendency: *a propensity to argue.*

proph·e·sy (prof′ə·sī) *v.* **proph·e·sied, proph·e·sy·ing**

To foretell the future; make predictions: *The monk prophesied disaster.*—**proph′e·si′er** *n.*

proph·et (prof′it) *n.*
1 A person who delivers divine messages or interprets the divine will: *the prophet Jeremiah.* **2** A person who foretells the future.
Spelling tip: Note the *ph* pronounced as *f.*

pro·phy·lac·tic (prō′fə·lak′tik *or* prof′ə·lak′tik) *adj., n.*
adj. Tending to protect against or ward off something, especially disease: *prophylactic measure.*
n. A medicine or appliance that tends to protect against or ward off something, especially disease.

pro·pi·tious (prō·pish′əs) *adj.*
1 Favorable; auspicious: *A propitious time for requesting a raise is when your boss is in a generous mood.* **2** Kindly disposed; gracious: *The propitious judge gave the penitent criminal a reduced sentence.*—**pro·pi′tious·ly** *adv.*

prop·o·si·tion (prop′ə·zish′ən) *n.*
1 A scheme or proposal offered for consideration or acceptance: *He decided to accept the company's proposition to buy his business and let him continue to manage it.* **2** Any matter or person to be dealt with: *a tough proposition.* **3** *In mathematics* A statement of a truth to be demonstrated (a *theorem*) or of an operation to be performed (a *problem*).—**prop′o·si′tion·al** *adj.*

pro·pound (prə·pound′) *v.*
To put forward for consideration, solution, etc.; suggest or submit: *At the meeting he propounded his own views for solving the city's problems.*

pro·pri·e·ty (prə·prī′ə·tē) *n.,* **pro·pri·e·ties** *pl.*
The character or quality of being proper; especially, accordance with recognized usage, custom, or principles: *The ethics committee questioned the propriety of the senator's action.*

pro ra·ta (prō rā′tə, prō rat′ə, *or* prō rä′tə)
In proportion: *The loss was shared pro rata by all the partners.*

pro·sa·ic (prō·zā′ik) *adj.*
1 Failing to arouse animation or interest; unimaginative; dull: *She was bored with her prosaic existence.* **2** Pertaining to or like prose.
—**pro·sa′i·cal·ly** *adv.*
Syn. 1 commonplace, tedious.
Ant. animated, interesting, lively.

pro·sce·ni·um prō·sē′nē·əm) *n.,* **pro·sce·ni·a** (prō·sē′nē·ə) *pl.*
In a theater, the part of the stage in front of the curtain: *The director came onto the proscenium to quiet the audience.*

pro·scribe (prō·skrīb′) *v.* **pro·scribed, pro·scrib·ing**
To prohibit: *The Bill of Rights proscribes illegal search and entry.*
Spelling tip: Don't confuse *proscribe* and *prescribe;* they are opposite in meaning. *Prescribe* means to set down as a rule to be followed: *Khaki uniforms are prescribed by Army regulations, but civilian clothes are often proscribed.*
Ant. prescribe, sanction, authorize, legalize.

pros·e·cute (pros'ə·kyo͞ot) *v.* **pros·e·cut·ed, pros·e·cut·ing**
To bring legal, especially criminal, proceedings against someone: *He was prosecuted for the assault.*

pros·e·lyte (pros'ə·līt) *n.; v.* **pros·e·lyt·ed, pros·e·lyt·ing**
n. A person who has been brought over to a new party, opinion, or, especially, religious belief: *He gained many proselytes by his preaching.*
v. To proselytize.

pros·e·lyt·ize (pros'ə·lit·īz') *v.* **pros·e·lyt·ized, pros·e·lyt·iz·ing**
To make a convert of: *The missionaries proselytized the heathen.*
Spelling tip: Remember that *proselytizing* has a *y.*
Syn. convert, recruit.

pros·per·ous (pros'pər·əs) *adj.*
1 Successful; flourishing: *a prosperous business.* **2** Auspicious; promising.
Syn. 1 thriving. **2** favorable.
Ant. 1 unsuccessful, failing. **2** unlucky, baneful.

pro·tag·o·nist (prō·tag'ə·nist) *n.*
A leading character in a play, story, contest, or situation: *The author is the protagonist in any autobiography.*

pro·té·gé (prō'tə·zhā) *n.*
A male under someone's special protection and patronage, especially for the furthering of his talent or career: *The patron helped his protégés by buying their paintings.*
Usage: A *protégée* is a female protégé.

pro·test (prō'test *n.,* prə·test' *v.*) *n., v.*
n. A solemn or formal declaration or objection: *The President is expected to send a strong protest to their ambassador.*
v. **1** To state formally, especially against expressed doubt: *He protested his innocence.* **2** To object, especially publicly: *He protested against the government policy.*
Syn. *v.* **1** declare, assert.

pro·to·col (prō'tə·kôl) *n.*
1 The rules of diplomatic and state etiquette: *It was against protocol for the ambassador to stand.* **2** The preliminary draft of an official document, especially a treaty: *The protocol had been signed by all parties.*

pro·to·type (prō'tə·tīp) *n.*
An original model on which subsequent forms are based: *The engineers expect to complete the prototype for the new plane this week.*

pro·tract (prō·trakt') *v.*
To draw out or lengthen in time; prolong: *to protract a visit.*
Syn. extend, continue.
Ant. shorten, curtail.

pro·trude (prō·tro͞od') *v.* **pro·trud·ed, pro·trud·ing**
To thrust out; to project outward: *His tongue was protruding.*
Syn. stick out, obtrude.
Ant. retract, draw back.

prove (pro͞ov) *v.* **proved, proved** or **prov·en, prov·ing**
1 To demonstrate to be true by evidence or argument: *He proved that he was out of town on the day of the murder.* **2** To test the quality or worth of: *Marines have proved themselves in many bitter battles.* **3** Turn out to be: *The illness proved fatal.*

prov·i·dent (prov'ə·dənt) *adj.*
Showing foresight, especially with respect to money.
Syn. thrifty, careful.
Ant. spendthrift.

pro·vin·cial (prə·vin'shəl) *adj., n.*
adj. **1** Of or pertaining to a province: *the provincial government.* **2** Rustic; uncultured: *His manners are rather provincial.*
n. **1** A native or inhabitant of a province. **2** A person who is rustic or uncultured.

pro·vi·so (prə·vī'zō) *n.,* **pro·vi·sos** or **pro·vi·soes** *pl.*
A stipulation, as in a contract or statute, limiting or modifying it, or rendering it conditional: *Her contract contained a proviso limiting the number of personal appearances she would have to make.*
Syn. condition.

prov·o·ca·tion (prov'ə·kā'shən) *n.*
Incitement; irritation: *He acted violently under extreme provocation.*
Syn. stimulus.

pro·voc·a·tive (prə·vok'ə·tiv) *adj.*
Serving to provoke, excite, or stimulate: *a provocative discussion about birth control.*—**pro·voc'a·tive·ly** *adv.*

prox·im·i·ty (prok·sim'ə·tē) *n.*
The state or fact of being near or next: *During rush hour people are jammed in close proximity on the subways.*
Syn. propinquity, nearness.
Ant. distance, remoteness.

prox·y (prok'sē) *n.,* **prox·ies** *pl.*
1 A person empowered by another to act for him: *He was a proxy for his absent brother at the baptism.* **2** The office or right to act for another, or the instrument conferring it: *The proxies have not yet been sent to the stockholders.*
Syn. 1 deputy, substitute.

psalm (säm) *n.*
A sacred song from the Old Testament Book of Psalms.

pseu·do·nym (so͞o'də·nim) *n.*
A fictitious name; pen name: *He wrote the novel under a pseudonym.*
Syn. alias, nom de plume.

psy·che (sī'kē) *n.*
The human soul; the mind; the intelligence.

psy·chi·a·try (sī·kī'ə·trē) *n.*
The branch of medicine that deals with the diagnosis, treatment, and prevention of mental disorders.—**psy·chi·at·ric** (sī'kē·at'·rik) *adj.,* **psy·chi'a·trist** *n.*

psy·chic (sī'kik) *adj.*
1 Pertaining to the mind or soul, as opposed to the body. **2** Related or sensitive to mental

phenomena unconnected with the five senses, such as telepathy or extrasensory perception: *The old lady claimed to be psychic and able to see into the future.*

psy·chol·o·gy (sī·kol′ə·jē) *n.*, **psy·chol·o·gies** *pl.*
1 The science of the human mind. 2 The aggregate of the emotions, behavior patterns, etc., considered characteristic of an individual, type, group, particular experience, etc.: *the psychology of love.*—**psy·chol′o·gist** *n.*

pueb·lo (pweb′lō *for defs. 1 and 2;* pwä′blō *for def. 3*) *n.*, **pueb·los** *pl.*
1 (Capital *P*) A member of one of the Indian tribes of Mexico and the southwest United States, as the Zuñi, Hopi, etc. 2 A communal abode or stone building of the Indians of the southwest United States. 3 A town or village of Indians or Spanish Americans, as in Mexico.

pu·er·ile (pyōō′ər·il *or* pyōō′rīl) *adj.*
Characteristic of childhood; juvenile: *the bad habit of making puerile jokes.*—**pu′er·ile·ly** *adv.*, **pu′er·il′i·ty** *n.*
Syn. childish, silly, immature.
Ant. adult, mature.

pu·gi·list (pyōō′jə·list) *n.*
One who fights with his fists; a boxer: *Joe Louis was a noted pugilist.*—**pu′gi·lism** *n.*
Syn. fighter, prize fighter.

pug·na·cious (pug·nā′shəs) *adj.*
Disposed to fight; quarrelsome: *a pugnacious boxer.*—**pug·na′cious·ly** *adv.*
Syn. bellicose, combative.
Ant. peaceful, calm, pacific.

pul·chri·tude (pul′krə·tōōd) *n.*
Beauty; grace; physical charm: *an outstanding example of feminine pulchritude.*—**pul′chri·tud′i·nous** *adj.*

pul·mo·nar·y (pul′mə·ner′ē) *adj.*
Of, pertaining to, or affecting the lungs: *pulmonary congestion.*

pul·sate (pul′sāt) *v.* **pul·sat·ed, pul·sat·ing**
Expand and contract rhythmically, as a pulse; vibrate: *The engine was still pulsating gently.*
Syn. beat, throb, palpitate.

pum·ice (pum′is) *n.*
Spongy lava used for removing stains from the hands and, in powdered form, for polishing.

punc·til·i·ous (pungk·til′ē·əs) *adj.*
Attentive to points of etiquette, etc.: *She was punctilious in setting the table for the formal dinner.*—**punc·til′i·ous·ness** *n.*, **punc·til′i·ous·ly** *adv.*
Syn. meticulous, scrupulous.
Ant. careless, offhand.

pun·dit (pun′dit) *n.*
A person who is learned or expert in any matter; also, a person who is inclined to offer authoritative opinions: *Almost all the pundits were proved wrong in predicting Truman's defeat.*
Syn. authority, expert.

pun·gent (pun′jənt) *adj.*

1 Having a sharp, pricking, or acrid taste or smell: *The curry was pungent rather than hot.* 2 Affecting the mind or feelings painfully, as if by sharp points; caustic; biting: *pungent sarcasm.*

pu·ni·tive (pyōō′nə·tiv) *adj.*
Inflicting punishment: *punitive damages.*
Syn. retributive, corrective.

pu·ny (pyōō′nē) *adj.* **pu·ni·er, pu·ni·est**
Small and feeble; insignificant: *He-men are not worried by puny showoffs.*
Syn. weak, sickly.

pur·ga·to·ry (pûr′gə·tôr′ē) *n.*
1 *In Roman Catholic theology* A place where the souls of the penitent dead expiate minor sins before going to heaven. 2 Any place or time of temporary suffering or expiation: *I went through purgatory when my mother-in-law came to stay.*

pur·loin (pûr·loin′) *v.*
To steal; filch: *The thief purloined the manuscript while its owner was away.*

pur·port (pûr′pôrt; *also* pər·pôrt′ *for v.*) *n., v.*
n. The meaning, significance, or intention of a document, speech, or action: *It was difficult to understand the purport of his words.*
v. To claim or profess, especially falsely: *It purported to be a letter from the President.*
Syn. *n.* import.

pur·pose (pûr′pəs) *n.*
1 An objective kept in mind during a course of action: *His purpose was to gain power.* 2 Practical advantage or result: *There is no purpose in going to town today.*
Syn. 1 aim, object, design.

pur·sue (pər·sōō′) *v.* **pur·sued, pur·su·ing**
1 To follow with intent to capture; chase: *The policeman pursued the thief.* 2 To follow persistently: *He pursued his search for knowledge.*

pur·vey·or (pər·vā′ər) *n.*
A person who furnishes supplies, especially food: *purveyor to the Royal Household.*

pu·sil·lan·i·mous (pyōō′sə·lan′ə·məs) *adj.*
Characterized by lack of courage: *too pusillanimous to complain.*
Syn. timid, cowardly, weak.

pu·tre·fy (pyōō′trə·fī) *v.* **pu·tre·fied, pu·tre·fy·ing**
To decay with a fetid odor; to rot: *The unrefrigerated meat slowly putrefied.*
Syn. decompose, spoil.

pyre (pīr) *n.*
A heap of combustible material on which a dead body is burned as a funeral rite: *to cremate the body on the pyre.*

py·ro·ma·ni·a (pī′rə·mā′nē·ə *or* pī′rə·mān′yə) *n.*
A compulsion to set things on fire.—**py′ro·ma′ni·ac** *adj. & n.*

Q

quack (kwak) *n., v.*
n. A harsh, croaking sound made by a duck,

or a similar sound: *the quacks of a man with laryngitis.*
v. To utter harsh, croaking sounds: *gossiping old women quacking away.*

qua·drille (kwə·dril′) *n.*
1 A five-figure square dance for four couples.
2 The music for this dance.

quad·ru·ped (kwod′rŏŏ·ped) *adj., n.*
adj. Having four feet: *quadruped mammals.*
n. A four-footed animal, especially a four-footed mammal: *Bears are quadrupeds.*

quaff (kwaf, kwof, *or* kwôf) *v.*
To drink, especially large amounts and with relish: *He quaffed the tankard of ale.*—**quaff′er** *n.*
Syn. swig, swill, gulp, drain.

quag·mire (kwag′mīr′ *or* kwog′mīr′) *n.*
1 A swamp or bog: *He got his boots muddy crossing the quagmire.* 2 A difficult situation from which it is hard to extricate oneself: *the quagmire of a war that neither side could win.*

qua·hog (kwô′hôg, kwô′hog, *or* kwə·hôg′) *n.*
An edible clam.
Spelling tip: This word is also spelled *quahaug.*
Syn. hard-shell clam, round clam.

quail (kwāl) *n.*, **quail** *or* **quails** *pl.*;
n. 1 A European game bird resembling the partridge and having a very short tail. 2 Any of various similar small American game birds, especially the bobwhite.

qual·i·fy (kwol′ə·fī) *v.* **qual·i·fied, qual·i·fy·ing**
1 To make competent or eligible for an occupation, office, privilege, etc.: *His fluent Russian qualifies him for the translator's job.*
2 To meet the requirements for or become eligible for something: *He qualified for the job by passing the exam.*

qualm (kwäm *or* kwôm) *n.*
A guilty or frightened feeling that makes a person reluctant or unhappy while doing or planning some act: *qualms about sky-diving.*

quan·ti·ty (kwon′tə·tē) *n.*, **quan·ti·ties** *pl.*
Amount, size, or number: *a small quantity of rice.*

quell (kwel) *v.*
1 To suppress by force: *The tyrant's army quelled the revolution.* 2 To stop, as pain or fear: *The medicine quelled his cough.*

ques·tion (kwes′chən) *n., v.*
n. 1 An inquiry, or the act of inquiring: *"Is it raining?"* is a question. 2 Uncertainty or disagreement: *No question about that!* 3 A subject being investigated, discussed, or argued about.
v. To ask a question: *Reporters questioned him.*

ques·tion·a·ble (kwes′chən·ə·bəl) *adj.*
Characterized by doubtful integrity, honesty, respectability, etc.: *a questionable reputation.*

ques·tion·naire (kwes′chə·nâr′) *n.*
A written or printed form consisting of a group of questions and submitted to a number of persons in order to obtain data for a survey, report, etc.

qui·es·cent (kwī·es′ənt) *adj.*
In a state of inactivity or rest: *The Black Plague was quiescent for centuries, but then it struck again.*
Syn. sleeping, dormant, passive.
Ant. active, turbulent, violent.

qui·et (kwī′ət) *adj., v., n.*
adj. 1 Making little or no noise: *a quiet baby.*
2 Peaceful: *a quiet day at the office.*
v. 1 To make silent: *to quiet a howling baby.*
2 To become softer or less boisterous (usually followed by *down*): *The party quieted down around midnight.*
n. A state of silence, calm, peace, etc.—
qui′et·ly *adv.*, **qui′et·ness** *n.*

qui·e·tude (kwī′ə·t(y)ōōd) *n.*
The quality or state of being calm: *the quietude of nuns.*
Syn. serenity, tranquillity, peace.
Ant. tension, frenzy, agitation.

quirk (kwûrk) *n.*
An odd mannerism, habit, eccentricity, etc.
Syn. idiosyncrasy, peculiarity.

quite (kwīt) *adv.*
1 To the fullest extent; completely or without the slightest uncertainty: *The rumor is quite true.* 2 To a great or considerable extent: *He is quite ill.*
Syn. 1 altogether, entirely. 2 very, exceedingly.

quiz (kwiz) *n.*, **quizzes** *pl.*; *v.* **quizzed, quiz·zing**
n. The act of questioning: *a quiz in geometry.*
v. To examine by asking questions: *The teacher quizzed the class.*

quiz·zi·cal (kwiz′i·kəl) *adj.*
Puzzled: *a quizzical glance.*—**quiz′zi·cal·ly** *adv.*
Syn. skeptical, curious.

quo·rum (kwôr′əm *or* kwō′rəm) *n.*
The number of members of a group who must be present to transact business, vote, etc. (usually a majority): *The Senate cannot vote unless a quorum of senators is present.*

quo·tient (kwō′shənt) *n.*
The number obtained by dividing one quantity by another: *When 10 is divided by 5, the quotient is 2.*

R

rab·id (rab′id) *adj.*
1 Affected with rabies; mad. 2 Fanatical; furious; violent: *He was rabid in defense of his principles.*

rac·on·teur (rak′on·tûr′) *n.*
A skilled teller of anecdotes: *As a raconteur, Oscar Wilde was unexcelled.*

ra·di·ate (rā′dē·āt) *v.* **ra·di·at·ed, ra·di·at·ing**
1 To emit or issue forth, as rays: *The sun radiates light and heat; Light and heat radiate from the sun.* 2 To diverge or spread from a central point: *Roads radiated from Rome to all parts of the empire.*

ra·di·us (rā′dē·əs) *n.*, **ra·di·i** (rā′dē·ī) *or* **ra·di·us·es** *pl.*
1 A line joining the center of a circle or sphere

to its circumference or surface. 2 A circular area or boundary measured by the length of its radius: *in a four-mile radius.*

rag·a·muf·fin (rag′ə·muf′in) *n.*
Anyone, especially a child, in dirty or ragged clothes.

rail·ler·y (rā′lər·ē) *n.,* **rail·ler·ies** *pl.*
Good-humored teasing.
Syn. banter, badinage.

raise (rāz) *v.* **raised, rais·ing**
1 To lift; elevate: *He raised one arm.* 2 To construct or build; erect: *Cheops raised a pyramid.* 3 To breed; grow: *We intend to raise corn.* 4 To gather together: *raise an army; raise more money for charity.*

ram·i·fi·ca·tion (ram′ə·fə·kā′shən) *n.*
A result, consequence, etc., stemming from a main source: *The police are still investigating the ramifications of the plot.*

ram·pant (ram′pənt) *adj.*
1 Spreading without control; unrestrained; raging: *Crime was rampant in the city.* 2 Growing unchecked: *Weeds were rampant in the garden.*

ram·part (ram′pärt) *n.*
1 A broad embankment surrounding a town or fort for its protection: *to take a walk along the ramparts.* 2 Any bulwark or defense: *the ramparts of democracy.*

ran·cid (ran′sid) *adj.*
Smelling or tasting like an oily substance that has begun to spoil: *The butter turned rancid in the hot weather.*

ran·cor (rang′kər) *n.*
Bitter and vindictive hatred; spitefulness: *He continued to bear rancor long after the quarrel.—***ran′cor·ous** *adj.*
Syn. malice, spite.

ran·dom (ran′dəm) *adj.*
Done or chosen without definite aim; chance: *a random sampling of opinion.*
Syn. casual, haphazard.
Ant. designed, purposeful.

range (rānj) *n.; v.* **ranged, rang·ing**
n. 1 The area in which anything moves, operates, or is distributed, as a plant, power, influence, studies, interests: *The range of the dandelion is worldwide; Mexico is in the U.S. range of influence; His range embraces all Oriental languages.* 2 The maximum distance which a projectile, airplane, etc., can travel. 3 A row, as of mountains. 4 A tract of land on which cattle, etc., roam and graze: *The cowboys rode the range looking for strays.* 5 A place for shooting at a mark: *rifle range.* 6 A stove used for cooking.
v. 1 To place or arrange in a definite order. 2 To move about or over a region, as in exploration. 3 To put cattle to graze on a range. 4 To roam.

ran·sack (ran′sak) *v.*
To search thoroughly, especially for plunder; pillage: *The burglars had ransacked the closets.*

rant (rant) *v.*
To speak in loud, violent, or extravagant language; rave: *The angry director ranted at the cast.*

ra·pa·cious (rə·pā′shəs) *adj.*
Greedy; grasping; extortionate: *rapacious loan sharks.*
Syn. predatory.

rap·ine (rap′in) *n.*
The taking of property by force, as in war; pillage.
Syn. plunder, looting.

rap·port (rə·pôr′) *n.*
Communication; relationship; harmony: *His interference disturbed the rapport we had established with the patients.*
Syn. sympathy, accord.

rar·e·fied (râr′ə·fīd) *adj.*
Pure, refined, thin, or rare: *the rarefied atmosphere of the high mountains.*

rar·i·ty (râr′ə·tē) *n.,* **rar·i·ties** *pl.*
1 The condition of being rare or uncommon: *a book of great rarity.* 2 Something rare or scarce: *The book is a rarity.*

ra·tion (rash′ən) *n., v.*
n. A fixed allowance, as of food or provisions, especially such an allowance issued to members of the army or navy.
v. To issue rations to.

ra·tion·al (rash′ən·əl) *adj.*
Able to reason; sensible; wise: *The decision was made by rational men.*

rat·tan (ra·tan′) *n.*
The long, tough, flexible stem of various palms, used to make furniture.

rau·cous (rô′kəs) *adj.*
1 Harsh-sounding; hoarse: *a raucous laugh.* 2 Boisterous; disorderly: *a raucous party.—***rau′cous·ness** *n.,* **rau′cous·ly** *adv.*
Syn. 1 strident, rough.
Ant. 1 soft, mild.

rav·age (rav′ij) *v.* **rav·aged, rav·ag·ing;** *n.*
v. To lay waste by pillaging; devastate: *The town had been ravaged by the invaders.*
n. Destructive action and its effects: *the ravages of time.*
Syn. despoil, devastate.

rav·en·ous (rav′ən·əs) *adj.*
Violently hungry; voracious: *the difficulty of feeding ten ravenous children.*
Syn. ravening, famished.
Ant. assuaged, full.

rav·ish (rav′ish) *v.*
1 To fill with delight; enrapture: *The visitor was ravished by the scenic beauty of the town.* 2 To rape.

raze (rāz) *v.* **razed, raz·ing**
To level to the ground; demolish: *The Romans razed Carthage.*
Spelling tip: When you *raise* something you are beginning it; when you *raze* it you come to the end, like *z.*
Syn. destroy, flatten.

ra·zor (rā′zər) *n.*
A sharp cutting implement used for shaving off hair, especially whiskers.

re·ac·tion·ar·y (rē·ak′shən·er′ē) *adj.; n.* **re·ac·tion·ar·ies** *pl.*
adj. Characterized by, pertaining to, or

having a desire to return to an earlier idea or condition, especially in politics: *a reactionary longing for the good old days.*
n. A person opposed to change.

read (rēd) *v.* **read** (red), **read·ing** (rē'ding)
1 To understand something written by interpreting the writing: *He could read at three.* **2** To speak written words out loud: *to read to the blind.* **3** To understand the significance of: *to read the sky; read palms.* **4** To indicate (said of a recording instrument): *The thermometer reads twenty below.*

read·i·ly (red'ə·lē) *adv.*
1 Without difficulty; promptly: *The book was readily available.* **2** Without reluctance; willingly: *He readily did what was required of him.*
Syn. 1 easily, speedily.

read·y (red'ē) *adj.* **read·i·er, read·i·est**
1 Completely prepared for use; finished: *Your order is ready; Dinner is ready.* **2** Quick to perceive or understand: *a ready wit.* **3** Likely or liable to: *The car was ready to collapse.*

re·al·is·tic (rē·ə·lis'tik) *adj.*
1 Having to do with the real and practical rather than the theoretical or imaginary: *a realistic foreign policy.* **2** Describing things in a lifelike way: *a realistic novel.*—**re·al·is'·ti·cal·ly** *adv.*

re·al·i·za·tion (rē'əl·i·zā'shən) *n.*
1 A clear understanding; complete appreciation: *a realization of a danger.* **2** The obtaining of money as a profit or return: *the realization of $500 on the sale.* **3.** The conversion into fact or action of plans, ambitions, fears, etc.: *the realization of his hopes.*

ream (rēm) *n.*
An amount of paper consisting of 480, 500, or 516 sheets.

re·bate (rē'bāt *or* ri·bāt') *n.*
A refund or discount: *There is a rebate for payment in cash.*

re·bel (ri·bel' *v.*; reb'əl *n., adj.*) *v.* **re·belled, re·bel·ling**; *n., adj.*
v. **1** To rise in armed resistance against the established government or ruler of one's country: *The American colonists rebelled against England.* **2** To fight against or disobey any authority or tradition: *to rebel against accepted beliefs.*
n. A person who rebels: *The rebels won the first fight.*
adj. Resisting an established ruler or authority: *The rebel generals planned a coup.*—**re·bel'lion** *n.,* **re·bel'lious** *adj.,* **re·bel'lious·ly** *adv.,* **re·bel'lious·ness** *n.*

re·cal·ci·trant (ri·kal'sə·trənt) *adj.*
Refusing to comply; obstinate or rebellious: *a recalcitrant student body.*—**re·cal'ci·trance, re·cal'ci·tran·cy** *n.*
Syn. defiant, stubborn.
Ant. cooperative, obedient, tractable, submissive.

re·cant (ri·kant') *v.*
To withdraw publicly something previously believed or defended: *to recant a heresy.*—**re'can·ta'tion, re·cant'er** *n.*

Syn. retract, renounce, deny, disavow.
Ant. reaffirm, confirm, defend, maintain.

re·ca·pit·u·late (rē'kə·pich'ŏŏ·lāt) *v.* **re·ca·pit·u·lat·ed, re·ca·pit·u·lat·ing**
To review briefly; sum up: *The judge recapitulated the evidence for the jury.*—**re'ca·pit'u·la'tion** *n.;* **re'ca·pit'u·la'tive, re'ca·pit'u·la·to'ry** *adj.*
Syn. summarize, restate, outline.

re·cede (ri·sēd') *v.* **re·ced·ed, re·ced·ing**
1 To move back; withdraw: *The tide recedes from the shore.* **2** To slope backward: *His forehead recedes.*

re·ceipt (ri·sēt') *n.*
1 A written acknowledgment that a sum of money has been paid, that certain goods have been delivered, etc. **2** The act of receiving: *the receipt of goods at warehouses.* **3** That which is received: *cash receipts.*

re·ceive (ri·sēv') *v.* **re·ceived, re·ceiv·ing**
1 To get, as a possession; acquire: *to receive a postcard; to receive a knighthood.* **2** To get knowledge of; learn about: *to receive the good news.* **3** To experience directly: *to receive a blow.* **4** To greet or welcome: *The emperor received the ambassadors.*

re·cess (rē'ses *or* ri·ses' *n.;* ri·ses' *v.*) *n.,* **re·cess·es** *pl.; v.*
n. **1** A depression or indentation in a surface, especially in a wall: *to build bookshelves in the recess in the wall.* **2** A period of time during which people stop working: *The schoolchildren played during recess.* **3** A withdrawn or inner place: *the recesses of the mind.*
v. To put in or as in a recess.

re·ces·sion (ri·sesh'ən) *n.*
1 A withdrawal: *the gradual recession of the tidal wave.* **2** A procession: *The congregation sang a hymn during the recession.* **3** A slight economic depression: *Unemployment increases during periods of recession.*

re·cid·i·vism (rə·sid'ə·viz'əm) *n.*
A tendency to repeat criminal acts and patterns of antisocial behavior: *the recidivism of a chronic offender.*—**re·cid'i·vist** *n.;* **re·cid'i·vis'tic** *or* **re·cid'i·vous** *adj.*
Syn. backsliding, incorrigibility.
Ant. reform, rehabilitation.

rec·i·pe (res'ə·pē) *n.*
1 Directions on how to make or prepare something, as food: *a recipe for chocolate cake.* **2** Any method for attaining a desired thing or goal: *Hard work is the recipe for success.*

re·cip·i·ent (ri·sip'ē·ənt) *n.*
A person or thing that receives: *the recipient of a national award.*

re·cip·ro·cal (ri·sip'rə·kəl) *adj.*
1 Shared or given by both sides: *their reciprocal love; an exchange of reciprocal insults.* **2** Done or given in return: *to expect a reciprocal favor when she lends a friend her car.*—**re·cip'ro·cal'i·ty, re·cip'ro·cal·ness** *n.;* **re·cip'ro·cal·ly** *adv.*
Syn. 1 mutual, corresponding. **2** equivalent.
Ant. 1 unilateral.

rec·luse (ri·klōōs' *or* rek'lōōs) *n.*
Someone who avoids all other people by shutting himself off from the world: *He was a recluse for twelve years.*—**re·clu'sive** *adj.*, **re·clu'sive·ness** *n.*
Syn. hermit, solitary.

rec·og·niz·a·ble (rek'əg·nī'zə·bəl) *adj.*
Capable of being recognized.

rec·og·nize (rec'əg·nīz) *v.* **rec·og·nized, rec·og·niz·ing**
1 To know or remember who or what someone or something is: *He didn't recognize the people at the next table; I recognize bad art when I see it.* 2 To acknowledge the existence or validity of and start to deal with: *The United States was among the first to recognize Israel.* 3 To show appreciation or awareness of: *His worth was soon recognized.*—**rec'og·ni'tion, rec'og·niz'er** *n.*

rec·on·cile (rek'ən·sīl) *v.* **rec·on·ciled, rec·on·cil·ing**
1 To bring back to friendship after estrangement: *to try to reconcile two friends who have quarreled.* 2 To cause to submit to or accept: *He is reconciled to his fate; Reconcile yourself to your lot.* 3 To make or show to be consistent: *to reconcile religion with science.*—**rec'on·cil'i·a'tion, rec'on·cile'ment, rec'on·cil'er** *n.*; **rec'on·cil'i·a·to'ry** *adj.*

rec·on·dite (rek'ən·dīt *or* ri·kon'dīt) *adj.*
Difficult to understand: *the recondite writings of theoretical physicists.*—**rec'on·dite'ly** *adv.*, **rec'on·dite'ness** *n.*
Syn. obscure, abstruse, arcane.
Ant. understandable, comprehensible.

re·con·nais·sance (ri·kon'ə·səns) *n.*
1 A preliminary examination or survey of territory. 2 The act of obtaining information of military value.

re·con·noi·ter (rē'kə·noi'tər *or* rek'ə·noi'tər) *v.*
To examine or survey, as for military or engineering purposes: *to reconnoiter the terrain.*

rec·ord (rek'ərd, *n.*; ri·kôrd' *v.*) *n. v.*
n. 1 An account that serves as evidence of a fact or event: *historical records; a photographic record.* 2 The known facts about a person or thing, regarded as a series of things done or achieved: *voting record.* 3 The best performance to date, as in a competitive sport: *the world's high-jump record.* 4 A phonograph disk: *to play an LP record.*
v. 1 To set down an authentic account: *The police stenographer recorded his confession verbatim.* 2 To register; tell: *The cardiograph recorded his heartbeat.* 3 To make a tape or phonograph record of: *to record the concert.*

re·crim·i·na·tion (ri·krim'ə·nā'shən) *n.*
An accusation made in answer to an accusation: *The angry salesmen exchanged recriminations.*—**re·crim'i·nate** *v.*; **re·crim'i·na·tive, re·crim'i·na·to'ry** *adj.*
Syn. countercharge.

re·cruit (ri·krōōt') *v., n.*
v. 1 To enlist men in an army, navy, etc.: *a campaign to recruit more soldiers.* 2 To cause to join an organization, etc.: *to recruit him to the cause.*
n. A newly enlisted member: *The recruits began their basic training.*

rec·ti·fy (rek'tə·fī) *v.* **rec·ti·fied, rec·ti·fy·ing**
To correct; adjust: *to rectify a mistake.*—**rec'ti·fi'a·ble** *adj.*, **rec'ti·fi·ca'tion** *n.*
Syn. remedy.

rec·ti·tude (rek'tə·tōōd *or* rek'tə·tyōōd) *n.*
Honesty; integrity; morality: *A man of rectitude does not renege on a promise.*
Ant. dishonesty.

re·cu·per·ate (ri·kōō'pə·rāt *or* ri·kyōō'pə·rāt) *v.* **re·cu·per·at·ed, re·cu·per·at·ing**
To recover, as from illness or unhappiness: *to recuperate slowly after an operation.*—**re·cu'per·a'tion** *n.*
Syn. convalesce, mend.
Ant. relapse, sink, weaken.

re·cur (ri·kûr') *v.* **re·curred, re·cur·ring**
To happen again at regular intervals: *a disease that recurs.*—**re·cur'rence** *n.*, **re·cur'rent** *adj.*, **re·cur'rent·ly** *adv.*

red her·ring (red her'ing) *n.*
1 A smoked herring. 2 Something introduced to draw attention away from the main subject.

red·o·lent (red'ə·lənt) *adj.*
1 Giving off a strong, pleasant fragrance; odorous: *to savor a redolent cup of coffee.* 2 Suggestive of: *a sudden disappearance redolent of mystery.*—**red'o·lence, red'o·len·cy** *n.*; **red'o·lent·ly** *adv.*
Syn. 1 fragrant, aromatic, odorous, savory.

re·doubt·a·ble (ri·dou'tə·bəl) *adj.*
Inspiring fear or dread; formidable: *a redoubtable enemy.*—**re·doubt'a·bly** *adv.*, **re·doubt'a·ble·ness** *n.*
Syn. fearsome, intimidating.

re·dress (ri·dres') *v., n.*
v. To set right, as a wrong; remedy: *to redress an injustice.*
n. Satisfaction for a wrong done; amends; reparation: *a redress of grievances.*

re·duc·i·ble (ri·dōōs'ə·bəl *or* ri·dyōōs'ə·bəl) *adj.*
Capable of being broken down: *All matter is reducible to molecules.*—**re·duc'i·bly** *adv.*, **re·duc'i·bil'i·ty** *n.*

re·dun·dant (ri·dun'dənt) *adj.*
Being more than is required: *"A high-pitched falsetto voice" is a redundant description.*—**re·dun'dant·ly** *adv.*, **re·dun'dan·cy** *n.*

reek (rēk) *v., n.*
v. To give off a strong, offensive smell: *to reek of stale cigar smoke.*
n. A strong, offensive smell: *the reek of dead fish.*

re·fer (ri·fûr') *v.* **re·ferred, re·fer·ring**
To turn or send to, as for information, help, advice, judgment, etc.: *to refer to an encyclopedia.*—**ref'er·a·ble, re·fer'ra·ble** *adj.*; **re·fer'ral, re·fer'rer** *n.*

ref·er·ence (ref′ər·əns *or* ref′rəns) *n.*
1 The act of referring: *a casual reference to a recent event.* 2 A source of information or help: *to consult encyclopedias and dictionaries for reference.* 3 A recommendation: *Her future employer asked for references.*

ref·er·en·dum (ref′ə·ren′dəm) *n.,* **ref·er·en·dums** *or* **ref·er·en·da** *pl.*
The presentation to the people of a proposed bill for decision by vote: *The bill was rejected in a nationwide referendum.*

re·flex (rē′fleks) *n.,* **re·flex·es** *pl.; adj.*
n. An involuntary response to a stimulus: *blinking and other reflexes.*
adj. Produced by such a response: *a reflex dilation of the pupils.*

re·frac·to·ry (ri·frak′tər·ē) *adj.*
Impossible or difficult to control or correct: *a refractory child.*—**re·frac′to·ri·ly** *adv.*

re·fur·bish (re·fûr′bish) *v.*
To restore to good condition: *to refurbish an old desk.*

re·fute (ri·fyo͞ot′) *v.* **re·fut·ed, re·fut·ing**
To prove incorrect or false: *The defense refuted the prosecution's argument.*
Syn. disprove, controvert.
Ant. prove, confirm, verify.

re·gal (rē′gəl) *adj.*
Royal or stately: *the regal palaces; her regal bearing.*

re·gale (ri·gāl′) *v.* **re·galed, re·gal·ing**
To entertain; amuse: *He regaled us with an account of his trip.*

re·gard (ri·gärd′) *v., n.*
v. 1 To look at or observe closely or attentively: *to regard something carefully.* 2 To think of: *I regard him as a friend.*
n. Respect; esteem: *to have regard for the law; to hold him in high regard.*

re·gard·less (ri·gärd′lis) *adj.*
Having no regard: *I'll do it regardless of the consequences!*

re·gat·ta (ri·gat′ə *or* ri·gä′tə) *n.*
A boat race or races: *to win the first race of the regatta.*

re·gime (ri·zhēm′) *n.*
A system or type of government: *The military regime lasted three years.*
Spelling tip: This word is also spelled *régime.*

reg·i·men (rej′ə·mən) *n.*
A systematic regulation of diet, exercises, etc., intended to improve health: *the regimen prescribed by his doctor.*

reg·i·ment (rej′ə·mənt) *n.*
A military unit larger than a battalion and smaller than a division: *the colonel in command of the regiment.*—**reg′i·men′tal** *adj.,* **reg′i·men·ta′tion** *n.*

reg·is·ter (rej′is·tər) *v., n.*
v. 1 To record officially: *All births and deaths are registered in the state archives.* 2 To indicate; show: *The scale registered 200 pounds; His face registered terror.* 3 To enter one's name in a record or list: *to register to vote.*
n. 1 An official record: *the births-and-deaths*

register. 2 A device for recording or indicating: *a cash register.*

reg·is·tra·tion (rej′is·trā′shən) *n.*
1 The act of entering in a register; also, such an entry. 2 The number of persons registered.

re·gret (ri·gret′) *v.* **re·gret·ted, re·gret·ting;** *n.*
v. To feel sorry about: *I regret my mistakes.*
n. A feeling of remorse or unhappiness about a past event: *When you look back have you any regrets?*—**re·gret′ful** *adj.,* **re·gret′ful·ly** *adv.,* **re·gret′ful·ness** *n.*

reg·u·lar (reg′yə·lər) *adj.*
Conforming to a rule, custom, or pattern; usual: *the regular weekly meeting; a man of regular habits.*—**reg′u·lar·ly** *adv.;* **reg′u·lar′i·ty, reg′u·lar·ness** *n.*
Syn. normal, even, orderly, steady.

re·hears·al (ri·hûr′səl) *n.*
A practice session before a public performance: *The dress rehearsal took place one week before opening night.*

reign (rān) *v., n.*
v. To rule over; control: *The Hapsburgs reigned over Austria.*
n. The time or duration of a sovereign's rule.
Spelling tip: *Rain, rein,* and *reign* all sound alike but they have different spellings and meanings. They are homophones.

re·im·burse (rē′im·bûrs′) *v.* **re·im·bursed, re·im·burs·ing**
To pay back money to; refund: *We will reimburse him for his travel expenses.*—**re′im·burs′a·ble** *adj.;* **re′im·burs′ment, re′im·burs′er** *n.*

rein (rān) *n., v.*
n. 1 One of two straps attached to a bit and used to guide or control a horse: *Pull on the reins to stop your pony.* 2 Any means of restraint or control: *The wage freeze will be a rein on inflation.*
v. To control with or as if with reins.

re·it·er·ate (rē·it′ə·rāt) *v.* **re·it·er·at·ed, re·it·er·at·ing**
To say again; repeat: *The angry man reiterated his warning of disaster.*—**re·it′er·a′tion** *n.*

re·ju·ve·nate (ri·jo͞o′və·nāt) *v.* **re·ju·ve·nat·ed, re·ju·ve·nat·ing**
To make youthful or vigorous again.—**re·ju′ve·na′tion** *n.*

re·lay (rē′lā) *n., v.*
n. 1 A fresh team or crew that replaces or relieves another: *to work in relays.* 2 A type of race. 3 An electric switch.
v. To pass on: *Please relay my message to your father.*

rel·e·gate (rel′ə·gāt) *v.* **rel·e·gat·ed, rel·e·gat·ing**
1 To send off or consign, as to an obscure position or place: *The old chair was relegated to a back office.* 2 To turn over to someone else: *Relegate all such problems to your assistant.*

rel·e·vant (rel′ə·vənt) *adj.*
Bearing upon; applicable: pertinent: *not relevant to the question.*—**rel′e·vance** *n.*

re·li·a·ble (re·lī′ə·bəl) *adj.*
Worthy of confidence; trustworthy: *a reliable employee; a reliable piece of information.*
—**re·li′a·bil′i·ty** *n.*, **re·li′a·bly** *adv.*

re·li·ance (re·lī′əns) *n.*
Confidence, trust, or dependence: *He admitted his reliance on his old friend.*

re·lief (ri·lēf′) *n.*
1 Deliverance from pain, anxiety, etc.: *The medicine gave him some relief.* 2 The person or thing that relieves: *The sentry was waiting for his relief.* 3 Assistance; aid: *receiving relief; on relief.* 4 A type of sculpture in which the figures are raised from the surface.

re·lieve (ri·lēv′) *v.* **re·lieved, re·liev·ing**
1 To bring relief to: *relieve a headache.* 2 To release, as from duty: *The watch was relieved at four bells.*

re·lig·ion (ri·lij′ən) *n.*
1 Any particular system of beliefs relating to faith and worship: *the Christian religion; Oriental religions.* 2 Belief in God or the supernatural.—**re·lig′ious** *adj.*

re·lin·quish (ri·ling′kwish) *v.*
To give up; abandon; surrender: *She relinquished her claim to the estate.*

re·ly (ri·lī′) *v.* **re·lied, re·ly·ing**
To place trust or confidence: *You can rely on me.*

re·me·di·a·ble (ri·mē′dē·ə·bəl) *adj.*
Capable of being cured or remedied: *Most childhood illnesses are remediable.*
Usage: Compare REMEDIAL.

re·me·di·al (ri·mē′dē·əl) *adj.*
Providing or intended to be used as a remedy or corrective measure: *There was great interest in the remedial reading project.*
Usage: *Remedial* refers to what remedies; *remediable* to what can be remedied.

re·mem·brance (ri·mem′brəns) *n.*
1 Memory; recollection: *He had no remembrance of his past life.* 2 Often *pl.* Keepsake; a memento or message of friendship or regard.

rem·i·nisce (rem′ə·nis′) *v.* **rem·i·nisced, rem·i·nisc·ing**
To recall incidents or events of the past.

rem·i·nis·cence (rem′ə·nis′əns) *n.*
1 The recalling to mind of past incidents or events; recollection. 2 The written or spoken account of one's past experiences: *The old friends exchanged reminiscences of college days.*
—**rem′i·nis′cent** *adj.*

re·miss (ri·mis′) *adj.*
Slack or careless in matters requiring attention; lacking energy; negligent: *He was remiss in settling his debts.*

re·mit (ri·mit′) *v.* **re·mit·ted, re·mit·ting**
1 To send, as money in payment for goods. 2 To pardon; forgive: *to remit a crime.*

re·mit·tance (ri·mit′əns) *n.*
The sending of money; also, the money sent: *He depended on a monthly remittance from home.*

re·mon·strate (ri·mon′strāt) *v.* **re·mon·strat·ed, re·mon·strat·ing**

To plead earnestly with, as in protest or reproof: *He remonstrated with the noisy children.*
Syn. expostulate, object, protest.

rend (rend) *v.* **rent** or **rend·ed, rend·ing**
To tear apart with violence; split; break: *He rent his garments; The silence was rent by a deafening explosion.*

ren·der (ren′dər) *v.*
1 To submit for action, approval, payment, etc.: *render a bill.* 2 To give or state formally: *render judgment.* 3 To melt down: *to render lard.*

ren·dez·vous (rän′dā·vōō) *n.*, **ren·dez·vous** *pl.*
1 An appointed place of meeting: *Under the station clock is a favorite rendezvous.* 2 A meeting by arrangement.
Syn. 1 meeting place. 2 assignation, appointment.

ren·e·gade (ren′ə·gād) *n.*
A traitor; deserter; turncoat: *A band of army renegades roamed the West.*

re·nege (ri·nig′) *v.* **re·neged, re·neg·ing**
1 In card games, to fail to follow suit when required to; revoke. 2 To fail to keep a promise: *He reneged on his offer to entertain the children.*

re·new (ri·nōō′) *v.*
1 To make new or like new again; restore. 2 To resume: *to renew an old quarrel.* 3 Replace: *renew our stock of supplies.* 4 To cause to continue in effect: *to renew a subscription.*
—**re·new′al** *n.*

re·nounce (ri·nouns′) *v.* **re·nounced, re·nounc·ing**
1 To give up, especially by a formal statement: *He renounced his inheritance.* 2 To disown; repudiate: *He renounced his daughter when she left home.*

ren·o·vate (ren′ə·vāt) *v.* **ren·o·vat·ed, ren·o·vat·ing**
To make new again; restore to good condition; repair: *The mansion was renovated at great expense.*—**ren′o·va′tion, ren′o·va′tor** *n.*

re·nown (ri·noun′) *n.*
Fame; celebrity: *a statesman of renown.*

re·nun·ci·a·tion (ri·nun′sē·ā′shən) *n.*
The act of renouncing or giving up: *His renunciation of high office was unexpected.*

rep·a·ra·tion (rep′ə·rā′shən) *n.*
The act of making amends; compensation, especially for war damage: *He promised to make reparation for his neglect; Reparations were demanded by the allies.*

re·pen·tance (ri·pen′təns) *n.*
Sorrow for past faults and a desire to reform; regret; contrition: *The judge saw no sign of repentance in the condemned man.*—**re·pen′tant** *adj.*

rep·er·toire (rep′ər·twär) *n.*
A list of plays, songs, etc., that a person or company is prepared to perform: *Many popular songs are not in her repertoire.*

rep·er·to·ry (rep′ər·tôr′ē) *n.*
1 Repertoire. 2 A place where things are gathered together; repository. 3 A collection.

rep·e·ti·tion (rep′ə·ti′shən) *n.*
The act of repeating; saying, doing, performing, etc., again: *He finally understood, after many repetitions.*

rep·e·ti·tious (rep′ə·tish′əs) *adj.*
Marked by repetition, especially tedious repetition: *Avoid a repetitious speech.*—**rep·e·ti′tious·ly** *adv.*; **rep·e·ti′tious·ness** *n.*

re·plen·ish (ri·plen′ish) *v.*
Fill up again; refill: *We must replenish our depleted stock of office supplies.*

re·plete (ri·plēt′) *adj.*
Abundantly supplied; well stocked: *a long novel replete with interesting characters; a life replete with adventure.*

rep·li·ca (rep′lə·kə) *n.*
A copy, as of an original picture or statue; duplicate; reproduction.

re·pos·i·to·ry (ri·poz′ə·tôr·ē) *n.*, **re·pos·i·to·ries** *pl.*
A place where things may be safely stored; warehouse; depository.

rep·re·hen·si·ble (rep′ri·hen′sə·bəl) *adj.*
Deserving blame or censure; deplorable: *Such behavior is morally reprehensible.*

re·prieve (ri·prēv′) *n.*; *v.* **re·prieved, re·priev·ing**
n. A temporary delay in carrying out the order of a court, especially a death sentence. *v.* 1 To issue an order for such a delay. 2 To relieve for a time from danger or trouble.

rep·ri·mand (rep′rə·mand) *v.*
To find fault with sharply or formally: *The judge reprimanded the young lawyer.*

rep·ro·bate (rep′rə·bāt) *n.*
A wicked or corrupt person; scoundrel.—**rep′ro·ba′tion** *n.*
Syn. profligate, scamp.

re·pud·i·ate (ri·pyoo′dē·āt) *v.* **re·pud·i·at·ed, re·pud·i·at·ing**
To refuse to accept as true or binding; disown: *He repudiated our agreement.*

re·pug·nance (ri·pug′nəns) *n.*
A strong dislike; distaste: *the repugnance which crudeness inspires.*—**re·pug′nant** *adj.*

rep·u·ta·ble (rep′yə·tə·bəl) *adj.*
Having a good reputation; estimable; honorable: *He was known as a hard-working, reputable man.*

rep·u·ta·tion (rep′yə·tā′shən) *n.*
1 The general estimation in which a person or thing is held by others, especially by a community; repute: *to be a man of high reputation.* 2 A particular credit or character ascribed to a person or thing: *a reputation for honesty.*

req·ui·site (rek′wə·zit) *adj., n.*
adj. Necessary; indispensable: *the skill requisite for driving a motorcycle.*
n. A necessity; requirement.

re·scind (ri·sind′) *v.*
To make void; repeal: *to rescind an order.*—**re·scind′a·ble** *adj.*
Syn. cancel, abrogate, revoke.

re·sem·ble (ri·zem′bəl) *v.* **re·sem·bled, re·sem·bling**
To be or look similar.

res·er·voir (rez′ər·vwôr *or* rez′ər·vwär) *n.*
1 A basin, either natural or artificial, for collecting and storing a large supply of water, as for use in a city. 2 A receptacle where some material, especially a liquid or gas, may be stored: *the mercury reservoir of a thermometer.* 3 A large supply of anything: *A computer is an amazing reservoir of data.*

res·i·due (rez′ə·doo *or* rez′ə·dyoo) *n.*
A remainder or surplus after a part has been removed or treated.

re·sign (ri·zīn′) *v.*
1 To give up a position, office, etc.: *He resigned his job and left town.* 2 To submit calmly: *She resigned herself to spending a boring evening.*

re·sil·ien·cy (ri·zil′yən·sē) *n.*
The quality or power of being resilient; elasticity.

re·sil·ient (ri·zil′yənt) *adj.*
1 Springing back to a former shape or position: *A rubber ball is resilient.* 2 Able to recover from trouble, sorrow, etc.: *a man of resilient character.*

res·in (rez′in) *n.*
1 A gummy, yellow-to-brown substance given off by certain plants, especially fir and pine trees, and used in making varnish, lacquer, etc. 2 Any of various synthetic substances with similar properties, used in making plastics.—**res′in·ous** *adj.*

re·solve (ri·zolv′) *v.* **re·solved, re·solv·ing**; *n.*
v. 1 To decide or determine: *He resolved to quit his job.* 2 To make clear; explain or solve: *to resolve a problem.* 3 To explain away; remove: *She resolved her doubts.*
n. A fixed determination: *a resolve to work hard.*

res·o·nant (rez′ə·nənt) *adj.*
1 Reflecting or prolonging sound: *a resonant wall.* 2 Resounding; ringing: *a resonant voice.*—**res′o·nant·ly** *adv.*

re·source (ri·sôrs′, ri·zors′, ri·sōrs′ *or* rē′sôrs) *n.*
1 A source of help or supply: *natural resources; financial resources.* 2 Skill or ingenuity in meeting any situation: *a man of resource and daring.*

re·spect·a·ble (ri·spek′tə·bəl) *adj.*
1 Deserving respect; being of good name or repute; respected: *respectable behavior.* 2 Fairly good; average: *Though respectable, their performance was worse than usual.* 3 Fairly large in number, quantity, size, quality, etc.: *a respectable amount of money.*—**re·spect′a·bly** *adv.*

re·spec·tive·ly (ri·spek′tiv·lē) *adv.*
Each in the order given: *The first three books go to John, James, and William, respectively.*

re·spir·a·to·ry (ri·spīr′ə·tôr′ē *or* res′pə·rə·tôr′ē) *adj.*
Having to do with breathing: *a respiratory disease.*

re·splen·dent (ri·splen′dənt) *adj.*
Vividly bright; splendid; gorgeous: *She was resplendent in her diamonds.*—**re·splen′dent·ly** *adv.*

re·sponse (ri·spons′) *n.*
An answer; reply; reaction: *The priest waited for the response from the congregation.*

re·spon·si·bil·i·ty (ri·spon′sə·bil′ə·tē) *n.*, **re·spon·si·bil·i·ties** *pl.*
1 The state of being responsible: *He denied any responsibility for his brother's actions.*
2 A person or thing for which one is responsible: *Her parents and children are her responsibilities.*

res·ti·tu·tion (res′tə·tōō′shən *or* res′tə·tyōō′shən) *n.*
The act of restoring or returning something that has been taken away or lost: *the restitution of the Indian lands.*

res·tive (res′tiv) *adj.*
1 Difficult to control; unruly: *a restive horse.*
2 Restless; uneasy: *a restive audience.*—**res′tive·ly** *adv.*

re·sume (ri·zōōm′) *v.* **re·sumed, re·sum·ing**
1 To begin again: *We will resume reading tomorrow.* 2 To take or occupy again: *to resume a position.*

rés·u·mé (rez′ŏŏ·mā′ *or* rez′ŏŏ·mā) *n.*
A summary, as of a person's employment record.

re·sur·gence (ri·sûr′jəns) *n.*
A rising again: *a resurgence of crime.*—**re·sur′gent** *adj.*

re·sus·ci·tate (ri·sus′ə·tāt) *v.* **re·sus·ci·tat·ed, re·sus·ci·tat·ing**
To bring or come back to life; revive from unconsciousness.—**re·sus′ci·ta′tion** *n.*
Spelling tip: Remember the *c* in this word.

re·tal·i·ate (ri·tal′ē·āt) *v.* **re·tal·i·at·ed, re·tal·i·at·ing**
To get even by returning like for like: *If you insult him, he will retaliate.*—**re·tal′i·a′tion** *n.*

re·ten·tive (ri·ten′tiv) *adj.*
Having the power to hold, keep, or remember: *a retentive mind; a retentive soil.*—**re·ten′tive·ly** *adv.*

ret·i·cent (ret′ə·sənt) *adj.*
Saying little; inclined to hesitate; uncommunicative.—**ret′i·cent·ly** *adv.*

ret·i·na (ret′ə·nə *or* ret′nə) *n.*, **ret·i·nas** *or* **ret·i·nae** (ret′ə·nē) *pl.*
The inner membrane at the back of the eyeball, that is sensitive to light and transmits the image to the optic nerve.

ret·i·nue (ret′ə·nōō *or* ret′ə·nyōō) *n.*
The group of persons attending a person of rank: *The movie star and her retinue arrived last night.*

re·trac·tion (ri·trak′shən) *n.*
The taking back of an assertion, accusation, admission, etc.: *He demanded a public retraction of the story.*

ret·ri·bu·tion (ret′rə·byōō′shən) *n.*
A deserved punishment given in return for a wrong done.

re·trieve (ri·trēv′) *v.* **re·trieved, re·triev·ing**
To get or bring back; regain; restore: *to retrieve a lost ball; to retrieve one's high spirits.*

ret·ro·ac·tive (ret′rō·ak′tiv) *adj.*
Having an effect on what is past: *a retroactive salary increase.*—**ret′ro·ac′tive·ly** *adv.*

ret·ro·spec·tive (ret′rə·spek′tiv) *adj.*
1 Looking back on the past. 2 Applying to the past: *a retrospective law.*—**ret′ro·spec′tive·ly** *adv.*

rev·eil·le (rev′i·lē) *n.*
A drum or bugle signal, notifying soldiers or sailors to wake up and start the day.

rev·e·la·tion (rev′ə·lā′shən) *n.*
A making known or something made known, especially when surprising: *His eloquence came as a revelation to me.*

rev·el·ry (rev′əl·rē) *n.*, **rev·el·ries** *pl.*
Noisy merrymaking.

re·ver·ber·ate (ri·vûr′bə·rāt) *v.* **re·ver·ber·at·ed, re·ver·ber·at·ing**
To echo back; resound: reecho: *The whole arena reverberated with the cheers.*—**re·ver′ber·a′tion** *n.*

rev·er·ence (rev′ər·əns) *n.*; *v.* **rev·er·enced, rev·er·enc·ing**
n. A feeling of profound respect often mixed with awe and affection; veneration.
v. To regard with respect; worship.

rev·er·ent (rev′ər·ənt) *adj.*
Feeling or showing reverence: *reverent pupils; a reverent genuflection.*—**rev′er·ent·ly** *adv.*

rev·er·ie (rev′ər·ē) *n.*
Dreamlike wandering of the mind; daydream: *Lost in reverie, she was startled by the sound of the doorbell.*

re·vile (ri·vīl′) *v.* **re·viled, re·vil·ing**
To attack with abusive language: *He reviled the traitor on the Senate floor.*

rev·o·ca·ble (rev′ə·kə·bəl) *adj.*
Capable of being taken back or canceled: *This license is revocable.*

re·vue (ri·vyōō′) *n.*
A type of musical comedy consisting of a series of loosely connected skits, songs, etc., often satirizing events and people.
Spelling tip: This word is also spelled *review.*

rhap·sod·ic (rap·sod′ik) *adj.*
1 Characteristic of a rhapsody: *a rhapsodic element of the symphony.* 2 Extravagantly enthusiastic; gushing: *The critics were rhapsodic about her performance.*
Syn. 2 rapt, rapturous.

rhap·so·dy (rap′sə·dē) *n.*, **rhap·so·dies** *pl.*
1 An extravagant or emotional utterance: *He went into a rhapsody about life in the woods.*
2 A musical composition irregular in form and very emotional: *Liszt's Hungarian rhapsodies.*

rhet·o·ric (ret′ə·rik) *n.*
1 The art of using elegant, forceful language: *Cicero and Aristotle wrote books on rhetoric.*
2 Language without honest meaning or intention: *It was mere rhetoric when he said he wanted reform; His crusade for reform is mere rhetoric.*—**rhe·tor·i·cal** (ri·tôr′i·kəl) *adj.*

rhi·noc·e·ros (rī·nos′ər·əs) *n.*
A large, plant-eating mammal having one or two horns on its nose and a very tough hide.

rhu·barb (rōō′bärb) *n.*
A plant having large leaves with thick leafstalks that are used in cooking.

rib·ald (rib′əld) *adj.*
Having to do with or using coarse language or vulgar jokes: *a ribald anecdote.*

ric·o·chet (rik′ə·shā′) *v.*
To bounce or rebound off a surface, as a bullet off a wall.

ri·dic·u·lous (ri·dik′yə·ləs) *adj.*
Absurd and unworthy of consideration: *a ridiculous fuss about a trifle.*

rife (rīf) *adj.*
Widespread: *Hunger is rife in the underdeveloped countries.*

right·eous (rī′chəs) *adj.*
Upright; just.—**right′eous·ly** *adv.*

rig·or (rig′ər) *n.*
1 Strictness; harshness; severity: *The judge interpreted the laws with rigor.* 2 Inclemency, as of weather; hardship: *the rigors of the northern climate.*

rinse (rins) *v.* **rinsed, rins·ing**
To clear soap, impurities, etc., from by using clear water: *Be sure and rinse the dishes after washing them.*

rise (rīz) *v.* **rose** or **ris·en, ris·ing**
1 Get up from a sitting, kneeling, or lying position. 2 To move, grow, or project upwards: *The sun is rising; The land rises near here.* 3 To swell in quantity or extent: *Dough rises.*

ris·qué (ris·kā′) *adj.*
Bordering on impropriety; off-color: *He embarrassed the company by telling a risqué story.* **Syn.** racy, ribald, suggestive.

rite (rīt) *n.*
A solemn or religious ceremony performed in a prescribed or established manner, or the words and acts accompanying it: *Easter rites.*

ri·val·ry (rī′vəl·rē) *n.,* **ri·val·ries** *pl.*
Competition: *They had engaged in friendly rivalry over the years.*

roan (rōn) *adj., n.*
adj. Having a color consisting of reddish or yellowish brown thickly speckled with white or gray.
n. A horse of this color.

ro·bot (rō′bət) *n.*
1 A mechanical man constructed to perform work in place of human beings. 2 A person who works dully or mechanically; automaton. **Etymology:** *Robots* was a term used by the Czech playwright Karel Capek for the mechanical men in his play *R.U.R.* (*Rossum's Universal Robots*).

ro·bust (rō·bust′) *adj.*
1 Possessing strength and endurance; sturdy; vigorous: *a robust physique; a robust plant.* 2 Rich or strong, as in flavor: *a robust soup.* 3 Crude or unpolished; without subtlety: *a robust humor; robust manners.*

rogue (rōg) *n.*
1 A dishonest person; knave: *The rogue stole all of my cash.* 2 A person who is innocently mischievous or playful; a rascal: *I saw you, you young rogue!* 3 A fierce and dangerous animal, separated from the herd.

room·mate (rōōm′māt′) *n.*
A person who shares a room or lodging with another or others: *They were roommates at prep school.*

ro·sa·ry (rō′zə·rē) *n.,* **ro·sa·ries** *pl.*
1 A string of beads for keeping count of prayers. 2 A series of prayers as counted on a rosary.

ros·trum (ros′trəm) *n.,* **ros·trums** or **ros·tra** *pl.*
A pulpit or platform for public speaking: *The speaker invited the heckler to join him on the rostrum.* **Syn.** dais.

ro·tate (rō′tāt) *v.* **ro·tat·ed, ro·tat·ing**
1 To turn or cause to turn on or as if on an axis: *The world is rotating at a rate of one revolution a day.* 2 To alternate in a definite order: *The farmer rotated his crops every year.* **Syn.** 1 revolve.

rote (rōt) *n.*
A mechanical way of doing something, as learning without understanding. **Usage:** *Rote* is usually always used in the phrase *by rote: to learn by rote; repeat by rote.*

ro·tund (rō·tund′) *adj.*
1 Chubby; spherical; plump: *a rotund countenance; a rotund little woman.* 2 Full-toned, as a voice or utterance; sonorous: *one of the usual rotund speeches by the senator.*

ro·tun·da (rō·tun′də) *n.*
A circular building or room with a dome.

rou·é (rōō·ā′) *n.*
A sensualist; debauchee: *aging roués attempting to recapture youth and vitality.*

rouge (rōōzh) *n.*
A cosmetic used to color the cheeks or lips red: *Her color owed more to rouge than good health.*

rough (ruf) *adj.*
1 Having an uneven or broken surface; not smooth, level, or polished: *a rough country; rough hands; rough cloth.* 2 Boisterous or tempestuous; stormy: *a rough passage.* 3 Brutal; disorderly: *a rough game; a rough customer.* 4 Approximate; not finished: *a rough estimate; a rough sketch.*
Spelling tip: Remember the *f* sound is spelled *gh.*

route (rōōt or rout) *n.*
1 The course taken in getting from one point to another: *We took the scenic route.* 2 The territory covered by a milkman, mailman, etc.: *That street is not on his route.*

rub·ble (rub′əl) *n.*
Rough pieces of stone, brick, etc., as that to which buildings are reduced when destroyed: *The explosion reduced the factory to rubble·*

rud·dy (rud'ē) *adj.* **rud·di·er, rud·di·est**
Having a reddish tinge or glow; rosy: *a ruddy complexion.*—**rud'di·ness** *n.*
Syn. florid, flushed, rubicund.

ru·di·ment (rōō'də·mənt) *n.*
A first principle, step, stage, or condition: *the rudiments of French.*
Syn. basic, fundamental, starter, beginning.

ru·di·men·ta·ry (rōō'də·men'tər·ē) *adj.*
1 Elementary: *a rudimentary knowledge of French.* **2** Imperfectly developed; vestigial: *a rudimentary tail.*
Syn. **1** fundamental, introductory. **2** embryonic, abortive.

ruf·fi·an (ruf'ē·ən *or* ruf'yən) *n.*
A lawless, brutal, cruel fellow: *a gang of ruffians.*
Syn. roughneck, rowdy, thug, hoodlum, hooligan.
Ant. gentleman.

ru·mi·nate (rōō'mə·nāt) *v.* **ru·mi·nat·ed, ru·mi·nat·ing**
1 To chew food previously swallowed and regurgitated, as a cow. **2** To think or reflect; ponder: *He ruminated over the evidence all day.*
Syn. **2** muse, deliberate.

rum·mage (rum'ij) *v.* **rum·maged, rum·mag·ing**
To search by turning over and disarranging the contents: *We rummaged the closet.*
Syn. ransack.

rum·mage sale (rum'ij sāl) *n.*
A sale of secondhand objects to obtain money for some charitable purpose.

ruse (rōōz) *n.*
An action intended to mislead or deceive; trick: *She thought of a clever ruse to avoid detection.*

ruth·less (rōōth'lis) *adj.*
Having no compassion; merciless: *a ruthless murderer.*—**ruth'less·ly** *adv.*; **ruth'less·ness** *n.*

S

sac·ri·fice (sak'rə·fīs) *n.; v.* **sac·ri·ficed, sac·ri·fic·ing**
n. **1** An offering to a god in worship or atonement: *the sacrifice of a lamb; human sacrifice.* **2** A giving up of one thing for another: *He made the sacrifice of a lucrative job in order to become a missionary.*
v. To make a sacrifice, as by offering something to a god or by relinquishing something: *He sacrificed his weekends for his sick friend.*

sac·ri·fi·cial (sak'rə·fish'əl) *adj.*
Being or having to do with a sacrifice: *a sacrificial lamb.*—**sac'ri·fi'cial·ly** *adv.*

sac·ri·lege (sak'rə·lij) *n.*
An act of disrespect for anything sacred.—**sac'ri·le'gious** *adj.*; **sac'ri·le'gious·ly** *adv.*; **sac'ri·le'gious·ness** *n.*
Syn. desecration, defilement.

sac·ro·sanct (sak'rō·sangkt) *adj.*
Exceedingly sacred: *Old ideas should not be treated as sacrosanct.*—**sac'ro·sanc'ti·ty** *n.*
Syn. holy, inviolable, sanctified.

sa·ga (sä'gə) *n.*
1 A medieval Scandinavian story of historical or legendary exploits: *the sagas of the Vikings.* **2** A long verse or prose narrative, often telling the history of a family.

sa·ga·cious (sə·gā'shəs) *adj.*
Characterized by wisdom and shrewdness: *to ask a sagacious man for advice.*—**sa·ga'cious·ly** *adv.*; **sa·ga'cious·ness** *n.*

sa·gac·i·ty (sə·gas'ə·tē) *n.*
Discernment and wisdom: *the sagacity of the wise old statesman.*
Syn. judgment, sense, perceptiveness.

sa·la·cious (sə·lā'shəs) *adj.*
Lewd; lustful; obscene: *a salacious man; a salacious joke.*—**sa·la'cious·ly** *adv.*; **sa·la'cious·ness** *n.*

sa·li·ent (sā'lē·ənt) *adj., n.*
adj. Standing out prominently; conspicuous or projecting: *the salient points of an argument; the salient features of the landscape.*
n. The part of a fortification, trench, etc., that extends toward the enemy: *the salient of the trench.*

sa·line (sā'lēn *or* sā'līn) *adj., n.*
adj. Made of, containing, or having to do with salt: *the saline taste of sea water; a saline solution.*
n. A metallic salt or a salt solution used in medicine and scientific research.—**sa·lin'i·ty** *n.*

sa·li·va (sə·lī'və) *n.*
The fluid secreted by the glands of the mouth.—**sal'i·var·y** *adj.*
Syn. spit, spittle, sputum.

sal·low (sal'ō) *adj.*
Of an unhealthy, yellowish color, said chiefly of the human skin: *a sallow complexion.*—**sal'low·ness** *n.*
Syn. wan, pallid.
Ant. ruddy, rosy.

sa·lon (sə·lon') *n.*
1 A formal room in which guests are received: *They entertained in the salon.* **2** The periodic gathering of a group of famous people in the house of a wealthy or prominent person: *the salon of Princess Matilde.* **3** A shop or establishment devoted to a specific purpose: *a beauty salon; a reducing salon.*

sa·lu·bri·ous (sə·lōō'brē·əs) *adj.*
Good for the health; healthful: *the salubrious sea air.*—**sa·lu'bri·ous·ly** *adv.*; **sa·lu'bri·ous·ness, sa·lu'bri·ty** *n.*
Syn. wholesome, invigorating.

sal·u·tar·y (sal'yə·ter'ē) *adj.*
1 Healthful: *the salutary effects of mountain air.* **2** Beneficial: *a salutary facing of the facts.*—**sal'u·tar'i·ly** *adv.*; **sal'u·tar'i·ness** *n.*
Syn. **1** salubrious, tonic, restorative. **2** helpful.

sa·lute (sə·lōōt') *n.; v.* **sa·lut·ed, sa·lut·ing**
n. A gesture of welcome or respect, as by raising the hand to the forehead, firing cannon, etc.: *the Boy Scout salute; a 20-gun salute.*
v. To make a salute: *The soldier saluted the general.*—**sa·lut'er** *n.*

sal·vage (sal′vij) *v.* **sal·vaged, sal·vag·ing;** *n.*
v. To save from destruction, as cargo from a shipwreck, papers from a fire, etc.: *to salvage part of the cargo.*
n. **1** The act of saving from destruction: *the salvage of furniture from a burning house.* **2** Something saved from destruction: *the salvage which the divers brought up from the wrecked ship.*—**sal′vage·a·ble** *adj.;* **sal′vag·er** *n.*

salve (sav) *n.; v.* **salved, salv·ing**
n. A thick, adhesive ointment which heals or soothes the pain of wounds, etc.: *to apply salve to the burn.*
v. To soothe or calm: *to salve one's conscience with good resolutions for the future.*

sanc·ti·mo·ni·ous (sangk′tə·mō′nē·əs) *adj.*
Making a pretense of piety or virtuousness: *his sanctimonious lecture on duty and ideals.*—**sanc′ti·mo′ni·ous·ly** *adv.;* **sanc′ti·mo′ni·ous·ness, sanc′ti·mo′ny** *n.*
Syn. hypocritical.

sanc·tu·ar·y (sangk′chōō·er′ē) *n.,* **sanc·tu·ar·ies** *pl.*
1 A holy or sacred place, especially a church or the part of a church where the main altar is located. **2** A place of refuge for people or animals: *a bird sanctuary.*

sand·wich (sand′wich *or* san′wich) *n., v.*
n. Two slices of bread with meat, cheese, or any other food between them: *a ham sandwich.*
v. To place or squeeze between two other things: *His small box was sandwiched between two suitcases.*
Spelling tip: Whichever way you pronounce this word, be sure to spell it with a *d.*
Syn. *v.* cram, wedge, insert.

san·guine (sang′gwin) *adj.*
1 Cheerful, confident, and optimistic: *A sanguine man sees the world through rose-colored glasses.* **2** Having a healthy, rosy color; ruddy. **3** Having the color of blood.—**san′guine·ly** *adv.;* **san′guine·ness** *n.;* **san′gui·nar′y** *adj.*
Syn. 1 buoyant, hopeful.
Ant. 1 gloomy, pessimistic, apprehensive.

sans (sanz, *French* säṅ) *prep.*
French Without: *She was in the habit of swimming sans suit.*
Syn. minus, lacking.
Ant. with, including, plus.

sap·phire (saf′īr) *n., adj.*
n. **1** A precious gem having a deep blue color: *a ring set with sapphires.* **2** The deep, pure blue color of this jewel.
adj. Having this color: *a sapphire gown.*

sar·casm (sär′kaz·əm) *n.*
1 The use of ironic or satirical remarks to express contempt or derision. **2** An ironical and mocking remark uttered as a taunt or scornful gibe.—**sar·cas′tic** *adj.;* **sar·cas′ti·cal·ly** *adv.*
Syn. 1 irony, mockery.

sar·don·ic (sär·don′ik) *adj.*
Scornful or derisive; sneering: *a sardonic expression.*—**sar·don′i·cal·ly** *adv.*
Syn. caustic, mocking, cynical, jaundiced.

sar·to·ri·al (sär·tôr′ē·əl *or* sär·tō′rē·əl) *adj.*
Pertaining to men's clothes: *the sartorial splendor of the Edwardian dandy.*—**sar·to′ri·al·ly** *adv.*

sat·el·lite (sat′ə·līt) *n.*
1 In astronomy, a celestial body (as a planet, moon, etc.) which revolves in orbit around a larger one. **2** A man-made object launched by means of a rocket into orbit around the earth or other celestial body. **3** A small nation whose political and economic policy is controlled by a great power: *East Germany is a satellite of Russia.*

sa·ti·e·ty (sə·tī′ə·tē) *n.*
The state of being completely or excessively satisfied; repletion or surfeit: *stuffed to satiety on Italian food.*

sat·ire (sat′īr) *n.*
Irony, wit, or parody used to expose follies, abuses, etc.; mockery: *political cartoons and other forms of satire.*—**sa·tir′ic, sa·tir′i·cal** *adj.;* **sat′i·rist** *n.*

sat·is·fy (sat′is·fī) *v.* **sat·is·fied, sat·is·fy·ing**
1 To please, gratify, appease, or fulfill: *The meal satisfied his hunger.* **2** To convince; free from doubt or anxiety: *Are you satisfied that I am telling the truth?*

sat·u·rate (sach′ə·rāt) *v.* **sat·u·rat·ed, sat·u·rat·ing**
To fill or permeate, as by soaking: *The dye slowly saturated the cloth.*—**sat′u·ra′tion** *n.*
Syn. impregnate, suffuse, drench.

sau·cy (sô′sē) *adj.* **sau·ci·er, sau·ci·est**
1 Insolent; disrespectful: *a saucy child talking rudely to her grandmother.* **2** Lively and amusing; piquant: *a sprightly, saucy gamin.*—**sau′ci·ly** *adv.;* **sau′ci·ness** *n.*
Syn. 1 impudent, impertinent, fresh. **2** pert.
Ant. 1 courteous, deferential, meek. **2** quiet, reserved, bland.

saun·ter (sôn′tər) *v., n.*
v. To walk in a leisurely or lounging manner; stroll: *to saunter along the riverbank.*
n. **1** A slow, aimless way of walking: *the saunter of a man with time to kill.* **2** An idle stroll: *a saunter through the woods.*

sa·voir-faire (sȧ·vwȧr·fâr′) *n. French*
Ability to say and do the right thing; polished and tactful manners: *a man with so little savoir-faire that he invariably does the wrong thing.*
Spelling tip: In French, *oi* is pronounced *wȧ.*
Syn. poise, polish, diplomacy, suavity.
Ant. gaucheness, tactlessness, boorishness.

sa·vor (sā′vər) *v., n.*
v. To taste or enjoy with pleasure: *to savor the bouquet of a delicious wine.*
n. Flavor; smell: *the savor of freshly brewed coffee.*

scal·pel (skal′pəl) *n.*
A small pointed knife with a very sharp, thin blade, used by surgeons.

scar·ab (skar'əb) *n.*
1 A large black beetle, held sacred in ancient Egypt. 2 A gem or ornament that represents this beetle.

scarce·ly (skârs'lē) *adv.*
1 Only just; barely: *I can scarcely see the house in the distance.* 2 Probably or certainly not: *He can scarcely be the author.*

scar·ci·ty (skâr'sə·tē) *n.*, **scar·ci·ties** *pl.*
Inadequate supply; insufficiency; lack: *a scarcity of fresh vegetables.*

scath·ing (skā'ŧhing) *adj.*
Painfully severe; bitter: *She wrote a scathing criticism of the project.*

scav·en·ger (skav'in·jər) *n.*
1 An animal that feeds on carrion, as the buzzard. 2 A person who searches refuse, garbage, etc., for usable material.

scene (sēn) *n.*
1 An area and all connected with it, as presented to view; a landscape: *A beautiful scene could be viewed from the window.* 2 The place in which the action of a drama is supposed to occur; setting. 3 The place and surroundings of any event: *the scene of the crime.* 4 A division of an act of a play. 5 A display of anger or excited feeling in front of others: *He made a scene in the shop.*

scent (sent) *n., v.*
n. 1 A distinctive odor, especially a pleasant one. 2 A residual odor by which a living being can be tracked. 3 Perfume: *I like the scent she wears.*
v. 1 To perceive by smell: *The dog scented his master.* 2 To form a suspicion of: *He scented his betrayal.* 3 To make fragrant; perfume: *The flowers scent the room.*

scep·ter (sep'tər) *n.*
A staff or wand carried as the badge of command or sovereignty.

sched·ule (skej'ool) *n.; v.* **sched·uled, sched·ul·ing**
n. 1 A list; catalogue; inventory: *a schedule of prices.* 2 A timetable: *a bus schedule.* 3 A detailed and timed plan for any procedure; program.
v. To place in or on a schedule: *to schedule an interview.*

schol·ar·ship (skol'ər·ship) *n.*
1 The mental attainments of a scholar; learning; erudition: *He was held in great respect because of his scholarship.* 2 A grant of money for a student to enable him to study.

sci·at·ic (sī·at'ik) *adj.*
Having to do with or affecting the hip or its nerves: *a sciatic vein.*

sci·ence (sī'əns) *n.*
1 Knowledge, generally obtained through observation and experimentation, logically arranged and systematized in general laws subject to verification. 2 Any branch of such knowledge, as mathematics, physics, etc.— **sci·en·tif·ic** *adj.*; **sci·en·tif'i·cal·ly** *adv.*; **sci'·en·tist** *n.*

scim·i·tar (sim'ə·tər) *n.*
A curved Oriental sword or saber.
Spelling tip: This word is also spelled *scimiter.*

scin·til·la (sin·til'ə) *n.*
A spark; trace; iota: *There was not a scintilla of truth in the story.*

scin·til·late (sin'tə·lāt) *v.* **scin·til·lat·ed, scin·til·lat·ing**
To sparkle; glitter; twinkle: *stars that scintillate in the sky.*

sci·on (sī'ən) *n.*
1 A child or descendant, especially of a prominent family. 2 A twig or shoot of a plant, especially for grafting.

scle·ro·sis (sklə·rō'sis) *n.*, **scle·ro·ses** (sklə·rō'sēz) *pl.*
The thickening and hardening of a tissue or part.

scone (skōn) *n.*
A round tea cake or biscuit usually eaten with butter.

scope (skōp) *n.*
1 Room or chance for development: *The job didn't give him enough scope to exercise his abilities.* 2 Range of view or activity; outlook: *a mind of limited scope.* 3 The area or sphere in which any activity takes place: *the scope of a scientific work.*

scoun·drel (skoun'drəl) *n.*
A mean, unprincipled person; rogue; villain.
Syn. rascal, knave, cad.

scourge (skûrj) *n.; v.* **scourged, scourg·ing**
n. 1 A whip. 2 A cause of suffering or trouble: *the scourge of disease; the scourge of war.*
v. 1 To whip severely; lash; flog. 2 To punish severely; chastise; afflict: *Attila's armies scourged the people of Europe.*

scru·pu·lous (skroo'pyə·ləs) *adj.*
Conscientious, exact, or careful: *a scrupulous person; a scrupulous account of all the expenses.*
Syn. meticulous, punctilious, fastidious.

scul·lion (skul'yən) *n.*
A servant who washes and scours dishes, pots, and kettles. This word is seldom used today.

scur·ri·lous (skûr'ə·ləs) *adj.*
Grossly and offensively abusive: *scurrilous language; scurrilous writing.* **scur'ri·lous·ly** *adv.*; **scur'ri·lous·ness, scur·ril'i·ty** *n.*

scythe (sīŧh) *n.*
A tool used for mowing, reaping, etc., consisting of a long, curved blade fixed at an angle to a long, bent handle.

sé·ance (sā'äns) *n.*
A meeting of persons seeking to communicate with the dead.

se·cede (si·sēd') *v.* **se·ced·ed, se·ced·ing**
To withdraw from a union, fellowship, or association, especially from a political or religious one.

se·ces·sion (si·sesh'ən) *n.*
The act of seceding; withdrawal from fellowship, especially from a political or religious association.—**se·ces'sion·ist** *n.*

sec·on·dar·y (sek′ən·der′ē) *adj.*
Of second rank, grade, importance, class, etc.: *secondary industries.*—**sec′on·dar′i·ly** *adv.*
Syn. auxiliary, subordinate.

sec·re·tar·y (sek′rə·ter′ē) *n.*, **sec·re·tar·ies** *pl.*
1 A person who writes letters, keeps records, etc., for an individual, business, etc. 2 An executive officer who presides over and manages a department of government: *the Secretary of State.* 3 A writing desk with a bookcase or cabinet on top.—**sec·re·tar·i·al** (sek′rə·târ′ē·əl) *adj.*

sec·u·lar (sek′yə·lər) *adj.*
1 Not religious or spiritual; temporal; worldly: *secular education.* 2 Not bound by monastic vows: *the secular clergy.*

se·cur·i·ty (si·kyŏŏr′ə·tē) *n.*, **se·cur·i·ties** *pl.*
1 The condition of being secure; freedom from danger, poverty, or apprehension. 2 A person or thing that secures or guarantees: *A diet rich in vitamin C is a security against scurvy.* 3 Something deposited or pledged as a guarantee for payment of money, etc.

se·date (si·dāt′) *adj.*
Habitually calm and unhurried; sober and decorous.—**se·date′ly** *adv.*; **se·date′ness** *n.*
Syn. placid, grave, composed, quiet.
Ant. excited, agitated.

sed·en·tar·y (sed′ən·ter′ē) *adj.*
1 Requiring much sitting or a habitual sitting posture: *Writers lead a sedentary life.* 2 Accustomed to much sitting: *sedentary people.*

se·duce (si·dōōs′ *or* si·dyōōs′) *v.* **se·duced, se·duc·ing**
To lead into wrongdoing; tempt: *He was seduced by dreams of wealth and power.*—**se·duc′er, se·duc·tion** (si·duk′shən) *n.*

seethe (sēth) *v.* **seethed, seeth·ing**
1 To boil. 2 To foam and bubble as if boiling: *The breakers seethed on the shore.* 3 To be agitated or excited, as by rage: *He seethed with anger.*

seg·re·gate (seg′rə·gāt) *v.* **seg·re·gat·ed, seg·re·gat·ing**
1 To place apart from others or the rest; isolate: *The safest way is to segregate the sick kitten.* 2 To set apart and force to use separate facilities, as in housing, schools, and transportation, because of racial, religious, or social differences.

seine (sān) *n.*; *v.* **seined, sein·ing**
n. A long fishnet hanging vertically in the water and having floats at the top edge and weights at the bottom.
v. To fish or catch with a seine.

seize (sēz) *v.* **seized, seiz·ing**
1 To take hold of suddenly; clutch; grasp: *The dog seized him by the leg.* 2 To take possession of by force: *The enemy seized the town.* 3 To take prisoner; capture; arrest. 4 To take advantage of immediately: *to seize an opportunity.*

sei·zure (sē′zhər) *n.*
1 The act of seizing. 2 A sudden or violent attack, as of a disease; fit; spell: *an epileptic seizure.*

sel·vage (sel′vij) *n.*
The edge of a woven fabric so finished that it will not ravel.
Spelling tip: This word is also spelled *selvedge.*

se·man·tics (si·man′tiks) *n.*
The study of the development of and the changes in the meanings of words.—**se·man′·tic** *adj.*

sem·blance (sem′bləns) *n.*
Outward appearance; likeness; look; aspect: *The room took on some semblance of order.*

semi- *prefix*
1 Not fully; partially; partly: *semiautomatic, semicivilized.* 2 Exactly half: *semicircle.* 3 Occurring twice (in the period specified): *semiweekly.*
Usage: *Semi-* in *semiweekly* and like words means twice a week, etc., and should not be confused with *bi-* in *biweekly*, etc., which usually means once every two weeks, etc.

sen·ate (sen′it) *n.*
1 A governing or legislative body. 2 (Capital S) The upper branch of national or state legislative bodies of the United States and other governments.

sen·a·tor (sen′ə·tər) *n.*
(Often capital S) A member of a senate.

se·nile (sē′nīl) *adj.*
1 Pertaining to, caused by, or characteristic of old age: *senile decay.* 2 Infirm; weak; doting.

se·nil·i·ty (si·nil′ə·tē) *n.*
Mental and physical weakness due to old age: *They watched for signs of senility.*

sen·ior (sēn′yər) *adj.*, *n.*
adj. 1 Older, often used to distinguish a father from his son: *John Smith, senior* (or *Sr.*). 2 Higher in rank or longer in service: *a senior partner.*
n. 1 The one who is older, higher in rank, or longer in service. 2 A student in the fourth year of a high school or college.

sen·sa·tion (sen·sā′shən) *n.*
1 The awareness resulting from the stimulation of any of the sense organs: *Honey gives a sensation of sweetness.* 2 A feeling that comes from the mind or the emotions: *a sensation of fear; a sensation of uneasiness.*

sen·sa·tion·al (sen·sā′shən·əl) *adj.*
Causing great excitement, interest, or shock: *a sensational play.*

sense (sens) *n.*; *v.* **sensed, sens·ing**
n. 1 Any of the physical powers by which an individual receives impressions of the external world, as taste, touch, hearing, smell, or sight. 2 Rational perception accompanied by feeling; realization; understanding: *a sense of wrong; a sense of duty.* 3 Normal power to think or understand; sound or natural judgment: *He has no sense; She is coming to her senses.*
v. To become aware of; feel; realize: *He sensed opposition.*

sen·si·ble (sen′sə·bəl) *adj.*
1 Having or showing good sense and understanding; reasonable: *sensible conduct; a*

sensible person. 2 Fully aware; cognizant *to: be sensible of the difficulties of a problem.*—**sen'si·bly** *adv.*

sen·so·ry (sen'sər·ē) *adj.*
Of or having to do with the senses or sensation: *sensory perception; sensory nerves.*

sen·ti·nel (sen'tə·nəl) *n.*
A watcher or guard; sentry.

sep·tic (sep'tik) *adj.*
Of, having to do with, caused by or causing infection: *a septic wound.*

sep·ul·cher (sep'əl·kər) *n.*
A tomb.
Spelling tip: This word is also spelled *sepulchre.*

se·ren·i·ty (si·ren'ə·tē) *n.,* **se·ren·i·ties** *pl.*
1 Repose; peacefulness: *His manner was one of great serenity.* 2 Clearness; brightness: *the serenity of an arctic night.*

serf (sûrf) *n.*
A person bound in servitude to the owner of the land he works on, as in feudal England.

se·ri·ous (sir'ē·əs) *adj.*
1 Grave and earnest in feeling; thoughtful: *He was so serious that no one believed he had a sense of humor.* 2 Not ironical or lying; sincere: *Are you serious?* 3 Of grave importance; weighty: *a serious problem; a serious accident.*—**se'ri·ous·ly** *adv.;* **se'ri·ous·ness** *n.*
Syn. 1 sober. 2 in earnest.
Ant. 1 frivolous, flighty. 2 joking, ironic. 3 unimportant, minor.

ser·rat·ed (ser'āt·əd) *adj.*
Toothed or notched like a saw: *Most roses have serrated leaves.*

ser·vile (sûr'vil) *adj.*
1 Like a slave; slavish: *a servile employee.* 2 Pertaining to or appropriate for slaves or servants: *servile employment.*—**ser·vil·i·ty** (sûr·vol'ə·tē) *n.*
Syn. 1 fawning, abject.

ses·a·me (ses'ə·mē) *n.*
1 An East Indian plant. 2 The seeds of this plant, used as food and as a source of a pale yellow oil.

sev·er·al (sev'ər·ol) *adj.*
1 Being of an indefinite number, not large but more than two: *Several people came up to ask for an autograph.* 2 Considered individually; pertaining to an individual; single; separate: *They went their several ways.*—**sev'er·al·ly** *adv.*

sham·bles (sham'bəlz) *n.*
1 A slaughterhouse. 2 Any scene of extensive destruction or disorder: *The room was a shambles after the fight.*
Usage: *Shambles* is usually treated as a singular noun.

sheaf (shēf) *n.,* **sheaves** (shēvz) *pl.*
A bundle of objects, especially stalks of cut grain, usually tied together: *a sheaf of barley; a sheaf of papers; a sheaf of arrows.*

sheik (shēk) *n.*
The head of an Arab tribe or clan.
Spelling tip: This word is also spelled *sheikh.*

shel·lac (shə·lak') *n.; v.* **shel·lacked, shel·lack·ing**
n. 1 A purified resinous material in the form of thin flakes. 2 A solution containing this material used as a protective coating on wood.
v. 1 To cover with shellac. 2 To defeat utterly.

shil·le·lagh (shi·lā'lē) *n.*
In Ireland, a thick club of oak or blackthorn.

shin·ing (shī'ning) *adj.*
1 Emitting or reflecting a continuous light; luminous: *shining morning face.* 2 Of unusual brilliance or excellence; conspicuous: *a shining example to us all.*

shoal (shōl) *n., v.*
n. 1 A school of fish: *a shoal of herring.* 2 An assemblage or multitude; throng: *Visitors came to the house in shoals.*
Syn. *n.* 2 crowd.

shoe (shoo) *n.,* **shoes** (shooz) *pl.; v.* **sho,d shoe·ing**
n. 1 An outer covering for the human foot. 2 Something resembling a shoe in position or use, as a horseshoe.
v. To furnish with shoes.

show (shō) *v.* **showed, shown** or **showed, show·ing;** *n.*
v. 1 To cause or permit to see or be seen: *They showed me their dog; She showed great talent.* 2 To explain something; teach: *Please show me how to solve this puzzle.*
n. An entertainment or performance: *a TV show.*

shriek (shrēk) *n., v.*
n. A sharp, shrill, generally uncontrollable outcry or scream: *a shriek in the night; a shriek of laughter.*
v. To utter such a wild cry: *She shrieked in horror when she saw the corpse.*

siege (sēj) *n.; v.* **sieged, sieg·ing**
n. 1 The act of surrounding a fortified place with the object of capturing it. 2 A steady attempt to win something. 3 A time of unpleasant illness or difficulty: *a siege of the flu.*
v. To try to capture, win, or gain something; besiege.

sieve (siv) *n.*
A utensil or apparatus for straining or sifting, consisting of a cylindrical container with a bottom of wire mesh, etc.

sign (sīn) *n., v.*
n. 1 A motion or action used instead of words to convey information or show respect: *She made a sign to the waiter to bring the check.* 2 A written mark having an arbitrary meaning: *the plus and minus signs.* 3 A board, placard, or other representation containing information of some kind: *a street sign; a neon sign.* 4 Any indication, trace, or evidence of a condition, state, etc.: *signs of poverty; sign of a struggle.* 5 An omen, portent, or miraculous occurrence. 6 Any of the twelve divisions of the zodiac.
v. 1 To write one's signature on: *to sign a contract.* 2 To engage by obtaining the signa-

ture to a contract: *to sign a new player.* **3** To communicate by gesture.

sig·nif·i·cant (sig·nif′ə·kənt) *adj.*
1 Having a meaning: *The porpoise was uttering apparently significant sounds.* **2** Conveying or having a more or less hidden meaning: *a significant glance.* **3** Important; momentous: *a significant event.*—**sig·nif′i·cance** *n.,* **sig·nif′i·cant·ly** *adv.*
Syn. 1 meaningful, indicative. **2** suggestive, expressive. **3** notable, weighty.
Ant. 1 meaningless. **3** unimportant, insignificant.

sil·hou·ette (sil′oo·et′) *n.; v.* **sil·hou·et·ted, sil·hou·et·ting**
n. **1** A portrait of a person with only the outline of the profile described, usually filled in with black. **2** The outline of a person or thing seen against a light or a light background.
v. To cause to appear in silhouette: *He was silhouetted against the sunlight.*

silt (silt) *n.*
Earthy sediment suspended in and carried by water.

sim·i·an (sim′ē·ən) *adj., n.*
adj. Pertaining to, resembling, or characteristic of apes and monkeys: *He had a simian appearance.*
n. An ape or monkey.

sim·i·le (sim′ə·lē) *n.*
A figure of speech expressing comparison or likeness by the use of such terms as *like, as, so,* etc.

sim·pli·fy (sim′plə·fī) *v.* **sim·pli·fied, sim·pli·fy·ing**
To make more simple.—**sim′pli·fi·ca′tion, sim′pli·fi′er** *n.*

sim·u·late (sim′yə·lāt) *v.* **sim·u·lat·ed, sim·u·lat·ing**
To pretend; feign: *an opossum simulating the appearance of death.*
Syn. counterfeit, imitate.

si·mul·ta·ne·ous (sī′məl·tā′nē·əs) *adj.*
Occurring, done, or existing at the same time: *Artificial snow is formed by the simultaneous ejection of compressed air and water.*—**si′mul·ta′ne·ous·ly** *adv.;* **si·mul·ta·ne·i·ty** (sī′məl·tə·nē′ə·tē) *n.*

sin·cere (sin·sir′) *adj.* **sin·cer·er, sin·cer·est**
1 Real; genuine: *with sincere regret.* **2** Free from hypocrisy; honest; faithful: *a sincere friend.*—**sin·cere′ly** *adv.*

si·ne·cure (sī′nə·kyoor) *n.*
An office or job involving little or no work and usually paying well.

sine qua non (sī′nē kwä non′) *Latin*
That which is indispensable; an essential: *Riches are becoming a sine qua non for running for public office.*
Etymology: *Sine qua non* means literally without which not.

singe (sinj) *v.* **singed, singe·ing**
To burn slightly or superficially, as when removing feathers or the ends of hairs; scorch.

sin·u·ous (sin′yoo·əs) *adj.*
Characterized by bends, curves, or folds; winding; undulating: *the sinuous curves of a python.*

site (sīt) *n.*
1 Place of location: *site of the battle.* **2** A plot of ground set apart for some specific use: *a building site.*
Spelling tip: Don't confuse this word with *cite* or *sight.*

sit·u·at·ed (sich′oo·ā′tid) *adj.*
1 Placed in a specified position: *The house is situated near the shore.* **2** Placed in certain circumstances or conditions: *He is well situated.*—**sit′u·a′tion** *n.*

skep·tic (skep′tik) *n.*
1 One who doubts the truth of any particular philosophical or religious doctrine, scientific theory, etc. **2** One who habitually doubts or is temperamentally prone to doubting the truth of something affirmed: *He was such a skeptic that he would check for himself when told that the sun had risen.*—**skep′ti·cal** *adj.*

skit·tish (skit′ish) *adj.*
1 Easily frightened; nervous: *a skittish horse.* **2** Capricious; uncertain; unreliable: *She is too skittish to be trusted with an important assignment.*—**skit′tish·ly** *adv.*

slan·der (slan′dər) *n., v.*
n. **1** A false statement maliciously made to injure someone's reputation: *To say that he was a thief would be a slander.* **2** In law, an oral false statement causing damage to a person's reputation, means of livelihood, etc.
v. To utter a slander about someone.
Usage: *Slander* is spoken defamation, libel written.
Syn. *n.* **1** calumny, defamation, lie. *v.* defame.

slea·zy (slē′zē) *adj.* **slea·zi·er, slea·zi·est**
1 Lacking firmness of texture or poorly made; flimsy: *a sleazy coat.* **2** Cheap, shoddy, or run-down: *a sleazy neighborhood.*

sleek (slēk) *adj.*
Smooth and glossy; polished: *sleek hair.*—**sleek′ly** *adv.*

sloth (slōth) *n.*
1 Disinclination to exertion; habitual indolence; laziness: *Sloth is one of the seven deadly sins.* **2** A slow-moving, tree-dwelling mammal of tropical America that hangs upside down from branches and sleeps most of the day.

slough (slou) *n.*
1 A place of deep mud or mire; bog; swamp. **2** A state of moral depravity or despair.

slov·en (sluv′ən) *n.*
One who is careless of dress or untidy; one habitually untidy.—**slov′en·ly** *adj.*

slug·gard (slug′ərd) *n.*
Someone habitually lazy or idle.
Syn. idler, lazybones, drone.

sluice (sloos) *n.; v.* **sluiced, sluic·ing**
n. An artificial waterway equipped with a valve or gate for regulating the flow.
v. To drench or wash down with water: *to sluice a concrete floor.*

smug (smug) *adj.* **smug·ger, smug·gest**
Characterized by self-satisfaction or complacency: *a smug supporter of the best causes; a smug look.*—**smug'ly** *adv.*; **smug'ness** *n.*

so·bri·quet (sō'bri·kā) *n.*
A nickname.
Spelling tip: This word is also spelled *soubriquet.*

soc·cer (sok'ər) *n.*
A form of football in which the ball is kicked or struck with the body or head toward the opponent's goal.

so·ci·ol·o·gy (sō'sē·ol'ə·jē *or* sō'shē·ol'ə·jē) *n.*
The study of human society, dealing with crime, marriage, education, etc.—**so'ci·ol'o·gist** *n.*

sof·ten (sôf'ən *or* sof'ən) *v.*
To make or become soft or softer.

so·journ (*v.* sō'jûrn *or* sō·jûrn'; *n.* sō'jûrn) *v., n.*
v. To stay or dwell temporarily; live for a time.
n. A temporary residence or stay.—**so'journ·er** *n.*

sol·ace (sol'is) *n.; v.* **sol·aced, sol·ac·ing**
n. Comfort in grief, trouble, or calamity; also, that which supplies such comfort: *He found solace in reading.*
v. To comfort or cheer in trouble, grief, or calamity.
Syn. *v.* console.

sol·der (sod'ər) *n., v.*
n. A fusible metal or alloy used for joining metallic objects.
v. To unite or repair with solder.

sol·dier (sōl'jər) *n., v.*
n. 1 A person serving in an army, especially an enlisted man. 2 One who serves loyally in any cause.
v. To be a soldier: *He soldiered in the Thirty Years' War.*

sol·emn (sol'əm) *adj.*
1 Arousing grave or serious thought; impressive; awe-inspiring: *solemn music.* 2 Grave; serious; earnest: *a solemn face.* 3 Characterized by ceremonial observances; religious; sacred: *Good Friday is a solemn day for Christians.*—**sol'emn·ly** *adv.*

so·lic·it (sə·lis'it) *v.*
To ask or ask for earnestly: *to solicit money for a church.* **so·lic'i·ta'tion, so·lic'i·tor** *n.*

so·lil·o·quy (sə·lil'ə·kwē) *n., pl.* **so·lil·o·quies** *pl.*
1 A talking to oneself; monologue. 2 In a play, a speech made by an actor to reveal his thoughts to the audience but not to the other actors.

so·lo (sō'lō) *n.,* **so·los** *pl., adj., adv.; v.* **so·loed, so·lo·ing**
n. 1 A musical composition or passage for a single voice or instrument. 2 Any performance accomplished alone.
adj. 1 Composed or written for, or executed by, a single voice or instrument. 2 Done by a single person: *a solo flight.*
adv. Without another person; alone: *to fly solo.*
v. To fly an airplane alone, especially for the first time.—**so'lo·ist** *n.*

sol·u·ble (sol'yə·bəl) *adj.*
1 Capable of being dissolved in a liquid: *Sugar is soluble in water.* 2 Capable of being solved or explained: *a soluble problem.*

so·lu·tion (sə·lōō'shən) *n.*
1 A mixture formed by dissolving one or more substances in another: *a salt-and-water solution.* 2 The act or process of making such a mixture. 3 The act or process of solving a difficulty, doubt, problem, etc. 4 The answer to a problem.

sol·vent (sol'vənt) *adj., n.*
adj. 1 Having enough money to pay one's debts: *a solvent person.* 2 Having the power of dissolving: *Water is a solvent agent.*
n. A substance capable of dissolving other substances: *Water is a solvent of salt.*

som·bre·ro (som·brâr'ō) *n.,* **som·bre·ros** *pl.*
A broad-brimmed hat, usually of felt, much worn in Spain, Latin America, and the southwestern United States.

som·nam·bu·list (som·nam'byə·list) *n.*
A person who walks in his sleep.—**som·nam'bu·lism** *n.*

so·no·rous (sə·nôr'əs *or* son'ər·əs) *adj.*
1 Loud and full-sounding; resonant: *a sonorous voice.* 2 Impressive in quality, effect, style, etc.: *a sonorous speech.*—**so·no'rous·ly** *adv.*

soothe (sōōth) *v.* **soothed, sooth·ing**
1 To restore to a quiet or normal state; calm: *He soothed the restive cattle.* 2 To mitigate, soften, or relieve: *She tried to soothe his grief.*

soph·o·more (sof'ə·môr) *n.*
A second-year student of an American high school or college which has a four-year course.

so·po·rif·ic (sō'pə·rif'ik, sop'ə·rif'ik) *adj., n.*
adj. Causing or tending to cause sleep: *a soporific story.*
n. A medicine that produces sleep.

sot·to vo·ce (sot'ō vō'chē)
Softly; in an undertone.

souf·flé (sōō·flā') *n.*
A light, baked dish made fluffy with beaten egg whites combined with the yolks, and often having cheese, mushrooms, or other ingredients.

soup·çon (sōōp·sôn') *n.*
A minute quantity; a taste: *A soupçon of salt added to the soup made the difference.*
Spelling tip: The difficulty here is the *o* pronounced as *s.*

source (sôrs *or* sōrs) *n.*
1 The spring or fountain from which a stream of water proceeds. 2 A person or thing from which information is obtained or from which something originates.

sou·ve·nir (sōō'və·nir') *n.*
Something that is kept as a reminder of a person, place, or event.
Syn. memento, remembrance.

sov·er·eign (sov'rən) *n., adj.*
n. Monarch; ruler.
adj. 1 Having supreme authority or power: *a sovereign prince.* 2 Free; independent; not

limited by external authority: *a sovereign state.*—**sov′er·eign·ly** *adv.*

sov·er·eign·ty (sov′rən·tē) *n.*, **sov·er·eign·ties** *pl.*
1 Supreme power or authority. 2 A sovereign state or similar political entity. 3 The status or dominion of a sovereign.

span·gle (spang′gəl) *n.*; *v.* **span·gled, span·gling**
n. 1 A small bit of sparkling metal, plastic, etc., used for decoration, as in a theatrical costume. 2 Any small sparkling object.
v. To adorn with or as if with spangles.

spate (spāt) *n.*
A sudden or vigorous outpouring: *a spate of words; a spate of feeling.*

spawn (spôn) *n.*, *v.*
n. 1 The eggs of fishes, amphibians, mollusks, etc. 2 The offspring of any animal.
v. 1 To produce spawn. 2 To give rise to; originate: *criminals spawned in the ghettos of our cities.*

speak (spēk) *v.* **spoke, spo·ken, speak·ing**
1 To say words; talk. 2 To express or convey ideas, opinions, etc., in this way: *to speak one's mind.* 3 To make a speech. 4 To use or be capable of using a language in conversation: *She speaks French fluently.*

spe·cial·ty (spesh′əl·tē) *n.*, **spe·cial·ties** *pl.*
1 A special occupation, craft, or study: *Pediatrics is his specialty.* 2 The condition of being special or of having peculiar characteristics.

spe·cie (spē′shē) *n.*
Coined money; coin.

spec·i·men (spes′ə·mən) *n.*
One of a group, or a part of something, taken as a sample of the whole: *a specimen of fish; a specimen of blood.*

spe·cious (spē′shəs) *adj.*
Apparently good, right, or true, but actually not so: *specious reasoning.*

spec·tac·u·lar (spek·tak′yə·lər) *adj.*
adj. Displaying unusual, exciting, or unexpected qualities, conditions, etc.: *a spectacular rescue.*—**spec·tac′u·lar·ly** *adv.*

spec·ta·tor (spek′tā·tər) *n.*
A person who is present at and watches some action or event, as a show, game, etc., without taking part in it.
Syn. onlooker, bystander, observer.

speech (spēch) *n.*
1 The ability to express thought and emotion by spoken words; the power of speaking: *He lost his speech.* 2 The act of speaking. 3 That which is spoken, as conversation, a saying or remark, or a public address or talk. 4 A characteristic way of speaking: *His speech is loud and unpleasant.*

sphinx (sfingks) *n.*, **sphinx·es** or **sphin·ges** (sfin′jēz) *pl.*
1 In Egyptian mythology, a wingless monster with a lion's body and the head of a man, ram, or hawk. 2 In Greek mythology, a winged monster with a woman's head and a lion's body, who killed those unable to guess her riddle. 3 A statue of a sphinx.

spin·et (spin′it *or* spi·net′) *n.*
1 A small musical instrument like a harpsichord. 2 A low upright piano.

sponge (spunj) *n.*; *v.* **sponged, spong·ing**
n. 1 A simple water animal with a highly porous body which lives in colonies. 2 The skeleton of certain of these animals, used for bathing, washing, etc., because of its power to absorb liquids; also, some other substances so used.
v. 1 To wipe, wet, or clean with a sponge. 2 *Informal* To get something without cost at the expense of others.

spon·sor (spon′sər) *n.*
1 A person who makes himself responsible for another person or thing: *the sponsor of a new bill in the Senate.* 2 A godparent. 3 A business firm that assumes all or part of the costs of a radio or television program advertising its products.—**spon′sor·ship** *n.*

spo·rad·ic (spô·rad′ik) *adj.*
Occurring from time to time; occasional: *sporadic appearances; We received reports of sporadic fighting.*—**spo·rad′i·cal·ly** *adv.*

spor·tive (spôr′tiv) *adj.*
Relating to or fond of sport or play; frolicsome: *a sportive disposition.*—**spor′tive·ly** *adv.*
Syn. playful, merry, gay.

sprock·et (sprok′it) *n.*
1 A projection, as on the rim of a wheel, for engaging with the links of a chain. 2 A wheel bearing such projections.

spume (spyōōm) *n.*; *v.* **spumed, spum·ing**
n. Froth, as on an agitated or effervescing liquid; foam; scum.
v. To foam; froth.

spu·ri·ous (spyōōr′ē·əs) *adj.*
Not genuine; false; illegitimate: *a spurious painting.*

squab·ble (skwob′əl) *v.* **squab·bled, squab·bling;** *n.*
v. To have a petty argument or quarrel: *They squabbled occasionally, but it was nothing serious.*
n. A petty argument or quarrel.

squan·der (skwon′dər) *v.*
To spend money, time, etc., wastefully; dissipate: *He squandered away his entire fortune.*—**squan′der·er** *n.*

squir·rel (skwûr′əl) *n.*
A small tree-dwelling rodent having a long bushy tail and feeding chiefly on nuts.

sta·bi·lize (stā′bə·līz) *v.* **sta·bi·lized, sta·bi·liz·ing**
1 To make firm or stable. 2 To keep from changing or fluctuating: *to stabilize prices.* 3 To secure or maintain the equilibrium of a ship or aircraft by means of a stabilizer.

sta·bi·liz·er (stā′bə·lī′zər) *n.*
A device or construction serving to stabilize a ship or aircraft.

stac·ca·to (stə·kä′tō) *adj., adv., n.,* **stac·ca·tos**
pl.
adj. Having or producing silence through
most of the written time value of each musical
note; very short or detached.
adv. In a staccato manner: *Play that part
staccato.*
n. A staccato style or passage.

stag·nant (stag′nənt) *adj.*
1 Standing still; not flowing: *stagnant water;
stagnant air.* **2** Foul from standing still, as
water. **3** Dull; sluggish: *a stagnant mind.*—
stag′nant·ly *adv.*

staid (stād) *adj.*
Steady and sober; sedate; modest: *staid
behavior.*

sta·lac·tite (stə·lak′tīt) *n.*
A long, tapering formation hanging from the
roof of a cave, produced by continuous
watery deposits containing certain minerals,
especially calcium carbonate.

sta·lag·mite (stə·lag′mīt) *n.*
A column, usually cylindrical or conical, on
the floor of a cave, the counterpart of a
stalactite, often fusing with it.

stal·wart (stôl′wərt) *adj., n.*
adj. **1** Strong and brawny; robust. **2** Resolute;
determined; unwavering. **3** Brave; courageous: *a stalwart warrior.*
n. A stalwart person, as an uncompromising
partisan in politics.—**stal′wart·ly** *adv.*

stam·i·na (stam′ə·nə) *n.*
Physical or moral capacity to withstand
hardship or difficulty; vitality; vigor;
strength.

stan·chion (stan′shən) *n.*
An upright bar that forms the main support
of a window, roof, etc.

stat·ic (stat′ik) *adj., n.*
adj. **1** At rest; dormant; not active, moving,
or changing: *static clouds.* **2** Of or having to do
with forces in equilibrium or to bodies at rest.
n. A disturbance, as in radio or television reception, caused by atmospheric or manmade
electrical interference; also, the noise produced by this.

sta·tion·ar·y (stā′shən·er′ē) *adj.*
Remaining in one place; fixed: *stationary
equipment.*
Usage: Do not confuse this word, which is an
adjective, with *stationery.*

sta·tion·er·y (stā′shən·er′ē) *n.*
Writing paper and envelopes; also, material
used in writing, as pens, pencils, etc.

sta·tis·tics (stə·tis′tiks) *n.pl.*
1 The science of collecting, classifying, and
tabulating numerical facts in order to use
them as a basis to obtain information about
some subject. **2** The numerical facts or the
information obtained: *Statistics show that air
fatalities are fewer than auto fatalities.*

stat·ue (stach′ōō) *n.*
A representation, as of a person or animal, in
marble, bronze, etc.

stat·ure (stach′ər) *n.*
1 Height, as of a person: *Although he was
slight in stature, he was very strong.* **2** Development; growth: *moral stature.*

sta·tus (stā′təs *or* stat′əs) *n.*
1 State, condition, or relation: *The status of
the economy is bad.* **2** Relative position or
rank.

sta·tus quo (stā′təs kwō *or* stat′əs kwō)
The state of affairs existing at a specified
time: *to maintain the status quo.*

stein (stīn) *n.*
A beer mug, as of earthenware.

stel·lar (stel′ər) *adj.*
1 Of or pertaining to the stars: *the silvery
stellar glow of summer skies.* **2** Of or pertaining to a prominent actor or actress or other
person in the arts: *a stellar role in a movie.*
Syn. 1 astral, starry. 2 star, leading, famous.

sten·cil (sten′səl) *n.; v.* **sten·ciled** *or* **sten·**
cilled, sten·cil·ing *or* **sten·cil·ling**
n. **1** A sheet, usually of paper, in which a
pattern is cut by means of spaces or dots,
through which applied paint or ink pene-
trates to a surface beneath: *to cut the outline
of a flower into a stencil.* **2** A decoration or the
like produced by the use of a stencil.
v. To mark with a stencil.

ste·nog·ra·phy (stə·nog′rə·fē) *n.*
The art of writing by the use of contractions
or arbitrary symbols; shorthand; also, the
transcription of shorthand notes.—**ste·nog′-**
ra·pher *n.;* **sten·o·graph·ic** (sten′ə·graf′ik)
adj.; **sten′o·graph′i·cal·ly** *adv.*

sten·to·ri·an (sten·tôr′ē·ən *or* sten·tō′rē·ən)
adj.
Extremely loud: *the drill sergeant's stentorian
voice.*
Syn. deafening, thunderous.
Ant. soft, low, weak.

ste·ve·dore (stē′və·dôr) *n.*
A person whose occupation is loading and
unloading cargoes of ships in port: *The
stevedores unloaded the cargo of machinery.*
Syn. longshoreman.

stig·ma (stig′mə) *n.,* **stig·mas** *or* **stig·ma·ta**
(stig·mä′tə *or* stig′mə·tə) *pl.*
1 A mark of disgrace or shame: *the stigma
of having been in prison.* **2** The wounds that
Christ received during the Passion and
Crucifixion; also, marks on the body corresponding to those wounds, said to be miraculously impressed on certain persons.

sti·let·to (sti·let′ō) *n.,* **sti·let·tos** *or* **sti·let·toes**
pl.
1 A small dagger with a slender blade. **2** A
small, sharp-pointed instrument used to
puncture eyelets in cloth that is to be em-
broidered.

stim·u·lant (stim′yə·lənt) *n.*
1 Something that increases or speeds up
activity of the body, as a drug: *Caffeine is a
general stimulant; a cardiac stimulant.* **2** An
alcoholic beverage.

stim·u·lus (stim′yə·ləs) *n.*, **stim·u·li** (stim′yə· lī) *pl.*
1 Anything that produces a response in some part of the body: *Pavlov's dog responded to the stimulus of the bell by drooling.* 2 Anything that rouses the mind or spirits; incentive: *Ambition is the stimulus that makes him work so hard.*

stint (stint) *v., n.*
v. To limit the amount or share of; to be stingy with: *Don't stint yourself.*
n. A task or fixed amount of work to be performed or a period of time spent doing a task or kind of work: *his stint in the army.*—**stint′ing·ly** *adv.*
Syn. *v.* skimp, grudge, deny. *n.* job.
Ant. *v.* indulge, pamper, surfeit.

sti·pend (stī′pend) *n.*
A regular, fixed allowance, salary, or pension.

stir·rup (stûr′əp *or* stir′əp) *n.*
An inverted, U-shaped piece of metal, leather, or wood with a flat footpiece, suspended from a horse's saddle to support the rider's foot.

sto·gy (stō′gē) *n.*, **sto·gies** *pl.*
A long, slender, inexpensive cigar: *to smoke a stogy.*
Spelling tip: This word is also spelled *stogie* or *stogey.*

stol·id (stol′id) *adj.*
Having or showing little or no emotion or sensitivity: *a dull, stolid man.*—**stol′id·ly** *adv.*; **sto·lid′i·ty, stol′id·ness** *n.*
Syn. phlegmatic, unresponsive, insensitive.
Ant. passionate, intense, volatile.

stop (stop) *v.* **stopped, stop·ping;** *n.*
v. 1 To come to a halt or make something come to a halt; to cease or arrest motion or progress: *He stopped to rest; The bus stopped; to stop a car.* 2 To cease doing something; quit: *to stop talking.* 3 To prevent the doing or completion of: *to stop a revolution.*
n. 1 A place where something stops: *a bus stop.* 2 The act or state of stopping.
Syn. *v.* 2 discontinue. 3 end, arrest. *n.* 1 terminus. 2 end, pause, standstill, termination.

strait (strāt) *n.*
1 A narrow passage of water connecting two larger bodies of water: *The Strait of Magellan across South America connects the Atlantic and Pacific.* 2 (*often pl.*) A position of difficulty or distress: *to be in financial straits.*
Syn. 2 predicament, jam, plight.

strat·a·gem (strat′ə·jəm) *n.*
A trick or ruse to win a battle, outwit an opponent, or obtain something by misleading or deceiving; a crafty maneuver: *a stratagem to lure the enemy troops into an ambush.*
Syn. wile, subterfuge, dodge.

stra·tum (strā′təm *or* strat′əm) *n.*, **stra·ta** (strā′tə *or* strat′ə) *or* **stra·tums** *pl.*
A layer, bed, or level: *a stratum of prehistoric remains; the lower strata of society.*

strength·en (strengk′thən *or* streng′thən) *v.*
To make or become strong or stronger: *The enemy strengthened their defense.*

stren·u·ous (stren′yoo·əs) *adj.*
Requiring strong effort or exertion: *strenuous exercise.*—**stren′u·ous·ly** *adv.*; **stren′u·ous·ness** *n.*
Syn. arduous, laborious.
Ant. easy, simple, light.

stri·at·ed (strī′āt·əd) *adj.*
Having stripes or parallel grooves resembling stripes: *a striated surface; striated muscle tissue.*—**stri′ate** *v.*; **stri·a′tion** *n.*
Syn. striped, veined, furrowed, streaked.

strict (strikt) *adj.*
1 Enforcing or observing harsh rules or absolute obedience to rules: *a strict disciplinarian; a strict curfew.* 2 Exact, complete, or precise: *the strict truth; strict secrecy; in the strict sense of the word.*—**strict′ly** *adv.*; **strict′ness** *n.*

stri·dent (strīd′nt *or* strīd′ənt) *adj.*
Having or making a high, harsh sound; shrill and grating: *the fishwife's strident voice.*—**stri′den·cy** *n.*; **stri′dent·ly** *adv.*
Syn. rasping, jarring.
Ant. soft, sweet, modulated.

strik·ing (strī′king) *adj.*
Compelling attention; eye-catching and impressive: *a striking woman.*—**strik′ing·ly** *adv.*
Syn. outstanding, arresting, imposing.
Ant. inconspicuous, indiscernible.

strych·nine (strik′nin *or* strik′nēn) *n.*
An extremely poisonous drug used in small doses as a stimulant or tonic.
Spelling tip: This word is also spelled *strychnin.*

stul·ti·fy (stul′tə·fī) *v.* **stul·ti·fied, stul·ti·fy·ing**
To make worthless or ineffectual; frustrate; invalidate: *The system tends to stultify our efforts to effect changes.*
Syn. nullify, blunt, dull, paralyze.
Ant. vitalize, stir, enliven.

stu·pe·fy (stoo′pə·fī *or* styoo′pə·fī) *v.* **stu·pe·fied, stu·pe·fy·ing**
To dull the senses or faculties of; stun: *to be stupefied by a blow.*—**stu′pe·fac′tion** *n.*
Syn. daze, bewilder, flabbergast.
Ant. sensitize, alert.

sty·lus (stī′ləs) *n.*, **sty·lus·es** (stī′ləs·iz) *or* **sty·li** (stī′lī) *pl.*
1 A pointed instrument for marking or engraving, as on carbons, stencils, etc.: *to cut lines into a stencil with a stylus.* 2 A phonograph needle.

sty·mie (stī′mē) *v.* **sty·mied, sty·my·ing**
To block or baffle: *The problem had him stymied.*
Spelling tip: This word is also spelled *stymy.*
Syn. thwart, frustrate.
Ant. help, assist, advance.

suave (swäv) *adj.*
Having a smooth, urbane manner; pleasantly polite: *the tactfulness of a suave diplomat.*—**suave′ly** *adv.*; **suave′ness, suav′i·ty** *n.*

sub·ju·gate (sub′joo·gāt) *v.* **sub·ju·gat·ed, sub·ju·gat·ing**
1 To impose rule or dominion over; conquer;

subdue: *Rome subjugated much of the ancient world.* 2 To bring under control in any way: *to subjugate one's feelings.*—**sub'ju·ga'tion, sub'ju·ga'tor** *n.*

sub·stance (sub'stəns) *n.*
1 The material of which anything is made or consists. 2 A substantial quality; solidity: *His ideas have substance.* 3 The essential part of anything said or written: *the substance of a speech.*

suc·ces·sor (sək·ses'ər) *n.*
A person or thing that comes after another; especially, a person who succeeds to a throne, property, or office.

suc·cinct (sək·singkt') *adj.*
Avoiding unnecessary words; briefly expressed: *He gave his views in a few succinct sentences.*—**suc·cinct'ly** *adv.*
Spelling tip: *Succinct* has three *c*'s.
Syn. terse, concise, laconic.
Ant. prolix, verbose, long-winded.

suc·cor (suk'ər) *n., v.*
n. Help or relief rendered in danger, difficulty, or distress.
v. To come to the help of; give succor.
Syn. *n.* aid, rescue, *v.* support.

suc·cumb (sə·kum') *v.*
1 To be overcome by force or persuasion; yield: *Poland succumbed under the might of Germany and Russia; Don't succumb to temptation.* 2 To die.

suede (swād) *n.*
A leather having a soft, velvetlike nap.
Spelling tip: This word is also spelled *suède.*

suf·fice (sə·fīs') *v.* **suf·ficed, suf·fic·ing**
To be sufficient or adequate; to meet the requirements or answer the purpose: *Two chickens will suffice if there are no more to be had.*

suf·fi·cient (sə·fish'ənt) *adj.*
Being all that is necessary for a particular purpose; adequate: *That is more than sufficient.*—**suf·fi'cient·ly** *adv.*
Syn. enough, satisfactory.

suf·frage (suf'rij) *n.*
1 The right to vote: *There was great resistance to woman suffrage.* 2 The vote in support of some measure or candidate: *The voters gave their suffrages to the proposal.*

suf·fuse (sə·fyōōz') *v.* **suf·fused, suf·fus·ing**
To spread over, as with a vapor, fluid, or color: *A blush suffused her cheeks; A lovely aroma suffused the room.*

sug·ar (shŏŏg'ər) *n., v.*
n. A sweet, crystalline substance obtained from the juice of various plants, especially the sugar cane and sugar beet.
v. 1 To form or produce sugar. 2 To sweeten or make agreeable.

su·i·ci·dal (sōō'ə·sīd'l) *adj.*
1 Of, having to do with, or leading to self-destruction: *The attempt to climb the mountain was suicidal.* 2 Fatal to one's prospects or interests; ruinous: *a suicidal political gesture.*

suit (sōōt) *n., v.*
n. 1 A matched set of garments consisting of a coat and trousers or skirt of the same material: *a tweed suit.* 2 A garment for a particular purpose: *a space suit.* 3 Any of the four sets of playing cards that make up a pack. 4 A proceeding in a court of law to settle a claim. 5 The courting of a woman.
v. To meet the requirements of; satisfy: *It suits all tastes; Suit yourself.* 2 To make appropriate; adapt: *Suit the action to the word.*

sul·ly (sul'ē) *v.* **sul·lied, sul·ly·ing**
To make soiled or tarnished; besmirch; defile: *I will not sully my lips with such words.*

sul·try (sul'trē) *adj.* **sul·tri·er, sul·tri·est**
1 Hot, moist, and still; close; oppressive: *sultry August days.* 2 Showing or suggesting passion; sensual: *sultry charms.*

sum·ma·rize (sum'ə·rīz) *v.* **sum·ma·rized, sum·ma·riz·ing**
To make a summary of; sum up: *He summarized his arguments in one sentence.*

sum·ma·ry (sum'ər·ē) *adj.; n.,* **sum·ma·ries** *pl.*
adj. 1 Dispensing with details or formalities; done with dispatch: *Summary justice is often a euphemism for lynching.* 2 Concise: *a summary account of the proceedings.*
n. Brief account; abridgment or abstract: *The onlooker gave a summary of what had happened.*—**sum·ma'ri·ly** *adv.*

sum·ma·tion (sum·ā'shən) *n.*
1 Addition. 2 A speech or portion of a speech summing up the principal points made, especially in a court of law.

sump·tu·ous (sump'chōō·əs) *adj.*
Involving lavish expenditure; luxurious; magnificent: *Our host provided a sumptuous feast.*
Syn. rich, costly.
Ant. frugal, simple, plain.

sun·dry (sun'drē) *adj.*
Of an indefinite small number; various; miscellaneous: *sundry expenditures.*
Syn. divers, several.

su·per·an·nu·at·ed (sōō'pər·an'yōō·ā'tid) *adj.*
1 Retired on account of age, especially with a pension: *Although superannuated, he still had influence in the firm.* 2 Too old to be useful or efficient: *superannuated men trying to find work.* 3 Obsolete; outdated: *superannuated equipment.*

su·per·cil·i·ous (sōō'pər·sil'ē·əs) *adj.*
Exhibiting contempt; arrogant: *His supercilious behavior offended his host.*
Etymology: *Supercilious* comes from the Latin word meaning eyebrow suggesting the raising of eyebrows by the *supercilious.*

su·per·fi·cial (sōō'pər·fish'əl) *adj.*
1 On, near, or affecting the surface only: *a superficial wound.* 2 Lacking depth or profundity; shallow: *a superficial person; a superficial writer.* 3 Marked by partial knowledge; slight; cursory: *a superficial analysis.*—**su·per·fi'cial·ly** *adv.*

su·per·flu·i·ty (sōō'pər·flōō'ə·tē) *n.*
1 An unnecessary thing. 2 Excess.

su·per·flu·ous (sŏō·pûr'flŏō·əs) *adj.*
More than is needed; redundant; needless: *burning superfluous corn; a superfluous question.*

su·per·im·pose (sŏō'pər·im·pōz') *v.* **su·per·im·posed, su·per·im·pos·ing**
To lay or impose upon something else: *He had superimposed his own touches on the painting.*—**su'per·im'po·si'tion** *n.*

su·per·in·ten·dent (sŏō'pər·in·ten'dənt) *n.*
1 A person whose function is to direct, manage, or supervise some particular work, organization, etc. 2 A janitor.

su·per·nu·mer·ar·y (sŏō'pər·nŏō'mə·rer'ē) *n.*, **su·per·nu·mer·ar·ies** *pl.*; *adj.*
n. 1 An extra person or thing. 2 An actor playing in crowd scenes.
adj. Being beyond a customary or necessary number; superfluous.

su·per·vise (sŏō'pər·vīz) *v.* **su·per·vised, su·per·vis·ing**
To have charge of directing employees, a project, etc.; superintend; oversee.

su·per·vi·sor (sŏō'pər·vī'zər) *n.*
A person who supervises or oversees; superintendent; inspector.—**su'per·vi'so·ry** *adj.*

su·pine (sŏō'pīn) *adj.*
1 Lying on the back with face turned upward: *The boxer lay supine as he was counted out.* 2 Having no interest or stamina: *The country was supine under the invader.*

sup·ple (sup'əl) *adj.* **sup·pler, sup·plest**
1 Easily bent; pliant; flexible: *a supple bow; boots made of supple leather.* 2 Readily adaptable; elastic: *a supple but strong intelligence.*—**sup'ple·ly** *adv.*
Ant. 2 rigid, narrow, fixed.

sup·ple·ment (*v.* sup'lə·ment; *n.* sup'lə·mənt) *v.*, *n.*
v. To make additions to: *You can supplement the rations with a bar of chocolate.*
n. Something that supplements, as an addition to a publication: *The article appeared in the Sunday supplement.*

sup·pli·cate (sup'lə·kāt) *v.* **sup·pli·cat·ed, sup·pli·cat·ing**
To ask for humbly or by earnest prayer or entreaty: *to supplicate mercy.*—**sup'pli·ca'tion** *n.*
Syn. entreat, beseech, implore.

sup·pose (sə·pōz') *v.* **sup·posed, sup·pos·ing**
1 To take for granted; assume; believe to be true; presume: *I suppose they are right; He supposed that the earth was flat.* 2 To assume for the sake of argument: *Suppose it isn't so?* 3 To expect or require: *She is supposed to make the beds.*

sup·press (sə·pres') *v.*
1 To put down; quell; crush: *to suppress a rebellion.* 2 To restrain; keep in; repress: *to suppress a yawn.* 3 To stop or prevent publication of: *to suppress a news story.*

sur·feit (sûr'fit) *v.*, *n.*
v. To feed or supply with too much of something; satiate: *surfeited with crackers.*

n. An excessive supply of anything: *a story with a surfeit of detail.*

sur·geon (sûr'jən) *n.*
A doctor who specializes in surgery.

sur·ly (sûr'lē) *adj.* **sur·li·er, sur·li·est**
Bad-tempered; rude; gruff: *a surly reply; a surly expression on his face.*—**sur'li·ly** *adv.*; **sur'li·ness** *n.*
Syn. crabbed, cross, churlish.

sur·mise (sûr·mīz') *v.* **sur·mised, sur·mis·ing;** *n.*
v. To make a doubtful supposition or conjecture; guess: *I surmised that she had been talking about me.*
n. 1 A thought or idea based on slight evidence; suspicion; guess: *It was a reasonable surmise that they were not going to buy the house.* 2 The act of surmising: *Surmise is no substitute for evidence.*

sur·plice (sûr'plis) *n.*
A loose white vestment worn over a cassock in many churches: *the choirboys in their surplices.*

sur·plus (sûr'plus) *n.*
An amount or quantity above that required for a particular purpose; excess: *The surplus will be given to charity.*

sur·rep·ti·tious (sûr'əp·tish'əs) *adj.*
Done or acting secretly; underhand; clandestine: *a surreptitious meeting.*—**sur'rep·ti'tious·ly** *adv.*
Syn. secret, furtive.
Ant. open, straightforward, plain.

sur·ro·gate (sûr'ə·gāt) *n.*
1 A substitute; deputy: *The cat became a surrogate for the puppies' mother.* 2 A judge of a court handling the probating of wills.

sur·round (sə·round') *v.*
To enclose; encircle: *The house was surrounded by open fields.*
Syn. encompass, environ.

sur·veil·lance (sər·vā'ləns) *n.*
Close watch kept over someone, as a prisoner or suspect; observation: *The suspected shoplifter was kept under surveillance.*

sus·pense (sə·spens') *n.*
An uncertain or doubtful situation or condition: *The movie had plenty of suspense.*—**sus·pense'ful** *adj.*

sus·pi·cious (sə·spish'əs) *adj.*
1 Inclined to suspect: *a suspicious man.* 2 Apt to arouse suspicion; questionable: *a suspicious move.* 3 Indicating suspicion: *a suspicious expression.*—**sus·pi'cious·ly** *adv.*

sus·te·nance (sus'tə·nəns) *n.*
Something that supports life or strength; food.
Syn. nourishment.

svelte (svelt) *adj.*
Slender; slim; willowy: *a svelte figure.*

swath (swoth) *n.*
A line or ridge of grass, grain, etc., as cut down by a mowing device.

swathe (swāᵺ) *v.* **swathed, swath·ing**
To bind or wrap, as in bandages: *to swathe a child in a blanket.*

swel·ter (swel'tər) *v.*
To suffer from oppressive heat; perspire; sweat.

syc·o·phant (sik'ə·fənt) *n.*
A person who uses flattery to gain favor; parasite.
Syn. toady.

syl·la·ble (sil'ə·bəl) *n.*
A word or part of a word that can be uttered by a single vocal effort: *The word "syllable" has three syllables.*

syl·la·bus (sil'ə·bəs) *n.,* **syl·la·bus·es** or **syl·la·bi** (sil'ə·bī) *pl.*
A brief summary of the main points of a course of study, subject, etc.

sym·bol (sim'bəl) *n.*
An emblem or sign representing something else: *The flag is a symbol of our country.*

sym·pho·ny (sim'fə·ne) *n.,* **sym·pho·nies** *pl.*
1 A composition for an orchestra, consisting usually of four movements. 2 A symphony orchestra. 3 An agreeable blend of sounds, colors, etc.: *a symphony in gray.*

sym·po·si·um (sim·pō'zē·əm) *n.,* **sym·po·si·ums** or **sym·po·si·a** (sim·pō'zē·ə) *pl.*
1 A meeting to discuss a particular subject. 2 A collection of comments or opinions on the same subject, as in a magazine.

symp·tom (sim'təm) *n.*
A sign, token, or indication of the existence of something, especially, an indication of the presence of disease.

syn·chro·nous (sin'krə·nəs) *adj.*
Occurring or moving at the same time or speed; coincident; simultaneous: *synchronous heartbeats.*

syn·od (sin'əd) *n.*
A regional church council called together to discuss matters of church doctrine and discipline.

syn·o·nym (sin'ə·nim) *n.*
A word that has the same or almost the same meaning as some other.

sy·non·y·mous (si·non'ə·məs) *adj.*
Equivalent or similar in meaning.—**sy·non'y·my** *n.*

syn·the·sis (sin'thə·sis) *n.,* **syn·the·ses** (sin'·thə·sēz) *pl.*
The assembling of separate parts into a whole.

syr·inge (sə·rinj') *n.; v.* **syr·inged, syr·ing·ing**
n. A device consisting of a narrow tube with a rubber bulb at one end into which a liquid may be drawn for ejection in a fine stream.
v. To cleanse or treat with a syringe.

T

tab·leau (tab'lō *or* ta·blō') *n.,* **tab·leaux** (tab'·lōz *or* tab'lō) or **tab·leaus** (tab'lōz) *pl.*
1 Any picture or scene. 2 A picturelike scene represented by silent and motionless persons standing in appropriate attitudes.

tac·it (tas'it) *adj.*
Not expressed but understood: *a tacit warning.*—**tac'it·ly** *adv.*
Syn. silent, implied, implicit.

tac·i·turn (tas'ə·tûrn) *adj.*
Habitually silent or reserved; disinclined to conversation.—**tac'i·tur'ni·ty** *n.;* **tac'i·turn·ly** *adv.*
Syn. uncommunicative.
Ant. communicative, talkative.

tac·tics (tak'tiks) *n.pl.*
1 (*Construed as singular*) The science and art of moving and handling troops in the presence of the enemy or for immediate objectives: *Tactics is a subject taught at West Point.*
2 Any means to gain an objective; methods: *He got his way by clever tactics.*—**tac'ti·cal** *adj.*

tac·tile (tak'til *or* tak'təl) *adj.*
Pertaining to the organs or sense of touch: *a tactile impression.*

tai·lor (tā'lər) *n., v.*
n. A person who makes garments to order or who repairs garments.
v. 1 To work at or make by tailoring: *to tailor a coat.* 2 To make, adjust, or adapt for a specific purpose: *The large-type, fully illustrated book was tailored for children.*
Spelling tip: Watch the *or* ending.

tal·is·man (tal'is·mən) *n.,* **tal·is·mans** *pl.*
Something supposed to produce extraordinary effects; a charm: *She said she wasn't superstitious, but she wore his class pin as a talisman while he was in the army.*
Syn. amulet, fetish.

tal·on (tal'ən) *n.*
The claw of a bird or other animal, especially of a bird of prey.

tan·gi·ble (tan'jə·bəl) *adj.*
1 Perceptible by touch; also, within reach by touch. 2 Definite; real; clear: *tangible results.*
Syn. 1 palpable, tactile.

tan·ta·lize (tan'tə·līz) *v.* **tan·ta·lized, tan·ta·liz·ing**
To tease or torment by showing something desired that is kept out of reach.

tan·ta·mount (tan'tə·mount) *adj.*
Having equivalent value, effect, or import; equivalent: *His decision not to defend himself is tantamount to his political suicide.*

tan·trum (tan'trəm) *n.*
A fit of rage or bad temper: *His tantrums are very childish.*

tap·es·try (tap'is·trē) *n.,* **tap·es·tries** *pl.*
An ornamental fabric used for hangings, with designs and pictures woven into it.

ta·ran·tu·la (tə·ran'chŏŏ·lə) *n.,* **ta·ran·tu·las** or **ta·ran·tu·lae** (tə·ran'chŏŏ·lē) *pl.*
A large, somewhat poisonous hairy spider of southern Europe.

tar·iff (tar'if) *n.*
1 A schedule of articles of merchandise with the rates of duty to be paid for their importation or exportation. 2 A duty, or duties collectively.
Spelling tip: Watch the double *f* and single *r*.

tar·pau·lin (tär·pô′lin *or* tär′pə·lin) *n.*
A waterproof canvas used to cover merchandise, athletic fields, etc.

tas·sel (tas′əl) *n.*; *v.* **tas·seled** *or* **tas·selled,
tas·sel·ing** *or* **tas·sel·ling**
n. A dangling ornament for curtains, cushions, etc., consisting of a tuft of loose threads or cords, or any similar object.
v. To provide or adorn with tassels.

tat·too (ta·tōō′) *v.*; *n.*, **tat·toos** *pl.*
v. To mark the skin with designs, etc., by pricking it and inserting indelible pigments.
n. A pattern or picture so made.

taw·dry (tô′drē) *adj.*
Showy and cheap: *tawdry costume jewelry from the dime store.*
Syn. gaudy, garish, flashy.

tech·nique (tek·nēk′) *n.*
A method, way, or manner of doing something: *new surgical techniques for heart transplants.*

tech·nol·o·gy (tek·nol′ə·jē) *n.*, **tech·nol·o·gies** *pl.*
The practical application of scientific knowledge and industrial skills: *There has been great progress in medical technology.*—**tech·no·log·i·cal** (tek′nə·loj′i·kəl) *adj.*

te·di·um (tē′dē·əm) *n.*
Boredom: *There was little to relieve the tedium of his lonely days.*—**te′di·ous** *adj.*; **te′di·ous·ly** *adv.*; **te′di·ous·ness** *n.*

te·mer·i·ty (tə·mer′ə·tē) *n.*
Foolish boldness; rashness: *The freshman had the temerity to question the dean's authority.*

tem·per·a·ment (tem′pər·ə·mənt *or* tem′prə·mənt) *n.*
A person's mental and emotional make-up: *He has a placid temperament and is not easily upset.*
Syn. disposition.

tem·po (tem′pō) *n.*, **tem·pos** *or* **tem·pi** (tem′·pī) *pl.*
1 *In music* Rate of speed: *This music should be played in a faster tempo.* **2** Pace: *the fast tempo of a big city.*

tem·po·rize (tem′pə·rīz) *v.* **tem·po·rized, tem·po·riz·ing**
To act or talk evasively so as to gain time or postpone making a decision: *The candidate was advised to temporize until more facts were available.*

ten·den·cy (ten′dən·sē) *n.*, **ten·den·cies** *pl.*
A leaning or inclination: *She has a tendency to gain weight during her vacations.*

ten·et (ten′it) *n.*
An opinion, doctrine, or principle accepted as true: *Respect for the rights of others is a tenet of most religions.*

ten·u·ous (ten′yōō·əs) *adj.*
Flimsy or delicate: *The old man retained a tenuous hold on life.*—**ten′u·ous·ly** *adv.*; **ten′·u·ous·ness** *n.*

tep·id (tep′id) *adj.*
Slightly warm; lukewarm: *a tepid bath.*—**tep′·id·ly** *adv.*; **tep′id·ness** *n.*

ter·ma·gant (tûr′mə·gənt) *n.*
A scolding or abusive woman: *His wife is a merciless termagant.*
Syn. shrew.

ter·mi·nate (tûr′mə·nāt) *v.* **ter·mi·nat·ed, ter·mi·nat·ing**
To end or bound.—**ter′mi·na′tion** *n.*

ter·mi·nol·o·gy (tûr′mə·nol′ə·jē) *n.*, **ter·mi·nol·o·gies** *pl.*
The technical terms used in science, art, trade, etc.: *It was difficult to understand the legal terminology.*

ter·rain (tə·rān′) *n.*
An area of land: *The rocky terrain surrounding the camp was barren and forbidding.*
Syn. territory, region.

terse (tûrs) *adj.* **ter·ser, ter·sest**
Short and to the point; concise: *a terse comment.*
Syn. pithy, succinct.
Ant. diffuse, wordy.

tes·ta·tor (tes·tā′tər) *n.*
Someone who makes a will or dies leaving a will.

tes·ty (tes′tē) *adj.* **tes·ti·er, tes·ti·est**
Irritable in manner or disposition; touchy: *The testy attitude of the guard discouraged us.*—**tes′ti·ly** *adv.*; **tes′ti·ness** *n.*

teth·er (teth′ər) *n.*, *v.*
n. A rope, etc., used for fastening an animal and keeping it within a defined area.
v. To fasten or confine by a tether.
Usage: The phrase *at the end of one's tether* means at the end of one's resources, patience, etc.

the·a·ter (thē·ə·tər) *n.*
1 A building or place adapted for the showing of plays, motion pictures, etc. **2** Any place or region that is the scene of events: *a theater of war.*
Spelling tip: This word is sometimes spelled, especially in Britain, *theatre.*

then (then) *adv.*
1 At that time: *I didn't know your name then.* **2** Soon or immediately afterward; next in space or time: *She looked at the window and then went away.* **3** In that case: *I will then, since you won't.* **4** Also; besides: *We have to buy food, and then there is the rent to pay.*

ther·a·peu·tic (ther′ə·pyōō′tik) *adj.*
Having healing properties; curative: *The sea air is therapeutic.*

ther·a·py (ther′ə·pē) *n.*, **ther·a·pies** *pl.*
The treatment of a disease or undesirable condition.

there·fore (thâr′for′ *or* thâr′fōr′) *adv.*, *conj.*
For that or this reason; on that ground or account; consequently: *He did not run fast enough, and therefore he lost the race.*
Syn. hence, accordingly, so.

ther·mo·nu·cle·ar (thûr′mō·nōō′klē·ər) *adj.*
Pertaining to or characterized by reactions involving the fusion of atomic nuclei at very high temperatures.

the·sau·rus (thə·sôr'əs) *n.*, **the·sau·ri** (thə·sôr'ī) *pl.*
A book containing a store of words; especially, a book of synonyms and antonyms arranged in categories.
Etymology: *Thesaurus* comes, through Latin, from the Greek *thesauros*, meaning treasure house, which is also the ultimate source of the word *treasure*.

the·sis (thē·sis) *n.*, **the·ses** (thē'sēz) *pl.*
1 A proposition to be maintained, especially by formal argument: *The thesis that all men are equal.* 2 A formal treatise on a particular subject, especially one presented to obtain a university degree.

though (thō) *conj.*
1 Notwithstanding the fact that: *Though it is windy, it is warm.* 2 Even if. 3 And yet (introducing a modifying statement added as an afterthought).

thought·ful (thôt'fəl) *adj.*
1 Full of thought, meditative: *a thoughtful expression.* 2 Attentive; considerate: *She is thoughtful of her friends.*—**thought'ful·ly** *adv.*, **thought'ful·ness** *n.*

thresh·old (thresh'ōld *or* thresh'hōld) *n.*
1 A plank or stone lying under the door of a building; doorsill: *He carried his bride across the threshold.* 2 The entrance or beginning of anything: *at the threshold of a new era.*

throes (thrōz) *n.pl.*
1 Violent pangs, especially of childbirth or death: *She suffered the throes of a painful delivery.* 2 Any violent or agonizing activity: *in the throes of revolution.*

through (thrōō) *prep., adv., adj.*
prep. 1 Into one side, end, or point, and out another: *a bullet through the heart.* 2 By means of: *I got the tickets through a friend.* 3 During the time or period of: *all through his life.*
adv. 1 To a termination or conclusion, especially a successful one: *to pull through.*
adj. Going from beginning to end without a stop or obstruction: *a through train.*

thwart (thwôrt) *v.*
To prevent someone from accomplishing something; frustrate: *He made it his business to thwart them.*
Syn. cross, foil, balk.

thy·roid (thī'roid) *n.*
A large gland situated in front of and on each side of the trachea (windpipe).

ti·ar·a (tē·är'ə) *n.*
1 An ornamental semicircular band of jewels, worn on the head by women. 2 The Pope's triple crown, worn on special occasions.

tim·bre (tim'bər *or* tam'bər) *n.*
The quality of a sound, apart from its pitch or intensity, that distinguishes it from another sound; tone color.
Spelling tip: Don't confuse timbre and timber (lumber).

ti·rade (tī·rād') *n.*
A long vehement speech, especially of censure: *Castro's three-hour tirade against the U.S.*

tis·sue (tish'ōō) *n.*
1 The substance of animal and plant organs formed by cells and cell-products: *The surgeon removed some bone tissue.* 2 A light or gauzy fabric. 3 A connected or interwoven series; network: *a tissue of lies.* 4 A light, absorbent paper, usually consisting of two or more layers, used to make disposable towels or handkerchiefs.

tit·u·lar (tich'ōō·lər *or* tit'yə·lər) *adj.*
1 Existing only in name: *the titular head of a political party.* 2 Of or having to do with a title.

to·geth·er (tōō·geth'ər *or* tə·geth'ər) *adv.*
1 Into union or contact with one another: *to gather together.* 2 In company or conjunction: *to live together.* 3 At the same time; simultaneously: *They answered together.* 4 In or into harmony or agreement: *The blue sofa and tan chairs go well together.*

tol·er·ance (tol'ər·əns) *n.*
1 Indulgence or forbearance in judging the opinions, customs, or acts of others; freedom from bigotry or from racial or religious prejudice. 2 The ability to endure large or increasing amounts of a drug or poison without ill effects.

tol·er·ant (tol'ər·ənt) *adj.*
Showing or having tolerance: *a tolerant attitude.*—**tol'er·ant·ly** *adv.*

tomb (tōōm) *n.*
A place or structure for the burial of the dead, as a vault, sepulcher, or grave.

to·mor·row (tə·môr'ō) *adv., n.*
adv. On or for the next day after today: *I will see you tomorrow.*
n. The next day after today: *Tomorrow is another day.*
Spelling tip: *Tomorrow* may be spelled with a hyphen: *to-morrow.*

to·night (tə·nīt') *adv., n.*
adv. In or during the present or coming night.
n. The present or coming night.
Spelling tip: *Tonight* may also be spelled with a hyphen: *to-night.*

ton·sil·li·tis (ton'sə·lī'tis) *n.*
Inflammation of the tonsils. **ton'sil·li'tic** *adj.*

too (tōō) *adv.*
1 In addition; likewise; also: *Are you going too?* 2 In excessive quantity or degree: *too good to be true.*

to·pog·ra·phy (tə·pog'rə·fē) *n.*, **to·pog·ra·phies** *pl.*
1 The physical features of a place, as the mountains, rivers, parks, etc. 2 The art of representing on a map the physical features of a place. **top·o·graph·ic** (top'ə·graf'ik) *adj.*

tor·na·do (tôr·nā'dō) *n.*, **tor·na·does** *or* **tor·na·dos** *pl.*
A whirling wind of exceptional violence, accompanied by a funnel-shaped cloud marking the narrow path of greatest destruction.

tor·pid (tôr′pid) *adj.*
1 Inactive, as a hibernating animal; dormant.
2 Sluggish, apathetic, dull: *The heat made us all feel torpid.*—**tor′pid·ly** *adv.*; **tor·pid·i·ty** (tôr·pid′ə·tē), **tor′pid·ness** *n.*

tor·toise (tôr′təs) *n.*
A turtle, especially one living on land.

tor·tu·ous (tôr′chōō·əs) *adj.*
1 With many bends and turns; twisting: *We followed a tortuous path through the swamp.*
2 Not straightforward; devious: *His tortuous policy involved many lies.*

to·tal·i·tar·i·an (tō·tal′i·târ′ē·ən) *adj.*
Designating or characteristic of a government controlled exclusively by one party or faction, and maintained by forbidding all other parties.

tou·pee (tōō·pā′) *n.*
A hairpiece worn to cover baldness or a bald spot.

tour·ni·quet (tōōr′nə·ket) *n.*
A device that stops the flow of blood through an artery by compression: *One of the first things she did was loosen the tourniquet.*

to·ward (tôrd) *prep.*
1 In the direction of: *looking toward the sea.*
2 With respect to; regarding: *animosity toward strangers.* **3** In anticipation of: *saving toward his retirement.* **4** Near: *toward evening.*
Spelling tip: *Towards,* which is common in British usage, is not wrong.

tox·ic (tok′sik) *adj.*
Pertaining to or caused by poison; poisonous: *toxic fumes.*—**tox′i·cal·ly** *adj.*, **tox·ic′i·ty** *n.*

tract·a·ble (trak′tə·bəl) *adj.*
1 Easily led or controlled; manageable: *a tractable pony; a mild and tractable child.*
2 Readily worked or handled; malleable: *Gold is more tractable than iron.*
Syn. 1 docile, compliant, amenable.
Ant. 1 obstinate, fractious, rebellious.

traf·fic (traf′ik) *n.; v.* **traf·ficked, traf·fick·ing**
n. **1** The movement or passage of vehicles, people, ships, etc., along a route: *There is a lot of traffic on the roads today.* **2** The business of buying and selling; trade: *the drug traffic.*
v. To engage in buying or selling, especially illegally.

trag·e·dy (traj′ə·dē) *n.,* **trag·e·dies** *pl.*
1 A sad or fatal event; disaster. **2** A serious or solemn play that has a sad ending.—**trag′·ic** *adj.*, **trag′i·cal·ly** *adv.*

traipse (trāps) *v.* **traipsed, traips·ing**
Informal To walk about in an idle or aimless manner: *I will not allow strangers to traipse through my home.*

trait (trāt) *n.*
A distinguishing feature or quality of character: *Generosity is an excellent trait.*

tram·mel (tram′əl) *n.; v.* **tram·meled** or **tram·melled, tram·mel·ing** or **tram·mel·ling**
n. **1** *Usually pl.* Anything that limits freedom or activity; an impediment; hindrance: *the trammels of prejudice.* **2** A shackle used in training horses. **3** A special net for catching fish.
v. To hinder or obstruct; restrict.

tran·quil (trang′kwil *or* tran′kwil) *adj.*
Calm; quiet; peaceful: *a tranquil life.*—**tran·quil′li·ty** or **tran·quil′i·ty** *n.*
Syn. placid, serene, still.

tran·sient (tran′shənt) *adj., n.*
adj. **1** Passing away quickly; of short duration; brief: *transient anger.* **2** Not permanent; temporary: *a transient guest.*
n. One who remains in a place for a short time.

tran·sit (tran′sit) *n.*
1 The act of passing over or through; passage. **2** The act of carrying across or through; conveyance: *The merchandise was smashed in transit.*

tran·si·to·ry (tran′sə·tôr′ē *or* tran′sə·tōr′ē) *adj.*
Existing for a short time only: *transitory pleasure.*
Syn. transient, passing, momentary.

trans·lu·cent (trans·lōō′sənt) *adj.*
Allowing the passage of light without being transparent: *Stained glass is usually translucent.*
Usage: A material is *translucent* when it allows some light to pass through without giving a clear view of objects on the other side. It is *transparent* when it permits a clear view. *Opaque* material is impervious to light.

trans·mis·sion (trans·mish′ən) *n.*
1 The act of passing on or sending: *the transmission of malaria by mosquitoes.* **2** That which is passed on or sent. **3** A device that sends power from the engine of an automobile to the driving wheels.

trans·mit (trans·mit′) *v.* **trans·mit·ted, trans·mit·ting**
1 To send from one place or person to another; convey: *to transmit a message.* **2** To pass on by heredity. **3** To send out by means of electromagnetic waves, as radio broadcasts.

trans·par·ent (trans·pâr′ənt) *adj.*
Admitting the passage of light and permitting a clear view of objects beyond.

tra·peze (trə·pēz′) *n.*
A short swinging bar, suspended by two ropes, used by gymnasts, etc.

trau·ma (trô′mə *or* trou′mə) *n.,* **trau·mas** or **trau·ma·ta** (trô′mə·tə *or* trou′mə·tə) *pl.*
A general condition of the body resulting from an injury or wound caused by shock, violence, etc.—**trau·mat′ic** *adj.*, **trau·mat′i·cal·ly** *adv.*

trav·ail (trav′āl *or* trə·vāl′) *n., v.*
n. **1** Strenuous physical or mental labor; toil.
2 The pain of childbirth.
v. **1** To toil or labor. **2** To suffer the pains of childbirth.

trav·erse (trav′ərs; *for v. and adv. also* trə·vûrs′) *v.* **trav·ersed, trav·ers·ing;** *n., adj.*
v. To pass over, across, or through: *The Indians traversed the plain.*
n. A part, as of a machine or structure,

placed across another part, as a crossbeam, transom, etc.

adj. Lying or being across; transverse.

treach·er·ous (trech'ər·əs) *adj.*
1 Not faithful; disloyal: *a treacherous act.* 2 Unreliable: *a treacherous jungle trail.*—**treach'er·ous·ly** *adv.*, **treach'er·ous·ness** *n.*
Syn. traitorous, false, faithless.
Ant. faithful, loyal, trusty.

treas·ure (trezh'ər) *n.; v.* **treas·ured, treas·ur·ing**
n. 1 Riches accumulated, especially in the form of money, jewels, or precious metals: *He found an old treasure buried in a cave.* 2 A person or thing that is regarded as valuable, precious, or rare: *My sons are my greatest treasure.*
v. 1 To store or hoard; accumulate. 2 To prize: *He treasures his art collection.*

treas·ur·er (trezh'ər·ər) *n.*
An officer of a state, city, corporation, society, etc., who has charge of funds or revenues.

treas·ur·y (trezh'ər·ē) *n.*, **treas·ur·ies** *pl.*
1 The place where private or public funds or revenues are received, kept, and paid out. 2 Public or private funds; money: *The church treasury was practically empty.* 3 Any collection of treasures.

trea·tise (trē'tis) *n.*
A formal and systematic written account of some subject: *a treatise on the history of steel-making.*

trek (trek) *n.; v.* **trekked, trek·king**
n. A journey, especially a slow one.
v. To travel, especially slowly and with difficulty.

tre·men·dous (tri·men'dəs) *adj.*
1 *Informal* Extraordinarily large: *a tremendous airplane.* 2 *Informal* Unusually great; amazing; wonderful: *She is a tremendous actress.*—**tre·men'dous·ly** *adv.*

trep·i·da·tion (trep'ə·dā'shən) *n.*
1 A state of agitation or alarm. 2 A trembling.

tres·tle (tres'əl) *n.*
1 A beam or bar supported by four legs, used to hold up platforms, etc. 2 An open, braced framework used to support a railway bridge, etc.

tri·bu·nal (tri·byoo'nəl *or* trī·byoo'nəl) *n.*
1 A court of justice. 2 The seat set apart for judges, magistrates, etc.

tri·fle (trī'fəl) *n.; v.* **tri·fled, tri·fling**
n. 1 Anything of little value or importance: *to quarrel over trifles.* 2 A small amount: *It costs only a trifle.*—**tri'fler** *n.*
v. To treat lightly or frivolously; dally: *to trifle with her affections.*

trip·tych (trip'tik) *n.*
A triple picture or carving on three hinged panels, often depicting a religious subject.

trite (trīt) *adj.* **trit·er, trit·est**
Made commonplace by repetition.
Syn. hackneyed, stereotyped.
Ant. fresh, original.

trom·bone (trom·bōn' *or* trom'bōn') *n.*
A brass musical instrument of the trumpet family but larger and lower in pitch than the trumpet.

tro·phy (trō'fē) *n.*, **tro·phies** *pl.*
Something representing a victory or success: *He had many hunting trophies.*

trou·ble (trub'əl) *n.; v.* **troub·led, troub·ling**
n. 1 Distress; worry; suffering: *He is always in trouble.* 2 Any difficulty, perplexity, or disturbance: *She has domestic troubles.* 3 Care, attention, work: *Take the trouble to do it correctly.* 4 A sick or diseased condition: *heart trouble.*
v. 1 To make or become distressed or worried: *The rising prices troubled her.* 2 To inconvenience: *May I trouble you for the sugar?*

trough (trôf) *n.*
1 A long, narrow, open container used to hold food or water for animals. 2 A gutter fixed to the roof of a house for carrying off rainwater.

trous·seau (troo'sō *or* troo·sō') *n.*, **trous·seaux** (troo'sōz *or* troo·sōz') *or* **trous·seaus** *pl.*
A bride's outfit, including clothing, linens, etc.

tru·an·cy (troo'ən·sē) *n.*, **tru·an·cies** *pl.*
The condition of being a truant; also, an act of being a truant.

tru·ant (troo'ənt) *n.*, *adj.*
n. A person who is absent without permission, as from school: *The dropout had a long history of being a truant.*
adj. Of or having to do with a truant or truancy.

truc·u·lent (truk'yə·lənt) *adj.*
Aggressively hostile; belligerent: *a truculent mood.*—**truc'u·lent·ly** *adv.*
Syn. angry, fierce, ruthless.
Ant. mild, inoffensive, gentle.

tru·ly (troo'lē) *adv.*
1 In agreement with fact; really: *That truly happened.* 2 With loyalty or faithfulness: *I love you truly.*

trun·cate (trung'kāt) *v.* **trun·cat·ed, trun·cat·ing**
To cut the top or end from: *to truncate a pyramid.*

try (trī) *v.* **tried, try·ing;** *n.;* **tries** *pl.*
v. 1 To undertake, endeavor: *The baby is trying to walk.* 2 To make experimental use of (often with *out*): *He tried out the new car.* 3 In law, To determine guilt or innocence by judicial trial: *He was arrested and tried almost immediately, which struck me as rather hasty.*
n. The act of attempting: *After ten tries he decided the battery was dead.*
Spelling tip: Remember that words ending in a *y* preceded by a consonant usually change the *y* to *i* before any suffix except one beginning with *i*. Thus *tried* and *tries*, but *trying.*

try·ing (trī'ing) *adj.*
Difficult: *It was a very trying time for the family.*

tryst (trist) *n.*
1 An appointment, as between lovers, to meet at a designated time and place. 2 The meeting place agreed upon.

tset·se (tset′sē) *n.*
A small, bloodsucking fly of southern Africa that transmits disease in cattle, horses, etc.

tung·sten (tung′stən) *n.*
A steel-gray, brittle metal much used in the manufacture of filaments for electric lamps and high-speed cutting tools.

tur·gid (tûr′jid) *adj.*
1 Unnaturally puffed out; swollen. 2 Bombastic, as language, style, etc.: *a turgid speech.*—**tur·gid·i·ty** (tûr·jid′ə·tē) *n.*
Usage: *Turgid* should not be confused with *turbid,* which means cloudy or muddy: *a turbid stream.*

tur·key (tûr′kē) *n.,* **tur·keys** *pl.*
A large American bird related to the pheasant.

tur·pi·tude (tûr′pə·t(y)ōōd) *n.*
Wickedness; vileness; depravity, or any action showing this: *the moral turpitude of Nero's times.*

tur·quoise (tûr′koiz *or* tûr′kwoiz) *n.*
1 A blue or greenish-blue precious stone. 2 A light greenish-blue color.

tur·ret (tûr′it) *n.*
1 A rotating armored tower, large enough to contain powerful guns, forming part of a warship, fort, tank, or airplane. 2 A small tower, often merely ornamental, rising above a larger structure, as on a castle.

ty·coon (tī·kōōn′) *n.*
A powerful business leader: *a Wall Street tycoon.*

ty·phoid (tī′foid) *n.*
An infectious disease caused by bacteria.

tyr·an·nize (tir′ə·nīz) *v.* **tyr·an·nized, tyr·an·niz·ing**
To rule unjustly or cruelly.—**tyr′an·ny** *n.*

ty·rant (tī′rənt) *n.*
A cruel and unjust ruler: *a defeated country at the mercy of a tyrant.*
Syn. despot, autocrat.

U

u·biq·ui·tous (yōō·bik′wə·təs) *adj.*
Existing, or seeming to exist, everywhere at once; omnipresent: *The television cameras, ubiquitous and demanding, overshadowed the entire convention.*—**u·biq′ui·tous·ly** *adv.;* **u·biq′ui·tous·ness, u·biq′ui·ty** *n.*

um·brage (um′brij) *n.*
A sense of injury; offense (used in the phrases *to give umbrage, to take umbrage*).

u·na·nim·i·ty (yōō′nə·nim′ə·tē) *n.*
Complete agreement in opinion, etc.: *We reached unanimity on all points.*

u·nan·i·mous (yōō·nan′ə·məs) *adj.*
1 In complete agreement; all of one mind; sharing the same views or sentiments: *The committee was unanimous in its decision.* 2 Showing or resulting from complete agree-

ment: *a unanimous vote.*—**u·nan′i·mous·ly** *adv.*

un·be·liev·a·ble (un′bə·lēv′ə·bəl) *adj.*
That cannot be believed; incredible; astounding.—**un′be·liev′a·bly** *adv.*

un·civ·i·lized (un·siv′ə·līzd) *adj.*
Not civilized; barbarous: *The benefits of Western culture were brought to the uncivilized tribes.*

un·con·scious (un·kon′shəs) *adj.*
1 Temporarily deprived of consciousness: *knocked unconscious by the blow.* 2 Unaware; ignorant: *unconscious of the impression he was making.* 3 Not known or felt to exist; unaccompanied by conscious effort: *an unconscious imitation.*

un·con·trol·la·ble (un′kən·trōl′ə·bəl) *adj.*
Beyond control; ungovernable.

unc·tu·ous (ungk′chōō·əs) *adj.*
1 Characterized by affectedly deep emotion; excessively smooth: *a smug, self-contented, unctuous man.* 2 Oily; greasy: *an unctuous clay.*—**unc′tu·ous·ly** *adv.,* **unc′tu·ous·ness** *n.*

un·doubt·ed·ly (un·dou′tid·lē) *adv.*
Without doubt; indubitably: *You are undoubtedly right.*

un·du·la·tion (un′d(y)ə·lā′shən) *n.*
1 A wavy motion or form; a gentle rise and fall: *the undulations of a rolling countryside.* 2 A wave.

un·dy·ing (un·dī′ing) *adj.*
Immortal, everlasting: *He pledged undying devotion.*

un·eas·y (un·ē′zē) *adj.* **un·eas·i·er, un·eas·i·est**
1 Disturbed; worried: *She was uneasy about the assignment.* 2 Embarrassed; awkward: *an uneasy laugh.* 3 Unstable: *an uneasy peace.*—**un·eas′i·ly** *adv.,* **un·eas′i·ness** *n.*

un·for·get·ta·ble (un′fər·get′ə·bəl) *adj.*
Not forgettable; memorable.—**un′for·get′ta·bly** *adv.*

un·in·tel·li·gi·ble (un′in·tel′ə·jə·bəl) *adj.*
Not intelligible; incomprehensible: *He could only make unintelligible sounds.*—**un′in·tel′li·gi·bly** *adv.*

un·man·age·a·ble (un·man′ij·ə·bəl) *adj.*
Not manageable; uncontrollable.

un·mit·i·gat·ed (un·mit′ə·gā′tid) *adj.*
1 Unrelieved: *unmitigated grief.* 2 Without qualification or condition; absolute; complete: *an unmitigated rogue.*

un·nec·es·sar·y (un·nes′ə·ser′ē) *adj.*
Not required or necessary; not essential.

un·par·al·leled (un·par′ə·leld) *adj.*
Without parallel; unmatched; unprecedented: *unparalleled effrontery.*

un·prec·e·dent·ed (un·pres′ə·den′tid) *adj.*
Being without precedent; preceded by no similar case; unheard of: *Such actions are unprecedented in this century.*

un·til (un·til′) *prep., conj.*
prep. 1 Up to the time of; till: *Wait until dark.* 2 Before: used with a negative: *not until seven.*
conj. 1 To the time when, place where, or de-

gree that: *until I die; until you reach the corner.* 2 Before: used with a negative: *Don't go until I come.*

un·u·su·al (un·yŏŏ′zhŏŏ·əl) *adj.*
Not usual, common, or ordinary; rare.—
un·u′su·al·ly *adv.*

un·wield·y (un·wēl′dē) *adj.*
Difficult to move or manage; clumsy; awkward: *He managed to get his unwieldy body out of the chair.*

up·braid (up·brād′) *v.*
To reproach for some wrongdoing: *She upbraided him for coming home late.*
Spelling tip: Remember the *b*, in pronunciation as well as spelling.
Syn. chide, scold, reprove.

ur·ban (ûr′bən) *adj.*
1 Of, having to do with, or characteristic of a city: *urban blight.* 2 Situated or dwelling in a town: *an urban population.*

ur·bane (ûr·bān′) *adj.*
Characterized by or having refinement or elegance; courteous; suave: *the urbane manners of a diplomat.*—**ur·ban′i·ty** (ûr·ban′ə·tē) *n.*, **ur·bane′ly** *adv.*
Etymology: *Urbane* and *urban* both come from the same Latin word, *urbanus*, meaning of the city.
Syn. polite, smooth.
Ant. rough, rustic, rude.

u·re·thra (yŏŏ·rē′thrə) *n.*, **u·re·thras** or **u·re·thrae** (yŏŏ·rē′thrē) *pl.*
The duct by which urine is discharged from the bladder of most mammals.

us·a·ble (yŏŏ′zə·bəl) *adj.*
Able to be used: *Most of the equipment is still usable.*
Spelling tip: This word is also spelled *useable.*

us·age (yŏŏ′sij) *n.*
1 Treatment: *worn by hard usage.* 2 A customary or habitual practice or way of doing something: *an act permitted by usage; ancient usage.* 3 The customary or standard way in which words, sounds, and grammatical forms in a language are used: *accepted American usage; the rules of good usage.* 4 A particular verbal expression or the application of such an expression.

use·ful (yŏŏs′fəl) *adj.*
Having a use: *a useful gadget; a useful bit of information.*—**use′ful·ly** *adv.*; **use′ful·ness** *n.*

u·su·al (yŏŏ′zhŏŏ·əl) *adj.*
Expected in the ordinary course of events; frequent; common; normal.—**u′su·al·ly** *adv.*, **u′su·al·ness** *n.*

u·surp (yŏŏ·zûrp′) *v.*
To seize and hold wrongfully; take possession of by force: *The military junta usurped the king's power and made him merely a figurehead.*—**u·surp′er**, **u′sur·pa′tion** *n.*

u·to·pi·a (yŏŏ·tō′pē·ə) *n.*
1 Any state, condition, or place of ideal perfection: *For two weeks I lived in Hawaii, my idea of utopia.* 2 An impractical scheme,

especially one for social improvement.—
u·top′i·an *adj.*

ux·o·ri·ous (uk·sôr′ē·əs) *adj.*
Showing extreme or foolish fondness for one's wife.—**ux·o′ri·ous·ly** *adv.*; **ux·o′ri·ous·ness** *n.*

V

va·can·cy (vā′kən·sē) *n.*, **va·can·cies** *pl.*
1 The state of being empty; emptiness: *the vacancy of her stare.* 2 An unoccupied place or position: *The apartment building has three vacancies.*—**va′cant** *adj.*, **va′cant·ly** *adv.*

va·cate (vā′kāt) *v.* **va·cat·ed**, **va·cat·ing**
To make empty by moving out of (as an apartment) or by giving up (as a job): *The old tenants vacated the apartment yesterday.*
Syn. quit, leave, withdraw.
Ant. take, occupy.

vac·ci·nate (vak′sə·nāt) *v.* **vac·ci·nat·ed**, **vac·ci·nat·ing**
To inoculate with a vaccine, especially to inoculate against smallpox: *The doctor vaccinated the child.*—**vac′ci·na′tion** *n.*

vac·cine (vak′sēn) *n.*
A preparation containing bacteria or viruses so treated as to give immunity from a disease when injected into someone; especially, a preparation containing the virus of cowpox and giving immunity from smallpox.

vac·il·late (vas′ə·lāt) *v.* **vac·il·lat·ed**, **vac·il·lat·ing**
To sway one way and the other, as in trying to make a decision; to waver: *She vacillated between wanting to be a blonde and a redhead.*—**vac′il·la′tion** *n.*

vac·u·um (vak′yŏŏ·əm *or* vak′yŏŏm) *n.*
1 A space absolutely devoid of matter, or space from which air and other gas has been exhausted to a very high degree: *to create an artificial vacuum by pumping out air.* 2 A void; emptiness; gap: *Her death left a vacuum in his life.*
Spelling tip: Remember to double the *u.*
Syn. 2 gap, emptiness.

va·gar·y (və·gâr′ē *or* vā′gər·ē) *n.*, **va·gar·ies** *pl.*
A wild fancy; extravagant notion: *the vagaries of a madwoman.*
Syn. caprice, whim, quirk.

va·grant (vā′grənt) *n.*, *adj.*
n. A person without a settled home; a tramp or wanderer; a vagabond: *A vagrant roaming the countryside.*
adj. Wandering about or having a wandering course: *a vagrant stream.*—**va′gran·cy** *n.*
Syn. *n.* beachcomber, hobo, bum. *adj.* vagabond, roaming.

val·e·dic·to·ry (val′ə·dik′tər·ē) *adj.*, *n.*, **val·e·dic·to·ries** *pl.*
adj. Having to do with leave-taking: *a valedictory speech.*
n. A parting address, as by a member of a graduating class: *He was chosen to deliver the valedictory.*

val·et (val′ā *or* val′it) *n.*
A gentleman's personal servant, or an em-

ployee, as in a hotel, who performs personal services for guests.

val·id (val'id) *adj.*
1 Legally binding: *a valid contract.* 2 Convincing; reasonable: *not a valid excuse for missing class.* 3 Based on proper logic: *a valid conclusion based on all the facts.*—**val'id·ly** *adv.*; **val'id·ness, va·lid'i·ty** *n.*
Syn. 1 lawful, legitimate. 2 bona fide.

va·lise (və·lēs') *n.*
A suitcase: *He carried a small valise.*
Syn. bag.

vap·id (vap'id *or* vā'pid) *adj.*
Without liveliness or flavor; insipid; flat and dull: *her vapid chatter.*—**vap'id·ly** *adv.*; **vap'id·ness, va·pid'i·ty** *n.*

ve·he·ment (vē'ə·mənt) *adj.*
1 Passionate or ardent; intense; fervent: *his vehement protestations of innocence.* 2 Full of energy; lively; vigorous: *vehement gestures; vehement applause.*—**ve'he·mence** or **ve'he·men·cy** *n.*; **ve'he·ment·ly** *adv.*
Syn. 1 fiery, feverish. 2 strenuous.
Ant. 1 calm, halfhearted. 2 listless.

ve·hi·cle (vē'ə·kəl) *n.*
1 Any device fitted with wheels or runners for conveying or transporting, as a car, sled, bicycle, etc. 2 A means of transmitting, communicating, expressing, etc.: *The play is a good vehicle for his comic talent.*—**ve·hic·u·lar** (vi·hik'yə·lər) *adj.*

ven·er·a·ble (ven'ər·ə·bəl) *adj.*
Worthy of or commanding reverence: *a venerable profession.*—**ven'er·a·ble·ness, ven'er·a·bil'i·ty** *n.*; **ven'er·a·bly** *adv.*
Syn. revered, esteemed, honored.

ven·geance (ven'jəns) *n.*
Revenge or the act of revenging; paying back or retaliating for an injury: *the bloody vengeance of the feuding mountain clans.*
Syn. reprisal, retaliation.
Ant. forgiveness.

ven·ti·late (ven'tə·lāt) *v.* **ven·ti·lat·ed, ven·ti·lat·ing**
1 To produce a circulation of air in; admit fresh air into: *to ventilate the room adequately.* 2 To expose to examination and discussion: *to ventilate long-standing grievances.*—**ven'ti·la'tion** *n.*

ve·ra·cious (və·rā'shəs) *adj.*
1 Habitually disposed to speak the truth; truthful: *a veracious man.* 2 Conforming to or expressing truth; true: *a veracious account.*—**ve·ra'cious·ly** *adv.*, **ve·ra'cious·ness** *n.*
Syn. 1 honest, trustworthy, reliable. 2 accurate, correct, unimpeachable.
Ant. 1 dishonest, unreliable. 2 false, adulterated, distorted.

ver·ba·tim (vər·bā'tim) *adj., adv.*
In the exact words; word for word: *a verbatim account; Repeat the conversation verbatim.*

ver·bi·age (vûr'bē·ij) *n.*
Excess of words; wordiness: *A simple idea buried under much verbiage.*

Syn. verbosity, prolixity.
Ant. conciseness, terseness.

ver·bose (vər·bōs') *adj.*
Using or containing a wearisome and unnecessary number of words; wordy: *a verbose, boring after-dinner speech.*—**ver·bos·i·ty** (vər·bos'ə·tē), **ver·bose'ness** *n.*; **ver·bose'ly** *adv.*
Syn. redundant, prolix, flatulent.
Ant. terse, pithy, condensed.

ver·nac·u·lar (vər·nak'yə·lər) *n.*
The common, everyday speech of the people, as opposed to the literary language: *to express oneself more clearly in the vernacular.*

ver·sus (vûr'səs) *prep.*
1 Against: *Brown versus the United States; Dempsey versus Tunney.* 2 Considered as the alternative of: *free trade versus tariffs.*
Usage: This word is abbreviated *v.* or *vs.*

ver·te·bra (vûr'tə·brə) *n.,* **ver·te·brae** (vûr'tə·brē) *pl.*
Any of the segmented bones of the spinal column.

ver·ti·cal (vûr'ti·kəl) *adj.*
Extending up and down; upright: *a vertical column of figures.*—**ver'ti·cal·ly** *adv.*
Syn. erect, plumb, perpendicular.
Ant. horizontal, flat.

ver·ti·go (vûr'tə·gō) *n.,* **ver·ti·goes** or **ver·tig·i·nes** (vər·tij'ə·nēz) *pl.*
Dizziness; any of a group of disorders in which a person feels as if he or his surroundings are whirling around.

vet·er·an (vet'ər·ən *or* vet'rən) *n.*
1 One who has had long experience in doing something: *Nixon is a veteran of many political campaigns.* 2 A former member of the armed forces: *the veterans of WWII.*

vi·a (vī'ə *or* vē'ə) *prep.*
By way of; by a route passing through: *He went to Boston via New Haven.*
Usage: *Via* not only refers to the route, but also can refer to the method of transportation: *We went via train.* This latter usage is informal.

vi·a·ble (vī'ə·bəl) *adj.*
1 Capable of living and developing normally, as a newborn infant, seed, etc. 2 Capable of working, as a plan; workable or practicable.

vi·and (vī'ənd) *n.*
1 An article of food, especially meat. 2 *pl.* Victuals; food, especially choice food or meat.
Syn. 2 provisions.

vi·car·i·ous (vī·kâr'ē·əs) *adj.*
1 Enjoyed, felt, etc., by a person as a result of his imagined participation in an experience not his own: *He got a vicarious thrill from reading adventure stories.* 2 Made or performed by substitution; suffered or done in place of another: *a vicarious sacrifice.*

vice (vīs) *n.*
1 Evil or wicked behavior: *Virtue is rewarded and vice punished.* 2 A grossly immoral habit.

vice·roy (vīs'roi) *n.*
A person who rules a country, colony, or province as a representative of his sovereign.

vi·ce ver·sa (vī′sə vûr′sə)
The order being changed; conversely: *She likes him, and vice versa.*

vi·cis·si·tude (vi·sis′ə·t(y)ōōd) *n.*
A sudden, unexpected change or variation, as of fortune (almost always used in the plural): *the vicissitudes of life.*—**vi·cis′si·tu′di·nous** *adj.*

vic·tim (vik′tim) *n.*
1 A living creature who is killed, injured, or subjected to suffering: *The money is being sent to the victims of the flood.* 2 A person who is swindled or tricked; a dupe.

vict·uals (vit′lz) *n.pl.*
Food for human beings, as prepared for eating: *The picnic victuals are in the hamper.*
Spelling tip: *Victuals* are sometimes spelled as they are pronounced—*vittles*—but this is an informal usage.

view (vyōō) *n., v.*
n. 1 Act of seeing; survey; inspection: *a private view.* 2 Power or range of vision: *Are the mountains in view yet?* 3 That which is seen; outlook; prospect: *the view from the bridge.* 4 Manner of looking at things; judgment; opinion: *my views on politics.*
v. 1 To examine; scrutinize: *He was asked to view the body and make an identification.* 2 To think of or consider: *His actions are viewed unfavorably.*

vig·i·lant (vij′ə·lənt) *adj.*
Alert, watchful: *If you wish to protect yourself, remain vigilant.*—**vig′i·lance** *n.*, **vig′i·lant·ly** *adv.*

vi·gnette (vin·yet′) *n.*
1 A short literary description marked by subtlety and delicacy: *vignettes of life in colonial days.* 2 An engraving, photograph, or the like whose background fades off gradually.

vil·i·fy (vil′ə·fī) *v.* **vil·i·fied, vil·i·fy·ing**
To abuse or characterize with defamatory language; to malign publicly: *The Nazi informer was vilified whenever he appeared in the street.*

vin·di·cate (vin′də·kāt) *v.* **vin·di·cat·ed, vin·di·cat·ing**
1 To clear of accusation, censure, suspicion, etc.: *He vindicated his name by proving he did not commit the crime.* 2 To maintain or defend successfully; justify: *The candidate vindicated his right to party support.*

vin·dic·tive (vin·dik′tiv) *adj.*
Having a spirit of revenge; spiteful: *The vindictive divorcée tried to turn her children against their father.*

vi·o·lence (vī′ə·ləns) *n.*
1 The quality or state of being violent; intensity; fury: *the violence of the storm.* 2 Violent or abusive use of force; injury; outrage: *robbery with violence.*

vi·ra·go (vi·rä′gō) *n.*, **vi·ra·goes** or **vi·ra·gos** *pl.*
A noisy, sharp-tongued woman; a shrew.

vir·ile (vir′əl) *adj.*
1 Having the characteristics of adult manhood; masculine. 2 Having qualities considered typically masculine; vigorous; sturdy: *virile prose.*—**vi·ril·i·ty** (və·ril′ə·tē) *n.*

vir·tue (vûr′chōō) *n.*
1 Moral excellence; righteousness; goodness. 2 Any admirable quality. 3 Purity; chastity.
Etymology. *Virtue* comes from a Latin word meaning manliness, strength, or bravery.

vir·tu·o·so (vûr′chōō·ō′sō) *n.*, **vir·tu·o·sos** or **vir·tu·o·si** *pl.*
A master of technique, especially in music.

vir·tu·ous (vûr′chōō·əs) *adj.*
Characterized by, exhibiting, or having the nature of virtue; morally pure and good; chaste.

vir·u·lent (vir′yə·lənt) *adj.*
1 Exceedingly harmful, poisonous, or infectious: *The family was plagued by a virulent disease.* 2 Full of bitterness and hate: *a virulent speech attacking slum lords.*—**vir′u·lence** *n.*, **vir′u·lent·ly** *adv.*

vis·cer·a (vis′ər·ə) *n.pl.*
The internal organs of the body, especially those of the great cavities of the body, as the stomach, lungs, heart, intestines, etc.

vis·cid (vis′id) *adj.*
1 Sticky or adhesive; viscous. 2 Having a sticky surface, as some leaves.

vis·cous (vis′kəs) *adj.*
Adhesive; semifluid; sticky: *Tar is a viscous liquid.*

vise (vīs) *n.*
A clamping device, usually of two jaws made to be closed together with a screw, lever, etc., used for grasping and holding objects being worked on.

vis·i·ble (viz′ə·bəl) *adj.*
Capable of being seen: *The ship was visible from the shore for a long time.*—**vis′i·bil′i·ty** *n.*, **vis′i·bly** *adv.*

vi·sor (vī′zər) *n.*
1 Something that shades the eyes, as the projecting piece at the front of a baseball cap. 2 A movable piece or part serving to protect against glare, etc., as on the windshield of an automobile.

vi·tals (vit′lz) *n.pl.*
1 The parts or organs of the body necessary to life. 2 The parts or qualities essential to the well-being of anything.

vi·ta·min (vī′tə·min) *n.*
Any of a group of organic substances found in minute quantities in most natural foodstuffs, and closely associated with the maintenance of a healthy body.
Spelling tip: This word is also spelled *vitamine.*

vit·re·ous (vit′rē·əs) *adj.*
Having to do with, obtained from, or resembling glass: *vitreous rocks.*

vit·ri·ol·ic (vit′rē·ol′ik) *adj.*
1 Corrosive, burning, or caustic. 2 Inclined to or marked by angry, caustic speech, criti-

cism, etc.: *a vitriolic review; a vitriolic opponent.*
Syn. 2 virulent, scathing, mordant.

vi·tu·per·a·tion (vī·tōō′pə·rā′shən) *n.*
Abusive language; censure: *a torrent of vituperation.*—**vi·tu′per·ate** *v.*, **vi·tu′per·a·tive** *adj.*
Syn. invective, abuse.

vi·va·cious (vi·vā′shəs *or* vī·vā′shəs) *adj.*
Full of life and spirit: *She was so vivacious before her illness.*

vi·vip·a·rous (vī·vip′ər·əs) *adj.*
Bringing forth living young, as most mammals.

vi·vi·section (viv′ə·sek′shən) *n.*
The dissection of and experimentation on living animals, especially for medical and scientific research.

vo·cif·er·ous (vō·sif′ər·əs) *adj.*
Making or characterized by a loud outcry; clamorous: *a vociferous minority.*—**vo·cif′er·ous·ly** *adv.*
Syn. strident, blatant, noisy.

vogue (vōg) *n.*
1 The prevalent way or fashion; style: *It's difficult to predict what will be in vogue this year.* **2** Popular favor; general acceptance: *Folk singers have had a great vogue recently.*

vol·a·tile (vol′ə·təl) *adj.*
1 Evaporating rapidly at ordinary temperatures: *volatile salts.* **2** Easily influenced; fickle; changeable; explosive: *a volatile girl; a volatile political situation.*

vo·ta·ry (vō′tər·ē) *n.*, **vo·ta·ries** *pl.*
1 A person bound by a vow or promise; a devout worshiper: *votaries of Artemis.* **2** A person devoted to some particular pursuit, worship, study, etc.: *a votary of the theater.*

vul·ner·a·ble (vul′nər·ə·bəl) *adj.*
1 Capable of being hurt or damaged. **2** Open to attack.—**vul′ner·a·bil′i·ty** *n.*

vul·ture (vul′chər) *n.*
1 A large bird that feeds mostly on decaying flesh. **2** A savagely greedy person.

W

waft (waft *or* wäft) *v.*
To carry or float gently or lightly through the air or over the water.

waive (wāv) *v.* **waived, waiv·ing**
1 To give up a claim to: *to waive an option on a piece of land.* **2** To put off; postpone; delay.

waiv·er (wā′vər) *n.*
1 The voluntary giving up of a right, privilege, or advantage. **2** The written evidence of such a surrender: *His client signed a waiver.*

wan (won) *adj.* **wan·ner, wan·nest**
Pale or faint, as from being ill or tired: *a wan complexion; a wan smile.*

wan·der (won′dər) *v.*
1 To move or travel about without destination or purpose; roam; rove: *to wander through the woods.* **2** To stray: *The dog has*

wandered away. **3** To extend in an irregular course; twist or meander: *A stream wanders through the fields of the estate.*—**wan′der·er** *n.*

war·rant (wôr′ənt *or* wor′ənt) *n.*, *v.*
n. **1** A legal paper authorizing arrest, search, seizure, etc. **2** Something that gives a right; sanction; justification: *What warrant do you have to make such a statement?*
v. To be sufficient grounds for; justify: *The facts warranted further investigation.*

was·sail (wos′əl *or* wo·sāl′) *n.*, *v.*
n. **1** An ancient festivity at which toasts were drunk. **2** The liquor prepared for such a festivity.
v. To take part in a wassail.

wat·tle (wot′l) *n.*; *v.* **wat·tled, wat·tling**
n. **1** A frame or structure of rods or twigs woven together, used for fences, walls, etc. **2** Flesh, often wrinkled and brightly colored, hanging from the throat of a turkey, chicken, etc., and of some reptiles.
v. **1** To weave or twist (twigs, branches, etc.) into a network. **2** To form, as baskets, by intertwining twigs.

way·bill (wā′bil′) *n.*
A list describing or identifying goods or naming passengers carried by a train, steamer, etc.

wear (wâr) *v.* **wore, worn, wear·ing**; *n.*
v. **1** To carry or have on the person, as a garment, ornament, etc,: *She wears glasses.* **2** To impair, waste, or consume by use or constant action. *The water had worn the stones.* **3** To cause or produce by scraping, rubbing, etc.: *to wear a hole in a coat.* **4** To withstand the effects of use, wear, etc., as specified: *The skirt wears well.* **5** To pass gradually or tediously: *The day wears on.*
n. **1** The act of wearing, or the state of being worn: *My shirt is the worse for wear.* **2** Material or articles of dress to wear: *silk for summer wear; men's wear.* **3** The destructive effect of use or work.—**wear′a·ble** *adj.*, **wear′er** *n.*

weath·er (weth′ər) *n.*, *v.*
n. The general atmospheric condition with respect to temperature, moisture, winds, etc.: *wet weather.*
v. **1** To expose or be exposed to the action of the weather: *to weather lumber.* **2** To pass through and survive: *to weather a storm.*

wel·ter (wel′tər) *v.*, *n.*
v. **1** To roll about; wallow. **2** To lie or be soaked in some fluid, as blood.
n. **1** A rolling movement, as of waves. **2** A commotion; turmoil.

where (hwâr) *adv.*, *conj.*, *pron.*
adv. **1** At or in what place, relation, respect, or situation: *Where is your car?* **2** To what place or end: *Where is he going?* **3** From what place, source, or cause: *Where did you learn that?* **4** At, in, or to which: *That's the place where I lost it.*
conj. To, at, or in the place to which or in which: *I live where the road ends.*
pron. What place: *Where does he come from?*

wher·ev·er (hwâr'ev'ər) *conj., adv.*
conj. In, at, or to whatever place: *Go wherever you wish.*
adv. Where (emphatic): *Wherever is my pen?*

wheth·er (hweth'ər) *conj.*
1 If it is the case that (used to introduce an indirect question, often with the negative being implied): *Tell me whether you are considering our plan.* **2** In either case when or if: *Whether she stays or leaves, we are still responsible for her.* **3** Either: *Whether by luck or ability, he passed the exam.*

which (hwich) *adj., pron.*
adj. What one of a certain group mentioned or implied: *Which toy do you want? Which is your house?*
pron. **1** That: *This is the story which he chose.* **2** The one, or ones, that: *He knows which I meant.*

while (hwīl) *n., conj.; v.* **whiled, whil·ing**
n. A short time; also, any period of time: *Stay and rest for a while.*
conj. **1** During the time that; as long as: *While in Paris he learned French.* **2** Although: *While he found fault, he also praised.*
v. To cause (time) to pass lightly and pleasantly: *He was whiling the time away.*

whim·si·cal (hwim'zi·kəl) *adj.*
1 Having eccentric ideas; capricious. **2** Oddly constituted; fantastic; quaint.—**whim'si·cal·ly** *adv.*

whis·tle (hwis'əl) *v.* **whis·tled, whis·tling,** *n.*
v. **1** To make a musical tone, usually shrill, by sending the breath through the teeth or through a small opening formed by puckering the lips. **2** To move with a whistling sound. **3** To blow or sound a whistle.
n. **1** A device for producing a shrill tone by the passage of air, steam, etc., through it. **2** Any whistling sound, as of a missile, the wind, etc.

whole (hōl) *adj., n.*
adj. **1** Entire; complete: *We traveled a whole day.* **2** Unbroken; sound; intact: *After the fire there was not one whole windowpane left in the building.*
n. All the parts making up a thing; totality: *He lost the whole of his estate.*

whol·ly (hō'lē) *adv.*
Completely; totally: *He will never be wholly pleased with the house.*

width (width) *n.*
1 Dimension or measurement of an object taken from side to side. **2** Something that has width, as a piece of cloth.

wield (wēld) *v.*
1 To handle, as a weapon or instrument. **2** To exercise authority, power, influence, etc.

win·try (win'trē) *adj.* **win·tri·er, win·tri·est**
Of or like the winter; cold; frosty.

wis·ter·i·a (wis·tir'ē·ə) *n.*
A woody twining shrub bearing clusters of blue, purple, or white flowers.
Spelling tip: This word is also spelled **wis·tar·i·a** (wis·târ'ē·ə).

with (with *or* with) *prep.*

1 In the company of: *I was walking with my cousin.* **2** Having; bearing: *a boy with a book.* **3** Against: *to fight with a burglar.* **4** Because of; as a consequence of: *to shiver with cold.* **5** In charge of; in possession of: *Leave the key with me.* **6** Using; by means of: *to dig with a spade.* **7** In the same direction as: *to swim with the current.* **8** In regard to; in the case of: *to sympathize with a child.* **9** In support of; of the same opinion as: *I am with you.*

with·er (with'ər) *v.*
1 To become or cause to become faded, lifeless, or dry: *The heat withered the roses.* **2** To make incapable of speech or action: *His scornful glance withered his opponent.*

with·hold (with·hōld' *or* with·hōld') *v.* **with·held, with·hold·ing**
1 To hold back; restrain: *Withhold your enthusiasm.* **2** To keep back; decline to grant: *He withheld his consent.*

wiz·ened (wiz'ənd) *adj.*
Dried up; shriveled; withered: *a wizened old crone.*

wob·ble (wob'əl) *v.* **wob·bled, wob·bling,** *n.*
v. **1** To move or cause to move unsteadily from side to side: *This desk wobbles.* **2** To show indecision or unsteadiness; waver; vacillate.
n. An unsteady, wobbling motion.

woe·ful (wō'fəl) *adj.*
Accompanied by or causing misery; direful; regrettable: *They lived in such woeful poverty.* —**woe'ful·ly** *adv.*
Syn. miserable.

wom·an (wŏm'ən) *n.,* **wom·en** (wim'in) *pl.*
1 An adult human female. **2** Women as a group.
Spelling tip: Notice that only one letter changes in the plural, despite the change in pronunciation: *a* becomes *e*.

won·drous (wun'drəs) *adj.*
Wonderful; marvelous: *such a wondrous tale.*

wont (wunt *or* wônt) *adj., n.*
adj. Doing habitually; accustomed; used: *He is wont to drink some port after dinner.*
n. Ordinary manner of doing or acting; habit: *It was his wont to take the dog for a walk.*
Syn. *n.* custom, practice.

woo (woo) *v.*
1 To seek the love and affection of, especially in order to marry; court: *Was ever woman in this humor wooed?* **2** To invite; solicit; seek: *Our aim is to woo the voters.*

wor·sted (wŏos'tid *or* wûr'stid) *n.*
1 Woolen yarn. **2** A fabric made from this yarn.

wrack (rak) *n.*
1 Ruin; destruction: used especially in the phrase **wrack and ruin**: *The house has gone to wrack and ruin.* **2** Wreckage or vegetation cast up on the shore: *wrack of the storm.*

wraith (rāth) *n.*
1 An apparition of a person thought to be alive, seen shortly before or shortly after his death. **2** Any shadowy apparition.
Syn. 2 phantom.

wrap (rap) *n.; v.* **wrapped** or **wrapt, wrap·ping**
n. An outer garment or cloak.
v. To enclose, pack, envelop, or conceal with folded or soft material: *to wrap a present; a hill wrapped in clouds.*

wrath (rath) *n.*
Extreme or violent anger; rage.

wreath (rēth) *n.,* **wreaths** (rēthz) *pl.*
1 A band or circle of flowers or greenery woven together: *The family sent a funeral wreath of roses.* **2** Any curled or spiral shape: *a wreath of smoke.*

wrench (rench) *v., n.*
v. **1** To twist or pull with force: *He wrenched the book out of her hand.* **2** To twist so as to cause strain or injury: *She wrenched her ankle.*
n. **1** A violent twist or pull: *He gave my arm a wrench.* **2** A sudden feeling of emotional distress, as that caused by parting: *It was a wrench to leave the old home.* **3** Any of various tools for twisting and turning bolts, nuts, pipes, etc.

wrest (rest) *v.*
1 To pull or force away by violent twisting or wringing: *He wrested the weapon from her.* **2** To extract by toil and effort: *wrest a living from the rocky soil.*

wres·tle (res'əl) *v.* **wres·tled, wres·tling**
1 To attempt to throw to the ground or force into a certain fallen position, especially in a contest with rules. **2** To struggle, as for mastery; contend: *to wrestle with one's conscience.*

wretch (rech) *n.*
1 A base, vile, or contemptible person. **2** A miserable or pitiable person.

wrig·gle (rig'əl) *v.,* **wrig·gled, wrig·gling** *n.*
v. **1** To twist in a sinuous manner; squirm: *She wriggled in her chair.* **2** To proceed by twisting and crawling: *He wriggled through the tunnel.* **3** To make one's way by evasive or indirect means: *He wriggled out of the situation by a lie.* **4** To cause to move in quick contortions: *wriggling her hips.*
n. A wriggling motion.

wrin·kle (ring'kəl) *n., v.* **wrin·kled, wrin·kling**
n. **1** A small ridge, crease, or fold, as on a smooth surface: *Your dress has a wrinkle in it.* **2** A small fold or ridge in the skin, usually produced by age or exposure to the elements.
v. To make or become contracted into a wrinkle or wrinkles.

wrist (rist) *n.*
The part or joint of the arm that lies between the hand and the forearm.

write (rīt) *v.* **wrote, writ·ten, writ·ing**
1 To trace or inscribe words, symbols, etc., on a surface with pen, pencil, or other means. **2** To communicate by writing, as in a letter: *He writes to her every day.* **3** To produce by writing: *He is writing a play.* **4** To be engaged in the occupation of writer: *I write for a living.*

writ·er (rī'tər) *n.*
A person who writes, especially someone who writes for a living: *He was hired as a writer by the film studio.*

writhe (rīth) *v.* **writhed, writh·ing**
1 To twist or distort the body, face, etc., as if in pain: *writhing in agony.* **2** To suffer mentally, as from anguish, embarrassment, etc.

wrong (rông) *adj., n., adv., v.*
adj. **1** Incorrect; mistaken; erroneous: *the wrong answer; I think you are wrong.* **2** Unsuitable; inappropriate: *the wrong clothes; the wrong job.* **3** Other than the right or most desirable: *the wrong way to do it; the wrong road.* **4** Not favored by conventional social standards: *the wrong side of town.* **5** Not morally right, proper, or just; immoral: *It is wrong to steal.*
n. **1** That which is wrong, as an evil or unjust action: *He can tell the difference between right and wrong; to do wrong.* **2** The state or condition of being wrong: *He is in the wrong.* **3** An invasion or violation of someone's legal rights.
adv. In a wrong direction, place, or manner; awry; amiss: *to go wrong.*
v. **1** To violate the rights of; inflict injuries upon: *He has been deeply wronged.* **2** To impute evil to unjustly; misrepresent: *If you think so, you wrong him.*

X

xen·o·phobe (zen'ə·fōb) *n.*
A person who hates or distrusts strangers or foreigners.

xy·lo·phone (zī'lə·fōn) *n.*
A musical instrument consisting of a row of wooden bars of different sizes that are sounded by being struck with mallets.—**xy'lo·phon·ist** *n.*

Y

yacht (yot) *n.*
A vessel specially built or fitted for racing or for private pleasure excursions.

yea (yā) *adv., n.*
adv. **1** *Archaic* Yes. **2** In reality; indeed; verily.
n. An affirmative vote or voter.

yeo·man (yō'mən) *n.,* **yeo·men** *pl.*
1 A petty officer in the U.S. Navy or Coast Guard who performs clerical duties. **2** In Britain, one who cultivates his own farm.

yield (yēld) *v., n.*
v. **1** Produce, give forth, or give in return: *The soil yields good crops; His investment yields a five percent return.* **2** Give up, as to a superior power; surrender: *to yield a fortress.*
n. The amount yielded; product; result: *an annual yield of 300 tons.*

Z

zeal·ot (zel'ət) *n.*
An immoderate partisan; a fanatic.

zeal·ous (zel′əs) *adj.*
Filled with or incited by great interest and devotion: *zealous workers.*
Syn. earnest, fervent, hardworking.
Ant. slack, unenthusiastic.

ze·nith (zē′nith) *n.*
1 The point of the heavens that is directly overhead, and opposite to the nadir. 2 The highest point or culminating point of power, fortunes, prosperity, etc.: *Venice was at her zenith as a sea power in the 15th century.*

zeph·yr (zef′ər) *n.*
1 The west wind. 2 Any soft, gentle wind. 3 A lightweight worsted or woolen yarn.

zin·ni·a (zin′ē·ə) *n.*
Any of several North American plants having brightly colored, showy flowers.

zo·ol·o·gy (zō·ol′ə·jē) *n.*
The science that deals with animals, their structure, evolution, classification, etc.—**zo·o·log·i·cal** (zō·ə·loj′ə·kəl) *adj.*, **zo·ol′o·gist** *n.*

INDEX

All the words, roots, prefixes, and suffixes defined in How To INCREASE YOUR WORD POWER are indexed by page number. This index includes words that appear in *Fun With Words, Quickie Quiz,* and *Exploring Words* features as well as those discussed in the text.

ag–, 14, 15, 94, 98, 140
again, 353
against, 353
agency, 14
agenda, 14, 390
agent, 14
aggravate, 98, 193
aggravate/ irritate, 499
aggression, 94
aggressive, 94
aggressor, 94
aggrieved, 335
agile, 15, 277, 374, 375
agility, 15
agitator, 271
agrarian, 191
agreeable, 296
agree to/agree with, 513
agronomist, 151
aisle, 293
aisle/isle, 481
–al, 16, 19, 21, 22, 35, 72, 94, 122, 200, 267, 275, 299–300, 301, 325
à la carte, 225
à la mode, 225
albatross, 191
Albuquerque, 381
alcoholism, 267
alfresco, 389
align, 27
allay, 17
all ready/already, 481
all together/ altogether, 481
allude/refer, 499
allusion, 27
allusion/ illusion, 481
–ally, 338, 339
almond, 292, 366
already/all ready, 481
altar/alter, 481
alter ego, 225
alternate, 373
altogether/all together, 481
altruist, 135
alumnus/alumni/ alumna/ alumnae, 500
am–, 18–19, 81
amalgamate, 191
amanuensis, 158
amateur, 18, 81
amateurish, 18
amateurishly, 18
amatory, 18, 19

ambi–, 71, 184, 196
ambidextrous, 71, 73, 184, 196
ambience, 196
ambiguous, 71, 196
ambitious, 196
ambivalence, 196
ambulate, 202, 236
amenable, 446
American, 270
ami–, 296
amiability, 18
amiable, 18, 296
amicability, 19
amicable, 19, 376, 446
amicably, 19
amity, 47
amnesia, 268
among, 371
among/ between, 500
amontillado, 389
amoral/immoral/ unmoral/ immortal, 506
amorous, 19
amount/number, 500
amour, 384
amphibian, 23
an/a, 499
–an, 270, 277–78
anachronism, 66
analysis, 268
analyze, 336
–ance, 267, 300, 302, 304, 306, 343
anchovy, 368
–ancy, 267, 302, 304
and, 515, 519
–ane, 270, 277
anecdote/antidote, 482
anesthetist, 85
angel, 25
angel/angle, 482
angina, 390
angle/angel, 482
Anglophile, 373, 375
Anglophobe, 47
anim–, 19–21, 124
animal, 19–20
animalistic, 20
animality, 20
animate, 20, 47
animated, 20
animation, 20
animosity, 20
Ankara, 381
annals, 21–22
annex, 193

annu–, 21–22
annual, 22, 200
annuity, 22, 47
annulment, 195
–ant, 160, 270, 278, 300, 302, 303–5
antagonism, 47
ante–, 42, 183, 198, 200
antebellum, 198
antecede, 198
antecedent, 42, 47, 198
antechamber, 183, 198
antedate, 198
anthrop–, 24, 230
anthropo–, 24, 71, 96
anthropologist, 24, 151
anthropology, 24, 66, 71, 271
anti–, 184, 198, 199–200, 245, 482
antiaircraft, 199
antibiotic, 199
anticlimax, 199
antidote, 47, 199
antidote/ anecdote, 482
antipasto, 389
antipathetic, 199
antipathy, 47, 199
antiquary, 151
antiseptic, 199
antisocial, 184
antithesis, 47
antitrust, 200
anxious/eager, 501
ap–, 127
aperture, 268
apostasy, 324
apostle, 292
apparatus, 353
apparent, 193
apparition, 193
appear, 193
appearance, 193
append, 27
appendicitis, 354
appetite, 127–28
appetizer, 128
appetizing, 128
applicable, 377
appreciable, 27
appreciate, 352
apprehension, 27
apprehensive, 319
appropriate, 27
appurtenance, 27, 306
apricot, 353
a priori, 403
apt/likely/liable, 501

apt–, 189
aquatic, 23
aquiline, 269
–ar, 270, 275, 307, 309, 311–12
arable, 301
arbitrary, 317
arboreal, 23
arch, 17, 368
arch–, 25, 26
–arch, 25
archaic, 369, 370
archangel, 25, 369
archbishop, 25
archenemy, 25
archeo–, 25, 96
archeological, 25
archeologist, 151
archeology, 25, 96, 345, 369
archetype, 367, 369
archi–, 25
archipelago, 369
architect, 26
architecture, 26
archives, 370
–archy, 25, 26
arctic, 292
ardor, 268
arduous, 342
Argyle, 61
aristocrat, 272
Armageddon, 197
arrive, 194
arrogance, 346
artistically, 338
–ary, 32, 178, 270, 275, 314–16
as/as if/like, 501
ascendancy, 324
ascetic, 135
ascribe, 182, 195
ask, 351
asked, 360
asparagus, 292, 361, 372
aspect, 195
aspersion, 195
aspirant, 195
aspiration, 27
assignment, 195
associate, 194, 373
association, 194
assure/ensure/ insure, 482
astronomy, 272
at–, 165
–ate, 20, 60, 65, 72, 93, 95, 133, 178, 251, 252, 258, 273, 276, 373
athlete, 292, 293, 348, 364, 365

718

incarcerate, 227
incarnate, 224,
    227
incendiary, 317
incense, 319
inception, 40
incessant, 223
inchoate, 370
incidence, 36,
    306
incident, 36
incidental, 36
incidentally, 36,
    338
incipience, 40
incipient, 40,
    227
includable, 52
include, 52
inclusion, 52
inclusive, 52
incognito, 355,
    378, 380
incoherent, 120
incomparable, 377,
    380, 446
    incomparable/
    uncompar-
    able, 510
incompetent, 129
incomplete, 131
inconceivable,
    335
incongruous, 223
inconsequential,
    224
inconspicuous,
    154
inconvenient, 169
incorporate, 56
increase, 57
incredible/
    incredulous,
    506
increment, 57
incubate, 60
incubator, 60
incumbency, 227
incumbent, 60,
    278
incur, 78
incursion, 227
indefensible, 296
indelible, 296
indemnity, 223
indescribable,
    182
indigenous, 342
indigestible, 93
indigestion, 93
indigo, 56
indispensable, 126
individual,
    476–77
indoctrinate, 78,
    106
indomitable, 223
–ine, 64, 275
inequitable, 224

inestimable, 298
inexorable, 223
infamous, 224,
    380
infantile, 373
infect, 75
infection, 75
infectious, 75
infer, 506
inference, 306
inferno, 403
infirm, 79–80
infirmary, 80
inflection, 90,
    295
influence, 82–83,
    267, 376
influential, 83
influx, 96
infraction, 90
infringe, 84, 227
infringement, 84
infuse, 86
–ing, 274–75,
    278, 318,
    325, 328,
    359, 371–72
ingenious, 89
ingénue, 385,
    387
ingenuous, 89,
    342
ingratiate, 227
ingratitude, 97
inhabitant, 270
inherent, 120,
    227
inhibit, 227
inhospitable, 380
inject, 102
injection, 102
injunction, 104
inmate, 373
innate, 226
innocuous, 269
inquire, 145
inquiry, 145,
    268, 377
inquisition, 145
inquisitive, 145,
    146
insatiable, 223,
    224, 346
inscribe, 149
inscription, 149
inscrutable, 298
insoluble, 301
inspect, 154
inspection, 154
inspector, 154
insufferable, 223
insular, 313
insult, 378
insuperable, 224
insure/ensure,
    482
intact, 156
intelligible, 296
intangible, 157

inter–, 45, 111,
    147, 226,
    227–28
interact, 33
interbreed, 226
intercept, 226
intercession, 45
intercollegiate,
    227
interdenomina-
    tional, 227
interdependent,
    227
interfere, 226
interject, 226
interjection, 120
interlocutor, 111
interlude, 226
intermezzo,
    227–28, 389
intermittent, 346
intern, 85
internecine, 227
internist, 85
interrupt, 147
interruption,
    147–48
intestate, 223
into/in, 506
in toto, 403
intra–, 183, 228
intramural, 183,
    228
intravenous, 228
intricacy, 324
intricate, 376
intro–, 69
introduce, 69
introduction, 69
introductory, 69,
    276
inundate, 461
invalidate, 223
inveigle, 335
invent, 170
invention, 170
inventive, 170
inventor, 170
invincible, 296
inviolate, 223
invisible, 176
invocation, 178
invoke, 177–78
involve, 180
involved, 180
involvement, 180
–ion, 29, 32, 65,
    83, 86, 94,
    104, 121,
    129, 133,
    139, 153,
    166, 176,
    250, 267,
    294–95, 325
ir–, 222, 224,
    295, 377
iridescent, 319
irony, 361
irreducible, 70

irrefutable, 298
irrelevance, 306
irreparable, 377,
    446
irresistible, 224,
    296
irretrievable, 335
irrevocable, 178,
    298, 377,
    380
irritate/
    aggravate,
    499
–ise, 336, 337
–ish, 117, 273,
    275, 341
isle/aisle, 481
islet, 280
–ism, 267
–ist, 270
it–, 196, 250
Italian, 357
–ite, 127, 271
itinerary, 360
its/it's, 491,
    497
–ity, 13, 18, 19,
    20, 21, 22,
    64, 98, 99,
    268
–ive, 15, 121,
    141, 173,
    277
–ize, 258, 273,
    337, 338

jac–, 102, 103,
    190
jai alai, 389
ject–, 102–3, 233
jeopardize, 367
jeremiad, 197
jetsam/flotsam,
    504
jeweler, 309
Jezebel, 197
join–, 103–4
joint–, 103
joyous, 277
Judas, 197
July, 162
junct–, 103, 104
junction, 104
juncture, 120
junta, 389
jur–, 237
just, 357
juvenile, 276,
    374, 375
juxtaposition, 101

kept, 360
kindergarten, 388
kind of, 362
kleptomaniac, 135
knockwurst, 388

monarchy, 26
monetary, 322
monit–, 115, 116
monitor, 116
monitory, 116
mono–, 87, 167,
    265
monocle, 167
monogamous, 101,
    265
monogamy, 87,
    167
monologue, 265,
    272
monotreme, 23
monument,
    115–16, 267
monumental, 116
–mony, 13,
    267–68,
moral/morale,
    493
morsel, 280
mortgage, 292,
    293, 366
mosaic, 318
mosaicked, 318
mosaicking. 318
Moscow, 382
mot–, 118–19
mother. 356
motif, 386
motivation, 144
motive, 144
motorist, 361
mountebank, 158
mov–, 118, 119
multitude, 268
mundane, 269
mural, 117, 228
mute, 243

nagging. 372
naive, 386
naiveté, 386
nappy, 243
nasc–, 121
nascent, 121
nat–, 121–22,
    124
natal, 144
Natchitoches, 381
nation, 121
national, 121
nationalism, 121
native, 121–22
nativity, 122
naval/navel, 493
nebulous, 342
neglig–, 296
negligence, 319
negligible, 296
    298
neither/either,
    514
nemesis, 108, 109
–ness, 268, 326,
    340, 341

neurologist, 85
New Yorker, 409
nex–, 193
nib, 414
nicotine, 162
niggardly, 269
nimrod, 158
nocturnal, 23
nomenclature,
    130
nominal, 130
nominate, 274
–nomy, 272
non–, 184, 232,
    265, 293
nonbelligerent, 93
nonchalance, 346
nonchalant, 232
noncomformist,
    232
nonentity, 232
nonflammable,
    184
nonpareil, 335
nonsense, 232
non sequitur, 390,
    403
nontransference,
    77
nor/or, 514
norm–, 186
nostalgic, 269
noticeable, 296
notoriety, 268
noun, 245
nov–, 265
novelty, 268
nuance, 386
nub, 414
nucleus, 345
number/amount,
    500

o–, 113
oaf, 414
Oahu, 382
ob–, 76, 113, 139,
    233, 234
obbligato, 389
obeisance, 335
obese, 233
obfuscate, 234
object, 233, 379
obligate, 234
oblique, 234, 358
oblong, 234
obnoxious, 234
obsession, 182
obsolete, 234
obstacle, 234
obstetrician, 85
obstetrics, 234
obstreperous, 234,
    269
obtrude, 233
obtuse, 234
oc–, 36, 62, 233,
    234

occasion, 36–37
occasional, 37
occident, 36
occidental, 36
occult, 235
occupy, 233
occur, 62–63
occurrence, 63
ocher, 56
oct–, 265
ocular–, 201
oculist/
    ophthal–
    mologist/
    optician/
    optometrist,
    508
of–, 76–77, 233,
    234
offend, 234
offer, 76–77
offering, 77
offertory, 77
often, 360, 366
of which, 518
–oid, 275, 276
Okinawa, 382
older/oldest, 503
–olent, 276, 277
–ology, 271
omission. 113
omit, 113
omni–, 167
omnipotent, 167
omniscience, 130
omniscient, 319
omnivorous, 130
on, 515
on–, 235
once, 364
onset, 235
onslaught, 235
onus, 342
op–, 139, 233,
    234, 235
operate, 361
ophthalmologist,
    85, 261, 520
ophthalmologist/
    oculist/
    optician/
    optometrist, 508
opponent, 140
opportune, 234
oppose, 139–40
opposite, 140–41
opposition, 140–
    41
oppress, 234
opprobrious, 343
opprobrium, 235
opt–, 189
optician/
    optometrist/
    ophthal–
    mologist/
    oculist, 508
optimist, 135
optometrist, 520

optometrist/
    optician/
    ophthal–
    mologist/
    oculist
    508
opulent, 277
or/nor, 514
–or, 16, 30, 89,
    111, 116,
    167, 241,
    268, 271,
    307, 308–9,
    310, 311–12
oral/verbal, 511
orbital, 252
ordin–, 252
ordinance, 306
orgy, 371, 372
orifice, 130
–orium. 30
orn–, 253
ort–, 186
orthodontist, 85
orthopedist, 85
–ory, 18, 271, 275
–ose, 276
ostensible, 296,
    298
ostentatious, 342
ought to, 362
–our, 307, 311–12
–ous, 19, 21, 196,
    276–77, 325,
    338, 340,
    342
out–, 235, 236
outermost, 235
outset, 236
outside, 236
over–, 184, 235,
    236
oversight, 236
overweight, 236
overwrought, 236
oviparous, 23
ovoid, 276

pachyderm, 23,
pacify, 274
Palestine, 382
palette, 117
pallid, 269
pamphlet, 364
panacea, 240
pandemonium,
    240
panic, 318
panicked, 318
panicking, 318
panicky, 318
panoply, 240
panorama, 240
par–, 193
paragon, 240
paralyze, 336
paranoia, 240
paranoid, 135

723